From Counting and Probability

Sequential Counting Principle (SCP)	If one event can occur in m ways, a second event can occur in n ways, a third event can occur in p ways, and so on, then the sequence of events can occur in $m \times n \times p \ldots$ ways.
$P(n, r) = \dfrac{n!}{(n-r)!}$	The number of permutations of n objects taken r at a time.
$C(n, r) = \dfrac{n!}{r!(n-r)!}$	The number of combinations of n objects taken r at a time.
$P(T') = 1 - P(T)$	The probability of the complement of an event.
$P(A \cup B) =$ $P(A) + P(B) - P(A \cap B)$	The probability of event A **or** event B.
$P(A \mid B) = \dfrac{P(A \cap B)}{P(B)}$	The probability of event A **given** event B.
$P(A \cap B) = P(A) \cdot P(B)$	The probability of event A **and** event B where A and B are independent.
Odds $f : u$ in favor of an event	Where f and u, respectively, represent the number favorable and unfavorable ways that an event can occur.
$E = a_1 p_1 + a_2 p_2 + \cdots + a_n p_n$	The expected value E for an event where a_1, $a_2, \ldots, a_n$ are the values that occur with probability p_1, p_2, $\ldots, p_n$.

From Statistics

Mean $\overline{x}$	The sum of a set of data values divided by the number of values.
Median	The middle value when data values are ranked in order of magnitude. If there are an even number of values, it is the mean of the two middle values.
Mode	1 ... set of d ...
Range	T ... d least v ...

$$s = \sqrt{\frac{(x_1 - \overline{x})^2 + (x_2 - \overline{x})^2 + \cdots + (x_n - \overline{x})^2}{n - 1}}$$

The standard deviation of a set of a data values $x_1, x_2, \ldots, x_n$.

$z = \dfrac{x - \overline{x}}{s}$ The z-score associated with the raw data value x where $\overline{x}$ is the mean and s is the standard deviation.

TOPICS IN
CONTEMPORARY MATHEMATICS

FIFTH EDITION

Ignacio Bello

Jack R. Britton

Hillsborough Community College

Professor Emeritus
University of South Florida

D. C. HEATH AND COMPANY
Lexington, Massachusetts   Toronto

Address editorial correspondence to:

D. C. Heath
125 Spring Street
Lexington, MA 02173

Acquisitions Editor: Charles Hartford
Developmental Editor: Philip Charles Lanza
Production Editor: Ron Hampton
Designer: Alwyn R. Velásquez
Art Editor: Gary Crespo
Production Coordinator: Richard Tonachel
Photo Researcher: Billie L. Ingram
Text Permissions Editor: Margaret Roll

Cover: Abstract of a Steinway framework and strings. © 1992 John F. Cooper.

International Standard Book Number: 0-669-28957-4

Library of Congress Catalog Number: 92-70365

10 9 8 7 6 5 4 3 2

In this fifth edition we have continued in our goal of introducing the student to the many interesting mathematical concepts that are used in our contemporary world. We have tried to bring out the basic ideas and techniques as simply and clearly as possible and have related these ideas to other areas—such as sociology, psychology, and business—that will be attractive to the reader. Whenever feasible, elementary applications are given; these can be found in a new section feature called Getting Started, throughout the text's discussion and examples, and in the lesson problem sets.

The more abstract and theoretical aspects of the subject matter have been de-emphasized. Instead, emphasis has been placed on the understanding and use of the various concepts that are introduced. An important aid to this goal will be found in the exercises, which include over 4100 problems ranging from the necessary routine drill to challenges for the better students. The reader will find considerable support and explanation in the over 500 worked-out examples.

What Is New in the Fifth Edition?

We have followed the valuable suggestions of users of previous editions and the many reviewers contributing to this fifth edition to clarify the exposition, expand the coverage, and, in general, improve the book.

◆ We have completely redesigned the format of the book, now in four colors, and provided hundreds of new examples and exercises.

◆ Each chapter now begins with a Preview feature detailing the material to be covered in the chapter and the ways in which the topics are related to each other.

◆ Each section now begins with a Getting Started feature. These applications offer a motivating introduction for the techniques and ideas to be covered, and are drawn from a vast array of fields.

◆ Problem-solving examples have been added in pertinent sections to emphasize problem-solving methods throughout the text. These special examples use a unique two-column format to describe the general problem-solving method and then demonstrate a specific use.

◆ A new exercise feature called In Other Words gives students the opportunity to use writing to clarify and express ideas, concepts, and procedures. Students will think, talk, and write mathematics when they work these problems, which are included in every exercise set.

◆ A set of Research Questions is included at the end of each chapter to help students master research and library techniques as well as to explore how the topics under discussion were developed. These questions can be assigned to individual students or as group projects. A Research Bibliography detailing sources for researching these questions is provided at the end of the book.

◆ We have added a new section on Infinite Sets and a section on Game Theory.

◆ The presentation of rational, real, and complex numbers has been consolidated into a single chapter.

◆ Chapter 7, Geometry, has been extensively revised, giving a more detailed treatment of angles, and placing perimeter and circumference in the same section.

◆ We have placed mathematical systems and matrices together in Chapter 8.

◆ We have revised Chapter 12, Consumer Mathematics, to reflect real-world changes.

◆ The metric system has been moved to Chapter 13.

◆ Revision of Chapter 14, Computers, now makes it more current and more applicable to other computer work touched on throughout the text.

◆ We have made many significant efforts to address the NCTM curriculum recommendations regarding communication (In Other Words), reasoning (Chapter 2), connections (Discovery features and Mathematical Systems), Algebra (Chapters 5 and 6), Geometry (Chapter 7), Statistics (Chapter 11), Probability (Chapters 9 and 10), mathematical structures (Chapter 8), and problem solving (throughout the book).

Suggested Courses Using this Book

The book is quite flexible, with a large selection of topics available to suit various courses. The entire book can be covered easily in a full year's course, while many alternative choices can be made for a two-quarter or a one-semester course. Here are some of the courses for which the book is suggested:

◆ General education or liberal arts mathematics (the text follows most of the CUPM [Committee on the Undergraduate Program in Mathematics] recommendations for liberal arts mathematics)

◆ Topics in contemporary mathematics courses

◆ College mathematics or survey of mathematics courses

◆ Introduction to mathematics or applications of mathematics courses

There are a few more advanced topics that may be included or omitted at the instructor's discretion. These choices will not affect the continuity of any chapter presentation or syllabus as a whole. The topics include the following sections: 1.6 Infinite Sets; 2.6 Implication; 2.9 Switching Networks; 6.7 Linear Programming; 7.8 Networks; and 8.8 Game Theory.

Supporting Material and Supplements

This text has an extensive support package that includes:

◆ An *Instructor's Guide* containing commentary and teaching suggestions for each chapter, suggested course syllabi, answers to even-numbered problems in the exercises, a variety of five test forms per chapter, as well as answers to all test questions in the guide.

◆ A *Student's Solutions and Study Guide* containing complete solutions to all odd-numbered problems in the exercises and to all the problems in the chapter Practice Tests.

◆ Algorithmic testing from ips Publishing offering a total of 200 algorithms for creating a nearly unlimited variety of test forms for each chapter of the text. Available in IBM PC and Macintosh versions.

◆ ESATEST II computerized testing which allows instructors to edit and print fixed-item tests. The full range of user features includes pull-down menus, dialog boxes, random or manual item selection, and export/import capability. Available in IBM PC and Macintosh versions.

◆ Preparing for the CLAST—Mathematics, which is a competency-based study guide that reviews and offers preparatory material for the CLAST (College Level Academic Skills Test) objectives required by the State of Florida for mathematics.

◆ Algorithmic CLAST software, also from ips Publishing, for preparing practice test forms covering every CLAST mathematics objective.

◆ Videotapes reviewing key topics in the text.

◆ A disk containing the computer programs given in the appendix, PROGRAMS IN BASIC, and suitable for interactively working the appropriate problems in the text.

A Word About Problem Solving

Problem solving has become a fixture in mathematics textbooks. Lead by the teachings of George Polya, and following the recommendations of the NCTM and the MAA, most mathematics books at this level cover the topic. Many texts, however, front-load much of their presentation in the first chapter; all of the techniques, procedures, and pedagogy are paraded in Chapter One and then promptly forgotten. We have chosen to integrate problem solving where it is needed, and consequently, where it can be taught and learned most effectively.

For example, a few of the strategies suggested by Polya himself call for making a table, writing an equation, making a diagram, and accounting for all possibilities. Why not wait to present these techniques in the chapters dealing with truth tables, algebra, geometry, and counting, respectively, where the pertinent methods can be effectively displayed, rather than laboriously creating artificial solutions only to demonstrate strategies by solving artificial problems?

The artificial approach, after all, is not problem solving; it is problem making. It will make problems for the instructor, for the student, and (one might argue) for society at large. As Professor Beberman put it: "I think in some cases we have tried to answer questions that students never raise and to resolve doubts they never had . . . ." Therefore, we have worked very hard to dispel the unfortunate notion gained by many students that mathematics is an artificial subject riddled with uninteresting and contrived problems. As an ongoing theme of this text, problem solving is presented purposefully in meaningful and appropriate contexts where students can best understand and appreciate its methods. Above all, we hope that this integrated approach will help students learn how to apply problem-solving techniques in the real world once the course is over.

Acknowledgments

We wish to thank the following reviewers of this fifth edition for their many valuable suggestions and constructive criticism. They are:

Isali Alsina, Kean College of New Jersey
Barbara Burrows, Santa Fe Community College
Stephen Eberhart, California State University—Northridge
John Emert, Ball State University
Wei Feng, University of North Carolina
Margaret Finster, Erie Community College
Patricia Gallagher, North Carolina State University
William Hobbs, Point Loma College
Lois Martin, Massasoit Community College
Sunny Norfleet, St. Petersburg Junior College
Jane Pickett, Hillsborough Community College
Rita Polston, Southern Illinois University
Scott Reed, College of Lake County
Hope Richards, Western Kentucky University
K. P. Satagopan, Shaw University
Burla Sims, University of Arkansas
Henry Smith, University of New Orleans
Ara Sullenberger, Tarrant County Junior College
Steve Sworder, Saddleback Community College

We also extend our continued appreciation to those reviewers who contributed to the success of earlier editions: Homer Austin, Salisbury State College; Gloria Arnold, University of Arkansas; James Bagby, Virginia Commonwealth University; John Christy, University of South Dakota; Barbara Cohen, West Los Angeles College; David Cusick, Marshall University; Duane Deal, Ball State University; Lucy Dechéne, Fitchburg State College; Benjamin Divers; Philip Downum, State University of New York; Margaret Hackworth, School Board, Pinellas County, Florida; Jim Hodge, College of Lake County; Charles Klein, Midland College; Calvin Lathan, Monroe Community College; Charles C. Miles, Hillsborough Community College; James O. Morgan, Southeastern Louisiana University; Curtis Olson, University of South Dakota; Edward T. Ordman, Memphis State College; Carol B. Ottinger, Mississippi University for Women; Josephine Rinaldo, School Board, Hillsborough County, Florida; Jean T. Sells, Sacred Heart University; Fay Sewell, Montgomery County Community College; Gary Tikriti, University of South Florida; John Vangor, Housatonic Community College; Harlie White, Jr., Campbellsville College.

We wish to express our particular appreciation to Dr. Heriberto Hernandez, who gave us invaluable help with the problems relating to medicine; Bill Albrecht, who created the computer programs appearing in the appendix; Barbara Burrows, our tireless reviewer, who offered invaluable comments and suggestions and kept us straight; Joe Clemente, who checked the accuracy of the problems while only complaining about his health; Gary Etgen, our final answer and page reader, who was both accurate and timely; Josephine Rinaldo, who proofread galleys and pages overnight and only doubted the accuracy of one of our probability problems; Prakash Sach, who did a wonderful job with several of the photos in the book; and to the following colleagues for all their helpful criticisms and suggestions: Diana Fernandez, James Gard, George Kosan, Chester Miles, Donald Clayton Rose, Donald Clayton Rose, II, and especially Charles Osborne, who worked every problem in the book and nearly missed his vacation. We would also like to thank the people involved in the preparation of the ancillary materials for the book: Alex Ambrioso, Marcus McWaters, Mark Oglesby, Rose Reyes, Robert Schatzow, T. Tran, and William Wilder. Without their professional and technical expertise we could have never finished the myriad of diagrams, charts, typing and proofreading involved.

Among the many people at D. C. Heath who have been involved with this project we would like to thank Philip Lanza, our developmental editor, who gave many suggestions and endured our needling and humor throughout the revision; Debbie Gruetzmacher, who believed in the project; Charlie Hartford, mathematics editor, who signed the project; Ron Hampton, who did a wonderful job with production; and the designer of the book Alwyn R. Velásquez. Last but not least, we wish to express our sincere thanks to the many users—students and instructors alike—of the previous editions. We hope that this fifth edition will please them even more. We always welcome students', professors', and readers' comments and suggestions. You may send them to us at the following address: Ignacio Bello, Hillsborough Community College, P.O. Box 5096, Tampa, Florida, 33675.

Ignacio Bello
Jack R. Britton

This new edition of *Topics in Contemporary Mathematics* contains a wide variety of features designed to help build the reader's understanding of mathematics by placing the work to be done **in context**. A student who utilizes the features in this book will gain a better understanding of the history behind each topic, how the topic relates to everyday life, how different topics in the course interrelate, and—most importantly—how to think about solving problems in the real world once the course is over.

The **features** in *Topics* have been carefully written to ensure that, while many are optional, they are **interrelated**. In addition, the text utilizes a new **four-color design** to highlight pedagogical features, emphasize each feature's function, and make them visually interesting.

Putting Material in Context

Chapter Preview

Each chapter begins with a list of topics for quick reference. The introduction that follows provides an overview of the material being studied, and explains the ways in which the topics are related.

The Human Side of Mathematics

Who devised this material or contributed to its development? Placed at the beginning of each chapter to serve as motivation and offer historical perspective, this feature helps to communicate the message that mathematics is a growing body of knowledge, that it is a human endeavor, and that every topic studied began as part of a problem solving process. Remarks on **Looking Ahead** link the biography to upcoming material.

CHAPTER

5

Equations, Inequalities, and Problem Solving

THE HUMAN SIDE OF MATHEMATICS

Karl Friedrich Gauss, who has been called the Prince of Mathematicians, was born in Brunswick, Germany, in 1777. His father was a poor laborer who did nothing to promote his son's talents. It was only by accident that Gauss became a mathematician.

Throughout his life, Gauss was noted for his ability to perform stupendous mental calculations. Before he was 3 years old, while watching his father make out a weekly payroll, he noted an error and told his father what the answer should be. A check of the account showed that the boy was correct.

At age 10 he met a mathematician named Bartels, who taught the boy some mathematics and brought his young friend to the attention of the Duke of Brunswick. The Duke was so impressed by Gauss that he made the boy his protégé.

Gauss entered the Caroline College in Brunswick at the age of 15, and in a short time began his research into higher arithmetic. When he left the College in 1795, he had already invented the method of least squares. He entered the University of

Karl Friedrich Gauss (1777–1855)

Archimedes, Newton, and Gauss, these three, are in a class by themselves among the great mathematicians, and it is not for ordinary mortals to attempt to range them in the order of merit.

E. T. Bell

Göttingen, where he spent three years completing his *Disquisitiones Arithmeticae (Arithmetical Researches)*. In 1798, he went to the University of Helmstedt, where he was awarded his Ph.D. His doctoral thesis gave the first proof of the fundamental theorem of algebra, that every algebraic equation has at least one root among the complex numbers.

His *Disquisitiones*, published in 1801, is regarded as the basic work in the theory of numbers. During his life he also made great contributions to astronomy, geodesy (the measurement of the Earth), geometry, theoretical physics, and complex numbers and functions. Along with his masterful theoretical research, he was also a well-known inventor; among other things, he made significant contributions to the invention of the electric telegraph in the early 1830s.

Looking Ahead: Much of Gauss's work in pure mathematics dealt with number theory, the concept of complex numbers (which we have seen in Chapter 4), and the solutions to algebraic equations, which is the focus of this chapter.

, and then use
o solve different
blems. We end
iscussing ratio,
variation, em-
ions to consu-
h as unit pric-

remember that
oy of ten who
er by adding
· + 100 with
Getting Started,
is doctoral dis-
vided the first
damental theo-
You can read
in The Human
ics.

Problem-Solving Skills
Problem Solving

Presented as an on-going theme throughout *Topics,* specific **Problem Solving** examples are clearly formatted using two columns. The left column uses the RSTUV method (Read, Select, Think, Use, and Verify) to guide the reader through the problem. In the right column, the solution is carefully developed. Similar standard examples follow and provide additional reinforcement.

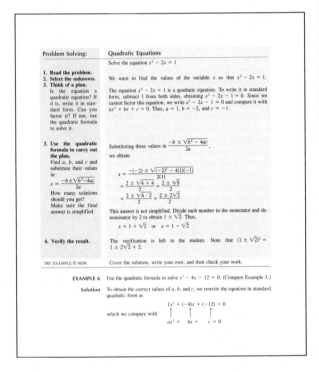

Using Your Knowledge

Interesting application problems help students generalize material they have learned and apply it immediately to similar real-life situations. They are included as an answer to that often asked question, "Why do I have to learn this, and what good is it?"

Discovery

More challenging problems are provided to further develop critical thinking and problem-solving skills. These are brief excursions into related topics, extensions, and generalizations.

Getting Started

Appearing at the beginning of every section, **Getting Started** is an application that demonstrates how the material relates to the real world. Hundreds of applications are used to introduce some of the techniques and ideas to be covered in each new section.

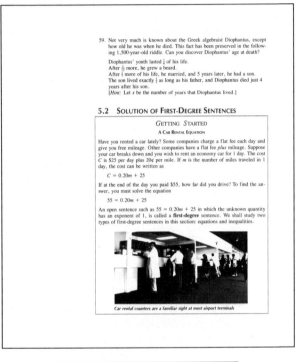

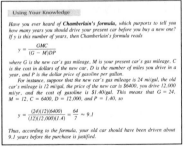

Using Your Knowledge

*Have you ever heard of **Chamberlain's formula,** which purports to tell you how many years you should drive your present car before you buy a new one? If y is this number of years, then Chamberlain's formula reads*

$$y = \frac{GMC}{(G - M)DP}$$

where G is the new car's gas mileage, M is your present car's gas mileage, C is the cost in dollars of the new car, D is the number of miles you drive in a year, and P is the dollar price of gasoline per gallon.

For instance, suppose that the new car's gas mileage is 24 mi/gal, the old car's mileage is 12 mi/gal, the price of the new car is $6400, you drive 12,000 mi/yr, and the cost of gasoline is $1.40/gal. This means that G = 24, M = 12, C = 6400, D = 12,000, and P = 1.40, so

$$y = \frac{(24)(12)(6400)}{(12)(12,000)(1.4)} = \frac{64}{7} \approx 9.1$$

Thus, according to this formula, your old car should have been driven about 9.1 years before the purchase is justified.

Discovery

82. A problem that comes from the Rhind papyrus, one of the oldest mathematical documents known, reads like this: "$\frac{2}{3}$ added and then $\frac{1}{3}$ taken away, 10 remains. . . ." The document then goes on to tell how to find the number with which you started. Can you discover what this number is? [*Hint:* If you let x be the unknown number, then the problem intends you to add $\frac{2}{3}x$ and then take away $\frac{1}{3}$ of the result to get a difference of 10.]

Examples, Exercise Sets, and Applications

The over 500 examples in *Topics* include a wide range of computational, drill, and applied problems selected to build confidence, competency, skill, and understanding.

Over 4100 carefully developed exercises provide extensive practice with drill and applied problems included in each section. Each exercise set is carefully graded to build student confidence in solving problems. Answers to odd-numbered exercises appear in the back of the text.

Extensive applications, a key strength of this text, are integrated throughout the examples and exercises, and have been carefully designed to show the relevance of the mathematics being studied.

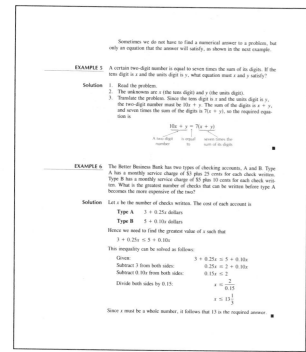

Calculator and Computer Corners

Another problem solving skill students should develop is the ability to understand how and when to utilize technology. These features provide essential background on how to solve problems using a calculator or a computer.

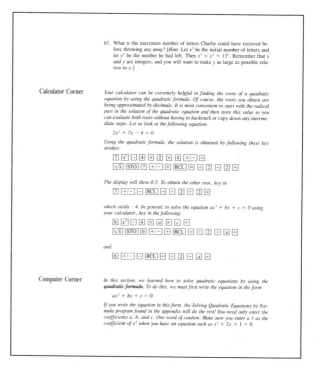

In Other Words

Useful as a writing exercise, or for class discussion, these brief questions provide the opportunity to think about and clarify ideas, concepts, and procedures.

In Other Words

47. In your own words define the *replacement set* for an equation.
48. In your own words define the *solution set* for an equation
49. If a real number a is in the replacement set of an equation, will it always be in the solution set? Explain.
50. If a number s is in the solution set of an equation, will it always be in the replacement set? Explain.

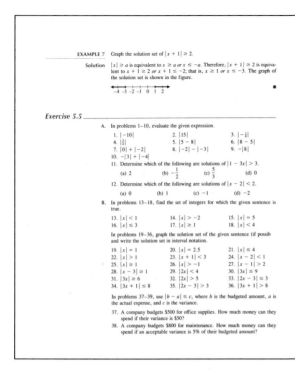

EXAMPLE 7   Graph the solution set of $|x + 1| \geq 2$.

Solution $|x| \geq a$ is equivalent to $x \geq a$ or $x \leq -a$. Therefore, $|x + 1| \geq 2$ is equivalent to $x + 1 \geq 2$ or $x + 1 \leq -2$; that is, $x \geq 1$ or $x \leq -3$. The graph of the solution set is shown in the figure.

$$-4 \quad -3 \quad -2 \quad -1 \quad 0 \quad 1 \quad 2$$

Exercise 5.5

A. In problems 1–10, evaluate the given expression.

1. $|-10|$ 2. $|15|$ 3. $|-\frac{1}{4}|$
4. $|\frac{3}{4}|$ 5. $|5 - 8|$ 6. $|8 - 5|$
7. $|0| + |-2|$ 8. $|-2| - |-3|$ 9. $-|8|$
10. $-|3| + |-4|$

11. Determine which of the following are solutions of $|1 - 3x| > 3$.

    (a) 2   (b) $-\frac{1}{2}$ (c) $\frac{5}{3}$ (d) 0

12. Determine which of the following are solutions of $|x - 2| < 2$.

    (a) 0   (b) 1   (c) -1 (d) -2

B. In problems 13–18, find the set of integers for which the given sentence is true.

13. $|x| < 1$ 14. $|x| > -2$ 15. $|x| = 5$
16. $|x| \leq 3$ 17. $|x| \geq 1$ 18. $|x| < 4$

In problems 19–36, graph the solution set of the given sentence (if possible and write the solution set in interval notation.

19. $|x| = 1$ 20. $|x| = 2.5$ 21. $|x| \leq 4$
22. $|x| > 1$ 23. $|x + 1| < 3$ 24. $|x - 2| < 1$
25. $|x| \geq 1$ 26. $|x| > -1$ 27. $|x - 1| > 2$
28. $|x - 3| \geq 1$ 29. $|2x| < 4$ 30. $|3x| \leq 9$
31. $|3x| \geq 6$ 32. $|2x| > 5$ 33. $|2x - 3| \leq 3$
34. $|3x + 1| \leq 8$ 35. $|2x - 3| > 3$ 36. $|3x + 1| > 8$

In problems 37–39, use $|b - a| \leq c$, where b is the budgeted amount, a is the actual expense, and c is the variance.

37. A company budgets $500 for office supplies. How much money can they spend if their variance is $50?

38. A company budgets $800 for maintenance. How much money can they spend if an acceptable variance is 5% of their budgeted amount?

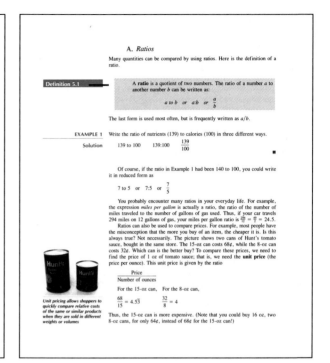

A. Ratios

Many quantities can be compared by using ratios. Here is the definition of a ratio.

Definition 5.1

A **ratio** is a quotient of two numbers. The ratio of a number a to another number b can be written as:

$$a \text{ to } b \quad \text{or} \quad a{:}b \quad \text{or} \quad \frac{a}{b}$$

The last form is used most often, but is frequently written as a/b.

EXAMPLE 1   Write the ratio of nutrients (139) to calories (100) in three different ways.

Solution   139 to 100   139:100 $\frac{139}{100}$

Of course, if the ratio in Example 1 had been 140 to 100, you could write it in reduced form as

$$7 \text{ to } 5 \quad \text{or} \quad 7{:}5 \quad \text{or} \quad \frac{7}{5}$$

You probably encounter many ratios in your everyday life. For example, the expression *miles per gallon* is actually a ratio, the ratio of the number of miles traveled to the number of gallons of gas used. Thus, if your car travels 294 miles on 12 gallons of gas, your miles per gallon ratio is $\frac{294}{12} = \frac{49}{2} = 24.5$.

Ratios can also be used to compare prices. For example, most people have the misconception that the more you buy of an item, the cheaper it is. Is this always true? Not necessarily. The picture shows two cans of Hunt's tomato sauce. The 15-oz can costs 68¢, while the 8-oz can costs 32¢. Which can is the better buy? To compare these prices, we need to find the price of 1 oz of tomato sauce; that is, we need the **unit price** (the price per ounce). This unit price is given by the ratio

$$\frac{\text{Price}}{\text{Number of ounces}}$$

For the 15-oz can,   For the 8-oz can,

$$\frac{68}{15} = 4.5\overline{3} \qquad \frac{32}{8} = 4$$

Thus, the 15-oz can is more expensive. (Note that you could buy 16 oz, two 8-oz cans, for only 64¢, instead of 68¢ for the 15-oz can!)

Unit pricing allows shoppers to quickly compare relative costs of the same or similar products when they are sold in different weights or volumes

Subsections Correlated to Exercise Sets

Before students can make decisions about how to solve a problem, they must first master the basic skills within each topic. To help the reader identify the different skills within a topic, each subsection is clearly titled and marked with an A, B, C, etc. These subsections are then correlated with the exercise sets to help students draw connections between subsection presentations and problems.

End-of-Chapter Study Aids

Summary

The Chapter Summary provides brief definitions and examples for key topics within a given chapter. Importantly, it also contains section references to encourage students to re-read sections, rather than memorizing a definition out of context.

34. The weight W of an object varies inversely as the square from the center of the Earth.
   (a) Write an equation of variation.
   (b) An astronaut weighs 121 pounds on the surface of the dius of the Earth is 3960 miles, find the value of k fo (Do not multiply out your answer.)
   (c) What will this astronaut weigh when she is 880 miles face of the Earth?

In Other Words

35. Explain the difference between a ratio and a proportion.
36. Explain the difference between direct variation and inverse

Section	Item	Meaning
5.3	Finite intervals	$a \leq x \leq b$ Cl
		$a < x < b$ Op
		$\left. \begin{array}{l} a \leq x < b \\ a < x \leq b \end{array} \right\}$ Ha
5.5A	Absolute value	The distance line from 0 to
5.6	Quadratic equation	A second-deg can be writter $ax^2 + bx +$
5.6C	Quadratic formula	The solutions $ax^2 + bx +$ $x = \frac{-b \pm \sqrt{}}{}$
5.6D	Pythagorean theorem	In any right square of the equal to the of the other
5.7		**Procedure for Solving Word Probler** 1. Read the problem carefully, and 2. Select a variable to represent thi 3. Translate the problem into the la 4. Use the rules of algebra to solve 5. Verify the solution.
5.8A	Ratio	A quotient of
5.8B	Proportion	An equality b
5.8C	Varies directly	y varies direc
5.8C	Varies inversely	y varies inver

Chapter 5 Summary

Section	Item	Meaning	Example
5.1	Variable	A symbol that may be replaced by any one of a set of numbers	x, y, z
5.1A	Open sentence	A sentence in which the variable can be replaced by a number	$x + 3 = 5; x -$
5.1A	Equation	Sentences in which the verb phrase is "="	$x + 7 = 9$
5.1A	Inequality	Sentences in which the verb is $>, <, \neq, \geq,$ or $\leq$	$x + 7 < 9; x >$
5.1A	Solution set	The set of elements of the replacement set that make the open sentence a true statement	{3} is the solutio $x + 2 = 5$ when replacement set whole numbers.
5.1A	Identities	Open sentences that are true for every number in the replacement set	$x + 0 = x; x +$ $a(b + c) = ab -$
5.2	First-degree sentence	An open sentence in which the unknown quantity has an exponent of 1 only	$x + 7 = 8 - 2$
5.2A	Elementary operations	Operations that may be performed on a sentence to obtain an equivalent sentence	Addition or subt number on both equation

Research Questions

These questions provide an additional opportunity to explore how various mathematical topics were developed. This reinforces the message begun with **The Human Side of Mathematics** that the body of mathematical knowledge has evolved through human thought, experience, and communication. **Research Questions** combine with **In Other Words** to provide a strong, interesting writing component to the course, and are an excellent opportunity for group learning as well.

Practice Test

These tests are designed to help students check their comprehension. Practice Tests can help to further develop problem-solving and test-taking skills. Answers to all Practice Test items appear at the back of the book.

Research Questions

Sources of information for these questions can be found in the Bibliography at the end of the book.

1. Write a short essay about Gauss's childhood.
2. Find out and write a report about Gauss's proof regarding regular polygons in his *Disquisitiones Arithmeticae*.
3. Write a short paragraph about Gauss's inventions.
4. Aside from being a superb mathematician, Gauss did some work in the field of astronomy. Report on some of Gauss's discoveries in the field of astronomy.
5. In 1807, a famous French mathematician paid Gauss's involuntary 2,000-franc contribution to the French government. Find out who this famous mathematician was and the circumstances of the payment.
6. Another French mathematician asked the general commanding the French troops to send an officer to see how Gauss was faring during the war. This mathematician had submitted some results in number theory to Gauss under a pen name. Write a report on this incident and try to find the circumstances, the pen name, and the real name of the mathematician.

Chapter 5 Practice Test

1. If the replacement set is the set of integers, solve the following equations:
   (a) $x + 7 = 2$ (b) $x - 4 = 9$
2. If the replacement set is the set of integers, find the solution set for each of the following inequalities:
   (a) $x + 5 > 4$ (b) $2 + x \geq -x - 1$
3. Solve: $2x + 2 = 3x - 2$
4. Solve: $2x + 8 \geq -x - 1$
5. Graph the solution set of each of the following:
   (a) $x - 3 \leq 0$ (b) $-2x + 4 > x + 1$
6. Graph the solution set (if it is not empty) of each of the following:
   (a) $x + 2 \geq 3$ and $x \leq 4$ (b) $x - 3 \geq 1$ and $x \leq 0$
7. Graph the solution set of each of the following:
   (a) $x < 0$ or $x - 2 < 1$ (b) $x + 2 < 3$ or $x - 1 > 2$
8. Solve the equation $|x| = 3$.
9. Graph the solution set of $|x| < 2$.

CONTENTS

Chapter 6   Functions and Graphs   389

Chapter 7   Geometry   467

TOPICS IN
CONTEMPORARY MATHEMATICS

The modern mathematical theory of sets is one of the most remarkable creations of the human mind. Because of the unusual boldness of some of the ideas found in its study, and because of some of the singular methods of proof to which it has given rise, the theory of sets is indescribably fascinating. But above this, the theory has assumed tremendous importance for almost the whole of mathematics.

HOWARD EVES

Who invented set theory, anyway? According to Burton's *History of Mathematics*, "the birth of set theory can be marked by Cantor's paper 'On a Property of the System of all the Real Algebraic Numbers.'" A number of mathematicians had studied finite sets, but Georg Ferdinand Ludwig Philip Cantor was one of the first to study and solve some of the problems in the theory of infinite sets. You can read about Cantor in *The Human Side of Mathematics* as you study sets yourself. We shall start by discussing **finite sets** and see how they can be described and written. Then we discuss **subsets** and the operations that can be performed with them and see how to visualize such operations by using **Venn diagrams** as shown in Section 1.4. We learn how to count the number of elements in a set and use this idea to analyze statistical surveys. We end the chapter with an optional section dealing with **cardinal numbers** and the "indescribably fascinating" **infinite sets.**

Sets

THE HUMAN SIDE OF MATHEMATICS

Georg F. L. P. Cantor made the first successful attempts to answer questions concerning infinite sets. Born in Russia in 1845, Cantor moved to Germany at the age of 11. At 15 he entered the Wiesbaden Gymnasium (a preparatory school), where he developed an abiding interest in mathematics. Cantor continued in mathematics, received his Ph.D. from the University of Berlin in 1867, and ended by making important contributions to some of the most abstract areas of mathematics.

Georg F. L. P. Cantor (1845–1918)

Intuition (male, female, or mathematical) has been greatly overrated. Intuition is the root of all superstition.

E. T. Bell

It was in the papers published between 1874 and 1884 that his most important contributions appeared. These papers attacked the basic questions of infinite sets—questions that concern the very heart of mathematical analysis. The entirely new methods he employed marked him as a creative mathematician of most unusual originality.

Unfortunately, Cantor received almost no recognition during this period of his life. He never attained his goal of a professorship at Berlin. Instead, he spent his entire professional career at the University of Halle, and did not become a full professor until 1879.

As often happens with original ideas, Cantor's work was rewarded by ridicule from many of his most famous contemporaries. Among these critics was the prominent mathematician Leopold Kronecker, who had been one of Cantor's instructors at the University of Berlin. As a result of the lack of recognition and acceptance of his work, Cantor suffered a series of breakdowns and eventually died in a mental institution in 1918.

It was only in the later years of his life that Cantor's ideas gained a measure of recognition from his colleagues. The importance of his contribution lay in his perception of the significance of the one-to-one correspondence principle and its logical consequences. Today, we know that much of the foundation of mathematics rests directly on Cantor's work.

Looking Ahead: In this chapter we will look at the ideas of sets and infinite sets, an area that was the main focus of Cantor's research and writings.

1.1   SETS

The idea of a **set** is familiar in everyday life. Do you have a **set** of dishes, a **set** of tools, or a **set** of books? Each of these sets is regarded as a unit.

Sets, however, need not consist of physical objects; they may well consist of abstract ideas. For instance, the *Ten Commandments* is a **set** of moral laws. The *Constitution* is the basic **set** of laws of the United States.

A. *Well-Defined Sets and Notation*

We study sets in this book not only because much of elementary mathematics can be based on this concept, but also because many mathematical ideas can be stated most simply in the language of sets.

Definition 1.1

> A **set** is a well-defined **collection** of objects called **elements**, or **members**, of the set.

The main characteristic of a set in mathematics is that it is **well defined.** This means that given any object, it must be clear whether that object is a member of the set. Thus, if we consider the set of even whole numbers, we know that every even whole number, such as 0, 2, 4, 6, etc., is an element of this set, but nothing else is. Thus, the set of even whole numbers is well defined. On the other hand, the set of funny comic sections in the daily newspaper is *not* well defined, because what one person thinks is funny may not agree with what someone else thinks is funny.

EXAMPLE 1   Which of the following descriptions define sets?

(a) Interesting numbers   (b) Multiples of 2
(c) Good writers   (d) Current directors of General Motors
(e) Numbers that can be substituted for x so that $x + 4 = 5$

Solution   Descriptions (b), (d), and (e) are well-defined. Descriptions (a) and (c) are *not* well defined, because people do not agree on what is "interesting" and what is "good." ∎

We use capital letters, such as A, B, C, X, Y, and Z, to denote sets, and lowercase letters, such as a, b, c, x, y, and z, to denote the elements of the set. It is customary, when practical, to list the elements of a set in braces and to separate these elements by commas. Thus, $A = \{1, 2, 3, 4\}$ means that "A is the set consisting of the elements 1, 2, 3, and 4." To indicate the fact that "4 is an element of the set A" or "4 is in A," we write $4 \in A$ (read "4 is an element of the set A"). To indicate that 6 is not an element of A, we write $6 \notin A$.

EXAMPLE 2   Let $X = \{$Eva, Mida, Jack, Janice$\}$. Which of the following are correct statements?

(a) Mida $\in X$ (b) Jack $\notin X$
(c) Janice $\in \{$Eva, Mida, Jack, Janice$\}$
(d) $E \in X$ (e) $X \in X$

Solution   Statements (a) and (c) are the only correct ones. ∎

B. *Describing Sets*

Sets may be defined in three ways:

1. By giving a **verbal description** of the set
2. By **listing** the elements of the set
3. By using **set-builder notation**

Peanuts. Reprinted by permission of UFS, Inc.

Description	List
The set of counting numbers less than 5	{1, 2, 3, 4}
The set of natural Earth satellites	{Moon}
The set of counting numbers	{1, 2, 3, . . .}.

The three dots, called an **ellipsis,** mean that the list goes on in the same pattern without end.

The set of odd counting numbers less than 15	{1, 3, 5, . . . , 13}

The three dots mean the odd numbers after 5 and before 13 are in the set but not listed.

The set of whole numbers less than or equal to 3.	{0, 1, 2, 3}

In set-builder notation, we use a defining property to describe the set. A vertical bar (|) is used to mean "such that." Thus, the preceding sets can be written as follows:

$\{x \mid x \text{ is a counting number less than 5}\}$	Read, "The set of all elements x, such that x is a counting number less than 5."
$\{x \mid x \text{ is a natural Earth satellite}\}$	Read, "The set of all elements x, such that x is a natural Earth satellite."
$\{x \mid x \text{ is a counting number}\}$	Read, "The set of all elements x, such that x is a counting number."
$\{x \mid x \text{ is an odd counting number less than 15}\}$	Read, "The set of all elements x, such that x is an odd counting number less than 15."
$\{x \mid x \text{ is a whole number less than or equal to 3}\}$	Read, "The set of all elements x, such that x is a whole number less than or equal to 3."

EXAMPLE 3   Write a verbal description for the following sets:

(a) {a, b, c, . . . , z} (b) {1, 3, 5, . . .} (c) {3, 6, 9, . . . , 27}

Solution   (a) The set of letters in the English alphabet
(b) The set of odd counting numbers
(c) The set of counting numbers that are multiples of 3 and less than or equal to 27. ∎

EXAMPLE 4   Write the following sets using the listing method and using set-builder notation:

(a) The set of digits in the number 1896
(b) The set of odd counting numbers greater than 6
(c) The set of counting numbers greater than 0 and less than 1
(d) The set of counting numbers that are multiples of 4

Solution	List	Set-Builder Notation
(a)	$\{1, 8, 9, 6\}$	$\{x \mid x$ is a digit in the number 1896$\}$
(b)	$\{7, 9, 11, \ldots\}$	$\{x \mid x$ is an odd counting number and $x > 6\}$ The symbol ">" means "greater than."
(c)	$\{\quad\}$	$\{x \mid x$ is a counting number and $0 < x < 1\}$ The symbol "<" means "less than" and $0 < x < 1$ can be read as "x is between 0 and 1."
(d)	$\{4, 8, 12, \ldots\}$	$\{x \mid x$ is a counting number that is a multiple of 4$\}$

A set with no elements, as in part (c) of Example 4, will be denoted by the symbol $\{\quad\}$ or $\emptyset$.

Definition 1.2   The symbol $\{\quad\}$ or $\emptyset$ represents the **empty**, or **null**, set.

EXAMPLE 5   Write the following sets using the listing method:

(a) $\{x \mid x$ is a counting number less than 10 and x is divisible by 4$\}$.
(b) $\{x \mid x$ is a counting number between 8 and 13 and x is divisible by 7$\}$.

Solution   (a) The counting numbers less than 10 that are divisible by 4 are 4 and 8. Hence, the required set is $\{4, 8\}$.
(b) None of the numbers between 8 and 13 is divisible by 7. Thus, the required set is empty and the answer may be written as $\{\quad\}$ or as $\emptyset$.

Note: It would *not* be correct to write $\{\emptyset\}$ for the answer to part *b*, because the set $\{\emptyset\}$ is not empty; it contains the element $\emptyset$.

C. *Equality of Sets*

Clearly, the order in which the elements of a set are listed does not affect membership in the set. Thus, if we are asked to write the set of digits in the year in which Columbus discovered America, we may write $\{1, 4, 9, 2\}$.

Someone else may write {1, 2, 4, 9}. Both are correct! Thus, we can see that {1, 4, 9, 2} = {1, 2, 4, 9}. Similarly, {a, b, c, d, e} = {e, d, c, b, a}.

Definition 1.3 ————

> In general, two sets are **equal,** denoted by $A = B$, if they have the same members (not necessarily listed in the same order).

For example, {1, 3, 2} = {1, 2, 3} and {20, $\frac{1}{2}$} = {$\frac{1}{2}$, 20}.

Notice also that repeated listings do not affect membership. For example, the set of digits in the year in which the *Declaration of Independence* was signed is {1, 7, 7, 6}. This set also may be written as {1, 6, 7}. Therefore, {1, 7, 7, 6} = {1, 6, 7}. In the same way, {a, a, b, b, c, c} = {a, b, c}, because the two sets have the same elements. By convention, we do not list an element more than once.

Exercise 1.1 —————————————————————————————

A. In problems 1–8, state whether the given set is well defined.

   1. The set of grouchy people
   2. The set of good tennis players in the United States
   3. The set of retired baseball players with a lifetime batting average of .400 or better
   4. The set of students taking mathematics courses at Yale University at the present moment
   5. $\{x \mid x$ is an odd counting number$\}$
   6. $\{x \mid x$ is an even counting number$\}$
   7. $\{x \mid x$ is a good college course$\}$
   8. $\{x \mid x$ is a bad instructor$\}$
   9. Let A = {Desi, Gidget, Jane, Dora}. Which of the following are correct statements?

     (a) $D \in A$ (b) Desi $\in A$
     (c) $A \in$ Jane   (d) $D \notin A$
     (e) Jane $\notin A$

In problems 10–14, let X = {a, b, x, y}. Fill the blank with $\in$ or $\notin$ to make the statement correct.

  10. a ——— X 11. x ——— X
  12. X ——— X 13. A ——— X
  14. {*bay*} ——— X

B. In problems 15–24, write a verbal description for the given set.

  15. {a, z}   16. {m, a, n}
  17. {Adam, Eve}   18. {Christopher Columbus}

19. $\{7, 2, 6, 3, 5, 4, 1\}$

20. $\{2, 6, 12, 20, 30\}$

21. $\{1, 3, 5, \ldots, 51\}$

22. $\{3, 6, 9, 12, \ldots, 36\}$

23. $\{1, 4, 7, 10, \ldots, 25\}$

24. $\{1, 6, 11, \ldots, 31\}$

The table of toxic substances found in the fat tissue of humans was compiled by the National Adipose Tissue Survey of the Public Health Service and will be used in problems 25 and 26.

Compound	Possible Sources of Exposure	Frequency in Test Subjects
Chloroform	Drinking water	76%
Dioxin	Wood treatment, herbicides, auto exhaust	100%
Heptachlor	Termite control	67%
Toluene	Gasoline	91%
Xylene	Gasoline, paints	100%

25. Which set of compounds was found in everybody's tissue?

26. Which set of compounds was found in less than 90% of the people?

In problems 27–36, list the elements in the given set.

27. $\{x \mid x$ is a counting number less than 8$\}$

28. $\{x \mid x$ is a counting number less than 2$\}$

29. $\{n \mid n$ is a whole number less than $7\frac{1}{2}\}$

30. $\{n \mid n$ is a whole number less than $8\frac{1}{4}\}$

31. $\{x \mid x$ is a counting number between 3 and 8$\}$

32. $\{x \mid x$ is a counting number between 2 and 7$\}$

33. $\{n \mid n$ is a counting number between 6 and 7$\}$

34. $\{n \mid n$ is a counting number between 8 and 10$\}$

35. $\{x \mid x$ is a counting number greater than 3$\}$

36. $\{x \mid x$ is a counting number greater than 0$\}$

In problems 37–44, a set is specified by certain conditions. List the elements in the set. In each of these problems, n is a counting number — that is, $n \in \{1, 2, 3, \ldots\}$.

37. $\{x \mid x = 5n\}$

38. $\{n \mid 3 < n < 7\}$

39. $\{n \mid n^2 < 0\}$

40. $\{x \mid x = n^2 \text{ and } 1 \leq n \leq 4\}$ (The symbol "$\leq$" means "less than or equal to.")

41. $\{n \mid n^3 < 15\}$

42. $\{n \mid 4 < n^2 < 40\}$

43. $\{n \mid 1 < n < 10, n \text{ is an even number}\}$

44. $\{x \mid x = 2n - 1\}$

Name	Volume	High	Low	Last	Chg.
WangB	1,593,900	$11\frac{5}{8}$	$10\frac{1}{2}$	$11\frac{1}{4}$	. . . .
Gull	1,493,800	$25\frac{1}{2}$	12	15	−10
WhrEnf	1,254,200	$13\frac{3}{4}$	13	$13\frac{5}{8}$	$+2\frac{1}{2}$
HomeSh	1,152,200	$6\frac{1}{8}$	$5\frac{1}{4}$	$5\frac{1}{2}$	$-\frac{3}{8}$
EchBg s	928,300	24	$22\frac{1}{2}$	$23\frac{3}{4}$	$+1\frac{1}{4}$
FAusPr	904,000	$8\frac{1}{2}$	$7\frac{1}{2}$	$7\frac{5}{8}$	$-\frac{1}{8}$
LorTel	896,500	$9\frac{3}{4}$	$8\frac{3}{8}$	$9\frac{1}{4}$	$+\frac{3}{8}$
ENSCO	778,800	$3\frac{1}{8}$	$2\frac{1}{2}$	$3\frac{1}{8}$	$+\frac{1}{2}$
WDigitl	776,100	$17\frac{1}{4}$	$15\frac{7}{8}$	$16\frac{3}{4}$	+1
TexAir	767,100	$12\frac{3}{8}$	$11\frac{1}{4}$	$11\frac{3}{4}$	$-\frac{1}{2}$

This listing gives the sales volume; high, low, and closing price; and net change in one week of ten stocks traded on the American Stock Exchange (AMEX) for more than $1.

Problems 45–54 refer to the stock listing in the margin. Use the information in this list of stocks for each of these problems.

List the elements in the following sets:

45. Stocks whose sales volume was greater than 1,300,000
46. Stocks whose sales volume was greater than 1,000,000
47. Stocks whose sales volume was less than 800,000
48. Stocks whose price went up more than $\frac{1}{2}$ point
49. Stocks that increased in price by more than 1 point
50. Stocks that increased in price by exactly $\frac{1}{2}$ point

For problems 51–54, study the "Last Chg." column and use set-builder notation to describe the following sets:

51. {HomeSh, FAusPr, LorTel, ENSCO}
52. {EchBg, WDigitl}
53. {EchBg}
54. {ENSCO}

In problems 55–58 list the elements in the given set:

55. The different letters in the word MISSISSIPPI
56. The planets of our solar system
57. All positive fractions having 1 for a numerator and a counting number as denominator
58. The U.S. astronauts who have landed on the planet Pluto
59. Which of the sets in problems 55–58 are empty?

C. In problems 60–63 state whether the sets A and B are equal:

60. $A = \{2n + 1 \mid n \text{ is a counting number}\}$,
    $B = \{2n - 1 \mid n \text{ is a counting number}\}$
61. $A = \{4n \mid n \text{ is a counting number}\}$,
    $B = \{2n \mid n \text{ is a counting number}\}$
62. $A = \{1, 1, 2, 2, 3\}$, $B = \{1, 2, 3\}$
63. $A = \{x \mid x \text{ is a cow that has jumped over the moon}\}$,
    $B = \{x \mid x \text{ is an astronaut who has landed on Pluto}\}$
64. Let $A = \{5\}$, $B = \{f, i, v, e\}$, $C = \{e, f, v, i\}$, and D be the set of letters in the word *repeat*. Find:
    (a) The set containing 5 elements
    (b) The set equal to B
    (c) The set of letters in the word *five*
65. Let $A = \{1, 2, 3, 4\}$, $B = \{4, 3, 2, 1\}$, and $C = \{4, 3, 2, 1, 0\}$. Fill in the blanks with "=" or "≠" to make a true statement:
    (a) A ____ B (b) A ____ C (c) B ____ C

66. Let $A = \{x \mid x$ is a counting number between 4 and 5$\}$, $B = \emptyset$, and $C = \{\emptyset\}$. Fill in the blanks with "$=$" or "$\neq$" to make a true statement:
    (a) A ____ B (b) A ____ C (c) B ____ C

67. Let A be the set of astronauts who have landed on Pluto, $B = \{0\}$, C be the empty set, and $D = \{\emptyset\}$. Write *true* or *false* for each of the following:
    (a) $A = B$ (b) $A = C$ (c) $B = C$
    (d) $A = D$ (e) $B = D$ (f) $C = D$

In Other Words

68. Find the definition for the word *set* in a dictionary. Does the definition contain the word *collection* or the word *thing*? Now, find the definitions of the words *collection* and *thing*. Why do you think it is almost impossible to give a formal definition for the word *set*?

69. Is "the set of all good students in your class" well defined? Why or why not? If not well defined, can you make it well defined?

70. Can you explain why:
    (a) $\emptyset \notin \emptyset$ (b) $\emptyset \in \{\emptyset\}$
    (c) $\emptyset \neq \{0\}$ (d) $\emptyset = \{\ \ \}$

Using Your Knowledge

Gepetto Scissore, a barber in the small town of Sevilla, who was naturally called the Barber of Sevilla, decided that as a public service he would shave all those men and only those men of the village who did not shave themselves. Let $S = \{p \mid p$ is a man of the village who shaves himself$\}$ and $D = \{p \mid p$ is a man of the village who does not shave himself$\}$.

71. If g represents Gepetto:
    (a) Is $g \in S$?   (b) Is $g \in D$?

*The preceding problem is a popularization of the **Russell paradox,** named after its discoverer, Bertrand Russell. In studying sets, it seems that one can classify sets as those that are members of themselves and those that are not members of themselves. Suppose that we consider the two sets of sets:*

$$M = \{X \mid X \in X, X \text{ is a set}\} \quad and \quad N = \{X \mid X \notin X, X \text{ is a set}\}.$$

72. Answer the following questions:
    (a) Is $N \in M$?   (b) Is $N \in N$?

Think about the consequences of your answers!

Discovery

You should find the following paradox amusing, puzzling, and perhaps even thought-provoking: Let us define a **self-descriptive word** *to be a word that makes good sense when put into both blanks of the sentence, "_____ is a(n) _____ word." Two simple examples of self-descriptive words are "English" and "short." Just try them out!*

Now define a **non-self-descriptive word** *to be a word that is not self-descriptive. Most words will fit into this category. Try it out again. Now consider the following questions:*

73. Let *S* be the set of self-descriptive words, and let *S'* be the set of non-self-descriptive words. How would you classify the word *non-self-descriptive*? Is it an element of *S*? Or is it an element of *S'*? You should get into difficulty no matter how you answer these questions. Think about it!

74. Let $A = \{1, 2, 3, \ldots\}$ and $B = \{\ \}$. Then proceed as follows:

   (a) Take the numbers 1 and 2 from *A* and place them in *B*.
   (b) At $\frac{1}{2}$ hr before noon, remove the largest number, 2, from *B* so that the number 1 remains.
   (c) Take the numbers 3 and 4 from *A* and place them in *B*.
   (d) At $\frac{1}{4}$ hr before noon, remove the largest number, 4, from *B* so that 1 and 3 remain.
   (e) Take the numbers 5 and 6 from *A* and place them in *B*.
   (f) At $\frac{1}{8}$ hr before noon, remove the largest number, 6, from *B* so that 1, 3, and 5 remain.

   If this procedure is continued, what will *B* consist of at noon?

75. In problem 74, amend steps (b), (d), and (f) by replacing "largest number" with "smallest number." Note that at $\frac{1}{2}$ hr before noon, the smallest number left in *B* is 2; at $\frac{1}{4} = \left(\frac{1}{2}\right)^2$ hr before noon, the smallest number left in *B* is 3; at $\frac{1}{8} = \left(\frac{1}{2}\right)^3$ hr before noon, the smallest number left in *B* is 4; and so on. Can you discover what the smallest number left in *B* is at $\left(\frac{1}{2}\right)^n$ hr before noon?

1.2   SUBSETS: A PROBLEM-SOLVING TOOL

GETTING STARTED

DISPATCHING EMERGENCY VEHICLES

Sets and subsets are used in many ways. For example, suppose that you are an anthropologist classifying all races of humankind. Can you use sets and subsets? We discuss how to do this in problems 41–46 of the Using Your Knowledge section in Exercise 1.2. Here is another application. If you are a police or sheriff's dispatcher with four cars, *a*, *b*, *c*, and *d*, available for assignment, what are your options in responding to an assistance call?

The guidelines used by the Tampa Sheriff's Department are:

Domestic disturbance	Send one car
Domestic disturbance, armed person	Send two cars
Disturbance in a public place (like a bar)	Send three cars
Disturbance with weapon or hostage situation	Send four cars

Keep in mind that other factors such as location, time, and availability enter into the picture. Moreover, if all units are busy and the call is of no immediate priority, you can opt to send no cars at this time. We solve this problem in the text and present some similar ones for you in Exercise 1.2, problems 25–34.

Sometimes, all the elements of a set A are also elements of another set B. For example, if A is the set of all students in your class, and B is the set of all students in your school, every element of A is also in B (because every student in your class is a student in your school). In such cases, we say that the set A is a **subset** of the set B. We denote this by writing $A \subseteq B$ (read, "A is a subset of B").

Definition 1.4

> The set A is a **subset** of B (denoted by $A \subseteq B$) if every element of A is also an element of B.

Thus, if $A = \{a, b\}$, $B = \{a, b, c\}$, and $C = \{b\}$, then $A \subseteq B$, $C \subseteq A$, $C \subseteq B$, and $A \subseteq A$.

It is a consequence of the definition of a subset that $A = B$ when both $A \subseteq B$ and $B \subseteq A$. Furthermore, for any set A, since every element of A is an element of A, we have $A \subseteq A$.

The definition of a subset may be restated in the following form:

Definition 1.5

> The set A is a **subset** of B if there is no element of A that is not an element of B.

From this it follows that $\emptyset \subseteq A$, because there is no element of $\emptyset$ that is not in A. This means that **the empty set is a subset of every set.**

A set A is said to be a **proper subset** of B, denoted by $A \subset B$, if A is a subset of B and $A \neq B$ (A is not equal to B). In other words, $A \subset B$ means that all elements of A are also in B, but B contains at least one element that is not in A. For example, if $B = \{1, 2\}$, the proper subsets of B are Ø, $\{1\}$, and $\{2\}$, but the set $\{1, 2\}$ itself is not a *proper* subset of B.

A. *Finding Subsets*

In everyday discussions, we are usually aware of the "universe of discourse," that is, the set of all things we are talking about. In dealing with sets, the universe of discourse is called the **universal set.**

Definition 1.6   The **universal set** $\mathcal{U}$ is the set of all elements under discussion.

Thus, if we agree to discuss the letters in the English alphabet, then $\mathcal{U} = \{a, b, c, \ldots, z\}$ is our universal set. On the other hand, if we are to discuss counting numbers, our universal set is $\mathcal{U} = \{1, 2, 3, \ldots\}$.

EXAMPLE 1   Find all the subsets of the set $\mathcal{U} = \{a, b, c\}$.

Solution   We have to form subsets of the set $\mathcal{U}$ by assigning some, none, or all of the elements of $\mathcal{U}$ to these subsets. We organize the work as follows:

Form all the subsets with no elements:	Ø.
Form all the subsets with 1 element:	$\{a\}, \{b\}, \{c\}$.
Form all the subsets with 2 elements:	$\{a, b\}, \{a, c\}, \{b, c\}$.
Form all the subsets with 3 elements:	$\{a, b, c\}$.

The set in this example has 3 elements and $2^3 = 2 \times 2 \times 2 = 8$ subsets. Similarly, a set such as $\{a, b\}$, containing 2 elements, has $2^2 = 2 \times 2 = 4$ subsets, namely, Ø, $\{a\}$, $\{b\}$, and $\{a, b\}$. The Discovery section of Exercise 1.5 shows another way of constructing all the subsets of a given set. It also shows that:

A set of n elements has 2^n subsets.

EXAMPLE 2   If $A = \{a_1, a_2, \ldots, a_8\}$, how many subsets does A have?

Solution   Because the set A has 8 elements, A has $2^8 = 256$ subsets.

EXAMPLE 3   List all the proper subsets of the set $\mathcal{U} = \{1, 2, 3\}$.

Solution   The proper subsets are Ø, $\{1\}$, $\{2\}$, $\{3\}$, $\{1, 2\}$, $\{1, 3\}$, and $\{2, 3\}$. By our definition of proper subsets, it is incorrect to include $\{1, 2, 3\}$ among the proper subsets of $\mathcal{U}$. Thus, a set with n elements has $2^n - 1$ proper subsets.

B. *Subsets and Problem Solving*

The ideas in the preceding examples can be applied to many practical problems. You have heard the slogans "Have it your way" and "We do it all for you." Now, suppose that you have a small hamburger place and you want to advertise that you have a great variety of burgers. If you have three condiments (catsup, mustard, and onions), how many different types of hamburgers can you prepare? (By the way, Wendy's did something similar some time ago. See problem 33 of Exercise 1.2.)

First, we need a procedure to solve **any** word problem. Here is our 5-step suggestion:

1. **R**ead the problem. Not once or twice but until you understand it.

2. **S**elect the unknown; that is, find out what the problem asks for.

3. **T**hink of a plan to solve the problem.

4. **U**se the techniques you are studying to carry out the plan.

5. **V**erify the answer.

Look at the first letter in each sentence. To help you remember the steps, we call it the **RSTUV** procedure. At the end of this section, we have additional tips on how to use this procedure.

Problem solving will be presented in a two-column format. Cover the answers in the right column (a 3-by-5 index card will do) and write *your own answers* so you can practice. After that, uncover the answers and check if you are right. We will then give you another example to try and provide you with its solution.

Problem Solving:	Finding Subsets
	List the different types of hamburgers that can be prepared if catsup (c), mustard (m), and onions (o) are available as condiments.
1. Read the problem.	Some problems must be read two or three times. Make sure you understand the problem before you attempt a solution.
2. Select the unknown.	We are looking for the *different* types of hamburgers that can be prepared if catsup, mustard, and onions are available.
3. Think of a plan. What is given? What do we do?	We are given a universal set $\mathcal{U} = \{c, m, o\}$ Find all the subsets of $\mathcal{U}$.

4. Use your knowledge to carry out the plan.

Find:

Subsets of 0 elements   Ø (1 hamburger with no condiments)

Subsets of 1 element   {c}, {m}, {o}. There are 3 hamburgers with only one condiment.

Subsets of 2 elements.   {c, m}, {c, o}, {m, o}. There are 3 hamburgers with 2 condiments.

Subsets of 3 element   {c, m, o}. One hamburger all the way.

5. Verify the answer.

The set $\mathcal{U} = \{c, m, o\}$ has 3 elements and $2^3 = 8$ different subsets, and we have found them all!

TRY EXAMPLE 4 NOW   Cover the solution, write your own, and then check your work.

___

EXAMPLE 4   A police dispatcher has 4 patrol cars a, b, c, and d available. List all the options for handling a particular call.

Solution

Send no cars: Ø

Send 1 car: {a}, {b}, {c}, {d}

Send 2 cars: {a, b}, {a, c}, {a, d}, {b, c}, {b, d}, {c, d}

Send 3 cars: {a, b, c}, {a, c, d}, {a, b, d}, {b, c, d}

Send 4 cars: {a, b, c, d}.

The total number of choices is $2^4 = 16$, and we included all of them.   ■

EXAMPLE 5   The Taste-T Noodle Company has 6 employees. The payroll department classifies these employees as follows:

P: Part-time employees who work 20 hr or less per week

F: Full-time employees who work more than 20 hr per week

H_5:   Employees paid at the rate of $5 per hour

H_6:   Employees paid at the rate of $6 per hour

O: Employees working over 40 hr per week and receiving a time-and-a-half rate for all hours worked over 40 per week

List the elements in the sets P, F, H_5, H_6, O, and $\mathcal{U}$. Use the employee numbers as the set elements and the data in the chart at the top of page 17.

Solution

$P = \{03, 06\}$

$F = \{01, 02, 04, 05\}$

$H_5 = \{02, 03, 04\}$

$H_6 = \{01, 05, 06\}$

$O = \{02, 05\}$

$\mathcal{U} = \{01, 02, 03, 04, 05, 06\}$ ■

WEEK ENDING ————————→

	NAME	EMPL. NO.	Status	Exemptions	HOURS							TOTAL HOURS	RATE	EARNINGS		
					SUN.	MON.	TUES.	WED.	THURS.	FRI.	SAT.			REGULAR	OVERTIME	OTHER
1	Amy Able	01	S	1		7	7	7	7	7	0	35	$6.00	$210 00		
2	Bernie Baker	02	M	2		8	8	8	8	8	4	44	$5.00	$200 00	$30 00	
3	Cindy Chan	03	M	2		0	0	0	0	0	8	8	$5.00	$40 00		
4	Donaldo Delleni	04	S	1		8	0	8	0	8	0	24	$5.00	$120 00		
5	Emilio Estéves	05	M	3		8	8	8	8	8	2	42	$6.00	$240 00	$18 00	
6	Felicia Fellini	06	S	1		0	4	4	4	4	0	16	$6.00	$96 00		
7																
8																
9		TOTALS														

Problem Solving:

Hints and Tips

Our problem solving procedure **(RSTUV)** contains 5 steps. The steps are given in the left column with hints and tips in the right.

1. Read the problem.

Mathematics is a language. As such you have to learn how to read it. You may not understand or even get through reading the problem the first time. Read it again and as you do, pay attention to "key" words or instructions such as *compute, draw, write, construct, make, show, identify, state, simplify, solve,* and *graph.* (Can you think of others?)

2. Select the unknown.

How can you answer a question if you do not know what the question is? One good way to look for the unknown is to look for the question mark "?" and read the material to its left. Try to determine what is given and what is missing.

3. Think of a plan.

Problem solving requires many skills and strategies. Some of them are: *look for a pattern, examine a related problem, make tables, pictures, diagrams, write an equation, work backwards,* and *make a guess.*

4. Use the techniques you are studying to carry out the plan.

If you are studying a mathematical technique, it is almost certain that you will have to use it in solving the given problem. Look for specific procedures that may be given to solve certain problems.

5. Verify the answer.

Look back and check the results of the original problem. Is the answer reasonable? Can you find it some other way?

Exercise 1.2 _____

A. In problems 1–6, list all the subsets and indicate which are proper subsets of the given set.

   1. $\mathcal{U} = \{a, b\}$ 2. $\mathcal{U} = \{1, 2, 3\}$
   3. $\mathcal{U} = \{1, 2, 3, 4\}$ 4. $\mathcal{U} = \{\emptyset\}$
   5. $\{1, 2\}$ 6. $\{x, y, z\}$
   7. How many subsets does the set $A = \{a, b, c, d\}$ have?
   8. How many proper subsets does the set $\{1, 2, 3, 4\}$ have?
   9. If $A = \{\frac{1}{1}, \frac{1}{2}, \frac{1}{3}, \ldots, \frac{1}{10}\}$, how many subsets does A have?
  10. How many proper subsets does the set A of problem 7 have?
  11. A set has 32 subsets. How many elements are there in this set?
  12. A set has 31 proper subsets. How many elements are there in the set?
  13. A set has 64 subsets. How many elements are there in the set?
  14. A set has 63 proper subsets. How many elements are there in the set?
  15. Is $\emptyset$ a subset of $\emptyset$? Explain.
  16. Is $\emptyset$ a proper subset of $\emptyset$? Explain.
  17. If A is the set of numbers that are divisible by 2 and B is the set of numbers that are divisible by 4, is $A \subseteq B$? Is $B \subseteq A$?
  18. Give an example of a set P and a set Q such that $P \in Q$ and $P \subseteq Q$.

In problems 19–24, fill in the blanks with $\in$, $\notin$, $\subset$, or $\not\subset$ so that the result is a correct statement.

  19. $\{2, 3\}$ _____ $\{3, 5, 2\}$
  20. 5 _____ $\{2, 4\}$
  21. $\{5\}$ _____ $\{2, 4\}$
  22. 31 _____ $\{1, 3, 5, \ldots\}$
  23. $\{2, 4, 6, \ldots\}$ _____ $\{1, 2, 3, \ldots\}$
  24. $\{1, 3, 5, \ldots\}$ _____ $\{1, 3, 5\}$

B. 25. The instructions on a vending machine say that you can use any combination of nickels, dimes, and quarters. If you have three coins—a nickel, a dime, and a quarter—how many different sums of money can you select? Use set notation to list all the choices you have. How many choices are there if you must use at least one coin with each choice?

    26. If you have five coins—a penny, a nickel, a dime, a quarter, and a half-dollar—how many different sums of money can you select? If you must use at least one coin, how many different sums can you select?

Suppose that television station WICU has 3 commercials available, c_1, c_2, and c_3.

27. How many choices are available if the station director may choose to have none, 1, 2, or 3 different commercials run, and is not concerned with the order in which they are run? [*Hint:* How many subsets does the set $\{c_1, c_2, c_3\}$ have?]

28. How many choices are available if the director decides to run either none or else all of the commercials?

29. How many choices are available if the director decides to have exactly 1 commercial?

30. How many choices are available if the director decides to run exactly 2 commercials?

31. Gino's Pizza offers the following set of toppings: $(C, M, O, P, S\}$, where C, M, O, P, and S mean Cheese, Mushrooms, Onions, Pepperoni, and Sausage. How many types of pizza can you order with:
    (a) One topping?
    (b) Two toppings?
    (c) Three toppings?

32. Referring to problem 31, how many different kinds of pizza with at least one topping can you order?

33. Some time ago, Wendy's Hamburger claimed that they could prepare your hamburger 256 ways. How many condiments do you need in order to be able to prepare 256 different hamburgers?

34. If Gino's Pizza decides to top Wendy's claim and advertises that they have 500 different types of pizza, what is the minimum number of toppings they should carry?

In Other Words

Can you explain why for any non-empty set A and universal set $\mathcal{U}$:

35. $A \subseteq A$

36. $A \not\subseteq A$

37. $\emptyset \subset A$

38. $\emptyset \subseteq A$

39. $A \subset \mathcal{U}$

40. Part 3 of the **R S T U V** procedure calls for you to **Think** of a plan of action to solve the problem. Here are some strategies you can include in your plan: Look for patterns, make a picture. Can you write three more strategies you think may help in problem solving?

Using Your Knowledge

The idea of a universal set and its subsets can be used in many applications. For example, the adjacent figure shows the human species as the universal set. As you can see from the diagram, there are 3 major racial groups: Caucasian (C), Mongoloid (M), and Negroid (N).

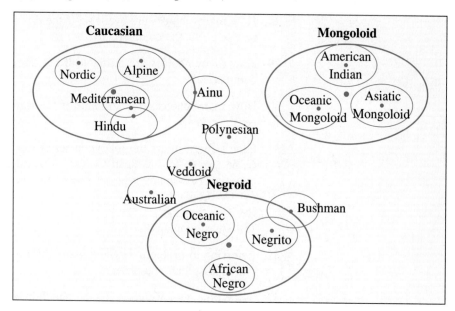

41. Name all the subraces (subsets) of the Caucasian race.
42. Name all the subraces (subsets) of the Mongoloid race.
43. Name all the subraces (subsets) of the Negroid race.
44. Name the 3 subraces (subsets) that do not belong to any of the 3 major races.
45. Name the subsets of the Caucasian race that have some members in common.
46. Name the subsets of the Negroid race that have some members in common.

Discovery

The empty set has only one subset (itself). A 1-element set has two subsets, the empty set and the 1-element set itself. As we saw in this section, a 2-element set has four subsets, and a 3-element set has eight subsets. In the table, the column under n shows the number of elements in the given set, the row labeled k gives the number of elements in the subset, and the last column, t, shows the total number of subsets for a given n-element set.

k \\ n	0	1	2	3	4	5	t
0	1						$1 = 2^0$
1	1	1					$2 = 2^1$
2	1	2	1				$4 = 2^2$
3	1		3	1			$8 = 2^3$
4	1						
5							

The other entries in the body of the table show the number of k-element subsets for a given n-element set. For example, to find the number of 2-element subsets for a given 3-element set, we go down the column under n to the number 3 and then across until we are under the entry k = 2, where we read 3. This tells us that a 3-element set has three 2-element subsets.

47. Fill in the missing items in the table.

48. It is possible to construct each row (after the first) of the table from the preceding row. For example, to go from the row n = 2 to the row n = 3, imagine that you have a set of 2 elements {a, b}. You know that this gives one empty subset, two 1-element subsets, and one 2-element subset: Ø, {a}, {b}, {a, b}. Now let us add another element, c, to the given set to form a 3-element set, {a, b, c}. How can we form the 2-element subsets of the new set from the subsets of the old set? The answer is that we can use the old 2-element subset {a, b} as one of the required subsets, and we can adjoin the new element, c, to each of the old 1-element subsets, {a} and {b}, to form the required subsets {a, c} and {b, c}. The three subsets obtained in this way are all the 2-element subsets of the new 3-element given set. Thus, we see that the number of 2-element subsets of a 3-element given set is the sum of the number of 1-element subsets and the number of 2-element subsets of a 2-element given set. Can you discover how this idea works in general so that you can build up the row n = 4 from the row n = 3?

49. Suppose that the symbol $\binom{n}{k}$ stands for the number of k-element subsets of an n-element given set. For instance, $\binom{3}{2}$ stands for the number of 2-element subsets of a 3-element given set. Can you discover a formula for $\binom{n+1}{k}$ in terms of the symbols for an n-element given set? [*Hint:* In problem 48, we found that $\binom{3}{2} = \binom{2}{1} + \binom{2}{2}$.]

50. Can you now discover how many 3-element subsets a 6-element given set has?

*The triangular array of numbers starting with the column under 0 in the table given above is known as **Pascal's triangle** in honor of Blaise Pascal (1623–1662), although we know now that the Chinese used it centuries before Pascal. This triangle is usually arranged as shown in the figure in the margin. Compare the entries in the table with those in the figure.*

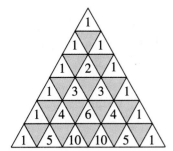

Pascal's triangle

Computer Corner

*We have shown you how to find all the subsets of a set of 2 or 3 elements. But can you find all the subsets of a set with 5 elements? A computer can! The power set program on page A2 of the appendix Programs in BASIC will find the 32 subsets in no time at all. The set consisting of all the subsets of a given set is called the **power set** of the original set.*

1. Use this program to check problems 1–7 in Exercise 1.2.

1.3   SET OPERATIONS

It is often important to ascertain which elements two given sets have in common. For example, the sets of symptoms exhibited by patients with too little sugar in the blood (hypoglycemia) or too much sugar in the blood (hyperglycemia) are as given in Table 1.1.

Table 1.1

Too Little Sugar in the Blood	Too Much Sugar in the Blood
Nausea (n)	Headache (h)
Visual disturbances (v)	Stomach cramps (s)
Trembling (t)	Nausea (n)
Headache (h)	Rapid breathing (r)

A. Intersections and Unions

We can clearly see that the set of symptoms *common* to both sets listed in Table 1.1 is $\{n, h\}$. The set $\{n, h\}$ is called the **intersection** of the two given sets.

Definition 1.7

If A and B are sets, the **intersection** of A and B, denoted by $A \cap B$ (read, "A intersection B"), is the set of all elements that are common to both A and B. That is,

$$A \cap B = \{x \mid x \in A \text{ and } x \in B\}$$

Thus, if $A = \{a, b, c, d\}$ and $B = \{b, d, e\}$, then $A \cap B = \{b, d\}$.

If we list all the symptoms mentioned in Table 1.1, we then obtain the set $\{n, v, t, h, s, r\}$. This set is called the **union** of the two given sets.

Definition 1.8

> If A and B are sets, the **union** of A and B, denoted by $A \cup B$ (read, "A union B"), is the set of all elements that are either in A or in B or in both A and B. That is,
>
> $$A \cup B = \{x \mid x \in A \text{ or } x \in B\}$$

Note that we use the **inclusive or,** that is, $x \in A$, $x \in B$, or x may be in both A and B.

Hence, if $A = \{1, 3, 4, 6\}$ and $B = \{3, 6, 7\}$, then $A \cup B = \{1, 3, 4, 6, 7\}$.

EXAMPLE 1   Let $A = \{a, b, c, d, e\}$ and $B = \{a, c, e, f\}$. Find:

(a) $A \cap B$ (b) $A \cup B$

Solution   (a) $A \cap B$ is the set of all elements common to both A and B. That is, $A \cap B = \{a, c, e\}$.

(b) $A \cup B$ is the set of all elements in A or B (or both). That is, $A \cup B = \{a, b, c, d, e, f\}$. Note that a, c, and e occur in both sets, yet we list each of these elements only once. ◼

Two sets with no elements in common are said to be **disjoint.** If sets A and B are disjoint, then $A \cap B = \emptyset$. For example, the sets $A = \{1, 2, 3\}$ and $B = \{4, 5\}$ are disjoint; they have no elements in common, that is, $A \cap B = \emptyset$.

B. *Complement of a Set*

We are often interested in the set of elements in the universal set under discussion but *not* in some specified set.

Definition 1.9

> Let $\mathcal{U}$ be the universal set, and let A be a subset of $\mathcal{U}$. The complement of A, denoted by A' (read, "A prime" or "A complement"), is the set of elements in $\mathcal{U}$ but not in A. That is, $A' = \{x \mid x \in \mathcal{U} \text{ and } x \notin A\}$. This set is also symbolized by $\mathcal{U} - A$.

For example, if $\mathcal{U}$ is the set of students in your school, and A is the set of those students who have taken algebra, then A' is the set of those students in your school who have not taken algebra. Similarly, if $\mathcal{U}$ is the set of all letters in the English alphabet, and $A = \{s, k, y,\}$, then A' is the set of all letters in the alphabet except s, k, and y.

EXAMPLE 2   Let $\mathcal{U} = \{1, 2, 3, 4, 5, 6\}$, $A = \{1, 3, 5\}$, $B = \{2, 4\}$. Find:

(a) A' (b) B' (c) $A' \cap B'$ (d) $A \cap B$

Solution   (a) $A' = \{2, 4, 6\}$ (b) $B' = \{1, 3, 5, 6\}$ (c) $A' \cap B' = \{6\}$
(d) $A \cap B = \emptyset$, because there are no elements common to
these two sets.   ■

Note that, because $\emptyset \subseteq \mathcal{U}$, and no element of $\mathcal{U}$ is an element of $\emptyset$, it follows that $\emptyset' = \mathcal{U}$ and $\mathcal{U}' = \emptyset$.

EXAMPLE 3   If A, B, and $\mathcal{U}$ are the same as in Example 2, find:

(a) $(A \cup B)'$ (b) $(A \cap B)'$ (c) $A' \cup B'$
(d) $A \cup (A \cup B)'$

Solution   (a) $A \cup B = \{1, 3, 5\} \cup \{2, 4\} = \{1, 2, 3, 4, 5\}$
Hence, $(A \cup B)' = \{6\}$.
[Note that in order to find $(A \cup B)'$, we first find $A \cup B$
and then take its complement.]
(b) $A \cap B = \{1, 3, 5\} \cap \{2, 4\} = \emptyset$
Hence, $(A \cap B)' = \mathcal{U} = \{1, 2, 3, 4, 5, 6\}$.
(c) $A' \cup B' = \{1, 3, 5\}' \cup \{2, 4\}'$
$= \{2, 4, 6\} \cup \{1, 3, 5, 6\}$
$= \{1, 2, 3, 4, 5, 6\}$
(d) $A \cup (A \cup B)' = \{1, 3, 5\} \cup \{6\} = \{1, 3, 5, 6\}$ ■

Notice that the answers to parts (b) and (c) are identical. Also, notice that the answers to Example 2c and Example 3a are identical. We can show for any sets A and B that $(A \cap B)' = A' \cup B'$ and $(A \cup B)' = A' \cap B'$. (See Exercise 1.4, problems 34a and 34b.)

It is also possible to form intersections, unions, and complements using more than two sets, as in the next example.

EXAMPLE 4   Let $\mathcal{U} = \{a, b, c, d, e, f\}$, $A = \{a, c, e\}$, $B = \{b, e\}$, and $C = \{a, b, d\}$. Find $(A \cup B) \cap C'$.

Solution   Since $A \cup B$ is in parentheses, we find $A \cup B$ first:

$$A \cup B = \{a, c, e\} \cup \{b, e\} = \{a, b, c, e\}$$

Then,

$$C' = \{c, e, f\}$$

Hence,

$$(A \cup B) \cap C' = \{a, b, c, e\} \cap \{c, e, f\}$$
$$= \{c, e\}$$ ■

C. *Difference of Two Sets*

In some cases, we might be interested in only part of a given set. For example, we might want to consider the set of all nonpoisonous snakes. If we let S be the set of all snakes and P be the set of all poisonous snakes, we are interested in the set of all snakes except (excluding) the poisonous ones. This set will be denoted by $S - P$.

Definition 1.10

> If A and B are two sets, the **difference** of A and B, denoted by $A - B$ (read, "A minus B"), is the set of all elements that are in A and not in B. That is, $A - B = \{x \mid x \in A \text{ and } x \notin B\}$.

Notice that

1. The definition of A' is a special case of Definition 1.10, because $\mathcal{U} - A = A'$. (See Definition 1.9.)
2. $A \cap B' = A - B$, because $A \cap B'$ is the set of all elements in A and not in B, and this is precisely the definition of $A - B$.

EXAMPLE 5   Let $\mathcal{U} = \{1, 2, 3, 4, 5, 6\}$, $A = \{1, 2, 3, 4\}$, and $B = \{1, 2, 5\}$. Find:

(a) $\mathcal{U} - A$ (b) A' (c) $A - B$ (d) $B - A$

Solution   (a) $\mathcal{U} - A$ is the set of all elements in $\mathcal{U}$ and not in A; that is, $\{5, 6\}$.
(b) A' is the set of all elements in $\mathcal{U}$ and not in A; that is, $\{5, 6\}$.
(c) $A - B$ is the set of all elements in A and not in B; that is, $\{3, 4\}$.
(d) $B - A$ is the set of all elements in B and not in A; that is, $\{5\}$.

D. *Applications*

EXAMPLE 6   A small, rural electric company has 10 employees who are listed by number as 01, 02, 03, . . . , 10. The company classifies these employees according to the work they do:

P: The set of part-time employees
F: The set of full-time employees
S: The set of employees who do shop work
O: The set of employees who do outdoor field work
I: The set of employees who do indoor office work

The payroll department lists these employees as follows:

$\mathcal{U} = \{01, 02, 03, 04, 05, 06, 07, 08, 09, 10\}$
$P = \{01, 02, 05, 07\}$
$F = \{03, 04, 06, 08, 09, 10\}$

$$S = \{01, 04, 05, 08,\}$$
$$O = \{03, 04, 06, 09\}$$
$$I = \{02, 05, 07, 10\}$$

Find and describe each of the following sets:

(a) $P \cap S$ (b) $O \cup S$ (c) $F \cap I$ (d) P'

(e) $F \cap (S \cup O)$ (f) $S' \cup (O' \cap I')$

Solution   (a) $P \cap S = \{01, 05\}$; the set of part-time employees who do shop work

(b) $O \cup S = \{01, 03, 04, 05, 06, 08, 09)$; the set of employees who do outside field work or shop work

(c) $F \cap I = \{10\}$; the set of full-time employees who do indoor office work

(d) $P' = \{03, 04, 06, 08, 09, 10\}$; the set of employees who are not part-time—that is, the set of full-time employees

(e) $F \cap (S \cup O) = \{03, 04, 06, 08, 09\}$; the set of full-time employees who do shop work or outside field work

(f) $S' \cup (O' \cap I') = \{01, 02, 03, 06, 07, 08, 09, 10\}$; the set of employees who do not do shop work combined with the set of employees who do neither outdoor field work nor indoor office work

Exercise 1.3 _____

A.   In problems 1–8, let $A = \{1, 2, 3, 4, 5\}$, $B = \{1, 3, 4, 6\}$, and $C = \{1, 6, 7\}$. Find:

1.   (a) $A \cap B$ (b) $A \cap C$ (c) $B \cap C$
2.   (a) $A \cup B$ (b) $A \cup C$ (c) $B \cup C$
3.   (a) $A \cap (B \cup C)$ (b) $A \cup (B \cap C)$
4.   (a) $(A \cap B) \cup C$ (b) $(A \cap B) \cup (A \cap C)$
5. $A \cup (B \cup C)$ 6. $(A \cup B) \cap (A \cup C)$
7. $A \cap (B \cap C)$ 8. $(A \cup B) \cap C$

In problems 9 and 10, let $A = \{\{a, b\}, c\}$, $B = \{a, b, c\}$, and $C = \{a, b\}$. Find:

9.   (a) $A \cap B$ (b) $A \cap C$
10. (a) $A \cup B$ (b) $A \cup C$

In problems 11–14, let $A = \{\{a, b\}, \{a, b, c\}, a, b\}$ and $B = \{\{a, b\}, a, b, c, \{b, c\}\}$. Which of the given statements are correct?

11. (a) $\{b\} \subseteq (A \cap B)$ (b) $\{b\} \in (A \cap B)$
12. (a) $\{a, b\} \subseteq (A \cap B)$ (b) $\{a, b\} \in (A \cap B)$
13. (a) $\{a, b, c\} \subseteq (A \cup B)$ (b) $\{a, b, c\} \in (A \cup B)$
14. (a) $3 \subseteq (A \cap B)$ (b) $3 \in (A \cap B)$

B. The sets $\mathscr{U} = \{a, b, c, d, e, f\}$, $A = \{a, c, e\}$, $B = \{b, d, e, f\}$, and $C = \{a, b, d, f\}$ will be used in problems 15–26. Find the specified set.

15. (a) A' (b) B' 16. (a) $A' \cap B'$ (b) $(A \cap B)'$

17. (a) $(A \cup B)'$ (b) $A' \cup B'$

18. (a) $(A \cup B) \cap C'$ (b) $(A \cup B)' \cap C$

19. (a) $(A \cap B) \cup C'$ (b) $C \cup (A \cap B)'$

20. (a) $A' \cup B$ (b) $A \cup B'$ 21. (a) $A' \cap B$ (b) $A \cap B'$

22. (a) $A' \cap (A \cup B')$ (b) $A \cup (A \cap B')$

23. (a) $C' \cup (A \cap B)'$ (b) $C' \cup (A \cup B)'$

24. (a) $(C \cup B)' \cap A$ (b) $(C \cup B) \cap A'$

C. 25. (a) $\mathscr{U} - A$ (b) $\mathscr{U} - B$ 26. (a) $A - B$ (b) $B - A$

In problems 27 and 28 let $\mathscr{U} = \{1, 2, 3, 4, 5\}$, $A = \{2, 3, 4\}$, and $B = \{1, 4, 5\}$. Find the specified set.

27. (a) B' (b) $\mathscr{U} - B$ 28. (a) $A - B$ (b) $B - A$

In problems 29–38, $\mathscr{U}$ is some universal set of which A is a subset. In each case find the indicated set in terms of A, $\mathscr{U}$, or $\emptyset$ alone.

29. $\emptyset'$ 30. $\mathscr{U}'$ 31. $A \cap \emptyset$ 32. $A \cap A$

33. $A \cap \mathscr{U}$ 34. $A \cup \emptyset$ 35. $A \cap A'$ 36. $A \cup A'$

37. $(A')'$ 38. $A \cup A$

39. If $A = \{1, 2, 3\}$, $B = \{2, 3, 4\}$, and $C = \{1, 3, 5\}$, find the smallest set that will serve as a universal set for A, B, and C.

D. Problems 40–45 refer to the following data: What traits do men and women like in each other? In an attempt to analyze factors in popularity, not only between members of the same sex but between men and women, a psychologist asked 676 college men and women to indicate a few persons whom they liked and to tell why they liked those persons.

Traits Men Liked in Women (M_w)	Traits Women Liked in Men (W_m)	Traits Men Liked in Men (M_m)	Traits Women Liked in Women (W_w)
Beauty	Intelligence	Intelligence	Intelligence
Intelligence	Consideration	Cheerfulness	Cheerfulness
Cheerfulness	Kindliness	Friendliness	Helpfulness
Congeniality	Cheerfulness	Congeniality	Loyalty

40. Find the smallest set that will serve as a universal set for M_w, W_m, M_m, and W_w.

41. Find the set of traits that are mentioned only once.

42. Find $M_w \cap W_w$.

43. Find $M_w \cap M_m$.

44. What set of traits is common to M_m and M_w?

45. Name the traits that are common to all four of the sets; that is, find $M_w \cap M_m \cap W_w \cap W_m$.

Boss behavior. In an article in the *Harvard Business Review,* 606 participants reported on 17 specific changes in their boss's behavior from one year to the next. Here are some of the traits that were most frequently mentioned in each of these years:

First Year	Second Year
Encourages suggestions	Is self-aware
Sets goals with me	Listens carefully
Gets me to have high goals	Follows up on action
Listens carefully	Gets me to have high goals
Is aware of others	Encourages suggestions
Is self-aware	Sets goals with me

Let S_1 be the set of traits mentioned in the first year, and let S_2 be the set of traits mentioned in the second year.

46. Find $S_1 \cap S_2$, the set of traits mentioned in both years.

47. What traits were mentioned only once?

48. Find the smallest set that will serve as a universal set for S_1 and S_2.

49. Find S_1' relative to the universal set found in problem 48.

50. Find S_2' relative to the universal set found in problem 48.

In problems 51–57 let
  $\mathcal{U}$ be the set of employees of a company,
  M be the set of males who are employees,
  F be the set of females who are employees,
  D be the set of employees who work in the data-processing department,
  T be the set of employees who are under 21,
  S be the set of employees who are over 65, and
  $\emptyset$ be the empty set.

In problems 51 and 52, find a single letter to represent the specified set:

51. (a) M' (b) F' 52. (a) $M \cup F$ (b) $M \cap F$ (c) $T \cap S$

In problems 53 and 54, describe verbally the specified set:

53. (a) $M \cap D$ (b) $F \cap T$

54. (a) $M \cap T'$ (b) $(T \cup S)'$ (c) $(D \cap T)'$

In problems 55–57, find a set representation for the given set:

55. Employees in data processing who are over 65
56. Female employees who are under 21
57. Male employees who work in data processing

In problems 58–60, write out in words the complement of the set in the specified problem.

58. problem 55.   59. problem 56.   60. problem 57.

For problems 61 and 62, refer to the data in Example 6. Find and describe the sets in each problem.

61. (a) $F \cap S$ (b) $P \cap (O \cup I)$
62. (a) $P \cap I$ (b) $P \cap O' \cap S'$

*I*n Other Words

In problems 63–66, a diagram is given showing certain relationships between sets *A* and *B* represented by the circular areas. State these relationships in your own words and find sets *A* and *B* that satisfy the conditions shown in the diagram. (*Hint:* In problem 63, *A* may be a set of cats and *B* a set of dogs.)

63.
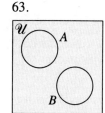

64.
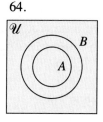

65.
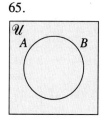

66.
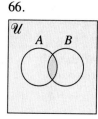

Using Your Knowledge

The ideas of sets, subsets, unions, intersections, and complements are used in zoology and in other branches of science. Here are some typical applications.

67. A zoology book lists the following characteristics of giraffes and okapis:

Giraffes	Okapis
Tall	Short
Long neck	Short neck
Long tongue	Long tongue
Skin-covered horns	Skin-covered horns
Native to Africa	Native to Africa

Let G be the set of characteristics of giraffes, and let O be the set of characteristics of okapis.

 (a) Find $G \cap O$.
 (b) What set of characteristics is common to okapis and giraffes?
 (c) Find the smallest set $\mathcal{U}$ that will serve as a universal set for G and O.
 (d) Find G'.
 (e) Find O'.

Problems 68 and 69 refer to the table below.

68. Let B be the set of characteristics of blind snakes, T be the set of characteristics of thread snakes, P be the set of characteristics of pipe snakes, and BP be the set of characteristics of boas and pythons. Find:

 (a) $B \cap T \cap P$
 (b) $B \cap T \cap P \cap BP$

69. If TL is the set of snakes with two lungs and SS is the set of snakes with spiny shields on the tail, find $TL \cap SS'$.

			Family	Number of Species	Common Name
With limb remnants	Burrowers	All teeth in upper jaw	Typhlopidae	200	Blind snakes
		All teeth in lower jaw	Leptotyphlopidae	40	Thread snakes
		Eyes with spectacle	Anilidae	10	Pipe snakes
No limb remnants	Surface dwellers		Boidae	100	Boas and pythons
	Two lungs	Spiny shield on tail	Uropeltidae	40	Shieldtails
			Xenopeltidae	1	Sunbeam snakes
	One lung	No poison fangs or back fanged	Colubridae	2500	Typical snakes
		Rigid fangs — Land	Elapidae	150	Cobras
		Rigid fangs — Sea	Hydrophidae	50	Seasnakes
		Folding fangs	Viperidae	80	Vipers

Discovery

Let the sets B_1 and B_2 be defined as follows:

(a) *Place the numbers 1 and 2 in B_1 and also in B_2.*

(b) *At $\frac{1}{2}$ hr before noon, take the smallest number — that is, 1 — from B_1 and the largest number — that is, 2 — from B_2. At this time, $B_1 \cap B_2 = \emptyset$.*

(c) *Place the numbers 3 and 4 in B_1 and also in B_2.*

(d) *At $\frac{1}{4}$ hr before noon, take the smallest number — that is, 2 — from B_1 and the largest number — that is, 4 — from B_2. At this time, $B_1 \cap B_2 = \{3\}$.*

(e) *Place the numbers 5 and 6 in B_1 and also in B_2.*

(f) *At $\frac{1}{8}$ hr before noon, take the smallest number — that is, 3 — from B_1 and the largest number — that is, 6 — from B_2. At this time, $B_1 \cap B_2 = \{5\}$.*

Continue this process.

70. Verify that at $\frac{1}{16}$ hr before noon, $B_1 \cap B_2 = \{5, 7\}$.

71. Verify that at $\frac{1}{32}$ hr before noon, $B_1 \cap B_2 = \{7, 9\}$.

72. Verify that at $\frac{1}{64}$ hr before noon, $B_1 \cap B_2 = \{7, 9, 11\}$.

Note that at $\frac{1}{16} = \left(\frac{1}{2}\right)^4$ hr before noon, the largest number in $B_1 \cap B_2$ was 7, and that at $\frac{1}{32} = \left(\frac{1}{2}\right)^5$ hr before noon, the largest number in $B_1 \cap B_2$ was 9.

73. Can you discover what will be the largest number in $B_1 \cap B_2$ at $\left(\frac{1}{2}\right)^n$ hr before noon?

74. Can you discover what the smallest number in $B_1 \cap B_2$ will be at $\left(\frac{1}{2}\right)^n$ hr before noon?

1.4   VENN DIAGRAMS

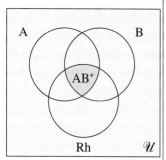

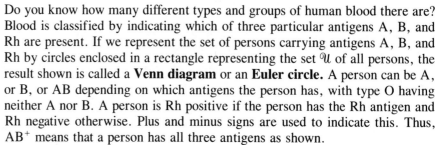

GETTING   STARTED

BLOOD TYPES AND VENN DIAGRAMS

Do you know how many different types and groups of human blood there are? Blood is classified by indicating which of three particular antigens A, B, and Rh are present. If we represent the set of persons carrying antigens A, B, and Rh by circles enclosed in a rectangle representing the set $\mathcal{U}$ of all persons, the result shown is called a **Venn diagram** or an **Euler circle.** A person can be A, or B, or AB depending on which antigens the person has, with type O having neither A nor B. A person is Rh positive if the person has the Rh antigen and Rh negative otherwise. Plus and minus signs are used to indicate this. Thus, AB^+ means that a person has all three antigens as shown.

What else can we do with Venn diagrams? You can show that the **Commutative, Associative,** and **Distributive Laws** familiar to you from arithmetic apply to sets by verifying that:

$$\left.\begin{array}{l} A \cup B = B \cup A \\ A \cap B = B \cap A \end{array}\right\} \quad \text{Commutative Laws}$$

$$\left.\begin{array}{l} A \cup (B \cup C) = (A \cup B) \cup C \\ A \cap (B \cap C) = (A \cap B) \cap C \end{array}\right\} \quad \text{Associative Laws}$$

$$\left.\begin{array}{l} A \cup (B \cap C) = (A \cup B) \cap (A \cup C) \\ A \cap (B \cup C) = (A \cap B) \cup (A \cap C) \end{array}\right\} \quad \text{Distributive Laws}$$

We do exactly this in problems 30–34 of Exercise 1.4.

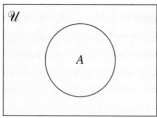

FIGURE 1.1

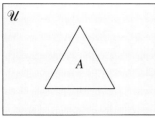

FIGURE 1.2

The ideas of sets, subsets, and the operations used to combine sets can be illustrated graphically by the use of diagrams called **Venn diagrams,** after John Venn (1834–1923), an English mathematician and logician. In these diagrams, we represent the universal set $\mathcal{U}$ by a rectangle, and we use regions enclosed by simple curves (usually circles) drawn inside the rectangle to represent the sets being considered. For example, if A is a subset of a universal set $\mathcal{U}$, we can represent this universal set by the set of points in the interior of the rectangle shown in Figure 1.1. The interior of the circle represents the set of points in A, while the set of points inside the rectangle and outside the circle represents the set A'. Obviously, closed figures other than circles may be used to represent the points of the set A. Figure 1.2 shows a Venn diagram in which A is represented by the points inside a triangle.

A. Drawing Venn Diagrams

We illustrate the idea of Venn diagrams in the following examples.

EXAMPLE 1   Let $\mathcal{U} = \{a, b, c, d, e\}$, $A = \{a, b, c\}$, and $B = \{a, e\}$. Draw a Venn diagram to illustrate this situation.

Solution

We draw a rectangle whose interior points represent the set $\mathcal{U}$ and two circles whose interior points represent the points in A and B. The completed diagram appears in Figure 1.3. We note that a is in both A and B, because $A \cap B = \{a\}$. Also, d is the only element that is not in A or in B, so $(A \cup B)' = \{d\}$. ∎

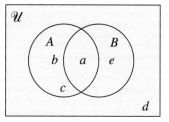

FIGURE 1.3

Intersections and unions of sets can be represented by Venn diagrams. For example, given two sets A and B, we can draw a Venn diagram to represent the region corresponding to $A \cap B$. We proceed as follows:

1. As usual, the points inside the rectangle represent $\mathcal{U}$, and the points inside the two circles represent A and B (Figure 1.4). Note that A and B overlap to allow for the possibility that A and B have points in common.
2. We shade the set A using vertical lines (Figure 1.5).
3. We shade the set B using horizontal lines (Figure 1.6). The region in which the lines intersect (cross-hatched in the diagram) is the region corresponding to $A \cap B$.

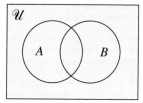

FIGURE 1.4

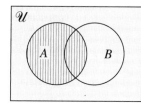

FIGURE 1.5

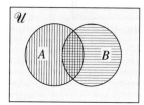

FIGURE 1.6
$A \cap B$

EXAMPLE 2

Draw a Venn diagram to represent the set $A' \cap B$.

Solution

We proceed as in Example 1:

1. We draw a rectangle and two circles as in Figure 1.7.
2. We shade the points of A' (the points in $\mathcal{U}$ and outside A) with vertical lines.
3. We shade the points of B with horizontal lines. Then $A' \cap B$ is represented by the cross-hatched region. ∎

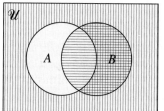

FIGURE 1.7
$A' \cap B$

We may associate with the formation of $A \cap B$ a command to shade the region representing the set to the left of the symbol $\cap$ one way and the region representing the set to the right of the symbol another way. For example, in finding $A \cap B$, because A is to the left of $\cap$, we shade region A vertically, and because B is to the right of the symbol $\cap$, we shade region B horizontally. As before, $A \cap B$ is represented by the region in which the lines intersect. (If $A \cap B = \varnothing$, A and B are said to be **disjoint**.) On the other hand, the operation $\cup$ may be thought of as a command to shade the regions representing the sets to the left and right of the symbol $\cup$ with the same type of lines (horizon-

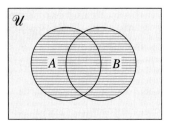

FIGURE 1.8

$A \cup B$

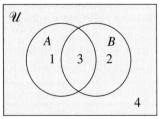

FIGURE 1.9

tal or vertical). Thus, in finding $A \cup B$, we shade A with, say, horizontal lines and shade B in the same way. The union of A and B will be the entire shaded region (see Figure 1.8).

A somewhat simpler procedure can be adopted in the construction of Venn diagrams. As before, we start with a rectangle and two circles representing the sets $\mathcal{U}$, A, and B, respectively. We then number the four regions into which the universal set is divided (see Figure 1.9.) The numbering of the regions is completely arbitrary. By referring to the figure, we can identify the various sets as follows:

> $A \cap B$ is the set of elements common to A and B — represented by region 3.
> $A' \cap B$ is the set of elements that are not in A and that are in B — represented by region 2.
> $A \cap B'$ is the set of elements in A and not in B — represented by region 1.
> $A \cup B$ is the set of elements in A or in B, or in both A and B — represented by regions 1, 2, 3.
> A' is the set of elements that are not in A — represented by regions 2 and 4.
> B' is the set of elements that are not in B — represented by regions 1 and 4.

B. *Verifying Equality*

Venn diagrams are convenient for analyzing problems involving sets as long as there are not many subsets of $\mathcal{U}$ to be considered. For example, referring to Figure 1.9, we note that $A \cap B$ is the set of points in A and in B (region 3); but $B \cap A$ is the set of points in B and in A (region 3). Hence, these two sets refer to the same region, and we can see that $A \cap B = B \cap A$.

If A, B, and C are subsets of $\mathcal{U}$, use the preceding method to verify the **distributive law** $A \cap (B \cup C) = (A \cap B) \cup (A \cap C)$.

EXAMPLE 3

Solution

We draw the rectangle and the circles representing the sets $\mathcal{U}$, A, B, and C, and number the regions 1, 2, 3, 4, 5, 6, 7, 8, as shown in Figure 1.10 in the margin. Note that when we had 2 sets, we used $2^2 = 4$ regions. In this example, we have 3 sets; hence, we need $2^3 = 8$ regions.

We first consider $A \cap (B \cup C)$:

(a) A is represented by regions 1, 3, 5, and 7.

(b) $B \cup C$ is represented by regions 2, 3, 4, 5, 6, and 7.

(c) $A \cap (B \cup C)$ is therefore represented by the regions common to the two sets in parts (a) and (b) — that is, by regions 3, 5, and 7.

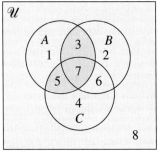

FIGURE 1.10

We next consider $(A \cap B) \cup (A \cap C)$:

(d) $(A \cap B)$ is represented by the regions common to the circles representing A and B — that is, by regions 3 and 7.

(e) $(A \cap C)$ is represented by the regions common to the circles representing A and C — that is, by regions 5 and 7.

(f) $(A \cap B) \cup (A \cap C)$ is therefore represented by all the regions found in parts (d) and (e) — that is, by regions 3, 5, and 7.

Because $A \cap (B \cup C)$ and $(A \cap B) \cup (A \cap C)$ are both represented by regions 3, 5, and 7, we see that

$$A \cap (B \cup C) = (A \cap B) \cup (A \cap C)$$

In problems 30, 31, and 34 we shall verify the **Commutative, Associative,** and **De Morgan's laws.**

C. *Applications*

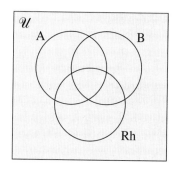

As we saw in Getting Started, human blood is grouped according to the presence of three antigens A, B, and Rh. Suppose that we want to use a Venn diagram to visualize all the different blood groups. We begin with three circles representing the sets of persons having antigens A, B, and Rh, respectively. As you can see, there are 8 different regions, so there are 8 different blood groups. Blood groups inside the set Rh will carry a plus sign (+), and those outside Rh will carry a minus sign (−). Blood with neither the A nor the B antigen will be labeled as type O.

EXAMPLE 4   Draw a Venn diagram to identify all possible blood groups.

Solution   The eight possible groupings of blood are A⁻, A⁺, B⁻, B⁺, AB⁻, AB⁺, O⁻, O⁺, where A⁺ means that the person has both A and Rh antigens, A⁻ means that the person has antigen A but not Rh, and similarly for the remaining symbols. Note that the circle labeled A represents the set of persons having the A antigen and A⁺, A⁻, AB⁺, or AB⁻ blood, and likewise for the other two circles.

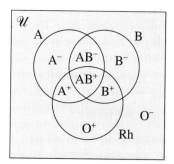

Human blood types

EXAMPLE 5   The ideas presented in this section have been used in recent years by forecasters in the National Weather Service. For example, in the accompanying map, rain, showers, snow, and flurries are indicated with different types of shadings. Find the states in which:

(a) It is warm and there are showers.
(b) It is warm and raining.
(c) It is warm only.
(d) It is snowing.
(e) There are snow flurries.

Solution   (a) Florida   (b) Texas   (c) California, Arizona
(d) North Dakota, Minnesota   (e) Minnesota

Exercise 1.4

A.   1. Let $\mathcal{U} = \{1, 2, 3, 4, 5\}$, $A = \{1, 2\}$, and $B = \{1, 3, 5\}$. Draw a Venn diagram to illustrate the relationship among these sets.

2. Do the same as in problem 1 for the sets $\mathcal{U} = \{a, b, c, d, e, f\}$, $A = \{a, b, c\}$, and $B = \{d, e, f\}$.

In problems 3–8, draw a Venn diagram to represent the specified set.

3. $A \cap B'$ 4. $A' \cup B'$ 5. $(A \cup B) - (A \cap B)$
6. $A \cup B'$ 7. $A' \cap B'$ 8. $(A \cup B) - A$

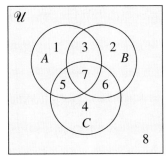

FIGURE 1.11

In problems 9–17 use the numbered regions of Figure 1.11 to identify the specified set:

9. $A - (B \cup C)$

10. $C \cap (A \cup B)$

11. $(A \cap B \cap C) - (A \cap B)$

12. $(A \cap B') \cup (A \cap C')$

13. $(A \cup B') \cap C$

14. $(A \cup B) - C$

15. $(A \cap B') \cup C$

16. $B \cap C' \cap A$

17. $(A \cup B \cup C)'$

In problems 18–25, draw a Venn diagram to illustrate the specified set:

18. $\{x \mid x \in A \text{ or } x \in B\}$

19. $\{x \mid x \notin A \text{ or } x \notin B\}$

20. $\{x \mid x \in A \text{ and } x \notin B\}$

21. $\{x \mid x \in A \text{ and } (x \in B \text{ and } x \notin C)\}$

22. $\{x \mid x \in A \text{ and } x \in B\}$

23. $\{x \mid x \notin A \text{ and } x \in B\}$

24. $\{x \mid x \in A \text{ or } (x \in B \text{ or } x \in C)\}$

25. $\{x \mid x \notin A \text{ and } (x \in B \text{ and } x \in C)\}$

B. In problems 26–29, draw a Venn diagram that satisfies the given equation:

26. $A \cap B = \emptyset$

27. $A \cap B = B$

28. $(A \cup B) \cap C = \emptyset$

29. $A \cap (A \cap B) = A$

In problems 30–34, use the numbered regions in Figure 1.11 to verify the given equalities.

30. (a) $A \cup B = B \cup A$
    (b) $A \cap B = B \cap A$
    (These two equations are called the **Commutative Laws** for set operations.)

31. (a) $A \cup (B \cup C) = (A \cup B) \cup C$
    (b) $A \cap (B \cap C) = (A \cap B) \cap C$
    (These two equations are called the **Associative Laws** for set operations.)

32. $A \cup (B \cap C) = (A \cup B) \cap (A \cup C)$
    [This equation and the equation $A \cap (B \cup C) = (A \cap B) \cup (A \cap C)$, which was verified in Example 3, are known as the **Distributive Laws** for set operations.

33. (a) $A \cup A' = \mathcal{U}$ (b) $A \cap A' = \emptyset$
    (c) $A - B = A \cap B'$

34. (a) $(A \cup B)' = A' \cap B'$ (b) $(A \cap B)' = A' \cup B'$
    (These two equations are known as **De Morgan's Laws**.)

35. Referring to Figure 1.11, the set of regions $\{3, 7\}$ represents which of the following?
    (a) $A \cap B$ (b) $A \cap B \cap C$ (c) $(A \cup B) \cap C$
    (d) $(A \cap B) \cup C$ (e) None of these

36. Referring to Figure 1.11, the set of regions {1, 2, 3} represents which of the following?
(a) $(A \cup B) \cap C$ (b) $(A \cup B) \cap C'$
(c) $(A \cap B) \cup C$ (d) $(A \cap B) \cup C'$
(e) None of these

37. Given $A \cap B = \{a, b\}$, $A \cap B' = \{c, e\}$, $A' \cap B = \{g, h\}$, and $(A \cup B)' = \{d, f\}$, use a Venn diagram to find:
(a) A, B, and $\mathcal{U}$ (b) $A \cup B$ (c) $(A \cap B)'$

38. Given $A \cap B = \{b, d\}$, $A \cup B = \{b, c, d, e\}$, $A \cap C = \{b, c\}$, and $A \cup C = \{a, b, c, d\}$, use a Venn diagram to find:
(a) A, B and C (b) $A \cap B \cap C$ (c) $A \cup B \cup C$

39. Draw a Venn diagram representing the most general situation for four sets A, B, C, and D. [*Hint:* There should be $2^4 = 16$ regions.]

40. Referring to the map in Example 5, find the states in which it is warm.

41. Referring to the map in Example 5, find the states in which it is warm and/or it is raining.

42. Referring to the map in Example 5, find the states in which it is warm and it is raining or there are showers.

In Other Words

In problems 43–46, write in words the set represented by the shaded region of the Venn diagram.

43.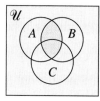
44.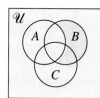
45.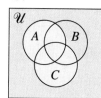
46.

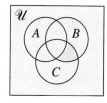

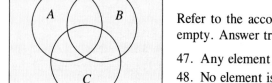

Refer to the accompanying diagram and assume none of the eight regions is empty. Answer true or false.

47. Any element in A is also in B.
48. No element is a member of A, B, and C.
49. Any element in $\mathcal{U}$ is also in C.
50. None of the statements in 47–49 are true.

Using Your Knowledge

In Example 4 of this section, blood was classified into eight different types. In blood transfusions, the recipient (the person receiving the blood) must have all or more of the antigens present in the donor's blood. For instance, an A^+ person cannot donate blood to an A^- person, because the recipient does not have the Rh antigen; but an A^- person can donate to an A^+ person. Refer to the Venn diagram in Example 4 and:

51. Identify the blood type of universal recipients.
52. Identify the blood type of universal donors.
53. May an AB^- person give blood to a B^- person?
54. May a B^- person give blood to an AB^- person?
55. May an O^+ person give blood to an O^- person?
56. May an O^- person give blood to an O^+ person?

Discovery

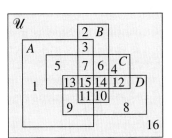

John Venn, the English logician who invented the diagrams introduced in this section, used them to illustrate his work, Symbolic Logic. *The Swiss mathematician Leonhard Euler (1707–1783) also used similar diagrams to illustrate his work. For this reason, Venn diagrams are sometimes called* **Euler circles.**

  We have seen in the preceding examples that if we have one set, the corresponding Venn diagram divides the universe into two regions. Two sets divide the universe into four regions, and three sets divide it into eight regions.

57. Can you discover the maximum number of regions into which four sets will divide the universe?
58. The diagram for a division of the universal set into the 16 regions corresponding to four given sets may look like that at left. Can you guess the maximum number of regions into which *n* sets will divide the universe?
59. Referring to the diagram for problem 58, find the regions corresponding to:
    (a) $A \cap B \cap C' \cap D$ (b) $(A \cup B \cup C)'$

1.5   THE NUMBER OF ELEMENTS IN A SET: A PROBLEM–SOLVING TOOL

*GETTING S*TARTED

TEST REGISTRATION AND COUNTING

When registering for the Test of English as a Foreign Language (TOEFL) or the Test of Spoken English (TSE), students must indicate which test they plan to take by checking one of the boxes on the envelope (below). Suppose that a total of 800 students are registered for the TOEFL exam and 500 students are registered for the TSE, with 200 of these students indicating that they are taking both tests. How many students are participating; that is, how many students are registered? To answer this question, we have to develop a notation indicating how many elements we have in each set. If F is the set of students registering for TOEFL and S is the set of students registered for TSE, we are asked to find the total number of registered students. (They can be taking TOEFL only, TSE only, or both.) We answer this question and more in Example 1. Similar problems are in Exercise 1.5, problems 7–9.

One of the simplest counting techniques involves the counting of elements in a given set. If A is any set, the number of elements in A is denoted by $n(A)$. For example, if $A = \{g, i, r, l\}$, then $n(A) = 4$. Likewise, if $B = \{@, \#, \$\}$ then $n(B) = 3$. We shall be interested here in counting the number of elements in sets involving the operations of union, intersection, and taking complements. The number $n(A)$ is frequently called the **cardinal number** of A.

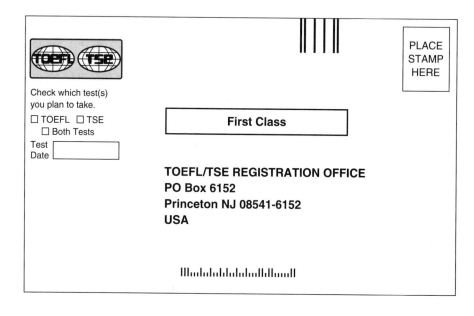

A. *Counting the Elements of a Set*

EXAMPLE 1   In a particular school, 800 students are registered for TOEFL, 500 are registered for TSE, and 200 are registered for both tests.

(a) What is the total number of registered students?
(b) How many students are taking TOEFL only?
(c) How many students are taking TSE only?

Solution   Let F be the set of students registering for TOEFL and S be the set of students registering for TSE. We first draw a Venn diagram with overlapping regions to show the information.

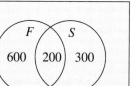

1. $S \cap F$ has 200 students. Write 200 in the region corresponding to $S \cap F$.

2. Since $n(F) = 800$ and 200 students are in the intersection of F and S, the number of students taking TOEFL only is $600 = 800 - 200$ as shown.

3. The number of students taking TSE only is $300 = 500 - 200$.
   (a) The number of registered students is

   $$n(F \cup S) = 600 + 200 + 300 = 1100$$

   (b) The number of students taking the TOEFL only is 600.
   (c) The number of students taking the TSE only is 300.

Note that

$$n(F \cup S) = n(F) + n(S) - n(S \cap F),$$

that is,

$$1100 = 800 + 500 - 200$$

■

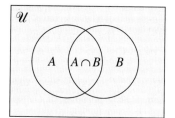

FIGURE 1.12
$A \cap B = \emptyset$

We now examine the problem of finding the number of elements in the union of two sets in a more general way. Let us assume that A and B are any two given sets. We must consider two possibilities:

1. $A \cap B = \emptyset$ (see Figure 1.12): In this case, $n(A \cup B) = n(A) + n(B)$.
2. $A \cap B \neq \emptyset$ (see Figure 1.13): In this case, we note that $A \cup B$ includes all the elements in A and all the elements in B, but each counted only once. It is thus clear that $n(A) + n(B)$ counts the elements in $A \cap B$ twice and so exceeds $n(A \cup B)$ by $n(A \cap B)$. Therefore, $n(A \cup B) = [n(A) + n(B)] - n(A \cap B)$, or

$$n(A \cup B) = n(A) + n(B) - n(A \cap B) \tag{1}$$

FIGURE 1.13
$A \cap B \neq \emptyset$

Notice that equation (1) is correct even if $A \cap B = \emptyset$, because in that case $n(A \cap B) = 0$.

EXAMPLE 2   If $n(A) = 20$, $n(B) = 30$, and $n(A \cap B) = 10$, find $n(A \cup B)$.

Solution   Using equation (1), we have

$$n(A \cup B) = n(A) + n(B) - n(A \cap B) = 20 + 30 - 10 = 40$$

It is possible to develop a formula similar to equation (1) for the case where three or more sets are considered. However, we will rely on the use of Venn diagrams to solve such problems.

B. Applications

Venn diagrams can be used to study surveys as shown next.

Problem Solving: **Surveys**

To estimate the number of persons interested in recycling aluminum cans, glass, and newspapers a company conducts a survey of 1000 people and finds out that:

200 recycle glass (G)	300 recycle paper (P)
450 recycle cans (C)	50 recycle cans and glass
15 recycle paper and glass	60 recycle cans and paper
10 recycle all three	

(a) How many people did not recycle at all?
(b) How many people recycle cans only?

1. **Read the problem.**
2. **Select the unknown.**
3. **Think of a plan.**

We want to find the number of people that did not recycle at all and the ones that recycle cans only.
Draw a Venn diagram with 3 overlapping circles labeled C, G, and P.

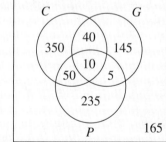

4. **Use the information to carry out the plan.**

Do we know how to distribute the 200 people that recycle glass inside the circle G?

No, we have to start with the 10 persons that recycle all three and place them in $C \cap G \cap P$. Since 15 recycle paper and glass, the intersection of P and G must have 15 people. We already have 10 in $C \cap G \cap P$, so we add 5 in the remainder of $P \cap G$.

Similarly, we place 50 more in the remainder of $C \cap P$ and 40 in the remainder of $C \cap G$. We now have 100 (10 + 50 + 40) persons in C, so we place 350 in the region corresponding to C only. Similarly, we place 145 in the region corresponding to G only and 235 in the region corresponding to P only.

We have 350 + 40 + 145 + 50 + 10 + 5 + 235 or 835 people inside the circles.

(a) Since 1000 persons were surveyed, 1000 − 835 or 165 persons are outside the three circles and did not recycle at all.
(b) 350 recycle cans only.

5. Verify the answer.   The sum of all the numbers in the diagram is 1000.

TRY EXAMPLE 3 NOW.   Cover the solution, write your own, and then check your work.

EXAMPLE 3   A survey of students at Prince Tom University shows that:

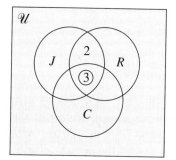

> 29 liked jazz.
> 23 liked rock.
> 40 liked classical music.
> 10 liked classical music and jazz.
> 13 liked classical music and rock.
> 5 liked rock and jazz.
> 3 liked rock, jazz, and classical music.

If there was a total of 70 students in the survey, find:

(a) The number of students who liked classical music only
(b) The number of students who liked jazz and rock, but not classical music.
(c) The number of students who did not like jazz, rock, or classical music

Solution   Read the problem carefully; there are three questions to be answered.

Select the letters J, R, and C to represent the set of students who liked jazz, rock, and classical music, respectively.

Think of a plan to solve the problem. Since the data indicates some overlap, we draw a Venn diagram as shown in the margin.

Use the Venn diagram to fill in the numbers in the figure as follows:

Since 3 students liked all three types of music, the region common to J, R, and C ($J \cap R \cap C$) must contain the number 3. Next, we see that 5 students liked jazz and rock, so that the region common to J and R ($J \cap R$) must contain a total of 5. But we already have 3 in $J \cap R \cap C$, a portion of $J \cap R$, so we must put 2 in the remainder of $J \cap R$. (See the figure, step 1.)

Similarly, since 13 students liked rock and classical music, the region common to R and C ($R \cap C$) must contain a total of 13. We already have 3 in

$\mathcal{U}$

Step 1

$J \cap R \cap C$, a portion of $R \cap C$, so we must put 10 in the remainder of $R \cap C$ (step 2).

Since 10 students liked classical music and jazz, the region common to C and J ($J \cap C$) must contain a total of 10. We already have 3 in a portion of this region ($J \cap R \cap C$), so the remainder of the region must contain $10 - 3 = 7$ (step 3).

Next, we see that 40 students liked classical music, and we have already accounted for $7 + 3 + 10 = 20$ of these. Thus, the remainder of region C, outside of regions J and R, must contain $40 - 20 = 20$ (step 4).

By proceeding in the same way, we can fill in the numbers for the remaining regions in the figure. From the completed diagram (step 5), we see that:

(a) 20 students liked classical music only.
(b) 2 students liked jazz and rock, but not classical music.
(c) Since the numbers inside the circles add up to 67, 3 students
     did not like jazz, rock, or classical music.   ∎

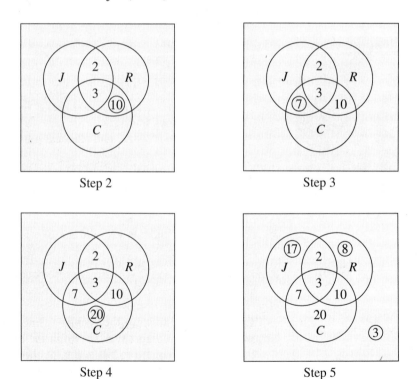

Step 2   Step 3

Step 4   Step 5

Verification is made by counting all elements in step 5 and making sure they add up to 70, the total number of students in the survey. Note that the problem solving strategy is to make a Venn diagram and fill it in, starting with the innermost region and then working step-by-step toward the outside as done in steps 1–5.

EXAMPLE 4

In a survey of 100 students, the numbers taking algebra (A), English (E), and philosophy (P) are as shown in Figure 1.14.

(a) How many students were taking algebra or English, but not both?

(b) How many students were taking algebra or English, but not philosophy?

(c) How many students were taking one or two of these courses, but not all three?

(d) How many students were taking at least two of these courses?

(e) How many students were taking at least one of these courses?

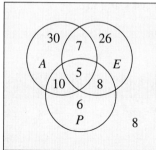

FIGURE 1.14

Solution

(a) Here, we want all the elements in A or E, but not in both. We read the numbers from the Venn diagram to get

$$30 + 10 + 26 + 8 = 74$$

Note that we have taken all the numbers in $A \cup E$ except those in $A \cap E$.

(b) Here, we need all the numbers in A or E that are not in P. From the diagram, we find

$$30 + 7 + 26 = 63$$

(c) The required number here is the number in the entire universal set, 100, minus the number taking all three courses, 5, or none of these courses, 8. Thus, the result is

$$100 - 5 - 8 = 87$$

(d) The number wanted here is the number in $(A \cap E) \cup (A \cap P) \cup (E \cap P)$, which is

$$7 + 5 + 10 + 8 = 30$$

(e) We can get the required number by taking the number in the universal set minus the number taking none of these courses. Thus, we find the result to be

$$100 - 8 = 92$$

■

EXAMPLE 5   The Safe-T Auto Insurance Company has classified a group of drivers as indicated in the table. Find the number of persons who:

(a) Are low risks under age 21   (b) Are not high risks and are over age 35

(c) Are under age 21   (d) Are low risks

	Under Age 21	Age 21–35	Over Age 35
Low risk	15	20	35
Average risk	25	15	10
High risk	50	10	30

Solution   (a) We see that there are **15** persons under the column labeled "Under Age 21" and in the row of "Low risk."

(b) There are 30 persons who are over age 35 and high risks, so the rest of the persons in the column labeled "Over Age 35" are not high risks. This number is 10 + 35 = **45**.

(c) We count all the persons in the column labeled "Under Age 21." The sum is 15 + 25 + 50 = **90**.

(d) We count the persons in the row labeled "Low risk." The sum is 15 + 20 + 35 = **70**.

Exercise 1.5

A.   1. Suppose that $n(A) = 15$, $n(B) = 20$, and $n(A \cap B) = 5$. Find $n(A \cup B)$.

2. Suppose that $n(A) = 12$, $n(B) = 6$, and $n(A \cup B) = 14$. Find $n(A \cap B)$.

3. Suppose that $n(A) = 15$, $n(A \cap B) = 5$, and $n(A \cup B) = 30$. Find $n(B)$.

4. There are 50 students in an algebra (A) class and 30 students in a chemistry (C) class. Find
   (a) $n(A)$ (b) $n(C)$
   (c) The total number of students taking either algebra or chemistry, if it is known that none of the students is taking both courses
   (d) The number of students taking algebra and/or chemistry if it is known that 10 students are taking both courses

5. Upon checking with 100 families, it was found that 75 families subscribe to *Time*, 55 to *Newsweek*, and 10 to neither magazine. How many subscribe to both?

6. If, on checking with 100 families, it was found that 83 subscribe to *Time,* 40 to *Newsweek,* and 30 to both magazines, how many subscribe to neither?

B. 7. In a survey of 100 students, the numbers taking various courses were found to be as follows: English, 60; mathematics, 40; chemistry, 50; English and mathematics, 30; English and chemistry, 35; mathematics and chemistry, 35; courses in all three areas, 25.
   (a) How many students were taking mathematics but neither English nor chemistry?
   (b) How many were taking mathematics and chemistry but not English?
   (c) How many were taking English and chemistry but not mathematics?

8. Mr. N. Roll, the registrar at Lazy U, has observed that, of the students:

   45% have a 9 A.M. class.
   45% have a 10 A.M. class.
   40% have an 11 A.M. class.
   20% have a 9 and a 10 A.M. class.
   10% have a 9 and an 11 A.M. class.
   15% have a 10 and an 11 A.M. class.
    5% have a 9, a 10, and an 11 A.M. class.

   (a) What percent of the students have only a 9 A.M. class at these times?
   (b) What percent of the students have no classes at these times?

9. The following table shows the distribution of employees at the Taste-T Noodle Company.
   (a) How many employees are there in the Purchasing Department?
   (b) How many skilled employees are there in the factory?
   (c) How many of the skilled employees are in the Janitorial Department?

Personnel Distribution

Department	Administrator (A)	Clerical (C)	Other (O)	Skilled (SK)	Semi-skilled (SS)	Unskilled (U)
Purchasing (P)	1	14	7	0	0	0
Quality control (Q)	11	7	6	21	53	11
Sales (S)	8	8	40	0	0	0
Manufacturing (M)	5	7	0	9	23	37
Janitorial (J)	3	0	0	6	8	11

10. Use the table in problem 9 to find the number of persons in the following sets:

   (a) $A \cap S$
   (b) $S \cup P$
   (c) $M \cap A' \cap SK'$
   (d) $S \cap A' \cap C'$

11. The table gives the estimated costs for a proposed computer system in 2-year intervals, projected over 10 years (figures in thousands of dollars).

Cost Projections

	Year				
Item	1–2	3–4	5–6	7–8	9–10
Data-processing equipment	215	240	260	295	295
Personnel	85	85	95	95	105
Materials	120	65	35	35	40
All others	90	85	90	95	120

(a) How much money would be spent on materials in the first 2 years?
(b) What would be the total cost at the end of the second year?
(c) What would be the cost of the data-processing equipment over the 10-year period?

12. In a survey of 100 investors, it was found that:

   5 owned utilities stock only.
   15 owned transportation stock only.
   70 owned bonds.
   13 owned utilities and transportation stock.
   23 owned transportation and bonds.
   10 owned utilities and bonds.
   3 owned all three kinds.

(a) How many investors owned bonds only?
(b) How many investors owned utilities and/or transportation stock?
(c) How many investors owned neither bonds nor utilities?

13. In a recent survey of readers of the *Times* and/or the *Tribune*, it was found that 50 persons read both the *Times* and the *Tribune*. If it is known that 130 persons read the *Times* and 120 read the *Tribune*, how many people were surveyed?

14. In a survey conducted in a certain U.S. city, the data in the following table were collected.

Income	White (W)	Black (B)	Other (O)
Over $10,000 (H)	50	15	10
$7,000–$10,000 (M)	40	25	15
Under $7,000 (L)	30	35	20

Find the number of people in:

(a) M (b) M' (c) $(O \cup B) \cap W'$
(d) $L \cup O'$ (e) $H \cap B'$

15. In a survey of 100 customers at the Royal Hassle Restaurant, it was found that:

    40 had onions on their hamburgers.
    35 had mustard on their hamburgers.
    50 had catsup on their hamburgers.
    15 had onions and mustard on their hamburgers.
    20 had mustard and catsup on their hamburgers.
    25 had onions and catsup on their hamburgers.
     5 had onions, mustard, and catsup on their hamburgers.

    (a) How many customers had hamburgers with onions only?
    (b) How many customers had plain hamburgers (no condiments)?
    (c) How many customers had only one condiment on their hamburgers?

16. A survey of 900 workers in a plant indicated that 500 owned their homes, 600 owned cars, 345 owned boats, 300 owned cars and houses, 250 owned houses and boats, 270 owned cars and boats, and 200 owned all three.

    (a) How many of the workers did not own any of the three items?
    (b) How many of the workers owned only two of the items?

17. A coffee company was willing to pay $1 to each person interviewed about his or her likes and dislikes on types of coffee. Of the persons interviewed, 200 liked ground coffee, 270 liked instant coffee, 70 liked both, and 50 did not like coffee at all. What was the total amount of money the company had to pay?

18. In a recent survey, a statistician reported the following data:

    15 persons liked brand A.
    18 persons liked brand B.
    12 persons liked brand C.
     8 persons liked brands A and B.
     6 persons liked brands A and C.
     7 persons liked brands B and C.
     2 persons liked all three brands.
     2 persons liked none of the three brands.

    When the statistician claimed to have interviewed 30 persons, he was fired. Can you explain why?

19. In problem 18, a truthful statistician was asked to find out how many people were interviewed. Can you tell what this statistician's answer was?

20. In an experiment, it was found that a certain substance could be of type x or type y (not both). In addition, it could have one, both, or neither of the characteristics m and n. The table gives the results of testing several samples of the substance. Let M and N be the sets with characteristic m and n, respectively, and let X and Y be the sets of type x and y, respectively. How many samples are in each of the following sets?

(a) $M \cap X$ (b) $(X \cup Y) \cap (M \cup N)$

(c) $(Y \cap M) - (Y \cap N')$ (d) $(X \cup Y) \cap (M \cup N')$

	m only	n only	m and n	Neither m nor n
x	6	9	10	20
y	7	11	15	9

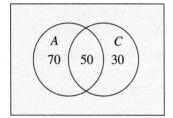

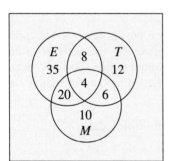

FIGURE 1.15

21. The number of students taking algebra (A) or calculus (C) is shown in Figure 1.15. Find:

(a) $n(A)$ (b) $n(C)$ (c) $n(A \cap C)$

22. Referring to Figure 1.15, find $n(A \cup C)$.

23. If the total number of students surveyed to obtain the data of problems 21 and 22 is 200, find:

(a) $n(A')$ (b) $n(C')$ (c) $n(A' \cap C')$

24. With the total number of students as in problem 23, find:

(a) $n(A' \cup C)$ (b) $n(A \cup C')$

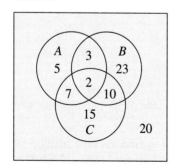

FIGURE 1.16

25. Upon checking with 100 investors to see who owned electric company stock (E), transportation stock (T), or municipal bonds (M), the numbers shown in Figure 1.16 were found.

(a) How many investors owned electric company or transportation stock but not both?

(b) How many owned electric company or transportation stock but not municipal bonds?

(c) How many had one or two of these types of investment but not all three?

(d) How many had at least two of these types of investment?

(e) How many had none of these?

26. A number of people were interviewed to find out who buys products A, B, and C regularly. The results are shown in Figure 1.17.

(a) How many buy product A?

(b) How many buy product A but not B?

(c) How many buy product B or C but not A?

(d) How many do not buy product C?

(e) How many people were interviewed?

FIGURE 1.17

*I*n Other Words

Classify the following statements as true or false. If true, explain why. If false, give a counterexample.

27. If $n(A) = n(B)$, then $A = B$
28. If $A = B$, then $n(A) = n(B)$
29. If $A - B = \varnothing$, then $n(A) = n(B)$
30. If $n(A) = n(B)$, then $A - B = \varnothing$

Using Your Knowledge

The cartoon shown below seems to indicate that it is impossible to have the morale statistics as follows:

> *58% want out (WO).*
> *14% hate his guts (HG).*
> *56% plan to desert (PD).*
> *8% are undecided (UD) (do not plan to do any of the above).*

However, a new statistician is hired and finds that in addition to the original information, the following statements are also true:

> *12% want to do only one thing — hate his guts.*
> *36% want to do exactly two things. Of these, 34% want out and plan to desert, and 2% hate his guts and want out.*

Of course, nobody in his right mind would do all three things.

31. Based on all the information, both old and new, draw a Venn diagram and show that it is possible to have the statistics quoted in the cartoon.

Reprinted with special permission of North America Syndicate, Inc.

Discovery

In Section 1.2 we discussed the subsets of a given set. It is interesting to diagram the formation of such subsets. We imagine that the elements of the given set are listed, and we look at each element in turn and decide whether or not to include it in the subset. For example, suppose that the given set is {a, b}. Then our diagram has two steps, as shown in the diagram at the left. This diagram makes it clear that there are 2 × 2, or 4, subsets in all.

The diagram at the right is for the three-element set {a, b, c}.

Diagrams like these are called **tree diagrams.** *The second tree diagram shows that a 3-element set has 2 × 2 × 2, or 8, subsets. Can you discover an easy way to explain this?*

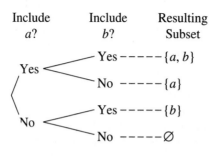

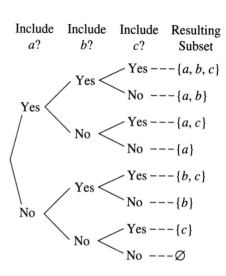

32. Can you discover the tree diagram for a 4-element set and its subsets?
33. Can you discover how to count the number of subsets of a 4-element set?
34. Can you now discover how to explain why an n-element set has

$$\underbrace{2 \times 2 \times 2 \times \cdots \times 2}_{n \text{ twos}}$$

or 2^n subsets?

1.6   INFINITE SETS

*Infrared map of Orion nebula
unveils new star formation*

GETTING STARTED

INFINITE SETS AND ONE-TO-ONE CORRESPONDENCES

Is the number of stars infinite? Mathematically speaking, if S is the set of all stars, what is $n(S)$? We do know that if $A = \{1, 2, 3\}$, then $n(A) = 3$. Now, suppose that $N = \{1, 2, 3, \ldots\}$, what is $n(N)$? To find $n(N)$ is to determine how many natural (counting) numbers there are! Georg Cantor studied this problem and assigned the **transfinite cardinal** $\aleph_0$ (read "aleph null"; $\aleph$ is the first letter of the Hebrew alphabet) to $n(N)$. Thus, $n(N) = \aleph_0$. Now, which set has more elements, $N = \{1, 2, 3, \ldots\}$ or $E = \{2, 4, 6, \ldots\}$?

At first, it seems that there should be twice as many natural numbers as there are even numbers. But consider the **one-to-one correspondence**

$$N = \{1, 2, 3, \ldots, n, \ldots\}$$
$$\updownarrow \; \updownarrow \; \updownarrow \qquad \updownarrow$$
$$E = \{2, 4, 6, \ldots 2n, \ldots\}$$

where every natural number n in N is paired with the even number $2n$ in E. Can you see that there are as many even numbers as there are natural numbers? We say that the two sets are **equivalent.** Moreover, there are as many natural numbers as there are fractions, but to see this you will have to get ahead of the game and look at the Discovery Section of Exercise 4.4. For now, you will learn how to use one-to-one correspondences to determine if sets are equivalent (see problems 1–5 in Exercise 1.6). In problems 16–20 you will even determine if a set is infinite!

What is an infinite set? In the years 1871–1884 Georg Cantor created a completely new mathematical discipline, **Set Theory.** Cantor asked himself: "What do we mean when we say of two finite sets that they consist of equally many things, that they have the same number, that they are equivalent?" The tool he used to answer this question was cardinal numbers and **one-to-one correspondences.**

A. *Equivalent Sets and Cardinal Numbers*

In Section 1.5 we learned that the **cardinal number** of a set A is the number of elements in A, denoted by $n(A)$ as before. Thus, if $A = \{a, b, c\}$, the cardinal number of A is $n(A) = 3$. To ascertain if two sets have the same cardinal number, we determine whether each element of A can be matched with a unique element of B and vice versa. That is, we check if there is a one-to-one correspondence between A and B.

EXAMPLE 1   Show that the sets $A = \{\#, \$, \&, *\}$ and $B = \{@, c, 2, ¢\}$ have the same cardinal number.

Solution   We have to show that there is a one-to-one correspondence between the elements of A and those of B. One such correspondence is given in Figure 1.6a. If, as before, $n(A)$ represents the number of elements in A, we see that $n(A) = n(B) = 4$.

■

FIGURE 1.6a

$$
\begin{array}{cccc}
\# & \$ & \& & \star \\
\updownarrow & \updownarrow & \updownarrow & \updownarrow \\
@ & c & 2 & ¢
\end{array}
$$

B. Equivalent Sets

Definition 1.11 ———

> If two sets A and B can be placed in a one-to-one correspondence with each other, the two sets are said to be equivalent, denoted by $A \sim B$.

Thus, the set of vowels V in the English alphabet is equivalent to the set of the first five counting numbers F, as can be seen by the correspondence

$$
\begin{array}{ccccc}
a & e & i & o & u \\
\updownarrow & \updownarrow & \updownarrow & \updownarrow & \updownarrow \\
1 & 2 & 3 & 4 & 5
\end{array}
$$

We then say that $V \sim F$.

EXAMPLE 2   Show that the set N of counting numbers and the set E of even counting numbers are equivalent.

Solution   We set up the correspondence

$$
\begin{array}{cccccccc}
1 & 2 & 3 & 4 & \ldots & n & n+1 & \ldots \\
\updownarrow & \updownarrow & \updownarrow & \updownarrow & & \updownarrow & \updownarrow & \\
2 & 4 & 6 & 8 & \ldots & 2n & 2(n+1) & \ldots
\end{array}
$$

■

Since the two sets can be placed in a one-to-one correspondence, $N \sim E$. In mathematics, when a set S is equivalent to the set N of counting numbers, S is called **denumerable.**

C. Infinite Sets

At first sight, it may seem strange that the set of counting numbers and a proper subset of itself (the set of even counting numbers) can be put in one-to-one correspondence. This apparent paradox puzzled mathematicians for years until it was resolved by Georg Cantor. Cantor defined an infinite set as follows.

Definition 1.12 ———

A set is **infinite** if it is equivalent to one of its proper subsets.

In his theory, he assigned the cardinal number $\aleph_0$ (read "aleph null") to the set of counting numbers; that is if $N = \{1, 2, 3, \ldots\}$, then $n(N) = \aleph_0$.

   With this convention it is possible to find the cardinal number of certain infinite sets. For example, because the set E of even counting numbers is equivalent to N, we must have $n(N) = n(E) = \aleph_0$.

   To show that N is infinite, note that N has the proper subset E that can be put in one-to-one correspondence with N. Thus, we conclude that N is an infinite set. In contrast to the cardinal number of a finite set, that of an infinite set is usually called a **transfinite cardinal number.**

EXAMPLE 3   Consider the set $S = \{1^2 = 1,\, 2^2 = 4,\, 3^2 = 9,\, \ldots n^2 \ldots\}$.

(a) Show that S is equivalent to N.
(b) Find the cardinality of S.
(c) Show that S is infinite.

Solution   (a) To show that S and N are equivalent, we set up a one-to-one correspondence between S and N as follows:

$$1 \quad 4 \quad 9 \ldots n^2 \ldots$$
$$\updownarrow \ \updownarrow \ \updownarrow \quad\ \updownarrow$$
$$1 \quad 2 \quad 3 \ldots n \ldots$$

Thus, S and N are equivalent; that is, $S \sim N$.

(b) Since S and N are equivalent and $n(N) = \aleph_0$, we have $n(N) = n(S) = \aleph_0$.

(c) To show that S is infinite, we must place S in one-to-one correspondence with one of its proper subsets. Here is such a correspondence:

$$1 \quad 4 \quad 9 \quad 16 \ldots \quad n^2 \ldots$$
$$\updownarrow \ \updownarrow \ \updownarrow \ \updownarrow \qquad\quad \updownarrow$$
$$4 \quad 9 \quad 16 \quad 25 \ldots (n+1)^2 \ldots$$

Note that
$$\{4, 9, 16, 25, \ldots, (n+1)^2, \ldots\} \subset \{1, 4, 9, 16, \ldots, n^2, \ldots\}. \quad \blacksquare$$

Exercise 1.6

A. In problems 1–5 show that the sets are equivalent by setting up a one-to-one correspondence between the two given sets.

1. The set N of counting numbers and the set O of odd counting numbers.

2. The set N of counting numbers and the set F of positive multiples of 5.

3. The set E of even counting numbers and the set G of even counting numbers greater than 100.

4. The set O of odd counting numbers and the set E of even counting numbers.

5. The set G of even counting numbers greater than 200 and the set T of even counting numbers greater than 300.

B. In problems 6–10, show that the two sets are equivalent.

6. $A = \{1, 2, 3, 4, 5\}$ and $B = \{a, b, c, d, e\}$
7. $P = \{2, 4, 8, 12\}$ and $Q = \{6, 12, 24, 36\}$
8. $W = \{0, 1, 2, 3, \ldots\}$ and $N = \{1, 2, 3, \ldots\}$
9. $I^- = \{-1, -2, -3, \ldots\}$ and $N = \{1, 2, 3, \ldots\}$
10. $N = \{1, 2, 3, \ldots\}$ and $F = \{\frac{1}{1}, \frac{1}{2}, \frac{1}{3}, \ldots\}$

In problems 11–15, find the cardinality of the given set.

11. $A = \{a, b, c, \ldots z\}$
12. $B = \{x \mid x \text{ is one of the Ten Commandments}\}$
13. $C = \{x \mid x \text{ is a star on the American flag}\}$
14. $D = \{\frac{1}{2}, \frac{1}{4}, \frac{1}{6}, \ldots\}$
15. $E = \{\frac{1}{1}, \frac{1}{4}, \frac{1}{9}, \ldots\}$

In problems 16–20, determine if the given set is finite.

16. $\{1, 2, 3, \ldots 999{,}999\}$
17. $\{100, 200, 300, \ldots\}$
18. $\{5, 10, 15, \ldots\}$
19. $\{\frac{1}{3}, \frac{2}{3}, \frac{3}{3}, \ldots\}$
20. $\{2^{64}, 2^{32}, 2^{16}, \ldots 2\}$

Use the sets $A = \{1, 2, 3, 4, 5, 6\}$, $B = \{a, b, c, d\}$, $C = \{w, x, y, z\}$, and $D = \{d, c, b, a\}$ to answer problems 21–23.

21. Which sets are equal and equivalent?
22. Which sets are equivalent but not equal?
23. Which sets are not equivalent and not equal?

*I*n Other Words

As you recall $n(N) = \aleph_0$ and $\aleph_0$ is called a **transfinite cardinal.** Can we perform arithmetic operations with these cardinals? Fill in the blank and justify your answer.

24. $\aleph_0 + 1 = $ _____   25. $\aleph_0 + \aleph_0 = $ _____

26. $2 \cdot \aleph_0 = $ _____   27. $\aleph_0 \cdot \aleph_0 = $ _____

28. Let $A = \{1, 3, 5, \ldots\}$ and $B = \{2, 4, 6, \ldots\}$.
As you recall, $n(A \cup B) = n(A) + n(B)$ if A and B are disjoint. Substitute A and B in the equation and state your result.

29. Consider the line segment shown. It is one unit long.

Draw an identical segment on a sheet of paper. Cut off the middle piece, the piece between $\frac{1}{3}$ and $\frac{2}{3}$, and paste it on a second sheet of paper. Then divide the piece between 0 and $\frac{1}{3}$ into three equal parts, each of length $\frac{1}{9}$. Cut off the middle piece, the piece between $\frac{1}{9}$ and $\frac{2}{9}$, and paste next to the first piece you pasted on the paper. Repeat the process with the piece between $\frac{2}{3}$ and 1. The middle piece you will cut off is the piece between $\frac{7}{9}$ and $\frac{8}{9}$. Paste this next to the second piece on the paper. Imagine that this process is continued.

(a) The points $\frac{1}{3}$, $\frac{2}{3}$, $\frac{1}{9}$, and $\frac{2}{9}$ are the first four points of the Cantor Set. What are the next two points?

(b) If you continue the foregoing pasting process, what do you think will be the total length of the pieces you pasted?

30. Do you think the Cantor Set and the set of all points on the line segment are equivalent? Explain.

Using Your Knowledge

Have you ever heard of the Infinity Hotel? It is a peculiar establishment indeed. The only prerequisite for employment is a thorough knowledge of infinite sets. In fact, the Employment Handbook consists entirely of the section you have just read. Even at that, Georg was hired as manager, and his first day on the job was a cinch.

The hotel soon filled all of its rooms, 1, 2, 3, . . . , n, n + 1, and so on. Trouble started on the second day with the arrival of a new guest. Where would Georg put this new guest? He thought about it for a split second, and then up went a neatly handwritten sign. Can you guess what it said?

If you are presently in room n, please move next door to room $n + 1$.

Where would the nice family in room 222 go? And what about the newcomer?

The third day things got more involved, for a group of eager customers arrived, in a Nexus Infinity, no less. Tensions were high at the hotel. Could Georg accommodate them all? No time was wasted. Without hesitation, the next sign went up. Do you know what it said?

If you are presently in room n, please move to room $2n$.

What an odd arrangement of rooms that would leave!
Use your knowledge to answer these questions.

31. On the second day, where would the family in room 222 go?

32. On the second day, in what room would the newcomer go?

33. What rooms were vacated for the people in the bus?

34. Where would the guest of problem 32 go the third day?

35. On the third day, where would the family in room 333 go?

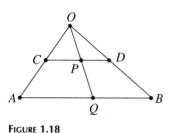

FIGURE 1.18

Discovery

*Here is one of the most striking results obtained by Cantor while studying the theory of **nondenumerable** sets (sets that cannot be put into one-to-one correspondence with the set of counting numbers). This result may appear incredible to you, but if you have mastered the idea of a one-to-one correspondence you should be able to prove it!*

    Two unequal line segments contain the same *number of points!*

    Cantor reasoned in the following manner: Two sets contain the same number of elements if and only if the elements can be paired off one-to-one. Then he diagrammed the two unequal line segments. (Call the line segments AB and CD as in Figure 1.18.) Notice that the line OPQ cuts CD at P, and AB at Q. We may regard P and Q as corresponding points.

36. Can you now discover the proof that there are as many points in *AB* as in *CD*?

Chapter 1 Summary

Section	Item	Meaning	Example
1.1A	{ }	Set braces	{1, 2, 3} is a set
1.1A	∈	Is an element of	$2 \in \{1, 2, 3\}$
1.1A	∉	Is not an element of	$4 \notin (1, 2, 3)$
1.1B	{1, 2}	List notation	
1.1B	{*x* | *x* has property *P*}	Set-builder notation	
1.1B	{ } or Ø	Empty, or null, set	The set of words that rhyme with "orange"
1.1C	*A* = *B*	*A* equals *B*	{1, 2} = {2, 1}
1.2	*A* ⊆ *B*	*A* is a subset of *B*	{1, 2} ⊆ {1, 2, 3}
1.2	*A* ⊂ *B*	*A* is a proper subset of *B*	{*a*} ⊂ {*a*, *b*}
1.2A	𝒰	Universal set	
1.3A	∩	Intersection	{1, 2, 3} ∩ {2, 3, 4} = {2, 3}
1.3A	∪	Union	{1, 2, 3, 4} ∪ {2, 3, 4} = {1, 2, 3, 4}
1.3B	*A*′	Complement	If 𝒰 = {1, 2, 3, 4, 5} and *A* = {1, 2}, then *A*′ = {3, 4, 5}.

1.3C	$A - B$	Set difference	If $A = \{1, 2, 3, 4, 5\}$ and $B = \{1, 2\}$, then $A - B = \{3, 4, 5\}$.
1.5	$n(A)$	Cardinal number of set A	If $A = \{a, b, c\}$ and $B = \{d, e\}$, then $n(A) = 3$ and $n(B) = 2$.
1.6B	$A \sim B$	A and B are equivalent	If $A = \{a, b\}$ and $B = \{1, 2\}$, they are equivalent.
1.6C	Infinite Sets	A set is infinite if it can be placed into one-to-one correspondence with one of its proper subsets	N is infinite since it can be placed into one-to-one correspondence with its proper subset E, the even numbers.

Research Questions

Sources of information for these questions can be found in the Bibliography at the end of the book.

1. Cantor's professor, and one of his most acerbic critics, was described as "A tiny man, who was increasingly self-conscious of his size with age." Who was he and what were his objections to Cantor's work?
2. The Ohio State Department of Education has a 16-item list of problem-solving strategies. The first three are: Look for a pattern, construct a table, and account for all possibilities. What are the other 13 strategies?
3. A brilliant mathematician and teacher, who taught at Princeton, Brown, Smith College, and Stanford, developed an extremely valuable problem-solving technique.
   (a) Who was this person?
   (b) List the four steps in his problem-solving technique.
   (c) List at least ten strategies found under step 2 of the problem-solving technique.
4. Venn diagrams were invented by John Venn. Write a paragraph about Venn's life and find out the name of the work in which these diagrams were first used. What is another name for Venn diagrams?
5. We have mentioned that Pascal's triangle was known to the Chinese centuries before Pascal. Find out how the Chinese, the Arabs, and the Persians dealt with the "arithmetic triangle" of Pascal.

Chapter 1 Practice Test

1. List the elements of the set:

   $\{x \mid x$ is a counting number between 2 and 10$\}$

2. Describe the following sets verbally and using set-builder notation:
   (a) $\{a, e, i, o, u\}$ (b) $\{2, 4, 6, 8\}$

3. List all the proper subsets of the set {$, ¢, %}.
4. Complete the following definitions by filling in the blanks with the symbol ∈ or ∉ :
   (a) $A \cup B = \{x \mid x \underline{\hspace{1cm}} A \text{ or } x \underline{\hspace{1cm}} B\}$
   (b) $A \cap B' = \{x \mid x \underline{\hspace{1cm}} A \text{ and } x \underline{\hspace{1cm}} B\}$
5. Complete the following definitions by filling in the blanks with the symbol ∈ or ∉ :
   (a) $A' = \{x \mid x \underline{\hspace{1cm}} \mathcal{U} \text{ and } x \underline{\hspace{1cm}} A\}$
   (b) $A - B = \{x \mid x \underline{\hspace{1cm}} A \text{ and } x \underline{\hspace{1cm}} B'\}$
6. Let $\mathcal{U} = \{$Ace, King, Queen, Jack$\}$, $A = \{$Ace, Queen, Jack$\}$, and $B = \{$King, Queen$\}$. Find:
   (a) A' (b) $(A \cup B)'$ (c) $A \cap B$
   (d) $\mathcal{U} - (A \cap B)'$
7. If, in addition to the sets in problem 6, we have $C = \{$Ace, Jack$\}$, find:
   (a) $(A \cap B) \cup C$ (b) $(A' \cup C) \cap B$
8. Draw a pair of Venn diagrams to show that $A - B = A \cap B'$.
9. Draw a Venn diagram to illustrate the set $A \cap B \cap C'$.
10. Find the sets of numbered regions in Figure 1.19 that represent the following sets:
    (a) $(A \cup B) \cap C'$ (b) $A' \cup (B' \cap C)$
11. Use the numbered regions in Figure 1.19 to verify that $(A \cap B) \cup C = (A \cup C) \cap (B \cup C)$.
12. Use the numbered regions in Figure 1.19 to verify that $(A \cap B)' = A' \cup B'$.
13. Refer to Figure 1.19 and determine which of the following sets (if any) is represented by regions 5, 6, 7.
    (a) $B - (A \cup C)$ (b) $(A \cup C) \cap B$
    (c) $(A \cap B \cap C) - (A \cap C)$ (d) $(A \cup C') \cap B$
14. Refer to Figure 1.19 and determine which of the following sets (if any) is represented by regions 6 and 7.
    (a) $A \cap B \cap C$ (b) $(A \cup C) \cap B$
    (c) $A \cap C$ (d) $(A \cap C) \cup B$

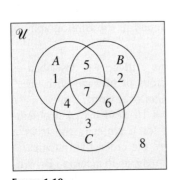

FIGURE 1.19

For problems 15–19, let $\mathcal{U} = \{1, 2, 3, 4, 5, 6, 7, 8\}$, $A = \{1, 3, 5, 7\}$, $B = \{2, 4, 6, 8\}$, and $C = \{1, 4, 5, 8\}$.

15. Fill in the blanks with ∈ or ∉ to make correct statements:
    (a) $2 \underline{\hspace{1cm}} A \cap B$ (b) $4 \underline{\hspace{1cm}} A \cup (B \cap C)$
    (c) $4 \underline{\hspace{1cm}} A \cap (B \cup C)$

16. Fill in the blanks with = or ≠ to make correct statements.
    (a) $n(A \cup C) \underline{\hspace{1cm}} 6$ (b) $n(B \cap C) \underline{\hspace{1cm}} 3$

17. Fill in the blanks with = or ≠ to make correct statements.
    (a) $(A \cup C) \cap B \underline{\hspace{1cm}} \{4, 8\}$
    (b) $(A \cap C) \cup B \underline{\hspace{1cm}} \{1, 2, 3, 5, 7, 8\}$

18. Let $n(A) = 25$ and $n(B) = 35$. Find $n(A \cup B)$ if:
    (a) $A \cap B = \emptyset$ (b) $n(A \cap B) = 5$

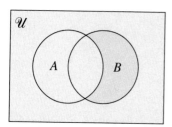

FIGURE 1.20

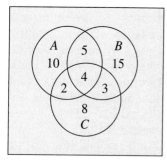

FIGURE 1.21

19. Let $n(A) = 15$, $n(B) = 25$, and $n(A \cup B) = 35$. Find:
    (a) $n(A \cap B)$ (b) $n(\mathcal{U})$ if $n(A' \cap B') = 8$

20. In Figure 1.20 the rectangular region represents the universal set $\mathcal{U}$, and the circular regions represent the subsets A and B of $\mathcal{U}$. Find an expression for the shaded region in the diagram.

21. Upon checking 200 students, it is found that 70 are taking French, 40 are taking German, 75 are taking Spanish, 10 are taking French and German, 30 are taking French and Spanish, 15 are taking German and Spanish, and 70 are taking no language. If it is known that no students are taking all three languages, draw a Venn diagram to determine the answers to the following questions:
    (a) How many are taking two languages?
    (b) How many are taking Spanish and no other language?
    (c) How many are taking Spanish and not French?

22. A survey of people to determine who buys products A, B, and C regularly gave the numbers shown in Figure 1.21.
    (a) How many people were surveyed?
    (b) How many buy product A but not B?
    (c) How many buy product B or C but not A?
    (d) How many buy both products B and C but not A?
    (e) How many do not buy either product B or product C?

Let D, C, and E be sets. In problems 23–25, choose the correct statement.

23. $D' \cup C' =$
    (a) $(D \cup C)'$
    (b) $(D \cap C)'$
    (c) $D \cap C$

24. $D \cup (C \cap E) =$
    (a) $(D \cup C) \cap E$
    (b) $D \cap (C \cup E)$
    (c) $(D \cup C) \cap (D \cup E)$

25. $D \cup (C \cup E) =$
    (a) $(D \cap C) \cap E$
    (b) $(D \cup C) \cap E$
    (c) $(D \cup C) \cup E$

26. Show that the sets $\{1, 3, \ldots, 2n - 1, \ldots\}$ and $\{2, 4, \ldots, 2n, \ldots\}$ have the same cardinal number.

27. Show that the sets $\{1, 2, \ldots, n, \ldots\}$ and $\{4, 16, \ldots, (2n)^2, \ldots\}$ are equivalent.

28. Find the cardinality of the set $\{1, 4, \ldots, n^2, \ldots, 144\}$.

29. Find the cardinality of the set $\{1, 4, \ldots, n^2, \ldots\}$.

30. Show that the set of all proper fractions with numerator 1 is infinite.

One of our most precious possessions is our ability to think and reason. Logic, the methods and principles used in distinguishing correct from incorrect thinking; logical thinking; and correct reasoning are used in many fields: law, insurance, science, and mathematics, to name a few. The study of logic dates back to the Greek philosopher Aristotle (384–322 B.C.), who systematized the principles of reasoning and laws of logic in his *Organon*.

We start this chapter with a basic concept in logic, **statements.** We learn how to write these statements and how to determine the conditions under which they are true or false. This idea goes back to the German mathematician and logician Gottlob Frege (1848–1925), who made the first effort to rewrite the established body of mathematics in logical symbolism.

To help us determine the truth or falsity of more complex statements, we develop a problem-solving tool called a **truth table** (Section 2.3), and then turn our attention to conditional and biconditional statements and their variations, as well as the related idea of implication. How do we determine if an argument is valid or invalid (Section 2.8)? We do this by using truth tables and the Euler diagrams of Section 2.7. We end the chapter with an important application of logic: switching circuits, or logic gates. All modern computers use Boolean logic, a system of logic devised by George Boole, the author of *The Mathematical Analysis of Logic*. You can read about Boole in The Human Side of Mathematics section that follows.

Logic

George Boole (1815–1864)

Others before Boole, notably Leibniz and De Morgan, had dreamed of adding logic to the domain of algebra; Boole did it.

E. T. Bell

THE HUMAN SIDE OF MATHEMATICS

George Boole, was born in Lincoln, England, on November 2, 1815. As a boy, thinking that a knowledge of Latin and Greek was the key to upper-class society, he taught himself both languages.

By age 16, Boole was educated enough to become an assistant teacher in an elementary school. Low wages forced him to lead a meager existence until at 20, he opened an elementary school.

Boole had received early instruction in the rudiments of mathematics from his father. As a teacher, Boole became deeply interested in learning more mathematics, which he again did on his own, even making his first original contribution to the subject with no aid from others.

Now his self-training in Latin and Greek proved its value. He sent a paper to the influential Scottish mathematician D. F. Gregory, who was so impressed with the style and content that he had the paper published. With Gregory's friendship, Boole was assured of the publication of his future work.

During the next few years, Boole became a friend of Augustus De Morgan a mathematician and a great logician. Influenced by De Morgan, Boole published a pamphlet, *The Mathematical Analysis of Logic,* in 1848. At age 34, Boole was appointed Professor of Mathematics at Queen's College in Cork, Ireland.

Then in 1854 at age 39, he published his masterpiece: *An Investigation of the Laws of Thought, on Which Are Founded the Mathematical Theories of Logic and Probabilities.*

In 1855, Boole married Mary Everest, niece of Sir George Everest, a professor of Greek at Queen's College and the individual for whom Mount Everest is named. With her, he lived a happy few years, honored and growing in fame. He died of pneumonia in December 1864.

Looking Ahead: Boole's work in logic and thought was instrumental in establishing modern symbolic logic, which is the focus of this chapter. He was primarily responsible for bringing the study of formal logic from the field of philosophy into that of mathematics.

2.1   STATEMENTS

Consider the following statements.

> Lessee shall not paint, paper, or otherwise redecorate or make alterations to the premises without the prior written consent of Lessor.

> Checking "Yes" will not change your tax or reduce your refund.

> Make sure your application is signed on page 3 and in the appropriate place on page 4.

Can you guess where these statements come from? Do you understand what they mean? In this section we study **statements,** that is, sentences that can be classified as true or false. The statements above were constructed using **conjunctions, disjunctions,** and **negations.** We shall study these types of statements and show you how to write them in symbols in Exercise 2.1, problems 9–16.

Now, look at the excerpt from a menu given below.

> **6. Country Fried Steak Breakfast**
>
> Includes 2 Eggs (any style), Country Fried Steak and Gravy, Grits or Breakfast Potatoes, Toast or Biscuits, and Fruit Jelly $4.99

Can you get the Eggs, Country Fried Steak and Gravy, Grits and Breakfast Potatoes, and Toast and Biscuit and Jelly? Not unless you pay extra! When translating statements containing commas into symbolic form, the commas indicate which simple statements are grouped together. Thus, using symbols, your breakfast menu may be translated as

$$e \wedge (s \wedge a) \wedge (g \vee p) \wedge (t \vee b) \wedge j$$

We will learn how to translate sentences into symbols and vice versa in the problems of Exercise 2.1.

The word *logic* is derived from the Greek word *logos,* which may be interpreted as "reason" or "discourse." The ancient Greeks are usually credited with initiating the study of our reasoning process. The principles discovered by the Greeks were first systematized by Aristotle (ca. 384–322 B.C.), and Aristotle's type of reasoning constitutes the traditional logic that has been studied and taught from his time to the present day. A simple illustration of Aristotelian logic goes as follows:

> All men are mortal.
> Socrates was a man.
> Therefore, Socrates was mortal.

This is a typical argument that is known as a **syllogism.**

Although the modern study of symbolic logic (the subject of this chapter) finds its roots in the works of such men as the German mathematician Leibniz (1647–1716), modern symbolism and algebraic-type operations were first systematically applied to logic in the works of George Boole (see the introduction to this chapter).

The study of logic has developed at an accelerated pace since Boole's analysis, and considerable progress toward an understanding of logical truth has been made. Whether we are trying to solve a problem, taking part in a debate, or working a crossword puzzle, we are engaged in a mental activity called "logical reasoning." This reasoning is usually expressed in terms of declarative sentences, and it is to the study of these sentences that we now turn our attention.

A. *Recognizing Statements*

In this and the following sections, we shall be concerned with certain types of declarative sentences called **statements** and the manner in which we can combine such sentences and arrive at valid conclusions.

> In general, a **statement** is a declarative sentence that can be classified as true or false, but not both simultaneously.

This capability of being classified as true or false makes statements different from questions, commands, or exclamations. Questions can be asked, commands given, and exclamations shouted, but only statements can be classified as true or false. The sentences in Example 1 are illustrations of statements.

EXAMPLE 1
(a) Boston is the capital of Massachusetts.
(b) 2 is even and less than 20.
(c) There are 5 trillion grains of sand in Florida.
(d) Either you study daily or you get an F in this course.
(e) If 2 is even, then $2 + 2$ is even.

Note that the truth or falsity of the first statement in Example 1 can be determined by a direct check, while the third one is true or false, even though there are no immediate or practical methods to determine its truth or falsity.

In contrast with the statements in Example 1, the following are illustrations of **nonstatements.**

EXAMPLE 2
(a) What time is it?
(b) Dagwood for president!
(c) Good grief, Charlie Brown!
(d) Close the door.
(e) This statement is false.

The sentences in Example 2 are not statements. Notice that if we assume that sentence (e) is true, then it is false, and if we assume that it is false, then it is true. Hence, the sentence cannot be classified as either true or false, so it is not a statement. A self-contradictory sentence of this type is called a **paradox.**

B. *Conjunction, Disjunction, and Negation*

Having explained what is meant by a statement, we now turn our attention to various combinations of statements. In Example 1, for instance, statements (a) and (c) have only one component each (that is, each says only one thing); while statement (b) is a combination of two components, namely, "2 is even," and "2 is less than 20." Statements (a) and (c) are **simple,** while statement (b) is **compound.**

As a further example, "John is 6 ft tall" is a simple statement. On the other hand, the statement, "John is 6 ft tall, *and* he plays basketball," is a compound statement, because it is a combination of the two simple statements, "John is 6 ft tall" and "he plays basketball."

As the reader may realize, there are many ways in which simple statements can be combined to form compound statements. Such combinations are formed by using words called **connectives** to join the statements. Two of the most important connectives are the words "and" and "or." Suppose we use the letters p and q to represent statements as follows:

p: It is hot today.
q: The air-conditioner in this room is broken.

Then we can form the following compound sentences:

p *and* q: It is hot today, *and* the air-conditioner in this room is broken.
p *or* q: It is hot today, *or* the air-conditioner in this room is broken.

In the study of logic, the word *and* is symbolized by $\wedge$ and the word *or* by $\vee$. Thus,

p **and** q is written $p \wedge q$
p **or** q is written $p \vee q$

Definition 2.1 ▬▬▬▬

> If two statement are combined by the word **and** (or an equivalent word), the resulting statement is called a **conjunction.** If the two statements are symbolized by p and q, respectively, then the conjunction is symbolized by $p \wedge q$.

EXAMPLE 3 Symbolize the following conjunctions:

(a) Tom is taking a math course, and Mary is taking a physics course.
(b) Ann is passing math, but she is failing English.

Solution (a) Let m stand for "Tom is taking a math course" and p stand for "Mary is taking a physics course." Then the given conjunction may be symbolized by $m \wedge p$.

(b) Let p stand for "Ann is passing math" and f stand for "she is failing English." The given conjunction is then symbolized by $p \wedge f$. Here, the word *but* is used in place of *and*.

Definition 2.2

If two statements are combined by the word **or** (or an equivalent word), the result is called a **disjunction.** If the two statements are symbolized by p and q, respectively, then the disjunction is symbolized by $p \vee q$.

EXAMPLE 4 Symbolize the disjunction, "We stop inflation, or we increase wages."

Solution Letting p stand for "We stop inflation" and q stand for "we increase wages," we can symbolize the disjunction by $p \vee q$.

Another construction important in logic is that of negating a given statement.

Definition 2.3

The **negation** of a given statement is a statement that is false whenever the given statement is true, and true whenever the given statement is false. If the given statement is denoted by p, its negation is denoted by $\sim p$. (The symbol $\sim$ is called a tilde.)

The negation of a statement can always be written by prefixing it with a phrase such as, "it is not the case that." Sometimes, the negation can be obtained simply by inserting the word *not* in the given statement. For example, the negation of the statement, "Today is Friday," can be written as,

"It is not the case that today is Friday."

Or as,

"Today is not Friday."

Similarly, if p stands for "It is hot today," then $\sim p$ (read, "not p") may be written either as "It is not hot today," or as "It is not the case that it is hot today."

In the preceding illustrations, we have negated simple statements. We often have to consider the negation of compound statements, as in the next example.

EXAMPLE 5   Let p be "the sky is blue," and let q be "it is raining." Translate the following statements into English:

(a) $\sim(p \wedge q)$ (b) $\sim p \wedge \sim q$ (c) $\sim q \wedge p$

Solution   (a) It is not the case that the sky is blue and it is raining.
Another form of the negation is: The sky is not blue or it is not raining.
(b) The sky is not blue and it is not raining.
(c) It is not raining and the sky is blue.

The two forms of the solution to part (a) of Example 5 illustrate the fact that the negation of $p \wedge q$ can be written either as $\sim(p \wedge q)$ or as $\sim p \vee \sim q$. Thus,

$$\sim(p \wedge q) \qquad \text{means} \qquad \sim p \vee \sim q$$

Similarly,

$$\sim(p \vee q) \qquad \text{means} \qquad \sim p \wedge \sim q$$

because the statement p *or* q is false when and only when p and q are *both* false. Thus, we have **De Morgan's laws:**

$$\sim(p \wedge q) \qquad \text{means} \qquad \sim p \vee \sim q$$
and
$$\sim(p \vee q) \qquad \text{means} \qquad \sim p \wedge \sim q$$

You should compare the preceding two laws with De Morgan's laws for sets $(A \cap B)' = A' \cup B'$ and $(A \cup B)' = A' \cap B'$.

EXAMPLE 6   Consider the two statements:

p: Sherlock Holmes is alive.
q: Sherlock Holmes lives in London.

Write the following statements in symbolic form:

(a) Sherlock Holmes is alive, and he lives in London.
(b) Either Sherlock Holmes is alive, or he lives in London.
(c) Sherlock Holmes is neither alive, nor does he live in London.
(d) It is not the case that Sherlock Holmes is alive and he lives in London.

Solution   (a) $p \wedge q$ (b) $p \vee q$ (c) $\sim p \wedge \sim q$ (d) $\sim (p \wedge q)$ ▪

Be sure to notice the use of parentheses to indicate which items are to be taken as a unit. Thus, in part (a) of Example 5 and in part (d) of Example 6, $\sim (p \wedge q)$ means the negation of the entire statement $(p \wedge q)$. It is important to distinguish $\sim (p \wedge q)$ from $\sim p \wedge q$. The latter means that only the statement p is negated. For example, if p is "John likes Mary," and q is "Mary likes John," then $\sim (p \wedge q)$ is "It is not true that John and Mary like each other." But $\sim p \wedge q$ is "John does not like Mary, but Mary likes John."

When translating statements containing commas into symbolic form, the commas indicate which simple statements are grouped together, as shown in the next example.

EXAMPLE 7   Write in symbolic form:

(a) "You are a full-time student (f) or over 21 (o), and a resident of the state (r)."

(b) "You are a full-time student, or over 21 and a resident of the state."

Solution   (a) $(f \vee o) \wedge r$ (b) $f \vee (o \wedge r)$ ▪

Note that statements (a) and (b) do not have the same meaning!

EXAMPLE 8   Let p be the statement "Tarzan likes Jane," and let q be the statement "Jane likes Tarzan." Symbolize and write in words:

(a) The negation of the conjunction of p and q.

(b) The disjunction of the negations of p and q.

(c) The conjunction of the negations of p and q.

(d) According to De Morgan's laws, what can you conclude about the statements in (a), (b), and (c)?

Solution   (a) The conjunction of p and q is $p \wedge q$. Thus, the negation of the conjunction of p and q is $\sim (p \wedge q)$. In words: It is not the case that Tarzan likes Jane and Jane likes Tarzan. That is, it is not the case that Tarzan and Jane like each other.

(b) The negations of p and q are $\sim p$ and $\sim q$, respectively. Thus, the disjunction of the negations of p and q is $\sim p \vee \sim q$. In words: Either Tarzan does not like Jane or Jane does not like Tarzan.

(c) $\sim p \wedge \sim q$. In words: Tarzan does not like Jane and Jane does not like Tarzan. That is, Tarzan and Jane dislike each other.

(d) By De Morgan's laws, the statements $\sim (p \wedge q)$ and $\sim p \vee \sim q$ in parts (a) and (b), respectively, have the same meaning. ▪

Statements involving the **universal quantifiers** *all, no,* and *every,* or the **existential quantifiers** *some* and *there exists at least one* are more complicated to negate. Here is a table that may help you.

Statement	Negation
All *a*'s are *b*'s	**Some** *a*'s **are not** *b*'s
No *a*'s are *b*'s	**Some** *a*'s **are** *b*'s

Thus, the following statements p and $\sim p$ are negations of each other as are q and $\sim q$.

p: **All** homeowners participate in recycling.

$\sim p$: **Some** homeowners **do not** participate in recycling, or "**Not** all homeowners participate in recycling."

q: **Some** of us will graduate.

$\sim q$: **None** of us will graduate.

Keep in mind that the definition of a negation (Definition 2.3) requires that the negation of a statement must be false whenever the statement is true, and must be true whenever the statement is false. You can check this by looking at statements q and $\sim q$ above.

EXAMPLE 9   Write the negation of:

(a) All of us like pistachio nuts.
(b) Nobody likes freezing weather.
(c) Some students work part-time.

Solution   (a) Some of us do not like pistachio nuts. An alternate form is: Not all of us like pistachio nuts.
(b) Somebody likes freezing weather.
(c) No student works part time.   ■

Exercise 2.1

A.   In problems 1–8, determine whether the sentence is a statement. Classify each sentence that is a statement as simple or compound. If it is compound, give its components.

1. Circles are dreamy.
2. Lemons and oranges are citrus fruits.
3. Jane is taking an English course, and she has four themes to write.
4. Apples are citrus fruits.
5. Do you like mathematics?

6. Walk a mile.

7. Students at Ohio State University are required to take either a course in history or a course in economics.

8. Today is Sunday, and tomorrow is Monday.

B. In problems 9–16, write the given statement in symbolic form using the indicated letter to represent the corresponding component.

9. This is April a, and income tax returns must be filed f.

10. Logic is a required subject for lawyers r but not for most engineers $\sim e$.

11. Dick Tracy is a detective d or a fictitious character in the newspaper f.

12. Snoopy is not an aviator $\sim a$, or the Sopwith Camel is an airplane p.

13. Violets are blue b, but roses are pink p.

14. The stock market goes up u; nevertheless, my stocks stay down d.

15. I will take art a or music m next term.

16. I will not drive to New York $\sim d$; however, I shall go by train t or by plane p.

In problems 17–20, let p be "Robin can type," and let q be "Robin takes shorthand." Write the given statement in symbolic form.

17. Robin can type and take shorthand.

18. Robin can type, but does not take shorthand.

19. Robin can neither type nor take shorthand.

20. It is not the case that Robin can type and take shorthand.

In problems 21–25, let p be "Dagwood loves Blondie," and let q be "Blondie loves Dagwood." Give a verbal translation of the given statement.

21. $p \vee \sim q$ 22. $\sim(p \vee q)$ 23. $p \wedge \sim q$

24. $\sim p \wedge \sim q$ 25. $\sim(p \wedge q)$

In problems 26–31, write the negation of the given sentence.

26. It is a long time before the end of the term.

27. Bill's store is making a good profit.

28. 10 is a round number.

29. My dog is a spaniel.

30. Your cat is not a Siamese.

31. I do not like to work overtime.

In problems 32–34, determine whether the statements p and q are negations of each other.

32. p: Sally is a very tall girl.   33. p: All squares are rectangles.
    q: Sally is a very short girl. q: Some squares are not rectangles.

34. p: All whole numbers are even.
    q: At least one whole number is not even.

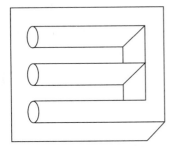

Some things are not what they appear to be

In problems 35–49, state the negation of the given statement.

35. All men are mortal.

36. Some women are teachers.

37. Some basketball players are not 6 ft tall.

38. Some things are not what they appear to be.

39. Either he is bald or he has a 10-inch forehead.

40. Nobody does not like Sara Lee.

41. Some circles are round

42. Some men earn less than $5 an hour, and some men earn more than $50 an hour.

43. Somebody up there loves me.

44. Nothing is certain but death and taxes.

45. Everybody likes to go on a trip.

46. No one can sue us under this coverage.

47. All persons occupying your covered auto are insured.

48. None of your contributions are deductible.

49. Some expenses are not subject to the 2% limit.

50. The statement "Not all people are awkward" is directly transformed into the statement "Some people are not awkward" by which one of the following logical equivalences?
    (a) "If p, then q" means the same as "if not q, then not p."
    (b) "All are not p" means the same as "none are p."
    (c) "Not all are p" means the same as "some are not p."
    (d) "Not (not p)" means the same as "p."

51. Consider the information: The chairperson of the city council told the members that if they declared a holiday, at least one of the ten banks in the city would remain open. The chairperson was mistaken. Which of the following (if any) is consistent with this information?
    (a) The council did not declare a holiday and all the banks remained closed.
    (b) The council did not declare a holiday and all the banks remained open.
    (c) The council declared a holiday and none of the banks remained closed.
    (d) The council declared a holiday and none of the banks remained open.

Write out problems 52–55 in symbolic form.

52. You are legally married m or divorced d, and currently enrolled e.

53. I am a dependent person d and my parents are residents p, or I have maintained legal residence in the state r.

54. *Excerpt from a Pell Grant brochure:* "You must be a U.S. citizen c or an eligible noncitizen n, and be enrolled as a degree-seeking student e."

55. *Excerpt from the Paul Douglas Teacher Scholarship:* "You must be a resident *r* and be ranked in the top 10% of your graduating class *t* or GED scores *g*."

*I*n Other Words

56. Let *p* be "Today is Friday." Let *q* be "Tomorrow is Saturday." Write the negation of each of the following in words:

    (a) $p \wedge q$
    (b) $p \wedge \sim q$
    (c) $p \vee q$

57. Let *p* be "The diagram is a square." Let *q* be "The diagram is a rectangle." Write the negation of each of the following in words:

    (a) $p \vee q$
    (b) $\sim p \wedge q$
    (c) $\sim p \vee \sim q$

2.2   TRUTH VALUES OF STATEMENTS

GETTING STARTED

TAX FORMS AND TRUTH VALUES

Have you ever *really* read the instructions for your 1040 tax form? For example, suppose you are interested in knowing if a person qualifies as your dependent. You turn to page 10 of the instruction booklet and it says that for someone to qualify as your dependent, he or she must pass five qualifying tests, including the following:

> **Test 3—Citizen or Resident**
>
> The person must have been a U.S. citizen *u* or resident alien *r*, a resident of Canada *c* or Mexico *m*, or your adopted child *a* who is not a U.S. citizen $\sim u$, but who lived with you all year in a foreign country *l*.

You got it? Here is some more bad news. This is only *one* of the *five* tests required to qualify a person as a dependent. For our purposes, let us just consider when a person qualifies under this test. First, translate the statement:

$$(u \vee r) \vee (c \vee m) \vee (a \wedge \sim u \wedge l)$$

As you recall, a disjunction is true when any of the components is true; thus, if any of the statements in parentheses is true, the test is satisfied. Can you think of three different conditions under which the test is satisfied? How can you make the third statement in parentheses true? In this section, you will learn to identify circumstances under which compound statements are true or false. Then you can do it yourself in problems 8–11 of Exercise 2.2.

We regard T (for true) and F (for false) as the possible **truth values** of a statement. Thus, the statement "George Washington was the first president of the United States" has the truth value T; and the statement "The moon is made of green cheese" has the truth value F.

One of the principal problems in logic is that of determining the truth value of a compound statement when the truth values of its components are known. In order to attack this problem, we must first assign appropriate truth values to such statements as $p \wedge q$, $p \vee q$, and $\sim p$. Although the symbols $\wedge$, $\vee$, and $\sim$ were introduced in Section 2.1, they were not completely defined there. We shall complete their definitions by assigning appropriate truth values to statements involving these symbols.

A. *The Conjunction*

Suppose you are offered a position in a firm that requires that:

> p: The applicant must be at least 18 years of age

and

> q: The applicant must be a college graduate

We can easily see that to be eligible for this position you must meet *both* requirements; that is, both p and q must be true. Thus, it seems desirable to say that for a conjunction to be true, both components must be true. Otherwise, the conjunction is false.

If we have a conjunction with two components, p and q, we have four possible pairs of truth values for these statements, namely:

1. p true, q true
2. p true, q false
3. p false, q true
4. p false, q false

Table 2.1 *Conjunction ($\wedge$)*

1	2	3
p	q	$p \wedge q$
T	T	T
T	F	F
F	T	F
F	F	F

As in the preceding example, it seems reasonable to assign the value T to the statement $p \wedge q$ only when both components are true. The assignment of these truth values can be summarized by means of a **truth table,** as shown in Table 2.1. This truth table is to be regarded as the definition of the symbol $\wedge$, and it expresses the fact that:

> The conjunction $p \wedge q$ is true when p and q are both true; otherwise, the conjunction is false.

Recall from Section 2.1 that other English words such as *but, nevertheless, still, however,* and so on, are sometimes used in place of the connective *and.* Thus, the statement "Mary is young but not under 15" is a conjunction. On the other hand, the statement "Mary and Sue are sisters" is not a conjunction (unless they are sisters in a sorority).

B. *The Disjunction*

As we shall see, there are two types of disjunctions, and we shall illustrate these by examples.

EXAMPLE 1

Let *p* be "I will pass this course."
Let *q* be "I will flunk this course."

Form the disjunction of *p* and *q*, and discuss its truth values.

Solution

The statement "I will pass this course, or I will flunk it" is the desired disjunction. This statement will be true only when *exactly* one of the components is true; it will be false otherwise.

■

EXAMPLE 2

Consider the two statements:

m: I will study Monday.
s: I will study Saturday.

Form the disjunction of *m* and *s*, and discuss its truth values.

Solution

The statement "I will study Monday, or I will study Saturday" is the required disjunction. It will be false only when both components are false; it will be true otherwise.

■

Table 2.2 *Disjunction* ($\lor$)

1	2	3
p	*q*	*p* $\lor$ *q*
T	T	T
T	F	T
F	T	T
F	F	F

If we compare the disjunctions in Examples 1 and 2, it is clear that in the statement contained in Example 1, only one of the two possibilities can occur: I will either pass the course or not. However, in Example 2, I have the possibility of studying Monday or Saturday, or even both. The meaning of the second usage is clarified by replacing the word *or* by *and/or*. Instead of arguing which usage should be called the disjunction of the two statements, we shall refer to the *or* used in Example 1 as the **exclusive or,** or the **exclusive disjunction.** On the other hand, the *or* used in Example 2 will be called the **inclusive or,** or the **inclusive disjunction,** and will be denoted by $\lor$. The truth table defining the symbol $\lor$ appears in Table 2.2 and expresses the important fact that:

> The inclusive disjunction *p* $\lor$ *q* (read, "*p* or *q*") is false only when *p* and *q* are both false; otherwise, it is true.

In the remainder of this chapter it will not be necessary to use the exclusive disjunction.

C. *Negations*

Finally, we shall consider the **negation** of a statement. In the English language, a negation is usually formed by inserting a *not* into the original statement. Of course, this is not the only way to negate a statement. A column by

Bill Gold, which appeared in the *Washington Post,* tells the story of a woman who offered a bus driver a $5 bill and asked for tokens. His reply? "I am sorry, lady, but there ain't no bus driver got no change or no tokens, no time, nowhere, no more."

EXAMPLE 3   Let *p* be the statement "I will be drafted." Express the statement $\sim p$ verbally, and discuss its truth values.

Solution   Either of the statements, "I will not be drafted" or "It is not the case that I will be drafted," is the negation of the statement *p* and may be symbolized by $\sim p$. Because every statement is either true or false (and not both), we see that $\sim p$ must be false whenever *p* is true, and $\sim p$ must be true whenever *p* is false. ∎

Table 2.3 *Negation* (~)

1	2
p	$\sim p$
T	F
F	T

Table 2.3 defines the negation symbol $\sim$. This table expresses the following definition:

$\sim p$ is false whenever *p* is true, and $\sim p$ is true whenever *p* is false.

EXAMPLE 4   Your driver's license will be renewed under the following conditions: You are a safe driver, have no physical disability, and are not addicted to drugs or intoxicants. Let *s* be the statement "You are a safe driver," *p* be the statement "You have a physical disability," and *q* be the statement "You are addicted to drugs or intoxicants." Write a statement in symbolic form whose truth will guarantee that your driver's license will be renewed.

Solution $s \wedge \sim p \wedge \sim q$ ∎

Exercise 2.2

In problems 1–4, let *p* be "Today is Friday," and let *q* be "Today is Monday."

1. Write in words the disjunction of the two statements.
2. Write in words the conjunction of the two statements.
3. Write in words the negation of the statement *p*.
4. Which of the statements in problems 1–3 always has the truth value *F*?

In problems 5–7, let *g* be "He is a gentleman," and let *s* be "He is a scholar." Write in words:

5. The disjunction of the two statements
6. The negation of the statement *g*
7. The conjunction of the two statements

In problems 8–10, use the two statements g and s of problems 5–7, and write in symbolic form:

8. He is not either a gentleman or a scholar.

9. He is a gentleman and a scholar.

10. He is neither a gentleman nor a scholar.

11. Consider the statements p and q:

   p: It is raining.
   q: I will go to the beach.

Write the statements in parts (a) and (b) in symbolic form.
(a) It is raining, but I will go to the beach.
(b) It is raining, or I will go to the beach.
(c) Assume that p is true and q is false. Find the truth values of the statements given in parts (a) and (b).

In problems 12–15, let p be "Mida is cooperative," and let q be "Desi is uncooperative." Write the given statement in symbolic form.

12. Mida and Desi are both cooperative.

13. Neither Desi nor Mida is uncooperative.

14. It is not the case that Mida and Desi are both uncooperative.

15. Either Mida is cooperative or Desi is uncooperative.

16. Assume that Mida is cooperative and Desi is uncooperative. Which of the statements in problems 12–15 are true?

In problems 17–21, suppose that p is true and q is false. Write the given statement in symbolic form, and find its truth value:

17. Either p or q 18. Either p or not q
19. Neither p nor q 20. p or q but not both
21. Not q and not p

In problems 22–25, consider the statements:

   g: I go to college.
   j: I join the army.

Suppose that g is false and j is true. Write the given statement in symbolic form, and find its truth value:

22. Either I go to college or I join the army.

23. I go to college, or I do not join the army.

24. I neither go to college, nor do I join the army.

25. I go to college or I join the army, but not both.

26. *An application to law*. A lawyer who specializes in damage suits arising out of automobile accidents knows that

   1. The court will decide in favor of his client when his client was not negligent and the other driver was negligent.
   2. The court will decide against his client when both drivers were negligent or when neither was negligent.

   Let c be the statement that the client was negligent, and let d be the statement that the other driver was negligent.
   (a) Use statement 1 to write a compound statement in symbolic form whose truth guarantees that the court will decide in favor of the client.
   (b) Use statement 2 to write a compound statement in symbolic form whose truth guarantees that the court will decide against the client.

27. A person is considered to have established his or her age for Social Security benefits when the person furnishes one of the following:

   1. Birth certificate b
   2. Church baptismal record c, giving the date of birth
   3. Early school record s and an employment record e, both giving the date of birth

Write in symbols (using the suggested abbreviations) the conditions under which a person has established his (or her) age.

28. *An application to medicine:* In diagnosing diseases, it is extremely important to recognize the symptoms that distinguish one disease from another (usually called the "differential diagnosis"). The *Diagnosis Treatment* handbook* states: "Many specific infectious diseases present initial manifestations indistinguishable from those of common respiratory disease. Vigilance is required to avoid diagnostic errors of omission." Next are listed some symptoms that may be present in a patient with a respiratory disease:

   s_1: Patient has a high white blood cell count.
   s_2: Patient has fever.
   s_3: Patient has nasal discomfort.
   s_4: Patient has a sore throat.
   s_5: Patient has a cough.
   s_6: Patient has a headache.
   s_7: Patient has a low white blood cell count.
   s_8: Patient has the influenza virus.

   In a certain hospital, it was found that:

   1. When s_8 was false, but s_1 and either s_4 or s_5 were true, the diagnosis was a cold.

*H. Brainerd, M. Chatton, and S. Margen, *Diagnosis Treatment*. Los Altos, Calif.: Lange Medical Publications, 1962, p. 102.

2. When s_8 was true, the diagnosis was influenza.
3. When s_8 was false, but s_7, s_6, s_4 and either s_2 or s_3 were true, the diagnosis was influenza.

    (a) State in symbolic form the statement whose truth implies that the diagnosis was a cold.
    (b) Do the same for influenza.

29. Here is a sign that appeared on a football stadium: "Students must present a valid student ID card i and agree to sit in the student section a, or else purchase a general admission ticket p." Write in symbols, using the suggested abbreviations, the conditions under which a student would *not* be admitted to the stadium.

30. A person can check books out of a certain county library under the following conditions: the person has a valid ID card c, and, in addition, either is a resident of the county r or else pays a \$12 annual fee p. Use the suggested symbols to write a statement in symbolic form whose truth would *not* permit a person to check books out of this library.

31. The Florida "Intangible Tax Return" states, "A Florida beneficiary having one or more property rights in a trust must file a return and pay a tax unless a Florida Intangible Tax Return was filed by the trustee." The state did not receive a return from Sam Slick, a Florida beneficiary with property rights in a trust. May the state assume that Sam was breaking the law?

Problems 32–36 give some income tax applications.

32. In case you do not file a joint return, the 1040 federal income tax form instructions states: "You may claim an exemption for your spouse only if your spouse had no income from U.S. sources and is not the dependent of another taxpayer." Ms. Mulberry filed a separate return from her spouse, who had no income at all, claiming him as an exemption. What additional true statement can you make about Ms. Mulberry's spouse?

33. In a recent set of income tax forms, in Schedule B, Interest and Dividend Income, it said that a taxpayer who was required to list interest in Part I i or dividends in Part II d, OR had a foreign account f or was a grantor of g or a transferor to a foreign trust t, must answer both questions in Part III. Use the suggested abbreviations and write in symbolic form the condition that would require the taxpayer to answer both questions in Part III. [*Hint:* You need two sets of parentheses.]

34. Refer to the statement in problem 33.
    (a) What is the minimum number of statements that have to be true in order for the taxpayer to have to answer both questions in Part III?
    (b) Name the five different statements such that if any one of them is true, the taxpayer must answer both questions in Part III.

35. The interest income section of Schedule D, Form 1040, states that a tax-payer who received interest that actually belongs to another person i, or received r or paid p interest on securities transferred between interest payment dates should see page 24. Write in symbolic form the condition that requires the taxpayer to see page 24.

36. Refer to the statement in problem 35, and write a statement in symbolic form—without using parentheses—that excuses the taxpayer from referring to page 24.

37. The Higher Education Act states that for a student to be eligible to apply for a loan, that student must be:

   1. Enrolled and in good standing, or accepted for enrollment, in an eligible school

   2. Registered for at least one-half of the normal full-time work load as determined by the school

   3. A citizen or national of the United States, or in the United States for other than a temporary reason

   Which of the following students are eligible to apply for a loan?

   (a) Sally has applied for admission to an eligible school and intends to register for a full-time load. She is a citizen of the United States.

   (b) Pedro has been accepted for enrollment in an eligible school and is registered for a full-time load leading to a Master's degree. Pedro is a citizen of Brazil and intends to return there after he earns the Master's degree.

   (c) Boris has been accepted for enrollment in an eligible school and is registered for a full-time load. Boris is a Russian refugee and has a permit to reside in the United States permanently.

   (d) Susan, who is a citizen of the United States, is enrolled and in good standing in an eligible school. Susan has a full-time job, so she is registered for only 7 credit hours. The full-time load at her school is 15 credit hours.

38. Refer to problem 32 and assume that all of the following filed separate returns. Which of them are allowed to claim the spouse as an exemption?

   (a) Mr. Ambrose, whose wife had no income of her own but is the dependent of her father, who is a taxpayer.

   (b) Mrs. Brown, whose husband has a large income from U.S. Treasury bonds.

   (c) Mr. Cary, whose wife has some income from an investment in Switzerland, but is otherwise dependent on her husband.

   (d) Mrs. Dolan, whose husband has no separate income, but is the dependent of his mother, who lives in Ireland and does not pay U.S. taxes.

In Other Words

Mathematics has a specialized vocabulary. For example, the negation of "9 is less than 3" is "9 is not less than 3," but it can also be "9 is greater than or equal to 3."

In problems 39–43 negate the statements without using the word *not.*

39. 7 is less than 5.

40. 8 is more than 9.

41. 0 is greater than 3.

42. $\frac{1}{3}$ is greater than or equal to 1.

43. $\frac{1}{2}$ is less than or equal to $\frac{1}{8}$.

44. Let *f* be "I will go fishing." Let *g* be "The sun is shining."
    (a) Write in words the conjunction of *f* and *g*.
    (b) The negation of *g*.
    (c) The disjunction of *f* and *g*.

45. For the statements given in problem 44, write in words the negation of the conjunction of *f* and *g*. State under what circumstances this negation would be true.

Using Your Knowledge

Here is an application of the material we have studied. The Higher Education Act states that any student is eligible to apply for a loan, provided the student is:
  (a) *Enrolled e and in good standing g, or accepted for enrollment a, at an eligible school.*
  (b) *Registered for at least one-half of the normal full-time work load as determined by the school h.*
  (c) *A citizen c or national n of the United States, or in the United States for other than a temporary purpose ~t.*

46. Translate requirements (a), (b), and (c) into symbolic form.

47. Can you discover the general compound statement whose truth implies that the student may apply for a loan?

48. A three-component statement whose truth implies that the student may apply for a loan is $a \wedge h \wedge c$. Can you discover two others?

Discovery

Consider the four statements:
  (a) $g \wedge s$ (b) $g \vee s$ (c) $\sim g \vee \sim s$ (d) $\sim g \wedge \sim s$

49. Make a table with the headings g, s, $g \wedge s$, $g \vee s$, $\sim g \vee \sim s$, and $\sim g \wedge \sim s$, and fill in all the possible combinations of truth values for the four statements.

50. Can you discover which of the four statements can be simultaneously true?

51. If you assume that two of the statements are true, can you discover the status (true or false) of the other two?

52. If you assume that two of the statements are false, can you discover the status (true or false) of the other two?

53. Can you discover a rule that gives the status (true or false) of the four statements in every possible case?

2.3   TRUTH TABLES: A PROBLEM-SOLVING TOOL

GETTING STARTED

A LOGIC PUZZLE

Have you ever heard of a logic puzzle? Here is one. Paloma, Janet, Kitty, and Julia are four talented, creative artists. One is a dancer, one a painter, one a singer, and one a writer (but not necessarily in that order).

1. Paloma and Kitty were in the audience the night the singer made her debut at a concert.
2. Both Janet and the writer have sat for portraits by the painter.
3. The writer, whose biography of Julia is on the best-seller list, is planning to write a biography of Paloma.
4. Paloma has never heard of Kitty.

What is each woman's field?

Our problem-solving strategy here is to make a **truth table** covering all possibilities and then use the four given facts to enter a series of T's or F's in the appropriate rows and columns.

	Dancer	Painter	Singer	Writer
Paloma			F	F
Janet		F		F
Kitty			F	T
Julia				F

From 1, neither Paloma nor Kitty can be the singer, so we enter F's opposite their names and in the appropriate column. From 2 we know that Janet is neither the painter nor the writer and from 3 we know that the writer is neither Paloma nor Julia. By looking at the last column, we can conclude that Kitty is the writer and we enter a T in the appropriate place. Can you finish the puzzle? A medical application using a similar problem-solving technique appears in the Using Your Knowledge section of Exercise 2.3. You will also find another puzzle in the Discovery section of the exercises.

In many cases, it is convenient to construct truth tables to determine the truth values of certain compound statements involving the symbols $\wedge$ (and), $\vee$ (or), and $\sim$ (not). These symbols were defined by truth tables in the preceding section. It is important to keep in mind that a conjunction $p \wedge q$ is true when p and q are both true and is false otherwise; a disjunction $p \vee q$ is false when p and q are both false and is true otherwise; and if p and $\sim p$ are negations of each other, then $\sim p$ is false whenever p is true, and $\sim p$ is true whenever p is false.

A. *Making Truth Tables*

EXAMPLE 1   Construct the truth table for the statement $\sim p \vee q$.

Solution   First, we break the statement down into its components to see what headings we need for the truth table. The statement $\sim p \vee q$ has the components $\sim p$ and q. We regard p and q as the primitive components, and we get the truth values of $\sim p$ from those of p. This breakdown suggests that the proper headings are p, q, $\sim p$, and $\sim p \vee q$, where the last two items are obtained from the preceding ones. We now construct the table in the margin, where the numbers at the top give the order in which the required statement is put together from p and q.

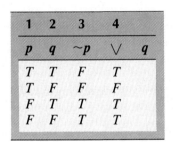

1	2	3	4	
p	q	$\sim p$	$\vee$	q
T	T	F	T	
T	F	F	F	
F	T	T	T	
F	F	T	T	

1. We write in columns 1 and 2 the four possible pairs of truth values for p and q.
2. Using column 1 as a reference, we negate the statement p to get the entries in column 3. Note that we simply write F in the rows where we wrote T for p, and we write T in the rows where we wrote F for p.
3. We combine columns 3 and 2 using the disjunction *or*, denoted by $\vee$. Recall (see Table 2.2) that a disjunction is false only when both its components are false; it is true otherwise. Thus, we write F in the second row of column 4, where both components, $\sim p$ and q, are false, and we write T in the other rows. This completes the table.   ∎

EXAMPLE 2   Let p be "I lie," and let q be "I would tell you." When will the statement "I do not lie or I would tell you" be false?

Solution   The statement under consideration can be symbolized as $\sim p \vee q$. From the table in Example 1, we see that $\sim p \vee q$ is false when p is true and q is false. Hence, the given statement is false when "I lie" and "I would not tell you."   ∎

EXAMPLE 3   Construct the truth table for the statement $\sim(p \wedge \sim q)$.

Solution   As in Example 1, the plan is to first break the given statement down into its primitive components. The statement $\sim(p \wedge \sim q)$ is the negation of $p \wedge \sim q$, which is the conjunction of the components p and $\sim q$. We can write the truth values of $\sim q$ from those of q, and p is itself a primitive component. Thus, the headings of the truth table will be p, q, $\sim q$, $p \wedge \sim q$, and $\sim(p \wedge \sim q)$. The table is filled out in the following steps, where the numbers at the top of the table are the column numbers:

1	2	5		4	3
p	q	$\sim(p$	$\wedge$		$\sim q)$
T	T	T		F	F
T	F	F		T	T
F	T	T		F	F
F	F	T		F	T

1. We write in columns 1 and 2 the four possible pairs of truth values for p and q.
2. Using column 2 as reference, we negate q to get column 3.
3. To get column 4, we combine columns 1 and 3, using the conjunction *and*, denoted by $\wedge$. Recall (see Table 2.1) that a conjunction is true only when both its components are true and is false otherwise. Thus, we write T in the second row of column 4, where p and $\sim q$ are both true, and we write F in the other rows.
4. We negate the truth values in column 4 to get those in column 5. The statement $\sim(p \wedge \sim q)$ has the truth values shown in column 5 of the table.

■

B. *Equivalent Statements*

Notice that the statements given in Examples 1 and 3 have exactly the same truth values, *TFTT*; hence, the two statements must have the same meaning (say the same thing).

Definition 2.4 ———— Two statements p and q that have identical truth values are said to be **equivalent** (denoted by $p \Leftrightarrow q$).

Accordingly, from Examples 1 and 3, we may write

$$\sim p \vee q \Leftrightarrow \sim(p \wedge \sim q)$$

Problem Solving:	**Equivalent Statements**
	Show that $p \wedge (q \vee r) \Leftrightarrow (p \wedge q) \vee (p \wedge r)$
1. Read the problem and select the unknown. We have to show that two statements are equivalent. What does this mean?	To show that two statements are equivalent we have to show that the statements have identical truth tables.
2. Think of a plan. Make a truth table for each of the statements. How many lines will each truth table have?	Because we have three primitive statements p, q, and r, each of which has two possible truth values, there are $2 \times 2 \times 2 = 8$ possible cases. Thus, the truth table must have 8 lines.

3. Use truth tables to carry out the plan.

Break the statement $p \wedge (q \vee r)$ into components and label the columns accordingly. Then proceed as in the previous examples to make the truth table.

The components of $p \wedge (q \vee r)$ are p and $(q \vee r)$, which breaks into the components q and r. Thus, the truth table must have columns for p, q, r, $(q \vee r)$, and $p \wedge (q \vee r)$.

The table is filled out in the same manner as the tables for our previous examples:

1. In the first three columns, we write the possible truth values for p, q, and r. In column 1, we enter four T's and four F's; in column 2, we enter two T's, two F's, two T's, and two F's; in column 3, we enter alternately one T and one F. This gives all the possible combinations of T's and F's for the three statements.

2. We combine columns 2 and 3 with a disjunction $\vee$ to obtain the truth values of $q \vee r$ in column 4. Because $q \vee r$ is false only when both q and r are false (rows 4 and 8), we enter F in rows 4 and 8 and T's in the remaining rows.

3. We combine columns 1 and 4 with a conjunction $\wedge$ to obtain the truth values of $p \wedge (q \vee r)$. Since a conjunction is true only when both components are true, we complete column 5 by writing T's in the first three rows and F's in the other rows. The given statement has the truth values shown in column 5 of the table.

1	2	3	5	4
p	q	r	$p \wedge$	$(q \vee r)$
T	T	T	T	T
T	T	F	T	T
T	F	T	T	T
T	F	F	F	F
F	T	T	F	T
F	T	F	F	T
F	F	T	F	T
F	F	F	F	F

Break the statement $(p \wedge q) \vee (p \wedge r)$ into components.

The components of $(p \wedge q) \vee (p \wedge r)$ are $(p \wedge q)$ and $(p \wedge r)$, and these two have components p, q, r, $(p \wedge q)$, and $(p \wedge r)$. The table is filled out in the same manner.

1	2	3	4	6	5
p	*q*	*r*	\(*(p ∧ q) ∨ (p ∧ r)*\)		
T	*T*	*T*	*T*	*T*	*T*
T	*T*	*F*	*T*	*T*	*F*
T	*F*	*T*	*F*	*T*	*T*
T	*F*	*F*	*F*	*F*	*F*
F	*T*	*T*	*F*	*F*	*F*
F	*T*	*F*	*F*	*F*	*F*
F	*F*	*T*	*F*	*F*	*F*
F	*F*	*F*	*F*	*F*	*F*

4. Verify the answer. Are the results of the two tables identical?

Since the final columns of the two tables (5 and 6, respectively) are identical, the two statements are equivalent.

TRY EXAMPLE 4 NOW.

Cover the solution, write your own, and then check your work.

EXAMPLE 4 (a) Show that $(\sim p \vee q) \wedge r \Leftrightarrow (\sim p \wedge r) \vee (q \wedge r)$.

(b) Let *p* be the statement "You recycle paper," let *q* be the statement "You recycle glass" and let *r* be the statement "You are an environmentalist." If we know that you recycle paper, under what condition(s) will the statement $(\sim p \vee q) \wedge r$ be true?

Solution (a) To show that $(\sim p \vee q) \wedge r \Leftrightarrow (\sim p \wedge r) \vee (q \wedge r)$ we have to show that the truth tables for both statements are identical. We first construct the table for $(\sim p \vee q) \wedge r$. The components for this statement are *p*, *q*, *r*, $\sim p$, and $(\sim p \vee q)$ as shown in the following table. The statement $(\sim p \vee q)$ is false only when $\sim p$ and *q* are both false. Thus, we enter *F*'s in rows 3 and 4 and *T*'s in the rest of the rows. Finally, $(\sim p \vee q) \wedge r$ is true only when both $(\sim p \vee q)$ and *r* are both true. We enter *T*'s in rows 1, 5, and 7 and *F*'s in the rest of the rows. The final truth values appear in column 7.

1	2	3	4	5	7	6
p	*q*	*r*	$\sim p$	\(*(~p ∨ q) ∧ r*\)		
T	*T*	*T*	*F*	*T*	*T*	*T*
T	*T*	*F*	*F*	*T*	*F*	*F*
T	*F*	*T*	*F*	*F*	*F*	*T*
T	*F*	*F*	*F*	*F*	*F*	*F*
F	*T*	*T*	*T*	*T*	*T*	*T*
F	*T*	*F*	*T*	*T*	*F*	*F*
F	*F*	*T*	*T*	*T*	*T*	*T*
F	*F*	*F*	*T*	*T*	*F*	*F*

The components for $(\sim p \wedge r) \vee (q \wedge r)$ are p, q, r, $\sim p$, $(\sim p \wedge r)$, and $(q \wedge r)$ as shown in the next table. Thus, $\sim p \wedge r$ is true only when $\sim p$ and r are both true (rows 5 and 7), while $(q \wedge r)$ is true only when both q and r are true (rows 1 and 5). Finally, $(\sim p \wedge r) \vee (q \wedge r)$ is false only when both $(\sim p \wedge r)$ and $(q \wedge r)$ are false (rows 2, 3, 4, 6, and 8). The final truth values are in column 7. Since columns 7 in both truth tables are identical, the statements are equivalent.

1	2	3	4	5	7	6
p	q	r	$\sim p$	\multicolumn{3}{c}{$(\sim p \wedge r) \vee (q \wedge r)$}
T	T	T	F	F	T	T
T	T	F	F	F	F	F
T	F	T	F	F	F	F
T	F	F	F	F	F	F
F	T	T	T	T	T	T
F	T	F	T	F	F	F
F	F	T	T	T	T	F
F	F	F	T	F	F	F

(b) Since p has truth value T (first 4 rows), $(\sim p \vee q) \wedge r$ is true only when q and r are also both true (row 1), that is, when the components "You recycle glass" and "You are an environmentalist" are both true. ∎

Exercise 2.3

A. In problems 1–14, construct a truth table for the given statement.

1. $p \vee \sim q$
2. $\sim(p \vee q)$
3. $\sim p \wedge q$
4. $\sim p \vee \sim q$
5. $\sim(p \vee \sim q)$
6. $\sim(\sim p \vee \sim q)$
7. $\sim(\sim p \wedge \sim q)$
8. $(p \vee q) \wedge \sim(p \wedge q)$
9. $(p \wedge q) \vee (\sim p \wedge q)$
10. $(p \wedge \sim q) \wedge (\sim p \wedge q)$
11. $p \wedge (q \vee r)$
12. $p \vee (q \wedge r)$
13. $(p \vee q) \vee (r \wedge \sim q)$
14. $[(p \wedge q) \vee (q \wedge \sim r)] \vee (r \wedge \sim s)$

15. Let p be "Mida is blonde," and let q be "Mida is 6 ft tall."
    (a) Under what conditions is the statement "Mida is blonde and 6 ft tall" true?
    (b) Under what conditions is the statement "Mida is blonde and 6 ft tall" false?

    (c) Under what conditions is the statement "Mida is blonde or 6 ft tall" true?

    (d) Under what conditions is the statement "Mida is blonde or 6 ft tall" false?

16. Let p be "Eva is a high school graduate," and let q be "Eva is over 16 years old."

    (a) Under what conditions is the statement "Eva is neither a high school graduate nor over 16 years old" true?

    (b) Under what conditions is the statement in part (a) false?

    (c) Under what conditions is the statement "Either Eva is a high school graduate or she is over 16 years old" true?

    (d) Under what conditions is the statement in part (c) false?

B. In problems 17–20, use truth tables to show that the two statements are equivalent.

17. $p \vee (q \wedge r)$ and $(p \vee q) \wedge (p \vee r)$

18. $p \wedge (q \vee r)$ and $(p \wedge q) \vee (p \wedge r)$

19. $\sim(p \vee q)$ and $\sim p \wedge \sim q$

20. $\sim(p \wedge q)$ and $\sim p \vee \sim q$

In problems 21–22, use truth tables to show the equivalence.

21. $(p \wedge q) \vee \sim p \Leftrightarrow q \vee \sim p$

22. $(p \vee q) \wedge (\sim p \vee \sim q) \Leftrightarrow (p \wedge \sim q) \vee (\sim p \wedge q)$

23. (a) Verify the entries in the following table:

p	q	$p \wedge q$	$p \wedge \sim q$	$\sim p \wedge q$	$\sim p \wedge \sim q$
T	T	T	F	F	F
T	F	F	T	F	F
F	T	F	F	T	F
F	F	F	F	F	T

    (b) Look at the last four columns of this table. Each of these columns has one T and three F's, and there is exactly one T on each line. This T occurs on the line where both components of the corresponding column heading are true. The headings of these last four columns are called **basic conjunctions.** By using these conjunctions, we can write statements having any given four-entry truth table. For instance, a statement with the truth table $TFFT$ is $(p \wedge q) \vee (\sim p \wedge \sim q)$. Explain this.

    (c) By forming disjunctions of the basic conjunctions, we can write statements with given truth tables as noted in part (b). Write a statement having truth table $FTTF$. Do the same for $FTTT$. Can you write a simpler statement for the truth table $FTTT$?

24. The ideas in problem 23 can be generalized to statements with any given number of components. Thus, the statement $p \wedge \sim q \wedge \sim r$ would have a truth table with a T on the line corresponding to p true, q false, and r false, and F's on the other seven lines. What would be the truth table for $(p \wedge \sim q \wedge r) \vee (\sim p \wedge \sim q \wedge \sim r)$?

25. Describe the circumstances under which the following statements have truth value T. [*Hint:* First write the statement in symbolic form.]
    (a) Billy goes to the zoo and feeds peanuts to the elephants or the monkeys.
    (b) I file my income tax return and pay the tax, or go to jail.

26. Describe the circumstances under which the following statements have truth value T (see the hint in problem 25):
    (a) John gets up before 7:00 A.M. and has cereal or pancakes for breakfast.
    (b) I do not drive over the speed limit and I obey the traffic signals, or I get a traffic ticket.

Table 2.4

p	q	$p * q$
T	T	F
T	F	F
F	T	F
F	F	T

In problems 27–29, let the connective $*$ be defined by Table 2.4. Construct the truth table for the given statement.

27. $(p \wedge q) * p$ 28. $(p \wedge \sim q) * q$ 29. $(p \vee q) * \sim p$

In problems 30–32, let the connective @ be defined by Table 2.5. Construct the truth table for the given statement.

30. $(p \wedge \sim q) @ p$ 31. $(p \wedge \sim q) @ q$ 32. $(p \vee q) @ \sim p$

Table 2.5

p	q	$p @ q$
T	T	F
T	F	T
F	T	T
F	F	T

In problems 33–35, use Tables 2.4 and 2.5 and find a statement that does not use either $*$ or @ and has the same truth table as the given statement.

33. $p * q$ 34. $\sim(p @ q)$ 35. $(p * q) @ \sim p$

36. The truth table for a statement compounded from two statements has $2^2 = 4$ rows, and the truth table for a statement compounded from three statements has $2^3 = 8$ rows. How many rows would the truth table for a statement compounded from four statements have? How many for five? For six? For n?

37. Use De Morgan's laws, problems 19 and 20,

$$\sim(p \vee q) \Leftrightarrow \sim p \wedge \sim q \text{ and } \sim(p \wedge q) \Leftrightarrow \sim p \vee \sim q$$

to determine which of the following statements is logically equivalent to "It is not true that Billie and Johnny are both boys."
    (a) Billie is a girl and Johnny is a boy.
    (b) Billie is a boy and Johnny is a girl.
    (c) Billie is a boy or Johnny is a boy.
    (d) Billie is a girl or Johnny is a girl.

38. Use De Morgan's laws, problems 19 and 20,

$$\sim(p \lor q) \Leftrightarrow \sim p \land \sim q \text{ and } \sim(p \land q) \Leftrightarrow \sim p \lor \sim q$$

to determine which of the following statements is logically equivalent to "It is not true that Jackie and Billie are both boys."
(a) Jackie is a girl or Billie is a boy.

(b) Billie is a girl or Jackie is a girl.

(c) Billie is a boy or Jackie is a boy.

(d) Jackie is a boy and Billie is a boy.

39. To be eligible for a position in a banking firm, an applicant must be at least 25 years old t, have a college degree in business administration d, and be married m. Assume that t, d, and m are true statements. Which of the following three applicants (if any) is eligible for the above position?

   Joe is married, has a college degree in fine arts, and is 26 years old.

   Mary is married, has a degree in business administration, and is 22 years old.

   Ellen has a degree in business administration, is 25 years old, and is single.

40. To qualify for a $40,000 loan, an applicant must have a gross income of $30,000 if single ($50,000 combined income if married) and assets of at least $10,000. Which of the following three applicants (if any) would qualify for the loan?

   Mr. Perez is married, with two children, and makes $35,000 on his job. His wife does not work.

   Ms. Jefferson and her husband have assets of $50,000. One makes $22,000; the other makes $19,000.

   Tran Quang is a bachelor and works at two jobs. He makes $28,000 on one job and $5,000 on the other; his only asset is a $7,000 Toyota.

In Other Words

In problems 41–42, use De Morgan's laws to write an equivalent statement using the word *or*.

41. We will not pay for damage due to wear and tear.

42. We will not pay for loss to TV antennas and awnings.

In problems 43–44, use De Morgan's laws to write an equivalent statement using the word *and*.

43. You may not deduct travel expenses or political contributions.

44. You may not deduct legal expenses or the cost of entertaining friends.

In problems 45 and 46, describe in words the circumstances under which the given statement has the truth value *F*. *(Hint:* First symbolize the statement.)

45. Lizzie goes to campus and studies in the library or attends a class.

46. Larry goes to campus and attends a class or he studies at home.

Using Your Knowledge

In medical practice, a method commonly used to diagnose certain food allergies is the food diary. This method uses a record form listing the foods eaten each day, as shown in the table.

	Date													
---	1	2	3	4	5	6	7	8	9	10	11	12	13	14
Indigestion occurred	×						×							×
Food														
Coffee	×	×	×	×	×	×	×	×	×	×	×	×	×	×
Eggs	×		×	×	×	×			×	×		×	×	×
Chicken	×						×	×			×		×	
Fish	×						×							×
Pork			×				×			×				

Since coffee was consumed every day by the person keeping this diary, and indigestion did not occur every day, coffee can be eliminated as a suspect.

Let e be "The person ate eggs."
Let c be "The person ate chicken."
Let f be "The person ate fish."
Let p be "The person ate pork."

Write a symbolic statement telling what the person ate:

47. On day 1   48. On day 7   49. On day 14

50. On all three days when indigestion occurred

51. Based on your answer to problem 50, which food do you think gives this person indigestion?

Discovery

In Logictown, there live four men, Mr. Baker, Mr. Carpenter, Mr. Draper, and Mr. Smith. One is a baker, one a carpenter, one a draper, and one a smith, but none follows the vocation corresponding to his name. A logician tries to find out who is who, and he obtains the following partially correct information:

Statement	I	II	III	IV
a	T	F	F	F
b	F	T	F	F
c	F	F	T	F
d	F	F	F	T

(a) *Mr. Baker is the smith.*
(b) *Mr. Carpenter is the baker.*
(c) *Mr. Draper is not the smith.*
(d) *Mr. Smith is not the draper.*

52. If it is known that three of the four statements are false, who is the carpenter? [*Hint:* Consider the four possible sets of truth values given for the statements in the table in the margin.]

Computer Corner

In this section, you learned how to write a statement with a given truth table (see problems 23 and 24). The computer can construct a statement corresponding to a given truth table, provided you enter the table. The Statement Generator Program appears in the Programs in BASIC appendix.

1. Use it to check the answer to problem 23(c) in Exercise 2.3.

2.4   THE CONDITIONAL AND THE BICONDITIONAL

GETTING STARTED

ON WHAT CONDITION?

Have you read your insurance policy or your income tax instructions lately? They contain many of the connectives we have studied and more. Here are some excerpts from an automobile insurance policy.

If the final recomputed premium exceeds the premium stated on the declarations page, you must pay the excess to Allstate.

(If you do not understand this, it may cost you money.) Here is another statement:

If an injured person unreasonably refuses to take the examination, we are not required to pay any subsequent personal injury protection benefits.

(On this one, failure to understand may cost you your benefits!)
    What about income taxes?

If you checked NO to any of the above questions, you may not take the earned income credit.

(Here you may make a mistake on your return, resulting in an audit.) Or what about this one?

If your return is more than 60 days late, the minimum penalty will be $100 or the amount of any tax you owe, whichever is smaller.

Do you know what the penalty will be?

Finally, let us look at a hypothetical application of conditional statements in the field of law. A man was being tried for participation in a robbery. Here is a partial transcript of the proceedings.

Prosecutor: "If the defendant is guilty, then he had an accomplice."

Defense Attorney: "That is not true!"

Judge: "In that case, I declare a mistrial. The defendant needs a new attorney."

The ability to apply logic to reasoning and argument is an important skill in the field of law

Table 2.6

p	*q*	*p* → *q*
T	*T*	*T*
T	*F*	*F*
F	*T*	*T*
F	*F*	*T*

Why? The attorney said that the statement "If the defendant is guilty *g*, then he had an accomplice *a*," or symbolically *g* → *a*, was not true; that is, *g* → *a* was false. Now, look at the second row of Table 2.6. When is a conditional false? When the antecedent (*g*, in this case) is true and the consequent (*a*, in this case) is false. What does that mean in terms of the defendant?

It is sometimes necessary to specify the conditions under which a given event will be true. For example, one might say, "If the weather is nice, then I will go to the beach." If we let *p* stand for "the weather is nice" and *q* stand for "I will go to the beach," then the preceding compound statement is of the form "If *p*, then *q*." Statements of this kind are called **conditional statements** and are symbolized by *p* → *q*. (Read, "if *p*, then *q*" or "*p* arrow *q*" or "*p* conditional *q*.") In *p* → *q*, statement *p* is sometimes called the **antecedent** and *q* the **consequent.**

A. *The Conditional*

To understand the truth table for the conditional, consider the sign in the margin. It promises, "If you stop here, your pain will too." Under what circumstances is this promise broken? Obviously, only if you *do* stop here and your pain *does not* stop. Thus, we should write *F* for *p* → *q* if *p* is true and *q* is false; otherwise, we should write *T*. Table 2.6 expresses these facts.

A chiropractor's sign makes use of a conditional statement

It shows that if p and q are both true, then $p \rightarrow q$ is true, and if p is true and q is false, then $p \rightarrow q$ is false. In the last two lines of the table, p is false so that it would be incorrect to say that $p \rightarrow q$ is false. Since we want a complete truth table, we have assigned the value T to $p \rightarrow q$ in these two lines. See problem 52, Exercise 2.4.

Note that "All p's are q's" is translated as "If it is a p, then it is a q." This idea will be used in Exercise 2.4, problems 35–39.

> The **conditional statement** $p \rightarrow q$ ("if p, then q") is false only when p is true and q is false; otherwise, it is true.

B. *The Biconditional*

In certain statements, the conditional is used twice, with the antecedent and the consequent of the first conditional reversed in the second conditional. For example, the statement "If money is plentiful, then interest rates are low, and if interest rates are low, then money is plentiful" uses the conditional twice in this manner. It is for this reason that such statements, which can be written in the form $(p \rightarrow q) \wedge (q \rightarrow p)$, are called **biconditionals.** The biconditional is usually symbolized by the shorter form $p \leftrightarrow q$, so that, by definition,

$$p \leftrightarrow q \Leftrightarrow (p \rightarrow q) \wedge (q \rightarrow p)$$

Table 2.7 is the truth table for the statement $(p \rightarrow q) \wedge (q \rightarrow p)$. This table is filled out in the usual way:

1. In columns 1 and 2, we write the four possible pairs of truth values for p and q.

2. We combine columns 1 and 2 with the conditional ($\rightarrow$) to form column 3. Since $p \rightarrow q$ is false only when p is true and q is false, we write F in the second line and T in the other lines.

3. We combine columns 2 and 1 — *in that order* — with the conditional ($\rightarrow$) to form column 4. Because $q \rightarrow p$ is false only when q is true and p is false, we write F in the third line and T in the other lines.

4. We combine columns 3 and 4 with the conjunction ($\wedge$) to form column 5. Since the conjunction is true only when both components are true, we write T in the first and fourth lines and F in the other two lines. This completes the table.

Table 2.7 shows that:

> The biconditional $p \leftrightarrow q$ is true when and only when p and q have the same truth values; it is false otherwise.

Table 2.7

1 2	3	5	4
p q	$(p \rightarrow q)$	$\wedge$	$(q \rightarrow p)$
T T	T	T	T
T F	F	F	T
F T	T	F	F
F F	T	T	T

EXAMPLE 1   Give the truth value of each of the following:

(a) If Tuesday is the last day of the week, then the next day is Sunday.
(b) If Tuesday is the third day of the week, then the next day is Sunday.
(c) If Tuesday is the third day of the week, then Wednesday is the fourth day of the week.
(d) If Tuesday is the last day of the week, then the next day is Wednesday.

Solution   All these statements are of the form $p \rightarrow q$, where p is the antecedent and q is the consequent. (Recall that the antecedent is the "if" part, and the consequent is the "then" part.)

(a) Because p is false, the statement $p \rightarrow q$ is true.
(b) Because p is true and q is false, the statement $p \rightarrow q$ is false.
(c) Because p and q are both true, the statement $p \rightarrow q$ is true.
(d) Because p is false, the statement $p \rightarrow q$ is true.

(Note the results in (a) and (d). The moral is that if you start off with a false assumption, then you can prove anything!) ■

EXAMPLE 2   Is the statement $(3 + 5 = 35) \leftrightarrow (2 + 7 = 10)$ true or false?

Solution   This statement is of the form $p \leftrightarrow q$, where p is "$3 + 5 = 35$" and q is "$2 + 7 = 10$." Since the biconditional $p \leftrightarrow q$ is true when p and q have the same truth value, and the p and q in this example are both false, the given statement is true. ■

EXAMPLE 3   Let p be "x is a fruit," and let q be "x is ripe." Under what conditions is the statement $p \rightarrow q$ false?

Solution   The statement $p \rightarrow q$ is a conditional statement, and thus is false only when p is true and q is false; hence, the given statement is false if x is a fruit that is not ripe. ■

EXAMPLE 4   Show that the statements $p \rightarrow q$ and $\sim p \lor q$ are equivalent; that is, show that $(p \rightarrow q) \Leftrightarrow (\sim p \lor q)$. Use the equivalence to write the statement "If you are under 18, then you must register" as a disjunction.

Solution   To show that two statements are equivalent, we must show that they have identical truth tables. The statement $p \rightarrow q$ is false only when p is true and q is false, (see the first truth table on page 96). To make a truth table for $\sim p \lor q$, we write the components p, q, $\sim p$ and $\sim p \lor q$ as shown in the second table.

The statement $\sim p \vee q$ is false only when both components are false (row 2); otherwise it is true. Since the final columns are identical, the statements are equivalent; that is, $(p \rightarrow q) \Leftrightarrow (\sim p \vee q)$.

1	2	3
p	q	$p \rightarrow q$
T	T	T
T	F	F
F	T	T
F	F	T

1	2	3	4
p	q	$\sim p$	$\sim p \vee q$
T	T	F	T
T	F	F	F
F	T	T	T
F	F	T	T

Let p be the statement "You are under 18" and q be the statement "You must register." Since $(p \rightarrow q) \Leftrightarrow (\sim p \vee q)$, the statement "If you are under 18, then you must register" can be written as the disjunction "You are not under 18 or you must register." ∎

The equivalence in Example 4,

$$(p \rightarrow q) \Leftrightarrow (\sim p \vee q)$$

is of great importance, because it allows us to handle a conditional statement in terms of the logical symbols for negation and disjunction. This equivalence will be used in several of the problems in Exercise 2.4 and later in this chapter. Note that since

$$(p \rightarrow q) \Leftrightarrow (\sim p \vee q)$$

the negation of $p \rightarrow q$ is equivalent to the negation of $\sim p \vee q$; that is, the negation of a conditional statement may be written:

$$\sim(p \rightarrow q) \Leftrightarrow \sim(\sim p \vee q)$$

See problem 40 in Exercise 2.4 for the simplification of the right-hand side of this equivalence.

Exercise 2.4

A. 1. Show that the statement $\sim q \to \sim p$ is equivalent to $p \to q$.

In problems 2 and 3, use truth tables to show the equivalences.

2. $p \to \sim q \Leftrightarrow \sim(p \land q)$ 3. $\sim p \to q \Leftrightarrow p \lor q$

In problems 4–7, give the truth value of the given statement.

4. If $2 + 2 = 22$, then $22 = 4$.
5. If $2 + 2 = 4$, then $8 = 5$.
6. If $2 + 2 = 22$, then $8 = 4 + 4$.
7. If $2 + 2 = 22$, then $4 = 26$.

In problems 8–11, find all the number replacements for x that make the given sentence true.

8. If $2 + 2 = 4$, then $x - 2 = 5$.
9. If $2 + 2 = 22$, then $x - 2 = 5$.
10. If $x + 2 = 6$, then $3 + 2 = 5$.
11. If $x + 2 = 6$, then $2 + 2 = 32$.
12. Let p be "I kiss you once," and let q be "I kiss you again." Under what conditions is the statement $p \to q$ false?
13. Under what condition is the statement "If you've got the time, we've got the beer" false?

In problems 14–16, construct a truth table for the given statement. Note the importance of the parentheses and the brackets to indicate the order in which items are grouped.

14. $[(p \to q) \to p] \to q$ 15. $(p \to q) \leftrightarrow (p \lor r)$
16. $(p \to q) \leftrightarrow (p \to \sim q)$

B. In problems 17 and 18, construct a truth table for the given statement.

17. $p \to (q \land r)$ 18. $(p \to q) \land (p \to r)$
19. Are the statements in problems 17–18 equivalent?

In problems 20–25, let p be "I will buy it," and let q be "It is a poodle." Translate the given statement into symbolic form.

20. If it is a poodle, then I will buy it.
21. If I will buy it, then it is a poodle.
22. It is a poodle if and only if I will buy it.
23. If it is not a poodle, then I will not buy it.
24. If I will not buy it, then it is not a poodle.
25. If it is a poodle, then I will not buy it.

In problems 26–28, let ~s be "You are out of Schlitz," and let ~b be "You are out of beer." Translate the given statement into symbolic form.

26. If you are out of Schlitz, you are out of beer.

27. If you are out of beer, you are out of Schlitz.

28. Having beer is equivalent to having Schlitz.

In problems 29–31, write each of the following statements in symbolic form using ~ and $\vee$. Also write the corresponding verbal statement. [*Hint:* $p \rightarrow q$ is equivalent to $\sim p \vee q$.]

29. If the temperature is above 80° *a*, then I will go to the beach *b*.

30. If Mida is home by 5 *h*, then dinner will be ready by 6 *r*.

31. If Eva has a day off *o*, then she will go to the beach *g*.

In Example 4 it was shown that $p \rightarrow q$ is equivalent to $\sim p \vee q$. In problems 32–34, use this equivalence to write the given statement as a disjunction.

32. If you work, you have to pay taxes.

33. If you got the time, we got the beer.

34. If you find a better one, then you buy it.

The statement "All even numbers are divisible by 2" can be translated as "If it is an even number, then it is divisible by 2." In general, the statement "All . . . are . . ." can be translated as "If it is a . . . , then it is a . . . ." In problems 35–39, use this idea to write the given statement in the if–then form:

35. All dogs are mammals.

36. All cats are felines.

37. All men are created equal.

38. All prime numbers greater than 2 are odd numbers.

39. All rectangles whose diagonals are perpendicular to each other are squares.

40. Because $p \rightarrow q$ is equivalent to $\sim p \vee q$ (see Example 4), the negation of $p \rightarrow q$ should be equivalent to the negation of $\sim p \vee q$. Show that the negation of $\sim p \vee q$ is $p \wedge \sim q$; that is, show that $\sim(\sim p \vee q)$ is equivalent to $p \wedge \sim q$.

41. From problem 40 it is clear that the negation of $p \rightarrow q$ is equivalent to $p \wedge \sim q$. Verify this by means of a truth table.

Problem 41 verified that the negation of $p \rightarrow q$ is $p \wedge \sim q$. This means that to negate an "if . . . , then . . ." statement, we simply assert the *if clause* and deny the *then clause*. For instance, the negation of the statement "If you are out of Schlitz, you are out of beer" is the statement "You are out of Schlitz, but you are not out of beer." In problems 42–44, write in words the negation of the given statement.

42. If you earn much money, then you pay heavy taxes.
43. If Johnny does not play quarterback, then his team loses.
44. If Alice passes the test, then she gets the job.

Refer to the instructions for problems 42–44. In problems 45–47, write out the negation of the given statement.

45. If I kiss you once, I kiss you again.
46. If Saturday is a hot day, I will go to the beach.
47. Evel Knievel will lose his life if he is careless.
48. From problem 41 we can see that $p \land \sim q$ has truth values *FTFF*. If you know that $p \land \sim q$ is the negation of $p \rightarrow q$, how can you define the truth table for $p \rightarrow q$?

In problems 49–51, write each of the following statements in the if–then form:

49. Johnny does not play quarterback or his team wins.
50. Alice fails the test or she gets the job.
51. Joe had an accident or he could get car insurance.

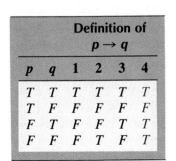

Definition of $p \rightarrow q$					
p	*q*	**1**	**2**	**3**	**4**
T	T	T	T	T	T
T	F	F	F	F	F
F	T	F	F	T	T
F	F	F	T	F	T

52. In defining $p \rightarrow q$, it is easy to agree that if *p* is true and *q* is true, then $p \rightarrow q$ is true; also, if *p* is true and *q* is false, then $p \rightarrow q$ is false. Assuming that the entries in the first two rows in the table in the margin are *TF*, respectively, we have four possible definitions for $p \rightarrow q$, as listed in the table.

   (a) Show that if we use definition 1, then $p \rightarrow q$ and $p \land q$ have the same truth table.
   (b) Show that if we use definition 2, then $p \rightarrow q$ and $p \leftrightarrow q$ have the same truth table.
   (c) Show that if we use definition 3, then $p \rightarrow q$ and *q* have the same truth table.

   Thus, the table shows that if we wish $p \rightarrow q$ to be different from $p \land q$, $p \leftrightarrow q$, and *q*, then we must use definition 4.

53. A mother promises her child, "If you eat the spinach and the liver, then you may go out to play." The child eats only the spinach, but the mother lets him out to play. Has she broken her original promise?

54. In place of the statement in problem 53, suppose the mother says, "If you do not eat the spinach and liver, then you may not go out to play." If the child eats only the spinach and the mother lets him out to play, has she broken her promise?

55. The Score Report Request Form for the Graduate Record Exam includes the following statements:

    1. If you entered a Future Test Date f, your score will be reported after scores from that date become available a.
    2. If you entered a Previous Test Date p, your scores will be reported from 2 to 4 weeks after this request is received t.

    Use the suggested abbreviations to write in symbolic form:
    (a) Statement 1   (b) Statement 2

56. Let p be the statement "Some Sunday newspapers are not printed on recycled paper" and let q be "Each year about 25 million trees are wasted." The statement $\sim p \rightarrow \sim q$ tells us an important fact. Write $\sim p \rightarrow \sim q$ in words.

57. Did you know that a four-passenger Ford Escort with a diesel engine gets about 50 miles to the gallon of fuel? If you switch from a car that gets 25 miles per gallon to one that gets 50 miles per gallon, you cut the dangerous emissions caused by your driving by about 50%. Let p be "You switch from a car that gets 25 miles per gallon to one that gets 50 miles per gallon," and let q be "You cut the dangerous emissions caused by your driving by 50%." Write the statement $\sim q \rightarrow \sim p$ in words. Is this statement true?

58. It has been found that if broadleaf trees are properly planted to shade a house, they can reduce the summer indoor temperatures by as much as 20 degrees. Let t be "Broadleaf trees are properly planted to shade a house," and let r be "They can reduce the summer indoor temperatures by as much as 20 degrees." Write the statement $\sim r \rightarrow \sim t$ in words.

59. Suppose that Joe Lipsworth says to his wife, "Honey, if I stay in good health and we have less than $600,000 in savings, then I will not retire until I reach age 70." Write out in words under what circumstances Joe can retire at age 65 without breaking this promise.

60. The Rollo Manufacturing Company has three positions open: (1) office manager, (2) assistant office manager, (3) assistant vice-president. Annie, Billie, and Carey are three women qualified for these positions. Suppose that the company president knows the following: If Carey gets position 1, then Annie must get position 2. If Billie gets position 1 or position 2, then Carey must get position 3. If Carey gets position 2 or position 3, then Billie must get position 1. Make a table with the headings 1, 2, and 3 and list the possible ways in which the three positions can be assigned.

61. Which of the following statements is logically equivalent to "If Mary is in Tampa, then she is in Florida"?
    (a) Mary is in Florida or she is in Tampa.
    (b) If Mary is not in Tampa, then she is not in Florida.
    (c) If Mary is in Florida, then she is in Tampa.
    (d) If Mary is not in Florida, then she is not in Tampa.

62. Which of the following statements is logically equivalent to "If you want to buy organic food, you have to let your grocer know"?
    (a) You want to buy organic food or you let your grocer know.
    (b) If you do not let your grocer know, then you do not want to buy organic food.
    (c) If you let your grocer know, then you want to buy organic food.
    (d) If you do not want to buy organic food, then you do not let your grocer know.

63. Which statement is the logical negation of "If you studied hard, you passed the course"?
    (a) If you didn't study hard, you didn't pass the course.
    (b) If you didn't pass the course, you didn't study hard.
    (c) You didn't study hard, but you passed the course.
    (d) You studied hard and you did not pass the course.

64. Which statement is the logical negation of "If it rains, we will not go to the beach"?
    (a) If it doesn't rain, then we will go to the beach.
    (b) It is raining and we do not go to the beach.
    (c) If we go to the beach, then it will not rain.
    (d) It is raining and we will go to the beach.

In Other Words

65. Assume that the chiropractor's advertisement, "If you stop here, your pain will too," found on page 93, is a true statement. Does it follow logically that if you did not stop your pain will not stop either? Explain.

66. Here is an excerpt from an automobile insurance policy: "If the loss is $50 or less, we will not make any payment." A policy holder suffers a $75 loss. What are the insurance company's options? Explain.

67. A sophomore college student reads the following statement: "If you are entering college for the first time, you are required to take the placement examination." Does the student have to take the placement examination? Explain.

Using Your Knowledge

A certain credit union issues the following memorandum with its monthly statement of account: Please carefully examine the enclosed memorandum. Report all differences to the Auditing Division. If no differences are reported in 10 days, we shall understand that the balance is correct as shown.

> *Let d be "A difference is found."*
> *Let r be "A report is made in 10 days."*
> *Let a be "The credit union makes the adjustment."*

68. Write in symbols: If a difference is found, then a report is made in 10 days.

69. Write in symbols: If a report is made in 10 days, the credit union makes the adjustment.

70. Write in symbols: If a difference is found, then a report is made in 10 days and the credit union makes the adjustment.

71. Does the statement in problem 70 indicate that the credit union will make no adjustment if a late report of differences is made?

Discovery

A logician is captured by a tribe of savages, whose chief makes the following offer: "One of these two roads leads to certain death and the other to freedom. You may select either road after asking any one question of one of these two warriors. I must warn you, however, that one of them is always truthful and the other always lies."

Let p be "The first read leads to freedom."
Let q be "You are telling the truth."

72. What should the question be? [*Hint:* We are to construct a question so that if *p* is true the answer is "Yes," and if *p* is false the answer is "No." Complete the table, and then refer to problem 23, Exercise 2.3, to find the desired question.]

p	*q*	Answer	Truth Table of Question to Be Asked
T	*T*	Yes	
T	*F*	Yes	
F	*T*	No	
F	*F*	No	

2.5 VARIATIONS OF THE CONDITIONAL

GETTING STARTED
CONDITIONAL STATEMENTS IN ADVERTISING

Can lawyers advertise in your state? Suppose that you are a lawyer and you want to subtly convey the message that you are a contingency lawyer; that is, you get paid a certain percentage of the money awarded in the cases you win. How would you word your message? You could say:

1. I win if you pay, or
2. Pay only if I win

Do the messages give you the impression that if you have enough money you can buy the wins? Here are two other wordings:

3. Paying is sufficient for winning, or
4. Winning is a necessary condition for paying

These two statements still place a lot of importance on paying. Probably the best message is the one in the photo:

5. If I do not win, you do not pay.

This lawyer's sign wisely emphasizes winning, not paying

Here the emphasis is on winning rather than paying. Do you realize that the five statements are equivalent? You will see why in this section when we discuss the different forms in which a conditional statement can be expressed.

In the preceding section, we observed that equivalent statements have identical truth tables and may be considered different forms of the same statement. In this section, we shall be concerned with some of the different forms in which the conditional statement $p \rightarrow q$ can be expressed.

A. *Converse, Inverse, and Contrapositive*

The conditional differs from conjunctions, disjunctions, and biconditionals in that the two components may *not* be interchanged to give an equivalent statement. Thus, $p \vee q \Leftrightarrow q \vee p$, $p \wedge q \Leftrightarrow q \wedge p$, but $p \rightarrow q$ is *not* equivalent to $q \rightarrow p$.* If we attempt to discover a statement that is equivalent to $p \rightarrow q$

---

*Recall that p and q are equivalent (denoted by $p \Leftrightarrow q$) if p and q have identical truth tables.

(that is, that has an identical truth table) and involves p and q and the conditional, or $\sim p$, $\sim q$, and the conditional, we find the following possibilities:

$q \to p$	**Converse** of $p \to q$
$\sim p \to \sim q$	**Inverse** of $p \to q$
$\sim q \to \sim p$	**Contrapositive** of $p \to q$

Table 2.8 shows the truth tables for these statements. Notice that $p \to q$ is equivalent to its contrapositive, $\sim q \to \sim p$ (because they have identical truth tables).

Table 2.8

p	q	Conditional $p \to q$	Converse $q \to p$	Inverse $\sim p \to \sim q$	Contrapositive $\sim q \to \sim p$
T	T	T	T	T	T
T	F	F	T	T	F
F	T	T	F	F	T
F	F	T	T	T	T

The contrapositive of a statement is used in proving theorems in which a direct proof is difficult, but the proof of the contrapositive is easy. Thus, to prove that "If n^2 is odd, then n is odd," we can prove the contrapositive "If n is not odd, then n^2 is not odd." That is, "If n is even, then n^2 is even." We do this in problem 45, Exercise 2.5.

EXAMPLE 1   Write in words the contrapositive of the statement "If n is an even integer, then n^2 is an even integer."

Solution   The given statement is of the form $p \to q$, where p is "n is an even integer" and q is "n^2 is an even integer." The contrapositive is $\sim q \to \sim p$, which translates into "If n^2 is not an even integer, then n is not an even integer." ∎

The contrapositive is also helpful in giving a different perspective to statements containing negatives. For example, the contrapositive of the statement "If you weren't at the party, then you were not invited" is "If you were invited, then you were at the party." The contrapositive says that everyone that was invited was at the party. This may not be clear from the original statement.

EXAMPLE 2   Let s be "You study every day," and let p be "You pass the course." Write symbolically and in words:

(a) The conditional "If s, then p."
(b) The converse of $s \to p$.
(c) The inverse of $s \to p$.
(d) The contrapositive of $s \to p$.

Solution
(a) The conditional "If s, then p" is symbolized by $s \rightarrow p$. In words, "If you study every day, then you pass the course."
(b) The converse of $s \rightarrow p$ is $p \rightarrow s$. In words, "If you pass the course, then you study every day."
(c) The inverse of $s \rightarrow p$ is $\sim s \rightarrow \sim p$. In words, "If you do not study every day, then you do not pass the course."
(d) The contrapositive of $s \rightarrow p$ is $\sim p \rightarrow \sim s$. In words, "If you do not pass the course, then you do not study every day." ∎

B. *Conditional Equivalents*

Table 2.9

Statement	Equivalent Forms
If p, then q.	p is sufficient for q
	q is necessary for p
	p only if q
	q, if p

Frequently in mathematics, the words **necessary** and **sufficient** are used in conditional statements. To say that p is sufficient for q means that when p happens (is true), q will also happen (is also true). Hence, "p is sufficient for q" is equivalent to "If p, then q."

Similarly, the sentence "q is necessary for p" means that if q does not happen, neither will p. That is, $\sim q \rightarrow \sim p$. The statement $\sim q \rightarrow \sim p$ is equivalent to $p \rightarrow q$, so the sentence "q is necessary for p" is equivalent to "If p, then q."

Finally, "p only if q" also means that if q does not happen, neither will p; that is, $\sim q \rightarrow \sim p$. The statement $\sim q \rightarrow \sim p$ is equivalent to $p \rightarrow q$, so the sentence "p only if q" is equivalent to $p \rightarrow q$. The equivalences discussed, together with the variation, "q, if p" are summarized in Table 2.9. To aid you in understanding this table, notice that in the statement $p \rightarrow q$, p is the sufficient condition (the antecedent) and q is the necessary condition (the consequent).

From Table 2.9, we see that the statements

p is necessary and sufficient for q
q is necessary and sufficient for p
q if and only if p

are all equivalent to the statement "p if and only if q" and may be symbolized by $p \leftrightarrow q$.

EXAMPLE 3
Let s be "You study regularly," and let p be "You pass this course." Translate the following statements into symbolic form:

(a) You pass this course only if you study regularly.

(b) Studying regularly is a sufficient condition for passing this course.

(c) To pass this course it is necessary that you study regularly.

(d) Studying regularly is a necessary and sufficient condition for passing this course.

(e) You do not pass this course unless you study regularly.
[*Hint:* p unless q means $\sim q \rightarrow p$.]

Solution   (a) $p \rightarrow s$

(b) Because s, studying regularly, is the sufficient condition, we write $s \rightarrow p$.

(c) Since s is the necessary condition, we write $p \rightarrow s$.

(d) $p \leftrightarrow s$ or $s \leftrightarrow p$

(e) Since not studying regularly is a sufficient condition for not passing, we write $\sim s \rightarrow \sim p$.   ■

Exercise 2.5

A. 1. Write in words the contrapositive of the statement "If n is not an even number, then n is not divisible by 2."

2. Let p be "You brush your teeth with Clean," and let q be "You have no cavities." Write the converse, contrapositive, and inverse of the statement $p \rightarrow q$, "If you brush your teeth with Clean, then you have no cavities."

B. In problems 3–5, let p and q be defined as in problem 2. Translate the following statements into symbolic form:

3. You have no cavities only if you brush your teeth with Clean.

4. Having no cavities is a sufficient condition for brushing your teeth with Clean.

5. To have no cavities, it is necessary that you brush your teeth with Clean.

In problems 6–14, write the given statement in the if–then form.

6. If I kissed you once, I will kiss you again.

7. To be a mathematics major it is necessary to take calculus.

8. A good argument is necessary to convince Eva.

9. A two-thirds vote is sufficient for a measure to carry.

10. To have rain, it is necessary that we have clouds.

11. A necessary condition for a stable economy is that we have low unemployment.

12. A sufficient condition for joining a women's club is being a woman.

13. Birds of a feather flock together.

14. All dogs are canines.

15. Use a truth table to show that, in general, the converse and the inverse of the statement $p \rightarrow q$ are equivalent (have identical truth tables).

In problems 16–18, let p be "I will pass this course," and let s be "I will study daily." Write the given statement in symbolic form.

16. Studying daily is necessary for my passing this course.

17. A necessary and sufficient condition for my passing this course is studying daily.

18. I will pass this course if and only if I study daily.

19. Write the converse, inverse, and contrapositive of the following statements.
    (a) If you do not eat your spinach, you will not be strong.
    (b) If you eat your spinach, you will be strong.
    (c) You will be strong only if you eat your spinach.

20. Which statements in problem 19 are equivalent?

In problems 21–25, write the converse of the given statement. State whether the converse is always true.

21. If an integer is even, then its square is divisible by 4.
22. If it is raining, then there are clouds in the sky.
23. In order to get a date, I must be neat and well-dressed.
24. If M is elected to office, then all our problems are over.
25. In order to pass this course, it is sufficient to get passing grades on all the tests.

In problems 26–30, write the contrapositive of the given statement.

26. In an equilateral triangle, the three angles are equal.
27. If the research is adequately funded, we can find a cure for cancer.
28. Black is beautiful.
29. All radicals want to improve the world.
30. Everyone wants to be rich.

31. The Score Report Request Form for the Graduate Record Exam includes the following statement: Use this box u only if your most recent scores were earned after October 1 a.
    (a) Use the suggested abbreviations to write the given statement in symbols.
    (b) Write the given statement in words using the "if . . . , then . . ." form.

32. The following statement appeared in an IRS Form 1040A: "If you want the IRS to figure your tax f, please stop here h and sign below s."
    (a) Use the given abbreviations to write the statement in symbolic form.
    (b) Write, in symbols, the contrapositive of the statement in part (a).

33. Here is a tip that may save you money on your tax return: If you rent your vacation home for less than 15 days a year f, you do not need to report the income $\sim r$.
    (a) Write the given statement in symbolic form using the suggested abbreviations.
    (b) Write, in symbols, the contrapositive of the statement in part (a).
    (c) Write, in words, the contrapositive of the statement in part (a).

34. The Dept. of Motor Vehicles of a certain state includes the following statement in its license renewal form: "If you do not enclose the correct fee ~e, your request will be returned r."
    (a) Use the given abbreviations to write the statement in symbolic form.
    (b) Write, in symbolic form, the contrapositive of the given statement.

35. Here is a statement found outside a certain establishment: "Under 18 not admitted without parent or guardian."
    (a) Write the statement in the "if . . . , then . . ." form.
    (b) Write the contrapositive of the statement in part (a).

36. Let d be "The postal service delivers your letter," and let p be "You use the proper postage stamps." Write in symbols:
    (a) For the postal service to deliver your letter, it is necessary that you use the proper postage stamps.
    (b) Using the proper postage stamps is a sufficient condition for the postal service to deliver your letter.
    (c) A necessary and sufficient condition for the postal service to deliver your letter is that you use the proper postage stamps.

In problems 37–40, use the suggested abbreviations to write the given statements in symbolic form.

37. (a) To keep wood from rotting k, it is necessary to use a preservative p.
    (b) Using a preservative is a necessary and sufficient condition to keep wood from rotting.
    (c) A sufficient condition to keep wood from rotting is that you use a preservative.

38. (a) To avoid a late penalty ~p, you must file your income tax return by April 15 f.
    (b) Filing your income tax return by April 15 is enough to avoid a late penalty.
    (c) A necessary and sufficient condition for avoiding a late penalty is that you file your income tax return by April 15.

39. (a) A necessary and sufficient condition for snow to be beautiful b is that it be clean c.
    (b) Snow must be clean in order for it to be beautiful.
    (c) Being clean is a sufficient condition for snow to be beautiful.

40. (a) A triangle is equilateral (has three equal sides) s if and only if it is equiangular (has three equal angles) a.
    (b) A rectangle is a square s only if its adjacent sides are equal e.
    (c) A necessary and sufficient condition for a quadrilateral (a four-sided plane figure) to be a rectangle r is that its angles are all right angles a.

41. The statement "If n is even, then $3n$ is even" is directly transformed into the statement "If $3n$ is not even, then n is not even" by which one of the following logical equivalences?
    (a) "Not (p and q)" is equivalent to "not p or not q."
    (b) "If p, then q" is equivalent to "(not p) or q."
    (c) "If p, then q" is equivalent to "if not q, then not p."

42. The statement "If it can be recycled, place in this container" is directly transformed into the statement "If it is not placed in this container, then it cannot be recycled" by which one of the following logical equivalences?
    (a) "If p, then q" is equivalent to "(not p) or q."
    (b) "If p, then q" is equivalent "if not q, then not p."
    (c) "Not (p and q)" is equivalent to "not p or not q."

43. Which of the following statements is *not* logically equivalent to "If the day is cool, I will go fishing"?
    (a) I will go fishing or the day is not cool.
    (b) If I go fishing, the day is cool.
    (c) If I do not go fishing, then the day is not cool.
    (d) The day is not cool or I go fishing.

44. Select the statement which is *not* logically equivalent to "If the class is cancelled, Mary will go to the library."
    (a) Mary will go to the library or the class is not cancelled.
    (b) It is not true that Mary will not go to the library and the class is cancelled.
    (c) If Mary does not go to the library, the class is cancelled.
    (d) If Mary does not go to the library, the class will not be cancelled.

45. Supply reasons for the steps in the following proof. To prove that if n^2 is odd, then n is odd, we shall prove the equivalent statement: "If n is even, then n^2 is even," the contrapositive of the given statement.
    (a) If n is even, then $n = 2k$, k an integer   Reason _____
    (b) $n^2 = (2k)^2$ Reason _____
    (c) $n^2 = 4k^2$ Reason _____
    (d) $n^2 = 2 \cdot 2k^2$, which is even   Reason _____

46. Follow the procedure in problem 45 and prove that: If n^2 is even, then n is even.

In Other Words

47. Explain the difference between the words *necessary* and *sufficient*

48. Write, in words, two statements of the form "If p, then q" using the word *sufficient*.

49. Write, in words, two statements of the form "If p, then q" using the word *necessary*.

50. Write, in words, two statements of the form "If p, then q" using the words *only if*.

The following properties are used by mathematicians and logicians. In problems 51–55, express the statements in symbols, and explain why they are true.

51. The contrapositive of the statement $\sim q \to \sim p$ is equivalent to $p \to q$.

52. The inverse of the inverse of $p \to q$ is equivalent to $p \to q$.

53. The contrapositive of the inverse of $p \to q$ is equivalent to $q \to p$.

54. The statement $r \lor s \lor \sim p \lor \sim q$ is equivalent to the contrapositive of $(p \land q) \to (r \lor s)$.

55. The statement $(\sim r \land \sim s) \lor (p \lor q)$ is equivalent to the converse of $(p \lor q) \to (r \lor s)$.

Table 2.10

	d	*c*	*p*	*i*
d	*d*	*c*	*p*	*i*
c	*c*	*d*	*i*	*p*
p	*p*	*i*	*d*	*c*
i	*i*	*p*	*c*	*d*

Some of the properties in problems 51–55 are summarized in Table 2.10 in the margin, where d stands for direct statement, c for converse, p for contrapositive, and i for inverse. Using the table, find:

56. The contrapositive of the contrapositive

57. The inverse of the inverse

58. The converse of the contrapositive

59. The inverse of the converse

60. The inverse of the contrapositive

2.6   IMPLICATION

GETTING STARTED

FAMILIAR QUOTES

Have you ever heard the statements "To be or not to be, that is the question" or "You cannot fish and cut bait"? Why do you think these statements are so forceful? The statement "to be or not to be" has the form $b \lor \sim b$, a statement that is always true. On the other hand, the statement "You fish and you cut bait" is a **contradictory** statement; it is always false. (You cannot do both simultaneously.) Statements that are *always true* are called **tautologies,** while those that are *always false* are **contradictions.**

Note that the negation of the contradictory statement "You fish and you cut bait" is a tautology that can be written as "You cannot fish and cut bait." We study these statements in this section. Finally, here is a sign in a popular restaurant:

Does the first statement imply the second one, or is it the other way around? As it turns out, these two statements are equivalent. We shall study **implications** and **equivalencies** in this section.

In Definition 2.4, two statements p and q were defined to be equivalent (symbolized by $p \Leftrightarrow q$) if they have identical truth tables. An alternate definition states that p is equivalent to q ($p \Leftrightarrow q$) if the biconditional $p \leftrightarrow q$ is always true. (Can you see why these definitions are really the same?)

A. *Tautologies and Contradictions*

Definition 2.5

A statement that is always true is called a **tautology.** A statement that is always false is called a **contradiction.**

EXAMPLE 1   Show by means of a truth table that the statement $p \vee \sim p$ is a tautology.

Solution   The truth table for $p \vee \sim p$ is given below.

p	$\sim p$	$p \vee \sim p$
T	F	T
F	T	T

We note that in every possible case, $p \vee \sim p$ is true; therefore, the statement $p \vee \sim p$ is a tautology.

■

EXAMPLE 2   Show by means of a truth table that the statement $p \wedge \sim p$ is a contradiction.

Solution   The truth table for $p \wedge \sim p$ is given in the margin. We note that in every possible case, $p \wedge \sim p$ is false; therefore, $p \wedge \sim p$ is a contradiction (always false).

p	$\sim p$	$p \wedge \sim p$
T	F	F
F	T	F

■

It is easy to restate the definition of equivalence in terms of a tautology.

Definition 2.6

> The statement p is equivalent to the statement q ($p \Leftrightarrow q$) if and only if the biconditional $p \leftrightarrow q$ is a tautology.

EXAMPLE 3   Show that the biconditional $\sim(p \wedge q) \leftrightarrow \sim p \vee \sim q$ is a tautology.

Solution   We can do this by an easy check.

1. If the left side, $\sim(p \wedge q)$, is true, then $p \wedge q$ is false. Thus, at least one of p and q is false, so that at least one of $\sim p$ and $\sim q$ is true. Therefore, the right side, $\sim p \vee \sim q$, is also true.
2. If the left side, $\sim(p \wedge q)$, is false, then $p \wedge q$ is true. Thus, both p and q are true, so that both $\sim p$ and $\sim q$ are false. Therefore, the right side, $\sim p \vee \sim q$, is also false.

Because both sides always have the same truth value, the biconditional is always true; that is, it is a tautology. (This also shows that the two sides of the biconditional are equivalent.)

■

B. *Implications*

Another relationship between statements that is used a great deal by logicians and mathematicians is that of **implication.**

Definition 2.7

> **Implication**
>
> The statement p is said to **imply** the statement q (symbolized by $p \Rightarrow q$) if and only if the conditional $p \rightarrow q$ is a tautology.

EXAMPLE 4   Show that $[(p \rightarrow q) \wedge p] \Rightarrow q$.

Solution   *First method.* By Definition 2.7, we must show that $[(p \rightarrow q) \wedge p] \rightarrow q$ is a tautology. A conditional is true whenever the antecedent is false, so we need to check only the cases where the antecedent is true. Thus, if $(p \rightarrow q) \wedge p$ is true, then $p \rightarrow q$ is true and p is true. But if p is true, then q is also true (why?), so both sides of the conditional are true. This shows that the conditional is a tautology and thus, $(p \rightarrow q) \wedge p$ implies q.

Second method. A different procedure, which some people prefer, uses truth tables to show an implication. In order to show that $a \Rightarrow b$, we need to show that $a \rightarrow b$ is a tautology. But this means only that the truth tables for a and b (in this order) must not have a line with the values *TF* (in the same order), because this is the only case in which $a \rightarrow b$ is false. Thus, we may simply examine the given truth table for $(p \rightarrow q) \wedge p$ and q to show the implication. Notice that in columns 2 and 3 of the table there is no row with *TF* (in this order). Thus, $[(p \rightarrow q) \wedge p] \Rightarrow q$.

		1	2	3
p	q	$p \rightarrow q$	$(p \rightarrow q) \wedge p$	q
T	T	T	T	T
T	F	F	F	F
F	T	T	F	T
F	F	T	F	F

■

EXAMPLE 5 Identify the combinations of truth values that may arise to determine whether $p \Rightarrow q$ or $q \Rightarrow p$, or neither, where p and q are as follows:

> p: The fruit is an apple.
> q: The fruit is not a pear.

Solution We make a truth table and give the verbal interpretation of each line:

p	q
T	T	The fruit is an apple and not a pear (possible).
T	F	The fruit is an apple and also a pear (impossible).
F	T	The fruit is not an apple and is not a pear (possible).
F	F	The fruit is not an apple and is a pear (possible).

Thus, we see that the only line of the truth table that cannot occur is the *TF* line. Hence, $p \Rightarrow q$.

■

Exercise 2.6

A. 1. Show by means of a truth table that the statement $(p \wedge q) \rightarrow p$ is a tautology. This demonstrates that $(p \wedge q) \Rightarrow p$.

2. Show by means of a truth table that the statement
$[(p \rightarrow q) \wedge (q \rightarrow r)] \rightarrow (p \rightarrow r)$
is a tautology. This demonstrates that
$[(p \rightarrow q) \wedge (q \rightarrow r)] \Rightarrow (p \rightarrow r)$.

3. Show by means of a truth table that the statement $p \leftrightarrow \sim p$ is a contradiction.

In problems 4–8, classify the given statement as a tautology, a contradiction, or neither:

4. $p \leftrightarrow p$
5. $(p \rightarrow q) \leftrightarrow (p \wedge \sim q)$
6. $(p \rightarrow q) \leftrightarrow (p \vee \sim q)$
7. $(p \rightarrow q) \leftrightarrow (\sim p \vee q)$
8. $(p \wedge \sim q) \wedge q$

B.   9. Find all implications that exist between the statements u, v, and w with truth values shown in the table in the margin.

In problems 10–18, make a truth table for p and q and use the combinations of truth values that may arise to determine whether $p \Rightarrow q$ or $q \Rightarrow p$, or neither. (See Example 5.)

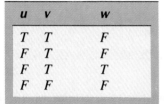

u	v	w
T	T	F
F	T	F
F	T	T
F	F	F

10. p: The number is positive.
    q: The number is negative.
11. p: The number is less than 0.
    q: The number is greater than or equal to 0.
12. p: The number is negative.
    q: The number is less than or equal to 0.
13. p: The course is a mathematics course.
    q: The course satisfies your mathematics requirement.
14. p: The animal is a dog.
    q: The animal is not a cat.
15. p: Jennie is tall or blonde.
    q: Jennie is either tall or blonde, but not both.
16. p: It rains every weekend.
    q: It never rains except on weekends.
17. p: To pass this course, I must average at least 70% on the tests.
    q: I will fail this course if and only if I do not average at least 70% on the tests.
18. p: To make money on the stock market, one must be willing to gamble.
    q: If one is willing to gamble, one will make money on the stock market.
19. Select the maximum number of consistent statements from the following set. *Note:* A set of statements is **consistent** if it is possible for all of them to be true at the same time. Make a truth table to see which of the given statements can be true simultaneously.
    (a) D is stupid.
    (b) D is careless.
    (c) D is careless, but not stupid.
    (d) If D is stupid, then D is careless.
    (e) D is careless if and only if D is stupid.
    (f) D is either stupid or careless, but not both.

In problems 20–26, two statements are given. Determine whether they are equivalent or if one implies the other, or neither.

20. $\sim(p \vee q)$; $\sim p \wedge \sim q$ 21. $\sim p \wedge q$; $p \rightarrow q$
22. $\sim p \rightarrow \sim q$; $\sim p \rightarrow q$ 23. $p \vee (p \wedge q)$; p
24. $p \wedge (p \vee q)$; p 25. $\sim p \vee \sim q$; $p \wedge \sim q$
26. $(p \wedge q) \rightarrow r$; $\sim p \vee \sim q \vee r$

In Other Words

27. Explain the difference between $p \rightarrow q$ and $p \Rightarrow q$.
28. Explain why a true statement is implied by any statement.
29. Explain why a false statement implies any statement.

Using Your Knowledge

*In describing sets using set-builder notation, the reader probably observed the close connection between a set and the statement used to define that set. If we are given a universal set $\mathcal{U}$, there is often a simple way in which to select a subset of $\mathcal{U}$ corresponding to a statement about the elements of $\mathcal{U}$. For example, if $\mathcal{U} = \{1, 2, 3, 4, 5, 6\}$ and p is the statement "The number is even," the set corresponding to this statement will be $P = \{2, 4, 6\}$; that is, P is the subset of $\mathcal{U}$ for which the statement p is true. The set P is called the **truth set** of p. Similarly, P' is the truth set of $\sim p$.*

Let $\mathcal{U} = \{a, b, c, d, e\}$. Then, let p be the statement "The letter is a vowel," let q be the statement "The letter is a consonant," and let r be the statement "The letter is the first letter in the English alphabet."

> *P, the truth set of p, is $\{a, e\}$.*
> *Q, the truth set of q, is $\{b, c, d\}$.*

Can you find:

> *R, the truth set of r?*
> *R', the truth set of $\sim r$?*

Because p and q are statements, $p \vee q$ and $p \wedge q$ are also statements; hence, they must have truth sets. To find the truth set of $p \vee q$, we select all the elements of $\mathcal{U}$ for which $p \vee q$ is true (that is, the elements that are vowels or consonants). Thus, the truth set of $p \vee q$ is $P \cup Q = \{a, b, c, d, e\} = \mathcal{U}$. Similarly, the truth set of $p \wedge q$ is the set of all elements of $\mathcal{U}$ that are vowels and consonants; that is, the truth set of $p \wedge q$ is $P \cap Q = \emptyset$.

30. With this information, complete the table in the margin.
31. If P, Q, and R are the truth sets of p, q, and r, respectively, find the truth sets of the following statements:

     (a) $q \wedge \sim r$ (b) $(p \wedge q) \wedge \sim r$

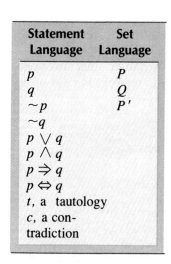

Statement Language	Set Language
p	P
q	Q
$\sim p$	P'
$\sim q$	
$p \vee q$	
$p \wedge q$	
$p \Rightarrow q$	
$p \Leftrightarrow q$	
t, a tautology	
c, a contradiction	

32. As in problem 31, find the truth sets of the following statements:

(a) $p \wedge \sim(q \vee r)$ (b) $(p \vee q) \wedge \sim(q \vee r)$

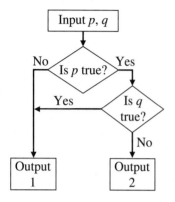

Input p, q

Is p true?   No   Yes

Is q true?   Yes   No

Output 1   Output 2

33. Here is a diagram for a machine that is set up to decide whether the statement $p \rightarrow q$ is true or false. What are the output decisions labeled Output 1 and Output 2?

34. Can you discover a similar diagram for a machine that will decide whether the statement $p \wedge q$ is true or false?

35. Can you discover a diagram for a machine that will decide whether the statement $p \vee q$ is true or false?

2.7   EULER DIAGRAMS

GETTING STARTED

INSURANCE POLICIES AND EULER DIAGRAMS

Sometimes statements in logic involve relationships between sets. Thus, a renewal provision of a life insurance policy states, "All life policies are renewable for additional term periods." This statement is equivalent to the following two statements:

1. If it is a life policy, then it is renewable for additional term periods.
2. The set of life policies is a subset of the set of all policies renewable for additional term periods.

Statements 1 and 2 can be visually represented by an Euler diagram (another name for a type of Venn diagram), as shown in Figure 2.1.

   In this section we shall discuss the techniques used to diagram statements and then use these diagrams to determine if a given argument is valid or invalid.

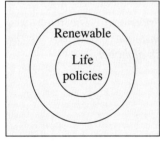

Renewable

Life policies

FIGURE 2.1

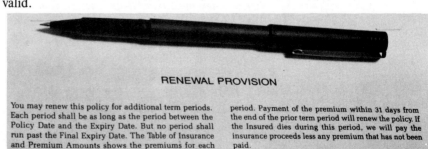

RENEWAL PROVISION

You may renew this policy for additional term periods. Each period shall be as long as the period between the Policy Date and the Expiry Date. But no period shall run past the Final Expiry Date. The Table of Insurance and Premium Amounts shows the premiums for each period. Payment of the premium within 31 days from the end of the prior term period will renew the policy. If the Insured dies during this period, we will pay the insurance proceeds less any premium that has not been paid.

A. *Drawing Euler Diagrams*

We shall now study the analysis of arguments by using Euler diagrams, a method that is most useful for arguments containing the words *all, some,* or *none.* In order to proceed, we must define what is meant by an **argument.**

Definition 2.8

> An **argument** is a set of statements, the **premises,** and a claim that another statement, the **conclusion,** follows from the premises.

We can represent four basic types of statements in Euler diagrams; these are illustrated in Figures 2.2–2.5.

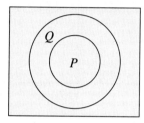

FIGURE 2.2
All P's are Q's

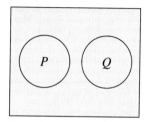

FIGURE 2.3
No P's are Q's

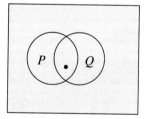

FIGURE 2.5
Some P's are not Q's

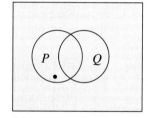

FIGURE 2.4
Some P's are Q's

The following examples discuss some simple arguments. Note that the premises are written on individual lines above a horizontal line; the conclusion is written below this line. This conclusion is preceded by the symbol ∴, which is read "therefore."

EXAMPLE 1   Consider the following argument:

> All men are mortal.
> Socrates is a man.
> ∴ Socrates is mortal.

(a) Identify the premises and the conclusion.
(b) Make an Euler diagram for the premises.

Solution   (a) The premises, which appear above the horizontal line, are "All men are mortal" and "Socrates is a man." The conclusion is "Socrates is mortal."

(b) To diagram the first premise, we begin by drawing a region to represent "mortals." Since all men are mortal, the region for "men" appears inside the region for mortals, as shown in Figure 2.6. The second premise, "Socrates is a man," indicates that "Socrates" goes inside the region representing "men." If s represents "Socrates," the diagram showing both premises appears in Figure 2.7.

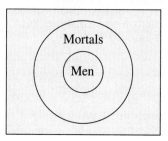 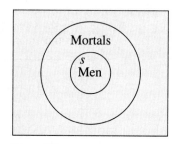

FIGURE 2.6   **FIGURE 2.7**   ■

B. *Valid Arguments*

If we use the premises in an argument to reach a conclusion, we would like the resulting argument to be **valid.**

Definition 2.9 ━━━━

> An argument is **valid** if the conclusion is true whenever the premises are assumed to be true. If an argument is not valid it is said to be **invalid.**

Thus, the argument shown in Figure 2.7 is valid because if Socrates is in the set of all men and the set of all men is inside the set of mortals, it must follow that Socrates is mortal.

EXAMPLE 2   Use an Euler diagram to test the validity of the following argument:

> All foreign cars are expensive.
> My car is expensive.
> ───────────────
> ∴ My car is a foreign car.

Solution   The first premise means that the set of all foreign cars is a subset of the set of expensive cars, while the second premise places "my car" (represented by m) within the set of expensive cars without specifying exactly where, as shown in the figure.

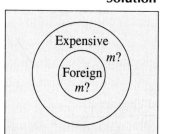

Since the information given is not enough to determine which alternative is correct — that is, m can be foreign or not — we say the argument is invalid.

            ■

EXAMPLE 3   Test the validity of the following argument:

>Some students are dangerous.
>All dangerous people are crazy.
>∴ Some students are not crazy.

Solution   The diagram in Figure 2.8 shows the premise, "Some students are dangerous," by two intersecting circles, with at least one student (represented by *s*) included in both circles. The second premise, "All dangerous people are crazy," can be shown by enclosing the set of dangerous people inside the set of crazy people, as in Figure 2.9 or as in Figure 2.10. Since we do not know which of these two drawings is correct, we cannot conclude that "some students are not crazy." Thus, the argument is invalid.

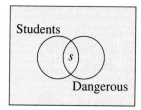
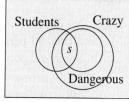
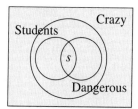

FIGURE 2.8   **FIGURE 2.9**   **FIGURE 2.10**   ■

EXAMPLE 4   Test the validity of the following argument:

>Some students are intelligent.
>All intelligent people are snobs.
>∴ Some students are snobs.

Solution   The first premise indicates that the set of students and the set of intelligent people have at least one element in common, represented by *s* (see the figure). Since all intelligent people are snobs, the set of intelligent people appears inside the circle of snobs. In this case, we can conclude that some students are snobs (that is, there is at least one student, *s*, who is also a snob). The argument is valid.

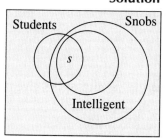

■

EXAMPLE 5   Determine the validity of the following argument:

>All persons taking the test outside the United States should not register.
>All persons not registered should write to the company.
>∴ Persons taking the test outside the United States should write to the company.

Solution

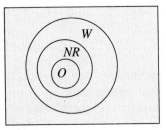

Let O be the set of all persons taking the test outside the United States, let *NR* be the set of all persons not registered for the test, and let *W* be the set of all persons that should write to the company. The first premise is diagramed by placing O inside *NR*, while the second premise indicates that *NR* is inside the set *W* (see the figure). It follows from the diagram that the set O is inside the set *W*. Thus, the argument is valid.   ∎

Exercise 2.7

In problems 1–6, state the premises and the conclusion for the given argument.

1. No misers are generous.
    Some old persons are not generous.
    ∴ Some old persons are misers.

2. No thieves are honest.
    Some dishonest people are convicted.
    ∴ Some thieves are convicted.

3. All diligent students get A's.
    All lazy students are not successful.
    ∴ All diligent students are lazy.

4. All students like logic.
    Robin likes logic.
    ∴ Robin is a student.

5. No kitten that loves fish is unteachable.
    No kitten without a tail will play with a gorilla.
    ∴ No unteachable kitten will play with a gorilla.

6. No birds are proud of their tails.
    Some birds cannot sing.
    ∴ Peacocks cannot sing.

In problems 7–20, use Euler diagrams to determine the validity of the given argument.

7. All professors are wise.
    Ms. Brown is a professor.
    ∴ Ms. Brown is wise.

8. All students are studious.
    Mr. Smith is studious.
    ∴ Mr. Smith is a student.

9. No drinkers are healthy.
    No joggers drink.
    ∴ No joggers are healthy.

10. All students are dedicated.
     All wealthy people are students.
     ∴ All wealthy people are dedicated.

11. All men are funny.
     Joey is a man.
     ∴ Joey is funny.

12. All football players are muscular.
     Jack is muscular.
     ∴ Jack is a football player.

13. All felines are mammals.
     No dog is a feline.
     ∴ No dogs are mammals.

14. Some students drink beer.
     All beer drinkers are dangerous.
     ∴ All students are dangerous.

15. No mathematics teacher is wealthy.
     No panthers teach mathematics.
     ∴ No panthers are wealthy.

16. All hippies have long hair.
     Some athletes are hippies.
     ∴ Some athletes have long hair.

17. All mathematics teachers have publications.
     Some Ph.D.'s have publications.
     ∴ Some Ph.D.'s are mathematics teachers.

18. All beer lovers like Schlitz.
     All people who like Schlitz get drunk.
     ∴ All beer lovers get drunk.

19. All heavy cars are comfortable to ride in.
     No car that is comfortable to ride in is shoddily built.
     ∴ No heavy car is shoddily built.

20. Some Nissan owners save money.
     Some fast drivers save money.
     ∴ Some fast drivers are Nissan owners.

In problems 21–25, use Euler diagrams to determine which (if any) of the given arguments are valid.

21. All bulldogs are ugly. This dog is ugly. So it must be a bulldog.

22. All peacocks are proud birds. This bird is not proud. Therefore, it is not a peacock.

23. All students who get A's in mathematics are drudges. This student got a B in mathematics. Hence, this student is not a drudge.

24. No Southerners like freezing weather. Joe likes freezing weather. Therefore, Joe is not a Southerner.

25. Some fishermen are lucky. Fred is unlucky. Therefore, Fred is not a fisherman.

26. Some students do well in history. Bobby failed history. Therefore, Bobby is not a student.

27. Given that
    i. All highway patrolmen direct traffic.
    ii. Persons who direct traffic must be obeyed.

    Use an Euler diagram to determine which conclusion(s) can be logically deduced.
    (a) Persons who direct traffic are highway patrolmen.
    (b) All highway patrolmen must be obeyed.
    (c) Some persons that direct traffic are not highway patrolmen.
    (d) None of the above.

28. All four of the following arguments have true conclusions, but one of the arguments is *not* valid. Use an Euler diagram to determine which argument is *not* valid.
    (a) All fish have gills and all trout are fish. Therefore, all trout have gills.
    (b) All trout have gills and all fish have gills. Therefore, all trout are fish.
    (c) All fish have tails and all trout are fish. Therefore, all trout have tails.
    (d) Every bird has a beak and the robin is a bird. Therefore, the robin has a beak.

In Other Words

29. Can a valid argument reach:
    (a) A true conclusion from true premises? Explain.
    (b) A false conclusion from true premises? Explain.

30. Can an invalid argument reach:
    (a) A true conclusion from true premises? Explain.
    (b) A false conclusion from true premises? Explain.

31. If an argument is invalid, does it have to have false premises? Explain and give examples.

32. Suppose an argument has a false conclusion. Which of the following statements should be true? Give reasons.
    (a) All premises are false.
    (b) Some premises are false.
    (c) The argument must be invalid.

33. Suppose all premises in an argument are true. If the argument is valid, what can you say about the conclusion?

34. Suppose all premises in an argument are false. If the argument is valid, What can you say about the conclusion?

Using Your Knowledge

At the beginning of this chapter, we mentioned a type of argument called a syllogism. The validity of this type of argument can be tested by using the knowledge you obtained about Venn diagrams in Chapter 1. We shall first diagram the four types of statements involved in these syllogisms.

As you recall, when we make a Venn diagram for two sets that are subsets of some universal set, we divide the region representing the universal set into four different regions, as shown in Figures 2.11–2.14.

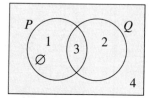

FIGURE 2.11
All P's are Q's

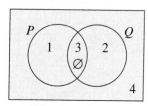

FIGURE 2.12
No P's are Q's

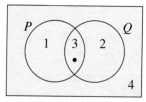

FIGURE 2.13
Some P's are Q's

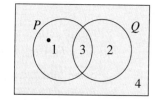

FIGURE 2.14
Some P's are not Q's

Figure 2.11 represents the statement, "All P's are Q's." Note that region 1 must be empty, because all P's are Q's.

Figure 2.12 represents the statement, "No P's are Q's." Note that region 3 must be empty, because no P's are Q's.

Figure 2.13 represents the statement, "Some P's are Q's." The dot in region 3 indicates that there is at least one P that is a Q.

Figure 2.14 represents the statement, "Some P's are not Q's." The dot in region 1 indicates that there is at least one P that is not a Q.
Similar considerations govern diagrams involving three sets, as you will see in the following illustration, where we examine the syllogism:

> *All kangaroos are marsupials.*
> *All marsupials are mammals.*
> *Therefore, all kangaroos are mammals.*

To diagram this argument, we draw a rectangle and three circles, and label the circles K (kangaroos), M (marsupials), and Ma (mammals). As before, these circles divide the rectangle (the universal set) into eight regions. The statement

"All kangaroos are marsupials" makes regions 1 and 5 empty (see Figure 2.15); whereas the statement *"All marsupials are mammals"* makes regions 2 and 3 empty. In order for the argument to be valid, regions 1 and 3 must be empty, because we wish to conclude that all kangaroos are mammals. Since the diagram shows that this is the case, the conclusion follows and the argument is valid.

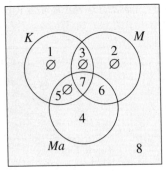

FIGURE 2.15   **FIGURE 2.16**

Using a similar technique and the diagram in Figure 2.16, we can show that the following argument is invalid:

Some intelligent people are attractive.
All models are attractive.
Therefore, some intelligent people are models.

To diagram the statement "Some intelligent people are attractive," we put dots in both regions 3 and 7, with a curved arrow symbol joining them. This indicates that the dot may be in region 3 or in region 7, or there may be dots in both, but we do not know which is the case. The second premise makes regions 4 and 5 empty. There is no statement in the argument that prevents region 7 from being empty. Thus, the conclusion could be false so the argument is invalid.

35–44. Use these ideas to examine the validity of the arguments in problems 11–20 of Exercise 2.7.

Use the same ideas to solve the following two problems:

45. Given the premises:

   No student who does not study will get an A in this course.
   Some students in this course do not study.

   Which of the following conclusions (if any) are valid?
   (a) Some students in this course will not get A's.
   (b) No students in this course will get A's.
   (c) All students in this course who do study will get A's.

46.   Given the premises:

Unless it rains, the grass will not grow.
If the grass grows, I will cut it.
It rains.

Which of the following conclusions (if any) are valid?
(a) I will cut the grass.
(b) The grass grows.
(c) If the grass does not grow, I will not cut it.

2.8   TRUTH TABLES AND VALIDITY OF ARGUMENTS

GETTING STARTED

FROM PREMISES TO VALID CONCLUSIONS

Here is an excerpt from the IRS instructions for Form 1040:

If you do not file your return by the due date, the penalty is usually 5% of the amount due for each month or part of a month your return is late, unless you have a reasonable explanation.

Now, suppose you filed your return one month late. Will there always be a penalty involved? Will it be 5% of the amount due? The answer is no in both cases. Do you see why?

In this section, we shall study how to determine if an argument is valid by writing the arguments in symbolic form and then using truth tables to determine their validity (problems 1–16, Exercise 2.8). Moreover, we shall discuss how to reach valid conclusions from given premises. Of course, you must be careful with the conclusions you reach. A sixth century B.C. paradox involving arguments claims that Epimenedis, the poet and prophet of Crete, made the statement:

All Cretans are liars.

What is paradoxical about that? First, rewrite the statement as

1. If it is a statement made by a Cretan, then it is not true. Also
2. The statement was made by a Cretan (Epimenedis). Thus
3. Statement 1 is not true.

But statement 3 makes statement 1 true! Do you see the problem? We shall stay away from such paradoxical arguments!

In the preceding section, a valid argument was defined as follows: An argument is **valid** if the conclusion is true whenever all the premises are assumed to be true. If an argument is not valid, it is said to be **invalid.** This definition suggests that a truth table can be used to check the validity of an argument. In order to construct such a truth table efficiently, the argument must be in symbolic form. The following examples illustrate the idea.

EXAMPLE 1   Write the following argument in symbolic form:

> If today is Sunday, then I will go to church.
> Today is Sunday.
> ∴ I will go to church.

Solution   Let s be "Today is Sunday," and let c be "I will go to church." Then the argument is symbolized as follows:

$$s \rightarrow c$$
$$\underline{s \qquad\quad}$$
$$\therefore c$$

■

EXAMPLE 2   Symbolize the following argument:

> A whole number is even or odd.
> This whole number is not even.
> ∴ This whole number is odd.

Solution   Let e be "A whole number is even," and let o be "A whole number is odd." Then the argument is symbolized as

$$e \lor o$$
$$\underline{\sim e \qquad}$$
$$\therefore o$$

■

A. *Problem Solving and Arguments*

To determine if an argument is valid, we follow this procedure

> 1. Write each premise in a separate line.
>
> 2. Write the conclusion after the premises and separate it by a horizontal line.
>
> 3. Make a truth table using a column for each premise and a column for the conclusion.
>
> 4. Check *only* the rows in which *all* premises are *true*. For the argument to be *valid,* the conclusion must also be *true*.

We illustrate this procedure next.

Problem Solving:	Determining Validity

Determine the validity of the following argument: If today is Sunday (s), then I will not go to school ($\sim g$). Today is not Sunday, so I will go to school.

1. Read the problem and select the unknown.
We are asked to determine if the given argument is valid.

2. Think of a plan.

Follow the 4-step procedure given.

3. Use the 4-step procedure.

1. Write each premise on a separate line. Draw a horizontal line after the last premise.

$$s \rightarrow \sim g \quad \text{(First premise)}$$
$$\underline{\sim s} \quad \text{(Second premise)}$$
$$\therefore g \quad \text{(Conclusion)}$$

2. Write the conclusion after the premises.

3. Make a truth table.

			Premise	Premise	Conclusion
s	g	$\sim g$	$s \rightarrow \sim g$	$\sim s$	g
T	T	F	F	F	T
T	F	T	T	F	F
F	T	F	T	T	T
F	F	T	T	T	F

4. Check the rows in which the premises $s \rightarrow \sim g$ and $\sim s$ are true.

Check rows 3 and 4. In the fourth row, both premises are true, but the conclusion g is false, so the argument is *invalid*.

TRY EXAMPLE 3 NOW.

Cover the solution, write your own, and then check your work.

EXAMPLE 3   Determine the validity of the argument in Example 2.

Solution   The argument is symbolized as

$$e \vee o$$
$$\underline{\sim e}$$
$$\therefore \quad o$$

We make a truth table for this argument with a column for each premise and a column for the conclusion as shown:

		Premise	Premise	Conclusion
e	o	$e \vee o$	$\sim e$	o
~~T~~	~~T~~	~~T~~	Ⓕ	~~T~~
~~T~~	~~F~~	~~T~~	Ⓕ	~~F~~
F	T	T	T	T
~~F~~	~~F~~	Ⓕ	~~T~~	~~F~~

← True premises
True conclusion

According to the definition of a valid argument, we need to examine only those rows of the table where all the premises are true. Consequently, we need to check only the third row of the truth table. (In rows 1, 2, and 4, at least one of the premises is false, and so these rows are crossed out.) For the argument to be valid, the remaining items in the conclusion column must all be T's. Thus, the table shows that the argument is valid.   ∎

EXAMPLE 4   Determine the validity of the following argument:

>Either the puppy is cute or I will not buy it.
>The puppy is cute.
>∴ I will buy it.

Solution   By writing p for "The puppy is cute" and b for "I will buy it," we can symbolize the argument in the form

$$p \vee \sim b$$
$$\underline{p \qquad\qquad}$$
$$\therefore b$$

Now, we construct the table for this argument:

			Premise	Premise	Conclusion
p	b	$\sim b$	$p \vee \sim b$	p	b
T	T	F	T	T	T
T	F	T	T	T	F
~~F~~	~~T~~	~~F~~	Ⓕ	Ⓕ	~~T~~
~~F~~	~~F~~	~~T~~	~~T~~	Ⓕ	~~F~~

← True premises
False conclusion

Next, we cross out all the rows where an F occurs in a premise column (rows 3 and 4 in the table). In the remaining rows, the premises are all true, so the remaining items in the conclusion column must all be T's if the argument is to be valid. Since there is an F in the second row of this column, the argument is invalid. ∎

EXAMPLE 5   Determine the validity of the following argument: You will not get overtime pay unless you work more than 40 hr per week. You work more than 40 hr per week. So you will get overtime pay.

Solution   To symbolize the argument, let p be "You get overtime pay," and let m be "You work more than 40 hr per week." Then, the argument is as follows:

$$p \rightarrow m \quad \text{Note: } \sim a \text{ unless } b \text{ means } a \rightarrow b. \text{ Why?}$$
$$\underline{m}$$
$$\therefore p$$

Notice that "You will not get overtime pay unless you work more than 40 hr per week" means that "If you get overtime pay, then you work more than 40 hr per week." The truth table for this argument is:

		Premise	Premise	Conclusion
p	m	$p \rightarrow m$	m	p
T	T	T	T	T
T	F	F	F	T
F	T	T	T	F
F	F	T	F	F

← True premises False conclusion

In the first and third rows of the table, both premises are true; but in the third row, the conclusion is false. Hence, the argument is invalid. ∎

EXAMPLE 6   Determine the validity of the following argument:

All dictionaries are useful books.
All useful books are valuable.
∴ All dictionaries are valuable.

Solution   We first write the argument in symbolic form. The statement "All dictionaries are useful books" is translated as "If the book is a dictionary d, then it is a useful book u." "All useful books are valuable" means "If the book is a useful book u, then it is valuable v." "All dictionaries are valuable" is translated as "If the book is a dictionary d, then it is valuable v." Thus, the argument is symbolized as

$$d \rightarrow u$$
$$\underline{u \rightarrow v}$$
$$\therefore d \rightarrow v$$

From the table, we see that whenever all the premises are true (rows 1, 5, 7, and 8), the conclusion is also true. Hence, the argument is valid. ∎

			Premise	Premise	Conclusion
d	u	v	$d \rightarrow u$	$u \rightarrow v$	$d \rightarrow v$
T	T	T	T	T	T
T	T	F	T	F	F
T	F	T	F	T	T
T	F	F	F	T	F
F	T	T	T	T	T
F	T	F	T	F	T
F	F	T	T	T	T
F	F	F	T	T	T

True premises
True conclusion

This problem can also be done by using an Euler diagram. Compare your results. ∎

EXAMPLE 7   Translate the argument in the cartoon into symbolic form and check its validity.

Peanuts. Reprinted by permission of UFS, Inc.

Solution   Let r be "You do not know how to read."
Let w be "You cannot read *War and Peace*."
Let h be "Leo Tolstoy will hate you."
Then the argument can be translated as follows:

$$r \rightarrow w$$
$$\underline{w \rightarrow h}$$
$$\therefore r \rightarrow h$$

Since the form of this argument is identical to that in Example 6, this argument is also valid. ∎

Examples 6 and 7 are illustrations of the fact that an argument of the form

$$p \to q$$
$$\underline{q \to r}$$
$$\therefore p \to r$$

is always valid.

In using a truth table to check the validity of an argument, it is to be emphasized that we need to examine only those rows where the premises are all true. This points out a basic logical principle: **If there is no case where the premises are all true, then the argument is valid regardless of the conclusion.**

This idea is used in the next example.

EXAMPLE 8   Determine the validity of the following argument:

It is raining now.
It is not raining now.
∴ It is raining now.

Solution   We let p be "It is raining now," and symbolize the argument to get

$$p$$
$$\underline{\sim p}$$
$$\therefore p$$

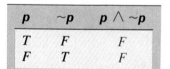

p	$\sim p$	$p \wedge \sim p$
T	F	F
F	T	F

From the table in the margin, we see that there is no case in which the conjunction of the premises, $p \wedge \sim p$, is true. Thus, the argument is valid. ∎

In many cases, we are confronted with arguments of the form

1. $p \to q$
2. $q \to r$
3. $r \to s$
4. $\therefore p \to s$

Four statements are involved in this argument, so the truth table to determine its validity will have $2^4 = 16$ rows. To construct such a table would be a tedious task, indeed. For this reason, we develop an alternative method for establishing the validity of such arguments. We first consider the premises $p \to q$ and $q \to r$. From these we can conclude (see Example 6) that $p \to r$. Hence, substituting our conclusion in the given argument, we have

2. $p \to r$
3. $\underline{r \to s}$
     $\therefore p \to s$

But this new argument again has the form of the one in Example 6, so we know it is valid.

In many cases, instead of determining the validity of an argument, we have to supply a valid conclusion for a given set of premises. Using the idea in Example 6, we can see that if the premises are $(p \rightarrow q)$, $(q \rightarrow r)$, . . . , $(x \rightarrow y)$, $(y \rightarrow z)$, a valid conclusion is $p \rightarrow z$. We illustrate this idea in the following examples.

EXAMPLE 9   Supply a valid conclusion using all the following premises:

1. $p \rightarrow q$
2. $q \rightarrow r$
3. $\sim s \rightarrow \sim r$

Solution   The third premise may be rewritten as $r \rightarrow s$, because a statement and its contrapositive are equivalent. Hence, the entire argument may be written as

1. $p \rightarrow q$
2. $q \rightarrow r$
3. $r \rightarrow s$

Thus, a valid conclusion using all the premises is $p \rightarrow s$.   ■

EXAMPLE 10   Suppose you know it to be true that:

1. If Alice watches TV, then Ben watches TV.
2. Carol watches TV if and only if Ben watches.
3. Don never watches TV if Carol is watching.
4. Don always watches TV if Ed is watching.

Show that Alice never watches TV when Ed is watching.

Solution   Let:

> a be "Alice watches TV"
> b be "Ben watches TV"
> c be "Carol watches TV"
> d be "Don watches TV"
> e be "Ed watches TV"

The argument above can be symbolized as follows:

1. $a \rightarrow b$
2. $c \leftrightarrow b$ or, equivalently, $2'$. $b \leftrightarrow c$
3. $c \rightarrow \sim d$
4. $e \rightarrow d$

If these premises are arranged in the order 1, $2'$, 3, and the contrapositive of 4, we obtain

1. $a \rightarrow b$	3. $c \rightarrow \sim d$
$2'$. $b \leftrightarrow c$	4. $\sim d \rightarrow \sim e$

Consequently, we may conclude that $a \rightarrow \sim e$; that is, "If Alice watches TV, then Ed does not watch TV," or, equivalently, "Alice never watches TV when Ed is watching." ∎

In our day-to-day reasoning, we do not make truth tables or check our arguments in any formal fashion. Instead, we (perhaps unconsciously) learn a few argument forms, which we use as we need them. The most commonly used of these argument forms are as follows:

Modus Ponens	**Modus Tollens**	**Hypothetical Syllogism**	**Disjunctive Syllogism**
$p \rightarrow q$	$p \rightarrow q$	$p \rightarrow q$	$p \vee q$
p	$\sim q$	$q \rightarrow r$	$\sim p$
$\therefore q$	$\therefore \sim p$	$\therefore p \rightarrow r$	$\therefore q$

The names of the first two of these are derived from the Latin and mean, respectively, "a manner of affirming" and "a manner of denying" (the parts of a conditional). The modus ponens and the two types of syllogism have already been discussed in this section; see Example 1, the problem solving example, and 2 and Example 6. It is left for the reader to show the validity of the modus tollens in problem 20 of Exercise 2.8.

Exercise 2.8

In problems 1–16, symbolize the argument using the suggested abbreviations. In each case, determine the validity of the given argument.

1. If you eat your spinach e, you can go out and play p.
   You did not eat your spinach.
   Therefore, you cannot go out and play.

2. If you eat your spinach e, you can go out and play p.
   You cannot go out and play.
   Therefore, you did not eat your spinach.

3. If you study logic s, mathematics is easy e.
   Mathematics is not easy.
   Therefore, you did not study logic.

4. I will learn this mathematics m, or I will eat my hat e.
   I will not eat my hat.
   Therefore, I will learn this mathematics.

5. The Good Taste Restaurant has good food g.
   Hence, the Good Taste Restaurant has good food, and I will recommend it to everyone r.

6. If prices go up u, management will scream s.
   If management screams, then supervisors will get tough t.
   Hence, if prices go up, supervisors will get tough.

7. If I work w, then I have money m.
   If I don't work, I have a good time g.
   Therefore, I have money or a good time.

8. Babies b are illogical i.
   Nobody is despised d who can manage a crocodile m.
   Illogical persons are despised.
   Hence, babies cannot manage crocodiles.

9. If you have the time t, we got the beer b.
   You have the time.
   So we got the beer.

10. Bill did not go to class this morning $\sim g$, because he wore a red shirt r, and he never wears a red shirt to class.

11. Where there is smoke s there is fire f.
    There is smoke.
    Hence, there is fire.

12. If you are enrolled e or have been accepted half-time at a college h, you may apply for a loan a.
    You have not been accepted half-time at a college.
    Hence, you may not apply for a loan.

13. You will be eligible for a grant e if you meet all the criteria m.
    You do not meet all the criteria.
    So you are not eligible for a grant.

14. We will pay for collision loss p only if collision coverage is afforded a.
    Collision coverage is not afforded.
    Hence, we will not pay for collision loss.

15. If spouse is also filing f, give spouse's Social Security number s.
    Spouse is not filing.
    Hence, do not give spouse's Social Security number.

16. Additional sheets of paper will not be attached $\sim a$ unless more space is needed m.
    More space is needed.
    Hence, additional sheets of paper are attached.

An argument is given in each of problems 17–21. Determine whether each argument is valid or invalid.

17. $p \lor q$
    $\underline{\sim p}$
    $\therefore \quad q$

18. $p \to q$
    $\underline{p}$
    $\therefore q$

19. $p \to q$
    $\underline{\sim p}$
    $\therefore \quad q$

20. $p \to q$
    $\underline{\sim q}$
    $\therefore \sim p$

21. $p \to q$
    $\underline{q \to r}$
    $\therefore \sim r \to \sim p$

In problems 22–31, find a valid conclusion using all the premises.

22. $p \rightarrow q$
$q \rightarrow r$
$\underline{r \rightarrow \sim s}$

23. $p \rightarrow q$
$\underline{\sim q \vee r}$
[*Hint*: $(\sim q \vee r) \leftrightarrow (q \rightarrow r)$]

24. $p \rightarrow q$
$s \rightarrow \sim r$
$t \rightarrow r$
$q \rightarrow u$
$\underline{\sim u \vee t}$

25. $p \rightarrow q$
$q \rightarrow r$
$\sim s \rightarrow \sim r$
$\underline{p}$

26. $p \rightarrow \sim q$
$r \rightarrow q$
$\underline{r}$

27. $\sim p \rightarrow q$
$\sim p \vee r$
$\underline{\sim r}$

28. If it rains, then the grass will grow.
A sufficient condition for cutting the grass is that it will grow.
The grass is cut only if it is higher than 8 inches.

29. The only books in this library that I do not recommend are unhealthy.
All bound books are well-written.
All romances are healthy in tone.
I do not recommend any of the unbound books.

30. All ducks can fly.
No land bird eats shrimp.
Only flightless birds do not eat shrimp.

31. If you are not patriotic, then you do not vote.
Aardvarks have no emotions.
You cannot be patriotic if you have no emotions.

32. Classify the arguments in problems 2, 4, 6, and 11 as modus ponens, modus tollens, hypothetical syllogism, or disjunctive syllogism.

In problems 33–36, two premises are given. In each problem, you are to select the conclusion that will make the entire argument valid.

33. If I drive to work, then I will not be late.
If I am not late, then I do not lose any pay.

(a) If I am not late, then I drive to work.
(b) If I do not lose any pay, then I drive to work.
(c) If I drive to work, then I do not lose any pay.
(d) If I do not drive to work, then I lose some pay.

34. If the Bears win the final game, then they will play in the NFL playoffs.
If they play in the NFL playoffs, their owners will make a good profit.

(a) If their owners made a good profit, then the Bears played in the NFL playoffs.
(b) If their owners made a good profit, then the Bears won the final game.

(c) If the Bears do not win the final game, then their owners will not make a good profit.

(d) If the Bears win the final game, then their owners will make a good profit.

35. If all persons pay their bills on time, then no collection agencies are needed.

Unfortunately, some collection agencies are needed.

(a) Some people pay their bills on time.

(b) Some people do not pay their bills on time.

(c) If there are no collection agencies, then all persons pay their bills on time.

(d) All people pay their bills on time.

36. If all students learn from their books alone, then no teachers are needed.

However, some teachers are needed.

(a) No students learn from their books alone.

(b) Some students learn from their books alone.

(c) If no teachers are needed, then all students learn from their books alone.

(d) Some students do not learn from their books alone.

37. If Bill studies economics, he will make money. If he studies business procedures, he will make good money. Bill studies economics but not business procedures. Which of the following (if any) is a logical conclusion?

(a) Bill does not make good money.

(b) Bill makes good money.

(c) Bill does not get a college degree.

38. All college graduates are educated. All educated people dress neatly. Jackie dresses neatly. Which of the following, if any, is a logical conclusion?

(a) Jackie is a college graduate.

(b) Jackie is not a college graduate.

(c) Jackie is educated.

In Other Words

The job of advertisers is to convince people to buy their products. Write the conclusion you think the advertisers want you to reach.

39. If you read X magazine, then you will not make bad financial decisions. You certainly do not want to make bad financial decision, so _____ .

40. If you do not join our fraternity (sorority), you will not be popular. You did join, so _____ .

41. The name of the fallacy in problem 39 is "affirming the consequent." Explain what this means.

42. The name of the fallacy in problem 40 is "denying the antecedent." Explain what this means.

Discovery

Consider the following premises taken from Symbolic Logic, *a book written by Lewis Carroll (logician, mathematician, and author of* Alice's Adventures in Wonderland):

> *No kitten that loves fish is unteachable.*
> *No kitten without a tail will play with a gorilla.*
> *Kittens with whiskers always love fish.*
> *No teachable kitten has green eyes.*
> *Kittens that have no whiskers have no tails.*

43. Find a valid conclusion using all the premises. [*Hint:* "No ____ is . . ." is translated as "If it is a ____ , then it is not a . . . .]"

2.9 SWITCHING NETWORKS: A PROBLEM–SOLVING TOOL

GETTING STARTED

COMPUTER CIRCUITS

Do you know how a computer works? All computers use a logic system devised by George Boole. The switches inside a computer chip can be arranged into a switching network or a system of gates delivering logical results. The most fundamental logic gates are called AND, OR, and NOT gates. The application of logic to electric circuits was pioneered by Claude E. Shannon of M.I.T and Bell Telephone Laboratories. The idea is to simplify circuits as much as possible by finding equivalent circuits in much the same way as we find equivalent statements. At Bell Laboratories, after several days' work, a group of engineers once produced a circuit with 65 contacts. Then an engineer, trained in symbolic logic, designed an equivalent circuit with 47 contacts in only *three hours*. In this section, you will learn about these circuits and simplify several yourself as in problems 16–20 of Exercise 2.9.

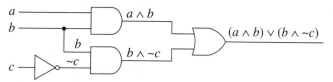

This logic diagram shows the inputs and outputs for a series of logic gates. From left to right, the gates shown are a NOT gate, two AND gates, and an OR gate. The lines that connect the gates represent the physical wires that actually connect "decision-making" devices on a circuit board or in an integrated circuit. For more information on logic gates see the Discovery section of Exercise 2.9.

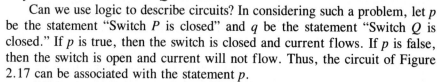

FIGURE 2.17

The theory of logic discussed in this chapter can be used to develop a theory of simple switching networks. A **switching network** is an arrangement of wires and switches that connect two terminals. A **closed** switch permits the flow of current, while an **open** switch prevents the flow. One may also think of a switch as a valve that controls the flow of water through a pipe, or as a drawbridge over a river controlling the flow of traffic along a road (see Figure 2.17).

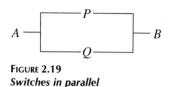

FIGURE 2.18
Switches in series

Two switches may be connected in **series** (in a line from left to right), as in Figure 2.18. In this network, the current flows between the **terminals** A and B only if both switches P and Q are closed.

Can we use logic to describe circuits? In considering such a problem, let p be the statement "Switch P is closed" and q be the statement "Switch Q is closed." If p is true, then the switch is closed and current flows. If p is false, then the switch is open and current will not flow. Thus, the circuit of Figure 2.17 can be associated with the statement p.

When two switches are connected in **series,** as in Figure 2.18, the current will flow only when both switches are closed. Thus, the circuit is associated with the statement $p \wedge q$. On the other hand, in Figure 2.19, current will flow when either P or Q is closed. The switches are connected in **parallel** and the statement corresponding to this circuit is $p \vee q$. What about the statement $\sim p$? This statement corresponds to P′, a switch that is open if P is closed and vice versa. Switches P and P′ are called **complementary.**

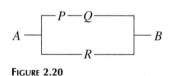

FIGURE 2.19
Switches in parallel

Series and parallel circuits can be combined to form more complicated networks, as shown in Figure 2.20. The network there corresponds to the statement (p $\wedge$ q) $\vee$ r. If you think of the switches as drawbridges, you can see that we are able to go from A to B when both P and Q are down (closed) or when R is down (closed). Now, all compound statements can be represented by switching networks. When switches open and close simultaneously, the switches will be represented by the same letter and will be called **equivalent.**

FIGURE 2.20

Problem Solving:

1. **Read the problem and select the unknown.**

2. **Think of a plan.** Find the components of $(p \vee q) \wedge r$ and the switches corresponding to each of the components.

Switching Networks

Construct a network corresponding to the statement $(p \vee q) \wedge r$.

We want to design a circuit starting at A, ending at B, and corresponding to $(p \vee q) \wedge r$.

The components of the conjunction $(p \vee q) \wedge r$ are $(p \vee q)$ and r. The parallel circuit containing the switches P and Q corresponds to the statement $(p \vee q)$, and the switch R corresponds to r.

3. Use your knowledge to carry out the plan.

Draw the switch corresponding to $(p \lor q)$.

corresponds to $(p \lor q)$

Draw the switch corresponding to r.

corresponds to r

Start at A and connect the two circuits in series to correspond to the connective $\land$. End at B.

corresponds to $(p \lor q) \land r$

TRY EXAMPLE 1 NOW.

Cover the solution, write your own, and then check your work.

EXAMPLE 1 Construct a network corresponding to the statement $(p \lor r) \land (q \lor r)$.

Solution The network associated with the given statement appears in Figure 2.21. The parallel circuit containing the switches P and R corresponds to the statement $p \lor r$. Similarly, the parallel circuit with the switches Q and R corresponds to the statement $q \lor r$. These two parallel circuits are connected in series to correspond to the connective $\land$, which joins the two statements $p \lor r$ and $q \lor r$. ∎

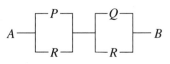

FIGURE 2.21

Notice that, in the networks of Figure 2.20 and 2.21, current will flow if P and Q are closed or if R is closed. For this reason, these two networks are said to be **equivalent**. In general, two networks are **equivalent** if their corresponding statements are equivalent. For example, the statement corresponding to the network in Figure 2.20 is $(p \land q) \lor r$ and that of Figure 2.21 is $(p \lor r) \land (q \lor r)$. The truth tables of these two statements are identical, so the networks of Figures 2.20 and 2.21 are equivalent.

Finally, we shall consider the design of certain networks having specified properties. An equivalent problem is that of constructing a compound statement having a specified truth table. The procedure used will involve the basic conjunctions given in Table 2.11. For example, a network associated with a statement having truth table *TTFF* will be the one corresponding to the statement $(p \land q) \lor (p \land \sim q)$. (See Exercise 2.3, problems 23 and 24.)

Table 2.11

p	q	Basic Conjunction
T	T	$p \land q$
T	F	$p \land \sim q$
F	T	$\sim p \land q$
F	F	$\sim p \land \sim q$

EXAMPLE 2 A toy designer plans to build a battery-operated kitten, with arms that can be lowered or raised and a purring mechanism. He wants his kitten to purr only when the *right* arm or *both* arms are raised; with any other arrangement, the purring mechanism is to be off. Construct a switching circuit that will do this.

Solution   Let p be the statement "The right arm is raised," and let q be the statement "The left arm is raised." The desired truth table is Table 2.12. We note that the cat will purr when p is true (rows 1 and 2). Hence, our network will correspond to a statement having truth table *TTFF*. We have just seen that one such statement is $(p \wedge q) \vee (p \wedge \sim q)$, so the network associated with this statement (see Figure 2.22) is a possible network for the toy kitten.   ∎

Table 2.12

		Desired
p	q	Truth Table
T	T	T
T	F	T
F	T	F
F	F	F

Notice that, in the network of Figure 2.22 current will flow when P is closed (because if Q is closed, current will flow through the top branch, and if Q is open, current will flow through the bottom branch). Hence, an equivalent network is the one given in Figure 2.23.

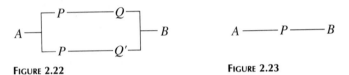

FIGURE 2.22   **FIGURE 2.23**

As indicated in problems 23 and 24 of Exercise 2.3, we can always write a statement corresponding to a given truth table as follows:

1. For each row with a T in the final column, write a conjunction using each variable with a T in its column and the negation of each variable with an F in its column.
2. Write the disjunction of these conjunctions.

For example, suppose that two rows of the given truth table are as given below and that all other rows end with an F.

p	q	r	Final Column	Desired Conjunction
T	T	F	T	$p \wedge q \wedge \sim r$
T	F	F	T	$p \wedge \sim q \wedge \sim r$

Then the desired conjunctions are as shown in the table, and the final desired statement is

$$(p \wedge q \wedge \sim r) \vee (p \wedge \sim q \wedge \sim r)$$

The corresponding network is shown in Figure 2.24. Of course, this procedure does not always give the simplest result for the given truth table. Thus, the statement obtained can be simplified to $p \wedge \sim r$, as you can verify by checking the network.

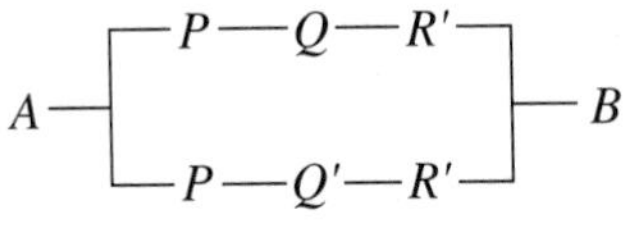

FIGURE 2.24

Exercise 2.9

In problems 1–6, construct a network corresponding to the given statement.

1. $(p \wedge q) \vee p$

2. $p \vee (q \wedge r)$

3. $(\sim p \wedge q) \vee (p \wedge \sim r)$

4. $(p \vee q) \wedge \sim r$

5. $[(p \vee \sim q) \vee q \vee (\sim p \vee q)] \vee q$

6. $[(p \vee \sim q) \vee q \vee (\sim p \vee q)] \wedge q$

In problems 7–11, find the compound statement corresponding to the network given.

7.

8.

9.

10.

11.

12. A switching network to control the launching of ICBMs is to be designed so that it can be operated by three generals. For democracy's sake, the Department of Defense assumes that in order to fire the missile, two of the three generals will have to close their switches. Design a network that will do this.

In problems 13–15, draw a pair of switching networks to indicate that the given statements are equivalent.

13. $p \vee p$ and p

14. $p \vee (q \wedge r)$ and $(p \vee q) \wedge (p \vee r)$

15. $(p \wedge q) \vee p$ and p

In problems 16–20, simplify the given network.

16.

17.

18.

19.

20.

A—P'—Q'—P—B

with A, P, Q, Q', B and P, Q

In Other Words

21. Explain the relationship between a series circuit with switches P and Q and the statement $p \wedge q$.
22. Explain the relationship between a parallel circuit with switches P and Q and the statement $p \vee q$.

Discovery

Computer Gates

Digital computers have circuits in which the flow of current is regulated by **gates,** *as shown below. These circuits respond to high (1) or low (0) voltages and can be described by* **logic statements.**

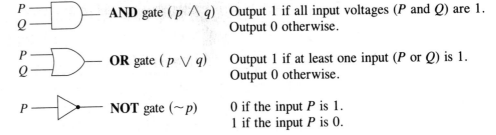

AND gate ($p \wedge q$) — Output 1 if all input voltages (P and Q) are 1. Output 0 otherwise.

OR gate ($p \vee q$) — Output 1 if at least one input (P or Q) is 1. Output 0 otherwise.

NOT gate ($\sim p$) — 0 if the input P is 1. 1 if the input P is 0.

Keep in mind that 1 and 0 correspond to high and low voltages, respectively.

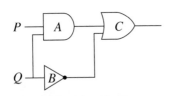

1	2	3	5	4
p	q	$(p \wedge q)$	$\vee$	$\sim q$
1	1	1	1	0
1	0	0	1	1
0	1	0	0	0
0	0	0	1	1

Logic diagrams show how the gates are connected. The outputs in these diagrams can be obtained in the same way in which truth tables are constructed, with 1's replacing the T's and 0's replacing the F's. For example, we can list the outputs for all possible inputs for the logic diagram shown in the margin as follows: The output of A is symbolized by $p \wedge q$ and the output of B by $\sim q$. Thus, the inputs of C correspond to $p \wedge q$ and $\sim q$. Since C is an OR gate, the final output can be symbolized by the statement $(p \wedge q) \vee \sim q$. If we construct the truth table for this statement using 1 for T and 0 for F, we obtain the table given in the margin. The table shows that the final output (column 5) is always a high (1) voltage except in the third row, where the input voltage corresponding to P is low (0) and that corresponding to Q is high (1). Since we have shown earlier that the statement $(p \wedge q) \vee \sim q$ is equivalent to

p $\vee$ ~*q, the given circuit can be simplified to
one corresponding to the latter statement. The
diagram for this circuit is

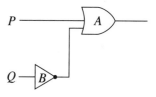

In problems 23–25, see if you can discover the final outputs for all possible inputs for the given diagrams.

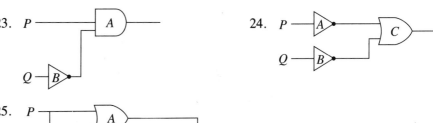

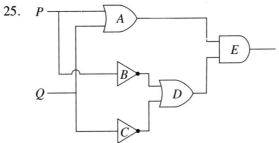

Chapter 2 Summary

Section	Item	Meaning	Example
2.1B	*p, q, r*, etc.	Statements	*p:* Today is Monday. *q:* The sky is blue.
2.1B	*p* $\wedge$ *q*	Conjunction (*p* **and** *q*)	Today is Monday, **and** the sky is blue.
2.1B	*p* $\vee$ *q*	Disjunction (*p* **or** *q*)	Today is Monday, **or** the sky is blue.
2.1B	~*p*	Negation (**not** *p*)	Today is **not** Monday.
2.2A, B, C		Truth tables for the statements *p* $\wedge$ *q*, *p* $\vee$ *q*, and ~*p*	

p	*q*	*p*$\wedge$*q*	*p*$\vee$*q*	~*p*
T	*T*	*T*	*T*	*F*
T	*F*	*F*	*T*	*F*
F	*T*	*F*	*T*	*T*
F	*F*	*F*	*F*	*T*

Section	Item	Meaning	Example
2.3B	$p \Leftrightarrow q$	The statements p and q are equivalent; that is, they have identical truth tables.	$\sim(p \vee q) \Leftrightarrow \sim p \wedge \sim q$
2.4A	$p \rightarrow q$	p conditional q	**If** today is Monday, **then** I will go to school.
2.4B	$p \leftrightarrow q$	p biconditional q	Today is Monday **if and only if** I go to school.
2.4A, B	<table><tr><td>p</td><td>q</td><td>$p \rightarrow q$</td><td>$p \leftrightarrow q$</td></tr><tr><td>T</td><td>T</td><td>T</td><td>T</td></tr><tr><td>T</td><td>F</td><td>F</td><td>F</td></tr><tr><td>F</td><td>T</td><td>T</td><td>F</td></tr><tr><td>F</td><td>F</td><td>T</td><td>T</td></tr></table>	Truth tables for the conditional and the biconditional	
2.5A	$q \rightarrow p$ $\sim p \rightarrow \sim q$ $\sim q \rightarrow \sim p$	Converse of $p \rightarrow q$ Inverse of $p \rightarrow q$ Contrapositive of $p \rightarrow q$	
2.5B	p is **sufficient** for q q is **necessary** for p p **only if** q q **if** p	Statements equivalent to "If p, then q."	
2.6A	A tautology	A statement that is always true	2 is even. $p \vee \sim p$
2.6A	A contradiction	A statement that is always false	2 is odd. $p \wedge \sim p$
2.6B	$p \Rightarrow q$	p implies q; the conditional $p \rightarrow q$ is a tautology.	The animal is a dog implies that the animal is a mammal.
2.7A	$p \rightarrow q$ $\underline{p}$ $\therefore q$	An argument (a set of statements, the premises, and a claim that another statement, the conclusion, follows from the premises)	
2.7B	Valid argument	An argument is valid if, whenever all the premises are true, the conclusion is also true.	All men are mortal. <u>Socrates is a man.</u> $\therefore$ Socrates is mortal.

Section	Item	Meaning
2.8	Modus ponens	$p \rightarrow q$ $\underline{p\ \ \ \ \ }$ $\therefore q$
2.8	Modus tollens	$p \rightarrow q$ $\underline{\sim q\ \ \ \ \ }$ $\therefore \sim p$
	Hypothetical syllogism	$p \rightarrow q$ $\underline{q \rightarrow r}$ $\therefore p \rightarrow r$
	Disjunctive syllogism	$p \vee q$ $\underline{\sim p\ \ \ \ \ }$ $\therefore \ \ q$

Research Questions

Sources of information for these questions can be found in the Bibilography at the end of the book.

1. Go to a logic book and find and discuss at least five different fallacies in logic. Give examples.
2. What is a paradox? Find at least two famous paradoxes in logic.
3. Find out what Boolean algebra is and how it relates to logic.
4. Find some newspaper or magazine articles using logic to persuade the reader.
5. Find some newspaper editorials using logic to persuade readers in important issues.
6. Write a paragraph about the author of the *Organon* and the material discussed in the book.
7. Write a report about the life and work of Gottlob Frege.
8. Find out and write a paper about the contributions of Claude Shannon to logic and his work in switching circuits.

Chapter 2 Practice Test

1. Which of the following are statements?
   (a) Green apples taste good.
   (b) 1991 was a leap year.
   (c) No fish can live without water.
   (d) Some birds cannot fly.
   (e) If it rains today, my lawn will get wet.
   (f) Can anyone answer this question?

2. Identify the components and the logical connective or modifier in each of the following statements. Write each statement in symbolic form using the suggested abbreviations.
   (a) If the number of a year is divisible by 4 (d), then the year is a presidential election year (p).
   (b) I love Bill (b), but Bill does not love me ($\sim m$).
   (c) A candidate is elected president of the United States (e) if and only if he receives a majority of the electoral college votes (m).
   (d) Janet can make sense out of symbolic logic (s), or she fails this course (f).
   (e) Janet cannot make sense out of symbolic logic ($\sim s$).

3. Let g be "He is a gentleman," and let s be "He is a scholar." Write in words:
   (a) $\sim(g \wedge s)$ (b) $\sim g \wedge s$

4. Write the negation of each of the following statements:
   (a) I will go to the beach or to the movies.
   (b) I will stay in my room and do my homework.
   (c) Pluto is not a planet.

5. Write the negation of each of the following statements:
   (a) All cats are felines.
   (b) Some dogs are well trained.
   (c) No dog is afraid of a mouse.

6. Write the negation of each of the following statements.
   (a) If Joey does not study, he will fail this course.
   (b) If Sally studies hard, she will make an A in this course.

7. In the table below, identify each entry under a, b, c, d, and e by matching it with the appropriate one of the following statements: $\sim p$, $p \rightarrow q$, $p \wedge q$, $p \vee q$, $p \leftrightarrow q$.

p	q	a.	b.	c.	d.	e.
T	T	T	T	F	T	T
T	F	F	F	F	F	T
F	T	F	F	T	T	T
F	F	T	F	T	T	F

8. Construct a truth table for the statement $(p \vee q) \wedge (\sim p \vee \sim q)$

9. Construct a truth table for the statement $(p \vee q) \rightarrow \sim p$

10. Which of the following statements is equivalent to $\sim p \vee q$?
    (a) $\sim p \wedge \sim q$ (b) $\sim(p \wedge \sim q)$

11. Under what conditions is the following statement true? "Sally is naturally beautiful, or she knows how to use makeup."

12. Is the following statement true or false? If $2 + 2 = 5$, then $2 \cdot 3 = 6$.

13. Construct the truth table for the statement $(p \rightarrow q) \leftrightarrow (q \vee \sim p)$

14. Write:
    (a) The converse   (b) The inverse   (c) The contrapositive
    of the statement "If you make a golf score of 62 once, you will make it again."

15. Let p be "You get overtime pay," and let m be "You work more than 40 hr per week." Symbolize the following statements:
    (a) If you work more than 40 hr per week, then you get overtime pay.
    (b) You get overtime pay only if you work more than 40 hr per week.
    (c) You get overtime pay if and only if you work more than 40 hr per week.

16. Let b be "You get a bank loan," and let c be "You have a good credit record." Symbolize the following statements:
    (a) For you to get a bank loan, it is necessary that you have a good credit record.
    (b) Your having a good credit record is sufficient for you to get a bank loan.
    (c) A necessary and sufficient condition for you to get a bank loan is that you have a good credit record.

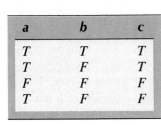

a	b	c
T	T	T
T	F	T
F	F	F
T	F	F

17. The table in the margin gives the truth values for three statements, a, b, and c. Find all the implications among these statements.

18. Which of the following statements are tautologies?
    (a) $p \wedge \sim p$ (b) $p \vee \sim p$
    (c) $(p \rightarrow q) \leftrightarrow (\sim q \vee p)$

19. Use an Euler diagram to check the validity of the following argument:

    All students study hard.
    John is not a student.
    ∴ John does not study hard.

20. Use an Euler diagram to check the validity of the following argument:

    No loafers work hard.
    Sally does not work hard.
    ∴ Sally is a loafer.

21. Use a truth table to check the validity of the argument in problem 19.

22. Use a truth table to check the validity of the argument in problem 20.

23. Use a truth table to check the validity of the following argument:

    If you win the race, you are a good runner.
    You win the race.
    ∴ You are a good runner.

24. Show that the following argument is invalid:

    $$p \rightarrow q$$
    $$\sim q \rightarrow \sim r$$
    $$\therefore \quad p \rightarrow \sim r$$

25. Construct a switching network that represents the statement

    $(p \rightarrow q) \wedge (\sim p \rightarrow \sim q)$.

This chapter will take you on a journey through time and number. Imagine yourself in Egypt 5,500 years ago, at a time when Egyptians used their fingers as standard counting units. To keep a record of counted objects, the Egyptians used short, straight strokes called **tally marks.** Thus, the numbers from 1 to 9 were represented by the proper number of tally marks, resulting in an additive system. In this system, the position of a numeral had no significance; ∩| and |∩ both represented 11. Number values were simply added. We continue our journey to Babylon, where we find the oldest system known in which the value of a numeral depends on its placement. Using 60 as the base, ▼▼ means $1 + 1 = 2$, but ▼ ▼ means $60 + 1 = 61$.

We then move on to the Roman numeral system, which uses base 10, as the Egyptians did, and constructs numerals by means of simple addition and subtraction.

XI means $10 + 1 = 11$, but IX is $10 - 1 = 9$. We then study our present decimal system, also called the Hindu-Arabic system. There, we also learn about exponents so that we can write numbers in expanded form. You will notice that the base we use is 10, though we will look at number systems using bases other than 10. You will be surprised to know that **binary** systems, using 2 as a base, were among the earliest systems invented. Even today, some South Sea Islanders have a binary system where counting by 2 means repeating the words for "one" and "two." For these islanders, *urapun* is 1, *okosa* is 2, *okosa urapun* 3, *okosa okosa* 4, and so on. How does the computer count? Well, for a computer 1_2 (one base two) is one, 10_2 (one zero base two) is two, 11_2 (one one base two) is three, and so on. Do you see the similarities?

From antiquity to the present day, the idea is the same!

Numeration Systems

THE HUMAN SIDE OF MATHEMATICS

One of the most influential mathematicians of the early Arab empire was Mohammed ibn Musa al-Khowarizmi (ca. A.D. 780–850). He was born in Khwarezm, the town that is now known as Kiva in Soviet Central Asia. As an adult, he was summoned to Baghdad and became the court astronomer. He wrote two books, one on algebra and one on the Hindu numeral system. These two books, when

Mohammed al-Khowarizmi (ca. A.D. 780–850)

translated into Latin in the twelfth century, exerted a tremendous influence on European mathematics.

In his book on the Hindu numerals, al-Khowarizmi touted the use of this system to merchants and mathematicians everywhere. However, it took 200 more years for these numerals to reach Spain, and it was not until the late thirteenth century that their use became widespread. It was the merchants who were won over by the ease of calculating in the new system and who were mainly responsible for its wide adoption.

Al-Khowarizmi's second book, *Hisah al-jabr w'almuqabala*, translated roughly as "the science of equations," gave us the word *algebra* (from *al-jabr*).

Our present-day symbols for the digits 1–9 originated with the Hindus. These numerals were de-

signed for a decimal (base 10) system of counting, named after the Latin word *decima*, meaning "tenth."

Why do we use a base of 10? There really is no reason except perhaps the number of fingers on a pair of human hands. We could just as well use a base of 5 or 12 or 20. Until about the fifteenth century, fractions were written using a positional system based on the number 60. This sexagesimal (base 60) system had been developed by the Mesopotamians more than 3000 years ago. The great disadvantage of this system was the need to represent 59 numerals. To get around this difficulty, the ancients used various combinations of two symbols, one representing our number one and the other representing our number ten.

It was not until about the year 500 that the Hindus devised a positional notation for the decimal system. They discarded the separate symbols for numbers greater than nine and standardized the symbols for the digits from 1 through 9. It was not until much later that the very important 0 symbol came into use. **Looking Ahead:** We will look at the ancient numeration systems and then at our familiar Hindu-Arabic system that al-Khowarizmi championed over 1000 years ago, centuries before its use became widespread.

3.1   EGYPTIAN, BABYLONIAN, AND ROMAN NUMERATION SYSTEMS

Napolean Bonaparte, French military leader and emperor of France, 1804–1815

GETTING STARTED

FROM EGYPTIANS TO TOLSTOY

The Egyptian system of numeration is additive; that is, the numeral ‖ represents $1 + 1 = 2$ and ‖‖ ∩ represents $1 + 1 + 1 + 10 = 13$. An additive system found in Leo Tolstoy's novel *War and Peace* gives each letter of the French alphabet the number shown in the table below. (Note there is no j.) Thus, the number associated with the name Sue is $90 + 110 + 5 = 205$.

a	b	c	d	e	f	g	h	i	k	l	m	n
1	2	3	4	5	6	7	8	9	10	20	30	40

o	p	q	r	s	t	u	v	w	x	y	z
50	60	70	80	90	100	110	120	130	140	150	160

Similarly, the number associated with the name Pierre, a character in the novel, is $60 + 9 + 5 + 80 + 80 + 5 = 239$. This character, Pierre Bezukhof, wondered what would be the number corresponding to the Emperor. So he wrote:

l'empereur Napoleon

and added the numbers for these letters, 20 for l, 5 for e, 30 for m, and so on. Can you find his answer? It was 666, the number of the beast prophesied in the Bible. Thus, Pierre reasoned that Napoleon must die. But who would vanquish the feared beast? He had some ideas:

l'empereur Alexandre?   La nation russe?

One was too low, the other too high. Can you find which is which? In desperation, Pierre wrote:

Comte Pierre Bezukhov.

Now the number was far away from what he wanted. He changed the spelling and added his nationality to get:

Le russe Besuhof

See if you can find his number. He knew that he was now near the coveted answer, and he finally wrote:

l'russe Besuhof

This gave him the desired answer, and he himself would take care of Napoleon! Can you find the final number that Pierre obtained and determine its relationship to Napoleon's number?

In this section we will examine some relationships among the Egyptian, the Babylonian, and the Roman numeral systems and our own decimal system.

During the period of recorded history (beginning about 4000 B.C.), people began to think about numbers as abstract concepts. That is, they recognized that two fruits and two arrows have something in common — a quantity called *two* — which is independent of the objects. The perception of this quantity was probably aided by the process of tallying. In different civilizations, different tallying methods have been found. For example, the Incas of Peru used knots in a string or rope to take the census, the Chinese used pebbles or sticks for computations, and the English used tally sticks as tax receipts. As a result of human efforts to keep records of numbers, the first numerals, reflecting the process of tallying, were developed. (A **numeral** is a symbol that represents a number. For example, the numeral 2 represents the number two.) Table 3.1 shows three ancient sets of numerals. The property shared by these three numeration systems is that they are **additive;** that is, the values of the written symbols are added to obtain the number represented.

Table 3.1 *Ancient Numerals*

	Egyptian	Sumerian	Mayan
1	I	I	•
2	II	II	••
3	III	III	•••
4	IIII	III I	••••
5	III II	III II	—
6	III III	III III	•̄
7	IIII III	III III I	•• ̄
8	IIII IIII	III III II	••• ̄
9	III III III	III III III	•••• ̄

A. *The Egyptian System*

Let us look at the Egyptian system in greater detail. The Egyptians used hieroglyphics (sacred picture writing) for their numerals. The first line of Table 3.2 shows these symbols and their probable numerical values. Convenient names for the hieroglyphics are given in the margin.

As you can see from Table 3.2, the Egyptians used a **base of 10.** That is, when the tallies were added and they reached 10, the 10 tallies were replaced by the symbol ∩. The Egyptians generally wrote their numbers from right to left, although they sometimes wrote from left to right, or even from top to bottom! Thus, the number 12 could have been represented by ‖ ∩ or by ∩ ‖. For this reason, we say that the Egyptian system is *not* a positional system. In contrast, our own **decimal system** (called **decimal** because we use a base of 10) is a **positional system.** In our system, the numerals 12 and 21 represent different numbers.

	Stroke
∩	Heel bone
	Scroll
	Lotus flower
	Pointing finger
	Fish
	Astonished man

Table 3.2 *Numerals*

Egyptian, about 3000 B.C						
I	∩					
1	10	100	1000	10,000	100,000	1,000,000

Babylonian, about 2000 B.C.						
0	1	10	12	20	60	600

Early Greek, about 400 B.C.						
I	Γ	Δ		H		
1	5	10	50	100	500	5000

Mayan, about 300 B.C.						
•	—	••	=	••	≡	
1	5	7	10	12	15	20

Tamil, Early Christian Era						
					ω	
1	2	3	5	6	10	1000

Hindu–Arabic, Contemporary						
0	1	2	3	4	5	6

Computation in the Egyptian system was based on the **additive principle.** For example, to add 24 to 48, the Egyptians proceeded as follows:

As you can see, before the computation was done, 10 of the strokes were replaced by a heelbone (see the names given in the margin with Table 3.2).

The Egyptians performed subtraction in a similar manner. Thus, to subtract 13 from 22, they proceeded as follows:

The procedure for Egyptian multiplication is explained in the Rhind papyrus (an ancient document found at Thebes and bought in Egypt by A. Henry Rhind and named in his honor). The operation was performed by **successive duplications.** Multiplying 19 by 7, for example, the Egyptians would take 19, double it, and then double the result. Then they would add the three numbers, thus:

$$
\begin{array}{lcc}
& \backslash 1 & 19 \\
& \backslash 2 & 38 \\
& \backslash 4 & \underline{76} \\
\text{Total} & 7 & 133
\end{array}
$$

The symbol \ is used to designate the submultipliers that add up to the total multiplier, in this case 7. In the Rhind papyrus, the problem 22 times 27 looks like this:

$$
\begin{array}{lcc}
& 1 & 27 \\
& \backslash\ 2 & 54 \\
& \backslash\ 4 & 108 \\
& 8 & 216 \\
& \backslash 16 & \underline{432} \\
\text{Total} & 22 & 594
\end{array}
$$

Again, the numbers to be added are only those in the lines with the symbol \.

EXAMPLE 1   Problem 79 of the Rhind papyrus states: "Sum the geometrical progression of five terms, of which the first term is 7 and the multiplier 7." It can be shown that the solution of the problem is obtained by multiplying 2801 by 7. Use the method of successive duplications to find the answer.

Solution

$$
\begin{array}{lcc}
& \backslash 1 & 2,801 \\
& \backslash 2 & 5,602 \\
& \backslash 4 & \underline{11,204} \\
\text{Total} & 7 & 19,607
\end{array}
$$

It is said that in later years the Egyptians adopted another multiplication technique generally known as **mediation and duplation.** This system consists of halving the first factor and doubling the second. For example, to find the product 19 × 7, we may successively halve 19, discarding remainders at each step, and successively double 7:

19 is odd →	19	⑦
9 is odd →	9	⑭
	4	28
	2	56
1 is odd →	1	(112)

Notice that half of 19 is regarded as 9, because all the remainders are discarded. The process is completed when a 1 appears in the left-hand column. Opposite each number in the left-hand column there is a corresponding number in the column of numbers being doubled. The product 19 × 7 is found by adding the circled numbers—those opposite the odd numbers in the column of halves. (Can you see why this works?) Thus 19 × 7 = 7 + 14 + 112 = 133.

EXAMPLE 2 Use the method of mediation and duplation to find the product 18 × 43.

Solution

	18	43
9 is odd →	9	(86)
	4	172
	2	344
1 is odd →	1	(688)

18 × 43 = 86 + 688 = 774 ■

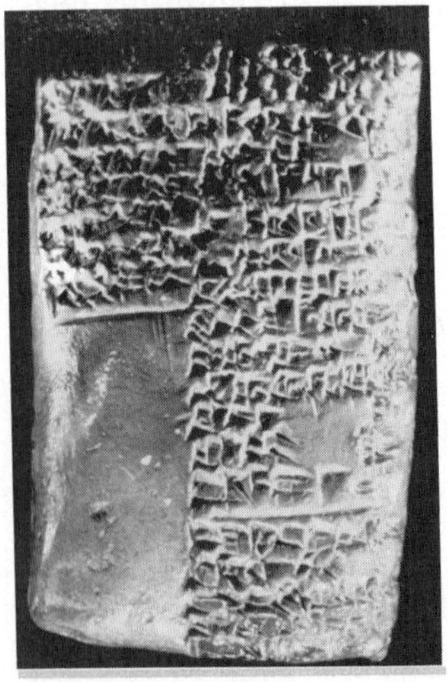

FIGURE 3.1
Sumerian clay tablets and inscriptions date back as far as 4000 B.C.

Additive numeral systems were devised to keep records of large numbers. As these numbers became larger and larger, it became evident that tallying them was difficult and awkward. Thus, numbers began to be arranged in groups and exchanged for larger units, as in the Egyptian system in which 10 tallies were exchanged for a heelbone (∩). The scale used to determine the size of the group to be exchanged (10 in the case of the Egyptians) was the **base** for the system. These additive systems were advantageous for record-keeping operations, but computation in these systems was extremely complicated. As problems became even more complex, a new concept evolved to help with computations, that of a **positional numeral system.** In such a system, a numeral is selected as the base, then symbols ranging from 1 to the numeral that is one less than the base are also selected. Numbers are then represented by placing the symbols in a specified order. For example, the Babylonians used a sexagesimal (base 60) system. In their system, a vertical wedge ▼ was used to represent 1 and the symbol ◀ represented 10. (These symbols first appeared on the clay tablets of the Sumerians and Chaldeans, but were later adopted by the Babylonians; see Figure 3.1.)

B. *The Babylonian System*

The Babylonian numerals, which may look odd to you, were simply wedge marks in clay. Figure 3.2 shows a few numerals. Notice that the same symbols are used for the numerals 1 and 60. To distinguish between them, a wider space was left between the characters. Thus, ▼▼▼ represents the numeral 3, while ▼ ▼▼ is 62.

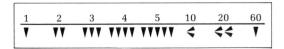

FIGURE 3.2
Babylonian numerals

EXAMPLE 3   Write the numbers 82, 733, and 4443 in Babylonian notation.

▼ ◀◀▼▼

Solution   82 = 1 × 60 + 22 = ▼ ◀◀▼▼

◀▼▼ ◀▼▼▼

733 = 12 × 60 + 13 = ◀▼▼ ◀▼▼▼

▼ ◀▼▼▼▼ ▼▼▼

4443 = 1 × 3600 + 14 × 60 + 3 = ▼ ◀▼▼▼▼ ▼▼▼   ∎

EXAMPLE 4   Write the given Babylonian numerals in decimal notation.

(a) ▼▼ ◀▼▼▼ (b) ◀ ▼▼▼▼▼ (c) ◀▼▼▼▼▼ (d) ▼▼ ◀▼ ◀▼▼

Solution   (a) ▼▼ ◀▼▼▼ = 2 × 60 + 13 = 133
(b) ◀ ▼▼▼▼▼ = 10 × 60 + 5 = 605
(c) ◀▼▼▼▼▼ = 10 + 5 = 15
(d) ▼▼ ◀▼ ◀▼▼ = 2 × 3600 + 11 × 60 + 12 = 7872   ∎

Note that the symbols in (b) and (c) are the same but the spacing is different. The lack of a symbol for zero in the Babylonian system was a significant shortcoming, which made it difficult to distinguish between numbers such as 605 and 15.

Our degree–minute–second system of measuring angles undoubtedly stems from the Babylonian division of a circle into 360 equal parts. Addition of angles in this system is essentially Babylonian-style addition.

The next example illustrates the method used by the Babylonians to add numbers.

EXAMPLE 5   Write in Babylonian notation and add 64 + 127.

Solution

$$\begin{array}{r} 64 \\ 127 \\ \hline 191 \end{array}$$ $191 = 3(60) + 11$

C. *The Roman System*

The Roman numeral system is still used today — for example, on the faces of clocks, for chapter numbers in books, on cornerstones of buildings, and for copyright dates on films and television shows. How did the Roman system work? The Roman symbol for the number one was I, which was repeated for two and three. Thus, II was 2 and III was 3. This is similar to the Egyptian system. However, unlike the Egyptians, the Romans introduced a special symbol for the number five. They then used another special symbol for ten, and repeated this symbol for 20 and 30. Other special symbols were used for 50, 100, 500, and 1000, as shown in Table 3.3.

Although both the Roman and Egyptian systems used the addition principle, the Romans went one step further and used the **subtraction principle** as well. For instance, instead of writing IIII for the number four, the Romans wrote IV with the understanding that the I (one) is to be *subtracted* from the V (five). In the Roman system, the value of a numeral is found by starting at the left and adding the values of the succeeding symbols to the right, unless the value of a symbol is less than that of the symbol to its right. In the latter case, the smaller value is *subtracted* from the larger one. Thus, XI = 10 + 1 = 11, but IX = 10 − 1 = 9. Only the numbers 1, 10, and 100 were allowed to be subtracted, and these only from numbers not more than two steps larger. For example, I could be subtracted from V to give IV = 4, or from X to give IX = 9, but could not be subtracted from C or L. Here are some other examples:

Table 3.3

Number	Roman Numeral
1	I
5	V
10	X
50	L
100	C
500	D
1000	M

Addition Principle

LX = 50 + 10 = 60
CX = 100 + 10 = 110
MC = 1000 + 100 = 1100

Subtraction Principle

XL = 50 − 10 = 40
XC = 100 − 10 = 90
CM = 1000 − 100 = 900

EXAMPLE 6   Write the following Roman numerals in decimal notation:

(a) DCXII   (b) MCMXLIX

Solution   (a) Since the value of each symbol is larger than that of the one to its right, we simply add these values:

DCXII = 500 + 100 + 10 + 1 + 1 = 612

(b) Here we must use the subtraction principle and write

$$M(CM)(XL)(IX) = 1000 + (1000 - 100) + (50 - 10) + (10 - 1)$$
$$= 1000 + 900 + 40 + 9$$
$$= 1949$$

The largest number that can be written using Roman numerals without using either the bar or the subtraction principle is

MMMDCCCLXXXVIII

What is this number in decimal notation?

Another way in which the Roman system went further than the Egyptian system is the use of a **multiplication principle** for writing larger numbers. A multiplication by 1000 was indicated by placing a bar over the entire numeral. Thus,

$$\overline{X} = 10 \quad \times 1000 = 10,000$$
$$\overline{LI} = 51 \quad \times 1000 = 51,000$$
$$\overline{DC} = 600 \quad \times 1000 = 600,000$$
$$\overline{M} = 1000 \times 1000 = 1,000,000$$

EXAMPLE 7 Write in Roman numerals:

(a) 33,008   (b) 42,120

Solution (a) 33 is written as XXXIII in Roman numerals, so 33,000 = $\overline{\text{XXXIII}}$. To write 33,008, we needed to add 8 more. Thus,

$$33,008 = 33,000 + 8 = \overline{\text{XXXIII}}\text{VIII}$$

(b) 42 = XLII, so 42,000 = $\overline{\text{XLII}}$. Since 120 = CXX, we see that

$$42,120 = \overline{\text{XLII}}\text{CXX}$$

Exercise 3.1

A. In problems 1–6, use the symbols given in Tables 3.1 and 3.2 to write each number in Egyptian notation.

1. 24   2. 54   3. 142
4. 1247   5. 835   6. 11,209

In problems 7–12, translate the Egyptian numerals into decimal notation.

7. ꩰ∩||| 8. 𐎓ꩰꩰꩰꩰꩰꩰꩰꩰꩰ||||
9. ꩰꩰꩰ∩∩|| 10. ∩∩∩∩||||
11. 𝒞𐎓ꩰꩰ∩∩∩|| 12. ꩰꩰꩰ∩∩∩|||
                         ꩰꩰꩰ∩∩ ||

In problems 13–16, write the numbers in Egyptian notation and perform the indicated operations.

13.   34   14.   148   15.   432   16.   1203
    + 23   + 45   − 143   − 502

Use the Egyptian method of successive duplications to find the product in each of problems 17–20.

17. 15 × 40   18. 25 × 15   19. 22 × 51   20. 21 × 63

Use the Egyptian method of mediation and duplation to find the product in each of problems 21–24.

21. 18 × 32   22. 15 × 32   23. 12 × 51   24. 40 × 61

B. In problems 25–34, write the given numbers in Babylonian notation.

25. 6   26. 24   27. 32   28. 64
29. 123   30. 144   31. 258   32. 192
33. 3733   34. 3883

In problems 35–40, write the given Babylonian numbers in decimal notation.

35. ▼ ◀◀◀▼▼   36. ◀▼▼▼ ◀▼▼
37. ▼▼▼ ◀▼▼   38. ◀▼▼▼▼ ▼▼▼
39. ▼ ◀▼▼ ▼▼   40. ▼▼ ◀▼ ▼▼▼▼

In problems 41–44, write the numbers in Babylonian notation and do the addition Babylonian style.

41.   32   42.   63   43.   133   44.   242
   + 43   + 81   + 68   + 181

C. In problems 45–50, write the numbers in decimal notation.

45. CXXVI   46. DCXVII   47. $\overline{\text{XLII}}$
48. $\overline{\text{XXX}}$DCI   49. $\overline{\text{XCCDV}}$ 50. $\overline{\text{LDDC}}$

In problems 51–56, write the numbers in Roman numerals.

51. 72   52. 631   53. 145
54. 1709   55. 32,503   56. 49,231

The following information will be used in problems 57–60.

Numerology, like astrology, is a pseudo-science concerning itself with birth dates, names, and other personal characteristics. A popular scheme used by numerologist Juno Jordan gives each letter the value of the number above it as shown.

1	2	3	4	5	6	7	8	9
A	B	C	D	E	F	G	H	I
J	K	L	M	N	O	P	Q	R
S	T	U	V	W	X	Y	Z	

The number associated with would be

J   a   m   e   s

$1 + 1 + 4 + 5 + 1 = 12 = 1 + 2 = \mathbf{3}.$

For the surname we have

B   r   o   w   n

$2 + 9 + 6 + 5 + 5 = 27 = 2 + 7 = \mathbf{9}.$

Thus, the final number for James Brown would be $\mathbf{3} + \mathbf{9} = 12 = 1 + 2 = \mathbf{3}$. What does this mean? Here are the characteristics supposedly held by persons with the given number.

1. Creative, inventive, positive
2. Gentle, imaginative, romantic
3. Ambitious, proud, independent
4. Rebels, unconventional
5. Mercurial, high-strung, risk-taker
6. Magnetic, romantic, artistic
7. Independent, individualistic
8. Lonely, misunderstood
9. Fighter, determined, leader

Thus, James Brown should be ambitious, proud, and independent! Do problems 57–60 just for fun. Don't take the results seriously!

57. Find the number for John Fitzgerald Kennedy.
58. Find the number for Sonya Kovalevski.
59. Find the number for Ringo Starr.
60. Find your own number.

In Other Words

61. Can you write 99 as IC in Roman numerals? Explain.
62. What are the differences between the Egyptian and our decimal system of numeration?
63. What are the differences between the Babylonian and our decimal system of numeration?
64. What are the differences between the Roman and our decimal system of numeration?
65. What are the differences between the Egyptian and the Babylonian systems of numeration?
66. Explain why it is difficult to distinguish between 605 and 15 in the Babylonian system.

Using Your Knowledge

The Rhind papyrus is a document that was found in the ruins of a small ancient building at Thebes. The papyrus was bought in 1858 by a Scottish antiquarian, A. Henry Rhind, and most of it is preserved in the British Museum where it was

A portion of the Rhind papyrus dating back to ca. 1650 B.C. It is the most extensive mathematical document from ancient Egypt.

named in Rhind's honor. The scroll was a handbook of Egyptian mathematics containing mathematical exercises and practical examples. Many of the problems were solved by the **method of false position.**

For example, one of the simple problems states: "A number and its one-fourth added together become 15. Find the number." The solution by false position goes like this: Assume that the number is 4. A number (4) and its one-fourth ($\frac{1}{4}$ of 4) added become 15; that is,

$$4 + \frac{1}{4}(4) \text{ must equal } 15$$

But

$$4 + \frac{1}{4}(4) = 5$$

and we need 15, which is three times the 5 we got. Therefore, the correct answer must be three times the assumed answer; that is, 3 × 4, or 12.

See if you can use the method of false position to solve the following problems.

67. A number and its one-sixth added together become 21. What is the number?

68. A number, its one-half, and its one-quarter add up to 28. Find the number.

69. If a number and its two-thirds are added, and from the sum one-third of the sum is subtracted, then 10 remains. What is the number?

Discovery

A Babylonian tablet giving the values of $n^3 + n^2$ for $n = 1$ to 30 was discovered a few years ago. The decimal equivalents of the first few entries in the table can be found as follows:

For $n = 1$, we have $1^3 + 1^2 = 2$.

For $n = 2$, we have $2^3 + 2^2 = 12$.

(Recall that $2^3 = 2 \times 2 \times 2 = 8$ and $2^2 = 2 \times 2 = 4$.)

For $n = 3$, we have $3^3 + 3^2 = 36$.

Complete the following:

$4^3 + 4^2 = \square$, $5^3 + 5^2 = \square$, $6^3 + 6^2 = \square$, $7^3 + 7^2 = \square$,

$8^3 + 8^2 = \square$, $9^3 + 9^2 = \square$, $10^3 + 10^2 = \square$

Using the preceding information, find the solution of

70. $n^3 + n^2 - 810 = 0$ 71. $n^3 + n^2 - 576 = 0$

72. There are many equations in which this method does not seem to work. For example, $n^3 + 2n^2 - 3136 = 0$. However, a simple transformation will reduce the sum of the first two terms to the familiar form $(\ \ )^3 + (\ \ )^2$. For example, let $n = 2x$. Now try to solve the following equation:

$$n^3 + 2n^2 - 3136 = 0$$

3.2 THE HINDU–ARABIC (DECIMAL) SYSTEM

GETTING STARTED

PACKAGING, GARBAGE, AND EXPONENTS

Do you know that in just one day, Americans throw out 1.5×10^5 tons of packaging material? How many pounds is that? Since 1 ton $= 2 \times 10^3$ lb, the amount of packaging material thrown out is:

$(1.5 \times 10^5) \times (2 \times 10^3)$ lb

How do we find this number? First, $1.5 \times 2 = 3$, so we need to find

$3 \times 10^5 \times 10^3$ lb

In this section, you will learn the laws of exponents for multiplication. These laws state that $a^m \times a^n = a^{m+n}$ and $a^m \div a^n = a^{m-n}$. Using the law for multiplication we get

$3 \times 10^5 \times 10^3 = 3 \times 10^{5+3} = 3 \times 10^8 = 300,000,000$ lb

The environmental stress created by landfills, such as this one, necessitates a greater awareness of waste management and recycling.

Thus, 300 million lb of packaging material is thrown out daily. Now, suppose a tractor trailer can carry a 15-ton load. How many tractor trailers do we need to carry out the packaging material? The answer is:

$$\frac{\text{Total weight of material}}{\text{weight per load}} = \frac{3 \times 10^8 \text{ lb}}{15 \text{ tons/load}}$$

Since 1 ton = 2000 lb, 15 tons = 30,000 lb = 3×10^4 lb. The answer is

$$\frac{3 \times 10^8 \text{ lb}}{3 \times 10^4 \text{ lb/load}} = \frac{10^8}{10^4} \text{ loads}$$

To find this answer, we need to divide 10^8 by 10^4. Using the law of exponents for division,

$$\frac{10^8}{10^4} = 10^{8-4} = 10^4$$

Thus, the number of tractor trailers needed is $1 \times 10^4 = 10,000$!

In this section, we shall work with exponents and see how to write standard numbers in expanded form containing exponents and vice versa. We will consider a few more environmental problems in Exercise 3.2, problems 44–50.

In this section, we will study our familiar **decimal system,** which is also called the **Hindu-Arabic system.** This numeration system is a positional system with 10 as its base, and it uses the symbols (called **digits**) 0, 1, 2, 3, 4, 5, 6, 7, 8, 9. Furthermore, each symbol in this system has a **place value;** that is the value represented by a digit depends on the position of that digit in the numeral. For instance, the digit 2 in the numeral 312 represents two ones, but in the numeral 321 the digit 2 represents two tens.

A. *Expanded Form*

To illustrate the idea further, we can write both numbers in **expanded form.**

$$312 = 3 \text{ hundreds} + 1 \text{ ten} + 2 \text{ ones}$$
$$= (3 \times 100) + (1 \times 10) + (2 \times 1)$$

$$321 = 3 \text{ hundreds} + 2 \text{ tens} + 1 \text{ one}$$
$$= (3 \times 100) + (2 \times 10) + (1 \times 1)$$

These numbers can also be written using exponential form, a notation introduced by the French mathematician René Descartes. As the name indicates, **exponential form** uses the idea of exponents. An **exponent** is a number that indicates how many times another number, called the **base,** is a factor in a product. Thus, in 5^3 (read, "5 cubed" or "5 to the third power") the exponent is 3, the base is 5, and $5^3 = 5 \times 5 \times 5 = 125$. Similarly, in 2^4, 4 is the exponent, 2 is the base, and $2^4 = 2 \times 2 \times 2 \times 2 = 16$. Based on this discussion, we state the following definition.

Definition 3.1 ────

If a is any number and n is any counting number, then a^n (read, "a to the nth power") is the product obtained by using a as a factor n times; that is,

$$a^n = \underbrace{a \times a \times \cdots \times a}_{n\ a's}$$

For any nonzero number a, we define $a^0 = 1$.

Using this definition, we can write: $1 = 10^0$, $10 = 10^1$, $100 = 10^2$, $1000 = 10^3$, $10,000 = 10^4$, and so on. Thus, in expanded form,

$$312 = (3 \times 100) + (1 \times 10) + (2 \times 1)$$
$$= (3 \times 10^2) + (1 \times 10^1) + (2 \times 10^0)$$

The exponent 1 usually is not explicitly written; we understand that $10^1 = 10$ and, in general, $a^1 = a$. Also, we used $10^0 = 1$ in the last term. With these conventions, we can write any number in expanded form.

EXAMPLE 1   Write 3406 in expanded form.

Solution $3406 = (3 \times 10^3) + (4 \times 10^2) + (0 \times 10) + (6 \times 10^0)$

Notice that we could have omitted the term (0×10), because $0 \times 10 = 0$. Using the same ideas, we can convert any number from expanded form into our familiar decimal form. ∎

EXAMPLE 2   Write $(5 \times 10^3) + (2 \times 10) + (3 \times 10^0)$ in ordinary decimal form.

Solution $(5 \times 10^3) + (2 \times 10) + (3 \times 10^0) = (5 \times 1000) + (2 \times 10) + 3$
$$= 5023$$
∎

B. *Operations in Expanded Form*

The idea of expanded form and place value can greatly simplify computations involving addition, subtraction, multiplication, and division. In the following examples, we present the usual way in which these operations are performed together with the steps depending on place value.

EXAMPLE 3   Add 38 and 61 in the usual way and in expanded form.

Solution
$$\begin{array}{r} 38 \\ + 61 \\ \hline 99 \end{array} \qquad \begin{array}{l} (3 \times 10) + (8 \times 10^0) \\ \underline{(6 \times 10) + (1 \times 10^0)} \\ (9 \times 10) + (9 \times 10^0) \end{array}$$

∎

EXAMPLE 4 Subtract 32 from 48 in the usual way and in expanded form.

Solution

$$
\begin{array}{r}
48 \\
-\ 32 \\
\hline
16
\end{array}
\qquad
\begin{array}{r}
(4 \times 10) + (8 \times 10^0) \\
-\ (3 \times 10) + (2 \times 10^0) \\
\hline
(1 \times 10) + (6 \times 10^0)
\end{array}
$$
∎

Before illustrating multiplication and division, we need to determine how to multiply and divide numbers involving exponents. For example, $2^2 \times 2^3 = (2 \times 2) \times (2 \times 2 \times 2) = 2^5$, and

$$a^m \times a^n = \underbrace{(a \times a \times a \times \cdots \times a)}_{m\ a's} \times \underbrace{(a \times a \times a \times \cdots \times a)}_{n\ a's}$$

$$= a^{m+n}$$

In order to divide 2^5 by 2^2 we can proceed as follows:

$$\frac{2^5}{2^2} = \frac{2 \times 2 \times 2 \times 2 \times 2}{2 \times 2} = 2 \times 2 \times 2 = 2^3$$

In general, if $m > n$,

$$a^m \div a^n = \frac{a^m}{a^n} = a^{m-n}$$

Laws of Exponents

$$a^m \times a^n = a^{m+n} \quad \text{and} \quad a^m \div a^n = \frac{a^m}{a^n} = a^{m-n}, \quad m > n$$

EXAMPLE 5 Perform the indicated operation and leave the answer in exponential form.

(a) $4^5 \times 4^7$ (b) $3^{10} \div 3^4$

Solution (a) $4^5 \times 4^7 = 4^{5+7} = 4^{12}$ (b) $3^{10} \div 3^4 = 3^{10-4} = 3^6$ ∎

Note that by Definition 3.1, we have, for example,

$$(2^3)^2 = 2^3 \times 2^3 = 2^{3+3} = 2^{3 \times 2} = 2^6 \quad \text{and}$$

$$(5^2)^4 = 5^2 \times 5^2 \times 5^2 \times 5^2 = 5^{2+2+2+2} = 5^{2 \times 4} = 5^8$$

In general,

$$(a^m)^n = a^{m \times n}$$

EXAMPLE 6 Show that $32^2 = 2^{10}$.

Solution Direct computation shows that $32 = 2^5$. Thus,

$$32^2 = (2^5)^2 = 2^{5 \times 2} = 2^{10}$$
∎

EXAMPLE 7 Multiply 32 and 21 in the usual way and in expanded form.

Solution

$$
\begin{array}{r}
32 \\
\times\ 21 \\
\hline
32 \\
64\ \ \\
\hline
672
\end{array}
$$

$$
\begin{array}{r}
(3 \times 10) + 2 \times 10^0 \\
\times\ (2 \times 10) + 1 \times 10^0 \\
\hline
(3 \times 10) + 2 \times 10^0 \\
(6 \times 10^2) + (4 \times 10)\ \ \\
\hline
(6 \times 10^2) + (7 \times 10) + 2 \times 10^0
\end{array}
$$

■

EXAMPLE 8 Divide 63 by 3 in the usual way and in expanded form.

Solution

$$
3\overline{)63}\quad\;\; \frac{21}{}
$$

$$
3\overline{)(6 \times 10) + 3 \times 10^0}\quad\;\; \frac{(2 \times 10) + 1 \times 10^0}{}
$$

■

Exercise 3.2

A. In problems 1–6, write the given number in expanded form.

1. 432
2. 549
3. 2307
4. 3047
5. 12,349
6. 10,950

In problems 7–15, write the given number in decimal form.

7. 5^0
8. $(3 \times 10) + (4 \times 10^0)$
9. $(4 \times 10) + (5 \times 10^0)$
10. $(4 \times 10^2) + (3 \times 10) + (2 \times 10^0)$
11. $(9 \times 10^3) + (7 \times 10) + (1 \times 10^0)$
12. $(7 \times 10^4) + (2 \times 10^0)$
13. $(7 \times 10^5) + (4 \times 10^4) + (8 \times 10^3) + (3 \times 10^2) + (8 \times 10^0)$
14. $(8 \times 10^9) + (3 \times 10^5) + (2 \times 10^2) + (4 \times 10^0)$
15. $(4 \times 10^6) + (3 \times 10) + (1 \times 10^0)$

B. In problems 16–19, add in the usual way and in expanded form.

16. $32 + 15$
17. $23 + 13$
18. $21 + 34$
19. $71 + 23$

In problems 20–23, subtract in the usual way and in expanded from.

20. $34 - 21$
21. $76 - 54$
22. $45 - 22$
23. $84 - 31$

In problems 24–35, perform the indicated operation and leave the answer in exponential form.

24. $3^5 \times 3^9$
25. $7^8 \times 7^3$
26. $4^5 \times 4^2$
27. $6^{19} \times 6^{21}$
28. $5^8 \div 5^3$
29. $6^{10} \div 6^3$
30. $7^{15} \div 7^3$
31. $6^{12} \div 6^0$
32. $(3^2)^4$
33. $(5^4)^3$
34. $(7^3)^5$
35. $(10^3)^{10}$

In problems 36–39, multiply in the usual way and in expanded form.

36. 41×23 37. 25×51
38. 91×24 39. 62×25

In problems 40–43, divide in the usual way and in expanded form.

40. $48 \div 4$ 41. $64 \div 8$
42. $93 \div 3$ 43. $72 \div 6$

In problems 44–50 write the answer in exponential form.

44. Each American produces about 4 lbs of garbage every day. If the U.S. population is assumed to be 25×10^7, how many pounds of garbage per day is produced nationwide?

45. If the *New York Times* printed one Sunday edition on recycled paper instead of new paper, 75,000 trees would be saved. How many trees would be saved if they did it for a month (4 editions)?

46. Americans use 3×10^7 gallons of motor oil every day. How many gallons per week is that?

47. Americans use 3×10^7 gallons of paint every day. How many gallons are used in 300 days?

48. An estimated 72×10^7 lead-acid batteries from automobiles are discarded each year. How many batteries per month is that?

49. Americans discard an estimated 240×10^7 automobile tires each year. How many tires per month is that?

50. Americans get rid of 7.2×10^7 cars each year. About how many cars per day is that? (*Hint:* $360 = 3.6 \times 10^2$.)

In Other Words

51. Explain what you must do to multiply a^m by a^n.
52. Explain what you must do to divide a^m by a^n.
53. Explain what you must do to raise a^m to the nth power.
54. By the laws of exponents

$$\frac{a^m}{a^n} = a^{m-n} \qquad \text{when } m > n.$$

when $m = n$,

$$\frac{a^m}{a^n} = \frac{a^m}{a^m}$$

What should the answer be? Explain. Based on your answer, how would you define a^0?

Discovery

The Rhind papyrus contains a problem that deals with exponents. Problem 79 is very difficult to translate, but historian Moritz Cantor formulates the problem as follows: "An estate consisted of seven houses; each house had seven cats; each cat ate seven mice; each mouse ate seven heads of wheat; and each head of wheat was capable of yielding seven hekat measures of grain: Houses, cats, mice, heads of wheat, and hekat measures of grain, how many of these in all were in the estate? Here is the solution:

Houses	$7 = 7^1$
Cats	$49 = 7^2$
Mice	$343 = 7^3$
Heads of wheat	$2,401 = 7^4$
Hekat measures	$\underline{16,807} = 7^5$
Total	*19,607*

Because the items in the problem correspond to the first five powers of 7, it was at first thought that the writer was introducing the terminology houses, cats, mice, and so on, for first power, second power, third power, and so on!

55. A similar problem can be found in *Liber Abaci,* written by Leonardo Fibonacci (A.D. 1170–1250). The problem reads as follows:

    There are seven old women on the road to Rome. Each woman has seven mules; each mule carries seven sacks; each sack contains seven loaves; with each loaf are seven knives; and each knife is in seven sheaths. Women, mules, sacks, loaves, knives, and sheaths, how many are there in all on the road to Rome?

    Can you find the answer?

56. A later version of the same problem reads as follows:

    As I was going to St. Ives
    I met a man with seven wives;
    Every wife had seven sacks;
    Every sack had seven cats;
    Every cat had seven kits.
    Kits, cats, sacks, and wives,
    How many were going to St. Ives?

    [*Hint*: The answer is not 2,800. If you think it is, then you did not read the first line carefully.]

3.3   NUMBER SYSTEMS WITH BASES OTHER THAN 10

GETTING STARTED

BINARY CARD MAGIC

Have you heard of binary cards? The set shown has a series of numbers on each card, the largest of which is 31. Let us say you have a smaller set of 3 cards.

Here they are:

    A 5 3 1 7
    B 6 3 2 7
    C 5 7 4 5

Now, pick a number, any number, from 1 to 7, say, 3.

Is it on card A? Yes. Note that the lowest number on A is 1.
Is it on card B? Yes. Note that the lowest number on B is 2.
Is it on card C? No.

The answer (that is, the number you picked) is $1 + 2$, the sum of the lowest numbers on the cards containing the number you picked. How does this work and why? It will be much easier to understand the trick if you know a little bit more about **binary** numbers, which we cover in this section. As a matter of fact, the Using Your Knowledge section in Exercise 3.3 explains how you can make your own set of cards and make the trick work.

A set of 5 binary cards

As you learned in Section 3.1, in a positional number system a number is selected as the base, and objects are grouped and counted using this base. In the decimal system, the base chosen was 10, probably because the fingers are a convenient aid in counting.

A. *Other Number Bases*

As we saw earlier, it is possible to use other numbers as bases for numeration systems. For example, if we decide to use 5 as our base (that is, count in groups of 5), then we can count the 17 asterisks below in this way:

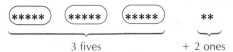

and we write 32_{five}.

If we select 8 as our base, the asterisks are grouped this way:

and we write 21_{eight}. Thus, if we use subscripts to indicate the manner in which we are grouping the objects, we may write the number 17 as follows:

$$17_{\text{ten}} = 32_{\text{five}} = 21_{\text{eight}}$$

Using groups of seven, we can indicate the same number of asterisks by

$$23_{\text{seven}} = 2 \text{ sevens} + 3 \text{ ones}$$

Note: In the following material, when no subscript is used it will be understood that the number is expressed in base 10.

EXAMPLE 1   Group 13 asterisks in groups of eight, five, and seven, and write the number 13 in:

(a) Base 8   (b) Base 5   (c) Base 7

Solution   (a) (✱✱✱✱✱✱✱)   ✱✱✱✱✱ $= 15_{\text{eight}}$
                    1 eight   + 5 ones

(b) (✱✱✱✱✱) (✱✱✱✱✱)   ✱✱✱ $= 23_{\text{five}}$
        2 fives   + 3 ones

(c) (✱✱✱✱✱✱)   ✱✱✱✱✱✱ $= 16_{\text{seven}}$
      1 seven   + 6 ones   ∎

B. *Changing to Base 10*

Now consider the problem of "translating" numbers written in bases other than 10 into our decimal system. For example, what number in our decimal system corresponds to 43_{five}? First, recall that in the decimal system, numbers can be

Recall that $a^0 = 1$ for $a \neq 0$. So, $10^0 = 1$ and $2 \times 10^0 = 2$.

written in expanded form. For example, $342 = (3 \times 10^2) + (4 \times 10) + (2 \times 10^0)$. As you can see, when written in expanded form, each digit in 342 is multiplied by the proper power of 10 (the base being used). Similarly, when written in expanded form, each digit in the numeral 43_{five} must be multiplied by the proper power of 5 (the base being used). Thus,

$$43_{\text{five}} = (4 \times 5^1) + (3 \times 5^0) = 23$$

EXAMPLE 2   Write the following numbers in decimal notation:

(a) 432_{five} (b) 312_{eight}

Solution   (a) $432_{\text{five}} = (4 \times 5^2) + (3 \times 5) + (2 \times 5^0) = 117$
(b) $312_{\text{eight}} = (3 \times 8^2) + (1 \times 8) + (2 \times 8^0) = 202$ ∎

In the seventeenth century, the German mathematician Gottfried Wilhelm Leibniz advocated the use of the **binary system** (base 2). This system uses only the digits 0 and 1, and the grouping is by twos. The advantage of the binary system is that each position in a numeral contains one of just two values (0 or 1). Thus, electric switches, which have only two possible states, *off* or *on,* can be used to designate the value of each position. Computers utilizing the binary system have revolutionized technology and the sciences by speedily performing calculations that would take humans years to complete. Hand-held calculators operate internally on the binary system.

A binary counter

Now consider how to convert numbers from base 2 to decimal notation. It will help you to keep in mind that in the binary system, numbers are built up by using blocks that are powers of the base 2:

$$2^0 = 1, \quad 2^1 = 2, \quad 2^2 = 4, \quad 2^3 = 8, \quad 2^4 = 16, \ldots$$

When we write 1101 in the binary system, we are saying in the yes/no language of the computer, "a block of 8, yes; a block of 4, yes; a block of 2, no; a block of 1, yes." Thus.

$$
\begin{aligned}
1101_{\text{two}} &= (1 \times 2^3) + (1 \times 2^2) + (0 \times 2^1) + (1 \times 2^0) \\
&= 8 + 4 + 0 + 1 \\
&= 13
\end{aligned}
$$

EXAMPLE 3   Write the number 10101_{two} in decimal notation.

Solution   We write

$$10101_{two} = (1 \times 2^4) + (0 \times 2^3) + (1 \times 2^2) + (0 \times 2^1) + (1 \times 2^0)$$
$$= 16 + 4 + 1$$
$$= 21$$

■

So far, we have used only bases less than 10, the most important ones being base 2 (**binary**) and base 8 (**octal**), which are used by computers. Bases greater than 10 also are possible, but then new symbols are needed for the digits greater than 9. For example, base 16 (**hexadecimal**) also is used by computers, with the "digits" A, B, C, D, E, and F used to correspond to the decimal numbers 10, 11, 12, 13, 14, and 15, respectively. We can change numbers from hexadecimal to decimal notation in the same way as we did for bases less than 10.

EXAMPLE 4   Write the number $5AC_{sixteen}$ in decimal notation.

Solution
$$5AC_{sixteen} = (5 \times 16^2) + (10 \times 16) + (12 \times 16^0)$$
$$= (5 \times 256) + (160) \qquad + 12$$
$$= 1280 \qquad + 160 \qquad + 12$$
$$= 1452$$

■

C. *Changing from Base 10*

Up to this point, we have changed numbers from bases other than 10 to base 10. Now we shall change numbers from base 10 to another base. A good method for doing this depends on successive divisions. For example, to change 625 to base 8, we start by dividing 625 by 8, obtaining 78 with a remainder of 1. We then divide 78 by 8, getting 9 with 6 remaining. Next, we divide 9 by 8, obtaining a quotient of 1 and a remainder of 1. We diagram these divisions as follows:

The answer is read upward as 1161_{eight} (see the arrow).

Why does this method work? Suppose we wish to find how many eights there are in 625. To find out, we divide 625 by 8. The quotient 78 tells us that there are 78 eights in 625, and the remainder tells us that there is 1 left over. Dividing the 78 by 8 (which is the same as dividing the 625 by $8 \times 8 = 64$) tells us that there are 9 sixty-fours in 625, and the remainder tells us that there are 6 eights left over. Finally, dividing the quotient 9 by 8 gives a new quotient of 1 and a remainder of 1. This tells us that there is 1 five hundred twelve $(8 \times 8 \times 8)$ contained in 625 with 1 sixty-four left over. Thus, we see that

$$625 = (1 \times 8^3) + (1 \times 8^2) + (6 \times 8) + (1 \times 8^0)$$
$$= 1161_{\text{eight}}$$

EXAMPLE 5   Change the number 33 to:

(a) Base 2   (b) Base 5

Solution   (a) 2 | 33

2 | 16   1
2 | 8   0
2 | 4   0
2| 2   0
   | 1   0

Thus, $33 = 100001_{\text{two}}$.

(b) 5 | 33

5| 6   3
   | 1   1

Thus, $33 = 113_{\text{five}}$.

EXAMPLE 6   Change the number 4923 to:

(a) Octal notation   (b) Hexadecimal notation

Solution   (a) 8 | 4923

8 | 615   3
8 | 76   7
8| 9   4
   | 1   1

Thus, $4923 = 11473_{\text{eight}}$.

(b) 16 | 4923

16 | 307   11
16| 19   3
   | 1   3

Thus, $4923 = 133B_{\text{sixteen}}$.

Exercise 3.3

A. In problems 1–4, write numerals in the bases indicated by the manner of grouping.

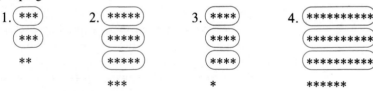

In problems 5–8, draw a diagram as shown in problems 1–4, and then write the given decimal number in the given base.

5. 15 in base 8

6. 15 in base 5

7. 15 in base 7

8. 15 in base 12

B. In problems 9–16, write the given number in decimal notation.

9. 42_{five}

10. 31_{five}

11. 213_{eight}

12. 563_{eight}

13. 11011_{two}

14. 101001_{two}

15. $123_{sixteen}$

16. $ACE_{sixteen}$

C. In problems 17–32, use the method of successive divisions.

17. Write the number 15 in base 5 notation.

18. Write the number 27 in base 5 notation.

19. Write the number 28 in binary notation.

20. Write the number 43 in binary notation.

21. Write the number 25 in hexadecimal notation.

22. Write the number 121 in hexadecimal notation.

23. Write the number 25 in base 6 notation.

24. Write the number 38 in base 6 notation.

25. Write the number 64 in base 7 notation.

26. Write the number 123 in base 7 notation.

27. Write the number 38 in octal notation.

28. Write the number 135 in octal notation.

29. Write the number 1467 in hexadecimal notation.

30. Write the number 145,263 in hexadecimal notation.

31. Write the number 73 in binary and in octal notation.

32. Write the number 87 in octal and in hexadecimal notation.

In Other Words

You may need a dictionary to answer questions 33–36.

33. What does binary mean? What does the prefix *bi* indicate?

34. What does octal mean? What does the prefix *oct* indicate?

35. What does hexadecimal mean? What does the prefix *hexa* indicate?

36. The binary system uses the numbers 0 and 1, the octal uses 0, 1, 2, 3, 4, 5, 6, and 7, and the hexadecimal uses 0, 1, 2, 3, 4, 5, 6, 7, 8, 9, A, B, C, D, E, F. Why do we need the A, B, C, D, E, and F?

Using Your Knowledge

Here is a trick that you can use to amaze your friends. Write the numbers from 1 to 7 in binary notation. They look like this:

Decimal	Binary
1	1
2	10
3	11
4	100
5	101
6	110
7	111

Now label three columns A, B, and C. In column A, write the numbers that have a 1 in the units place when written in binary notation. In column B, write the numbers that have a 1 in the second position from the right when written in binary notation; and in column C, write the numbers with 1's in the third position from the right.

A	B	C
1	2	4
3	3	5
5	6	6
7	7	7

Ask someone to think of a number between 1 and 7 and tell you in which columns the number appears. Say the number is 6 (which appears in columns B and C). You find the sum of the numbers at the top of columns B and C. This sum is 2 + 4 = 6, and you have the desired number!

37. Can you explain why this works?

38. If you extend this trick to cover the first 15 numbers, how many columns do you need?

39. Can you discover how to do the trick with 31 numbers?

Calculator Corner

Converting from Base *b* to Base 10

For convenience and to save space, we shall write the base b as an ordinary decimal rather than spelling it out. Thus, for example, 47_8 means exactly the same thing as 47_{eight}. Suppose that 4735_8 is to be converted to base 10. We know that

$$4735_8 = (4 \times 8^3) + (7 \times 8^2) + (3 \times 8) + 5$$

Since the three quantities in parentheses are all divisible by 8, we may rewrite the expression to get

$$4735_8 = 8 \times [(4 \times 8^2) + (7 \times 8) + 3] + 5$$

Next, we see that the two quantities in parentheses inside the brackets are divisible by 8, so we may rewrite again to get

$$4735_8 = 8 \times [8 \times \{(4 \times 8) + 7\} + 3] + 5$$

Now we can evaluate the last expression by a simple step-by-step procedure. Start with the innermost parentheses, multiply 4 by the base 8 and add 7 to the result. Then, multiply the last result by 8 and add 3 to the product. Finally, multiply the preceding result by 8 and add 5 to the product. The final sum is the required answer.

The arithmetic can be done on the calculator by keying in the following.

$$\boxed{4} \; \boxed{\times} \; \boxed{8} \; \boxed{+} \; \boxed{7} \; \boxed{=} \; \boxed{\times} \; \boxed{8} \; \boxed{+} \; \boxed{3} \; \boxed{=} \; \boxed{\times} \; \boxed{8} \; \boxed{+} \; \boxed{5} \; \boxed{=}$$

The calculator will show the result 2525.

Notice that we multiplied the first octal digit, 4, by the base, 8, and added the next octal digit, 7. Then we multiplied the result by the base and added the next octal digit, 3. Finally, we multiplied by the base again and added the last octal digit, 5.

This procedure holds for any base. Thus, to convert from any base b to base 10:

1. *Multiply the first digit of the number by b, and add the second digit to the result.*

2. *Multiply the preceding result by b, and add the third digit of the given numeral.*

3. *Continue the same procedure until you have added the last digit of the given numeral.*

The calculator will show the final answer. Be sure that you work from left to right in using the digits of the given numeral.

As another example, let us convert the hexadecimal numeral $BF3_{16}$ to base 10. Recall that the hexadecimal digits B and F are the numbers 11 and 15, respectively, in decimal notation, so you key in the following:

$$\boxed{1} \; \boxed{1} \; \boxed{\times} \; \boxed{1} \; \boxed{6} \; \boxed{+} \; \boxed{1} \; \boxed{5} \; \boxed{=} \; \boxed{\times} \; \boxed{1} \; \boxed{6} \; \boxed{+} \; \boxed{3} \; \boxed{=}$$

Your calculator should show the result 3059.

Convert each of the following to decimal notation:

1. 1101_2 2. 231_4

3. 423_5 4. 752_8

5. 3572_8 6. 873_9

7. $A3C_{16}$ 8. $93DC_{16}$

Computer Corner

*We have already learned how to convert from one base to another using a calculator. But there is a faster way! Use a computer. We have three different programs that will convert numbers from one base to another. The Converting from Base 10 program converts numbers from base 10 to any other base. The Converting to Base 10 program converts numbers from any base to base 10, and the Base Converter Program (X, Y < 11) converts from **any** base to **any** other base, as long as both bases are less than 11. All three programs are in the appendix, Programs in BASIC.*

3.4 BINARY, OCTAL, AND HEXADECIMAL CONVERSION

GETTING STARTED

PHOTOGRAPHS FROM SPACE AND THE BINARY SYSTEM

Do you know how spacecraft send pictures back to Earth? It is not done by using photographic film. Instead, the image is broken into tiny dots called **pixels.** Thus, a photo may be divided into 1000 pixels horizontally and 500 vertically. Each of these pixels is then assigned a **binary number** representing its brightness, 0 for white, 111111 for black, and binary values in between for various shades of gray. An electronic message carrying the assigned pixel color values is then sent back to Earth, where it is converted into a photograph. In this section, you will learn how to convert numerals from one system to another. If you want to know more about the photo transmission process discussed here, do problems 33–37 in the Discovery section of Exercise 3.4.

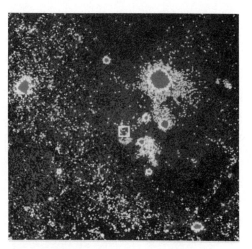

This NASA photo shows an International Ultraviolet Explorer pixellated view of the Supernova 1987a

The octal and hexadecimal systems are used by computers to store data and instructions. Sometimes, operators must convert between these two systems and the binary system.

A. *Binary and Octal Conversion*

Table 3.4

Binary	Octal
000	0
001	1
010	2
011	3
100	4
101	5
110	6
111	7

For the octal system, the procedure is simplified by using Table 3.4. This table tells us, for example, that $101_2 = 5_8$ and that $6_8 = 110_2$. Notice that three-digit binary numbers correspond to one-digit octal numbers throughout. Accordingly, to convert from binary to octal, we simply break the given binary number into groups of three, starting from the right, and then write the octal equivalent for each group of three digits. (Consult Table 3.4 when doing this.) Thus, to convert 11010_2 to octal, 11010_2 is broken into groups of three digits (a 0 is attached at the left), and the octal equivalent for each group is written as follows:

$$\text{We attached this } 0 \rightarrow \underset{\downarrow}{011} \quad \underset{\downarrow}{010}$$
$$3 \qquad 2$$

We then have $11010_2 = 32_8$.

EXAMPLE 1   Convert 11101110_2 to octal notation.

Solution   We break the given number into groups of three and write the octal equivalent of each group (a 0 was attached to the leftmost group):

$$\underset{\downarrow}{011} \quad \underset{\downarrow}{101} \quad \underset{\downarrow}{110}$$
$$3 \qquad 5 \qquad 6$$

Thus, $11101110_2 = 356_8$. ∎

To change from octal to binary, the procedure can be reversed as in the next example.

EXAMPLE 2   Convert 5732_8 to binary notation.

Solution   Using Table 3.4, we write the binary equivalents of 5, 7, 3, and 2. Thus,

$$\underset{101}{\overset{5}{\downarrow}} \quad \underset{111}{\overset{7}{\downarrow}} \quad \underset{011}{\overset{3}{\downarrow}} \quad \underset{010}{\overset{2}{\downarrow}}$$

and $5732_8 = 101111011010_2$. ∎

B. *Binary and Hexadecimal Conversion*

Conversions between hexadecimal and binary are done in the same way, except that we need a table giving the relationship between binary and hexadecimal numbers (Table 3.5, below). This table tells us, for example, that below $1001_2 = 9_{16}$ and that $D_{16} = 1101_2$. Note that each four-digit binary number in Table 3.5 corresponds to a one-digit hexadecimal number. Thus, the conversions will use groups of four binary digits for each hexadecimal digit, as shown in the following examples.

Table 3.5

Binary	Hexadecimal	Binary	Hexadecimal
0000	0	1000	8
0001	1	1001	9
0010	2	1010	A
0011	3	1011	B
0100	4	1100	C
0101	5	1101	D
0110	6	1110	E
0111	7	1111	F

EXAMPLE 3   Convert 1101110_2 to hexadecimal notation.

Solution   We divide the digits in the binary numeral into groups of four, starting from the right, and write under these groups the corresponding hexadecimal digits. (Consult Table 3.5 to do this.) Thus,

$$
\begin{array}{cc}
0110 & 1110 \\
\downarrow & \downarrow \\
6 & E
\end{array}
$$

so that $1101110_2 = 6E_{16}$ ∎

To change from hexadecimal to binary notation, we reverse the procedure in Example 3, as shown next.

EXAMPLE 4   Convert $9AD_{16}$ to binary notation.

Solution   Using Table 3.5, we find the binary equivalents of 9, A, and D. Thus,

$$
\begin{array}{ccc}
9 & A & D \\
\downarrow & \downarrow & \downarrow \\
1001 & 1010 & 1101
\end{array}
$$

so that $9AD_{16} = 100110101101_2$.   ∎

C. *Octal and Hexadecimal Conversion*

To convert between octal and hexadecimal notation, we first convert the given numeral to binary notation and then convert this result to the desired notation, as illustrated in the next examples.

EXAMPLE 5   Convert $9AD_{16}$ to octal notation.

Solution   From Example 4, we have $9AD_{16} = 100110101101_2$. Converting this binary numeral to octal (Table 3.4), we obtain

$$
\begin{array}{cccc}
100 & 110 & 101 & 101 \\
\downarrow & \downarrow & \downarrow & \downarrow \\
4 & 6 & 5 & 5
\end{array}
$$

Thus, $100110101101_2 = 4655_8$, so that $9AD_{16} = 4655_8$.

EXAMPLE 6   Convert 357_8 to hexadecimal notation.

Solution   1. First, convert the given numeral to binary form (Table 3.4):

$$
\begin{array}{ccc}
3 & 5 & 7 \\
\downarrow & \downarrow & \downarrow \\
011 & 101 & 111
\end{array}
$$

Thus, $357_8 = 11101111_2$.

2. Now, convert 11101111_2 to hexadecimal notation (Table 3.5):

$$
\begin{array}{cc}
1110 & 1111 \\
\downarrow & \downarrow \\
E & F
\end{array}
$$

Therefore, $357_8 = EF_{16}$

Exercise 3.4

A. In problems 1–4, convert each numeral to octal notation.

1. 110111_2 2. 101101_2 3. 1101101_2 4. 10111101_2

In problems 5–8, convert each numeral to binary notation.

5. 65_8 6. 57_8 7. 306_8 8. 472_8

B. In problems 9–12, convert each numeral to hexadecimal notation.

9. 110111_2 10. 101101_2 11. 1101101_2 12. 10111101_2

In problems 13–16, convert each numeral to binary notation.

13. 95_{16} 14. $8B_{16}$ 15. $7CD_{16}$ 16. $A9C_{16}$

C. In problems 17 and 18, convert each numeral to octal notation.

17. 109_{16} 18. $2BF_{16}$

In problems 19 and 20, convert each numeral to hexadecimal notation.

19. 537_8 20. 6235_8

In problems 21 and 22, convert each numeral to octal and to hexadecimal notation.

21. 365   22. 457

In Other Words

In ASCII (American Standard Code for Information Interchange), characters are numbered in **binary notation.** The characters A–O are prefixed by 0100 and numbered in order, starting with A = 0001, B = 0010, C = 0011, D = 0100, and so on. The characters P–Z are numbered in order starting with P = 0000 and prefixed by 0101. In problems 23–25, write the message in words.

23. 01001000   01000101   01001100   01001100   01001111.
    What decimal number corresponds to each of the letters?

24. 01000011   01000001   01001100   01001100
    01001101   01000101
    What decimal number corresponds to each of the letters?

25. 01001000   01000101   01001100   01010000
    01001001
    01000001   01001101
    01001100   01001111   01010011   01010100
    What decimal number corresponds to each of the letters?

Using Your Knowledge

Since $4 = 2^2$, the ideas presented in this section should apply to conversions back and forth between the binary system and the base 4 system of numeration. The digits of the base 4 system are 0, 1, 2, and 3, and all these can be obtained as sums formed from the numbers 0, 1, and 2. Thus, we can construct a table for base 4 numerals similar to the tables for octal and hexadecimal numerals, as shown in the margin. The table tells us that we can use exactly the same ideas for conversion between the base 4 and the binary system as we did for the octal and hexadecimal systems. For instance, we can convert from binary to base 4 notation as illustrated, where we change 11110_2 to base 4:

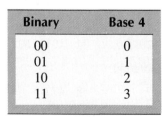

Binary	Base 4
00	0
01	1
10	2
11	3

$$
\begin{array}{ccc}
01 & 11 & 10 \\
\downarrow & \downarrow & \downarrow \\
1 & 3 & 2
\end{array}
$$

This shows that $11110_2 = 132_4$.

26. Show how to change 132_4 to binary notation.
27. Show how to change 312_4 to binary notation.
28. Convert 203_4 to binary notation.
29. Convert 1101111_2 to base 4 notation.
30. Convert 1010101_2 to base 4 notation.
31. Convert 301_4 to octal notation.
32. Convert 223_4 to hexadecimal notation.

Discovery

On July 14, 1965, a camera installed on the spacecraft Mariner IV *took the first pictures of the planet Mars and sent them by radio signals back to Earth. On Earth, a computer received the pictures in the form of binary numerals consisting of six bits. (A **bit** is a binary digit.) The shade of each dot in the final picture was determined by six bits.*

The numeral 000000_2 (0 in base 10) indicated a white dot, and the numeral 111111_2 (63 in base 10) indicated a black dot. The 62 numerals between represented various shades of gray between white and black. To make a complete picture, 40,000 dots, each described by six bits, were needed!

33. If one of the numerals received was 110111_2, can you discover the corresponding decimal numeral?
34. Does the dot corresponding to the numeral received in problem 33 represent a shade of gray closer to white or to black?
35. Can you discover what binary numeral would represent the lightest shade of gray that is not white?
36. Can you discover what binary numeral would represent the darkest shade of gray that is not black?
37. Can you discover what binary numeral would represent the shade numbered 31?

Calculator Corner

You can convert numbers from one base to another provided you have a calculator with a key displaying the desired bases. For instance, to convert 11101110_2 to octal (Example 1), you need $\boxed{\text{bin}}$ and $\boxed{\text{oct}}$ (or equivalent) keys. First, set the calculator in the binary mode by pressing $\boxed{\text{2nd}}$ $\boxed{\text{mode}}$ $\boxed{\text{bin}}$ (Some calculators do not require you to press $\boxed{\text{2nd}}$.). Enter the number 11101110_2 and enter $\boxed{\text{2nd}}$ $\boxed{\text{mode}}$ $\boxed{\text{oct}}$. The answer 356_8 appears on the screen. Conversely, to change 5732_8 to binary (Example 2), we place the calculator in the octal mode (press $\boxed{\text{2nd}}$ $\boxed{\text{mode}}$ $\boxed{\text{oct}}$), enter 5732, and change it to binary by pressing $\boxed{\text{2nd}}$ $\boxed{\text{mode}}$ $\boxed{\text{bin}}$. In this case, an error message appears because the answer (101111011010_2) has twelve digits and the calculator can enter only ten digits. This problem cannot be done on the calculator. Instead, let us change 472_8 to binary. As before, place the calculator in the oc-

tal mode by pressing $\boxed{\text{2nd}}$ $\boxed{\text{mode}}$ $\boxed{\text{oct}}$ *and enter* 472_8. *We then convert to binary by entering* $\boxed{\text{2nd}}$ $\boxed{\text{mode}}$ $\boxed{\text{bin}}$. *The answer* 100111010_2 *appears on the screen.*

1. Use a calculator to check the answers to problems 1–19 in Exercise 3.4.

Computer Corner

The conversion of numbers involving binary, octal, and hexadecimal bases requires the use of Tables 3.4 and 3.5. We can avoid using these tables if we use the Base Converter Program (X, Y < 17) found in the appendix, Programs in BASIC. This program converts a number with a given base to a number with a specified base as long as both bases are less than 17.

1. Use the program to check problems 1, 3, 5, 7, 9, 11, 13, 15, and 17 in Exercise 3.4.

3.5   BINARY ARITHMETIC

GETTING STARTED

MODEMS AND ASCII CODE

Do you know what a modem is? It is a device that transmits data to or from a computer via telephone. How does one work? Let us say you are writing a message starting with the letter A in your computer. A stream of digital bits with 0 volts for binary 0 and a constant voltage for 1 flows from the computer into the modem carrying the American Standard Code for Information Interchange (ASCII) code for the letter A: 01000001. At the receiving end, the signal is demodulated, that is, changed back, and resumes its original form, a series of pulses representing 0's and 1's resulting in 01000001, the letter A. You can learn how these letters are encoded in different bases by doing problems 27–32 in Exercise 3.5.

Now that we know how to represent numbers in the binary system, we look at how computations are done in that system. First, we can construct addition and multiplication tables like the ones for base 10 arithmetic. See Tables 3.6 and 3.7 below.

Table 3.6 *Binary Addition*

+	0	1
0	0	1
1	1	10

Table 3.7 *Binary Multiplication*

×	0	1
0	0	0
1	0	1

The only entry that looks peculiar is the 10 in the addition table, but recall that 10_2 means 2_{10}, which is exactly the result of adding $1 + 1$. (Be sure to read 10 as "one zero" not as "ten.")

A. *Addition*

Binary addition is done in the same manner as addition in base 10. We line up the corresponding digits and add column by column.

EXAMPLE 1   Add 1010_2 and 1111_2.

Solution

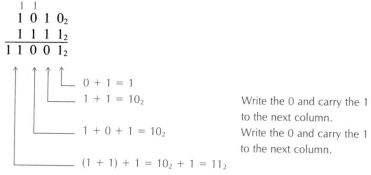

Thus, $1010_2 + 1111_2 = 11001_2$.

■

EXAMPLE 2   Perform the additiion $1101_2 + 110_2 + 11_2$.

Solution   We shall omit the subscript 2 in the computation, but keep in mind that all numerals are binary.

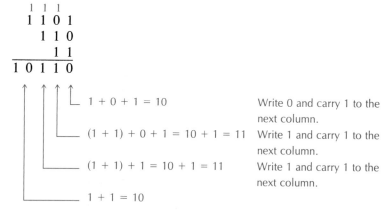

Thus, $1101_2 + 110_2 + 11_2 = 10110_2$.

■

B. *Subtraction*

To substract in the binary system, we line up corresponding digits and subtract column by column, "borrowing" as necessary.

EXAMPLE 3   Perform the subtraction $1111_2 - 110_2$.

Solution   Again, we omit the subscript 2 in the computation:

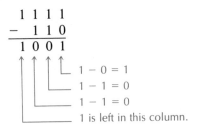

$$
\begin{array}{r}
1\ 1\ 1\ 1 \\
-\ \ 1\ 1\ 0 \\
\hline
1\ 0\ 0\ 1
\end{array}
$$

$1 - 0 = 1$
$1 - 1 = 0$
$1 - 1 = 0$
1 is left in this column.

This shows that $1111_2 - 110_2 = 1001_2$. You can check this by adding $1001_2 + 110_2$ to get 1111_2. ∎

Example 3 did not require "borrowing," but the next example does.

EXAMPLE 4   Subtract 101_2 from 1010_2.

Solution

$$
\begin{array}{r}
0\ \ 10\ 0\ 10 \\
1\ 0\ 1\ 0 \\
-\ 1\ 0\ 1 \\
\hline
1\ 0\ 1
\end{array}
$$

$0 - 1$ requires borrowing; then, $10 - 1 = 1$.
$0 - 0 = 0$
$0 - 1$ requires borrowing; then, $10 - 1 = 1$.

The result is $1010_2 - 101_2 = 101_2$. You can check this answer by adding $101_2 + 101_2$ to get 1010_2. ∎

C. *Multiplication*

Multiplication in the binary system also is done in a manner similar to that for base 10, as the following examples illustrate.

EXAMPLE 5   Multiply $101_2 \times 110_2$.

Solution

$$
\begin{array}{r}
1\ 1\ 0 \\
\times\ 1\ 0\ 1 \\
\hline
1\ 1\ 0 \\
0\ 0\ 0 \\
1\ 1\ 0 \\
\hline
1\ 1\ 1\ 1\ 0
\end{array}
$$

← Start from the right and multiply by 1.
← Indent and multiply by 0.
← Indent and multiply by the left-hand 1.
← Add the above products.

The result shows that $101_2 \times 110_2 = 11110_2$. Note that we could abbreviate a little by omitting the two leftmost 0's in the second partial product and writing the third product on the same line. ∎

EXAMPLE 6   Multiply 1110_2 by 110_2.

Solution

$$
\begin{array}{r}
1\ 1\ 1\ 0 \\
\times\ 1\ 1\ 0 \\
\hline
1\ 1\ 1\ 0\ 0 \\
1\ 1\ 1\ 0 \\
\hline
1\ 0\ 1\ 0\ 1\ 0\ 0
\end{array}
$$

← Multiply by 0, and write one 0. Then multiply by 1, using the same line.
← Indent two places and multiply by 1.
← Add the partial products.

The computation shows that $110_2 \times 1110_2 = 1010100_2$. ∎

D. *Division*

The procedure used for division in the base 10 system also can be used in the binary system. This is illustrated next.

EXAMPLE 7   Divide 1011_2 by 10_2.

Solution

$$
\begin{array}{r}
1\ 0\ 1 \\
10\,\overline{)\,1\ 0\ 1\ 1} \\
-1\ 0 \\
\hline
1\ 1 \\
-1\ 0 \\
\hline
1
\end{array}
$$

Step 1.
Step 2.
Step 3.
←—— Remainder

Step 1. $1 \times 10 = 10$. Write 1 in the quotient above the 10. Then subtract.
Step 2.   Bring down the next digit. 10 does not go into 1, so write 0 in the quotient and bring down the final digit.
Step 3. $1 \times 10 = 10$. Write 1 in the quotient and then subtract to get the remainder.

The computation shows that $1011_2 \div 10_2 = 101_2$ with remainder 1. You can check this answer by multiplying 101_2 by 10_2 and adding 1 to the product. Thus,

$$(10_2 \times 101_2) + 1 = 1010_2 + 1 = 1011_2$$

showing that the answer is correct. ∎

EXAMPLE 8   Divide 110111_2 by 101_2.

Solution

$$
\begin{array}{r}
1\ 0\ 1\ 1 \\[2pt]
1\ 0\ 1\ \overline{)\ 1\ 1\ 0\ 1\ 1\ 1} \\
\end{array}
$$

Step 1. $\longrightarrow$ $-1\ 0\ 1$

Step 2. $\longrightarrow$ $1\ 1\ 1$

Step 3. $\longrightarrow$ $-1\ 0\ 1$

Step 4. $\longrightarrow$ $1\ 0\ 1$

Step 5. $\longrightarrow$ $-1\ 0\ 1$

0 $\longleftarrow$ Remainder

Step 1. $1 \times 101 = 101$. Write 1 in the quotient above the 110. Then subtract.

Step 2.   Bring down the next digit. 101 does not go into 11, so write 0 in the quotient and bring down the next digit.

Step 3. $1 \times 101 = 101$. Write 1 in the quotient. Then subtract.

Step 4.   Bring down the final digit.

Step 5. $1 \times 101 = 101$. Write 1 in the quotient and then subtract to get the remainder.

The division here is exact; the quotient is 1011_2 and the remainder is 0.

You can check the answer by multiplying the quotient 1011_2 by the divisor 101_2. Thus,

$$
\begin{array}{r}
1\ 0\ 1\ 1 \\
\times\quad 1\ 0\ 1 \\
\hline
1\ 0\ 1\ 1 \\
1\ 0\ 1\ 1\ 0 \\
\hline
1\ 1\ 0\ 1\ 1\ 1
\end{array}
$$

Therefore, the answer is correct.   ■

Exercise 3.5

A. In problems 1–6, perform the indicated additions.

1. 111_2
    $+\ \ 10_2$

2. 111_2
    $+\ 101_2$

3. 1101_2
    $+\ 110_2$

4. 1111_2
    $+\ 1101_2$

5. 110_2
    $+\ 101_2$
    $+\ 111_2$

6. 1101_2
    $+1110_2$
    $+\ 101_2$

B. In problems 7–12, perform the indicated subtractions.

7. 111_2
    $-\ \ 10_2$

8. 110_2
    $-\ \ 11_2$

9. 1000_2
    $-\ 111_2$

10.	1101_2	11.	1111_2	12.	1010_2
	$-\ 111_2$		$-\ 101_2$		$-\ 101_2$

C. In problems 13–18, multiply as indicated.

13.	110_2	14.	101_2	15.	1111_2
	$\times\ 11_2$		$\times\ 10_2$		$\times\ 11_2$

16.	1110_2	17.	1011_2	18.	1011_2
	$\times\ 111_2$		$\times\ 101_2$		$\times\ 111_2$

D. In problems 19–24, divide as indicated.

19. $10_2 \overline{)1101_2}$ 20. $11_2 \overline{)1101_2}$ 21. $11_2 \overline{)1110_2}$

22. $11_2 \overline{)11011_2}$ 23. $101_2 \overline{)111011_2}$ 24. $111_2 \overline{)1110111_2}$

In Other Words

25. Why are the operations of addition and multiplication easier in base 2?

26. In our decimal system, we need to know 81 multiplication facts. (1×1, 1×2, . . . 9×9). How many multiplication facts do you need to know:

   (a) in base 2?   (b) in base 5?

Using Your Knowledge

In ASCII (American Standard Code for Information Interchange) the characters A–O are prefixed by 0100 and numbered in order starting with A = 0001, B = 0010, C = 0011, and so on. The characters P–Z are numbered in order starting with P = 0000 and prefixed by 0101.

*   In problems 27–32, use the ASCII to write the binary, then the decimal, and the hexadecimal code for the letters.*

		Binary	Decimal	Hexadecimal
27.	A	___	___	___
28.	I	___	___	___
29.	Q	___	___	___
30.	V	___	___	___
31.	X	___	___	___
32.	Z	___	___	___

In problems 33 and 34, change the hexadecimal numerals representing letters to binary and then use the ASCII to write the message.

33.   48   45   4C   50

34.   49
          44   4F
          4E   4F   54
          47   45   54
          49   54

Calculator Corner

Some scientific calculators will perform operations in different bases. Thus, to add $1101_2 + 110_2 + 11_2$ (Example 2), we place the calculator in the binary made by pressing 2nd mode bin *and proceed as in regular addition by entering $1101 + 110 + 11 =$. The answer will appear on the screen as 10110. You can do addition, subtraction, and multiplication in the same manner, but you must be careful with division. Thus, in Example 7 we divided 1011_2 by 10_2. The answer is 101_2 with a remainder of 1. To do this on your calculator, enter* 2nd mode bin *(now you are in binary) and $1011 \div 10$. The calculator will give you the quotient 101 but not the remainder. To discover that there is a remainder, you must check your division by multiplying the quotient (101_2) by the divisor (10_2). The result is 1010_2, not 1011_2, so the remainder must be 1. The moral of the story is that when doing division problems in different bases, you must check the problem by multiplication and, during this process, find the remainder.*

1. Use your calculator to find the remainder (if any) in problems 19, 21, and 23 of Exercise 3.5.

3.6   OCTAL AND HEXADECIMAL ARITHMETIC

GETTING STARTED

NATIVE AMERICAN ARITHMETIC

When counting in the decimal system, you can use ten fingers. In the binary system you use two fingers. What would you use in an octal system? The answer is not at your fingertips, but *between* your fingers! The Yuki Indians of California use the spaces between their fingers for counting. Thus, some of their counting is in base 4 and some is in base 8 (octal or octonary). In this section, we shall study octal and hexadecimal arithmetic.

A Yuki Indian poses in traditional dance costume, ca. 1900

Arithmetic in the base 8 and base 16 systems can be done with addition and multiplication tables in much the same way as in the base 10 system. We consider the octal system first and construct the required tables (Tables 3.8 and 3.9).

Table 3.8 *Octal Addition Table*

+	0	1	2	3	4	5	6	7
0	0	1	2	3	4	5	6	7
1	1	2	3	4	5	6	7	10
2	2	3	4	5	6	7	10	11
3	3	4	5	6	7	10	11	12
4	4	5	6	7	10	11	12	13
5	5	6	7	10	11	12	13	14
6	6	7	10	11	12	13	14	15
7	7	10	11	12	13	14	15	16

Table 3.9 *Octal Multiplication Table*

×	0	1	2	3	4	5	6	7
0	0	0	0	0	0	0	0	0
1	0	1	2	3	4	5	6	7
2	0	2	4	6	10	12	14	16
3	0	3	6	11	14	17	22	25
4	0	4	10	14	20	24	30	34
5	0	5	12	17	24	31	36	43
6	0	6	14	22	30	36	44	52
7	0	7	16	25	34	43	52	61

A. *Octal Addition*

To add octal numbers, we align corresponding digits and add column by column, carrying over from column to column as necessary.

As in the preceding section, we shall omit the subscripts in the computations, but keep in mind the system with which we are working.

EXAMPLE 1 Add: $673_8 + 52_8$

Solution

```
    1
  6 7 3
+   5 2
  7 4 5  ←——— 3 + 2 = 5
  ↑ ↑
  │ └————— 7 + 5 = 14 (Table 3.8)     Write 4 and carry 1. (Read
  │                                    14 as "one-four" not as
  │                                    "fourteen.")
  └——————— 1 + 6 = 7
```

Thus, $673_8 + 52_8 = 745_8$.

EXAMPLE 2   Do the addition: $705_8 + 374_8$

Solution

$$
\begin{array}{r}
\overset{1\ \ 1}{7\ 0\ 5} \\
+\ 3\ 7\ 4 \\
\hline
1\ 3\ 0\ 1
\end{array}
$$

← $5 + 4 = 11$ (Table 3.8)   Write 1 and carry 1.

$1 + 0 + 7 = 10$ (Table 3.8)   Write 0 and carry 1.

$1 + (7 + 3) = 1 + 12 = 13$ (Table 3.8)

The required sum is 1301_8.   ▪

B. *Octal Multiplication*

EXAMPLE 3   Multiply 46_8 by 5_8.

Solution

$$
\begin{array}{r}
4\ 6 \\
\times\ \ \ 5 \\
\hline
2\ 7\ 6
\end{array}
$$

← $5 \times 6 = 36$ (Table 3.9)   Write 6 and carry 3.

$5 \times 4 = 24$ (Table 3.9)   Add the 3 to get 27.

The answer is 276_8. [*Note:*   You can check the answer by converting all the numbers to base 10. Thus, since $46_8 = 38$ and $5_8 = 5$, in base 10, we have $5 \times 38 = 190$. We also find that $276_8 = 190$, so the answer checks.]   ▪

EXAMPLE 4   Multiply 237_8 by 14_8.

Solution

$$
\begin{array}{r}
2\ 3\ 7 \\
\times\ \ 1\ 4 \\
\hline
1\ 1\ 7\ 4 \\
2\ 3\ 7 \\
\hline
3\ 5\ 6\ 4
\end{array}
$$

$4 \times 7 = 34$ (Table 3.9)   Write 4 and carry 3.

$4 \times 3 = 14$ (Table 3.9); $14 + 3 = 17$ Write 7 and carry 1.

$4 \times 2 = 10$ (Table 3.9); $10 + 1 = 11$

$1 \times 237 = 237$

Addition of the partial products gives the final answer, 3564_8. The check is left to you.   ▪

C. *Octal Subtraction and Division*

Subtraction and division also can be done by using tables as in the following examples.

EXAMPLE 5 Subtract 56_8 from 747_8.

Solution

```
    6  14
    7  4  7
 −     5  6
    6  7  1
```
← $7 − 6 = 1$ (Table 3.8 shows $6 + 1 = 7$.)

$4 − 5$ requires borrowing. Change the leftmost 7 to 6 and add 10 to the 4. Then subtract. To get this result, refer to Table 3.8, go down the left-hand column under $+$ to the 5 and read across to 14. The 7 in the top line above the 14 is the required number.

Bring down the 6.

The final answer is 671_8. You can check this answer by adding $56_8 + 671_8$ to get 747_8. ∎

EXAMPLE 6 Subtract as indicated: $643_8 − 45_8$

Solution

```
    5  13
    3  13
    6  4  3
 −     4  5
    5  7  6
```
← $3 − 5$ requires borrowing. Change the 4 to 3 and add 10 to the first 3 to give 13. Then subtract: $13 − 5 = 6$ (Table 3.8).

$3 − 4$ requires borrowing. Change the 6 to 5 and add 10 to the 3 to give 13. Then subtract: $13 − 4 = 7$ (Table 3.8).

Bring down the 5.

The result shows that $643_8 − 45_8 = 576_8$. This can be checked by addition as in Example 5. ∎

EXAMPLE 7 Divide 765_8 by 24_8.

Solution

```
          3  1
    2  4 )7  6  5
          7  4
          2  5
          2  4
             1
```
← $3 × 24 = 74$ (Table 3.9). Write 3 in the quotient above the 76.

Subtract and bring down the 5.

$1 × 24 = 24$

Subtract to get the remainder.

This computation shows that $765_8 ÷ 24_8 = 31_8$ with a remainder of 1_8. This can be checked by multiplying 31_8 by 24_8 and adding 1 to the product. ∎

EXAMPLE 8   Do the indicated division: $4357_8 \div 21_8$

Solution

$$
\begin{array}{r}
2\ 0\ 6 \\
2\ 1\overline{)4\ 3\ 5\ 7} \\
4\ 2 \\
\overline{1\ 5\ 7} \\
1\ 4\ 6 \\
\overline{1\ 1}
\end{array}
$$

← $2 \times 21 = 42$. Write 2 in the quotient above the 43.

← Subtract and bring down the 5. 21 does not go into 15, so write 0 in the quotient and bring down the 7.

$6 \times 21 = 146$ (Table 3.9). Write 6 in the quotient.

Subtract to get the remainder.

The computation shows that the quotient is 206_8 and the remainder is 11_8.

As before, the answer can be checked by multiplying the quotient by the divisor and adding the remainder. Thus,

$$
\begin{array}{r}
206 \\
\times\quad 21 \\
\hline
206 \\
414 \\
\hline
4346 \\
+\quad 11 \\
\hline
4357
\end{array}
$$

which shows the answer is correct.   ■

D. *Hexadecimal Addition and Multiplication*

To do arithmetic in the hexadecimal system, we first construct the addition and multiplication tables, as shown in Tables 3.10 and 3.11. These tables furnish the "number facts" we need to do the computations.

Table 3.10 *Hexadecimal Addition Table*

+	0	1	2	3	4	5	6	7	8	9	A	B	C	D	E	F
0	0	1	2	3	4	5	6	7	8	9	A	B	C	D	E	F
1	1	2	3	4	5	6	7	8	9	A	B	C	D	E	F	10
2	2	3	4	5	6	7	8	9	A	B	C	D	E	F	10	11
3	3	4	5	6	7	8	9	A	B	C	D	E	F	10	11	12
4	4	5	6	7	8	9	A	B	C	D	E	F	10	11	12	13
5	5	6	7	8	9	A	B	C	D	E	F	10	11	12	13	14
6	6	7	8	9	A	B	C	D	E	F	10	11	12	13	14	15
7	7	8	9	A	B	C	D	E	F	10	11	12	13	14	15	16
8	8	9	A	B	C	D	E	F	10	11	12	13	14	15	16	17
9	9	A	B	C	D	E	F	10	11	12	13	14	15	16	17	18
A	A	B	C	D	E	F	10	11	12	13	14	15	16	17	18	19
B	B	C	D	E	F	10	11	12	13	14	15	16	17	18	19	1A
C	C	D	E	F	10	11	12	13	14	15	16	17	18	19	1A	1B
D	D	E	F	10	11	12	13	14	15	16	17	18	19	1A	1B	1C
E	E	F	10	11	12	13	14	15	16	17	18	19	1A	1B	1C	1D
F	F	10	11	12	13	14	15	16	17	18	19	1A	1B	1C	1D	1E

Table 3.11 *Hexadecimal Multiplication Table*

×	0	1	2	3	4	5	6	7	8	9	A	B	C	D	E	F
0	0	0	0	0	0	0	0	0	0	0	0	0	0	0	0	0
1	0	1	2	3	4	5	6	7	8	9	A	B	C	D	E	F
2	0	2	4	6	8	A	C	E	10	12	14	16	18	1A	1C	1E
3	0	3	6	9	C	F	12	15	18	1B	1E	21	24	27	2A	2D
4	0	4	8	C	10	14	18	1C	20	24	28	2C	30	34	38	3C
5	0	5	A	F	14	19	1E	23	28	2D	32	37	3C	41	46	4B
6	0	6	C	12	18	1E	24	2A	30	36	3C	42	48	4E	54	5A
7	0	7	E	15	1C	23	2A	31	38	3F	46	4D	54	5B	62	69
8	0	8	10	18	20	28	30	38	40	48	50	58	60	68	70	78
9	0	9	12	1B	24	2D	36	3F	48	51	5A	63	6C	75	7E	87
A	0	A	14	1E	28	32	3C	46	50	5A	64	6E	78	82	8C	96
B	0	B	16	21	2C	37	42	4D	58	63	6E	79	84	8F	9A	A5
C	0	C	18	24	30	3C	48	54	60	6C	78	84	90	9C	A8	B4
D	0	D	1A	27	34	41	4E	5B	68	75	82	8F	9C	A9	B6	C3
E	0	E	1C	2A	38	46	54	62	70	7E	8C	9A	A8	B6	C4	D2
F	0	F	1E	2D	3C	4B	5A	69	78	87	96	A5	B4	C3	D2	E1

EXAMPLE 9   Add: $2B4_{16} + A1_{16}$

Solution

$$
\begin{array}{r}
\overset{1}{} \\
2\ B\ 4 \\
+\ \ A\ 1 \\
\hline
3\ 5\ 5
\end{array}
$$

$3\ 5\ 5 \longleftarrow 4 + 1 = 5$

$B + A = 15$ (Table 3.10)   Write 5 and carry 1.

$1 + 2 = 3$

The answer is 355_{16}. (You can check this by converting to base 10.) ∎

EXAMPLE 10   Add: $1AB2_{16} + 2CD3_{16}$

Solution

$$
\begin{array}{r}
\overset{1}{}\ \overset{1}{} \\
1\ A\ B\ 2 \\
+\ 2\ C\ D\ 3 \\
\hline
4\ 7\ 8\ 5
\end{array}
$$

$4\ 7\ 8\ 5 \longleftarrow 2 + 3 = 5$

$B + D = 18$ (Table 3.10)   Write 8 and carry 1.

$(A + C) + 1 = 16 + 1 = 17$ (Table 3.10)   Write 7 and carry 1.

$1 + 1 + 2 = 4$

The answer is 4785_{16}. (You can check this by converting to base 10.) ∎

EXAMPLE 11   Multiply $1A2_{16}$ by B_{16}.

Solution

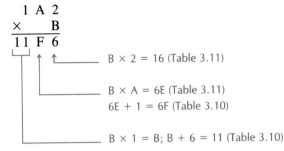

$$\begin{array}{r} 1\ A\ 2 \\ \times\ \ \ B \\ \hline 11\ F\ 6 \end{array}$$

$B \times 2 = 16$ (Table 3.11)   Write 6 and carry the 1.

$B \times A = 6E$ (Table 3.11)
$6E + 1 = 6F$ (Table 3.10)   Write F and carry the 6.

$B \times 1 = B$; $B + 6 = 11$ (Table 3.10)

The answer is $11F6_{16}$.   ■

EXAMPLE 12   Multiply $2B4_{16}$ by $B1_{16}$.

Solution

$$\begin{array}{r} 2\ B\ 4 \\ \times\ \ B\ 1 \\ \hline 2\ B\ 4 \\ 1\ D\ B\ C \\ \hline 1\ D\ E\ 7\ 4 \end{array}$$

$\longleftarrow 1 \times 2B4 = 2B4$

$\longleftarrow B \times 4 = 2C$ (Table 3.11); write C and carry the 2. Then, $B \times B = 79$ (Table 3.11); $79 + 2 = 7B$ (Table 3.10); write B and carry the 7. Then, $B \times 2 = 16$ (Table 3.11); $16 + 7 = 1D$ (Table 3.10).

$B + C = 17$ (Table 3.10); write 7 and carry the 1.
$(2 + B) + 1 = D + 1 = E$ (Table 3.10)

The answer is $1DE74_{16}$.   ■

Exercise 3.6

A. In problems 1–4, do the indicated additions.

1. $531_8 + 47_8$ 2. $425_8 + 364_8$
3. $7256_8 + 634_8$ 4. $5732_8 + 747_8$

B. In problems 5–8, do the indicated multiplications.

5. $57_8 \times 6_8$ 6. $45_8 \times 7_8$
7. $216_8 \times 32_8$ 8. $312_8 \times 65_8$

C. In problems 9–12, do the indicated subtractions.

9. $534_8 - 25_8$ 10. $617_8 - 47_8$
11. $3264_8 - 756_8$ 12. $4763_8 - 654_8$

In problems 13–16, do the indicated divisions.

13. $317_8 \div 7_8$ 14. $4355_8 \div 5_8$
15. $4215_8 \div 15_8$ 16. $7342_8 \div 31_8$

D. In problems 17–20, do the indicated additions.

17. $3CB_{16} + 4C_{16}$ 18. $4FE_{16} + 35_{16}$

19. $98D_{16} + 2B_{16}$ 20. $CBD_{16} + AF_{16}$

In problems 21–24, do the indicated multiplications.

21. $2C5_{16} \times 3B_{16}$ 22. $4DE_{16} \times 12_{16}$

23. $6F3_{16} \times AB_{16}$ 24. $29A_{16} \times E0F_{16}$

In Other Words

25. Explain why it is easier to add and multiply in the binary than in the hexadecimal system.

26. Why is it easier to write a number in expanded form in the decimal system than in the binary or hexadecimal system?

Using Your Knowledge

You know that we used decimals in the base 10 system with the understanding that the place values to the right of the decimal point are

$$\frac{1}{10^1}, \quad \frac{1}{10^2}, \quad \frac{1}{10^3}, \quad etc.$$

For example, the decimal numeral 23.759 stands for

$$(2 \times 10) + 3 + \frac{7}{10^1} + \frac{5}{10^2} + \frac{9}{10^3}$$

The same idea is used in other number systems. Thus, in the binary system, the numeral

$$11.101_2 = (1 \times 2) + 1 + \frac{1}{2^1} + \frac{1}{2^2} + \frac{1}{2^3}$$

In the octal system, the numeral

$$73.524_8 = (7 \times 8) + 3 + \frac{5}{8^1} + \frac{2}{8^2} + \frac{4}{8^3}$$

To convert numbers from binary or octal form to decimal form, it is convenient to have the values

$$\frac{1}{2} = 0.5, \quad \frac{1}{4} = 0.25, \quad \frac{1}{8} = 0.125, \quad etc.$$

For instance,

$$1.111_2 = 1 + 0.5 + 0.25 + 0.125 = 1.875$$
$$3.5_8 = 3 + (5 \times 0.125) = 3.625$$

Change to decimal form:

27. 10.101_2 28. 11.011_2 29. 10.001_2

30. 21.4_8 31. 72.6_8 32. 31.7_8

Calculator Corner

Some scientific calculators are able to perform arithmetic in different bases. (You need a key displaying the desired base.) Thus, to add $673_8 + 52_8$ (Example 1), we place the calculator in the octal mode by pressing $\boxed{\text{2nd}}$ $\boxed{\text{mode}}$ $\boxed{\text{oct}}$ *and entering the indicated operation 673 + 52 =, as in regular addition. The answer 745 will appear on the calculator screen. Keep in mind that when doing division the calculator will not provide the remainder. Thus, if you divide 765_8 by 24_8 (Example 7), the calculator gives the quotient as 31. Is there a remainder? If you multiply the quotient 31_8 by the divisor 24_8, the result is 764_8 and not 765_8. Thus, the remainder must be 1.*

What about the hexadecimal system? First, you need a $\boxed{\text{hex}}$ *key and A, B, C, D, E, F buttons to represent the numbers 10, 11, 12, 13, 14, and 15, respectively. You can then multiply $1A2_{16}$ by B_{16} (Example 11) by entering* $\boxed{\text{2nd}}$ $\boxed{\text{mode}}$ $\boxed{\text{hex}}$ $\boxed{\text{1A2}}$ $\boxed{\times}$ $\boxed{\text{B}}$ $\boxed{=}$
The calculator gives the answer 11F6.

1. Use your calculator to find the remainder (if any) in problems 13 and 15, Exercise 3.6.

Chapter 3 Summary

Section	Item			Meaning
	Egyptian	Babylonian	Roman	
3.1	|	▼	I	One
3.1	|||||	▼▼▼▼▼	V	Five
3.1	∩	◄	X	Ten
3.1	∩∩∩∩∩	◄◄◄◄	L	Fifty
3.1	ჲ		C	One hundred
3.1	ჲჲჲჲჲ		D	Five hundred
3.1	ſ		M	One thousand

Section	Item			Meaning	Example
	Egyptian	Babylonian	Roman		
3.1	⌒		$\overline{X}$	Ten thousand	
3.1	⌒		$\overline{C}$	One hundred thousand	
3.1	𝄪		$\overline{M}$	One million	
3.2A	a^n			$\underbrace{a \times a \times \cdots \times a}_{n\ a\text{'s}}$	$10^3 = 10 \times 10 \times 10$
3.2A	$(2 \times 10^2) + (4 \times 10^1) + (5 \times 10^0)$			Expanded form of 245	
3.2B	$a^m \times a^n = a^{m+n}$			Law of exponents	$5^3 \times 5^6 = 5^9$
3.2B	$a^m \div a^n = a^{m-n}$			Law of exponents	$4^7 \div 4^2 = 4^5$
3.3A	43_{five}			$(4 \times 5) + (3 \times 5^0)$	
3.3B	10001_{two}			$(1 \times 2^4) + (1 \times 2^0)$	
3.3B	$A_{16}, B_{16}, C_{16}, D_{16}, E_{16}, F_{16}$			10, 11, 12, 13, 14, 15	
3.3B	17_{eight}			$(1 \times 8) + (7 \times 8^0)$	

Research Questions

Sources of information for these questions can be found in the Bibliography at the end of the book.

1. Write a report on the Egyptian numeration system.

2. Trace the development of the Babylonian numeration system, with special emphasis on the base used.

3. Write a report on the Sumerian numeration system.

4. Write a report on the Mayan numeration system and find out how 0's were used in their system.

5. Write a report on the life and works of Mohammed al-Khowarizmi, with special emphasis on the books he wrote.

6. Write a report on A. Henry Rhind and the Rhind papyrus.

7. Find out and report on the uses of binary arithmetic in computers.

8. Write a report on Leonardo Fibonacci and his book the *Liber Abaci*.

9. Find out and write a report about the development and use of ASCII.

Chapter 3 Practice Test

1. Write in Egyptian numerals:
   (a) 63   (b) 735

2. Write in decimal notation:
   (a) ∩∩||| (b) ꝥ∩∩|

3. Write in Babylonian numerals:
   (a) 63   (b) 735

4. Write in decimal notation:
   (a) ▼ ◄◄▼▼   (b) ▼▼ ◄▼

5. Do the multiplication 23×21 using:
   (a) The Egyptian method of successive duplication
   (b) The Egyptian method of mediation and duplation

6. Write in Roman numerals:
   (a) 53   (b) 42   (c) 22,000

7. Write in decimal notation:
   (a) LXVII   (b) $\overline{\text{XLVIII}}$

8. Write in expanded form:
   (a) 2507   (b) 189

9. Write in decimal notation:
   (a) $(3 \times 10^3) + (7 \times 10^2) + (2 \times 10^0)$
   (b) $(5 \times 10^4) + (9 \times 10^3) + (4 \times 10)$

10. Do the following computations in the usual way and in expanded form:
    (a) $75 + 32$ (b) $56 - 24$

11. Perform the indicated operations, leaving the answer in exponential form:
    (a) $3^4 \times 3^8$ (b) $2^9 \div 2^3$

12. Do the following computations in the usual way and in expanded form:
    (a) 83×21 (b) $54 \div 7$

13. Change to decimal notation:
    (a) 203_4 (b) 143_5 (c) 1101_2

14. Change to decimal notation:
    (a) 152_8 (b) $A2C_{16}$

15. Convert the number 33 to:
    (a) Base 5   (b) Base 6

16. Convert to binary notation:
    (a) 39   (b) 527

17. Convert the number 47 to:
    (a) Base 8   (b) Base 16

18. (a) Convert 1011101_2 to octal notation.
    (b) Convert 327_8 to binary notation.

19. (a) Convert 1011101_2 to hexadecimal notation.
    (b) Convert $2BD_{16}$ to binary notation.

20. (a) Convert $2B_{16}$ to octal notation.
    (b) Convert 27_8 to hexadecimal notation.

21. Do the indicated computations in the binary system:

    (a) $\quad 1101_2$ (b) $\quad 1101_2$
    $\quad + \ 101_2 \qquad\qquad - \ 111_2$

22. Do the indicated computations in the binary system:

    (a) $1101_2 \times 11_2$ (b) $10110_2 \div 11_2$

23. Do the following computations in the octal system:

    (a) $632_8 + 46_8$ (b) $37_8 \times 5_8$

24. Do the following computations in the octal system:

    (a) $632_8 - 46_8$ (b) $572_8 \div 6_8$

25. Do the following computations in the hexadecimal system:

    (a) $2BC_{16} + 5D_{16}$ (b) $3C4_{16} \times 2B_{16}$

In the last chapter, you took a journey through time and the numbers of antiquity. Now we shall explore more recent developments in the history of mathematics by studying the **natural** or **counting** numbers, their properties, and uses. We will also look closely at some special natural numbers: the **primes.** Since ancient times, mathematicians have been fascinated by the divisors of numbers, and on that basis classified the numbers as abundant, perfect, or deficient. Prime numbers have only two divisors, themselves and 1. The search for prime numbers continues today using supercomputers, and the results are used in sophisticated areas such as cryptography.

As useful as they are, the natural numbers are not enough for everyday life. We need numbers to measure such things as sub-zero temperatures, yardage losses in a football game, and financial losses in the stock market. In other words, we need **negative** numbers, which we shall introduce when we study the **integers.** Further, division of one integer by another yields a new number, a **rational** number. Rational numbers can also be written as decimals.

You might imagine that the rationals would be the end of this numerical journey. However, the Pythagoreans, an ancient Greek secret society, made a stunning discovery. The *irrational numbers* defied their knowledge of number properties, as they could not write them as the ratio of two whole numbers. The union of the rationals and the irrationals yields the **real numbers.** One of the most interesting real numbers is π, and we shall trace different attempts to find its value. Finally, the real numbers are a part of a larger set, the set of **complex numbers.** These numbers allow us to solve equations of the form $x^2 = -1$ through the introduction of a new unit $i = \sqrt{-1}$. In the next chapter we will find out how all these numbers are used in a new world: algebra.

The Real and the Complex Numbers

**Leopold Kronecker
(1823–1891)**

In short, Kronecker was an artist who used mathematical formulas as his medium.

E. T. BELL

THE HUMAN SIDE OF MATHEMATICS

Leopold Kronecker was born on December 7, 1823, in Liegnitz, Prussia. The boy's early education was under a private tutor who was supervised by Leopold's father, a well-educated man whose love of philosophy was handed on to his son.

Throughout his schooling, Kronecker's performance was many-sided and brilliant. He mastered Greek, Latin, Hebrew, and philosophy with ease, though it became obvious that his greatest talent was in mathematics. In addition to his formal studies, he took music lessons and became an accomplished pianist and vocalist.

In 1841, Kronecker entered the University of Berlin, where he began to specialize in mathematics. His dissertation for the Ph.D. degree was accepted in 1845 when he was 22 years old. His doctoral work was in the theory of numbers and involved algebraic problems stemming from the attempt to construct a regular polygon of n sides with only a straightedge and compass.

In that same year, a rich uncle died, leaving Leopold to manage a large estate and to run a bank-ing business for his cousin (whom he married in 1848). He was an extremely successful businessman, having a genius for making the right friends and investments.

Despite his diversion to business and finance, Kronecker did not neglect his mathematics. He finished an outstanding memoir on the theory of equations, which was published in 1853. Throughout his mathematical work, much of it in number theory and theory of equations, he tried to make concise and expressive formulas tell the whole story. Most of Kronecker's papers have a strong arithmetical flavor; he wanted to explain everything in terms of the whole numbers and in a finite number of steps, something that has had a great influence on modern mathematics.

In 1883 the University of Berlin offered Kronecker a professorship, which he accepted and held until his death in December 1891, at the age of 68.

Looking Ahead: Kronecker's work in number systems and number theory led him to remark that "God made the integers, all else is the work of man." In this chapter we will look at number systems from the natural numbers to the real and complex numbers.

4.1   THE NATURAL, OR COUNTING, NUMBERS

GETTING STARTED

"THAT'S ABOUT A GOOGOL . . . BUT WHO'S COUNTING?"

In this section we shall study the numbers we use for counting, 1, 2, 3, and so on. These numbers were adopted in most European countries in the early sixteenth century, and we still use them for three important functions: counting, ordering, and identifying. The lowest number used for counting is 1. Is there any highest counting number? You may have heard of a **googol**, a number introduced by Edward Kasner, whose nine-year-old nephew allegedly coined the term. How big is the **googol**? A 1 followed by 100 zeros (10^{100}). What about the Buddhist **asankhyeya**, a 1 followed by 140 zeros (10^{140}). Lexicographically, the highest natural number is the **centillion**, a 1 followed by 303 zeros (10^{303}), but the same nine year old that introduced the **googol** gave us the **googolplex**, a 1 followed by a googol of zeros ($10^{10^{100}}$).

The counting numbers obey the Commutative, Associative, and Distributive Laws under multiplication and addition. All of these properties (and more) are used to solve this puzzle:

Take your age and multiply it by 2; add 5; multiply by 50; subtract 365; add the loose change in your pocket (under a dollar); then add 115. The first two figures in the answer give your age, and the last two the change in your pocket!

Can you figure why this works? You might be able to do it faster if you let *a* represent your age and then multiply by 2; add 5; multiply by 50; and so on.

Look at the numbers on the keys of your calculator. They can be used to form a special set of numbers, called the set N of **natural,** or **counting, numbers** $\{1, 2, 3, \ldots\}$. In this section, we shall discuss some uses and properties of the set of natural numbers.

A. *Using the Natural Numbers*

The natural numbers can be used in three different ways: As cardinals (for counting or showing how many), as ordinals (for indicating order in a series), or for identification. Thus, the number of elements in $A = \{a, b, c, d\}$ is 4. We then say that the **cardinal number of A** is 4 and write $n(A) = 4$. Here, the number 4 is used as a **cardinal number.**

Numbers can also be used to assign an **order,** or position, to the elements of a set, that is, to indicate which element is **first, second, third,** and so on. We then refer to these numbers as **ordinal numbers.** Finally, numbers can be used for **identification.** Your Social Security number, your passport number, and your savings account number are used for identification purposes.

EXAMPLE 1 Determine whether the underlined word is used as a cardinal or an ordinal number, or for identification.

(a) If she kissed you once, would she kiss you <u>two</u> times?
(b) My account number is <u>123456</u>.
(c) This is my <u>first</u> and last warning.

Solution (a) Cardinal   (b) Identification   (c) Ordinal ∎

B. *Properties of the Natural Numbers*

Suppose you are given two natural numbers. Regardless of what these numbers are, you know that if you add or multiply them, the results are again natural numbers. Try it. This property is described by saying that *the set of natural numbers is closed under addition and under multiplication.*

Definition 4.1

> If an operation is defined on a set and the result of this operation is always an element of the set, then the set is said to be **closed** under this operation.

EXAMPLE 2 Show that the set {0, 1} is closed under ordinary multiplication.

Solution In the table in the margin, we show the operation table for the given set. For any two elements of the set, the result after multiplication is in the set, so the given set is closed under the operation of multiplication. Note that you need to look only at the body of the table. If all the entries are in the original set, then the set is closed under the operation. It is not closed otherwise. (See the next example.) ∎

×	0	1
0	0	0
1	0	1

EXAMPLE 3 Show that the set {0, 1} is not closed under the operation of addition.

Solution In the table in the margin, we show the operation table for the given set. The addition of 1 and 1 yields 2, which is not a member of the original set, so the given set is not closed under the operation of addition. ∎

+	0	1
0	0	1
1	1	2

Notice that the set of natural numbers is not closed under subtraction (because, for example, $3 - 5 = -2$, which is not a natural number) or division (because $3 \div 2$ is not a natural number).

Which multiplication would you rather do?

$$\begin{array}{r} 123 \\ \times\ \ 49 \\ \hline \end{array} \quad \text{or} \quad \begin{array}{r} 49 \\ \times\ 123 \\ \hline \end{array}$$

The first one is probably easier to do, but the answer is actually the same, because when multiplying or adding numbers, the **order** is not important, that is, $123 \times 49 = 49 \times 123$ and $123 + 49 = 49 + 123$. How would you add

328 + 193 + 7? It is easier to add 193 + 7, obtain 200, and add this result to 328. To show that we are adding 193 and 7 **first,** we use parentheses and write 328 + (193 + 7). If we add 328 and 193 first, we write (328 + 193) + 7. It does not matter which numbers we **group** together; the answer is the same, that is, 328 + (193 + 7) = (328 + 193) + 7. We summarize our discussion in the following table, where a, b, and c represent any natural numbers. The symbols "+" and "×" denote the usual binary operations, associating a unique result to each pair of elements in N.

Property	Name	Example
$a + b = b + a$	Commutative Property of Addition	$10 + 15 = 15 + 10$
$a \times b = b \times a$	Commutative Property of Multiplication	$2 \times 8 = 8 \times 2$
$a + (b + c) = (a + b) + c$	Associative Property of Addition	$3 + (6 + 2) = (3 + 6) + 2$
$a \times (b \times c) = (a \times b) \times c$	Associative Property of Multiplication	$4 \times (5 \times 3) = (4 \times 5) \times 3$

The method of proving the two Associative Properties is indicated in the Discovery section of Exercise 4.1.

There is another very important property of addition and multiplication. Suppose we are asked to find the product of 4 and $(10 + 6)$, which is denoted by $4(10 + 6)$ or by $4 \cdot (10 + 6)$, where the raised dot is used in place of the times sign. We can find the product by adding 10 and 6 first, getting

$$4 \cdot (10 + 6) = 4 \cdot 16 = 64$$

However, we get the same result by multiplying by 4 first:

$$4 \cdot (10 + 6) = 4 \cdot 10 + 4 \cdot 6 = 40 + 24 = 64$$

In general, if a, b, and c are natural numbers, then

$$a \times (b + c) = (a \times b) + (a \times c)$$

This property is called the **Distributive Property of Multiplication over Addition.** Note that $a(b + c)$ means $a \times (b + c)$. This notation and the fact that $a \times b$ is usually written ab will be used throughout this book.

> **Distributive Property**
>
> If a, b, and c are any natural numbers, then
>
> $$a(b + c) = ab + ac$$

Note that the Distributive Property is used in ordinary multiplication. For example, to multiply 14 by 21, we may write

$$14 \cdot 21 = 14(20 + 1) = 14 \cdot 20 + 14 \cdot 1$$
$$= 280 + 14 = 294$$

We can check the Closure and Commutative Properties of Addition by examining an addition table such as Table 4.1. Because all the entries in this table are natural numbers (no new numbers are introduced), the set N is closed with respect to addition.

Table 4.1

+	1	2	3	4	...
1	2	3	4	5	...
2	3	4	5	6	...
3	4	5	6	7	...
4	5	6	7	8	...
⋮	⋮	⋮	⋮	⋮	⋱

To check commutativity, we draw a diagonal from the upper left-hand corner to the lower right and note that each entry is identical to the entry that is symmetrically placed with respect to this diagonal. Thus, the entry in the first row, fourth column and that in the fourth row, first column are identical. When this happens for every entry in the table, the operation is commutative (assuming that the entries in the top row and the left-hand column are listed in the same order).

EXAMPLE 4 Consider the set $A = \{a, b, c\}$ and the operation $*$ as defined by the table in the margin.

(a) Is the set closed under $*$? Why?

(b) Is the set commutative under $*$? Why?

(c) Is the set associative under $*$? Why?

*	a	b	c
a	a	c	b
b	b	a	c
c	c	b	a

Solution

(a) A set is closed under the operation $*$ if the result of the operation is always an element of the set. Examining the table shows that all entries are in set A; thus A is closed under $*$.

(b) To be commutative, the table must be symmetric with respect to the diagonal shown. In our case, $a * b = c$ but $b * a = b$, which shows that $*$ is not commutative.

(c) No. For instance, $a * (b * c) = a * c = b$, but $(a * b) * c = c * c = a$. ∎

Exercise 4.1

A. In problems 1–5, identify the underlined items as cardinal numbers, as ordinal numbers, or for identification only.

1. My telephone number is <u>123-7643</u>.
2. This is the <u>second</u> problem in this exercise.
3. It takes <u>two</u> to tango.
4. <u>One</u>, <u>two</u>, <u>three</u>, go!
5. <u>First</u> National Bank is number <u>one</u>.
6. Three numbers are circled on the check shown here. Identify each of these numbers as a cardinal number, an ordinal number, or for identification only.

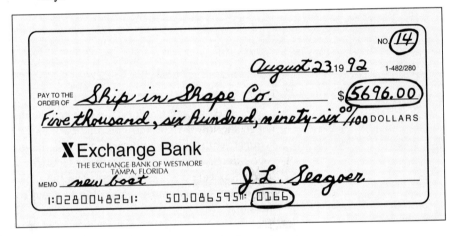

B. 7. Construct a multiplication table similar to Table 4.1 and answer the following questions on the basis of your table.
   (a) Would you say that multiplication is a binary operation? Why?
   (b) Would you say that the set of natural numbers is closed under multiplication? Why?
   (c) Is multiplication of natural numbers commutative? Why?

8. Consider the set $A = \{0, 1, 2, 3\}$ and the operation $\oplus$ as given by the table in the margin.
   (a) Is $\oplus$ a binary operation? Why?
   (b) Is the set A closed under $\oplus$? Why?
   (c) Is $\oplus$ commutative? Why?

$\oplus$	0	1	2	3
0	0	1	2	3
1	1	2	3	1
2	2	3	1	2
3	3	1	2	3

In problems 9–12, use the distributive property to multiply the following:

9. $4(3 + 8)$
10. $5(9 + 6)$
11. $8(3 + 8)$
12. $9(4 + 9)$

Sometimes, the Distributive Property can be used to simplify multiplication. For example, $8 \cdot 19 = 8(10 + 9) = 8 \cdot 10 + 8 \cdot 9 = 80 + 72 = 152$. In problems 13–16, use this technique to compute the following:

13. $6 \cdot 17$ 14. $8 \cdot 16$ 15. $7 \cdot 23$ 16. $9 \cdot 18$

17. Is the set of even natural numbers, $E = \{2, 4, 6, \ldots\}$, closed under addition? Under multiplication?

18. Is the set of odd numbers, $O = \{1, 3, 5, \ldots\}$, closed under addition? Under multiplication?

*	*a*	*b*	*c*
a	*b*	*c*	*a*
b	*c*	*a*	*b*
c	*a*	*b*	*c*

19. Consider the set $A = \{a, b, c\}$ and the operation $*$ as given by the table in the margin.
    (a) Is $*$ a binary operation? Why?
    (b) Is the set A closed under $*$? Why?
    (c) Is $*$ commutative? Why?
    (d) Is $*$ associative? Why?

⊗	0	1	2
0	1	2	0
1	2	0	1
2	0	1	2

20. Consider the set $A = \{0, 1, 2\}$ and the operation $\otimes$ as given by the table in the margin. Show that this set with the operation $\otimes$ has exactly the same properties as the set described in problem 19; only the notation is different.

In problems 21–32, state which of the properties discussed in this section is being applied.

21. (a) $7 + (5 + 3) = 7 + (3 + 5)$ (b) $7 + (5 + 3) = (7 + 5) + 3$
22. (a) $3(4 \times 8) = (3 \times 4) \times 8$ (b) $3(4 \times 3) = 3 \times (3 \times 4)$
23. (a) $3(4 + 8) = 3 \times 4 + 3 \times 8$ (b) $3(4 + 8) = 3 \times (8 + 4)$
24. (a) $5 \cdot (7 \cdot 9) = (7 \cdot 9) \cdot 5$ (b) $3 \cdot (4 \cdot 7) = (7 \cdot 4) \cdot 3$
25. (a) $(5 + 9) \cdot 3 = 5 \cdot 3 + 9 \cdot 3$ (b) $(5 + 9) \times 3 = 3(5 + 9)$
26. (a) $5(a + b) = 5a + 5b$ (b) $5(a + b) = 5(b + a)$
27. (a) $3(2a + b) = 6a + 3b$ (b) $3(2a + b) = (2a + b)(3)$
28. (a) $9a + 3b = 3b + 9a$ (b) $9a + 3b = 3(3a + b)$
29. (a) $a(b + c) = (b + c)a$ (b) $a(b + c) = ab + ac$
30. (a) $a(b + c) = a(c + b)$ (b) $(b + c)a = a(b + c)$
31. (a) $ab + ac = ac + ab$ (b) $ab + ac = ab + ca$
32. (a) $a(bc) = (ab)c$ (b) $a(bc) = (bc)a$

33. After adding a column of numbers such as

$$\begin{array}{r} 17 \\ 3 \\ 9 \\ \underline{8} \end{array}$$

from top to bottom, one can check the result by adding from bottom to top. Which of the properties discussed in this section guarantees the validity of the check?

In problems 34–39, use the Distributive Property to fill in each blank with the correct number:

34. $4(3 + 5) = (4 \cdot 3) + (4 \cdot$ _____ $)$
35. $5(6 + 7) = (5 \cdot$ _____ $) + (5 \cdot 7)$
36. $8(4 + 6) = ($ _____ $\cdot 4) + (8 \cdot 6)$
37. _____ $(2 + 5) = (3 \cdot 2) + (3 \cdot 5)$
38. $8(9 +$ _____ $) = (8 \cdot 9) + (8 \cdot 4)$
39. $7($ _____ $+ 5) = (7 \cdot 9) + (7 \cdot 5)$

40. The Taste-T Noodle Company has 3 secretaries and 6 sales representatives. If each of them makes $280 a week, the weekly payroll can be calculated by multiplying 280 by 9. It could also be calculated by first finding the total payroll for the secretaries and adding this to the total payroll for the sales representatives. Which of the properties discussed in this section guarantees that the final results will be the same?

41. A grocer found that a shelf containing canned beans held 4 layers of cans, and each layer contained 5 rows of 3 cans. He counted the cans in each row (3) and the number of rows (5) and found that he had 15 cans per layer. Then he multiplied the result by 4, and knew he had $(5 \times 3) \times 4 = 60$ cans. His son noticed that there were 4 cans in each pile. There were 3 cans in each row so each row had $4 \cdot 3 = 12$ cans. He then multiplied by the number of rows and obtained $(4 \times 3) \times 5 = 60$ cans. Which of the properties discussed in this section guarantees that the total, calculated either way, will be the same?

42. Refer to the figure below. Person A claims that there are 3 rows of 5 objects in front of him, while person B says that there are 5 rows of 3 objects in front of her. Which property discussed in this section guarantees that they both see the same total number of objects?

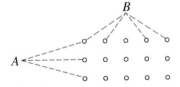

In Other Words

43. We already know that multiplication is distributive over addition. Is addition distributive over multiplication? Explain.

44. Is multiplication distributive over subtraction? That is, does $a(b - c) = (a \cdot b) - (a \cdot c)$? Explain.

45. Is subtraction distributive over multiplication? That is, does $a - (b \times c) = (a - b) \times (a - c)$? Explain.

Discovery

*As we have seen, the cardinal number of a set A is the number of elements in A and is denoted by n(A). Thus, if A = {@, #, %, &, *} and B = {a, b, c}, then n(A) = 5 and n(B) = 3. The addition of 5 and 3 can be defined using the sets A and B and noting that 5 + 3 = n(A) + n(B). Since*

$$A \cup B = \{@, \#, \%, \&, *, a, b, c\},$$

then n(A ∪ B) = 8 and n(A) + n(B) = n(A ∪ B). In general, we use the following definition:

> *If A and B are two sets such that n(A) = a, n(B) = b, and A ∩ B = ∅, then*
>
> $$a + b = n(A \cup B)$$

Note that we require A ∩ B to be empty, because, for example, if A = {x, y, z} and B = {y, z, u, v}, n(A) = 3, n(B) = 4, and n(A) + n(B) = 4 + 3 = 7. But n(A ∪ B) = n({x, y, z, u, v}) = 5; that is, n(A ∪ B) ≠ n(A) + n(B). Using these ideas, we can prove the Commutative Property of Addition for natural numbers, a + b = b + a, as follows:

> *i. Let A and B be disjoint sets such that n(A) = a and n(B) = b; that is, A has a elements and B has b elements.*
> *ii. By the above definition, a + b = n(A ∪ B).*
> *iii. By the Commutative Law for set union, A ∪ B = B ∪ A.*
> *iv. By the above definition, b + a = n(B ∪ A).*
> *v. From steps ii, iii, and iv, it follows that*
>
> $$a + b = n(A \cup B) = n(B \cup A) = b + a.$$
>
> *vi. Therefore, a + b = b + a.*

46. Can you discover the proof for the Associative Law of Addition?

*The multiplication of natural numbers can be defined in terms of sets. Thus, if you are taking three classes, x, y, and z, and there are two exams in each class, the number of exams you will have is 3 · 2 = 6. If the exams in each of the classes are identified as 1 and 2, the set of all exams will be {(x, 1), (x, 2), (y, 1), (y, 2), (z, 1), (z, 2)}, where (x, 1) denotes the first exam in class x, (x, 2) the second exam in class x, and so on. The number of elements in this set is 6. If the set of classes is A = {x, y, z} and the set of exams is B = {1, 2}, the set {(x, 1), (x, 2), (y, 1), (y, 2), (z, 1), (z, 2)} is called the **Cartesian product** of A and B and is denoted by $A \times B$. As you can see from this example, 2 · 3 = n(A) · n(B) = 6 and n(A × B) is also 6.*

47. Can you discover a definition for the product of any two natural numbers *a* and *b*?

48. Using the definition from problem 47, can you discover the proof of the Commutative Law for Multiplication?

49. Using the definition from problem 47, can you discover the proof of the Associative Law for Multiplication?

4.2   PRIME NUMBERS AND THEIR USES

GETTING STARTED

EMIRPS AND PRIMES

Do you know what an "emirp" is? It is a prime number that turns into another prime number when its digits are reversed; 13 and 31, 37 and 73 are emirps. A **prime number** is a number that has exactly two distinct factors, itself and 1. Prime numbers are used in cryptography, the encoding of secret messages. The lowest prime is 2 and the highest known prime is $391{,}581 \times 2^{216{,}193} - 1$, discovered by the "Amdahl Six" in Santa Clara, California, on August 6, 1989. Here you will learn about prime and composite numbers, factors and divisors and their uses.

Five members of the "Amdahl Six," from left to right: Sergio E. Zarantonello, B. K. Parady, Joel F. Smith (seated), Gene Ward Smith, and Landon Curt Noll

The proper divisors of a number have fascinated mathematicians as far back as the Pythagoreans, a group of scholars in ancient Greece, who actually classified numbers according to the sum of their proper divisors (all of the divisors, except the number itself). Thus, if the sum of the proper divisors is:

(a) *More* than the number, the number is *abundant* (12 and 20).
(b) *Equal* to the number, the number is *perfect* (6 and 28).
(c) *Less* than the number, the number is *deficient* (14 and 15).

You will learn more about these numbers in the Discovery section of Exercise 4.2. Can all numbers be written as a sum of primes: $10 = 5 + 5$, $18 = 11 + 7$, and $21 = 19 + 2$? (See problem 71, Exercise 4.2.) Here is another problem: 17 is prime and 19 is prime, their difference is 2. 43 is prime and 41 is prime, their difference is 2. These pairs of numbers are called **twin primes.** Are there infinitely many twin primes? Nobody knows!

How can we find if the number of primes is infinite? (See problem 9, Exercise 4.2) One way is to find a formula that generates primes. Here is one such formula: $n^2 - n + 17$. When $n = 1$, $1 - 1 + 17 = 17$, a prime number. When $n = 2$, $2^2 - 2 + 17 = 4 - 2 + 17 = 19$, a prime number. Will this formula generate primes all the time? Can you find another formula?

Suppose there are 40 students in your class and you wish to divide them into 5 equal groups. Each group will have 8 students, and no student will be left out. Thus, we say that 40 divided by 5 is exactly 8 with no remainder. In other words, 5 is an **exact divisor** of 40 or, more briefly, 5 is a **divisor** or **factor** of 40. Similarly, 63 divided by 7 is exactly 9, so 7 is a divisor or factor of 63. However, 7 is not a divisor or factor of 60, because 60 is not exactly divisible by 7.

A. *Prime and Composite Numbers*

If 40 is written as a product of factors, the product — for example, 5×8 — is called a **factorization** of 40. The 5 and the 8 are factors (divisors) of 40, and the number 40 is a **multiple** of each of these factors. Note that the 8 has divisors other than 8 and 1 (2 and 4), but the only divisors of 5 are itself and 1. We say that 5 is a prime number.

Definition 4.2

> A natural number with exactly two distinct divisors (1 and itself) is called a **prime number**, or is said to be **prime**.
> Any number with more than two distinct divisors is called a **composite number**, or is said to be **composite**.

According to Definition 4.2, 5 is a prime number but 40 and 8 are composite. Notice that the number 1 is neither prime nor composite, because it has only one divisor (itself).

In the third century B.C., the Greek mathematician Eratosthenes devised the following procedure to find prime numbers: He listed all the numbers from 2 up to a given number (say, from 2 through 50 as in Figure 4.1). He concluded that 2 is prime, but every multiple of 2 (4, 6, 8, etc.) is composite, because it is divisible by 2. He then circled 2 as a prime and crossed out all multiples of 2. Next, because 3 is prime, he circled it, and crossed out all following multiples of 3. Similarly, he circled 5 (the next prime), and crossed out its multiples. He continued this process until he reached 11. We note that all the multiples of 11 (11 · 2, 11 · 3, 11 · 4) were eliminated earlier when the multiples of 2 and 3 were crossed out. Similarly, the multiples of any prime larger than 11 also were eliminated. Hence, all the numbers left in the table are primes. Eratosthenes then circled those numbers. If the table had gone as far as 200, he would have had to continue his stepwise exclusion of composite numbers until he came to 17, the first prime whose square exceeds 200. (Can you explain why?) Because it sifts out prime numbers, the preceding method is called the **Sieve of Eratosthenes.**

	②	③	4	⑤	6	⑦	8	9	10
⑪	12	⑬	14	15	16	⑰	18	⑲	20
21	22	㉓	24	25	26	27	28	㉙	30
㉛	32	33	34	35	36	㊲	38	39	40
㊶	42	㊸	44	45	46	㊼	48	49	50

FIGURE 4.1

Note that the set of primes is not finite; that is, there is no largest prime. This fact is proved in problem 9 of Exercise 4.2.

The applications of prime numbers that we shall consider depend on a theorem that we state below without proof.

> **Fundamental Theorem of Arithmetic**
>
> Every composite number can be expressed as a unique product of primes (disregarding the order of the factors).

Thus,

$$180 = 2 \cdot 2 \cdot 3 \cdot 3 \cdot 5 = 2^2 \cdot 3^2 \cdot 5$$

and

$$92 = 2 \cdot 2 \cdot 23 = 2^2 \cdot 23$$

B. Factorization

The prime factorization of a composite number can be found by "dividing out" the prime factors of the number, starting with the smallest factor. Thus,

$$40 = 2 \cdot 20 = 2 \cdot 2 \cdot 10 = 2 \cdot 2 \cdot 2 \cdot 5 = 2^3 \cdot 5$$

and

$$63 = 3 \cdot 21 = 3 \cdot 3 \cdot 7 = 3^2 \cdot 7$$

We can write these computations using repeated division as follows:

Divide by 2 →	2	40		Divide by 3 →	3	63
Divide by 2 →	2	20		Divide by 3 →	3	21
Divide by 2 →	2	10		Divide by 7 →	7	7
Divide by 5 →	5	5				1
		1				

Reading downward, as indicated by the arrows, we get

$$40 = 2 \cdot 2 \cdot 2 \cdot 5 = 2^3 \cdot 5 \quad \text{and} \quad 63 = 3 \cdot 3 \cdot 7 = 3^2 \cdot 7$$

as before.

EXAMPLE 1   Write 1440 as a product of primes.

Solution
```
2|1440
 2|720
  2|360
   2|180
    2|90
     3|45
      3|15
       5|5
         1
```

Hence, $1440 = 2 \cdot 2 \cdot 2 \cdot 2 \cdot 2 \cdot 3 \cdot 3 \cdot 5 = 2^5 \cdot 3^2 \cdot 5$.

EXAMPLE 2   Is the number 197 prime or composite?

Solution   To answer this question, we must determine whether 197 has factors other than 1 and itself. Thus, we try dividing by the consecutive prime numbers 2, 3, 5, 7, 11, 13, ... Since 197 is not even, it is not divisible by 2. It is also not divisible by 3 or 5 or 7 or 11 or 13, as you can find by actual trial. Where do we stop?

In trying to divide 197 by 3, 5, 7, 11, and 13, you should notice that the quotient is greater than the trial divisor each time (for example, dividing 197 by 3 gives a quotient of 65). The Sieve of Eratosthenes (Figure 4.1) gives the next prime as 17. If we try to divide 197 by 17, we get a quotient (11) that is *less* than 17 and a remainder showing that 17 is not a factor of 197. Consequently, we need go no further (can you see why?), and we have shown that 197 is prime.   ■

C. *Divisibility Rules*

Finding the prime factorization of a number or determining whether the number is prime or composite may require a number of trial divisions. Some of these divisions can be avoided if we know the **divisibility rules** given in Table 4.2.

Table 4.2

Divisible By	Test	Example
2	The number ends in 0, 2, 4, 6, or 8.	345,678 ends in 8, so it is divisible by 2.
3	The sum of its digits is divisible by 3.	258 is divisible by 3, since $2 + 5 + 8 = 15$, which is divisible by 3.
5	The number ends in 0 or 5.	365 ends in 5, so it is divisible by 5.

There are other rules for divisibility by larger primes, but most people feel these rules are too complicated to bother with; it is easier to check by direct division.

EXAMPLE 3   Which of the following numbers are divisible by 2, 3, or 5?

(a) 8925   (b) 39,120   (c) 2553

Solution   (a) 8925 is not divisible by 2.

$8 + 9 + 2 + 5 = 24$, which is divisible by 3; hence 8925 is divisible by 3.

Since 8925 ends in 5, it is divisible by 5.

(b) 39,120 is divisible by 2, 3, and 5. Note that $3 + 9 + 1 + 2 = 15$, which is divisible by 3.

(c) 2553 is not divisible by 2 or 5, but is divisible by 3 because the sum of its digits is divisible by 3.   ■

Problem Solving:	**Divisibility**

How many numbers leave a remainder of 2 when divided into 50 and a remainder of 3 when divided into 63?

1. Read the problem. What do "remainder" and "divided into" mean?

3 divided into 50 means $\dfrac{50}{3}$. The answer is 16 with a remainder of 2.

2. Select the unknown.

We want to find all numbers with the property stated in the problem.

3. Think of a plan. What can you say when a number leaves a remainder of 2 when divided into 50? What about when the remainder is 3 if divided into 63?

If the remainder is 2 when the number is divided into 50, then $50 - 2 = 48$ is divisible by the number.

Similarly, $63 - 3 = 60$ is divisible by the number. Moreover, the number must be larger than 3, the larger of the two remainders.

4. Use the information to carry out the plan. We need the divisors of 48 and 60 larger than 3.

The divisors of 48 larger than 3 are:

$$48 \quad 24 \quad 16 \quad 12 \quad 8 \quad 6 \quad 4.$$

Of these, the divisors of 48 *and* 60 larger than 3 are: 12 6 4. Thus, there are exactly three numbers that meet the given condition.

5. Verify the answer.

If 12, 6, and 4, respectively, are divided into 50, the remainder is 2. If 12, 6, and 4 are divided into 63, the remainder is 3. Try it!

TRY EXAMPLE 4 NOW.

Cover the solution, write your own, and then check your work.

EXAMPLE 4

Find the smallest multiple of 5 that leaves a remainder of 2 when divided by 3 and a remainder of 6 when divided by 7.

Solution

We write all the multiples of 5 larger than 6, the larger of the two remainders, and select the ones that satisfy the two given conditions.

Multiples of 5	10	15	20	25	30	35 . . .
Remainder when divided by 3	1	0	$\boxed{2}$	1	0	2 . . .
Remainder when divided by 7	3	1	$\boxed{6}$	4	2	0 . . .

The desired number is 20.

■

D. *Greatest Common Factor*

The number 5 is the **greatest common factor** of 15 and 35. We abbreviate greatest common factor by GCF and write GCF(15, 35) = 5. A fraction a/b is said to be in **simplest form** if GCF(a, b) = 1. In this case, we say that a and b are **relatively prime.** If GCF(a, b) ≠ 1, the fraction is reduced to lowest terms by dividing a and b by their GCF. The most commonly used way of finding the GCF of a set of numbers is as follows:

> **How to Find the GCF**
>
> 1. Write the prime factorization of each number.
> 2. Select *all* the primes that occur in *all* the factorizations, applying to each such prime the smallest exponent to which it occurs.
> 3. The product of the factors selected in step 2 is the GCF of all the numbers.

It will be easier for you to see if you write the same primes in a column as in the next example.

EXAMPLE 5   Find GCF(216, 234). and then reduce $\frac{216}{234}$ to lowest terms.

Solution   **Step 1.** We write the prime factorization of each number:

$$216 = 2^3 \cdot 3^3$$
$$234 = 2 \cdot 3^2 \cdot 13$$

Pick the one with the smallest exponent in each column.

Step 2. We select the *common* prime factors with their *smallest* exponents; these factors are 2 and 3^2.

Step 3. GCF(216, 234) = $2 \cdot 3^2$ = 18.   ■

To reduce the fraction $\frac{216}{234}$ to lowest terms we divide out GCF(216, 234), which we found to be 18. Thus, we write

$$\frac{216}{234} = \frac{18 \cdot 12}{18 \cdot 13} = \frac{12}{13}$$

(Notice that you can get the 12 and the 13 from the respective prime factorization. Just use all the factors except those in the GCF.)

E. *Least Common Multiple*

A second use of prime factorization occurs in the addition of fractions, where we need to find a common denominator. For example, to add $\frac{3}{8}$ and $\frac{5}{12}$, we must first select a common denominator for the two fractions. Such a denominator is any natural number that is exactly divisible by both 8 and 12. Thus, we could use $8 \cdot 12 = 96$. However, it is usually most efficient to use the **least** (smallest) **common denominator (LCD).** In our case, we note that

$$8 = 2^3 \quad \text{and} \quad 12 = 2^2 \cdot 3.$$

To have a common multiple of 8 and 12, we must include 2^3 and 3, at the very least. Thus, we see that the LCM (least common multiple) of 8 and 12 is $2^3 \cdot 3 = 24$, so that the LCD of $\frac{3}{8}$ and $\frac{5}{12}$ is 24.

The procedure that we used to find LCM(8, 12) can be generalized to find the LCM of any two or more natural numbers.

How to Find the LCM

1. Write the prime factorization of each number.
2. Select every prime that occurs, to the highest power to which it occurs, in these factorizations.
3. The product of the factors selected in step 2 is the LCM.

EXAMPLE 6   Find LCM(18, 21, 28) and use it to add $\frac{1}{18} + \frac{1}{21} + \frac{1}{28}$.

Solution   **Step 1.**

Pick the one with the greatest exponent in each column.

$$18 = 2 \cdot 3^2$$
$$21 = \quad\; 3 \cdot 7$$
$$28 = 2^2 \quad\;\; \cdot 7$$

Step 2. We select every prime factor (not just the common factors) with the greatest exponent to which it occurs, obtaining 2^2, 3^2, and 7.

Step 3. LCM(18, 21, 28) $= 2^2 \cdot 3^2 \cdot 7 = 252$. ∎

We now use the LCM of 252 to replace the given fractions by equivalent fractions with 252 as their common denominator. To obtain these equivalents, we refer to the factored forms of the denominators and the LCM. Since the LCM is

$$252 = 2^2 \cdot 3^2 \cdot 7$$

and

$$18 = 2 \cdot 3^2$$

we have to multiply 18 by $2 \cdot 7 = 14$ to get 252. Hence, we multiply the fraction $\frac{1}{18}$ by 1 in the form $\frac{14}{14}$ to get

$$\frac{1 \times 14}{18 \times 14} = \frac{14}{252}$$

The same procedure can be used for the other two fractions.

$$\frac{1}{18} = \frac{14}{252} \qquad \frac{1}{21} = \frac{1 \times 12}{21 \times 12} = \frac{12}{252} \qquad \frac{1}{28} = \frac{1 \times 9}{28 \times 9} = \frac{9}{252}$$

Then we add:

$$\frac{1}{18} + \frac{1}{21} + \frac{1}{28} = \frac{14}{252} + \frac{12}{252} + \frac{9}{252} = \frac{14 + 12 + 9}{252} = \frac{35}{252}$$

Since $35 = 5 \times 7$ and $252 = 36 \times 7$, we can reduce the last fraction by dividing out the 7. This gives a final answer of $\frac{5}{36}$. ∎

EXAMPLE 7   Do the subtraction: $\frac{7}{24} - \frac{5}{84}$

Solution   To do this subtraction, we have to change the fractions to equivalent fractions with a common denominator. We factor the denominators to get

$$24 = 2^3 \cdot 3$$
$$84 = 2^2 \cdot 3 \cdot 7$$

Thus, the LCM is $2^3 \cdot 3 \cdot 7 = 168$. Consequently, we multiply the first fraction by $\frac{7}{7}$ and the second by $\frac{2}{2}$ to get

$$\frac{7}{24} - \frac{5}{84} = \frac{7 \cdot 7}{24 \cdot 7} - \frac{5 \cdot 2}{84 \cdot 2}$$

$$= \frac{49 - 10}{168} = \frac{39}{168} = \frac{3 \cdot 13}{3 \cdot 56} = \frac{13}{56}$$ ∎

F. *Applications*

EXAMPLE 8   A motorist on a 2500-mile trip drove 500 miles the first day, 600 miles the second day, and 750 miles the third day. What (reduced) fraction of the total distance did he drive each of these days?

Solution   First day: $\dfrac{500}{2500} = \dfrac{1 \times 500}{5 \times 500} = \dfrac{1}{5}$

Second day: $\dfrac{600}{2500} = \dfrac{6 \times 100}{25 \times 100} = \dfrac{6}{25}$

Third day: $\dfrac{750}{2500} = \dfrac{3 \times 250}{10 \times 250} = \dfrac{3}{10}$ ∎

The procedures used to find the GCF and LCM of two or more numbers are very similar. If you are asked to find the GCF *and* LCM of two numbers, you can use the procedure below, which we use to find the GCF and LCM of 42, 28, and 210.

$$
\begin{array}{c|ccc}
2 & 42 & 28 & 210 \\
7 & 21 & 14 & 105 \\
3 & 3 & ② & 15 \\
\hline
& 1 & 2 & 5
\end{array}
$$

The LCM is $2 \times 7 \times 3 \times 1 \times 2 \times 5 = 420$

Finding the GCF and LCM

1. Write the numbers in a horizontal line and divide them by a prime divisor that is common to them all.
2. Repeat the procedure with the quotients until there is no longer any common divisor.
3. The products of all the divisors in steps 1 and 2 is the GCF (in the example, $2 \times 7 = 14$).
4. Divide by a prime factor common to two or more numbers. If any of the numbers is not divisible by this prime, circle the number and carry it down to the next line.
5. The LCM is the product of all divisors in steps 1, 2, and 4 and the numbers in the final row.

Exercise 4.2

A.
1. Continue the Sieve of Eratosthenes (Figure 4.1 on page 212), and find all the primes between 50 and 100.

Use Figure 4.1 and the results of problem 1 to find how many primes there are between:

2. 1 and 25   3. 25 and 50   4. 50 and 75   5. 75 and 100

6. Refer to Figure 4.1 and find:
   (a) The smallest prime   (b) An even prime

7. Refer to Figure 4.1.
   (a) Find a pair of primes that are consecutive counting numbers.
   (b) Can there be a second pair of primes that are consecutive counting numbers? Why?

8. Primes that differ by 2 are called **twin primes.** The smallest twin primes are 3 and 5. Refer to Figure 4.1 and find two other pairs of twin primes.

9. To show that there is no largest prime, Euclid (in about 300 B.C.) gave the following *proof by contradiction:* Assume that there is a largest prime; call

it P. Now form a number, say, m, by taking the product of all the primes from 2 through P and adding 1 to the result. This gives $m = (2 \cdot 3 \cdot 5 \cdot 7 \cdot \cdots \cdot P) + 1$

(a) m is not divisible by 2. Why?
(b) m is not divisible by 3. Why?
(c) m is not divisible by 5. Why?
(d) m is not divisible by any of the primes from 2 through P. Why?
(e) m is greater than P, so cannot be a prime. Why?
(f) m cannot be a composite number. Why?

Now we have a contradiction! Since m is a natural number greater than 1, it must be either prime or composite. But if our assumption that P is the largest prime is correct, then m cannot be either prime or composite. Therefore, the assumption is invalid, and there is no largest prime.

B. In problems 10–15, find all the factors (divisors) of the given number.

| 10. 28 | 11. 50 | 12. 119 |
| 13. 128 | 14. 1365 | 15. 1001 |

In problems 16–21, find the prime factorization of the given number. If the number is prime, state so.

| 16. 24 | 17. 41 | 18. 82 |
| 19. 91 | 20. 191 | 21. 148 |

In problems 22–25, find the natural number whose prime factorization is given.

| 22. $2 \cdot 3^2 \cdot 5^2$ | 23. $2 \cdot 5 \cdot 7^2$ |
| 24. $2 \cdot 3 \cdot 5 \cdot 11$ | 25. $2^4 \cdot 3 \cdot 5^2$ |

C. In problems 26–27, determine whether the given numbers are divisible by 2, 3, or 5.

| 26. (a) 468 | (b) 580 | (c) 795 | (d) 3942 |
| 27. (a) 6345 | (b) 8280 | (c) 11,469,390 | |

28. Find the smallest whole number multiple of 4 that leaves a remainder of 1 when divided by either 5 or 7.

29. How many whole numbers leave a remainder of 1 when divided into either 23 or 45?

D. In problems 30–39, find the GCF of the given numbers. If two numbers are relatively prime, state so.

30. 14 and 210	31. 135 and 351
32. 315 and 350	33. 147 and 260
34. 368 and 80	35. 282 and 329
36. 12, 18, and 30	37. 12, 15, and 20
38. 285, 315, and 588	39. 100, 200, and 320

In problems 40–46, reduce the given fractions to lowest terms.

40. $\dfrac{80}{92}$ 41. $\dfrac{62}{88}$ 42. $\dfrac{140}{280}$

43. $\dfrac{156}{728}$ 44. $\dfrac{315}{420}$ 45. $\dfrac{96}{384}$ 46. $\dfrac{716}{4235}$

E. In problems 47–56, find the LCM of the given numbers and use it to add the fractions.

47. 15 and 55; $\dfrac{1}{15} + \dfrac{1}{55}$ 48. 17 and 136; $\dfrac{1}{17} + \dfrac{1}{136}$

49. 32 and 124; $\dfrac{3}{32} + \dfrac{1}{124}$ 50. 124 and 155; $\dfrac{3}{124} + \dfrac{1}{155}$

51. 180 and 240; $\dfrac{1}{180} + \dfrac{1}{240}$ 52. 284 and 568; $\dfrac{3}{284} + \dfrac{1}{568}$

53. 12, 18, and 30; $\dfrac{1}{12} + \dfrac{1}{18} + \dfrac{1}{30}$ 54. 12, 15, and 20; $\dfrac{1}{12} + \dfrac{1}{15} + \dfrac{1}{20}$

55. 285, 315, and 588; $\dfrac{1}{285} + \dfrac{1}{315} + \dfrac{1}{588}$

56. 100, 200, and 320; $\dfrac{1}{100} + \dfrac{1}{200} + \dfrac{1}{320}$

F. 57. A recipe for *flan* (an egg custard) calls for $2\frac{1}{2}$ cups of sugar for the mixture itself and $\frac{1}{8}$ cup of sugar for the caramel. How much sugar is needed for this recipe?

58. A Simplicity pattern calls for $\frac{3}{4}$ yd of material for the dress and $\frac{1}{8}$ yd of the same material for the collar. How much material is needed?

59. The baseboards must be installed in a room 10 ft by $9\frac{1}{4}$ ft. If the door uses $3\frac{1}{8}$ ft of space that does not require baseboard, how much baseboard is needed?

60. My house is $36\frac{1}{8}$ ft long. If I increase the length by adding another room of dimensions $10\frac{1}{4}$ ft by $10\frac{1}{4}$ ft, how long will the remodeled house be?

61. My lot is $100\frac{3}{4}$ ft wide. If the city takes an easement $16\frac{1}{8}$ ft wide off one side of the lot, what is the width of the remaining lot?

62. A cyclist traveled only $\frac{1}{6}$ of his route yesterday because of inclement weather. He decides to go $\frac{3}{8}$ of the route today and $\frac{2}{7}$ tomorrow. How much more will he have to go to finish his route the day after tomorrow?

63. A survey by the National Opinion Research Center indicated that $\frac{3}{100}$ of the workers were dissatisfied with their jobs, $\frac{1}{100}$ were a little dissatisfied, and $\frac{9}{25}$ were moderately satisfied. The rest were very satisfied. What fraction of the workers is that?

64. In a recent year, $410 billion was spent on health care in the United States. Of this amount, $\frac{1}{10}$ went for drugs, eyeglasses, and necessities; $\frac{1}{4}$ for professional services; $\frac{2}{25}$ for nursing homes; $\frac{3}{20}$ for miscellaneous; and the rest for hospital costs. What fraction of the money went for hospital costs?

65. A car depreciates an average of $\frac{1}{4}$ of its value the first year, $\frac{3}{20}$ the second, and $\frac{1}{10}$ the third. What fraction of its original value is the car worth after the third year?

66. A book store owner spent $\frac{3}{5}$ of her initial investment on bookcases, $\frac{1}{10}$ on office machines, and the rest on books. What portion of her initial investment was spent on books?

67. The operating ratios for hardware stores in the United States suggest that $\frac{3}{5}$ of their sales go to pay for merchandise, $\frac{1}{4}$ for expenses, and the rest is profit. What portion of sales is profit?

68. Do you know what is in your trash? $\frac{1}{5}$ is yard waste; $\frac{1}{10}$ is food waste; $\frac{1}{4}$ is metal, glass, and plastics; $\frac{1}{8}$ is wood, rubber, and miscellaneous. The rest is paper and cardboard, which can be recycled. What fraction of the garbage is paper and cardboard?

69. How do you use your water indoors? On the average, $\frac{3}{10}$ goes for shower and bathing, $\frac{1}{5}$ goes for laundry, $\frac{1}{20}$ is lost to leaky toilets, $\frac{3}{20}$ goes for dishwashing and faucets. Where does the rest go? Toilet flushing! What fraction of the water is used for toilet flushing?

70. Mathematicians dream of finding a formula that will yield an infinite number of primes only when natural numbers are substituted into the formula. No such formula has ever been found, but there are formulas that give a large number of primes. One such formula is $n^2 - n + 41$. This formula gives primes for all natural numbers n less than 41. For example,

    For $n = 1$, $1^2 - 1 + 41 = 41$, a prime.
    For $n = 2$, $2^2 - 2 + 41 = 4 - 2 + 41 = 43$, a prime.
    For $n = 3$, $3^2 - 3 + 41 = 9 - 3 + 41 = 47$, a prime.

    (a) What prime do you get for $n = 4$?
    (b) What prime do you get for $n = 5$?
    (c) What number do you get for $n = 41$?
    (d) Is the number obtained in part (c) prime?

71. There are many **conjectures** (unproved theories) regarding primes. One of these was transmitted to Euler in 1742 by C. Goldbach. Goldbach conjectured that every even natural number, except 2, could be written as the sum of two primes. Thus, $4 = 2 + 2$, $6 = 3 + 3$, $8 = 3 + 5$, $10 = 5 + 5$, and so on.

    (a) Write 100 as the sum of two primes.
    (b) Write 200 as the sum of two primes. [*Hint:* Look at the examples above.]

72. In 1931, the Russian mathematician Schnirelmann proved that every natural number can be written as the sum of not more than 300,000 primes. Another mathematician,. I. M. Vinogradoff, has proved that every sufficiently large natural number can be expressed as the sum of at most four primes!

    (a) Try to write 20 as the sum of three primes.
    (b) Try to write 43 as the sum of four primes.

In Other Words

73. Look at Definition 4.1 and explain why the number 1 cannot be classified either as a prime number or as a composite number.

74. In view of your explanations in problem 73, how would you classify the number 1?

75. To determine that 211 is prime, we start by trying to divide by 2, 3, 5, and 7. What is the highest prime you will have to try in order to determine that 211 is prime? Explain.

76. Explain why Euclid's proof that there is no largest prime (problem 9) also shows that the number of primes is infinite.

Using Your Knowledge

The validity of the divisibility by 3 rule can be shown by using some of the properties of the natural numbers. For example, consider the number 2853. Since $10 = 9 + 1$, $100 = 99 + 1$, and $1000 = 999 + 1$, we may write

$$2853 = 2(999 + 1) + 8(99 + 1) + 5(9 + 1) + 3$$
$$= 2 \cdot 999 + 2 + 8 \cdot 99 + 8 + 5 \cdot 9 + 5 + 3$$
$$= 2 \cdot 999 + 8 \cdot 99 + 5 \cdot 9 + (2 + 8 + 5 + 3)$$

(We have used the Distributive Property first and then the Commutative and Associative Properties of Addition.)

    Now, as you can see, the first three terms of the last expression are all divisible by 3, because 999, 99, and 9 are all divisible by 3. Thus, the number is divisible by 3 if and only if the sum of the numbers in parentheses is divisible by 3. But the numbers in parentheses are exactly the digits 2, 8, 5, and 3 of the number 2853. Since the sum of these digits is 18, which is exactly divisible by 3, the number 2853 is also divisible by 3.

    The reasoning we have used for 2853 applies to any natural number. Hence, the divisibility by 3 rule is valid.

77. If some of the digits of a number are 3's, 6's, or 9's, you can omit these in figuring the sum of the digits to check for divisibility by 3. For example, 2,963,396,607 is divisible by 3, because $2 + 7 = 9$ is divisible by 3. Explain this.

78. Is 5,376,906,391 divisible by 3?

79. The way in which we wrote

$$2853 = 2(999 + 1) + 8(99 + 1) + 5(9 + 1) + 3$$

shows that 2853 is divisible by 9 if and only if the sum of its digits is divisible by 9. Explain this.

Here are some other simple divisibility rules for the natural numbers:

Divisible By	If and Only If
4	The last two digits of the number form a number divisible by 4.
6	The number is divisible by both 2 and 3.
8	The last three digits of the number form a number divisible by 8.
9	The sum of the digits of the number is divisible by 9.
10	The number ends in 0.
12	The number is divisible by both 3 and 4.

The rule for divisibility by 8 may be obtained as follows: Consider the number 2,573,649,336. This can be written in the form 2,573,649 × 1000 + 336. Since 1000 is divisible by 8, the entire number is divisible by 8 if and only if the 336 is. Since 336 is divisible by 8, the given number is also divisible by 8. This reasoning applies to the natural numbers in general. Therefore, the rule is valid.

80. Which of the following numbers are divisible by 9? By 6?

    (a) 405   (b) 676
    (c) 7,488   (d) 309,907,452

81. Which of the following numbers are divisible by 4? By 8?

    (a) 1,436   (b) 21,408
    (c) 347,712 (d) 40,924

82. Which of the following numbers are divisible by 10? By 12?

    (a) 4,920   (b) 943
    (c) 52,341,120 (d) 60,210

Discovery

*A natural number is said to be **perfect** if the number is the sum of its proper divisors. (The **proper divisors** of a number include all its divisors except the number itself.) For example, 6 is a perfect number because the proper divisors of 6 are 1, 2, and 3, and 1 + 2 + 3 = 6.*

Some historians believe that the Pythagoreans were the first to define perfect numbers. In any event, it is certain that the Pythagoreans knew about these numbers and endowed them with mystical properties. In the ancient Greek numerology, 6 was regarded as the most beautiful of all numbers; it is not only a perfect number (equal to the sum of its proper divisors), but it is also the product of all its proper divisors: 6 = 1 × 2 × 3.

83. Can you discover why 6 is the smallest perfect number? This fact may be what led St. Augustine in about the year 400 to assert, "God created all things in 6 days because 6 is a perfect number."

84. The next perfect number after 6 is a number between 25 and 30. Can you discover what number this is?

85. The third perfect number is 496. Can you find its proper divisors and so prove that 496 is a perfect number?

86. In about the year 800, Alcuin remarked that the whole human race descended from the 8 souls of Noah's Ark, and he regarded this as imperfect. Can you discover why?

*When the sum of the proper divisors of a number is less than the number, the number is called **deficient**. For example, 4 is a deficient number because its proper divisors are 1 and 2, and 1 + 2 = 3, which is less than 4. Similarly, 7 is a deficient number, because it has only 1 as a proper divisor.*

87. If n is any prime number, can you discover whether n is a deficient number?

88. It is known that there are infinitely many prime numbers. Can you use this fact to prove that there are infinitely many deficient numbers?

Computer Corner

Do you want to see the Sieve of Eratosthenes being constructed by a computer before your very own eyes? If you type and run the Sieve of Eratosthenes Program found in the appendix Programs in BASIC, the computer will show all the numbers up to 320 first, then eliminate those divisible by 2, those divisible by 3, and so on, until only the primes that are less than 320 are left on the screen. If you want a faster program, the Prime Searcher Program will list directly all the primes up to a desired number. You'll also find The Prime Factorization Program that will factor a number as a product of primes.

On the following page we have programs that find the GCF and LCM of two numbers. There, you can also find a program that reduces fractions.

4.3   THE WHOLE NUMBERS AND THE INTEGERS

This thermometer shows one very familiar application of negative numbers

GETTING STARTED

THOSE ABSURD NUMBERS!

Look at the thermometer in the photo. It uses **zero, positive,** and **negative** numbers to measure temperature. The set $\{. . . -2, -1, 0, 1, 2 . . .\}$ is called the set of **integers** and will be studied in this section. In the twelfth century, the Chinese discovered negative numbers for counting purposes, using red rods for positive quantities and black rods for negatives. However, most mathematicians of the sixteenth and seventeenth centuries refused to accept negative numbers. In fact, Nicolas Chuquet and Michael Stifel both referred to negative numbers as **absurd** numbers. What can we do with the integers? We can add, subtract, and multiply them and get more integers. Note in particular that the set of integers is closed under subtraction. This is not true of the natural numbers that we studied earlier. Here are some other quantities that use integers for their measure:

The lowest temperature ever recorded on Earth: $-129°F$. (Vostock, Antarctica).

The income for the movie *Heaven's Gate*: $-\$57$ million.

The stock loss incurred by Ray A. Kroc on July 8, 1974: $-\$65$ million.

The lowest temperature ever recorded in the atmosphere: $-225°F$.

What about operations with integers? The solution of the next three problems involves operations with integers. The greatest temperature ranges are in Vekrhoyanks, near Siberia, where temperatures vary from $98°F$ to $-94°F$. How many degrees difference is that?

The greatest temperature variation in one day occurred in Browning, Montana, on January 23–24, 1916, when the temperature went from $44°F$ to $-56°F$. But this is not as spectacular as the most freakish rise that occurred in Spearfish, South Dakota, on January 22, 1943. On this day, the temperature rose from $-40°F$ to $45°F$ in two minutes. In each of these cases, to find the range in temperatures requires subtraction of a negative number. This section will discuss such operations with integers.

The set of natural numbers N and the operations of addition, subtraction, multiplication, and division form a **mathematical system.** We have already discussed many properties of this system, but there is one more property that leads to some interesting and important ideas.

A. *Whole Number Properties*

As you can see from the cartoon, the number 1 has the unique property that multiplication of any natural number *a* by 1 gives the number *a* again. Because the **identity** of the number *a* is preserved under multiplication by 1, the number 1 is the **multiplicative identity,** and this property is the **identity property for multiplication.**

Reprinted with special permission of King Features Syndicate, Inc.

Identity Property for Multiplication

If *a* is any natural number, then

$$a \cdot 1 = 1 \cdot a = a$$

It can be shown (problem 49, Exercise 4.3) that 1 is the only element with this property.

Is there an **additive identity**? That is, is there an element *z* such that $a + z = a$ for every *a* in *N*? There is no such element in *N*. This lack of an additive identity spoils the usefulness of *N* in many everyday applications of arithmetic. The Babylonians realized this difficulty and simply used a space between digits as a zero place-holder, but it was not until about A.D. 1400 that the Hindu-Arabic system popularized the idea of zero. The Hindus used the word *sunya* (meaning "void"), which was later adopted by the Arabs as *sifr,* or "vacant." This word passed into Latin as *zephirum* and became, over the years, zero.

The number zero (0) provides us with an **identity for addition.** Therefore, we enlarge the set *N* by adjoining to it this new element. The set consisting of all the natural numbers and the number 0, that is, the set {0, 1, 2, 3, . . .}, is called the set of **whole numbers** and is denoted by the letter *W*. It is an important basic assumption that the set *W* obeys the same fundamental laws of arithmetic as do the natural numbers. Moreover, adding 0 to a whole number does not change the identity of the whole number. Thus, we have the following:

> **Identity Property for Addition**
>
> If a is any whole number, then
>
> $$0 + a = a \qquad \text{and} \qquad a + 0 = a$$

As with the number 1, we can prove (problem 50, Exercise 4.3) that the number 0 is unique. It also can be shown that if a is any natural number, then

$$a - 0 = a, \qquad 0 \cdot a = 0, \quad \text{and} \quad 0 \div a = \frac{0}{a} = 0$$

The proofs for these facts are in problems 51–53, Exercise 4.3. Note that $a \div 0$ is **not** defined.

The importance of 0 is also evident in algebra. When solving an equation such as

$$(x - 1)(x - 2) = 0$$

we argue that either $x - 1 = 0$ or else $x - 2 = 0$, and conclude that $x = 1$ or $x = 2$. This argument is based on the following theorem:

Theorem 4.1

> If $a \cdot b = 0$, then $a = 0$ or $b = 0$.

Proof Assume that $a \neq 0$. Divide both sides by a:

$$\frac{a \cdot b}{a} = \frac{0}{a} = 0$$

Since

$$\frac{a \cdot b}{a} = b$$

then $b = 0$.

A similar argument shows that if $b \neq 0$, then $a = 0$. Of course, if a and b are both 0, the theorem is obviously true. ∎

B. *The Set of Integers*

The set W is extremely useful when the idea of "How many?" is involved. However, the whole numbers are inadequate even for some simple everyday problems. For instance, the below-zero temperature on a winter's day cannot be described by a whole number, and the simple equation $x + 3 = 0$ has no solution in W. Because similar problems occur repeatedly in the applications of mathematics, the set of whole numbers is extended to include the **negative numbers,** $-1, -2, -3, \ldots$. This new set, called the set of **integers,** is denoted by the letter I, so that $I = \{\ldots, -3, -2, -1, 0, 1, 2, 3, \ldots\}$. Note that the set I consists of three subsets:

1. The **positive integers:** 1, 2, 3, . . .
2. The number **0**
3. The **negative integers:** $-1, -2, -3, \ldots$

We make the important assumption that the set I obeys the same basic laws of arithmetic as do the natural numbers. However, some of the properties of the set I must be examined more closely. First, you must realize that with the set I, an important concept has been added to the idea of a number, the concept of *direction.*

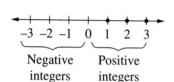

Negative integers   Positive integers

FIGURE 4.2

A **number line** offers a good representation for this concept. Thus, we draw a horizontal straight line, choose any point on it, and label that point 0. We then measure successive equal intervals to the right and to the left of 0 (see Figure 4.2). The endpoints of the intervals to the right of 0 are labeled with the positive integers in order $1, 2, 3, \ldots$. Those to the left of 0 are labeled with the negative integers in order $-1, -2, -3, \ldots$. The resulting picture is called a number line. Note that the number line continues indefinitely in the positive (right) and negative (left) directions. We graph the integers 1, 2, and 3 by adding dots to the number line, as shown in Figure 4.2.

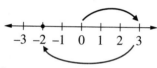

FIGURE 4.3

We can give a physical interpretation of addition using the number line. For example, $3 + 2$ may be regarded as a move of 3 units from 0 in the positive direction (right) followed by a move of 2 units more in the positive direction (right). The terminal point is 5. Similarly, $3 + (-5)$ may be interpreted as a move of 3 units in the positive direction followed by a move of 5 units in the negative direction (left). The terminal point is -2 (see Figure 4.3). Thus

$$3 + (-5) = -2$$

Using the same idea,

$$3 + (-3) = 0$$

Note that the numbers 3 and -3 are the **same distance** from 0 on the number line, but in **opposite directions.** Thus, 3 and -3 are **opposites.** Similarly, 5 and -5, and -12 and 12 are opposites. This fact can be easily verified, since $5 + (-5) = 0$ and $(-12) + 12 = 0$. Because of this, 5 and -5, and -12 and 12 are also known as **additive inverses.** This discussion can be summarized as follows:

Additive Inverse Property

If n is any integer, then there exists an integer $-n$ such that

$$n + (-n) = 0 \qquad \text{and} \qquad (-n) + n = 0$$

n and $-n$ are said to be **additive inverses (opposites)** of each other.

It can be proved (see problem 54, Exercise 4.3) that each integer has exactly one additive inverse.

The operation of subtraction can also be represented on the number line. For instance, $3 - 5$ may be thought of as a move of 3 units from 0 in the positive (right) direction, followed by a move of 5 units in the negative (left) direction. The terminal point is -2. Thus, we have $3 - 5 = -2$. Notice that this is the same result we found for $3 + (-5)$ (see Figure 4.3); that is,

$$3 - 5 = 3 + (-5)$$

The minus sign is used in two different ways in this last equation: On the left side of the equal sign, it means to subtract 5 from 3; on the right, it means that -5 is the integer 5 units in the negative direction from 0.

EXAMPLE 1   Illustrate the subtraction $-3 - (-4)$ on the number line.

Solution   This subtraction may be considered as a move of 3 units to the left of 0, followed by a move of 4 units to the right (in the opposite direction from that indicated by the -4). The terminal point is 1 unit to the right of 0, as indicated in the figure, so we have $-3 - (-4) = 1$. Notice that this is the same result as $-3 + 4 = 1$.

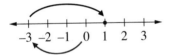

This discussion should convince you that subtraction may be viewed as the opposite of addition, and any subtraction problem can be transformed into an addition problem, as shown next.

Subtraction Problem	Equivalent Addition Problem
$3 - 1$	$3 + (-1)$
$10 - 7$	$10 + (-7)$
$-3 - 5$	$-3 + (-5)$
$2 - (-3)$	$2 + 3$

This motivates the following definition:

Definition of Subtraction

If a and b are any integers, the **subtraction** of b from a is defined as

$$a - b = a + (-b)$$

This means that subtracting b from a is the same as adding the inverse (opposite) of b to a.

EXAMPLE 2   Change the subtraction problem $4 - 3$ to an equivalent addition problem and illustrate on the number line.

Solution   By the above definition, $4 - 3 = 4 + (-3)$. On the number line, we think of this as a move of 4 units to the right, followed by a move of 3 units to the left. The result, as shown in the figure, is 1.

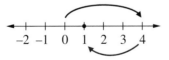

We assume that the reader is familiar with the operations of addition and subtraction of integers. However, the rules for the multiplication of integers usually have been memorized without any attempt to see or understand their development. We now give these results and prove one of them.

1. The product of two positive integers is positive.
2. The product of a positive integer and a negative integer is negative.
3. The product of two negative integers is positive.

Table 4.3 summarizes these results. Note that the product of integers with *like* signs is *positive*; with *unlike* signs the product is *negative*.

Table 4.3

Rule of Signs in Multiplication	Example
1. Positive × Positive = Positive	$4 \times 3 = 12$
2. Positive × Negative = Negative	$4 \times (-3) = -12$
3. Negative × Negative = Positive	$(-4) \times (-3) = 12$

Problem Solving:	**Signed Number Properties**
	If n is a negative odd integer, what kind of number is $(n - 2)^3$?
1. Read the problem. What are the negative odd integers?	The negative odd integers are: $-1, -3, -5, \ldots$
2. Select the unknown.	We want to know what type of number is $(n - 2)^3$.
3. Think of a plan. What kind of number is $n - 2$? Try it when n is $-1, -3, -5$, and so on. What does $(n - 2)^3$ mean?	If n is a negative odd integer, n can be $-1, -3, -5 \ldots$. Thus, $n - 2$ can be $-3, -5, -7 \ldots$; that is $n - 2$ is also a negative odd integer. $(n - 2)^3$ means $(n - 2)(n - 2)(n - 2)$.

4. Use the laws of signs to carry out the plan.

If $(n - 2)$ is negative, $(n - 2)(n - 2)$ is positive $[(-) \times (-) = (+)]$ and $(n - 2)(n - 2)(n - 2)$ is negative. $[(-) \times (-) \times (-) = (-)]$ Thus, $(n - 2)^3$ is a negative odd integer.

5. Verify the answer. Take some examples and see if it works.

If $n = -1$. Then $n - 2 = -1 - 2 = -3$ and $(-3)^3 = (-3)(-3)(-3) = -27$, which is a negative odd integer.

TRY EXAMPLE 3 NOW.

Cover the solution, write your own, and then check your work.

EXAMPLE 3

If n is a negative even integer, what kind of number is $(n + 1)^3$?

Solution

If n is a negative even integer, n can be $-2, -4, -6, \ldots$. Thus, $n + 1$ can be $-1, -3, -5, \ldots$; that is, $n + 1$ is a negative odd integer. Now,

$$(n + 1)^3 = (n + 1)(n + 1)(n + 1)$$
$$(-) \quad (-) \quad (-)$$

which is a negative odd integer. So $(n + 1)^3$ is a negative odd integer. ∎

The next theorem illustrates the way in which we can prove the rule of signs.

Theorem 4.2

If a and b are positive, then

$$(a) \quad \times \quad (-b) \quad = \quad -(ab)$$
Positive   Negative   Negative

Before proceeding with the proof, we note that in Theorem 4.2, a is a positive number, $-b$ is negative (because b is positive), $a \cdot b$ is positive (by property 1), and hence, $-(ab)$ is negative. Thus, Theorem 4.2 states that a positive number (a) times a negative number $(-b)$ yields a negative number $-(ab)$.

Proof

i. $b + (-b) = 0$ — Definition of inverse

ii. $a[b + (-b)] = a \cdot 0 = 0$ — Multiplying both sides of the equation by a and recalling that $a \cdot 0 = 0$

iii. $a \cdot b + a(-b) = 0$ — Distributive Law

iv. By step iii, the additive inverse of $a \cdot b$ is $a(-b)$, but because $a \cdot b$ is positive, its additive inverse is also $-(ab)$.

v. However, the additive inverse of a number is unique, so we conclude that $a(-b) = -(ab)$. ∎

We now summarize the properties of the integers under the operations of addition and multiplication.

Properties of Addition

1. The integers are closed with respect to addition. (The sum of any two integers a and b is always an integer.)
2. The integers are commutative with respect to addition. (For any two integers a and b, $a + b = b + a$.)
3. The integers are associative with respect to addition. [For any three integers a, b, and c, $a + (b + c) = (a + b) + c$.]
4. The integers have a unique identity (the number 0) for addition. ($a + 0 = a$ and $0 + a = a$.)
5. Each integer has a unique additive inverse. [$a + (-a) = 0$.]

Properties of Multiplication

1. The integers are closed with respect to multiplication. (The product of two integers a and b is always an integer.)
2. The integers are commutative with respect to multiplication. (For any two integers a and b, $a \cdot b = b \cdot a$.)
3. The integers are associative with respect to multiplication. [For any three integers a, b, and c, $a \cdot (b \cdot c) = (a \cdot b) \cdot c$.]
4. The integers have a unique identity (the number 1) for multiplication. ($1 \cdot a = a$ and $a \cdot 1 = a$.)
5. Not all the integers have multiplicative inverses. For example, the multiplicative inverse for 3 would be a number b such that $3 \cdot b = 1$. But there is no such integer as b.

Besides these properties, the integers have the distributive property of multiplication over addition. Thus,

$$a(b + c) = ab + ac \quad \text{and} \quad (a + b)c = ac + bc$$

C. Order of Operations

Suppose you wish to evaluate the expression $8 - 3 \times 5$. Which evaluation is correct?

$$8 - 3 \times 5 = 5 \times 5 = 25 \quad \text{or} \quad 8 - 3 \times 5 = 8 - 15 = -7$$

In this example, -7 is the correct evaluation. To avoid this sort of ambiguity, there is an agreed and established order in which operations are to be per-

You can remember the order of operations if you remember
Please
 Excuse
  My **D**ear
   Aunt **S**ally

formed. In such calculations, we always use the following order of operations:

1. Evaluate quantities inside **p**arentheses.
2. Do all **e**xponentiations.
3. Do all **m**ultiplications and **d**ivisions in order from left to right.
4. Do all **a**dditions and **s**ubtractions in order from left to right.

EXAMPLE 4   Evaluate $7 \times 8 \div 4 \times 10^2 - 3(-5 + 2) \times 10^3$.

Solution $7 \times 8 \div 4 \times 10^2 - 3(-5 + 2) \times 10^3$

Step 1. $= 7 \times 8 \div 4 \times 10^2 - 3(-3) \times 10^3$

Step 2. $= 7 \times 8 \div 4 \times 100 - 3(-3) \times 1000$

Step 3. $= 56 \div 4 \times 100 - (-9) \times 1000$

$= 14 \times 100 - (-9000)$

$= 1400 - (-9000)$

Step 4. $= 1400 + 9000 = 10{,}400$ ∎

Exercise 4.3

A. In problems 1–4, graph the indicated set of numbers.

1. The integers between 4 and 9, inclusive
2. The integers between −5 and 6, inclusive
3. The whole numbers between −2 and 5, inclusive
4. The natural (counting) numbers between −2 and 4, inclusive

In problems 5–8, find the additive inverse of the given number.

5. 3   6. 47   7. −8   8. −1492

B. In problems 9–16, illustrate on the number line the indicated operation.

9. $4 - 5$ 10. $-3 - 2$ 11. $4 - 2$ 12. $3 + 4$
13. $-5 + 4$ 14. $4 - 4$ 15. $3 + (-5)$ 16. $5 + (-2)$

In problems 17–28, write each problem as an equivalent addition problem and find the answer.

17. $3 - 8$ 18. $8 - 3$ 19. $3 - 4$ 20. $-3 - 4$
21. $-5 - 2$ 22. $-3 - 5$ 23. $5 - (-6)$ 24. $6 - (-3)$
25. $-3 - (-4)$ 26. $-5 - (-6)$ 27. $-5 - (-3)$ 28. $-10 - (-5)$

In problems 29–34, find each product.

29. (a) $(-5) \times 3$ (b) $(-8) \times 9$

30. (a) $(-3) \times (-4)$ (b) $(-9) \times (-3)$

31. (a) $4 \times (-5)$ (b) $3 \times (-13)$

32. (a) $0 \times (-4)$ (b) $(-0) \times 0$

33. (a) $3 \times (4) \times (-5)$ (b) $5 \times (-4) \times (3)$

34. (a) $-2 \times (-3) \times (-1)$ (b) $-4 \times (-5) \times (-7)$

35. If n is a negative odd integer, what kind of a number is $(n - 1)^3$?

36. If n is a positive odd integer, what kind of a number is $(n + 1)^5$?

C. In problems 37–46, perform the indicated operations.

37. (a) $-3(4 + 5)$ (b) $-4(4 - 5)$

38. (a) $-2(-3 + 1)$ (b) $-5(-4 + 2)$

39. (a) $-5 + (-5 + 1)$ (b) $-8 + (-2 + 5)$

40. (a) $-2(4 - 8) - 9$ (b) $-3(5 - 7) - 11$

41. $(-2 - 4)(-3) - 8(5 - 4)$

42. $(-3 - 5)(-2) + 8(3 + 4 - 5)$

43. $6 \times 2 \div 3 + 6 \div 2 \times (-3)$

44. $8 \div 2 \times 4 - 8 \times 2 \div 4$

45. $4 \times 9 \div 3 \times 10^3 - 2 \times 10^2$

46. $5 \times (-2) \times 3^2 + 6 \div 3 \times 5 \times 3^2$

47. The highest point on Earth is Mount Everest, 9 km above sea level. The lowest point is the Marianas Trench, 11 km below sea level. Use signed numbers to find the difference in altitude between these two points.

48. Julius Caesar died in 44 B.C. Nero is said to have set Rome afire in A.D. 64. Use signed numbers to find how many years elapsed between Caesar's death and the burning of Rome.

49. Supply reasons for steps 1, 3, and 4 in the following proof by contradiction that 1 is the unique multiplicative identity: Suppose there is another multiplicative identity, say, m, possibly different from 1. Then for every element a of N:

Step 1. $m \cdot a = a$
Step 2. $m \cdot 1 = 1$ Substituting 1 for a
Step 3. $m \cdot 1 = m$
Step 4.   Therefore, $m = 1$.

50. Fill in the blanks in the following proof that 0 is the unique additive identity: Assume that there are two additive identity elements, say, 0 and z. Then:
    (a) $0 + z = z$, because 0 is an additive _____ .
    (b) $0 + z = 0$, because z is an additive _____ .
    (c) Therefore, $z = 0$, because they are both equal to _____ .
    This shows that the assumed two identity elements are the same; that is, 0 is the unique additive identity.

51. Supply reasons for steps 1, 3, and 5 in the following proof that $a - 0 = a$:

    Step 1. $a - 0 = a + (-0)$

    Step 2. $= [a + (-0)] + 0$ Because 0 is the additive identity

    Step 3. $= a + [(-0) + 0]$

    Step 4. $= a + 0$ Because 0 and -0 are additive inverses of each other

    Step 5. $= a$

52. Fill in the blanks in the following proof that $0 \cdot a = 0$:
    (a) $0 \cdot a = [1 + (-1)] \cdot a$ Because 1 and -1 are _____ inverses
    (b) $= 1 \cdot a + (-1) \cdot a$ By the _____ property
    (c) $= a + (-a)$ Multiplying and using the rule of signs
    (d) $= 0$ Because a and $-a$ are _____

53. Fill in the blanks in the following proof that for $a \neq 0, \dfrac{0}{a} = 0$:

    (a) Let the quotient $\dfrac{0}{a} = q$. Then by the definition of division, $q \cdot a = 0$.
    (b) $q \cdot a + a = 0 + a$ by _____ to both sides.
    (c) $q \cdot a + a = a$, because 0 is the additive _____ .
    (d) $q \cdot 1 + 1 = 1$ by dividing both sides by a.
    (e) Therefore, $q + 1 = 1$, because $q \cdot 1 =$ _____ .
    (f) Consequently, $q = 0$, because the additive _____ is _____ .

54. Fill in the blanks in the following proof that each integer has only one additive inverse, $-n$: Suppose that the integer n has another such inverse, say, x. Then because $n + (-n) = 0$,
    (a) $x = x + [n + (-n)]$ 0 is the _____ identity.
    (b) $= (x + n) + (-n)$ _____ law of addition
    (c) $= (n + x) + (-n)$ _____ law of addition
    (d) $= 0 + (-n)$ x was assumed to be an additive inverse of n.
    (e) $= -n$ 0 is the _____ .

55. Supply reasons for steps 1, 3, and 5 in the following alternative proof that $a \cdot 0 = 0$:

Step 1. $0 + 0 = 0$

Step 2. $a \cdot (0 + 0) = a \cdot 0$ Multiplying both sides by a

Step 3. The left side,
$$a \cdot (0 + 0) = a \cdot 0 + a \cdot 0$$

Step 4. Therefore,
$$a \cdot 0 + a \cdot 0 = a \cdot 0$$ Substituting from step 3 into step 2

Step 5. Hence, $a \cdot 0 = 0$.

56. Supply reasons for steps 1, 3, 4, and 6 in the following proof that $(-a)(-b) = ab$:

Step 1. $a + (-a) = 0$

Step 2. $[a + (-a)](-b) = 0$ Multiplying both sides by $(-b)$ and using $0 \cdot (-b) = 0$

Step 3. $(a)(-b) + (-a)(-b) = 0$

Step 4. $(a)(-b) = -ab$

Step 5. $-ab + (-a)(-b) = 0$ Substituting from step 4 into step 3

Step 6. Hence, $(-a)(-b)$ is the additive inverse of $-ab$.

Step 7. Therefore, $(-a)(-b) = ab$.   The additive inverse of a number is unique.

*I*n Other Words

57. Write in your own words, the rule of signs:

Positive $\times$ Positive = Positive

58. Write in your own words, the rule of signs:

Positive $\times$ Negative = Negative

59. Write in your own words, the rule of signs:

Negative $\times$ Negative = Positive

60. Two numbers having the *same* sign are said to have *like* signs. If two numbers have *different* signs, they have *unlike* signs. Use the words *like* and *unlike* to summarize the rules of signs given in Table 4.3.

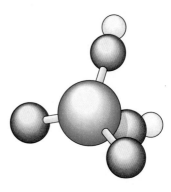

A sulfuric acid molecule

Using Your Knowledge

The oxidation number (or valence) of a molecule is found by using the oxidation numbers of the atoms present in the molecule. For example, the oxidation number of hydrogen (H) is +1, that of sulfur (S) is +6, and that of oxygen (O) is −2. Thus, we can get the oxidation number of sulfuric acid (H_2SO_4) as follows:

$$H_2SO_4$$

$$2(+1) + (+6) + 4(-2) = 2 + 6 - 8 = 0$$

Use this idea to find the oxidation number of:

61. Phosphate, PO_4, if the oxidation number of phosphorus (P) is +5 and that of oxygen (O) is −2.
62. Sodium dichromate, $Na_2Cr_2O_7$, if the oxidation number of sodium (Na) is +1, that of chromium (Cr) is +6, and that of oxygen (O) is −2
63. Baking soda, $NaHCO_3$, if the oxidation number of sodium (Na) is +1, that of hydrogen (H) is +1, that of carbon (C) is +4, and that of oxygen (O) is −2

Discovery

***Nomographs** are graphs that can be drawn to perform various numerical operations. For example, the nomograph in the figure can be used to do addition and subtraction. To add any two numbers, we locate one of the numbers on the lower scale and the other number on the upper scale. We then connect these by a straight line. The point where the line crosses the middle scale gives the result of the addition. The figure shows the sum −2 + 4 = 2.*

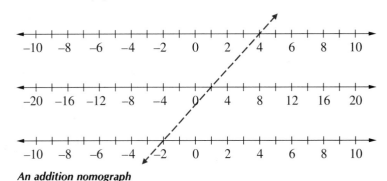

An addition nomograph

64. Can you discover how to subtract on a nomograph?

Calculator Corner

*Most scientific calculators perform operations in **algebraic order;** that is, they perform multiplications and divisions first, followed by additions and subtractions. Thus, if you enter* ⌑3⌑⌑+⌑⌑5⌑⌑×⌑⌑2⌑⌑=⌑ *in an algebraic calculator, the answer is 13. (If you do not get this answer, you have to multiply 5 × 2 first and*

*then add 3 to the result.) Of course, if you have an expression such as
−3(−5 + 2), remember that the parentheses represent an indicated multiplication. Thus, you must enter this expression as*

$$\boxed{-}\ \boxed{3}\ \boxed{\times}\ \boxed{(}\ \boxed{-}\ \boxed{5}\ \boxed{+}\ \boxed{2}\ \boxed{)}\ \boxed{=}$$

Practice this concept by evaluating the expression from Example 3 on your calculator:

$$7 \times 8 \div 4 \times 10^2 - 3(-5 + 2) \times 10^3$$

(Recall that $10^2 = 10 \times 10$ and $10^3 = 10 \times 10 \times 10$.)

1. Use your calculator to check the answers to problems 43, 45, and 46 in Exercise 4.3.

4.4   THE RATIONAL NUMBERS

GETTING STARTED

ON PYRAMIDS AND BASKETBALL

The picture shows the great pyramid at Giza, erected about 2600 B.C. by Khufu, whom the Greeks called Cheops. The Greek historian Herodotus claimed that the ratio $\frac{b}{a}$, where b is one half of the base and a is the altitude of one of the face triangles, is the Golden Ratio,

$$\frac{\sqrt{5} - 1}{2}$$

an irrational number that can be approximated by 0.6180339 . . . . How close were the Egyptians to this ratio? Actual measurements show that $b = 377.89$ ft and $a = 611.85$ ft. Substituting in $\frac{b}{a}$ will tell you how close!

*In Egypt, near Cairo, an old man stops to pray near the Great
Pyramid at Giza*

Here is a more modern application of ratios. During the 1953–1954 basketball season the NBA had a problem with the game: it was boring! Fans wanted plenty of action, shooting, and scoring, but if a team had an early lead, their best ball handler would dribble in the backcourt until he was fouled. How could the game be speeded up? Danny Biasone, the owner of an obscure team from upstate New York called the Syracuse Nationals, thought that more shots could be encouraged by limiting the time a team could have the ball. But how many seconds should be allowed between shots? He figured out that in a fast-paced game a team would take about 60 shots during the 48 minutes the game lasted (4 quarters of 12 minutes each). He then looked at the ratio:

$$\frac{\text{seconds}}{\text{shots}}$$

Now, the number of shots for both teams combined would be 2×60, and the number of seconds in each game is 48×60. Thus, the ratio becomes

$$\frac{\text{seconds}}{\text{shots}} = \frac{48 \times 60}{2 \times 60} = \frac{24}{1}$$

and now you know how the 24-second shot clock was born!

In this section we shall study the rational numbers, numbers that can be written in the form $\frac{a}{b}$ where a and b are integers, and the operations that can be performed using these numbers.

In Section 4.3 we extended the set of natural numbers and obtained the set of integers. As we saw, in studying multiplication of integers, not all the integers have multiplicative inverses; for instance, there is no integer b such that $3 \cdot b = 1$. Just as the lack of an additive identity and additive inverses impairs the usefulness of the set of natural numbers, so does the lack of multiplicative inverses impair the usefulness of the set of integers.

A. *Rational Numbers*

The difficulty lies in the fact that the set of integers is not closed under division; division of two integers can produce fractions such as $\frac{3}{4}$, $\frac{5}{7}$, $\frac{8}{3}$, and so on. Thus, we extend the system of integers to include such fractions and call the resulting system the set of **rational numbers.** The set of rational numbers is symbolized by the letter Q. (Note that a common fraction is often called a *ratio;* hence the name rational numbers.)

Definition 4.3

A **rational number** is a number that can be put in the form

$$\frac{a}{b}$$

where a and b are integers and $b \neq 0$

Thou shalt not divide by zero

Cartoon by Paul Kicklighter

Here are some important facts about rational numbers:

1. Every integer is a rational number, because the integers can be written in the form $\ldots, -\frac{2}{1}, -\frac{1}{1}, \frac{0}{1}, \frac{1}{1}, \frac{2}{1}, \ldots$.

2. The integer a in Definition 4.3 is called the **numerator,** and the integer b is called the **denominator.**

3. The restriction $b \neq 0$ is a necessary one. By the definition of division, if $a/b = c$, then $a = bc$. So, if $b = 0$, this means that $a = 0$. Thus, if $a \neq 0$, then the attempted division by 0 leads to a contradiction. If $a = 0$, then the equation $0 = 0 \cdot c$ is true for every number c; that is, the quotient c is not uniquely defined. The only way to avoid this dilemma is to **forbid division by 0.**

4. Definition 4.3 includes the words "a number that *can* be put in the form a/b, where a and b are integers and $b \neq 0$." Why couldn't we say "a number of the form a/b, where a and b are integers and $b \neq 0$"? To answer this question, consider the number $0.333 \ldots$. This number is *not* of the form a/b, but because $0.333 \ldots = \frac{1}{3}$, it *can* be put in the form a/b, where $a = 1$ and $b = 3$. Similarly, $1\frac{3}{4}$ is not of the form a/b. But because $1\frac{3}{4} = \frac{7}{4}$, the number *can* be put in the form a/b, where $a = 7$ and $b = 4$. From this discussion we may conclude that $0.333 \ldots$ and $1\frac{3}{4}$ are rational numbers.

How do we recognize the fact that $\frac{1}{3}$ and $\frac{3}{9}$ represent the same rational number? To do this we need to define equality of rational numbers.

Definition 4.4

$$\frac{a}{b} = \frac{c}{d} \qquad \text{if and only if} \qquad ad = bc$$

Thus, $\frac{1}{3} = \frac{3}{9}$ because $1 \cdot 9 = 3 \cdot 3$, and $\frac{1}{8} = \frac{4}{32}$ because $1 \cdot 32 = 8 \cdot 4$. Using Definition 4.4, we can prove the following useful result:

Theorem 4.3

$$\frac{a}{b} = \frac{ak}{bk} \qquad k \neq 0$$

Proof $\frac{a}{b} = \frac{ak}{bk}$ if and only if $a(bk) = b(ak)$ By Definition 4.4

But this equality is true, because we can use the associative and commutative laws of multiplication for the integers to show that $a(bk) = b(ak)$. ∎

Theorem 4.3 enables us to reduce $\frac{4}{6}$ by writing $\frac{4}{6} = (2 \cdot 2)/(3 \cdot 2)$ and "canceling" the 2's to obtain $\frac{4}{6} = \frac{2}{3}$. The theorem also assures us that if we multiply the numerator and denominator of a fraction by the same nonzero number k, the fraction is unchanged in value. Thus,

$$\frac{1}{2} = \frac{1 \cdot 2}{2 \cdot 2} = \frac{2}{4} \quad \text{and} \quad \frac{1}{8} = \frac{1 \cdot 3}{8 \cdot 3} = \frac{3}{24}$$

EXAMPLE 1   Use Theorem 4.3 to reduce $\frac{10}{30}$.

Solution $\frac{10}{30} = \frac{1 \cdot 10}{3 \cdot 10} = \frac{1}{3}$

EXAMPLE 2   Using Theorem 4.3, find a rational number with a denominator of 12 and equal to $\frac{5}{6}$.

Solution $\frac{5}{6} = \frac{5 \cdot 2}{6 \cdot 2} = \frac{10}{12}$

B. *Operations with Rational Numbers*

We now define the operations of addition, subtraction, multiplication, and division of rational numbers.

Definition 4.5

The **product** of two rational number a/b and c/d is defined by

$$\frac{a}{b} \cdot \frac{c}{d} = \frac{ac}{bd}$$

Thus,

$$\frac{2}{7} \cdot \frac{3}{5} = \frac{2 \cdot 3}{7 \cdot 5} = \frac{6}{35}$$

Definition 4.6

The **sum** of two rational numbers a/b and c/d is defined as

$$\frac{a}{b} + \frac{c}{d} = \frac{ad + bc}{bd}$$

For example,

$$\frac{2}{7} + \frac{3}{5} = \frac{(2 \cdot 5) + (7 \cdot 3)}{7 \cdot 5} = \frac{10 + 21}{35} = \frac{31}{35}$$

We can arrive at this definition by noting that

$$\frac{a}{b} = \frac{ad}{bd} \qquad \text{and} \qquad \frac{c}{d} = \frac{bc}{bd}$$

by Theorem 4.3. We then write

$$\frac{a}{b} + \frac{c}{d} = \frac{ad}{bd} + \frac{bc}{bd}$$

$$= \frac{ad + bc}{bd} \qquad \text{The fractions have a common denominator.}$$

[*Note:* If $d = b$, it is easy to show that Definition 4.6 gives

$$\frac{a}{b} + \frac{c}{b} = \frac{a + c}{b}$$

as we should expect.]

Definition 4.7

The **difference** of two rational numbers a/b and c/d is defined as

$$\frac{a}{b} - \frac{c}{d} = \frac{a}{b} + \frac{-c}{d} = \frac{ad - bc}{bd}$$

Thus,

$$\frac{1}{3} - \frac{1}{4} = \frac{1}{3} + \frac{-1}{4} = \frac{(1 \cdot 4) - (3 \cdot 1)}{3 \cdot 4} = \frac{4 - 3}{12} = \frac{1}{12}$$

Now suppose that we want to do the addition $\frac{3}{4} + \frac{1}{16}$. Using Definition 4.7, we proceed as follows:

$$\frac{3}{4} + \frac{1}{16} = \frac{(3 \cdot 16) + (4 \cdot 1)}{4 \cdot 16} = \frac{48 + 4}{64} = \frac{52}{64} = \frac{13}{16}$$

However, it is easier to use the fact that

$$\frac{3}{4} = \frac{3 \cdot 4}{4 \cdot 4} = \frac{12}{16}$$

and thus,

$$\frac{3}{4} + \frac{1}{16} = \frac{12}{16} + \frac{1}{16} = \frac{13}{16}$$

The number 16 is the **least common denominator (LCD)** of $\frac{3}{4}$ and $\frac{1}{16}$. Recall from Section 4.2 that this number is the LCM of the given denominators, so it can be obtained by following the procedure discussed in Section 4.2. The next example illustrates the use of this idea.

EXAMPLE 3   Perform the addition: $\frac{3}{8} + \frac{7}{36}$.

Solution   We first find the LCM of 8 and 36 by using the procedure given in Section 4.2:

$$\begin{array}{l} 8 = 2^3 \\ \underline{36 = 2^2 \cdot 3^2} \\ \text{LCM} = 2^3 \cdot 3^2 = 72 \end{array}$$

As you can see, LCM(8, 36) = 72. Thus,

$$\frac{3}{8} = \frac{3 \cdot 9}{8 \cdot 9} = \frac{27}{72} \qquad \text{and} \qquad \frac{7}{36} = \frac{7 \cdot 2}{36 \cdot 2} = \frac{14}{72}$$

so that

$$\frac{3}{8} + \frac{7}{36} = \frac{27}{72} + \frac{14}{72} = \frac{41}{72}$$

■

To define division, we introduce the idea of a *reciprocal*.

Definition 4.8

The **reciprocal** of a rational number $\frac{a}{b}$ is $\frac{b}{a}$, where $a \neq 0$ and $b \neq 0$.

Note that

$$\frac{a}{b} \cdot \frac{b}{a} = 1$$

Thus, the product of any nonzero rational number and its reciprocal is 1. For this reason, the reciprocal of a rational number is also called its **multiplicative inverse**.

EXAMPLE 4   Find the reciprocal of:

(a) $\frac{1}{3}$ (b) $-\frac{3}{4}$ (c) $1\frac{3}{8}$

Solution   (a) The reciprocal of $\frac{1}{3}$ is $\frac{3}{1} = 3$.

(b) The reciprocal of $-\frac{3}{4}$ is $-\frac{4}{3}$. Note that $(-\frac{3}{4})(-\frac{4}{3}) = (-1)(-1)(\frac{3}{4})(\frac{4}{3}) = 1$.

(c) We first write $1\frac{3}{8}$ in the form a/b. Because $1\frac{3}{8} = \frac{11}{8}$, the reciprocal of $1\frac{3}{8}$ is $\frac{8}{11}$.

■

Note: The reciprocal of any negative rational number can be handled as in part (b) of Example 4. This shows that the reciprocal of a negative number is always negative.

Definition 4.9

The **quotient** of two rational numbers a/b and c/d is defined as

$$\frac{a}{b} \div \frac{c}{d} = \frac{a}{b} \cdot \frac{d}{c} \qquad c \neq 0$$

Briefly, we say, "Invert the divisor and multiply." Thus,

$$\frac{1}{3} \div \frac{2}{7} = \frac{1}{3} \cdot \frac{7}{2} = \frac{7}{6} \qquad \text{and} \qquad \frac{4}{5} \div \frac{3}{5} = \frac{4}{5} \cdot \frac{5}{3} = \frac{4 \cdot 5}{3 \cdot 5} = \frac{4}{3}$$

We can check Definition 4.9 by multiplying the quotient, $(a/b) \cdot (d/c)$, by the divisor, c/d, to obtain the dividend, a/b. Thus,

$$\left(\frac{a}{b} \cdot \frac{d}{c}\right) \cdot \frac{c}{d} = \frac{a}{b} \cdot \left(\frac{d}{c} \cdot \frac{c}{d}\right) = \frac{a}{b} \cdot 1 = \frac{a}{b}$$

as required.

As a consequence of these definitions of the basic operations, the set of rational numbers under addition and multiplication is closed and has the associative, commutative, and distributive properties. It also has an additive identity (0) and additive inverses. With respect to multiplication, the rational numbers have a multiplicative identity (1), and every rational number, except 0, has a multiplicative inverse (its reciprocal).

It can be shown that the definitions we have given are the only possible ones if we require that the rational numbers obey the same basic laws of arithmetic as do the integers. (Just imagine how unpleasant it would be if $\frac{1}{2} + \frac{1}{4} \neq \frac{1}{4} + \frac{1}{2}$.)

From the preceding definitions and Theorem 4.3, we can obtain some additional important results. By the definition of the rational number -1, we know that $-1 = \frac{-1}{1}$, and by Theorem 4.3

$$\frac{-1}{1} = \frac{(-1)(-1)}{(1)(-1)} = \frac{1}{-1}$$

Therefore,

$$-\frac{a}{b} = -1 \cdot \frac{a}{b} = \frac{-1}{1} \cdot \frac{a}{b} = \frac{-a}{b}$$

Similarly,

$$-\frac{a}{b} = -1 \cdot \frac{a}{b} = \frac{1}{-1} \cdot \frac{a}{b} = \frac{a}{-b}$$

Thus, we have the important conclusion that

$$-\frac{a}{b} = \frac{-a}{b} = \frac{a}{-b}$$

Furthermore, because $1 = \dfrac{1}{1} \cdot \dfrac{-1}{-1} = \dfrac{-1}{-1}$, we see that

$$\frac{a}{b} = \frac{-1}{-1} \cdot \frac{a}{b} = \frac{-a}{-b}$$

If you think of a and b as positive numbers, you can see that the rule of signs in division is exactly the same as that in multiplication: The quotient of two numbers with like signs is positive and of two numbers with unlike signs is negative. For example,

$$\frac{9}{3} = \frac{-9}{-3} = 3 \quad \text{and} \quad \frac{-9}{3} = \frac{9}{-3} = -3$$

If the operations under discussion involve **mixed numbers,** first write the mixed numbers as fractions. Thus, to add $2\frac{3}{4} + \frac{5}{6}$, note that $2\frac{3}{4} = 2 + \frac{3}{4} = \frac{8}{4} + \frac{3}{4} = \frac{11}{4}$. A simpler way to do this (in just one step) is

$$2\frac{3}{4} = \frac{2 \cdot 4 + 3}{4} = \frac{11}{4}$$
$$\uparrow \qquad\quad \uparrow$$
$$\text{Same denominator}$$

Thus,

$$2\frac{3}{4} + \frac{5}{6} = \frac{11}{4} + \frac{5}{6} = \frac{33}{12} + \frac{10}{12} = \frac{43}{12} = 3\frac{7}{12}$$

Note that to convert the fraction $\frac{43}{12}$ to a mixed number, we divide 43 by 12 (the answer is 3) and write the remainder 7 as the numerator of the remaining fraction, with the denominator unchanged.

EXAMPLE 5 Perform the indicated operations:

(a) $3\frac{1}{4} + 4\frac{1}{6}$ (b) $5 - 2\frac{1}{7}$ (c) $3\frac{1}{4} \times (-8)$

(d) $21 \div (-4\frac{1}{5})$

Solution (a) We first change the mixed numbers to fractions:

$$3\frac{1}{4} = \frac{13}{4} \quad \text{and} \quad 4\frac{1}{6} = \frac{25}{6}$$

We then obtain the LCD, which is 12, and change the fractions to equivalent ones with 12 as a denominator. We then have

$$3\frac{1}{4} + 4\frac{1}{6} = \frac{13}{4} + \frac{25}{6} = \frac{39}{12} + \frac{50}{12} = \frac{89}{12} = 7\frac{5}{12}$$

(b) Changing the $2\frac{1}{7}$ to $\frac{15}{7}$, and 5 to $\frac{35}{7}$, we write

$$5 - 2\frac{1}{7} = \frac{35}{7} - \frac{15}{7} = \frac{20}{7} = 2\frac{6}{7}$$

(c) Write $3\frac{1}{4}$ as $\frac{13}{4}$, and recall that the product of two numbers with unlike signs is negative. We have

$$3\frac{1}{4} \times (-8) = \frac{13}{\cancel{4}_{1}} \times (-\cancel{8}^{-2}) = -26$$

(d) Change the $-4\frac{1}{5}$ to $-\frac{21}{5}$, invert, and then multiply to get

$$21 \times \left(-\frac{5}{21}\right) = -5$$

(Note that the answer is negative.)

Exercise 4.4

A. In problems 1–4, identify the numerator and denominator of the given rational number.

1. $\dfrac{3}{4}$ 2. $\dfrac{4}{5}$ 3. $\dfrac{3}{-5}$ 4. $\dfrac{-4}{5}$

In problems 5–7, identify which rational numbers are equal by using Definition 4.4.

5. (a) $\dfrac{17}{41}$ (b) $\dfrac{289}{697}$ (c) $\dfrac{714}{1682}$ 6. (a) $\dfrac{438}{529}$ (b) $\dfrac{19}{23}$ (c) $\dfrac{323}{391}$

7. (a) $\dfrac{11}{91}$ (b) $\dfrac{111}{911}$ (c) $\dfrac{253}{2093}$

In problems 8–10, reduce the given rational number.

8. $\dfrac{14}{21}$ 9. $\dfrac{95}{38}$ 10. $\dfrac{42}{86}$ 11. $\dfrac{21}{48}$

12. $\dfrac{15}{12}$ 13. $\dfrac{30}{28}$ 14. $\dfrac{22}{33}$ 15. $\dfrac{52}{78}$

16. $\dfrac{224}{84}$

B. It is possible to add and subtract rational numbers by converting them to equivalent rational numbers with the same denominator. In problems 17–19, express each sum as a sum of rational numbers with a denominator of 18.

17. $\frac{2}{9} + \frac{1}{6} + \frac{7}{18}$ 18. $\frac{7}{3} + \frac{7}{9} + \frac{5}{6}$ 19. $\frac{1}{3} + \frac{1}{6} + \frac{1}{9}$

In problems 20–82, perform the indicated operations and reduce the answer (if possible).

20. $\frac{1}{7} + \frac{1}{3}$ 21. $\frac{1}{7} + \frac{1}{9}$ 22. $\frac{2}{7} + \frac{3}{11}$ 23. $\frac{3}{4} + \frac{5}{6}$

24. $\frac{1}{12} + \frac{7}{18}$ 25. $\frac{3}{17} + \frac{7}{19}$ 26. $\frac{1}{3} - \frac{1}{7}$ 27. $\frac{1}{7} - \frac{1}{9}$

28. $\frac{2}{7} - \frac{3}{11}$ 29. $\frac{3}{4} - \frac{5}{6}$ 30. $\frac{7}{18} - \frac{1}{12}$ 31. $\frac{7}{19} - \frac{3}{17}$

32. $\frac{3}{4} \times \frac{2}{7}$ 33. $\frac{2}{5} \times \frac{5}{3}$ 34. $\frac{7}{9} \times \frac{3}{8}$ 35. $\frac{3}{4} \div \frac{2}{7}$

36. $\frac{2}{5} \div \frac{5}{3}$ 37. $\frac{7}{9} \div \frac{3}{8}$ 38. $\left(\frac{-2}{5}\right) \times \frac{4}{9}$

39. $\left(-\frac{6}{7}\right) \times \left(-\frac{3}{11}\right)$ 40. $\frac{4}{5} \div \left(\frac{-7}{9}\right)$ 41. $\left(-\frac{3}{4}\right) \div \left(-\frac{7}{6}\right)$ 42. $\frac{3}{4} \div \left(-\frac{1}{5}\right)$

43. $\frac{1}{8} \div \left(-\frac{3}{4}\right)$ 44. $\left(-\frac{1}{4}\right) + \left(-\frac{1}{7}\right)$ 45. $\left(-\frac{1}{8}\right) + \left(\frac{1}{4}\right)$

46. $\left(\frac{1}{3} + \frac{1}{4}\right) + \frac{7}{8}$ 47. $\frac{3}{8} - \left(\frac{1}{4} - \frac{1}{8}\right)$ 48. $\left(\frac{1}{5} \times \frac{1}{4}\right) \times \frac{3}{7}$

49. $\frac{1}{2} \times \left(\frac{7}{8} \times \frac{7}{5}\right)$ 50. $\frac{1}{2} \div \left(\frac{1}{8} \div \frac{1}{4}\right)$ 51. $\left(\frac{1}{2} \div \frac{1}{8}\right) \div \frac{1}{4}$

52. $\frac{3}{4} + \frac{1}{2}\left(\frac{3}{2} + \frac{1}{4}\right)$ 53. $\frac{2}{3}\left(\frac{1}{2} + \frac{3}{4}\right) + \frac{2}{3}$ 54. $\frac{1}{2}\left(\frac{3}{4} - \frac{1}{2}\right) - \frac{1}{12}$

55. $\frac{1}{3}\left(\frac{3}{2} - \frac{1}{5}\right) - \frac{1}{30}$ 56. $\frac{1}{2}\left(\frac{5}{2} - \frac{1}{3}\right) - \frac{5}{12}$ 57. $1\frac{1}{2} + \frac{1}{7}$ 58. $5 - 1\frac{1}{3}$

59. $\frac{1}{4} \times 1\frac{1}{7}$ 60. $5 \div \left(-2\frac{1}{2}\right)$ 61. $3\frac{1}{4} + \frac{1}{6}$ 62. $4 - 2\frac{1}{4}$

63. $\frac{1}{5} \times 2\frac{1}{7}$ 64. $6 \div \left(-1\frac{1}{5}\right)$ 65. $-3 + 2\frac{1}{4}$

66. $-\frac{2}{3} - (-2)$ 67. $(-8) \times 2\frac{1}{4}$ 68. $7 \div \left(-2\frac{1}{3}\right)$

69. $-2 + 1\frac{1}{5}$ 70. $-\frac{3}{4} - (-3)$ 71. $(-9) \times 3\frac{1}{3}$

72. $\left(-\frac{1}{6}\right) \div \left(-\frac{5}{7}\right)$ 73. $7\frac{1}{4} + \left(-\frac{1}{8}\right)$ 74. $-3\frac{1}{8} - (-2)$

75. $\left(-1\frac{1}{4}\right) \times \left(-2\frac{1}{10}\right)$ 76. $\left(-1\frac{1}{8}\right) \div \left(-2\frac{1}{4}\right)$

77. $\frac{1}{2} \times \frac{1}{6} - \frac{1}{3} + \frac{1}{4}$ 78. $\frac{3}{8} - 6\left(\frac{1}{4} - \frac{1}{8}\right)$

79. $\frac{1}{3} - \frac{1}{3} \times \frac{2}{3} \div \frac{2}{5}$ 80. $\frac{1}{2} \div \frac{1}{4} - \frac{3}{4}$

81. $\left(2\frac{1}{2}\right) \times \left(-3\frac{1}{4}\right) - \left(-7\frac{1}{8}\right) \div 3$ 82. $\left(-6\frac{2}{3}\right) \div (-4) + \left(2\frac{1}{10}\right) \times (-2)$

Applications

83. The normal body temperature is $98\frac{6}{10}$ degrees Fahrenheit. Carlos had the flu and his temperature was $101\frac{6}{10}$ degrees. How many degrees above normal is that?

84. An average human brain weighs approximately $3\frac{1}{8}$ lb. The brain of the writer Anatole France weighed only $2\frac{1}{4}$ lb. How much under the average was that?

85. As stated in problem 84, the average human brain weighs approximately $3\frac{1}{8}$ lb. The heaviest brain ever recorded was that of Ivan Sergeevich Turgenev, a Russian author. His brain weighed approximately $4\frac{7}{16}$ lb. How much above the average is this weight?

86. A board $\frac{3}{4}$ inch thick is glued to another board $\frac{5}{8}$ inch thick. If the glue is $\frac{1}{32}$ inch thick, how thick is the result?

87. A recent survey found that $\frac{3}{10}$ of the American people work long hours and smoke, while another $\frac{1}{5}$ are overweight. What fraction of the people is neither of these?

88. Human bones are $\frac{1}{4}$ water, $\frac{9}{20}$ minerals, and the rest living tissue. What fraction of human bone is living tissue?

89. Americans spend $3\frac{1}{2}$ billion on daily newspapers and $1\frac{2}{5}$ billion on Sunday newspapers. How many billions of dollars are spent on newspapers?

90. Americans work an average of $46\frac{3}{5}$ hr per week, while Canadians work $38\frac{9}{10}$. How many more hr per week do Americans work on average?

91. Do husbands help with the household chores? A recent survey estimated that husbands spend about $7\frac{1}{2}$ hr during weekdays helping around the house, $2\frac{3}{5}$ hr on Saturday, and 2 hr on Sunday. How many hr do husbands work around the house during the entire week?

In Other Words

92. Why do you think the set of rational numbers is symbolized by the letter Q?

93. You know that $\frac{3}{3} = 1$, $\frac{2}{2} = 1$ and $\frac{1}{1} = 1$. Is $\frac{0}{0} = 1$? Why or why not?

94. The Golden Ratio mentioned in Getting Started is of the form

$$\frac{b}{a} = \frac{\sqrt{5} - 1}{2}$$

but it does not satisfy the definition of a rational number. Why?

Using Your Knowledge

Road maps and other maps are drawn to **scale.** *The scale on a map shows what distance is represented by a certain measurement on the map. For example, the scale on a certain map is*

1 inch = 36 miles

Thus, if the distance on the map is $2\frac{1}{4}$ inches from Indianapolis to Dayton, the actual distance is

$$36 \times 2\frac{1}{4} = 36 \times \frac{9}{4} = (9 \times 4) \times \frac{9}{4} = 81 \text{ miles}$$

95. Find the actual distance from Indianapolis to Cincinnati, a distance of $3\frac{1}{2}$ inches on the map.

96. Find the actual distance from Indianapolis to Terre Haute, a distance of $3\frac{1}{4}$ inches on the map.

97. If the actual distance between two cities is 108 miles, what is the distance on the map?

98. If the actual distance between two cities is 162 miles, what is the distance on the map?

Discovery

Let us try to discover how many positive rational numbers there are. We arrange the first few fractions as shown below:

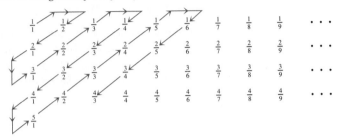

99. Can you discover the next two rows in this array?

100. Notice that the number $\frac{1}{5}$ appears in the first row, fifth column. Can you discover where the number $\frac{37}{43}$ will be?

101. By following the path indicated in the array, we can set up a correspondence between the set of natural numbers N and the set of positive rational numbers. The first few terms look like this:

1	2	3	4	5	6	7	8	9	10	11	$\cdots$
$\updownarrow$	$\updownarrow$	$\updownarrow$	$\updownarrow$	$\updownarrow$	$\updownarrow$	$\updownarrow$	$\updownarrow$	$\updownarrow$	$\updownarrow$	$\updownarrow$	
1	$\frac{1}{2}$	$\frac{2}{1}$	$\frac{3}{1}$	$\frac{1}{3}$	$\frac{1}{4}$	$\frac{2}{3}$	$\frac{3}{2}$	$\frac{4}{1}$	$\frac{5}{1}$	$\frac{1}{5}$	$\cdots$

You will notice that in this pairing we skipped $\frac{2}{2}$, $\frac{4}{2}$, $\frac{3}{3}$, and $\frac{2}{4}$. Can you discover why?

102. The correspondence indicated in problem 101 can be continued indefinitely. If we assign a cardinal number to the set N of natural numbers, say, $n(N) = \aleph_0$ *(aleph zero)*, so that we can speak of the "number of natural numbers" as being $\aleph_0$, what would $n(Q^+)$ be? That is, how many positive rational numbers are there?

103. Based on your answer to problem 102, would you say that there are more or fewer rational numbers than natural numbers?

Computer Corner

Some calculators will perform operations with fractions; however, most of them will convert fractions to decimals and then perform the operations, giving answers in decimal form. But a computer can be programmed to do calculations involving fractions. The Addition of Fractions and Addition of (Reduced) Fractions programs in the Programs in BASIC appendix add fractions. (One program reduces the answer, the other one does not.) Note that the addition is done by using Definition 4.5 without converting to decimals, thus eliminating round-off errors.

4.5 DECIMALS

GETTING STARTED

ADVERBS, ADJECTIVES, AND DECIMALS

How fast does a snail move? We can express the answer as a decimal. Many measurements involving decimals are so small or so large that they must be written in a special way called **scientific notation,** which you will study in Part B of this section. Here are some speeds in decimal form and in scientific notation:

Speed at which a snail moves	$0.0310 = 3.10 \times 10^{-2}$ mi/hr
Brisk walking speed of a person	$5.72 = 5.72 \times 10^{0}$ mi/hr
Fast running speed for a man	$16.70 = 1.67 \times 10^{1}$ mi/hr
Speed of a peregrine falcon	$168 = 1.68 \times 10^{2}$ mi/hr
Speed of an SR-71A plane	$2193 = 2.193 \times 10^{3}$ mi/hr

Decimals are used in many ways. For example, social scientists often try to quantify different characteristics of people or things. Thus, psychologists and linguists have a numerical way to indicate the difference between *nice* and *very nice* or between *unpleasant* and *very unpleasant*. Suppose you assign a positive number (+2, for example) to the adjective *nice* and a negative number (say, −2) to *unpleasant* and a positive number greater than 1 (say, +1.25) to *very*. Then, *very nice* is quantified as

Very nice
↓   ↓

$(1.25) \cdot (2) = 2.50$ (1.25) and (2) are multiplied.

and *very unpleasant* is

Very unpleasant
↓   ↓

$(1.25) \cdot (-2) = -2.50$

Here are some adverbs and adjectives and their average numerical values, as rated by several panels of college students. (Values differ from one panel to another.)

Adverbs				Adjectives			
Slightly	0.54	Very	1.25	Wicked	−2.5	Good	3.1
Rather	0.84	Extremely	1.45	Disgusting	−2.1	Lovable	2.4
Decidedly	1.16			Average	−0.8		

Now you are able to quantify phrases such as *extremely disgusting* and *very wicked*. Which of the two phrases is worse? If you do the multiplication, you will know and if you get the correct answer you are 4.495!

As you probably know, the number $\frac{1}{2}$ can be written in decimal form, that is, as 0.5. Because all rational numbers can be written in the form a/b, it is always possible to change a rational number a/b to its decimal form by simply dividing a by b. For example, $\frac{1}{2} = 0.5$, $\frac{1}{8} = 0.125$, And $\frac{1}{4} = 0.25$. Of course, if the denominator of a fraction is already a power of 10 (10, 100, 1000, and so on), then the fraction can easily be written as a decimal. Thus,

$$\frac{7}{10} = 0.7, \qquad \frac{19}{100} = 0.19, \quad \text{and} \quad \frac{17}{1000} = 0.017$$

You should keep in mind that the successive places to the right of the decimal point have the place values

$$\frac{1}{10^1}, \quad \frac{1}{10^2}, \quad \frac{1}{10^3}, \quad \frac{1}{10^4}, \cdots$$

The exponent on the 10 is the number of the place. For example, the underlined digit in 2.567\underline{9}4 has the place value $1/10^4$, because the 9 is in the fourth decimal place.

A. *Decimals in Expanded Form*

You learned in Section 3.2 that a positive integer can always be written in expanded form, as, for instance,

$$361 = (3 \times 10^2) + (6 \times 10^1) + (1 \times 10^0)$$

Can we do something like this for a decimal, say, 3.52? You know that

$$0.5 = \frac{5}{10} \qquad \text{and} \qquad 0.02 = \frac{2}{100}$$

so

$$3.52 = (3 \times 10^0) + \left(5 \times \frac{1}{10^1}\right) + \left(2 \times \frac{1}{10^2}\right)$$

This is somewhat awkward, so to make it more convenient, we define **negative exponents** as follows:

$$10^{-1} = \frac{1}{10^1} = \frac{1}{10}, \qquad 10^{-2} = \frac{1}{10^2} = \frac{1}{100}, \qquad 10^{-3} = \frac{1}{10^3} = \frac{1}{1000}, \cdots$$

Definition 4.10

In general, if n is a positive integer and $a \neq 0$,

$$a^{-n} = \frac{1}{a^n}$$

The definition of negative exponents gives a good pattern:

$10^3 = 1000$

$10^2 = 100$

$10^1 = 10$

$10^0 = 1$

$10^{-1} = \dfrac{1}{10}$

$10^{-2} = \dfrac{1}{100}$

$10^{-3} = \dfrac{1}{1000}$

and so on.

It can be shown that **negative exponents obey exactly the same laws as positive exponents.**

Using these negative exponents, you can write, for example,

$$3.52 = (3 \times 10^0) + (5 \times 10^{-1}) + (2 \times 10^{-2})$$

and

$$362.754 = (3 \times 10^2) + (6 \times 10^1) + (2 \times 10^0) +$$
$$(7 \times 10^{-1}) + (5 \times 10^{-2}) + (4 \times 10^{-3})$$

which looks like a very natural generalization of the expanded form that we used for positive exponents.

EXAMPLE 1

(a) Write 25.603 in expanded form.

(b) Write $(7 \times 10^2) + (2 \times 10^0) + (6 \times 10^{-1}) + (9 \times 10^{-4})$ in standard decimal form.

Solution

(a) $25.603 = (2 \times 10^1) + (5 \times 10^0) + (6 \times 10^{-1}) +$
$(0 \times 10^{-2}) + (3 \times 10^{-3})$
$= (2 \times 10^1) + (5 \times 10^0) + (6 \times 10^{-1}) +$
(3×10^{-3})

(b) Notice that the exponent in 10^{-n} tells you that the first nonzero digit comes in the nth decimal place. With this in mind, we have

$$(7 \times 10^2) + (2 \times 10^0) + (6 \times 10^{-1}) + (9 \times 10^{-4}) = 702.6009$$ ∎

B. *Scientific Notation*

In science and in other areas, there frequently occur very large or very small numbers. For example, a red cell of human blood contains 270,000,000 hemoglobin molecules, and the mass of a single carbon atom is 0.000 000 000 000 000 000 000 019 9 gram. Numbers in this form are difficult to write and to work with, so they are written in *scientific notation*.

Definition 4.11

A number is said to be in **scientific notation** if it is written in the form

$$m \times 10^n$$

where m is a number greater than or equal to 1 and less than 10, and n is an integer.

For any given number, the m is obtained by placing the decimal point so that there is exactly one nonzero digit to its left. The n is then the number of places that the decimal point must be moved from its position in m to its original position; it is positive if the point must be moved to the right, and negative if the point must be moved to the left. Thus,

$5.3 = 5.3 \times 10^0$	Decimal point in 5.3 must be moved 0 places.
$87 = 8.7 \times 10^1 = 8.7 \times 10$	Decimal point in 8.7 must be moved 1 place to the right to get 87.
$68{,}000 = 6.8 \times 10^4$	Decimal point in 6.8 must be moved 4 places to the right to get 68,000.
$0.49 = 4.9 \times 10^{-1}$	Decimal point in 4.9 must be moved 1 place to the left to get 0.49.
$0.072 = 7.2 \times 10^{-2}$	Decimal point in 7.2 must be moved 2 places to the left to get 0.072.
$0.0003875 = 3.875 \times 10^{-4}$	Decimal point in 3.875 must be moved 4 places to the left to get 0.0003875.

EXAMPLE 2   Write in scientific notation:

(a) 270,000,000

(b) 0.000 000 000 000 000 000 000 019 9

Solution   (a) $270{,}000{,}000 = 2.7 \times 10^8$

(b) $0.000\ 000\ 000\ 000\ 000\ 000\ 000\ 019\ 9 = 1.99 \times 10^{-23}$ ■

EXAMPLE 3   Write in standard decimal notation:

(a) 2.5×10^{10} (b) 7.4×10^{-6}

Solution   (a) $2.5 \times 10^{10} = 25{,}000{,}000{,}000$

(b) $7.4 \times 10^{-6} = 0.0000074$ ■

We noted earlier in this section that negative exponents obey the same laws as positive exponents. You can verify this quite easily in simple cases. For example,

$$10^4 \times 10^{-2} = 10{,}000 \times \frac{1}{100} = 100 = 10^2 = 10^{4+(-2)}$$

$$10^{-2} \times 10^{-3} = 0.01 \times 0.001 = 0.00001 = 10^{-5} = 10^{-2+(-3)}$$

The laws of exponents can be used to do calculations with numbers in scientific notation.

EXAMPLE 4 Do the following calculation, and write the answer in scientific notation:
$(5 \times 10^4) \times (9 \times 10^{-7})$

Solution

$$(5 \times 10^4) \times (9 \times 10^{-7}) = (5 \times 9) \times (10^4 \times 10^{-7})$$
$$= 45 \times 10^{4-7}$$
$$= 45 \times 10^{-3}$$
$$= 4.5 \times 10^1 \times 10^{-3}$$
$$= 4.5 \times 10^{1-3}$$
$$= 4.5 \times 10^{-2}$$ ∎

C. *Operations with Decimals*

We have already studied the operations of addition, subtraction, multiplication, and division with whole numbers, integers, and fractions. We now consider the same operations with decimals. To add or subtract decimals, we proceed as with whole numbers, making sure that the numbers to be added have the same number of decimal places. Thus, to add 5.1 and 2.81, we attach a 0 to 5.1 so that it has two decimal places and then add. To see why this works, we write the numbers in expanded form and add as follows:

$$5.10 = 5 + \tfrac{1}{10} + \tfrac{0}{100}$$
$$\underline{2.81 = 2 + \tfrac{8}{10} + \tfrac{1}{100}}$$
$$7.91 = 7 + \tfrac{9}{10} + \tfrac{1}{100}$$

In practice, we place the numbers to be added in a vertical column *with the decimal points aligned,* and then add or subtract as required. The rules for "carrying" in addition and "borrowing" in subtraction are justified here also, as shown by the expanded forms in the next examples.

EXAMPLE 5 (a) Add 4.81 and 3.7
(b) Subtract 6.53 from 8.71

Solution (a) We attach a 0 to the 3.7, align the decimal points, and add.

Short Form	**Expanded Form**

$$
\begin{array}{l}
\quad 4.81 \\
\underline{+\ 3.70} \leftarrow \text{Attach a 0} \\
\quad 8.51
\end{array}
$$

$$
\begin{array}{rl}
& 4 + \tfrac{8}{10} + \tfrac{1}{100} \\
+ & 3 + \tfrac{7}{10} + \tfrac{0}{100} \\
\hline
& 7 + \tfrac{15}{10} + \tfrac{1}{100} \\
= & 7 + \tfrac{10}{10} + \tfrac{5}{10} + \tfrac{1}{100} \\
= & 8 + \tfrac{5}{10} + \tfrac{1}{100} \\
= & 8.51
\end{array}
$$ ∎

(b) **Short Form**   **Expanded Form**

$$8.71 \qquad 8 + \tfrac{7}{10} + \tfrac{1}{100} = 8 + \tfrac{6}{10} + \tfrac{11}{100}$$

$$\underline{-6.53} \qquad \underline{-6 + \tfrac{5}{10} + \tfrac{3}{100} = 6 + \tfrac{5}{10} + \tfrac{3}{100}}$$

$$2.18 \qquad\qquad\qquad 2 + \tfrac{1}{10} + \tfrac{8}{100} = 2.18$$

Note: In the first line of the expanded form, we wrote

$$\tfrac{7}{10} = \tfrac{6}{10} + \tfrac{1}{10} = \tfrac{6}{10} + \tfrac{10}{100}$$

and then combined the hundredths.   ∎

To understand the rule for multiplying decimals, look at the following example, where the decimals are first replaced by equivalent fractions.

EXAMPLE 6   Multiply 0.37×7.2.

Solution $$0.37 \times 7.2 = \frac{37}{100} \times \frac{72}{10} = \frac{37 \times 72}{1000}$$

The numerator 37×72 tells us that the 37 and the 72 are to be multiplied as usual for whole numbers. The 1000 in the denominator tells us that the final answer will have three decimal places, the sum of the number of decimal places in the two factors. Thus, we can multiply the 0.37 and the 7.2 just as if they were whole numbers and then place the decimal point so that there are three decimal places in the product. The short form of the multiplication follows:

$$0.37 \leftarrow \text{2 decimal places}$$
$$\underline{\times\quad 7.2} \leftarrow \text{1 decimal place}$$
$$74$$
$$\underline{259}$$
$$2.664 \leftarrow 2 + 1 = 3 \text{ decimal places}$$

∎

In general, we multiply two decimals as if they were whole numbers and then place the decimal point so that the number of decimal places is equal to the sum of the number of decimal places in the two factors.

If signed numbers are involved, the rules of signs apply. Thus,

$$(-0.37) \times 7.2 = -2.664$$
$$0.37 \times (-7.2) = -2.664$$
$$(-0.37) \times (-7.2) = 2.664$$

A division involving decimals is easier to understand if the divisor is a whole number. If the divisor is not a whole number, we can make it so by moving the decimal point to the right the same number of places in both the divisor and the dividend. This procedure can be justified as in the next example.

EXAMPLE 7   A $6\frac{1}{2}$ ounce can of tuna fish is on sale for 55¢. What is the cost per ounce to the nearest tenth of a cent?

Solution   The cost per ounce can be obtained by dividing the total cost by the number of ounces. Thus, we have to find 55 ÷ 6.5, and we can make the divisor a whole number by writing the division in fractional form:

$$\frac{55}{6.5} = \frac{550}{65}$$ Multiply numerator and denominator by 10.

This is equivalent to moving the decimal point one place to the right in both the divisor and the dividend. Now, we divide in the usual way:

$$\begin{array}{r} 8.46 \\ 65\overline{)550.00} \\ \underline{520} \\ 30\ 0 \\ \underline{26\ 0} \\ 4\ 00 \\ \underline{3\ 90} \\ 10 \end{array}$$

To two decimal places, the cost per ounce is 8.46¢. Therefore, to the nearest tenth of a cent, the answer is 8.5¢.   ■

Again, if signed numbers are involved, the rules of signs apply. For example,

$$\frac{-14}{2.5} = -5.6 \qquad \frac{14}{-2.5} = -5.6 \qquad \frac{-14}{-2.5} = 5.6$$

Problem Solving: Applications to Decimals

Bank A offers a checking account costing $3.00 per month plus $0.20 per check after the first 10 checks. Bank B offers unlimited checking for a $6.00 charge.
(a) Which bank is cheaper if you write 20 checks per month?
(b) How many checks do you have to write so that the cost is the same in both banks?

1. **Read the problem.**

2. **Select the unknown.**   We want to find out which bank is cheaper if you write 20 checks per month and when the cost is the same for both banks.

3. **Think of a plan.**
   Find the cost of writing 20 checks in bank A and in bank B.

   Bank A costs $3 plus $0.20 for each check over 10. For 20 checks, 10 are free, 10 cost $0.20 each.

4. Use the information to find the answers.

Which bank is cheaper if you write 20 checks?

When is the cost the same?

The cost of writing 20 checks in bank A is $3 + 10 \cdot 0.20 = $3 + $2 = $5. The cost in bank B is $6. Bank A is cheaper.

The cost is $6 in bank A when you pay the $3 monthly charge and you spend an additional $3 on checks. Since checks are $0.20 each, you can write $\dfrac{\$3.00}{\$0.20} = 15$ checks plus the 10 free ones for a total of 25 checks.

Thus the cost is the same ($6) when you write 25 checks.

5. Verify the answer.

The cost of writing 25 checks in bank A is $3 + 15 \cdot 0.20 = $3 + $3 = $6, the same fee as in bank B.

TRY EXAMPLE 8 NOW.

Cover the solution, write your own, and then check your work.

EXAMPLE 8

Suppose you need to rent a car for a 3-day, 400-mile trip. Your choice of rental companies is as follows:

Company A: $50 per day, with free, unlimited mileage.

Company B: $25 per day, plus $0.20 per mile.

(a) Which company offers the best deal for your trip?

(b) How many miles do you have to travel for the 3-day trip to cost the same with either company?

Solution

Let us look at the cost for each company.

Company A   charges $50 each day for three days or
3 × $50 = $150

Company B   costs 3 × $25 + 0.20 × 400 = $75 + $80 = $155.

(a) It is less expensive to rent from company A.

(b) The 3-day charge for A is $150 and for B is $75. The $75 difference ($150 − $75) can to be used to pay the mileage with company B. Since the cost is $0.20 per mile, the number of miles we can travel is

$$\frac{75}{0.20} = 375 \text{ miles.}$$

Verifying that the cost is the same can be done by looking at the cost for company B, $75 + 0.20 × 375 = $75 + $75 = $150, the same cost as for company A.

■

D. *Rounding*

In Example 7, we **rounded off** the quotient 8.4̲6 to one decimal place to get 8.5. This type of procedure is necessary in many practical problems and is done in the following way:

> **To Round Off Numbers**
>
> 1. Underline the digit in the place to which you are rounding.
> 2. If the first digit to the right of the underlined digit is 5 or more, add 1 to the underlined digit. Otherwise, do not change the underlined digit.
> 3. Drop all digits to the right of the underlined digit, attaching 0's to fill in the place values if necessary.

For instance, to round off 8.46 to one decimal place, that is, to the tenths place:

1. Underline the 4: 8.4̲6

2. The digit to the right of the underlined digit is 6 (greater than 5). So add 1 to the underlined digit.

3. Drop all digits to the right of the underlined digit. The result is 8.5.

If it is necessary to round off 2632 to the hundreds place, you should underline the 6 to show 2̲632. Since the next digit is 3 (less than 5), the underlined 6 is unchanged and the 32 is replaced by 00 to give 2600.

In many applications, the numbers are obtained by measurement and are usually only approximate numbers correct to the stated number of decimal places. When calculations are performed with approximate numbers, two rules are customarily used to avoid presenting results with a false appearance of accuracy. The rule for addition and subtraction is:

> The result of an addition or subtraction of approximate numbers should be given to the number of decimal places possessed by the approximate number with the *least* number of decimal places.

EXAMPLE 9   The three sides of a triangle are measured to be approximately 26.3, 7.41, and 20.64 cm long, respectively. What is the perimeter of the triangle?

Solution   The perimeter is the total distance around the triangle, so we must add the lengths of the three sides. We get

$$\begin{array}{r} 26.3 \\ 7.41 \\ +\ 20.64 \\ \hline 54.35 \end{array}$$

However, the least precise of the measurements is 26.3, with just one decimal place. Therefore, we round off the answer to 54.4 cm.   ■

Before giving the rule that is used when multiplying or dividing approximate numbers, we must explain what is meant by the **significant digits** of a number.

> 1. The digits 1, 2, 3, 4, 5, 6, 7, 8, 9 are always significant.
> 2. The digit 0 is significant if it is preceded and followed by other significant digits.
> 3. The digit 0 is significant unless its only purpose is to place the decimal point.

Thus, all the digits in the numbers 2.54 and 1.73205 are significant. However, the number 0.00721 has only three significant digits: 7, 2, and 1; the 0's in this number do nothing except place the decimal point. There is one ambiguous case left. For example, how many significant digits does the number 73,200 have? We cannot answer this question unless we know more about the final 0's. To avoid this type of difficulty, we write 73,200 in the form

$$7.32 \times 10^4, \quad \text{if three digits are significant}$$
$$7.320 \times 10^4, \quad \text{if four digits are significant}$$
$$7.3200 \times 10^4, \quad \text{if all five digits are significant}$$

EXAMPLE 10   State the number of significant digits in each of the following:

(a) 0.50 in.   (b) 0.05 lb

(c) 8.2×10^3 liters   (d) 8.200×10^3 km

Solution   (a) 0.50 has two significant digits.

(b) 0.05 has one significant digit. The 0 before the 5 only places the decimal point.

(c) 8.2×10^3 has two significant digits.

(d) 8.200×10^3 has four significant digits.   ∎

We can now state the multiplication and division rule for approximate numbers:

> The result of a multiplication or division of approximate numbers should be given with the same number of significant digits as are possessed by the approximate number with the *fewest* significant digits.

For instance, if we wish to convert 6 centimeters to inches, we note that 1 cm is approximately 0.394 in. Therefore, we multiply

$$6 \times 0.394 = 2.364$$

However, 0.394 has only three significant digits, so we must round our answer to three significant digits. Our final result is

6 cm ≈ 2.36 in.   ≈ means "approximately equal to"

Notice carefully that the 6 in 6 cm is an *exact,* not an approximate, number.

EXAMPLE 11   Two adjacent sides of a rectangular lot are measured to be approximately 91.5 ft and 226.6 ft. Find the area of this lot.

Solution   The area of a rectangle of sides a and b is $A = ab$. Thus, we have

$$A = 91.5 \times 226.6$$
$$= 20{,}733.90$$

However, the 91.5 has only three significant digits, so our answer must be rounded to three significant digits. This gives 20,700 sq. ft for the area. A better form for the answer is 2.07×10^4 sq. ft. Use of scientific notation frequently helps to display only the significant digits of the answer. ∎

Exercise 4.5

A.   In problems 1–4, write the given number in expanded notation.

1. 692.087
2. 30.2959
3. 0.00107
4. 4.30008

In problems 7–8, write the given number in standard decimal notation.

5. $(5 \times 10^3) + (2 \times 10^1) + (3 \times 10^{-1}) + (9 \times 10^{-2})$
6. $(4 \times 10^2) + (5 \times 10^0) + (6 \times 10^{-2}) + (9 \times 10^{-4})$
7. $(4 \times 10^{-3}) + (7 \times 10^{-4}) + (2 \times 10^{-6})$
8. $(2 \times 10^{-1}) + (5 \times 10^{-2}) + (4 \times 10^{-4})$

B.   In problems 9–12, write the given number in scientific notation.

9. 935
10. 0.372
11. 0.0012
12. 3,453,000

In problems 13–16, write the given numbers in standard notation.

13. 8.64×10^4
14. 9.01×10^7
15. 6.71×10^{-3}
16. 4.02×10^{-7}

In problems 17–22, simplify and write the answer in scientific notation.

17. $0.0346 \div 1{,}730{,}000$
18. $0.00741 \times 225{,}000$
19. $(3.1 \times 10^5) \times (2.2 \times 10^{-6})$
20. $(4.9 \times 10^{-2}) \times (3.5 \times 10^{-1})$

21. $\dfrac{(2 \times 10^6)(6 \times 10^{-5})}{4 \times 10^3}$

22. $\dfrac{(8 \times 10^2)(3 \times 10^{-2})}{24 \times 10^{-3}}$

23. The most plentiful form of sea life known is the nematode sea worm. It is estimated that there are

    40,000,000,000,000,000,000,000,000

    of these worms in the world's oceans. Write this number in scientific notation.

24. Sir Arthur Eddington claimed that the total number of electrons in the universe is 136×2^{256}. It can be shown that 2^{256} is approximately 1.16×10^{77}. Use this result to write Eddington's number in scientific notation.

In problems 25–30, write the answer in scientific notation.

25. The width of the asteroid belt is 2.8×10^8 km. The speed of *Pioneer 10* in passing through this belt was 1.4×10^5 km/hr. Thus, *Pioneer 10* took

    $$\dfrac{2.8 \times 10^8}{1.4 \times 10^5} \text{ hr}$$

    to go through the belt. How many hours was that?

26. The mass of the Earth is 6×10^{21} tons. The Sun is about 300,000 times as massive. Thus, the mass of the Sun is $(6 \times 10^{21}) \times 300,000$ tons. How many tons is that?

27. The velocity of light can be measured by knowing the distance from the Sun to the Earth (1.47×10^{11} m) and the time it takes for sunlight to reach the Earth (490 sec). Thus, the velocity of light is

    $$\dfrac{1.47 \times 10^{11}}{490} \text{ m/sec}$$

    How many meters per second is that?

28. United States oil reserves are estimated to be 3.5×10^{10} barrels. Production amounts to 3.2×10^9 barrels per year. At this rate, how long would U.S. oil reserves last? (Give answer to the nearest year.)

29. The world's oil reserves are estimated to be 6.28×10^{11} barrels. Production is 2.0×10^{10} barrels per year. At this rate, how long would the world's oil reserves last? (Give answer to the nearest year.)

30. Scientists have estimated that the total energy received from the Sun each minute is 1.02×10^{19} calories. Since the area of the Earth is 5.1×10^8 km² (square kilometers), the amount of energy received per square centimeter of Earth's surface per minute (the solar constant) is

    $$\dfrac{1.02 \times 10^{19}}{(5.1 \times 10^8) \times 10^{10}} \qquad Note: \quad 1 \text{ km}^2 = 10^{10} \text{ cm}^2$$

    How many calories per square centimeter is that?

C. In problems 31–38, perform the indicated operations.

31. (a) $3.81 + 0.93$ (b) $-3.81 + (-0.93)$
32. (a) $18.64 - 0.983$ (b) $-18.64 - 0.983$
33. (a) $2.08 - 6.238$ (b) $3.07 - 8.934$
34. (a) 2.48×2.7 (b) $(-2.48) \times (-2.7)$
35. (a) $(-0.03) \times (-1.5)$ (b) $(-3.2) \times (-0.04)$
36. (a) $10.25 \div 0.05$ (b) $2.16 \div 0.06$
37. (a) $(-0.07) \div 1.4$ (b) $(-0.09) \div (-4.5)$
38. (a) $(-1.8) \div (0.09)$ (b) $3.6 \div (-0.012)$

39. The revenues (in millions) of City Investing were derived from the following sources: manufacturing, $926.3; printing, $721.21; international, $488.34; housing, $674; food services, $792.45; insurance, $229.58. Find the total revenue.

40. Ann rented a car at a cost of $25 per day plus $0.15 per mile traveled. What was her cost for a 2-day trip of 700 miles?

41. A 6-ounce can of orange juice concentrate costs $0.48 and a 12-ounce can costs $0.89. How much is saved by buying 36 ounces of the more economical size?

42. A worker was paid $4.50 per hr for a 40-hr week. The worker was paid an additional $1.50 per hr for each hr over 40 hr per week. How much did the worker earn in 3 weeks if he worked 43 hr the first week, 42 hr the second week, and 45 hr the third week?

43. George, Harry, and Joe played poker one evening. Joe won $25.75, which was the total amount lost by George and Harry. If George lost $7.25 more than Harry, how much did each lose?

44. A library charged for an overdue book at the rate of 10 cents for the first day and 5 cents for each additional day. If Mabel paid a fine of 75 cents for an overdue book, how many days overdue was the book?

45. A bookstore ordered 30 books for a certain course. Each book, which cost the bookstore $25, was to be sold for $31.50. A service charge of $3 was to be paid for each unsold book returned. If the bookstore sold 28 of the books and returned the other two, what was its gross profit?

D. 46. Round the measure 45.49 meters to the nearest meter.

47. Round 3,265 ounces to the nearest hundred ounces.

48. The sides of a triangular lot are measured to be 392.1, 307.25, and 507 ft. Find the perimeter of the lot to the correct number of decimal places.

49. The mileage indicator on a car read 18,327.2 miles at the beginning of a trip. It read 18,719.7 at the end. How far did the car go?

50. A business reported annual sales of $8.5 million. If the expenses were reported as $6.52 million, find the profit to the correct number of decimal places.

51. The average weekly circulation of *TV Guide* is 19,230,000 copies. If each copy is sold for 75¢, how much money (on the average) do sales amount to each week?

52. On October 17, 1965, the *New York Times* contained a total of 946 pages. If the thickness of one sheet of newspaper is 0.0040 inch, find (to the correct number of decimal places) the thickness of this edition of the paper.

53. A light-year is about 5.878×10^{12} miles. The *Great Galaxy* in *Andromeda* is about 2.15 million light-years away. How many miles is the *Great Galaxy* from us? (Write your answer in scientific notation.) By the way, this galaxy is the most remote heavenly body visible to the naked eye.

54. Lionel Harrison drove the 1,900 miles from Oxford, England, to Moscow in a Morris Minor fitted with a 62-gallon tank. If he used all the 62 gallons of gas, how many miles per gallon did he get? (Round the answer to the nearest tenth.)

55. Stuart Bladon holds the record for the greatest distance driven without refueling, 1150.3 miles on 19.41 gallons of fuel. To the correct number of decimal places, how many miles per gallon is that?

56. The highest average yardage gain for a football season belongs to Beattie Feathers. He gained 1004 yards in 101 carries. What was his average number of yards per carry? (Answer to the nearest tenth of a yard.)

57. In 1925, a 3,600-revolution-per-minute (rpm) motor was attached to a gramaphone with a 46 : 1 gear ratio. The resulting speed was $\frac{3600}{46}$ rpm. What is this ratio to the nearest whole number? This ratio gave birth to a new kind of record, and if you find the answer, you will find what kind of record we mean.

58. The longest and heaviest freight train on record was one about 21,120 ft in length and consisting of 500 coal cars. To the nearest ft, how long was each coal car?

In Other Words

59. Explain in your own words some of the advantages of decimals over ordinary fractions.

60. Explain why, when multiplying two decimals, the number of decimal places in the answer is equal to the sum of the number of decimal places in the two factors.

Using Your Knowledge

In doing numerical computations, it is often worth making an estimate of the answer to avoid bad errors. (Even if you use a calculator, you might hit a wrong key!) In many instances, a good estimate may be all that is needed. For example, suppose we want to find the area of a rectangular lot that is measured to be 98.2 ft wide by 347 ft deep. The area of a rectangle of sides a and b is A = ab. If we round 98.2 to 100 and the 347 to 340, then we have a quick estimate of 34,000 square feet for the area of the lot.

Using a calculator to multiply the given dimensions yields an answer of 34,075.4. Rounding to three significant digits (to agree with the accuracy of the dimensions), gives 34,100 square feet. Thus, our estimate is off by only 100 square feet.

61. Edie goes to the grocery store and picks up four items costing $1.98, $2.35, $2.85, and $4.20. Before going to the checkout counter, Edie wants an estimate of her total purchases. Which of the following is the best estimate?
    (a) $9   (b) $11
    (c) $13   (d) $8

62. Jasper has a room that is 15 feet wide and 24.5 feet long. He wants to put in flooring that costs $10.25 per square yard. Which of the following is the best estimate of the total cost?
    (a) $300   (b) $400
    (c) $350   (d) $3,500

Calculator Corner

If your calculator has a $\boxed{\text{sci}}$ *key or its equivalent, then you can convert numbers to scientific notation automatically. Thus, to write 270,000 in scientific notation, enter* $\boxed{2}\ \boxed{7}\ \boxed{0}\ \boxed{0}\ \boxed{0}\ \boxed{0}\ \boxed{=}$ *and* $\boxed{\text{2nd}}\ \boxed{\text{sci}}$ *. If you do not have a* $\boxed{\text{sci}}$ *key, you must know to enter numbers in scientific notation by using the* $\boxed{\text{exp}}$ *key. Thus, to enter 270,000, you have to know that*

$$270,000 = 2.7 \times 10^5$$

and enter $\boxed{2}\ \boxed{.}\ \boxed{7}\ \boxed{\text{exp}}\ \boxed{5}$ *. The display shows 2.7 05.*

To perform operations in scientific notation (without a $\boxed{\text{sci}}$ *key), we enter the numbers as discussed. Thus, to find (5 × 10⁴) × (9 × 10⁻⁷) (as we did in Example 4), enter* $\boxed{(}\ \boxed{5}\ \boxed{\text{exp}}\ \boxed{4}\ \boxed{)}\ \boxed{\times}\ \boxed{(}\ \boxed{9}\ \boxed{\text{exp}}\ \boxed{7}\ \boxed{\pm}\ \boxed{)}\ \boxed{=}$ *. The display will give the answer as 4.5 −02, that is 4.5 × 10⁻². If you have a* $\boxed{\text{sci}}$ *key or if you can place the calculator in scientific mode, then enter* $\boxed{5}$ $\boxed{\text{exp}}\ \boxed{4}\ \boxed{\times}\ \boxed{9}\ \boxed{\text{exp}}\ \boxed{7}\ \boxed{\pm}\ \boxed{=}$ *(no need to use parentheses), and the same result as before will appear in the display.*

1. Use your calculator to check problems 13, 15, 17, and 19 in Exercise 4.5.

The operations of addition, subtraction, multiplication, and division involving decimals are easy to perform with a calculator. You just press the appropriate numbers and indicated operations and the calculator does the rest! However, you must know how to round off answers using the rules we have discussed. Thus, in Example 9, you enter 26.3 + 7.41 + 20.64, but you have to know that the answer must be rounded off to 54.4.

4.6   RATIONAL NUMBERS AS DECIMALS: PERCENTS

GETTING STARTED

STOCK PRICES AND FRACTIONS

The fractional part of the price of gas is usually listed as $\frac{9}{10}$ of a cent. Can you imagine the problems that would arise if it were $\frac{3}{7}$ or $\frac{7}{11}$? It would be extremely difficult to change $\frac{3}{7}$ and $\frac{7}{11}$ to a decimal to find the total price. (Try dividing 3 by 7 or 7 by 11.) Now, look at the fractional parts in the stock listing shown. The denominators are 2's, 4's or 8's. Now, try writing $\frac{1}{8}$, $\frac{2}{8} = \frac{1}{4}$, $\frac{3}{8}$, $\frac{4}{8} = \frac{1}{2}$, $\frac{5}{8}$, $\frac{6}{8} = \frac{3}{4}$ or $\frac{7}{8}$ as decimals. It is much easier! What do you think the denominators of all the fractions that are easy to convert to decimals (10, 2, 4, and 8) have in common? The answer is contained in a theorem included in this section. As a matter of fact, after you read and understand the theorem, you will be able to tell if a fraction has a terminating or a nonterminating decimal representation (problems 25–30, Exercise 4.6). You will also learn to write this representation and even change a terminating or nonterminating repeating decimal to a fraction (problems 43–58, Exercise 4.6.)

We end this section by studying a special type of decimal, **percents.**

MOST ACTIVE ISSUES			
NYSE	VOLUME	CLOSE	CHANGE
AT&T	3,122,600	37³/₈	− ¹/₈
PepsiCo	2,811,700	29⁵/₈	+ ¹/₂
Boeing Co	2,708,800	50	− 1¹/₈
Tenneco Inc	2,301,700	40¹/₂	− 2¹/₈
Heinz (HJ) Co	1,912,600	37³/₄	− ¹/₂
Marion Merrell	1,832,000	36³/₄	+ 3
Syntex Corp	1,669,300	42	− ³/₈
Kemper Corp	1,654,500	30	− 1³/₈
IBM	1,587,900	101³/₈	+ 1³/₄
Salomon Inc	1,542,300	25	+ ⁷/₈
Westinghouse	1,495,300	22¹/₄	+ ¹/₈
Campbell Soup	1,449,400	76³/₄	+ 1
General Elec	1,442,900	70³/₈	+ ¹/₈
Limited Inc	1,300,800	25¹/₂	+ ³/₄
Telefonos Mex	1,239,700	37³/₄	+ ⁷/₈

As we mentioned in Section 4.5, a rational number can always be written in decimal form. If the number is a fraction, we divide the numerator by the denominator, obtaining either a terminating or a nonterminating decimal.

A. *Terminating and Nonterminating Decimals*

Numbers such as $\frac{1}{2}$, $\frac{1}{8}$, and $\frac{1}{5}$ are said to have **terminating decimal representations** because division of the numerator by the denominator terminates (ends). However, some rational numbers — for example, $\frac{1}{3}$ — have **infinite repeating decimal representations.** Such a representation is obtained by dividing the numerator of the fraction by its denominator. In the case of $\frac{1}{3}$, we obtain

$$
\begin{array}{r}
0.333\ \ldots \\
3\overline{)1.0} \\
\underline{9} \\
10 \\
\underline{9} \\
10 \\
\underline{9} \\
1 \ \text{etc.}
\end{array}
$$

For convenience, we shall write 0.333 . . . as $0.\bar{3}$. The bar over the 3 indicates that the 3 repeats indefinitely. Similarly,

$\frac{1}{7} = 0.142857142857\ldots = 0.\overline{142857}$.

EXAMPLE 1   Write as decimals and state the value in the second decimal place:

(a) $\dfrac{3}{4}$ (b) $\dfrac{2}{3}$

Solution   (a) Dividing 3 by 4, we obtain

$$
\begin{array}{r}
0.75 \\
4\overline{)3.0} \\
\underline{28} \\
20 \\
\underline{20} \\
0
\end{array}
$$

Thus, $\frac{3}{4} = 0.75$, and the value in the second decimal place is $\frac{5}{100}$.

(b) Dividing 2 by 3, we obtain

$$
\begin{array}{r}
0.666\ \ldots \\
3\overline{)2.0} \\
\underline{1\ 8} \\
20 \\
\underline{18} \\
20 \\
\underline{18} \\
2 \ \text{etc.}
\end{array}
$$

Thus, $\frac{2}{3} = 0.666 \ldots = 0.\overline{6}$, and the value in the second decimal place is $\frac{6}{100}$. ∎

You should be able to convince yourself of the truth of the following theorem, which indicates which rational numbers have terminating decimal representations.

Theorem 4.4 —— A rational number a/b (in lowest terms) has a terminating decimal expansion if and only if b has no prime factors other than 2 and 5.

Notice that b does not have to have 2 *and* 5 as factors; it might have only one of them as a factor, or perhaps neither, as in the following illustrations:

$$\frac{1}{25} = 0.04$$

Since $25 = 5 \times 5$, $\frac{1}{25}$ has a terminating decimal expansion.

$$\frac{1}{4} = 0.25$$

Since $4 = 2 \times 2$, $\frac{1}{4}$ has a terminating decimal expansion.

$$\frac{8}{1} = 8.0$$

The denominator is 1, which has no prime factors, so $\frac{8}{1}$ has a terminating decimal expansion. Of course, if the rational number is given as a mixed number — for example, $5\frac{1}{2}$ — we could first convert it to $\frac{11}{2}$ and notice that the denominator has only 2 as a factor. Thus $5\frac{1}{2} = \frac{11}{2}$ has a terminating decimal expansion.

The stock markets use the fractions with denominators 2, 4, 8, and 16 because these fractions have simple terminating decimal forms. The denominators are powers of 2 and

Of the first twenty counting numbers, only 7, 17, and 19 have reciprocals with the maximum possible number of digits in the repeating part of their decimal representations:

$\frac{1}{7} = 0.\overline{142857}$

$\frac{1}{17} = 0.\overline{0588235294117647}$

$\frac{1}{19} = 0.\overline{052631578947368421}$

$$\frac{1}{2^n} = (0.5)^n$$

so there will be exactly n decimal places.

It is easy to see that every rational number has an infinite repeating decimal representation. In the case of a terminating decimal, we can agree simply to adjoin an infinite string of 0's. For example, $\frac{3}{4} = 0.75\overline{0}$, $\frac{1}{20} = 0.05\overline{0}$, and so on. If the rational number a/b has no terminating decimal representation, then it must have a repeating decimal representation, as we can see by carrying out the division of a by b. The only possible remainders are $1, 2, 3, \ldots, b - 1$. Therefore, after at most $(b - 1)$ steps of the division, a remainder must occur for the second time. Thereafter, the digits of the quotient must repeat. The following division illustrates the idea:

$$
\begin{array}{r}
1.692307 \\
13\overline{)22} \\
\underline{13} \\
90 \\
\underline{78} \\
120 \\
\underline{117} \\
30 \\
\underline{26} \\
40 \\
\underline{39} \\
100 \\
\underline{91} \\
\mathbf{9}
\end{array}
$$

Notice that the remainder **9** occurs just before the digit 6 appears in the quotient and occurs again just after the digit 7 appears in the quotient. Thus, the repeating part of the decimal must be 692307, and $\frac{22}{13} = 1.\overline{692307}$.

B. *Changing Infinite Repeating Decimals to Fractions*

The preceding discussion shows that **every rational number can be written as an infinite repeating decimal.** Is the converse of this statement true? That is, does every infinite repeating decimal represent a rational number? If the repeating part is simply a string of 0's so that the decimal is actually terminating, it can be written as a rational number with a power of 10 as the denominator. For example, $0.73 = \frac{73}{100}$, $0.7 = \frac{7}{10}$, and $0.013 = \frac{13}{1000}$. If the decimal is repeating but not terminating, then we can proceed as in the next example.

EXAMPLE 2   Write $0.\overline{23}$ as a quotient of integers.

Solution   If $x = 0.232323\ldots$, then $100x = 23.232323\ldots$. Now we can remove the repeating part by subtraction as follows:

$$
\begin{array}{r}
100x = 23.232323\ldots \\
(-) x = 0.232323\ldots \\
\hline
99x = 23
\end{array}
$$

Then, dividing by 99, we get

$$
x = \frac{23}{99}
$$

Here is the procedure.

■

> **Changing an Infinite Repeating Decimal to a Fraction**
>
> 1. Let x = the given decimal.
> 2. Multiply by a power of 10 to move the decimal point to the right of the first sequence of digits that repeats.
> 3. If the decimal point is not at the left of the first repeating sequence of digits, multiply by a power of 10 to place it there.
> 4. Subtract the result of step 3 from that of step 2.
> 5. Divide by the multiplier of x in the result of step 4 to get the desired fraction.

The idea in steps 2 and 3 is to line up the repeating parts so they drop out in the subtraction in step 4.

EXAMPLE 3   Write 3.5212121 . . . as a quotient of two integers.

Solution

1. Let x = 3.5212121 . . . .   We want the decimal point here.
2. Since we want the decimal point to the right of the first 21, we multiply by 1000:

$$1000x = 3521.212121 \ldots$$

3. In this step, we want the decimal point to the left of the first 21,

3.5212121 . . .   Here

so we multiply x by 10:

$$10x = 35.212121 \ldots$$

4. $1000x = 3521.212121 \ldots$
   $(-)\quad 10x = \quad\ \ 35.212121 \ldots$
   $\overline{\qquad 990x = 3486}$ The decimal parts drop out.

5. We divide by 990 to get

$$x = \frac{3486}{990} = \frac{581 \cdot 6}{165 \cdot 6} = \frac{581}{165}$$

∎

This discussion can be summarized as follows: **Every rational number has a repeating decimal representation, and every repeating decimal represents a rational number.**

If we use the procedure of Examples 2 and 3 for the repeating decimal 0.999 . . . , we come out with the result

$$0.999 \ldots = 1$$

If you are bothered by this result, here are some examples that may convince you of its truth.

(a) $\frac{1}{3} = 0.333 \ldots$
  $\frac{2}{3} = 0.666 \ldots$
  What is the result when you add these two equations?

(b) $\frac{4}{9} = 0.444 \ldots$
  $\frac{5}{9} = 0.555 \ldots$
  What is the result when you add these two equations?

(c) $\frac{1}{9} = 0.111 \ldots$
  What do you get by multiplying both sides of this equation by 9? (You can try it on your calculator! Begin by entering 1, then press $\boxed{\div}\ \boxed{9}\ \boxed{\times}\ \boxed{9}\ \boxed{=}$ and watch the display.)

C. *Percent*

In many of the daily applications of decimals, information is given in terms of **percents.** The interest rate on a mortgage may be 12% (read, "12 percent"), the Dow Jones stock average may increase by 2%, your savings account may earn interest at 6%, and so on. The word "percent" comes from the Latin words *per* and *centum* and means "by the hundred." Thus, 12% is the same as $\frac{12}{100}$ or the decimal 0.12.

> **Changing a Percent to a Decimal**
>
> Move the decimal point in the number two places to the left and omit the % symbol.

EXAMPLE 4   Write as a decimal:

(a) 18%   (b) 11.5%   (c) 0.5%

Solution   (a) 18% = 0.18   (b) 11.5% = 0.115   (c) 0.5% = 0.005   ∎

To change a decimal to a percent, we just reverse the procedure.

> **Changing a Decimal to a Percent**
>
> Move the decimal point two places to the right and affix the percent sign.

EXAMPLE 5   Change to a percent: (a) 0.25   (b) 1.989

Solution   (a) 0.25 = 25%   (b) 1.989 = 198.9%   ∎

> **Changing a Fraction to a Percent**
>
> Divide the numerator by the denominator, and then convert the resulting decimal to a percent.

EXAMPLE 6   Write as a percent: (a) $\frac{2}{5}$ (b) $\frac{3}{7}$ (Give answer to one decimal place.)

Solution   (a) $\frac{2}{5} = 0.40 = 40\%$ (b) $\frac{3}{7} = 0.42856$ By ordinary division

$$= 0.429 \quad \text{Rounded to three decimal places}$$

$$= 42.9\%$$

■

EXAMPLE 7   When you buy popcorn at the theater, you get popcorn, butter substitute, and a bucket. Which of these is the most expensive? The bucket! Here are the approximate costs to a theater: popcorn, 5¢; butter substitute, 2¢; bucket, 25¢.

     (a) Find, to two decimal places, the percent of the total cost for each of these components.

     (b) If the average profit on this popcorn is 86% of the cost, how much is that?

Solution   (a) Cost of popcorn is $\frac{5}{32} = 0.15625$, or 15.63%.

       Cost of butter substitute is $\frac{2}{32} = 0.0625$, or 6.25%.

       Cost of bucket is $\frac{25}{32} = 0.78125$, or 78.13%.

     (b) 86% of 32 = $0.86 \times 32 = 27.52$, or nearly 28¢.

■

EXAMPLE 8   Theater concession stands make 25% of all the popcorn sales in the United States. If these stands make about 250 million sales annually, about how many popcorn sales are made per year in the United States?

Solution   We know that 25% of all sales is about 250 million. If we let s be the total number of sales, then

$$0.25s = 250 \text{ million}$$

Thus, dividing both sides by 0.25, we get

$$s = \frac{250 \text{ million}}{0.25}$$

$$= 1{,}000 \text{ million, or about 1 billion sales per year.}$$

■

D. *Percent Increase or Decrease*

EXAMPLE 9   (a) In a certain company, male engineers' salaries began at $23,000, while female engineers began at $15,500. To the nearest percent, how much higher were male engineers' salaries?

(b) According to the *Almanac of Jobs and Salaries,* the average starting salary offers for bachelor degree candidates in engineering was $30,300 while for those in computer sciences it was $27,600. To the nearest percent, how much more was the offer for engineers?

Solution (a) The difference in salaries is $23,000 − $15,500 = $7500. Thus, the male engineers earned

$$\frac{7500}{15,500} = 0.484 \qquad \boxed{7}\,\boxed{5}\,\boxed{\div}\,\boxed{1}\,\boxed{5}\,\boxed{5}\,\boxed{=}$$

or a whopping 48% more. (Note that the female engineers' salary was in the denominator of the fraction, because that salary was the basis for comparison.)

(b) Here, the salary difference is $30,300 − $27,600 = $2700. Thus, the engineers earned

$$\frac{2700}{27,600} = 0.0978 \qquad \boxed{2}\,\boxed{7}\,\boxed{\div}\,\boxed{2}\,\boxed{7}\,\boxed{6}$$

or 9.78% more than computer scientists.   ∎

Exercise 4.6

A. In problems 1–24, write the given number in decimal form.

1. $\frac{9}{10}$	2. $\frac{3}{10}$	3. $\frac{11}{10}$	4. $\frac{27}{10}$
5. $\frac{17}{100}$	6. $\frac{38}{100}$	7. $\frac{121}{100}$	8. $\frac{3520}{100}$
9. $\frac{3}{1000}$	10. $\frac{143}{1000}$	11. $\frac{1243}{1000}$	12. $\frac{25360}{1000}$
13. $\frac{3}{5}$	14. $\frac{7}{8}$	15. $\frac{9}{16}$	16. $\frac{15}{32}$
17. $\frac{5}{8}$	18. $\frac{5}{4}$	19. $\frac{5}{7}$	20. $\frac{7}{6}$
21. $\frac{4}{15}$	22. $6\frac{1}{4}$	23. $7\frac{1}{7}$	24. $3\frac{2}{3}$

B. In problems 25–30, determine whether the given number has a terminating decimal expansion. If it does, give the expansion.

25. $\frac{3}{16}$	26. $\frac{3}{14}$	27. $\frac{1}{64}$
28. $\frac{4}{28}$	29. $\frac{31}{3125}$	30. $\frac{9}{250}$

In problems 31–42, rewrite the given repeating decimal, using a bar and as few digits as possible written out.

31. 0.555555 . . .	32. 0.777777 . . .	33. 0.646464 . . .
34. 0.737373 . . .	35. 0.235235 . . .	36. 0.930930 . . .
37. 0.215555 . . .	38. 0.7132222 . . .	39. 0.079353535 . . .
40. 0.23515151 . . .	41. 5.070707 . . .	42. 9.23373737 . . .

In problems 43–58, write the given number as a fraction (a quotient of two integers). Reduce if possible.

43. $0.\overline{8}$ 44. $0.\overline{6}$ 45. $0.\overline{31}$ 46. $0.\overline{21}$
47. $0.\overline{114}$ 48. $0.\overline{102}$ 49. $2.\overline{31}$ 50. $5.\overline{672}$
51. $1.\overline{234}$ 52. $0.0\overline{17}$ 53. $1.2\overline{7}$ 54. $2.4\overline{8}$
55. $0.45\overline{75}$ 56. $0.23\overline{15}$ 57. $0.\overline{2016}$ 58. $0.201\overline{6}$

C. In problems 59–67, write the given percent as a decimal.

59. 29%   60. 23.4%   61. 0.9%   62. 56.9%
63. 45.69%   64. 0.008%   65. 34.15%   66. 93.56%
67. 0.0234%

In problems 68–76, write the given decimal as a percent.

68. 0.38   69. 3.45   70. 9.998   71. 0.567
72. 0.0045   73. 9.003   74. 0.0004   75. 0.0045
76. 0.0008

In problems 77–80. write the given fraction as a percent.

77. $\frac{3}{5}$ 78. $\frac{4}{7}$ (to one decimal place)
79. $\frac{5}{6}$ (to one decimal place)   80. $\frac{7}{8}$
81. Find 13% of 70.
82. What is 110% of 90?
83. 24 is what percent of 72?
84. 15 is 30% of what number?
85. 100 is what percent of 80?
86. Find $12\frac{1}{4}$% of 320.

87. In a recent year, about 16,300,000 cars were sold by the U.S. auto industry. Of these, 8,214,671 were made in the United States. What percent is that? (Answer to one decimal place.)

88. One of the most expensive British standard cars is the Rolls-Royce Phantom VI, quoted at \$312,954. An armor-plated version was quoted at \$560,000. What percent more does the armor plating cost?

89. By weight, the average adult is composed of 43% muscle, 26% skin, 17.5% bone, 7% blood, and 6.5% organs. If a person weighs 150 lb:
    (a) How many lb of muscle does the person have?
    (b) How many lb of skin does the person have?

90. Referring to problem 89:
    (a) How many lb of bone does the person have?
    (b) How many lb of organs does the person have?

91. A portable paint compressor is priced at $196.50. If the sales tax rate is 5.5%, what is the tax?

92. The highest recorded shorthand speed was 300 words per minute for 5 minutes with 99.64% accuracy. How many errors were made?

93. In a recent year, the United States had 168,607,000 cars. This represented about 37.9% of the total world stock of cars. How many cars were in the world stock?

94. In a recent year, 41.2 million households with televisions watched the Superbowl. This represented 47.1% of homes with televisions in major cities. How many homes with televisions are there in major cities?

D. 95. If 25 is increased to 30, what is the percent increase?

96. If 32 is decreased to 28, what is the percent decrease?

97. If you increase 28 by 25% of itself, what is the result?

98. If you decrease 24 by $16\frac{1}{2}$% of itself, what is the result?

99. Joe Long is a computer programmer. His salary was increased by $8,000. If his previous salary was $28,000, what was his percent increase? (Answer to the nearest percent.)

100. Felicia Perez received a $1,750 annual raise from the state of Florida. If her salary was $25,000 before the raise, what percent raise did she receive?

101. Joseph Clemons had a salary of $20,000 last year. This year, his salary was increased to $22,000. What percent increase is this?

102. Here are some professions and the average salaries earned by males and females. To the nearest percent, how much more did males make?

	Male	Female
(a) Doctors and dentists	$90,000	$72,000
(b) Elementary and high school teachers	$21,600	$17,280
(c) Sales clerks	$18,000	$ 9,180

103. Andy was told that if he would switch to the next higher grade of gasoline, his mileage would increase to 115% of his present mileage of 22 mi/gal. What would be his increased mileage?

104. Gail learned that a new hairdresser's fees were only 80% of her present hairdresser's fees. If her present fees are $25 per month, what would be her monthly savings if she changed to the new hairdresser?

105. A furniture dealer sold two small sets of furniture for $391 each. On one set he made 15% and on the other he lost 15%. What was his net profit or loss on the two sets?

*I*n Other Words

Answer true (T) or false (F) for each of the following statements and give reasons to support each answer.

106. (a) Some repeating decimals are not rational numbers.
     (b) All counting numbers are rational numbers.
     (c) Some integers are not rational numbers.
     (d) 0.20200200020000 . . . is a repeating decimal.
     (e) All terminating decimals are rational numbers.

Discovery

In this section we developed a procedure for expressing an infinite repeating decimal as a quotient of two integers. For example,

$$0.\overline{3} = 0.333 \ldots = \tfrac{3}{9}$$
$$0.\overline{6} = 0.666 \ldots = \tfrac{6}{9}$$
$$0.\overline{21} = 0.212121 \ldots = \tfrac{21}{99}$$
$$0.\overline{314} = 0.314314314 \ldots = \tfrac{314}{999}$$

107. From these examples, can you discover how to express $0.\overline{4} = 0.444 \ldots$ as a quotient of integers?

108. Can you express $0.\overline{4321}$ as a quotient of integers?

*If we have a repeating decimal with one digit as a **repetend** (the part that repeats), the number can be written as a fraction by dividing the repetend by 9. For example, $0.\overline{7} = \tfrac{7}{9}$. If the number has two digits in the repetend, the number can be written as a fraction by dividing the repetend by 99. For example, $0.\overline{21} = \tfrac{21}{99}$.*

Use this idea to check your results in problems 43–48, Exercise 4.6.

Calculator Corner

Most operations in this section can be done with a calculator. For example, to change a fraction to a decimal, divide the numerator by the denominator. But can you find the decimal expansion for $\tfrac{3}{14}$? If the calculator has ten decimal places, then when you divide 3 by 14 the answer is given as 0.214285714, and you must know that the repeating part is 142857.

Note that you can check the decimal expansion of a fraction by simply leaving your answer in the calculator and multiplying by the denominator.

Some calculators have a $\boxed{\%}$ key that changes percents to decimals. You can determine whether your calculator does this by entering 11.5 $\boxed{\text{2nd}}$ $\boxed{\%}$. The answer should appear as 0.115 (Example 4b).

1. Use your calculator to check problems 59–67 in Exercise 4.6.

4.7 THE REAL NUMBERS

GETTING STARTED

PI (π) THROUGH THE AGES

One of the most unusual and interesting real numbers is π (the Greek letter pi, pronounced "pie"), which is the ratio of the circumference to the diameter of a circle, that is,

$$\pi = \frac{C}{d}.$$

What is the numerical value of π? Actually, there have been many versions. In 1800–1600 B.C. the Babylonians gave π a value of 3. The Hebrews used the same approximation in the Old Testament (1 Kings 7:23, written in 650 B.C. but dating back to 900 B.C.). It reads, "And he made a molten sea, 10 cubits from one brim to the other: it was round all about . . . : and a line of 30 cubits did compass it round about." More recent findings (a tablet in Susa) indicate that the Babylonians might have used $3\frac{1}{8} = 3.125$ as the value for π. The Egyptians used the approximation $4 \times (\frac{8}{9})^2 = 3.1605$ in the Rhind papyrus, an ancient document written in 1650 B.C.

In the first century, Liu Hsin used 3.1547, while Chang Hen (A.D. 78–139) used the value $\sqrt{10}$, which is approximately 3.1622, or the fraction $\frac{92}{29}$, which is about 3.1724. In the third century B.C., Archimedes approximated π by drawing a circle between two polygons of 6, 12, 24, 48 and 96 sides. As the number of sides increased, the perimeter of the polygons approximated the circumference of the circle and showed that π was between $3\frac{10}{71}$ and $3\frac{1}{7}$. This same method was employed by Liu Hui to find his best value for π, namely, 3.14159. Tsu Chung-Chi (A.D. 430–501) refined the method and obtained boundaries of 3.1415926 and 3.1415727, giving the fraction $\frac{22}{7}$ as the "inaccurate" value for π and $\frac{355}{113}$, a value correct to six decimals, as the "accurate" value. (No fraction with a denominator less than 113 gives a closer approximation for π.) How close can you get to π? Get a soda can, measure around it and divide by the distance across the top. What do you get? What about using computers to find a more accurate approximation? The latest approximation for π (done with both an IBM and a Cray-2) has 1,011,196,691 decimal places!

In Section 4.3, we presented the usefulness and beauty of the set of integers. The Pythagoreans, an ancient Greek secret society (ca. 540–500 B.C.), were so certain that the entire universe was made up of the whole numbers that they classified them into categories such as "perfect" and "amicable." They labeled the even numbers as "feminine" and the odd numbers as "masculine," except 1, which was the generator of all other numbers. (At that time, the symbol for marriage was the number 5, the sum of the first feminine number, 2, and the first masculine number, 3.) In the midst of these charming fantasies, the discovery of a new type of number was made — a type of number so unexpected that the brotherhood tried to suppress their discovery. They had found the numbers that we call **irrational numbers** today.

Here is a general idea of what happened: Suppose you draw a number line 2 units long (see Figure 4.4):

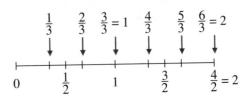

FIGURE 4.4

We divide the unit interval into 2 equal parts and graph $\frac{1}{2}$, $\frac{2}{2} = 1$, $\frac{3}{2}$, and $\frac{4}{2} = 2$. We then proceed in the same way and divide the unit interval into three parts, marking $\frac{1}{3}$, $\frac{2}{3}$, $\frac{3}{3} = 1$, $\frac{4}{3}$, $\frac{5}{3}$, and $\frac{6}{3} = 2$ as shown. For any whole number q, we can divide the unit interval into q equal parts and then graph $1/q$, $2/q$, and so on. It seems reasonable to assume that this process continued indefinitely would assign a rational number to every point on the line.

Now, suppose we construct a unit square and draw its diagonal as shown in Figure 4.5. Turn this diagonal (called the **hypotenuse** of the resulting triangle) clockwise to coincide with the number line extending from 0 to a point marked P. What rational number corresponds to P? None! Why? Because the required number is not obtainable by dividing any whole number by another whole number; it is not a rational number.

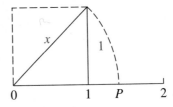

FIGURE 4.5

Ironically enough, Pythagoras himself had proved the famous theorem bearing his name: *The square of the hypotenuse of a right triangle is equal to the sum of the squares of the other two sides.* If we let x be the length of this hypotenuse (the diagonal of the square in Figure 4.5), the theorem says that

$$x^2 = 1^2 + 1^2 = 2$$

so that

$$x = \sqrt{2} \qquad \text{Square root of 2, a positive number that when squared yields 2}$$

The Pythagoreans were able to prove that $\sqrt{2}$ is not obtainable by dividing any whole number by another, that is, that $\sqrt{2}$ is not a rational number. To do so, they used a method of proof called *reductio ad absurdum,* meaning "reduction to the absurd" (we now call this **proof by contradiction**). Their proof may have gone as follows:

Proof Assume that $\sqrt{2}$ is a rational number, say, a/b, in lowest terms; that is, a and b have no common factor other than 1. Thus,

1. $$\sqrt{2} = \frac{a}{b}$$
2. Multiply by b: $\sqrt{2}\,b = a$
3. Square both sides: $(\sqrt{2}\,b)^2 = a^2$
4. Simplify: $2b^2 = a^2$

5. Thus, a^2 is an even number, and since only even numbers have squares that are even, a is an even number. Suppose $a = 2c$.
6. Substitute $a = 2c$ in step 4:
$$2b^2 = (2c)^2 = 4c^2$$
7. Divide by 2: $b^2 = 2c^2$

8. This last equation says that b^2 is an even number, so that b is an even number.
9. Now, we have a contradiction: Step 5 says that a is even, and step 8 says that b is even, which means that a and b would have the common factor 2, contrary to our assumption. Hence, our assumption is invalid, and $\sqrt{2}$ is not a rational number. ∎

Numbers that are not rational are called **irrational.**

A. *Square Roots*

The proof above can be generalized to show that the only numbers with rational square roots are the **perfect squares:**

$\sqrt{1} = 1$ because $1^2 = 1$

$\sqrt{4} = 2$ because $2^2 = 4$

$\sqrt{9} = 3$ because $3^2 = 9$

and so on. The square roots of all other natural numbers are irrational.

EXAMPLE 1 Classify as rational or irrational:

(a) $\sqrt{36}$ (b) $\sqrt{44}$ (c) $\sqrt{81}$

Solution (a) $\sqrt{36} = 6$; it is rational   (b) $\sqrt{44}$ is irrational.
(c) $\sqrt{81} = 9$; it is rational. ∎

B. *Irrational Numbers and Decimal Numbers*

Irrational numbers such as $\sqrt{2}$ can be approximated to any finite number of decimal places. But these decimal numbers can never repeat (as in $\frac{1}{7}$) or terminate (as in $\frac{1}{2}$), because if they did, they would be rational numbers. For example,

$$\sqrt{2} = 1.4142 \ldots \qquad \text{or} \qquad \sqrt{2} = 1.414213 \ldots$$

We use this idea to define irrational numbers.

Definition 4.12

> An **irrational number** is a number that has a **nonterminating, nonrepeating** decimal representation.

For example, 0.909009000 . . . (the successive sets of digits are 90, 900, 9000, etc.) is nonterminating and nonrepeating, and thus is irrational. Another irrational number is the decimal 1.23456789101112 . . . , where we continue writing the digits of the successive counting numbers. Here again, although there is a definite pattern, the decimal is nonrepeating and nonterminating.

The set consisting of all decimals, terminating or nonterminating, repeating (that is, the rational numbers) and nonterminating, nonrepeating (that is, the irrational numbers) is called the set R of **real numbers.** (Keep in mind that the rationals can be written as quotients of two integers and the irrationals cannot.) The set R includes all the numbers we have studied: the natural numbers, the integers, the rational numbers, and the irrational numbers. The rationals and the irrationals completely cover the number line: To each point on the line there corresponds a unique real number, and to each real number there corresponds a unique point.

EXAMPLE 2   Classify the following numbers as rational or irrational:

(a) 0.35626262 . . .   (b) 0.305300530005 . . .   (c) 0.12345678
(d) $-\frac{1}{3}$ (e) $\sqrt{65}$ (f) $\sqrt{144}$

Solution   (a) A repeating decimal; therefore, rational
(b) A nonrepeating, nonterminating decimal; therefore, irrational
(c) A terminating decimal; therefore, rational
(d) A fraction; therefore, rational
(e) Irrational
(f) $\sqrt{144} = 12$, which is rational   ■

Looking at the decimal approximations of $\sqrt{2}$ given earlier, we can see that 1.4 is less than $\sqrt{2}$ but 1.5 is greater; that is, $\sqrt{2}$ is between 1.4 and 1.5. Can we always find an irrational number between any two rational numbers? In order to answer this question, we must first make the ideas of **less than** ($<$) and **greater than** ($>$) more precise, as in the following definition.

Definition 4.13 ———

If a and b are real numbers, then:

1. $a < b$ if and only if there is a positive number c such that $a + c = b$.
2. $b > a$ if and only if $a < b$.

Thus, $3 < 5$ because $3 + 2 = 5$; $-4 < -1$ because $-4 + 3 = -1$; $5 > 3$ because $3 < 5$; and $\frac{1}{3} = 0.333 \ldots < \frac{1}{2} = 0.5$ because $\frac{1}{3} + \frac{1}{6} = \frac{1}{2}$.

A basic property of the real numbers is given by the following statement.

The Trichotomy Law

If a and b are any real numbers, then exactly one of the following relations must occur:

$$a = b \tag{1}$$

$$a < b \tag{2}$$

$$a > b \tag{3}$$

Thus, if $a \not> b$ (a is not greater than b), then $a \le b$ (a is less than or equal to b). And if $a \not< b$ (a is not less than b), then $a \ge b$ (a is greater than or equal to b).

It is not difficult to compare two rational numbers, but what about comparing an irrational number such as $\sqrt{48}$ and a rational number such as 6.9? You know that the numbers are close because $\sqrt{49} = 7$, which is close to 6.9, but can we fill in the blank with $<$ or $>$ to obtain a correct statement in the expression

$$\sqrt{48} \underline{\hspace{1cm}} 6.9?$$

By squaring both sides we get the equivalent comparison

$$48 \underline{\hspace{1cm}} (6.9)^2 = 47.61$$

which shows that the $>$ symbol is the correct choice. Thus,

$$\sqrt{48} > 6.9.$$

EXAMPLE 3 Insert $<$, $>$, or $=$ to make a correct statement.

(a) $\sqrt{60} \underline{\hspace{1cm}} 7.7$ (b) $\sqrt{30} \underline{\hspace{1cm}} 5.5$

Solution (a) As before, we write $\sqrt{60} \underline{\hspace{1cm}} 7.7$
Squaring both sides, $60 \underline{\hspace{1cm}} (7.7)^2 = 59.29$
Since $60 > 59.29$, we have $\sqrt{60} > 7.7$

(b) Squaring both sides, we get $30 \underline{\hspace{1cm}} (5.5)^2 = 30.25$
Since $30 < (5.5)^2 = 30.25$, $\sqrt{30} < 5.5$ ∎

We now return to the question "Can we always find an irrational number between any two rational numbers? The answer is affirmative. For example, to find an irrational number between $\frac{1}{3}$ and $\frac{1}{2}$, we first write $\frac{1}{3}$ and $\frac{1}{2}$ as decimals:

$$\frac{1}{2} = 0.5$$

$$\frac{1}{3} = 0.333 \ldots$$

Obviously, the number 0.4 is between 0.5 and 0.333 . . . ; however, this number is not irrational. We now add a nonrepeating, nonterminating part to this number as shown:

$$\frac{1}{2} = 0.5$$
$$\quad 0.4101001000 \ldots \quad \text{Nonterminating, nonrepeating}$$
$$\frac{1}{3} = 0.333 \ldots$$

The number 0.4101001000 . . . is bigger than 0.333 . . . , smaller than 0.5, and irrational. We could have found infinitely many other numbers using a similar technique. Can you find two more?

EXAMPLE 4   Find:

(a) A rational number between 0.121 and 0.122
(b) An irrational number between 0.121 and 0.122

Solution   (a) The rational number 0.1215 is between 0.121 and 0.122 as shown:

0.121
0.1215
0.122

(b) The irrational number 0.121567891011 . . . is between 0.121 and 0.122 as shown:

0.121
0.121567891011 . . .   Nonterminating, nonrepeating
0.122   ■

In the preceding discussion we have seen that we are able to find an irrational number between any two given rational numbers. We can show that it is indeed possible to find a rational number between *any* two given rational numbers. For example, given the rational numbers $\frac{4}{7}$ and $\frac{5}{7}$, we write

$$\frac{4}{7} = \frac{4 \cdot 2}{7 \cdot 2} = \frac{8}{14} \quad \text{and} \quad \frac{5}{7} = \frac{5 \cdot 2}{7 \cdot 2} = \frac{10}{14}$$

We can now see by inspection that one rational number between $\frac{4}{7}$ and $\frac{5}{7}$ is $\frac{9}{14}$. If the two given rationals do not have the same denominator, then we can proceed as in the next example.

EXAMPLE 5 Find a rational number between $0.\overline{4}$ and $\frac{6}{13}$.

Solution Since $0.\overline{4} = \frac{4}{9}$, the problem is equivalent to that of finding a rational number between $\frac{4}{9}$ and $\frac{6}{13}$. We can do this easily by changing to fractions with common denominators. Thus,

$$\frac{4}{9} = \frac{4 \cdot 13}{9 \cdot 13} = \frac{52}{117} \quad \text{and} \quad \frac{6}{13} = \frac{6 \cdot 9}{13 \cdot 9} = \frac{54}{117}$$

Therefore, an obvious choice for the number we seek is $\dfrac{53}{117}$. ∎

C. *The Number* π

There is one more important irrational number that caused the Pythagoreans further difficulties. The number π introduced in Getting Started as the ratio of the circumference of a circle C to its diameter d is itself an irrational number, $3.14159 \ldots$. Use of the symbol π was probably inspired by the first letter in the Greek word *periphereia*, meaning "periphery." Thus,

$$\frac{C}{d} = \pi$$

or, solving for the circumference,

$$C = \pi d$$

Actually proving that π is irrational is a very difficult mathematical problem and we shall simply accept the fact. As we have already noted, the value of π has been approximated by various people throughout the ages, and different methods have been used to calculate the value of π to a large number of decimal places. Today, this value is known to millions of decimal places. Here is the value to a mere 32 places:

$$\pi = 3.141\ 592\ 653\ 589\ 793\ 238\ 462\ 643\ 383\ 279\ 50$$

In most applications, however, we use only two decimal places, 3.14, but if greater accuracy is desired, the value 3.1416 is customarily used.

EXAMPLE 6 A manufacturer of cylindrical tanks wants to put a reinforcing steel strap around a 2-ft-diameter tank. The strap is to be 2 in. longer than the circumference to allow for riveting the overlap. How long should the strap be? (Answer to the nearest 0.1 in.)

Solution We use the formula $C = \pi d$, taking π as 3.14. Thus,

$$C = 3.14 \times 2 \text{ ft}$$
$$= 3.14 \times 2 \times 12 \text{ in.}$$
$$= 75.4 \text{ in.}$$

Adding the 2-in. overlap, we get the required length to be 77.4 in. ∎

Problem Solving:	**Circumferences and Diameters**
	The fence around a bullring in Spain is 450 ft long and has a 20-ft-wide gate. What is the diameter of this bullring?
1. Read the problem.	
2. Select the unknown.	We want to find the diameter of the bullring.
3. Think of a plan. We need to find the diameter of a circle (the bullring) when we know its circumference.	Since the fence is 450 ft long and there is a 20-ft gate, the circumference C must be 450 + 20 or 470 ft. We also know that $C = \pi d$.
4. Use $C = \pi d$ and solve for $d = C/\pi$ to find the diameter.	Solve for $d = \dfrac{C}{\pi}$ where $C = 470$. Thus $$d = \frac{C}{\pi} = \frac{470}{3.14} = 149.68.$$ Since the value for π has three significant digits, we round the answer 149.68 to three significant digits, obtaining $d = 150$ ft.
5. Verify the answer.	The circumference of a circle with a 150-ft diameter is $C = 3.14 \cdot 150 = 471$ or about 470 ft as required.
TRY EXAMPLE 7 NOW.	Cover the solution, write your own, and then check your work.

EXAMPLE 7   A rectangular piece of silver approximately 0.5 in. by 6.75 in. is to be formed into a circular bracelet. If the band is bent so that its ends are exactly one-half inch apart, what will be the diameter of the bracelet? (Use the approximate value 3.14 for π.)

Solution   The circumference C of a circle is given by $C = \pi d$, where d is the diameter. The total circumference of the bracelet will be 6.75 + 0.5 in. (the length of the piece of silver plus the 0.5-in. gap). Since $C = \pi d$, solving for d gives

$$d = \frac{C}{\pi} = \frac{6.75 + 0.5}{3.14} = \frac{7.25}{3.14} = 2.3089$$

Since the 7.25 and 3.14 both have only three significant digits, we round our answer to three significant digits, giving $d = 2.31$ in. ∎

Exercise 4.7

A–B In problems 1–20, classify the given numbers as rational or irrational.

1. $\sqrt{120}$

2. $\sqrt{121}$

3. $\sqrt{125}$

4. $\sqrt{169}$

5. $\sqrt{\frac{9}{16}}$

6. $\sqrt{\frac{9}{15}}$

7. $\frac{3}{5}$

8. $-\frac{22}{7}$

9. $-\frac{5}{3}$

10. -0

11. $0.232323\ldots$

12. $0.023002300023\ldots$

13. $0.121231234\ldots$

14. 0.121231234

15. $6\frac{1}{4}$

16. $\sqrt{6\frac{1}{4}}$

17. $0.24681012\ldots$

18. 0.1122334455

19. 3.1415

20. π

In problems 21–32, evaluate the given expression.

21. $\sqrt{16}$

22. $\sqrt{49}$

23. $\sqrt{64}$

24. $-\sqrt{144}$

25. $\sqrt{81}$

26. $\sqrt{256}$

27. $-\sqrt{169}$

28. $-\sqrt{25}$

29. $\sqrt{196}$

30. $\sqrt{225}$

31. $-\sqrt{81}$

32. $-\sqrt{121}$

In problems 33–46 insert $<$, $>$, or $=$, as appropriate.

33. 3 _____ 4

34. 17 _____ 11

35. $\frac{1}{5}$ _____ $\frac{1}{4}$

36. $\frac{12}{19}$ _____ $\frac{11}{17}$

37. $\frac{5}{7}$ _____ $\frac{10}{14}$

38. $1\frac{2}{3}$ _____ $\frac{8}{6}$

39. $\sqrt{20}$ _____ 4.5

40. $3.777\ldots$ _____ $\sqrt{15}$

41. $0.333\ldots$ _____ $0.333444\ldots$

42. 0.101001000 _____ $0.1101001000\ldots$

43. $0.999\ldots$ _____ 1

44. $0.333\ldots + 0.666\ldots$ _____ 1

45. $3(0.333\ldots)$ _____ 1

46. 0.112233 _____ $0.111222333\ldots$

47. Find a rational number between 0.31 and 0.32.

48. Find a rational number between 0.28 and 0.285.

49. Find an irrational number between 0.31 and 0.32.

50. Find an irrational number between 0.28 and 0.285.

51. Find a rational number between $0.101001000\ldots$ and $0.102002000\ldots.$

52. Find a rational number between $0.303003000\ldots$ and $0.304004000\ldots.$

53. Find an irrational number between 0.101001000 . . . and 0.102002000 . . . .

54. Find an irrational number between 0.303003000 . . . and 0.304004000 . . . .

55. Find a rational number between $\frac{3}{11}$ and $\frac{4}{11}$.

56. Find a rational number between $\frac{7}{9}$ and $\frac{9}{11}$.

57. Find an irrational number between $\frac{4}{9}$ and $\frac{5}{9}$.

58. Find an irrational number between $\frac{2}{11}$ and $\frac{3}{11}$.

59. Find a rational number between $0.\overline{5}$ and $\frac{2}{3}$.

60. Find a rational number between 0.1 and $0.\overline{1}$.

In problems 61 and 62, list the given numbers in order from smallest to largest.

61. 0.21, 0.212112111 . . . , 0.21211, 0.2121, 0.21212

62. 3.14, 3.1414, 3.141411411 . . . , 3.141, 3.1

C. In problems 63–68, use the approximate value 3.14 for π.

63. The largest circular crater in northern Arizona is 5200 ft across. If you were to walk around this crater, how many miles would you walk? (1 mi = 5,280 ft.)

64. The Fermi National Accelerator Laboratory has a circular atom smasher that is 6562 ft in diameter. Find the distance in miles that a particle travels in going once around in this accelerator. (1 mi = 5,280 ft.)

65. The U.S. Department of Energy is studying the possibility of building a circular superconductivity collider that will be 52 mi in diameter. How far would a particle travel in going once around this collider? Give your answer to the nearest mile.

66. The smallest functional phonograph record, a rendition of "God Save the King," is $1\frac{3}{8}$ in. in diameter. To the nearest hundredth of an inch, what is the circumference of this record?

67. The diameter of a circular running track is increased from 90 yards to 100 yards. By how many yards is the length of the track increased? Give your answer to the nearest yard.

68. You are asked to build a circular running track of length one quarter of a kilometer. To the nearest meter, what radius would you use? (Recall that a kilometer is 1,000 meters.)

In Other Words

69. Explain in your own words how you can tell a rational from an irrational number.

70. If the rational numbers were used to mark the points on a straight line, what points would be missed? Give three examples.

Using Your Knowledge

The figure shows an interesting spiral made up of successive right triangles. This spiral can be used to construct lengths corresponding to the square roots of the integers on the number line. For example, the second triangle has sides 1 and $\sqrt{2}$, so if the hypotenuse is of length x, then

$$x^2 = 1^2 + (\sqrt{2})^2$$
$$= 1 + 2 = 3$$

Therefore, $x = \sqrt{3}$.

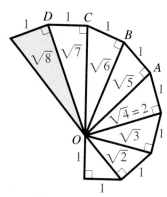

71. Verify that the ray *OB* is of length $\sqrt{6}$.

72. Verify that the ray *OD* is of length $\sqrt{8}$.

73. Find the length of the hypotenuse of the triangle shown in color.

74. If the triangles are numbered 1, 2, 3, . . . , starting with the lowest triangle in the figure, what would be the number of the triangle whose hypotenuse is of length $\sqrt{17}$?

Calculator Corner

If your calculator has a pi (π) key, then calculations involving π can easily be done on the calculator. For example, to find the radius of a circle with a circumference of 96 feet, all you need do is key in

$$\boxed{96}\ \boxed{\div}\ \boxed{\pi}\ \boxed{\div}\ \boxed{2}\ \boxed{=}$$

The calculator will show the answer 15.278875, which, to the nearest $\frac{1}{100}$ ft, rounds to 15.28 ft.

1. Use the π key on your calculator to check the answers to problems 63–68, Exercise 4.7.

4.8   RADICALS AND COMPLEX NUMBERS

GETTING STARTED

THE "RADICAL" NOTION OF SUPERSONIC SPEED

How fast can this plane travel? The answer is classified information but it exceeds twice the speed of sound (747 mi/hr). It is then said that the plane's speed is more than Mach 2. The formula for calculating the Mach number is

$$M = \sqrt{\frac{2}{\gamma}} \sqrt{\frac{P_2 - P_1}{P_1}}$$

where P_1 and P_2 are air pressures. This expression can be simplified by multiplying both radical expressions and rationalizing the denominator. In this section we will add, subtract, multiply, and divide radical expressions — that is, expressions containing radicals.

In the preceding section, we studied irrational numbers of the form $\sqrt{n}$, where n is a positive number but not a perfect square. You may recall that we did this with the help of the Pythagoreans, who solved the equation $x^2 = 2$. Numbers of the form $\sqrt{n}$ are called **radicals.** We study next some simple operations on radicals.

A. *Simplifying Radicals*

The velocity v (in feet per second) of an object in free-fall depends on the distance d that it has fallen. The formula is

$$v = \sqrt{32d}$$

Thus, after an object has fallen 1 ft ($d = 1$), its velocity is $\sqrt{32}$ ft/sec, and after 2 ft ($d = 2$), it is $\sqrt{64}$ ft/sec. The number $\sqrt{32}$ is an irrational number, because 32 is not a perfect square, but 64 is a perfect square ($8^2 = 64$), so that $\sqrt{64} = 8$ is a rational number. Note that $\sqrt{32}$ is positive. We interpret $\sqrt{n}$ to mean the positive square root of n. Can we simplify $\sqrt{32}$? We say that $\sqrt{n}$ is in **simplest form** if n has no factor (other than 1) that is a perfect square. Using this definition, we can see that $\sqrt{32}$ is not in simplest form, because the perfect square 16 is a factor of 32. The simplification can be done using the following property:

> If a and b are nonnegative real numbers, then
> $$\sqrt{a \cdot b} = \sqrt{a} \cdot \sqrt{b}$$

Thus,

$$\sqrt{32} = \sqrt{16 \cdot 2} = \sqrt{16} \cdot \sqrt{2} = 4\sqrt{2}$$

In general, the simplest form of a number involving the radical sign $\sqrt{}$ is obtained by using the perfect squares 1, 4, 9, 16, 25, 36, 49, 64, 81, 100, and so on, as factors under the radical and then using the property given above, as in the next example.

EXAMPLE 1   Simplify if possible:

(a) $\sqrt{75}$ (b) $\sqrt{70}$

Solution   (a) The largest perfect square dividing 75 is 25. Thus, we write
$$\sqrt{75} = \sqrt{25 \cdot 3} = \sqrt{25} \cdot \sqrt{3} = 5\sqrt{3}$$

(b) There is no perfect square (except 1) that divides 70. (Try dividing by 4, 9, 16, 25, 36.) Thus, $\sqrt{70}$ cannot be simplified any further.

∎

The property $\sqrt{a \cdot b} = \sqrt{a} \cdot \sqrt{b}$ can be used to **rationalize** the denominator of certain expressions, that is, to free the denominator of radicals. Thus, if we wish to rationalize the denominator in the expression $6/\sqrt{3}$, we use the fundamental principle of fractions and multiply the numerator and the denominator of the fraction by $\sqrt{3}$, as follows:

$$\frac{6}{\sqrt{3}} = \frac{6 \cdot \sqrt{3}}{\sqrt{3} \cdot \sqrt{3}} = \frac{6 \cdot \sqrt{3}}{\sqrt{9}} = \frac{6 \cdot \sqrt{3}}{3} = 2\sqrt{3}$$

EXAMPLE 2   Rationalize the denominator in the expression $5/\sqrt{10}$.

Solution   We multiply the numerator and the denominator by $\sqrt{10}$ and then simplify. Thus,

$$\frac{5}{\sqrt{10}} = \frac{5 \cdot \sqrt{10}}{\sqrt{10} \cdot \sqrt{10}} = \frac{5 \cdot \sqrt{10}}{\sqrt{100}} = \frac{5 \cdot \sqrt{10}}{10} = \frac{\sqrt{10}}{2}$$

∎

B. *Multiplication and Division of Radicals*

Can we simplify $\sqrt{\frac{3}{4}}$? (This is one of the two answers you will get if you solve the equation $x^2 = \frac{3}{4}$.) This time, the perfect square 4 appears in the denominator, so to simplify the expression, we use the following property:

If a and b are positive numbers, then

$$\sqrt{\frac{a}{b}} = \frac{\sqrt{a}}{\sqrt{b}}$$

Thus,

$$\sqrt{\frac{3}{4}} = \frac{\sqrt{3}}{\sqrt{4}} = \frac{\sqrt{3}}{2}$$

EXAMPLE 3   Simplify:

(a) $\sqrt{\dfrac{32}{25}}$ (b) $\sqrt{\dfrac{36}{7}}$

Solution   (a) $\sqrt{\dfrac{32}{25}} = \dfrac{\sqrt{32}}{\sqrt{25}} = \dfrac{\sqrt{32}}{5} = \dfrac{\sqrt{16 \cdot 2}}{5} = \dfrac{4 \cdot \sqrt{2}}{5}$

(b) $\sqrt{\dfrac{36}{7}} = \dfrac{\sqrt{36}}{\sqrt{7}} = \dfrac{6}{\sqrt{7}}$

But now we must rationalize the denominator by multiplying the numerator and the denominator of the fraction $6/\sqrt{7}$ by $\sqrt{7}$, obtaining

$$\frac{6 \cdot \sqrt{7}}{7}$$

as our final answer. An easier way to get this result would be to multiply the numerator and the denominator of the original fraction $\frac{36}{7}$ by 7 first, obtaining

$$\sqrt{\frac{36}{7}} = \sqrt{\frac{36 \cdot 7}{7 \cdot 7}} = \frac{\sqrt{36 \cdot 7}}{\sqrt{7 \cdot 7}} = \frac{6\sqrt{7}}{7}$$

Keep this in mind when working the exercises!   ■

The two properties we have presented can serve as the definitions for the multiplication and division of radicals. Thus,

$$\sqrt{6} \cdot \sqrt{2} = \sqrt{12} \qquad \text{Using the first property to multiply}$$
$$= \sqrt{4 \cdot 3} = 2\sqrt{3} \qquad \text{Using the first property to simplify}$$

Similarly,

$$\frac{\sqrt{32}}{\sqrt{2}} = \sqrt{\frac{32}{2}} = \sqrt{16} = 4 \quad \text{Using the second property}$$

EXAMPLE 4 Perform the indicated operations and simplify: (a) $\sqrt{6} \cdot \sqrt{3}$ (b) $\dfrac{\sqrt{40}}{\sqrt{5}}$

Solution (a) $\sqrt{6} \cdot \sqrt{3} = \sqrt{18} = \sqrt{9 \cdot 2} = 3\sqrt{2}$

(b) $\dfrac{\sqrt{40}}{\sqrt{5}} = \sqrt{\dfrac{40}{5}} = \sqrt{8} = \sqrt{4 \cdot 2} = 2\sqrt{2}$

C. Addition and Subtraction of Radicals

The addition and subtraction of radicals can be accomplished using the distributive law. Note that radicals may be combined only when their radicands (the quantity under the radical sign) are the same. Thus, to add $5\sqrt{2} + 3\sqrt{2}$ or subtract $5\sqrt{2} - 3\sqrt{2}$, we write:

$$5\sqrt{2} + 3\sqrt{2} = (5 + 3)\sqrt{2} = 8\sqrt{2}$$

or

$$5\sqrt{2} - 3\sqrt{2} = (5 - 3)\sqrt{2} = 2\sqrt{2}$$

Sometimes, you may have to use the properties we mentioned before the additions or subtractions can be accomplished. Thus, to add $\sqrt{48} + \sqrt{27}$, we use the first property to write $\sqrt{48} = \sqrt{16 \cdot 3} = 4\sqrt{3}$ and $\sqrt{27} = \sqrt{9 \cdot 3} = 3\sqrt{3}$. We then have

$$\sqrt{48} + \sqrt{27} = 4\sqrt{3} + 3\sqrt{3} = 7\sqrt{3}$$

EXAMPLE 5 Perform the indicated operations:

(a) $\sqrt{50} - \sqrt{8}$ (b) $\sqrt{75} + \sqrt{48} - \sqrt{147}$

Solution (a) $\sqrt{50} - \sqrt{8} = \sqrt{25 \cdot 2} - \sqrt{4 \cdot 2}$
$$= 5\sqrt{2} - 2\sqrt{2}$$
$$= 3\sqrt{2}$$

(b) $\sqrt{75} + \sqrt{48} - \sqrt{147} = \sqrt{25 \cdot 3} + \sqrt{16 \cdot 3} - \sqrt{49 \cdot 3}$
$$= 5\sqrt{3} + 4\sqrt{3} - 7\sqrt{3}$$
$$= 2\sqrt{3}$$

D. Applications

EXAMPLE 6 The greatest speed s (in miles per hour) at which a bicyclist can safely turn a corner of radius r ft is $s = 4\sqrt{r}$. Find the greatest speed at which a bicyclist can safely turn a corner with a 20-ft radius, and write the answer in simplest form.

Solution $s = 4\sqrt{r} = 4\sqrt{20} = 4\sqrt{4 \cdot 5} = 4 \cdot 2\sqrt{5} = 8\sqrt{5}$ mph

This is slightly less than 18 mph.   ■

E. *The Set of*
Complex Numbers

As we have seen, the real numbers include all the rational and irrational numbers. The set of real numbers is so vast that it includes every number that corresponds to a point on the number line. At first glance, it seems that this set of numbers would contain the solution for any possible equation, but this is not the case! If we consider the equation $x^2 = -1$, we seek a number that, when multiplied by itself, equals -1. No real number will satisfy this equation, because every real number multiplied by itself results in a nonnegative product. This means that the set R is not closed with respect to the operation of taking square roots. To avoid this difficulty, sixteenth-century mathematicians expanded the set of real numbers and created a new set of numbers called the **complex numbers.** In this system, we are allowed to take the square root of a negative number. In 1545, Girolamo Cardano, an Italian mathematician, used the square root of a negative number to solve the following problem: Find two numbers whose sum is 10 and whose product is 40. The answer?

$$5 + \sqrt{-15} \quad \text{and} \quad 5 - \sqrt{-15}$$

As you can see, if you add these numbers, their sum is 10. But what about their product? If we use ordinary multiplication and the rules we have studied, we obtain

$$
\begin{array}{r}
5 + \sqrt{-15} \\
\times\ 5 - \sqrt{-15} \\
\hline
25 + 5\sqrt{-15} \\
-\ 5\sqrt{-15} - (-15) \\
\hline
25 \qquad\qquad\quad + 15 = 40
\end{array}
$$

Note that the definition of the product of two radicals given in Part A does not apply to the product $\sqrt{-15} \times \sqrt{-15}$ because the number under the radical sign is negative. Here we are using the fact that $\sqrt{-15}$ is just a symbol for one of the square roots of -15. The great mathematician Leonhard Euler introduced the following notation for the square root of a negative number:

$$i = \sqrt{-1} \quad \text{so that} \quad i^2 = -1$$

Then, the square root of any other negative number can be expressed in terms of i. For example,

$$\sqrt{-4} = (\sqrt{-1})(\sqrt{4}) = (i)(2) = 2i$$

and

$$\sqrt{-7} = (\sqrt{-1})(\sqrt{7}) = (i)(\sqrt{7}) = \sqrt{7}\,i$$

Similarly, if c is any positive number, then $\sqrt{-c}$ is expressed in the form $\sqrt{c}\,i$ or $i\sqrt{c}$.

EXAMPLE 7   Express in the form bi, where b is a real number:

(a) $\sqrt{-25}$ (b) $\sqrt{-19}$

Solution   (a) $\sqrt{-25} = \sqrt{25}\,i = 5i$ (b) $\sqrt{-19} = \sqrt{19}\,i$ ∎

Any number of the form bi, where b is a nonzero real number, is called a **pure imaginary** number. For example,

$$i, \quad 3i, \quad -5i, \quad \tfrac{4}{7}i, \quad \sqrt{2}\,i, \quad \text{and} \quad \pi i$$

are pure imaginary numbers. We then define a **complex number** as the indicated sum of a real number and a pure imaginary number.

Definition 4.14

> The set C of **complex numbers** is defined as follows:
>
> $$C = \{a + bi \mid a \text{ and } b \text{ are real numbers}\}$$

Note that if $a = 0$, $a + bi = 0 + bi = bi$ is a pure imaginary number. If $b = 0$, we define $0 \cdot i$ to be 0, so that every real number can be written in the form $a + 0i$. With this convention, every real number may be regarded as a complex number — that is, the real numbers are a subset of the set C.

EXAMPLE 8   Classify the given numbers by making a check mark in the appropriate row:

Set	$5 + 3i$	$7i$	$-\tfrac{3}{4}$	$\sqrt{5}\,i$
Real number				
Pure imaginary number				
Complex number				

Solution   The correct check marks are shown below:

Set	$5 + 3i$	$7i$	$-\tfrac{3}{4}$	$\sqrt{5}\,i$
Real number			✓	
Pure imaginary number		✓		✓
Complex number	✓	✓	✓	✓

∎

You should be warned that the adjective *imaginary* is a most unfortunate choice of words and must not be taken literally. The complex numbers have many *real* practical applications. Electric circuit analysis and mechanical vibration analysis are two of these applications. If you thought imaginary numbers were imaginary in the popular sense of that word, then you would be very surprised (not to say shocked) if you stuck your finger into a 110-volt electric socket with the power on and felt the "imaginary" current!

This completes our discussion of the relationship of the various sets of numbers that we have studied. In particular, we see that

$$N \subset W \subset I \subset Q \subset R \subset C$$

as shown in Figure 4.6.

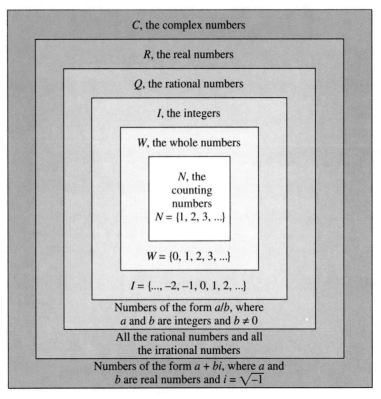

FIGURE 4.6

EXAMPLE 9   Classify the given numbers by making a check mark in the appropriate row:

Set	$\sqrt{4}$	$\sqrt{5}\,i$	$\sqrt{2}$	$3 + 5i$
Natural numbers				
Integers				
Rational numbers				
Irrational numbers				
Real numbers				
Complex numbers				

Solution The correct check marks are shown below:

Set	$\sqrt{4}$	$\sqrt{5}\,i$	$\sqrt{2}$	$3 + 5i$
Natural numbers	✓			
Integers	✓			
Rational numbers	✓			
Irrational numbers			✓	
Real numbers	✓		✓	
Complex numbers	✓	✓	✓	✓	■

Exercise 4.8

A. In problems 1–12, simplify as much as possible.

1. $\sqrt{90}$
2. $\sqrt{72}$
3. $\sqrt{122}$

4. $\sqrt{175}$
5. $\sqrt{180}$
6. $\sqrt{162}$

7. $\sqrt{200}$
8. $\sqrt{191}$
9. $\sqrt{384}$

10. $\sqrt{486}$
11. $\sqrt{588}$
12. $\sqrt{5000}$

In problems 13–18, rationalize the denominator.

13. $\dfrac{3}{\sqrt{7}}$
14. $\dfrac{6}{\sqrt{5}}$
15. $\dfrac{-\sqrt{2}}{\sqrt{5}}$

16. $\dfrac{-\sqrt{3}}{\sqrt{7}}$
17. $\dfrac{4}{\sqrt{8}}$
18. $\dfrac{3}{\sqrt{27}}$

B. In problems 19–27, simplify the given expression.

19. $\sqrt{\dfrac{3}{49}}$
20. $\sqrt{\dfrac{7}{16}}$
21. $\sqrt{\dfrac{4}{3}}$

22. $\sqrt{\dfrac{25}{11}}$
23. $\sqrt{\dfrac{8}{49}}$
24. $\sqrt{\dfrac{18}{25}}$

25. $\sqrt{\dfrac{18}{50}}$
26. $\sqrt{\dfrac{24}{75}}$
27. $\sqrt{\dfrac{32}{125}}$

In problems 28–36, perform the indicated operations and simplify.

28. $\sqrt{7} \cdot \sqrt{8}$
29. $\sqrt{5} \cdot \sqrt{50}$
30. $\sqrt{10} \cdot \sqrt{5}$

31. $\dfrac{\sqrt{28}}{\sqrt{2}}$
32. $\dfrac{\sqrt{22}}{\sqrt{2}}$
33. $\dfrac{\sqrt{10}}{\sqrt{250}}$

34. $\dfrac{\sqrt{10}}{\sqrt{490}}$
35. $\dfrac{\sqrt{33}}{\sqrt{22}}$
36. $\dfrac{\sqrt{18}}{\sqrt{12}}$

C. In problems 37–50, perform the indicated operations and simplify.

37. $\sqrt{3} + \sqrt{12}$

38. $\sqrt{32} - \sqrt{8}$

39. $\sqrt{125} + \sqrt{80}$

40. $\sqrt{24} - \sqrt{150}$

41. $\sqrt{3^2 + 4^2}$

42. $\sqrt{5^2 + (12)^2}$

43. $\sqrt{(13)^2 - (12)^2}$

44. $\sqrt{(25)^2 - (24)^2}$

45. $6\sqrt{7} + \sqrt{7} - 2\sqrt{7}$

46. $\sqrt{3} + 11\sqrt{3} - 3\sqrt{3}$

47. $5\sqrt{7} - 3\sqrt{28} - 2\sqrt{63}$

48. $3\sqrt{28} - 6\sqrt{7} - 2\sqrt{175}$

49. $-3\sqrt{45} + \sqrt{20} - \sqrt{5}$

50. $-5\sqrt{27} + \sqrt{12} - 5\sqrt{48}$

D. 51. A playing field is 80 meters wide and 100 meters long. If Marcie ran diagonally across this field from one corner to the opposite corner, how far did she run? Leave your answer in simplest radical form.

52. The hypotenuse of a right triangle is 10 inches long and one of the sides is 7 inches long. Is the other side longer or shorter than the 7 inch side? Justify your answer.

53. The time t (in seconds) it takes an object dropped from a certain distance (in feet) to hit the ground is

$$t = \sqrt{\frac{\text{Distance in feet}}{16}}$$

Find the time it takes an object dropped from a height of 50 ft to hit the ground, and write the answer in simplified form.

54. The time t (in seconds) it takes an object dropped from a certain distance (in meters) to hit the ground is

$$t = \sqrt{\frac{\text{Distance in meters}}{5}}$$

Find the time it takes an object dropped from a height of 160 meters to hit the ground, and write the answer in simplified form.

55. The compound interest r that is paid when you borrow $\$P$ and pay $\$A$ at the end of 2 years is

$$r = \sqrt{\frac{A}{P}} - 1$$

Find the rate when $100 is borrowed and the amount paid at the end of the 2 years is $144.

56. When you are at an altitude of a ft above the Earth, your view V_m (in miles) extends as far as a circle called the *horizon* and is given by

$$V_m = \sqrt{\frac{3}{2}a}$$

The greatest altitude reached in a manned balloon is 123,800 ft and was attained by Nicholas Piantanida.
(a) In simplified form, what was the view in miles from this balloon?
(b) If $\sqrt{1857} \approx 43$, what was the view in miles?

E. In problems 57–62, express the given number in the form bi, where b is a real number.

57. $\sqrt{-49}$ 58. $\sqrt{-55}$ 59. $\sqrt{-63}$
60. $\sqrt{-64}$ 61. $\sqrt{-100}$ 62. $\sqrt{-144}$

In problems 63–68, express the given number in the form $i\sqrt{b}$, where $\sqrt{b}$ is in simplified form.

63. $\sqrt{-50}$ 64. $\sqrt{-32}$ 65. $\sqrt{-200}$
66. $\sqrt{-98}$ 67. $\sqrt{-48}$ 68. $\sqrt{-80}$

In problems 69–73, classify the given numbers by making a check mark in the appropriate row:

Set	69. $9i$	70. $7 - 4i$	71. $-\frac{5}{8}$	72. $\sqrt{18}\,i$	73. $0.8i$
Real numbers					
Pure imaginary numbers					
Complex numbers					

In problems 74–80, classify the given numbers by making a check mark in the appropriate row.

Set	74. $-\frac{3}{8}$	75. 0	76. $\sqrt{3}$	77. $\sqrt{9}$	78. 5	79. $\sqrt{3}\,i$	80. $-2 + i$
Natural numbers							
Whole numbers							
Integers							
Rational numbers							
Irrational numbers							
Real numbers							
Complex numbers							

*I*n Other Words

81. Explain why we cannot use the definition $\sqrt{a} \cdot \sqrt{b} = \sqrt{ab}$ when a and b are negative numbers.

82. Explain why every real number is a complex number.

Using Your Knowledge

At the beginning of the next section we shall see that after the man in the pic-ture had fallen 1 ft, his velocity was $\sqrt{32} = 4\sqrt{2}$ ft/sec. Can you estimate what $\sqrt{32}$ is? Mathematicians use a method called **interpolation** *to approxi-mate this answer. Since we know that $\sqrt{25} = 5$ and $\sqrt{36} = 6$, $\sqrt{32}$ should be between 5 and 6. If we place $\sqrt{25}$, $\sqrt{32}$, and $\sqrt{36}$ in a column, the inter-polation is done as shown in the diagram:*

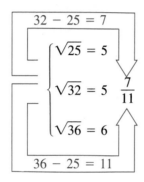

Thus, $\sqrt{32}$ is approximately $5\frac{7}{11}$. If we wish, we can write this answer as a decimal by dividing 7 by 11, obtaining $0.\overline{63}$ and writing the approximation as $5.\overline{63}$. (If you use a calculator to find the square root of 32, the actual answer is 5.6569.)

Use this knowledge to approximate the following roots. Give each answer as a mixed number and then to two decimal places.

83. $\sqrt{40}$ 84. $\sqrt{68}$

85. $\sqrt{85}$ 86. $\sqrt{108}$

Discovery

To define the addition or subtraction of complex numbers, we would like to keep the real and the imaginary parts separated. Can you discover how to add and subtract $a + bi$ and $c + di$?

Use your definition to do the following problems.

87. Find the sum of $7 + 13i$ and $11 + 6i$.

88. Simplify: $(8 - 9i) - (-3 + 6i)$.

89. Simplify: $(7 + \sqrt{12}i) - (5 - \sqrt{3}i)$.

90. Simplify: $(\sqrt{8} - 2i) + (-\sqrt{32} + 4i)$.

Calculator Corner

Some scientific calculators perform complex number calculations. For example, to add $(3 - 8i) + (-5 + 2i)$, you place the calculator in the complex number mode (press $\boxed{\text{mode}}$ $\boxed{\text{cplx}}$). Now, recall that $3 - 8i$ is written in the form $a + bi$, so $a = 3$ and $b = -8$. Similarly, in the complex number $-5 + 2i$, $a = -5$ and $b = 2$. Thus, to add these two numbers, enter the sequence

$$\boxed{3}\ \boxed{a}\ \boxed{8}\ \boxed{\pm}\ \boxed{b}\ \boxed{+}\ \boxed{5}\ \boxed{\pm}\ \boxed{a}\ \boxed{2}\ \boxed{b}\ \boxed{=}$$

The display shows the real part -2. To find the imaginary part, press $\boxed{b}$. The display shows -6. Thus, the complete answer is $-2 - 6i$.

4.9 NUMBER SEQUENCES

GETTING STARTED

THE 12 DAYS OF CHRISTMAS AND PROGRESSIONS

Do you know the song "The Twelve Days of Christmas"? How many gifts do you get each day? What is the total number of gifts you receive? If you sing along you will recall that the song goes like this:

Day 1:	A partridge in a pear tree.	1 gift
Day 2:	A partridge in a pear tree, two turtle doves.	1 + 2 gifts
Day 3:	A partridge in a pear tree, two turtle doves, three French hens.	1 + 2 + 3 gifts

On the twelfth day, you get $1 + 2 + 3 + \cdots + 11 + 12$ gifts. This sum is an **arithmetic progression.** Can you add it quickly?

According to a story told by E. T. Bell, in late eighteenth-century Germany, a precocious boy of ten was admitted to the class in arithmetic where none of the children were expected to know about progressions. "It was easy for the heroic Buttner (the teacher) to give out a long problem in addition whose answer he could find by a formula in a few seconds. The problem was of the following sort:

"$1 + 2 + 3 + 4 + \cdots + 98 + 99 + 100$"

The student who first got the answer was to lay his slate on the table; the next laid his slate on top of the first, and so on. Buttner had barely finished stating the problem when the boy flung his slate on the table. "Ligget se'" (there it lies), he said in his peasant dialect. The rest of the hour, while the class worked on the problem, the boy sat with his hands folded, favored now and then by a sarcastic glance from Buttner, who imagined the boy to be just another blockhead. At the end of the period, Buttner looked over the answers.

On the boy's slate there apeared but a single number. Do you know what that number was? In later years, the boy confessed to having recognized the pattern:

$$1 + 2 + 3 + 4 + \cdots + 97 + 98 + 99 + 100$$

101

in which the sum of each pair of numbers is 101. Since there are 50 pairs of numbers, the total sum would be $50 \times 101 = 5,050$, the number on the tablet. In this section we will show you the magic formula so you too can add arithmetic progressions! By the way, you will get 6×13 gifts on the twelfth day of Christmas, but only if you have been good. What about the boy? Karl Friedrich Gauss became one of the most renowned European mathematicians of his time.

The photograph shows a skydiver plunging toward the ground. Do you know how far he will fall in the first 5 seconds? A free-falling body travels about 16 feet in the first second, 48 feet in the next second, 80 feet in the third second, and so on. The number of feet traveled in each successive second is:

16, 48, 80, 112, 144, . . .

This list of numbers is an example of a **number sequence.** In general, a list of numbers having a first number, a second number, a third number, and so on, is called a **sequence;** the numbers in the sequence are called the **terms.** Here are some examples of sequences:

(a) The odd positive integers $1, 3, 5, 7, \ldots$
(b) The positive multiples of 3 $3, 6, 9, 12, \ldots$
(c) The powers of 10 $10^1, 10^2, 10^3, \ldots$
(d) The interest on the first three $\$8.33, \$8.11, \$7.89, \ldots$
     payments on a $10,000 car
     being paid over 3 years at 12%
     annual interest

A. *Arithmetic Sequences*

The sequences **(a), (b),** and **(d)** given above are *arithmetic sequences.* An **arithmetic sequence,** or **arithmetic progression,** is a sequence in which each term after the first is obtained by *adding* a quantity called the **common difference** to the preceding term. Thus,

$$16, \quad 48, \quad 80, \quad 112, \quad 144, \ldots$$

is an arithmetic sequence in which each term is obtained by adding the common difference 32 to the preceding term. This means that the common difference for an arithmetic sequence is just the difference between any two consecutive terms.

EXAMPLE 1   Find the common difference in each sequence.

(a) $7, 37, 67, 97, \ldots$ (b) $10, 5, 0, -5, \ldots$

Solution   (a) The common difference is $37 - 7 = 30$ (or $67 - 37$, or $97 - 67$).
(b) The common difference is $5 - 10 = -5$ (or $0 - 5$, or $-5 - 0$).   ∎

It is customary to denote the first term of an arithmetic sequence by a_1 (read, "*a* sub 1"), the common difference by d, and the *n*th term by a_n. Thus, in the sequence $16, 48, 80, 112, 144, \ldots$, we have $a_1 = 16$ and $d = 32$. The second term of the sequence, a_2, is

$$a_2 = a_1 + 32 = 16 + 32 = 48$$

Since each term is obtained from the preceding one by adding 32,

$$a_3 = a_2 + 32 = (a_1 + 32) + 32 \quad = a_1 + 2 \cdot 32 = 80$$

$$a_4 = a_3 + 32 = (a_1 + 2 \cdot 32) + 32 = a_1 + 3 \cdot 32 = 112$$

$$a_5 = a_4 + 32 = (a_1 + 3 \cdot 32) + 32 = a_1 + 4 \cdot 32 = 144$$

By following this pattern, we find the **general term** a_n to be

$$a_n = a_1 + (n - 1) \cdot d$$

EXAMPLE 2   Consider the sequence 7, 10, 13, 16, ... Find:

(a) a_1, the first term   (b) d, the common difference
(c) a_{11}, the 11th term   (d) a_n, the nth term

Solution   (a) The first term a_1 is 7.
(b) The common difference d is $10 - 7 = 3$.
(c) The 11th term is $a_{11} = 7 + (11 - 1) \cdot 3 =$
  $7 + 10 \cdot 3 = 37$.
(d) $a_n = a_1 + (n - 1) \cdot d = 7 + (n - 1) \cdot 3 = 4 + 3n$ ∎

B. *Sum of an Arithmetic Sequence*

Let us go back to our original problem of finding how far the skydiver falls in 5 seconds. The first five terms of the sequence are 16, 48, 80, 112, and 144; thus, we need to find the sum

$$16 + 48 + 80 + 112 + 144$$

Since successive terms of an arithmetic sequence are obtained by adding the common difference d, the sum S_n of the first n terms is

$$S_n = a_1 + (a_1 + d) + (a_1 + 2d) + (a_1 + 3d) + \cdots + a_n \tag{1}$$

We can also start with a_n and obtain successive terms by subtracting the common difference d. Thus, with the terms written in reverse order,

$$S_n = a_n + (a_n - d) + (a_n - 2d) + \cdots + a_1 \tag{2}$$

Adding equations (1) and (2), we find that the d's drop out, and we obtain

$$2S_n = (a_1 + a_n) + (a_1 + a_n) + \cdots + (a_1 + a_n)$$
$$= n(a_1 + a_n)$$

Thus,

$$S_n = \frac{n(a_1 + a_n)}{2}$$

We are now able to determine the sum S_5, the distance the skydiver dropped in 5 sec. The answer is

$$S_5 = \frac{5(16 + 144)}{2} = 400 \text{ ft}$$

C. *Geometric Sequences*

The sequence 10, 100, 1000, and so on, is *not* an arithmetic sequence, since there is no common difference. This sequence is obtained by *multiplying* each term by 10 to get the next term. Such sequences are called geometric sequences. A **geometric sequence,** or **geometric progression,** is a sequence in which each term after the first is obtained by multiplying the preceding term by a number called the **common ratio,** r. Thus, the common ratio can be found by taking the ratio of two successive terms. For example, in the sequence 8, 16, 32, . . . the first term a_1 is 8 and the common ratio is $16/8 = 2$ (or $32/16$). Thus, the first n terms in a geometric sequence are

$$a_1, a_1r, a_1r^2, a_1r^3, \ldots a_1r^{n-1}$$

EXAMPLE 3 Consider the sequence $1, \frac{1}{10}, \frac{1}{100}, \frac{1}{1000}, \ldots$. Find:

(a) a_1 (b) r (c) a_n

Solution (a) a_1 is the first term, 1.
(b) r is the common ratio of any two successive terms. Thus,

$$r = \frac{1/10}{1} = \frac{1}{10}$$

(c) $a_n = a_1r^{n-1} = 1 \cdot \left(\frac{1}{10}\right)^{n-1} = \frac{1}{10^{n-1}}$ ■

D. *Sum of a Geometric Sequence*

Can we find the sum S_n of the first n terms in a geometric sequence?

By definition: $S_n = a_1 + a_1r + a_1r^2 + \cdots + a_1r^{n-1}$
Multiply by r: $rS_n = a_1r + a_1r^2 + a_1r^3 + \cdots + a_1r^n$
Subtract: $S_n - rS_n = a_1 - a_1r^n = a_1(1 - r^n)$
By the Distributive Law: $S_n(1 - r) = a_1(1 - r^n)$
Divide by $1 - r$:

$$S_n = \frac{a_1(1 - r^n)}{1 - r}$$

Thus, the sum of the first three powers of 10, that is, $10 + 10^2 + 10^3$, can be found by noting that $a_1 = 10$, $r = 10^2/10 = 10$, and

$$S_3 = \frac{10(1 - 10^3)}{1 - 10} = \frac{(10)(-999)}{-9} = 1110$$

as expected.

EXAMPLE 4 The first term of a geometric sequence is $\frac{1}{5}$, and $r = \frac{1}{2}$, Find:

(a) a_5, the fifth term   (b) S_5, the sum of the first five terms

Solution (a) The nth term in a geometric sequence is a_1r^{n-1}; thus,

$$a_5 = \left(\frac{1}{5}\right)\left(\frac{1}{2}\right)^{5-1} = \left(\frac{1}{5}\right)\left(\frac{1}{2}\right)^4 = \left(\frac{1}{5}\right)\left(\frac{1}{16}\right) = \frac{1}{80}$$

(b) The sum of the first n terms of a geometric sequence is
$S_n = a_1(1 - r^n)/(1 - r)$, so

$$S_5 = \frac{(\frac{1}{5})[1 - (\frac{1}{2})^5]}{1 - \frac{1}{2}} = \frac{\frac{1}{5}[\frac{31}{32}]}{\frac{1}{2}} = \frac{62}{160} = \frac{31}{80}$$

∎

E. *Infinite Geometric Sequences*

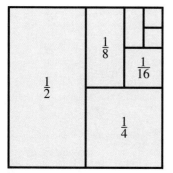

$$\frac{1}{8} \quad \frac{1}{16} \quad \frac{1}{2} \quad \frac{1}{4}$$

***What do you think is the sum of
the sequence $\frac{1}{2} + \frac{1}{4} + \frac{1}{8} + \cdots$?***

Let us now return to the repeating decimals we discussed in Section 4.5. These decimals can be written using an **infinite geometric sequence.** Thus, the decimal 0.333 . . . can be written as

$$0.333 \cdots = \frac{3}{10} + \frac{3}{100} + \frac{3}{1000} + \cdots$$

where the common ratio is $\frac{1}{10}$. The sum of the first n terms of this sequence is

$$S_n = \frac{a_1(1 - r^n)}{1 - r} = \frac{a_1}{1 - r} \cdot (1 - r^n)$$

where $a_1 = \frac{3}{10}$ and $r = \frac{1}{10}$. If we want to find the sum of *all* the terms, we note that as n increases, $(\frac{1}{10})^n$ becomes very small. Thus, S_n is very close to

$$\frac{a_1}{1 - r} = \frac{\frac{3}{10}}{1 - \frac{1}{10}} = \frac{\frac{3}{10}}{\frac{9}{10}} = \frac{1}{3}$$

that is, 0.333 . . . $= \frac{1}{3}$. We can generalize this discussion to obtain the following result:

> If r is a number between -1 and 1, the sum of the infinite geometric sequence $a_1, a_1r, a_1r^2, \ldots$ is
> $$S = \frac{a_1}{1 - r}$$

EXAMPLE 5   Use the sum of an infinite geometric sequence to write the repeating decimals as fractions.

(a) 0.666 . . .   (b) 0.121212 . . .   (c) 3.222 . . .

Solution   (a) $0.666 \ldots = \frac{6}{10} + \frac{6}{100} + \frac{6}{1000} + \cdots$

This is a geometric sequence with first term $a_1 = \frac{6}{10}$ and ratio $r = \frac{1}{10}$. The sum of this sequence is

$$\frac{a_1}{1 - r} = \frac{\frac{6}{10}}{1 - \frac{1}{10}} = \frac{\frac{6}{10}}{\frac{9}{10}} = \frac{6}{9} = \frac{2}{3}$$

Thus, 0.666 . . . $= \frac{2}{3}$.

(b) $0.121212 \ldots = \dfrac{12}{100} + \dfrac{12}{10,000} + \cdots$

This is a geometric sequence with $a_1 = \frac{12}{100}$, $r = \frac{1}{100}$, and sum

$$\frac{a_1}{1 - r} = \frac{\frac{12}{100}}{1 - \frac{1}{100}} = \frac{\frac{12}{100}}{\frac{99}{100}} = \frac{12}{99} = \frac{4}{33}$$

Thus, $0.121212 \ldots = \frac{4}{33}$.

(c) $3.222 \ldots = 3 + \dfrac{2}{10} + \dfrac{2}{100} + \dfrac{2}{1000} + \cdots$

The repeating part, $0.222 \ldots$ is a geometric sequence with $a_1 = \frac{2}{10}$, $r = \frac{1}{10}$, and sum

$$\frac{a_1}{1 - r} = \frac{\frac{2}{10}}{1 - \frac{1}{10}} = \frac{\frac{2}{10}}{\frac{9}{10}} = \frac{2}{9}$$

Thus, $3.222 \ldots = 3\frac{2}{9} = \frac{29}{9}$.

Problem Solving: Number Sequences

Suppose you have two job offers for a 2-week (14 day) trial period. Job A starts at $50 per day with a $50 raise each day. Job B starts at 50 cents per day and your salary is doubled every day. Find the total amount paid by each of the jobs at the end of the 14 days.

1. Read the problem.

2. Select the unknown.

We need to find the total amount each of the jobs pays.

3. Think of a plan.

Find the amount job A pays at the end of 14 days. Then find the amount job B pays at the end of 14 days.

The pay for job A starts at $50 ($a_1 = 50$) and increases by $50 each day ($d = 50$). The salary for the 14th day is $a_{14} = 50 + 13 \cdot 50 = 700$. The pay for job B starts at $0.50 ($a_1 = 0.50$) and doubles every day ($r = 2$).

4. Use the formula for the sum of an arithmetic and a geometric progression to

For job A the sum of the arithmetic progression for 14 days is

$$S_{14} = \frac{n(a_1 + a_n)}{2} = \frac{14 \cdot 750}{2} = \$5250$$

find the amount each job pays for 14 days.

For job B the sum of the geometric progression for 14 days is

$$S_{14} = \frac{a_1(1 - r^n)}{1 - r} = \frac{0.50(1 - 2^{14})}{1 - 2}$$

$$= \frac{0.50(1 - 2^{14})}{-1}$$

$$= 0.50(2^{14} - 1)$$

$$= 0.50\,(16,383)$$

$$= \$8191.50$$

Job B pays much more!

5. Verify your answer.

The verification is left for the student.

TRY EXAMPLE 6 NOW.

Cover the solution, write your own, and then check your work.

EXAMPLE 6　The game of chess is said to have originated in Persia. Legend has it that the Shah (or king) was so happy that he offered the inventor of the game anything he wanted. The inventor asked that one grain of wheat be placed on the first square of the chessboard, two grains on the second, four on the third, and so on. If there are 64 squares on a chessboard:

(a) How many grains were to be placed on the 64th square?

(b) What is the total number of grains the inventor would receive?

Solution　(a) The number of grains in each square is shown:

Square 1　Square 2　Square 3　Square 4 . . .　Square 64

　1　　　　2　　　$4 = 2^{3-1}$　　$8 = 2^{4-1}$　　　$2^{63} = 2^{64-1}$

(b) The sum of the geometric progression 1, 2, 4, . . . 2^{63} where $a_1 = 1$ and $r = 2$ (since the number of grains is doubled every day) is

$$S_{64} = \frac{1(1 - 2^{64})}{1 - 2} = \frac{1 - 2^{64}}{-1}$$

$$= 2^{64} - 1$$

By the way, since 2^{10} is about 1000, $2^{60} = (2^{10})^6$ is about $(1,000)^6$ or 1,000,000,000,000,000,000 (one quintillion). ∎

Exercise 4.9

A. In problems 1–10, an arithmetic sequence is given. Find the first term, the common difference d, the 10th term, and the nth term.

   1. 7, 13, 19, 25, . . .   2. 3, 6, 9, 12, . . .
   3. 43, 34, 25, 16, . . .   4. 3, -1, -5, -9, . . .
   5. 2, -3, -8, -13, . . .   6. $\frac{2}{3}, \frac{5}{6}, 1, \frac{7}{6}, \ldots$
   7. $\frac{-5}{6}, \frac{-1}{3}, \frac{1}{6}, \frac{2}{3}, \ldots$ 8. $\frac{-1}{4}, \frac{1}{4}, \frac{3}{4}, \frac{5}{4}, \ldots$
   9. 0.6, 0.2, -0.2, -0.6, . . .   10. 0.7, 0.2, -0.3, -0.8, . . .

B. In problems 11–20, find S_{10} and S_n for the sequences given in problems 1–10.

C. In problems 21–26, a geometric sequence is given. Find the first term, the common ratio r, the tenth term, and the nth term.

   21. 3, 6, 12, 24, . . .   22. 5, 15, 45, 135, . . .
   23. $\frac{1}{3}$, 1, 3, 9, . . .   24. $\frac{1}{5}$, 1, 5, 25, . . .
   25. 16, -4, 1, $\frac{-1}{4}$, . . .   26. 3, -1, $\frac{1}{3}$, $\frac{-1}{9}$, . . .

D. In problems 27–32, find S_{10} and S_n for the sequences given in problems 21–26. Give answers in simplified exponential form.

E. In problems 33–36, find the sum of the infinite geometric sequence.

   33. 6, 3, $\frac{3}{2}, \frac{3}{4}, \ldots$ 34. 12, 4, $\frac{4}{3}, \frac{4}{9}, \ldots$
   35. -8, -4, -2, -1, . . .   36. 9, -3, 1, $\frac{-1}{3}$, . . .

   In problems 37–40, use sequences to write the given repeating decimal as a fraction.

   37. 0.777 . . .   38. 1.555 . . .
   39. 2.101010 . . .   40. 1.272727 . . .

   41. A property valued at $30,000 will depreciate $1,380 the first year, $1,340 the second year, $1,300 the third year, and so on.
       (a) What will be the depreciation the tenth year?
       (b) What will be the value of the property at the end of the tenth year?

   42. Strikers at a plant were ordered to return to work and were told they would be fined $100 the first day they failed to do so, $150 the second day, $200 the third day, and so on. If the strikers stayed out for 10 days, what was their fine?

   43. A well driller charges $50 for the first foot; for each succeeding foot, the charge is $5 more than that for the preceding foot. Find:
       (a) The charge for the 10th ft
       (b) The total charge for a 50-ft well

44. When dropped on a hard surface, a Super Ball takes a series of bounces, each one being about $\frac{9}{10}$ as high as the preceding one. If a Super Ball is dropped from a height of 10 ft, find:
    (a) How high it will bounce on the 10th bounce
    (b) The approximate distance the ball travels before coming to rest
        [*Hint:* Draw a picture.]

45. If $100 is deposited at the end of each year in a savings account paying 10% compounded annually, at the end of 5 years the compound amount of each deposit is:

    $$100, \quad 100(1.10), \quad 100(1.10)^2, \quad 100(1.10)^3, \quad 100(1.10)^4$$

    How much money is in the account right after the last deposit? [*Hint:* $(1.10)^5 = 1.61051$.]

46. Sally's father told her that if she was well behaved, he would put a nickel in her piggy bank at the end of one week, two nickels at the end of two weeks, four nickels at the end of three weeks, and so on, doubling the number of nickels each successive week. At this rate, in how many weeks would a single deposit amount to over $6?

47. In the Getting Started for this section, we discussed the pattern

    $$1 + 2 + 3 + 4 + \cdots + 97 + 98 + 99 + 100$$

    101

    where the sum of each pair is 101 and there are $\frac{100}{2} = 50$ pairs. Thus, the total sum is 50×101. Generalize this idea to find:

    $$1 + 2 + 3 + \cdots + (n - 1) + n$$

48. (a) Use the ideas of problem 47 to find the sum:

    $$2 + 4 + 6 + \cdots + (2n - 2) + 2n$$

    (b) You can check the answer to part (a) by doubling the answer you get for problem 47. Why? Did you get the same answer?

*I*n Other Words

49. What is the difference between an arithmetic sequence and a geometric sequence?

50. Explain why the Fibonacci sequence 1, 1, 2, 3, 5 is neither an arithmetic sequence nor a geometric sequence.

Using Your Knowledge

Leonardo Fibonacci, one of the greatest mathematicians of the Middle Ages, wrote a book called the Liber Abaci. In this book, Fibonacci proposed the following problem: Let us suppose you have a 1-month-old pair of rabbits, and assume that in the second month, and every month thereafter, they produce a new pair. If each new pair does the same, and none of the rabbits die, can we find out how many pairs of rabbits there will be at the beginning of each month?

*The figure illustrates what happens in the first 5 months. The rabbits shown in color indicate newborn pairs of rabbits. As you can see, the number of pairs of rabbits at the beginning of each of the 5 months is: 1, 1, 2, 3, 5. The resulting sequence is called a **Fibonacci sequence.***

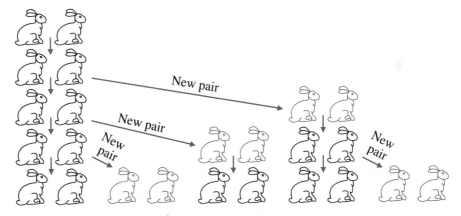

51. Is the sequence an arithmetic sequence? A geometric sequence?
52. What is the relationship between the first two terms of the sequence and the third term?
53. Look at the second and third terms of the sequence. What is their relationship to the fourth term?
54. Based on the pattern found in problems 52 and 53, write the first 10 terms of the Fibonacci sequence.

Chapter 4 Summary

Section	Item	Meaning	Example
4.1	$N = \{1, 2, 3, \ldots\}$	The natural numbers	Any counting numbers such as 10, 27, 38, and so on
4.1A	$n(A)$	The cardinal number of A	If $A = \{a, b\}$, then $n(A) = 2$.
4.1A	1st, 2nd, 3rd, . . .	Ordinal numbers	This is the *first* one.
4.1A	123-45-6789	Number used for identification	A Social Security number

Section	Item	Meaning	Example
4.1B	$+, -, \times, \div$	Binary operations that associate with any two elements of the set a unique result	Addition, subtraction, multiplication, and division are binary operations
4.1B	Closed set	A set is closed if, when an operation is performed on elements of the set, the result is also an element of the set.	The natural numbers are closed under multiplication.
4.1B	$a + b = b + a$	Commutative Property of Addition	$3 + 5 = 5 + 3$
4.1B	$a \times b = b \times a$	Commutative Property of Multiplication	$6 \times 7 = 7 \times 6$
4.1B	$a + (b + c) = (a + b) + c$	Associative Property of Addition	$4 + (2 + 5) = (4 + 2) + 5$
4.1B	$a \times (b \times c) = (a \times b) \times c$	Associative Property of Multiplication	$2 \times (4 \times 7) = (2 \times 4) \times 7$
4.1B	$a \cdot (b + c) = a \cdot b + a \cdot c$	Distributive Property	$3 \cdot (4 + 7) = 3 \cdot 4 + 3 \cdot 7$
4.2A	Prime number	A number with exactly two divisors, 1 and itself	2, 3, 5, 7, 11, etc.
4.2A	Composite	A number with more than two divisors	4, 33, 50, etc.
4.2B	$12 = 2^2 \cdot 3$	Prime factorization of 12	
4.2D	GCF	Greatest common factor	18 is the GCF of 216 and 234.
4.2E	LCM	Least common multiple	252 is the LCM of 18, 21, and 28.
4.3A	$a \cdot 1 = 1 \cdot a = a$	Identity property for multiplication	$1 \cdot 97 = 97$ and $83 \cdot 1 = 83$
4.3A	$W = \{0, 1, 2, \ldots\}$	The set of whole numbers	
4.3A	$0 + a = a + 0 = a$	Identity property for addition	$0 + 13 = 13$ and $84 + 0 = 84$
4.3B	$I = \{\ldots, -1, 0, 1, \ldots\}$	The set of integers	
4.3B	$\xleftarrow{\hspace{0.5em}\underset{-2\ -1\ \ 0\ \ 1\ \ 2}{+\ +\ +\ +\ +}\hspace{0.5em}}\rightarrow$	The number line	
4.3B	$n + (-n) = 0$	Additive inverse property	$3 + (-3) = 0$ and $(-5) + 5 = 0$

Section	Item	Meaning	Example
4.3B	$a - b = a + (-b)$	Definition of subtraction	$3 - 7 = 3 + (-7)$
4.4A	$Q = \left\{ r \,\middle|\, r = \dfrac{a}{b}, \right.$ $\left. a, b \in I, b \neq 0 \right\}$	The set of rational numbers	$\frac{3}{5}, -\frac{7}{3}, 3\frac{1}{2}$
4.5B	$\dfrac{b}{a}$	The reciprocal, or multiplicative inverse, of a/b	$\frac{3}{4}$ and $\frac{4}{3}$ are reciprocals
4.5A	$a^{-n} = \dfrac{1}{a^n}$	Definition of negative exponents	$4^{-2} = \dfrac{1}{4^2}$
4.5B	$m \times 10^n$, where m is greater than or equal to 1 and less than 10, and n is an integer	Scientific notation	7.4×10^{-6}
4.6A	$0.\overline{142857}$	A nonterminating, repeating decimal	$0.\overline{142857} =$ $0.142857142857 \ldots$
4.6C	$\%$	Percent sign	
4.7	Irrational number	A number that is not rational	$\sqrt{2}, 3\sqrt{5}, \pi$
4.7B	Irrational number	A number that has a nonterminating, nonrepeating decimal representation	$0.101001000 \ldots$
4.7B	R	Real numbers	
4.7C	$C = \pi d$	Circumference of a circle	
4.8A	$\sqrt{}$	Radical sign	
4.8A	$\sqrt{a \cdot b} = \sqrt{a} \cdot \sqrt{b}$		$\sqrt{32} = \sqrt{16 \cdot 2} =$ $\sqrt{16} \cdot \sqrt{2} = 4\sqrt{2}$
4.8B	$\sqrt{\dfrac{a}{b}} = \dfrac{\sqrt{a}}{\sqrt{b}}$		$\sqrt{\dfrac{2}{7}} = \dfrac{\sqrt{2}}{\sqrt{7}}$
4.8E	i	$\sqrt{-1}$	
4.8E	C	Complex numbers	
4.8E	$a + bi$	A complex number	$3 + 4i$
4.9	d	The common difference of an arithmetic sequence	In the sequence, 4, 9, 14, . . . , $d = 5$.

Section	Item	Meaning	Example
4.9A	$a_n = a_1 + (n - 1) \cdot d$	The nth term of an arithmetic sequence	In the above sequence, $a_n = 4 + (n - 1) \cdot 5 = 5n - 1$.
4.9B	$S_n = \dfrac{n(a_1 + a_n)}{2}$	The sum of the first n terms of an arithmetic sequence	In the above sequence, $S_5 = \dfrac{5(4 + 24)}{2} = 70$
4.9C	r	The common ratio of a geometric sequence	The common ratio of 5, 10, 20, . . . is $r = 2$.
4.9C	$a_n = a_1 r^{n-1}$	The nth term of a geometric sequence	In the sequence 5, 10, 20, . . . , $a_n = 5 \cdot 2^{n-1}$.
4.9D	$S_n = \dfrac{a_1(1 - r^n)}{1 - r}$	The sum of the first n terms of a geometric sequence	For the sequence 5, 10, 20, . . . , $S_4 = \dfrac{5(1 - 2^4)}{1 - 2} = 75$
4.9E	$\dfrac{a_1}{1 - r}$	The sum of the infinite geometric sequence $a_1, a_1 r, a_1 r^2, \ldots$, where r is between -1 and 1	The sum of the sequence 2, 1, $\frac{1}{2}, \frac{1}{4}, \ldots$ is $S = \dfrac{2}{1 - 1/2} = 4$

Research Questions

Sources of information for these questions can be found in the Bibliography at the end of the book.

1. Write a report about the introduction of the terms **googol** and **googolplex** in mathematics.

2. Make a report about the discovery of the largest known prime number. (See the *Guinness Book of World Records* for starters.)

3. Write a report about the discovery of negative numbers and the popularization of 0.

4. The first perfect number is 6 and the next is 28. Write a report about the religious implications of perfect numbers and find out what the next two perfect numbers are.

5. Find out and report on Euclid's formula for perfect numbers.

6. Trace the evolution of different approximations for π including the early Hebrew approximations and the approximation of π by using the perimeter of a polygon.

7. In the Discovery section in Exercise 4.4 we have a "diagonalization" process that shows that there are as many natural numbers as there are rational numbers. This development is due to Cantor. Write a report on Cantor's "diagonalization" process.

8. Find out some instances where the terms in the Fibonacci sequence appear in nature.

Chapter 4 Practice Test

1. Tell whether the underlined item is used as a cardinal number, an ordinal number, or for identification.
   (a) Sally came in third in the 100-yard dash.
   (b) Bill's lottery ticket won two dollars.
   (c) Jane's auto license number was 270-891 .

2. Consider the set $A = \{0, 1, 2\}$ and the operation table in the margin.
   (a) Is the set A closed under $*$? Why?
   (b) Is the operation commutative? Why?

$*$	0	1	2
0	0	1	2
1	1	2	0
2	2	0	1

3. What properties of the system of natural numbers are used in the following equations?
   (a) $8 + 9 + 2 = 8 + 2 + 9$
   (b) $8 \times 12 = 8(10 + 2) = 80 + 16$
   (c) $5 \times 27 \times 4 = 5 \times 4 \times 27$

4. Write 1,220 as a product of primes.

5. Is 143 prime or composite?

6. Of the numbers 2345, 436, 387, and 1,530, identify those divisible by:
   (a) 2   (b) 3   (c) 5

7. Find the GCF of 216 and 254 and reduce the fraction 216/254 to lowest terms.

8. Find the LCM of 18, 54, and 60 and perform the indicated operations: $\frac{1}{18} + \frac{1}{54} - \frac{1}{60}$

9. A father left $\frac{1}{4}$ of his estate to his daughter, $\frac{1}{2}$ to his wife, and $\frac{1}{8}$ to his son. If the rest went for taxes, what fraction of the estate was that?

10. Change to an equivalent addition problem and give the result:
    (a) $8 - 19$ (b) $8 - (-19)$
    (c) $-8 - 19$ (d) $-8 - (-19)$

11. Evaluate $4 \times 12 \div 3 \times 10^3 - 2(-6 + 4) \times 10^4$.

12. Find a rational number with a denominator of 16 and equal to $\frac{3}{4}$.

13. Find the reciprocal of:
    (a) $\frac{2}{3}$ (b) $-\frac{4}{7}$ (c) $2\frac{5}{8}$ (d) -8

14. Perform the indicated operations:
    (a) $\frac{7}{8} \times (-\frac{5}{16})$ (b) $-\frac{7}{8} \div (-\frac{5}{16})$

15. (a) Write 23.508 in expanded form.
    (b) Write $(8 \times 10^2) + (3 \times 10^0) + (4 \times 10^{-2})$ in decimal form.

16. Do the following calculation and write the answer in scientific notation:
    $(6 \times 10^4) \times (8 \times 10^{-6})$

17. Perform the indicated operations:
    (a) $6.73 + 2.8$ (b) $9.34 - 4.71$
    (c) 0.29×6.7 (d) $17.36 \div 3.1$

18. The three sides of a triangle are measured to be 18.7, 6.25, and 19.63 centimeters long, respectively. What is the perimeter of the triangle?

19. The dimensions of a college basketball court are 93.5 by 50.6 feet. What is the area of this court?

20. Write as decimals:
    (a) $\frac{3}{4}$ (b) $\frac{1}{15}$

21. Write as a quotient of two integers:
    (a) $0.\overline{12}$ (b) $2.6555 \ldots$

22. Write as a decimal:
    (a) 21% (b) 9.35% (c) 0.26%

23. Write as a percent:
    (a) 0.52 (b) 2.765
    (c) $\frac{3}{5}$ (d) $\frac{2}{11}$ (Answer to one decimal place.)

24. A 2-liter bottle of soda sells for 86¢ and costs the store 48¢. Find, to two decimal places, the percent of profit on the cost.

25. About 4 million women make between $25,000 and $50,000 annually. This represents 15% of all working women. About how many working women are there?

26. Classify as rational or irrational:
    (a) $\sqrt{49}$ (b) $\sqrt{45}$ (c) $\sqrt{121}$
    (d) $0.41252525 \ldots$ (e) $0.212112111 \ldots$ (f) $0.246810 \ldots$

27. Find:
    (a) A rational number between $0.\overline{2}$ and 0.25
    (b) An irrational number between $0.\overline{2}$ and 0.25

28. The diameter of a circular hamburger is 4 in. To the nearest tenth of an inch, what is the circumference of this hamburger? (Use $\pi = 3.14$.)

29. The circumference of a basketball is 29.5 inches. Find the diameter. (Use $\pi = 3.14$.)

30. Simplify if possible:
    (a) $\sqrt{96}$ (b) $\sqrt{58}$
31. Simplify:
    (a) $\dfrac{4}{\sqrt{20}}$ (b) $\sqrt{\dfrac{48}{49}}$
32. Perform the indicated operations and simplify:
    (a) $\sqrt{8} \cdot \sqrt{6}$ (b) $\dfrac{\sqrt{56}}{\sqrt{7}}$
33. Perform the indicated operations:
    (a) $\sqrt{90} - \sqrt{40}$ (b) $\sqrt{32} + \sqrt{18} - \sqrt{50}$
34. Express in the form bi, where b is a real number:
    (a) $\sqrt{-36}$ (b) $\sqrt{-43}$
35. Classify the given numbers by making a check mark in the appropriate row:

Set	(a) $2 + 7i$	(b) $-3i$	(c) $-\frac{2}{5}$	(d) $\sqrt{3}\, i$
Real numbers				
Pure imaginary numbers				
Complex numbers				

36. Classify the given numbers by making a check mark in the appropriate row:

Set	(a) $\sqrt{16}$	(b) $\sqrt{7}\, i$	(c) $\sqrt{5}$	(d) $9 - 2i$
Natural numbers				
Integers				
Rational numbers				
Irrational numbers				
Real numbers				
Complex numbers				

37. Classify as an arithmetic or geometric sequence:
    (a) 2, 4, 8, 16, . . .   (b) 5, 8, 11, 14, . . .
38. Find the sum of the first ten terms of 9, 13, 17, 21, ...
39. Find the sum of the first five terms of the sequence $1, \frac{1}{2}, \frac{1}{4}, \frac{1}{8}, \ldots$
40. Use the sum of an infinite geometric sequence to write the following repeating decimals as fractions:
    (a) 0.444 . . .   (b) 0.212121 . . .   (c) 2.555 . . .

As promised, we are now ready to begin our introduction to algebra. Do you know where the word *algebra* comes from? It is the European derivation of *al-jabr*, part of the title of al-Khowarizmi's treatise *Hisab al-jabr w'al muqabalah*, "the science of reunion and reduction." The study of algebra starts with its foundations: open sentences, statements, equations, and inequalities. We will learn how to solve first-degree equations and inequalities in Section 5.2, graph the results of the solutions of inequalities (Sections 5.3–5.5). Next, we study quadratic equations and their methods of solution, factoring and the quadratic formula, and then use this information to solve different types of word problems. We end the chapter by discussing ratio, proportion, and variation, emphasizing applications to consumer problems such as unit pricing.

Now, do you remember that precocious little boy of ten who amazed his teacher by adding $1 + 2 + 3 + \cdots + 100$ with lightning speed? (Getting Started, Section 4.9). In his doctoral dissertation he provided the first proof of the fundamental theorem of algebra. You can read more about him in The Human Side of Mathematics.

Equations, Inequalities, and Problem Solving

THE HUMAN SIDE OF MATHEMATICS

Karl Friedrich Gauss, who has been called the Prince of Mathematicians, was born in Brunswick, Germany, in 1777. His father was a poor laborer who did nothing to promote his son's talents. It was only by accident that Gauss became a mathematician.

Throughout his life, Gauss was noted for his ability to perform stupendous mental calculations. Before he was 3 years old, while watching his father make out a weekly payroll, he noted an error and told his father what the answer should be. A check of the account showed that the boy was correct.

At age 10 he met a mathematician named Bartels, who taught the boy some mathematics and brought his young friend to the attention of the Duke of Brunswick. The Duke was so impressed by Gauss that he made the boy his protégé.

Gauss entered the Caroline College in Brunswick at the age of 15, and in a short time began his research into higher arithmetic. When he left the College in 1795, he had already invented the method of least squares. He entered the University of

Karl Friedrich Gauss (1777–1855)

Archimedes, Newton, and Gauss, these three, are in a class by themselves among the great mathematicians, and it is not for ordinary mortals to attempt to range them in the order of merit.

E. T. Bell

Göttingen, where he spent three years completing his *Disquisitiones Arithmeticae (Arithmetical Researches)*. In 1798, he went to the University of Helmstedt, where he was awarded his Ph.D. His doctoral thesis gave the first proof of the fundamental theorem of algebra, that every algebraic equation has at least one root among the complex numbers.

His *Disquisitiones*, published in 1801, is regarded as the basic work in the theory of numbers. During his life he also made great contributions to astronomy, geodesy (the measurement of the Earth), geometry, theoretical physics, and complex numbers and functions. Along with his masterful theoretical research, he was also a well-known inventor; among other things, he made significant contributions to the invention of the electric telegraph in the early 1830s.

Looking Ahead: Much of Gauss's work in pure mathematics dealt with number theory, the concept of complex numbers (which we have seen in Chapter 4), and the solutions to algebraic equations, which is the focus of this chapter.

5.1   OPEN SENTENCES AND STATEMENTS

GETTING STARTED

CRICKETS, ANTS, AND TEMPERATURES

Does temperature affect animal behavior? You must know about bears hibernating in the winter and the languid nature of students in the spring. But what about the behavior of crickets and ants? Can you tell if crickets will stop chirping before ants stop crawling? In Exercise 5.1 you will find (problem 38) that the number N of chirps a cricket makes per minute satisfies the equation. $N = 4(F - 40)$, where F is the temperature in degrees Fahrenheit. What happens as the temperature increases? In problem 41 we find that the speed S (in cm/sec) for certain types of ants is $S = \frac{1}{6}(C - 4)$, where C is the temperature in degrees Celsius. What happens as the temperature decreases? Finally, problem 43 states that the relationship between Fahrenheit and Celsius temperature is given by $F = \frac{9}{5}C + 32$. Armed with this information, can you tell if crickets stop chirping before ants stop crawling?

For some types of ants, the speed at which they move varies directly with changes in temperature.

Elementary algebra was first treated in a systematic fashion by the Arabs during the period before the Renaissance, when Europe was almost at a standstill intellectually. By the early 1600s, algebra had become a fairly well-developed branch of mathematics, and mathematicians were beginning to discover that a marriage of algebra and geometry could be highly beneficial to both subjects.

It has been said that algebra is arithmetic made simple, and it is true that a small amount of elementary algebra enables us to solve many problems that would be quite difficult by purely arithmetic means. In this chapter we shall learn some of the simpler algebraic techniques that are used in problem solving.

We have already made frequent use of various symbols, usually letters of the alphabet, as place-holders for the elements of a set of numbers. For example, we wrote

$$a + b = b + a \qquad a, b \text{ real numbers}$$

as a symbolic way of stating the commutative property of addition. Of course, we mean that a and b may each be replaced by any real number. In this case the set of real numbers is the **replacement set** for a and b. A symbol that may be replaced by any one of a set of numbers is called a **variable.**

Letters of the alphabet as well as symbols such as $\square$ are often used to indicate variables in arithmetic. The study of sentences and expressions involving variables is, however, a part of algebra.

In algebra, as in arithmetic, the commonly used **verb phrases** are

$=$	is equal to	$\neq$	is not equal to
$>$	is greater than	$\geq$	is greater than or equal to
$<$	is less than	$\leq$	is less than or equal to

By using these verb phrases along with specific numbers and variables joined by the usual operations from arithmetic, we can form many types of sentences. Some examples of simple algebraic sentences are

1. $x - 1 = 3$
2. $x - 2 \neq 4$
3. $x - 1 \geq 3$
4. $x + 7 < 9$

A. *Equations and Inequalities*

In the four preceding sentences, x is a variable — that is, a place-holder for the numbers by which it may be replaced. Until x is replaced by a number, none of these sentences is a statement, because it is neither true nor false. For this reason, we call such sentences **open sentences.** Because only one variable is involved, we may refer to the sentences as **open sentences in one variable.** Sentences in which the verb phrase is $=$ are called **equations;** if the verb phrase is any of the others we have listed, then the sentence is called an **inequality.**

In order to study an open sentence in one variable, we obviously must know what is the replacement set for that variable. We are interested in knowing for which of the possible replacements the sentence is a true statement. The set of elements of the replacement set that make the open sentence a true statement is called the **solution set** for the given replacement set.

EXAMPLE 1

Suppose the replacement set for x is $\{2, 4, 6\}$. For each of the following open sentences, find the solution set:

(a) $x - 1 = 3$ (b) $x - 2 \neq 4$

(c) $x - 1 \geq 3$ (d) $x + 7 < 9$

Solution

(a) We substitute the elements of the replacement set into the open sentence $x - 1 = 3$:

For $x = 2$, we get $2 - 1 = 1$, not 3.

For $x = 4$, we get $4 - 1 = 3$, which makes the sentence a true statement.

For $x = 6$, we get $6 - 1 = 5$, not 3.

Thus, $x = 4$ is the only replacement that makes the sentence $x - 1 = 3$ a true statement, so the solution set is $\{4\}$.

(b) We make the permissible replacements into the open sentence $x - 2 \neq 4$:

For $x = 2$, we get $2 - 2 = 0$, which is not equal to 4, so the sentence is a true statement.

For $x = 4$, we get $4 - 2 = 2$, which is not equal to 4, so the sentence is a true statement.

For $x = 6$, we get $6 - 2 = 4$, which does not satisfy the "$\neq 4$," so the sentence is a false statement.

Thus, the solution set is $\{2, 4\}$.

(c) Making the permissible replacements into $x - 1 \geq 3$:

For $x = 2$, we get $2 - 1 = 1$, which is less than 3, not greater than or equal to 3. Hence, the sentence is a false statement.

For $x = 4$, we get $4 - 1 = 3$, which satisfies the "≥ 3," so that the sentence is a true statement.

For $x = 6$, we get $6 - 1 = 5$, which satisfies the "≥ 3," so that the sentence is a true statement.

The solution set is thus $\{4, 6\}$.

(d) Making the permissible replacements into $x + 7 < 9$:

For $x = 2$, we get $2 + 7 = 9$, which is not less than 9, so the sentence is a false statement.

For $x = 4$, we get $4 + 7 = 11$, which is not less than 9, so the sentence is a false statement.

For $x = 6$, we get $6 + 7 = 13$, which is not less than 9, so the sentence is a false statement.

Since none of the replacements make the sentence $x + 7 < 9$ a true statement, the solution set is $\emptyset$.

EXAMPLE 2   Find the solution set for the inequality $x + 7 < 9$ if x is an integer.

Solution   The replacement set for the inequality $x + 7 < 9$, x is an integer, is the set of integers. Of this set, the integer 1 is the largest for which $x + 7 < 9$, because $1 + 7 = 8$, which is less than 9; but $2 + 7 = 9$, which *not* less than 9. The solution set is the set of all integers less than or equal to 1, that is, the set $\{\ldots, -3, -2, -1, 0, 1\}$. Test for yourself that the integers less than 1 satisfy the given inequality.

■

EXAMPLE 3   Find the solution set for $2(y - 2) = -4 + 2y$ if y is a real number.

Solution   We work with the left-hand side of the given sentence. By the distributive property, for any real number y,

$$2(y - 2) = 2y - 4$$

Then, by the commutative property of addition, for any real number y,

$$2y - 4 = -4 + 2y$$

which is the same as the right-hand side of the given sentence. Thus, the equation $2(y - 2) = -4 + 2y$ is true for all real numbers, so the solution set is the set of all real numbers.

■

Open sentences that are true statements for every number in the replacement set are called **identities.** Thus, the equation given in Example 3 is an identity as is the equation $x + 1 = 1 + x$, x a real number.

B. *Applications*

In the preceding examples, we learned how to determine whether a given number **satisfies** an equation or an inequality. This idea can be used to do some detective work, as you will see in the next example.

EXAMPLE 4   The relationship between the length f of the human female femur bone and the height H of the female is given (in centimeters) by the formula

$$H = 1.95f + 72.85$$

Suppose the police find a female femur bone 40 cm long. If a missing girl is known to be 120 cm tall, can the bone belong to her?

Solution   If the bone belongs to the missing girl (120 cm tall), its length f must satisfy the equation

$$120 = 1.95f + 72.85$$

But the right side, for $f = 40$, is

$$1.95(40) + 72.85 = 150.85$$

Since $120 \neq 150.85$, the bone does *not* belong to the missing girl.

■

Exercise 5.1

A. In problems 1–4, determine which of the given numbers are solutions of the given inequality.

1. $2 + x \leq 2 - x$
   - (a) 2
   - (b) −2
   - (c) 0
   - (d) 5

2. $3x + 1 < 2x + 4$
   - (a) $\frac{1}{3}$
   - (b) 4
   - (c) 0
   - (d) 3

3. $3x - 2 \geq 2x - 1$
   - (a) 0
   - (b) 3
   - (c) −2
   - (d) 1

4. $x > 3 - 2x$
   - (a) 1
   - (b) 2
   - (c) 0
   - (d) −2

In problems 5–20 let the replacement set be the set of positive integers. Find the solution set.

5. $x + 2 = 4$ 6. $x + 3 = 7$ 7. $x + 2 \geq 2$ 8. $x + 1 \geq 1$

9. $x + 3 < x$ 10. $x < x + 2$ 11. $x + 4 \leq 7$ 12. $x + 1 \leq 5$

13. $x - 1 < 5$ 14. $x - 2 < 1$ 15. $x + 1 \neq 7$ 16. $3 + x \neq 4$

17. $x + 3 < 3$ 18. $x - 1 < 1$ 19. $x - 5 = 18$ 20. $x - 3 = 2$

In problems 21–36, let the replacement set be the set of all integers. Find the solution set.

21. $x + 1 = 5$ 22. $x + 4 < 0$ 23. $2 + x \leq x + 2$

24. $x - 5 = \frac{1}{2}$ 25. $x + 3 = 2$ 26. $x + 2 = 2$

27. $x + 1 > 3$ 28. $x + 3 > 1$ 29. $x - 1 > 0$

30. $x + 1 < 3$ 31. $x + \frac{1}{2} = 2$ 32. $x - \frac{1}{2} \neq 0$ 33. $x + 2 = 2$

34. $x + 2 \neq 2$ 35. $x - 3 \leq 4$ 36. $x + 1 \geq 2$

B. 37. The relationship between the length h of the human male humerus bone and the height H of the male is given (in centimeters) by the formula

$$H = 2.89h + 70.64$$

Can a 36-cm humerus bone belong to a man 174.68 cm tall?

38. The number of chirps N that a cricket makes per minute satisfies the equation

$$N = 4(F - 40)$$

where F is the temperature in degrees Fahrenheit. A farmer claimed that a cricket chirped 150 times a minute when the temperature was 80°F. Is this possible?

39. Referring to problem 38, if the temperature was 77.5°F, how many chirps per minute would the cricket make?

40. At what temperature will the cricket of problem 38 stop chirping?

41. The speed S (in centimeters per second) at which a certain type of ant crawls is $S = \frac{1}{6}(C - 4)$, where C is the temperature in degrees Celsius. Find the ant's speed when the temperature is 10°C.

42. At what temperature will the ant in problem 41 stop crawling? Now, can you tell if the cricket stops chirping before the ant stops crawling?

43. The relationship between Fahrenheit and Celsius temperature is $F = \frac{9}{5}C + 32$. The freezing point in the Celsius scale occurs at 0°C. What temperature is that on the Fahrenheit scale?

44. Water boils at 100°C. What temperature is that on the Fahrenheit scale?

45. The perimeter P of a rectangle of height h and base b is given by the formula

$$P = 2(b + h)$$

A wire of length 20 cm is to be bent into a rectangle of height 4 cm. What will be the length of the base of the rectangle?

46. In Example 4, the equation relating a girl's 120-cm height to the length of her femur bone was given.
    (a) If you subtract 72.85 from both sides, what equation results?
    (b) How long should the girl's femur bone be?

In Other Words

47. In your own words define the *replacement set* for an equation.

48. In your own words define the *solution set* for an equation

49. If a real number a is in the replacement set of an equation, will it always be in the solution set? Explain.

50. If a number s is in the solution set of an equation, will it always be in the replacement set? Explain.

Using Your Knowledge

The ideas presented in this section can be used to solve many problems that involve certain simple formulas. For example, the weekly salary of a salesperson is given by

(Salary) plus (Commission) equals (Total pay)

$$S \quad + \quad C \quad = \quad T$$

51. If a salesperson made $66 on commissions and her total pay was $176, what was her salary?

52. If a salesperson's salary was $150 and his total pay amounted to $257, what was his commission?

One's bank balance is given by

(Deposits) minus (Withdrawals) equals (Balance)

$$D \quad - \quad W \quad = \quad B$$

53. If a person deposited $304 and her balance was $102, how much money did she withdraw?

54. If a person withdrew $17 and her balance was $39, how much money did she deposit?

The ideal weight W (in pounds) of a man is related to his height H (in inches) by the formula

$$W = 5H - 190$$

55. If a man weighs 200 lb, what should his height be?

56. What should be the weight of a man whose height is 5 ft 10 in.?

Discovery

Here are some problems just for fun!

57. Sally has 20 coins, all dimes and quarters. She wishes the dimes were quarters and the quarters were dimes, because she would then have $1.20 more than she has now. Can you discover how many of each coin she has?

58. A clever little child who knows her addition and multiplication tables for the integers from 1 through 5 uses finger reckoning to multiply numbers between 5 and 10. On one hand she extends the number of fingers equal to the excess of one of the numbers over 5, and does the same with the second number on her other hand. She then finds the product of the two numbers corresponding to the unextended fingers on her two hands. The units digit of this product is the units digit of the final answer. The sum of the tens digit of this product plus her extended fingers is the tens digit of the final answer. For example, to multiply 6 and 7, she extends one finger on her left hand and two fingers on her right hand. She now has four unextended fingers on her left hand and three unextended fingers on her right hand. The product $4 \times 3 = 12$. The units digit 2 is the units digit of the final answer. The sum of the tens digit and the extended fingers is $1 + 1 + 2 = 4$. The 4 is the tens digit of the final answer, 42. Try it! Can you discover why this works?

59. Not very much is known about the Greek algebraist Diophantus, except how old he was when he died. This fact has been preserved in the following 1,500-year-old riddle. Can you discover Diophantus' age at death?

Diophantus' youth lasted $\frac{1}{6}$ of his life.
After $\frac{1}{12}$ more, he grew a beard.
After $\frac{1}{7}$ more of his life, he married, and 5 years later, he had a son.
The son lived exactly $\frac{1}{2}$ as long as his father, and Diophantus died just 4 years after his son.
[*Hint:* Let x be the number of years that Diophantus lived.]

5.2 SOLUTION OF FIRST-DEGREE SENTENCES

GETTING STARTED

A CAR RENTAL EQUATION

Have you rented a car lately? Some companies charge a flat fee each day and give you free mileage. Other companies have a flat fee *plus* mileage. Suppose your car breaks down and you wish to rent an economy car for 1 day. The cost C is $25 per day plus 20¢ per mile. If m is the number of miles traveled in 1 day, the cost can be written as

$$C = 0.20m + 25$$

If at the end of the day you paid $55, how far did you drive? To find the answer, you must solve the equation

$$55 = 0.20m + 25$$

An open sentence such as $55 = 0.20m + 25$ in which the unknown quantity has an exponent of 1, is called a **first-degree** sentence. We shall study two types of first-degree sentences in this section: equations and inequalities.

Car rental counters are a familiar sight at most airport terminals

In the preceding section, we learned how to determine if a certain number satisfies an equation. Now we shall learn how to find these numbers, that is, how to solve equations by finding equivalent equations whose solution is obvious.

A. *Solving Equations*

First, we consider what operations may be performed on a sentence to obtain an equivalent sentence — that is, one with exactly the same solution set as the original sentence. Such operations are called **elementary operations.**

For the equation

$$a = b$$

the following elementary operations yield equations **equivalent** to the original equation:

1. **Addition** $a + c = b + c$
2. **Subtraction** $a - c = b - c$
3. **Multiplication** $a \times c = b \times c$ $c \neq 0$
4. **Division** $a \div c = b \div c$ $c \neq 0$

Briefly stated, we may add or subtract the same number on both sides, or multiply or divide both sides by the same nonzero number. To solve an equation, we use the elementary operations as needed to obtain an equivalent equation of the form

$$x = n \quad \text{or} \quad n = x$$

where the number n is the desired solution. For example, to solve the equation

$$55 = 0.20m + 25$$

we must get the m all by itself on one side of the equation. Hence, we proceed as follows:

Subtract 25: $55 - 25 = 0.20m + 25 - 25$

or $30 = 0.20m$

$$\frac{30}{0.20} = \frac{0.20m}{0.20}$$

Divide by 0.20

or $150 = m$

Thus, if you paid $55 at the end of the day, you drove 150 miles.

EXAMPLE 1   Solve the equation $x + 2 = 5$.

Solution   To solve the equation, we first want to get the variable x by itself on one side. Therefore, we subtract 2 from both sides to eliminate the "$+2$" on the left-hand side:

$$x + 2 - 2 = 5 - 2$$

which simplifies to

$$x = 3$$

The solution set is {3}. We used elementary operation 2. ■

EXAMPLE 2 Solve the equation $2x - 1 = x - 5$.

Solution First, we add 1 to both sides to eliminate the "-1" on the left side:

$$2x - 1 + 1 = x - 5 + 1$$

or

$$2x = x - 4$$

Then, to eliminate the x on the right side, we subtract x from both sides to get

$$2x - x = x - 4 - x$$

or

$$x = -4$$

The solution set is {-4}. Here, we have used elementary operations 1 and 2. ■

Note: In the second operation of the solution to Example 2, we subtracted x from both sides. The only restriction on the addition or subtraction of an expression whose value depends on the value of x is that this expression be a real number for each element of the replacement set of the given equation. It is possible to get into trouble if this is not so. For instance, the equation

$$x + 1 = 2$$

has the solution set {1}. If we add $1/(x - 1)$ to both sides, to get

$$x + 1 + \frac{1}{x - 1} = 2 + \frac{1}{x - 1}$$

then we have an equation that is not equivalent to the given equation, because neither side of the new equation is defined for $x = 1$. (Why?)

EXAMPLE 3 Solve the equation $2x - 8 = 5x - 6$.

Solution Because the coefficient of x *on* the right is greater than that on the left, we subtract $2x$ on both sides to get

$$2x - 8 - 2x = 5x - 6 - 2x$$

or

$$-8 = 3x - 6$$

To eliminate the "−6" on the right side, we add 6 to both sides to obtain

$$-8 + 6 = 3x - 6 + 6$$

or

$$-2 = 3x$$

Since the 3 on the right multiplies the x, we divide both sides by 3:

$$\frac{-2}{3} = \frac{3x}{3}$$

That is,

$$-\frac{2}{3} = x \quad \text{or} \quad x = -\frac{2}{3}$$

The solution set is $\{-\frac{2}{3}\}$, and we have used elementary operations 1, 2, and 4. ■

To help you in solving an equation, we suggest the following procedure:

Procedure to Solve an Equation

1. If there are fractions, multiply each term on both sides of the equation by the LCD of the fractions.

2. Simplify both sides of the equation, if necessary. (Remove parentheses and combine like terms.)

3. Add or subtract the same expression (terms) on both sides so that the variable occurs on one side only.

4. Add or subtract the same numbers on both sides so that only the variable term is left on one side.

5. If the coefficient of the variable is not 1, divide both sides by this coefficient.

6. The resulting equation is of the form $x = a$ (or $a = x$), where the number a is the solution of the equation.

7. Check your answer by substituting it into the original equation. Both sides must simplify to the same number.

EXAMPLE 4   Solve the equation $2(x + 1) = 5(x - 2) + 18$.

Solution   We follow the suggested procedure for the given equation:

$$2(x + 1) = 5(x - 2) + 18$$

1. Simplify both sides:

    $$2x + 2 = 5x - 10 + 18$$

    or

    $$2x + 2 = 5x + 8$$

2. Since the coefficient of x is greater on the right than on the left, we subtract $2x$ on both sides to get

    $$2x + 2 - 2x = 5x + 8 - 2x$$

    or

    $$2 = 3x + 8$$

3. To eliminate the   on the right-hand side, we subtract 8 on both sides:

    $$2 - 8 = 3x + 8 - 8$$

    or

    $$-6 = 3x$$

4. Divide both sides by 3:

    $$\frac{-6}{3} = \frac{3x}{3}$$

5. Or

    $$-2 = x$$

    Thus, the solution is $x = -2$.

6. *Check*. For $x = -2$, the left side of the given equation becomes

    $$2(-2 + 1) = 2(-1) = -2$$

    and the right side becomes

    $$5(-2 - 2) + 18 = 5(-4) + 18$$
    $$= -20 + 18 = -2$$

    Since the two sides agree, the solution checks. ∎

An expression of the form $ax + b$, where a and b are real numbers and $a \neq 0$, is called a **first-degree (or linear) expression in x,** and an equation of the form

$$ax + b = 0 \qquad a \neq 0$$

is called a **first-degree (or linear) equation in x.** The methods we have used in Examples 1–4 always suffice to solve first-degree equations.

EXAMPLE 5   Solve for p:

$$1 + 3 \times 2p = 7 + \frac{3(2p)^2}{3p}$$

Solution   First we simplify the given equation by doing the indicated multiplications and divisions.

$$1 + 3 \times 2p = 7 + \frac{3(2p)^2}{3p}$$

$$1 + 6p = 7 + \frac{4p^2}{p} \quad \left(\text{Since } \frac{\cancel{3}(2p)^2}{\cancel{3}p} = \frac{4p^2}{p}\right)$$

$$1 + 6p = 7 + 4p$$

$$1 + 2p = 7 \quad \text{(Subtract } 4p \text{ from both sides.)}$$

$$2p = 6 \quad \text{(Subtract 1 from both sides.)}$$

$$p = 3 \quad \text{(Divide both sides by 2.)}$$

Check: For $p = 3$, the left side becomes

$$1 + 3 \times 6 = 19$$

and the right side becomes

$$7 + \frac{3(6^2)}{9} = 7 + \frac{36}{3} = 7 + 12 = 19.$$

Since the two sides agree, the answer $p = 3$ is correct.   ∎

B. *Solving Inequalities*

An **inequality of the first degree in x** is an inequality of the form

$$ax + b < 0 \qquad a \neq 0$$

or of the form

$$ax + b > 0 \qquad a \neq 0$$

We can solve such inequalities by means of elementary operations that produce equivalent inequalities. These operations are as follows:

For the inequality

$$a < b$$

the following elementary operations yield inequalities **equivalent** to the original inequality:

1. **Addition** $a + c < b + c$
2. **Subtraction** $a - c < b - c$
3. **Multiplication** $ac < bc$ for $c > 0$
                              $ac > bc$ for $c < 0$
4. **Division** $\dfrac{a}{c} < \dfrac{b}{c}$ for $c > 0$
                              $\dfrac{a}{c} > \dfrac{b}{c}$ for $c < 0$

Briefly stated, we may add or subtract the same number on both sides. The sense of the inequality is **unchanged** if both sides are multiplied or divided by the same *positive* number. The sense of the inequality is **reversed** if both sides are multiplied or divided by the same *negative* number. For instance, if both sides of $-2 < 1$ are multiplied by -3, we get $6 > -3$. Similarly, if both sides of $-9 < -6$ are divided by -3, the result is $3 > 2$.

The preceding operations have been stated for the inequality $a < b$, but the same operations are valid for $a > b$. You can convince yourself of the validity of these operations by noting that the geometric equivalent of $a < b$ is **a precedes b on the number line.** (The diagram in Figure 5.1 will clarify this idea.) *Note:* Since $a \leq b$ means $a < b$ or $a = b$, the elementary operations listed above may also be used for inequalities of the type $a \leq b$ and $a \geq b$.

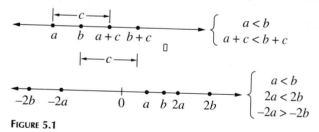

FIGURE 5.1

Linear (first-degree) inequalities can be solved by a procedure similar to that used for equations. This is illustrated in the next examples, where x represents a real number.

EXAMPLE 6   Solve the inequality $3x + 2 > x + 6$.

Solution   1. The two sides are already in simplified form.
2. Subtract x from both sides:

$$3x + 2 - x > x + 6 - x$$
$$2x + 2 > 6$$

3. Subtract 2 from both sides:

$$2x + 2 - 2 > 6 - 2$$
$$2x > 4$$

4. Divide both sides by 2:

$$\frac{2x}{2} > \frac{4}{2}$$
$$x > 2$$

5. The solution set is $\{x \mid x > 2\}$.

6. A partial check can be made by substituting a number from the proposed solution set into the original inequality. For instance, 3 is in the set $\{x \mid x > 2\}$. For $x = 3$, the left side becomes

$$3(3) + 2 = 11$$

and the right side becomes

$$3 + 6 = 9$$

Since $11 > 9$, $x = 3$ does satisfy the inequality. Because the solution set contains infinitely many numbers, we cannot check by substituting one number at a time. However, if the number selected did *not* check, then something would be wrong, and we could check the work to find the error. ∎

EXAMPLE 7   Solve the inequality $2x - 3 < 5x + 7$.

Solution
1. The two sides are already in simplified form.
2. Subtract $5x$ from both sides:

$$2x - 3 - 5x < 5x + 7 - 5x$$
$$-3x - 3 < 7$$

3. Add 3 to both sides:

$$-3x - 3 + 3 < 7 + 3$$
$$-3x < 10$$

4. Divide both sides by -3:

$$x > -\frac{10}{3}$$

5. The solution set is $(x \mid x > -\frac{10}{3})$. Be sure to notice that **division by -3 reversed the sense of the inequality.**
6. The check is left for you to do. An easy number to use is 0.

If, in step 2, you were to subtract $2x$ from both sides of the inequality, you would avoid dividing by a negative number later. However, in this case, the answer would be $-\frac{10}{3} < x$. If you are asked what x is, then you must write the equivalent answer $x > -\frac{10}{3}$. Which way should you do it? Whichever way you understand best!

∎

EXAMPLE 8   Solve the inequality $-\frac{1}{2}x < \frac{1}{2} + x$

Solution   This time we want to eliminate the fractions and the minus sign on the left. This is done by multiplying both sides by -2. Since this multiplier is negative, the inequality sign is reversed. Here are the steps.
Given:

$$-\frac{1}{2}x < \frac{1}{2} + x$$

$$(-2)\left(-\frac{1}{2}\right)x > (-2)\left(\frac{1}{2} + x\right)$$

or $\qquad\qquad x > -1 - 2x$

Now we add $2x$ to both sides to get

$\qquad 3x > -1$

Then we divide both sides by 3 to obtain the answer

$$x > -\frac{1}{3}$$

The solution set is $\left\{ x \mid x \text{ is a real number and } x > -\frac{1}{3} \right\}$.

∎

C. *Applications*

One of the most important ideas in elementary mathematics is that of **percent.** Basically, there are three types of problems involving percent. These may be illustrated as follows:

1. 40% of 60 is what number?
2. What percent of 50 is 10?
3. 20 is 40% of what number?

All these problems (which, incidentally, can be stated in different ways) can be solved easily by using what we have learned in this section. The basic idea is that "$r\%$ of n is p" translates into the equation

$\qquad 0.01\ rn = p \qquad$ Recall that $r\% = \dfrac{r}{100} = 0.01\ r \qquad\qquad$ (1)

Each type of percent problem can be solved by substituting the known data into equation (1) and then solving for the unknown as follows:

EXAMPLE 9   40% of 60 is what number?

Solution   Here, $r = 40$, $n = 60$, and p is unknown. Equation (1) becomes

$$0.01 \times 40 \times 60 = p$$

or

$$0.40 \times 60 = p$$

This gives

$$p = 24$$

EXAMPLE 10   What percent of 50 is 10?

Solution   Here, r is unknown, $n = 50$, and $p = 10$. Equation (1) becomes

$$0.01 \times 50r = 10 \quad \text{or} \quad 0.50r = 10$$

To find r, divide both sides by 0.50 to get

$$r = 20$$

So, 10 is 20% of 50.

EXAMPLE 11   20 is 40% of what number?

Solution   Here, $r = 40$, $p = 20$, and n is unknown. Equation (1) becomes

$$0.01 \times 40n = 20 \quad \text{or} \quad 0.40n = 20$$

Dividing by 0.40, we find that $n = 50$.

Exercise 5.2

A. 1. Determine which of the following are solutions of $2x - 1 = 3$.
   (a) -1 (b) 1   (c) 2   (d) 0

2. Determine which of the following are solutions of $\frac{1}{5}(3x - 2) = 2$.

   (a) -1 (b) 0   (c) 2   (d) 4

In problems 3–28, solve the given equation.

3. $x + 10 = 15$ 4. $x - 5 = 8$
5. $2x - 1 = 5$ 6. $3x + 1 = 4$

7. $2x + 2 = x + 4$

8. $3x + 1 = x - 3$

9. $3x + 1 = 4x - 8$

10. $2x + 3 = 3x - 1$

11. $7 = 3x + 4$

12. $22 = 4x + 2$

13. $4 = 3x - 2$

14. $1 = 5x - 8$

15. $7n + 10 - 2n = 4n - 2 + 3n$

16. $13a - 6 + a = 5a + 3 + 3a$

17. $2(x + 5) = 13$

18. $6(x + 2) = 17$

19. $\frac{1}{2}(x - 2) = 5$

20. $\frac{2}{3}(5x - 4) = 1$

21. $3(x + 1) - x = 2(9 - x)$

22. $14y - 14 - 3y = 10y - 6(1 - y)$

23. $8(x - 1) = x + 2$

24. $x + 6 = 6(x - 1)$

25. $\frac{1}{4}(x - 2) = \frac{1}{3}(x - 4)$

26. $\frac{1}{2}(3x - 1) = \frac{2}{5}(3x + 1)$

27. $3 \times 2p + 5 = 37 - \frac{4p^2}{2p}$

28. $15 + \frac{12t^2}{3t} = 3 \times 3t - 5$

B. Find the solution set for each of the following if the replacement set is the set of real numbers.

29. $x - 3 < 1$

30. $x - 2 < 2$

31. $x - 4 > -1$

32. $x + 3 > -2$

33. $2x - 1 > x + 2$

34. $3x - 3 > 2x + 1$

35. $2x + 3 \leq 9 + 5x$

36. $x + 8 \geq 2x - 1$

37. $x + 1 > \frac{1}{2}x - 1$

38. $x - 1 < \frac{1}{2}x + 2$

39. $x \geq 4 + 3x$

40. $x - 1 \leq 5 + 3x$

41. $\frac{1}{3}x - 2 \geq \frac{2}{3}x + 1$

42. $\frac{1}{4}x + 1 \leq \frac{3}{4}x - 1$

43. $2x - 2 > x + 1$

44. $3x - 2 > 2x + 2$

45. $x + 3 > \frac{1}{2}x + 1$

46. $x + 1 < \frac{1}{2}x + 4$

47. $x \geq 2 + 4x$

48. $x - 2 \leq 6 + 3x$

49. $2x + 1 < 2x$

50. $5x \leq 5x + 4$

51. $8x + 2 \leq 3(x + 4)$

52. $9x + 3 \leq 4(x + 2)$

53. $3(x + 4) > -5x - 4$

54. $5(x + 2) < -3x + 2$

55. $-2(x + 1) \geq 3x - 4$

56. $-3(2 - x) \geq 5x - 7$

57. $a(x - 1) \leq a(2x + 3)$ with $a < 0$

58. $b(1 - 2x) > 5b - 4bx$ with $b < 0$

Applications

59. 40% of 80 is what number?

60. Find 15% of 60.

61. 315 is what percent of 3150?

62. 8 is what percent of 4?

63. What percent of 40 is 5?

64. 20 is what percent of 30?

65. 30% of what number is 60?

66. 10 is 40% of what number?

67. North America has approximately 7% of the world's oil reserves. If the North American reserves represent 47 billion barrels of oil, what are the world's oil reserves? (Round your answer to the nearest billion.)

68. In a recent year, about 280 million tons of pollutants were released into the air in the United States. If 47% of this amount was carbon monoxide, how many tons was that?

69. On a 60-item test, a student got 40 correct. What percent is that? (Round to the nearest percent.)

70. The price of an article on sale was 90% of the regular price. If the sale price was $18, what was the regular price?

71. Two stores sell an item that they normally price at $140. Store A advertises a sale price of 25% off the regular price, and store B advertises a sale price of $100. Which is the lower price?

72. The ABC Savings & Loan loans the Adams family $40,000 toward the purchase of a $48,000 house. What percent of the purchase price is the loan?

Write the given information as an inequality.

73. The temperature t in your refrigerator is between 20°F and 40°F.

74. The height h (in ft) of any mountain is always less than or equal to that of Mt. Everest, 29,028 ft.

75. My salary s for this year will exceed $23,000.

76. The gas mileage m (in miles) per gallon of gas is between 18 and 22, depending on your driving.

77. The number of possible eclipses e in a year varies from 2 to 7, inclusive.

*I*n Other Words

78. Explain what was done in each step in the solution of the following equation:

$$(2x + 1) - 1 = 14 - (x - 1)$$

Step 1 $\qquad 2x + 1 - 1 = 14 - x + 1$

Step 2 $\qquad\qquad\quad 2x = 15 - x$

Step 3 $\qquad\qquad\quad 3x = 15$

Step 4 $\qquad\qquad\quad\ \ x = 5$

Using Your Knowledge

We can use our knowledge and the facts we have learned in this section to solve problems like this one: 60% of the calories in a McDonald's biscuit with sausage and eggs are fat calories (calories derived from the fat in the food). If there are 351 fat calories in this product, what is the total number of calories in a McDonald's biscuit with sausage and eggs? Let this number be c. Since 60% of c is 351, we have:

$$60\% \cdot c = 351$$
$$0.60c = 351$$
$$60c = 35{,}100 \qquad \text{Multiplying both sides by 100.}$$
$$c = \frac{35{,}100}{60} = 585 \text{ Dividing by 60.}$$

Thus, there are 585 total calories in a McDonald's biscuit with sausage and eggs. (See the Fast-Food Guide *for a wealth of nutritional information on fast foods.)*

79. Of the total calories in a McDonald's apple pie, 50% are fat calories. If there are 125 fat calories in a McDonald's apple pie, how many total calories are there in the apple pie?

80. Of the total calories in a Big Mac, 55% are fat calories. If 313.5 of the calories in a Big Mac are fat calories, how many total calories are there in a Big Mac?

81. The Burger King Whopper also contains 55% fat calories. If 343.75 of the calories in a Whopper are fat calories, how many total calories are there in a Whopper?

Discovery

82. A problem that comes from the Rhind papyrus, one of the oldest mathematical documents known, reads like this: "$\frac{2}{3}$ added and then $\frac{1}{3}$ taken away, 10 remains. . . ." The document then goes on to tell how to find the number with which you started. Can you discover what this number is? [*Hint:* If you let x be the unknown number, then the problem intends you to add $\frac{2}{3}x$ and then take away $\frac{1}{3}$ of the result to get a difference of 10.]

83. Mr. C usually takes the 5 o'clock train from the city and is met at the station by Mrs. C, who then drives him home. One day Mr. C took the 4 o'clock train, and when he reached his station, he started walking home. Mrs. C met him on the way and drove him the rest of the way home. If they reached home 20 min earlier than usual, how long did Mr. C walk? [*Hint:* You do not need any algebra for this problem. Just draw a diagram to see on what portion of the trip Mrs. C saved the 20 min.]

84. There is a peculiar three-digit number. It ends with a 4. If the 4 is moved to the front, the new number is as much greater than 400 as the original number was less than 400. Can you discover what was the original number? [*Hint:* If the digits of a three-digit number are a, b, c, then the number is $100a + 10b + c$. If you simply move the c to the front, the new number is $100c + 10a + b$.]

5.3   GRAPHS OF ALGEBRAIC SENTENCES

GETTING STARTED

IN KING SOLOMON'S GARDEN

In ancient history it is said that King Solomon was the wisest of men. There is a legend that goes like this: One day when he was resting in his palace garden, Solomon, who was so wise that he could even understand the language of all animals and plants, heard gentle voices close to him. Upon further inspection he discovered two snails in a solemn meeting.

> *The first snail said, "Brother, see'st thou yon straight pole that riseth upright from the ground 30 cubits high?" And the second snail answered, "Yea, even so do I."*
>
> *"It is my desire," said the first snail, "to climb to the very top of it. How long thinketh thou it will take me?"*
>
> *"That certainly shall depend on the speed with which thou climbest."*
>
> *"It is not as simple as that," said the would-be climber, "I can ascend but 3 cubits during the day, but in the evening I fall asleep and slip back 2 cubits so that, in effect, I move up but one cubit every 24 hours."*
>
> *"Tis plain then," said the second snail, "that thou will take 30 days to reach the top of the pole. Why dost thou plague me with such a simple problem? Prithee be silent and allow me to sleep."*
>
> *King Solomon smiled. He alone knew whether the second snail was right.*

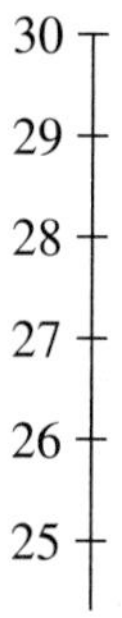

What do you think? [*Hint:* It will obviously take the snail 25 days to reach 25 cubits of height. From then on, draw a graph on the number line in the margin and find the number of days it really took the snail to get to the top.]

In this section we learn how to graph algebraic sentences (equations and inequalities) on the number line.

The solution set of an open sentence in one variable can always be represented by a set of points on the number line. This set of points is often called the **graph** of the equation or the inequality, as the case may be. We shall illustrate various types of graphs in the following examples.

EXAMPLE 1   Graph the solution set of the equation $x + 1 = 0$, where the replacement set is the set of integers.

Solution   Subtracting 1 from both sides, we see that the solution set is the singleton set $\{-1\}$. The graph consists of the single point -1 on the number line. We draw a solid dot to indicate this graph (see Figure 5.2).

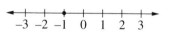

−3 −2 −1 0 1 2 3

FIGURE 5.2
The singleton set {−1}

EXAMPLE 2   Graph the solution set of the inequality $x + 1 \leq 0$, where the replacement set is the set of integers.

Solution   Subtracting 1 from both sides yields the equivalent inequality $x \leq -1$. Thus, the solution set is the set of all integers that are less than or equal to -1, that is, the set $\{\ldots, -3, -2, -1\}$. To show this graph we draw dots at the corresponding points of the number line (see Figure 5.3).

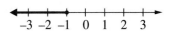

FIGURE 5.3
$\{\ldots, -3, -2, -1\}$

EXAMPLE 3   Graph the solution set of the inequality $x + 1 \leq 0$, where x is a real number.

Solution   Proceeding as in Example 2, we see that the solution set is the set of all real numbers less than or equal to -1, that is, $\{x \mid x \leq -1, x \text{ real}\}$. We display this set by drawing a heavy line starting at -1 on the number line and going to the left. The point at -1 is marked with a solid dot to show that it is included in the set (see Figure 5.4).

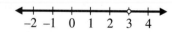

FIGURE 5.4
The set $\{x \mid \leq -1\}$

EXAMPLE 4   Graph the solution set of the inequality $x + 2 \neq 5$, where x is a real number.

Solution   The number 3 is the only replacement for x such that $x + 2 = 5$, so the solution set is all real numbers except 3, that is, $\{x \mid x \neq 3, x \text{ real}\}$. The graph consists of the entire number line except for the point 3. In Figure 5.5, the graph is shown in color and the point 3 is marked with an open circle to indicate its exclusion from the solution set.

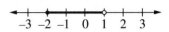

FIGURE 5.5
The set $\{x \mid x \neq 3\}$

EXAMPLE 5   Graph the solution set of the inequality $-2 \leq x < 1$, where the replacement set is the set of real numbers.

Solution   The solution set consists of all the real numbers between -2 and 1, with the -2 included and the 1 excluded. The graph is shown in color in Figure 5.6.

FIGURE 5.6
The set $\{x \mid -2 \leq x < 1\}$

     The piece of the number line such as that in Figure 5.6 is called a **finite interval** (or a **line segment**). The endpoints are -2 and 1. We call the interval **closed** if both endpoints are included, **open** if both endpoints are excluded, and **half-open** if only one of the endpoints is included. The interval in Figure 5.6 is half-open.

If a and b are real numbers with $a < b$, then the various types of finite intervals and how they are written in interval notation are as shown in Figure 5.7.

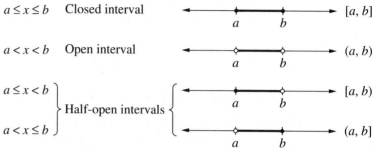

FIGURE 5.7
Finite intervals

The notation for **infinite** intervals is discussed in the Using Your Knowledge section of Exercise 5.3.

Exercise 5.3

In problems 1–8, take x to be an integer and graph the solution set of the given sentence.

1. $x + 2 = 4$ 2. $x - 1 = 3$ 3. $x + 1 \geq 2$
4. $x + 2 < 5$ 5. $x - 3 \neq 1$ 6. $-3 < x \leq 2$
7. $-2 \leq x \leq 4$ 8. $-2 < x < 4$

In problems 9–26, take x to be a real number and graph the solution set of the given sentence.

9. $x < 4$ 10. $x \geq 2$ 11. $x - 2 \leq 0$
12. $x - 2 \geq 4$ 13. $-2 \leq x \leq 4$ 14. $x - 3 \neq 1$
15. $x + 2 > 5$ 16. $x - 2 = 1$ 17. $-1 < x < 2$
18. $x \geq 3$ 19. $x + 4 < 5$ 20. $x + 5 < 4$
21. $x + 1 < x$ 22. $x + 1 > x$ 23. $2x + 3 < x + 1$
24. $-x + 5 \leq 2x + 2$ 25. $3x - 7 \geq -7$ 26. $2x + 5 < 5$

*I*n Other Words

27. Use the word *between* to indicate what numbers are represented in the given graph.

(a)    (b)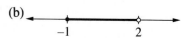

(c)    (d)

-1   2   -1   2

Using Your Knowledge

The graph of the inequality $x \leq -1$ in Example 3 is an **infinite interval** *on the number line and can be written as $(-\infty, -1]$ using interval notation. The symbol $-\infty$ (read, "negative infinity") does not represent a number; it simply means that the interval includes all numbers less than or equal to -1. The square bracket on the right indicates that -1 is part of the interval. The interval $(-\infty, -1]$ is called a* **half-open interval.** *If -1 were not included, we would write the* **open interval** *as $(-\infty, -1)$. Note that the interval notation for $\{x \mid x > -2\}$ is $(-2, \infty)$ where the ∞ (read, "infinity") symbol indicates that the interval includes all numbers greater than -2 (-2 itself is* not *included in the interval). The interval is an open interval. Here are some types of* **infinite intervals,** *their notation, and their graphs.*

Set Notation	Interval Notation	Graph
$\{x \mid a < x\}$	$(a, +\infty)$	←————○———→ a
$\{x \mid x < b\}$	$(-\infty, b)$	←———○————→ b
$\{x \mid a \leq x\}$	$[a, +\infty)$	←————•———→ a
$\{x \mid x \leq b\}$	$(-\infty, b]$	←———•————→ b

Use interval notation to write:

28. $\{x \mid x \geq -4\}$
29. $\{x \mid x < 5\}$
30. $\{x \mid x \leq -6\}$
31. $\{x \mid x > 9\}$
32. $\{x \mid 3 < x < 7\}$
33. $\{x \mid -4 \leq x < -1\}$
34. $\{x \mid 0 < x \leq 8\}$
35. $\{x \mid -1 \leq x \leq 10\}$

Discovery

Can we discover a base 6, three-digit number that has its first and third digits reversed when expressed in base 5? Here is how to go about it. Let the digits in base 6 be a, b, c. Then, we want to have

$$abc_6 = cba_5$$

But, in expanded notation, this means

$$(a \times 6^2) + (b \times 6) + c = (c \times 5^2) + (b \times 5) + a$$

that is,

$$36a + 6b + c = 25c + 5b + a$$

By substracting a, 5b, and c from both sides, we get

$$35a + b = 24c$$

Since a, b, and c are to be digits in base 5 notation, the domain of the equation is the set {0, 1, 2, 3, 4}. Also, to have actual three-digit numbers, the a and the c must not be 0. Now, we use trial and error to solve the equation.

(a) *Try c = 1. Then 35a + b = 24. If a ≥ 1, then b would be negative. Thus, there is no solution for c = 1.*

(b) *Try c = 2. Then 35a + b = 48. If a = 1, b would be 13, which is not in the domain. If a ≥ 2, b would be negative. Thus, there is no solution for c = 2.*

(c) *Try c = 3. Then 35a + b = 72. If a = 1, b would be 37, which is not in the domain. If a = 2, we get 70 + b = 72, so that b = 2. Therefore, a = 2, b = 2, c = 3 is a solution, and $223_6 = 322_5$.*
If a ≥ 3, b would be negative.

(d) *Try c = 4. Then 35a + b = 96. You can show that there is no solution for b in the domain for any permissible value of a.*

The only solution is that found in step (c).

Check. *Convert to base 10:*

$$223_6 = (2 \times 36) + (2 \times 6) \times 3 = 87$$
$$322_5 = (3 \times 25) + (2 \times 5) + 2 = 87$$

Thus, the answer is correct.

36. Can you discover a base 10, three-digit number that has its digits reversed when expressed in base 9?

37. Can you discover a base 9, three-digit number that has its digits reversed when expressed in base 7?

38. Can you discover a base 9, three-digit number that has its digits reversed when expressed in base 5?

39. Can you discover a base 7, three-digit number that has its digits reversed when expressed in base 5?

40. Show that there is no base 5, three-digit number that has its digits reversed when expressed in base 3.

5.4 COMPOUND SENTENCES

What can you conclude from the information in the cartoon? To find the answer, you have to know how to translate the given information into symbols. The second panel says that Bill is taller than Frank *and* Frank is taller than Joe.

In symbols, we can write $B > F$ and $F > J$. In mathematics, an inequality using the word *and* as a connective is a **compound** inequality. If you know how to solve these inequalities, you will be able to finish the problem in the Using Your Knowledge section of Exercise 5.4.

In this section we consider compound algebraic sentences consisting of two or more simple sentences of the type that occurred in the preceding sections. We shall be concerned with the connectives *and* and *or* used in exactly the same sense as in Chapter 2.

A. *Sentences with* and

As we work with finding the solution sets of compound sentences, note that if no replacement set is specified, we assume that the replacement set consists of all real numbers for which the members of the inequalities are defined.

EXAMPLE 1   Consider the sentence $x + 1 < 3$ and $x - 1 > -1$. Find its solution set.

Solution   The sentence given here is a compound sentence of the type $p \wedge q$ (p and q), where p is $x + 1 < 3$ and q is $x - 1 > -1$. Such a sentence as $p \wedge q$ is true only when both p and q are true. Consequently, the solution set of the compound sentence is the **intersection** of the solution sets of the two components.

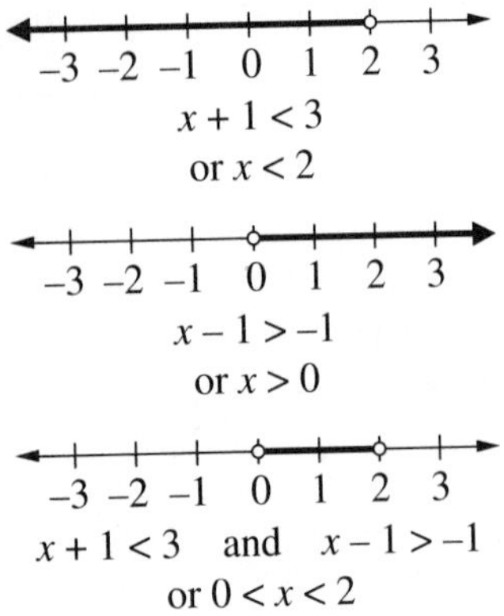

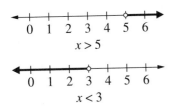

$x + 1 < 3$
or $x < 2$

$x - 1 > -1$
or $x > 0$

$x + 1 < 3$ and $x - 1 > -1$
or $0 < x < 2$

FIGURE 5.8

We have

$$x + 1 < 3 \qquad \text{and} \qquad x - 1 > -1$$
$$x + 1 - 1 < 3 - 1 \quad \text{and} \quad x - 1 + 1 > -1 + 1$$
$$x < 2 \qquad \text{and} \qquad x > 0$$

Rewriting the second inequality, we see that x must satisfy the conditions

$$0 < x \quad \text{and} \quad x < 2$$

Thus, the solution set can be written in set notation as

$$\{x \mid 0 < x\} \cap \{x \mid x < 2\}$$

or, more efficiently, $\{x \mid 0 < x < 2\}$.

  This result is most easily seen in Figure 5.8.   ■

You can obtain this result by first graphing $x + 1 < 3$, or equivalently, $x < 2$ (see the figure), then graphing $x - 1 > -1$, or equivalently $x > 0$. The intersection of these two graphs consists of all numbers between 0 and 2, as shown.

EXAMPLE 2   Find the solution set of $x - 1 > 4$ and $x + 2 < 5$.

Solution   We have

$$x - 1 > 4 \qquad \text{and} \qquad x + 2 < 5$$
$$x - 1 + 1 > 4 + 1 \quad \text{and} \quad x + 2 - 2 < 5 - 2$$
$$x > 5 \qquad \text{and} \qquad x < 3$$

$x > 5$

$x < 3$

FIGURE 5.9

Since there are no numbers satisfying both of these conditions (see Figure 5.9), there are no solutions; the solution set is empty.   ■

EXAMPLE 3   Find the solution set of the sentence $x \leq 5$ and $x + 1 \geq 0$ if x is an integer.

Solution   If x is an integer, then the solution set of $x \leq 5$ is the set of all integers less than or equal to 5. Similarly, the solution set of $x + 1 \geq 0$ is the set of all integers greater than or equal to -1. The intersection of these two sets is the set $\{-1, 0, 1, 2, 3, 4, 5\}$, which is the desired solution set (see Figure 5.10).

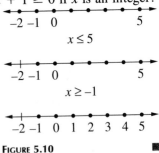

$x \leq 5$

$x \geq -1$

FIGURE 5.10   ■

B. *Sentences with* or

EXAMPLE 4   Find the solution set of the sentence $x + 1 < 5$ or $x - 1 > 6$.

Solution   The replacement set is the set of all real numbers. (Why?) Because this is a sentence of the type $p \lor q$ (p or q), we know that the solution set is the **union** of the solution sets of the two components. We have

$$x + 1 < 5 \quad \text{or} \quad x - 1 > 6$$

$$x < 4 \quad \text{or} \qquad x > 7$$

Thus, the required solution set is

$$\{x \mid x < 4\} \cup \{x \mid x > 7\}$$

or stated in another way,

$$\{x \mid x < 4 \quad \text{or} \quad x > 7\}$$

The graph in Figure 5.11 illustrates the solution.

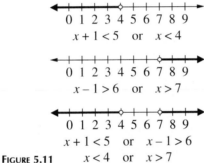

$$x + 1 < 5 \quad \text{or} \quad x < 4$$

$$x - 1 > 6 \quad \text{or} \quad x > 7$$

$$x + 1 < 5 \quad \text{or} \quad x - 1 > 6$$

FIGURE 5.11 $x < 4 \quad \text{or} \quad x > 7$ ■

Exercise 5.4

A–B.   In problems 1–8, let the replacement set be the set of integers. Give the solution set by listing its elements.

1. $x \le 4$ and $x - 1 \ge -2$ 2. $x > 0$ and $x \le 5$
3. $x + 1 \le 7$ and $x > 2$ 4. $x > -5$ and $x - 1 < 0$
5. $2x - 1 > 1$ and $x + 1 < 4$ 6. $x - 1 < 1$ or $3x - 1 > 11$
7. $x < -5$ or $x > 5$ 8. $x \ge 0$ or $x < -2$

In problems 9–26, let the replacement set be the set of real numbers. Graph the solution set unless it is the empty set.

9. $x + 1 \ge 2$ and $x \le 4$ 10. $x \le 5$ and $x > -1$
11. $x > 2$ and $x < -2$ 12. $x + 2 \le 4$ or $x + 2 \ge 6$
13. $x - 1 > 0$ and $x + 1 < 5$ 14. $x \le 0$ or $x > 3$
15. $x \le x + 1$ and $x \ge 2$ 16. $x + 2 \ge -2$ or $x < 0$
17. $x - 2 \ge 2$ and $x < 0$ 18. $x + 3 \le 0$ or $x - 1 > 0$

19. $x \geq 0$ and $x - 1 \geq 2$

20. $x \geq 0$ and $x - 1 \leq 2$

21. $x < 0$ or $x - 1 < 2$

22. $x < 0$ and $x - 1 > 2$

23. $x + 1 > 2$ and $x - 2 < 3$

24. $x - 1 > 3$ and $x + 1 > 2$

25. $x - 1 > 0$ or $x + 2 < 4$

26. $x + 1 > 2$ or $x - 1 < 2$

*I*n Other Words

27. What set of numbers is represented in the given graph.

(a)    (b)

(c)    (d)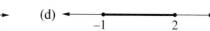

28. What set of numbers is represented in the given graph?

(a)   (b)

(c)   (d)

Using Your Knowledge

Translate each statement into an equation or an inequality:

29. Joe is 5 ft (60 in.) tall.

30. Bill is taller than Frank.

31. Frank is 3 in. shorter than Sam.

32. Frank is taller than Joe.

33. Sam is 6 ft 5 in. (77 in.)

34. According to the statement in problem 30, Bill is taller than Frank, and according to the statement in 32, Frank is taller than Joe. Write these two statements as an inequality of the form $a > b > c$.

35. Based on the answer to problem 34 and the fact that you can obtain Frank's height by using the results of problems 31 and 33, what can you really say about Bill's height?

5.5   SENTENCES INVOLVING ABSOLUTE VALUES

GETTING STARTED

BUDGET VARIANCE AND ABSOLUTE VALUE

Have you ever been on a budget? Businesses and individuals usually try to predict how much money will be spent on certain items over a given period of time, but it is almost impossible to know exactly the final expenditures in different categories. For example, suppose you budget $120 for a month's utilities. Any heat wave or cold snap might make your actual expenses jump to

For most families and individuals it is important to budget expenses and keep track of monthly finances

$150. The $30 difference, representing a 25% increase $\left(\frac{30}{120} = 25\%\right)$ might be an acceptable **variance.** To keep your budget "on target" you can make several variance checks during the year, possibly at the end of each month. Now, suppose b represents the budgeted amount for a certain item, a represents the actual expense, and you want to be within $10 of your estimate. The item will **pass** the variance test if the actual expenses a are within $10 of the budgeted amount b, that is, if

$$-10 \le b - a \le 10$$

Is there a way to write this information using a single inequality? We can if we use **absolute values.** The absolute value of a number x, denoted by $|x|$ (read, "the absolute value of x") is its numerical value with the sign disregarded. For example $|-3| = 3$ and $|+7| = 7$. Thus, $-10 \le b - a \le 10$ is equivalent to $|b - a| \le 10$. Do you see why?

In general, if a and b are as before, a certain item will pass the variance test if $|b - a| \le c$, where c is the variance. The quantity c can be a definite amount, or a percent of the budget. Now, suppose you budget $50 for gas and you want to be within 10% of your budget. How much gas money can you spend and still be within your variance? Intuitively, you can see that if you spend between $45 and $55 you will be within your 10% variance.

The amount of variance is given by

$$0.10 \cdot 50 = 5$$

and $|b - a| \le c$ becomes $|50 - a| \le 5$ or

$$-5 \le 50 - a \le 5$$

Subtracting 50 from each member,

$$-55 \le -a \le -45$$

Multiplying each term by -1,

$$55 \ge a \ge 45$$

or

$$45 \le a \le 55$$

The answer that we expected! In problems 37–39 of Exercise 5.5, you will solve some more problems having to do with variance.

A. *Absolute Value*

Sometimes we need to solve equations or inequalities that involve absolute values. The **absolute value** of a number x is defined to be the distance on the number line from 0 (the origin) to x, and is denoted by $|x|$ (read, "absolute value of x"). For example, the number 2 is 2 units away from 0, so $|2| = 2$. The number -2 is also 2 units away from 0, so $|-2| = 2$. (See Figure 5.12.)

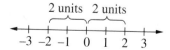

FIGURE 5.12

Similarly, we see that $|8| = 8$, $|\tfrac{1}{2}| = \tfrac{1}{2}$, $|-5| = 5$, and $|-\tfrac{1}{4}| = \tfrac{1}{4}$. In general, if x is any real nonnegative number $(x \geq 0)$, then $|x|$ is simply x itself. But if x is a negative number $(x < 0)$, then $|x|$ is the corresponding positive number obtained by reversing the sign of x. Thus,

The **absolute value** of x is given by

$$|x| = \begin{cases} x & \text{if } x \geq 0 \\ -x & \text{if } x < 0 \end{cases}$$

B. *Equations and Inequalities with Absolute Values*

EXAMPLE 1   Find and graph the solution set of $|x| = 2$.

Solution   We look for all numbers that are 2 units away from the origin (the 0 point). Since 2 and -2 are the only two numbers that satisfy this condition, the solution set of the equation $|x| = 2$ is $\{2, -2\}$. The graph of this set is shown in Figure 5.13. Note that this solution set can be described by the compound sentence $x = 2$ or $x = -2$.

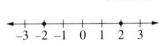

FIGURE 5.13

EXAMPLE 2   Find and graph the solution set of the inequality $|x| < 2$.

Solution   Here we look for all real numbers x that are less than 2 units away from 0. Since 2 and -2 are each exactly 2 units away from 0, we need all points between -2 and 2, that is, all numbers that satisfy the inequality

$$-2 < x < 2$$

FIGURE 5.14

The solution set is thus $\{x \mid -2 < x < 2\}$. The graph appears in Figure 5.14.

In general, if a is any positive number, then

$|x| < a$ is equivalent to $-a < x < a$

EXAMPLE 3   Graph the solution set of $|x| \leq 4$.

Solution   Since $|x| \leq 4$ is equivalent to $-4 \leq x \leq 4$, the graph of the solution set is as shown in the figure.

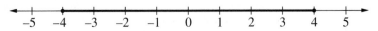

EXAMPLE 4 Find the solution set of the inequality $|x - 1| < 4$.

Solution Since $|x| < a$ is equivalent to $-a < x < a$,

$|x - 1| < 4$ is equivalent to $-4 < x - 1 < 4$

As in the case of equations, we still want to have x alone; so in the middle member of the inequality, we need to add 1. Of course, we must do the same to all the members. Thus, we get

$-4 + 1 < x - 1 + 1 < 4 + 1$

or

$-3 < x < 5$

Thus, the solution set is $\{x \mid -3 < x < 5\}$ or $(-3, 5)$ in interval notation. ∎

EXAMPLE 5 Find and graph the solution set of $|x| \geq 3$.

Solution The solution set of $|x| = 3$ consists of all points that are exactly 3 units away from 0. Hence, the solution set of $|x| \geq 3$ consists of all points that are 3 or more units away from 0. As you can see from the figure, these points can be described by the compound sentence

$x \geq 3$ or $x \leq -3$

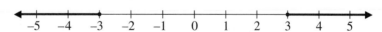

We may therefore write the solution set of $|x| \geq 3$ in the form

$\{x \mid x \geq 3\} \cup \{x \mid x \leq -3\}$

Note that the answer may also be written in the form $\{x \mid x \geq 3 \text{ or } x \leq -3\}$ or in interval notation $(-\infty, -3] \cup [3, \infty)$. ∎

The idea in Example 5 can be generalized as follows:

> If $a \geq 0$, then $|x| > a$ is equivalent to the compound sentence
>
> $x > a$ or $x < -a$

Note: Be sure to remember to reverse the inequality sign for the $-a$, as in the next examples.

EXAMPLE 6 Graph the solution set of $|x| > 2$.

Solution $|x| > 2$ is equivalent to the compound sentence $x > 2 \text{ or } x < -2$. The graph of the solution set appears in the figure.

∎

EXAMPLE 7   Graph the solution set of $|x + 1| \geq 2$.

Solution $|x| \geq a$ is equivalent to $x \geq a$ *or* $x \leq -a$. Therefore, $|x + 1| \geq 2$ is equivalent to $x + 1 \geq 2$ *or* $x + 1 \leq -2$; that is, $x \geq 1$ *or* $x \leq -3$. The graph of the solution set is shown in the figure.

Exercise 5.5

A.   In problems 1–10, evaluate the given expression.

1. $|-10|$
2. $|15|$
3. $|-\frac{1}{8}|$
4. $|\frac{3}{4}|$
5. $|5 - 8|$
6. $|8 - 5|$
7. $|0| + |-2|$
8. $|-2| - |-3|$
9. $-|8|$
10. $-|3| + |-4|$

11. Determine which of the following are solutions of $|1 - 3x| > 3$.

    (a) 2   (b) $-\dfrac{1}{2}$ (c) $\dfrac{5}{3}$ (d) 0

12. Determine which of the following are solutions of $|x - 2| < 2$.

    (a) 0   (b) 1   (c) -1 (d) -2

B.   In problems 13–18, find the set of integers for which the given sentence is true.

13. $|x| < 1$
14. $|x| > -2$
15. $|x| = 5$
16. $|x| \leq 3$
17. $|x| \geq 1$
18. $|x| < 4$

In problems 19–36, graph the solution set of the given sentence (if possible) and write the solution set in interval notation.

19. $|x| = 1$
20. $|x| = 2.5$
21. $|x| \leq 4$
22. $|x| > 1$
23. $|x + 1| < 3$
24. $|x - 2| < 1$
25. $|x| \geq 1$
26. $|x| > -1$
27. $|x - 1| > 2$
28. $|x - 3| \geq 1$
29. $|2x| < 4$
30. $|3x| \leq 9$
31. $|3x| \geq 6$
32. $|2x| > 5$
33. $|2x - 3| \leq 3$
34. $|3x + 1| \leq 8$
35. $|2x - 3| > 3$
36. $|3x + 1| > 8$

In problems 37–39, use $|b - a| \leq c$, where b is the budgeted amount, a is the actual expense, and c is the variance.

37. A company budgets $500 for office supplies. How much money can they spend if their variance is $50?

38. A company budgets $800 for maintenance. How much money can they spend if an acceptable variance is 5% of their budgeted amount?

39. George budgets $300 for miscellaneous monthly expenses. His actual expenses for one month amounted to $290. Was he within a 5% budget variance?

40. Write the absolute value inequality that corresponds to the given graph.

In Other Words

41. Write in words: $|x| < a$ is equivalent to $-a < x < a$.
42. Write in words: $|x| > a$ is equivalent to $x < a$ or $x > -a$.

5.6 QUADRATIC EQUATIONS

GETTING STARTED

FIRE FIGHTING AND FACTORING QUADRATICS

How much water is the engine pumping if the friction loss is 36 lb/in.^{2}? You can find out by solving the equation

$$2g^2 + g - 36 = 0 \qquad (g \text{ in hundreds of gal/min})$$

This equation is a **quadratic equation in standard form.** It can be solved by **factoring,** that is, by undoing the multiplication that yielded $2g^2 + g - 36$, writing $(2g + 9)(g - 4) = 0$ and then reasoning that if the product of $(2g + 9)$ and $(g - 4)$ is 0, at least one of the factors must be 0, that is, $2g + 9 = 0$ or $g - 4 = 0$. The first equation gives $g = -\dfrac{9}{2}$, an impossible answer, since g represents hundreds of gallons per minute. The second equation gives $g = 4$ (hundred gallons per minute), an acceptable answer. But wouldn't it be nice if we had a formula that we could use to give us the answer? Fortunately, we do have such a formula. It is called the **quadratic formula,** and we will use it in this section to solve quadratic equations.

Tampa firefighters use high-pressure water cannons and hoses to bring a house fire under control

In the preceding sections we discussed the solution of first-degree sentences. We now turn our attention to a certain type of **second-degree** sentence that is called a *quadratic equation.*

A **quadratic equation** is a second-degree sentence whose standard form is

$$ax^2 + bx + c = 0$$

where a, b, c are real numbers and $a \neq 0$.

We first consider quadratic equations where the second-degree expression $ax^2 + bx + c$ can be written as a product of two first-degree expressions. Suppose that we have the product $(x + p)(x + q)$. Then, by the distributive property $a(b + c) = ab + ac$, with $a = x + p$ and $b + c = x + q$, we get

$$(x + p)(x + q) = (x + p)x + (x + p)q$$
$$= x^2 + px + qx + pq$$
$$= x^2 + (p + q)x + pq$$

A good way to remember this multiplication is to remember the **FOIL** method.

To multiply $(x - 1)(x + 2)$, we write:

1. Multiply **F**irst terms: $(x - 1)(x + 2) = x^2 \ldots$

2. Multiply **O**utside terms: $(x - 1)(x + 2) = x^2 + 2x \ldots$

3. Multiply **I**nside terms: $(x - 1)(x + 2) = x^2 + 2x - x \ldots$

4. Multiply **L**ast terms: $(x - 1)(x + 2) = x^2 + \underline{2x - x} - 2$

5. Combine like terms: $(x - 1)(x + 2) = x^2 + x - 2$

A. *Factoring Quadratic Expressions*

These ideas can sometimes be "reversed" to write a quadratic expression in the product (factored) form. For example, in order to write $x^2 + 5x + 6$ in factored form, we try to find two numbers p and q so that $pq = 6$ and $p + q = 5$. By inspection, we see that $p = 2$ and $q = 3$ will work. Therefore,

$$x^2 + 5x + 6 = (x + 2)(x + 3)$$

To **factor** an expression means to write it as a product of lower-degree expressions, as in the above illustration.

EXAMPLE 1   Factor:

(a) $x^2 + x - 2$ (b) $x^2 - 2x - 8$

Solution   (a) We must find two numbers whose product is -2 and whose sum is 1. By inspection, we see that these numbers are 2 and -1. Thus,

$$x^2 + x - 2 = (x + 2)(x - 1)$$

Note that $2x - x = x$.

(b) Here we need two numbers whose product is -8 and whose sum is -2. By inspection we see that these numbers are -4 and 2. Thus,

$$x^2 - 2x - 8 = (x - 4)(x + 2)$$

Note that $-4x + 2x = -2x$.

B. *Solving Quadratic Equations by Factoring*

The next examples show how factoring can sometimes be used to solve quadratic equations.

EXAMPLE 2 Solve the equation $x^2 + 5x + 6 = 0$.

Solution By the preceding discussion, we see that an equivalent equation is

$$(x + 2)(x + 3) = 0$$

With 0 on one side of the equation, we can make use of the property of the real number system that says that **a product of two real numbers is 0 if and only if at least one of them is 0.** Thus, the preceding equation is true if and only if

$$x + 2 = 0 \quad \text{or} \quad x + 3 = 0$$
$$x = -2 \quad \text{or} \quad x = -3$$

The solution set of the given equation is $\{-3, -2\}$.

Check By substitution in the left side of the given equation, we find for $x = -3$, $x^2 + 5x + 6 = (-3)^2 + 5(-3) + 6 = 9 - 15 + 6 = 0$. This checks the solution $x = -3$. For $x = -2$, we get $x^2 + 5x + 6 = (-2)^2 + 5(-2) + 6 = 4 - 10 + 6 = 0$, which checks the solution $x = -2$. ∎

EXAMPLE 3 Solve the equation $x^2 - 4x - 12 = 0$.

Solution We try to write the left side in the product form by finding p and q so that $pq = -12$ and $p + q = -4$. A little trial and error using factors of 12 shows that $p = -6$, $q = 2$ will work. Thus, an equivalent equation is

$$(x - 6)(x + 2) = 0$$

If $x - 6 = 0$, then $x = 6$. If $x + 2 = 0$, then $x = -2$. The solution set is $\{-2, 6\}$. (The reader may check this solution set as in Example 2.) ∎

EXAMPLE 4 Solve the equation $x^2 - 9 = 0$.

Solution The equation $x^2 - 9 = 0$ can be solved by factoring since the difference of two squares, $x^2 - p^2$, can always be written as the product

$(x - p)(x + p)$. [Checking this multiplication, we get

$$(x - p)(x + p) = x^2 \underbrace{- px + px}_{0} - p^2 = x^2 - p^2.]$$

Thus,

$$x^2 - 9 = 0 \text{ becomes}$$

$$(x - 3)(x + 3) = 0$$

which gives the solution $\{-3, 3\}$. We can avoid factoring by adding 9 to both sides, obtaining

$$x^2 = 9$$

Taking the square roots of both sides, we have

$$x = \pm 3$$

so the solution set is $\{-3, 3\}$, as before.   ■

EXAMPLE 5   Solve the equation $3x^2 + 2 = 50$.

Solution   We first subtract 2 from both sides, obtaining

$$3x^2 = 48$$

We then divide both sides by 3 to get

$$x^2 = 16$$

As in Example 4, we find the solution set by taking square roots of both sides. This gives the solution set $\{-4, 4\}$.   ■

C. *The Quadratic Formula*

The solutions of a quadratic equation in standard form

$$ax^2 + bx + c = 0 \qquad a \neq 0$$

are given by the **quadratic formula,**

$$x = \frac{-b \pm \sqrt{b^2 - 4ac}}{2a}$$

The derivation of this formula is given in Exercise 5.6, problem 55. The symbol $\pm$ in the formula means that there are two solutions, one with the plus sign and the other with the minus sign. If the quantity under the radical sign, $b^2 - 4ac$, is positive, there are two real number solutions. If $b^2 - 4ac$ is 0, the two solutions are the same, so that there is actually just one solution, $-b/2a$. If the quantity $b^2 - 4ac$ is negative, then the two solutions are both nonreal complex numbers.

Problem Solving:	Quadratic Equations

Solve the equation $x^2 - 2x = 1$

1. Read the problem.
2. Select the unknown.

We want to find the values of the variable x so that $x^2 - 2x = 1$.

3. Think of a plan.
Is the equation a quadratic equation? If it is, write it in standard form. Can you factor it? If not, use the quadratic formula to solve it.

The equation $x^2 - 2x = 1$ is a quadratic equation. To write it in standard form, subtract 1 from both sides, obtaining $x^2 - 2x - 1 = 0$. Since we cannot factor this equation, we write $x^2 - 2x - 1 = 0$ and compare it with $ax^2 + bx + c = 0$. Thus, $a = 1$, $b = -2$, and $c = -1$.

3. Use the quadratic formula to carry out the plan.
Find a, b, and c and substitute their values in
$$x = \frac{-b \pm \sqrt{b^2 - 4ac}}{2a}$$
How many solutions should you get? Make sure the final answer is simplified.

Substituting these values in $\dfrac{-b \pm \sqrt{b^2 - 4ac}}{2a}$,

we obtain

$$x = \frac{-(-2) \pm \sqrt{(-2)^2 - 4(1)(-1)}}{2(1)}$$
$$= \frac{2 \pm \sqrt{4 + 4}}{2} = \frac{2 \pm \sqrt{8}}{2}$$
$$= \frac{2 \pm \sqrt{4 \cdot 2}}{2} = \frac{2 \pm 2\sqrt{2}}{2}$$

This answer is *not* simplified. Divide each number in the numerator and denominator by 2 to obtain $1 \pm \sqrt{2}$. Thus,

$$x = 1 + \sqrt{2} \quad \text{or} \quad x = 1 - \sqrt{2}$$

4. Verify the result.

The verification is left to the student. Note that $(1 \pm \sqrt{2})^2 = 1 \pm 2\sqrt{2} + 2$.

TRY EXAMPLE 6 NOW.

Cover the solution, write your own, and then check your work.

EXAMPLE 6 Use the quadratic formula to solve $x^2 - 4x - 12 = 0$. (Compare Example 3.)

Solution To obtain the correct values of a, b, and c, we rewrite the equation in standard quadratic form as

$$1x^2 + (-4)x + (-12) = 0$$

which we compare with

$$ax^2 + \quad bx + \quad c = 0$$

Now, we see that $a = 1$, $b = -4$, and $c = -12$. Thus,

$$x = \frac{-(-4) \pm \sqrt{(-4)^2 - (4)(1)(-12)}}{(2)(1)}$$

$$= \frac{4 \pm \sqrt{16 + 48}}{2} = \frac{4 \pm \sqrt{64}}{2} = \frac{4 \pm 8}{2}$$

so that

$$x = \frac{4 + 8}{2} = \frac{12}{2} = 6 \quad \text{or} \quad x = \frac{4 - 8}{2} = \frac{-4}{2} = -2$$

Hence, the solution set is $\{-2, 6\}$, which agrees with our results from Example 3. ■

EXAMPLE 7   Solve the equation $3x^2 + x - 5 = 0$.

Solution   We compare

$$ax^2 + bx + c = 0 \quad \text{and} \quad 3x^2 + x - 5 = 0$$

to see that $a = 3$, $b = 1$, and $c = -5$. Hence,

$$x = \frac{-1 \pm \sqrt{1^2 - 4(3)(-5)}}{2(3)} = \frac{-1 \pm \sqrt{61}}{6}$$

The solution set is

$$\left\{ \frac{-1 - \sqrt{61}}{6}, \frac{-1 + \sqrt{61}}{6} \right\}$$

These numbers cannot be expressed exactly in any simpler form. By using the table of square roots in the back of the book (or a calculator), we find that $\sqrt{61} \approx 7.81$. This gives the approximate solutions -1.47 and 1.14. ■

EXAMPLE 8   Solve the equation $2x^2 - 2x = -1$.

Solution   In order to use the quadratic formula, we must first write the equation in the standard quadratic form. We can do this by adding 1 to both sides of the given equation to obtain

$$2x^2 - 2x + 1 = 0$$

which we compare with

$$ax^2 + bx + c = 0$$

Thus, $a = 2$, $b = -2$, and $c = 1$. Now, we can substitute into the quadratic formula to find

$$x = \frac{-(-2) \pm \sqrt{(-2)^2 - 4(2)(1)}}{2(2)} = \frac{2 \pm \sqrt{-4}}{4}$$

Recall that $\sqrt{-4} = 2i$ (Section 4.8), so the solutions are

$$x = \frac{2 \pm 2i}{4} = \frac{2(1 \pm i)}{4} = \frac{1 \pm i}{2}$$

The solution set is

$$\left\{ \frac{1 + i}{2}, \frac{1 - i}{2} \right\}$$

∎

Examples 6–8 display the tremendous advantage of the quadratic formula over other methods of solving quadratic equations. It is not necessary to attempt to write the left side as a product of first-degree expressions. You need only recognize the values of a, b, c and make a direct substitution into the quadratic formula. Note that if the equation is easily factorable, you should solve it by factoring.

D. *The Pythagorean Theorem*

Quadratic equations can be used to find the lengths of the sides of right triangles using the **Pythagorean theorem,** which we state next.

Pythagorean Theorem

In any right triangle (a triangle with one 90° angle), the square of the longest side (hypotenuse) is equal to the sum of the squares of the other two sides (the legs). In symbols:

$$c^2 = a^2 + b^2$$

It is interesting to note that there are infinitely many triples of whole numbers (a, b, c) that satisfy the equation $c^2 = a^2 + b^2$. Such triples are called **Pythagorean triples,** and we will find some of them next.

EXAMPLE 9 The length of the three sides of a right triangle are consecutive integers. What are these lengths?

Solution Let the length of the shortest side be x. Since the lengths of the sides are consecutive integers, we have:

Length of the shortest side	x
Length of the next side	$x + 1$
Length of the hypotenuse	$x + 2$

See the diagram. By the Pythagorean theorem

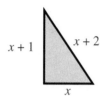

$$(x + 2)^2 = (x + 1)^2 + x^2$$

$x^2 + 4x + 4 = x^2 + 2x + 1 + x^2$ Multiply.

$x^2 + 4x + 4 = 2x^2 + 2x + 1$ Simplify.

$0 = x^2 - 2x - 3$ Subtract x^2, $4x$, and 4 from both sides.

$x^2 - 2x - 3 = 0$ Write in standard form.

$(x - 3)(x + 1) = 0$ Factor.

$x - 3 = 0$ or $x + 1 = 0$ Use the zero-factor property.

$x = 3$ or $x = -1$ Solve $x - 3 = 0$ and $x + 1 = 0$.

Since the lengths of the sides must be positive, we discard the negative answer, -1. Thus, the shortest side is 3 units, so that the other two sides are 4 and 5 units. ■

Note that if you have one Pythagorean triple of the form $(a, a + 1, c)$, you can find another by substituting the a and c of the original triple into

$$(3a + 2c + 1, 3a + 2c + 2, 4a + 3c + 2)$$

For instance, if we let $a = 3$, $b = 4$, and $c = 5$, we find

$$(3 \cdot 3 + 2 \cdot 5 + 1, 3 \cdot 3 + 2 \cdot 5 + 2, 4 \cdot 3 + 3 \cdot 5 + 2) =$$
$$(20, 21, 29)$$

as another such triple. If we now let $a = 20$, $b = 21$, $c = 29$, then we get the next such triple: $(119, 120, 169)$. Using $c^2 = a^2 + (a + 1)^2$, we can show that

$$(3a + 2c + 1)^2 + (3a + 2c + 2)^2 = (4a + 3c + 2)^2$$

which proves that there are infinitely many Pythagorean triples of the form $(a, a + 1, c)$.

Exercise 5.6

A. In problems 1–10, factor the given expression.

1. $x^2 + 6x + 8$ 2. $x^2 + 7x + 10$ 3. $x^2 - x - 12$
4. $x^2 - 3x - 10$ 5. $x^2 + 7x - 18$ 6. $x^2 - 12x + 11$
7. $x^2 - 10x + 25$ 8. $x^2 - 8x + 16$ 9. $x^2 + 10x + 25$
10. $x^2 + 16x + 64$

B. In problems 11–14, determine which of the numbers $-4, -3, -1, 0, \dfrac{1}{2}, 1, \dfrac{3}{2},$ 2, 3, 4 satisfy the given equation.

11. $x^2 + x - 4 = 2$ 12. $x(x + 3)(x + 4) = 0$
13. $(x - 5)(x + 3) = -12$ 14. $(1 + 2x)(5 - 2x) = 8$

In problems 15–30, solve the given equation.

15. $(x - 2)(x - 4) = 0$ 16. $(x + 2)(x + 3) = 0$

17. $(x + 2)(x - 3) = 0$ 18. $(x + 5)(x - 6) = 0$

19. $x(x - 1)(x + 1) = 0$ 20. $(x + 1)(x + 2)(x - 3) = 0$

21. $(2x - 1)(x + 2) = 0$ 22. $(3x + 5)(4x + 7) = 0$

23. $x^2 - 16 = 0$ 24. $3x^2 - 27 = 0$

25. $5x^2 = 125$ 26. $4x^2 + 1 = 65$

27. $(3x - 6)(2x + 3)(5x - 8) = 0$ 28. $2x(x + 7)(2x - 3) = 0$

29. $6x^2 - 1 = 215$ 30. $4x^2 + 1 = 50$

C. In problems 31–38, rewrite the given equation with the left side factored. Then use your result to solve the equation.

31. $x^2 - 12x + 27 = 0$ 32. $x^2 - 6x + 8 = 0$

33. $x^2 - 8x - 20 = 0$ 34. $x^2 - 9x - 36 = 0$

35. $x^2 + 19x - 20 = 0$ 36. $x^2 + 5x - 24 = 0$

37. $x^2 - x - 12 = 0$ 38. $x^2 - x - 30 = 0$

In problems 39–54, solve by using the quadratic formula.

39. $2x^2 + 3x - 5 = 0$ 40. $3x^2 - 7x + 2 = 0$

41. $2x^2 + 5x - 7 = 0$ 42. $4x^2 - 7x - 15 = 0$

43. $x^2 + 5x + 3 = 0$ 44. $2x^2 + 7x - 4 = 0$

45. $5x^2 - 8x + 2 = 0$ 46. $3x^2 + 5x + 1 = 0$

47. $7x^2 - 6x = -1$ 48. $7x^2 - 12x = -5$

49. $9x^2 - 6x + 2 = 0$ 50. $4x^2 - 8x + 5 = 0$

51. $2x^2 + 2x = -1$ 52. $2x^2 - 6x = -5$

53. $4x^2 = -8x - 5$ 54. $2x^2 = 2x - 5$

55. The following procedure can be used to obtain the quadratic formula. Suppose that the quadratic equation is given in the standard form

$$ax^2 + bx + c = 0 \qquad a \neq 0$$

Then

$$ax^2 + bx = -c \quad \text{Why?}$$

Now multiply both sides by $4a$ to get

$$4a^2x^2 + 4abx = -4ac$$

By adding b^2 to both sides, we get

$$4a^2x^2 + 4abx + b^2 = b^2 - 4ac$$

The left side of this equation is the square of $(2ax + b)$. (Verify this!) Thus, we have

$$(2ax + b)^2 = b^2 - 4ac$$

Next, take the square roots of both sides to get

$$2ax + b = \pm\sqrt{b^2 - 4ac}$$

From this equation, we get

$$2ax = -b \pm \sqrt{b^2 - 4ac} \qquad \text{\textit{Explain}}$$

and

$$x = \frac{-b \pm \sqrt{b^2 - 4ac}}{2a} \qquad \text{\textit{Explain}}$$

(These solutions can be checked in the original equation.)

D. Solve problems 56–60 using the Pythagorean theorem.

56. The sides of a right triangle are consecutive even integers. Find their lengths.

57. The hypotenuse of a right triangle is 4 cm longer than the shortest side and 2 cm longer than the remaining side. Find the dimensions of the triangle.

58. The hypotenuse of a right triangle is 16 in. longer than the shortest side and 2 in. longer than the remaining side. Find the dimensions of the triangle.

59. The hypotenuse of a right triangle is 8 in. longer than the shortest side and 1 in. longer than the remaining side. Find the dimensions of the triangle.

60. People have been interested in right triangles for thousands of years. The right triangle relationship $a^2 + b^2 = c^2$ seems to have been known to the Babylonians and the ancient Egyptians. Among the interesting problems about right triangles is this one: Find the right triangles with integer sides, such that the hypotenuse is 1 unit longer than one of the legs. We can solve this problem by letting the legs be x and y units long, so that the hypotenuse is $y + 1$ units long. Then, we have

$$x^2 + y^2 = (y + 1)^2$$

(a) Solve this equation for x^2. You should find $x^2 = 2y + 1$. Since x and y are to be positive integers, $2y + 1$ is an odd integer. This means that x^2 is an odd integer, so that x must also be an odd integer. You can see that $x \neq 1$, because this would make $y = 0$ (no triangle!). However, if x is any odd integer greater than 1, there is a right triangle with the desired relationship between the sides. If you choose $x = 3$, and solve $x^2 = 2y + 1$ for y, you find $y = 4$. This gives you the well-known 3-4-5 right triangle.

(b) Make a table of the next four of these triangles.

In Other Words

The solutions of the quadratic equation $ax^2 + bx + c = 0$ $(a \neq 0)$ are

$$x = \frac{-b \pm \sqrt{b^2 - 4ac}}{2a}$$

61. What kind of an answer do you get if $b^2 - 4ac = 0$?

62. What kind of an answer do you get if $b^2 - 4ac > 0$?

63. What kind of an answer do you get if $b^2 - 4ac < 0$?

Using Your Knowledge

The distance h (in feet) traveled in t sec by an object dropped from a point above the surface of the Earth is given by the formula

$$h = 16t^2$$

64. An object is dropped from the top of a 64-ft building. How long does it take the object to hit the ground?

65. A man jumps from a height of 28 ft into a tank of water. How long does it take him to hit the water?

66. An object is dropped from a height of 144 ft. How long does it take for the object to hit the ground?

Discovery

Charlie Brown received a chain letter. Several days later, after receiving more letters, he found that the number he had received was a perfect square. (The numbers 1^2, 2^2, 3^2, and so on, are perfect squares.) Charlie decided to throw away some of the letters, and being very superstitious, he threw away 13^2 of them. To his surprise, he found that the number he had left was still a perfect square.

Peanuts. Reprinted by permission of UFS, Inc.

67. What is the maximum number of letters Charlie could have received before throwing any away? [*Hint:* Let x^2 be the initial number of letters and let y^2 be the number he had left. Then $x^2 = y^2 + 13^2$. Remember that x and y are integers, and you will want to make y as large as possible relative to x.]

Calculator Corner

Your calculator can be extremely helpful in finding the roots of a quadratic equation by using the quadratic formula. Of course, the roots you obtain are being approximated by decimals. It is most convenient to start with the radical part in the solution of the quadratic equation and then store this value so you can evaluate both roots without having to backtrack or copy down any intermediate steps. Let us look at the following equation:

$$2x^2 + 7x - 4 = 0$$

Using the quadratic formula, the solution is obtained by following these key strokes:

$$\boxed{7}\;\boxed{x^2}\;\boxed{-}\;\boxed{4}\;\boxed{\times}\;\boxed{2}\;\boxed{\times}\;\boxed{4}\;\boxed{+/-}\;\boxed{=}$$
$$\boxed{\sqrt{x}}\;\boxed{STO}\;\boxed{7}\;\boxed{+/-}\;\boxed{+}\;\boxed{RCL}\;\boxed{=}\;\boxed{\div}\;\boxed{2}\;\boxed{\div}\;\boxed{2}\;\boxed{=}$$

The display will show 0.5. To obtain the other root, key in

$$\boxed{7}\;\boxed{+/-}\;\boxed{-}\;\boxed{RCL}\;\boxed{=}\;\boxed{\div}\;\boxed{2}\;\boxed{\div}\;\boxed{2}\;\boxed{=}$$

which yields −4. In general, to solve the equation $ax^2 + bx + c = 0$ using your calculator, key in the following:

$$\boxed{b}\;\boxed{x^2}\;\boxed{-}\;\boxed{4}\;\boxed{\times}\;\boxed{a}\;\boxed{\times}\;\boxed{c}\;\boxed{=}$$
$$\boxed{\sqrt{x}}\;\boxed{STO}\;\boxed{b}\;\boxed{+/-}\;\boxed{+}\;\boxed{RCL}\;\boxed{=}\;\boxed{\div}\;\boxed{2}\;\boxed{\div}\;\boxed{a}\;\boxed{=}$$

and

$$\boxed{b}\;\boxed{+/-}\;\boxed{-}\;\boxed{RCL}\;\boxed{=}\;\boxed{\div}\;\boxed{2}\;\boxed{\div}\;\boxed{a}\;\boxed{=}$$

Computer Corner

In this section, we learned how to solve quadratic equations by using the **quadratic formula.** *To do this, we must first write the equation in the form*

$$ax^2 + bx + c = 0$$

If you write the equation in this form, the Solving Quadratic Equations by Formula program found in the appendix will do the rest! You need only enter the coefficients a, b, and c. One word of caution: Make sure you enter a 1 as the coefficient of x^2 when you have an equation such as $x^2 + 2x + 1 = 0$.

5.7   WORD PROBLEMS

GETTING   STARTED

PUTTING ON THE BRAKES

Do you remember the **RSTUV** procedure that we studied in Chapter 1? We are certainly going to need it in this section, but we shall make a small modification. It has been our experience that the most difficult task in solving word problems is *translating* the problem into the language of algebra. Because of this, the third step of our procedure will emphasize this idea of translation. What types of problems will we be working? There are many of them, including some that may save your life! For example, do you know what the stopping distance d is for a car traveling v miles per hour if the driver has a reaction time of t seconds? Now, suppose you are driving a car at 20 mi/hr and you are 42 ft away from an intersection. If your reaction time is 0.6 sec, can you stop the car in time? See Example 3 and problems 27–34 in Exercise 5.7 and you will be able to tell!

In the preceding sections, we learned how to solve certain kinds of equations. Now, we are ready to apply this knowledge to solve problems. These problems will be stated in words, and are consequently called **word** or **story problems.** Word problems frighten many students, but you should not panic. We have a surefire method for tackling such problems.

Let us start with a problem that you might have heard about. Do you know the name of the heaviest glider in the world? It is the space shuttle *Columbia!* Here is a problem concerning this glider.

The Columbia, one of three active space shuttles in the NASA program, lifts off from Cape Kennedy, Florida

Problem Solving: ## Word Problems

When fully loaded, the space shuttle *Columbia* and its payload weigh 215,000 lb. The *Columbia* itself weighs 85,000 lb more than the payload. What is the weight of each?

1. Read the problem carefully and decide what it asks for.

The problems aks for the weight of each, that is, the weight of the *Columbia* and the weight of the payload.

2. Select a variable to represent the unknown.

Let *p* represent the weight of the payload in pounds. Since the *Columbia* weighs 85,000 lb more than the payload, the *Columbia* weighs $p + 85,000$.

3. Think of a plan. Can you translate the information into an equation or inequality?

We translate the first sentence in the problem: The *Columbia* and its payload weigh 215,000

$$(p + 85,000) + p = 215,000$$
$$p + 85,000 + p = 215,000$$
$$2p + 85,000 - 85,000 = 215,000 - 85,000$$
$$2p = 130,000$$
$$p = 65,000$$

4. Use algebra to solve for the unknown.

Thus, the payload weighs 65,000 lb and the *Columbia* $65,000 + 85,000$ or 150,000 lb.

5. Verify the answer.

To verify the answer, note that the combined weight of the *Columbia* and its payload is $150,000 + 65,000$ or 215,000 lb, as stated in the problem.

TRY EXAMPLE 1 NOW.

Cover the solution, write your own, and then check your work.

EXAMPLE 1

Angie bought a 6-month, $10,000 certificate of deposit. At the end of the 6 months, she received $650 simple interest. What rate of interest did the certificate pay?

Solution

1. Read the problem. It asks for the rate of simple interest.

2. Select the variable *r* to represent this rate.

3. Translate the problem. Here, we need to know that the formula for simple interest is

$$I = Prt$$

where *I* is the amount of interest, *P* is the principal, *r* is the interest rate, and *t* is the time in years. For our problem, $I = \$650$, $P = \$10,000$, *r* is unknown, and $t = \frac{1}{2}$ year. Thus, we have

$$650 = (10{,}000)(r)(\tfrac{1}{2})$$

or

$$650 = 5000r$$

4. Use algebra to solve the equation:

$$650 = 5000r$$

Divide by 5000: $\frac{650}{5000} = r$

Express decimally: $r = 0.13 = 13\%$

Hence, the certificate paid 13% simple interest.

5. Verify the answer. Is the interest earned on a $10,000, 6-month certificate at a 13% rate $650? Evaluating Prt, we have

$$(10{,}000)(0.13)(\tfrac{1}{2}) = 650$$

Since the answer is yes, 13% is correct.

■

The next problem may save you some money. When you rent a car, you may be able to choose either a mileage rate or a flat rate. For example, if you wish to rent an intermediate sedan for 1 day, you can pay $25 plus 20¢ for each mile traveled, or a $50 flat rate. Which is the better deal? That depends on how far you plan to go. Let's be more specific. How many miles could you travel for $50 if you used the mileage rate? We shall find the answer in the next example.

EXAMPLE 2   Jim Jones rented an intermediate sedan at $25 per day plus 20¢ per mile. How many miles can Jim travel for $50?

Solution   Again, we proceed by steps:

1. Read the problem carefully. We are looking for the number of miles Jim can travel for $50.
2. Select m to represent this number of miles.
3. Translate the problem into an equation. To do this, you must realize that Jim is paying 20¢ for each mile plus $25 for the day. Thus, if Jim travels

1 mi, the cost is $0.20(1) + 25$
2 mi, the cost is $0.20(2) + 25$
m mi, the cost is $0.20m + 25$

Because we want to know how many miles Jim can drive for $50, we must put the cost for m miles equal to $50, which gives the equation

$$0.20m + 25 = 50$$

4. Use algebra to solve the equation

$$0.20m + 25 = 50$$

Subtract 25: $0.20m = 25$

Multiply by 100: $20m = 2500$ This gets rid of the decimal.

Divide by 20: $m = \frac{2500}{20} = 125$

Thus, Jim can travel 125 mi for $50.

5. Verify that $(0.20)(125) + 25 = 50$. (We leave this to you.)   ∎

From this information, you can deduce that if you want to rent an intermediate sedan for 1 day and plan to drive over 125 mi, then the flat rate is the better of the two options.

Talking about distances, we think that the next example could save some lives. Have you seen the Highway Patrol booklet that indicates the **braking distance** b (in ft) that it takes to stop a car after the brakes are applied? This information is usually given in a chart, but there is a formula that gives close estimates under normal driving conditions. The braking distance formula is

$$b = 0.06v^2$$

where v is the speed of the car (in mi/hr) when the brakes are applied. Thus, if you are traveling 20 mi/hr, you will travel

$$b = 0.06(20^2) = 0.06(400) = 24 \text{ ft}$$

after you apply the brakes.

EXAMPLE 3

A car traveled 150 ft *after* the brakes were applied. (It might have left a skid mark that long.) How fast was the car going when the brakes were applied?

Solution

1. Read the problem carefully.

2. Select the variable v to represent the velocity.

3. Translate: The braking distance $b = 150$, and the braking distance formula reads $b = 0.06v^2$. Thus, we have the equation

$$0.06v^2 = 150$$

4. Use algebra to solve the last equation:

Multiply by 100: $6v^2 = 15,000$ This gets rid of the decimal.

Divide by 6: $v^2 = \frac{15,000}{6} = 2500$

Take square roots: $v = 50 \quad \text{or} \quad -50$

Since the -50 makes no sense in this problem, we discard it. Thus, the car was going 50 mi/hr when the brakes were applied.

5. Verify the answer by substituting 50 for v in the braking distance formula.

■

You have probably noticed the frequent occurrence of certain words in the statements of word problems. Because these words are used frequently, Table 5.1 presents a brief mathematics dictionary to help you translate them properly.

Table 5.1 *Mathematics Dictionary*

Words	Translation	Example	Translation
Add More than Sum Increased by Added to	+	Add n to 7 7 more than n The sum of n and 7 n increased by 7 7 added to n	$n + 7$
Subtract Less than Minus Difference Decreased by Subtracted from	−	Subtract 9 from x 9 less than x x minus 9 Difference of x and 9 x decreased by 9 9 subtracted from x	$x - 9$
Of The product Times Multiply by	×	$\frac{1}{2}$ of a number x The product of $\frac{1}{2}$ and x $\frac{1}{2}$ times a number x Multiply $\frac{1}{2}$ by x	$\frac{1}{2}x$
Divide Divided by The quotient	÷	Divide 10 by x 10 divided by x The quotient of 10 and x	$\dfrac{10}{x}$
The same, yields, gives, is, equals	=		

The next example shows how some of these words are used in a word problem.

EXAMPLE 4   If 7 is added to twice the square of a number n, the result is 9 times the number. Find n.

Solution   1. Read the problem.
2. Select the unknown: n in this case.
3. Translate the problem.

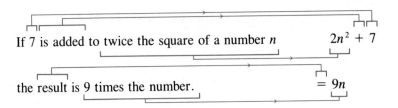

If 7 is added to twice the square of a number n $2n^2 + 7$

the result is 9 times the number. $= 9n$

4. Use algebra to solve the equation:

$$2n^2 + 7 = 9n$$

Since this equation has both a squared term and a first-degree term, we solve it as a quadratic equation, first putting it in the standard form $ax^2 + bx + c = 0$. Hence, we subtract $9n$ from both sides to get

$$2n^2 - 9n + 7 = 0$$

Then, we use the quadratic formula with $a = 2$, $b = -9$, and $c = 7$ to get the value of n:

$$n = \frac{-(-9) \pm \sqrt{(-9)^2 - 4(2)(7)}}{2(2)}$$

$$= \frac{9 \pm \sqrt{81 - 56}}{4} = \frac{9 \pm \sqrt{25}}{4}$$

$$= \frac{9 \pm 5}{4}$$

$$= \frac{9 + 5}{4} \quad \text{or} \quad \frac{9 - 5}{4}$$

$$= \frac{14}{4} \quad \text{or} \quad \frac{4}{4}$$

$$= \frac{7}{2} \quad \text{or} \quad 1$$

5. Verification for $n = \frac{7}{2}$:

$$2\left(\frac{7}{2}\right)^2 + 7 = 2 \times \frac{7}{2} \times \frac{7}{2} + 7 = \frac{49}{2} + 7 = \frac{63}{2}$$

and

$$9 \times \frac{7}{2} = \frac{63}{2}$$

Thus, we see that if 7 is added to twice the square of $\frac{7}{2}$, the result is 9 times 7/2. The verification for $n = 1$ is left for you to do. We have now shown that the number n can be either 7/2 or 1. ∎

Sometimes we do not have to find a numerical answer to a problem, but only an equation that the answer will satisfy, as shown in the next example.

EXAMPLE 5 A certain two-digit number is equal to seven times the sum of its digits. If the tens digit is x and the units digit is y, what equation must x and y satisfy?

Solution 1. Read the problem.
2. The unknowns are x (the tens digit) and y (the units digit).
3. Translate the problem. Since the tens digit is x and the units digit is y, the two-digit number must be $10x + y$. The sum of the digits is $x + y$, and seven times the sum of the digits is $7(x + y)$, so the required equation is

$$10x + y = 7(x + y)$$

A two digit   is equal   seven times the
number   to   sum of its digits

EXAMPLE 6 The Better Business Bank has two types of checking accounts, A and B. Type A has a monthly service charge of $3 plus 25 cents for each check written. Type B has a monthly service charge of $5 plus 10 cents for each check written. What is the greatest number of checks that can be written before type A becomes the more expensive of the two?

Solution Let x be the number of checks written. The cost of each account is

Type A $3 + 0.25x$ dollars

Type B $5 + 0.10x$ dollars

Hence we need to find the greatest value of x such that

$$3 + 0.25x \leq 5 + 0.10x$$

This inequality can be solved as follows:

Given:	$3 + 0.25x \leq 5 + 0.10x$
Subtract 3 from both sides:	$0.25x \leq 2 + 0.10x$
Subtract $0.10x$ from both sides:	$0.15x \leq 2$
Divide both sides by 0.15:	$x \leq \dfrac{2}{0.15}$
	$x \leq 13\dfrac{1}{3}$

Since x must be a whole number, it follows that 13 is the required answer.

Exercise 5.7

1. Write an equation that is equivalent to the description: The product of 4 and a number m is the number increased by 18.

2. Given three consecutive, positive, even integers, write an inequality that is equivalent to the statement: The product of the smallest integer, say, $2n$, and the largest integer is always less than the square of the middle integer.

3. The tens digit of a two-digit number is 3 more than the units digit. If the number itself is 26 times the units digit, write an equation to find x, the tens digit.

4. The square of a number x, decreased by twice the number itself, is 10 more than the number. Write an equation expressing this statement.

In problems 5–14, write the given statement as an equation, and then solve it.

5. If 4 times a number is increased by 5, the result is 29. Find the number.

6. Eleven more than twice a number is 19. Find the number.

7. The sum of 3 times a number and 8 is 29. Find the number.

8. If 6 is added to 7 times a number, the result is 69. Find the number.

9. If the product of 3 and a number is decreased by 2, the result is 16. Find the number.

10. Five times a certain number is 9 less than twice the number. What is the number?

11. Two times the square of a certain number is the same as twice the number increased by 12. What is the number?

12. If 5 is subtracted from half the square of a number, the result is 1 less than the number itself. Find the number.

13. One-third the square of a number decreased by 2 yields 10. Find the number.

14. One-fifth the square of a certain number, plus 2 times the number, is 15. What is the number?

In problems 15–36, use the RSTUV method to obtain the solution.

15. The space shuttle *Columbia* consists of the orbiter, the external tank, two solid-fuel boosters, and fuel. At the time of lift-off, the weight of all these components was 4.16 million lb. The tank and the boosters weighed 1.26 million lb less than the orbiter and fuel. What was the weight of the orbiter and fuel?

16. The external tank and the boosters of the *Columbia* weighed 2.9 million lb, and the boosters weighed 0.34 million lb more than the external tank. Find the weight of the tank and of the boosters.

17. Russia and Japan have the greatest number of merchant ships in the world. The combined total is 15,426 ships. If Japan has 2,276 ships more than Russia, how many ships does each have?

18. Mary is 12 years old and her brother Joey is 2 years old. In how many years will Mary be just twice as old as Joey?

19. The cost of renting a car is $18 per day plus 20¢ per mile traveled. Margie rented a car and paid $44 at the end of the day. How many miles did Margie travel?

20. In baseball, the slugging average of a player is obtained by dividing his total bases (1 for a single, 2 for a double, 3 for a triple, and 4 for a home run) by his official number of times at bat. José Cataña has 2 home runs, 1 triple, 2 doubles, and 9 singles. His slugging average is 1.2. How many times has he been at bat?

21. Peter buys a $10,000, 3-month certificate of deposit. At the end of the 3 months, he receives interest of $350. What was the rate of interest on the certificate?

22. A loan company charges $588 for a 2-year loan of $1,400. What simple interest rate is the loan company charging?

23. The cost of renting a sedan for 1 day is $(0.25m + 20)$ dollars, where m is the number of miles traveled.
    (a) How many miles could you drive for $71?
    (b) If you plan to make a 60-mi round trip, should you use a $40 flat rate or the mileage rate?

24. The Greens need to rent a station wagon to move some furniture. If the round trip distance is 50 mi, should the Greens use a $50 flat rate or a rate of $40 per day plus 22 cents per mile?

25. If P dollars is invested at r percent compounded annually, then at the end of 2 years, the amount will have grown to

$$A = P(1 + r)^2$$

At what rate of interest will $1,000 grow to $1,210 in 2 years?

26. Use the formula in problem 25 to find at what rate of interest $1,000 will grow to $1,440 in 2 years.

27. As given in the text, the braking distance b (in feet) for a car traveling v miles per hour is

$$b = 0.06v^2$$

After the driver applied the brakes, a car traveled 54 ft. How fast was the car going when the brakes were applied?

28. The **reaction distance** r (in ft) is the distance a car travels while the driver is moving his or her foot (reacting) to apply the brakes. The formula for this distance is

$$r = 1.5tv$$

where t is the driver's reaction time (in sec) and v is the speed of the car (in miles per hour). A car going 30 mi/hr travels 22.5 ft while the driver is reacting to applying the brakes. What is the driver's reaction time?

Use the following information in problems 29–34. The stopping distance d (in feet) for a car traveling v miles per hour when the driver has a reaction time of t is given by

$$d = 1.5tv + 0.06v^2$$

29. A car is traveling 30 mi/hr. If the driver's reaction time is 0.5 sec, what is the stopping distance?

30. The reaction time of a driver is 0.5 sec. If the stopping distance is 187.5 ft, how fast is the car going?

31. An automobile going 20 mi/hr is 42 ft away from an intersection when the traffic light turns red. If the automobile stops right at the intersection, what is the driver's reaction time?

32. You may have heard about the reflecting collars that can save the life of a dog or a cat. If your car's headlights will illuminate objects up to 200 ft away and you are driving 50 mi/hr when you see a dog on the road at the edge of the illuminated distance, what must be your reaction time if you can stop just short of hitting the dog?

33. Loren, who has a reaction time of $\frac{2}{3}$ sec, was taking a driving test. When the examiner signaled for a stop, she stopped her car in 44 ft. How fast was she going at the instant of the stop signal?

34. Pedro reacts very quickly. In fact, his reaction time is 0.4 sec. When driving on a highway, Pedro saw a danger signal ahead and tried to stop. If his car traveled 120 ft before stopping, how fast was he going when he saw the signal?

35. Two consecutive integers are such that 6 times the smaller is less than 5 times the larger. Find the largest integers for which this is true.

36. A wallet contains 20 bills, all $1 and $5 bills. If the total value is less than $80, what is the greatest possible number of $5 bills? What is the largest total value possible?

37. Americans use about 60 billion aluminum cans each year. Approximately two-thirds as many of these cans are either thrown away or left to litter the landscape as are recycled. About how many billion aluminum cans are not recycled?

38. Many businesses use computer printers to make paper copies. It is estimated that American businesses make about 350 billion such copies each year. If $\frac{9}{16}$ as many copies are thrown into the waste as are saved, about how many billion copies are wasted? By the way, it takes about 11 million trees to make that wasted paper.

In Other Words

39. When reading a word problem, what is the first thing you should try to determine?

40. How can you verify the answer in a word problem?

Using Your Knowledge

Have you ever heard of **Chamberlain's formula,** *which purports to tell you how many years you should drive your present car before you buy a new one? If y is this number of years, then Chamberlain's formula reads*

$$y = \frac{GMC}{(G - M)DP}$$

where G is the new car's gas mileage, M is your present car's gas mileage, C is the cost in dollars of the new car, D is the number of miles you drive in a year, and P is the dollar price of gasoline per gallon.

For instance, suppose that the new car's gas mileage is 24 mi/gal, the old car's mileage is 12 mi/gal, the price of the new car is $6400, you drive 12,000 mi/yr, and the cost of gasoline is $1.40/gal. This means that G = 24, M = 12, C = 6400, D = 12,000, and P = 1.40, so

$$y = \frac{(24)(12)(6400)}{(12)(12,000)(1.4)} = \frac{64}{7} \approx 9.1$$

Thus, according to the formula, your old car should have been driven about 9.1 years before the purchase is justified.

Now try these:

41. Suppose the new car's gas mileage is 32 mi/gal, the old car's gas mileage is 10 mi/gal, the price of the new car is $7,000, you drive 15,000 mi/year, and the cost of gasoline is $1.30/gal. How many years should your old car have been driven to justify buying the new one?

42. Suppose that G, M, D, and P have the same values as in problem 41, and you have driven your present car for 5 years. What price (to the nearest $10) would you be justified in paying for the new car?

43. Disregarding such factors as depreciation, maintenance, replacement cost, and so on, under what conditions does Chamberlain's formula yield unrealistic values for y?

5.8   RATIO, PROPORTION, AND VARIATION

GETTING STARTED

JUNK FOOD AND RATIOS

You have probably heard the term "junk food," but do you know what foods fall into this category? The U.S. Department of Agriculture suggests looking at the *ratio* of nutrients to calories and multiplying the result by 100. The actual procedure totals the RDA's (recommended daily allowances) for the first eight nutrients listed on the label, divides by the number of calories in one serving, and multiplies by 100. For instance, the sum of the first eight nutrients for the cereal label shown is 139, and the number of calories in one serving is 100. Thus, the ratio of nutrients to calories is

$$\frac{139}{100} \times 100 = 139$$

If the answer is less than 32, the nutritional value of the food is in question.

NUTRITION INFORMATION

SERVING SIZE: 1 OZ. (28.4 g, ABOUT 4 BISCUITS)

SERVINGS PER PACKAGE: 20

	CEREAL	WITH $\frac{1}{2}$ CUP VITAMINS A & D SKIM MILK
CALORIES	100	140*
PROTEIN	3 g	7 g
CARBOHYDRATE	24 g	30 g
FAT	0 g	0 g*
CHOLESTEROL	0 mg	0 mg*
SODIUM	5 mg	65 mg
POTASSIUM	80 mg	280 mg

PERCENTAGE OF U.S. RECOMMENDED DAILY ALLOWANCES (U.S. RDA)

PROTEIN	4	15
VITAMIN A	25	30
VITAMIN C	25	25
THIAMIN	25	30
RIBOFLAVIN	25	35
NIACIN	25	25
CALCIUM	**	15
IRON	10	10
VITAMIN D	10	25
VITAMIN B$_6$	25	25
FOLIC ACID	25	25
PHOSPHORUS	8	20
MAGNESIUM	8	10
ZINC	10	15
COPPER	4	6

*WHOLE MILK SUPPLIES AN ADDITIONAL 30 CALORIES, 4 g FAT, AND 15 mg CHOLESTEROL.

**CONTAINS LESS THAN 2% OF THE U.S. RDA OF THIS NUTRIENT.

In this section, we shall study many kinds of ratios and their uses. For example, we shall study unit pricing (see Example 2) to make you a more aware consumer. We will then learn how to compare ratios by studying proportions and end the section by looking at different types of variation.

You have probably heard of the student-teacher ratio or the gear ratio in your automobile.

A. *Ratios*

Many quantities can be compared by using ratios. Here is the definition of a ratio.

Definition 5.1

> A **ratio** is a quotient of two numbers. The ratio of a number a to another number b can be written as:
>
> $$a \text{ to } b \quad or \quad a{:}b \quad or \quad \frac{a}{b}$$

The last form is used most often, but is frequently written as a/b.

EXAMPLE 1 Write the ratio of nutrients (139) to calories (100) in three different ways.

Solution   139 to 100   139:100 $\dfrac{139}{100}$

Of course, if the ratio in Example 1 had been 140 to 100, you could write it in reduced form as

$$7 \text{ to } 5 \quad or \quad 7{:}5 \quad or \quad \frac{7}{5}$$

You probably encounter many ratios in your everyday life. For example, the expression *miles per gallon* is actually a ratio, the ratio of the number of miles traveled to the number of gallons of gas used. Thus, if your car travels 294 miles on 12 gallons of gas, your miles per gallon ratio is $\frac{294}{12} = \frac{49}{2} = 24.5$.

Ratios can also be used to compare prices. For example, most people have the misconception that the more you buy of an item, the cheaper it is. Is this always true? Not necessarily. The picture shows two cans of Hunt's tomato sauce, bought in the same store. The 15-oz can costs 68¢, while the 8-oz can costs 32¢. Which can is the better buy? To compare these prices, we need to find the price of 1 oz of tomato sauce; that is, we need the **unit price** (the price per ounce). This unit price is given by the ratio

$$\frac{\text{Price}}{\text{Number of ounces}}$$

For the 15-oz can,   For the 8-oz can,

$$\frac{68}{15} = 4.5\overline{3} \qquad \frac{32}{8} = 4$$

Thus, the 15-oz can is more expensive. (Note that you could buy 16 oz, two 8-oz cans, for only 64¢, instead of 68¢ for the 15-oz can!)

Unit pricing allows shoppers to quickly compare relative costs of the same or similar products when they are sold in different weights or volumes

EXAMPLE 2

A 4-oz can of mushrooms costs 74¢, while an 8-oz can of the same brand costs $1.44. Find the cost per ounce for:

(a) The 4-oz can   (b) The 8-oz can

(Round answers to the nearest tenth of a cent.)

Solution

(a) For the 4-oz can, the cost per ounce is

$$\frac{74}{4} = 18.5 \text{ cents}$$

(b) For the 8-oz can, the cost per ounce is

$$\frac{144}{8} = 18 \text{ cents}$$

∎

Note that if we wish to find which of the two cans in Example 2 is the better buy, we do not have to look at the unit prices. Two 4-oz cans would cost us $1.48 for 8-oz, while the 8-oz can costs only $1.44.

B. *Proportion*

Let us return to the problem of the car that traveled 294 miles on 12 gallons of gas. How many miles would this car go on 10 gallons of gas? The ratio of miles per gallon for the car is $\frac{294}{12}$ or $\frac{49}{2}$. If we let m be the number of miles the car would travel on 10 gallons of gas, the ratio of miles per gallon would be $m/10$. Since the two ratios must be equal,

$$\frac{49}{2} = \frac{m}{10}$$

This equation, which is an equality between two ratios, is called a **proportion.**

Definition 5.2

> A **proportion** is an equality between two ratios that can be written as $\dfrac{a}{b} = \dfrac{c}{d}$.

To solve the proportion

$$\frac{49}{2} = \frac{m}{10}$$

which is simply an equation involving fractions, we proceed as before.

1. Multiply both sides by 10 so the m is by itself on the right.

$$\frac{49}{2} \cdot 10 = \frac{m}{10} \cdot 10$$

2. Simplify: $245 = m$
3. Thus, the car can go 245 mi on 10 gal of gas.

Proportions can often be solved by a shortcut method that depends on the definition of equality of fractions:

$$\text{If } \frac{a}{b} = \frac{c}{d} \text{ then } ad = bc$$

Thus, to solve the proportion

$$\frac{3}{4} = \frac{15}{x}$$

We use the cross-products, and write

$$3 \cdot x = 15 \cdot 4$$
$$3x = 60$$
$$x = 20$$

EXAMPLE 3 The ratio of your foot length to your height (in inches) is 1 to 6.7. In 1951, Eric Shipton published photographs of what he thought were the Abominable Snowman's footprints. Each footprint was 23 inches long. How tall is the Abominable Snowman?

Solution We use the five-step procedure outlined in Section 5.7.

1. Read the problem carefully.

2. Select a variable to represent the unknown. Here, we let h be the height of the Abominable Snowman.

3. Translate the problem: Since the original ratio is 1/6.7, the ratio for the Snowman is 23/h. But these ratios must be equal, so

$$\frac{1}{6.7} = \frac{23}{h}$$

4. Use cross-products to solve the equation:
$$1 \cdot h = 6.7 \cdot 23$$
$$h = 154.1 \text{ inches} = 12 \text{ ft, } 10.1 \text{ in.}$$

5. Verify your answer: If we substitute $h = 154.1$ in the original proportion, we obtain

$$\frac{1}{6.7} = \frac{23}{154.1}$$

which is a true statement since $1 \cdot 154.1 = 6.7 \cdot 23$. ∎

C. *Variation*

Sometimes we say that a variable is **proportional to** or **varies directly as** another variable x. For example, the number m of miles you drive a car is proportional to or varies directly as the number g of gallons of gas used. This means that the ratio m/g is a constant, the miles per gallon the car attains. In general, we have the following definition:

Definition 5.3

> y **varies directly as** x if there is a constant k such that
> $$y = kx$$

EXAMPLE 4   The length L of a moustache varies directly as the time t.

(a) Write an equation of variation.
(b) The longest moustache on record was owned by Masuriya Din. His moustache grew to 56 inches (on each side) over a 14-year period. Find k and explain what it represents.

Solution   (a) Since the length L varies directly as the time t,

$$L = kt$$

(b) We know that when $L = 56$, $t = 14$. Thus,

$$56 = k \cdot 14$$
$$4 = k$$

This means that the moustache grew 4 in. each yr.   ∎

Sometimes, as a quantity increases, a related quantity decreases proportionately. For example, the more time you spend practicing a task, the less time it will take you to do the task. In this case, we say that the quantities **vary inversely** as each other.

Definition 5.4

> y **varies inversely as** x if there is a constant k such that
> $$y = \frac{k}{x}$$

EXAMPLE 5   The speed s that a car travels is inversely proportional to the time t it takes to travel a given distance.

(a) Write the equation of variation.
(b) If a car travels at 60 miles per hour for 3 hours, what is k, and what does it represent?

Solution   (a) The equation is

$$s = \frac{k}{t}$$

(b) We know that $s = 60$ when $t = 3$. Thus,

$$60 = \frac{k}{3}$$
$$k = 180$$

In this case, k represents the distance traveled.

EXAMPLE 6   Have you ever heard one of those loud "boom" boxes or a car sound system that makes your stomach tremble? The loudness L of sound is inversely proportional to the square of the distance d that you are from the source.

(a) Write an equation of variation.
(b) The loudness of rock music coming from a boom box 5 feet away is 100 decibels. Find k.
(c) If you move to 10 feet away from the boom box, how loud is the sound?

Solution   (a) The equation is

$$L = \frac{k}{d^2}$$

(b) We know that $L = 100$ for $d = 5$, so that

$$100 = \frac{k}{5^2} = \frac{k}{25}$$

Multiplying both sides by 25, we find that $k = 2500$.

(c) Since $k = 2500$,

$$L = \frac{2500}{d^2}$$

When $d = 10$,

$$L = \frac{2500}{10^2} = 25 \text{ decibels}$$

Exercise 5.8

A.   1. The *Voyager* was the first plane to fly nonstop around the world without refueling. At the beginning of the trip, the fuel in the 2000-pound plane weighed 7000 pounds. Write the ratio of fuel to plane weight in three different ways.

2. During the last 6 years of his life, Vincent Van Gogh produced 700 drawings and 800 oil paintings. Write the ratio of drawings to oil paintings in three different ways.

3. The first suspension bridge built in England has a 70-foot span. The world's longest suspension bridge, the Verrazano Narrows Bridge in New York, is 4260 feet long. Write the ratio of the span of the first suspension bridge to that of the Verrazano Narrows Bridge in three different ways.

4. A woman has a 28-inch waist and 34-inch hips. Write the waist-to-hip ratio in three different ways. (If the waist-to-hip ratio is over 1.0 for men or over 0.8 for women, the risk of heart attack or stroke is five to ten times greater than for persons with a lower ratio.)

5. The reduced transmission ratio in an automobile is the ratio of engine speed to drive-shaft speed. Find the reduced transmission ratio for an engine running at 2,000 revolutions per minute when the drive-shaft speed is 600 revolutions per minute.

6. Most job seekers can expect about 6 job leads and/or interviews for every 100 resumes they mail out. What is the ratio of job leads and/or interviews to resumes?

7. The average American car is driven 12,000 miles a year and burns 700 gallons of gas. How many miles per gallon does the average American car get? (Give the answer to the nearest whole number.)

8. Are generic products always cheaper than name brands? Not necessarily! It depends on where you buy. On comparing two cans of mushrooms, the name brand 8-oz can costs $1.09 and the generic 4-oz can costs 53¢.
   (a) To the nearest tenth of a cent, what is the cost per ounce of the name brand 8-oz can?
   (b) To the nearest tenth of a cent, what is the cost per ounce of the generic 4-oz can?
   (c) Which can is the better buy?
   (d) In Example 2, the 4-oz can cost 18.5¢ per ounce. Which is the better buy, the generic can here or the 4-oz can of Example 2?

9. As a consumer, you probably believe that cheaper is always better. But be careful. Here is a situation that should give you food for thought!
   (a) Dermassage dishwashing liquid costs $1.31 for 22 oz. To the nearest cent, what is the cost per ounce?
   (b) White Magic dishwashing liquid costs $1.75 for 32 oz. To the nearest cent, what is the cost per ounce?
   (c) Based on price alone, which is the better buy, Dermassage or White Magic?

   But how much do you use per wash? *Consumer Reports* estimated that it costs 10¢ for 10 washes with Dermassage and 18¢ for the same number of washes with White Magic. Thus, Dermassage is more economical.

10. Is cheaper still better? Here is another problem. A&P Wool Washing Liquid costs 79¢ for 16 oz. Ivory Liquid is $1.25 for 22 oz.
    (a) To the nearest cent, what is the price per ounce of the A&P Wool Washing Liquid?
    (b) To the nearest cent, what is the price per ounce of the Ivory Liquid?
    (c) Based on price alone, which is the better buy?

    But wait. How much do you have to use? According to *Consumer Reports*, it costs 17¢ for 10 washes with the A&P Wool Washing Liquid, while Ivory Liquid is only 12¢ for 10 washes!

B. In problems 11–16, solve the given proportion.

11. $\dfrac{x}{9} = \dfrac{4}{3}$ 12. $\dfrac{x}{6} = \dfrac{5}{12}$ 13. $\dfrac{8}{x} = \dfrac{4}{3}$

14. $\dfrac{6}{x} = \dfrac{18}{7}$ 15. $\dfrac{3}{8} = \dfrac{9}{x}$ 16. $\dfrac{3}{5} = \dfrac{9}{x}$

17. A machine manufactures 9 toys every 2 hours. Let n be the number of toys it completes in 40 hours. Write a proportion using this information and the ratio of n to 40.

18. A woman has several rectangular flower beds that she wants to be of equal area. If L feet is the length of a bed that is 3 feet wide, and the length is 10 feet when the width is 2 feet, write a proportion using the ratio of L to 10.

19. When flying a hot-air balloon, you get $\frac{1}{2}$ hour of flight time for each 20-pound tank of propane gas. How many tanks of gas do you need for a 3-hour flight?

20. When serving shrimp, you need $\frac{1}{2}$ pound of cooked shrimp without the shell to make 3 servings. How many pounds of cooked shrimp do you need for 90 servings?

21. The official ratio of width to length for the U.S. flag is 10 to 19. If a flag is 35 inches wide, how long should it be?

22. Do you like tortillas? Tom Nall does. As a matter of fact, he ate 74 tortillas in 30 minutes! How many could he eat in 45 minutes at that rate?

23. A certain pitcher allowed 10 runs in the last 32 innings he pitched. At this rate, how many runs would he allow in 9 innings? (The answer is called the ERA, or earned run average, for the pitcher and is usually given to two decimal places.)

24. Do you know what a xerus is? It is a small rodent that looks like a cross between a squirrel and a chipmunk. The ratio of tail to body length in one of these animals is 4 to 5. If the body of a xerus is 10 inches long, how long is its tail?

25. A zoologist tagged and released 250 fish into a lake. A few days later, 53 fish were taken at random locations from the lake and 5 of them were found to be tagged. Approximately how many fish are there in the lake?

C. 26. The amount of annual interest I received on a savings account is directly proportional to the amount of money m you have in the account.
(a) Write an equation of variation.
(b) If $480 produced $26.40 in interest, what is k?
(c) How much annual interest would you receive if the account had $750?

27. The number of revolutions R a record makes as it is being played varies directly with the time t that it is on the turntable.
(a) Write an equation of variation.
(b) A record that lasted $2\frac{1}{2}$ minutes made 112.5 revolutions. What is k?
(c) If a record makes 108 revolutions, how long does it take to play it?

28. The distance d an automobile travels after the brakes have been applied varies directly as the square of its speed s.
(a) Write an equation of variation.
(b) If the stopping distance for a car going 30 miles per hour is 54 feet, what is k?
(c) What is the stopping distance for a car going 60 miles per hour?

29. The weight of a person varies directly as the cube of the person's height h (in inches). The **threshold weight** T (in pounds) for a person is defined as "the crucial weight, above which the mortality risk for the patient rises astronomically."
(a) Write an equation of variation relating T and h.
(b) If $T = 196$ when $h = 70$, find k.
(c) To the nearest pound, what is the threshold weight for a person 75 inches tall?

30. To remain popular, the number S of new songs a rock band needs to produce each year is inversely proportional to the number y of years the band has been in the business.
(a) Write an equation of variation.
(b) If, after 3 years in the business, the band needs 50 new songs, how many songs will it need after 5 years?

31. When a camera lens is focused at infinity, the f-stop on the lens varies inversely with the diameter d of the aperture (opening).
(a) Write an equation of variation.
(b) If the f-stop on a camera is 8 when the aperture is $\frac{1}{2}$ inch, what is k?
(c) Find the f-stop when the aperture is $\frac{1}{4}$ inch.

32. Boyle's law states that if the temperature is held constant, then the pressure P of an enclosed gas varies inversely as the volume V. If the pressure of the gas is 24 pounds per square inch when the volume is 18 cubic inches, what is the pressure if the gas is compressed to 12 cubic inches?

33. For the gas of problem 32, if the pressure is 24 pounds per square inch when the volume is 18 cubic inches, what is the volume if the pressure is increased to 40 pounds per square inch?

34. The weight W of an object varies inversely as the square of its distance d from the center of the Earth.
   (a) Write an equation of variation.
   (b) An astronaut weighs 121 pounds on the surface of the Earth. If the radius of the Earth is 3960 miles, find the value of k for this astronaut. (Do not multiply out your answer.)
   (c) What will this astronaut weigh when she is 880 miles above the surface of the Earth?

*I*n Other Words

35. Explain the difference between a ratio and a proportion.
36. Explain the difference between direct variation and inverse variation.

Chapter 5 Summary

Section	Item	Meaning	Example
5.1	Variable	A symbol that may be replaced by any one of a set of numbers	x, y, z
5.1A	Open sentence	A sentence in which the variable can be replaced by a number	$x + 3 = 5; x - 1 < 7$
5.1A	Equation	Sentences in which the verb phrase is "="	$x + 7 = 9$
5.1A	Inequality	Sentences in which the verb is $>, <, \neq, \geq$, or $\leq$	$x + 7 < 9; x > 8; x \neq 9$
5.1A	Solution set	The set of elements of the replacement set that make the open sentence a true statement	$\{3\}$ is the solution set of $x + 2 = 5$ when the replacement set is the set of whole numbers.
5.1A	Identities	Open sentences that are true for every number in the replacement set	$x + 0 = x; x + 2 = 2 + x;$ $a(b + c) = ab + ac$
5.2	First-degree sentence	An open sentence in which the unknown quantity has an exponent of 1 only	$x + 7 = 8 - 2x; 20 = 3m$
5.2A	Elementary operations	Operations that may be performed on a sentence to obtain an equivalent sentence	Addition or subtraction of a number on both sides of an equation

Section	Item	Meaning	Example
5.3	Finite intervals	$a \le x \le b$ Closed interval	$[a, b]$
		$a < x < b$ Open interval	(a, b)
		$\left.\begin{array}{l} a \le x < b \\ \\ a < x \le b \end{array}\right\}$ Half-open intervals	$[a, b)$ $(a, b]$
5.5A	Absolute value	The distance on the number line from 0 to the number	$\|3\| = 3;\ \|-7\| = 7;\ \left\|\frac{-2}{3}\right\| = \frac{2}{3}$
5.6	Quadratic equation	A second-degree sentence that can be written in the form $ax^2 + bx + c = 0,\ a \ne 0$	$x^2 - 7x = 6;$ $8x^2 - 3x - 4 = 0$
5.6C	Quadratic formula	The solutions of the equation $ax^2 + bx + c = 0$ are $$x = \frac{-b \pm \sqrt{b^2 - 4ac}}{2a}$$	The solutions of the equation $x^2 - 4x - 12 = 0$ are -2 and 6.
5.6D	Pythagorean theorem	In any right triangle, the square of the hypotenuse c is equal to the sum of the squares of the other two sides.	If a, b, and c are the sides, $a^2 + b^2 = c^2$.

5.7

Procedure for Solving Word Problems

1. **R**ead the problem carefully, and decide what it asks for (the unknown).
2. **S**elect a variable to represent this unknown.
3. **T**ranslate the problem into the language of algebra.
4. **U**se the rules of algebra to solve for the unknown.
5. **V**erify the solution.

Section	Item	Meaning	Example
5.8A	Ratio	A quotient of two numbers	The ratio of 5 to 7 is $\frac{5}{7}$.
5.8B	Proportion	An equality between two ratios	$\frac{5}{7} = \frac{10}{14}$
5.8C	Varies directly	y varies directly as x if $y = kx$	
5.8C	Varies inversely	y varies inversely as x if $y = k/x$	

Research Questions

Sources of information for these questions can be found in the Bibliography at the end of the book.

1. Write a short essay about Gauss's childhood.

2. Find out and write a report about Gauss's proof regarding regular polygons in his *Disquisitiones Arithmeticae*.

3. Write a short paragraph about Gauss's inventions.

4. Aside from being a superb mathematician, Gauss did some work in the field of astronomy. Report on some of Gauss's discoveries in the field of astronomy.

5. In 1807, a famous French mathematician paid Gauss's involuntary 2,000-franc contribution to the French government. Find out who this famous mathematician was and the circumstances of the payment.

6. Another French mathematician asked the general commanding the French troops to send an officer to see how Gauss was faring during the war. This mathematician had submitted some results in number theory to Gauss under a pen name. Write a report on this incident and try to find the circumstances, the pen name, and the real name of the mathematician.

Chapter 5 Practice Test

1. If the replacement set is the set of integers, solve the following equations:
   (a) $x + 7 = 2$ (b) $x - 4 = 9$

2. If the replacement set is the set of integers, find the solution set for each of the following inequalities:
   (a) $x + 5 > 4$ (b) $2 + x \geq -x - 1$

3. Solve: $2x + 2 = 3x - 2$

4. Solve: $2x + 8 \geq -x - 1$

5. Graph the solution set of each of the following:
   (a) $x - 3 \leq 0$ (b) $-2x + 4 > x + 1$

6. Graph the solution set (if it is not empty) of each of the following:
   (a) $x + 2 \geq 3$ *and* $x \leq 4$ (b) $x - 3 \geq 1$ *and* $x \leq 0$

7. Graph the solution set of each of the following:
   (a) $x < 0$ *or* $x - 2 < 1$ (b) $x + 2 < 3$ *or* $x - 1 > 2$

8. Solve the equation $|x| = 3$.

9. Graph the solution set of $|x| < 2$.

10. Graph the solution set of $|x + 2| < 1$.

11. Graph the solution set of $|x - 2| < 2$.

12. Graph the solution set of $|x| > 2$.

13. Graph the solution set of $|x - 2| > 3$.

14. Factor:
    (a) $x^2 + 3x + 2$ (b) $x^2 - 3x - 4$

15. Solve:
    (a) $(x - 1)(x + 2) = 0$ (b) $x(x - 1) = 0$

16. Solve by factoring: $x^2 + 7x + 10 = 0$.

17. Solve by factoring: $x^2 - 3x - 10 = 0$.

18. Use the quadratic formula to solve: $2x^2 + 3x - 5 = 0$.

19. Use the quadratic formula to solve: $3x^2 + 5x - 2 = 0$.

20. Solve:
    (a) $9x^2 - 16 = 0$ (b) $25x^2 - 4 = 0$

21. The hypotenuse of a right triangle is 9 cm longer than one of the legs and 2 cm longer than the other leg. Find the dimensions of the triangle.

22. A certain two-digit number is equal to five times the sum of its digits. If the tens digit is x and the units digit is y, write an equation that x and y must satisfy.

23. Suppose you rent a car for 1 day at the rate of $21 per day plus 21¢ per mile. How many miles could you drive for a rental charge of $63?

24. Three times the sum of two consecutive integers is 45. What are the integers?

25. A pair of consecutive integers is such that 12 times the smaller is more than 9 times the larger. What is the least pair of integers for which this is true?

26. On a certain day, the New York Stock Exchange reported that 688 stocks went up, 801 went down, and 501 were unchanged.
    (a) Write the ratio of losers to gainers in three different ways.
    (b) What is the ratio of losers to the total number of stocks?

27. Sally has two rings, one that is 9 years old and one that is 35 years old. In how many years will the older ring be twice as old as the newer one?

28. A supermarket is selling a certain kind of cracker for 50¢ for an 8-oz box and 76¢ for a 12-oz box.
    (a) Find the unit price for each box.
    (b) Which is the better buy?

29. A piggy bank contains 20 coins, all dimes and nickels. If the total value of the coins is more than $1.20, what is the least possible number of dimes in the bank?

30. We know that corresponding sides of similar rectangles are proportional. One rectangle is 5 ft by 8 ft, and the short side of a similar rectangle is 9 ft long.
    (a) Write a proportion for the length, x ft, of the long side of the second rectangle.
    (b) Find the missing length.

31. The cost C of fuel per hour for running an airplane is directly proportional to the square of the speed.
    (a) Write an equation of variation.
    (b) If the cost is $100 per hour for a speed of 150 miles per hour, find the value of k.
    (c) Find the cost per hour for a speed of 180 miles per hour.

32. The time t of exposure needed to photograph an object at a fixed distance from the camera is inversely proportional to the intensity I of the illumination.
    (a) Write an equation of variation.
    (b) If the correct exposure is $\frac{1}{30}$ sec when I is 300 units, find the value of k.
    (c) If I is increased to 600 units, what is the correct exposure time?

In Chapter 5 we studied first- and second-degree equations with *one* variable. In this chapter, we shall study similar equations with *two* variables. The main feature here, however, is an introduction to some simple ideas that belong to the area that is called **analytic geometry,** a blend of algebra and geometry in which algebra is used to study geometry and geometry is used to study algebra. The key to this combination is a workable system of associating **points in the plane** with **ordered pairs of numbers.**

We start the chapter by studying sets of ordered pairs called **relations,** concentrating on a special type of relation called a **function.** We learn about function notation and how to represent relations and functions by means of graphs. We also study the formula giving the distance between any two points in the Cartesian plane and the slope (inclination) of a line passing through these two points. We explore the different ways in which the equations of a line can be written depending on the information that is given, and learn how to solve systems of linear equations with two unknowns by using algebraic or graphical methods.

We use graphing to represent linear inequalities and to solve systems of inequalities. Graphing is then used to study **linear programming** and maximizing or minimizing profits or losses by using the **simplex** algorithm, a method of solution for systems of linear inequalities developed by George B. Dantzig in the late 1940s.

Functions and Graphs

René Descartes (1596–1650)

But there are other men who attain greatness because they embody the potentiality of their own day and magically reflect the future. They express the thoughts that will be everybody's two or three centuries after them. Such a one was Descartes.

Thomas Huxley

THE HUMAN SIDE OF MATHEMATICS

René Descartes was born March 31, 1596, near Tours, France.

Frail health caused René's formal education to be delayed until he was 8. His father enrolled him in a Jesuit school, where it was noticed that the boy needed more than normal rest and was advised to stay in bed as long as he liked in the morning. Descartes followed this advice, and made a lifelong habit of staying in bed late whenever he could.

Descartes was trained to be a gentleman, educated in Latin, Greek, and rhetoric. However, he soon developed a healthy skepticism toward all he was taught. He left school at 17, so disenchanted with his studies that he took an interlude of pleasure, settling in Paris. He then moved to the suburb of St. Germain, where he worked on mathematics for 2 years.

At the age of 32, Descartes was persuaded to prepare his researches for publication. At 38, he compiled what was to be one grand treatise on the world, but fear of ecclesiastic displeasure with his conclusions caused him to refrain from having it printed.

In 1637 at age 41, his friends persuaded him to print his masterpiece known as *The Method*. It included an essay on geometry, that is probably the single most important thing that Descartes ever did. His *analytic geometry* (a combination of algebra and geometry) revolutionized the realm of geometry and made much of modern mathematics possible.

In the spring of 1649, Queen Christine of Sweden summoned Descartes. He arrived in Sweden to discover that she expected him to teach her philosophy every day at five o'clock in the morning in the ice-cold library of her palace. He soon caught "inflammation of the lungs," from which he died on February 11, 1650, at the age of 54.

Looking Ahead: The Cartesian coordinate system, a legacy of the work of René Descartes, is introduced in Section 6.1 and used throughout this chapter in studying functions and graphs.

6.1   RELATIONS AND FUNCTIONS

GETTING STARTED

FUNCTIONS FOR FASHIONS

James C. Penney opened his first dry goods store in Kemmerer, Wyoming in 1902. Today, the J. C. Penney Company is one of the nation's largest retailers.

Did you know that women's clothing sizes are getting smaller? According to the J. C. Penney Catalog for winter 1991, "Simply put, you will wear one size smaller than before." Is there a relationship between the new sizes and waist size? Look at the table. It gives a $1\frac{1}{2}$-inch leeway for waist sizes. In this table, let us consider the first number in the waist sizes corresponding to different dress sizes, that is 30, 32, 34, 36. For sizes 14 to 22, the waist size is 16 inches more than the dress size. If we wish to formalize this relationship, we can write:

$w(s) = s + 16$ (Read, "w of s equals s plus 16")

What would be the waist size of a woman that wears size 14? It would be

$w(14) = 14 + 16 = 30$

For size 16,

$w(16) = 16 + 16 = 32$

and so on. It works! Can you do the same for hip sizes? If you get

$h(s) = s + 26.5$

you are on the right track. Examples 8 and 9 and problems 36 and 37 will give you more practice with relationships between number pairs.

Women's Sizes
Women's Petite: 4′11″–5′3″   Women's: 5′3 ½″–5′7½″

WOMEN'S PETITE SIZE	14WP	16WP	18WP	20WP	22WP	24WP	26WP	28WP	30WP	32WP
WOMEN'S SIZE	—	16W	18W	20W	22W	24W	26W	28W	30W	32W
BUST	38-39½	40-41½	42-43½	44-45½	46-47½	48-49½	50-51½	52-53½	54-55½	56-57½
WAIST	30-31½	32-33½	34-35½	36-37½	38-40	40½-42½	43-45	45½-47½	48-50	50½-52½
HIPS	40½-42	42½-44	44½-46	46½-48	48½-50	50½-52	52½-54	54½-56	56½-58	58½-60

The word *relation* might remind you of members of your family — parents, brothers, sisters, cousins, and so on. We have already studied relations such as "is a subset of," "is less than," and "is equivalent to." Relations can be expressed by using ordered pairs.

Let us first consider an example of an ordered pair of numbers, $(4, -3)$. We say "ordered pair" because there are two numbers and the order of these numbers is important. Thus, the first number is 4 and the second is -3, and we distinguish $(4, -3)$ from $(-3, 4)$. That is,

$$(4, -3) \neq (-3, 4)$$

because the order of the two numbers is different in these pairs. You should not confuse this with the idea of equality of sets of numbers, where the order is not considered and we write $\{4, -3\} = \{-3, 4\}$. The use of parentheses for ordered pairs and braces for sets should serve to warn you that they are not the same.

In mathematics, we often call the first number of an ordered pair the **x value**, or **abscissa**, and the second number the **y value**, or **ordinate.** The pair is symbolized by (x, y), and the equation

$$(x, y) = (2, -5)$$

means that $x = 2$ and $y = -5$. In general,

$$(x, y) = (a, b) \quad \text{if and only if} \quad x = a, y = b$$

There are many problems in which we need to study sets of ordered pairs. For convenience, we call such a set a *relation*.

Definition 6.1

A **relation** is a set of ordered pairs.

For instance, the set $R = \{(4, -3), (2, -5), (-3, 4)\}$ is a relation in which all the pairs have been specifically listed. Notice that the set of first members is $\{-3, 2, 4\}$ and the set of second members is $\{-5, -3, 4\}$. The listing in the relation R shows how the elements of the first set are associated with the elements of the second set to form the ordered pairs of the given relation. Different ways of associating the elements of the two sets will, of course, result in different relations. Thus,

$$S = \{(-3, -5), (2, -3), (4, 4)\}$$

is an example of a relation different from R but formed from the same two sets of first and second numbers.

Relations as simple as the preceding two are usually not of particular interest. In most cases, we shall be concerned with a set of pairs $\{(x, y)\}$, where a **rule** is given for finding the y value for a given x value. For example,

$$Q = \{(x, y) \mid y = 4 - 2x, x \text{ an integer}\}$$

is a relation in which the ordered pairs are (x, y) such that x is an integer and $y = 4 - 2x$. For instance, the pair $(1, 2)$ is an element of Q, because if $x = 1$, then $y = 4 - 2 = 2$. Thus, a y value of 2 is paired with an x value of 1. Other elements of Q are $(0, 4)$, $(-1, 6)$, and $(3, -2)$. In each case, we replace x by an integer and calculate y from the formula (or rule) $y = 4 - 2x$ to construct an element of Q. Clearly, Q has infinitely many elements.

A. *Domain and Range*

In the description of the relation Q above, the replacement set for the variable x was prescribed as the set of integers. The set of all possible x values is called the **domain** of the relation. Thus, the domain of Q is the set of integers. Corresponding to any x value from the domain, the y value can be computed by using the rule given for this relation, $y = 4 - 2x$, as we have seen. The set of all possible y values is called the **range** of the relation. The range of the relation Q is the set of all even integers. (Can you see why?) The relations R and S above both have the domain $\{-3, 2, 4\}$ and the range $\{-5, -3, 4\}$.

Unless otherwise specified, the domain of a relation is taken to be the largest set of real numbers that can be substituted for x and that result in real numbers for y. The range is then determined by the rule of the relation.

For example, if

$$Q = \{(x, y) \mid y = \sqrt{x}\}$$

then we may substitute any *nonnegative* real number for x and obtain a real number for y. But x cannot be replaced by a negative number. (Why?) Thus, the domain is the set of all nonnegative real numbers, and the range, in this case, is the same set. Why?

EXAMPLE 1   Find the domain and the range of the relation

$$R = \{(x, y) \mid y = 2x\}$$

Solution   The variable x can be replaced by any real value, because 2 times any real number is a real number. Hence, the domain is $\{x \mid x \text{ a real number}\}$. The range is also the set of real numbers, because every real number is 2 times another real number. Thus, the range is $\{y \mid y \text{ a real number}\}$.   ∎

EXAMPLE 2   Find the domain and the range of the relation

$$S = \{(x, y) \mid y = x^2 + 1\}$$

Solution   The variable x can be replaced by any real value, because the result of squaring a real number and adding 1 is again a real number. Thus, the domain of S is $\{x \mid x \text{ a real number}\}$. The square of a real number is never negative, $x^2 \geq 0$, so $x^2 + 1 \geq 1$. Hence, the rule $y = x^2 + 1$ implies $y \geq 1$. Consequently, the range of S is $\{y \mid y \geq 1\}$.   ∎

EXAMPLE 3   Find the domain and the range of the relation

$$R = \{(x, y) \mid y \leq x, x \text{ and } y \text{ positive integers less than } 5\}$$

Solution The domain as described is {1, 2, 3, 4}. For $x = 1$, $y = 1$; for $x = 2$, $y = 1$ or 2; for $x = 3$, $y = 1$, 2, or 3; for $x = 4$, $y = 1$, 2, 3, or 4. Thus, the range is also {1, 2, 3, 4}. We can list the ordered pairs that are elements of R:

$$\{(1, 1), (2, 1), (2, 2), (3, 1), (3, 2), (3, 3), (4, 1), (4, 2), (4, 3), (4, 4)\}$$

■

B. *Functions*

In many areas of mathematics and its applications, the most important kind of relation is one where to each element in the domain there corresponds one and only one element in the range. The relation in Example 1, $R = \{(x, y) \mid y = 2x\}$, is an illustration of such a relation. It is clear here that for each x value there corresponds exactly one y value, because the rule is $y = 2x$. On the other hand, the relation given in Example 3 is not this type of relation, because to each of the x values 2, 3, and 4 there corresponds more than one y value.

Definition 6.2

> A **function** is a relation where to each domain value there corresponds exactly one range value.

All of us bump into functions every day: the correspondence between the weight of a letter and the amount of postage you pay, the correspondence between the cost of a piece of meat and the number of pounds it weighs, the correspondence between the number of miles per gallon that you get and the speed at which you drive. These are all simple examples of functions. You can undoubtedly think of many more.

EXAMPLE 4 Is the relation $\{(x, y) \mid y = 2x + 3, x \text{ a real number}\}$ a function? Explain.

Solution If x is a real number, then y is the unique real number $2x + 3$. For instance, if $x = 2$, then $y = 2(2) + 3 = 7$; if $x = -\frac{1}{2}$, then $y = 2(-\frac{1}{2}) + 3 = 2$. Clearly, for each real x value, the expression $2x + 3$ gives one and only one y value. Thus, the given relation has exactly one range value corresponding to each domain value and is therefore a function.

■

EXAMPLE 5 Is the relation $\{(x, y) \mid x = y^2 + 1\}$ a function? Explain.

Solution For this relation the domain is $\{x \mid x \geq 1\}$. Why? If we take $x = 5$, then the rule $x = y^2 + 1$ gives $5 = y^2 + 1$, or $y^2 = 4$. Thus, $y = 2$ or -2, because $2^2 = (-2)^2 = 4$. So the pairs (5, 2) and (5, -2) both are elements of this relation. The fact that there are two range values (2 and -2) for the domain value 5 shows that the given relation is not a function.

■

C. *Function Notation*

We often use letters such as f, F, g, G, h, and H to designate functions. Thus, for the relation in Example 4 we use set notation to write

$$f = \{(x, y) \mid y = 2x + 3\}$$

because we know this relation to be a function. Another very commonly used notation to denote the range value that corresponds to a given domain value x is $f(x)$. (This is usually read, "f of x.")

The $f(x)$ notation, called **function notation,** is quite convenient, because it denotes the value of the function for the given value of x. For example, if

$$f(x) = 2x + 3$$

then

$$f(1) = 2(1) + 3 = 5$$
$$f(0) = 2(0) + 3 = 3$$
$$f(-6) = 2(-6) + 3 = -9$$
$$f(4) = 2(4) + 3 = 11$$
$$f(a) = 2(a) + 3 = 2a + 3$$
$$f(w + 2) = 2(w + 2) + 3 = 2w + 7$$

and so on. Whatever appears between the parentheses in $f(\ )$ is to be substituted for x in the rule that defines $f(x)$.

Instead of describing a function in set notation, we frequently say, "the function defined by $f(x) = \ldots$" where the three dots are to be replaced by the expression for the value of the function. For instance, "the function defined by $f(x) = 2x + 3$" has the same meaning as "the function $f = \{(x, y) \mid y = 2x + 3\}$."

EXAMPLE 6   Let $f(x) = 3x + 5$. Find:

   (a) $f(4)$ (b) $f(2)$
   (c) $f(2) + f(4)$ (d) $f(x + 1)$

Solution   (a) Since $f(x) = 3x + 5$,

$$f(4) = 3 \cdot 4 + 5 = 12 + 5 = 17$$

(b) $f(2) = 3 \cdot 2 + 5 = 6 + 5 = 11$

(c) Since $f(2) = 11$ and $f(4) = 17$,

$$f(2) + f(4) = 11 + 17 = 28$$

(d) $f(x + 1) = 3(x + 1) + 5 = 3x + 8$ ■

EXAMPLE 7   A function g is defined by $g(x) = x^3 - 2x^2 + 3x - 4$. Find:

(a) $g(2)$ (b) $g(-3)$ (c) $g(2) - g(-3)$

Solution   (a) $g(2) = 2^3 - 2(2^2) + 3(2) - 4 = 8 - 8 + 6 - 4 = 2$

(b) $g(-3) = (-3)^3 - 2(-3)^2 + 3(-3) - 4$
$$= -27 - 18 - 9 - 4 = -58$$

(c) $g(2) - g(-3) = 2 - (-58) = 60$ ■

In the preceding problems, we have evaluated a specified function. Sometimes, as was the case in Getting Started, we must find the function as shown next.

EXAMPLE 8   Consider the ordered pairs (2, 6), (3, 9), (1.2, 3.6) and (2/5, 6/5). There is a functional relationship $y = f(x)$ between the numbers in each pair. Find $f(x)$ and use it to fill in the missing numbers in the pairs (_____, 12), (_____, 3.3), and (5, _____).

Solution   The given pairs are of the form (x, y). A close examination reveals that each of the y's in the pairs is three times the corresponding x, that is, $y = 3x$ or $f(x) = 3x$. Now, in each of the ordered pairs (_____, 12), (_____, 3.3), and (5, _____) the y value must be three times the x value. Thus,

$$(\underline{}, 12) = (4, 12)$$

$$(\underline{}, 3.3) = (1.1, 3.3) \quad \text{and}$$

$$(5, \underline{}) = (5, 15)$$ ■

D. *Applications*

In recent years, aerobic exercises such as jogging, swimming, bicycling, and roller blading have been taken up by millions of Americans. To see if you are exercising too hard (or not hard enough), you should stop from time to time and take your pulse to determine your heart rate. The idea is to keep your rate within a range known as the **target zone,** which is determined by your age. The next example explains how to find the **lower limit** of your target zone.

Roller bladers benefit from a low-impact, highly aerobic workout

EXAMPLE 9   The lower limit L (heartbeats per minute) of your target zone is a function of your age a (in years) and is given by

$$L(a) = -\tfrac{2}{3}a + 150$$

Find the value of L for a person who is:

(a) 30 years old   (b) 45 years old

Solution   (a) We need to find $L(30)$, and because

$$L(a) = -\tfrac{2}{3}a + 150$$
$$L(30) = -\tfrac{2}{3}(30) + 150$$
$$= -20 + 150 = 130$$

This result means that a 30-year-old person should try to attain at least 130 heartbeats per minute while exercising.

(b) Here, we want to find $L(45)$. Proceeding as before, we obtain

$$L(45) = -\tfrac{2}{3}(45) + 150$$
$$= -30 + 150 = 120$$

(Find the value of L for your own age.)   ■

Exercise 6.1 _____

A.   In problems 1–14, find the domain and the range of the given relation. [*Hint:* Remember that you cannot divide by 0.]

1. $\{(1, 2), (2, 3), (3, 4)\}$ 2. $\{(3, 1), (2, 1), (1, 1)\}$

3. $\{(1, 1), (2, 2), (3, 3)\}$ 4. $\{(4, 1), (5, 2), (6, 1)\}$

5. $\{(x, y) \mid y = 3x\}$ 6. $\{(x, y) \mid y = 2x + 1\}$

7. $\{(x, y) \mid y = x + 1\}$ 8. $\{(x, y) \mid y = 1 - 2x\}$

9. $\{(x, y) \mid y = x^2\}$ 10. $\{(x, y) \mid y = 2 + x^2\}$

11. $\{(x, y) \mid y^2 = x\}$ 12. $\{(x, y) \mid x = 1 + y^2\}$

13. $\left\{(x, y) \mid y = \dfrac{1}{x}\right\}$ 14. $\left\{(x, y) \mid y = \dfrac{1}{x - 2}\right\}$

Find the domain and the range of the relation given in each of problems 15–22. List the ordered pairs in each relation.

15. $\{(x, y) \mid y = 2x,\ x$ an integer between -1 and 2, inclusive$\}$

16. $\{(x, y) \mid y = 2x - 1,\ x$ a counting number not greater than 5$\}$

17. $\{(x, y) \mid y = 2x - 3,\ x$ an integer between 0 and 4, inclusive$\}$

18. $\{(x, y) \mid y = \tfrac{1}{x},\ x$ an integer between 1 and 5, inclusive$\}$

19. $\{(x, y) \mid y = \sqrt{x},\ x = 0, 1, 4, 9, 16,$ or 25$\}$

20. $\{(x, y) \mid y \leq x + 1,\ x$ and y positive integers less than 4$\}$

21. $\{(x, y) \mid y > x,\ x$ and y positive integers less than 5$\}$

22. $\{(x, y) \mid 0 < x + y < 5,\ x$ and y positive integers less than 4$\}$

B. In problems 23–30, decide whether the given relation is a function. State the reason for your answer in each case.

23. $\{(x, y) \mid y = 5x + 6\}$

24. $\{(x, y) \mid y = 3 - 2x\}$

25. $\{(x, y) \mid x = y^2\}$

26. $\{(x, y) \mid x + 1 = y^2\}$

27. $\{(x, y) \mid y = \sqrt{x}, x \geq 0\}$

28. $\{(x, y) \mid x = \sqrt{y}, y \geq 0\}$

29. $\{(x, y) \mid x = y^3\}$

30. $\{(x, y) \mid y = x^3\}$

C. 31. A function f is defined by $f(x) = 3x + 1$. Find:

(a) $f(0)$ (b) $f(2)$ (c) $f(-2)$

32. A function g is defined by $g(x) = -2x + 1$. Find:

(a) $g(0)$ (b) $g(1)$ (c) $g(-1)$

33. A function F is defined by $F(x) = \sqrt{x - 1}$. Find:

(a) $F(1)$ (b) $F(5)$ (c) F(26)

34. A function G is defined by $G(x) = x^2 + 2x - 1$. Find:

(a) $G(0)$ (b) $G(2)$ (c) $G(-2)$

35. A function f is defined by $f(x) = 3x + 1$. Find:

(a) $f(x + h)$ (b) $f(x + h) - f(x)$ (c) $\dfrac{f(x + h) - f(x)}{h}, h \neq 0$

36. Given are the ordered pairs: (2, 1), (6, 3), (9, 4.5), and (1.6, 0.8). There is a simple functional relationship, $y = f(x)$, between the numbers in each pair. What is $f(x)$? Use this to fill in the missing number in the pairs (_____ , 7.5), (_____ , 2.4), and (_____ , $\frac{1}{7}$).

37. Given are the ordered pairs: $(\frac{1}{2}, \frac{1}{4})$, (1.2, 1.44), (5, 25), and (7, 49). There is a simple functional relationship, $y = g(x)$, between the numbers in each pair. What is $g(x)$? Use this to fill in the missing number in the pairs $(\frac{1}{4},$ _____ $)$, (2.1, _____), and (_____ , 64).

38. Given that $f(x) = x^3 - x^2 + 2x$, find

(a) $f(-1)$ (b) $f(-3)$ (c) $f(2)$

39. If $g(x) = 2x^3 + x^2 - 3x + 1$, find

(a) $g(0)$ (b) $g(-2)$ (c) $g(2)$

D. 40. The Fahrenheit temperature reading F is a function of the Celsius temperature reading C. This function is given by

$$F(C) = \tfrac{9}{5}C + 32$$

(a) If the temperature is 15°C, what is the Fahrenheit temperature?

(b) Water boils at 100°C. What is the corresponding Fahrenheit temperature?

(c) The freezing point of water is 0°C or 32°F. How many Fahrenheit degrees below freezing is a temperature of $-10°C$?

(d) The lowest temperature attainable is $-273°C$; this is the zero point on the absolute temperature scale. What is the corresponding Fahrenheit temperature?

41. Refer to Example 9. The **upper limit** U of your target zone when exercising is also a function of your age a (in years), and is given by

$$U(a) = -a + 190$$

Find the highest safe heart rate for a person who is:

(a) 50 years old   (b) 60 years old

42. Refer to Example 9 and problem 41. The target zone for a person a years old consists of all the heart rates between $L(a)$ and $U(a)$, inclusive. Thus, if a person's heart rate is R, that person's target zone is described by $L(a) \le R \le U(a)$. Find the target zone for a person who is:

(a) 30 years old   (b) 45 years old

43. The ideal weight w (in pounds) of a man is a function of his height h (in inches). This function is defined by

$$w(h) = 5h - 190$$

(a) If a man is 70 in. tall, what should his weight be?
(b) If a man weighs 200 lb, what should his height be?

44. The cost C in dollars of renting a car for 1 day is a function of the number m of miles traveled. For a car renting for $20 per day and 20¢ per mile, this function is given by

$$C(m) = 0.20m + 20$$

(a) Find the cost of renting a car for 1 day and driving 290 miles.
(b) If an executive paid $60.60 after renting a car for 1 day, how many miles did she drive?

45. The pressure P (in lb/ft^2) at a depth of d ft below the surface of the ocean is a function of the depth. This function is given by

$$P(d) = 63.9d$$

What is the pressure on a submarine at a depth of:

(a) 10 ft?   (b) 100 ft?

46. If a ball is dropped from a point above the surface of the Earth, the distance s (in meters) that the ball falls in t seconds is a function of t. This function is given by

$$s(t) = 4.9t^2$$

Find the distance that the ball falls in:

(a) 2 sec   (b) 5 sec

47. The function $S(t) = \frac{1}{2}gt^2$ gives the distance that an object falls from rest in t sec. If S is measured in feet, then the gravitational constant, g, is approximately 32 ft/sec². Find the distance that the object will fall in:
(a) 3 sec   (b) 5 sec

48. An experiment, carefully carried out, showed that a ball dropped from rest fell 64.4 ft in 2 sec. What is a more accurate value of g than that given in problem 47?

49. The kinetic energy (E) of a moving object is measured in Joules and is given by the function $E(v) = \frac{1}{2}mv^2$, where m is the mass in kilograms and v is the velocity in meters per second. An automobile of mass 1,200 kg is going at a speed of 36 km/hr. What is the kinetic energy of the automobile?

50. If the kinetic energy of the automobile in problem 49 is 93,750 Joules, how fast (km/hr) is the automobile traveling?

51. The centripetal (radial) force (F) of an object moving in a circle of radius r is measured in Newtons and is given by the formula $F = \dfrac{mv^2}{r}$, where m is the mass in kilograms, v is the velocity in meters per second, and r is the radius in meters. Find the centripetal force needed to keep an object of mass 144 kg, moving on a circular track of radius 50 m at a speed of 30 km/hr.

52. If it takes 25,000 Newtons to keep the object of problem 51 moving in a circle at a speed of 30 km/hr, what is the radius of the circle?

53. Decide if the given relation is a function and state the reason for your answer. If the given relation is a function, what is its domain?
(a) $\{(x, y) \mid x = y^2 + 2y\}$
(b) $\{(x, y) \mid x = \sqrt{y - 1}, \ y \geq 1\}$

In Other Words

54. Consider the function $f(x) = \dfrac{1}{x^2 - 1}$. What numbers are excluded from the domain and why?

55. Consider the function $g(x) = \sqrt{x - 1}$. What numbers are excluded from the domain and why?

56. Consider the function $h(x) = \dfrac{x}{\sqrt{x + 1}}$. What numbers are excluded from the domain and why?

Using Your Knowledge

57. There are many interesting functions that can be defined using the ideas of this section. Let's return to the cricket from Section 5.1 whose chirping frequency is a function of the temperature. The table below shows the number of chirps per minute and the temperature in degrees Fahrenheit. Can you find a function that relates the number (c) of chirps per minute and the temperature x?

Temperature (°F)	40	41	42	43	44
Chirps Per Minute	0	4	8	12	16

58. The function relating the number of chirps per minute of the cricket and the temperature is given by $f(x) = 4(x - 40)$. If the temperature is 80°F, how many chirps per minute will you hear from your friendly house cricket?

Time Elapsed (sec)	Distance (ft)
1	$16 = 16 \times 1$
2	$64 = 16 \times 4$
3	$144 = 16 \times 9$
4	$256 = 16 \times 16$
5	$400 = 16 \times 25$
6	$576 = 16 \times 36$

59. An interesting function in physics was discovered by Galileo Galilei. This function relates the distance an object (dropped from a given height) travels and the time elapsed. The table in the margin shows the time (in seconds) and the distance (in feet) traveled by a rock dropped from a tall building. Can you find the relationship between the number of seconds elapsed, t, and the distance traveled, $f(t)$?

60. Assume that a rock took 10 sec to reach the ground when dropped from a helicopter. Using the results of problem 59, can you find the height of the helicopter?

Discovery

A special kind of relation that is important in mathematics is called an **equivalence relation.** *A relation R is an equivalence relation if it has the following three properties:*

(a) **Reflexive property.** *If a is an element of the domain of R, then (a, a) is an element of R.*

(b) **Symmetric property.** *If (a, b) is an element of R, then (b, a) is an element of R.*

(c) **Transitive property.** *If (a, b) and (b, c) are both elements of R, then (a, c) is an element of R.*

A very simple example of an equivalence relation is

$$R = \{(x, y) \mid y = x, x \text{ an integer}\}$$

To show that R is an equivalence relation, we check the above three properties:

(a) **Reflexive.** *If a is an integer, then a = a, so (a, a) is an element of R.*

(b) **Symmetric.** *Suppose that (a, b) belongs to R. Then, by the definition of R, a and b are integers and b = a. But if b = a, then a = b, so (b, a) also belongs to R.*

(c) **Transitive.** *Suppose that (a, b) and (b, c) both belong to R. Then b = a and c = b, so c = a. Hence, (a, c) also belongs to R.*

Because R has all three properties, it is an equivalence relation.
*   The pairs in a relation do not have to be numbers, and some interesting relations occur outside the field of numbers. For example,*

$$R = \{(x, y) \mid y \text{ is a member of the same family as } x, x \text{ is a person}\}$$

is a relation. Is R an equivalence relation?
*   We check the three properties as before:*

(a) **Reflexive.** *Given a person A, is (A, A) an element of R? Yes, A is obviously a member of the same family as A.*

(b) **Symmetric.** *Suppose that (A, B) is an element of R. Then B is a member of the same family as A. But then A is a member of the same family as B, so (B, A) is an element of R.*

(c) **Transitive.** *Suppose that (A, B) and (B, C) both belong to R. Then A, B, C are all members of the same family. Thus, (A, C) is an element of R.*

Again, we see that R has all three properties, so it is an equivalence relation.

Can you discover which of the following are equivalence relations?

61. $R = \{(x, y) \mid x \text{ and } y \text{ are triangles and } y \text{ is similar to } x\}$
    [*Note:* Here, *is similar to* means *has the same shape as.*]

62. $R = \{(x, y) \mid x \text{ and } y \text{ are integers and } y > x\}$

63. $R = \{(x, y) \mid x \text{ and } y \text{ are positive integers and } y \text{ has the same } parity \text{ as } x\}$;
    that is, y is odd if x is odd and y is even if x is even

64. $R = \{(x, y) \mid x \text{ and } y \text{ are boys and } y \text{ is the brother of } x\}$

65. $R = \{(x, y) \mid x \text{ and } y \text{ are positive integers and when } x \text{ and } y \text{ are divided by } 3, y \text{ leaves the same remainder as } x\}$

66. $R = \{(x, y) \mid x \text{ is a fraction } a/b, \text{ where } a \text{ and } b \text{ are integers } (b \neq 0), \text{ and } y \text{ is an equivalent fraction } ma/mb, \text{ where } m \text{ is a nonzero integer}\}$

6.2   GRAPHING RELATIONS AND FUNCTIONS

GETTING STARTED

BATTEN DOWN AND BUCKLE UP

The idea of an ordered pair is widely used in many areas. For example, the map in the figure shows the track and position of hurricane Carmen. As you can see, the storm center was near longitude 91° and latitude 25°. If we agree to write this information as an ordered pair of numbers showing the longitude (east–west distance) first and the latitude (north–south distance) second, then the location of the storm is (91, 25). These numbers are called the **coordinates** of the hurricane. On the same map, the coordinates of New Orleans are (90, 30).

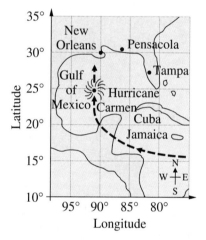

Hurricanes are a concern to people who live in coastal regions. What about something important to everyone, like wearing seat belts? Suppose you wish to make a graph showing that seat belt use is increasing nationwide. From 1982 to 1991 your information is as follows:

Year	% Using
1982	11
1983	12
1984	12
1985	20
1986	37
1987	41
1988	45
1989	46
1990	49
1991	50

How would you make the graph? You can start with a horizontal line marked with the years 1982 to 1991 and a vertical line perpendicular to the year line and labeled with the percents 0, 10, 20, 30, 40, and 50. Then the ordered pair (1982, 11) is graphed by starting at 1982 on the horizontal axis, moving up to 11 on the vertical axis, and graphing the point (1982, 11). Follow the same procedure for the rest of the points and connect the points with line segments. You will obtain a graph similar to the one shown.

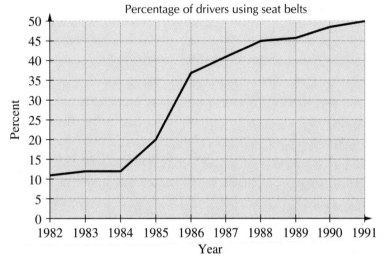

Source: Traffic Safety Now, Inc., observations of 43,000 drivers in 19 cities.

In many areas of mathematics, we need to take into account the possibility that negative numbers are included in our graph data. Because of that, our graphs use a coordinate system like the one shown in Figure 6.1. In this section you will learn about graphs of relations and functions.

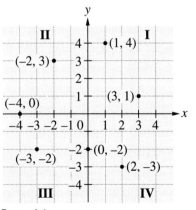

FIGURE 6.1
Cartesian coordinate system

We shall now study a method for drawing pictures of relations and functions. Figure 6.1 shows two number lines drawn perpendicular to each other. The horizontal line is labeled x and is called the **x axis.** The vertical line is labeled y and is called the **y axis.** The intersection of the two axes is the **origin.** We mark a number scale with the 0 point at the origin on each of the axes. The four regions into which the plane is divided by these axes are called **quadrants** and are numbered I, II, III, IV, as shown in Figure 6.1. This diagram forms a **Cartesian coordinate system** (named after René Descartes). We can make pictures of relations on such a coordinate system.

Figure 6.1 shows the usual way in which the positive directions along the axes are chosen. On the x axis, to the right of the origin is positive and to the left is negative. On the y axis, up from the origin is positive and down is negative. To locate a point (x, y), we go x units horizontally along the x axis and then y units in the vertical direction. For instance, to locate $(-2, 3)$, we go 2 units horizontally in the negative direction along the x axis and then 3 units up, parallel to the y axis. Several points are plotted in Figure 6.1.

A. *Graphs of Relations*

The Cartesian coordinate system furnishes us with a one-to-one correspondence between the points in the plane and the set of all ordered pairs of numbers; that is, corresponding to a given ordered pair there is exactly one point, and corresponding to a given point there is exactly one ordered pair. The **graph** of a relation is the set of points corresponding to the ordered pairs of the relation.

EXAMPLE 1   Find the graph of the relation

$$R = \{(x, y)\,|\,y = 2x, x \text{ an integer between } -1 \text{ and } 2, \text{ inclusive}\}$$

Solution   The domain of R is $\{-1, 0, 1, 2\}$. By using the rule of R, $y = 2x$, we can find the ordered pairs $(-1, -2)$, $(0, 0)$, $(1, 2)$, and $(2, 4)$ that belong to R. Note that since $y = 2x$, the y coordinate is always *twice* the x coordinate. The graph of the relation is shown in the figure below.   ∎

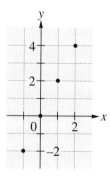

EXAMPLE 2   Graph the relation

$$T = \{(x, y) \mid y^2 = x, y \text{ an integer between } -3 \text{ and } 3, \text{ inclusive}\}$$

Solution   We are given the range $\{y \mid y$ an integer between -3 and 3, inclusive$\}$, and by squaring each of these integers, we find the domain, $\{0, 1, 4, 9\}$. The set of pairs $\{(0, 0), (1, 1), (1, -1), (4, 2), (4, -2), (9, 3), (9, -3)\}$ is thus the relation T. The graph of the relation consists of the seven dots shown in the figure below. If the domain of this relation had been $x \geq 0$, the graph would be a curve called a **parabola** (shown dashed in the figure).

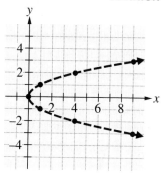

■

B. *Graphs of Functions*

Since a function is simply a special kind of relation, a function can also be graphed on a Cartesian coordinate system. It is customary to represent the x values along the horizontal axis and the $f(x)$, or y, values along the vertical axis.

Because a function has just one value for each value of x in the domain, the graph of the function cannot be cut in more than one point by any vertical line. Thus, we have a simple **vertical line test** for a function. If the graph of a relation is known, we can tell by inspection whether the relation is a function. For example, the parabola in the figure for Example 2 is the graph of a relation, but that relation is *not* a function because any vertical line to the right of the y axis cuts the graph in two points. On the other hand, if we had defined the range of the relation so that its graph were only the lower (or only the upper) portion of the parabola, then the relation would be a function.

EXAMPLE 3   Graph the function f defined by $f(x) = 2 - 3x$ if the domain is the set $\{-1, 0, 1, 2\}$.

Solution   We calculate the values of the function using the rule $f(x) = 2 - 3x$ to obtain the values in the table. The figure shows the graph.

■

x	$y = f(x)$	Ordered Pair
-1	5	$(-1, 5)$
0	2	$(0, 2)$
1	-1	$(1, -1)$
2	-4	$(2, -4)$

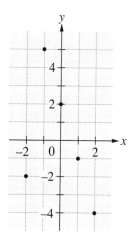

There is something remarkable about the set of points graphed in this figure. Can you see what it is? The points all lie on a straight line!

EXAMPLE 4   Graph the function g defined by $g(x) = 2 - x^2$ if the domain is the set of real numbers.

Solution   The rule $g(x) = 2 - x^2$ tells us that to find the range value corresponding to an x value we must square the x value and subtract the result from 2. Using this procedure for integral values of x between -3 and 3 inclusive, we obtain the values in the table. We then graph the ordered pairs and join them with a smooth curve as shown in the figure. Notice that the graph is a parabola, as in Example 2.

x	$y = g(x)$	Ordered Pair
-3	-7	$(-3, -7)$
-2	-2	$(-2, -2)$
-1	1	$(-1, 1)$
0	2	$(0, 2)$
1	1	$(1, 1)$
2	-2	$(2, -2)$
3	-7	$(3, -7)$

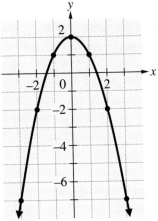

C. *Applications*

EXAMPLE 5   Long-distance telephone costs are functions of time. The dial-direct rate for a Tampa to Los Angeles call made during business hours is given in the margin. Of course, if you talk for a fraction of a minute, you will be charged for the whole minute, so the words "or fraction thereof" should be understood to be included in each column. Find the cost of a call lasting:

Mon.–Fri.	8 A.M.–5 P.M.
Initial minute $0.36	additional minute $0.28

(a) 1 min or less
(b) More than 1 min but not more than 2 min
(c) More than 2 min but not more than 3 min
(d) More than 3 min but not more than 4 min
(e) Draw a graph showing the results of parts a, b, c, and d.

Solution   We make a table of values, as in Examples 3 and 4. This table gives the answers for parts (a), (b), (c), and (d);

	Time, t	Cost, c
(a)	$0 < t \le 1$	$0.36
(b)	$1 < t \le 2$	$0.36 + (1)($0.28) = $0.64
(c)	$2 < t \le 3$	$0.36 + (2)($0.28) = $0.92
(d)	$3 < t \le 4$	$0.36 + (3)($0.28) = $1.20

(e) The graph is shown in the figure. The open circles in the figure indicate that the left-hand endpoints of the line segments are not included in the graph. The solid dots mean that the right-hand endpoints are included.

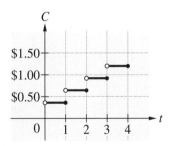

EXAMPLE 6   The **greatest integer function** is often denoted by the symbol $[\![x]\!]$ and is defined by the rule: $[\![x]\!]$ = the greatest integer that is less than or equal to x.

For example, $[\![2.56]\!] = 2$, $[\![3]\!] = 3$, $[\![0.623]\!] = 0$, $[\![-2.5]\!] = -3$, and so on. Graph $f(x) = [\![x]\!]$.

Solution   The domain of this function is the set of all real numbers. The definition tell us that if x is *between* two consecutive integers, then $[\![x]\!]$ is the lesser of the two integers. Thus, if n is an integer, and $n \leq x < n + 1$, then $[\![x]\!] = n$. We can list some values as in the table. The graph of these values appears in the figure. The open dots in the figure indicate that the right-hand endpoints of the line segments are not included in the graph; the solid dots indicate that the left-hand endpoints are included.

x	$f(x) = [\![x]\!]$
$-3 \leq x < -2$	-3
$-2 \leq x < -1$	-2
$-1 \leq x < 0$	-1
$0 \leq x < 1$	0
$1 \leq x < 2$	1
$2 \leq x < 3$	2
$3 \leq x < 4$	3

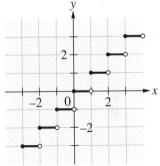

Graph of the greatest integer function $f(x) = [x]$

Functions like those in Examples 5 and 6 are called **step functions.**

If you are curious about a possible connection between the functions in Examples 5 and 6, you should look at problem 35 of Exercise 6.2.

Exercise 6.2

A.   In problems 1–10, graph the given relation.

1. $\{(x, y) \,|\, y = x$, an integer between -1 and 4, inclusive$\}$
2. $\{(x, y) \,|\, y = -x$, x an integer between -1 and 4, inclusive$\}$
3. $\{(x, y) \,|\, y = 2x + 1$, x an integer between 0 and 5, inclusive$\}$
4. $\{(x, y) \,|\, x + 2y = 3$, x an odd integer between 0 and 10$\}$

5. $\{(x, y) \mid 2x - y = 4, x \text{ an integer between } -2 \text{ and } 2, \text{ inclusive}\}$
6. $\{(x, y) \mid y = x^2, x \text{ an integer between } -3 \text{ and } 3, \text{ inclusive}\}$
7. $\{(x, y) \mid y = \sqrt{x}, x = 0, 1, 4, 9, 16, 25, \text{ or } 36\}$
8. $\{(x, y) \mid x = \sqrt{y}, x \text{ an integer between } 0 \text{ and } 3, \text{ inclusive}\}$
9. $\{(x, y) \mid x + y < 5, x, y \text{ nonnegative integers}\}$
10. $\{(x, y) \mid y > x, x \text{ and } y \text{ positive integers less than } 4\}$

B. In problems 11–18, graph the given function for the given domain (the replacement set for x).

11. $f(x) = x + 1, x$ an integer between -3 and 3, inclusive
12. $f(x) = 3x - 1, x$ an integer between -1 and 3, inclusive
13. $g(x) = x^2 + 1, x$ an integer between -3 and 3, inclusive
14. $h(x) = -x^2, x$ an integer between -3 and 3, inclusive
15. $F(x) = x^2 - 2, x$ an integer between -3 and 3, inclusive
16. $f(x) = [\![x]\!] + 1, -3 \le x \le 3$
17. $g(x) = [\![x]\!] - 1, -3 \le x \le 3$
18. $h(x) = -[\![-x]\!], -3 \le x \le 3$

C. 19. Anthropologists can determine a person's height in life by using the person's skeletal remains as a clue. For example, the height (in centimeters) of a man with a humerus bone of length x cm can be obtained by multiplying 2.89 by x and adding 70.64 to the result.
   (a) Find a function $h(x)$ that gives the height of a man whose humerus bone is x cm long.
   (b) Use your function h from part (a) to predict the height of a man whose humerus bone is 34 cm long.

20. A plumber charges \$25 per hour plus \$30 for the service call. If $c(h)$ is the function representing the total charges, and h is the number of hours worked, find:
   (a) $c(h)$
   (b) The total charges when the plumber works for 2, 3, or 4 hours
   (c) Graph the points obtained in part (b).

21. A finance company will lend you \$1,000 for a finance charge of \$20 plus simple interest at 1% per month. This means that you will pay interest of $\frac{1}{100}$ of \$1,000, that is, \$10 per month in addition to the \$20 finance charge. The total cost of the loan can be expressed as a function $F(x)$, where x is the number of months before you repay the loan.
   (a) Find $F(x)$.
   (b) Find the total cost of borrowing the \$1,000 for 8 months.

22. A bank charges 2% per month on a high-risk loan. If this is simple interest, describe the function that gives the cost $C(x)$ of borrowing \$5,000 for x months. (Compare problem 21.)

23. One of the depreciation (loss of value) methods approved by the IRS is the **straight-line method.** Under this method, if a $10,000 truck is to be fully depreciated in 5 years, the yearly depreciation will be $\frac{1}{5}$ of $10,000, that is, $2,000.
    (a) Write an equation that defines the depreciated value V of the truck as a function of the time t in years.
    (b) Draw a graph of this function.

24. The rates for a Tampa to Atlanta dial-direct telephone call during business hours are: 33¢ for the first minute or fraction thereof, and 27¢ for each additional minute or fraction thereof. Find the cost C of a call lasting:
    (a) 1 minute or less
    (b) More than 1 minute but not more than 2 minutes
    (c) More than 2 minutes but not more than 3 minutes
    (d) Draw a graph of the results of parts (a), (b), and (c).

25. The cost of a Boston to Nantucket dial-direct telephone call during business hours is given for positive integer values of t by

    $$C(t) = 0.55 + 0.23(t - 1)$$

    (a) Draw a graph of $C(t)$ for $0 < t \le 5$.

    (b) Santiago made a call from Boston to his friend Jessica in Nantucket. If the call cost Santiago $3.31, how long did they talk?

In Other Words

26. What is the graph of a function?
27. Is every relation a function? Explain why or why not.
28. Is every function a relation? Explain why or why not.
29. Why does the vertical line test work?
30. Why is the greatest integer function called a "step" function?

Using Your Knowledge

*U.S. first class postage charges can be described by a **step function** similar to the greatest integer function of Example 6. If the weight of a letter is x oz, where $0 < x \le 11$, then the postage is 29¢ for the first ounce or fraction thereof plus 23¢ for each additional ounce or fraction thereof.*

31. Complete the table in the margin.

32. To describe the first-class postage function by a formula, we first need to look at the function $f(x) = [\![1 - x]\!]$. Compare Example 6 and make a table for values of x between 0 and 12, using unit intervals $0 < x \le 1$, $1 < x \le 2$, etc. You should get $f(x) = 0$ for $0 < x \le 1$, $f(x) = -1$ for $1 < x \le 2$, etc.

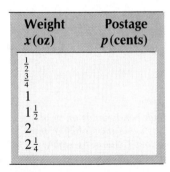

Weight x(oz)	Postage p(cents)
$\frac{1}{2}$	
$\frac{3}{4}$	
1	
$1\frac{1}{2}$	
2	
$2\frac{1}{4}$	

33. The function that describes the first-class postage is

$$p(x) = 29 - 23[\![1 - x]\!] \qquad 0 < x \le 11$$

Use the results of problem 32 to graph the function p.

34. Show that $p(x) = 29 + 23[\![x - 1]\!]$ is not correct for the postage function. (Try it for $x = 1.5$.)

35. Show that the telephone call cost function of Example 5 is described by $C(t) = 0.36 - 0.28[\![1 - t]\!]$

36. Use the function $C(t)$ in problem 35 to find the cost of a call lasting
(a) 1 min.   (b) $3\frac{1}{2}$ min.

Discovery

Have you ever seen a pendulum clock? An Italian scientist named Galileo Galilei made various discoveries about swinging weights, and these discoveries led to the invention of the pendulum clock. Galileo discovered that there was a relationship between the time of the swing of a pendulum and its length. The table shows corresponding values of these two quantities. (The unit length is about 25 cm.)

Time of Swing $f(x)$	Length of Pendulum (x)
1 sec	1 unit
2 sec	4 units
3 sec	9 units
4 sec	16 units
5 sec	25 units

37. Judging from the table, what do you think is the rule connecting the time, $f(x)$, of the swing and the length, x, of the pendulum?

38. From the pattern given in the table, can you find the length of a pendulum that takes 6 sec for a swing?

39. Can you find the length of a pendulum that takes 100 sec for a swing?

40. The University of South Florida has a Foucault pendulum in its physics building. This pendulum takes 7 sec for a swing. Can you find the length of the pendulum?

This Foucault pendulum is on display in the visitor's entrance lobby of the United Nations General Assembly building in New York

6.3 LINEAR FUNCTIONS
AND RELATIONS

GETTING STARTED

FITNESS AND GRAPHING FUNCTIONS

Have you been to a fitness center lately? Some of them display a graph showing your desirable heart rate **target zone** based on your age. The idea is to elevate your heart rate so that it is within a prescribed range. If your heart races during exercise, the consequences may be fatal. Thus, it is recommended that your heart rate (pulse) does not exceed 190 beats per minute regardless of age. For a 70-year-old, the recommended upper limit is 120 beats per minute. We enter this information in the table to the left. Now, suppose $U(a)$ is the upper limit in heartbeats per minute for a person whose age is a; can we find $U(a)$? If we assume that $U(a)$ is linear, it must be defined by an equation of the form $U(a) = ma + b$. We now find m and b. According to the chart, when $a = 0$, $U(a) = 190$.

a	Pulse
0	190
70	120

Thus,

$$U(0) = m \cdot 0 + b = 190$$

and

$$b = 190$$

Also from the chart,

$$U(70) = 120$$

Thus,

$$U(70) = m \cdot 70 + 190 = 120$$

Subtracting 190,

$$70m = -70$$

Solving for m,

$$m = -1$$

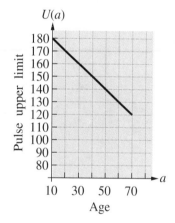

Since $m = -1$ and $b = 190$, $U(a) = -1a + 190$, that is, $U(a) = -a + 190$. To graph $U(a)$ between 10 and 70, let $a = 10$, $U(10) = -10 + 190 = 180$. Graph (10, 180). The point (70, 120) is in the chart, so we plot it and draw a straight line through (70, 120) and (10, 180). The result is the graph for $U(a)$. In Section 6.6, Example 6, we also graph $L(a)$, the lower limit in heartbeats per minute. The region between the two graphs is the **target zone** for the heart rate while exercising. You will find more problems like this one in problems 33–35 of Exercise 6.3.

A relation of the form

$$\{(x, y) \mid y = ax + b\}$$

where a and b are real numbers, always defines a function. (Why?) A function of this special form is called a **linear function,** because its graph is a straight line. We shall learn here how to draw the graph of a linear function.

A. *Graphs of Vertical and Horizontal Lines*

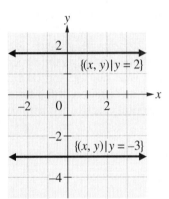

FIGURE 6.2

Let us look first at the case in which $a = 0$. Then the rule of the function is $y = b$ for *all real values of x*. Note that x is unrestricted (any real number) but for any value of x, $y = b$. This means that the graph consists of all points such as $(0, b)$, $(-1, b)$, $(\sqrt{2}, b)$, $(10.26, b)$, and so on. Thus, the graph is a straight line parallel to the x axis and b units from this axis. If $b > 0$, the line will be above the x axis; and if $b < 0$, the line will be below the x axis. (What if $b = 0$?) Figure 6.2 shows the graphs of $\{(x, y) \mid y = b\}$ for $b = -3$ and for $b = 2$.

A relation such as $\{(x, y) \mid x = c\}$, where c is a real number, is not a function, because y may have any real value. For instance, if $R = \{(x, y) \mid x = 2\}$, then $(2, -1)$, $(2, 0)$, $(2, 1.75)$, and so on, are all ordered pairs belonging to R. Because x has the fixed value 2, all these points are on the line parallel to and 2 units to the right of the y axis. In general, the equation $x = c$ (or the relation $\{(x, y) \mid x = c\}$) has for its graph a vertical line, that is, a line parallel to and c units from the y axis.

In summary:

> The graph of the function $\{(x, y) \mid y = b\}$ or, equivalently, of the equation $y = b$, is a **horizontal** line parallel to the x axis and b units from it.
> The graph of the relation $\{(x, y) \mid x = c\}$ or, equivalently, of the equation $x = c$, is a **vertical** line parallel to the y axis and c units from it.

EXAMPLE 1   Graph   (a) $y = -2$ (b) $x = 2$

Solution   (a) The graph of $y = -2$ is a horizontal line parallel to the x axis and two units below it. Note that for any x you choose, y is always -2. The graph is shown in the figure.

(b) The graph of $x = 2$ is a vertical line parallel to the y axis as shown in the figure.

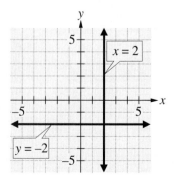

B. *Graphs of Linear Equations*

We will now show you the general procedure that can be used to draw the graph of a linear function in the form $f = \{(x, y) \mid y = ax + b\}$ or, equivalently, $f(x) = ax + b$.

Problem Solving:	**Graphing Linear Equations**

Graph the function defined by $f(x) = 3x - 6$.

1. Read the problem.

2. Select the unknown.
What are we looking for?

We want to draw the graph of $f(x) = 3x - 6$. To do this we need to find ordered pairs (x, y) that satisfy the relation $f = \{(x, y) \mid y = 3x - 6\}$.

3. Think of a plan.
Is the graph a straight line? If it is, we know that two points will determine the line.

The function is of the form $y = ax + b$, so its graph is a line. To graph this function, we find two points on the line and draw a line through them. The result will be the graph of the function.

4. Use the preceding idea to carry out the plan. Find two points and then join them with a line. (Try to use points that are easy to graph.)

For ease of computation, we let $x = \mathbf{0}$, obtaining $y = 3 \cdot \mathbf{0} - 6$ or $y = -6$. Thus, $(0, -6)$ is one of the points. For $y = \mathbf{0}$, we have $\mathbf{0} = 3x - 6$ or $6 = 3x$, that is, $x = 2$. This makes $(2, 0)$ another point on the line. Now, graph $(0, -6)$ and $(2, 0)$ and draw a line through them. The result is the graph of $f(x) = 3x - 6$.

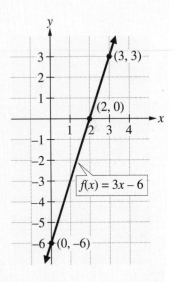

5. Verify your answer
How can you do this?

Select a point on the line, say, $(3, 3)$, and verify that it satisfies the equation $y = 3x - 6$. If $x = \mathbf{3}$, $y = \mathbf{3}$, $\mathbf{3} = 3 \cdot \mathbf{3} - 6$ is a true statement.

The x coordinate of the point where the line crosses the x axis is called the **x intercept** of the line. Similarly, the y coordinate of the point where the line crosses the y axis is called the **y intercept.** For $f(x) = 3x - 6$, the x intercept is 2 and the y intercept is -6. Note that, in general, we may say either graph the function f, where $f(x) = ax + b$, or graph the equation $y = ax + b$.

TRY EXAMPLE 2 NOW.

Cover the solution, write your own, and then check your work.

EXAMPLE 2 Graph the equation $y = -2x + 4$.

Solution Since the equation is of the form $y = ax + b$, its graph is a straight line. We find the y intercept by letting $x = 0$, obtaining $y = -2 \cdot \mathbf{0} + 4$ or $y = 4$. We then graph the point $(0, 4)$. For $y = 0$, we have $\mathbf{0} = -2x + 4$ or $x = 2$. Graph the point $(2, 0)$. We then draw a straight line through $(0, 4)$ and $(2, 0)$ to get the graph of $y = -2x + 4$. For verification, select a point on the line, say, $(1, 2)$. Substituting $x = \mathbf{1}$ and $y = \mathbf{2}$ into $y = -2x + 4$, we have $\mathbf{2} = -2(\mathbf{1}) + 4$, a true statement. ∎

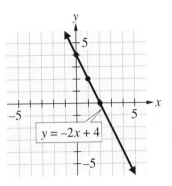

Now that we know how to graph lines, we might wonder whether there are any other relations whose graphs are straight lines. We can show that the relation described by $\{(x, y) \mid ax + by = c\}$, where a and b are not both 0, is always a linear relation. If $b \neq 0$, we can solve the equation $ax + by = c$ for y, obtaining

$$by = -ax + c$$

$$y = -\frac{a}{b}x + \frac{c}{b}$$

Because a, b, and c are all real numbers, this equation is the rule for a linear function. If $b = 0$, then

$$0 = -ax + c$$

so that

$$x = +\frac{c}{a}$$

which is the rule for a linear relation (not a function), corresponding to a vertical line $\frac{c}{a}$ units from the y axis. Because of these facts, the equation $ax + by = c$, with a and b not both 0, is called a **linear equation;** its graph is always a straight line, which can be drawn using our familiar intercept procedure, as shown next.

EXAMPLE 3 Graph the equation $2x + 3y = 6$.

Solution Because the equation $2x + 3y = 6$ is a linear equation, we know that its graph is a straight line. Thus, any two points on the line will determine the line. For $x = 0$, we have $3y = 6$, or $y = 2$, so the point $(0, 2)$ is on the line. For $y = 0$, we get $x = 3$, so $(3, 0)$ is a second point on the line. We graph these two points and draw a straight line through them to get the graph shown in the figure.

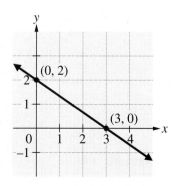

C. *Applications*

In order to make sensible decisions in problem solving and in certain consumer problems, it is helpful to be able to make a quick sketch of a linear function. Such a situation is illustrated in the next example.

EXAMPLE 4

Suppose the cost of renting a cellular phone from company A is $200 a month plus $1 per minute of air time (the time spent talking on the phone). If m is the number of minutes of air time and $C_1(m)$ is the corresponding cost in dollars, then

$$C_1(m) = 200 + m$$

For company B the cost is $100 a month plus $2 per minute of air time. If $C_2(m)$ is the corresponding cost, then

$$C_2(m) = 100 + 2m$$

(a) Graph C_1 and C_2 on the same set of axes.

(b) When will the cost be the same for either company?

(c) If cost is the only consideration, which company would you rent from if you are planning to have more than 100 minutes of air time per month?

Solution

(a) Since C_1 and C_2 are both linear functions of m, their graphs are straight lines. For $m = 0$, $C_1(0) = 200$, so $(0, 200)$ is on the graph of C_1. For $m = 100$, $C_1(100) = 300$, so $(100, 300)$ is also on this graph. We draw a line through these two points as shown in the figure. Similarly, for $m = 0$, $C_2(0) = 100$ and for $m = 100$, $C_2(100) = 300$. Thus, the two points $(0, 100)$ and $(100, 300)$ are on the graph of C_2. Again, we draw a line through these two points as shown.

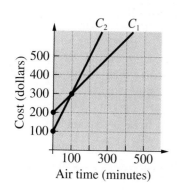

(b) Since both lines pass though the point $(100, 300)$, it is clear that the cost is the same for both companies when 100 minutes of air time are used.

(c) You can see from the graph that company A will cost less if you are planning to have more than 100 minutes of air time. ∎

D. *Distance Between Two Points*

In this section we have learned that the line $y = b$ is a line parallel to the x axis and b units from it (see Figure 6.2). Similarly, the line $x = a$ is a line parallel to and a units from the y axis (see Example 1). It is not difficult to find the distance between two points on a horizontal or on a vertical straight line, that is, on a line $y = b$ or on a line $x = a$.

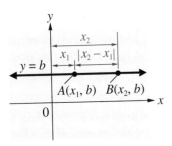

FIGURE 6.3

Suppose that we have two points, say, A and B, on the same horizontal line, the line $y = b$ in Figure 6.3. Then their coordinates would be (x_1, b) and (x_2, b), as in the figure. Because x_1 and x_2 are the **directed distances** of the respective points from the y axis, the length of AB is $|x_2 - x_1|$. Denoting this length by $|AB|$, we have the formula

$$|AB| = |x_2 - x_1| \tag{1}$$

Similarly, if the two points C and D are on the same vertical line, their coordinates are (a, y_1) and (a, y_2), and the length of CD is

$$|CD| = |y_2 - y_1| \tag{2}$$

To obtain a formula for the distance between *any* two points, we use the **Pythagorean theorem:**

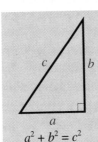

If a triangle is a right triangle (has one 90° angle), then the square of the hypotenuse c equals the sum of the squares of the other two sides a and b, that is, $a^2 + b^2 = c^2$ (see Figure 6.4).

$a^2 + b^2 = c^2$

FIGURE 6.4
The Pythagorean theorem

The Pythagorean theorem will be discussed in greater detail in Section 7.6.

In Figure 6.5, $A(x_1, y_1)$ and $B(x_2, y_2)$ represent two general points. The line BC is drawn parallel to the y axis and the line AC is drawn parallel to the x axis, so ABC is a right triangle with right angle at C.

Because A and C are on the same horizontal line, they must have the same y coordinates. Likewise, B and C are on the same vertical line, so they have the same x coordinates. Thus, the coordinates of C must be (x_2, y_1). By the Pythagorean theorem, the length of AB is given by $|AB| = \sqrt{|AC|^2 + |BC|^2}$. By equations (1) and (2), $|AC| = |x_2 - x_1|$ and $|BC| = |y_2 - y_1|$. Thus, we have:

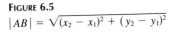

FIGURE 6.5
$|AB| = \sqrt{(x_2 - x_1)^2 + (y_2 - y_1)^2}$

The distance between two points $A(x_1, y_1,)$ and $B(x_2, y_2)$ is given by
$$|AB| = \sqrt{(x_2 - x_1)^2 + (y_2 - y_1)^2}. \tag{3}$$

EXAMPLE 5   Find the distance between the points $A(2, -3)$ and $B(8, 5)$.

Solution   By equation (3),

$$|AB| = \sqrt{(8 - 2)^2 + [5 - (-3)]^2}$$
$$= \sqrt{6^2 + 8^2} = \sqrt{36 + 64} = \sqrt{100} = 10$$

The distance between A and B is 10 units.   ■

EXAMPLE 6   Find the distance between the points $A(-1, -4)$ and $B(-3, 5)$.

Solution   As in the preceding example, we find

$$|AB| = \sqrt{[-3 - (-1)]^2 + [5 - (-4)]^2}$$
$$= \sqrt{(-2)^2 + 9^2} = \sqrt{4 + 81} = \sqrt{85}$$

With the aid of a table of square roots (or a calculator), we could express this result in decimal form. However, the indicated root form, $\sqrt{85}$ units, is adequate for our purposes.

EXAMPLE 7   Use the distance formula to show that $A(-3, -6)$, $B(5, 0)$, and $C(1, 2)$ are the vertices of a right triangle.

Solution   We know that a triangle is a right triangle if the square of one side equals the sum of the squares of the other two sides. This suggests that we find the squares of the sides of the triangle and then see whether two of the squares add up to the third. Using the distance formula, we find

$$|AB|^2 = [5 - (-3)]^2 + [0 - (-6)]^2 = 8^2 + 6^2 = 100$$

$$|BC|^2 = (1 - 5)^2 + (2 - 0)^2 = (-4)^2 + 2^2 = 20$$

$$|AC|^2 = [1 - (-3)]^2 + [2 - (-6)]^2 = 4^2 + 8^2 = 80$$

Thus, $|AB|^2 = |BC|^2 + |AC|^2$. So ABC is a right triangle with AB as its hypotenuse.

EXAMPLE 8   Determine if the triangle with vertices at $A(2, 7)$, $B(6, 0)$, and $C(12, 3)$ is a right triangle (see the figure).

Solution
$$|AB|^2 = (6 - 2)^2 + (0 - 7)^2 = 16 + 49 = 65$$

$$|BC|^2 = (12 - 6)^2 + (3 - 0)^2 = 36 + 9 = 45$$

$$|AC|^2 = (12 - 2)^2 + (3 - 7)^2 = 100 + 16 = 116$$

There is no side whose square is the sum of the squares of the other two sides. Therefore, the triangle is not a right triangle. In fact, you should note that the longest side is the only potential hypotenuse of a right triangle. You need only check whether the square of the longest side equals the sum of the squares of the other two sides.

Exercise 6.3

A–B. 1. In the table, the entries in the two columns have a common, simple linear relationship, $y = ax$. Find the missing entry.

x	y
3	2.25
2	1.5
$\frac{1}{2}$	$\frac{3}{8}$
?	3

2. In the table, the entries in the two columns have a common, simple quadratic relationship, $y = ax^2$. Find the missing entry.

x	y
$\frac{1}{2}$	$\frac{1}{2}$
1	2
2	8
?	50

In problems 3–18, graph the given linear function or equation.

3. $f(x) = 3x + 6$

4. $f(x) = 2x + 5$

5. $f(x) = 3$

6. $f(x) = -2$

7. $x = -1$

8. $x = 4$

9. $f(x) = -x + 2$

10. $f(x) = -2x - 4$

11. $g(x) = -3x - 6$

12. $g(x) = -2x + 6$

13. $3x + 2y = 6$

14. $4x + 3y = 12$

15. $-2x + 3y = 6$

16. $-3x + 2y = 12$

17. $4x - 3y = 12$

18. $3x - 5y = 15$

C. In problems 19–28, find the distance between the given points.

19. $(2, 4)$ and $(-1, 0)$

20. $(3, -2)$ and $(8, 10)$

21. $(-4, -5)$ and $(-1, 3)$

22. $(5, 7)$ and $(-2, 3)$

23. $(4, -8)$ and $(1, -1)$

24. $(-2, -2)$ and $(6, -4)$

25. $(3, 0)$ and $(3, -2)$

26. $(4, -1)$ and $(6, -1)$

27. $(-2, 3)$ and $(-2, 7)$

28. $(1, -5)$ and $(8, -5)$

In problems 29–32, take the three given points as the vertices of a triangle. Determine whether the triangle is a right triangle, an isosceles (two sides equal) triangle, or a scalene (no sides equal) triangle. Note that a triangle can be a right triangle and isosceles or scalene.

29. $(2, 2)$, $(0, 5)$, $(-20, -12)$ 30. $(2, 2)$, $(0, 5)$, $(-19, -12)$

31. $(2, 2)$, $(-4, -14)$, $(-20, -8)$ 32. $(0, 0)$, $(6, 0)$, $(3, 3)$

D.
33. Elite Catering charges $500 to plan a banquet plus $25 per plate. Society Catering's charges are $1,000 for the planning and $20 per plate. Let $E(x)$ and $S(x)$ represent the cost of a banquet for x persons catered by Elite and Society, respectively,
    (a) Find $E(x)$ and $S(x)$.
    (b) Graph $E(x)$ and $S(x)$ on the same set of axes.
    (c) Find the number of persons for which the cost is the same with either company.

34. The costs (in dollars) of a repair call taking x hours or fraction thereof from companies A and B are, respectively,

    $$C_1(x) = 20x + 30 \quad \text{and} \quad C_2(x) = 10x + 50.$$

    (a) Graph C_1 and C_2 on the same set of axes.
    (b) For how many hours is the cost the same for either company?

35. Economy telephone calls to Spain from Tampa, Florida, have to be made between 6 P.M. and 7 A.M. The rates for calls dialed direct during those hours are $1.16 for the first minute or fraction thereof and 65¢ for each additional minute or fraction thereof.
    (a) Let t (in minutes) be the duration of a call, and make a table of the cost $C(t)$ for $0 < t \le 5$.
    (b) Draw a graph of $C(t)$ for $0 < t \le 5$.

36. Use the rates described in problem 35.
    (a) José wanted to call his dad in Spain during the economy hours, but José had only $5. How long a call could he make without exceeding his $5?
    (b) Maria called her mother in Spain during the economy hours and was charged $7.01. How long was Maria's call?

In Other Words

37. Suppose the three vertices of a triangle are $A(a_1, a_2)$, $B(b_1, b_2)$, and $C(c_1, c_2)$. Explain in detail how you can determine whether the triangle is a right triangle.

38. Explain in detail how you can use the Problem Solving procedure given in this section to graph $y = b$.

39. Explain in detail how you can use the Problem Solving procedure given in this section to graph $x = c$.

40. Explain in detail the steps you will use in graphing $f(x) = ax + b$, then look at the Discovery problem and see if your steps are similar.

Discovery

*The ideas developed in this section for graphing lines can be summarized by means of a flowchart. A **flowchart** is a pictorial representation describing the logical steps that have to be taken in order to perform a task.*

The basic component of a flowchart is a box that contains a command. For example, $\boxed{x \to 0}$ instructs one to take x, a previously given quantity, and let it be equal to 0. In some cases, this instruction is given as

> Let $x = 0$

The figure shows a flowchart that can be used to find the graph of any line not passing through the origin. An example of how it works is given at the right for the line $y = 2x + 6$.

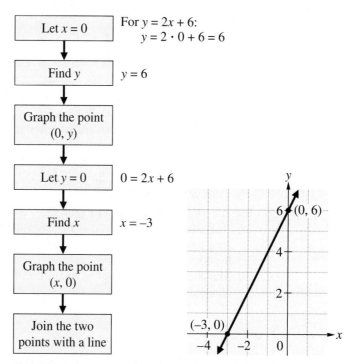

Let $x = 0$ For $y = 2x + 6$:
                    $y = 2 \cdot 0 + 6 = 6$

Find y $y = 6$

Graph the point $(0, y)$

Let $y = 0$ $0 = 2x + 6$

Find x $x = -3$

Graph the point $(x, 0)$

Join the two points with a line

Flowchart for graphing a line

Use the flowchart technique to graph the linear relations described by the following problems in Exercise 6.3.

41. Problem 3   42. Problem 4   43. Problem 9   44. Problem 10
45. Problem 11   46. Problem 12   47. Problem 13   48. Problem 14
49. Problem 15   50. Problem 16   51. Problem 17   52. Problem 18

Calculator Corner

You can use a calculator to find the distance between two points. For example, to find the distance between (2, −3) and (8, 5), you must use equation (3). Here are the steps you need. Press:

$$(\boxed{(} \boxed{8} \boxed{-} \boxed{2} \boxed{)} \boxed{x^2} \boxed{+} \boxed{(} \boxed{5} \boxed{-} \boxed{3} \boxed{\pm} \boxed{)} \boxed{x^2} \boxed{=} \boxed{\sqrt{}}$$

(or $\boxed{2\text{nd}}$ $\boxed{\sqrt{x}}$ *) Note that in this case the answer appears as 10. If you work Example 6 using a calculator, your answer will be 9.219544457, an approximation for* $\sqrt{85}$.

53. Try problems 19, 21, 23, 25, and 27 with your calculator.

Computer Corner

The Distance Between Two Points Program in the Programs in BASIC appendix will find the distance between two points when the points are entered. Following the notation in equation (3), you must enter x_1, y_1, x_2, *and* y_2. *The program does the rest. Notice that the answer to Example 6 in the text would appear as* sqrt(85) = 9.219544. *The program gives answers to six decimal places.*

54. Try problems 19, 21, 23, 25, and 27 on the computer.

6.4 EQUATIONS OF A LINE

GETTING STARTED

A GRAPHIC LOOK AT ENGINE DEPOSITS

Study the advertisement shown below. It shows that engine deposits increase if you do *not* use Texaco gasoline and decrease if you do. How fast do the deposits increase or decrease? To find out we can look at the ratio of deposit

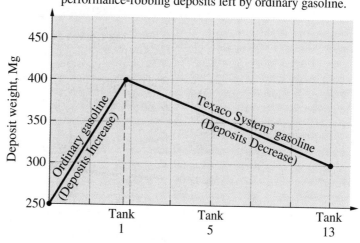

In the BMW test, Texaco's new System³ gasoline removed performance-robbing deposits left by ordinary gasoline.

weight (in mg) to tanks of gas. Without Texaco gas, the deposits increased from 250 mg to 400 mg when using approximately one tank of gas. Thus,

$$\frac{\text{mg of deposit}}{\text{tanks of gas}} = \frac{400 - 250}{1} = 150 \frac{\text{mg}}{\text{tank}}.$$

How fast did the deposits decrease? They went from 400 mg to 300 mg after using about 12 tanks of Texaco. The ratio of decrease is given by

$$\frac{\text{mg of deposit}}{\text{tanks of gas}} = \frac{300 - 400}{13 - 1} = -\frac{100}{12} = -8\frac{1}{3} \frac{\text{mg}}{\text{tank}}$$

The ratio of mg of deposit to tanks of gas, or in general the ratio of rise (difference in y values) to run (difference in x values) for a line, is called the **slope** of the line. The slope of the increasing line is 150 mg/tank while the slope of the decreasing line is $-8\frac{1}{3}$ mg/tank. Note that the slope of an *increasing* line (rising from left to right) is *positive* and the slope of a *decreasing* line (falling from left to right) is *negative*. Now, one more point. The two lines look almost perpendicular to each other, so if one has slope m, the other one must have slope $-\frac{1}{m}$ (see problem 46 in Exercise 6.4). Is this the case? If not, what is wrong? Think of how you can redraw the graph more accurately to reflect the actual situation.

Obviously, the best investment in the graph is the tax-exempt account. Can you tell when the account produces the most money? Since the line is

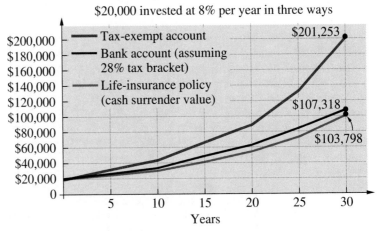

$20,000 invested at 8% per year in three ways

Note: Life-insurance policy is single-premium, variable-life coverage for a 35-year-old male. Assumes interest on other accounts is reinvested.

FIGURE 6.6

"steeper" during the last five years, that is when the account will produce the most. The annual amount produced in the last five years is approximately

$$\frac{200{,}000 - 140{,}000}{30 - 25} = \frac{60{,}000}{5} = 12{,}000$$

That is, the rate of change in the account over the last five years is about $12,000 per year. In general, when we look at a line graph and speak of its "rate of change," we are referring to the **slope** of the line.

A. *Slope*

In mathematics, an important feature of a straight line is its *steepness*. We can measure the steepness of a nonvertical line by means of the ratio of the **vertical rise (or fall)** to the corresponding **horizontal run.** We call this ratio the **slope.** For example, a staircase that rises 3 ft in a horizontal distance of 4 ft is said to have a slope of $\frac{3}{4}$ (see Figure 6.7).

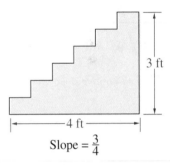

Slope $= \frac{3}{4}$

FIGURE 6.7

In general, we use the following definition.

Definition 6.3

A line going through two points (x_1, y_1) and (x_2, y_2), where $x_1 \neq x_2$, has **slope** m, where

$$m = \frac{y_2 - y_1}{x_2 - x_1}$$

Figure 6.8 shows the horizontal run $x_2 - x_1$ and the vertical rise $y_2 - y_1$ used in calculating the slope. We do not define slope for a vertical line. The slope of a horizontal line is obviously 0, because all points on such a line have the same y values.

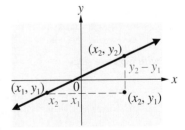

The slope of a line:

$$m = \frac{y_2 - y_1}{x_2 - x_1}, \quad x_1 \neq x_2$$

FIGURE 6.8

EXAMPLE 1   Find the slope of the line that goes through the points $(0, -6)$ and $(3, 3)$.

Solution   The two given points are shown in the figure. Suppose we choose $(x_1, y_1) = (0, -6)$ and $(x_2, y_2) = (3, 3)$. Then we get

$$m = \frac{3 - (-6)}{3 - 0} = \frac{9}{3} = 3$$

If we choose $(x_1, y_1) = (3, 3)$ and $(x_2, y_2) = (0, -6)$, then

$$m = \frac{-6 - 3}{0 - 3} = \frac{-9}{-3} = 3$$

As you can see, it makes no difference which point is labeled (x_1, y_1) and which is labeled (x_2, y_2). Since an interchange of the two points simply changes the sign of both the numerator and the denominator in the slope formula, the result is the same in both cases. ∎

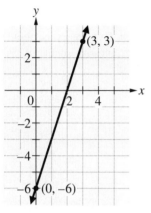

Line with positive slope

EXAMPLE 2   Find the slope of the line that goes through the two points $(3, -4)$ and $(-2, 3)$. See the figure.

Solution   We take $(x_1, y_1) = (-2, 3)$ so that $(x_2, y_2) = (3, -4)$. Then

$$m = \frac{-4 - 3}{3 - (-2)} = -\frac{7}{5}$$

∎

Examples 1 and 2 are illustrations of the fact that a line that rises from left to right has a **positive slope** and one that falls from left to right has a negative slope. Note that the slope of a line gives **the change in y per unit change in x.**

B. *Equations of Lines*

The slope of a line can be used to obtain an equation of the line. For example, suppose the line goes through a point $P_1(x_1, y_1)$ and has slope m. See Figure 6.9. We let $P(x, y)$ be any second point (distinct from P_1) on the line. Then, by Definition 6.3, the slope of the line in terms of these two points is

$$\frac{y - y_1}{x - x_1} = m$$

Line with negative slope

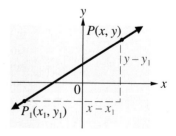

FIGURE 6.9

Multiplying both sides by $(x - x_1)$, we get $y - y_1 = m(x - x_1)$.

> The **point-slope form** of the equation of a line with slope m and passing through the point (x_1, y_1) is
>
> $$y - y_1 = m(x - x_1) \tag{1}$$

This equation must be satisfied by the coordinates of every point on the line.

EXAMPLE 3   Find an equation of the line that goes through the point $(2, -3)$ and has slope $m = -4$.

Solution   Using the point-slope equation (1), we get

$$y - (-3) = -4(x - 2)$$
$$y + 3 = -4x + 8$$
$$y = -4x + 5$$

An important special case of equation (1) is that in which the given point is the point where the line intersects the y axis. Let this point be denoted by $(0, b)$. Then b is called the **y intercept** of the line. Using equation (1), we obtain

$$y - b = m(x - 0)$$

and, by adding b to both sides, we get $y = mx + b$.

> The **slope–intercept form** of the equation of a line with slope m and y intercept b is
>
> $$y = mx + b \tag{2}$$

Notice that the answer to Example 3 was given in the slope–intercept form. This form is convenient for reading off the slope and the y intercept of the line. Thus, the answer to Example 3 immediately tells us that the slope of the line is -4 and the y intercept is 5 (see Figure 6.10).

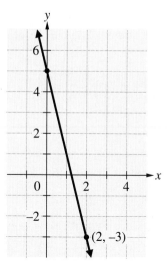

FIGURE 6.10
$y = -4x + 5$

EXAMPLE 4   Find the slope and the y intercept of the line with equation $6x + 3y = 5$.

Solution   By equation (2), the slope–intercept form of the equation of a line is $y = mx + b$, where m is the slope and b is the y intercept. We can solve the given equation for y by subtracting $6x$ from both sides and then dividing by 3. This procedure gives

$$y = -2x + \tfrac{5}{3}$$

an equation in the slope–intercept form. Thus, the slope m of the given line is -2 and the y intercept is $\tfrac{5}{3}$.

The procedure of Example 4 can be followed for any equation of the form $Ax + By = C$, where $B \neq 0$, to obtain an equation in the slope–intercept form. If $B = 0$, then we can divide by A to get $x = C/A$, an equation of a line parallel to the y axis. Thus, we see that every equation of the form

$$Ax + By = C \tag{3}$$

where A, B, and C are real numbers and A and B are not both 0, is an equation of a straight line.

On the other hand, we can show that every straight line has an equation of the form $Ax + By = C$. Any line that is not parallel to the y axis has a slope–intercept equation $y = mx + b$, which can be written in the form $mx - y = -b$ by subtracting b and y from both sides. This last equation is of the form $Ax + By = C$, with $A = m$, $B = -1$, and $C = -b$. For example, the equation $y = 2x + 5$ can be written in the form $2x - y = -5$ by subtracting 5 and y from both sides. This equation is the special case of $Ax + By = C$ with $A = 2$, $B = -1$, and $C = -5$. A line parallel to the y axis has an equation $x = a$, which is already of the form $Ax + By = C$, with $A = 1$, $B = 0$, and $C = a$. Thus, we see that every straight line can be described by the equation $Ax + By = C$.

> The **general form** of the equation of a straight line is
>
> $$Ax + By = C \tag{3}$$

EXAMPLE 5   Find the general form of the equation of the line that passes through $(6, 2)$ and $(3, -2)$.

Solution   We first find the slope of the line:

$$m = \frac{-2 - 2}{3 - 6} = \frac{-4}{-3} = \frac{4}{3}$$

Then, using the point–slope form, we find the equation

$$y - 2 = \tfrac{4}{3}(x - 6)$$
$$3y - 6 = 4x - 24$$
$$4x - 3y = 18$$

We can check this answer by seeing that $(6, 2)$ and $(3, -2)$ are both solutions of the equation. ∎

The ideas of Example 5 can often be used to obtain a simple formula that summarizes a group of data in a convenient form. For example, Table 6.1 shows the desirable weight range corresponding to a given height for men and for women.

Table 6.1

Height (in.)	Men's Weight (lb)	Women's Weight (lb)
62	108–134	98–123
63	112–139	102–128
64	116–144	106–133
65	120–149	110–138
66	124–154	114–143
67	128–159	118–148
68	132–164	122–153
69	136–169	126–158
70	140–174	130–163
71	144–179	134–168
72	148–184	138–173
73	152–189	
74	156–194	
75	160–199	
76	164–204	

Can we find an equation giving the relationship between height and weight? First, we must realize two things:

1. Men are heavier, so there will be one equation for men and another equation for women.
2. Even for men, the table gives only a weight *range*. For instance, a 76-in. (6-ft 4-in.) man should weigh between 164 and 204 lb.

Hence, to write an equation requires ideally that we be more specific, as in the next example.

EXAMPLE 6   Find an equation that gives the relationship between a man's height h (in inches) and his weight w (in pounds) using the lower weights in Table 6.1 as the desirable ones.

Solution   If we examine the heights and the corresponding weights in the table, we see that the heights increase by 1 in. from one entry to the next and the corresponding weights increase by 4 lb. This means that all the points (62, 108), (63, 112), . . . , (76, 164) lie on one straight line, because the slope of a line connecting any consecutive pair of these points is the same as the slope of the line connecting any other consecutive pair. Thus, we want to find the equation of this line. The slope of the line is easily obtained by using the first pair of points (62, 108) and (63, 112):

$$m = \frac{112 - 108}{63 - 62} = 4$$

Then, we can use the point–slope form of the equation to obtain

$$w - 108 = 4(h - 62)$$
$$w - 108 = 4h - 248$$
$$w = 4h - 140$$

You can check this against entries in the table. For example, for a 72-in. (6-ft) man, the equation gives

$$w = 4(72) - 140$$
$$= 288 - 140 = 148$$

which agrees with the table entry.   ■

C. *Parallel Lines*

Since the slope of a line determines its direction, it is obvious that **two lines with the same slope and different *y* intercepts are parallel lines.** The next example makes use of this idea.

EXAMPLE 7   Show that $3y = x + 2$ and $2x - 6y = 7$ describe parallel lines.

Solution   We solve each equation for y to obtain

$$y = \tfrac{1}{3}x + \tfrac{2}{3} \quad \text{and} \quad y = \tfrac{1}{3}x - \tfrac{7}{6}$$

These equations show that both lines have slope $\tfrac{1}{3}$. The y intercepts are different, so the lines are parallel.   ■

At this point, many students ask, "Which formula should we use in the problems?" Table 6.2 tells you which formula to use, depending on what information is given. Study this table before you attempt the problems in Exercise 6.4.

Table 6.2

To Find the Equation of a Line, Given:	Use
Two points (x_1, y_1) and (x_2, y_2), $x_1 \neq x_2$	Point-slope form: $y - y_1 = m(x - x_1)$, where $m = (y_2 - y_1)/(x_2 - x_1)$
A point (x_1, y_1) and the slope m	Point-slope form: $y - y_1 = m(x - x_1)$
The slope m and the y intercept b	Slope–intercept form: $y = mx + b$

The resulting equation can always be written in the general form: $Ax + By = C$.

Problem Solving:

Finding the Equation of a Line

Find the equation of the line parallel to $2y = 6x + 5$ and passing through $(1, 2)$.

1. **Read the problem.**
2. **Select the unknown.**

We are asked to find the line parallel to $2y = 6x + 5$ and passing through $(1, 2)$.

3. **Think of a plan.**
   Find the slope of the given line and use it in finding the equation of the new line.
4. **Use one of the formulas to find the equation.**
   Which formula can you use?

If the new line is to be parallel to $2y = 6x + 5$, or equivalently, $y = 3x + \dfrac{5}{2}$, the new line must have slope $m = 3$. Since the line passes through the point $(1, 2)$, we use the point-slope formula

$$y - y_1 = m(x - x_1)$$

with $m = 3$ and $(x_1, y_1) = (1, 2)$ obtaining

$$y - 2 = 3(x - 1)$$

5. **Verify the solution.**

To verify our answer, solve for y in $y - 2 = 3(x - 1)$ obtaining $y = 3x - 1$. This equation has slope 3, thus is parallel to the given line, and passes through $(\mathbf{1, 2})$ since $\mathbf{2} - 2 = 3(\mathbf{1} - 1)$.

TRY EXAMPLE 8 NOW.

Cover the solution, write your own, and then check your work.

EXAMPLE 8 Find the equation of a line parallel to $3y = -6x + 8$ and with y-intercept -3.

Solution The line $3y = -6x + 8$ has slope -2. (Why?) Since we want to find a line parallel to $3y = -6x + 8$, the new line must also have slope $m = -2$. We now have the slope and y intercept of the line we want. Using the slope–intercept form $y = mx + b$ with $m = -2$ and $b = -3$, we obtain *the desired equation $y = -2x - 3$.* ∎

Exercise 6.4

A. In problems 1–10, find the slope of the line that passes through the two given points.

1. $(1, 2)$ and $(3, 4)$
2. $(1, -2)$ and $(-3, -4)$
3. $(0, 5)$ and $(5, 0)$
4. $(3, -6)$ and $(5, -6)$
5. $(-1, -3)$ and $(7, -4)$
6. $(-2, -5)$ and $(-1, -6)$
7. $(0, 0)$ and $(12, 3)$
8. $(-1, -1)$ and $(-10, -10)$
9. $(3, 5)$ and $(-2, 5)$
10. $(4, -3)$ and $(2, -3)$

B. In problems 11–16, find the slope–intercept form (if possible) of the equation of the line that has the given properties (m is the slope).

11. Passes through $(1, 2)$; $m = \frac{1}{2}$
12. Passes through $(-1, -2)$; $m = -2$
13. Passes through $(2, 4)$; $m = -1$
14. Passes through $(-3, 1)$; $m = \frac{3}{2}$
15. Passes through $(4, 5)$; $m = 0$
16. Passes through $(3, 2)$; slope is not defined (does not exist)

In problems 17–26, find:

   (a) The slope　　　　(b) The y intercept

of the graph of the given equation.

17. $y = x + 2$
18. $2x + y = 3$
19. $3y = 4x$
20. $2y = x + 4$
21. $x + y = 14$
22. $y - 4x = 8$
23. $y = 6$
24. $2y = 16$
25. $x = 3$
26. $3x = -6y + 9$

In problems 27–32, find the general form of the equation of the straight line through the two given points.

27. $(1, -1)$ and $(2, 2)$
28. $(-3, -4)$ and $(-2, 0)$
29. $(3, 2)$ and $(2, 3)$
30. $(3, 0)$ and $(0, 5)$
31. $(0, 0)$ and $(1, 10)$
32. $(-4, -1)$ and $(-4, 3)$

33. Use Table 6.1 to find a formula relating the height h of a man and his ideal weight w given by the *second* number in the weight column. See Example 6.
34. Use Table 6.1 to find a formula relating the height h of a woman and her weight w as given by the *first* number in the weight column. See Example 6.
35. Repeat problem 34 using the *second* number in the weight column.
36. Based on your answer to problem 35, if a woman weighs 183 pounds, how tall should she be? (This is not given in Table 6.1.)

C. In problems 37–42, determine whether the given lines are parallel.

37. $y = 2x + 5$; $4x - 2y = 7$
38. $y = 4 - 5x$; $15x + 3y = 3$
39. $2x + 5y = 8$; $5x - 2y = -9$
40. $3x + 4y = 4$; $2x - 6y = 7$
41. $x + 7y = 7$; $2x + 14y = 21$
42. $y = 5x - 12$; $y = 3x - 8$

43. Find an equation of the line that passes through the point $(1, -2)$ and is parallel to the line $4x - y = 7$.

44. Find an equation of the line that passes through the point $(2, 0)$ and is parallel to the line $3x + 2y = 5$.

45. It is shown in analytic geometry that two lines, $a_1x + b_1y = c_1$ and $a_2x + b_2y = c_2$, are perpendicular if and only if

$$a_1a_2 + b_1b_2 = 0$$

that is, **two lines are perpendicular if and only if the sum of the products of the corresponding coefficients of x and y in the general form of the equations is 0.** This leads to a very easy way of writing an equation of a line that is perpendicular to a given line. For instance, if the given line is $3x + 5y = 8$, then $5x - 3y = c$ for each real number c is a line perpendicular to the given line. This is obvious because $(3)(5) + (5)(-3) = 0$. Notice that all we need to do to form the left side of the second equation is interchange the coefficients of x and y in the first equation and change the sign of one of these coefficients. If we wish to have the second line pass through a specified point, we select the value of c so that this happens. Thus, if the second line is to pass through $(3, 2)$, then c has to be selected so that $(3, 2)$ is in the solution set of the equation. Hence,

$$5(3) - 3(2) = c \quad \text{or} \quad c = 9$$

The line $5x - 3y = 9$ passes through $(3, 2)$ and is perpendicular to the line $3x + 5y = 8$. In each of the following problems, find an equation of the line that is perpendicular to the given line and passes through the given point.

(a) $2x + 5y = 7$; $(2, 0)$ (b) $y = 2x - 3$; $(1, 1)$

(c) $x - 2y = 3$; $(2, -2)$ (d) $4x + 5y = 9$; $(1, 1)$

46. If the lines $y = m_1x + b_1$, $m_1 \neq 0$, and $y = m_2x + b_2$ are perpendicular, then $m_2 = -1/m_1$. Show this by referring to problem 45. This leads to the simple statement that **the slopes of perpendicular lines are negative reciprocals of each other.** Why do we need the condition $m_1 \neq 0$?

47. A line passes through the two points $(0, 0)$ and $(100, 200)$. A second line passes through the two points $(0, 10)$ and $(790, -405)$. Can you see how to determine whether these are perpendicular lines? [*Hint:* Look at problem 46.]

*I*n Other Words

48. Explain why it is impossible to find the slope of a vertical line.

49. Explain why the slope of any horizontal line is 0.

50. Refer to problem 46. If $m_1 = 0$, then the first equation becomes $y = b_1$. What lines are perpendicular to this line? Explain. What are the equations of these perpendicular lines?

Using Your Knowledge

51. The idea of slope is used in economics in the **consumption possibility** line. For simplicity, we assume that a man has a total of $10 per day to spend. He is confronted with fixed prices for each food and clothing unit. The cost of food is $2 per unit and that of clothing is $1 per unit. If it is known that the man will spend the entire $10 on some combination of food and clothing, make a graph depicting this situation. [*Hint:* Use the x axis to represent the number of units of food and the y axis to represent the number of units of clothing.]

52. In problem 51, what is the interpretation of the point $(0, 10)$?

53. In problem 51, what is the interpretation of the point $(5, 0)$?

54. What does the slope of the line obtained in problem 51 tell about the ratio of the cost of food units to the cost of clothing units?

55. If the total cost y of producing x units of a product is assumed to be linear, then it can be written as

    $$y = mx + b$$

    where m is the cost of producing 1 unit (the *marginal cost*) and b is the **fixed cost,** which does not depend on the number of units produced. Find the total cost y of a product whose production cost is $2 per unit and whose fixed cost is $2,000.

56. Refer to problem 55. If the total cost y changes from $1,200 to $1,350 as the number x increases from 400 to 700, find the fixed cost b and the marginal cost m. [*Hint*: The line must pass through the two points $(400, 1200)$ and $(700, 1350)$.]

Discovery

Squaresville

The Fun and Games Club of Squaresville is having a treasure hunt. The figure shows a map of a portion of the town. The blocks are all square (of course!) and all of the same size. The instructions for the hunt are as follows: Draw two lines, one line passing through the intersection of Central Avenue and Main Street and through the intersection of 20th Street East and 10th Avenue North, the second line passing through the intersection of Central Avenue and 35th Street East and through the intersection of 40th Street East and 15th Avenue North. The treasure is in the red brick house at the intersection of these two lines.

Unfortunately, the treasure is in a new part of the town and there are no maps covering the area. Furthermore, no one on the treasure hunt has thought to bring any graph paper.

57. Can you locate the treasure without doing any drawing?

Computer Corner

You learned in this section that you can find the equation of a line if:

(a) Two points are given
(b) A slope and a point are given

The Equation of a Line Program in the Programs in BASIC appendix combines these two features; that is, you can provide two points, or a slope and a point, and the program will give you the equation of the corresponding line. To do Example 3, simply enter the points (2, −3) and the slope −4. As before, the answer is given in slope–intercept form.

58. Work problems 11, 13, and 15 using this program.

6.5 TWO LINEAR EQUATIONS IN TWO VARIABLES

GETTING STARTED

INSURANCE AND SYSTEMS OF EQUATIONS

The graph shows the total amount (in billions of dollars) of life insurance in force for a 10-year period. Can you tell from the graph in what year Metropolitan Life and Prudential had the same amount of insurance in force? This happened during the eighth year. This is because the value representing the total life insurance in force for each of the companies is the same (approximately $200 billion) in the middle of the eighth year. If we agree to denote the year by x and the total life insurance in force by y, the point $(x, y) = (8.5, 200)$ represents the point at which the two curves *intersect*. The coordinates of the point of intersection (if there is one) are the common solution of both equa-

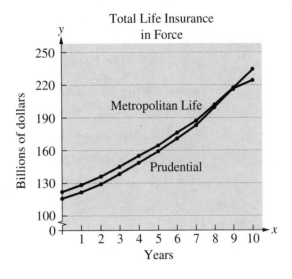

Total Life Insurance
in Force

tions. Suppose that for company A the total life insurance in force, y, at the end of x years is $y = 10x + 110$, and for company B it is $y = 5x + 120$. We can find the year when both companies had the same amount of life insurance in force by graphing these two equations and locating the point of intersection. In this section, we will learn how to find the solution of a system of equations with two unknowns using the method of graphing.

There are many applications of algebra that require the solution of a **system of linear equations.** We shall consider only the simple case of two equations in two variables. (Applications that require the solution of such systems appear in Section 6.7.)

As we have seen, a linear equation $Ax + By = C$ has a straight line for its graph. Hence, two such equations will graph into two straight lines in the plane. Two distinct lines in the plane can either *intersect* at a point or else be *parallel* (have no intersection). If the lines intersect, then the coordinates of the point of intersection are called the **solution of the system of equations.** If the lines are parallel, then, of course, the system has no solution.

A. *Solution by Graphing*

One way to solve a system of two equations in two variables is to graph the two lines and read the coordinates of the point of intersection from the graph. The next two examples illustrate this graphical method.

EXAMPLE 1   Use the graphical method to find the solution of the system

$$2x - y = 4$$

$$x + y = 5$$

Solution   We graph the two equations as shown in the figure. The point of intersection of the two lines appears to be (3, 2). We check this set of coordinates in the given system: For $x = 3$ and $y = 2$,

$$2x - y = 2 \cdot 3 - 2 = 4$$

$$x + y = 3 + 2 = 5$$

Thus, the two equations are both satisfied, and the desired solution is $x = 3$, $y = 2$, or (3, 2).

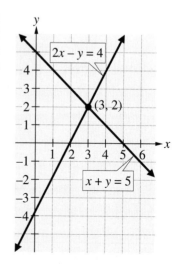

EXAMPLE 2   If you are about to build a house, you might consider two types of heating:

1. Solar heating, which requires a $10,000 initial investment and a $200 annual cost
2. Oil heating, with a $2000 initial investment and an annual cost of $1000

(a) Write an equation giving the total cost y (in dollars) of solar heating over x years.
(b) Repeat part (a) for the oil heating.
(c) Graph the equations obtained in parts (a) and (b) for a period of 12 years.
(d) When will the total costs for the two systems be equal?

Solution   (a) The cost y of solar heating is given by $y = 10{,}000 + 200x$.
(b) The cost y of oil heating is given by $y = 2000 + 1000x$.
(c) Note that the x coordinate represents the number of years and the y coordinate represents the number of dollars in the corresponding total cost. For the solar heating equation, we find the two points $(0, 10{,}000)$ and $(5, 11{,}000)$. These two points and the line through them are shown in color in the figure. For the oil heating equation, we find the two points $(0, 2{,}000)$ and $(5, 7{,}000)$. These two points and the line through them are also shown in the figure.

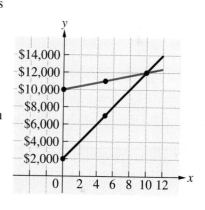

(d) As you can see from the figure, the lines intersect at the point where $x = 10$ and $y = 12{,}000$. Thus, the total costs are equal at the end of 10 years. (After 10 years, the total cost for solar heating is much less than that for oil heating.) ■

One word of warning: You should always check apparent solutions by substituting the respective values of x and y back into the original equations. **Picture (graph) solutions often give only approximations of actual solutions.**

B. *Solution by Algebraic Methods*

If the solution of the system is a pair of simple numbers that can be read exactly from the graph, then the graphical method is quite satisfactory. Naturally, you should always check a proposed solution in the given equations. Unfortunately, most systems will have solutions that are not easy to read exactly from the graph, and for such systems an algebraic method of solving is needed. There is a quite simple method that is best explained by means of examples, as follows.

EXAMPLE 3   Solve the system of Example 1 by algebraic means.

Solution   The point (x, y) where the lines $2x - y = 4$ and $x + y = 5$ intersect is the intersection of the solution sets of the two equations. This means that the number pair consisting of the x value and the y value of this point must satisfy both equations. Hence, we may use the following procedure: Since the y terms in the two equations are the same except for sign, we add the two equations term by term to eliminate the y terms and get an equation in one variable:

$$\begin{array}{r} 2x - y = 4 \\ x + y = 5 \\ \hline 3x \qquad = 9 \end{array}$$

Thus, $x = 3$. By substituting this x value into the second equation, we get

$$3 + y = 5 \quad \text{or} \quad y = 2$$

We have now found the same solution as before, $(3, 2)$.   ∎

If both variables occur in both equations, we can proceed as follows:

> 1. Eliminate one of the variables:
>   (a) Multiply one or both equations by nonzero constants, if necessary, so that the resulting coefficients for one of the variables are of equal magnitude and opposite in sign in the two respective equations.
>   (b) Add corresponding terms of the two equations.
> 2. Solve the resulting linear equation for the remaining variable.
> 3. Substitute the solution back into one of the original equations to find the value of the second variable.

This procedure is illustrated in the next example.

EXAMPLE 4   Find the point of intersection of the two lines $3x - 2y = 19$ and $2x + 5y = -19$.

Solution   **Step 1a** We multiply the first equation by 5 and the second by 2 to get

$$\begin{array}{r} 15x - 10y = 95 \\ 4x + 10y = -38 \end{array} \qquad \text{opposites}$$

Step 1b We then add the two equations to get

$$19x = 57$$

Step 2 Solving for x gives $x = 3$.

Step 3 We substitute $x = 3$ into the first of the given equations to obtain

$$3 \cdot 3 - 2y = 19$$
$$9 - 2y = 19$$
$$-2y = 10$$
$$y = -5$$

The point of intersection is thus $(3, -5)$. ∎

EXAMPLE 5 Solve the following system (if possible):

$$2x - y = 5$$
$$4x - 2y = 7$$

Solution **Step 1a** We multiply the first equation by -2 to obtain the system

$$-4x + 2y = -10$$
$$4x - 2y = 7$$

Step 1b Upon adding these two equations, we get the *impossible* result

$$0 = -3$$

Thus, the system has no solution. The lines represented by the two equations are parallel. ∎

Notice that the method of addition of the equations (used in Examples 4 and 5) will detect parallel lines as in Example 5 by arriving at an *impossible* result: $0 = $ a nonzero number.

EXAMPLE 6 Solve the following system (if possible):

$$2x - y = 5$$
$$4x - 2y = 10$$

Solution **Step 1a** We multiply the first equation by 2 to get

$$4x - 2y = 10$$

which is exactly the second equation. Thus, we see that the two equations represent the same line, and every solution of one of these equations satisfies the other. If we put $x = a$ in the first equation and then solve for y to get $y = 2a - 5$, we can write the general solution of the system as $(a, 2a - 5)$, where a is any real number. ∎

Exercise 6.5

A. In problems 1–6, find the solution of the given system by the graphical method.

1. $x + y = 3$; $2x - y = 0$ 2. $x + y = 5$; $x - 4y = 0$

3. $2x - y = 10$; $3x + 2y = 1$ 4. $2x - 3y = 1$; $x + 2y = 4$

5. $3x + 4y = 4$; $2x - 6y = 7$ 6. $y = 5x - 12$; $y = 3x - 8$

B. In problems 7–30, find the solution of the given system by the method of addition that was used in Examples 4 and 5. If there is no solution, state so.

7. $x + y = 3$; $2x - y = 0$ 8. $x + y = 5$, $x - 4y = 0$

9. $x + y = 6$; $3x - 2y = 8$ 10. $2x - y = 5$; $5x + 3y = 18$

11. $2x - y = 10$; $3x + 2y = 1$ 12. $2x - 3y = 1$; $x + 2y = 4$

13. $5x + y = 4$; $15x + 3y = 8$ 14. $2x - y = -5$; $4x - 2y = -10$

15. $2x + 5y = 12$; $5x - 3y = -1$ 16. $2x + 3y = 9$; $11x + 7y = 2$

17. $3x + 4y = 4$; $2x - 6y = 7$ 18. $y = 5x - 12$; $y = 3x - 8$

19. $11x + 3 = -3y$; $5x + 2y = 5$ 20. $10x + 6y = 1$; $5x = 9 - 3y$

21. $x = 2y - 3$; $x = -2y - 1$ 22. $y = 4x - 2$; $4x = 2y + 3$

23. $2x + 3y + 11 = 0$; $5x + 6y + 20 = 0$

24. $3x + y = 4$; $2x = 4y - 9$ 25. $3x - 12y = -8$; $2x + 2y = 3$

26. $4x + 8y = 7$; $3x + 4y = 6$ 27. $r - 4s = -10$; $2r - 8s = 13$

28. $3r + 4s = 15$; $4r - s = 20$ 29. $6u - 2v = -27$; $4u + 3v = 8$

30. $8w - 13z = 3z + 4$; $12w - 3 = 18z$

31. Company A will cater a banquet for x guests at a cost of y dollars where

$$y = 8x + 1000.$$

For company B the cost is

$$y = 10x + 800.$$

(a) Use the method of addition to find the number of guests for which the two costs are equal.

(b) Graph the two equations on the same set of axes from $x = 0$ to $x = 200$.

(c) For which company is the cost less if there are more than the number of guests you found in part (a)?

32. A solar hot water heating system requires an initial investment of $5400 and an annual cost of $50. An electric hot water heating system requires an initial investment of $1,000 and an annual cost of $600. Let y dollars be the total cost at the end of x years.
    (a) Write an equation giving the total cost of the solar heating system.
    (b) Write an equation giving the total cost of the electric heating system.
    (c) Graph the two equations you found in parts (a) and (b) on the same set of axes from $x = 0$ to $x = 10$.
    (d) Use the method of addition to solve the system of equations.
    (e) How long will it take for the total cost of the solar heat to become less than the total cost of the electric heat?

33. The supply y of a certain item is given by the equation $y = 2x + 8$, where x is the number of days elapsed. If the demand is given by $y = 4x$, in how many days will the supply equal the demand?

34. The supply of a certain item is $y = 3x + 8$, where x is the number of days elapsed. If the demand is given by $y = 4x$, in how many days will the supply equal the demand?

35. A company has 10 units of a certain item and can manufacture 5 items each day. If the demand for the items is $y = 7x$, where x is the number of days elapsed, in how many days will the demand equal the supply?

36. Clonker Manufacturing has 12 clonkers in stock. They manufacture 3 other clonkers each day. If the clonker demand is 7 each day, in how many days will the supply equal the demand?

*I*n Other Words

37. Describe the steps you would use in solving a system of two linear equations in two unknowns by graphing.

38. Write a word problem that will have the system of equations

$$x + 2y = 20$$

$$x - y = 5$$

as a model.

Using Your Knowledge

Linear systems can sometimes be used to solve word problems. Here is an illustration. Suzie has 15 coins, all nickels and dimes, in a peculiar combination. If the nickels were quarters and the dimes were nickels, the amount of money that Suzie has would be unchanged. How many of each coin does she have?

If we let x be the number of nickels and y be the number of dimes that Suzie has, then we see that $x + y = 15$, the total number of coins. Furthermore, the amount of money she has is $(5x + 10y)$ cents. Now, if the nickels *were quarters and the dimes were nickels, the amount would be (25x + 5y) cents. The problem says that the amount would be unchanged, so we must have*

$$25x + 5y = 5x + 10y$$

or

$$20x - 5y = 0 \qquad \text{By subtracting 5x and 10y from both sides}$$

and

$$4x - y = 0 \qquad \text{By dividing both sides by 5}$$

Thus, we have the system

$$x + y = 15$$
$$4x - y = 0$$

By adding the equations, term by term, we obtain

$$5x = 15 \quad \text{or} \quad x = 3$$

If x = 3 is substituted into the first equation, it gives 3 + y = 15, or y = 12. Hence Suzie has 3 nickels and 12 dimes. (You can check that 3 quarters and 12 nickels will give the same amount of money.)

Try to use these ideas to solve the following problems.

39. Ronnie has $2.95 in nickels and dimes. If the nickels were dimes and the dimes were nickels, Ronnie would have exactly $1.00 more. How many of each coin does he have?

40. Josie has invested $10,000 in two types of bonds. Type A pays a 7% dividend and type B pays a 6% dividend. If the total dividend amounts to $640, how much has Josie invested in each type of bond?

41. A bank has a $10 monthly service charge plus 10¢ per check written. A second bank charges $20 per month plus 6¢ per check. Find the number of checks that have to be written so that the cost is the same in both banks.

42. Tickets for a dance were sold to men for $3 and to women for $2. If 130 tickets were sold for $340, how many of each were sold?

43. Admission to a certain movie was $2.50 for adults and $1.50 for children. If 300 tickets were sold for a total of $550, how many adult tickets and how many children's tickets were sold?

Computer Corner

*The Solving Systems of Equations program will solve a system of two or three linear equations when you enter the **coefficients** of the variables and the numbers to the right of the equal signs. Note that in Example 3, you must enter a 1 for the coefficients of x and y in x + y = 5. If the system has **infinitely many solutions** or **no solution**, the computer replies, "I can't solve this one."*

44. Try the odd-numbered problems from 7 to 29 in Exercise 6.5.

6.6   LINEAR INEQUALITIES

GETTING STARTED

RHYME AND REASON

Do you like poetry? Perhaps you will understand the graphing of inequalities if we do it in verse.

How to Graph a Linear Inequality, by Julie Ashmore[*]

Look here, my children, and you shall see
How to graph an inequality.
Here's a simple inequality to try:
x plus 2 is less than *y*. $x + 2 < y$
First, make the "less than" "equal to";
So now *y* equals *x* plus 2. $y = x + 2$
Then pick a point for *x*: say, 10;
Now plug that single constant in.
Add 10 plus 2 and you'll get *y*; $x = 10, y = 10 + 2$
See if this pair will satisfy!
x: 10, *y*: 12; you'll find it's right,   (10, 12)
So graph this point to expedite.
Now find a second ordered pair   See the figure.
That fits in your equation there.
x: 3, *y*: 5 will do quite well.   (3, 5)
And it's correct, as you can tell
Plot this point, and then you've got
To draw a line from dot to dot.   See the figure.
Make it neat and make it straight;
A ruler's edge I'd advocate.
The next step's hard! You've got to choose
Which side of this line you must use.
Change "equal to" back to "less than," $x + 2 < y$
Just as it was when you began.
Pick a point on one side! I
Use 3 for *x* and 1 for *y*.   (3, 1)
Is 1 greater than 3 plus 2?
No! This side will never do! $3 + 2 \not< 1$
On the other side, let's try
1 for *x* and 4 for *y*.   (1, 4)
1 plus 2 (which equals 3)
Is less than 4, as you can see. $1 + 2 = 3 < 4$
Shade in the side that dot is on;
We've one more step to come upon.   See the figure.
Do the points upon your line
Fit the equation I assigned?
Use 1 and 3 for this last test;   (1, 3)
They're "equal to," but they're not "less."
Make your line dotted to show this is true. $1 + 2 = 3$
And that is *all* you have to do!   See the figure.

*Julie Ashmore was a young student in the John Burroughs School in St. Louis, Missouri, when she wrote this verse.

In this section we want to discover how to graph a relation in which the rule is a linear inequality, that is, an inequality of the type $ax + by + c \geq 0$.

A. *Graphing Linear Inequalities*

Let us look at the relation $\{(x, y) \mid 2x + 3y - 6 \geq 0\}$. We already know how to graph the straight line $2x + 3y = 6$, and this is a big start on our present problem. Figure 6.11 shows the graph of the straight line and several points not on the line. We know that any point on the line has coordinates (x, y) such that $2x + 3y - 6 = 0$. In Table 6.3 we have evaluated the linear expression $2x + 3y - 6$ and compared it with 0 at each of the points in the figure. Notice that for all the points on one side of the line, $2x + 3y - 6$ is less than 0 (negative), and for all points on the other side of the line, $2x + 3y - 6$ is greater than 0 (positive). These results lead us to guess that $2x + 3y - 6 < 0$ for all points below the line and that $2x + 3y - 6 > 0$ for all points above the line. This guess is correct; it is a fact that all the points above the line do satisfy the inequality $2x + 3y - 6 > 0$, and no points below the line satisfy this inequality. We shall not prove this. The shaded region in Figure 6.11 plus the line $2x + 3y = 6$ is the graph of the relation $\{(x, y) \mid 2x + 3y - 6 \geq 0\}$.

Table 6.3

Point	$2x + 3y - 6$
$(1, 3)$	$5 > 0$
$(3, 3)$	$9 > 0$
$(4, 1)$	$5 > 0$
$(-3, 1)$	$-9 < 0$
$(0, 0)$	$-6 < 0$
$(-2, -2)$	$-16 < 0$
$(3, -1)$	$-3 < 0$

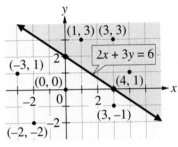

FIGURE 6.11
$\{(x, y) \mid 2x + 3y - 6 \geq 0\}$

We know that a straight line in a plane divides the plane into three sets of points, the line itself and the two **half-planes,** one half-plane on one side and the other half-plane on the other side of the line. We regard the line as belonging to neither half-plane. The two half-planes are disjoint sets; no point of one set is shared by the other set. Geometrically speaking, we cannot connect a point in one half-plane and a point in the other half-plane by a continuous line (or curve) in the plane without crossing the line that separates one half-plane from the other. It is proved in more advanced mathematics that this intuitive geometric fact has an important algebraic counterpart, namely: **If an equation of the line is $ax + by = c$, then for every point in one half-plane, the linear expression $ax + by - c$ is positive (> 0), and for every point in the other half-plane, $ax + by - c$ is negative (< 0).**

This result makes it quite easy to graph a linear inequality, as shown next.

Problem Solving: Graphing Linear Inequalities

Graph the linear inequality $2x < 3y - 6$.

1. Read the problem.
2. Select the unknown.

We need to find the solution set for the linear inequality $2x < 3y - 6$, that is, find its graph.

3. Think of a plan.
First, graph $2x = 3y - 6$. Select a test point and check to see if it satisfies the inequality.

We start by graphing $2x = 3y - 6$. When $x = 0$, then $y = 2$, so graph $(0, 2)$. When $y = 0$, then $x = -3$, so graph $(-3, 0)$. Join $(0, 2)$ and $(-3, 0)$ with a **dotted** line, since the graph of $2x = 3y - 6$ is not actually part of the solution set. To find the points satisfying $2x < 3y - 6$, find out if $(0, 0)$ satisfies $2x < 3y - 6$.

4. Use the test point to find the solution set.
What do you have to do after you check to see if the test point satisfies the inequality $2x < 3y - 6$?

When $x = 0$ and $y = 0$, $2x < 3y - 6$ becomes

$$2 \cdot 0 < 3 \cdot 0 - 6$$

or

$$0 < -6$$

which is false. Thus, $(0, 0)$ and all points below the line $2x = 3y - 6$ are *not* in the solution set of $2x < 3y - 6$, The solution set must consist of all points *above* the line $2x = 3y - 6$. Remember that to emphasize the fact that points on the line $2x = 3y - 6$ are *not* part of the solution set, the line itself is shown dashed.

5. Verify the solution.

The verification that the points in the shaded region satisfy the inequality $2x < 3y - 6$ is left to the student.

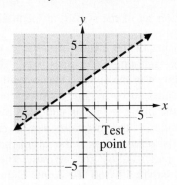

TRY EXAMPLE 1 NOW.   Cover the solution, write your own, and then check your work.

Example 1 illustrates the solution of an inequality that involves the less than or equal to sign. Notice carefully that the line corresponding to the equals sign is a part of the solution and is drawn solid in the graph.

EXAMPLE 1   Graph the linear inequality $3x - 4y \leq 12$.

Solution   We first draw the graph of the line $3x - 4y = 12$ (see the figure). We know that our answer requires one of the half-planes determined by this line. To find which of the half-planes is required, we may select any point not on the line and check whether it satisfies the original inequality. If the origin is not on the line, then $(0, 0)$ is a good choice, because it is so easy to check. Does $(0, 0)$ satisfy the inequality $3x - 4y \leq 12$? Yes, because $3(0) - 4(0) = 0 < 12$. Thus, the half-plane containing $(0, 0)$ is the one we need. This half-plane is shaded in the figure.

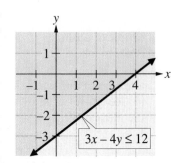

■

B. *Solving Systems of Inequalities by Graphing*

The solution set of a system of linear inequalities in two variables can often be found as in the next example, where the individual inequalities are first solved separately and then the final shading shows the intersection of these solution sets. This intersection is the solution set of the system.

EXAMPLE 2   Graph the solution set of the system of inequalities $-2 \leq x \leq 3$.

Solution   Our system consists of the inequalities $-2 \leq x$ and $x \leq 3$. We first graph the lines $x = -2$ and $x = 3$ as shown in the figure. The inequality $-2 \leq x$ is satisfied by all the points on or to the right of the line $x = -2$ as indicated by the arrows. Similarly, the inequality $x \leq 3$ is satisfied by all the points on or to the left of the line $x = 3$ as indicated by the arrows. The given system is satisfied by all the points common to these two regions, that is, all the points on either line or between the two lines. The solution set is shown shaded in the figure.

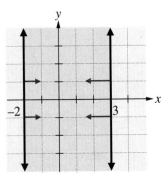

■

EXAMPLE 3　Graph the solution set of the system of inequalities

$$x + 2y \leq 5$$
$$x - y < 2$$

Solution　We first graph the lines $x + 2y = 5$ and $x - y = 2$, as shown in the figure. The inequality $x + 2y \leq 5$ is satisfied by the points *on or below* the line $x + 2y = 5$, as indicated by the arrows attached to the line. The inequality $x - y < 2$ is satisfied by the points *above* the line $x - y = 2$, as indicated by the arrows attached to the line. This line is drawn dashed to indicate that the points on it do *not* satisfy the inequality $x - y < 2$. The solution set of the system is shown in the figure by the shaded region and the portion of the solid line forming one boundary of this region. The point of intersection of the two lines is *not* in the solution set.

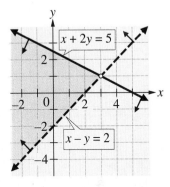

We can also graph the solution set of a system consisting of more than two inequalities, as illustrated by the next example.

EXAMPLE 4　Graph the solution set of the system of inequalities.

$$x + 2y \leq 6$$
$$3x + 2y < 10$$
$$x \geq 0$$
$$y \geq 0$$

Solution　We first graph the lines $x + 2y = 6$, $3x + 2y = 10$, $x = 0$, $y = 0$, as in the figure. The inequality $x + 2y \leq 6$ is satisfied by the set of points on or below the line $x + 2y = 6$, as indicated by the arrows attached to the line. The inequality $3x + 2y < 10$ is satisfied by the set of points below the line $3x + 2y = 10$. Notice that this line is drawn dashed to show that it does not satisfy the given inequality. The set of inequalities $x \geq 0$ and $y \geq 0$ is satisfied by points in the first quadrant or points on the portions of the axes bounding the first quadrant. The solution set of the system can easily be identified; it is the shaded region plus the solid portions of the boundary lines.

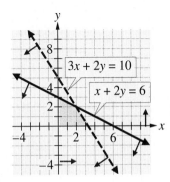

EXAMPLE 5   Graph the solution set of the system of inequalities $x + 1 \geq 0$ or $y - 2 \leq 0$.

Solution   We first graph the lines $x + 1 = 0$ and $y - 2 = 0$ as shown in the figure. The inequality $x + 1 \geq 0$ is satisfied by the points on or to the right of the line $x + 1 = 0$ as indicated by the arrows attached to this line. The inequality $y - 2 \leq 0$ is satisfied by the points on or below the line $y - 2 = 0$ as indicated by the arrows attached to this line. Since this is an "or" set of inequalities, the solution consists of all the points that are on or to the right of the line $x + 1 = 0$ and all the points that are on or below the line $y - 2 = 0$. The shaded region in the figure shows this set of points.

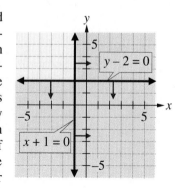

■

C. Applications

In Section 6.1, we mentioned the target zone used to gauge your effort when performing aerobic exercises. This target zone is determined by your pulse rate p and your age a and is found in the next example.

EXAMPLE 6   The target zone for aerobic exercise is defined by the following inequalities, in which a is the age in years and p is the pulse rate:

$$10 \leq a \leq 70$$

$$p \geq -\tfrac{2}{3}a + 150 \qquad \text{Lower limit}$$

$$p \leq -a + 190 \qquad \text{Upper limit}$$

Graph these inequalities and label the resulting target zone.

Solution   Since a is between 10 and 70, inclusive, it is convenient to label the horizontal axis starting at 10, using 10-unit intervals, and ending at 70. The vertical axis is used for the pulse rate p, and we start at 70 (the normal pulse rate) and go up to 200, as shown in the figure. We then graph the line $p = -\tfrac{2}{3}a + 150$ after finding the two points (30, 130) and (60, 110). Notice that because of the $-\tfrac{2}{3}a$, values of a that are divisible by 3 are most convenient to use. The inequality $p \geq -\tfrac{2}{3}a + 150$

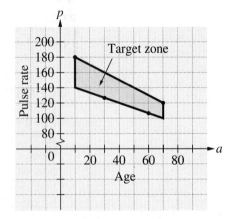

is satisfied for all points that are *on or above* this line. Next, we graph the line $p = -a + 190$. Two points easy to find on this line are (10, 180) and (70, 120). The inequality $p \leq -a + 190$ is satisfied by all points that are *on or below* this line. The target zone is shaded in the figure.   ■

Exercise 6.6

A. Graph the linear inequalities in problems 1–10.

1. $x + 2y \geq 2$	2. $x - 2y > 0$	3. $x \leq 4$
4. $y \leq 3$	5. $3x - y < 6$	6. $3x + 4y \geq 12$
7. $2x + y \leq 4$	8. $2x - 3y < 0$	9. $4x + y > 8$
10. $x - 4y \leq 4$		

B. In problems 11–26, graph the solution set of the system of inequalities.

11. $-4 \leq x < 3$	12. $2 \leq y \leq 5$
13. $x \leq -1 \ or \ x > 1$	14. $y < 0 \ or \ y > 3$
15. $x - y \geq 2; x + y \leq 6$	16. $x + 2y \leq 3; x \leq y$
17. $2x - 3y \leq 6; 4x - 3y \geq 12$	18. $2x - 5y \leq 10; 3x + 2y \leq 6$
19. $2x - 3y \leq 5; x \geq y; y \geq 0$	20. $x \leq 2y; 2x \geq y; x + y < 4$
21. $x + 3y \leq 6; x \geq 0; y \geq 0$	22. $2x - y \leq 2; y \geq 1; x \geq \frac{1}{2}$

23. $x \geq 1; y \geq 1; x - y \leq 1; 3y - x < 3$
24. $x - y \geq -2; x + y \leq 6; x \geq 1; y \geq 1$
25. $x + y \geq 1; x \leq 2; y \geq 0; y \leq 1$
26. $1 < x + y < 8; x < 5; y < 5$

In problems 27–30, select the set of conditions (a) or (b) that corresponds to the shaded region in the given figure.

27.

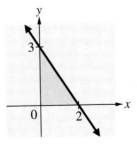

(a) $3x + 2y \leq 6, x \leq 2$
    and $y \leq 3$
(b) $3x + 2y \leq 6, x \geq 0$
    and $y \geq 0$

28.

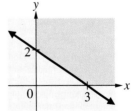

(a) $2x + 3y \geq 6, x \geq 3$
    and $y \geq 2$
(b) $2x + 3y \geq 6, x \geq 0$
    and $y \geq 0$

29.

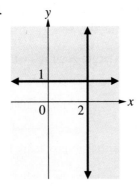

(a) $x \geq 2$ or $y \geq 1$
(b) $x \geq 2$ and $y \geq 1$

30.

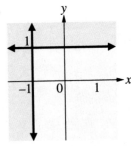

(a) $x \leq -1$ and $y \geq 1$
(b) $x \leq -1$ or $y \geq 1$

31. Which shaded region corresponds to the set of inequalities $x + y \geq 1$ and $x - y \leq 1$?

(a)

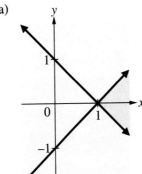

(b)

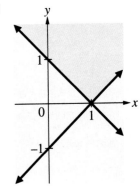

(c)

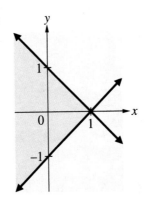

(d)

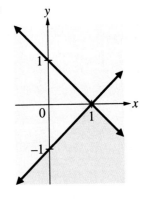

32. Write the set of inequalities that corresponds to the shaded region in the figure. Explain.

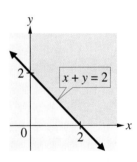

C. 33. The desirable weight range corresponding to a given height for a man is shown in Table 6.1. We found the equation for the lower weights in terms of the height to be $w = 4h - 140$. The equation for the upper weights is $w = 5h - 176$. Thus, the desirable weights for men from 62 to 76 inches in height satisfy the system of inequalities

$$62 \leq h \leq 76$$

$$w \geq 4h - 140$$

$$w \leq 5h - 176$$

Graph this system of inequalities and shade the region corresponding to the range of desirable weights. Be sure to take the horizontal axis as the h axis.

34. The desirable weight range corresponding to a given height for a woman is also shown in Table 6.1. The equation for the lower weights in terms of the height h is $w = 4h - 150$ and for the upper weights is $w = 5h - 187$. Thus, the desirable weights for women from 62 to 72 inches in height satisfy the system of inequalities

$$62 \leq h \leq 72$$

$$w \geq 4h - 150$$

$$w \leq 5h - 187$$

Graph this system of inequalities and shade the region corresponding to the range of desirable weights. Be sure to take the horizontal axis as the h axis.

In Other Words

35. Describe the steps you would take to graph the inequality $ax + by > c$.
36. Describe the graph of the inequality $y < mx + b$.
37. Describe the graph of the inequality $x \geq k$.
38. Describe the graph of the inequality $y < k$.

Using Your Knowledge

Suppose you want to find two integers x and y with y > 1 and such that the sum of the two integers is less than 10 and the difference 3x − 2y is greater than 6. Here is an easy way to find the possible pairs (x, y):

39. Graph the corresponding system of inequalities:

$$y > 1$$
$$x + y < 10$$
$$3x - 2y > 6$$

You should end up with a shaded region in the plane. Mark each integer point (point with integer coordinates) within this region, and then just read the coordinates. These are the possible pairs of integers.

40. Find all the pairs of integers (x, y) such that x is greater than 1, the sum of the two integers is less than 12, and the difference $2y - x$ is at least 8.

Discovery

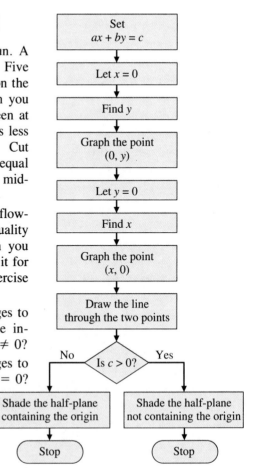

41. Here is a problem just for fun. A square is 2 in. on a side. Five points are marked inside or on the perimeter of the square. Can you show that the distance between at least two of the five points is less than or equal to $\sqrt{2}$? [*Hint:* Cut the square up into four equal squares by connecting the midpoints of the opposite sides.]

42. The figure to the right is a flowchart for graphing the inequality $ax + by > c$, $abc \neq 0$. Can you explain why this works? Try it for some of the problems in Exercise 6.6.

43. Can you discover what changes to make in the flowchart if the inequality is $ax + by < c$, $c \neq 0$?

44. Can you discover what changes to make in the flowchart if $c = 0$?

6.7 LINEAR PROGRAMMING

GETTING STARTED

"YOU WANT A COKE WITH THAT?"

Are you on a steady diet of burgers and fries? Are you also watching your fat and protein intake? A regular hamburger contains about 11 grams of fat and 12 grams of protein. Your daily consumption of fat and protein should be about 56 and 51 grams, respectively. (You can check this out in the *Fast Food Guide* by Jacobson and Fritschner.) Suppose that a regular hamburger costs 39 cents and regular fries are 79 cents. How many of each could you eat so that you meet the recommended fat and protein intake and, at the same time, minimize the cost? We enter the given information in the following table, where h and f represent the number of hamburgers and fries, respectively.

	Hamburgers	French Fries	Total
Fat (gm)	11	12	$11h + 12f$
Protein (gm)	12	3	$12h + 3f$
Cost (cents)	39	79	$39h + 79f$

Since the recommended amounts of fat and protein are 56 and 51 gm, respectively, we have the system of equations

$$11h + 12f = 56$$

$$12h + 3f = 51$$

In the first equation when $h = 0$, $f = 56/12 = 14/3$. Graph $(0, 14/3)$. When $f = 0$, $h = 56/11$. Graph $(56/11, 0)$. Join the two points with a line. Similarly, graph the second equation.

Now, look at the graph. The shaded region is called the **feasible region,** and the minimum or maximum for a linear function (such as the cost function given by $C = 39h + 79f$) occurs at one of the corner points. We first approximate $(0, 14/3)$ to $(0, 5)$ and then try each of the points.

For $(0, 5)$,

$$C = 39 \cdot 0 + 79 \cdot 5 = \$3.95$$

For $(0, 17)$,

$$C = 39 \cdot 0 + 79 \cdot 17 = \$13.43$$

For $(4, 1)$,

$$C = 39 \cdot 4 + 1 \cdot 79 = \$2.35$$

Thus, the most economical way to meet your fat and protein intake by eating hamburgers and fries is to eat 4 hamburgers and 1 order of fries for $2.35 (not necessarily all at once!)

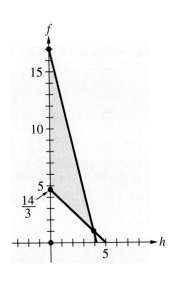

There are many problems that require us to find better ways of accomplishing a given objective. For example, there are many ways of conserving energy, but some of these ways are more costly than others. Consequently, we may be interested in minimizing the cost of our energy requirements. If the equations and inequalities involved in such a problem are linear, then we have a **linear programming problem.**

Most practical linear programming problems involve a large number of variables and are solved on a digital computer using a scheme known as the **simplex algorithm.** The simplex method of solving such problems was developed by George B. Dantzig in the late 1940s as a tool for the solution of some complex problems in allocating supplies for the U.S. Air Force. Linear programming problems are of great importance today in business and in the social sciences.

Although we shall not consider the simplex method, we shall solve some simple problems that illustrate the variety of applications of linear programming methods. The concepts we employ are basic even for the larger problems that are beyond the scope of this book.

As an example of a linear programming problem, let us assume that Sew & Sew, Inc. manufactures pants and vests. The profit on each pair of pants is $6 and on each vest is $5. The pants use 2 yd of material and the vests use 1.5 yd of material each. Because of production limitations, Sew & Sew can manufacture not more than 10 of these garments per day, and cannot use more than 18 yd of material per day. If Sew & Sew can sell all the pants and vests they make, find the number of each garment they should produce per day to **maximize their profit.**

One way of presenting a linear programming problem so that it is easier for our minds to grasp is to put the data into tabular form. For the Sew & Sew problem, we tabulate the data and make some minor calculations as shown in the table in the margin. We can now see that the total profit, say, P, is

	Pants	Vests
Number produced	x	y
Yards used	$2x$	$1.5y$
Profit $	$6x$	$5y$

$$P = 6x + 5y \text{ dollars}$$

Thus, P is a linear function of x and y, and we wish to determine x and y so that P has its maximum value.

Next, we must express the restrictions in the problem in terms of x and y. The first restriction is that Sew & Sew produce not more than 10 garments per day. Since they produce x pants and y vests, the total number of garments is $x + y$. Thus,

$$x + y \leq 10$$

A second restriction is that they use not more than 18 yd of material per day. This means that

$$2x + 1.5y \leq 18$$

Another restriction is that x and y cannot be negative. This gives the so-called **positivity conditions**

$$x \geq 0 \qquad y \geq 0$$

We can summarize our problem as follows: We want to maximize the linear function P given by

$$P = 6x + 5y$$

subject to the **constraints** (that is, the restrictions)

$$x + y \leq 10 \tag{1}$$

$$2x + 1.5y \leq 18 \tag{2}$$

$$x \geq 0 \qquad y \geq 0 \tag{3}$$

To make a start on the solution of this problem, we graph the solution set of the system of inequalities (1), (2), and (3), just as we did in the preceding section. This gives the shaded region in Figure 6.12. Each point (x, y) in this region represents a combination of garments that satisfies all the constraints. For this reason, the region is called the **feasible region.**

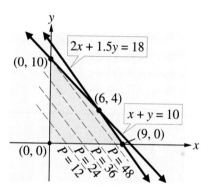

FIGURE 6.12

We need to select a point from the feasible region that will maximize the expression $6x + 5y$. In order to do this, let us examine the equation $6x + 5y = P$. For a given value of P, this is an equation of a straight line, which in slope–intercept form is

$$y = -\frac{6}{5}x + \frac{P}{5}$$

This equation shows that the slope is $-\frac{6}{5}$ regardless of the value of P. Hence, for a set of values of P, we get a set of parallel straight lines. Furthermore, for positive increasing values of P, the lines move out away from the origin. (This follows because the y intercept is $P/5$.) The dashed lines in Figure 6.12 are the graphs of $6x + 5y = P$ for the values $P = 12$, 24, 36, and 48. The smaller the value of P, the closer is the line to the origin.

These considerations make plausible the following basic theorem for feasible regions that are **convex** (nonreentrant) polygons, that is, regions such that the points of the line segment joining any two points on the boundary lie entirely inside the region or else on the boundary. See Figure 6.13.

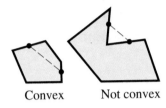

Convex   Not convex

FIGURE 6.13

Theorem 6.1 ————

If the feasible region is a convex (nonreentrant) polygon, then the desired maximum (or minimum) value of a linear function occurs at a corner point (vertex) of the region.

To make use of this theorem, we need only check the values of P at the vertices of the polygon. These vertices are indicated in Figure 6.12 and can, of course, be found by solving the appropriate pairs of linear equations. By direct calculation, we find the values in the table in the margin. Thus, Sew & Sew should produce 6 pants and 4 vests per day to maximize their profit.

Vertex	$P = 6x + 5y$	
(0, 0)	0	
(9, 0)	54	
(6, 4)	56	←— Max.
(0, 10)	50	

EXAMPLE 1 Little Abner raises ducks and geese. He is too lazy to take care of more than 30 birds altogether, but wants to make as much profit as possible (naturally). It costs him $1 to raise a duck and $1.50 to raise a goose, and he has only $40 to cover this cost. If Little Abner makes a profit of $1.50 on each duck and $2 on each goose, what is his maximum profit?

Solution Letting x and y be the number of ducks and geese, respectively, that Little Abner should raise, we tabulate the given information as follows:

	Ducks	Geese
Number	x	y
Cost	$1.00 each	$1.50 each
Profit	$1.50 each	$2.00 each
Total cost	$$x$	$1.5y$
Total profit	$1.5x$	$2y$

It appears that Little Abner's total profit from both ducks and geese is P, where

$$P = 1.5x + 2y$$

The constraints are (in the order stated in the problem):

$x + \quad y \le 30$ Too lazy to raise more than 30 birds   (4)

$x + 1.5y \le 40$ Has only \$40 to cover his costs   (5)

Although it is not stated, we must also obey the positivity conditions

$x \ge 0 \quad\quad \ge 0$ (6)

We proceed as before to find the feasible region by graphing the system of inequalities (4), (5), and (6), as shown in the figure. We then find the vertices and check them in the profit function:

Vertex	$P = 1.5x + 2y$
$(0, 0)$	0
$(30, 0)$	45
$(10, 20)$	55 ←Max.
$(0, \frac{80}{3})$	$53\frac{1}{3}$

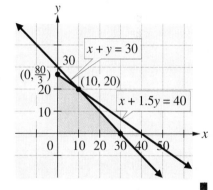

By raising 10 ducks and 20 geese, Little Abner will make the maximum possible profit, \$55.

If you have been thinking while studying the preceding problems, you have undoubtedly wondered what to do if the desired maximum (or minimum) occurs at a vertex with noninteger coordinates. In the case of two-variable problems, if the solution must be in integers, we can try the integer points inside the feasible region that are nearest to this vertex (see Getting Started) and select the point that gives the desired maximum (or minimum). For many-variable problems, more complicated techniques, which are beyond the scope of this book, must be used.

Exercise 6.7

1. Find the minimum value of $C = 2x + y$ subject to the constraints

$$x \ge 1$$
$$x \le 4$$
$$y \le 4$$
$$x - 3y \le -2$$

2. Find the maximum value of $P = x + 4y$ subject to the constraints
$$y - x \leq 0$$
$$x \leq 4$$
$$y \geq 0$$
$$x + 2y \leq 6$$

3. Find the minimum value of $W = 4x + y$ subject to the constraints
$$x + y \geq 1$$
$$2y - x \leq 1$$
$$x \leq 1$$

4. Find the minimum value of $C = 2x + 3y$ subject to the constraints
$$2x + y \geq 18$$
$$x + y \geq 12$$
$$3x + 2y \leq 34$$

5. Find the minimum value of $C = x + 2y$ subject to the constraints
$$8 \leq 3x + y \leq 10$$
$$x \geq 1$$
$$y \geq 2$$

6. Find the maximum value of $P = 2x + 3y$ subject to the constraints
$$y - x \leq 2$$
$$x + y \leq 4$$
$$0 \leq x \leq 3$$
$$y \geq 0$$

7. Find the maximum value of $P = x + 2y$ subject to the constraints
$$2x + y \geq 6$$
$$0 \leq y \leq 4$$
$$0 \leq x \leq 2$$

8. Find the maximum value of $P = 4x + 5y$ subject to the constraints
$$y - x \leq 2$$
$$x - y \leq 2$$
$$x + y \leq 6$$
$$x \geq 0$$
$$y \geq 0$$

9. The E-Z-Park storage lot can hold at most 100 cars and trucks. A car occupies 100 ft^2 and a truck 200 ft^2, and the lot has a usable area of 12,000 ft^2. The storage charge for a car is $20 per month and for a truck is $35 per month. How many of each should be stored to bring E-Z-Park the maximum revenue?

10. The Zig-Zag Manufacturing Company produces two products, zigs and zags. Each of these products has to be processed through all three machines, as shown in the table. If Zig-Zag makes $12 profit on each zig and $8 profit on each zag, find the number of each that the company should make in order to maximize its profit.

Machine	Hours Available	Hours/Piece Zigs	Zags
I	Up to 100	4	12
II	Up to 120	8	8
III	Up to 84	6	0

11. The Kwik-Pep Vitamin Company wishes to prepare two types of vitamin tablets. The first type of tablet contains

1 milligram (mg) of vitamin B_1
1 mg of vitamin B_2

while the second type of tablet contains

1 mg of vitamin B_1
2 mg of vitamin B_2

The profit on the two types of tablets is as follows:

2¢ for each tablet of the first type
3¢ for each tablet of the second type

In manufacturing two bottles of tablets, one of each type, but with the same number of tablets, Kwik-Pep wants to use no more than 100 mg of vitamin B_1 and 150 mg of vitamin B_2. How many tablets should be packed in each bottle to obtain the largest profit?

12. A nutritionist is designing a meal for one of her patients. The meal must include two vegetables, A and B, but not more than 100 gm of each. Suppose that each 10-gm portion of A contains 2 units of iron and 2 units of vitamin B_{12}, and each 10-gm portion of B contains 1 unit of iron and 5 units of vitamin B_{12}. The number of calories in each 10-gm portion of these vegetables is 5 for A and 3 for B. If the patient needs at least 20 units of iron and 36 units of vitamin B_{12} in the meal, how many grams of each vegetable should the nutritionist include to satisfy the iron and vitamin requirements while minimizing the number of calories in the meal?

13. The Jeri Tonic Company wishes to manufacture Jeri Tonic so that each bottle contains at least 32 units of vitamin A, 10 units of vitamin B, and 40 units of vitamin C. To supply the vitamins, the company uses additive X, which costs 20¢ per ounce and contains 16 units of vitamin A, 2 units of B, and 4 of C; and additive Y, which costs 40¢ per ounce and contains 4 units of vitamin A, 2 units of B, and 14 of C. If the total amount of additives is not to exceed 10 oz, how many ounces of each additive should the company put into each bottle to minimize its cost?

14. The Write-Right Paper Company operates two factories that manufacture three different grades of paper. There is a demand for each grade, and the company has contracts to supply 16 tons of low-grade, 5 tons of medium-grade, and 20 tons of high-grade paper, all in not more than 8 working days. It costs $1000 per day to operate the first factory and $2000 per day to operate the second factory. In one day's operation, factory number 1 produces 8 tons of low-grade, 1 ton of medium-grade, and 2 tons of high-grade paper, while factory number 2 produces 2 tons of low-grade, 1 ton of medium-grade, and 7 tons of high-grade paper. For how many days should Write-Right operate each factory in order to minimize its cost of filling these contracts?

15. Two oil refineries produce three grades of gasoline, A, B, and C. The refineries operate so that the various grades they produce are in a fixed proportion. Refinery I produces 1 unit of A, 3 units of B, and 1 unit of C per batch, and refinery II produces 1 unit of A, 4 units of B, and 5 units of C per batch. The price per batch is $300 from refinery I and $500 from refinery II. A dealer needs 100 units of A, 340 units of B, and 150 units of C. If the maximum number of batches he can get from either refinery is 100, how should he place his orders to minimize his cost?

16. A local television station is faced with a problem. It found that program A with 20 min of music and 1 min of commercials draws 30,000 viewers, while program B with 10 min of music and 1 min of commercials draws 10,000 viewers. The sponsor insists that at least 6 min per week be devoted to his commercials, and the station can afford no more than 80 min of music per week. How many times per week should each program be run to obtain the maximum number of viewers?

17. A fruit dealer ships her fruit north on a truck that holds 800 boxes of fruit. She must ship at least 200 boxes of oranges, which net her 20¢ profit per box; at least 100 boxes of grapefruit, which net her 10¢ profit per box; and at most 200 boxes of tangerines, which net her 30¢ profit per box. How should she load the truck for maximum profit? [*Hint:* If she ships x boxes of oranges and y boxes of grapefruit, then she ships $800 - x - y$ boxes of tangerines.]

18. Mr. Jones has a maximum of $15,000 to invest in two types of bonds. Bond *A* returns 8% and bond *B* returns 10% per year. Because bond *B* is not as safe as bond *A*, Jones decides that his investment in bond *B* will not exceed 40% of his investment in bond *A* by more than $1,000. How much should he invest at each rate to obtain the maximum number of dollars in interest per year?

19. Growfast Nursery is adding imported fruit trees and oriental shrubs to its existing line of nursery products. The trees yield a profit of $6 each, and the shrubs a profit of $7 each. The trees require 2 ft^2 of display space per tree, and the shrubs require 3 ft^2 per shrub. In addition, it takes 2 min to prepare a tree for display, and 1 min to prepare a shrub. The space and time constraints are as follows:
(a) At most 12 ft^2 of display space is available.
(b) At most 8 min of preparation time is available.
If Growfast can sell all the trees and shrubs it displays, how many trees and how many shrubs should Growfast display each day to maximize its profit? (Assume that it is possible to arrange a display only once per day.)

20. The Excelsior Mining Company operates two mines, EMC no. 1 and EMC no. 2. EMC no. 1 produces 20 tons of lead ore and 30 tons of low-grade silver ore per day of operation. EMC no. 2 produces 15 tons of lead ore and 35 tons of low-grade silver ore per day of operation. Lead ore sells for $14 per ton and low-grade silver ore sells for $34 per ton. The company can sell at most 630 tons of the low-grade silver ore per month, but it can sell all the lead ore it produces. However, there is no space available for stockpiling any silver ore. The company employs one crew and operates only one of the mines at a time. Furthermore, union regulations stipulate that the crew not be worked in excess of 20 days per month. How many days per month should Excelsior schedule for each mine so that the income from the sale of the ore is a maximum?

21. The ABC Fruit Juice Company wants to make an orange–grapefruit drink and is concerned with the vitamin content. The company plans to use orange juice that has 2 units of vitamin A, 3 units of vitamin C, and 1 unit of vitamin D per ounce, and grapefruit juice that has 3 units of vitamin A, 2 units of vitamin C, and 1 unit of vitamin D per ounce. Each can of the orange–grapefruit drink is to contain not more than 15 oz and is to have at least 26 units of vitamin A, 30 units of vitamin C, and 12 units of vitamin D. If the per-ounce cost of the orange juice is 4¢ and of the grapefruit juice is 3¢:
(a) How many ounces of each should be put into a can if the total cost of the can is as low as possible?
(b) What is the minimum cost per can?
(c) What is the vitamin content per can?

22. Joey likes a mixture of Grape-nuts, Product 19, and Raisin Bran for his breakfast. Here is some information about these cereals (each quantitiy in the table is per ounce):

	Grape-nuts	Product 19	Raisin Bran
Calories	100	110	90
Fat	1 gm	0	1gm
Sodium	195 mg	325 mg	170 mg

Joey is on a low-sodium diet and tries to make up 12 oz of the mixture so that the number of calories is at least 1,200 but not over 1,500, the total amount of fat is not more than 10 gm, and the sodium content is minimized. Can he do it? If so, what are the per-ounce quantities of calories, fat, and sodium in his mixture? [*Hint:* If he uses x oz of Grape-nuts and y oz of Product 19, then he must use $12 - x - y$ oz of Raisin Bran.]

*I*n Other Words

In a linear programming problem, describe in your own words what is meant by:

23. (a) Constraint
    (b) Feasible region

24. (a) Positivity condition
    (b) Convex polygon

Discovery

25. Suppose there is a championship prize fight. Gary the Gambler is tired of losing money and wants to hedge his bets so as to win at least $100 on the fight. Gary finds two gambling establishments: A, where the odds are 5 to 3 in favor of the champion, and B, where the odds are 2 to 1 in favor of the champion. What is the least total amount of money that Gary can bet, and how should he place it to be sure of winning at least $100? You can do this as a linear programming problem. First, let x dollars be placed on the champion to win with A, and y dollars on the challenger to win with B. Then, verify the following:
    (a) If the champion wins, Gary wins $\frac{3}{5}x$ dollars and loses y dollars, for a net gain of $(\frac{3}{5}x - y)$ dollars.
    (b) If the challenger wins, then Gary loses x dollars and wins $2y$ dollars, for a net gain of $(-x + 2y)$ dollars.

(c) The problem now is to minimize $x + y$ subject to the constraints

$$\tfrac{3}{5}x - y \geq 100$$
$$-x + 2y \geq 100$$
$$x \geq 0$$
$$y \geq 0$$

Solve this problem.

26. Show that there is no feasible region if Gary reverses his bets and places x dollars on the challenger to win with A, and y dollars on the champion to win with B.

Chapter 6 Summary

Section	Item	Meaning	Example
6.1	Relation	A set of ordered pairs	$S = \{(3, 2), (5, 2), (7, 4)\}$.
6.1A	Domain	The set of all possible x values of a relation	The domain of S is $\{3, 5, 7\}$.
6.1A	Range	The set of all possible y values of a relation	The range of S is $\{2, 4\}$.
6.1B	Function	A relation such that to each domain value there corresponds exactly one range value	$\{(x, y) \mid y = 2x\}$
6.1C	$f(x)$	Function notation	$f(x) = 3x + 2$
6.2A	Graph of a relation	The set of points corresponding to the ordered pairs of a relation	
6.2C	$[\![x]\!]$	The greatest integer $\leq x$	$[\![2.59]\!] = 2$; $[\![-2.59]\!] = -3$
6.3A	x intercept	x coordinate of the point where the line crosses the x axis ($y = 0$)	The x intercept of $y = 2x - 4$ is 2.

Section	Item	Meaning	Example
6.3A	y intercept	y coordinate of the point where the line crosses the y axis ($x = 0$)	The y intercept of $y = 2x - 4$ is -4.
6.3B	Linear equation	An equation that can be written in the form $ax + by = c$	$3x + 5y = -2$; $3y = 2x - 1$
6.3D	Distance formula	$d = \sqrt{(x_2 - x_1)^2 + (y_2 - y_1)^2}$	The distance between $(3, 5)$ and $(5, 12)$ is $\sqrt{53}$.
6.4A	Slope of a line	$m = \dfrac{y_2 - y_1}{x_2 - x_1}$	The slope of the line through $(3, 5)$ and $(5, 12)$ is $\frac{7}{2}$.
6.4B	Point–slope equation	$y - y_1 = m(x - x_1)$	$y - 5 = \frac{7}{2}(x - 3)$ is the point–slope equation of the line described above.
6.4B	Slope–intercept equation	$y = mx + b$ (m is the slope, b is the y intercept)	
6.4B	General equation of a line	$Ax + By = C$	
6.4C	Parallel lines	Two lines with the same slope and different y intercepts	$y = 2x + 5$ and $y = 2x - 3$ are equations of parallel lines.
6.7	Convex polygon	A nonreentrant polygon	

Research Questions

Sources of information for most of these questions can be found in the Bibliography at the end of the book.

1. Some historians claim that the official birthday of analytic geometry is November 10, 1619. Investigate and write a report on why this is so and the events that led Descartes to the discovery of analytic geometry.

2. Find out what led Descartes to make his famous pronouncement "*Je pense, donc je suis*" (I think, therefore I am) and write a report about the contents of one of his works, *La Geometrie*.

3. She was nineteen, a capable ruler, a good classicist, a remarkable athlete, an expert hunter and horsewoman. Find out who this queen was and what connections she had with Descartes.

4. Upon her arrival at the University of Stockholm, one newspaper reporter wrote "Today we do not herald the arrival of some vulgar, insignificant prince of noble blood. No, the Princess of Science has honored our city with her arrival." Write a report identifying this woman and discussing the circumstances leading to her arrival in Sweden.

5. When she was six years old, the "princess's" room was decorated with a unique type of wallpaper. Write a paragraph about this wallpaper and its influence on her career.

6. In 1888, the "princess" won the Prix Bordin offered by the French Academy of Sciences. Write a report about the contents of her prize-winning essay and the motto that accompanied it.

7. Write a report on the simplex algorithm and its developer.

Chapter 6 Practice Test

1. Find the domain and range of the relation

$$R = \{(5, 3), (3, -1), (2, 2), (0, 4)\}$$

2. Find the domain and range of the relation

$$R = \{(x, y) \mid y = -3x\}$$

3. Find the domain and range of the relation

$$R = \{(x, y) \mid y \geq x, x \text{ and } y \text{ are positive integers less than 5}\}$$

4. Which of the following relations are functions?
   (a) $\{(x, y) \mid y^2 = x\}$
   (b) $\{(3, 1), (4, 1), (6, 1)\}$
   (c) $\{(x, y) \mid y = x^2\}$

5. A function is defined by $f(x) = x^2 - x$. Find:
   (a) $f(0)$
   (b) $f(1)$
   (c) $f(-2)$

6. For a car renting for $15 per day plus 10¢ per mile, the cost for 1 day is

$$C(m) = 15 + 0.10m \text{ dollars}$$

where m is the number of miles driven. If a person paid $35.30 for 1 day's rental, how far did the person drive?

7. Graph the relation

$$R = \{(x, y) \mid y = 3x, x \text{ is an integer between } -1 \text{ and } 3, \text{ inclusive}\}$$

8. Graph the relation

$$Q = \{(x, y) \mid x + y < 3, x \text{ and } y \text{ are nonnegative integers}\}$$

9. Graph the function defined by $g(x) = 2x^2 - 1$, x is an integer and $-2 \leq x \leq 2$.

10. Graph the function defined by $f(x) = 2x - 6$.

11. Graph the equation $3x - 2y = 5$.

12. Find the distance between the two given points:
    (a) $(4, 7)$ and $(7, 3)$
    (b) $(-3, 8)$ and $(-3, -2)$

13. Determine whether the triangle with vertices at $A(2, 0)$, $B(4, 4)$, and $C(1, 3)$ is a right triangle.

14. (a) Find the slope of the line that goes through the two points $(-1, -3)$ and $(9, -2)$.
    (b) Find the general equation of the line in part (a).

15. (a) Find the slope–intercept form of the equation of the line that goes through the point $(3, -1)$ and has slope of -2.
    (b) Find the slope–intercept form of the equation $2y = 4 - 8x$. What is the slope and what is the y intercept of the line?

16. Determine whether the two given lines are parallel. If they are not parallel, find the coordinates of the point of intersection.
    (a) $2x + y = 1$; $12x + 3y = 4$
    (b) $y = 2x - 5$; $4x - 2y = 7$

17. Find the general equation of the line that passes through the point $(1, -2)$ and is parallel to the line $2x - 3y = -5$.

18. Find the point of intersection of the lines

$$3x + 2y = 9 \quad \text{and} \quad 2x - 3y = 19$$

19. Graph the solution set of the inequality $4x - 3y \le 12$.

20. Graph the solution set of the system of inequalities

$$x + 3y \le 6 \quad \text{and} \quad x - y \ge 2$$

21. Graph the solution set of the system of inequalities

$$x + 2y \le 3$$

$$x \le y$$

$$x \ge 0$$

22. Solve the following system if possible. If not possible, explain why.

$$y = 2x - 3$$

$$6x - 3y = 9$$

23. Find the maximum value of $C = x + 2y$ subject to the constraints

$$3x + y \leq 8$$
$$x \leq 1$$
$$y \geq 2$$
$$x \geq 0$$

24. Find the minimum value (if possible) of $P = 3y - 2x$ subject to the constraints

$$y - x \leq 2$$
$$x + y \leq 4$$
$$x \leq 3$$
$$x \geq 0$$
$$y \geq 0$$

25. Two machines produce the same item. Machine A can produce 10 items per hour and machine B can produce 12 items per hour. At least 420 of the items must be produced each 40-hr week, but the machines cannot be operated at the same time. If it costs \$20/hr to operate A and \$25/hr to operate B, determine how many hours are required per week to operate each machine in order to meet the production requirement at minimum machine cost.

This chapter is devoted to the study of **geometry.** The word *geometry* literally means earth (*geo*) measurements (*metry*). You might have studied geometry in the past as a collection of theorems and proofs. We will not do that here. Instead, we will concentrate on measurements involving *linear*, *square*, and *cubic* units.

We start with some undefined terms (points, lines, planes), see how they relate to each other, and use linear measures to measure distances and perimeters of many-sided figures called **polygons.** We then discuss how to measure and classify *angles* by their measures, and we classify triangles by the number of equal sides they contain. We will relate these ideas to many other topics, including motorcycle riding, satellite trajectories, angles formed by veins in leaves, and traffic signs.

We study *similar* triangles, *similar* figures, and *circumferences* of circles and their many applications: hat sizes, ring sizes, and so on. We then study *areas* of polygons (squares, rectangles, parallelograms, and triangles) and circles and the Pythagorean theorem. Next, we look at *surface area* and *volumes* of three-dimensional objects such as cubes, cylinders, cones, pyramids, and spheres and end the chapter with a classic problem, called the Bridges of Königsberg, solved by Leonhard Euler in 1736.

THE HUMAN SIDE OF MATHEMATICS

One of the most famous mathematicians of all time is Euclid, who taught in about 300 B.C. at the university in Alexandria, the main Egyptian seaport. Unfortunately, very little is known about Euclid personally; even his birthdate and birthplace are unknown. However, two stories about him seem to have survived. One concerns the Emperor Ptolemy, who asked if there was no easy way to learn geometry and received Euclid's reply, "There is no royal road to geometry." The other story is about a student who studied geometry under Euclid and, when he had mastered the first theorem, asked, "But what shall I get by learning these things?" Euclid called a slave and said, "Give him a penny, since he must make gain from what he learns."

Geometry evolved from the more or less rudimentary ideas of the ancient Egyptians (about 1500 B.C.), who were concerned with practical problems involving measurement of areas and volumes. The Egyptians were satisfied with the geometry that was needed to construct buildings and pyramids; they cared little about mathematical derivations or proofs of formulas.

Euclid (flourished 300 B.C.)
Euclid alone has looked on Beauty bare.

Edna St. Vincent Millay

The geometry of the Greeks, which is said to have begun with Thales about 600 B.C., was very different from that of the Egyptians. The Greek geometers tried to apply the principles of Greek logic to the study of geometry and to prove theorems by a sequence of logical steps that proceeded from certain basic assumptions to a conclusion.

Euclid's greatest contribution was his collection and systematization of most of the Greek mathematics of his time. His reputation rests mainly on his work titled *Elements,* which contains geometry, number theory, and some algebra. Most American textbooks on plane and solid geometry contain essentially the material in the geometry portions of Euclid's *Elements*. No work, except the Bible, has been so widely used or studied, and probably no work has influenced scientific thinking more than this one. Over a thousand editions of *Elements* have been published since the first printed edition appeared in 1482, and for more than 2,000 years this work has dominated the teaching of geometry.

Looking Ahead: Many of the geometric concepts that were the focus of Euclid's studies and writings also constitute the topics in this chapter.

7.1   POINTS, LINES, AND PLANES

GETTING STARTED

PUTTING GEOMETRY TO SOUND USE

The stereo and a speaker in the diagram are to be installed in the opposite corners of a 12 ft by 12 ft room. How much speaker wire is needed if the stereo is 3 ft high and the speaker is to be at a height of 6 ft? One way of connecting the two is to run the wire diagonally across the floor as shown in Figure 7.1. If the speaker is at A and the stereo is at D, and AB, BC, and CD denote the respective lengths of the line segments in the figure, then the total length of the wire is

$$AB + BC + CD$$

By the Pythagorean theorem,

$$BC^2 = 12^2 + 12^2 = 2 \cdot 12^2$$

and

$$BC = \sqrt{2 \cdot 12^2} = 12\sqrt{2}$$

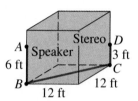

FIGURE 7.1

or about 17 ft.

Thus, the length of the wire is $(6 + 17 + 3) = 26$ ft. Is this the shortest wire possible? Let us look at the problem a little differently. Suppose the room is a perfect cube 12 ft on a side (Figure 7.2). Let's cut along each corner from ceiling to floor (Figure 7.3) and flatten it out. A scale drawing of the room without the ceiling is shown in Figure 7.4. What is the length AD of the wire?

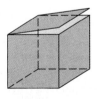

FIGURE 7.2

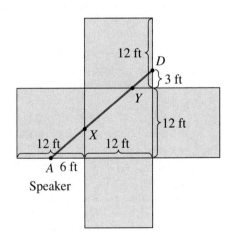

FIGURE 7.4

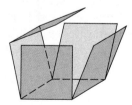

FIGURE 7.3

Since A, X, Y, and D are collinear (on the same line), we can find AD directly by using the Pythagorean theorem. From the diagram,

$$AD^2 = (6 + 12)^2 + (12 + 3)^2$$
$$= 18^2 + 15^2$$
$$= 324 + 225 = 549$$

Thus, $AD = \sqrt{549} = 23.4$ ft. Can you draw a diagram like Figure 7.1 and sketch the location of the wire? In this section, we shall learn more about lines, line segments, and distances.

The basic elements of Euclidean geometry are **points, lines,** and **planes.** These three words cannot be precisely defined, because this would require the use of other words that are also undefined. For example, we can say that a line is a set of points. But what is a point? A point is that which has no dimension. But, again, what is dimension? However, since all other geometric terms are defined on the basis of these three words, we must develop an intuitive idea of their meaning.

A. *Points and Lines*

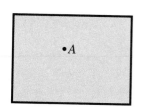

FIGURE 7.5

A **point** may be regarded as a location in space. A point has no breadth, no width, and no length. We can picture a point as a small dot, such as A in Figure 7.5. (The sharper the pencil, the better the picture.)

A **line** is a set of points, and each point of the set is said to be on the line. You may think of a line as the path of a point moving in a fixed direction in space. A line extends without end in both its directions. Here are some properties that may help to clarify what is meant by the word *line*.

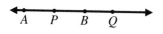

FIGURE 7.6
The line AB

1. Two distinct points A and B determine a line AB (Figure 7.6). In other words, **one and only one line can be drawn through the two points.** If P and Q are points on the line AB, then the line PQ is the same as the line AB. Thus, **a line may be named by any two of its points.** We designate the line AB by the symbol $\overleftrightarrow{AB}$ (read, "the line AB"). Points on the same line are said to be **collinear.** If A, B, P, and Q are collinear, then, for example, $\overleftrightarrow{AB} = \overleftrightarrow{PQ}$.

2. **Any point A on a line separates the line into three sets: the point A itself and two half-lines, one on each side of A.** The half-lines do not include the point A, although A is regarded as an endpoint of both (see Figure 7.7). The two half-lines may be termed half-line AB and half-line AC, respectively, and are designated by $\overset{\circ}{\overrightarrow{AB}}$ and $\overset{\circ}{\overrightarrow{AC}}$. The open circle at the end of the arrow in the symbol $\overset{\circ}{\overrightarrow{AB}}$ indicates that the half-line does *not* include the point A.

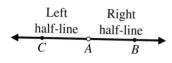

FIGURE 7.7

It is sometimes convenient to consider the set of points consisting of a half-line and its endpoint. Such a set is called a **ray.** The ray consisting of $\overrightarrow{AB}$

and the point A will be designed by $\overrightarrow{AB}$. The ray consisting of the half-line $\overset{\circ}{\overrightarrow{BA}}$ and the point B will be denoted by $\overrightarrow{BA}$. Note that $\overrightarrow{AB} \neq \overrightarrow{BA}$ because rays are named using the endpoint first.

A **line segment** AB consists of the points A and B and all the points between A and B. We designate this segment by $\overline{AB}$. Note that $\overline{AB} = \overline{BA}$.

Figure 7.8 shows the figures and notations we have described.

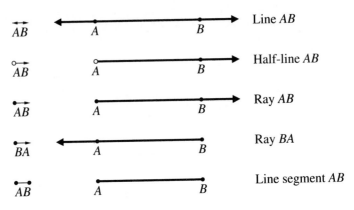

$\overleftrightarrow{AB}$ Line AB

$\overset{\circ}{\overrightarrow{AB}}$ Half-line AB

$\overrightarrow{AB}$ Ray AB

$\overrightarrow{BA}$ Ray BA

$\overline{AB}$ Line segment AB

FIGURE 7.8

EXAMPLE 1   Refer to Figure 7.9 and state what each of the following describes:

(a) $\overrightarrow{AC} \cap \overrightarrow{CA}$ (b) $\overrightarrow{AB} \cap \overrightarrow{BD}$

(c) $\overrightarrow{AC} \cup \overrightarrow{BD}$ (d) $\overrightarrow{AB} \cap \overrightarrow{CD}$

(e) $\overleftrightarrow{BC} \cap \overleftrightarrow{BA}$ (f) $\overrightarrow{AB} \cup \overrightarrow{BD}$

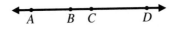

FIGURE 7.9

Solution   (a) Figure 7.10 shows the two rays $\overrightarrow{AC}$ and $\overrightarrow{CA}$. The set of points they have in common is the segment $\overline{AC}$. Thus, $\overrightarrow{AC} \cap \overrightarrow{CA} = \overline{AC}$.

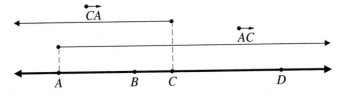

FIGURE 7.10

(b) You can see from Figure 7.11 that the segment $\overline{AB}$ and the ray $\overrightarrow{BD}$ have only the point B in common. Therefore, $\overline{AB} \cap \overrightarrow{BD} = \{B\}$.

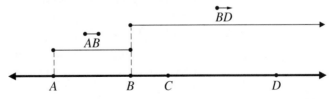

FIGURE 7.11

(c) Figure 7.12 shows that the union of the segment $\overline{AC}$ and the ray $\overrightarrow{BD}$ is the ray $\overrightarrow{AD}$. Thus, $\overline{AC} \cup \overrightarrow{BD} = \overrightarrow{AD}$.

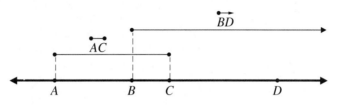

FIGURE 7.12

(d) Figure 7.13 shows that the segments $\overline{AB}$ and $\overline{CD}$ have no points in common. Hence, $\overline{AB} \cap \overline{CD} = \varnothing$.

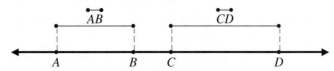

FIGURE 7.13

(e) Since $\overleftrightarrow{BC}$, $\overleftrightarrow{BA}$, and $\overleftrightarrow{AD}$ are all symbols for the same line, we have

$$\overleftrightarrow{BC} \cap \overleftrightarrow{BA} = \overleftrightarrow{AD}$$

(f) As we can see in the lines shown above, the union of the segment $\overline{AB}$ and the segment $\overline{BD}$ is the segment $\overline{AD}$, so we may write

$$\overline{AB} \cup \overline{BD} = \overline{AD}$$

■

B. *Planes*

As with the terms *point* and *line,* we give no formal definition of a **plane.** To help you visualize a plane, you can think of the surface of a very large flat floor or of a straight wall extending indefinitely in all directions. Here are some basic properties of planes:

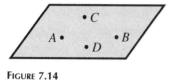

FIGURE 7.14

1. **Any three noncollinear (not on the same line) points determine one and only one plane.** We often name planes by giving three noncollinear points in the plane—for example, *ABC* in Figure 7.14. A set of points all in the same plane are called **coplanar.** In Figure 7.14 the point *D* is in the plane *ABC,* so the points *A, B, C,* and *D* are coplanar.

2. **Every pair of distinct points in a given plane determines a line that lies entirely in the plane.** For example, if a line were drawn through the points *A* and *B* in Figure 7.14, every point of the line would lie in the plane *ABC.* (A builder uses this property to test the flatness of a floor or a wall by placing a straightedge on the surface and determining whether every point of the straightedge touches the surface.)

3. **Any line *m* in a plane separates the plane into three parts: the line *m* itself and two half-planes.** The points of *m* do not belong to either half-plane, although the line is often called the *edge* of both half-planes. As indicated by the shading in Figure 7.15, we regard the points of the plane that are on one side of *m* as forming one of the half-planes and the points of the plane on the other side of *m* as forming the other half-plane.

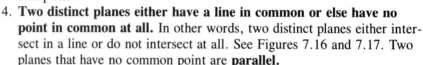

4. **Two distinct planes either have a line in common or else have no point in common at all.** In other words, two distinct planes either intersect in a line or do not intersect at all. See Figures 7.16 and 7.17. Two planes that have no common point are **parallel.**

FIGURE 7.15
Two half-planes

If a line is not in a given plane, then there are two possibilities:

(a) The line **intersects** the plane in exactly one point. For instance, line *m* in plane 2 of Figure 7.16 intersects plane 1 in the point *P.*

(b) The line is *parallel* to the plane. In Figure 7.17, any line such as *n* in plane 3 will be parallel to plane 4.

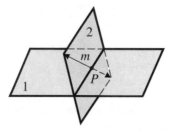

FIGURE 7.16
Intersecting planes

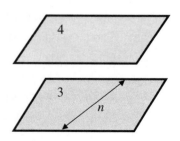

FIGURE 7.17
Parallel planes

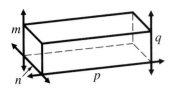

FIGURE 7.18

A rectangular box

If two distinct lines in space are given, then there may or may not be a plane that contains both lines. If the lines are parallel or if they intersect, then there is exactly one plane that contains both lines. If the lines are neither parallel nor intersecting, so that no plane can contain both lines, then they are called **skew** lines. A simple example of skew lines is the line of intersection of the ceiling and the front wall of an ordinary rectangular classroom, and the line of intersection of the floor and one of the side walls. Figure 7.18 shows a rectangular box. The edges determine various straight lines. For instance, lines m and n intersect at a vertex (corner) of the box; m and p are skew lines; m and q are parallel lines, that is, coplanar lines that *never* intersect.

Exercise 7.1

A. In problems 1 and 2, draw a line or a portion of a line that corresponds to the given symbol.

1. (a) $\overrightarrow{PQ}$ (b) $\overset{\circ}{\underset{\circ}{\overrightarrow{QP}}}$ (c) $\overleftrightarrow{QP}$

2. (a) $\overleftarrow{PQ}$ (b) $\overset{\circ}{\overrightarrow{QP}}$ (c) $\overleftrightarrow{PQ}$

In problems 3–14, use Figure 7.19 and determine what each union or intersection describes.

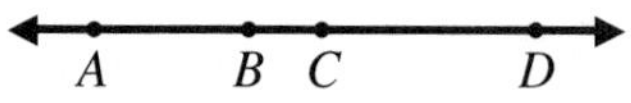

3. $\overrightarrow{AB} \cap \overrightarrow{BC}$ 4. $\overrightarrow{AC} \cap \overrightarrow{BC}$ 5. $\overrightarrow{AC} \cup \overrightarrow{BC}$

6. $\overrightarrow{AD} \cup \overrightarrow{CB}$ 7. $\overrightarrow{AC} \cap \overrightarrow{DA}$ 8. $\overrightarrow{BD} \cap \overrightarrow{DC}$

9. $\overrightarrow{AC} \cup \overrightarrow{DC}$ 10. $\overrightarrow{AC} \cup \overrightarrow{DB}$ 11. $\overrightarrow{BA} \cap \overrightarrow{CD}$

12. $\overleftrightarrow{CB} \cap \overleftrightarrow{CD}$ 13. $\overleftrightarrow{AC} \cap \overrightarrow{DC}$ 14. $\overleftrightarrow{AB} \cap \overrightarrow{DB}$

15. Let A, B, C, and D be four points, no three of which are collinear. How many straight lines do these points determine? Name each of these lines.

16. Suppose that A, B, C, D, and E are five points, no three of which are collinear. How many straight lines do these points determine? Name each of these lines.

17. If the four points in problem 15 are not coplanar (do not lie in the same plane), how many planes do the four points determine? Name each of these planes.

18. If no four of the five points in problem 16 are coplanar, how many planes do the five points determine? Name each of these planes.

19. Figure 7.20 represents a triangular pyramid.
    (a) Name all the edges.
    (b) State which pairs of edges determine skew lines.
    (c) Do any of the edges determine parallel lines?

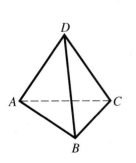

FIGURE 7.19

FIGURE 7.20

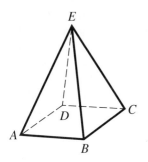

FIGURE 7.21

20. Figure 7.21 represents a pyramid with a square base *ABCD*.
    (a) Name all the edges of the pyramid.
    (b) Which pairs of edges determine parallel lines?
    (c) Which determine skew lines?
    (d) Which lines are intersecting?

B. Determine whether each of the following statements seems to be true or false in Euclidean geometry. You will find it helpful to use pencils, pieces of cardboard, walls, floors, and so on, to represent lines and planes.

21. Given any plane *ABC* and any point *P* not on *ABC*, there is exactly one plane that contains *P* and is parallel to plane *ABC*.

22. Given any line *m* and any point *P* not on *m*, there is exactly one plane that contains *P* and is parallel to *m*.

23. Given any line *m* and any point *P* not on *m*, there is exactly one line that contains *P* and is parallel to *m*.

24. Given any plane *ABC* and any point *P* not on *ABC*, there are any number of lines containing *P* and parallel to *ABC*.

25. Given any line *m* and any point *P* not on *m*, there are any number of lines that contain *P* and are skew to *m*.

26. Given any plane *ABC* and any line *m* parallel to *ABC*, there is exactly one plane that contains *m* and intersects *ABC*.

27. Two nonparallel lines always determine a plane.

28. Given any line *m* and any point *P* not on *m*, there is exactly one plane that contains both *m* and *P*.

29. Given a plane *ABC* and a line *m* that intersects *ABC*, there is a plane that contains *m* and that does not intersect *ABC*.

30. If a plane intersects two parallel planes, the lines of intersection are parallel.

Problems 31–38 refer to Figure 7.22, which represents a triangular pyramid *ABCD* with its base on the plane *ABC*.

31. Are the points *A*, *R*, and *D* collinear or noncollinear?
32. Are the points *R*, *S*, and *T* collinear or noncollinear?
33. Are the points *B*, *C*, *D*, and *T* coplanar or noncoplanar?
34. Are the points *A*, *C*, *D*, and *T* coplanar or noncoplanar?
35. Are lines *AB* and *CD* skew lines?
36. Name a line that is skew to the line *AD*.
37. Name the line that is coplanar with the lines *BC* and *CD*.
38. If a line is drawn through the points *R* and *T*, what three lines would be skew to the line *RT*?

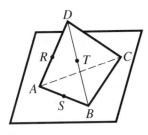

FIGURE 7.22

Use the following information in problems 39–41. The definition of *line segment* contains the word *between*. "Point *B* is between points *A* and *C*" means that *A*, *B*, and *C* are collinear and the distance from *A* to *C* is the sum of the distance from *A* to *B* and the distance from *B* to *C*, that is, $AB + BC = AC$ as illustrated

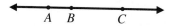

39. In Figure 7.23, point *Q* is between points *P* and *R*.
    (a) What relationship must the three points have?
    (b) Write an equation using the distances *PQ*, *QR*, and *PR*.
    (c) If *B* is between *A* and *C*, we write *A-B-C*. How would you write the fact that *Q* is between *P* and *R* in two different ways?

40. Points *S*, *T*, and *U* are collinear. Which point is between the other two if:
    (a) $UT + TS = US$　　　　　　(b) $UT = US + ST$

41. If point *B* is between points *A* and *C*, we can write $AB + BC = AC$. Write two other equations each containing all three lengths.

P　Q　　　　　　R

FIGURE 7.23

In Other Words

42. You have heard the saying "The shortest distance between two points is a straight line." Explain why this is technically incorrect.

43. Name three undefined geometric terms.

44. Find the word *point* in a dictionary. How many definitions does the word have? In your own words, give three definitions that may apply to geometry.

45. Describe the different ways in which a ray and a plane can intersect.

46. Describe the different ways in which a line and a ray can intersect.

Using Your Knowledge

Suppose you have a large number of points, and no three of them are collinear. Can you calculate how many distinct lines these points determine? Let us say there are 10 points in all. Then you can select any one of them as a first point, which means there are 10 such choices. Having made a choice, you can select a second point from the remaining 9 points, so that there are 9 choices possible for the second point. Since for each of the 10 first choices, there are 9 second choices, there are 10 × 9, or 90, ways of choosing a first point and then a second point. Will there be 90 distinct lines? No, because if you select a point A for the first point and a point B for the second point, the line is the same line as if you had chosen B first and A second. This means that of the 90 lines, half are duplicates of the other half. Thus, the number of distinct lines is (10 × 9)/2, or 45.

Use this idea to answer the following questions. Assume in each case that no three of the points are collinear.

47. If the number of points is 20, how many distinct lines are determined?
48. If the number of points is 50, how many distinct lines are determined?
49. If the number of points is *n*, how many distinct lines are determined?

Now suppose that you have a large number of points, no four of which are coplanar. Can you calculate how many distinct planes these points determine? Try it for 10 points. As you just saw, 10 points determine (10 × 9)/2, or 45, distinct lines. It takes 2 of the 10 points to determine one of these lines, and you can use any one of the remaining 8 points to pair with the line to determine a plane. Thus, for each of the 45 lines, 8 planes are determined; but these planes are not all distinct. You can check that only one-third are distinct by noting that if a line AB and a point C are selected, this gives the same plane as the line AC and the point B or the line BC and the point A. Hence, the number of distinct planes is (10 × 9 × 8)/(2 × 3), or 120.

Use these ideas to answer the following questions. Assume in each case that no four of the points are coplanar.

50. If the number of points is 20, how many distinct planes are determined?
51. If the number of points is *n*, how many distinct planes are determined?

Discovery

52. Figure 7.24 is called a **complete quadrangle.** It is a model for which the following three statements are true:

  i. There are exactly four lines.
  ii. Each pair of lines has exactly one point in common.
  iii. Every point of intersection is on exactly two lines.

  Can you discover how to show that any model of lines and points satisfying properties i, ii, and iii also satisfies statements (a), (b), and (c) below?
  (a) There are exactly six points of intersection (*A, B, C, D, E, F* in the figure).
  (b) There are exactly three such points on each line.
  (c) For each point of intersection, there is exactly one other point of intersection that does not lie on the same line with it. (For instance, the point *D* in the figure is the only point not on the same line with *A*.)

53. Can you write the statements that correspond to statements i, ii, and iii of problem 52 if the words *line* and *point* are interchanged throughout? Can you discover a simple figure for which the three new statements are true? What do statements (a), (b), and (c) become with this interchange of "line" and "point"?

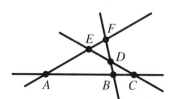

FIGURE 7.24
A complete quadrangle

54. Draw a pyramid with a triangular base. Can you discover with what words to replace *line* and *point* in problem 52 so that the pyramid is an appropriate model? Check to see whether the statements that correspond to statements (a), (b), and (c) are true for the pyramid.

55. In problem 52, replace the word *line* by *club* and the word *point* by *member*. If statements i, ii, and iii are true, will statements (a), (b), and (c) also be true? Justify your answer.

7.2 ANGLES

GETTING STARTED

GETTING THE RIGHT ANGLE

Have you heard the expression "I am looking at it from a new angle"? In algebra, we measured the inclination of a line using the *slope* of a line. In geometry, we measure the inclination of a line by measuring the *angle* the line makes with the horizontal with an instrument called a **protractor.** (See Figures 7.31 and 7.32 on page 479.) Angles are everywhere. We can see angles in things as large as the cables on a suspension bridge, or as small as the veins in a plant leaf. The figure here shows the angles in the flight path of the *Ranger 9* lunar probe. The Leaning Tower of Pisa in the picture has an angle of inclination of about 5° (read, "5 degrees") from the vertical. Thus the tower makes an 85° *acute* angle (an angle that is less than 90°) with the ground. How did we know that? Because if the tower were completely vertical, it would make a 90° angle, that is, a *right* angle with the ground. Can you find the angle that the left side of the tower makes with the ground? Your answer will be an *obtuse* angle, an angle that measures more than 90°. In this section we shall study angles (right, acute, and obtuse), the ways in which angles are named, and some relationships among them.

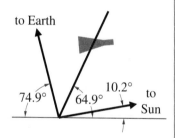

Ranger 9 *terminal trajectory orientation and glide path. (NASA)*

Construction of the Tower of Pisa began in 1174 and settling was already noticeable after only three of its eight stories were built. Work was delayed as engineers sought unsuccessfully to correct the problem. Still leaning, the tower was completed in the 14th century.

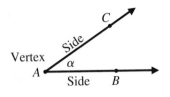

FIGURE 7.25

One of the most important concepts in mathematics is that of a *plane angle*. In elementary geometry, we think of a *plane angle* as the figure formed by two rays with a common endpoint, as in Figure 7.25. The common endpoint (A in Figure 7.25), is called the **vertex** of the angle, and the two rays ($\overrightarrow{AB}$ and $\overrightarrow{AC}$ in the figure) are called the **sides** of the angle. We often use the symbol ∠ (read, "angle") in naming angles. The angle in Figure 7.25 can be named in three ways:

1. By using a letter or a number inside the angle. Thus, we would name the angle in Figure 7.25 ∠α (read, "angle alpha").

2. By using the vertex letter only, such as ∠A in Figure 7.25.

3. By using three letters, one from each ray and with the vertex letter in the middle. The angle in Figure 7.25 would be named ∠BAC or ∠CAB.

EXAMPLE 1   Consider the angle in Figure 7.26:

(a) Name the angle in three different ways.

(b) Name the vertex of the angle.

(c) Name the sides of the angle.

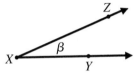

FIGURE 7.26

Solution   (a) The angle can be named ∠β (Greek letter beta), ∠X, or ∠YXZ (or ∠ZXY).

(b) The vertex is the point X.

(c) The sides are the rays $\overrightarrow{XZ}$ and $\overrightarrow{XY}$.

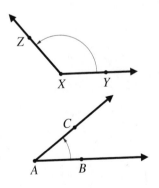

FIGURE 7.27

For most practical purposes, we need to have a way of measuring angles. We first consider the amount of **rotation** needed to turn one side of an angle so that it *coincides with* (falls exactly on top of) the other side. Figure 7.27 shows two angles, ∠CAB and ∠ZXY, with curved arrows to indicate the rotation needed to turn the rays $\overrightarrow{AB}$ and $\overrightarrow{XY}$ so that they coincide with the rays $\overrightarrow{AC}$ and $\overrightarrow{XZ}$, respectively. Clearly, the amount needed for ∠ZXY is greater than that for ∠CAB. To find how much greater, we have to measure the amounts of rotation.

The most common unit of measure for an angle is the *degree*. We can trace the degree system back to the ancient Babylonians, who were responsible for the base 60 system of numeration. The Babylonians considered a *complete revolution* of a ray as indicated in Figure 7.28 and divided that into 360 equal parts. Each part is **one degree,** denoted by **1°**. Thus, a complete revolution is equal to 360°. One-half of a complete revolution is 180° and gives us an angle that is called a **straight angle** (see Figure 7.29). One-quarter of a complete revolution is 90°, giving a **right angle** (Figure 7.30). Notice the small square at Y to denote that this is a right angle.

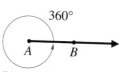

FIGURE 7.28

A complete revolution

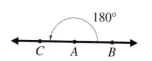

FIGURE 7.29

The straight angle CAB

FIGURE 7.30

The right angle XYZ

EXAMPLE 2 Through how many degrees does the hour hand of a clock move in going from:

(a) 1 to 2 o'clock?

(b) 1 to 4 o'clock?

(c) 12 to 5 o'clock?

(d) 12 to 9 o'clock?

Solution (a) One complete revolution is 360°, and the face of the clock is divided into 12 equal parts. Thus, the hour hand moves through

$$\frac{360°}{12} = 30°$$

in going from 1 to 2 o'clock.

(b) From 1 to 4 o'clock is 3 hr. Since a 1-hr move corresponds to 30°, a 3-hr move corresponds to 3(30°) = 90°. (Thus, the hour hand moves through one right angle.)

(c) From 12 to 5 o'clock is 5 hr. Hence, the hour hand moves through 5(30°) = 150°.

(d) From 12 to 9 o'clock is 9 hr, so the hour hand moves through 9(30°) = 270°.

In practice, the size of an angle is measured with a protractor (see Figure 7.31). The protractor is placed with its center at a vertex of the angle and the straight side of the protractor along one side of the angle as in Figure 7.32 The measure of ∠BAC is then read as 70° (because it is obviously less than 90°) and the measure of ∠DAC is read as 110°. Surveying and navigational instruments, such as a sextant, use the idea of a protractor to measure angles very precisely.

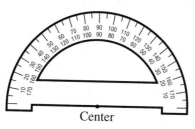

FIGURE 7.31

A protractor

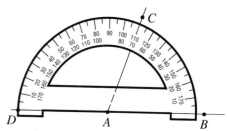

FIGURE 7.32

Measuring an angle

We have already named two angles: a *straight angle* (180°) and a *right angle* (90°). Certain other angles are classified as follows:

1. An **acute angle** is an angle of measure *greater* than 0° and *less* than 90°.
2. An **obtuse angle** is an angle of measure *greater* than 90° and *less* than 180°.

In Figure 7.32, ∠*BAC* is an acute angle and ∠*DAC* is an obtuse angle.

Geometric figures frequently appear in highway signs. Do you know what the sign in Figure 7.33 means? It is an advance warning for a railroad crossing. The angles *B* and *D* that are marked in Figure 7.34 are called *vertical angles*. In general, when two lines intersect, the opposite angles so formed are called **vertical angles.** Two pairs of vertical angles are shown in Figure 7.35. Since the sides of angle *C* are just extensions of the sides of angle *A*, these two angles are of equal size. You can complete a mathematical proof of this fact in problem 41, Exercise 7.2.

FIGURE 7.33

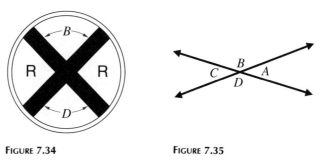

FIGURE 7.34   **FIGURE 7.35**

Thus, in Figure 7.35, the measure of angle *A*, denoted by $m \angle A$, is the same as that of angle *C*. This fact is simply written as $m \angle A = m \angle C$. Similarly, $m \angle B = m \angle D$.

In Figure 7.35, angles *A* and *B* together form a straight angle, so the sum of their measures must be 180°. For this reason, *A* and *B* are called *supplementary angles.*

> In general, any two angles whose measures add up to 180° are called **supplementary angles.**

Other pairs of supplementary angles in Figure 7.35 are *B* and *C*, *C* and *D*, and *A* and *D*. Figure 7.35 illustrates the obvious fact that *supplements of the same angle are equal.* For example, angles *A* and *C* are both supplements of ∠*B*.

EXAMPLE 3   Refer to Figure 7.35:

(a) If the measure of ∠*A* is 25°, what are the measures of the other three angles?
(b) If the two lines are to be drawn so that ∠*B* is twice the size of ∠*A*, what should the measure of ∠*A* be?

Solution   (a) Angles A and B are supplementary, so their measures add to 180°. Hence, the measure of $\angle B$ is 180° minus the measure of $\angle A$, that is, $180° - 25° = 155°$. Since $m \angle D = m \angle B$, the measure of $\angle D$ is also 155°. Also, $m \angle C = m \angle A$, so the measure of $\angle C$ is 25°.

(b) We let the measure of angle A be $x°$. Then the measure of angle B is $2x°$. Because angles A and B are supplementary, we must have

$$x + 2x = 180$$
$$3x = 180$$
$$x = 60$$

Thus, if we make $\angle A$ a 60° angle, $\angle B$ will be a 120° angle, twice the size of $\angle A$. ∎

If you drive a motorcycle, you should look closely at Figure 7.36; it tells you to cross the railroad tracks at right angles (because there is less danger of a wheel catching in the tracks). Now, look at angles A, B, C, and D that we have marked on the right side of Figure 7.36. What can you say about angles B and D? Since they are vertical angles, they are of equal measure. (Similarly, angles A and C are of equal measure.) As you can see, the railroad track crosses

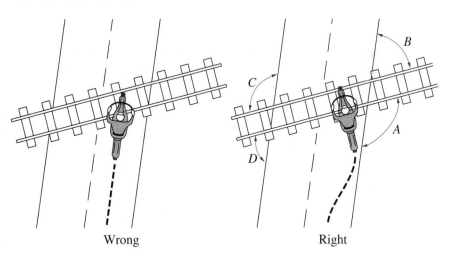

Wrong   Right

FIGURE 7.36

the two parallel black lines in the figure. In geometry, a line that crosses two or more other lines is called a **transversal.** Thus, each railroad track is a transversal of the pair of parallel black lines. If a transversal crosses a pair of parallel lines, some of the resulting angles are of equal measure. See Figure 7.37. The exact relationships are:

Corresponding Angles Are of Equal Measure:

$$m\angle A = m\angle E \qquad m\angle B = m\angle F$$
$$m\angle C = m\angle G \qquad m\angle D = m\angle H$$

Alternate Interior Angles Are of Equal Measure:

$$m\angle A = m\angle G \qquad m\angle D = m\angle F$$

Alternate Exterior Angles Are of Equal Measure:

$$m\angle B = m\angle H \qquad m\angle C = m\angle E$$

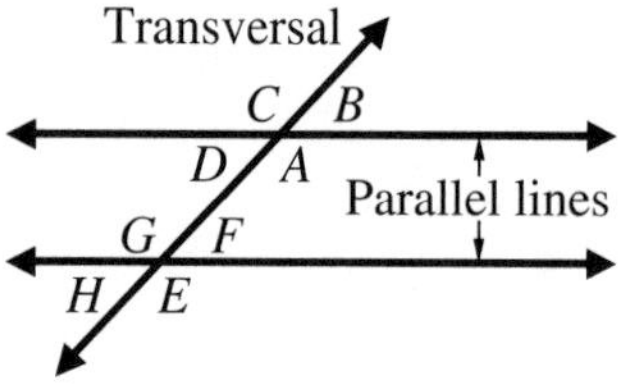

In Figure 7.37, angles A and B form a straight angle and are thus supplementary. Because $m\angle B = m\angle F$, it follows that angles A and F are also supplementary. The same idea applies to angles D and G as well as to angles B and E and angles C and H. We can summarize these facts by saying: **Interior angles on the same side of the transversal are supplementary, and exterior angles on the same side of the transversal are also supplementary.**

The next example will help to clarify and fix this information in your mind.

FIGURE 7.37

Corresponding Angles:
A *and* **E, B** *and* **F**
C *and* **G, D** *and* **H**
Alternate Interior Angles:
A *and* **G, D** *and* **F**
Alternate Exterior Angles:
B *and* **H, C** *and* **E**

EXAMPLE 4　In Figure 7.38, find the measure of the angle:

(a) Y　(b) Z　(c) X　(d) R　(e) S　(f) T　(g) U

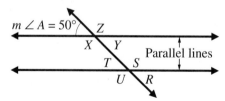

FIGURE 7.38

Solution　(a) Since Y and A are vertical angles, $m\angle Y = m\angle A = 50°$.

(b) Angles A and Z are supplementary, so
$$m\angle Z = 180° - 50° = 130°.$$

(c) X and Z are vertical angles. Thus, $m\angle X = m\angle Z = 130°$.

(d) R and A are alternate exterior angles. Hence,
$$m\angle R = m\angle A = 50°.$$

(e) S and Y are interior angles on the same side of the transversal and so are supplementary. Therefore,
$$m\angle S = 180° - m\angle Y = 130°.$$

(f) T and A are corresponding angles. Thus,
$$m\angle T = m\angle A = 50°.$$

(g) U and A are exterior angles on the same side of the transversal. Thus, $m\angle U = 180° - m\angle A = 130°.$

∎

Parallel lines and the associated angles allow us to obtain quite easily one of the most important results in the geometry of triangles. In Figure 7.39, *ABC* represents any triangle. The line *XY* has been drawn through the point *C* parallel to the side *AB* of the triangle. Note that $\angle 1 = \angle 2$ and $\angle 3 = \angle 4$, because they are respective pairs of alternate interior angles. Furthermore, angles 2, 5, and 4 form a straight angle, so

$$m\angle 2 + m\angle 5 + m\angle 4 = 180°$$

By substituting $\angle 1$ for $\angle 2$ and $\angle 3$ for $\angle 4$, we obtain

$$m\angle 1 + m\angle 5 + m\angle 3 = 180°$$

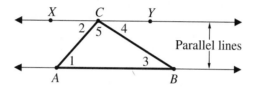

FIGURE 7.39

Thus, we have shown that **the sum of the measures of the angles of any triangle is 180°.**

EXAMPLE 5

(a) In a triangle *ABC*, $m\angle A = 47°$ and $m\angle B = 59°$. Find the measure of $\angle C$.

(b) Is it possible for a triangle *ABC* to be such that $\angle A$ is twice the size of $\angle B$, and $\angle C$ is three times the size of $\angle B$?

Solution

(a) Because $m\angle A + m\angle B + m\angle C = 180°$, we have

$$47° + 59° + m\angle C = 180°$$
$$m\angle C = 180° - 47° - 59°$$
$$= 180° - 106° = 74°$$

(b) To answer this question, let $m\angle B = x°$, so $m\angle A = 2x°$ and $m\angle C = 3x°$. Then, since the sum of the angles is 180°,

$$x + 2x + 3x = 180$$
$$6x = 180$$
$$x = 30, \qquad 2x = 60, \qquad 3x = 90$$

This means that there is such a triangle, and $m\angle A = 60°$, $m\angle B = 30°$, and $m\angle C = 90°$. (Note that this is a right triangle because one of the angles is a right angle.)

In part (b) of Example 5, we found angles A and B to be of measure 60° and 30°, respectively, so $m \angle A + m \angle B = 90°$.

> Two angles whose sum is 90° are called **complementary angles,** and each angle is called the **complement** of the other.

EXAMPLE 6   (a) Find the complement of a 38° angle.
(b) Can two complementary angles be such that one is three times the size of the other?

Solution   (a) For an angle to be the complement of a 38° angle, its measure must be $90° - 38° = 52°$.
(b) Let the smaller angle be of measure $x°$, so the larger is of measure $3x°$. Since the angles are to be complementary,

$$x + 3x = 90$$
$$4x = 90$$
$$x = \tfrac{90}{4} = 22\tfrac{1}{2}, \qquad 3x = 67\tfrac{1}{2}$$

The answer is yes, and the angles would be of measure $22\tfrac{1}{2}°$ and $67\tfrac{1}{2}°$. ∎

Two lines that intersect at right angles are said to be *perpendicular* to each other. The lines are called **perpendicular lines.** For example, two adjacent outside edges of a page of this book are perpendicular to each other.

Exercise 7.2

Problems 1–14 refer to Figure 7.40. Note that perpendicular lines are indicated by small boxes.

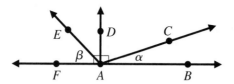

FIGURE 7.40

1. Name in another way:
   (a) $\angle\alpha$ (b) $\angle EAF$

2. Name in another way:
   (a) $\angle CAB$ (b) $\angle\beta$

3. List all the acute angles in the figure.

4. List all the right angles in the figure.

5. List all the obtuse angles in the figure.

6. Name an angle that is the complement of:
   (a) $\angle\alpha$ (b) $\angle\beta$

7. Name an angle that is the complement of
   (a) $\angle EAF$ (b) $\angle BAC$

8. Name an angle that is supplementary to:
   (a) $\angle\alpha$ (b) $\angle\beta$

9. Name an angle that is supplementary to:
   (a) $\angle BAD$ (b) $\angle EAF$

10. If $m\angle\alpha = 15°$, find $m\angle CAD$.

11. If $m\angle\beta = 55°$, find $m\angle DAE$.

12. If $m\angle DAE = 35°$, find $m\angle\beta$.

13. If $m\angle CAD = 75°$, find $m\angle\alpha$.

14. If $m\angle\alpha = 15°$, and $m\angle\beta = 55°$, find $m\angle CAE$.

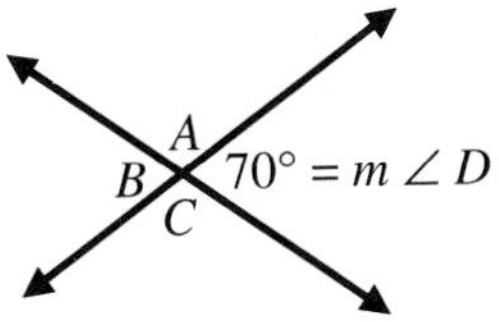

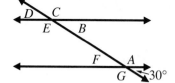

FIGURE 7.41

Problems 15–22 refer to the two intersecting lines shown in Figure 7.41.

15. Name the angle that is vertical to the 70° angle.

16. Name the two angles that are each supplementary to the 70° angle.

17. Find $m\angle A$.

18. Find $m\angle B$.

19. What is the measure of an angle complementary to the 70° angle?

20. Find the sum of the measures of angles A, B, and C.

21. Find the sum of the measures of angles A and C.

22. If $m\angle D = x°$ (instead of 70°), write an expression for the measure of $\angle A$.

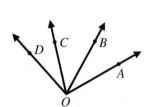

FIGURE 7.42

Problems 23–25 refer to the two parallel lines and the transversal shown in Figure 7.42.

23. Find:
    (a) $m\angle A$ (b) $m\angle B$ (c) $m\angle C$

24. Find:
    (a) $m\angle D$ (b) $m\angle E$ (c) $m\angle F$

25. Name all the angles that are supplementary to $\angle B$.

26. Refer to the angles shown in Figure 7.43.
    (a) If $m\angle AOB = 30°$ and $m\angle AOC = 70°$, find $m\angle BOC$.
    (b) If $m\angle AOB = m\angle COD$, $m\angle AOD = 100°$, and $m\angle BOC = 2x°$, find $m\angle COD$ in terms of x.

27. If $m\angle A = 41°$, find $m\angle B$ if:
    (a) The two angles are complementary
    (b) The two angles are supplementary

FIGURE 7.43

28. If $m\angle A = 19°$, find $m\angle B$ if:
    (a) The two angles are complementary
    (b) The two angles are supplementary

29. Given that $m\angle A = (3x + 15)°$, $m\angle B = (2x - 5)°$, and the two angles are complementary, find x.

30. Rework problem 29 if the two angles are supplementary.

In problems 31–34, the figures show the number of degrees in each angle in terms of x. Use algebra to find x and the measure of each angle.

31.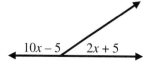

32.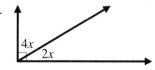

33.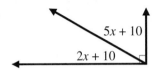

34.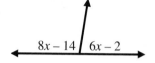

35. Through how many degrees does the hour hand of a clock move in going from:
    (a) 11 o'clock to 12 o'clock?   (b) 11 o'clock to 5 o'clock?

36. Through how many degrees does the hour hand of a clock move in going from:
    (a) 12 o'clock to 7 o'clock?   (b) 12 o'clock back to 12 o'clock?

37. In a triangle ABC, $m\angle A = 37°$ and $m\angle C = 53°$. Find $m\angle B$.

38. In a triangle ABC, $m\angle B = 67°$ and $m\angle C = 105°$. Find $m\angle A$.

39. In a triangle ABC, $m\angle A = (x + 10)°$, $m\angle B = (2x + 10)°$, and $m\angle C = (3x + 10)°$. Find x.

40. In a triangle ABC, $m\angle A$ is 10° less than $m\angle B$, and $m\angle C$ is 40° greater than $m\angle B$. Find the measure of each angle.

41. Refer to Figure 7.35. Complete the first two equations and give the reason for each step in the following proof that vertical angles are of equal measure.

    i. $m\angle A + m\angle B =$ _____   iii. $m\angle A + m\angle B = m\angle C + m\angle B$
    ii. $m\angle C + m\angle B =$ _____   iv. $m\angle A = m\angle C$

In Other Words

42. We have classified four types of angles according to their measures.
    (a) Name the four types of angles.
    (b) Define each of these in your own words.

43. We have already defined an acute and an obtuse angle. Look at the definition of acute and obtuse in a dictionary and explain:
    (a) What does "an acute" pain mean?
    (b) What does "obtuse intelligence" mean?

44. Describe and show sketches of how
    (a) a line can intersect an angle.
    (b) two angles can intersect.

Using Your Knowledge

Angles are extremely important in surveying and in navigation. With the knowledge you have gained in this section, you should be able to do the following problems.

45. A surveyor measured a triangular plot of ground and reported the three angles as 48.2°, 75.9°, and 56.1°. How much of an error did the surveyor make?

In land surveying, angles are measured with respect to due north and due south. For example, a direction of N 30° W means a direction that is 30° west of due north, and S 60° E means a direction that is 60° east of due south. Surveyors use acute angles only. In aerial navigation, angles are always measured clockwise from due north. A navigator's bearing of 90° corresponds to due east, 180° to due south, and 270° to due west. Thus, a navigator's bearing of 225° would correspond to a surveyor's bearing of S 45° W.

46. Write a navigator's bearing of 135° in the surveyor's terminology.
47. Write a navigator's bearing of 310° in the surveyor's terminology.
48. Write the direction S 40° W as a navigator's bearing.
49. Write the direction N 40° W as a navigator's bearing.

7.3 TRIANGLES AND OTHER POLYGONS

Soap bubbles exhibit various polygonal shapes when closely packed

GETTING STARTED
SOAP BUBBLE POLYGONS

Look at the soap bubbles in the photo. What do you notice about the shapes shown? First, all of them are made up of line segments that do not cross themselves, and second, each shape can be traced by starting and ending at one point. Such shapes, called **polygons,** will be studied in this section.

Plane polygons can be named according to the number of sides. Thus, a *3-sided* polygon is a *tri*angle and a *4-sided* polygon is a *quadr*ilateral. Later, you will learn how to name polygons with 5, 6, 7, and 8 sides.

How many polygons do you see in the picture?

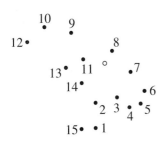

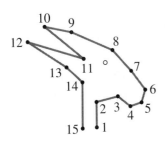

FIGURE 7.44

As you recall, the sum of the measures of the angles in a triangle is 180°. Because a quadrilateral can always be divided into two triangles, the sum of the measures of the angles is 360°. Can we find the sum of the measures of the angles in polygons with 5, 6, 7, and, in general, n sides? See if you can discover a pattern.

Number of Sides	Sum of the Angles
3-sided polygon	$1 \cdot 180°$
4-sided polygon	$2 \cdot 180°$
5-sided polygon	?

The answer should be $3 \cdot 180°$. Why? Read part C of this section on page 494 and you will see!

A popular children's puzzle consists of joining in order a set of numbered dots by straight line segments to form a path from the first to the last point. An example of such a puzzle and its solution is shown in Figure 7.44. (What is pictured, an antelope or a bird?)

A. *Broken Lines and Polygons*

A path (such as the one shown in the puzzle) consisting of a sequence of connected straight line segments is called a **broken line.** Such a path can be traced without lifting the pencil from the paper. Certain broken line paths have two characteristics that are of interest to us in this section:

1. A **simple path** is a path that does *not* cross itself.
2. A **closed path** is one that starts and ends at the same point.

The path in the solution of the puzzle in Figure 7.44 is simple but not closed. Figure 7.45 shows four broken lines. The paths in I, II, and IV are simple, but path III is not simple. Moreover, paths III and IV are closed; paths I and II are not closed.

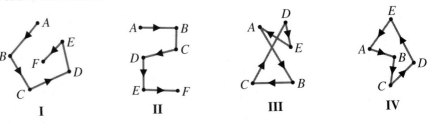

FIGURE 7.45
Broken lines

Any path that consists of a simple closed broken line is called a **polygon.**
Path IV, *ABCDE*, in Figure 7.45 is an example of a polygon. The line segments of the path are the **sides** of the polygon, and the endpoints of the sides
are the **vertices.** A polygon is said to be *convex* if no line segment *XY* joining
any two points on the path ever extends outside the polygon (see Figure 7.46).
The points *X* and *Y* may be any two points not on the same side of the
polygon. Except for its endpoints, the line segment *XY* lies entirely inside the
polygon. (Of course, if *X* and *Y* were on the same side, then the segment
would lie on that side.)

FIGURE 7.46
Convex polygon

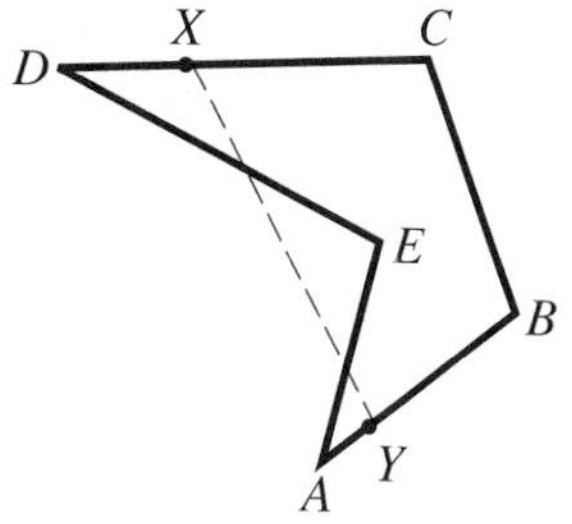

FIGURE 7.47
Concave polygon

A polygon that is not convex is called a *concave,* or *reentrant,* polygon
(see Figure 7.47). Here a portion of the line segment *XY* lies outside the
polygon—something that never occurs in a convex polygon.

EXAMPLE 1   Consider the polygon *ABCDE* in Figure 7.48:

(a) Name its sides.   (b) Name its vertices.

(c) Is this a concave or a convex polygon?

Solution   (a) The sides are *AB*, *BC*, *CD*, *DE*, and *EA*.

(b) The vertices are *A*, *B*, *C*, *D*, and *E*.

(c) This is a reentrant, or concave, polygon.

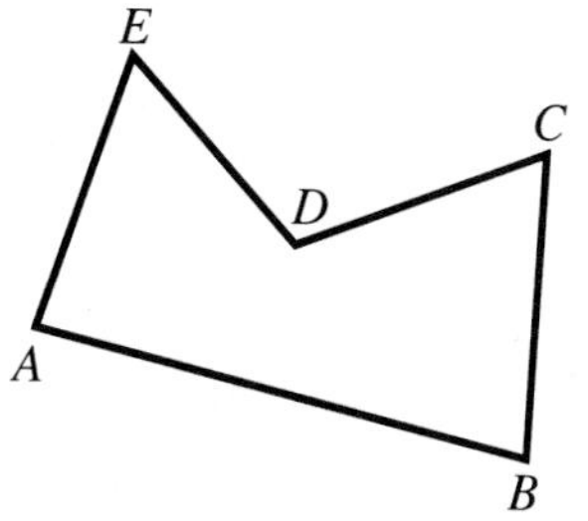

■

Plane polygons are customarily named according to the number of sides.
Here are some of the usual names:

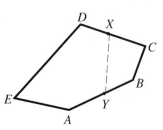

FIGURE 7.48

Sides	Name	Sides	Name
3	Triangle	8	Octagon
4	Quadrilateral	9	Nonagon
5	Pentagon	10	Decagon
6	Hexagon	12	Dodecagon
7	Heptagon		

As you probably know, traffic signs are most often in the shape of a
polygon. For example, the stop sign is in the shape of an octagon. In fact, it is

in the shape of a *regular* octagon. A **regular polygon** is a polygon with all its sides of equal length and all its angles of equal size. A regular triangle has three equal sides and three 60° angles; it is called an **equilateral triangle.** A regular quadrilateral has four equal sides and four 90° angles. You undoubtedly know that it is called a **square.** No special names are given to other regular polygons.

EXAMPLE 2   Some standard traffic signs are shown below.

(a) Which ones are regular polygons?
(b) Name the shape of the school sign.
(c) Name the shape of the yield sign.
(d) Name the shape of the warning sign.

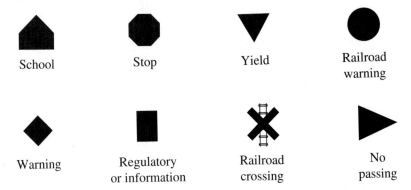

School   Stop   Yield   Railroad warning

Warning   Regulatory or information   Railroad crossing   No passing

Solution   (a) The stop sign, the yield sign, and the warning sign are all in the shape of regular polygons.
(b) The school sign has five sides, so it is in the shape of a pentagon (but not a regular pentagon).
(c) The yield sign has three equal sides; it is in the shape of an equilateral triangle.
(d) The warning sign has four equal sides and four equal angles; it is in the shape of a regular quadrilateral, a square.

FIGURE 7.49

Can you see the triangular region? It is an optical illusion. The triangle exists only in your mind.

B. *Triangles and Quadrilaterals*

Triangles are often classified according to their angles, as shown in Table 7.1.

Triangles are also classified according to the number of equal sides, as shown in Table 7.2

Note that the angles opposite the equal sides of an **isosceles triangle** are of equal measure. (See the Using Your Knowledge section of Exercise 7.3.) Moreover, an **equilateral triangle** is also **equiangular;** it has three 60° angles. The triangle that you see in the optical illusion in Figure 7.49 is an equilateral triangle.

Table 7.1

Definition	Illustration	Example
Right triangle: A triangle containing a right angle.	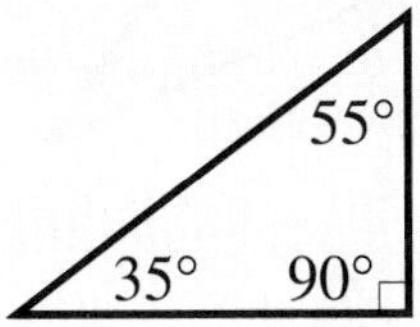 55° 35° 90°	 (barn illustration)
Acute triangle: A triangle in which all the angles are acute.	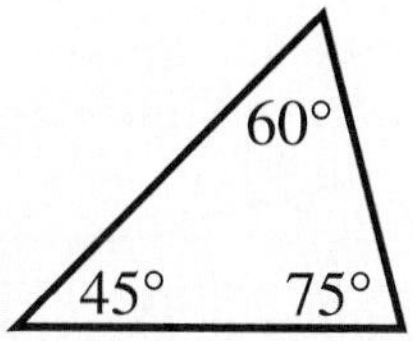 60° 45° 75°	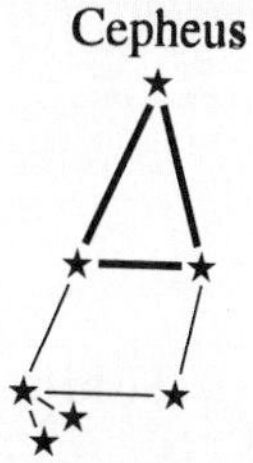 Cepheus (constellation illustration)
Obtuse triangle: A triangle containing an obtuse angle.	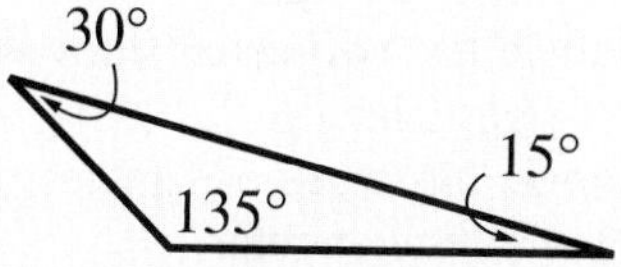 30° 135° 15°	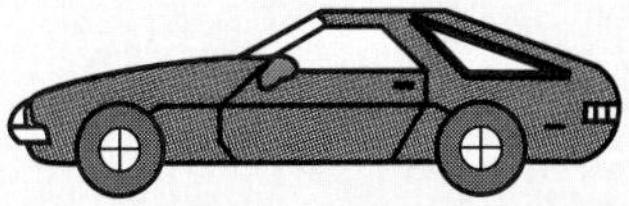 (car illustration)

Table 7.2

Definition	Illustration	Example
Scalene triangle: A triangle with **no** equal sides. (Note that the sides are labelled I, II, and III to show that the lengths of the sides are different.)	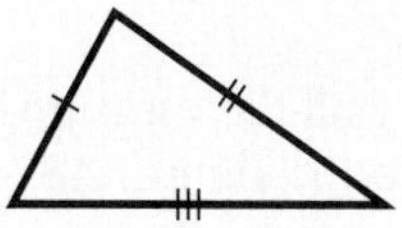 (scalene triangle illustration)	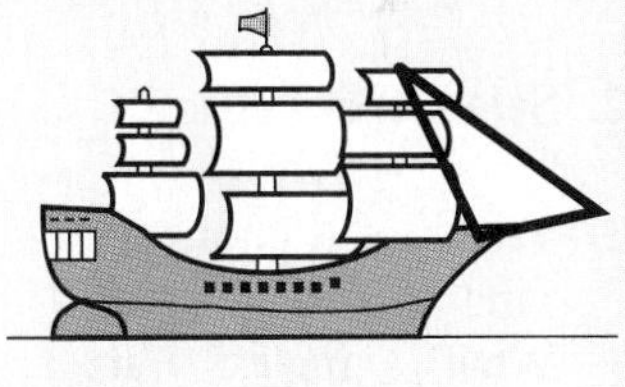 (ship illustration)
Isosceles triangle: A triangle with **exactly** two equal sides.	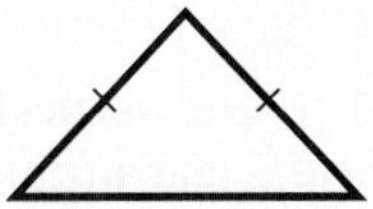 (isosceles triangle illustration)	 HCC (pennant illustration) YIELD (yield sign illustration)
Equilateral triangle: A triangle with **all** three sides equal.	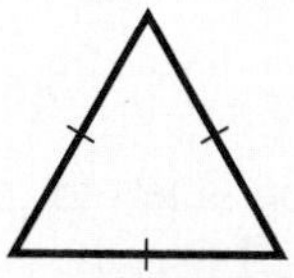 (equilateral triangle illustration)	

EXAMPLE 3   Classify the given triangles according to their angles and their sides.

(a)    (b)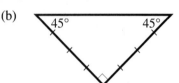

(c)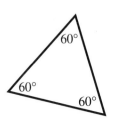

Solution   (a) The triangle has an obtuse angle and no equal sides; it is an obtuse, scalene triangle.

(b) The triangle has two equal sides and a right angle; it is an isosceles right triangle.

(c) The triangle has three 60° angles; it is an equilateral triangle, which is also equiangular.

Problem Solving:	**Finding the Measure of an Angle**

Find the measure of angle β.

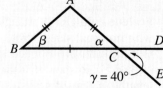

1. Read the problem.

2. Select the unknown.

3. Think of a plan. Find the equal sides. What angles are given? Are there any vertical angles?

We want to find the measure of angle β.
According to the figure, $AB = AC$ and $\gamma = 40°$.

4. Use the fact that α and γ are vertical angles to find α. Look at the angles opposite the equal sides.

Since α and γ are vertical angles, they must be equal, that is, $\alpha = \gamma = 40°$. Angle α and angle β are opposite the equal sides of $\triangle ABC$ (triangle ABC); hence, they must also be of equal measure. Thus, the measure of angle β is 40°.

5. Verify the solution.

The verification is left to the student.

TRY EXAMPLE 4 NOW.   Cover the solution, write your own, and then check your work.

EXAMPLE 4 In $\triangle ABC$, $AB = AC$ and $m\angle DCE = 37°$. Find $m\angle A$.

Solution $\angle ACB$ and $\angle DCE$ are vertical angles, so $m\angle ACB = m\angle DCE = 37°$. $\angle ACB$ and $\angle B$ are opposite the equal sides of $\triangle ABC$ and are thus of equal measure. So $m\angle B = 37°$. Since

$$m\angle A = 180° - m\angle ACB - m\angle ABC,$$
$$m\angle A = 180° - 37° - 37°$$
$$= 106°$$

∎

We have already learned how to name different polygons according to the number of sides. Certain quadrilaterals (four-sided polygons) also have special names, as shown in Table 7.3.)

Table 7.3

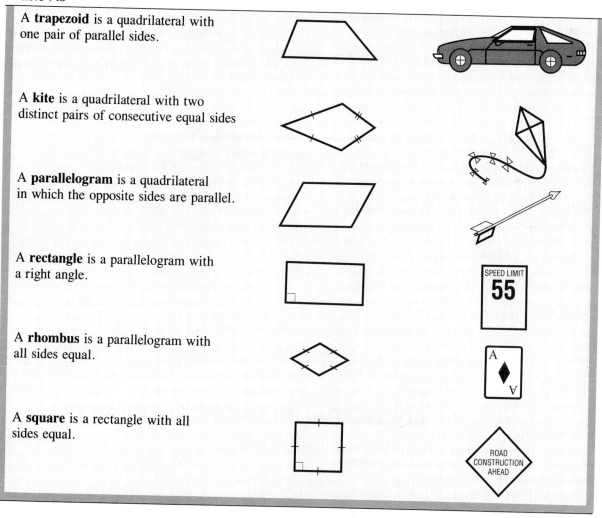

A **trapezoid** is a quadrilateral with one pair of parallel sides.

A **kite** is a quadrilateral with two distinct pairs of consecutive equal sides

A **parallelogram** is a quadrilateral in which the opposite sides are parallel.

A **rectangle** is a parallelogram with a right angle.

A **rhombus** is a parallelogram with all sides equal.

A **square** is a rectangle with all sides equal.

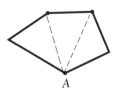

A

FIGURE 7.50

C. *Angles of a Polygon*

In Section 7.2, we learned that the sum of the measures of the three angles of any triangle is 180°. We can use this idea to find the corresponding sum S for any convex polygon. For example, suppose the polygon is a pentagon as shown in Figure 7.50. Select any vertex, say, A, and draw lines from A to each nonadjacent vertex, as shown by the dashed lines in the figure. The resulting number of triangles is three (two less than the five sides of the polygon), and the number of degrees in the angles of these three triangles is $3 \times 180° = 540°$.

This result can be generalized to any convex polygon; if the polygon has n sides, there will be $n - 2$ triangles. We have the following result:

> The sum S of the measures of the interior angles of any convex polygon with n sides is given by
>
> $$S = (n - 2)180°$$

Furthermore, if the polygon is a regular polygon, then the angles are all equal. In this case, the measure of a single angle of the polygon is just the preceding result divided by n, the total number of angles. This idea is illustrated in the next example.

EXAMPLE 5   Find the measure of an angle of a regular heptagon.

Solution   Since a heptagon has seven sides, the formula gives

$$S = (7 - 2)180° = 5 \times 180° = 900°$$

Because the polygon is regular, each angle has measure

$$\frac{900°}{7} = 128\frac{4}{7}°$$

∎

Exercise 7.3

A.   In problems 1 and 2, sketch a broken line path as described.

   1. (a) Closed but not simple   (b) Simple but not closed

   2. (a) Both simple and closed   (b) Neither simple nor closed

In problems 3–7, use the alphabet as printed here.

ABCDEFGHIJKLMNOPQRSTUVWXYZ

   3. Which letters form a path that is:
      (a) Simple?   (b) Closed?

   4. Which letters form a path that is:
      (a) Closed but not simple?   (b) Simple but not closed?

5. Which letters form a path that is:
   (a) Simple and closed?
   (b) Neither simple nor closed?

6. If the lowest points of the legs of the letter M are joined by a straight line segment, will the resulting polygon be concave or convex?

7. If the highest points of the legs of the letter V are joined by a straight line segment, will the resulting polygon be concave or convex?

8. Refer to the traffic signs in Example 2, and name the shape of:
   (a) The information sign
   (b) The no passing sign

B. In problems 9–16, name the given quadrilaterals.

9.

10.

11.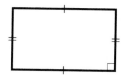

12.

13.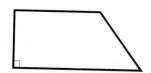

14.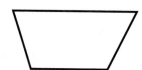

15.

16.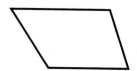

In problems 17–24, classify the given triangles as scalene, isosceles, or equilateral, and as acute, right, or obtuse.

17.

18.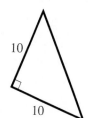

19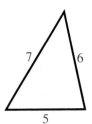

20.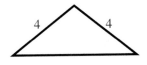

21.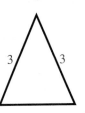

22.

23.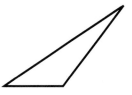

24.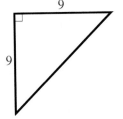

In problems 25–28, use the following table, which lists all possible triangle classifications. For example, IR stands for an isosceles right triangle, SO stands for a scalene obtuse triangle, and so on. The problems ask you to draw certain types of triangles. In any case where you think no such triangle exists, write "impossible."

	Acute	Right	Obtuse
Scalene	SA	SR	SO
Isosceles	IA	IR	IO
Equilateral	EA	ER	EO

25. Draw an example of type:
    (a) SA   (b) IA   (c) EA

26. Draw an example of type:
    (a) SR   (b) IR   (c) ER

27. Draw an example of type:
    (a) SO   (b) IO   (c) EO

28. Which of the triangles in the table are impossible?

29. In the given figures, $AC = BC$. Find the measures of the three angles of $\triangle ABC$.

(a)

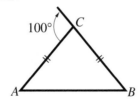

(b)

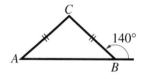

30. $ABCD$ is a parallelogram. Find the measure of $\angle BAD$.

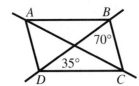

31. In the given figure, AE and BD are parallel and CE is perpendicular to BD. Find $m \angle BCD$.

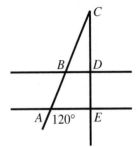

32. For the given figure, find $m \angle C$. What type of triangle is $\triangle ABC$?

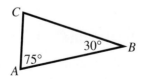

C. 33. Find the sum of the measures of the angles of a regular polygon with 14 sides.

34. Find the sum of the measures of the angles of a regular polygon with 20 sides.

In problems 35–40, find the measure of one angle of the indicated polygon.

35. A regular pentagon
36. A regular hexagon
37. A regular octagon
38. A regular nonagon
39. A regular decagon
40. A regular dodecagon

41. The information in Table 7.2 can be shown as the **family tree** or **hierarchy** shown in Figure 7.51, where each name includes all the shapes below it to which it is connected.
    (a) Use set notation to show the relationship between the set P of all polygons, the set T of all triangles, and so on.
    (b) Draw a Venn diagram to show the relationship between P, T, I, and E.

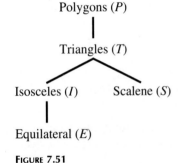

Polygons (P)

Triangles (T)

Isosceles (I)   Scalene (S)

Equilateral (E)

FIGURE 7.51

42. Show a family tree or hierarchy for the quadrilaterals in Table 7.3. Here are the first two steps:

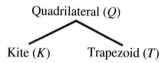

43. Draw a Venn diagram to represent the hierarchy shown in problem 42.

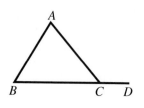

FIGURE 7.52

In Other Words

44. In Figure 7.52, $\angle ACD$ is called an **exterior angle** of $\triangle ABC$. In relation to this angle, $\angle A$ and $\angle B$ are called the **remote interior angles.** Can you find a relationship between the measures of an exterior angle and its corresponding two remote interior angles? Write out this relationship in words and explain.

45. In geometry we say that two figures are **congruent** if they have the same size and shape.
    (a) Do you think all angles have the same size?
    (b) Do you think all angles have the same shape?
    (c) Do you think that two angles that have the same size must have the same shape?

Using Your Knowledge

In geometry, if two figures are congruent (symbolized by $\cong$), they can be placed one on the other to coincide exactly. In the case of two polygons, congruence means that the corresponding sides of the polygons are equal and the corresponding angles are of equal measure. If the polygons are triangles, there are three useful statements about congruence:

*(1) **The SSS statement:** If the three sides of one triangle are equal to the corresponding sides of a second triangle, the triangles are congruent. This statement says that if $\overrightarrow{AB} = \overrightarrow{DE}$, $\overrightarrow{BC} = \overrightarrow{EF}$, and $\overrightarrow{AC} = \overrightarrow{DF}$, then $\triangle ABC \cong \triangle DEF$. (Corresponding parts of the triangles are marked in the following figures.)*

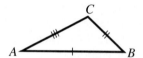
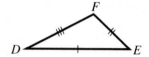

*(2) **The SAS statement:** If two sides and the included angle of one triangle are equal to the corresponding two sides and the included angle of a second triangle, the triangles are congruent.*

This statement says that if $\overrightarrow{AB} = \overrightarrow{DE}$, $\overrightarrow{AC} = \overrightarrow{DF}$, and $m\angle BAC = m\angle EDF$, then $\triangle ABC \cong \triangle DEF$.

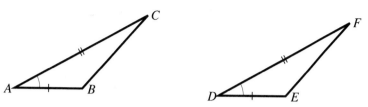

(3) **The ASA statement:** *If two angles and the included side of one triangle are equal to the corresponding two angles and the included side of a second triangle, the triangles are congruent.*
This statement says that if $m\angle A = m\angle D$, $m\angle B = m\angle E$, and $\overrightarrow{AB} = \overrightarrow{DE}$, then $\triangle ABC \cong \triangle DEF$.

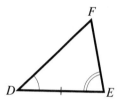

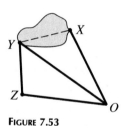

FIGURE 7.53

These three statements are useful in surveying and in construction problems. For example, to measure the distance across a swamp (see Figure 7.53), a surveyor was able to sight the points X and Y from a point O, and he could measure the distance from O to X. He then used his transit to lay out $\angle YOZ = \angle YOX$ and laid out $\overrightarrow{OZ} = \overrightarrow{OX}$. Finally, he measured the length of $\overrightarrow{ZY}$, which gave him the distance across the swamp. Why? Since $\overrightarrow{OX} = \overrightarrow{OZ}$, $\overrightarrow{OY} = \overrightarrow{OY}$, and $m\angle YOZ = m\angle YOX$, the SAS statement applies and $\triangle OXY \cong \triangle OZY$. Therefore, the corresponding sides $\overrightarrow{ZY}$ and $\overrightarrow{XY}$ equal.
Try to use these ideas to solve the following problems:

46. A parallelogram *ABCD* is cut in two along the diagonal *AC*. Which of the SSS, SAS, ASA statements guarantees that the two triangles so formed are congruent?

47. A carpenter needs a pair of shelf braces. He cuts a wooden rectangle in half along one of the diagonals. Explain why this gives him two congruent right triangles for his braces.

48. Sonya wants to find the distance across a river. She finds a point *A* on one bank where she can sight a tree *T* directly across the river on the other bank. (See Figure 7.54.) She walks 40 yd along the stream in a direction perpendicular to the line $\overleftrightarrow{AT}$, and arrives at a point *B*, where she can sight the tree *T* again. Using a surveyor's transit, and with the help of an assistant, she locates a point *C* on the line $\overleftrightarrow{AT}$ and such that $m\angle ABC = m\angle ABT$. She then finds the length of $\overrightarrow{AC}$ to be 67 yd and concludes this to be the distance across the river. Justify Sonya's answer.

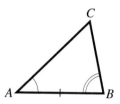

FIGURE 7.54

49. Can you see why an AAS statement is not needed?

50. Can you see why an SSA statement doesn't work? Make some sketches to show this. Keep in mind that SSA means that the angle is not between the two sides.

Discovery

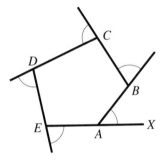

FIGURE 7.55

*If you extend each side of a convex polygon in one direction, as shown in the figure in the margin, you form a set of exterior angles of the polygon. An **exterior angle** is an angle between the extension of one side and the next side of the polygon. For instance, ∠XAB in Figure 7.55 is one such angle.*

Imagine yourself walking around the perimeter of the polygon. Every time you come to a vertex you must turn through the exterior angle at that vertex to stay on the perimeter of the polygon. When you finish your trip and arrive back at your starting point, you will have made a complete revolution. Therefore, it follows that the sum of the measures of one set of exterior angles is 360°.

If the polygon is regular, then all the exterior angles are equal. Thus, if we know the measure of one exterior angle, we can discover the number of sides of the polygon. For instance, if the measure of one exterior angle of a regular polygon is 30°, we let n be the number of sides. Then we know that $n \times 30° = 360°$. To discover how many sides the polygon has, we just have to solve the equation

$$30n = 360$$

This gives $n = 12$, so that the polygon is a dodecagon. Use this idea to find the number of sides of a regular convex polygon if one exterior angle has measure:

51. 60°   52. 24°   53. 72°   54. 15°

55. It is not possible for an exterior angle of a regular convex polygon to have measure 25°. Can you discover why?

7.4 SIMILAR TRIANGLES

GETTING STARTED

USING SIMILAR FIGURES IN CHARTS AND GRAPHS

The Social Security graph shows the number of workers needed to pay for the benefits of one worker in different years. Does the graph accurately depict the situation? Look at the figures for 1975 and 2005. Should these figures be **similar** (same shape, different size) or **identical**? To make the graph accurate, we can draw the height of the figures to **scale**. Since the drawings for the years 1960 and 2035 represent 5.1 and 1.9 workers, respectively, the height of the

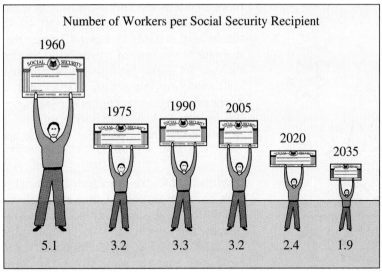

Number of Workers per Social Security Recipient

Source: Social Security Administration

figures for 1960 should be $\frac{5.1}{1.9}$ or 2.7 times the height of the figures for 2035. The 2035 figures measure about 0.5 in., so the 1960 figures should measure about 1.4 in. Is the diagram about right? Measure and see! What about the figures for the Social Security cards themselves? Are they **similar**?

Now, let us turn to the soft drink graph. Since Diet Coke represents 28.8% of the market while Diet 7-Up is 6.7%, Diet Coke should be $\frac{28.8}{6.7} = 4.3$

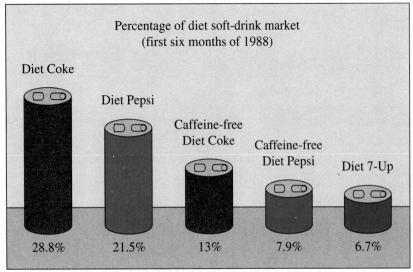

Percentage of diet soft-drink market
(first six months of 1988)

Source: *Beverage World*; survey of national chain food stores

times as tall as the Diet 7-Up (0.5 in.), that is, 2.2 in. The Diet Coke can is actually 1.5 in. tall. Why? Since soft drinks are measured by volume, perhaps the drawing is trying to depict 4.3 times the **volume** of the 7-Up can. (The formula for the volume of a cylinder in Section 7.7 will show you that this is not the case!) Clearly, the concept of similarity is important when dealing with scale models of things such as spacecraft, cars, office buildings, and bridges. Architects, engineers, clothes designers, and scientists use scale models to see how objects look without having to make them to actual size. In this section we will study similar polygons and their applications.

FIGURE 7.56

In everyday life, we learn to recognize objects such as buildings and automobiles more on account of their shape than their size. Geometric figures with exactly the same shape, but not necessarily the same size, are called **similar figures.** The six-pointed stars in Figure 7.56 are similar polygons.

Look at the two similar triangles $\triangle ABC$ and $\triangle DEF$ in Figure 7.57. Because they have the same shape, the corresponding angles are equal. In the figure, $m \angle A = m \angle D$, $m \angle B = m \angle E$, and $m \angle C = m \angle F$. The corresponding sides of the two triangles are $\overleftrightarrow{AB}$ and $\overleftrightarrow{DE}$, $\overleftrightarrow{BC}$ and $\overleftrightarrow{EF}$, and $\overleftrightarrow{AC}$ and $\overleftrightarrow{DF}$. Notice that the length of each side of $\triangle DEF$ is one-half the length of the corresponding side of $\triangle ABC$.

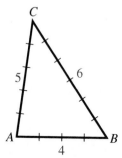

FIGURE 7.57

Definition 7.1

Two triangles are **similar** (denoted by $\triangle ABC \sim \triangle DEF$) if and only if they have equal corresponding angles and the corresponding sides are proportional.

Recall that the ratio of two numbers, a and b, is the fraction a/b. For Figure 7.57, we have

$$\frac{DE}{AB} = \frac{EF}{BC} = \frac{DF}{AC} = \frac{1}{2}$$

as the ratio of corresponding sides.

EXAMPLE 1   Two similar triangles are shown in Figure 7.58. Find d and f for $\triangle DEF$.

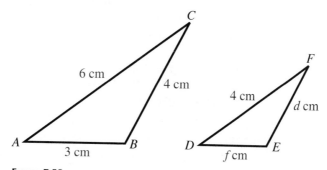

FIGURE 7.58

Solution   Since $\triangle ABC \sim \triangle DEF$, the corresponding sides must be proportional. Thus,

$$\frac{DE}{AB} = \frac{EF}{BC} = \frac{DF}{AC}$$

so that

$$\frac{f}{3} = \frac{d}{4} = \frac{4}{6}$$

Since $\frac{4}{6} = \frac{2}{3}$, we have

$$\frac{d}{4} = \frac{2}{3} \quad \text{and} \quad \frac{f}{3} = \frac{2}{3}$$

Solving these equations for d and f, we get

$$d = \frac{8}{3} = 2\frac{2}{3} \quad \text{and} \quad f = \frac{6}{3} = 2$$

∎

For similar triangles, we have statements analogous to the SSS, SAS, and ASA statements for congruent triangles (see the Using Your Knowledge section in Exercise 7.3).

1. **The AA statement:** If two angles of a triangle are equal to the corresponding two angles of a second triangle, the triangles are similar.

Note that if there are two pairs of equal angles, then the remaining pair must also be equal. (Remember that the sum of the measures of the angles of any triangle is 180°.) Thus, the two triangles would have the same shape.

2. **The SAS similarity statement:** If an angle of one triangle is equal to an angle of a second triangle, and if the sides including this angle are proportional, then the triangles are similar.

The proof of this statement is given in the Discovery section of Exercise 7.4.

EXAMPLE 2   Wally wanted to find the distance across a lake, so he located a point A from which he could sight points B and C on opposite ends of the lake. See Figure 7.59. With a surveyor's sextant, Wally found that $m\angle A = 35°$. He was able to measure $\overrightarrow{AB}$ and $\overrightarrow{AC}$ as 400 m and 300 m, respectively. He took this data to his office and drew a triangle that he labeled $A_1 B_1 C_1$ with $m\angle A_1 = 35°$, $\overrightarrow{A_1 B_1} = 40$ cm and $\overrightarrow{A_1 C_1} = 30$ cm. He then measured $\overrightarrow{B_1 C_1}$ and found it to be 23.1 cm long. How could Wally use all this information to find the distance across the lake?

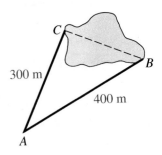

FIGURE 7.59

Solution   Since Wally made $m\angle A_1 = m\angle A$, and he used the same scale (10 m/cm) for $\overrightarrow{A_1 B_1}$ and $\overrightarrow{A_1 C_1}$, he knows that $\triangle A_1 B_1 C_1 \sim \triangle ABC$. Therefore, if the length of BC is x meters, then

$$\frac{400}{40} = \frac{300}{30} = \frac{x}{23.1}$$

so that

$$\frac{x}{23.1} = 10 \quad \text{and} \quad x = 231$$

Thus, Wally found the distance across the lake to be 231 m.   ■

3. **The SSS similarity statement:** If the ratios of the lengths of the three sides of one triangle to the lengths of the corresponding sides of a second triangle are all the same, the triangles are similar.

   The proof of this statement is also left for the Discovery section of Exercise 7.4.

EXAMPLE 3   Polly, who worked in an architect's office, had to make a scale drawing of a panel in the shape of a parallelogram. The base of the panel was 10 ft long, the adjacent side was 4 ft long, and the longer diagonal was 12 ft long. Polly drew a parallelogram, $ABCD$, with the base $AB = 5$ cm, the adjacent side $BC = 2$ cm, and the longer diagonal $AC = 6$ cm (see Figure 7.60). Why is her parallelogram similar to the panel parallelogram?

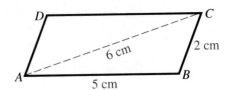

FIGURE 7.60

Solution Let A_1, B_1, C_1, D_1 be the vertices of the panel corresponding to the points A, B, C, D in Polly's drawing. Since Polly used the scale 1 cm per 2 ft for her drawing, the ratios of the corresponding lines are all the same. Thus, triangle $A_1 B_1 C_1$ is similar to triangle ABC, and triangle $A_1 D_1 C_1$ is similar to triangle ADC. Therefore, the corresponding angles of these triangles are equal, so that the corresponding angles of the two parallelograms are equal. Because corresponding sides have the same ratio and corresponding angles are equal, the two parallelograms are similar. ∎

Exercise 7.4

1. Which (if any) of the rectangles below are similar?

   (a) 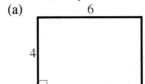 (b) 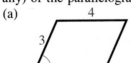 (c)

2. The marked angles in the parallelograms below are all equal. Which (if any) of the parallelograms are similar?

   (a) 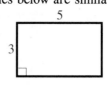 (b) (c)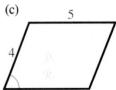

3. Which (if any) of the following triangles are similar?

   (a) 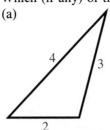 (b) 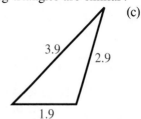 (c)

4. The marked angles in the following triangles are all equal. Which (if any) aof the triangles are similar?

   (a) 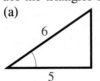 (b) (c)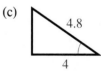

5. The following triangles are similar. Find the lengths marked x and y.

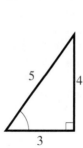
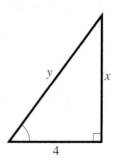

6. The following parallelograms are similar. Find the length of the diagonal PR.

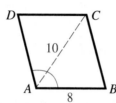
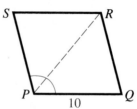

Problems 7–10 refer to Figure 7.61. In this figure, PQ is parallel to AB. In each problem, certain lengths are given. Find the indicated missing length.

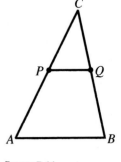

	AP	PC	BQ	BC
7.	3	4	6	?
8.	5	4	?	6
9.	2	?	3	5
10.	?	4	4	8

FIGURE 7.61

11. The sides of a triangle measure 6, 9, and 12 cm, respectively. The longest side of a similar triangle measures 7 cm. Find the lengths of the other two sides of the smaller triangle.

12. In problem 11, if the length of the shortest side of the smaller triangle is 5 cm, find the lengths of the other two sides.

13. The sides of a triangle measure 2, 3, and 4 in., respectively. The perimeter of a similar triangle is 36 in. long. Find the length of each side of the second triangle.

14. Jackie has a piece of wire 18 in. long. She wants to bend this into a triangle similar to a triangle whose sides are 3 in., 4 in., and 5 in. long, respectively. What must be the dimensions of her triangle?

15. A telephone pole casts a shadow 30 ft long at the same time that a 5-ft fence post casts a shadow 8 ft long. How tall is the telephone pole?

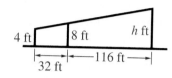

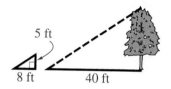

FIGURE 7.62

16. Betty wants to measure the height of a flagpole. She puts up a vertical post 8 ft tall and moves back in line with the flagpole and the post until her line of sight hits the tops of both post and pole. (See Figure 7.62.) If the known distances are as shown in the figure, what height does Betty find for the flagpole?

17. Ronny wants to find the height of a tree standing on level ground. He places a 5-ft stake vertically so that the sun throws a shadow of the tree and the stake as shown in the diagram. He then measures the lengths of the shadows, with the results shown in Figure 7.63. Why are the two triangles similar? What height did Ronny find for the tree?

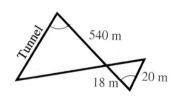

FIGURE 7.63

18. Gail wants to measure the distance AB across a small lake. (See Figure 7.64.) She walks 240 m away in a direction perpendicular to the line AB to a point C from which she can sight the point B. She then walks back 80 m along CA to a point P, and then walks in a direction perpendicular to CA to a point Q in line with B and C. She finds that $PQ = 60$ m. With this data, what does Gail find for the distance AB?

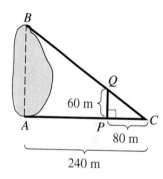

FIGURE 7.64

19. Sonny, the surveyor, needs to find the length of a tunnel to be bored through a small hilly area. He makes the marked angles equal and finds the measurements shown in Figure 7.65. What length should Sonny find for the tunnel?

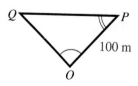

FIGURE 7.65

20. To find the distance between two points P and Q separated by an inaccessible area, Andy makes the measurements shown in Figure 7.66. He returns to his office and draws $\triangle ABC$ with $m\angle A = m\angle O$, $m\angle B = m\angle P$, and $\overleftrightarrow{AB} = 10$ cm. He then measures $\overleftrightarrow{BC}$, finding it to be 18 cm. What length would Andy find for PQ?

FIGURE 7.66

In Other Words

21. Explain why the two triangles in Figure 7.65 are similar.

22. When a boat, car, or plane is manufactured, a model of it is constructed first. Explain what the model and the actual structure have in common.

23. Some distances are not easy to measure directly (the distance across a lake, as we have shown). Describe in your own words a situation in which indirect measurements using similar triangles are used.

24. Johnny claims that he has drawn two similar triangles. He says the sides of the first triangle are 4 cm, 5 cm, and 7 cm long and that the corresponding sides of the second triangle are 8 cm, 10 cm, and 12 cm long. Betty says that Johnny is making a mistake. Write out a complete explanation and justification for Betty's claim.

Using Your Knowledge

You can use what you know about similar triangles to prove the following important result:

> *A line parallel to one side of a triangle and cutting the other two sides, divides these sides proportionally.*

In Figure 7.67, if PQ is parallel to AB, then

$$\frac{AC}{PC} = \frac{BC}{QC}$$

This follows because $\triangle ABC \sim \triangle PQC$. *But* $AC = AP + PC$ *and* $BC = BQ + QC$, *so by substituting for AC and BC, we get*

$$\frac{AP + PC}{PC} = \frac{BQ + QC}{QC}$$

or

$$\frac{AP}{PC} + \frac{PC}{PC} = \frac{BQ}{QC} + \frac{QC}{QC}$$

which is the same as

$$\frac{AP}{PC} + 1 = \frac{BQ}{QC} + 1$$

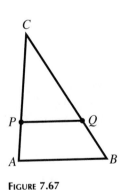

FIGURE 7.67

Therefore,

$$\frac{AP}{PC} = \frac{BQ}{QC}$$

This result can be used to show that:

> *On any two transversals, parallel lines cut off segments whose lengths are proportional.*

In Figure 7.68, $\overleftrightarrow{AC}$ and $\overleftrightarrow{PR}$ are two transversals, cut by the three parallel lines $\overleftrightarrow{AP}$, $\overleftrightarrow{BQ}$, and $\overleftrightarrow{CR}$. The dashed line is drawn joining P and C and intersecting $\overleftrightarrow{BQ}$ at the point labeled S. In $\triangle CPR$, the segment SQ is parallel to CR, so that

$$\frac{PS}{SC} = \frac{PQ}{QR}$$

In $\triangle ACP$, the line segment BS is parallel to AP, so that

$$\frac{PS}{SC} = \frac{AB}{BC}$$

Since AB/BC and PQ/QR are both equal to PS/SC, the desired proportion follows; that is,

$$\frac{AB}{BC} = \frac{PQ}{QR}$$

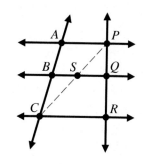

FIGURE 7.68

___ *Here is an application of this result. In Figure 7.69, the lengths of $\overline{LM}$, $\overline{MN}$, and $\overline{RS}$ are as shown. The length x of ST must be such that*

$$\frac{x}{5} = \frac{3}{2}$$

Therefore,

$$x = \frac{15}{2} = 7.5$$

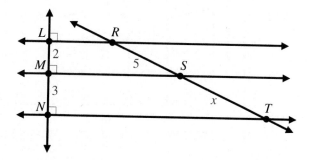

FIGURE 7.69

Use these ideas to solve the following problems.

25. The marked angles in Figure 7.70 are all equal. Find the value of x and the value of y.

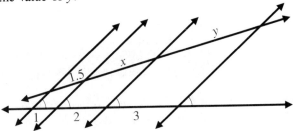

FIGURE 7.70

26. Bobby marks points A, B, and C on one transversal so that $AB = 1$ cm and $BC = 3$ cm. He then marks corresponding points D, E, and F on a second transversal so that $DE = 3$ cm and $EF = 5$ cm. If Bobby draws the lines AD, BE, and CF, will these lines be parallel? Explain.

FIGURE 7.71

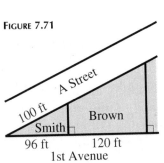

27. Mr. Smith and Ms. Brown own the lots shown in Figure 7.71. A survey of Mr. Smith's lot showed a frontage of 100 ft on A Street and 96 ft on 1st Avenue. Ms. Brown measured her 1st Avenue frontage to be 120 ft. How much frontage does Brown have on A Street?

28. The owners of the four lots in Figure 7.72 are the Allens (A), the Bakers (B), the Cooks (C), and the Danes (D). The county agrees to pave L Street between 1st Avenue and 2nd Avenue if the property owners pay for the cost of the materials, with each owner to pay a share proportional to the owner's frontage on L Street. If the frontage figures are as shown in the diagram, find what fraction of the cost of materials each owner will have to pay.

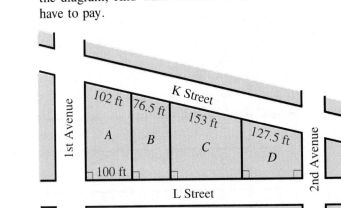

FIGURE 7.72

Discovery

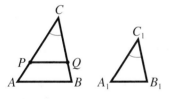

FIGURE 7.73

In order to prove the SAS similarity statement, let the two triangles be ABC and $A_1B_1C_1$ in Figure 7.73. Suppose that

$$m\angle C = m\angle C_1 \quad and \quad \frac{AC}{A_1C_1} = \frac{BC}{B_1C_1}$$

We want to prove that: $\triangle ABC \sim \triangle A_1B_1C_1$.

Suppose that $\triangle ABC$ is the larger of the two triangles. Mark a point P on AC so that $PC = A_1C_1$. Then draw a line PQ parallel to AB and meeting BC at Q.

29. $m\angle CPQ = m\angle A$ and $m\angle CQP = m\angle B$. Why?
30. Therefore, $\triangle PQC \sim \triangle ABC$. Can you discover the reason for this?

31. Now, $\dfrac{AC}{PC} = \dfrac{BC}{QC}$ Why?

32. Since $PC = A_1C_1$, it follows that

$$\frac{AC}{A_1C_1} = \frac{BC}{B_1C_1} = \frac{BC}{QC}$$

Why? Remember that the equality of the first two fractions was given.

33. From the equality of the second two fractions, we see that $B_1C_1 = QC$. Why?
34. The SAS congruence statement tells us that $\triangle PQC \cong \triangle A_1B_1C_1$. Can you discover why?
35. It now follows that $\triangle ABC \sim \triangle A_1B_1C_1$. Why?
36. The SSS similarity statement can be proved in about the same way as the preceding proof. Can you discover how to put the proof together?

7.5 PERIMETER AND CIRCUMFERENCE

GETTING STARTED

HATS, RINGS, AND CIRCUMFERENCES

Do you know your hat size? If you don't, you will be glad to know that it is supposed to be about the same as your ring size! (See *Rules of Thumb* by Tom Parker.) How can that be? The ancient Greeks discovered that if they divided the circumference C of a circle by the length of its diameter d, they always obtained approximately the same number, π, regardless of the size of the circle. You can verify this by measuring the circumference (the distance around) of a soda can and dividing by its diameter. The answer should be about 3.14. The formula used to do this is the same one used by the Greeks, $\frac{C}{d} = \pi$. Now, back to rings and hats. The average man's head is about 23 in. in circumference. If you divide 23 by π (3.14), that is, $\frac{23}{\pi}$, the answer is the diameter $d = 7.32$. Unfortunately, hats are sized in increments of $\frac{1}{8}$ in. What size, to the nearest $\frac{1}{8}$ in., is the closest to 7.32 in.? We know that $7\frac{2}{8} = 7\frac{1}{4} = 7.25$ and can easily find $7\frac{3}{8} = 7.375$. Thus, $7\frac{3}{8}$ is the closest to our measure of $d = 7.32$ in. Now you know that your hat size is really the "average diameter" of your head in inches. How can this be the same as your ring size? Assume that your hat size is 7 (in. in diameter). What would a 7 ring size measure? According to a jewelry handbook, the diameter d of a ring (in in.) is given by

$$d = 0.458 + 0.032s$$

where s is the ring size When $s = 7$,

$$d = 0.458 + 0.032 \cdot 7 = 0.682 \text{ in.}$$

Since the diameter of the ring, and hence of the finger, is 0.682 in., the circumference of the finger should be $C = 3.14 \cdot 0.682 = 2.14$ in. You can repeat this little experiment by measuring your own head, dividing by π, and obtaining your hat size. Now, substitute your hat size for s in the formula and multiply the result by π. The answer you get should be the same as the circumference of your finger! What if it is not even close? Keep in mind that hat sizes and ring sizes should be the same for an *average* person. If you lose or gain weight, the circumference of your finger decreases or increases, respectively, but your head size does not.

In this section we study circles and the perimeters of circles, called **circumferences,** and the different applications we can solve using these ideas.

In geometry, units of length are used to measure distances along lines and are consequently called **linear measures.** Table 7.4 shows the standard units of length in the U.S customary system and the metric system.

Table 7.4 *Standard Units of Length*

U.S. System	Metric System
inch (in.)	millimeter (mm) = 0.001 m
foot (ft) = 12 in.	centimeter (cm) = 0.01 m
yard (yd) = 3 ft	meter (m) = base unit
mile (mi) = 1760 yd	kilometer (km) = 1,000 m
= 5280 ft	

Note that the metric system is a simple decimal system in contrast to the awkward conversions in the U.S. system. Although you will not be asked to convert from one of these systems to the other in this chapter, you should know that the U.S. inch is legally defined to be exactly 2.54 centimeters long. Here are a few simple conversions to help you see the relationship between metric and U.S. lengths.

1 in. = 2.54 cm	1 cm = 0.39 in.
1 yd = 0.91 m	1 m = 1.09 yd
1 mi = 1.61 km	1 km = 0.62 mi

So a centimeter is about 4/10 of an inch, a meter is just a bit longer than a yard, and a kilometer is about 2/3 of a mile.

A. *Polygonal Paths*

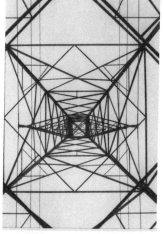

How many kinds of polygons can you see in this view looking up through the center of a tower that supports power lines?

Many of the applications of geometry involve finding the length of a polygonal path. For instance, fencing a field, laying tile around a rectangular pool, or finding the amount of baseboard needed for a room all involve measuring around polygons. The distance around a plane figure is generally called the **perimeter** of the figure. In the case of a polygon, the perimeter is just the sum of the lengths of the sides. Table 7.5 gives the formulas for the perimeters in terms of the sides for some of the polygons we have discussed. Note that perimeters are always expressed in linear measures.

Table 7.5

Name	Geometric Shapes	Perimeter
Triangle		$P = s_1 + s_2 + b$
Trapezoid		$P = s_1 + s_2 + b_1 + b_2$
Parallelogram		$P = 2L + 2W$
Rectangle		$P = 2L + 2W$
Square		$P = 4s$

EXAMPLE 1   The *Mona Lisa* by Leonardo da Vinci was assessed at $100 million for in-
surance purposes. The picture measures 30.5 by 20.9 in. Find the perimeter of
this picture.

Solution   Because the picture is rectangular, its perimeter is given by

$$P = 2L + 2W$$

where $L = 30.5$ and $W = 20.9$. Thus,

$$P = 2(30.5) + 2(20.9)$$
$$= 102.8 \text{ in.}$$

∎

The ideas we have been studying here can be combined with the algebra
you know to solve certain kinds of problems. Here is an interesting problem.

EXAMPLE 2   The largest recorded poster was a rectangular greeting card 166 ft long and
with a perimeter of 458.50 ft. How wide was this poster?

Solution   The perimeter of a rectangle is $P = 2L + 2W$ and we know that $L = 166$ and
$P = 458.50$. Thus, we can write

$$2(166) + 2W = 458.50$$
$$332 + 2W = 458.50$$
$$2W = 126.50$$
$$W = 63.25$$

Thus, the poster was 63.25 ft wide.

∎

EXAMPLE 3   John and Emily Gardener want to fence in a small, rectangular plot for Emily's
kitchen garden. John has 20 m of fencing and decides that the length of the
plot should be one and one-half times its width. What will be the dimensions
of Emily's garden plot?

Solution   We let x meters be the width of the plot. Then the length must be $\frac{3}{2}x$ m. We
know the perimeter is to be 20 m, so

$$2L + 2W = P$$
$$2(\tfrac{3}{2}x) + 2x = 20$$
$$3x + 2x = 20$$
$$5x = 20$$
$$x = 4, \qquad \tfrac{3}{2}x = 6$$

Emily's plot will be 6 m long and 4 m wide.

∎

B. *Circles*

You are probably familiar with the geometric figure that we call a circle. The circle has been of great interest ever since prehistoric times; it always has been used for many decorative and practical purposes. Here is a modern definition:

Definition 7.2

> A **circle** is the set of all coplanar points at a given fixed distance (the **radius**) from a given point (the **center**).

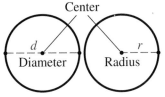

FIGURE 7.74

Figure 7.74 shows two circles with the radius and the diameter indicated. Note that the **diameter** consists of two collinear radii, so that $d = 2r$; that is, the length of the diameter is twice the length of the radius.

The perimeter of a circle is known as the **circumference.** We noted earlier that the length of the circumference of a circle is given by the formula

$$C = \pi d = 2\pi r$$

The irrational number $\pi \approx 3.14159$ was discussed in Section 4.7. Unless otherwise noted, you may use the approximate value 3.14 for the problems in this book.

EXAMPLE 4 Andy has a circular swimming pool with a diameter of 25 ft. To keep his little boy from falling into the water, Andy wants to put a low wire fence around the circumference of the pool. How much fencing does he need?

Solution We use $C = \pi d$ to get

$$C \approx (3.14)(25) = 78.5 \text{ ft}$$

Since 3.14 is a little less than π, Andy should play safe and get 79 ft of fencing.

■

EXAMPLE 5 According to the *Guinness Book of World Records,* one of the largest beef hamburgers had a circumference of 27.50 ft. Find the diameter of this hamburger to the nearest hundredth of a foot. Use $\pi \approx 3.14$.

Solution Since the circumference of a circle is $C = \pi d$, we have

$$27.50 \approx 3.14d$$

Dividing by 3.14, we find

$$d = 8.76 \qquad \text{to the nearest hundredth}$$

Thus, the diameter of this mammoth beef hamburger was about 8.76 ft. (It also weighed 2859 lb.) [*Note:* If you used a more accurate value of π, you would find the diameter to be 8.75 ft to the nearest hundredth of a foot.]

■

Exercise 7.5

A. In problems 1–8, find the perimeter of the given polygon.

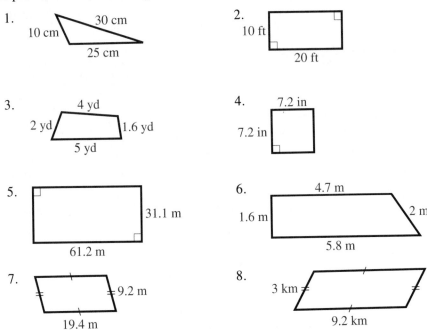

1. 10 cm, 30 cm, 25 cm

2. 10 ft, 20 ft

3. 4 yd, 2 yd, 1.6 yd, 5 yd

4. 7.2 in, 7.2 in

5. 31.1 m, 61.2 m

6. 4.7 m, 1.6 m, 2 m, 5.8 m

7. 9.2 m, 19.4 m

8. 3 km, 9.2 km

9. If one side of a regular pentagon is 6 cm long, find the perimeter of the pentagon.

10. If one side of an octagonal stop sign is 6 in. long, what is the perimeter of the stop sign?

11. The largest rectangular omelet ever cooked was 30 ft long and had an 80-ft perimeter. How wide was it?

12. Do you have a large swimming pool? If you were to walk around the largest pool in the world, in Casablanca, Morocco, you would walk more than 1 km. To be exact, you would go 1,110 m. If the pool is 480 m long, how wide is it?

13. A baseball diamond is actually a square. A batter who hits a home run must run 360 ft around the bases. What is the distance to first base?

14. The playing surface of a football field is 120 yd long. A player jogging around the perimeter of this surface covers 346 yd. How wide is the playing surface?

15. Have you seen the largest scientific building in the world? It is in Cape Canaveral, Florida. If you were to walk around the perimeter of this building, you would cover 2,468 ft. If this rectangular building is 198 ft longer than it is wide, what are its dimensions?

16. The largest regular hexagon that can be cut from a circular sheet of cardboard has each side equal to the radius of the circle. If you cut such a hexagon from a sheet of radius 5 in., how much shorter is the perimeter of the hexagon than the circumference of the circle?

In problems 17–24, find the circumference. First, give the answer in terms of π, then calculate the approximate answer using $\pi \approx 3.14$.

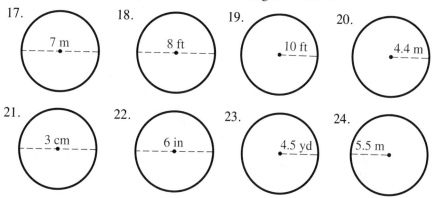

17. 7 m

18. 8 ft

19. 10 ft

20. 4.4 m

21. 3 cm

22. 6 in

23. 4.5 yd

24. 5.5 m

In the following problems, first give an exact answer in terms of π, then calculate the required approximate answer using $\pi \approx 3.14$.

25. The diameter of a bicycle tire is 61 cm. Through what distance does the bicycle go when the wheel makes one complete turn? Give your answer to the nearest centimeter.

26. The lid on a garbage can has a diameter of 17 in. Find the length of the circumference of this lid. Give your answer to the nearest tenth of an inch.

27. The minute hand of a clock is 8 cm long. How far does the tip of the hand move in 1 hr? Give your answer to the nearest tenth of a centimeter.

28. The dial on a rotary telephone has a radius of 4.5 in. How far does a point on the rim of this dial travel when the dial makes three-fourths of a complete revolution?

29. Shirley wants to put a low, decorative wooden border around her circular flower bed. If the radius of the bed is 4 ft, how long must the border be? Give your answer to the nearest tenth of a foot.

30. A long-playing record has a radius of 6 in. How far does a point on the rim move when the record goes around once? Give your answer to the nearest tenth of an inch.

31. The circumference of a circle is 15π cm. Find the diameter and the radius of this circle.

32. A thin metal rod 8 ft long is to be bent into a circular hoop. Find the radius of this hoop to the nearest tenth of an inch.

33. To make a wedding band for a man who wears a size 12 ring, a strip of gold 7 cm long is needed. Find the diameter of this ring.

34. One of the largest pizzas ever made had a circumference of 251.2 ft. What was its diameter?

35. You already know from problem 30 that a long-playing record has a 6 in. radius. However, do you know the circumference of the smallest functional record? It is an amazing $4\frac{1}{8}$ in.! Find the diameter of this tiny record to the nearest hundredth of an inch.

36. The outside diameter of a motorcycle tire is 26 in. How many revolutions does the tire make in one *mile*? Round the answer to the nearest whole number. [*Hint:* 1 mi. = 5,280 ft.]

37. A motorcycle tire is guaranteed for 20,000 mi. Use the information from problem 36 to find out for how many revolutions the tire is guaranteed.

38. The largest doughnut ever made weighed 2,099 lb and had a 70-ft circumference. To the nearest whole number, what is the diameter of the smallest pan in which the doughnut could fit?

39. A circular pool is enclosed by a square deck 20 yd on each side. If the distance between the edge of the deck and the pool is 2 yd as shown, how far is it around the pool?

40. It takes about an hour to walk around the Colosseum in Rome. At this rate, how long would it take you to walk straight through along a diameter? (Assume the Colosseum is perfectly round and give the answer to the nearest minute.)

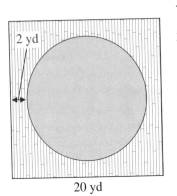

2 yd

20 yd

In Other Words

41. Which do you think is the better illustration of a circle: a perfectly round penny or a bicycle tire? (See Definition 7.2.)

42. The formula $C = 1.44 + 0.1\,s$ gives the circumference C (in inches) of a ring of size s. Explain how you would use this formula to find your ring size.

43. If two tires, one new and one worn, are installed on a car, which one will turn more times per mile? Explain your answer.

44. If your calculator has a π key, use this to calculate the answer to problem 30. In your own words, explain the discrepancy between the answer you obtained following the instructions for this problem and the new answer your calculator gave.

Discovery

A pencil compass and a straightedge are the traditional tools for making geometric constructions. Do you know how to draw an equilateral triangle? Just decide how long you want the sides to be. Draw a line segment, say, AB, of this length (see Figure 7.75). Open a pencil compass to this radius. Then, putting the point at one end, say, A, draw an arc. Place the point at B and

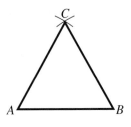

FIGURE 7.75
An equilateral triangle

draw another arc that intersects the first as shown. Where the two arcs intersect is the third vertex of the equilateral triangle.

It is also quite easy to construct a regular hexagon. Again, decide on the length of the side. Draw a circle with this length as radius. Then use this radius to mark off six equidistant points on the circle. These points are the vertices of the hexagon (see Figure 7.76). Can you see why this works? [Hint: Look at triangle OAB.]

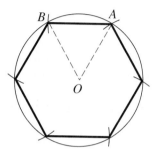

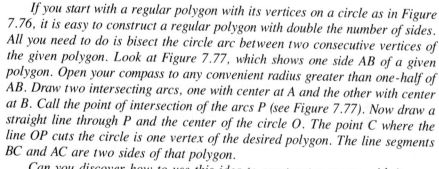

FIGURE 7.76
A regular hexagon

FIGURE 7.77

If you start with a regular polygon with its vertices on a circle as in Figure 7.76, it is easy to construct a regular polygon with double the number of sides. All you need to do is bisect the circle arc between two consecutive vertices of the given polygon. Look at Figure 7.77, which shows one side AB of a given polygon. Open your compass to any convenient radius greater than one-half of AB. Draw two intersecting arcs, one with center at A and the other with center at B. Call the point of intersection of the arcs P (see Figure 7.77). Now draw a straight line through P and the center of the circle O. The point C where the line OP cuts the circle is one vertex of the desired polygon. The line segments BC and AC are two sides of that polygon.

Can you discover how to use this idea to construct a square with its vertices on a given circle? You can start by drawing any diameter of the circle. The ends of this diameter will be two vertices of the square. Use the method of construction shown in Figure 7.77 to find two points, each equidistant from the ends of the diameter and one on each half of the circle. These points will be the other two vertices of the square (see Figure 7.78).

There is a rather complicated way to construct a regular pentagon and a regular decagon with straightedge and compass. We shall not consider this here. But it is interesting to know that mathematicians have proved that it is impossible to construct a regular heptagon or a regular nonagon with straightedge and compass alone.

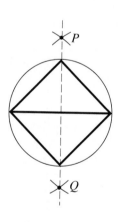

FIGURE 7.78

45. Use the preceding ideas to construct a regular octagon with its vertices on a given circle.

46. Use the preceding ideas to construct a regular dodecagon with its vertices on a given circle.

Calculator Corner

Many calculators come equipped with a $\boxed{\pi}$ *key (to access it, you may have to press* $\boxed{2nd}$ $\boxed{\pi}$*) that gives a nine-decimal-place approximation for* π*. If you use this approximation to solve Example 5, the answer obtained when dividing 27.50 by* π *comes out to be 8.75352187, or 8.75 to the nearest hundredth of a foot, as mentioned in the text.*

47. Rework problems 25, 26, 30, 32, and 34 of Exercise 7.5 on your calculator.

7.6   AREA MEASURE AND THE PYTHAGOREAN THEOREM

GETTING STARTED

PIZZA AREA

What is your telephone area code? What areas were severely affected by storms last year? The idea of **area** occurs in many contexts, but in geometry **area** is measured by defining a **unit region**. For example, a square whose side is **1 unit in length** has an area of **one square unit.** To measure larger areas, we measure how many **unit squares** are contained in the given region. In this section we develop formulas that give the area of several polygons as well as the area of a circle.

Now, suppose you want to find the area covered by the giant, 111-ft-diameter pizza made by Pizza Hut in Singapore on June 9, 1990. You will learn later that the formula for the area A of a circle of radius r is $A = \pi r^2$. Since the diameter of the pizza is 111 ft, its radius is 55.5 ft and its area $A = \pi \cdot 55.5^2 = 3080.25 \pi$ or about 9,670 ft^2!

In the same way, we can use areas to do some comparison shopping for pizzas. Suppose Pizza Hut sells medium pizzas (12 in. in diameter) with one topping for \$7.99. If we assume that the ingredients are of equal quality and the pizzas of equal thickness, is it better to buy one of these pizzas or get two 10-in. pizzas for \$4.99 each? We can compare by finding out how much we pay per square inch. The area of the \$7.99 pizza is $A = \pi \cdot (6 \text{ in.})^2 = 36 \pi$ or about 113 in.^{2} Thus, the price per square inch is $\frac{7.99}{113} = 0.07$, that is, about 7¢/in.^{2} On the other hand, the area of one 10-in. pizza is $A = \pi \cdot (5)^2 = 25 \pi$ or about 78.5 in.^{2} Thus, the area of two pizzas will be 157 in.^{2} and the price per square inch $\frac{2 \cdot 4.99}{157}$ or about 6.37¢/in.^{2} In this case, smaller is better; you pay less per square inch if you buy the two small pizzas. By the way, at 7¢/in.^{2}, how much would the 111-ft-diameter pizza be worth? Close to \$100,000! Check this out by keeping in mind that 1 square foot (1 ft)^2 is exactly 144 in^2. Here are two more questions for you. How many 12-in. pizzas are there in the Singapore pizza, and if you assume that a 12-in. pizza serves 8 people, how many people can be served with the Singapore pizza? Think of areas and use the techniques we just developed to find the answers.

Now consider the question of how much glass might be used in the construction of a skyscraper. If you think a moment, you will realize that the meaning of the question is not clear. Are you looking for the number of pieces of glass, the number of pounds of glass, or what? Let us be more specific and say that we want to know the total *area* covered by the glass in this building. In order to answer questions like this, we must have a good understanding of what we mean by *area*.

A. *Area of a Polygon*

We start by choosing the **unit region** to be that of a **square,** each of whose sides is **1 unit in length,** and we say that this region has an **area of 1 square unit** (see Figure 7.79). The side of the unit square may be 1 in., 1 ft, 1 mi, 1 cm, 1 m, and so on. The corresponding units of area are the square inch (in.²), the square foot (ft²), the square mile (mi²), the square centimeter (cm²), the square meter (m²), and so on.

Some of the commonly used units of area are given in the following table. Note that **area** is always measured in **square** units.

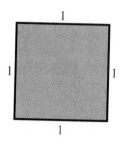

FIGURE 7.79
The unit of area measure

Standard Units of Area

U.S. System	Metric System
Square inch (in.²)	Square millimeter (mm²)
Square foot (ft²)	Square centimeter (cm²)
Square yard (yd²)	Square meter (m²)
Square mile (mi²)	Square kilometer (km²)

In everyday language, the area measure of a plane region is the *number of these unit regions contained in the given region.* Thus, suppose that we have a square with side 2 units long. Then, as shown in Figure 7.80, we can draw lines joining the midpoints of the opposite sides and dividing the square into 2 × 2 = 4 unit squares. We say that the area of the square is 4 square units. Similarly, for a rectangle that is 3 units by 4 units, we can draw lines parallel to the sides that divide the rectangle into 3 × 4 = 12 unit squares (see Figure 7.81). We say that the area of the rectangle is 12 square units.

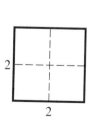

FIGURE 7.80
Area = 4 square units

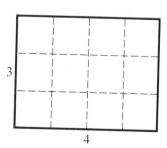

FIGURE 7.81
Area = 12 square units

The previous illustrations show how the area measure can be found if the sides of the rectangle are whole numbers. In order to avoid a complicated mathematical argument, we define the area of a rectangle of sides b units long and h units long to be bh square units (see Figure 7.82). Written as a formula, with A standing for area, this means

$$A = bh \qquad \text{Area of a rectangle}$$

Notice that we are following the usual custom of saying "area of a rectangle" to mean "area of a rectangular region." Similarly, we shall say "area of a polygon" to mean "area of a polygonal region."

Knowing the area of a rectangle, we can find the area of a parallelogram. The idea is to construct a rectangle with the same area as the parallelogram. As Figure 7.83 shows, we simply cut the right triangle ADE from one end of the parallelogram and attach it to the other end. This forms a rectangle $CDEF$

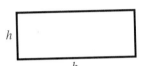

FIGURE 7.82
Area = bh

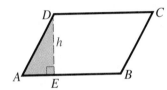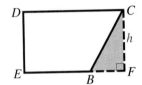

FIGURE 7.83

with the same area as the parallelogram. Since the base and height are the same for both figures, it follows that the area of a parallelogram of base b and height h is

$$A = bh \qquad \text{Area of a parallelogram}$$

(Be sure to note that h is the perpendicular height, not just a side of the parallelogram.)

It is now an easy matter to find the area of any triangle. Suppose that triangle ABC in Figure 7.84 is given. We draw a line through C parallel to AB and a line through A parallel to BC. These lines meet at a point D, and the quadrilateral $ABCD$ is a parallelogram. Clearly, the segment AC is a diagonal of the parallelogram and divides the parallelogram into two equal pieces. Because the area of parallelogram $ABCD$ is bh, the area of the triangle ABC is $\frac{1}{2}bh$. Thus, we have a formula for the area of any triangle with base b and height h:

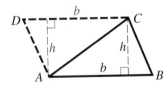

FIGURE 7.84

$$A = \tfrac{1}{2}bh \qquad \text{Area of a triangle}$$

Note: If the angle B in Figure 7.84 is a right angle, the parallelogram obtained is a rectangle. This does not change the final result.

EXAMPLE 1 Find the area of the triangle shown in Figure 7.85.

Solution This triangle has a base of 4 in. and a height of 1.5 in. Thus,

$$A = \tfrac{1}{2}(4)(1.5) = 3 \text{ in.}^2 \qquad \blacksquare$$

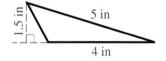

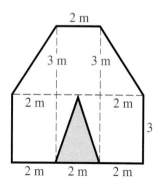

FIGURE 7.85

> The formulas we have developed can be used for finding the areas of many polygonal regions. This is done by subdividing these regions into nonoverlapping rectangular and/or triangular regions, finding the areas of these subdivisions, and adding the results. This procedure is illustrated in the next example.

EXAMPLE 2 Find the area of the region given in Figure 7.86.

Solution We subdivide the region as shown:
The area of the lower rectangle is $6 \times 3 = 18 \text{ m}^2$. The area of the shaded triangle is $\tfrac{1}{2}(2 \times 3) = 3 \text{ m}^2$. The upper two triangles both have area 3 m^2 and the upper rectangle has area $2 \times 3 = 6 \text{ m}^2$. Thus, the required area is

$$18 - 3 + 3 + 3 + 6 = 27 \text{ m}^2$$

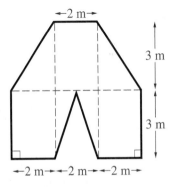

FIGURE 7.86 $\blacksquare$

Thus far, we have been concerned entirely with the areas of polygonal regions. How about the circle? Can we find the area of a circle by using one of the preceding formulas? Interestingly enough, the answer is yes. The required area can be found by using the formula for the area of a rectangle. Here is how you can go about it. Look at Figure 7.87. Cut the lower half of the circular region into small equal slices called **sectors,** and arrange them as shown in the figure. Then cut the remaining half of the circle into the same number of slices

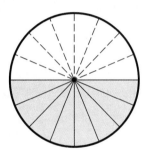

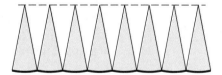

FIGURE 7.87

and arrange them along with the others as shown in Figure 7.88. The result is approximately a parallelogram whose longer side is of length πr (half the circumference of the circle) and whose shorter side is r (the radius of the circle).

One-half the circumference

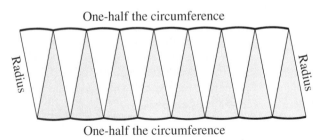

One-half the circumference

FIGURE 7.88

The more pieces you cut the circle into, the more accurate this approximation becomes. You should also observe that the more pieces you use, the more nearly the parallelogram becomes a rectangle of length πr and height r. Mathematicians have proved that the area of the circle is actually the same as the area of this rectangle, that is, $(\pi r)(r)$, or πr^2. Thus, we arrive at the formula for the area of a circle of radius r:

$$A = \pi r^2 \qquad \text{Area of a circle}$$

EXAMPLE 3

The circular dish for the Arecibo radiotelescope has a radius of 500 ft. What area does the dish cover? (Use $\pi \approx 3.14$.)

Solution

Here, $r = 500$, so

$$A = \pi (500)^2$$
$$= \pi (250,000) \approx 785,000 \text{ ft}^2$$

■

Your knowledge of algebra can be used in conjunction with the geometric formulas you have just studied. This is illustrated in the next example.

EXAMPLE 4

The Fermi National Accelerator Laboratory has the atom smasher shown in the photo. The smasher covers an area of 1.1304 mi^2. What is the diameter of this atom smasher? Use $\pi \approx 3.14$, and give the answer to the nearest hundredth of a mile.

The large circle is the main accelerator at the Fermi National Accelerator Laboratory at Batavia, Illinois. A proton beam travels around this circle at 50,000 times a second, producing highly energized particles used in nuclear research.

Solution The formula for the area of a circle of radius r is

$$A = \pi r^2$$

Here, $A = 1.1304$ and $\pi \approx 3.14$. Thus,

$$1.1304 \approx 3.14 r^2$$
$$r^2 \approx \frac{1.1304}{3.14} = 0.36$$
$$r \approx 0.60 \text{ mi}$$

Thus, the diameter is about 1.20 mi. If your calculator has a square root key, you can do this calculation by keying in $\boxed{1.1304}$ $\boxed{\div}$ $\boxed{3.14}$ $\boxed{=}$ $\boxed{\sqrt{x}}$ ∎

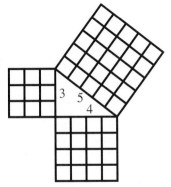

FIGURE 7.89
$5^2 = 3^2 + 4^2$

B. *The Pythagorean Theorem*

The solution of Example 4 required taking the square root of both sides of an equation. The same technique is used in many problems involving the sides of a right triangle. One of the most famous and important theorems of all time is the **Pythagorean theorem,** which says, **"The square on the hypotenuse (the longest side) of a right triangle is equal to the sum of the squares on the other two sides."** Figure 7.89 illustrates the theorem for a 3-4-5 right triangle.

It is important to note that the converse of the Pythagorean theorem is also true. (The proof, which can be constructed with a little trignometry, is omitted.) We can include both theorems in the following statement:

> A triangle is a right triangle if, and only if, the square of one of the sides is the sum of the squares of the other two sides.

The perpendicular sides of a right triangle are often called legs. In Figure 7.90, the legs are labeled a and b, and the hypotenuse is labeled c. Given a right triangle with legs a and b and hypotenuse c, the Pythagorean theorem states that

$$c^2 = a^2 + b^2$$

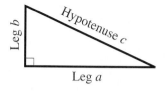

FIGURE 7.90

The early Egyptians, and even the Babylonians, knew some special cases of this result; in particular, they knew the result illustrated in Figure 7.89. However, the ancient Greeks seem to have been the first to prove the general theorem. There are many different proofs of the theorem, some of which depend on areas in a simple fashion. Here is one of these proofs.

The area of the large square in Figure 7.91 is c^2. The area of the small square is $(a - b)^2 = a^2 - 2ab + b^2$, and the area of each of the four right triangles is $\frac{1}{2}ab$. Thus,

$$c^2 = a^2 - 2ab + b^2 + (4)(\tfrac{1}{2}ab)$$
$$= a^2 - 2ab + b^2 + 2ab$$
$$= a^2 + b^2$$

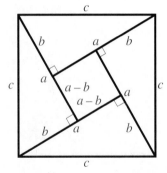

FIGURE 7.91

EXAMPLE 5   Find the length of the hypotenuse of a right triangle whose legs are 5 and 12 units long.

Solution   We use the Pythagorean theorem to get

$$c^2 = a^2 + b^2$$
$$= 5^2 + 12^2 = 25 + 144 = 169$$

Therefore, $c = \sqrt{169} = 13$.

Exercise 7.6

A. In problems 1–12, find the area of the given region.

1.
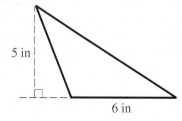

2.
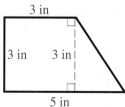

3.
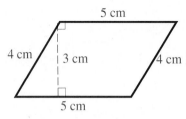

4.
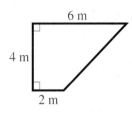

5.
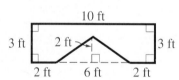

6.
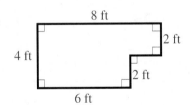

7.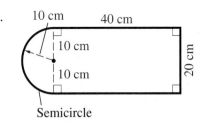

8.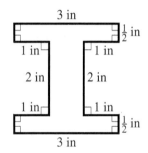

9.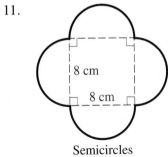

Semicircle

10.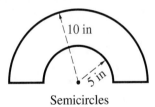

Semicircle

11.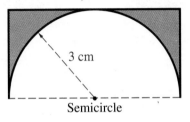

Semicircles

12.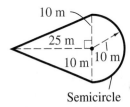

Semicircles

In problems 13–16, find the shaded area.

13.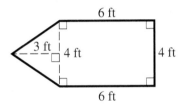

Semicircle

14.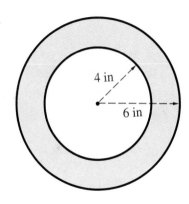

15.

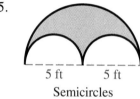

Semicircles

16.

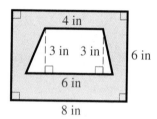

B. 17. The diagonal of a rectangle is 17 ft long, and one of the sides is 15 ft long. How long is the other side?

18. A rectangle is 24 cm long and 7 cm wide. How long is its diagonal?

19. The base of an isosceles triangle is 16 in. long and the equal sides are each 17 in. long. Find the height h of the triangle, that is, the perpendicular distance from the base to the opposite vertex.

20. The two diagonals of a rhombus are 4 cm and 8 cm long, respectively. Find the length s of the sides of the rhombus. Diagonals are perpendicular.

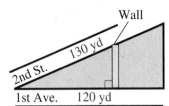

21. A concrete wall is to be constructed on a triangular lot as shown in the diagram. If the estimated cost of the wall is $12 per linear foot, what is the estimated total cost of the wall?

22. A telephone pole is supported by two cables attached to points on the pole 15 ft above ground and to points on the level ground 8 ft from the foot of the pole. What is the total length of the two cables?

23. The base of a parallelogram is 12 ft long, the height is 8 ft, and the shorter diagonal is 10 ft long. How long are the other sides of the parallelogram?

24. The base of a parallelogram is 10 cm long, the height is 5 cm, and the longer diagonal is 13 cm long. How long is the shorter diagonal?

25. The playing surface of a football field is 120 yd long and $53\frac{1}{3}$ yd wide. How many square yards of artificial turf are needed to cover this surface?

26. The floors of three rooms in a certain house measure 9 by 10 ft, 12 by 12 ft, and 15 by 15 ft, respectively.
    (a) How many square yards of carpet are needed to cover these three floors?
    (b) If the price of the carpet is $14/yd^2, how much would it cost to cover these floors?

27. A rectangular room is to have 288 ft^2 of floor space. If the room is 16 ft long, how wide must it be?

28. The Louisiana Superdome covers an area of 363,000 ft^2. Find the diameter of this round arena to the nearest foot. Use $\pi \approx 3.14$.

29. The largest cinema screen in the world is in the Pictorium Theater in Santa Clara, California; it covers 6,720 ft^2. If this rectangular screen is 70 ft tall, how wide is it?

30. The area of the biggest pizza was about 5,024 ft^2. What was its diameter?

31. What is the area of a circular region whose diameter is 8 cm? (Leave your answer in terms of π.)

32. Find the height of a triangle of area 70 in.^{2} if its base is 20 in. long.

33. Glass for picture frames costs $3/ft^2. If the cost of the glass for a rectangular frame is $4.50 and the frame is one and one-half times as long as it is wide, find the dimensions in inches.

34. Diazinon is a toxic chemical used for insect control in grass. Each ounce of this chemical, diluted in 3 gal of water, covers 125 ft^2. The transportation department used 32 oz of Diazinon to spray the grass in the median strip of a highway. If the strip was 16 ft wide, how long was it?

35. John Carpenter has a tabletop that is 4 ft wide by 5 ft long. He wants to cut down the length and the width both by the same amount so as to decrease the area by $4\frac{1}{4}$ ft^2. What would be the new dimensions?

36. In problem 35, suppose John wants to decrease the 4-ft side and increase the 5-ft side by the same amount so as to decrease the area by $\frac{3}{4}$ ft^2. What would be the new dimensions?

37. Show that the area of an equilateral (all sides equal) triangle of side s is $s^2 \cdot \sqrt{3}/4$. [*Hint:* A perpendicular from one vertex to the opposite side bisects that side.]

38. What happens to the area of a triangle:
    (a) If the length of its base is doubled?
    (b) If both base and height are doubled in length?

39. What happens to the area of a rectangle if both its dimensions are:
    (a) Doubled?   (b) Tripled?
    (c) Multiplied by a constant k?

40. Use the result of problem 37 to find the area of a regular hexagon whose side is 4 in. long.

41. The circumference of a circle and the perimeter of a square are both 20 cm long. Which has the greater area, and by approximately how much?

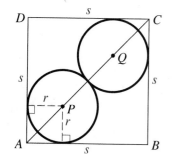

FIGURE 7.92

42. In Figure 7.92, the two circles have their centers on the diagonal AC of the square $ABCD$. The circles just touch each other and the sides of the square, as shown in the figure. If the side of the square is of length s, find the total area of the two circles in terms of s.

43. A regular octagon is to be formed by cutting equal isosceles right triangles from the four corners of a square. If the side of the square is of length a, and the equal sides of the isosceles triangles are of length s, show that

$$s = \frac{2 - \sqrt{2}}{2}a.$$

In Other Words

44. Which of the following triangles are right triangles? Explain your reasoning.
    (a) Sides 3, 5, 6   (b) Sides 5, 12, 13
    (c) Sides 7, 24, 25   (d) Sides 9, 10, 15

45. What will be the most appropriate U.S. units (in.^{2}, yd^2, mi^2) and metric units (cm^2, m^2, and km^2) for measuring:
    (a) The area of a nickel
    (b) The area of your state
    (c) The area of your classroom
    (d) The area of a house

46. Explain in your own words the difference between a 2-in. square and 2 in.^{2}

Using Your Knowledge

You can use what you learned in this section to help you solve some commonly occurring problems. Do the following problems to see how.

47. A gallon of Lucite wall paint costs $14 and covers 450 ft^2. Three rooms in a house measure 10 by 12 ft, 14 by 15 ft, and 12 by 12 ft, and the ceiling is 8 ft high.
    (a) How many gallons of paint are needed to cover the walls of these rooms if you make no allowance for doors and windows?
    (b) What will be the cost of the paint? (The paint is sold by the gallon only.)

48. Figure 7.93 shows the front of a house. House paint costs $17/gal and covers 400 ft^2.
    (a) What is the minimum number of gallons of paint needed to cover the front of the house? (The paint is sold by the gallon only.)
    (b) How much will the paint for the front of the house cost?

49. A house and lot are shown in Figure 7.94. The entire lot, except for the buildings and the drive, is lawn. A bag of lawn fertilizer costs $4 and covers 1,200 ft^2 of grass.
    (a) What is the minimum number of bags of fertilizer needed for this lawn?
    (b) What will be the cost of the fertilizer?

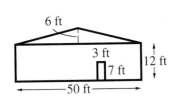

FIGURE 7.93

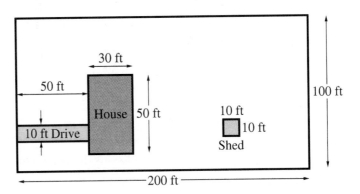

FIGURE 7.94

50. A small pizza (11-in. diameter) costs $5 and a large pizza (15-in. diameter) costs $8. Use $\pi \approx 3.14$ and find, to the nearest square inch:
    (a) The area of the small pizza
    (b) The area of the large pizza
    (c) Which is the better deal, two small pizzas or one large pizza?

51. A frozen apple pie of 8-in. diameter sells for $1.25. The 10-in.-diameter size sells for $1.85.
    (a) What is the unit price (price per square inch), to the nearest hundredth of a cent, of the 8-in. pie?
    (b) What is the unit price of the 10-in. pie?
    (c) Which pie gives you the most for your money?

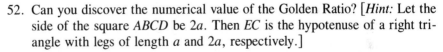

Discovery

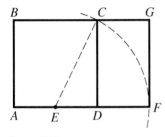

FIGURE 7.95

*Artists and architects, past and present, have used the **Golden Ratio** in their art and their architecture. Do you know what the Golden Ratio is? Begin with a square (shaded in Figure 7.95). Let E be the midpoint of the base AD. Put the point of your pencil compass at E and the pencil point at C, and draw the circular arc as shown. Extend AD to meet this arc and call the point of intersection F. Now draw a line perpendicular to AF at F and extend BC to meet this perpendicular at G. The rectangle ABGF is known as the **Golden Rectangle**. Its proportions are supposed to be particularly pleasing to the eye. The ratio of the longer to the shorter side of this rectangle is the Golden Ratio.*

52. Can you discover the numerical value of the Golden Ratio? [*Hint:* Let the side of the square *ABCD* be 2a. Then *EC* is the hypotenuse of a right triangle with legs of length a and 2a, respectively.]

Artists are interested in the areas of their paintings and sometimes meet with the problem of drawing a rectangle of height h that will have the same area as that of a given rectangle. Figure 7.96 shows the problem. The given rectangle is of length L and width W, and the artist wants a rectangle of height h that will have the same area. Of course, you could find the area LW and divide by h to get the second dimension of the desired rectangle. But the artist can do the job

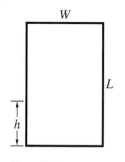

FIGURE 7.96

very quickly without any arithmetic at all! Here is how: Look at Figure 7.97. Draw a line across the given rectangle at height h (line BD in the figure). Next, draw a line through A and C and extend the top line of the rectangle to meet line AC at point F. Then drop a perpendicular from F to the extended base of the given rectangle. The rectangle ABDE is

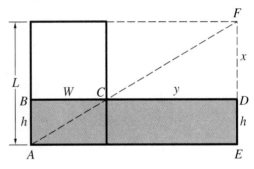

FIGURE 7.97

the desired rectangle. Can you discover why? Look at Figure 7.97 again. The triangle ABC and FDC are similar (have exactly the same shape). Corresponding sides of similar triangles are always in the same ratio. Thus,

$$\frac{y}{W} = \frac{x}{h}$$

53. Can you discover how to use this result to show that the area of rectangle *ABDE* is equal to the area of the original rectangle? [*Hint:* What is the area of the rectangle taken away from the given rectangle? What is the area of the rectangle added on?]

54. Draw a careful diagram of a rectangle 4 cm wide and 6 cm high. Use the construction described above to find a rectangle 5 cm high and with the same area. If you do this very carefully, the result will help convince you that this is a neat construction.

7.7 VOLUME AND SURFACE AREA

GETTING STARTED

FROM THE GROCER'S SHELF

Which of the two bottles on the right side of the picture has more ketchup? Which has more sauce, the bottle on the left, or the can? As it turns out, both ketchup bottles hold the same amount. They have the same **volume.** The volume of sauce in the can and in the bottle is also the same. One of the ketchup bottles has greater **surface area,** which sometimes gives the false impression that it has greater volume and holds more. We have already studied perimeter (the length of the **boundary** of a polygon) and area (the space **enclosed** by the polygon).

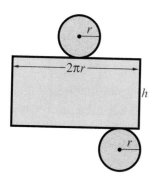

FIGURE 7.98

The counterparts for perimeter and area in three dimensions are **surface area** and **volume.** Like perimeters, **surface area** measures a **boundary,** the surface of a three-dimensional figure, while **volume,** like area, measures the space **enclosed** by the figure. Keep in mind, however, that perimeter is measured in **linear** units, surface areas in **square** units, and volume in **cubic** units.

How can we find the surface area of the can or, in general, the surface area of a **cylinder**? If a vertical cut is made down the side of the can and the metal flattened, it would form a rectangle whose length is the same as the circumference of the can ($2\pi r$) and whose width is the height h of the can (see Figure 7.98).

The area of this rectangle would be $2\pi r \cdot h$. Then we find the area of the top and bottom lids, πr^2 for each, to obtain the total surface area for the can, or, in general, for a cylinder of radius r and height h. Thus,

$$S = 2\pi rh + 2\pi r^2$$

Now, how could you determine whether a can and a bottle hold the same volume? (No fair reading the label!) One way is to fill the can with water and then pour it into the bottle. If the bottle is exactly filled, they have the same volume. We will study volumes and surface areas in this section.

The photograph shows the Transamerica Pyramid in San Francisco. At 853 feet in height (48 stories) it is the tallest building on the city's skyline. The pyramid portion of the structure is built on a square base and is thus an example of a *square pyramid*. Pyramids are one example of solids bounded by polygons.

The Transamerica Corporation building in San Francisco, more commonly called the Transamerica pyramid

A. *Three-Dimensional Figures*

A solid bounded by plane polygons is called a **polyhedron.** The polygons are the **faces** of the polyhedron, the sides of the polygons are the **edges,** and the vertices of the polygons are the **vertices** of the polyhedron. The Egyptian pyramids are polyhedrons with five faces, one of which is a square (the base) and the others are triangles. A square pyramid has eight edges and five vertices. The Transamerica Pyramid is a striking example of the use of a square pyramid in the design of a modern building.

A **convex polyhedron** is one that lies entirely to one side of the plane of each of its faces. A polyhedron that is not convex is called **concave,** or **reentrant.** The polyhedrons shown in Figure 7.99 are a **cube,** a **rectangular parallelepiped,** a six-sided polyhedron with triangular faces (illustration III), and a seven-sided polyhedron (illustration IV). The first three polyhedrons are convex, and the fourth is concave (reentrant).

If two faces of a polyhedron lie in parallel planes and if the edges that are not in these planes are all parallel to each other, then the polyhedron is called a

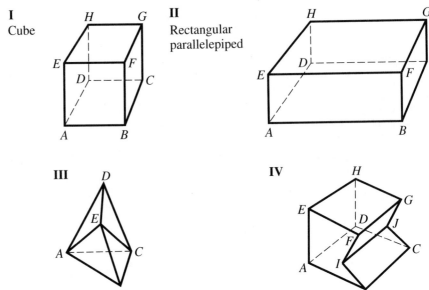

FIGURE 7.99
Polyhedrons

prism. In Figure 7.99, illustrations I, II, and IV all illustrate prisms. The faces of a prism that are in the two parallel planes are called the **bases.** The parallel lines joining the bases are the **lateral edges.** The two bases of a prism are congruent polygons. Figure 7.100 shows a **triangular prism.**

If all but one of the vertices of a polyhedron lie in one plane, then the polyhedron is a **pyramid.** The face that lies in this one plane is the **base,** and the remaining vertex is the **vertex of the pyramid.** Figure 7.101 shows a pentagonal pyramid; the base is a pentagon. Prisms and pyramids are named by the shapes of their bases.

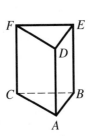

FIGURE 7.100
Triangular prism

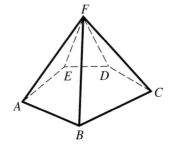

FIGURE 7.101
Pentagonal pyramid

EXAMPLE 1   Name the edges and the vertices of the pyramid in Figure 7.101.

Solution   The edges are the line segments *AB, BC, CD, DE, EA, FA, FB, FC, FD,* and *FE.* The vertices are the points *A, B, C, D, E,* and *F.*   ∎

B. *Formulas for Volume and Surface Area*

The *volume* of a three-dimensional region is measured in terms of a *unit volume*, just as area is measured in terms of a unit area. For the unit volume, we choose the region enclosed by a *unit cube*, as shown in Figure 7.102. Some of the commonly used units of volume are given in the following table. Note that *volume* is always measured in *cubic* units.

Standard Units of Volume

U.S. System	Metric System
Cubic inch (in.^{3})	Cubic millimeter (mm^3)
Cubic foot (ft^3)	Cubic centimeter (cm^3)
Cubic yard (yd^3)	Cubic meter (m^3)

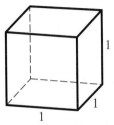

FIGURE 7.102
Unit cube:
Volume = 1 cubic unit

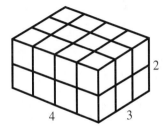

FIGURE 7.103
$V = 4 \times 3 \times 2 = 24$ *cubic units*

Volumes may be considered in a manner similar to that used for areas. If a rectangular parallelepiped (box) is such that the lengths of its edges are all whole numbers, then the region can be cut up by planes parallel to the faces, as in Figure 7.103. In general, we define the volume of a rectangular box of length *l*, width *w*, and height *h* to be *lwh*. Thus,

$$V = lwh = \text{length} \times \text{width} \times \text{height} \qquad \text{Volume of a rectangular box}$$

The surface area of a rectangular box is the sum of the areas of the six faces. Thus, for the dimensions *l*, *w*, *h*, the surface area *S* is

$$S = 2lw + 2lh + 2wh$$

For the rectangular box in Figure 7.103, we have

$$S = 2(4 \times 3) + 2(4 \times 2) + 2(3 \times 2)$$
$$= 24 + 16 + 12$$
$$= 52 \text{ square units}$$

Table 7.6 gives the formulas for the volume and the surface area of some commonly occurring three-dimensional figures.

Table 7.6

Name	Figure	Volume (V)	Surface Area (S)
Cube		$V = a^3$	$S = 6a^2$
Rectangular box		$V = lwh$	$S = 2(lw + lh + wh)$
Cylinder		$V = \pi r^2 h$	$S = 2\pi rh + 2\pi r^2$
Cone		$V = \dfrac{1}{3}\pi r^2 h$ *	$S = \pi r^2 + \pi rs$
Sphere		$V = \dfrac{4}{3}\pi r^3$	$S = 4\pi r^2$

* The formula for the volume of a circular cone can be verified by pouring water or sand from a hollow cone into a cylinder of the same base and height. This will check the coefficient $\frac{1}{3}$.

EXAMPLE 2 You are probably familiar with the Rubik's Cube puzzle like the one shown in the photograph below. Each of the little cubes is 3/4 in. on a side.

(a) Find the volume of Rubik's Cube.
(b) Find the surface area if no allowance is made for the dips between the small cubes.

Solution (a) Since there are three little cubes in a row, the edge of the large cube is

$$(3)\left(\frac{3}{4}\right) = \frac{9}{4} \text{ in.}$$

Using the formula for the volume of a cube, we get

$$V = a^3 = \left(\frac{9}{4}\right)^3 = \frac{729}{64} \text{ in.}^3$$

or, expressed as a decimal,

$$v = 11.390625 \quad \text{or about} \quad 11.4 \text{ in.}^3$$

(b) The formula for the surface area of a cube gives

$$S = 6a^2 = 6\left(\frac{9}{4}\right)^2 = \frac{243}{8} \quad \text{or about 30.4 in.}^2$$

Let us denote the area measure of the base of a prism or a pyramid by B and the height by h. It is shown in solid geometry that the formulas for the volumes of these figures are

$V = Bh$	Volume of a prism
$V = \frac{1}{3}Bh$	Volume of a pyramid

EXAMPLE 3 If a crocoite crystal is in the form of a prism with a triangular base of height 3 cm and base length 2.6 cm, and if the crystal is 30 cm long, what is its volume?

Solution First we find B, the area of the base of the prism. Since the base is a triangle of base length 2.6 cm and height 3 cm,

$$B = \frac{1}{2}(2.6)(3) = 3.9 \text{ cm}^2$$

Then we use the formula for the volume of a prism to obtain

$$V = Bh = (3.9)(30) = 117 \text{ cm}^3$$

EXAMPLE 4   Figure 7.104 shows a polyhedron that consists of a rectangular box sur-mounted by a square pyramid with the top of the box for its base. The dimensions of the polyhedron are shown in the figure.

(a) Find the volume of the polyhedron.
(b) Find the total surface area.

Solution   (a) The volume of the rectangular box portion in Figure 7.104 is

$$V = lwh = (3)(3)(5) = 45 \text{ ft}^3$$

The volume of the pyramid is

$$V = \frac{1}{3}Bh = \frac{1}{3}(3 \times 3)(2) = 6 \text{ ft}^3$$

Thus, the entire volume is 51 ft³.

(b) The area of the base of the figure is

$$B = 3 \times 3 = 9 \text{ ft}^2$$

The area of the four sides of the rectangular box portion is

$$A_1 = 4(3 \times 5) = 60 \text{ ft}^2$$

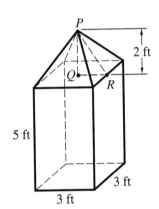

FIGURE 7.104

To find the area of the four triangular faces of the pyramid we must first find the altitude of the triangles. To do this, draw a line PQ from the top vertex and perpendicular to the base of the pyramid. This line will meet the base at its midpoint Q. Then draw a second line QR from the foot of the perpendicular to the midpoint of an edge of the base. Finally, draw the line PR. The triangle PQR is a right triangle, whose hypotenuse PR is the desired altitude. Thus, we have

$$PR = \sqrt{2^2 + \left(\frac{3}{2}\right)^2} = \sqrt{4 + \frac{9}{4}} = \sqrt{\frac{25}{4}} = \frac{5}{2} \text{ ft}$$

Consequently, the area of the four triangular faces of the pyramid is

$$A_2 = 4 \times \frac{1}{2}bh = 4 \times \frac{1}{2}(3)\left(\frac{5}{2}\right) = 15 \text{ ft}^2$$

The total surface area of the polyhedron is

$$B + A_1 + A_2 = 9 + 60 + 15 = 84 \text{ ft}^2 \qquad \blacksquare$$

EXAMPLE 5   Natasha is inflating a toy globe. Suppose the globe is a perfect sphere. What would be the diameter of the globe when the number of square inches of its surface area is equal to the number of cubic inches of its volume?

Solution Let r in. be the radius of the globe. Then the surface area is $4\pi r^2$ in.^{2} and the volume is $\frac{4}{3}\pi r^3$ in.^{3} The number of units of surface area is to be equal to the number of units of volume, so

$$\frac{4}{3}\pi r^3 = 4\pi r^2$$

$$\frac{1}{3}r = 1 \qquad \text{(Divide both sides by } 4\pi r^2.\text{)}$$

$$r = 3$$

Since the diameter is twice the radius, the required diameter is 6 in. ■

EXAMPLE 6 The water tank for a small town is in the shape of a cone (vertex down) surmounted by a cylinder, as shown in Figure 7.105. If a cubic foot of water is about 7.5 gal, what is the capacity of the tank in gallons? (Use $\pi \approx 3.14$.)

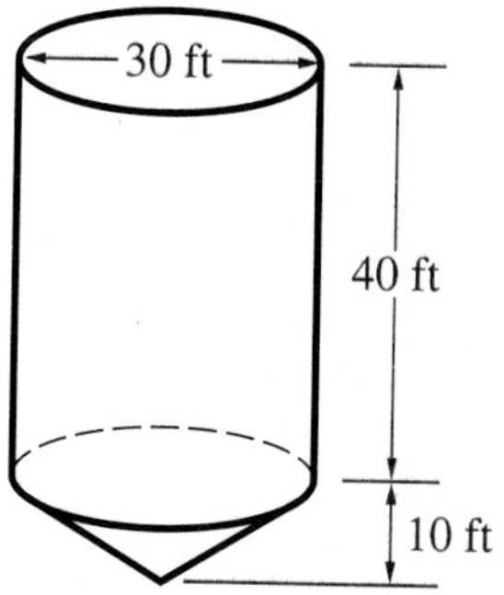

FIGURE 7.105

Solution For the cylindrical portion of the tank, $r = 15$ and $h = 40$, so that

$$V = \pi(15)^2(40) = 9000\pi \text{ ft}^3$$

For the conical portion, $r = 15$ and $h = 10$. Thus,

$$V = \tfrac{1}{3}\pi(15)^2(10) = 750\pi \text{ ft}^3$$

The total volume is the sum of these—that is, 9750π ft^3. Using 7.5 gal/ft^3 and 3.14 for π, we get

$$\begin{aligned} 9750\pi \text{ ft}^3 &\approx (9750)(3.14)(7.5) \text{ gal} \\ &\approx 230{,}000 \text{ gal} \end{aligned}$$

■

EXAMPLE 7 A solid metal sphere of radius 3 m just fits inside a cubical tank. If the tank is full of water and the sphere is slowly lowered into the tank until it touches bottom, how much water is left in the tank?

Solution The amount of water left in the tank is the difference between the volume of the tank and the volume of the sphere. Thus, since the length of any edge of the cube equals the diameter of the sphere, the required volume is

$$\begin{aligned} V &= 6^3 - \tfrac{4}{3}\pi(3^3) \\ &= 216 - 36\pi \\ &\approx 103 \text{ m}^3 \end{aligned}$$

■

Exercise 7.7

A. 1. Refer to Figure 7.99, illustration III. Name:
(a) The vertices   (b) The edges

2. Refer to Figure 7.100 and repeat problem 1.
3. Refer to Figure 7.99, illustration IV, and name the bottom face.
4. Refer to Figure 7.99, illustration IV, and name the left-hand back face.

In each of problems 5–8, make a sketch of the figure.

5. A triangular pyramid
6. A triangular prism surmounted by a triangular pyramid with the top base of the prism as the base of the pyramid
7. A six-sided polyhedron that is convex and is not a parallelepiped
8. An eight-sided polyhedron with triangular faces
9. (a) If the edges of a cube are doubled in length, what happens to the volume?
(b) What if the lengths are tripled?

B. 10. A pyramid has a rectangular base. Suppose that the edges of the base and the height of the pyramid are all doubled in length. What happens to the volume?
11. Find (a) the volume V and (b) the total surface area S of a rectangular solid that is 20 in. long, 10 in. wide, and 8 in. high.
12. A rectangular solid is constructed by putting together two cubes each of edge x ft. If the number of cubic feet in the total volume is equal to the number of square feet in the total external surface area of this solid, what is the value of x?
13. A solid consists of a cube of side $6x$ surmounted by a regular square pyramid whose base is the top face of the cube and whose height is $4x$. Find a formula for
(a) The volume of this solid.
(b) The total external surface area of this solid.
14. A cylindrical can is to have the area of its curved surface equal to the sum of the areas of its base and its top. What must be the relation between the height and the diameter of this can?
15. A pentagonal prism has a base whose area is 10 in.^{2} If the prism is 5 in. high, what is its volume?
16. The base of a prism is a triangle whose base is 3 ft and whose height is 4 ft. If the prism is 5 ft high. What is its volume?
17. The edge of the base of a square pyramid is 4 in. long, and the pyramid is 6 in. high. Find the volume of the pyramid.

18. A convex polyhedron consists of two pyramids with a common base that is an equilateral triangle 3 in. on a side. The height of one of the pyramids is 2 in. and the height of the other is 4 in. What is the volume of the polyhedron?

19. A container consists of a cube 10 cm on an edge surmounted by a pyramid of height 15 cm and with the top face of the cube as its base. How many liters does this container hold? (*Hint:* 1 liter = 1000 cm^3.)

20. The Great Pyramid of Egypt (the Pyramid of Cheops) is huge. It is 148 m high, and its square base has a perimeter of 930 m. What is the volume of this pyramid?

In problems 21–24, find the volume and the total surface area of:
(a) The circular cylinder of given radius and height
(b) The circular cone of given radius and height

Use the approximate value 3.14 for π.

21. Radius 5 in., height 9 in.

22. Radius 10 cm, height 6 cm

23. Radius 3 ft, height 4 ft

24. Radius 6 cm, height 12 cm

25. Find the volume of a sphere of radius 6 in.

26. Find the volume of a sphere of radius 12 cm.

27. The Peachtree Plaza Hotel tower in Atlanta, Georgia, is 70 stories high. If the height of this cylinder is 754 ft and its diameter is 116 ft, what is the volume?

28. A grain silo is in the shape of a cone, vertex down, surmounted by a cylinder. If the diameter of the cylinder is 10 ft, the cylinder is 30 ft high, and the cone is 10 ft high, how many cubic yards of grain does the silo hold?

29. A pile of salt is in the shape of a cone 12 m high and 32 m in diameter. How many cubic meters of salt are in the pile?

30. The fuel tanks on some ships are spheres of which only the top halves are above deck. If one of these tanks is 120 ft in diameter, how many gallons of fuel does it hold? Use 1 ft^3 ≈ 7.5 gal.

31. A popular-sized can in American supermarkets is 3 in. in diameter and 4 in. high (inside dimensions). About how many grams of water will one of these cans hold? (Recall that 1 cm^3 of water weighs 1 gm, and 1 in. = 2.54 cm.)

32. An ice cream cone is 7 cm in diameter and 10 cm deep (see Figure 7.106). The inside of the cone is packed with ice cream and a hemisphere of ice cream is put on top. If ice cream weighs $\frac{1}{2}$ g/cm^3, how many grams of ice cream are there in all?

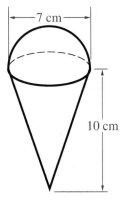

FIGURE 7.106

33. The circumference of a baseball, soccer ball, and basketball are 9 in., 27 in., and 30 in., respectively. Find:
    (a) The surface area and volume of each.
    (b) How does the surface area of a baseball compare to that of a basketball?
    (c) How does the volume of a baseball compare to that of a soccer ball?

34. A cylindrical storage tank for gasoline has a 300-ft-diameter and is 200 ft high.
    (a) Find the capacity of this tank if one cubic foot of gasoline equals 7.5 gal.
    (b) How many gallons of paint are needed to paint the exterior and top of this tank with two coats of paint if a gallon of paint covers 400 ft^2?

35. A bowling ball has a 27-in. circumference and weighs 16 lb.
    (a) Find the volume of the ball before the holes are drilled.
    (b) If three cylindrical holes with diameters 1.25 in., 1 in., and 1 in., respectively, each 2.5 inches deep, are drilled into the ball, what is the weight of the ball now?

36. A basketball with a 30-in. circumference is tightly packed into a cubical box for shipment.
    (a) What is the volume of the ball?
    (b) What is the smallest possible volume for the box?
    (c) What percent of the space in the box is occupied by the basketball?

37. A grocery bag has a 7 in. by 12 in. base and is 17 in. high.
    (a) What is the volume of the bag?
    (b) What is the minimum surface area for the bag?
    (c) A ton of recycled paper will save 17 trees. If one bag weighs 2 oz, how many bags are needed to save 34 trees?

38. A building contractor is constructing a second-story concrete floor 100 ft long, 50 ft wide, and 12 in. thick.
    (a) How much concrete is needed?
    (b) A concrete truck carries 6 yd^3 of concrete. How many truckloads are needed for the job?
    (c) If the concrete is to be hoisted by a crane in a cone-shaped bucket 4 ft in diameter and 5 ft high, how many buckets of concrete are needed?

*I*n Other Words

39. Explain in your own words why lengths are measured in linear units, areas in square units, and volume in cubic units.

40. Explain in your own words what happens to the volume and surface area of a sphere if the diameter is doubled.

41. Is the number of cubic units in the volume of a sphere always larger than the number of square units in its surface area? Explain in your own words why or why not.

42. Suppose the radius of a circular cone is doubled and the height is halved. Explain in your own words what happens to the volume.

Discovery

43. A **regular polyhedron** is one whose faces are all congruent regular polygons, that is, regular polygons of exactly the same shape and size. The appearance of such a polyhedron at any vertex is identical with its appearance at any other vertex; the same is true at the edges. The early Greeks discovered that only five regular polyhedrons are possible. Can you repeat this discovery? Consider the regular polygons one at a time: equilateral triangles, squares, regular pentagons, and so on. In case you use squares, how many squares can you put together at a vertex to form a polyhedron? Look at a cube. This is the only regular polyhedron with squares for its faces. The regular polyhedrons are as follows:
    (a) A **tetrahedron** with four equilateral triangles for faces
    (b) A **cube** with six squares for faces
    (c) An **octahedron** with eight equilateral triangles for faces
    (d) A **dodecahedron** with 12 pentagons for faces
    (e) An **icosahedron** with 20 equilateral triangles for faces

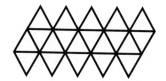

FIGURE 7.107

44. Copy the pattern of equilateral triangles in Figure 7.107 on a piece of stiff cardboard. Cut around the outside edges and fold on the heavy lines. You can build an icosahedron by holding the cut edges together with transparent tape. There are five triangles at each vertex.

45. Count the number of faces (F), vertices (V), and edges (E) for each of the figures listed in the accompanying table. Compare the value of E with the value of $F + V$ and see if you can discover Euler's famous formula for polyhedrons.

Figure	F	V	E
7.99, II			
7.99, III			
7.99, IV			
7.100			
7.101			

46. Can you check the formula you got in problem 45 by using the diagram in problem 44?

Calculator Corner

When higher exponents are present in an expression, calculators with a $\boxed{y^x}$
*key are especially helpful. As the notation indicates, this key raises a number y
to a power x. For instance, to perform the calculations in Example 7, we enter*

$\boxed{6}$ $\boxed{y^x}$ $\boxed{3}$ $\boxed{-}$ $\boxed{4}$ $\boxed{\times}$ $\boxed{\pi}$ $\boxed{\times}$ $\boxed{3}$ $\boxed{y^x}$ $\boxed{3}$ $\boxed{\div}$ $\boxed{3}$ $\boxed{=}$

The result is given as 102.9026645, or about 103 m³.

47. Rework problem 25 using your calculator.

7.8   NETWORKS

GETTING STARTED

CROSSING THAT BRIDGE

What do you think the following activities have in common: urban engineers mapping traffic patterns, chemists modeling complex molecules, managers creating the organizational charts for a large corporation, the drawing of your family tree? Each of the models consists of **points** (locations, atoms, job positions, people) connected by lines. The study of these "graphs" is now called **network theory.**

A famous puzzle problem known as the **Bridges of Königsberg** probably started the study of the traversability of networks. There was a river flowing through the city, and in the river were two islands (*A* and *D*) connected to each other and to the city by seven bridges (*a, b, c, d, e, f, g*), as shown in Fig. 7.108. The people of the city loved a Sunday walk and thought it would be fun to follow a route that would take them across each of the seven bridges exactly once. But they found that no matter where they started or what path they took, they could not cross each bridge exactly once.

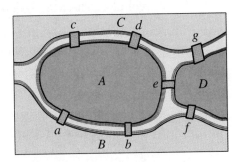

FIGURE 7.108

The great Swiss mathematician Leonhard Euler solved the problem in 1736. First, he redrew the map by making islands *A* and *D* smaller and lengthening the bridges (Figure 7.109). He also made shores *B* and *C* smaller (Figure 7.110). These changes only distort the picture but *do not* change the problem. Then, in a stroke of genius, Euler thought of land areas *A, B, C,* and *D* as

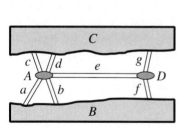

FIGURE 7.109

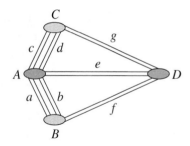

FIGURE 7.110

points and bridges *a* through *g* as **arcs** connecting them. The resulting **network** is diagrammed in Figure 7.111. Euler's question became: *Can all the arcs be traced with a pencil only once without lifting the pencil off the paper?* If the answer to a problem like this is yes, the network is called **traversable.**

In a network, the **points** are the endpoints of arcs and are called **vertices** (singular **vertex**). Euler noticed that if a path goes through a vertex, the vertex must have two arcs: one in, one out. Thus, if a network has an odd vertex, it *must* be the starting or finishing point for a traversable path. But all four vertices in the Königsberg network are odd! Thus, the network is *not* traversable. We will study more about networks, traversability, and the Bridges of New York in this section.

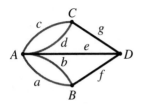

FIGURE 7.111

Any connected set of line segments or arcs is called a **network.** (For the purposes of this section, your intuitive notion of what an arc is will be sufficient.) If the network can be drawn by tracing each line segment or arc exactly once without lifting the pencil from the paper, the network is said to be **traversable.** Any simple network (one that does not cross itself) is traversable. If the network is both simple and closed, then you may choose any point of the network as the starting point, and this point will also be the terminal point of the drawing. If the network is simple but not closed, then you must start at one of the endpoints and finish at the other. Figure 7.112 shows several examples of simple networks that are either closed or not closed.

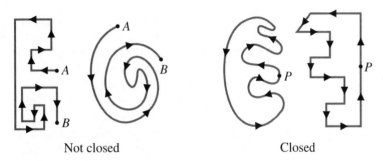

Not closed   Closed

FIGURE 7.112
Simple networks

Let us examine the network in Figure 7.111 more closely. The number of edges for vertex A is 5; it is an odd vertex. As a matter of fact, all vertices in Figure 7.111 are odd. Figure 7.113 shows another network in which A and D are odd vertices but B and C are even. Since every arc has two endpoints, it is impossible for a network to have an odd number of odd vertices. Thus, a network may have 0, 2, 4, 6, . . . , any even number of odd vertices. Notice that there were four odd vertices in the Königsberg problem and two odd vertices in Figure 7.113.

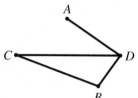

FIGURE 7.113

EXAMPLE 1   Which of the networks below is (are) traversable? If a network is traversable, indicate your beginning and ending points.

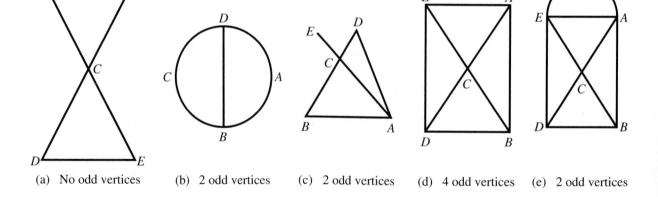

(a) No odd vertices   (b) 2 odd vertices   (c) 2 odd vertices   (d) 4 odd vertices   (e) 2 odd vertices

Solution   (a) The network in (a) is traversable. You can start at any point and you will end at that same point.
(b) The figure in (b) is traversable, but you must start at one of the odd vertices B or D. If you start at B you end at D, and if you start at D you end at B.
(c) The figure in (c) is traversable. This time you must start at A or E (the odd vertices).
(d) The figure in (d) is not traversable. (Do you know why?)
(e) The figure in (e) is traversable. You can start at one of the odd vertices, D or B, and end at the other.

From what you have studied so far, can you make any generalizations about the traversability of a network? Here are the conclusions Euler reached.

> **Traversability Rules**
>
> 1. A network with *no* odd vertices is traversable. You can start at any point and you will end at that same point.
> 2. A network with exactly *two* odd vertices is traversable. You must start at one of the odd vertices and end at the other.
> 3. A network with *more* than *two* odd vertices is not traversable.

EXAMPLE 2   The city of New York is composed of five boroughs as shown in Figure 7.114: Bronx (*B*), Brooklyn and Queens (*B–Q*), Manhattan (*M*), and Staten Island (*SI*), connected by a network of bridges and tunnels, some of them passing through Randall's Island (*RI*) and some leading to New Jersey (*NJ*). Determine if you could take a tour going over each bridge and through each tunnel exactly once. (Since there is no water separating Brooklyn and Queens, we called this land mass *B–Q*.)

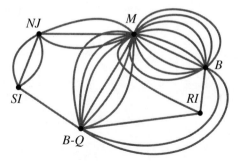

FIGURE 7.114

Solution   The network is shown in Figure 7.114. Note that the only *two* odd vertices are Manhattan (19) and Randall's Island (3), so the network is traversable. Your path must start at one of these two odd vertices and end at the other. ∎

EXAMPLE 3   Figure 7.115 shows a house floor plan with six rooms (*A, B, C, D, E,* and *F*) with the openings representing doors. Is it possible to take a walk through the house and pass through each door exactly once?

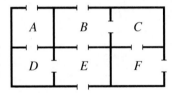

FIGURE 7.115

Solution Think of each room and the outdoors as a vertex and the corresponding number of doors as the number of paths to that vertex. Since there are only two odd vertices, *B* and *E*, the network is traversable, but you must start at one of the odd vertices and end at the other as shown in Figure 7.116. ∎

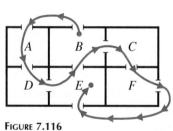

FIGURE 7.116

Network theory has many practical applications. It is of great importance in computer science and technology; it is also used to solve problems in the design of city streets, to analyze traffic patterns, to find the most efficient routes for garbage collection, and so on. Networks are also used in connection with PERT (Program Evaluation and Review Technique) diagrams in planning complicated projects. These diagrams help to determine how long a project will take and when to schedule different phases of the project.

Exercise 7.8

In problems 1–10, find:
(a) The number of even vertices
(b) The number of odd vertices
(c) Whether the network is traversable and which vertices are possible starting points if the network is traversable

1.

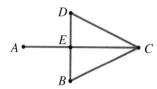

2.

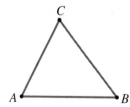

3.

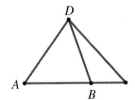

4.

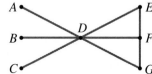

5.

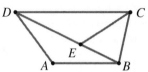

6.

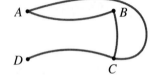

7.

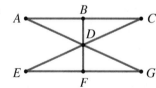

8.

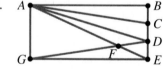

9. The network formed by the edges of a square pyramid
10. The network formed by the edges of a rectangular box
11. Use a network to find whether it is possible to draw a simple connected broken line that crosses each line segment of Figure 7.117 exactly once. The line segments are those that join successive dots.

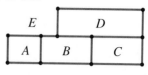

FIGURE 7.117

12. Repeat problem 11 for Figure 7.118.

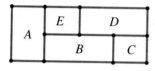

FIGURE 7.118

In problems 13–20, use the traversability rules to determine if it is possible to take a walk through the house and pass through each door exactly once. Which of the paths must start and end outside?.

13.
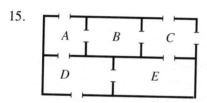

14.
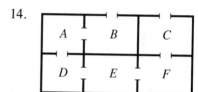

15.
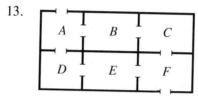

16.
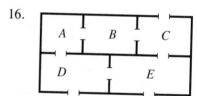

17.
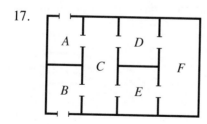

18.
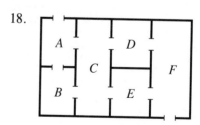

19.
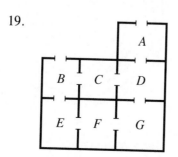

20.
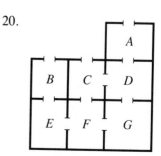

21. Use a network to find whether it is possible to take a walk through the building with the floor plan in Figure 7.119 and pass through each doorway exactly once. Is it possible if you must start and end outside?

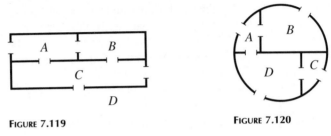

FIGURE 7.119   **FIGURE 7.120**

22. Repeat problem 21 for the floor plan in Figure 7.120.

*I*n Other Words

23. Explain in your own words why it is impossible for a network to have an odd number of odd vertices. (Try to construct one.)

24. Explain in your own words how a network can be used to plan a bus route that can be traversed without traveling any paths twice.

Discovery

A plane curve that does not cross itself is called **simple,** *just as in the case of a broken line. A* **closed curve** *is one that starts and ends at the same point. A* **simple closed curve divides the plane into two parts, the region interior and the region exterior to the curve.** *This important statement is the* **Jordan curve theorem,** *a very deep theorem and one that is very difficult to prove in spite of the fact that it seems so obvious.*

Which dot is inside?

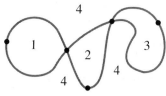

FIGURE 7.121

A nonsimple closed curve

*A closed curve that is not simple divides the plane into three or more parts. We call the points where the curve crosses itself **vertices**. Any other points on the curve may also be designated as vertices. We mark the vertices with black dots as in Figure 7.121, where five vertices are indicated. The regions into which the plane is divided are numbered 1, 2, 3, 4 in the figure. The simple curves with vertices as endpoints and containing no other endpoints are called **arcs**. In the figure, there are seven arcs. Can you count them?*

For the networks below, fill in the table with the number of vertices (V), regions (R) into which the plane is divided, and arcs (A) for each figure. (Line segments connecting vertices are also called arcs.) See if you can discover a formula for A in terms of V and R. This formula is one form of the **Euler formula for networks.**

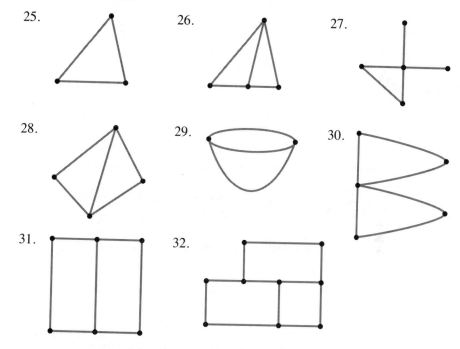

Figure	Vertices (V)	Regions (R)	Arcs (A)
25			
26			
27			
28			
29			
30			
31			
32			

Chapter 7 Summary

Section	Item	Meaning	Example
7.1A	Collinear	On the same line	
7.1A	$\overleftrightarrow{AB}$	The line AB	
7.1A	Ray, $\overrightarrow{AB}$	A half-line and its endpoint A	The ray AB:
7.1A	Line segment AB, $\overline{AB}$	The points A and B and the part of the line between A and B	The line segment AB:
7.1B	Coplanar	On the same plane	
7.1B	Skew lines	Lines that are not coplanar	
7.2	Plane angle	The figure formed by two rays with a common endpoint	
7.2	Vertex of an angle	The common point of the two rays	
7.2	Sides of the angles	The rays forming the angle	
7.2	Degree	$\frac{1}{360}$ th of a complete revolution	
7.2	Straight angle	One-half of a complete revolution	
7.2	Right angle	One-quarter of a complete revolution	
7.2	Vertical angles	The opposite angles formed by two intersecting lines	
7.2	Supplementary angles	Angles whose measures add to $180°$	

Section	Item	Meaning	Example
7.2	Transversal	A line that crosses two or more other lines	
7.2	Complementary angles	Angles whose measures add to 90°	
7.2	Perpendicular lines	Lines that intersect at right angles	
7.3A	Broken line	A sequence of connected straight line segments	
7.3A	Simple path	A path that does not cross itself	
7.3A	Closed path	A path that starts and ends at the same point	
7.3A	Polygon	A simple, closed, broken line	
7.3A	Sides (of polygon)	The line segments of the path	
7.3A	Vertices (of polygon)	The endpoints of the sides of the polygon	
7.3A	Convex polygon	A polygon that is not reentrant	
7.3A	Concave polygon	A polygon that is reentrant	
7.3A	Regular polygon	A polygon with all sides of equal length and all angles of equal size	

Section	Item	Meaning	Example
7.3A	Equilateral triangle	A triangle with three equal sides	
7.3B	Acute triangle	All three angles are acute	
7.3B	Right triangle	One of the angles is a right angle	
7.3B	Obtuse triangle	One of the angles is an obtuse angle	
7.3B	Scalene triangle	No equal sides	
7.3B	Isosceles triangle	Two equal sides	
7.3B	Trapezoid	A quadrilateral with two parallel and two nonparallel sides	
7.3B	Parallelogram	A quadrilateral with both pairs of opposite sides parallel	
7.3B	Rhombus	A parallelogram with four equal sides	
7.3B	Rectangle	A parallelogram whose angles are right angles	
7.3B	Square	A rectangle with four equal sides	
7.3B	Perimeter	Distance around a polygon	
7.3C	$S = (n - 2) \cdot 180°$	Sum of the measures of the angles of a polygon of n sides	

Section	Item	Meaning	Example
7.4	Similar figures	Figures with exactly the same shape	
7.5	Circle	The set of all coplanar points at a given fixed distance (the radius) from a point (the center)	
7.5	Circumference, $C = \pi d = 2\pi r$	The perimeter of a circle of diameter d (radius r)	
7.6	$A = bh$	The area of a rectangle of base b and height h	
7.6	$A = bh$	The area of a parallelogram of base b and height h	
7.6	$A = \frac{1}{2}bh$	The area of a triangle of base b and height h	
7.6	$A = \pi r^2$	The area of a circle of radius r	
7.6	Pythagorean theorem, $c^2 = a^2 + b^2$	The square of the hypotenuse c of a right triangle equals the sum of the squares of the other two sides, a and b	
7.7A	Polyhedron	A solid bounded by plane polygons	
7.7A	Convex polyhedron	One that lies entirely on one side of the plane of each of its faces	
7.7A	Concave polyhedron	One that is not convex	
7.7A	Prism	A polyhedron, two of whose faces are parallel and whose edges not on these faces are all parallel	
7.7A	Pyramid	A polyhedron with all but one of its vertices in one plane	

Section	Item	Meaning	Example
7.7B	$V = a^3$ $S = 6a^2$	Volume (V) and surface area (S) of a cube of edge a	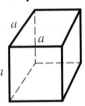
7.7B	$V = lwh$ $S =$ $2(lw + lh + wh)$	Volume (V) and surface area (S) of a rectangular box of length l, width w, and height h	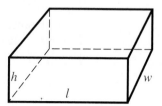
7.7B	$V = \pi r^2 h$ $S = 2\pi rh + 2\pi r^2$	Volume (V) and surface area (S) of a circular cylinder of radius r and height h	
7.7B	$V = \dfrac{1}{3}\pi r^2 h$ $S = \pi r^2 + \pi rs$	Volume (V) and surface area (S) of a circular cone of radius r, height h, and slant height s	
7.7B	$V = \dfrac{4}{3}\pi r^3$ $S = 4\pi r^2$	Volume (V) and surface area (S) of a sphere of radius r	
7.8	Network	A connected set of line segments or curves	
7.8	Traversable network	One that can be drawn by tracing each line segment or curve exactly once without lifting the pencil from the paper	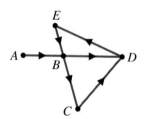

Research Questions

Sources of information for these questions can be found in the Bibliography at the end of the book.

1. Write a report about the author of the phrase "There is no royal road to geometry" and the person's other contributions to geometry.
2. Write a paragraph about Thales of Miletus (640–546 B.C.) and his contributions to geometry.
3. Write a report on how surveyors and navigators use geometry. Read one of the following articles from *The World of Mathematics* by James Newman and write a report on its relevance to the geometry we have studied.
   (a) Commentary on Descartes and analytical geometry
   (b) Commentary on a famous problem
   (c) Projective geometry
4. Write a report on Camille Jordan (1838–1922), his discoveries in topology, and how they relate to geometry.
5. The Pythagorean theorem reveals three numbers (3, 4, 5) such that $a^2 + b^2 = c^2$. Write a report on the evolution of this theorem through different ages and civilizations.
6. In 1637, Pierre de Fermat scribbled a note proposing that there are no positive integers a, b, and c so that $a^n + b^n = c^n$, when $n > 2$. Write a report on Fermat's last theorem and the false proof of the theorem offered in March 1988.
7. Charlotte Angas Scott (1858–1931) wrote *An Introductory Account of Certain Modern Ideas and Methods in Plane Analytical Geometry*. Write a report on her work and her life.
8. Grace Chisholm Young (1868–1944) developed some interesting material in the field of solid geometry. In her *First Book of Geometry,* she included many diagrams that were to be cut and folded to make three-dimensional figures. Find out about this and make some of the figures that Young described.

Chapter 7 Practice Test

1. Refer to the line shown below and state what each of the following describes:
   (a) $\overleftrightarrow{WY} \cap \overrightarrow{XZ}$ (b) $\overleftrightarrow{WY} \cap \overrightarrow{YZ}$ (c) $\overrightarrow{WX} \cup \overrightarrow{XZ}$

2. Let A, B, C, and D be four points, no three of which are collinear. How many straight lines do these points determine? Name each of these lines. Would you change your answers if the four points were not coplanar?

3. Sketch a triangular prism. Label the vertices and then name the edges that are:

   (a) Parallel lines   (b) Skew lines   (c) Intersecting lines

4. Is it true that two skew lines always determine a plane? Explain.

5. Sketch a broken line that is:

   (a) Simple but not closed   (b) Closed but not simple

6. Through how many degrees does the hour hand of a clock turn in going from:

   (a) 12 to 4 o'clock?   (b) 3 to 5 o'clock?

7. If $\angle A$ and $\angle B$ are supplementary angles, and $m\angle A = 3 \times m\angle B$, find the measures of the two angles.

8. In the figure below, lines PQ and RS are parallel. Find:

   (a) $m\angle C$ (b) $m\angle E$ (c) $m\angle D$

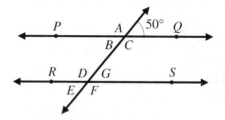

9. (a) In a triangle ABC, $m\angle A = 38°$ and $m\angle B = 43°$. Find $m\angle C$.

   (b) In a triangle ABC, $m\angle A = m\angle B = 2 \times m\angle C$. Find the measures of the three angles.

10. Angles A and B are the acute angles of a right triangle, and $m\angle A = 4 \times m\angle B$. Find $m\angle A$ and $m\angle B$.

11. What is the measure of one of the interior angles of a regular polygon with:

    (a) Nine sides?   (b) Ten sides?

12. A rectangular plot of ground is to be enclosed with 120 yd of fencing. If the plot is to be twice as long as it is wide, what must be its dimensions?

13. Triangles ABC and XYZ are similar, with $m\angle A = m\angle X$ and $m\angle B = m\angle Y$. If AB, BC, and AC are 2 in., 3 in., and 4 in. long, respectively, and XY is 3 in. long, find the lengths of YZ and XZ.

14. The center of a circle is also the center of a square of side 2 cm. The circle passes through the four vertices of the square. Find the circumference of the circle. (Leave your answer in terms of π.)

15. In problem 14, find the area of the region that is inside the circle and outside the square. (Leave your answer in terms of π.)

16. If you rolled up an $8\frac{1}{2}$ by 11 in. sheet of paper into the largest possible cylinder $8\frac{1}{2}$ in. high, what would be the diameter of the cylinder? Leave your answer in terms of π.

17. A window is in the shape of a rectangle surmounted by an isosceles triangle. The window is 3 ft wide, 6 ft high at the center, and 4 ft high on the sides. Find the total area of the window.

18. A rectangle is 84 ft long and 13 ft wide. Find the length of its diagonal.
19. A window is in the shape of a rectangle surmounted by a semicircle. The width of the window is 3 ft, which is also the diameter of the circle, and the height of the rectangular part is 4 ft. Find the total area of the window.
20. A circle of diameter 2 in. has its center at the center of a square of side 2 in. Find the area of the region that is inside the square and outside the circle.
21. Find the total surface area of a rectangular box whose base is 3 ft wide and 5 ft long and whose height is 2 ft.
22. A solid consists of a cone and a hemisphere mounted base to base. If the radius of the common base is 2 in. and the volume of the cone is equal to the volume of the hemisphere, what is the height of the cone?
23. In problem 22, suppose the area of the curved surface of the hemisphere equals the area of the curved surface of the cone. What is the height of the cone?
24. A sphere and a cylinder have the same radius, 10 in. If the total surface area of the cylinder equals the surface area of the sphere, what is the height of the cylinder?
25. The area of a regular hexagon is $(3\sqrt{3}/2)s^2$, where s is the length of the side. A circular cylinder of radius s and a regular hexagonal prism of side s have the same height. What is the ratio of the volume of the prism to the volume of the cylinder?
26. The base of a prism is a triangle whose base is 5 ft and whose height is 3 ft. If the prism is 4 ft high, what is its volume?

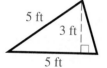

27. The triangle shown in the margin is the base of a pyramid that is 4 ft high. What is the volume of this pyramid?
28. Draw two networks, each with five vertices, such that one of them is traversable and the other is not traversable.

In this chapter we will study different mathematical systems. First, we consider rectangular arrays of numbers called **matrices** and the operations that can be performed with these matrices, as well as their applications. As it turns out, matrices can be used to solve systems of linear equations by using *elementary row operations*. They can also be used to code and decode messages, a method employed by intelligence services around the world.

We then start the study of mathematical systems by considering *clock arithmetic* in a 12- or 5-hour clock and generalize the idea to *modular* arithmetic We continue with a discussion of abstract mathematical systems, followed by a study of two mathematical structures called **groups** and **fields,** and end the chapter with a study of game theory, a subject with numerous applications to business, games of chance, and military science.

Mathematical Systems
and Matrices

Sophie Germain 1776–1831

THE HUMAN SIDE
OF MATHEMATICS

Sophie Germain was born in Paris in 1776. As a child she spent many hours in her father's library. There, she came across the legend of Archimedes, who was so engrossed in the study of a geometric figure he had drawn, that he failed to respond to a Roman soldier. "The soldier flew into a passion, unsheathed his glorious sword, and dispatched the unarmed veteran geometer of seventy-five." How fascinating the problem must have been, Germain reasoned, to command such intense concentration! From that point she was determined to learn all she could about mathematics.

In 1794 the Ecole Polytechnic was founded but women were not admitted as regular students. She obtained Lagrange's lectures from her friends, and at the end of the course, handed her observations to the professor under the pen name M. le Blanc. So impressed was Lagrange with the originality of the notes that he wanted to meet the author. After discovering that the author was a woman, Lagrange praised Germain as "a promising young analyst."

In 1801, facinated by Gauss's work on the theory of numbers, Germain began sending him the results of her own mathematical investigations, again using her pen name. When her identity was revealed in 1807, Gauss wrote: *But how to describe to you my admiration and astonishment at seeing my esteemed correspondent M. Le Blanc metamorphose himself into this illustrious personage [Sophie Germain] who gives such a brilliant example of what I would find it difficult to believe.*

Sophie Germain won the French Academy's prize under her own name. It was the high point of her career. She died at age 55, a short time before she was to receive her honorary doctor's degree from the University of Gottingen.

Looking Ahead: Some of Germain's communication with Gauss involved her work in modular arithmetic, which is also our focus in Section 8.5.

8.1   MATRIX OPERATIONS

GETTING STARTED
APPLICATIONS OF MATRICES

The information in the chart is presented as a rectangular array of numbers. Thus, the entry in the third row, fourth column tells us that a 176-pound person would burn off 250 calories by gardening for one hour. In mathematics, when such arrays are enclosed in brackets, the result is called a **matrix.** In this section, we shall study matrices, their addition, subtraction, and multiplication.

Suppose you wish to know how many calories are burned in 3 hours using the same activities and weights listed in the matrix. You simply multiply each entry by 3. For example, the entry in the fourth row, third column should be 750, telling you that a 154-lb person would burn 750 calories by mowing the lawn for 3 hr.

Matrices have a wide range of applications including spreadsheets, inventory analysis, and communications. For example, the diagram (illustrated in the figure) shows part of a complex computer communication network. Since there are eight nodes, we use the 8 by 8 matrix on page 563 to list the communication links between the nodes. The fact that node 1 can communicate directly with nodes 2, 4, and 5 is represented by entering 1's in the second, fourth, and fifth columns and 0's in the remaining columns of the first row as listed. Similarly, the second row has 1's in the first, third, and

How Fast You Burn Off Calories*

Weight (in pounds)

Moderate activity	110	132	154	176	187	209
	Calories burned per hour					
Housework	175	210	245	285	300	320
Making bed	165	185	210	230	245	255
Gardening	155	190	215	250	265	280
Mowing lawn	195	225	250	280	295	305
Watching TV	60	70	80	85	90	95
Golf (foursome)	210	240	270	295	310	325
Tennis	335	380	425	470	495	520
Bowling	210	240	270	300	310	325
Jogging	515	585	655	725	760	795
Walking briskly	355	400	450	500	525	550
Dancing	350	395	445	490	575	540
Cycling	190	215	245	270	280	295

*Read down the column closest to your weight for approximate use of calories per hour.

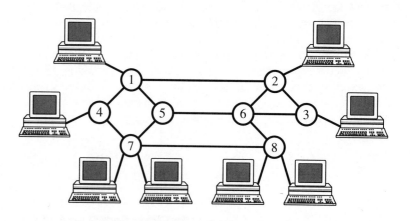

sixth columns, since node 2 communicates directly with nodes 1, 3, and 6. Can you complete the rest of the matrix?

$$
\begin{array}{c}
 \\
1 \\
2 \\
3 \\
4 \\
5 \\
6 \\
7 \\
8
\end{array}
\begin{array}{cccccccc}
1 & 2 & 3 & 4 & 5 & 6 & 7 & 8 \\
\left[\begin{array}{cccccccc}
0 & 1 & 0 & 1 & 1 & 0 & 0 & 0 \\
1 & 0 & 1 & 0 & 0 & 1 & 0 & 0 \\
 & & & & & & & \\
 & & & & & & & \\
 & & & & & & & \\
 & & & & & & & \\
 & & & & & & & \\
 & & & & & & &
\end{array}\right]
\end{array}
$$

We can also construct a matrix representing all the *two*-step communication possibilities. For example, node 2 *can* communicate with 5 in two steps (2 to 6 and 6 to 5). You can find all the two-step communications when you learn to multiply matrices.

Table 8.1

	Regular	Deluxe
Bolts	5	3
Clamps	2	4
Screws	7	10

Since the late 1940s, matrices have become an important tool in business and the social sciences, just as they have been in the physical sciences and technology since some decades before that. Matrices can be used to store information. For example, suppose the ABC Sports Company manufactures two types of billiard tables, regular and deluxe. Each of these models requires bolts, clamps, and screws according to Table 8.1. If we remember that the rows are labeled bolts, clamps, and screws, in that order, then the rectangular array of numbers

$$
R = \begin{bmatrix} 5 & 3 \\ 2 & 4 \\ 7 & 10 \end{bmatrix}
$$

gives all the necessary information regarding the assembly requirements of each billiard table.

Definition 8.1

A rectangular array of numbers enclosed in square brackets (or, sometimes, parentheses) is called a **matrix.** (The plural is **matrices.**) The entries in a matrix are called its **elements.**

The matrix

$$
\begin{bmatrix} a_{11} & a_{12} \\ a_{21} & a_{22} \\ a_{31} & a_{32} \end{bmatrix}
$$

where the subscripts give the **row** and **column** of each element, has 3 rows and 2 columns. We speak of it as a 3 by 2 (3 × 2) matrix. The number of rows and the number of columns in a matrix are called the **dimensions** of the matrix. Thus, a matrix with m rows and n columns is an **m × n** matrix.

For convenience, we often denote matrices by single capital letters, such as A, B, C. We might write

$$A = \begin{bmatrix} 1 & 2 \\ -3 & 0 \end{bmatrix} \qquad B = \begin{bmatrix} 1 \\ 3 \\ 5 \end{bmatrix} \qquad C = \begin{bmatrix} 1 & 0 & -2 & 4 \end{bmatrix}$$

Of these, A is a 2×2 matrix, B is a 3×1 matrix, and C is a 1×4 matrix. A matrix such as B, consisting of a single column, is called a **column matrix.** Likewise, a matrix such as C, consisting of a single row, is called a **row matrix.** A matrix such as A, having the same number of columns as rows, is called a **square matrix.**

Definition 8.2

Two matrices A and B are said to be **equal** ($A = B$) if and only if the corresponding elements are equal. (This means that they have the same dimensions, and that each element of A equals the element of B in the same row and column.)

For example, if

$$A = \begin{bmatrix} 1 & 2 \\ -3 & 0 \end{bmatrix} \qquad B = \begin{bmatrix} 1 & 4 \\ -3 & 0 \end{bmatrix} \qquad C = \begin{bmatrix} 1 & 2 \\ -3 & 0 \end{bmatrix}$$

then $A \neq B$, because the element in the first row, second column of A is 2 and that in B is 4. On the other hand, $A = C$, because each element of A is the same as the corresponding element of C.

A. *Addition, Subtraction, and Multiplication by a Number*

Suppose that the ABC Sports Company makes 5 of each of its 2 models of billiard tables. Of course, it would need 5 times as many bolts, clamps, and screws as for just one of each. It is easily seen that the matrix of parts requirements for 5 of each table is obtained by multiplying each element of the original matrix by 5 to get

$$\begin{bmatrix} 5 \times 5 & 5 \times 3 \\ 5 \times 2 & 5 \times 4 \\ 5 \times 7 & 5 \times 10 \end{bmatrix} = \begin{bmatrix} 25 & 15 \\ 10 & 20 \\ 35 & 50 \end{bmatrix}$$

If we write R for the original parts requirement matrix, then it is natural to write $5R$ for the new matrix. Thus,

$$5R = 5\begin{bmatrix} 5 & 3 \\ 2 & 4 \\ 7 & 10 \end{bmatrix} = \begin{bmatrix} 25 & 15 \\ 10 & 20 \\ 35 & 50 \end{bmatrix}$$

This idea motivates the definition of multiplication of a matrix by a real number.

Definition 8.3

If A is a matrix and k is a real number, then the **multiplication of A by k,** symbolized by kA or Ak, is the operation that multiplies every element of A by k.

Thus, if

$$A = \begin{bmatrix} 1 & 2 \\ -3 & 0 \end{bmatrix}$$

then

$$-2A = \begin{bmatrix} (-2) \times 1 & (-2) \times 2 \\ (-2) \times (-3) & (-2) \times 0 \end{bmatrix} = \begin{bmatrix} -2 & -4 \\ 6 & 0 \end{bmatrix}$$

EXAMPLE 1 If

$$A = \begin{bmatrix} 1 & x \\ 0 & y \end{bmatrix} \quad \text{and} \quad B = \begin{bmatrix} 2 & 6 \\ 0 & -10 \end{bmatrix}$$

find x and y to satisfy the equation $2A = B$.

Solution Substituting for A and B in the equation $2A = B$, we get

$$2\begin{bmatrix} 1 & x \\ 0 & y \end{bmatrix} = \begin{bmatrix} 2 & 6 \\ 0 & -10 \end{bmatrix}$$

Thus,

$$\begin{bmatrix} 2 & 2x \\ 0 & 2y \end{bmatrix} = \begin{bmatrix} 2 & 6 \\ 0 & -10 \end{bmatrix}$$

By Definition 8.2 then,

$$2x = 6 \quad \text{and} \quad 2y = -10$$

Hence, $x = 3$ and $y = -5$.

Suppose that a work crew at the ABC Sports Company assembles 6 of each of their billiard tables during the first half of the day and 5 of each during the second half. (They get a little bit tired of regulars and deluxes before the day is over.) What is the matrix of parts requirements for the day's work?

We see that the matrix $6R$ will be the appropriate matrix for the first half-day, and that $5R$ will be the matrix for the second half-day. Thus,

$$6R = \begin{bmatrix} 30 & 18 \\ 12 & 24 \\ 42 & 60 \end{bmatrix} \begin{matrix} \text{Bolts} \\ \text{Clamps} \\ \text{Screws} \end{matrix} \quad \text{and} \quad 5R = \begin{bmatrix} 25 & 15 \\ 10 & 20 \\ 35 & 50 \end{bmatrix} \begin{matrix} \text{Bolts} \\ \text{Clamps} \\ \text{Screws} \end{matrix}$$

are the matrices for the parts requirements for the two half-days. It is easy to see that the total requirements can be found by adding the corresponding elements as follows:

$$\begin{bmatrix} 30 + 25 & 18 + 15 \\ 12 + 10 & 24 + 20 \\ 42 + 35 & 60 + 50 \end{bmatrix} = \begin{bmatrix} 55 & 33 \\ 22 & 44 \\ 77 & 110 \end{bmatrix}$$

It seems perfectly natural to regard this as $6R + 5R$, the "sum" of the two matrices. These and similar considerations motivate the following definition of addition of matrices.

Definition 8.4

The **sum** of two matrices A and B *of the same dimensions* is written $A + B$ and is the matrix obtained by adding corresponding elements of A and B.

EXAMPLE 2   If

$$A = \begin{bmatrix} 2 & 1 \\ 3 & 4 \end{bmatrix} \quad \text{and} \quad B = \begin{bmatrix} 1 & 5 \\ 4 & 2 \end{bmatrix}$$

find:

(a) $A + B$ (b) $2A + 3B$

Solution   (a) $A + B = \begin{bmatrix} 2 + 1 & 1 + 5 \\ 3 + 4 & 4 + 2 \end{bmatrix} = \begin{bmatrix} 3 & 6 \\ 7 & 6 \end{bmatrix}$

(b) $2A + 3B = \begin{bmatrix} 4 & 2 \\ 6 & 8 \end{bmatrix} + \begin{bmatrix} 3 & 15 \\ 12 & 6 \end{bmatrix} = \begin{bmatrix} 7 & 17 \\ 18 & 14 \end{bmatrix}$

Definition 8.5

If A and B are two matrices of the same dimensions, then the **difference** $A - B$ is given by $A - B = A + (-1)B$, which is the same as the matrix formed by subtracting each element of B from the corresponding element of A.

EXAMPLE 3 If A and B are as in Example 2, find $2A - 3B$.

Solution With $2A$ and $3B$ as in Example 2, we have

$$2A - 3B = \begin{bmatrix} 4 & 2 \\ 6 & 8 \end{bmatrix} - \begin{bmatrix} 3 & 15 \\ 12 & 6 \end{bmatrix}$$

$$= \begin{bmatrix} 4 - 3 & 2 - 15 \\ 6 - 12 & 8 - 6 \end{bmatrix} = \begin{bmatrix} 1 & -13 \\ -6 & 2 \end{bmatrix}$$

B. *Matrix Multiplication*

Let us return to the ABC Sports Company and recall that the assembly requirement matrix was

$$R = \begin{matrix} & \text{Regular} & \text{Deluxe} \\ \text{Bolts} & \\ \text{Clamps} \\ \text{Screws} \end{matrix} \begin{bmatrix} 5 & 3 \\ 2 & 4 \\ 7 & 10 \end{bmatrix}$$

Suppose now that Jane's work crew assembles regulars and Jim's workers assemble deluxes. Jane turns out 18 regulars, and Jim turns out 16 deluxes per day. We can specify the total output by means of the column matrix

$$C = \begin{bmatrix} 18 \\ 16 \end{bmatrix} \begin{matrix} \text{Regular} \\ \text{Deluxe} \end{matrix}$$

Can we use these matrices to calculate how many bolts, clamps, and screws are needed for the daily output of Jane's and Jim's workers? Yes! We proceed as follows: To calculate the number of bolts, we use a "row–column" type of multiplication, as indicated by the following scheme:

$$[5 \quad 3] \begin{bmatrix} 18 \\ 16 \end{bmatrix} = 5 \times 18 + 3 \times 16 = 90 + 48 = 138$$

Similarly, we find the number of clamps to be

$$[2 \quad 4] \begin{bmatrix} 18 \\ 16 \end{bmatrix} = 2 \times 18 + 4 \times 16 = 36 + 64 = 100$$

and the number of screws to be

$$[7 \quad 10] \begin{bmatrix} 18 \\ 16 \end{bmatrix} = 7 \times 18 + 10 \times 16 = 126 + 160 = 286$$

Next, let us write the result of our computation in the briefer form

$$\begin{matrix} \text{Bolts} \\ \text{Clamps} \\ \text{Screws} \end{matrix} \begin{bmatrix} 5 & 3 \\ 2 & 4 \\ 7 & 10 \end{bmatrix} \begin{bmatrix} 18 \\ 16 \end{bmatrix} = \begin{bmatrix} 138 \\ 100 \\ 286 \end{bmatrix} \begin{matrix} \text{Bolts} \\ \text{Clamps} \\ \text{Screws} \end{matrix}$$

If we call the daily parts requirement matrix D, then we can write

$$RC = D$$

and regard the RC as a type of product. Notice that this product is a column matrix in which the first element is obtained from a row–column multiplication using the first row of R. Similarly, the second element is obtained in the same way using the second row of R, and likewise for the third element.

Now, suppose the ABC Sports Company needs to produce 18 regular and 16 deluxe billiard tables today and 10 regular and 20 deluxe tables tomorrow. To represent the production matrix P for the 2 days, we write

$$\begin{matrix} & \text{Today} & \text{Tomorrow} \\ P = & \begin{bmatrix} 18 & 10 \\ 16 & 20 \end{bmatrix} & \begin{matrix} \text{Regular} \\ \text{Deluxe} \end{matrix} \end{matrix}$$

How many bolts, clamps, and screws are needed in the next 2 days? We need to make the computation for tomorrow only, since we have already done it for today. Thus,

$$\begin{bmatrix} 5 & 3 \\ 2 & 4 \\ 7 & 10 \end{bmatrix} \begin{bmatrix} 10 \\ 20 \end{bmatrix} = \begin{bmatrix} 5 \times 10 + 3 \times 20 \\ 2 \times 10 + 4 \times 20 \\ 7 \times 10 + 10 \times 20 \end{bmatrix} = \begin{bmatrix} 110 \\ 100 \\ 270 \end{bmatrix}$$

If we denote the final requirement matrix by W, then it is natural to write

$$\begin{bmatrix} 5 & 3 \\ 2 & 4 \\ 7 & 10 \end{bmatrix} \begin{bmatrix} 18 & 10 \\ 16 & 20 \end{bmatrix} = \begin{bmatrix} 138 & 110 \\ 100 & 100 \\ 286 & 270 \end{bmatrix}$$

or

$$RP = W$$

where each element in W is calculated by the following rule: **The element of W in the ith row and jth column is the row–column product of the ith row of R and the jth column of P.**

For example, the element of W in the first row, second column position is the row–column product of the first row of R and the second column of P; that is,

$$[5 \quad 3]\begin{bmatrix} 10 \\ 20 \end{bmatrix} = 5 \times 10 + 3 \times 20 = 110$$

You should check all the elements of W to be sure you understand the rule.

Definition 8.6

The matrix $W = RP$ is called the **product** of the matrices R and P in that order, and the calculation of W according to the rule given above is called **matrix multiplication.**

The preceding discussion can easily be generalized to the multiplication of two matrices A and B. Suppose that A has as many columns as B has rows. Then we can do a row–column multiplication with any row of A and any column of B. Thus, we have the following definition:

Definition 8.7

The matrices A and B are said to be **conformable** with respect to multiplication in the order AB if the number of columns in A is the same as the number of rows in B. In this case, each element of the product AB is formed as follows: The element in row i and column j of AB is the row–column product of the ith row of A and the jth column of B.

If two matrices are not conformable, then we do not attempt to define their product. Notice that A and B might be conformable for multiplication in the order AB and not in the order BA. Thus, if A is $m \times n$ and B is $n \times k$, then A and B are conformable for multiplication in the order AB, but not in the order BA unless $m = k$. Note that AB will be an $m \times k$ matrix. For instance, if A is 2×3 and B is 3×4, then we can form AB, and it will be a 2×4 matrix; but we cannot form BA.

Note: *Even when the matrices are conformable for both orders of multiplication, there is no reason why the results need to be equal. In fact, it is generally true that $AB \neq BA$.*

This failure of matrix multiplication to be commutative was one of the exciting properties of matrices to the mathematicians who first studied them.

EXAMPLE 4   Let

$$A = \begin{bmatrix} 2 & 1 & 0 \\ 3 & 2 & 4 \end{bmatrix} \quad \text{and} \quad B = \begin{bmatrix} 1 & 4 \\ 3 & 1 \\ 2 & 3 \end{bmatrix}$$

Calculate the product AB.

Solution   Because A is 2×3 and B is 3×2, we may proceed according to Definition 8.7 to get the 2×2 product matrix

$$AB = \begin{bmatrix} 2 & 1 & 0 \\ 3 & 2 & 4 \end{bmatrix} \begin{bmatrix} 1 & 4 \\ 3 & 1 \\ 2 & 3 \end{bmatrix}$$

$$= \begin{bmatrix} 2 \times 1 + 1 \times 3 + 0 \times 2 & 2 \times 4 + 1 \times 1 + 0 \times 3 \\ 3 \times 1 + 2 \times 3 + 4 \times 2 & 3 \times 4 + 2 \times 1 + 4 \times 3 \end{bmatrix}$$

$$= \begin{bmatrix} 5 & 9 \\ 17 & 26 \end{bmatrix}$$

■

EXAMPLE 5   Using the same matrices as in Example 4, form the product BA (if possible).

Solution   We first check that B has as many columns as A has rows (two in each case). This shows that the matrices are conformable for multiplication in the order BA. Thus, by Definition 8.7 we get the 3×3 matrix

$$BA = \begin{bmatrix} 1 & 4 \\ 3 & 1 \\ 2 & 3 \end{bmatrix} \begin{bmatrix} 2 & 1 & 0 \\ 3 & 2 & 4 \end{bmatrix}$$

$$= \begin{bmatrix} 1 \times 2 + 4 \times 3 & 1 \times 1 + 4 \times 2 & 1 \times 0 + 4 \times 4 \\ 3 \times 2 + 1 \times 3 & 3 \times 1 + 1 \times 2 & 3 \times 0 + 1 \times 4 \\ 2 \times 2 + 3 \times 3 & 2 \times 1 + 3 \times 2 & 2 \times 0 + 3 \times 4 \end{bmatrix}$$

$$= \begin{bmatrix} 14 & 9 & 16 \\ 9 & 5 & 4 \\ 13 & 8 & 12 \end{bmatrix}$$

■

Examples 4 and 5 offer unassailable evidence that in general $AB \neq BA$. If A and B were both square matrices of the same size, do you think that $AB = BA$ always? Try it for some simple 2×2 matrices!

C. *The Identity Matrix*

Is there an identity for matrix multiplication? The answer is yes. For example, the multiplication of any 2×2 matrix A by

$$I = \begin{bmatrix} 1 & 0 \\ 0 & 1 \end{bmatrix}$$

gives the matrix A back again. We find that

$$IA = AI = A \quad \text{Try it for } \begin{bmatrix} a & b \\ c & d \end{bmatrix}$$

It can be shown that I is the only matrix that has this property for *all* 2×2 matrices. Because of this uniqueness, I is called the **multiplicative identity** for 2×2 matrices.

Similarly for 3×3 matrices, the multiplicative identity is the matrix

$$I = \begin{bmatrix} 1 & 0 & 0 \\ 0 & 1 & 0 \\ 0 & 0 & 1 \end{bmatrix}$$

The **main diagonal** of a square matrix is the diagonal set of numbers running from the upper left corner to the lower right corner of the matrix. The two identity matrices, one for 2×2 and the other for 3×3 matrices, are particular examples of the general result that the $n \times n$ identity matrix is the $n \times n$ matrix with 1's on the main diagonal and 0's for all other elements.

Addition properties of matrices are discussed in the Discovery section of Exercise 8.1.

Exercise 8.1

A. For problems 1–6, suppose that

$$A = \begin{bmatrix} 2 & 1 \\ 0 & -1 \end{bmatrix} \qquad B = \begin{bmatrix} -2 & 4 \\ 3 & 1 \end{bmatrix} \qquad C = \begin{bmatrix} 3 & 5 \\ 2 & 0 \end{bmatrix}$$

1. Find:
   (a) $4A$ (b) $-3B$ (c) $C - B$
2. Find:
   (a) $2A + B$ (b) $4A + 3B$ (c) $2A - C$
3. Find:
   (a) $A + B + C$ (b) $A + B - C$
4. Find:
   (a) $A - B + 2C$ (b) $2A + 2B - C$
5. Find:
   (a) $7A + 4B - 2C$ (b) $2A - 2B - 3C$
6. Find:
   (a) $5A + 4B - 4C$ (b) $4A - 2B - 4C$

For problems 7–12, suppose that

$$A = \begin{bmatrix} 1 & -1 & 2 \\ 3 & 0 & -2 \\ 4 & 2 & 1 \end{bmatrix} \qquad B = \begin{bmatrix} -1 & 2 & 1 \\ 4 & 3 & -1 \\ 0 & 1 & -1 \end{bmatrix} \qquad C = \begin{bmatrix} 0 & -1 & 3 \\ 1 & -2 & 4 \\ 3 & -3 & 0 \end{bmatrix}$$

7. Find:
   (a) $A + B$ (b) $A - B$ (c) $A - C$

8. Find:
   (a) $2A$ (b) $-2B$ (c) $-3C$

9. Find:
   (a) $2A + 3B$ (b) $-2A + 3B$

10. Find:
    (a) $4A + 4B$ (b) $4A - 4B$

11. Find:
    (a) $3A - 2C$ (b) $B + C$

12. Find:
    (a) $3A + B - 4C$ (b) $5A + 2B + 3C$

B. In problems 13–20, use

$$A = \begin{bmatrix} 1 & -2 & 1 \\ 2 & 0 & 2 \\ -1 & 1 & 3 \end{bmatrix} \quad B = \begin{bmatrix} 3 & 2 & 0 \\ 1 & 1 & -1 \\ 2 & 0 & 1 \end{bmatrix} \quad C = \begin{bmatrix} 1 & 0 & 2 \\ 3 & 2 & 1 \\ 2 & 0 & 1 \end{bmatrix}$$

and evaluate the given expression.

13. AB 14. AC 15. BA

16. CA 17. $(A - B)(A + B)$ 18. $(A - C)(A + C)$

19. $A^2 - B^2$ 20. $A^2 - C^2$

C. 21. If I is the 2×2 identity matrix, find I^2.

22. If n is a positive integer, is it true that $I^n = I$? Why?

In problems 23–27, verify that $AB = I$, and calculate BA.

23. $A = \begin{bmatrix} 2 & 1 \\ 1 & 1 \end{bmatrix}$; $B = \begin{bmatrix} 1 & -1 \\ -1 & 2 \end{bmatrix}$

24. $A = \begin{bmatrix} -2 & 3 \\ 1 & -1 \end{bmatrix}$; $B = \begin{bmatrix} 1 & 3 \\ 1 & 2 \end{bmatrix}$

25. $A = \begin{bmatrix} 2 & 5 \\ 1 & 3 \end{bmatrix}$; $B = \begin{bmatrix} 3 & -5 \\ -1 & 2 \end{bmatrix}$

26. $A = \begin{bmatrix} 1 & 0 & 1 \\ 0 & 1 & 1 \\ 1 & 0 & 0 \end{bmatrix}$; $B = \begin{bmatrix} 0 & 0 & 1 \\ -1 & 1 & 1 \\ 1 & 0 & -1 \end{bmatrix}$

27. $A = \begin{bmatrix} 1 & 0 & 1 \\ 0 & 2 & -1 \\ 2 & 1 & 2 \end{bmatrix}$; $B = \begin{bmatrix} 5 & 1 & -2 \\ -2 & 0 & 1 \\ -4 & -1 & 2 \end{bmatrix}$

28. Let R be the row matrix [2 1]. Is it possible for there to be a 2×2 matrix, say, J, such that $JR = RJ = R$? Explain.

29. If A is a nonsquare matrix of dimensions $m \times n$, do you think there could be a square matrix J such that $AJ = JA = A$? Explain.

30. Find all possible 2×2 matrices A such that $A = 3A$.

31. A square matrix A is called **idempotent** if $A^2 = A$. All identity matrices and all zero matrices (elements all 0's) are idempotent. Show that the following matrices are also idempotent:

    (a) $\begin{bmatrix} 1 & 2 \\ 0 & 0 \end{bmatrix}$ (b) $\begin{bmatrix} \frac{1}{2} & \frac{1}{2} \\ \frac{1}{2} & \frac{1}{2} \end{bmatrix}$

32. A square matrix A is called **nilpotent** if there is a positive integer n such that A^n is a zero matrix (elements all 0's). Show that the following matrices are nilpotent:

    (a) $\begin{bmatrix} 2 & 1 \\ -4 & -2 \end{bmatrix}$ (b) $\begin{bmatrix} 0 & 0 & 1 \\ 2 & 0 & 3 \\ 0 & 0 & 0 \end{bmatrix}$

33. The E-Z Rest Furniture Company makes armchairs and rocking chairs in three models each: E, an economy model; M, a medium-priced model; L, a luxury model. Each month, the company turns out 20 model E armchairs, 15 model M armchairs, 10 model L armchairs, 12 model E rockers, 8 model M rockers, and 5 model L rockers.
    (a) Write this information as a 2×3 matrix.
    (b) Use your answer in part (a) to obtain a matrix showing the total production for 6 months.

34. Suppose the costs of materials for E-Z Rest's armchairs (see problem 33) are \$30 for model E, \$35 for model M, and \$45 for model L; and for the rockers, \$35 for model E, \$40 for model M, and \$60 for model L.
    (a) Write this information as a 3×2 matrix.
    (b) Suppose that costs increase by 20%. Write the new matrix by multiplying your answer in part (a) by 1.2.

35. At the end of 6 months, the E-Z Rest Furniture Company (see problem 33) has sold armchairs as follows: 90 model E, 75 model M, and 50 model L. They also sold rockers as follows: 60 model E, 20 model M, and 30 model L. Use matrix methods to obtain a matrix showing how many of each item are left at the end of the 6 months. Use your answer to problem 33 and assume that there was no unsold stock at the beginning of the period.

36. The ABC Sports Company figures that the bolts, clamps, and screws used in assembling its billiard tables cost, respectively, 5¢, 10¢, and 2¢ each. Show that the cost of these assembly materials for each table is obtained by carrying out the multiplication CR, where C is the **cost matrix** [5   10   2] and R is the assembly requirement matrix given at the beginning of this section.

37. The ABC Sports Company has the projected production schedule shown in the table below for the 5 months preceding December.

	July	Aug.	Sept.	Oct.	Nov.
Regular	100	200	300	400	300
Deluxe	50	100	200	200	300

Let M be the matrix with these numbers as the elements, and let R be the same as in problem 36. Use these matrices to find the schedule of assembly requirements for the 5 months so you can fill in the missing items in the following table:

	July	Aug.	Sept.	Oct.	Nov.
Bolts	650				
Clamps		800			
Screws			4100		

38. Let A be the matrix of assembly requirements you calculated in problem 37, and let C be the cost matrix of problem 36. Calculate CA to find the cost of assembly materials for each of the 5 months.

39. Tom, Dick, and Harry are in a computer network whose communication matrix C is as shown. The 1's in the first row indicate that Tom can communicate with Dick and Harry directly.

$$\begin{array}{c} \quad\;\; \textbf{T}\;\; \textbf{D}\;\; \textbf{H} \\ \begin{array}{c} \textbf{T} \\ \textbf{D} \\ \textbf{H} \end{array} \left[\begin{array}{ccc} 0 & 1 & 1 \\ 1 & 0 & 0 \\ 1 & 0 & 0 \end{array} \right] = C \end{array}$$

(a) Find C^2, the matrix of possible two-step communications in the network.

(b) What does the 2 in the first row, first column mean?

(c) How many two-step communications between two different people are shown in C^2?

40. Complete the matrix in Getting Started and find how many two-step communications between two different nodes are possible in the network. Label the original matrix A and the two-step matrix A^2. (You can look at the diagram at the beginning of the section to verify that you are correct.)

41. Let the point (a, b) in the XY plane be represented by the column matrix

$$\begin{bmatrix} a \\ b \end{bmatrix}$$

Then the right triangle with its vertices at $(1, 0)$, $(1, 2)$, and $(0, 2)$ can be represented by the matrix

$$\begin{bmatrix} 1 & 1 & 0 \\ 0 & 2 & 2 \end{bmatrix}$$

Draw this triangle. Then multiply this matrix by the matrix

$$\begin{bmatrix} -2 & 0 \\ 0 & 2 \end{bmatrix}$$

to get the vertices of another triangle. Draw the new triangle and explain what the multiplication did to the original triangle.

In Other Words

42. The system of matrices with the operations of addition, subtraction, and multiplication is a mathematical system. Name and discuss all of the *differences* you see between the system of matrices and the real numbers. (For example, if a and b are any real numbers, $a + b = b + a$. Is this true for any two matrices A and B?)

Using Your Knowledge

Here are six special 2 × 2 matrices:

$$r_1 = \begin{bmatrix} 1 & 0 \\ 0 & -1 \end{bmatrix} \quad r_2 = \begin{bmatrix} -1 & 0 \\ 0 & 1 \end{bmatrix} \quad r_3 = \begin{bmatrix} 0 & 1 \\ 1 & 0 \end{bmatrix}$$

$$R_1 = \begin{bmatrix} 0 & -1 \\ 1 & 0 \end{bmatrix} \quad R_2 = \begin{bmatrix} -1 & 0 \\ 0 & -1 \end{bmatrix} \quad R_3 = \begin{bmatrix} 0 & 1 \\ -1 & 0 \end{bmatrix}$$

It is interesting to see what effect these matrices have when they multiply a column matrix,

$$P = \begin{bmatrix} a \\ b \end{bmatrix}$$

that represents a point (a, b) in the XY plane. For example,

$$r_1 \times P = \begin{bmatrix} 1 & 0 \\ 0 & -1 \end{bmatrix} \begin{bmatrix} a \\ b \end{bmatrix} = \begin{bmatrix} a \\ -b \end{bmatrix}$$

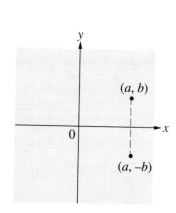

which represents the point $(a, -b)$, the reflection of (a, b) across the X axis (see Figure 8.1). Because the matrices r_1, r_2, and r_3 all correspond to reflec-

FIGURE 8.1

tions across certain lines in the plane, we may think of these three matrices as **reflectors.**

Similarly,

$$R_1 \times P = \begin{bmatrix} 0 & -1 \\ 1 & 0 \end{bmatrix}\begin{bmatrix} a \\ b \end{bmatrix} = \begin{bmatrix} -b \\ a \end{bmatrix}$$

represents the point $(-b, a)$, *which can be obtained from the point* (a, b) *by a rotation of* $90°$ *around the origin (see Figure 8.2). Because all three of the matrices* R_1, R_2, *and* R_3 *correspond to rotations in the plane, we may think of them as* **rotators.**

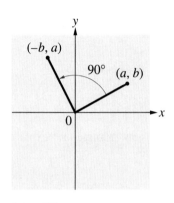

FIGURE 8.2

What is accomplished by each of the following?

43. $r_2 \times P$ 44. $r_3 \times P$ 45. $R_2 \times P$ 46. $R_3 \times P$

47. A triangle with its vertices at (2, 1), (3, 1), and (3, 2) can be represented by the matrix

$$T = \begin{bmatrix} 2 & 3 & 3 \\ 1 & 1 & 2 \end{bmatrix}$$

Form the products $r_1 \times T$, $r_2 \times T$, and so on. Then draw graphs to show the effect of each multiplication.

48. Consider another special matrix

$$K = \begin{bmatrix} k & 0 \\ 0 & k \end{bmatrix}$$

What happens to the triangle in problem 47 if you form the product $K \times T$? Try this for $k = 2$.

Discovery

We want to discover here in what ways the set S of 2×2 *matrices behaves like the set I of integers under addition and multiplication. To do this, we consider the following questions:*

49. Is S closed with respect to addition? [*Hint:* Is the sum of two 2×2 matrices a 2×2 matrix?]

50. Is S associative with respect to addition?

51. Can you find an additive identity for the set S?
    Hint: If

$$A = \begin{bmatrix} 1 & 3 \\ 4 & 6 \end{bmatrix}$$

find a matrix B so that

$$\begin{bmatrix} 1 & 3 \\ 4 & 6 \end{bmatrix} + \begin{bmatrix} & \\ & \end{bmatrix} = \begin{bmatrix} 1 & 3 \\ 4 & 6 \end{bmatrix}$$

52. Does every matrix in S have an additive inverse? For example, if

$$A = \begin{bmatrix} 1 & 2 \\ -3 & 4 \end{bmatrix}$$

try to find a matrix B so that

$$\begin{bmatrix} 1 & 2 \\ -3 & 4 \end{bmatrix} + \begin{bmatrix} & \\ & \end{bmatrix} = \begin{bmatrix} 0 & 0 \\ 0 & 0 \end{bmatrix}$$

53. Is $A + B = B + A$ for any two 2×2 matrices in S?

54. Consider the set S of 2×2 matrices.
    (a) Is S closed with respect to multiplication?
    (b) Is S associative with respect to multiplication?
    (c) Can you find a multiplicative identity for the set S?

55. The inverse of a 2×2 matrix A is defined to be a matrix B such that $AB = BA = I$, where I is the 2×2 identity matrix. Can you show that the matrix given below has no inverse?

$$A = \begin{bmatrix} 1 & 2 \\ 0 & 0 \end{bmatrix}$$

56. Can you discover whether the matrix given below has an inverse?

$$A = \begin{bmatrix} 2 & 4 \\ 1 & 2 \end{bmatrix}$$

Computer Corner

The Matrix Addition or Subtraction Program adds or subtracts matrices and The Matrix Multiplication Program multiplies matrices, provided you enter the numbers in the rows and columns (see the Programs in BASIC appendix). Work problems 7, 11b, 13, 14, 15, 16, 26, and 27 in this section using these programs.

8.2 SYSTEMS OF LINEAR EQUATIONS

GETTING STARTED
ONCE UPON A MATRIX

Have you ever read *Alice in Wonderland*? Do you know who wrote this book? The answer is Lewis Carroll. Although better known as the author of this popular tale, Carroll was also a mathematician and logician. He also wrote another book called *Through the Looking Glass*. In this book, a conversation between the characters Tweedledee and Tweedledum included the following exchange:

Tweedledee: The sum of your weight and twice mine is 361 pounds.
Tweedledum: Contrariwise, the sum of your weight and twice mine is 360 pounds.

Alice meets Tweedledee and Tweedledum in Through the Looking Glass

If Tweedledee weighs x pounds and Tweedledum weighs y pounds, recall from Section 6.5 that the two sentences can be translated as

$$2x + y = 361$$

$$x + 2y = 360$$

Do you remember how to solve this system? We are going to do it again, but this time we shall also write the equivalent operations using matrices. Follow each of the steps very carefully.
Given:

$$\begin{array}{l} 2x + y = 361 \\ x + 2y = 360 \end{array} \quad \left[\begin{array}{cc|c} 2 & 1 & 361 \\ 1 & 2 & 360 \end{array}\right]$$

Multiply the second equation by -2

$$\begin{array}{l} 2x + y = 361 \\ -2x - 4y = -720 \end{array} \quad \left[\begin{array}{cc|c} 2 & 1 & 361 \\ -2 & -4 & -720 \end{array}\right]$$

Add the two equations

$$\begin{array}{l} 2x + y = 361 \\ -3y = -359 \end{array} \quad \left[\begin{array}{cc|c} 2 & 1 & 361 \\ 0 & -3 & -359 \end{array}\right]$$

Divide the second equation by -3

$$\begin{array}{l} 2x + y = 361 \\ \phantom{2x + {}} y = 119\frac{2}{3} \end{array} \quad \left[\begin{array}{cc|c} 2 & 1 & 361 \\ 0 & 1 & 119\frac{2}{3} \end{array}\right]$$

Now, you can substitute $119\frac{2}{3}$ for y in the equation $2x + y = 361$ and solve for x. Did you notice that the operations performed on the equations were identical to those performed on the matrices? The matrices used are called the **augmented matrices,** and they can be more quickly written because the variables are omitted. In this section we shall solve systems of three equations using matrices.

In Chapter 6 we considered systems of two linear equations in two unknowns and discoverd how to solve such systems. There are many practical applications that require the consideration of m linear equations in n unknowns. We shall not try to be so general here; instead, we shall look in detail only into the case of three equations in three unknowns. The techniques we shall use are applicable to all the more general cases.

Let the unknowns be x, y, z, and let the equations be

$$a_1x + b_1y + c_1z = d_1$$
$$a_2x + b_2y + c_2z = d_2 \qquad (1)$$
$$a_3x + b_3y + c_3z = d_3$$

The a's, b's, and c's are usually called the **coefficients;** they, along with the d's, are assumed to be specific known numbers.

Define three matrices A, X, and D as follows:

$$A = \begin{bmatrix} a_1 & b_1 & c_1 \\ a_2 & b_2 & c_2 \\ a_3 & b_3 & c_3 \end{bmatrix} \qquad X = \begin{bmatrix} x \\ y \\ z \end{bmatrix} \qquad D = \begin{bmatrix} d_1 \\ d_2 \\ d_3 \end{bmatrix}$$

Then, system (1) can be written in the brief form

$$AX = D \qquad (2)$$

where on the left we mean that the 3×3 matrix A multiplies the column matrix X. This operation yields the column matrix D whose elements are the right-hand sides of the equations from the given system. Because the equation $AX = D$ implies that corresponding elements are equal, this equation represents system (1) exactly. We can go back and forth, as it suits us, from one form to the other.

For example, let the system of equations be

$$2x - y + z = 3$$
$$x + y \qquad = -1 \qquad (3)$$
$$3x - y - 2z = 7$$

Then, by writing

$$A = \begin{bmatrix} 2 & -1 & 1 \\ 1 & 1 & 0 \\ 3 & -1 & -2 \end{bmatrix} \qquad X = \begin{bmatrix} x \\ y \\ z \end{bmatrix} \qquad D = \begin{bmatrix} 3 \\ -1 \\ 7 \end{bmatrix}$$

we can symbolize the given set of equations by

$$AX = D \qquad (4)$$

(Be sure to verify this!)

The matrix A is called the **matrix of the system** (or sometimes, the matrix of coefficients). The matrix formed by adjoining the column matrix D to the matrix A is denoted by the symbol $[A \mid D]$ and is called the **augmented matrix.** For system (3), the augmented matrix is

$$[A \mid D] = \left[\begin{array}{ccc|c} 2 & -1 & 1 & 3 \\ 1 & 1 & 0 & -1 \\ 3 & -1 & -2 & 7 \end{array} \right]$$

We may regard this symbol as a listing of the detached coefficients of the system. The vertical line takes the place of the equals signs and separates the coefficients matrix from the column of right-hand terms.

Suppose we wish to solve system (3). This means that we wish to find all sets of values of (x, y, z) that make all three equations true. We first need to consider what changes can be made in the system to yield an **equivalent system,** a system that has exactly the same solutions as the original system. We need to consider only three simple operations:

> **Elementary Operations on Systems of Equations**
>
> 1. **The order of the equations may be changed.** This clearly cannot affect the solutions.
>
> 2. **Any of the equations may be multiplied by any nonzero real number.** If (m, n, p) is a solution of $ax + by + cz = d$, then, for $k \neq 0$, it is also a solution of $kax + kby + kcz = kd$, and conversely. (Why?)
>
> 3. **Any equation of the system may be replaced by the sum (member by member) of itself and any other equation of the system.** (You can show this by doing problem 11 of Exercise 8.2.)

These three **elementary operations** are used to simplify systems of equations and to find their solutions. Let us use them to solve system (3).

Step 1. In the second equation of the system, x and y have unit coefficients, so we interchange the first two equations to get the following more convenient arrangement:

$$x + y \qquad\quad = -1$$
$$2x - y + z = \quad 3$$
$$3x - y - 2z = \quad 7$$

Step 2. To make the coefficients of x in the first two equations the same in absolute value but opposite in sign, multiply both sides of the first equation by -2:

$$-2x - 2y = +2$$

Step 3. To eliminate x between the first and second equations, add the equation obtained in step 2 to the second equation to get

$$-3y + z = 5$$

and restore the first equation by dividing out the -2. The system now reads

$$
\begin{aligned}
x + y &= -1 \\
-3y + z &= 5 \\
3x - y - 2z &= 7
\end{aligned}
\tag{5}
$$

We proceed next in a similar way to eliminate x between the first and third equations.

Step 4. Multiply the first equation of system (5) by -3:

$$-3x - 3y = 3$$

Step 5. Add this last equation to the third equation to get

$$-4y - 2z = 10$$

and restore the first equation by dividing out the -3. The system now reads

$$
\begin{aligned}
x + y &= -1 \\
-3y + z &= 5 \\
-4y - 2z &= 10
\end{aligned}
\tag{6}
$$

We now eliminate y between the second and third equations in the following way:

Step 6. Multiply the second equation of system (6) by -4 and the third equation by 3 to get

$$
\begin{aligned}
12y - 4z &= -20 \\
-12y - 6z &= 30
\end{aligned}
$$

Step 7. Add the last two equations to get

$$-10z = 10$$

and restore the second equation by dividing out the -4. The system is now

$$
\begin{aligned}
x + y &= -1 \\
-3y + z &= 5 \\
-10z &= 10
\end{aligned}
\tag{7}
$$

Step 8. It is very easy to solve system (7): The third equation immediately gives $z = -1$. Then, by substitution into the second equation, we get

$$-3y - 1 = 5$$
$$-3y = 6$$
$$y = -2$$

By substituting $y = -2$ into the first equation in (7), we find

$$x - 2 = -1$$
$$x = 1$$

Thus, the solution of the system is $x = 1$, $y = -2$, $z = -1$. This is easily checked in the given set of equations.

A general system of the same form as system (7) may be written

$$ax + by + cz = d$$
$$ey + fz = g \qquad (8)$$
$$hz = k$$

A. *Solution by Matrices*

A system such as system (8), in which the first unknown, x, is missing from the second and third equations, and the second unknown, y, is missing from the third equation, is said to be in **echelon form.** A system in echelon form is quite easy to solve. The third equation immediately yields the value of z. Back-substitution of this value into the second equation yields the value of y. Finally, back-substitution of the values of y and z into the first equation yields the value of x. Briefly, we say that we solve the system by **back-substitution.**

Every system of linear equations can be brought into echelon form by the use of the elementary operations. It remains only to organize and make the procedure more efficient by employing the augmented matrix.

Let us compare the augmented matrices of systems (3) and (7):

$$\begin{bmatrix} 2 & -1 & 1 & | & 3 \\ 1 & 1 & 0 & | & -1 \\ 3 & -1 & -2 & | & 7 \end{bmatrix} \qquad (3)$$

$$\begin{bmatrix} 1 & 1 & 0 & | & -1 \\ 0 & -3 & 1 & | & 5 \\ 0 & 0 & -10 & | & 10 \end{bmatrix} \qquad (7)$$

The augmented matrix for system (7) shows that the system is in echelon form because it has only 0's below the main diagonal of the coefficient matrix. We should be able to obtain the second matrix from the first by performing operations corresponding to the elementary operations on the equations. These operations are called **elementary row operations** and always yield matrices of equivalent systems. Such matrices are called **row-equivalent.** If two matrices A and B are row-equivalent, we shall write $A \sim B$. The elementary row operations are:

Elementary Row Operations on Matrices

1. A change of order of the rows
2. Multiplication of all the elements of a row by any nonzero number
3. Replacement of any row by the element-by-element sum of itself and any other row

---

We illustrate the procedure by showing the transition from the matrix of system (3) to that of system (7). To symbolize the steps, we use the notation R_1, R_2, and R_3 for the respective rows of the matrix, along with the following typical abbreviations:

Notation	Meaning
1. $R_1 \leftrightarrow R_2$	Interchange R_1 and R_2.
2. $2 \times R_1$	Multiply each element of R_1 by 2.
3. $2 \times R_1 + R_2 \to R_2$	Replace R_2 by $2 \times R_1 + R_2$.

Thus, we write

$$\begin{bmatrix} 2 & -1 & 1 & | & 3 \\ 1 & 1 & 0 & | & -1 \\ 3 & -1 & -2 & | & 7 \end{bmatrix} \sim \begin{bmatrix} 1 & 1 & 0 & | & -1 \\ 2 & -1 & 1 & | & 3 \\ 3 & -1 & -2 & | & 7 \end{bmatrix}$$
$$R_1 \leftrightarrow R_2$$

Next, we proceed to get 0's in the second and third rows of the first column:

$$\begin{bmatrix} 1 & 1 & 0 & | & -1 \\ 2 & -1 & 1 & | & 3 \\ 3 & -1 & -2 & | & 7 \end{bmatrix} \sim \begin{bmatrix} 1 & 1 & 0 & | & -1 \\ 0 & -3 & 1 & | & 5 \\ 0 & -4 & -2 & | & 10 \end{bmatrix}$$
$$-2 \times R_1 + R_2 \to R_2$$
$$-3 \times R_1 + R_3 \to R_3$$

To complete the procedure, we get a 0 in the third row of the second column:

$$\begin{bmatrix} 1 & 1 & 0 & | & -1 \\ 0 & -3 & 1 & | & 5 \\ 0 & -4 & -2 & | & 10 \end{bmatrix} \sim \begin{bmatrix} 1 & 1 & 0 & | & -1 \\ 0 & -3 & 1 & | & 5 \\ 0 & 0 & -10 & | & 10 \end{bmatrix}$$
$$-4 \times R_2 + 3 \times R_3 \to R_3$$

Verify the result, which is the augmented matrix of system (7). Of course, once we obtain this last matrix, we can solve the system by back-substitution, as before.

We shall now give additional illustrations of this procedure, but these will help you only if you take a pencil and paper and carry out the detailed row operations as they are indicated.

EXAMPLE 1   Solve the system

$$2x - y + 2z = 3$$
$$2x + 2y - z = 0$$
$$-x + 2y + 2z = -12$$

Solution   The augmented matrix is

$$
\begin{bmatrix}
2 & -1 & 2 & 3 \\
2 & 2 & -1 & 0 \\
-1 & 2 & 2 & -12
\end{bmatrix}
\sim
\begin{bmatrix}
2 & -1 & 2 & 3 \\
0 & 3 & -3 & -3 \\
0 & 3 & 6 & -21
\end{bmatrix}
$$

$$-R_1 + R_2 \rightarrow R_2$$
$$R_1 + 2 \times R_3 \rightarrow R_3$$

$$
\sim
\begin{bmatrix}
2 & -1 & 2 & 3 \\
0 & 1 & -1 & -1 \\
0 & 0 & 9 & -18
\end{bmatrix}
$$

$$-R_2 + R_3 \rightarrow R_3$$
$$\tfrac{1}{3} \times R_2 \rightarrow R_2$$

This last matrix is in echelon form and corresponds to the system

$$2x - y + 2z = 3$$
$$y - z = -1$$
$$9z = -18$$

We solve this system by back-substitution. The last equation immediately yields $z = -2$. The second equation then becomes

$$y + 2 = -1$$

so that

$$y = -3$$

The first equation then becomes

$$2x + 3 - 4 = 3$$

so that

$$x = 2$$

The final answer, $x = 2$, $y = -3$, $z = -2$, can be checked in the given system. ∎

EXAMPLE 2 Solve the system

$$2x - y + 2z = 3$$
$$2x + 2y - z = 0$$
$$4x + y + z = 5$$

Solution

$$\begin{bmatrix} 2 & -1 & 2 & | & 3 \\ 2 & 2 & -1 & | & 0 \\ 4 & 1 & 1 & | & 5 \end{bmatrix} \sim \begin{bmatrix} 2 & -1 & 2 & | & 3 \\ 0 & 3 & -3 & | & -3 \\ 0 & 3 & -3 & | & -1 \end{bmatrix}$$

$$-R_1 + R_2 \rightarrow R_2$$
$$-2 \times R_1 + R_3 \rightarrow R_3$$

$$\sim \begin{bmatrix} 2 & -1 & 2 & | & 3 \\ 0 & 3 & -3 & | & -3 \\ 0 & 0 & 0 & | & 2 \end{bmatrix}$$

$$-R_2 + R_3 \rightarrow R_3$$

The final matrix is in echelon form, and the last line corresponds to the equation

$$0x + 0y + 0z = 2$$

which is false for all values of x, y, z. Hence, the given system has *no solution.* ∎

Note: *It is important to notice that if reduction to echelon form introduces any row with all 0's to the left and a nonzero number to the right of the vertical line, then the system has no solution.*

EXAMPLE 3 Solve the system

$$2x - y + 2z = 3$$
$$2x + 2y - z = 0$$
$$4x + y + z = 3$$

Solution

$$\begin{bmatrix} 2 & -1 & 2 & | & 3 \\ 2 & 2 & -1 & | & 0 \\ 4 & 1 & 1 & | & 3 \end{bmatrix} \sim \begin{bmatrix} 2 & -1 & 2 & | & 3 \\ 0 & 3 & -3 & | & -3 \\ 0 & 3 & -3 & | & -3 \end{bmatrix}$$

$$-R_1 + R_2 \rightarrow R_2$$
$$-2 \times R_1 + R_3 \rightarrow R_3$$

$$\sim \begin{bmatrix} 2 & -1 & 2 & | & 3 \\ 0 & 3 & -3 & | & -3 \\ 0 & 0 & 0 & | & 0 \end{bmatrix}$$

$-R_2 + R_3 \rightarrow R_3$

The last matrix is in echelon form, and the last line corresponds to the equation

$$0x + 0y + 0z = 0$$

which is true for all values of x, y, z. Thus, any solution of the first two equations will be a solution of the system. The first two equations are

$$2x - y + 2z = 3$$
$$3y - 3z = -3$$

This system is equivalent to

$$2x - y = 3 - 2z$$
$$y = -1 + z \quad \text{(Solve the second equation for } y\text{)}$$

Suppose we let $z = k$, where k is any real number. Then the last equation gives $y = -1 + k$. Substitution into the first equation results in

$$2x + 1 - k = 3 - 2k$$

so that

$$2x = 2 - k$$
$$x = 1 - \tfrac{1}{2}k$$

Thus, if k is any real number, then $x = 1 - \tfrac{1}{2}k$, $y = k - 1$, $z = k$ is a solution of the system. You should verify this by substitution into the original system. We see that the system in this example has infinitely many solutions, because the value of k may be quite arbitrarily chosen. For instance, if $k = 2$, then the solution is $x = 0$, $y = 1$, $z = 2$; if $k = 5$, then $x = -\tfrac{3}{2}$, $y = 4$, $z = 5$; if $k = -4$, then $x = 3$, $y = -5$, $z = -4$; and so on. ∎

If in the final echelon form there is no row with all 0's to the left and a nonzero number to the right of the vertical line, but there is a row with all 0's both to the left and to the right, then the system has infinitely many solutions.

Examples 1, 2, and 3 illustrate the three possibilities for three linear equations in three unknowns. The system may have **a unique solution** as in Example 1; the system may have **no solution** as in Example 2; the system may have **infinitely many solutions** as in Example 3. The final echelon form of the matrix always shows which case is at hand.

B. Applications

Problem Solving:

Matrices and Nutrition

A dietitian wants to arrange a diet composed of three basic foods A, B, and C. The diet must include 170 units of calcium, 90 units of iron, and 110 units of vitamin B. The table gives the number of units per ounce of each of the needed ingredients contained in each of the basic foods.

	Units per Ounce		
	Food A	Food B	Food C
Calcium	15	5	20
Iron	5	5	10
Vitamin B	10	15	10

If a, b, and c are the number of ounces of basic foods A, B, and C taken by an individual, find the number of ounces of each of the basic foods needed to meet the diet requirements.

1. Read the problem.
2. Select the unknown.

We want to find the values of a, b, and c, the number of ounces of basic foods A, B, and C taken by an individual.

3. Think of a plan.
What is the amount of calcium needed?

Since the individual gets 15 units of calcium from A, 5 from B, and 20 from C, the amount of calcium is:

$$15a + 5b + 20c = 170$$

What is the amount of iron needed?

The amount of iron is:
$$5a + 5b + 10c = 90$$

What is the amount of Vitamin B needed?

The amount of vitamin B is:
$$10a + 15b + 10c = 110$$

Write the equations obtained using matrices.

The simplified system of three equations and three unknowns, obtained by dividing each term in each of the equations by 5, is written as:

How can you simplify each of the three original equations?

$$\begin{bmatrix} 3 & 1 & 4 & | & 34 \\ 1 & 1 & 2 & | & 18 \\ 2 & 3 & 2 & | & 22 \end{bmatrix}$$

4. Use matrices to solve the system.

$$\begin{bmatrix} 3 & 1 & 4 & | & 34 \\ 1 & 1 & 2 & | & 18 \\ 2 & 3 & 2 & | & 22 \end{bmatrix} \sim \begin{bmatrix} 1 & 1 & 2 & | & 18 \\ 3 & 1 & 4 & | & 34 \\ 2 & 3 & 2 & | & 22 \end{bmatrix}$$
$$R_1 \leftrightarrow R_2$$

$$\sim \begin{bmatrix} 1 & 1 & 2 & | & 18 \\ 0 & -2 & -2 & | & -20 \\ 0 & 1 & -2 & | & -14 \end{bmatrix} \sim \begin{bmatrix} 1 & 1 & 2 & | & 18 \\ 0 & 1 & 1 & | & 10 \\ 0 & 1 & -2 & | & -14 \end{bmatrix}$$

$$R_2 - 3R_1 \rightarrow R_2 \qquad\qquad \frac{R_2}{-2} \rightarrow R_2$$

$$R_3 - 2R_1 \rightarrow R_3$$

$$\sim \begin{bmatrix} 1 & 1 & 2 & | & 18 \\ 0 & 1 & 1 & | & 10 \\ 0 & 0 & -3 & | & -24 \end{bmatrix}$$

$$R_3 - R_2 \rightarrow R_3$$

From the third row, $-3c = -24$ or $c = 8$. Substituting in the second row, we have $b + 8 = 10$ or $b = 2$. Finally, substituting in the first row, we have $a + 2 + 2(8) = 18$ or $a = 0$.

5. Verify the solution.

Substitute $a = 0$, $b = 2$, and $c = 8$ into the first equation, obtaining $15 \cdot 0 + 5 \cdot 2 + 20 \cdot 8 = 10 + 160 = 170$. You should use the same procedure to check the second and third equations.

TRY EXAMPLE 4 NOW.

Cover the solution, write your own, and then check your work.

EXAMPLE 4

Tom Jones, who was building a workshop, went to the hardware store and bought 1 lb each of three kinds of nails: small, medium, and large. After doing part of the work, Tom found that he had underestimated the number of small and large nails he needed. So he bought another pound of the small nails and 2 lb more of the large nails. After doing some more of the construction, he again ran short of nails and had to buy another pound of each of the small and the medium nails. Upon looking over his bills, he found that the hardware store had charged him \$2.10 for nails the first time, \$2.30 the second time, and \$1.20 the third time. The prices for the various sizes of nails were not listed. Find these prices.

Solution

We let $x\,\phi$/lb, $y\,\phi$/lb, and $z\,\phi$/lb be the prices for the small, medium, and large nails, respectively. Then, we know that

$$
\begin{aligned}
x + y + z &= 210 \\
x \quad\;\; + 2z &= 230 \\
x + y \quad\;\; &= 120
\end{aligned}
$$

We solve this system as follows:

$$\begin{bmatrix} 1 & 1 & 1 & | & 210 \\ 1 & 0 & 2 & | & 230 \\ 1 & 1 & 0 & | & 120 \end{bmatrix} \sim \begin{bmatrix} 1 & 1 & 1 & | & 210 \\ 0 & 1 & -1 & | & -20 \\ 0 & 0 & 1 & | & 90 \end{bmatrix}$$

$$R_1 - R_2 \rightarrow R_2$$
$$R_1 - R_3 \rightarrow R_3$$

Size	Price per Pound
Small	50¢
Medium	70¢
Large	90¢

The second matrix is in echelon form, and the solution of the system is easily found by back-substitution to be $x = 50$, $y = 70$, $z = 90$, giving the schedule of prices shown in the margin. ∎

Exercise 8.2

A. In problems 1–10, find all the solutions (if there are any).

1. $x + y - z = 3$
   $x - 2y + z = -3$
   $2x + y + z = 4$

2. $x + 2y - z = 5$
   $2x + y + z = 1$
   $x - y + z = -1$

3. $2x - y + 2z = 5$
   $2x + y - z = -6$
   $3x + 2z = 3$

4. $x + 2y - z = 0$
   $2x + 3y = 3$
   $2y + z = -1$

5. $3x + 2y + z = -5$
   $2x - y - z = -6$
   $2x + y + 3z = 4$

6. $4x + 3y - z = 12$
   $2x - 3y - z = -10$
   $x + y - 2z = -5$

7. $x + y + z = 3$
   $x - 2y + z = -3$
   $3x + 3z = 5$

8. $x + y + z = 3$
   $x - 2y + 3z = 5$
   $5x - 4y + 11z = 20$

9. $x + y + z = 3$
   $x - 2y + z = -3$
   $x + z = 1$

10. $x - y - 2z = -1$
    $x + 2y + z = 5$
    $5x + 4y - z = 13$

11. Show that elementary operation 3 yields an equivalent system. [*Hint:* Consider the first two equations of system (1) in the text. Show that if (m, n, p) satisfies both these equations, then it satisfies the system consisting of the first equation and the sum of the first two equations, and conversely.]

B. 12. The sum of $8.50 is made up of nickels, dimes, and quarters. The number of dimes is equal to the number of quarters plus twice the number of nickels. The value of the dimes exceeds the combined value of the nickels and the quarters by $1.50. How many of each coin are there?

13. The Mechano Distributing Company has three types of vending machines, which dispense snacks as listed in the table below. Mechano fills all the machines once a day and finds them all sold out before the next day. The total daily sales are: candy, 760; peanuts, 380; sandwiches, 660. How many of each type of machine does Mechano have?

		Vending Machine Type	
Snack	I	II	III
Candy	20	24	30
Peanuts	10	18	10
Sandwiches	0	30	30

14. Suppose the total daily income from the various types of machines in problem 13 is as follows: type I, $32.00; type II, $159.00; type III, $192.00. What is the selling price for each type of snack? (Use the answers for problem 13.)

Table 8.2

	Type of Fertilizer		
Chemical	I	II	III
A	6%	8%	12%
B	6%	12%	8%
C	8%	4%	12%

15. Gro-Kwik Garden Supply has three types of fertilizer, which contain chemicals A, B, C in the percentages shown in Table 8.2. In what proportions must Gro-Kwik mix these three types to get an 8-8-8 fertilizer (one that has 8% of each of the three chemicals)?

16. Three water supply valves, A, B, C, are connected to a tank. If all three valves are opened, the tank is filled in 8 hr. The tank can also be filled by opening A for 8 hr and B for 12 hr, while keeping C closed, or by opening B for 10 hr and C for 28 hr, while keeping A closed. Find the time needed by each valve to fill the tank by itself. [*Hint:* Let x, y, z, respectively, be the fractions of the tank that valves A, B, C can fill alone in 1 hr.]

17. A 2 by 2 matrix $\begin{bmatrix} a & b \\ c & d \end{bmatrix}$ is said to be **nonsingular** if $ad - bc \neq 0$. Determine whether the following matrices are nonsingular.

(a) $\begin{bmatrix} 1 & 2 \\ 2 & 4 \end{bmatrix}$
(b) $\begin{bmatrix} 2 & -3 \\ 3 & 5 \end{bmatrix}$
(c) $\begin{bmatrix} 0 & 2 \\ 2 & 4 \end{bmatrix}$

18. The definition in problem 17 is important because every nonsingular matrix has a unique multiplicative inverse. To find the inverse of the matrix $\begin{bmatrix} a & b \\ c & d \end{bmatrix}$, you have to find a matrix $\begin{bmatrix} x & y \\ z & w \end{bmatrix}$ such that $\begin{bmatrix} a & b \\ c & d \end{bmatrix}\begin{bmatrix} x & y \\ z & w \end{bmatrix} = \begin{bmatrix} 1 & 0 \\ 0 & 1 \end{bmatrix}$. This means that you must solve the systems

$$ax + bz = 1$$

$$cx + dz = 0$$

and

$$ay + bw = 0$$

$$cy + dw = 1$$

To solve the first system, we can write

$$\begin{bmatrix} a & b & | & 1 \\ c & d & | & 0 \end{bmatrix} \sim \begin{bmatrix} ac & bc & | & c \\ ac & ad & | & 0 \end{bmatrix} \sim \begin{bmatrix} ac & bc & | & c \\ 0 & ad-bc & | & -c \end{bmatrix}$$

Now, we see that the second equation has a unique solution if and only if $ad - bc \neq 0$.

Use these ideas to find the inverse of

(a) $\begin{bmatrix} 3 & 2 \\ 2 & 1 \end{bmatrix}$ (b) $\begin{bmatrix} 1 & -2 \\ 2 & 1 \end{bmatrix}$

Using Your Knowledge

Instead of stopping with the echelon form of the matrix and then using back-substitution to solve a system of equations, many people prefer to transform the matrix of coefficients into the identity matrix and then read off the solution by inspection. If the final augmented matrix reads

$$\begin{bmatrix} 1 & 0 & 0 & | & a \\ 0 & 1 & 0 & | & b \\ 0 & 0 & 1 & | & c \end{bmatrix}$$

then the solution of the system is $x = a$, $y = b$, $z = c$. You need only read the column to the right of the vertical line.

Suppose, for example, that we have reduced the augmented matrix to the form

$$\begin{bmatrix} 2 & -1 & 2 & | & 3 \\ 0 & 3 & -3 & | & -3 \\ 0 & 0 & 2 & | & 5 \end{bmatrix} \tag{1}$$

We can now divide R_2 by 3 and R_3 by 2 to obtain

$$\begin{bmatrix} 2 & -1 & 2 & | & 3 \\ 0 & 1 & -1 & | & -1 \\ 0 & 0 & 1 & | & \frac{5}{2} \end{bmatrix} \tag{2}$$

To get 0's in the off-diagonal places of the matrix to the left of the vertical line, we first add R_2 to R_1 to get the new R_1:

$$\begin{bmatrix} 2 & 0 & 1 & | & 2 \\ 0 & 1 & -1 & | & -1 \\ 0 & 0 & 1 & | & \frac{5}{2} \end{bmatrix} \tag{3}$$

Next, we subtract R_3 from R_1 and add R_3 to R_2, with the result

$$\begin{bmatrix} 2 & 0 & 0 & | & -\frac{1}{2} \\ 0 & 1 & 0 & | & \frac{3}{2} \\ 0 & 0 & 1 & | & \frac{5}{2} \end{bmatrix} \tag{4}$$

Finally, we divide R_1 by 2 to obtain

$$\begin{bmatrix} 1 & 0 & 0 & | & -\frac{1}{4} \\ 0 & 1 & 0 & | & \frac{3}{2} \\ 0 & 0 & 1 & | & \frac{5}{2} \end{bmatrix} \tag{5}$$

from which we can see by inspection that the solution of the system is $x = -\frac{1}{4}$, $y = \frac{3}{2}$, $z = \frac{5}{2}$.

Keep in mind that after you bring the augmented matrix into echelon form, you perform additional elementary operations to get 0's in all the off-diagonal places of the coefficient matrix and 1's on the diagonal. Of course, we assume that the system has a unique solution. If this is not the case, you will see what the situation is when you obtain the echelon form and you will also see that it is impossible to transform the coefficient matrix into the identity matrix if the system does not have a unique solution. Use these ideas to solve problems 1–10 in Exercise 8.2.

Computer Corner

It is rather tedious to use the methods described in this section to solve a system of equations. The Matrix Reduction Program in the appendix will give you practice solving equations using a computer. The program employs the three elementary row operations we have mentioned in the text, but you must learn how to translate the notation in the text to that used in the program. For example, when working Example 1, the second step is $R_1 + 2 \times R_3 \rightarrow R_3$. In the program, you must multiply $2 \times R_3$ first, and then add $R_1 + R_3$. It will save a lot of time and writing to do the problems using this program.

8.3   THE INVERSE OF A MATRIX

GETTING STARTED

INTRIGUE AND INVERSES

Have you read Edgar Allan Poe's short story "The Gold Bug," or Arthur Conan Doyle's Sherlock Holmes story "The Adventure of the Dancing Men"? If so, you will recall the major role played by the mysterious coded messages. In both stories, the codes were broken by statistical methods, methods that frequently work with *simple substitution codes*. A simple substitution code is one that replaces each letter of the alphabet by a single symbol and uses this same symbol for the same letter each time.

For simplicity, let us number the letters of the alphabet from 1 to 26 in the usual order, and let us indicate a space between words by the number 27.

1. a	**5.** e	**9.** i	**13.** m	**17.** q	**21.** u	**25.** y
2. b	**6.** f	**10.** j	**14.** n	**18.** r	**22.** v	**26.** z
3. c	**7.** g	**11.** k	**15.** o	**19.** s	**23.** w	**27.** space
4. d	**8.** h	**12.** l	**16.** p	**20.** t	**24.** x	

Suppose we want to encode the message:

Meet me tonight.

We first write the message, replacing letters and spaces by the assigned numbers and disregarding the punctuation, to get

13.5.5.20.27.13.5.27.20.15.14.9.7.8.20.27.

Next we choose a 2 × 2 matrix that has an inverse. How do we know if a matrix has an inverse? You will learn that in a moment. For now, we write

$$M = \begin{bmatrix} 2 & 3 \\ 1 & 2 \end{bmatrix}$$

The **inverse** M^{-1} of M is

$$M^{-1} = \begin{bmatrix} 2 & -3 \\ -1 & 2 \end{bmatrix}$$

You can verify this because

$$MM^{-1} = M^{-1}M = I$$

Since we have chosen a 2 × 2 matrix, we break the message up into successive pairs of numbers, which we write as column matrices:

$$\begin{bmatrix} 13 \\ 5 \end{bmatrix} \begin{bmatrix} 5 \\ 20 \end{bmatrix} \begin{bmatrix} 27 \\ 13 \end{bmatrix} \begin{bmatrix} 5 \\ 27 \end{bmatrix} \begin{bmatrix} 20 \\ 15 \end{bmatrix} \begin{bmatrix} 14 \\ 9 \end{bmatrix} \begin{bmatrix} 7 \\ 8 \end{bmatrix} \begin{bmatrix} 20 \\ 27 \end{bmatrix}$$

We then multiply each column matrix by M to get

$$\begin{bmatrix} 41 \\ 23 \end{bmatrix} \begin{bmatrix} 70 \\ 45 \end{bmatrix} \begin{bmatrix} 93 \\ 53 \end{bmatrix} \begin{bmatrix} 91 \\ 59 \end{bmatrix} \begin{bmatrix} 85 \\ 50 \end{bmatrix} \begin{bmatrix} 55 \\ 32 \end{bmatrix} \begin{bmatrix} 38 \\ 23 \end{bmatrix} \begin{bmatrix} 121 \\ 74 \end{bmatrix}$$

The coded message is simply the list of numbers in these matrices:

41.23.70.45.93.53.91.59.85.50.55.32.38.23.121.74

The intended receiver of this message has the magic key, M and M^{-1}. Because M is 2 × 2, the receiver knows that he or she has to separate the message into 2 × 1 column matrices and multiply each matrix by M^{-1}. This converts the message into its original numbered form, which the receiver can easily read. But to decode the message, you have to know how to find M^{-1}. You will learn how to find the inverse of a matrix in this section.

In Section 8.1, we defined the multiplicative identity matrix I, which behaves in matrix multiplication like the integer 1 does in ordinary arithmetic multiplication. In arithmetic, we defined the multiplicative inverse of a number $a \neq 0$ to be a second number a^{-1} such that

Note that $a^{-1} = 1/a$ for $a \neq 0$.

$$a \cdot a^{-1} = a^{-1} \cdot a = 1$$

This suggests a corresponding definition for matrices.

Definition 8.8

Let A be a square matrix. If there exists a second matrix A^{-1} such that

$$AA^{-1} = A^{-1}A = I$$

then A^{-1} is called the **inverse** of A.

Notice that the superscript $^{-1}$ is not an exponent. The symbol A^{-1} simply stands for the inverse of A. It is clear that if A^{-1} exists, then A and A^{-1} are inverses of each other.

The practical importance of the inverse matrix lies in the fact that a system of n linear equations in n unknowns, symbolized as in Section 8.2 by

$$AX = D$$

can easily be solved if the matrix A^{-1} is known. Thus, by premultiplying both sides by A^{-1}, we get

$$A^{-1}AX = A^{-1}D$$

Because $A^{-1}A = I$ and $IX = X$, we can see that

$$X = A^{-1}D$$

Thus, to get the solution, we only need to premultiply the column matrix of the right-hand terms by the inverse (if it exists) of the coefficient matrix.

Let us now consider the problem of finding A^{-1} for a specific 2×2 matrix, say,

$$A = \begin{bmatrix} 2 & 3 \\ 1 & 2 \end{bmatrix}$$

Suppose that

$$A^{-1} = \begin{bmatrix} x & z \\ y & w \end{bmatrix}$$

Then by the definition of A^{-1}, it follows that $AA^{-1} = I$, or

$$\begin{bmatrix} 2 & 3 \\ 1 & 2 \end{bmatrix} \begin{bmatrix} x & z \\ y & w \end{bmatrix} = \begin{bmatrix} 1 & 0 \\ 0 & 1 \end{bmatrix}$$

By multiplying out the matrices on the left and equating corresponding elements on both sides of the equation, we get the following two systems:

$$\left.\begin{array}{l} 2x + 3y = 1 \\ x + 2y = 0 \end{array}\right\} \tag{1}$$

$$\left.\begin{array}{l} 2z + 3w = 0 \\ z + 2w = 1 \end{array}\right\} \tag{2}$$

We see at once that the left sides of the two systems are the same except for the unknowns (x, y) in system (1) being replaced by (z, w) in system (2). This suggests that we can use matrices to solve the two systems in one set of operations. We write the augmented matrices together as follows:

$$\left[\begin{array}{cc|cc} 2 & 3 & 1 & 0 \\ 1 & 2 & 0 & 1 \end{array}\right]$$

where the first column after the vertical bar is the column of right-hand members of system (1) and the second column is that for system (2). Together, these two columns constitute the identity matrix.

We first reduce the matrix on the left to echelon form:

$$\left[\begin{array}{cc|cc} 2 & 3 & 1 & 0 \\ 1 & 2 & 0 & 1 \end{array}\right] \sim \left[\begin{array}{cc|cc} 2 & 3 & 1 & 0 \\ 0 & -1 & 1 & -2 \end{array}\right]$$
$$R_1 - 2 \times R_2 \to R_2$$

We then try to reduce the matrix on the left to the identity matrix, because this will give the values of x, y, z, w by inspection. Thus,

$$\left[\begin{array}{cc|cc} 2 & 3 & 1 & 0 \\ 0 & -1 & 1 & -2 \end{array}\right] \sim \left[\begin{array}{cc|cc} 2 & 0 & 4 & -6 \\ 0 & -1 & 1 & -2 \end{array}\right]$$
$$3 \times R_2 + R_1 \to R_1$$

$$\sim \left[\begin{array}{cc|cc} 1 & 0 & 2 & -3 \\ 0 & 1 & -1 & 2 \end{array}\right]$$
$$\tfrac{1}{2} \times R_1 \to R_1$$
$$-R_2 \to R_2$$

This last matrix tells us that $x = 2$, $y = -1$, $z = -3$, and $w = 2$. Since

$$A^{-1} = \left[\begin{array}{cc} x & z \\ y & w \end{array}\right]$$

we have

$$A^{-1} = \left[\begin{array}{cc} 2 & -3 \\ -1 & 2 \end{array}\right]$$

We can check this by multiplying A by A^{-1}:

$$A^{-1}A = \begin{bmatrix} 2 & -3 \\ -1 & 2 \end{bmatrix}\begin{bmatrix} 2 & 3 \\ 1 & 2 \end{bmatrix}$$

$$= \begin{bmatrix} 2 \times 2 - 3 \times 1 & 2 \times 3 - 3 \times 2 \\ -1 \times 2 + 2 \times 1 & -1 \times 3 + 2 \times 2 \end{bmatrix}$$

$$= \begin{bmatrix} 1 & 0 \\ 0 & 1 \end{bmatrix} = I$$

You should verify that AA^{-1} also is I.

The preceding method is applicable not only to 2×2 matrices, but in general to $n \times n$ matrices. Of course, there is more work for the higher-order matrices. In practical applications, where the matrices are quite large, the procedure is carried out on a computer. The method itself is quite simply described:

Finding the Inverse of a Matrix

1. Write an augmented matrix consisting of the given square matrix on the left of the vertical bar and the identity matrix on the right of the bar.

2. By means of elementary row operations, reduce (if possible) the given matrix to the identity matrix. When this is accomplished, the matrix that appears on the right of the bar is the desired inverse.

This procedure is always possible if the given matrix has an inverse. It is, of course, not possible otherwise. For instance, if

$$A = \begin{bmatrix} 1 & 1 \\ 2 & 2 \end{bmatrix}$$

we would find

$$\begin{bmatrix} 1 & 1 & | & 1 & 0 \\ 2 & 2 & | & 0 & 1 \end{bmatrix} \sim \begin{bmatrix} 1 & 1 & | & 1 & 0 \\ 0 & 0 & | & -2 & 1 \end{bmatrix}$$
$$-2 \times R_1 + R_2 \rightarrow R_2$$

Obviously, it is not possible to reduce the left-hand matrix to the identity matrix! This means that the given matrix has no inverse.

EXAMPLE 1   Find the inverse (if it exists) for the matrix

$$A = \begin{bmatrix} 1 & -2 \\ 2 & 3 \end{bmatrix}$$

Solution   We write

$$\begin{bmatrix} 1 & -2 & | & 1 & 0 \\ 2 & 3 & | & 0 & 1 \end{bmatrix} \sim \begin{bmatrix} 1 & -2 & | & 1 & 0 \\ 0 & 7 & | & -2 & 1 \end{bmatrix}$$

$$-2 \times R_1 + R_2 \rightarrow R_2$$

$$\sim \begin{bmatrix} 1 & -2 & | & 1 & 0 \\ 0 & 1 & | & -\frac{2}{7} & \frac{1}{7} \end{bmatrix}$$

$$\tfrac{1}{7} \times R_2 \rightarrow R_2$$

$$\sim \begin{bmatrix} 1 & 0 & | & \frac{3}{7} & \frac{2}{7} \\ 0 & 1 & | & -\frac{2}{7} & \frac{1}{7} \end{bmatrix}$$

$$2 \times R_2 + R_1 \rightarrow R_1$$

Hence,

$$A^{-1} = \begin{bmatrix} \frac{3}{7} & \frac{2}{7} \\ -\frac{2}{7} & \frac{1}{7} \end{bmatrix}$$

∎

EXAMPLE 2   Use the result of Example 1 to solve the system

$$x - 2y = -6$$
$$2x + 3y = 37$$

Solution   We can symbolize this system by

$$AX = D$$

where

$$A = \begin{bmatrix} 1 & -2 \\ 2 & 3 \end{bmatrix} \qquad X = \begin{bmatrix} x \\ y \end{bmatrix} \qquad D = \begin{bmatrix} -6 \\ 37 \end{bmatrix}$$

As you will recall, the solution is given by

$$X = A^{-1}D = \begin{bmatrix} \frac{3}{7} & \frac{2}{7} \\ -\frac{2}{7} & \frac{1}{7} \end{bmatrix} \begin{bmatrix} -6 \\ 37 \end{bmatrix}$$

$$= \frac{1}{7} \begin{bmatrix} 3 & 2 \\ -2 & 1 \end{bmatrix} \begin{bmatrix} -6 \\ 37 \end{bmatrix}$$

$$= \frac{1}{7} \begin{bmatrix} 56 \\ 49 \end{bmatrix} = \begin{bmatrix} 8 \\ 7 \end{bmatrix}$$

Thus, $x = 8$ and $y = 7$. (You do not have to take our word for this. You can check this solution in the given equations!)

∎

EXAMPLE 3   Find the inverse (if it exists) for the matrix

$$A = \begin{bmatrix} 1 & 0 & 1 \\ 1 & 1 & 3 \\ 0 & 1 & 3 \end{bmatrix}$$

Solution   We write

$$\left[\begin{array}{ccc|ccc} 1 & 0 & 1 & 1 & 0 & 0 \\ 1 & 1 & 3 & 0 & 1 & 0 \\ 0 & 1 & 3 & 0 & 0 & 1 \end{array}\right] \sim \left[\begin{array}{ccc|ccc} 1 & 0 & 1 & 1 & 0 & 0 \\ 0 & 1 & 2 & -1 & 1 & 0 \\ 0 & 1 & 3 & 0 & 0 & 1 \end{array}\right]$$

$$-R_1 + R_2 \rightarrow R_2$$

$$\sim \left[\begin{array}{ccc|ccc} 1 & 0 & 1 & 1 & 0 & 0 \\ 0 & 1 & 2 & -1 & 1 & 0 \\ 0 & 0 & 1 & 1 & -1 & 1 \end{array}\right]$$

$$-R_2 + R_3 \rightarrow R_3$$

$$\sim \left[\begin{array}{ccc|ccc} 1 & 0 & 0 & 0 & 1 & -1 \\ 0 & 1 & 0 & -3 & 3 & -2 \\ 0 & 0 & 1 & 1 & -1 & 1 \end{array}\right]$$

$$-R_3 + R_1 \rightarrow R_1$$
$$-2 \times R_3 + R_2 \rightarrow R_2$$

Since the matrix on the left has been reduced to the identity matrix, the matrix on the right is the desired inverse. Thus,

$$A^{-1} = \begin{bmatrix} 0 & 1 & -1 \\ -3 & 3 & -2 \\ 1 & -1 & 1 \end{bmatrix}$$

You can check this result by showing that $AA^{-1} = I$.   ∎

EXAMPLE 4   Use the result of Example 3 to solve the system

$$x + z = 5$$
$$x + y + 3z = 7$$
$$ y + 3z = 4$$

Solution   If we symbolize the system by $AX = D$, where A is the matrix given in Example 3, then the solution is given by

$$X = A^{-1}D = \begin{bmatrix} 0 & 1 & -1 \\ -3 & 3 & -2 \\ 1 & -1 & 1 \end{bmatrix}\begin{bmatrix} 5 \\ 7 \\ 4 \end{bmatrix} = \begin{bmatrix} 3 \\ -2 \\ 2 \end{bmatrix}$$

Thus, the solution is $x = 3$, $y = -2$, $z = 2$. You can check this solution in the given system of equations. ∎

Exercise 8.3

In problems 1–8, find the inverse (if it exists) of the given matrix.

1. $\begin{bmatrix} 2 & 4 \\ 3 & 5 \end{bmatrix}$ 2. $\begin{bmatrix} -1 & 0 \\ 3 & 1 \end{bmatrix}$ 3. $\begin{bmatrix} 5 & -1 \\ 8 & 2 \end{bmatrix}$ 4. $\begin{bmatrix} 3 & -5 \\ 2 & -3 \end{bmatrix}$

5. $\begin{bmatrix} 2 & 3 \\ 4 & 6 \end{bmatrix}$ 6. $\begin{bmatrix} 3 & 4 \\ -1 & 2 \end{bmatrix}$ 7. $\begin{bmatrix} -1 & 0 \\ 0 & -1 \end{bmatrix}$ 8. $\begin{bmatrix} 2 & 2 \\ 4 & 4 \end{bmatrix}$

9. Use your answer to problem 1 to solve the system

   $2x + 4y = 14$

   $3x + 5y = 16$

10. Use your answer to problem 3 to solve the system

    $5x - y = 2$

    $8x + 2y = 3$

11. Use your answer to problem 4 to solve the system

    $3x - 5y = -1$

    $2x - 3y = 0$

12. Use your answer to Problem 6 to solve the system

    $3x + 4y = -3$

    $-x + 2y = 11$

In problems 13–16, decide whether the two given matrices are inverses of each other.

13. $\begin{bmatrix} 1 & 2 & 3 \\ 0 & 1 & 2 \\ 0 & 1 & 3 \end{bmatrix}$ and $\begin{bmatrix} 1 & -3 & 1 \\ 0 & 3 & -2 \\ 0 & -1 & 1 \end{bmatrix}$

14. $\begin{bmatrix} 1 & 3 & 0 \\ 0 & 1 & 1 \\ 1 & 4 & 2 \end{bmatrix}$ and $\begin{bmatrix} -2 & -6 & 3 \\ 1 & 2 & -1 \\ -1 & -1 & 1 \end{bmatrix}$

15. $\begin{bmatrix} 1 & 1 & 1 \\ -1 & -1 & -2 \\ 2 & 3 & 3 \end{bmatrix}$ and $\begin{bmatrix} 3 & 0 & -1 \\ -1 & 1 & 1 \\ -1 & -1 & 0 \end{bmatrix}$

16. $\begin{bmatrix} 1 & 0 & 1 \\ 1 & 1 & 0 \\ 0 & 1 & 1 \end{bmatrix}$ and $\begin{bmatrix} 1 & 1 & 0 \\ 0 & 1 & 1 \\ 1 & 0 & 1 \end{bmatrix}$

17. Find the inverse of the matrix

$$\begin{bmatrix} 1 & 2 & -4 \\ 0 & 1 & -1 \\ 1 & -1 & 0 \end{bmatrix}$$

18. Find the inverse of the matrix

$$\begin{bmatrix} 1 & 0 & -2 \\ 1 & 1 & 0 \\ 0 & 1 & 3 \end{bmatrix}$$

19. Find the inverse of the matrix

$$\begin{bmatrix} 1 & 3 & -1 \\ 0 & 2 & 1 \\ -1 & 1 & 2 \end{bmatrix}$$

20. Find the inverse of the matrix

$$\begin{bmatrix} 2 & -1 & 0 \\ 1 & 2 & -1 \\ -1 & -1 & 2 \end{bmatrix}$$

21. Show that the following matrix has no inverse:

$$\begin{bmatrix} 1 & 2 & 1 \\ -1 & 0 & 1 \\ 1 & 4 & 3 \end{bmatrix}$$

22. Show that the following matrix has no inverse:

$$\begin{bmatrix} 1 & 2 & 1 \\ 1 & 1 & 1 \\ 1 & 0 & 1 \end{bmatrix}$$

23. Use your answer to problem 17 to solve the system

$$\begin{aligned} x + 2y - 4z &= 16 \\ y - z &= 4 \\ x - y &= 1 \end{aligned}$$

24. Use your answer to problem 18 to solve the system

$$\begin{aligned} x \quad\quad - 2z &= 0 \\ x + y \quad\quad &= 5 \\ y + 3z &= 7 \end{aligned}$$

25. Use your answer to problem 19 to solve the system

$$\begin{aligned} x + 3y - z &= 3 \\ 2y + z &= 11 \\ -x + y + 2z &= 14 \end{aligned}$$

26. Use your answer to problem 20 to solve the system

$$\begin{aligned} 2x - y \quad\quad &= 4 \\ x + 2y - z &= 3 \\ -x - y + 2z &= 3 \end{aligned}$$

27. You are given the magic key

$$C = \begin{bmatrix} 1 & -3 & 1 \\ 0 & 3 & -2 \\ 0 & -1 & 1 \end{bmatrix} \quad \text{and} \quad C^{-1} = \begin{bmatrix} 1 & 2 & 3 \\ 0 & 1 & 2 \\ 0 & 1 & 3 \end{bmatrix}$$

(a) Use the procedure shown in Getting Started to decode the following message:

2.−9.12.−31.18.0.19.−11.10.24.−18.13.24.−25.13.

(b) Use the matrix C to encode the message *MATH CAN BE FUN*.

In Other Words

28. Use the variables x, y and z, w to write the equations that you would get from the second row of

$$\left[\begin{array}{cc|cc} 1 & 1 & 1 & 0 \\ 0 & 0 & -1 & 1 \end{array}\right]$$

Now, can you explain why

$$\begin{bmatrix} 1 & 1 \\ 2 & 2 \end{bmatrix}$$

has no inverse?

29. Explain in your own words why a nonsquare matrix cannot have an inverse.

30. When we look for the inverse of a certain matrix A, the last step looks like this

$$\left[\begin{array}{cc|cc} 1 & 1 & 1 & 0 \\ a & b & a & b \end{array}\right]$$

Explain when and why A has no inverse.

If you are like most people, at this point you are probably not greatly impressed with the idea of solving a system of linear equations by using the inverse of the coefficient matrix. Why go to the trouble of finding the inverse matrix, when you can solve the system directly with less work?

Let us recall problem 15 of Exercise 8.2: Gro-Kwik Garden Supply has three types of fertilizer, which contain chemicals A, B, and C in the percentages shown in Table 8.2. In what proportions must Gro-Kwik mix these three types to get an 8-8-8 fertilizer (one that has 8% of each of the three chemicals)?

For convenience, let us assume that the mixture is to be put up in 100-lb sacks. If x, y, z are the number of pounds of type I, II, and III, respectively, required per sack, then

$$0.06x + 0.08y + 0.12z = 8$$

$$0.06x + 0.12y + 0.08z = 8$$

$$0.08x + 0.04y + 0.12z = 8$$

No matter what the required mix is, the left sides of these equations will be the same; only the right-hand numbers will change. So if we have the inverse

Table 8.2

Chemical	Type of Fertilizer		
	I	II	III
A	6%	8%	12%
B	6%	12%	8%
C	8%	4%	12%

of the coefficient matrix, then we can find the values of x, y, z for any possible mix without having to go through the process of solving the equations each time.

   This problem is a very much simplified illustration of an important practical application of the inverse of a matrix. In actual practice, the number of components of the mix may be quite large, so hand calculation would be out of the question. The inverse of the coefficient matrix may be stored on a computer. When the requirements of the desired mix are known, the information can be put into a computer, which will multiply the matrix of right-hand numbers by the inverse of the coefficient matrix, and quickly turn out the desired answers.

31. If A denotes the coefficient matrix of the above system of equations, verify that

$$A^{-1} = \frac{25}{8}\begin{bmatrix} -14 & 6 & 10 \\ 1 & 3 & -3 \\ 9 & -5 & -3 \end{bmatrix}$$

32. Suppose that an 8-10-6 mix of the fertilizer is required. Can you see how to use the matrix A^{-1} in problem 31 to find how many pounds of each type to put in per 100 lb of mix? Be sure to check your answers.

Computer Corner

The Inverse Finder Program in the appendix finds the inverse of a 2 × 2 or 3 × 3 matrix, provided you enter the original matrix. Thus, to work Example 1, just enter the numbers in the original matrix. If the matrix has no inverse, the program tells us, "No inverse." Use the program to verify the examples in this section.

8.4   MATHEMATICAL SYSTEMS AND CLOCK ARITHMETIC

GETTING STARTED

ALL IN DUE TIME

"Oh, Mr. Chronos, I wish I had a job like yours—making clocks for eight hours every day. My boss makes us come early to work—6, 7, or 8 o'clock in the morning—and doesn't let us go unitl 5 or 6 at night. And then, he doesn't even pay the overtime!"

   "I have the perfect clock for you," said Chronos knowingly as he reached for a nearby clock that showed the numbers from I to VIII around its face. "Each hour on this clock lasts as long as a normal hour. The difference is that it takes only eight hours for the little hand to make a complete revolution around the clock's face, instead of the twelve hours it takes on a normal clock."

Chronos explained further, "You see, you can set both hands at 8 when you get in to work, and when they reach 8 again you can leave!"

"But what about keeping track of overtime hours?"

"It is then simply the number of hours showing on the clock."

"Why is that, Mr. Chronos?"

"Because by this clock, VIII + II = II, just as VIII + III = III. Do you see?" (If you don't see why, think of 12 + 2 or 12 + 3 on a normal clock.)

"Well," concluded the customer, "that clock's good for on-the-job, but hardly a practical one to use at home."

"On the contrary," Chronos replied. "If I set both hands at VIII when midnight arrives on Sunday, then I will know, for instance, that if the clock says IV on Wednesday afternoon, then it really is . . . ."

Can you figure out what would be the rest of Mr. Chronos' reply? In this section we use a clock to create a mathematical system complete with the usual operations of addition, subtraction, multiplication, and division. We will even work with an unusual five-hour clock in the Discovery section.

In earlier chapters of this book, we made frequent reference to *mathematical systems*. For example, in Chapter 4 we defined the set of natural numbers together with the operations of addition and multiplication. We then discussed certain properties of the set of natural numbers with respect to these operations. The set of natural numbers, together with the operations of addition and multiplication, constitutes a mathematical system.

In general, a *mathematical system* consists of the following items:

1. A *set of elements*
2. One or more *operations*
3. One or more *relations* that enable us to compare the elements in the set
4. Some *rules, axioms, or laws* that the elements in the set satisfy

For example, when we refer to the system of integers, we have

1. *Elements.* The elements of this system are the integers in the set
   $I = \{. . . , -2, -1, 0, 1, 2, . . .\}$.

2. *Operations.* Within the system of integers, we can always perform the operations of addition, subtraction, and multiplication. We can sometimes divide, but most often the result of dividing one integer by another is not an integer. The set of integers is not closed under division.

3. *Relations.* We have three possible relations between any two integers a and b:

   $a < b \qquad a > b \qquad a = b$

4. *Rules or laws.* Addition and multiplication in the system of integers satisfy the Commutative and the Associative laws, as well as the Distributive Law.

Most of the mathematical systems we have discussed involve an *infinite* number of elements. In this section, we shall study a mathematical system that contains only a *finite* number of elements. If you become thoroughly familiar with the workings of a finite system, you will be able to generalize this knowledge and apply it to other systems.

As you are aware, the numbers on the face of a clock are used to tell the time of the day or night. The set of numbers used for this purpose is

$$S = \{1, 2, 3, 4, 5, 6, 7, 8, 9, 10, 11, 12\}.$$

We shall define addition on this set by means of an addition table, but we first present some examples to justify the entries in the table.

If it is now 11A.M., and you have to go to class in 3 hours, it is obvious that you have to go to class at 2 P.M. For this reason, we define $11 \oplus 3 = 2$, where $\oplus$ (read, "circle plus") is the operation of clock addition. If your class were to meet in 5 hours, and it was now 10 A.M., you would have to go to class at 3 P.M., so $10 \oplus 5 = 3$.

EXAMPLE 1   Find the following sums in clock arithmetic:

(a) $8 \oplus 3$ (b) $8 \oplus 7$ (c) $11 \oplus 12$

Solution   (a) $8 \oplus 3$ means 3 hours after 8 o'clock, so $8 \oplus 3 = 11$ (see Figure 8.3).

(b) $8 \oplus 7$ means 7 hours after 8 o'clock. Thus, $8 \oplus 7 = 3$ (see Figure 8.4).

(c) $11 \oplus 12$ means 12 hours after 11 o'clock. Thus, $11 \oplus 12 = 11$.

FIGURE 8.3   FIGURE 8.4

We can now construct a table for the addition facts in clock arithmetic, as shown in Table 8.3. You should verify the entries in this table before proceeding further.

Of course, other operations can be defined on this set. For example, the clock difference $3 \ominus 4$ (read, "3 circle minus" 4) is a number n with the property that $3 = 4 \oplus n$. By looking at Table 8.3 we can see that the number 11

Table 8.3 *Addition in Clock Arithmetic*

$\oplus$	1	2	3	4	5	6	7	8	9	10	11	12
1	2	3	4	5	6	7	8	9	10	11	12	1
2	3	4	5	6	7	8	9	10	11	12	1	2
3	4	5	6	7	8	9	10	11	12	1	2	3
4	5	6	7	8	9	10	11	12	1	2	3	4
5	6	7	8	9	10	11	12	1	2	3	4	5
6	7	8	9	10	11	12	1	2	3	4	5	6
7	8	9	10	11	12	1	2	3	4	5	6	7
8	9	10	11	12	1	2	3	4	5	6	7	8
9	10	11	12	1	2	3	4	5	6	7	8	9
10	11	12	1	2	3	4	5	6	7	8	9	10
11	12	1	2	3	4	5	6	7	8	9	10	11
12	1	2	3	4	5	6	7	8	9	10	11	12

satisfies this equation, because $3 = 4 \oplus 11$. Accordingly, we state the following definition:

Definition 8.9

$$a \ominus b = n \quad \text{if and only if} \quad a = b \oplus n$$

With this definition, $4 \ominus 6 = 10$, because $4 = 6 \oplus 10$.

If a is a positive number, we can define $-a$ in clock arithmetic as the number obtained by going counterclockwise a hours. With this convention, it follows that

$$-a = 12 - a$$

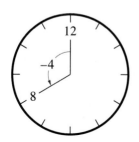

FIGURE 8.5

For example, $-4 = 12 - 4 = 8$, which agrees with Figure 8.5.

With this definition of $-a$, it also follows that

$$a \ominus b = a \oplus (-b)$$

which may be regarded as an alternate way to define circle minus.

EXAMPLE 2   Find a number n so that:

(a) $n \oplus 5 = 3$ (b) $2 \ominus 3 = n$

Solution   (a) We inspect the fifth row in Table 8.3. We have to find a
number n so that when we add n to 5 we obtain 3. The
answer is 10, because $10 \oplus 5 = 3$.

(b) $2 \ominus 3 = 2 \oplus (-3) = 2 \oplus (12 - 3) = 2 \oplus 9 = 11$.
(You can check in the table that $3 \oplus 11 = 2$.) ∎

As usual, multiplication can be defined in terms of addition. Thus,
$3 \otimes 5 = (5 \oplus 5) \oplus 5 = 10 \oplus 5 = 3$, so $3 \otimes 5 = 3$.

Definition 8.10

$$a \otimes b = \underbrace{b \oplus b \oplus b \oplus \cdots \oplus b}_{a \text{ times}}$$

(The symbol $\otimes$ is read, "circle times.")

With this definition, $4 \otimes 3 = 3 \oplus 3 \oplus 3 \oplus 3 = 12$ and $2 \otimes 8 = 8 \oplus 8 = 4$.

Notice that a quicker way to obtain the answer is to multiply the two numbers by ordinary arithmetic, divide by 12, and take the remainder as the answer. (If the remainder is 0, the answer is 12, the zero point on a clock.) For example, $6 \otimes 5 = 6$, because $6 \times 5 = 30$ and 30 divided by 12 equals 2 with a remainder of 6. Similarly, $6 \otimes 4 = 12$, because $6 \times 4 = 24$, and 24 divided by 12 is 2 with a 0 remainder.

EXAMPLE 3   Find the following products in clock arithmetic:

(a) $3 \otimes 5$ (b) $4 \otimes 8$ (c) $9 \otimes 9$

Solution   (a) $3 \otimes 5 = 3$, because $3 \times 5 = 15$, which divided by 12 is 1 with a remainder of 3.

(b) $4 \otimes 8 = 8$, because $4 \times 8 = 32$ and 32 divided by 12 is 2 with a remainder of 8.

(c) $9 \otimes 9 = 9$, because $9 \times 9 = 81$, which divided by 12 is 6 with a remainder of 9.   ■

Division is defined in clock arithmetic in terms of multiplication. For example, $\frac{4}{8} = 2$ because $4 = 8 \otimes 2$, and $\frac{3}{5} = 3$ because $3 = 5 \otimes 3$.

Definition 8.11

$$\frac{a}{b} = n \quad \text{if and only if} \quad a = b \otimes n$$

In discussing multiplication in clock arithmetic, we noted that 12 in this arithmetic corresponds to 0 in ordinary arithmetic. To show further that 12 behaves like 0 in ordinary arithmetic, let us try to find a number n such that

$$\frac{1}{12} = n$$

This equation is true only if $1 = 12 \otimes n$. But there is no n in clock arithmetic such that $12 \otimes n = 1$. So, in clock arithmetic, we cannot divide by 12, just as in ordinary arithmetic we cannot divide by 0.

EXAMPLE 4 Find the following quotients in clock arithmetic:

(a) $\frac{2}{7}$ (b) $\frac{8}{8}$ (c) $\frac{3}{4}$

Solution   (a) $\frac{2}{7} = n$ if and only if $2 = 7 \otimes n$. Thus, we wish to find an n such that $7 \otimes n = 2$, because $n = 2$ satisfies the given equation, $\frac{2}{7} = 2$. Note that the answer $n = 2$ can be found by trial and error; that is, we let $n = 1$ and see if $7 \otimes 1 = 2$. We then let $n = 2$ and check to see if $7 \otimes 2 = 2$. Because $7 \otimes 2 = 2$, the desired number has been obtained.

(b) $\frac{8}{8} = n$ if and only if $8 = 8 \otimes n$, an equation that is satisfied by $n = 1$, $n = 4$, $n = 7$, and $n = 10$. Note that unlike ordinary division problems, in which the answer is unique, in clock arithmetic a division problem may have many solutions.

(c) $\frac{3}{4} = n$ if and only if $3 = 4 \otimes n$. There is no n such that $3 = 4 \otimes n$, so the problem $\frac{3}{4} = n$ has no solution.   ∎

Exercise 8.4

In problems 1–8, find the sum in clock arithmetic.

1. $9 \oplus 7$ 2. $2 \oplus 8$ 3. $8 \oplus 3$ 4. $5 \oplus 7$
5. $7 \oplus 8$ 6. $9 \oplus 9$ 7. $8 \oplus 11$ 8. $12 \oplus 3$

In problems 9–14, find the difference in clock arithmetic.

9. $8 \ominus 3$ 10. $5 \ominus 8$ 11. $9 \ominus 12$ 12. $6 \ominus 9$
13. $8 \ominus 7$ 14. $1 \ominus 12$

In problems 15–22, find all n satisfying the given equation in clock arithmetic.

15. $n \oplus 7 = 9$ 16. $n \oplus 8 = 2$ 17. $2 \oplus n = 1$
18. $7 \oplus n = 3$ 19. $3 \ominus 5 = n$ 20. $2 \ominus 4 = n$
21. $1 \ominus n = 12$ 22. $3 \ominus 7 = n$

In problems 23–28, find the indicated products in clock arithmetic.

23. $4 \otimes 3$ 24. $3 \otimes 8$ 25. $9 \otimes 2$ 26. $3 \otimes 9$
27. $2 \otimes 8$ 28. $12 \otimes 3$

29. Make a table of multiplication facts in clock arithmetic.

In problems 30–34, find the indicated quotients in clock arithmetic.

30. $\frac{9}{7}$ 31. $\frac{3}{5}$ 32. $\frac{3}{9} = n$
                                                                          [*Hint:* There are three answers.]

33. $\frac{1}{11}$ 34. $\frac{1}{12}$

In problems 35–40, find all n satisfying the given equations in clock arithmetic.

35. $\dfrac{n}{5} = 8$

36. $\dfrac{n}{2} = 4$

37. $\dfrac{n}{2} \oplus 4 = 8$

38. $\dfrac{n}{7} = 9$

39. $\dfrac{2}{n} = 3$

40. $\dfrac{12}{12} = n$

41. Clock arithmetic can also be defined on the 8-hour clock mentioned in the Getting Started presentation where we agreed that, for example, II + VII = I.
    (a) Make an addition table for this clock arithmetic.
    (b) Is the set $S = \{$I, II, III IV, V, VI, VII, VIII$\}$ closed under this addition operation? Explain.

42. Is the addition operation for the 8-hour clock commutative? Explain.

43. Is there any element of the set S in problem 41 that does not have an inverse under addition? Explain.

In Other Words

44. Find out about "military" or "international" or "airline" time. How many hours does a military clock have? Discuss the advantages of "military" time over "regular" time.

45. In algebra, if a and b are real numbers and $a \cdot b = 0$, then $a = 0$ or $b = 0$.
    (a) In your own words, write an equivalent theorem for clock arithmetic.
    (b) How many numbers a and b can you find so that $a \otimes b = 12$?

46. In your own words, write all the similarities and differences between clock arithmetic and regular arithmetic.

Discovery

Clock arithmetic can also be defined on the 5-hour clock in Figure 8.6. We agree that on this clock $1 \oplus 4 = 0$ (not 5).

47. Can you discover the addition table for 5-hour clock arithmetic?

48. Is the set $S = \{0, 1, 2, 3, 4\}$ closed with respect to clock arithmetic?

49. Is the operation $\oplus$ commutative?

50. Is there any element of S that does not have an inverse with respect to $\oplus$?

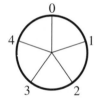

FIGURE 8.8

8.5   MODULAR ARITHMETIC

GETTING STARTED

AIRBILLS, MONEY ORDERS, AND CHECKING DIGITS

Look at the Federal Express airbill with tracking number 9048724285. Now, divide 904872428 (the number to the left of 5) by 7. The remainder is 5. Now, try it with airbill 0054604362. When you divide 5460436 by 7, the remainder is 2. Next, consider the postal money order number 42888671414. Divide the number to the left of the last 4 by 9 this time. The remainder is 4. In mathematics, when we divide a by b and the remainder is c, we say that a is congruent to c modulo b and write

$$a \equiv c \ (\text{mod } b)$$

The relationships in the Federal Express airbills can be written as:

$$904872428 \equiv 5 \ (\text{mod } 7) \quad \text{and} \quad 005460436 \equiv 2 \ (\text{mod } 7)$$

while that in the money order is $4288867141 \equiv 4 \ (\text{mod } 9)$. In this section we will study modular arithmetic, its operations and relationships, as well as some applications. (See problems 39–44 and the Using Your Knowledge section of Exercise 8.5.)

The last number in the airbill and the money order is sometimes called the **checking digit** or **CD** for short. Checking digits are used in a variety of situations. Airline tickets, UPS packages, and driver's licenses, for example, use

checking digits to encode information. Why? For security reasons. Suppose you try to change the postal money order amount from $5.00 to $500. The post office *knows* that money order number 42888671414 is for $5.00, so if the amount were altered, the checking number would have to be altered as well. Do you know what other numbers would work? Mathematically, we must solve the equation $x \equiv 4$ (mod 9). Practically, x must somewhat resemble 42888671414. (For example, $22 \equiv 4$ (mod 9) because when 22 is divided by 9 the remainder is 4, but money order 22 was probably used a long time ago.) Can you find "better" numbers that will work without changing the CD number? Note that the CD number 4 is written under three bars ||| so that an erasure or alteration of the CD will disturb the bars, exposing the fraud.

In Section 8.4, the four fundamental operations were defined on the 12-hour clock. These operations can be generalized to a kind of mathematical system called **modular arithmetic.** This system can be defined on the set of integers as follows:

Definition 8.12

Two integers a and b are said to be **congruent modulo m,** denoted by $a \equiv b$ (mod m), if $a - b$ (or $b - a$) is a multiple of m (m an integer).

Thus, $14 \equiv 4$ (mod 5), because $14 - 4 = 10$, which is a multiple of 5; and $2 \equiv 18$ (mod 4), because $18 - 2 = 16$, which is a multiple of 4.

EXAMPLE 1   Are the following statements true or false?

(a) $4 \equiv 1$ (mod 3)   (b) $7 \equiv 2$ (mod 4)   (c) $1 \equiv 6$ (mod 5)

Solution   (a) True, because $4 - 1 = 3$, a multiple of 3.
(b) False, because $7 - 2$ is *not* a multiple of 4.
(c) True, because $6 - 1 = 5$, a multiple of 5.   ■

The addition of two numbers in modular arithmetic is very simple. For example, in arithmetic modulo 5, $3 + 3 \equiv 1$, because $3 + 3 = 6 \equiv 1$ (mod 5). Thus, to add nonnegative numbers in a system modulo m, we proceed as follows:

Addition modulo m

1. Add the numbers in the ordinary way.
2. If the sum is less than m, the answer is the sum obtained.
3. If the sum is greater than or equal to m, the answer is the remainder obtained upon dividing the sum by m.

Table 8.4 *Addition Modulo 5*

+	0	1	2	3	4
0	0	1	2	3	4
1	1	2	3	4	0
2	2	3	4	0	1
3	3	4	0	1	2
4	4	0	1	2	3

For example, in modulo 8

$3 + 4 \equiv 7$ (mod 8), because $3 + 4 = 7$ is less than 8.

$3 + 5 \equiv 0$ (mod 8), because $3 + 5 = 8$, which divided by 8 leaves a 0 remainder.

$3 + 7 \equiv 2$ (mod 8), because $3 + 7 = 10$, which divided by 8 is 1 with a remainder of 2.

We now define addition in modular arithmetic for modulo 5, as shown in Table 8.4.

When adding numbers in modular arithmetic, we may want to use the following theorem:

Theorem 8.1

If $a \equiv b$ (mod m) and $c \equiv d$ (mod m), then

$$a + c \equiv b + d \,(\text{mod } m)$$

For example, to add 18 and 31 (mod 5), we can use the facts that

$18 \equiv 3$ (mod 5) and $31 \equiv 1$ (mod 5)

to obtain

$18 + 31 \equiv 4$ (mod 5)

Proof The theorem can be proved by using the meanings of the two congruences. Thus,

$a \equiv b$ (mod m)   means $a - b = km$, k an integer

$c \equiv d$ (mod m)   means $c - d = pm$, p an integer

Hence,

$$(a - b) + (c - d) = km + pm = (k + p)m$$

Also,

$$(a - b) + (c - d) = (a + c) - (b + d)$$

so that

$$(a + c) - (b + d) = (k + p)m$$

That is, $(a + c) - (b + d)$ is a multiple of m, which means that

$a + c \equiv b + d$ (mod m)

Table 8.5 *Multiplication Modulo 5*

×	0	1	2	3	4
0	0	0	0	0	0
1	0	1	2	3	4
2	0	2	4	1	3
3	0	3	1	4	2
4	0	4	3	2	1

To multiply two numbers in arithmetic modulo 5, we multiply the numbers in the ordinary way. If the product is less than 5, the answer is this product. If the product is greater than 5, the answer is the remainder when the product is divided by 5. For example, $4 \times 4 \equiv 1$, because the product $4 \times 4 = 16$, which leaves a remainder 1 when divided by 5. The table for multiplication modulo 5 is shown in Table 8.5.

Subtraction in modular arithmetic is defined as follows:

$$a - b \equiv c \ (\text{mod } m) \quad \text{if and only if} \quad a \equiv b + c \ (\text{mod } m)$$

Thus, $3 - 4 \equiv 4 \ (\text{mod } 5)$, because $3 \equiv (4 + 4) \ (\text{mod } 5)$; and $2 - 4 \equiv 3$, because $2 \equiv (4 + 3) \ (\text{mod } 5)$.

EXAMPLE 2   Find:

(a) $(4 - 1) \ (\text{mod } 5)$ (b) $(2 - 3) \ (\text{mod } 5)$ (c) $(1 - 4) \ (\text{mod } 5)$

Solution   (a) $4 - 1 \equiv 3 \ (\text{mod } 5)$
(b) $2 - 3 \equiv n \ (\text{mod } 5)$ if and only if $2 \equiv (3 + n) \ (\text{mod } 5)$. From Table 8.4, $3 + 4 \equiv 2 \ (\text{mod } 5)$. Thus, $2 - 3 \equiv 4 \ (\text{mod } 5)$.
(c) $1 - 4 \equiv n \ (\text{mod } 5)$ if and only if $1 \equiv 4 + n \ (\text{mod } 5)$. From Table 8.4, we see that $1 \equiv 4 + 2 \ (\text{mod } 5)$. Thus, $1 - 4 \equiv 2 \ (\text{mod } 5)$.   ∎

We examine Table 8.6 to find what properties the set $S = \{0, 1, 2, 3, 4\}$ has under the operation of addition modulo 5.

1. All entries in the table are elements of S, so S is *closed* with respect to addition (mod 5).

2. The operation of addition (mod 5) is *associative*. (This fact is a consequence of the properties of ordinary addition, because division by 5 and taking the remainder may be done after the ordinary addition is done.)

3. The operation of addition (mod 5) is *commutative*; that is, if x and y are any elements of S, then $x + y \equiv y + x \ (\text{mod } 5)$. This can easily be checked by inspecting Table 8.6. As you can see, the results of the operations $2 + 4$ and $4 + 2$ appear in positions that are *symmetric* with respect to a diagonal line drawn from top left to bottom right of the table. If this type of symmetry is present for any operation table, that is, if the top half of the table is the reflection of the bottom half across the diagonal, then the operation is commutative.

Table 8.6 *Addition Modulo 5*

+	0	1	2	3	4
0	0	1	2	3	4
1	1	2	3	4	0
2	2	3	4	0	1
3	3	4	0	1	2
4	4	0	1	2	3

4. The *identity* for addition modulo 5 is 0, because for any x in S, $x + 0 = x$; that is, $0 + 0 = 0$, $1 + 0 = 1$, $2 + 0 = 2$, $3 + 0 = 3$, and $4 + 0 = 4$.

5. Every element has an additive *inverse* (mod 5). The inverse of 0 is 0, because $0 + 0 \equiv 0 \ (\text{mod } 5)$. The inverse of 1 is 4, because $1 + 4 \equiv 0 \ (\text{mod } 5)$. The inverse of 2 is 3, because $2 + 3 \equiv 0 \ (\text{mod } 5)$. The inverse of 3 is 2, because $3 + 2 \equiv 0 \ (\text{mod } 5)$. The inverse of 4 is 1, because $4 + 1 \equiv 0 \ (\text{mod } 5)$.

As we have seen in the preceding discussion, modular arithmetic is a mathematical system in which two operations are defined on the same set. For the set $S = \{0, 1, 2, 3, 4\}$, we defined addition and multiplication modulo 5 as shown in Tables 8.4 and 8.5. Are there any properties that involve both operations? The answer is yes. For example, to find $3 \times (2 + 4)$ (mod 5), we can proceed in one of two ways:

1. $3 \times (2 + 4) \equiv 3 \times (1) \equiv 3$ (mod 5)
2. $3 \times (2 + 4) \equiv (3 \times 2) + (3 \times 4) \equiv 1 + 2 \equiv 3$ (mod 5)

To get the answer in the second way, we used a property that involves both addition and multiplication. This property is called the Distributive Property; it is true in general that if a, b, and c are elements of S, then

$$a \times (b + c) \equiv (a \times b) + (a \times c) \pmod{m}$$

because $a \times (b + c) - (a \times b) - (a \times c) = 0$ in ordinary arithmetic.

EXAMPLE 3   Find a replacement for n that will make the given sentence true in arithmetic modulo 5.

(a) $4 \times (3 + 1) \equiv (4 \times n) + (4 \times 1)$
(b) $n \times (1 + 3) \equiv (2 \times 1) + (2 \times 3)$

Solution   (a) By the distributive property, $4 \times (3 + 1) \equiv (4 \times 3) + (4 \times 1)$. Thus, $n = 3$ will make the sentence $4 \times (3 + 1) \equiv (4 \times n) + (4 \times 1)$ true.

(b) By the distributive property, $2 \times (1 + 3) \equiv (2 \times 1) + (2 \times 3)$. Thus, $n = 2$ will make the sentence $n \times (1 + 3) \equiv (2 \times 1) + (2 \times 3)$ true. ■

EXAMPLE 4   Find a replacement for n that will make the given sentence true.

(a) $3 + n \equiv 2$ (mod 5)   (b) $\frac{3}{4} \equiv n$ (mod 5)

Solution   (a) By inspection of Table 8.4 (or 8.6), we see that $3 + 4 \equiv 2$ (mod 5). Thus, $n = 4$ will make the sentence $3 + n \equiv 2$ (mod 5) true.

(b) $\frac{3}{4} \equiv n$ (mod 5) is true if and only if $3 \equiv 4 \times n$ (mod 5). By inspection of Table 8.5, we see that $4 \times 2 \equiv 3$ (mod 5). Hence, $n = 2$ will make the sentence $\frac{3}{4} \equiv n$ (mod 5) true. ■

In Examples 3 and 4, we have given answers in the set $\{0, 1, 2, 3, 4\}$. If we allow n to be any integer that makes the given congruence true, then each answer can be modified by adding or subtracting any desired multiple of 5. This is justified by the addition theorem (Theorem 8.1) proved earlier. For instance, in Example 4a, all the possible integer answers would be given by $n \equiv 4$ (mod 5). This means that n could have any of the values . . . , -6, -1, 4, 9, 14, . . . ; each of these would make the congruence $3 + n \equiv 2$ (mod 5) true.

Exercise 8.5

In problems 1–6, classify the given statement as true or false.

1. $2 \equiv 4 \pmod 3$
2. $5 \equiv 2 \pmod 3$
3. $6 \equiv 7 \pmod 5$
4. $5 \equiv 3 \pmod 2$
5. $8 \equiv 9 \pmod{10}$
6. $12 \equiv 8 \pmod 4$

In problems 7–10, find the indicated sums.

7. $(3 + 4) \pmod 5$
8. $(2 + 9) \pmod{10}$
9. $(3 + 1) \pmod 5$
10. $(3 + 6) \pmod 7$

In problems 11–14, find the indicated products.

11. $(4 \times 2) \pmod 5$
12. $(4 \times 3) \pmod 5$
13. $(2 \times 3) \pmod 5$
14. $(3 \times 3) \pmod 5$

In problems 15–18, find the indicated differences.

15. $(2 - 4) \pmod 5$
16. $(3 - 4) \pmod 5$
17. $(1 - 3) \pmod 5$
18. $(0 - 2) \pmod 5$

In problems 19–34, find a value of n in the set $\{0, 1, 2, 3, 4\}$ that will make the given congruence true.

19. $4 \times (3 + 0) \equiv (4 \times 3) + (4 \times n) \pmod 5$
20. $2 \times (1 + 3) \equiv (2 \times 1) + (n \times 3) \pmod 5$
21. $2 \times (0 + 3) \equiv (2 \times n) + (2 \times 3) \pmod 5$
22. $4 \times (1 + n) \equiv (4 \times 1) + (4 \times 2) \pmod 5$
23. $2 + n \equiv 3 \pmod 5$
24. $n + 3 \equiv 1 \pmod 5$
25. $2 \times n \equiv 4 \pmod 5$
26. $3 \equiv 2 \times n \pmod 5$
27. $n - 3 \equiv 4 \pmod 5$
28. $2 \equiv n - 1 \pmod 5$
29. $3 \equiv n - 4 \pmod 5$
30. $n - 2 \equiv 1 \pmod 5$
31. $\dfrac{n}{2} \equiv 4 \pmod 5$
32. $\dfrac{n}{3} \equiv 2 \pmod 5$
33. $\frac{3}{4} \equiv n \pmod 5$
34. $\frac{1}{2} \equiv n \pmod 5$

In problems 35–38, use Table 8.5 and multiplication modulo 5.

35. Is the set $S = \{0, 1, 2, 3, 4\}$ closed with respect to $\times$?
36. Is the set operation $\times$ commutative?
37. Is there an identity for the operation $\times$? If so, what is this identity?
38. Find the inverse (if possible) of:
    (a) 0   (b) 1   (c) 2   (d) 3   (e) 4

A modulo 7 arithmetic is suggested by the fact that a week has 7 days. If one wants to know what day of the week it will be 29 days from Wednesday, we can follow the sequence Wednesday, Thursday, Friday, etc. However, we know that in 28 days it will be Wednesday again, so in 29 days it will be Thursday.

In problems 39–44, state what day of the week it will be:

39. 30 days from a Monday
40. 140 days from a Tuesday
41. 150 days from a Wednesday
42. 80 days from a Thursday
43. 350 days from a Friday
44. 440 days from a Saturday
45. Construct an addition table for the set {0, 1, 2, 3} (mod 4).
46. Construct a multiplication table for the set and modulus of problem 45.

In Other Words

47. Suppose you are tracking a package for Federal Express. The customer claims that the package number is 0005234981 or 0005234983. Which is correct? Explain your answer.

48. In your own words, detail the similarities between clock arithmetic using a 5-hour clock and arithmetic modulo 5.

Using Your Knowledge

Look at the back cover of this book. What did you find? The ISBN (International Standard Book Number) is a ten-digit number that encodes certain information about the book. (Some books show the ISBN only on the copyright page.) For this book the ISBN is 0-669-28957-4. The following diagram shows the reference of each part of the ISBN:

The book

English-speaking country 0-669-28957-**4**

Publisher

*But what about the **4** at the right end? This digit is a check digit that is used to verify orders. The check number is obtained from the other digits as follows: Write the numbers 10, 9, 8, 7, 6, 5, 4, 3, 2 above the first nine digits of the ISBN, and then multiply each of these digits by the number above it and add the results.*

10	9	8	7	6	5	4	3	2
↓	↓	↓	↓	↓	↓	↓	↓	↓
0	6	6	9	2	8	9	5	7
↓	↓	↓	↓	↓	↓	↓	↓	↓

$$(10 \cdot 0) + (9 \cdot 6) + (8 \cdot 6) + (7 \cdot 9) + (6 \cdot 2) + (5 \cdot 8) + (4 \cdot 9) + (3 \cdot 5) + (2 \cdot 7)$$
$$= 0 + 54 + 48 + 63 + 12 + 40 + 36 + 15 + 14$$
$$= 282$$

*To get the check number (**4** in our ISBN), divide the sum 282 by 11 and take the remainder, r = 7. The check number c is the solution of c + r ≡ 0 (mod 11), that is, c + 7 ≡ 0 (mod 11) for the replacement set {0, 1, 2, . . . , 10}. Since 4 + 7 = 11 ≡ 0 (mod 11), we see that the check number is c = **4**. Note that the easy way to get the check number is to subtract the remainder r from 11.*

Use these ideas to solve the following problems. Note that if the check number is 10, it is written as the Roman numeral X.

49. If the first nine digits of the ISBN are 0-06-040613, find the check number.

50. If the first nine digits of the ISBN are 0-517-53052, find the check number.

51. Find the check number for ISBN 0-312-87867.

52. The last digit of the book number in the ISBN 0-060-4098■3 was blurred as indicated. What must this digit be?

53. Find what the blurred digit must be in the ISBN 0-03-0589■4-2.

54. Find what the blurred digit must be in the ISBN 0-716■-0456-0.

Discovery

The idea of modular arithmetic can be used to create modular designs. To construct a modulo 5 design, we first choose a multiplier (say, 2) so that we will get what is called a (5, 2) design. Then we proceed as follows:

(a) *Write the multiplication table for mod 5 arithmetic (see Table 8.5).*

(b) *Draw a circle and divide the circumference into four equal parts, labeling the points 1, 2, 3, 4 as shown in Figure 8.7.*

(c) *From Table 8.5, we read*

$$2 \times \overset{\frown}{1} \equiv 2 \,(mod\ 5)$$

$$2 \times \overset{\frown}{2} \equiv 4 \,(mod\ 5)$$

$$2 \times \overset{\frown}{3} \equiv 1 \,(mod\ 5)$$

$$2 \times \overset{\frown}{4} \equiv 3 \,(mod\ 5)$$

(d) *We now connect 1 and 2, 2 and 4, 3 and 1, and 4 and 3, as in Figure 8.8.*

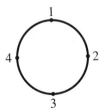

FIGURE 8.6

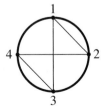

FIGURE 8.7

55. Can you discover how the design (5, 3) looks?

56. Can you discover why (5, 3) and (5, 2) are identical? [*Hint:*   Look at the "multipliers" (mod 5).]

57. The designs (19, 9) and (21, 10) are shown in the figure below. Can you draw the design (19, 17)?

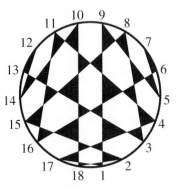
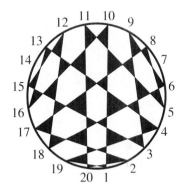

The (19, 9) modular design   The (21, 10) design

58. Can you discover why (19, 9) and (19, 17) are identical?

59. Draw the (13, 3) design. Can you discover for what value of m the $(13, m)$ design is the same as the (13, 3) design?

Sophie Germain tried to discover whether a congruence of the type $x^3 \equiv 2 \pmod{p}$, p a prime, has a solution. Let us look at the congruence $x^3 \equiv y \pmod{p}$, where x takes on the values 0, 1, 2, 3, . . . , and p is a prime. There is a value of y for each value of x but, because the modulus is p, the values of y repeat after each p values of x. For example, if $p = 3$, then the congruence becomes $x^3 \equiv y \pmod{3}$.

If $x = 0$, then $0^3 \equiv 0 \pmod{3}$, and $y = 0$
If $x = 1$, then $1^3 \equiv 1 \pmod{3}$, and $y = 1$
If $x = 2$, then $2^3 = 8 \equiv 2 \pmod{3}$, and $y = 2$.

Since the modulus is 3, if we go on to greater values of x, the values of y simply repeat the sequence 0, 1, 2. Thus, the congruence $x^3 \equiv 2 \pmod{3}$ has infinitely many solutions: $x = 2, 5, 8, . . . , 3n + 2, ...$

60. Determine whether the following congruences have infinitely many or no solutions. (Note that if the modulus is p, you have to check only the values $x = 0, 1, 2, . . . , p - 1$.)

(a) $x^3 \equiv 2 \pmod{5}$

(b) $x^3 \equiv 2 \pmod{7}$

(c) $x^3 \equiv 2 \pmod{11}$

8.6 ABSTRACT MATHEMATICAL SYSTEMS

GETTING STARTED

EVENS, ODDS, AND MATHEMATICAL SYSTEMS

Suppose you encounter the mysterious table

+	E	O
E	E	O
O	O	E

What do you think this table represents? If you think for a moment, you will see that the table exhibits the fact that if you add two even numbers the answer is even, the addition of an even and an odd yields an odd, the sum of an odd and an even is odd, and an odd added to another odd is even. As you recall from Section 8.5, a mathematical system consists of a set of elements, {E, O} in this case, one or more operations (+ here), one or more relations (=), and some rules, axioms, or laws that the elements in the set satisfy (E + O = O, for example). In this section we shall study mathematical systems in general. To prepare for this study, can you finish defining the operation ×?

×	E	O
E	E	
O		

If you do it successfully, you are ready to start studying abstract mathematical systems.

In this section we shall concentrate on the rules and laws that are obeyed by abstract mathematical systems. To illustrate the ideas involved, we shall define a set $A = \{a, b, c, d, e\}$ and an operation ∗, which we shall call *star*. The operations on the set A can be defined by a table similar to the one used to define

Table 8.7

∗	a	b	c	d	e
a	b	c	d	e	a
b	c	d	e	a	b
c	d	e	a	b	c
d	e	a	b	c	d
e	a	b	c	d	e

Table 8.8

∗	a	b	c	d	e
a	b	c	d	e	a
b	c	d	e	a	b
c	d	e	a	b	c
d	e	a	b	c	d
e	a	b	c	d	e

addition of natural numbers, or addition in modulo 5. Suppose that the operation $*$ is defined by Table 8.7.

To perform the operation star on any pair of elements, say, b and c, we find the element that is in the b row and the c column (rows are horizontal and columns are vertical), as shown in Table 8.8. From this table we can see that $b * c = e$. Similarly, $a * b = c$ and $c * d = b$.

EXAMPLE 1   Use Table 8.7 to find the result of each of the following operations:

   (a) $b * e$ (b) $d * b$ (c) $(a * b) * c$

Solution   (a) $b * e$ corresponds to the entry in the b row, e column; that is, $b * e = b$.

   (b) $d * b$ corresponds to the entry in the d row, b column; that is, $d * b = a$.

   (c) We wrote $(a * b)$ in parentheses, so we must find $(a * b)$ first. Thus, $(a * b) * c = c * c = a$.   ▧

By proceeding as in Example 1, we can find the result $x * y$ for all elements x and y that are in S, and it is evident that the result is also in S. The name that we give to this property is *closure*.

Definition 8.13   A set A is **closed** under the operation $*$ if, for all a and b in A, $a * b$ is also in A.

Intuitively, we say that the set A is closed under the operation $*$ if the operation is always possible, and if no new elements are introduced in the table defining the operation. For example, the set of natural numbers is closed under the operation of addition, because for any two natural numbers a and b, $a + b$ is also a natural number. On the other hand, the set of natural numbers is not closed under subtraction since, for example, $5 - 7 = -2$, which is not a natural number.

EXAMPLE 2   Consider the sets $A = \{0, 1\}$ and $B = \{1, 2\}$. Are these sets closed under ordinary multiplication?

Solution   The set A is closed under multiplication, because all possible products $0 \times 0 = 0$, $0 \times 1 = 0$, $1 \times 0 = 0$, and $1 \times 1 = 1$ are in A. On the other hand, the set B is not closed under multiplication, because $2 \times 2 = 4$, which is not in B.   ▧

Another important property previously discussed in connection with the natural numbers is *associativity*.

Definition 8.14 ——

An operation $*$ defined on a set A is **associative** if, for all a, b, and c in A,

$$(a * b) * c = a * (b * c)$$

For example, the intersection of sets that we studied in Chapter 1 is associative, because for any three sets A, B, C, we have

$$A \cap (B \cap C) = (A \cap B) \cap C.$$

EXAMPLE 3   In Table 8.7, check to see if

(a) $(a * b) * d = a * (b * d)$ (b) $(c * a) * e = c * (a * e)$

Solution   (a) Table 8.7 gives $a * b = c$, so $a * b$ may be replaced by c to get $(a * b) * d = c * d$. Then, because the figure gives $c * d = b$, we see that $(a * b) * d = b$. Similarly, we find that $a * (b * d) = a * a = b$. The result in both cases is b, so $(a * b) * d = a * (b * d)$.

(b) Again, by using Table 8.7, we find that $(c * a) * e = d * e = d$ and $c * (a * e) = c * a = d$. Because the result is d in both cases, we have $(c * a) * e = c * (a * e)$.   ■

Can we conclude from Example 3 that the operation $*$ is associative? The answer is no, because we have not checked all the possibilities. Try some other possibilities and state whether or not you think $*$ is associative.

The next property we shall discuss is the *Commutative Property*.

Definition 8.15 ——

An operation $*$ defined on a set A is **commutative** if, for every a and b in A,

$$a * b = b * a$$

For example, the intersection of sets that we studied in Chapter 1 is commutative, because for any two sets A and B, $A \cap B = B \cap A$.

EXAMPLE 4   In Table 8.7, check to see if:

(a) $b * d = d * b$ (b) $e * c = c * e$

Solution   (a) $b * d = a$ and $d * b = a$; thus, $b * d = d * b$.
(b) $e * c = c$ and $c * e = c$; thus, $e * c = c * e$.   ■

Can we conclude from Example 4 that the operation $*$ is commutative? Again, the answer is no, because we have not checked all the possibilities. However, there is a simple check that we can make. Since the top half of the table is the reflection of the bottom half across the diagonal, the operation is commutative.

As we learned in Chapter 4, the set of integers has an additive identity (0), with the property that for any integer a, $a + 0 = a = 0 + a$. Similarly, 1 is the identity for multiplication, because $a \cdot 1 = a = 1 \cdot a$. The idea of an *identity* can be generalized by means of the following definition:

Definition 8.16

An element e in a set A is said to be an **identity** for the operation $*$ if, for each element x in A,

$$x * e = x = e * x$$

For example, for the operator $*$ defined on the set $A = \{a, b, c, d, e\}$ in Table 8.7, the identity element is e, as you can easily check. Notice that the column directly under the identity element e is identical with the column at the far left, and the row opposite the element e is identical with the row across the top of the table. This appearance of the operation table is characteristic for any set that has an identity element under the operation.

EXAMPLE 5 Let $A = \{a, b, c\}$, and let $*$ be an operation defined on A. If c is the identity element, what do you know about the table that defines the operation $*$?

Solution From the preceding discussion, we can complete a partial table like Table 8.9. The column at the far right is identical to the column at the far left; the row across the bottom is identical to the row across the top.

Table 8.9

$*$	a	b	c
a			a
b			b
c	a	b	c

Closely related to the idea of an identity is the idea of an *inverse*. For example, the additive inverse of 3 is -3, because $3 + (-3) = 0$ (the additive identity). Similarly, the multiplicative inverse of 3 is $\frac{1}{3}$, because $3 \times \frac{1}{3} = 1$ (the multiplicative identity). In order to find the inverse of a number a under addition, we need a number b so that $a + b = 0$; similarly, to find the inverse of a number a under multiplication, we need a number b so that $a \times b = 1$. These ideas can be summarized by the following definition:

Definition 8.17

If a and b are in A, we say that **a is the inverse of b** under the operation $*$, if $a * b = e = b * a$, where e is the identity.

EXAMPLE 6 Consider Table 8.10, which defines the operation #. Find:

(a) The identity   (b) The inverse of a (c) The inverse of b

Solution (a) The identity is b, because the column under b is identical to the column at the far left and the row opposite b is identical to the row across the top.

(b) We have to find an element to place in the box so that $a \# \square = b$. From the table we can see that this element is a, because $a \# a = b$. Thus, a is its own inverse.

(c) We have to find an element to place in the box so that $b \# \square = b$. From the table we can see that this element is b, because $b \# b = b$. So, b is its own inverse.

Table 8.10

#	a	b
a	b	a
b	a	b

EXAMPLE 7   Consider the operation # defined by Table 8.11.

(a) Is there an identity element?
(b) Do any of the elements have inverses?
(c) Is the operation commutative?

Note that this table of operations corresponds to rotations in the plane as shown in Figure 8.9.

Table 8.11

#	a	b	c
a	c	a	b
b	b	c	a
c	a	b	c

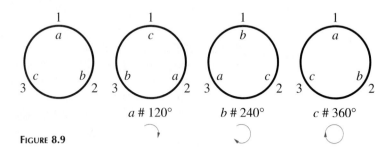

FIGURE 8.9

Solution   (a) There is no column identical to the column under #, so there is no identity element.
(b) Since there is no identity element, there are no inverses.
(c) The operation is not commutative. For example,

$$a \# b = a \quad \text{but} \quad b \# a = b$$

As in the case of modular arithmetic, there is a property that involves two operations. This property is called the *distributive property* and is defined as follows:

Definition 8.18

> The operation * defined on a set A is said to be **distributive** over the operation # if, for all, a, b, and c in A, we have
>
> $$a * (b \# c) = (a * b) \# (a * c)$$

For example, the operation of multiplication defined on the set of real numbers is distributive over addition because, for any real numbers a, b, and c,

$$a \times (b + c) = (a \times b) + (a \times c)$$

On the other hand, addition is *not* distributive over multiplication because

$$a + (b \times c) \neq (a + b) \times (a + c)$$

as shown by the example

$$3 + (4 \times 5) = 3 + 20 = 23$$

$$(3 + 4) \times (3 + 5) = 7 \times 8 = 56$$

Thus,

$$3 + (4 \times 5) = 23 \neq (3 + 4) \times (3 + 5) = 56$$

Now, let us consider two operations, F and S, defined on the set of natural numbers as follows: If a and b are any two natural numbers, then:

1. $a\,F\,b$ means to select the *first* of the two numbers.
2. $a\,S\,b$ means to select the *smaller* of the two numbers. (If $a = b$, then $a\,S\,a$ is defined to be a.)

Thus, 3 F 5 = 3, 5 F 3 = 5, and 4 F 1 = 4. Similarly, 3 S 5 = 3, 5 S 3 = 3, 4 S 1 = 1, and 2 S 2 = 2.

EXAMPLE 8   Is the operation F distributive over S?

Solution   Recall that $a\,F\,b$ means to select the first of the numbers and that $a\,S\,b$ means to select the smaller of the two numbers a and b (if the numbers are the same, select the number). To show that F distributes over S, we have to show that

$$a\,F\,(b\,S\,c) = (a\,F\,b)\,S\,(a\,F\,c)$$

We know that $a\,F\,(b\,S\,c) = a$ (because a is the first number). Also, $a\,F\,b = a$ and $a\,F\,c = a$, so

$$(a\,F\,b)\,S\,(a\,F\,c) = a\,S\,a = a$$

Thus,

$$a\,F\,(b\,S\,c) = (a\,F\,b)\,S\,(a\,F\,c)$$

which shows that F is distributive over S.   ■

Exercise 8.6

Consider the set $S = \{a, b, c\}$ and the operation @ defined by Table 8.12. Problems 1–7 refer to this table.

Table 8.12

@	a	b	c
a	c	a	b
b	a	b	c
c	b	c	a

1. Find:
   (a) $a\,@\,b$ (b) $b\,@\,c$ (c) $c\,@\,a$

2. Find:
   (a) $a\,@\,(b\,@\,c)$ (b) $(a\,@\,b)\,@\,c$
   (c) Are the results in parts (a) and (b) identical?

3. Find:
   (a) $b\,@\,(a\,@\,b)$ (b) $(b\,@\,a)\,@\,b$
   (c) Are the results in parts (a) and (b) identical?

4. Find:
   (a) $(a\,@\,b)\,@\,a$ (b) $a\,@\,(b\,@\,a)$
   (c) Are the results in parts (a) and (b) identical?

5. Find:
   (a) $b @ c$ (b) $c @ b$
   (c) Are the results in parts (a) and (b) identical?

6. Is the operation @ a commutative operation? Explain.

7. Is the set S closed with respect to the operation @? Explain

8. Suppose a F b means to select the first of two numbers a and b, as in Example 8 of this section. Let $A = \{1, 2, 3\}$.
   (a) Make a table that will define the operation F on the set A.
   (b) Is A closed under the operation F?
   (c) Is the operation F commutative?
   (d) For any three natural numbers a, b, and c, show that

   $$a \text{ F } (b \text{ F } c) = (a \text{ F } b) \text{ F } c$$

9. Let the operation F be defined as in problem 8, and let N be the set of natural numbers.
   (a) Is the set N closed under the operation F? Explain.
   (b) Is the operation F associative? Explain.
   (c) Is the operation F commutative? Explain.

10. Let S be the set of all multiples of 5 (0, 5, 10, etc.).
    (a) Is the set S closed with respect to ordinary multiplication?
    (b) Is the operation of ordinary multiplication commutative on S? Explain.
    (c) Is the operation of ordinary multiplication associative on S? Explain.

11. Are the following sets closed under the given operation?
    (a) The odd numbers under addition
    (b) The odd numbers under multiplication
    (c) The even numbers under addition
    (d) The even numbers under multiplication

12. Give an example of an operation under which the set $\{0, 1\}$ is
    (a) Not closed   (b) Not associative   (c) Not commutative

Let $S = \{\emptyset, \{a\}, \{b\}, \{a, b\}\}$. Table 8.13 will be used in problems 13–18. The entries in the table represent the set intersection of the elements in the corresponding rows and columns.

Table 8.13 **Table for Problems 13–18**

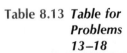

∩	Ø	{a}	{b}	{a, b}
Ø	Ø	Ø	Ø	Ø
{a}	Ø	{a}	Ø	{a}
{b}	Ø			
{a, b}	Ø			

13. Supply the missing entries in Table 8.13.

14. Find:
    (a) $(\{a\} \cap \{b\}) \cap \{a, b\}$ (b) $\{a\} \cap (\{b\} \cap \{a, b\})$
    (c) Are the results in parts (a) and (b) identical?

15. Find:
    (a) $(\{b\} \cap \{a, b\}) \cap \{a\}$ (b) $\{b\} \cap (\{a, b\} \cap \{a\})$
    (c) Are the results in parts (a) and (b) identical?

Table 8.14 *Table for Problem 19*

L	1	2	3	4
1				4
2			3	
3		3		
4	4			4

16. In Chapter 1 we learned that for any three sets A, B, and C, $A \cap (B \cap C) = (A \cap B) \cap C$. On the basis of this result, would you say that the operation $\cap$ defined in Table 8.13 is associative?

17. Is the set S closed with respect to the operation $\cap$? Explain.

18. Is the operation $\cap$ commutative? How can you tell?

19. Suppose that $a \text{ L } b$ means to select the larger of the two numbers a and b (if the numbers are the same, select the number).
    (a) Complete Table 8.14.
    (b) If there is an identity element, what is it?

Table 8.15 will be used in problems 20 and 21.

Table 8.15 *Table for Problems 20 and 21*

S	1	2	3	4
1	1	1	1	1
2	1	2	2	2
3	1	2	3	3
4	1	2	3	4

20. Does the set $A = \{1, 2, 3, 4\}$ have an identity? If so, what is this identity?

21. Find the inverses of:
    (a) 1   (b) 2   (c) 3   (d) 4

22. Consider the set $S = \{-1, 0, 1\}$ and the operation of ordinary multiplication. Complete Table 8.16.

23. Does the set $S = \{-1, 0, 1\}$ have an identity under multiplication? If so, what is this identity?

24. For the set $S = \{-1, 0, 1\}$ under the operation of multiplication, find the inverse (if possible) of:
    (a) 1   (b) -1 (c) 0

25. If $\mathcal{U}$ is the set of all subsets of any non-empty set A:
    (a) Find the identity element for the operation of set intersection ($\cap$).
    (b) Can you find more than one identity?

Table 8.16 *Table for Problems 22–24*

×	−1	0	1
−1			
0			
1			

Table 8.17 will be used in problems 26–28.

26. Is the set $S = \{0, 1, 2, 3\}$ closed under the operation @?

27. Does the set S have an identity with respect to the operation @? If so, what is this identity?

28. Find the inverse (if it exists) of:
    (a) 0   (b) 1   (c) 2   (d) 3

Table 8.17 *Table for Problems 26–28*

@	0	1	2	3
0	0	1	2	3
1	1	2	3	0
2	2	3	0	1
3	3	0	1	2

In problems 29–32, let F be defined as in problem 8 and let $a \text{ L } b$ mean to select the larger of the two numbers a and b (if $a = b$, assume $a \text{ L } b = a$) as in problem 19.

29. Find:
    (a) 3 F (4 L 5)   (b) 4 F (5 L 6)

30. Find:
    (a) 4 L (4 F 5)   (b) 5 L (6 F 7)

31. Does the distributive property $a \text{ F } (b \text{ L } c) = (a \text{ F } b) \text{ L } (a \text{ F } c)$ hold for all real numbers a, b, c? Explain.

32. Does the distributive property $a \, \mathrm{L} \, (b \, \mathrm{F} \, c) = (a \, \mathrm{L} \, b) \, \mathrm{F} \, (a \, \mathrm{L} \, c)$ hold for all real numbers a, b, c? Explain.

33. In ordinary arithmetic, is multiplication distributive over subtraction?

34. In ordinary arithmetic, is division distributive over subtraction? [*Hint:* Look at two forms: $a \div (b - c) = (a \div b) - (a \div c)$ and $(a - b) \div c = (a \div c) - (b \div c)$.]

35. In the arithmetic of fractions, is multiplication distributive over addition?

36. In the arithmetic of fractions, is addition distributive over multiplication?

In Other Words

Suppose you are given a set S and a table defining the operation ◆. Explain in your own words the procedure for determining:

37. If the set S is closed under the operation ◆.

38. If the operation ◆ is commutative.

39. If there is an identity for the operation ◆.

40. If two elements, say, a and b, are inverses of each other.

Using Your Knowledge

The distributive property can be used to shorten the labor in certain multiplication problems. For instance, the product of 6 and 999 can easily be found by writing

$$6 \times 999 = 6 \times (1000 - 1) = 6000 - 6 = 5994$$

Use this idea to calculate the following products:

41. 6×9999 42. 8×99 43. 7×59

44. 8×999 45. 4×9995 46. 3×9998

Discovery

The distributive property can be used in an interesting way in number puzzles. Have you ever seen a magician ask a person in the audience to think of a number and do several things with it? Then, without knowing the original number, the magician knows the number with which the person ended up! Here is one of these puzzles:

Think of a number.
Add 3 to it.
Triple the result.
Subtract 9.
Divide by the number with which you started.
The result is 3.

Here are the calculations of four persons who selected different numbers.

	First	**Second**	**Third**	**Fourth**
Think of a number:	*4*	*6*	*8*	*10*
Add 3 to it:	*7*	*9*	*11*	*13*
Triple the result:	*21*	*27*	*33*	*39*
Subtract 9:	*12*	*18*	*24*	*30*
Divide by the number with which you started:	*3*	*3*	*3*	*3*

The result is always 3!

47. Can you discover why the puzzle works? [*Hint:* Let x be the number you select and work through the puzzle.]

48. Can you discover the result of the following puzzle?

Think of a number.
Add 2 to it.
Double the result.
Subtract 4.
Divide by the number with which you started.
The result is _____ .

8.7 GROUPS AND FIELDS

GETTING STARTED

APPLICATIONS OF GROUP THEORY

What do you think of when the word *group* is mentioned? It might mean a study *group,* *group* discussions, a tactical *group,* or a *group* of friends. In mathematics, the word *group* means a type of system with operations, rules, and axioms. Groups also satisfy some properties we have mentioned before: commutative, associative, and closure, for example. Have you seen any groups yet? The even numbers under addition and the real numbers under multiplication are examples of groups. Groups are even used in physics. A rudimentary model for an atom includes the nucleus at the middle and electrons spinning around in orbits, much as the Earth orbits the sun. An electron can move from orbit 1 to 3 and then from 3 to 6 in two jumps, but it could also go from 1 to 6 in one jump. These electron jumps (from 1 to 3 and 3 to 6, for example) actually form a group.

As you know, an important function of mathematics is to produce models that sometimes can be solved using algebraic equations. We know how to solve first- and second-degree equations. It was Nicolo de Brescia, an Italian mathematician, who discovered how to solve third-degree equations. Then, the general fourth-degree equation was solved in the sixteenth century; but it took Evariste Galois and **group theory** to produce a proof that general equations of degree higher than four could not be solved using a finite number of steps. In this section we study *groups* and *fields* and we will exhibit several examples of these useful and interesting mathematical structures.

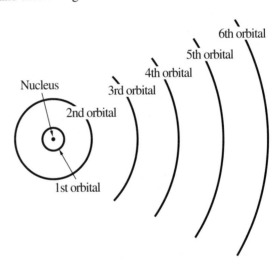

Hypothetical circular orbits in an atomic model

Interest in mathematical systems such as those we studied in Section 8.6 started in the early nineteenth century with the study of groups.

Definition 8.19

A **group** is a mathematical system consisting of a set S and an operation * with the following four properties:

1. **Closure** property

2. **Associative** property

3. There is an **identity** element.

4. Each element of S has an **inverse** in S.

If the system also has the **commutative** property, then the group is called a **commutative** (or **abelian**) **group.**

For example, the set of integers with the operation of addition has the following properties.

Closure	The sum of two integers is always an integer.
Associative	If a, b, c are integers, then $a + (b + c) = (a + b) + c$.
Identity	The integer 0 is the identity element such that $0 + a = a + 0 = a$ for every integer a.
Inverse	If a is an integer, then $-a$ is an integer such that $a + (-a) = 0$.
Commutative	If a and b are integers, then $a + b = b + a$.

Thus, the set of integers is a commutative group under addition.

Although group theory was developed by many mathematicians, the French mathematician Evariste Galois is usually considered the pioneer in this field. However, the origin of group theory can be traced back to the efforts of the Babylonians in solving equations of degree greater than 2. At the time of the Renaissance, the Italian mathematicians Girolamo Cardano and Nicolo de Brescia, commonly referred to as *Tartaglia* ("the stammerer"), made the first successful attempts to solve equations of third and fourth degree. After their discoveries, it seemed natural to pursue methods to solve equations of degree 5 and higher. At this point, Galois investigated the general properties of the equations involved, as well as the properties of their solutions. These ideas led to the theory of groups.

EXAMPLE 1   Does the set $S = \{0, 1, 2, 3, 4\}$, together with the operation of addition modulo 5, form a commutative group?

Solution   The system has the five properties (closure, associative, identity, inverse, and commutative) as shown following Example 2 in Section 8.5, so the set S together with the operation of addition modulo 5 forms a commutative group. ∎

EXAMPLE 2   Does the set $S = \{0, 1, 2, 3, 4\}$, together with the operation of multiplication modulo 5, form a commutative group?

Solution   The multiplication table for this system is shown in Table 8.18. We check the five properties.

1. The set S is *closed,* because all the entries in the table are elements of S.

2. The operation is *commutative,* because the reflection of the bottom half of the table along the diagonal is identical to the top part.

3. The operation is *associative.*

4. The *identity* for this system is 1.

Table 8.18 *Multiplication Modulo 5*

×	0	1	2	3	4
0	0	0	0	0	0
1	0	1	2	3	4
2	0	2	4	1	3
3	0	3	1	4	2
4	0	4	3	2	1

5. All the elements, except 0, have *inverses*. Zero does not
have an inverse because there is no number a in S such that
$0 \times a \equiv 1$.

The inverse of 1 is 1 ($1 \times 1 \equiv 1$).
The inverse of 2 is 3 ($2 \times 3 \equiv 1$).
The inverse of 3 is 2 ($3 \times 2 \equiv 1$).
The inverse of 4 is 4 ($4 \times 4 \equiv 1$).

Since the system does not have an inverse for 0, the system is not a group under the operation of multiplication modulo 5.   ∎

EXAMPLE 3   If the number 0 is omitted from the set in Example 2, is the resulting system a
commutative group?

Solution   The multiplication table for this system would be Table 8.18 with the 0 row
and the 0 column omitted. From the discussion in Example 2, we see that this
system has all the required properties and is thus a commutative group.   ∎

The Distributive Law discussed in Section 8.6 is the only property we
have studied that involves two operations. We now turn our attention to a kind
of mathematical system, called a *field*, which consists of a set S and two operations.

Definition 8.20

A **field** is a mathematical system consisting of a set S and two operations,
say, * and #, defined on S and having the following properties:

1. *Closure* property
2. *Associative* property
3. *Identity* property
4. *Inverse* property (except that there is no inverse for the identity
   with respect to *)
5. *Commutative* property
6. *Distributive* property of # with respect to *

Problem Solving: Groups and Fields

Show that the system consisting of the set $S = \{0, 1, 2, 3, 4\}$ and the operations of addition and multiplication modulo 5 is a field.

1. Read the problem.
2. Select the unknown.   We have to show that the set S together with the operations + and × modulo 5 form a field.

3. Think of a plan.
   What do we have to   Thus, we have to show that + and × have the closure, associative, iden-
   show?   tity, inverse, commutative, and distributive properties.

4. Use the results of Examples 1 and 2 to verify that the operations of + and × modulo 5 satisfy the properties stated in Definition 8.20.

According to Example 1, the operation + modulo 5 has the closure, associative, identity, inverse, and commutative properties, while Example 2 shows that the operation × modulo 5 has the closure, commutative, associative, identity, and inverse properties (except that 0 has no inverse). Finally, × is distributive over + in the set of real numbers. Thus, × is distributive over + in the set S.

5 Verify the solution.

You can examine Tables 8.4 and 8.18 and verify the properties mentioned. In general, it can be shown that if p is any prime number, then the integers modulo p form a field under + and × .

TRY EXAMPLE 4 NOW.

Cover the solution, write your own, and then check your work.

EXAMPLE 4

Let $S = \{$Odd, Even$\}$, and let + and × be two operations defined by Tables 8.19 and 8.20. You may recognize that these operations correspond to adding or multiplying odd and even numbers. For instance, an odd number added to an even number gives an odd number; thus, Odd + Even = Odd. Similarly, Even × Even = Even. Does the set $S = \{$Odd, Even$\}$ form a field under the + and × operations?

Solution

1. **Closure:** The tables show that S is closed under the two operations.
2. **Associative:** Both operations are associative. For example,
   Odd + (Odd + Even) = Odd + Odd = Even, and
   (Odd + Odd) + Even = Even + Even = Even, so that
   Odd + (Odd + Even) = (Odd + Odd) + Even. (You can check the other cases in the same way.)
3. **Commutative:** The two tables show that both operations are commutative.
4. **Identity:** The identity for + is Even, because the column under Even in Table 8.19 is identical to the column at the far left, and the row adjacent to Even is identical to the top row. You can check in the same way that the identity for × is Odd.
5. **Inverse:** The inverse of Even under + is Even because Even + Even = Even. The inverse of Odd under + is Odd, because Odd + Odd = Even. The inverse of Odd under × is Odd because Odd × Odd = Odd. There is no inverse of Even under × (see Definition 8.20, part 4).
6. **Distributive:** The distributive property of × over + holds because it holds for multiplication over addition for the real numbers.

Thus, the set $S = \{$Odd, Even$\}$ with the operations + and × satisfies all the requirements of Definition 8.20, so the system is a field. ∎

Table 8.19

+	Odd	Even
Odd	Even	Odd
Even	Odd	Even

Table 8.20

×	Odd	Even
Odd	Odd	Even
Even	Even	Even

Exercise 8.7

1. Let $S = \{a, b, c\}$, and let $*$ be defined by Table 8.21. Is S a group with respect to the operation $*$?

In problems 2–13, determine whether the given set under the given operation forms a group. For each that is not a group, give one specific example of a condition that is not satisfied.

Table 8.21 *Table for Problem 1*

*	a	b	c
a	b	c	a
b	c	a	b
c	a	b	c

2. The odd integers under the operation of addition
3. The odd integers under the operation of multiplication
4. The even integers under the operation of addition
5. The even integers under the operation of multiplication
6. The positive integers under the operation of addition
7. The positive integers under the operation of multiplication
8. The integers under the operation of addition
9. The integers under the operation of multiplication
10. The real numbers under the operation of multiplication
11. The real numbers under the operation of addition
12. The set $\{-1, 0, 1\}$ under the operation of addition
13. The set $\{-1, 0, 1\}$ under the operation of multiplication
14. Complete Table 8.22 so that the result will be a group under the given operation.
15. Let $S = \{a, b, c, d, e\}$, and let $\#$ be defined on S by Table 8.23. Is the set S under the operation $\#$ a group? If not, give one specific example of a condition that is not satisfied.

Table 8.22 *Table for Problem 14*

#	a	b	c
a			b
b		b	c
c			

In problems 16–20, determine whether the given sets form a field under the operations of addition and multiplication.

16. The set of positive odd integers
17. The set of positive even integers
18. The set of integral multiples of 5
19. The set of integral multiples of 2
20. The set of all real numbers

Table 8.23 *Table for Problem 15*

#	a	b	c	d	e
a	a	b	c	d	e
b	b	e	a	c	d
c	d	c	e	a	b
d	c	d	b	e	a
e	e	a	d	b	c

In Other Words

21. Explain a procedure you can use to verify that the operation $*$ of problem 1 is associative. How many cases do you have to check to be convinced that $*$ is associative?
22. Suppose that an associative operation $\cdot$ is defined for every pair of elements of a set S and that S is closed under this operation. There is a theo-

rem that can save work when trying to show that this system is a group. This theorem says that if there is an identity element e in S such that $e \cdot x = x$ for every element x of S and if every element x of S has an inverse $x^\wedge$ in S such that $x^\wedge \cdot x = e$, then the system is a group. Explain the procedure you would follow to use this theorem to solve problem 1. How many cases do you have to check now?

Using Your Knowledge

If you studied Section 8.3, then you can use what you learned there to answer the following questions. First, however, we define a nonsingular matrix.

> *A square matrix A with an inverse A^{-1} is said to be a **nonsingular matrix**.*

The importance of this definition lies in the fact that every nonsingular matrix has a unique multiplicative inverse. You can see why this is so, because to find the inverse of a matrix A, you must solve a system of linear equations of which A is the matrix of coefficients. This system has a unique solution if and only if A has an inverse.

23. Consider the set of all 2×2 matrices under the operation of matrix addition. Is this system a group? If so, is it a commutative group? Explain.

24. Consider the set of all nonsingular 2×2 matrices under the operation of matrix multiplication. Is this system a group? If so, is it a commutative group? Explain.

25. If you adjoined the matrix

$$\begin{bmatrix} 0 & 0 \\ 0 & 0 \end{bmatrix}$$

to the set of matrices in problem 24, and considered the operations of matrix addition and multiplication, would the system be a field? Explain.

26. Consider the set of all matrices of the special form

$$\begin{bmatrix} a & b \\ -b & a \end{bmatrix}$$

where a and b are real numbers. Is this set a field under matrix addition and multiplication? [*Hint:* You must determine whether the inverse of a matrix in this set is also in the set, and do not forget to check the commutative property of multiplication.]

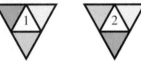

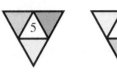

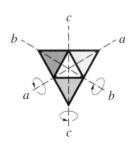

FIGURE 8.10
Rotations of a triangle

Discovery

There is an interesting problem in group theory that is related to the orientations of a triangle in a plane. Figure 8.10 shows the six different orientations that can be obtained by the use of one or more of the following operations.

Operation 1.   *Leave the triangle as is.*
Operation 2.   *Turn the triangle over using the a–a axis.*
Operation 3.   *Rotate the triangle 120° counterclockwise in its own plane.*
Operation 4.   *Turn the triangle over using the b–b axis.*
Operation 5.   *Rotate the triangle 120° clockwise in its own plane.*
Operation 6.   *Turn the triangle over using the c–c axis.*

You can check what we are going to do very easily by cutting an equilateral triangle out of a piece of paper and identifying the small triangles as shown in the figure. Then draw three axes a–a, b–b, c–c on another sheet of paper, which is to be kept in a fixed position. As you can verify, starting with orientation 1, each operation will give the correspondingly numbered new orientation. For instance, operation 5 changes orientation 1 into orientation 5; operation 4 changes orientation 1 into orientation 4.

Let us define an operator C that corresponds to changing from one orientation to another by means of the preceding operations. We could use a symbol such as 3 C 2 to mean that we apply operation 3 to orientation 2. Then the statement 3 C 2 = 6 means that operation 3 applied to orientation 2 gives orientation 6. You should verify that it does. We can also make a table to display the results as shown below, where the numbers in the body of the table give the final orientation in each case. From Table 8.24, we can read 2 C 4 = 3, 3 C 3 = 5, and so on.

27. Can you fill in the rest of Table 8.24?
28. Can you discover the identity for the operator C?
29. You can see from the table that C does not have the commutative property. For instance, 3 C 2 ≠ 2 C 3; the first of these gives 6, and the second gives 4. However, as seems plausible from the physical interpretation

Table 8.24

C	Starting Orientation					
	1	**2**	**3**	**4**	**5**	**6**
1	1	2	3	4	5	6
2	2	1	4	3	6	5
3	3	6	5	2	1	4
4						
5						
6						

Operation

of rotating the triangle in various ways, C does have the associative property. You need not prove this, but do verify it in a few cases. For example, (3 C 4) C 6 = 2 C 6 = 5, and 3 C (4 C 6) = 3 C 3 = 5. Can you now discover if the set {1, 2, 3, 4, 5, 6} is a group with respect to the operation C? (If it is, then it is an illustration of a noncommutative group.)

8.8 GAME THEORY

GETTING STARTED

HAVE IT YOUR WAY

Have you noticed that when a fast food chain such as McDonald's opens a restaurant, another fast food chain, maybe Burger King, starts a competing restaurant within a couple of blocks? Why do you think this happens? Either both chains conduct extensive fast-food demand, demographic, and location surveys, reach the same conclusion, and target the same population, or one of the chains does most of the research and the other just follows. Now, suppose McDonald's and Burger King wish to open restaurants. They can decide to open on opposite sides of town (*O*) or in a central location (*C*) near each other. If they both open on opposite sides of town (*O*), or in a central location (*C*) near each other, each will get 50% of the targeted business. If McDonald's opens in the central location (*C*) and Burger King on another location (*O*), McDonald's gets 70% of the business (and Burger King 30%). However, if McDonald's is on the other side of town (*O*) and Burger King is in the central location (*C*), McDonald's gets 40% of the business (and Burger King 60%). What should each of the franchisers do to insure their greatest incomes? The percentage gains or losses for McDonald's can be the entries in a **payoff matrix,** and the optimal strategies can be obtained by examining the rows and columns in this matrix.

It is not unusual to see competing fast-food franchises in close proximity to one another

Column

$$\begin{array}{c} & H \quad T \\ \textbf{Row} \begin{array}{c} H \\ T \end{array} & \begin{bmatrix} +1 & -1 \\ -1 & +1 \end{bmatrix} \end{array}$$

To see how such a situation can be represented by a matrix, let us look at the simpler game of matching pennies. In this game, two players *R* and *C* each toss a penny. If they match, (*HH* or *TT*), *R* keeps both pennies but if they do not, *C* keeps both pennies. In the matrix representation for this game, the column headings H and T represent the outcomes (Heads or Tails) for *C*, the row headings represent the outcomes for *R*, and the matrix entries give the payoffs for *R*. Note that row 1, column 1 corresponds to the outcome HH, and since there is a match, *R* wins one penny (+1). On the other hand, in row 2, column 1, the outcomes are TH and, since there is no match, *R* loses a penny (−1).

Now, for which of these situations (choosing a location or matching pennies) do you think it is easier to develop a winning strategy? Surprisingly enough, it will be shown in this section that it is easier to develop a winning strategy for the restaurant situation.

In business, economics, sciences, and the military, decisions have to be made in competitive situations that are similar to games played according to formal rules. The branch of mathematics that deals with the analysis of competition and conflict is called **game theory** and was started because of the efforts of John von Neumann, Emil Borel, and Oskar Morgenstern. **Two-person games (or matrix games)** are those that have only two adversaries or players always making intelligent choices. Matching pennies and the selection of a restaurant location by two different franchises are examples of two-person games. Let us construct the **payoff matrix** denoting the percentage gains for McDonald's as described in Getting Started. Here is the information we need:

1. If McDonald's selects O or C, and Burger King chooses the same location, each will get 50% of the business.

2. If McDonald's picks C and Burger King O, McDonald's gets 70% (and Burger King 30%).

3. If McDonald's selects O, and Burger King C, McDonald's gets 40% (and Burger King 60%).

From (1), we can enter 50 in row 1, column 1 and row 2, column 2.
From (2), we can enter 70 in row 1, column 2.
From (3), we can enter 40 in row 2, column 1.

$$\begin{array}{c} \textbf{Burger King} \\ \begin{array}{cc} C & O \end{array} \\ \textbf{McD} \begin{array}{c} C \\ O \end{array} \begin{bmatrix} 50 & 70 \\ 40 & 50 \end{bmatrix} \end{array}$$

This game and the penny-matching game are **constant-sum** games, since the sum of the payoffs is a constant (in the McDonald's–Burger King game, the McDonald's percentage plus the Burger King percentage is a constant 100%). In the penny matching game the sum of the payoffs is 0. Thus, matching pennies is called a **zero-sum** game.

A. *Saddle Points*

In game theory players seek an **optimal strategy,** a strategy that maximizes the player's gain or minimizes his loss. What should the strategy for McDonald's (the row player) be? To select row 1 or row 2? If they select row 1, they have a chance of getting 70% of the business! But the Burger King people will then pick column 1, and each will end up with 50%. Certainly, row 1 is better than row 2 for McDonald's, since the best they can do in row 2 is 50%, but it is also possible to end up with only 40% if Burger King picks column 1. Thus, the best strategy for McDonald's is to **select row 1.** If we think of McDonald's as player R, the row player, this discussion suggests the following method for developing an **optimal pure strategy** for player R.

> **Optimal Pure Strategy for Player R**
> 1. Circle the smallest element in each row.
> 2. Choose the row that has the largest of the circled values.

Note that this strategy guarantees the greatest gain to R, independent of the other player's choice.

What strategy should Burger King follow? If they select column 2, McDonald's will certainly select row 1, giving McDonald's 70% of the business. Thus, the best strategy for Burger King is to **select column 1.**

> **Optimal Pure Strategy for Player C**
> 1. Box the largest element in each column.
> 2. Choose the column with the smallest boxed number.

In this game, the **optimal pure strategy** for McDonald's is to **select row 1** and the **optimal pure strategy** for Burger King is to **select column 1.** Note that 50 is both the **smallest** element in its row and the **largest** element in its column. 50 is called a **saddle point** and it is the **value** of this game.

Definition 8.21

A matrix game is **strictly determined** if there is an entry in the payoff matrix that is both the smallest element in its row and the largest element in its column. Such an entry is called a **saddle point** for the game and the **value** of the game is the value of this saddle point.

EXAMPLE 1 If the entries represent payoff values for the row player, determine which of the following matrices define a strictly determined game and find the value of the game.

(a) $\begin{bmatrix} 1 & 3 & -2 \\ -1 & 0 & 4 \\ 2 & -3 & 1 \end{bmatrix}$ (b) $\begin{bmatrix} -2 & 1 & -3 \\ 3 & 4 & 1 \\ -2 & -4 & -1 \end{bmatrix}$ (c) $\begin{bmatrix} 2 & 3 & 2 & 4 \\ 1 & 4 & -3 & 3 \\ 1 & -1 & 0 & -1 \\ 2 & 4 & 2 & 5 \end{bmatrix}$

Solution (a) For the row player:

1. Circle the smallest element in each row.
   $(-2, -1, \text{ and } -3)$
2. The row player's optimal strategy is to choose the row that has the largest circled value, that is, the row containing -1 (**row 2**).

$\begin{bmatrix} 1 & 3 & \boxed{-2} \\ \boxed{-1} & 0 & 4 \\ 2 & \boxed{-3} & 1 \end{bmatrix}$ ← **Choose row 2**

For the column player:

1. Box the largest element in each column.
   (2, 3, and 4)
2. The column player's optimal strategy is to choose the column with the smallest boxed number, that is, the column containing 2 (**column 1**).

$$\begin{bmatrix} 1 & \boxed{3} & -2 \\ -1 & 0 & \boxed{4} \\ \boxed{2} & -3 & 1 \end{bmatrix}$$

Choose ⟶
column 1

Since there is no value that is both the smallest element in its row and the largest in its column, there is no saddle point. This game is **not strictly determined.**

(b) The row player circles -3, 1 and -4. Since 1 is the **largest** of the three numbers, the row player selects **row 2.** The row player's optimal strategy is to select the row containing 1 (**row 2**).

$$\begin{bmatrix} -2 & 1 & ⦸3 \\ 3 & 4 & ①1 \\ -2 & ⦸4 & -1 \end{bmatrix} \leftarrow \textbf{Choose row 2}$$

The column player boxes 3, 4, and 1. Since 1 is the **smallest** of the three numbers, the optimal strategy for the column player is to select **column 3,** the column containing 1.

$$\begin{bmatrix} -2 & 1 & -3 \\ \boxed{3} & \boxed{4} & \boxed{1} \\ -2 & -4 & -1 \end{bmatrix}$$

↑
Choose
column 3

Since the 1 in the second row, third column is both the **smallest** element in its row and the largest element in its column (it is **circled and boxed**), this is a saddle point. The value of this strictly determined game is 1.

(c) The row player circles the **smallest** numbers in each row, **2** (twice) in row 1, -3 in row 2, -1 (twice) in row 3 and **2** (twice) in row 4. Since 2 is the largest of 2, -3, -1 and 2, the row player should select row 1 or row 4 (each containing 2 twice).

The column player boxes the **largest** number(s) in each column, the **2**'s in column 1, the **4**'s in column 2, the **2**'s in column 3, and **5** in column 4. The column player should select column 1 or 3.

Since the number 2 (columns 1 and 3) is both the smallest element in rows 1 and 4 and the largest element in columns 1 and 3, the game is **strictly determined** and its value is 2, occurring at four different saddle points. Note that 2 is both circled and boxed each time.

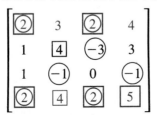

As you can see from Example 1c, a game can have more than one saddle point (four in this case), but they must have the same value.

B. *Mixed Strategies*

The penny-matching game discussed in Getting Started does not have a saddle point. How can we develop a strategy to play this game a large number of times? Clearly, player R should not always play the same strategy (say, H) for if he did, player C might always play T and win! So, R must play H some fraction p of the time and win $(+1)$ and T the rest, or $1 - p$ of the time, and lose (-1). What can C do? Let us look at the payoff matrix.

If C always chooses H, R's expected payoff is:

$$E_H = (p)(1) + (1 - p)(-1) = 2p - 1$$

If C always chooses T, R's expected payoff is:

$$E_T = (p)(-1) + (1 - p)(1) = -2p + 1$$

Column

$$\begin{array}{c} \\ \textbf{Row} \end{array} \begin{array}{c} H \\ T \end{array} \begin{array}{cc} H & T \\ \begin{bmatrix} +1 & -1 \\ -1 & +1 \end{bmatrix} \end{array}$$

Note that these two equations can be obtained by multiplying $[p \quad 1 - p]$ by the first and second columns, respectively, in the payoff matrix. Since the expected payoff for R should be the same, regardless of C's choice.

$$E_H = E_T$$

or

$$2p - 1 = -2p + 1$$

Solving for p

$$p = \frac{1}{2}$$

This means that if C chooses H, R's expected payoff will be

$$E_H = 2p - 1 = 2\left(\frac{1}{2}\right) - 1 = 0$$

and if C chooses T, R's expected payoff will be:

$$E_T = -2p + 1 = -2\left(\frac{1}{2}\right) + 1 = 0$$

EXAMPLE 2   At the present time most restaurants have a smoking section (S) and a non-smoking section (N). Suppose that the average smoker spends $15 per meal, and the average non-smoker $10. A customer enters a restaurant and the manager has designated smoking and non-smoking sections. If the person is a smoker and the smoking section is open, the restaurant makes $15, but if only the non-smoking section is open, the smoker leaves and the restaurant makes nothing. If the customer is a non-smoker and only the smoking section is available, the non-smoker will leave and the restaurant will make nothing, while if the person is a non-smoker and the non-smoking section is open, the restaurant will make $10.

(a) Construct the payoff matrix for the manager.
(b) Is there a saddle point for this game?
(c) What proportion of the customers should the manager expect to be smokers and what proportion non-smokers?

Solution   (a) If we use the row for the manager's choice and the columns for the customer's choice, the payoff matrix is:

$$
\begin{array}{c}
\textbf{Customer} \\
\begin{array}{cc}
S & N
\end{array} \\
\textbf{Manager}\;
\begin{array}{c}
S \\ N
\end{array}
\begin{bmatrix}
\$15 & 0 \\
0 & \$10
\end{bmatrix}
\end{array}
$$

(b)

$$
\begin{array}{c}
\textbf{Customer} \\
\begin{array}{cc}
S & N
\end{array} \\
\textbf{Manager}\;
\begin{array}{c}
S \\ N
\end{array}
\begin{bmatrix}
\boxed{\$15} & \boxed{0} \\
\boxed{0} & \boxed{\$10}
\end{bmatrix}
\end{array}
$$

There is no saddle point for this matrix.

(c) Let p be the proportion of customers that are smokers and $1 - p$ the proportion that are non-smokers. The manager's expectation from a smoking customer is:

$$E_s = p(15) + (1 - p)(0) = 15p$$

The manager's expectation from a nonsmoking customer is:

$$E_N = p(0) + (1 - p)(10) = 10 - 10p$$

To make each customer's payoff be the same, we must have

$$E_S = E_N$$
$$15p = 10 - 10p$$
$$25p = 10$$

or $$p = \frac{2}{5}$$

Thus, the manager should expect $\frac{2}{5}$ of his customers to be smokers and $\frac{3}{5}$ to be non-smokers.

EXAMPLE 3 How hard do you study for your tests? It probably depends on the subject and your instructor's reputation. The payoff matrix gives the average grade expectations for students when a test that can be classified as Hard (H), Medium (M), or Easy (E) is given.

Instructor

$$\text{Student} \quad \begin{matrix} & H & M & E \\ H \\ M \\ E \end{matrix} \begin{bmatrix} 70 & 80 & 90 \\ 75 & 70 & 80 \\ 50 & 60 & 70 \end{bmatrix}$$

Based on this information, what type of test should students expect?

Solution First, we note that there is no saddle point. Think of the students and the instructor as competitors in a two person game. Certainly, the students would never choose row 3, since all the grades there are lower than the corresponding grades in row 1. Thus, the students eliminate row 3. (We say that row 1 **dominates** row 3). The result is:

Instructor

$$\text{Student} \quad \begin{matrix} & H & M & E \\ H \\ M \end{matrix} \begin{bmatrix} 70 & 80 & 90 \\ 75 & 70 & 80 \end{bmatrix}$$

On the other hand, the instructor would never let the students make 90s and 80s, that is, would never choose column 3. (Note that both columns 1 and 2 **dominate** column 3, since their corresponding values are smaller than those in column 3). Thus, we can eliminate column 3 from further consideration, leaving the 2 × 2 matrix

Instructor

$$\text{Student} \quad \begin{matrix} & H & M \\ H \\ M \end{matrix} \begin{bmatrix} 70 & 80 \\ 75 & 70 \end{bmatrix}$$

Now, let h be the proportion of the times a hard test is given. Then $1 - h$ of the time the test will not be hard. The student's expectation for a hard test is:

$$E_h = h(70) + (1 - h)(75)$$

The student's expectation for not having a hard test is:

$$E_n = h(80) + (1 - h)(70)$$

Thus,

$$h(70) + (1 - h)(75) = h(80) + (1 - h)(70)$$

or $\qquad -5h + 75 = 10h + 70$

Solving for h,

$$h = \frac{1}{3}$$

Thus, based on the information given, the students should expect a hard test $\frac{1}{3}$ of the time and a medium test $\frac{2}{3}$ of the time. No easy tests are given! ∎

Exercise 8.8

In problems 1–8 decide whether the payoff matrix represents a strictly determined game. If the game is strictly determined, find the optimal pure strategy for each player and the value of the game.

1. $\begin{bmatrix} 4 & 5 \\ 2 & 3 \end{bmatrix}$

2. $\begin{bmatrix} 3 & 1 \\ 2 & 0 \end{bmatrix}$

3. $\begin{bmatrix} 5 & 2 \\ 3 & 4 \end{bmatrix}$

4. $\begin{bmatrix} -3 & 2 \\ 0 & -3 \end{bmatrix}$

5. $\begin{bmatrix} 6 & 6 & 4 \\ 2 & -5 & -10 \\ 5 & 5 & -15 \end{bmatrix}$

6. $\begin{bmatrix} 10 & -3 & -8 \\ 12 & -2 & 5 \\ 8 & 0 & 4 \end{bmatrix}$

7. $\begin{bmatrix} 1 & 6 & -2 \\ 3 & 5 & 2 \\ 4 & 5 & 4 \end{bmatrix}$

8. $\begin{bmatrix} 5 & 1 & 2 \\ 8 & 0 & -4 \\ 4 & 1 & 3 \end{bmatrix}$

In problems 9–12,

    (a) Determine whether there is a saddle point.
    (b) Find the mixed strategy for the row player.

9. $\begin{bmatrix} 2 & 1 \\ -1 & 4 \end{bmatrix}$

10. $\begin{bmatrix} 3 & 2 \\ 2 & 4 \end{bmatrix}$

11. $\begin{bmatrix} 3 & -2 \\ -1 & 0 \end{bmatrix}$

12. $\begin{bmatrix} 10 & 5 \\ 6 & 12 \end{bmatrix}$

13. Use the given payoff matrix to find the optimal mixed strategy and the value of the game for the row player.

$$\begin{bmatrix} 6 & 0 \\ 2 & 4 \\ 0 & 3 \end{bmatrix}$$

14. Use the given payoff matrix to find the optimal mixed strategy and the value of the game for the row player.

$$\begin{bmatrix} 5 & 30 \\ 0 & 20 \\ 25 & 15 \end{bmatrix}$$

15. You are preparing for a test, but you don't know whether it is an essay test or a multiple choice test. You can spend 2 hours or 4 hours studying for this test and the table shows the probable scores that you would make. Based on this table, what should you do?

		Essay	Multiple Choice
Study	2hr	70	80
	4hr	85	75

16. John must prepare for an English test and for a math test. He decides to study 3 hours for one of the tests and 2 hours for the other test. The table shows the probable scores he would make. What should he do?

	English	Math
English 2hr Math 3hr	80	85
English 3hr Math 2hr	90	75

17. Ann is planning to invest some of her savings in bonds, stocks, and money market funds. Her expected return will depend on whether interest rates rise or fall during the year. The table shows the expected returns. Find Ann's optimum investment strategy and the corresponding expected return.

	Interest Rates	
	Rise(%)	Fall(%)
Bonds	6	11
Stocks	10	12
Money market	15	10

18. When stocks increase in price on a certain day, their prices tend to decrease the next day and vice versa. The payoff matrix shows the pertinent percents. In the long run, what fraction of the time will the stock increase in price?

Tomorrow's Price

		Increase	Decrease
Today's	Increase	0.2	0.8
Price	Decrease	0.6	0.4

19. Two gas stations R and C are competing with each other at a certain location. The percentage of the business captured by each station is dependent on the price and given in the payoff matrix:

Station C

		$1.00	$1.10
Station R	$1.00	60%	50%
	$1.10	30%	70%

How should station R price its gasoline?

20. Manhattan is divided into three sectors: Uptown (U), Midtown (M), and Lower (L). The proportions of the time that a taxicab operating in Manhattan picks up a passenger in any sector and drops the passenger off in any sector are given by the payoff matrix.

Drop Off

		U	M	L
	U	0.5	0.4	0.1
Pick Up	M	0.3	0.6	0.1
	L	0.2	0.3	0.1

What is the expected percent of fares going from upper Manhattan to a different sector?

21. Car manufacturers' ads rely on the performance or safety of the cars being advertised. Market studies show that ads based on performance are effective for 70% of the young buyers and 20% of the old buyers, while ads based on safety are effective for 80% of the old buyers and 40% of the young buyers. If this process is viewed as a game between the manufacturer and buyers,

  (a) Give the payoff matrix for the game.

  (b) In what proportion should the two kinds of ads be mixed for maximum effectiveness?

22. You and your friend play a game with pennies and nickels. Each of you puts down a coin. If the coins match, you take both, and if they do not match, your friend takes both. Write the matrix for this game. What is your optimal mixed strategy and what is your corresponding expected pay-off for this game?

23. A farmer has a large acreage planted in strawberries. A freeze is predicted and the farmer must decide whether to turn on his water sprays to protect the crop. He estimates that if there is a freeze and he turns on the sprays, he will save the crop and be able to sell it for $6000. If there is no freeze, he will be out the $400 in water and pumping costs. If he does not turn on the sprays and there is a freeze, he will lose $4000, but if there is no freeze, he can sell the crop for $4000. Make a matrix to show these figures and find the farmer's optimal mixed strategy and his corresponding expected payoff.

In Other Words

24. Why do you think the value of a strictly determined game is called a saddle point?

25. Explain why, when a row i dominates another row j in a payoff matrix, j can be eliminated.

26. Explain why, when a column i dominates a column j in a payoff matrix, j can be eliminated.

Using Your Knowledge

We are now ready to use your knowledge in love games. A young student is planning to send flowers, poems, or candy to his sweetheart but there are several things to take into account. She may be allergic to flowers or on a very strict diet. The payoff matrix for the situation is:

		Sweetheart's Response	
		Allergic	On a diet
	Flowers	−3	4
He Sends	Poems	2	5
	Candy	3	−2

27. Which of the rows is dominated by row 2?

28. Which row can be eliminated?

29. What is the optimal mixed strategy for the student?

30. What is the student's expected value for this love game?

Chapter 8 Summary

Section	Item	Meaning	Example
8.1	Matrix	A rectangular array of numbers enclosed in square brackets (or parentheses)	$\begin{bmatrix} 3 & 4 \\ 5 & 6 \end{bmatrix}$
8.1	$A = B$	The corresponding elements of matrices A and B are equal.	$\begin{bmatrix} 2 & 4 \\ 5 & 6 \end{bmatrix} = \begin{bmatrix} \frac{6}{3} & 2 \cdot 2 \\ 3 + 2 & 6 \end{bmatrix}$
8.1A	kA	Multiplication of each element of the matrix A by the number k	$3\begin{bmatrix} 1 & 2 \\ 3 & 4 \end{bmatrix} = \begin{bmatrix} 3 & 6 \\ 9 & 12 \end{bmatrix}$
8.1A	$A + B$	The sum of the matrices A and B	$\begin{bmatrix} 1 & 2 \\ 3 & 4 \end{bmatrix} + \begin{bmatrix} 4 & 5 \\ 3 & 2 \end{bmatrix} = \begin{bmatrix} 5 & 7 \\ 6 & 6 \end{bmatrix}$
8.1B	AB	The product of the matrices A and B	$[3 \quad 4]\begin{bmatrix} 1 & 2 \\ 0 & 5 \end{bmatrix} = [3 \quad 26]$
8.1C	I	The identity matrix	For a 2×2 matrix, $I = \begin{bmatrix} 1 & 0 \\ 0 & 1 \end{bmatrix}$
8.3	A^{-1}	The inverse of the matrix A	If $A = \begin{bmatrix} 2 & 3 \\ 1 & 2 \end{bmatrix}$, then $A^{-1} = \begin{bmatrix} 2 & -3 \\ -1 & 2 \end{bmatrix}$
8.4	Mathematical system	A set of elements with one or more operations, relations, and rules, axioms, or laws	The set of integers with the four fundamental operations
8.5	$a \equiv b \pmod{m}$	$a - b$ is a multiple of m	$3 \equiv 8 \pmod 5$
8.6	Closure property	A set S is closed under an operation $*$ if, for all a and b in A, $a * b$ is in A.	
8.6	Associative property	An operation $*$ is associative if, for all a, b, c in A, $(a * b) * c = a * (b * c)$.	
8.6	Commutative property	An operation $*$ is commutative if, for all a and b in A, $a * b = b * a$.	

Section	Item	Meaning	Example
8.6	Identity	An element e is an identity for $*$ if, for every a in A, $a * e = a = e * a$.	
8.6	Inverse	An element b is the inverse of a if $a * b = e = b * a$ (e is the identity for $*$).	
8.6	Distributive property	The operation $*$ is distributive over the operation $\#$ if, for every a, b, c in A, $a * (b \# c) = (a * b) \# (a * c)$.	
8.7	Group	A mathematical system consisting of a set S and an operation $*$ that has the closure, associative, identity, and inverse properties	
8.7	Commutative group	A group with the commutative property	
8.7	Field	A set S and the operations $*$ and $\#$ with the closure, associative, commutative, and identity properties; the distributive property of $\#$ with respect to $*$; and the inverse property (except that there is no inverse for the identity with respect to $*$)	
8.8	Zero-sum game	A game in which the payoff to one player is the opposite of the payoff of the opposing player.	
8.8a	Optimal Strategy	A strategy that maximizes the player's gain or minimizes his loss.	
8.8a	Strictly determined game	A game in which the payoff game matrix has a saddle point	
8.8a	Saddle point	A point in the payoff matrix that is both the smallest element in its row and the largest element in its column	

Research Questions

Sources of information for these questions can be found in the Bibliography at the end of the book.

1. Write a report on the uses of matrices in science with particular emphasis on the work of Werner Heisenberg, W. J. Duncan, and A. R. Collar.
2. Find out which mathematician first introduced the term *matrix*.
3. Who received the 1973 Nobel Prize for economics and how did he use matrices?
4. Write a report on how matrices are used in game theory and the contribution of John von Neumann to this field.
5. In 1858 Arthur Cayley, an English mathematician, published *A Memoir on the Theory of Matrices*. What was discussed in this book, and what was the name of the only theorem appearing in the book?
6. In the Human Side of Mathematics it was stated that Sophie Germain won a French Academy prize for one of her research papers. Write a short report detailing the name of this paper and its content.
7. Emmy Noether (1882–1935) was a creative mathematician who made significant contributions to the area of abstract algebra. Write a short report about the life of this famous woman.

Chapter 8 Practice Test

1. Given the three matrices below, find x and y so that $2A + B = C$.

$$A = \begin{bmatrix} 2 & x \\ 3 & y \end{bmatrix} \qquad B = \begin{bmatrix} 2 & -1 \\ 3 & 2 \end{bmatrix} \qquad C = \begin{bmatrix} 6 & 5 \\ 9 & 10 \end{bmatrix}$$

2. If

$$A = \begin{bmatrix} 4 & -5 \\ 1 & -1 \end{bmatrix} \quad \text{and} \quad B = \begin{bmatrix} -1 & 5 \\ -1 & 4 \end{bmatrix}$$

calculate AB and BA.

3. To build three types of zig-zag toys, the Zee-Zee Toy Company requires materials as listed below. Suppose that Zee-Zee decides to build 20 type I, 25 type II, and 10 type III zig-zag toys. Use matrices to find the number of units of frames, wheels, chains, and paint needed for the job.

Type	Frames	Wheels	Chains	Paint
I	1	2	1	1
II	1	3	2	1
III	4	4	2	2

4. Zee-Zee finds that frames cost $2 each, wheels $1 each, chains 75¢ each, and paint 50¢ per unit. Use matrices to find the total cost of these items for each type of zig-zag toy in problem 3.

For problems 5–9, suppose that

$$A = \begin{bmatrix} 2 & 0 & 1 \\ 2 & -1 & 3 \\ 4 & 1 & 2 \end{bmatrix} \quad \text{and} \quad B = \begin{bmatrix} -2 & 1 & 0 \\ 4 & 3 & -2 \\ 1 & 2 & -1 \end{bmatrix}$$

5. Find $2A - 3B$.

6. Find $A + B$.

7. Find AB and BA.

8. Find $(A + B)^2$.

9. Verify that

$$A^{-1} = \frac{1}{4} \begin{bmatrix} 5 & -1 & -1 \\ -8 & 0 & 4 \\ -6 & 2 & 2 \end{bmatrix}$$

10. Find M^{-1} if

$$M = \begin{bmatrix} 3 & 1 \\ 2 & -1 \end{bmatrix}$$

11. Use the method of reducing the augmented matrix to echelon form to solve the system $AX = D$, where

$$A = \begin{bmatrix} 2 & 0 & 1 \\ 2 & -1 & 3 \\ 4 & 1 & 2 \end{bmatrix} \quad X = \begin{bmatrix} x \\ y \\ z \end{bmatrix} \quad D = \begin{bmatrix} 1 \\ 9 \\ 0 \end{bmatrix}$$

12. Use the matrix A^{-1} of problem 9 to solve the system of problem 11.

13. Use matrices to solve the system

$$x + 3y = 19$$
$$y + 3z = 10$$
$$z + 3x = -5$$

14. Find the inverse of the matrix

$$\begin{bmatrix} -1 & 1 & 0 \\ 4 & 3 & -2 \\ 2 & 2 & -1 \end{bmatrix}$$

15. Use your answer to problem 14 to solve the system

$$-x + y = 5$$
$$4x + 3y - 2z = 7$$
$$2x + 2y - z = 5$$

16. Show that the following matrix has no inverse:

$$\begin{bmatrix} 3 & 3 & 3 \\ 4 & 2 & 0 \\ 3 & 3 & 3 \end{bmatrix}$$

17. On counting the money in her piggy bank, Sally found that she had 122 coins, all nickels, dimes, and quarters. If the total value of the coins was $15, and the total value of the quarters was four times the total value of the nickels, how many of each kind of coin did Sally have?

18. The augmented matrix of a system of three equations in the three unknowns x, y, z is reduced to the following form:

$$\left[\begin{array}{ccc|c} 2 & 1 & 1 & 1 \\ 0 & 3 & 2 & 4 \\ 0 & 0 & 1 & 2 \end{array}\right]$$

Find the solution of the system.

19. Suppose the reduced matrix in problem 18 read as follows:

$$\left[\begin{array}{ccc|c} 2 & 1 & 1 & 1 \\ 0 & 3 & 2 & 4 \\ 0 & 0 & 0 & 2 \end{array}\right]$$

What can be said about the system of equations?

20. Suppose the reduced matrix in problem 18 read as follows:

$$\left[\begin{array}{ccc|c} 2 & 1 & 1 & 1 \\ 0 & 3 & 2 & 4 \\ 0 & 0 & 0 & 0 \end{array}\right]$$

In problems 21–22, find the answer in 12-hour clock arithmetic.

21. (a) $3 \oplus 11$ (b) $8 \oplus 9$ (c) $3 \ominus 9$ (d) $5 \ominus 12$

22. (a) $3 \otimes 5$ (b) $6 \otimes 8$ (c) $\frac{3}{11}$ (d) $\frac{5}{6}$

23. Are the following statements true or false?
    (a) $5 \equiv 2 \pmod 3$ (b) $9 \equiv 5 \pmod 4$
    (c) $9 \equiv 2 \pmod 6$

24. Find the value of n.
    (a) $3 + 2 \equiv n \pmod 5$ (b) $4 \times 3 \equiv n \pmod 5$
    (c) $2 - 4 \equiv n \pmod 5$ (d) $\frac{3}{2} \equiv n \pmod 5$

In problems 25 and 26, find all possible replacements for n for which the given
congruence is true.

25. (a) $6 + n \equiv 1 \pmod 7$ (b) $3 - n \equiv 4 \pmod 7$

26. (a) $2n \equiv 1 \pmod 3$ (b) $\dfrac{n}{2} \equiv 2 \pmod 3$

Problems 27–31 refer to the operation * defined by the table in the margin.

*	#	$	%	¢
#	#	$	%	¢
$	$	%	¢	#
%	%	¢	#	$
¢	¢	#	$	%

27. Is the set $S = \{\#, \$, \%, ¢\}$ closed with respect to the operation * ? Ex-
plain.

28. Use the table to find the result of each of the following operations:
    (a) $(\$ * ¢) * \#$ (b) $\$ * (¢ * \#)$ (c) $(\$ * \#) * (\% * ¢)$

29. Is the operation * commutative? Explain.

30. Find the identity element for the operation * .

31. Find the inverse of:
    (a) #   (b) $ (c) %   (d) ¢

@	$	#	&
$	&	$	#
#	#	&	$
&	$	#	&

32. The table in the margin defines the operation @.
   (a) Find the identity element if there is one.
   (b) Does any element have an inverse?
   (c) Is the operation commutative?

In problems 33 and 34, suppose that a S b means to select the second of the two numbers a and b, and a L b means to select the lesser of the two numbers (if the numbers are equal, select the number).

33. Is S distributive over L? Explain.
34. Is L distributive over S? Explain.
35. Is the set $\{0, 1, 2\}$ together with addition modulo 3 a commutative group? Explain.
36. Is the set $\{1, 2\}$ together with multiplication modulo 3 a commutative group? Explain.
37. Is the set of all rational numbers along with the ordinary operations of addition and multiplication a field? Explain.

$\oplus$	0	1
0	0	1
1	1	0

$\otimes$	0	1
0	0	0
1	0	1

Problems 38–40 refer to the set $\{0, 1\}$ and the operations $\oplus$ and $\otimes$ as defined by the tables in the margin.

38. Is the set $\{0, 1\}$ together with the operation $\oplus$ a group?
39. Is the set $\{0, 1\}$ together with the operation $\otimes$ a group?
40. Is the set $\{0, 1\}$ together with the two operations $\oplus$ and $\otimes$ a field?

In problems 41–43, determine which of the following payoff matrices represent strictly determined games and find their values.

41. $\begin{bmatrix} -2 & 0 & 8 \\ 1 & 3 & -2 \\ 2 & -3 & 1 \end{bmatrix}$ 42. $\begin{bmatrix} -2 & -4 & -1 \\ -4 & 2 & -6 \\ 3 & 4 & 1 \end{bmatrix}$ 43. $\begin{bmatrix} 1 & 2 & 1 & 4 \\ 1 & -1 & 0 & 1 \\ 2 & 8 & -6 & 6 \\ 2 & 3 & 2 & 4 \end{bmatrix}$

44. In the following strictly determined game, find the optimal pure strategy for player R and give the payoff when both players use their optimal strategy.
$$\begin{bmatrix} 4 & -6 \\ 2 & -7 \end{bmatrix}$$

45. The Hills Area Rapid Transit (HART) is planning a new rapid transit system. Planners estimate that 60% of the commuters presently using HART will continue to do so next year but that 40% of them will switch to using their own cars. On the other hand, the planners predict that 30% of commuters presently using their own cars this year will switch to HART but 70% will continue to use cars.
   (a) Give the payoff matrix for the game.
   (b) What is the expected percentage of commuters using HART next year?

We use counting every day. "How many shopping days are left until Christmas?" or "How many students are in your class?" In this chapter, we shall study how to determine the number of ways in which more complicated events can occur without actually counting them. For example, do you know in how many ways 6 numbers can be picked from a set of 49 numbers? The answer is 13,983,816. You can see that your chances of picking the right numbers to win a lottery jackpot are pretty slim. The counting methods discussed in this chapter are:

1. **Tree diagrams,** a useful technique when the number of outcomes is small.

2. The **sequential counting principle,** a method based on generalizations made about tree diagrams.

3. **Permutations,** a procedure that counts the number of ordered arrangements that can be made with r objects selected from a set of n objects.

4. **Combinations,** a method that counts arrangements, like permutations, but is used when the order is not important.

All of these counting techniques will be extremely useful when we discuss probability in the next chapter. Make sure you master the techniques in this chapter before you go on.

Counting Techniques

**Gottfried Wilhelm Leibniz
(1646–1716)**

In his dream of a "universal characteristic" Leibniz was well over two centuries ahead of his age.

E. T. Bell

THE HUMAN SIDE OF MATHEMATICS

Gottfried Wilhelm Leibniz was born in Leipzig, Germany, in 1646. At an early age, he had mastered the then current textbook knowledge of mathematics, philosophy, theology, and law. By the time he was 20, he had already begun to have ideas for a kind of *universal mathematics,* which later developed into the symbolic logic of George Boole.

When, supposedly because of his youth, he was refused the doctor of laws degree at the University of Leipzig, he moved to Nuremberg. There, a brilliant dissertation on a historical method of teaching law earned him the doctorate at the University of Altdorf in 1666. The rest of his career was spent in the diplomatic service for the estate of the Duke of Brunswick at Hanover.

In 1672, while on a diplomatic visit to Paris, he met physicist Christian Huygens, whom he persuaded to teach him some mathematics. Then, in 1673, on a visit to London, he became acquainted with some British mathematicians and he exhibited his calculating machine (the first mechanical device that could do multiplication). This and some of his earlier work earned him a foreign membership in the Royal Society.

Leibniz's appointment at Hanover allowed him ample time to devote to his favorite studies, and he produced an enormous number of papers on a variety of subjects. His writings on philosophy were highly regarded, and he made contributions to law, religion, history, literature, and logic. In 1682, he helped establish a journal, the *Acta Eruditorum,* of which he became editor-in-chief. Most of his mathematical papers appeared in this journal from 1682 to 1692.

Looking Ahead: Leibniz's outstanding achievements in mathematics were his discovery of *calculus* (independent of Isaac Newton) and his work on *combinatorial analysis,* which involves counting techniques, the subject of this chapter.

9.1   THE SEQUENTIAL COUNTING PRINCIPLE (SCP): A PROBLEM-SOLVING TOOL

GETTING STARTED

TREES AND BREAKFAST POSSIBILITIES

Why does it seem nearly impossible to win the lottery, or open a combination lock by just guessing at the numbers? Because the number of possibilities is so large. Let us consider an easier problem. At breakfast, the server asks: how do you want your eggs? Fried (f), poached (p), or scrambled (s)? Rye (r) or white toast (w)? Juice (j) or coffee (c)? How many choices do you have? To answer this type of question we may try a tree diagram, a picture that details the possibilities at each step. In this case, the diagram will be a *three*-step process (pick eggs, toast, and beverage). The first step will have three branches indicating the 3 different ways in which you can order your eggs, as shown in Figure 9.1. Each of the three branches will have two branches (rye or white) and each of these branches will have two other branches (coffee or juice). The total number of possibilities corresponds to the number of branches, $3 \times 2 \times 2 = 12$. By tracing each path from left to right you can see all possible combinations. For example, the third choice in the list is *fwc* (fried egg, white toast, and coffee).

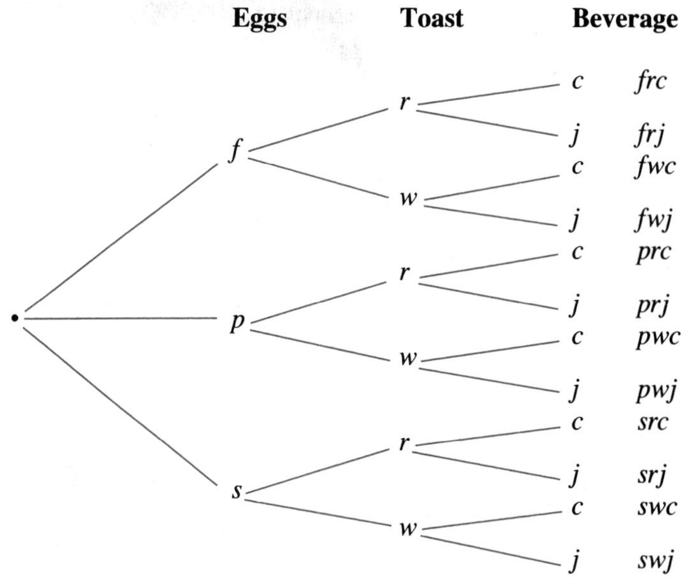

Eggs   **Toast**   **Beverage**

		c — frc
	r	
f		*j* — frj
		c — fwc
	w	
		j — fwj
		c — prc
	r	
p		*j* — prj
		c — pwc
	w	
		j — pwj
		c — src
	r	
s		*j* — srj
		c — swc
	w	
		j — swj

FIGURE 9.1

Let us look at an easier lottery example called Cash 3 played with three identical urns, each containing ten balls numbered from 0 to 9. A ball is chosen from the first urn (10 choices), then another one from the second urn (10 choices), and a third ball from the last urn (10 choices). How many possibilities are there in all? If we drew the tree diagram, it would have $10 \times 10 \times 10 = 1000$ branches, the number of possibilities for Cash 3. What about the combination lock? Since there are 40 possible numbers to choose as your first number, 40 for the second, and 40 for the third, the total number of possibilities is $40 \times 40 \times 40 = 64{,}000$. That is why it is nearly impossible to open the lock just by picking numbers at random!

In this section we will study tree diagrams and then develop a formula for counting the number of possibilities associated with different events.

Counting is not always as easy as 1, 2, 3. For example, can you tell in how many different ways Funky Winkerbean can answer the questions on a true/false test? There are many situations in which the answer to the question, "How many?" is the first step in the solution of a problem. In Section 1.2, we counted the number of subsets of a given set, and in Section 1.5, we used Venn diagrams to count the number of elements of various sets. In this chapter, we shall consider a few counting techniques that are important in many applications and that we shall use in Chapter 10 when we study probability.

FUNKY WINKERBEAN by Tom Batiuk

Reprinted With special permission of North America Syndicate, Inc.

A. *Tree Diagrams*

Let us return to Funky Winkerbean. He is still taking a true/false test and guessing at the answers. If we assume that there are just two questions and that Funky answers both, in how many different ways can he respond?

In order to answer this question, we have to find all the possible ways in which the two questions can be answered. We do this by constructing a **tree diagram,** as shown in Figure 9.2. In the figure, the first set of branches of the tree shows the two ways in which the first question can be answered (*T* for true, *F* for false), while the second set of branches shows the ways in which the second question can be answered. By tracing each path from left to right, we find that there are four end results, which correspond to the $2 \times 2 = 4$ ways in which the two questions can be answered. The four possibilities are *TT*, *TF*, *FT*, and *FF*.

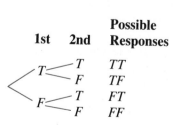

1st	2nd	Possible Responses
T	*T*	*TT*
	F	*TF*
F	*T*	*FT*
	F	*FF*

FIGURE 9.2

The tree diagram technique is used again in the next example.

EXAMPLE 1   A woman desires to purchase a car. She has a choice of two body styles (convertible or hardtop) and three colors (red, blue, or green). Make a tree diagram and find how many choices she has.

Solution   We make a tree diagram as in the Funky Winkerbean problem. As shown in Figure 9.3, for each of the body styles, convertible (c) or hardtop (h), the women has three choices of color, red (r), blue (b), or green (g). Thus, she has $2 \times 3 = 6$ choices.

Body Style	Color	Possible Choices
c	r	Convertible, red
	b	Convertible, blue
	g	Convertible, green
h	r	Hardtop, red
	b	Hardtop, blue
	g	Hardtop, green

FIGURE 9.3

B. *Sequential Counting Principle (SCP)*

In Example 1, we found that if there are 2 ways to do a thing (select a body style) and 3 ways to do a second thing (select a color), then there are $2 \times 3 = 6$ ways of doing the two things in succession in the stated order. This example illustrates a basic principle:

Sequential Counting Principle (SCP)

If an event can occur in m ways and a second event can then occur in n ways, then the sequence of two events can occur in $m \times n$ ways.

(The SCP is sometimes called the **FCP, fundamental counting principle.**)

Note that it is assumed that the second event can occur in n ways for *each* of the ways that the first event can occur.

For example, the number of ways in which two cards can be drawn in succession from a pack of 52 cards is $52 \times 51 = 2652$, because the first card can be drawn in 52 ways, while the second card can be drawn in only 51 ways. If the first card is returned to the deck (before the second card is drawn), then the answer is 52×52.

EXAMPLE 2   Johnny's Homestyle Restaurant has 12 different meals and 5 different desserts on the menu. How many meal choices followed by a dessert does a customer have?

Solution   There are 12 choices for the meal and 5 choices for the dessert. Thus, by the SCP, there are $12 \times 5 = 60$ choices in all.   ∎

The SCP can be extended to cases in which 3, 4, or more things occur in succession. Thus, if the customer in Example 2 also has the choice of selecting a cookie (vanilla, chocolate, or almond) to go with the dessert, then the number of choices the customer has is

$$12 \times 5 \times 3 = 180$$

We now state a more general sequential counting principle.

> **Sequential Counting Principle (SCP)**
>
> If an event can occur in m ways and a second event can then occur in n ways, and a third event can then occur in r ways, and so on, then the sequence of events can occur in $m \times n \times r \times \cdots$ ways.

EXAMPLE 3   In the cartoon on page 361, Charlie Brown has just received a chain letter. If he sends this letter to 6 of his friends, and these 6 friends send letters to 6 of their friends, and all these people send letters to 6 of their friends, how many letters will be sent?

Solution   Charlie Brown sends 6 letters, and each of the people receiving one of these sends 6 letters. Thus, by the SCP, these 6 people send a total of $6 \times 6 = 36$ letters. Then, each of the 36 people receiving one of these sends 6 letters. Again by the SCP, these 36 people send a total of $6 \times 6 \times 6 = 216$ letters. Therefore, the total number of letters is

$$6 + (6 \times 6) + (6 \times 6 \times 6) = 258$$ ∎

EXAMPLE 4   Alice and Betsy agreed to meet at 2:00 P.M. and go shopping in one of the three clothing stores in their hometown. However, they forgot to specify which store. If Alice and Betsy were both on time and each went to one of the three stores, find

(a) The number of ways in which they could miss each other.
(b) The number of ways in which they could meet.

Solution   (a) Alice could go to any one of the 3 stores and Betsy could go to either of the remaining 2 stores.
Thus, by the SCP, there would be

$$3 \times 2 = 6$$

ways in which they could miss each other.

(b) In order to meet, they would both have to go to the same one of the 3 stores. Thus, there are just 3 ways in which they could meet. ▪

Sometimes it is advantageous to use a diagram to represent the individual events in a sequence of events. For example, suppose we want to find out how many different combinations of telephone numbers are possible. Since phone numbers consist of a three digit area code, followed by a seven digit number (ten digits in all), we must find the number of ways in which the squares in the diagram can be filled.

That number is $10 \times 10 \times 10 \cdots \times 10 = 10^{10}$ or 10 billion numbers. But wait, there are some restrictions:

1. The area code cannot begin with 0 or 1 (Why?)
2. The second digit in the area code must be 0 or 1
3. The seven digit number after the area code cannot begin with 0 or 1

Now, how many telephone numbers are possible? To solve this new problem we will again use the preceding diagram to represent the individual numbers to be picked in the sequence as shown.

Problem Solving: The Sequential Counting Principle

How many telephone numbers can be made using the three given restrictions?

1. Read the problem.
2. Select the unknown.
3. Think of a plan.
We have to find the number of choices we have to fill each of the 10 boxes.
4. Use the SCP to carry out the plan.
How many numbers can we place in the first box?
In the second box?
In the third box?
In the fourth box?
In each of the remaining six boxes?
5. Verify the solution.

Pay particular attention to the three given restrictions. We want to find the number of phone numbers that are possible under the given conditions.
The idea is to find the number of ways in which each of the 10 boxes can be filled and then use the SCP to find the total number of possibilities. Note that special restrictions apply to box 1 (no 0's or 1's), box 2 (must be 0 or 1) and box 4 (no 0's or 1's).

The first restriction permits us to use **8** numbers (2, 3, 4, 5, 6, 7, 8, 9) in box 1, the second restriction lets us use **2** numbers (0, 1) in box 2, there are no restrictions for the third box so we can use 10 numbers in box 3, the third restriction allows **8** numbers in box 4 (no 0's or 1's) and **10** numbers in each of the remaining 6 boxes. Using the SCP the number of different telephone numbers is:

$$(\boxed{8}\,\boxed{2}\,\boxed{10})\ \boxed{8}\ \boxed{10}\ \boxed{10}\ —\ \boxed{10}\ \boxed{10}\,\boxed{10}\ \boxed{10}$$

$$128 \times 10^7 = 1{,}280{,}000{,}000$$

TRY EXAMPLE 5 NOW.

Cover the solution, write your own, and then check your work.

EXAMPLE 5   A game consists of 4 cubes, each with 6 different words or phrases inscribed, one on each face. If it is assumed that the cubes are arranged with a pronoun coming first, then an auxiliary verb, then a verb, and finally an adverb, find how many different phrases can be formed.

Solution   We make 4 boxes representing the 4 events:

There are 6 choices for each of the boxes (each cube has 6 sides), so we enter a 6 in each box:

| 6 | 6 | 6 | 6 |

The number of possibilities, by the SCP, is $6 \times 6 \times 6 \times 6 = 6^4 = 1296$. ∎

EXAMPLE 6   A slot machine has three dials, each having 20 symbols, as listed in Table 9.1. If the symbols are regarded as all different:

(a) How many symbol combinations are possible on the three dials?

(b) In how many ways can we get 3 bars? (The biggest payoff.)

Table 9.1

Symbol	Dial 1	Dial 2	Dial 3
Bar	1	3	1
Bell	1	3	3
Cherry	7	7	0
Lemon	3	0	4
Orange	3	6	7
Plum	5	1	5

Solution   (a) We make 3 boxes representing the 3 dials:

There are 20 choices for each of the boxes (each dial has 20 symbols), so we enter a 20 in each box:

| 20 | 20 | 20 |

The number of possibilities is $20 \times 20 \times 20 = 8000$.

(b) The number of different ways we can get 3 bars is $1 \times 3 \times 1 = 3$, because we have one bar on the first dial, three on the second, and one on the third.

∎

The Clearwater Hilton Inn has a free chance coupon that works like this: When you check out, ask the desk clerk to hand you the three dice. Pick your lucky number and give them a toss. If your number comes up, the room charges are canceled. Does this sound easy? Look at the next example.

COUPON

FREE CHANCE

This coupon is better than all the rest! When you check out, ask the clerk to hand you the three dice. Pick your lucky number and give them a toss. If your number comes up, the room charges for your entire stay are on us!!!

(Validated Coupon Issued At Check In)

EXAMPLE 7   Suppose that one of three dice is black, one is green, and one is red.

(a) If we distinguish the result of a toss by both numbers and colors, how many different results are possible?
(b) If you picked 4 as your lucky number, in how many ways could you get a sum of 4?

Solution   (a) We make three boxes, one for each die (singular of dice), to represent the possible outcomes:

☐ ☐ ☐
Black Green Red

There are six choices for each box because a die can come up with any number from 1 to 6. So we enter a 6 in each box:

6   6   6
Black Green Red

By the SCP, there are $6 \times 6 \times 6 = 216$ outcomes possible.

(b) The simplest way to solve this part of the problem is to reason that in order to get a sum of 4, one of the three dice must come up 2 and the other two dice must come up 1. Thus, the only choice we have is which die is to come up 2. This means that there are only *three* ways to get a sum of 4 out of the 216 possible outcomes. (See the tree diagram in Figure 9.4.)

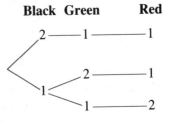

FIGURE 9.4

EXAMPLE 8   Zip codes start with a five digit number.

(a) How many different five-digit zip codes are possible?
(b) How many are possible if 0 is not to be used as the first digit?

Solution   (a) We make five boxes, each to be filled with the number of choices for that digit:

Since there are 10 digits (0, 1, 2, 3, 4, 5, 6, 7, 8, 9), there are 10 choices for each box:

$$\boxed{10}\;\boxed{10}\;\boxed{10}\;\boxed{10}\;\boxed{10}$$

Thus, by the SCP, there are $10 \times 10 \times 10 \times 10 \times 10$, that is,

$$10^5 = 100,000$$

different five-digit zip codes possible.

Note that this result gives a good estimate of the number of cities and towns in the United States. (Towns too small to have their own zip code make up for cities and towns that have more than one zip code.)

(b) If we cannot use a 0 for the first digit, we will have only 9 choices for the first box, but the others will still have 10 choices. Again, by the SCP, there are $9 \times 10 \times 10 \times 10 \times 10$, that is,

$$9 \times 10^4 = 90,000$$

different possible five-digit zip codes that do not start with a 0.

EXAMPLE 9   Two cards are drawn in succession and without replacement from a deck of 52 cards. Find:

(a) The number of ways in which we can obtain the ace of spades and the king of hearts, in that order.
(b) The total number of ways in which two cards can be dealt.

Solution   (a) There is one way of selecting the ace of spades and one way of selecting the king of hearts. Thus, there is $1 \times 1 = 1$ way of selecting the ace of spades and the king of hearts, in that order.

(b) There are 52 ways of selecting the first card and 51 ways of selecting the second card. Thus, there are $52 \times 51 = 2652$ ways in which the two cards can be dealt.

Exercise 9.1

A. 1. A man has 2 suits and 4 shirts. Use a tree diagram to find how many different outfits he can wear.

2. At the end of a meal in a restaurant, Elsie wants to have pie à la mode (pie topped with ice cream) for dessert. There are 5 flavors of ice cream—chocolate, vanilla, strawberry, peach, and coffee—and there are 2 kinds of pie—apple and cherry. Make a tree diagram to find how many choices Elsie has.

B. 3. Research Associates selects 4 people and asks their preferences regarding 2 different styles of blue jeans. If it is important to know which person prefers which style, how many different outcomes are possible?

4. In 1935, a chain letter fad started in Denver, Colorado. The scheme worked like this: You would receive a letter with a list of 5 names, send a dime to the person at the top of the list, cross that name out, and add your name to the bottom of the list. Suppose you received one of these letters today and sent it to 5 other persons, each of whom sends it to 5 other persons, each of whom sends it to 5 others, and so on.
(a) How many letters will have your name on the list?
(b) How much money will you receive if the chain is not broken?

5. Refer to the slot machine in Example 6, and determine in how many ways you can get:
(a) 3 bells   (b) 3 oranges   (c) 3 plums

6. An ordinary deck of playing cards contains 52 cards, 26 red and 26 black. If a card is dealt to each of 2 players, find in how many different ways this can be done if:
(a) Both cards are red
(b) Both cards are black
(c) One card is black and the other is red

7. In poker, a pair of aces with any other pair is a good hand.
(a) In how many ways can you get a pair of aces when 2 cards are dealt from the deck?
(b) If the two pairs are aces and eights, the hand is considered to be unlucky! In how many ways can you get a pair of aces and then a pair of eights, in that order, when 4 cards are dealt from the deck? (This superstition dates back to 1876 when Wild Bill Hickok was shot dead by Jack McCall during a poker game. What hand was Wild Bill holding when he fell dead? A pair of aces and a pair of eights!)

8. Mr. C. Nile and Mr. D. Mented agreed to meet at 8:00 P.M. in one of the Spanish restaurants in Ybor City. They were both punctual, and they both remembered the date agreed upon. Unfortunately, they forgot to specify

the name of the restaurant. If there are 5 Spanish restaurants in Ybor City, and each man goes to one of these, find:
(a) The number of ways in which they could miss each other
(b) The number of ways in which they could meet

9. In how many ways can 1 man and 1 woman, in that order, be selected from 5 men and 6 women?

10. How many different sets of 2 initials can be constructed from the letters of the English alphabet?

11. How many different sets of 3 initials can be constructed from the letters of the English alphabet?

12. A man wants to buy a ring. Suppose that he has 2 choices of metals (gold and silver) and 3 choices of stones (diamond, emerald, and ruby). How many choices does he have?

13. The Good Taste Restaurant has 7 entrees, 6 vegetables, and 9 desserts on its menu. If you want to order 1 entree, 1 vegetable, and 1 dessert, how many choices do you have?

14. An airline recently introduced their newest hub. There are 2 flights from Tampa to Dayton and 2 flights from Dayton to Lansing. In how many ways can you fly from Tampa to Lansing, via Dayton?

15. An airline has 8 flights from Miami to Washington and 2 flights from Washington to Dayton. In how many ways can you fly from Miami to Dayton, via Washington?

16. In Connecticut, auto license plates carry 3 digits followed by 3 letters.
(a) How many arrangements are possible for the 3 letters?
(b) How many arrangements are possible for the 3 numbers?
(c) How many different license plates can be made using 3 numbers followed by 3 letters?

17. How many two-digit numbers are there in the set of natural numbers? [*Hint:* 10 is a two-digit number, but 01 is not.]

18. How many three-digit numbers are there in the set of natural numbers?

19. Social Security numbers consist of nine digits. If the first digit cannot be 0, how many Social Security numbers are possible?

20. Telephone numbers within the same area code consist of seven digits. For local calls, the first digit cannot be a 0 or a 1. How many local telephone numbers are possible?

21. A combination lock has 40 numbers on its face. To open this lock, you move right to a certain number, then left to another number, and finally right again to a third number. If no number is used twice, what is the total number of combinations?

22. Romano's Restaurant has 6 items that you can add to your pizza. The dessert menu lists 5 different desserts. If you want a pizza with one of the 6 items added and a dessert, how many choices do you have?

Problems 23–30 refer to the menu below.

Family Dinners

FOR 2 PERSONS 13.00 — Select 1 from Group A and 1 from Group B
FOR 3 PERSONS 18.00 — Select 1 from Group A and 2 from Group B
FOR 4 PERSONS 24.00 — Select 2 from Group A and 2 from Group B
FOR 5 PERSONS 30.00 — Select 2 from Group A and 3 from Group B
FOR 6 PERSONS 36.00 — Select 3 from Group A and 3 from Group B

Entree

EGG ROLL (One Per Person)

Soup: ROAST PORK WONTON or EGG DROP
(Served Individually)

A	**B**
SHRIMP WITH LOBSTER SAUCE	CHICKEN CHOW MEIN
CHOW HAR KEW	SHRIMP CHOW MEIN
BUTTERFLY SHRIMP	CHICKEN CHOP SUEY
CHOW GAI KEW	SHRIMP CHOP SUEY
WOR SUE GAI	BEEF CHOP SUEY
MOO GOO GAI PAN	BEEF WITH BEAN SPROUT
LEMON CHICKEN	ROAST PORK EGG FOO YOUNG
GREEN PEPPER STEAK	ROAST PORK LO MEIN
WOR SUE OPP (PRESSED DUCK)	BARBECUED SPARERIBS
SWEET & SOUR PORK	

Served with fried rice and hot tea
Group A in Exchange for Group B—$1.50 extra
CHOICE OF DESSERTS
PINEAPPLE CHUNKS, ALMOND COOKIES, KUMQUATS, FORTUNE COOKIES.
EXTRA SERVICE ON ANY FAMILY DINNER INCLUDING SOUP $1.00

---

23. If Billy decides to get an item from group *A*, a soup, and a dessert, how many choices does he have?

24. If Sue decides to get an item from group *B*, a soup, and a dessert, how many choices does she have?

25. If Pedro decides to get an item from group *A* or *B*, a soup, and a dessert, how many choices does he have?

26. If Bob and Sue decide to have the family dinner, which includes soup and dessert, one item from group *A*, and one item from group *B*, how many choices do they have?

27. If Sam and Sally are having the same type family dinner as Bob and Sue in problem 26, and Sally decides to get an item from group *A*, so Sam must get an item from group *B*, how many choices do they have?

28. In problem 27, if Sam does not want to eat shrimp, how many choices do they have?

29. In problem 27, if Sam wants to avoid all the varieties of chop suey, how many choices do they have?

30. In problem 27, if Sam does not want the roast pork, how many choices do they have?

31. Write out all the different ways in which the elements of the set {a, b, c} can be matched in pairs with the elements of the set {@, &, %} if the order in each pair is important. For example, the pair (a, @) is different from the pair (@, a).

32. Use the ideas of problem 31 to determine how many different couples Escort Dating Service can select if they have 120 men and 210 women registered with the service.

*I*n Other Words

33. The SCP indicates that if one event can occur in *m* ways **and** another event in *n* ways, then the sequence of events can occur in $m \times n$ ways. State an equivalent principle when a single event can occur in *m* ways **or** in *n* ways.

34. Many states are changing the configuration of their license plates. Florida, for example, changed from 3 digits followed by 3 letters to 3 letters followed by 2 digits and one letter. Explain why you think this change was made.

Using Your Knowledge

35. If a word is any arrangement of 4 letters, how many 4-letter words can be formed from the letters *B, O, N, K*?

36. How many 3-letter words can be formed from the letters *B, O, N, K*?

37. In problem 11 we found the number of different sets of 3 initials that are possible. If a town has 27,000 inhabitants, each with exactly 3 initials, can you show that at least two of the inhabitants have the same initials?

Discovery

In a recent trial in Sweden, the owner of a car was charged with overtime parking. The policeman who accused the man had noted the position of the air valves on the front and rear tires on the curb-side of the car and ascertained that one valve pointed to the place occupied by 12 o'clock on a clock (directly upward) and the other one to 3 o'clock. (In both cases the closest hour was selected.) After the allowed time had elapsed, the car was still there, with the valves pointing to 12 and 3 o'clock. In court, however, the man claimed that he had moved the car and returned later. The valves just happened to come to rest in the same position as before! At this time an expert was called to compute the probability of such an event happening.

If you were this expert and you assumed that the two wheels move independently of each other, could you use the SCP to find the following?

38. The number of ways in which the front air valve could come to rest

39. The number of ways in which the front *and* rear air valves could come to rest

The defendant, by the way, was acquitted! The judge remarked that if all four wheels had been checked (assuming that they moved independently) and found in the same position as before, he would have rejected the claim as too improbable and convicted the man.

40. Again, assume you are the expert and find the number of positions in which the four air valves could come to rest.

41. The claim that the two wheels on an automobile move independently is not completely warranted. For example, if the front air valve points to 12 and the rear (on the same side) points to 3, after a complete revolution of the front wheel, where will the rear air valve be? (Assume no slippage of the wheels.)

42. Based on your answer to problem 41, how many positions were possible for the two wheels on the curb-side of the car if the owner did move it and did return later?

9.2   PERMUTATIONS

GETTING STARTED

PERMUTATIONS IN THE MEDICAL LAB

Have you heard of animal research in medical labs? The possibility of adverse reactions and side-effects makes experimenting with medicines risky to test on humans, so lab animals are used for these tests. For example, some patients take blood-pressure medicines, blood-thinners, and cholesterol-lowering medicines. To test for adverse reactions or differences in the way individual medicines work, a lab may want to experiment with animals by giving them 3 different medicines chosen from a group of 5 medicines and studying the results. How many lab animals are needed to perform the experiment?

In mathematics, an ordered arrangement of r objects selected from n objects without repetition is called a **permutation.** The number of such permutations is denoted by

$$P(n, r)$$
available   chosen

Here we want to find $P(5, 3)$, the number of permutations of 3 of the 5 objects. To do so, we can use the sequential counting principle. Since we wish to select 3 medicines from among 5, there are 5 choices of medicines for the first selection, 4 for the second and 3 for the third. Thus, the number of

These laboratory rats are being tested for the effects of a mutagen agent

---

ways in which we can select 3 objects from a group of 5 (in our case, the number of lab animals needed for testing) is $5 \times 4 \times 3 = 60$. Note that the first animal may be given medications A, B, and C in that *order*. If the researcher decides to use medications A, C, and B, a different animal is needed because the order in which medicines is given is extremely important. Thus, we have found that the number of permutations of 5 objects, taken 3 at a time, is 60. We will study **permutations** in this section and develop a new type of notation, called **factorial** notation, that will help us write and compute permutations more efficiently.

In Section 9.1 we used the sequential counting principle (SCP) to determine the number of ways in which a sequence of events could happen. A special case of this principle occurs when we want to count the possible *arrangements* of a given set of elements.

EXAMPLE 1   In how many different orders can we write the letters in the set $\{a, b, c\}$ if no letter is repeated in any one arrangement?

Solution   We have three choices for the first letter, two for the second, and one for the third. By the SCP, the number of arrangements is $3 \times 2 \times 1 = 6$. ∎

A. *Permutations*

If we are asked to display the arrangements in Example 1, we can draw the tree diagram shown in Figure 9.5, in which each path corresponds to one such arrangement. There are six paths, so the total number of arrangements is 6. Notice that in this example *abc* and *acb* are treated as different arrangements, because the order of the letters is not the same in the two arrangements. This type of arrangement, in which the *order is important*, is called a *permutation*.

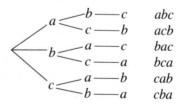

FIGURE 9.5

Definition 9.1

An ordered arrangement of n distinguishable objects, taken r at a time and with no repetitions, is called a **permutation** of the objects. The **number** of such permutations is denoted by $P(n, r)$. *The notation $_nP_r$ sometimes is used instead of $P(n, r)$.*

In Example 1, we saw that the number of permutations of the letters in the set $\{a, b, c\}$ is $3 \times 2 \times 1 = 6$. Thus, $P(3, 3) = 6$. A notation that is convenient to represent $3 \times 2 \times 1$ is 3! (read, "3 factorial").

Definition 9.2

The symbol **n!** (read, "**n factorial**"), where n is a positive integer, represents the product of n and each positive integer less than n,

$$n! = n \times (n - 1) \times (n - 2) \times \cdots \times 3 \times 2 \times 1$$

Thus,

$$4! = 4 \times 3 \times 2 \times 1 = 24$$

and

$$5! = 5 \times 4 \times 3 \times 2 \times 1 = 120$$

EXAMPLE 2   Compute:

(a) $6!$ (b) $7!$ (c) $\dfrac{6!}{3!}$

Solution   By Definition 9.2,

(a) $6! = 6 \times 5 \times 4 \times 3 \times 2 \times 1 = 720$
(b) $7! = 7 \times 6 \times 5 \times 4 \times 3 \times 2 \times 1 = 5040$
(c) $\dfrac{6!}{3!} = \dfrac{6 \times 5 \times 4 \times \cancel{3} \times \cancel{2} \times \cancel{1}}{\cancel{3} \times \cancel{2} \times \cancel{1}} = 120$ Note that $\dfrac{6!}{3!} \neq 2$. ∎

EXAMPLE 3   Wreck-U Car Club organizes a race in which five automobiles, A, B, C, D, and E, are entered. If there are no ties:

(a) In how many ways can the race finish?
(b) In how many ways can the first three positions come in?

Solution   (a) The number of ways in which the race can finish if there are no ties is the number of permutations of 5 things taken 5 at a time. By Definition 9.1, this number is $P(5, 5)$, so, by the SCP,

$$P(5, 5) = 5 \cdot 4 \cdot 3 \cdot 2 \cdot 1 = 5! = 120$$

(b) Here we need the number of ordered arrangements of 3 out of the 5 cars, that is, the number of permutations of 5 things taken 3 at a time. Again, by Definition 9.1, this number is $P(5, 3)$, and by the SCP,

$$P(5, 3) = 5 \cdot 4 \cdot 3 = 60$$

∎

By Definition 9.1, $P(n, r)$ is the number of permutations of n objects using r of these objects at a time. We can now obtain formulas to compute these numbers.

1. If we use all n of the objects, we must find $P(n, n)$. We can think of n boxes to be filled with n objects, as shown in Figure 9.6. We have n choices for the first box, $(n - 1)$ choices for the second box, $(n - 2)$

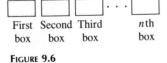

First Second Third nth
box   box   box   box

FIGURE 9.6

choices for the third box, and so on, until we come to the last box, when there will be only 1 object left. By the SCP, we have:

The number of permutations of n objects, n at a time:
$$P(n, n) = n(n - 1)(n - 2) \cdot \cdots \cdot (3)(2)(1) = n!$$

2. The procedure used to evaluate $P(n, n)$ can be applied to $P(n, r)$. We think of r boxes to be filled by r of the n objects. There are n choices for the first box, $n - 1$ choices for the second box, $n - 2$ choices for the third box, and so on, until there are $n - r + 1$ choices for the rth box. Thus, by the SCP:

The number of permutations of n objects, r at a time:
$$P(n, r) = n(n - 1)(n - 2) \cdot \cdots \cdot (n - r + 1)$$

You should keep in mind that the n in $P(n, r)$ is the number of objects available and the r is the number of spaces to be filled. (Notice that if $r = n$, then the preceding two formulas agree exactly.)

The symbols $_nP_r$, $P_{n,r}$, and P_r^n are sometimes used to represent the number of permutations of n things, r at a time.

Some calculators have a factorial ($n!$) key and a $P(n, r)$ or $_nP_r$ key. By following the instructions for the calculator, you can get answers to many of the following examples and problems without all the detailed arithmetic.

EXAMPLE 4   Compute:

(a) $P(6, 6)$ (b) $P(7, 3)$ (c) $P(6, 2)$

Solution   (a) Here we use the formula for $P(n, n)$ with $n = 6$:
$$P(6, 6) = 6 \cdot 5 \cdot 4 \cdot 3 \cdot 2 \cdot 1 = 6! = 720$$

(b) Here we are finding the number of permutations of 7 objects, taken 3 at a time. We use the formula for $P(n, r)$ with $n = 7$ and $r = 3$:
$$P(7, 3) = 7 \cdot 6 \cdot 5 = 210$$

(c) We proceed as in part (b), but with $n = 6$ and $r = 2$:
$$P(6, 2) = 6 \cdot 5 = 30$$ ∎

By using the definitions of $n!$ and $(n - r)!$, we can obtain the useful formula

$$P(n, r) = \frac{n!}{(n - r)!} \qquad r < n$$

We can verify this formula as follows:

$$\frac{n!}{(n-r)!} =$$

$$\frac{n(n-1)(n-2) \cdots \cdots (n-r+1)(n-r) \cdots \cdots (3)(2)(1)}{(n-r) \cdots \cdots (3)(2)(1)}$$

$$= n(n-1)(n-2) \cdots \cdots (n-r+1) = P(n, r)$$

as the formula states. Notice that for $r < n$,

$$P(n, n) = n(n-1)(n-2) \cdots \cdots (n-r+1)[(n-r)!]$$
$$= P(n, r)[(n-r)!]$$

We want this formula to hold also in the case $n = r$; that is, we want

$$P(n, n) = P(n, n)(0!)$$

For this reason, 0! is defined to be 1:

$$0! = 1$$

EXAMPLE 5   Use the preceding formula for $P(n, r)$ to compute the answer to part (b) of Example 4.

Solution $$P(7, 3) = \frac{7!}{(7-3)!} = \frac{7!}{4!}$$

$$= \frac{7 \times 6 \times 5 \times 4 \times 3 \times 2 \times 1}{4 \times 3 \times 2 \times 1}$$

$$= 7 \times 6 \times 5 = 210$$

B. *The Complementary Counting Principle*

The number of elements in a set A can sometimes be calculated more easily by an indirect rather than a direct method. If $\mathcal{U}$ is the universal set, the number of elements in A can be obtained by subtracting the number of elements in A' from the number in $\mathcal{U}$. This gives us the **complementary counting principle,**

$$n(A) = n(\mathcal{U}) - n(A')$$

EXAMPLE 6   Out of four dogs, how many ways are there to have *at least* one male?

Solution   The only alternative to having at least one male is having no males; that is, the four dogs are all females, which is just one of all the possible cases. Since there are four places to fill, with two choices for each place (male or female), the total number of possible arrangements is

$$n(\mathcal{U}) = 2 \times 2 \times 2 \times 2 = 2^4 = 16$$

Thus,

$$n(\text{At least one male}) = 16 - n(\text{No males})$$
$$= 16 - 1 = 15$$

C. *The Additive Counting Principle*

Another useful counting principle is the **additive counting principle,** giving the number of elements in the union of two sets, which we obtained in Section 1.5. If A and B are two sets, then

$$n(A \cup B) = n(A) + n(B) - n(A \cap B)$$

The use of this formula is illustrated in the next example.

EXAMPLE 7   How many two-digit numbers are divisible by 2 or by 5?

Solution   Let A be the set of two-digit numbers divisible by 2, and let B be the set of two-digit numbers divisible by 5. For two-digit numbers divisible by 2, the first digit can be any digit from 1 to 9 (9 choices), and the second digit can be 0, 2, 4, 6, or 8 (5 choices). Thus,

$$n(A) = 9 \times 5 = 45$$

For two-digit numbers divisible by 5, the first digit can be any digit from 1 to 9 (9 choices), and the second digit can be 0 or 5 (2 choices). Thus,

$$n(B) = 9 \times 2 = 18$$

Since $A \cap B$ is the set of numbers divisible by both 2 and 5, the first digit can still be any digit from 1 to 9 (9 choices), and the second digit can only be 0 (1 choice). Thus,

$$n(A \cap B) = 9 \times 1 = 9$$

and the desired number is

$$n(A \cup B) = n(A) + n(B) - n(A \cap B)$$
$$= 45 + 18 - 9 = 54$$

That is, the number of two-digit numbers divisible by either 2 or 5 is 54.

Exercise 9.2

A.   1. In how many different orders can the letters in the set $\{a, b, c, d\}$ be written?

2. In how many different ways can 4 people be seated in a row?

3. If 6 horses are entered in a race and they all finish with no ties, in how many ways can they come in?

4. In how many different ways can 7 people be lined up at the checkout counter in a supermarket?

5. An insurance agent has a list of 5 prospects. In how many different orders can the agent phone these 5 prospects?

6. If the agent in problem 5 decides to phone 3 of the prospects today and the other 2 prospects tomorrow, in how many ways can the agent do this?

In problems 7–20, compute the given number.

7. $8!$

8. $10!$

9. $9!$

10. $\dfrac{10!}{7!}$

11. $\dfrac{11!}{8!}$

12. $\dfrac{8!}{2!6!}$

13. $\dfrac{9!}{5!4!}$

14. $P(9, 4)$

15. $P(10, 2)$

16. $\dfrac{P(6, 3)}{4!}$

17. $\dfrac{P(5, 2)}{2!}$

18. $2 \cdot P(8, 3)$

19. $3 \cdot P(8, 5)$

20. $4 \cdot P(3, 3)$

21. A student is taking 5 classes, each of which uses 1 book. In how many ways can she stack the 5 books she must carry?

22. Suppose 10 people are entered in a race. If there are no ties, in how many ways can the first 3 places come out?

23. A basketball coach must choose 4 players to play in a particular game. (The team already has a center.) In how many ways can the remaining 4 positions be filled if the coach has 10 players who can play any position?

24. Rework problem 23 if the coach does not have a center already and must fill all 5 positions from the 10 players.

25. In how many ways can 3 hearts be drawn from a standard deck of 52 cards?

26. In how many ways can 2 kings be drawn from a standard deck of 52 cards?

27. In how many ways can 2 red cards be drawn from a standard deck of 52 cards?

28. In how many ways can 4 diamonds be drawn from a standard deck of 52 cards?

29. How many three-digit numbers can be formed from the digits, 1, 3, 5, 7, and 9 with no repetitions allowed?

30. How many even three-digit numbers can be formed from the digits 2, 4, 5, 7, and 9 with no repetitions allowed? [*Hint:* Try filling the units place first.]

31. A red die and a green die are tossed. In how many ways is it possible for both dice to come up even numbers? (Distinguish between the two dice.)

32. In problem 31, in how many ways is it possible for one of the dice to come up an odd number and the other to come up an even number?

B. 33. Out of 5 children, in how many ways can a family have *at least* 1 boy?

34. If two dice are tossed; in how many ways can at least one of the dice come up a 6? [*Hint:* There are five ways in which a single die can come up not a 6.]

Six coins are tossed; in how many ways can you have:

35. No tails

36. At least one tail

37. At least two heads

38. At most one head

C. 39. How many of the first 100 natural numbers are multiples of 2 or multiples of 5?

40. How many of the first 100 natural numbers are multiples of 2 or multiples of 3?

In Other Words

41. Give at least two reasons why 0! had to be defined as 1.

42. How would you define $P(n, 0)$? Verify your answer by finding $P(n, 0)$ using the formula for $P(n, r)$

43. In your own words, what is the additive counting principle?

44. Explain under what circumstances it is advantageous to use the additive counting principle.

| **Using Your Knowledge** |

If you are interested in horse racing, here are some problems for you.

45. Five horses are entered in a race. If there are no ties, in how many ways can the race end?

46. In problem 45, if we know that 2 horses are going to be tied for first place (say, *A* and *B*), in how many ways can the race end?

47. It seems unlikely that if 5 horses are entered in a race, 3 of them will be tied for first place. However, this actually happened! In the Astley Stakes, at Lewes, England, in August 1880, Mazurka, Wandering Nun, and Scobell triple dead-heated for first place. If it is known that these 3 horses tied for first place, in how many ways could the rest of the horses finish?

48. You probably answered 2 in response to problem 47, because it is unlikely that there will be a tie for fourth place. However, the other 2 horses, Cumberland and Thora, *did* tie for fourth place. If ties are allowed, in how many different ways could Cumberland and Thora have finished the race in the preceding problem?

Discovery

In this section we learned that the number of permutations of n distinct objects is n!. Thus, if we wish to seat 3 people across the table from you, the number of possible arrangements is 3!. However, if 3 persons were to be seated at a circular table, the number of possible arrangements is only 2! = 2. If the persons are labeled A, B, and C, the two arrangements look like those in Figure 9.7.

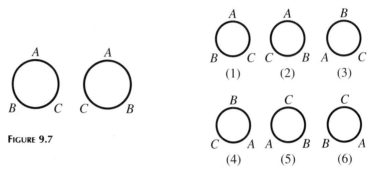

FIGURE 9.7

FIGURE 9.8

At first glance it may seem that there should be 3! = 6 different arrangements, like those in Figure 9.8. However, a closer look will reveal that arrangements (1), (4), and (5) are identical; in all of them B is to the right and C to the left of A. Similarly, (2), (3), and (6) are identical, because in every case C is to the right and B is to the left of A. To avoid this difficulty, if we have, say, 4 persons to be seated at a circular table, we seat one of them and use this person as a reference. The rest of the people can be seated in 3! ways. We have the following relationship:

Number of Persons	Number of Different Ways They Can Be Seated Around a Circular Table
3	2!
4	3!

49. From this discussion, can you discover in how many ways *n* persons can be seated around a circular table?

50. In how many ways can 4 people (including *A* and *B*) be seated at a circular table so that *A* and *B* are facing each other?

51. In problem 50, find the number of ways in which the people can be seated so that *A* and *B* are *not* facing each other.

52. In problem 50, find the number of ways in which the people can be seated so that *A* and *B* are next to each other.

Calculator Corner

Many calculators have a factorial $\boxed{x!}$ or $\boxed{n!}$ key. Thus, to find 6!, you first enter the number 6; then activate the factorial key. The steps are:

$$\boxed{6}\ \boxed{2\text{nd}}\ \boxed{x!}\quad\text{or}\quad\boxed{6}\ \boxed{\text{inv}}\ \boxed{x!}$$

In addition, some calculators even have a key that will calculate $P(n, r)$, the $\boxed{_n P_r}$ key. To enter the n and the r, you must use other special keys. If the $\boxed{a}$ and $\boxed{b}$ keys are those special keys on your calculator and you wish to find $P(7, 3)$, as in Example 4(b), you enter

$$\boxed{7}\ \boxed{a}\ \boxed{3}\ \boxed{b}\ \boxed{2\text{nd}}\ \boxed{_n P_r}\quad\text{The answer is 210.}$$

1. Use your calculator to check the answers to problems 7 and 14.

Computer Corner

The Programs in BASIC appendix features several programs that can lessen the labor when working with factorials and permutations. For example, do you know what 30! is? The Factorial Program for Large n will actually tell you in 5 seconds (using an AT&T 6300). If you are impatient, the Factorial Program (n < 30) will tell you instantly (but you have to know how to read scientific notation because the answer comes out as 2.652529E32, which means 2.652529×10^{32}. Finally, the Permutations and Combinations Formula Program will compute $P(n, r)$, provided you enter n and r. Again, the answer is in scientific notation.

1. Use these programs to check the answers to problems 7 and 14.

9.3 COMBINATIONS

GETTING STARTED

PLANETARY CONJUNCTIONS AND COMBINATIONS

Have you heard of planetary conjunctions? When two or more planets, as seen from the Earth, are in the same direction (celestial longitude) as the Sun, we have what is known as a planetary conjunction. In certain cultures planetary conjunctions were believed to exert special influences on events. According to Hindu tradition, a special dreaded conjunction was that of the seven planetary

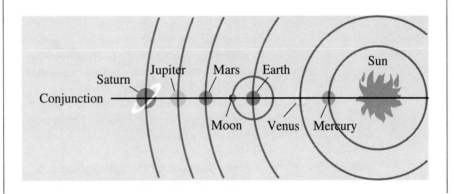

bodies known to man at that time (Sun, Moon, Mercury, Venus, Mars, Jupiter, and Saturn), an event that was supposed to occur every 26,000 years and result in the end of the world.

Rabbi Ben Ezra, a Jewish scholar, used an original computational method to show that the number of possible conjunctions of two or more of these planetary bodies is 120. How did he do it? Using *permutations* and *combinations*, Ben Ezra reasoned that the number of conjunctions of two planets was $P(7, 2) = 42$, but a conjunction of the Sun and Moon, for example, was the same as a conjunction of the Moon and Sun. Since there were 2! ways of arranging two planets, he divided $P(7, 2)$ by 2! to obtain the correct result, 21. For three planets, the number of conjunctions was $P(7, 3) = 210$, but this number must be divided by $3! = 6$ to account for repetitions, thus the number of possible conjunctions involving three planets is 35.

In mathematics, a set of objects that can be selected while disregarding their order is called a **combination** of the objects. The number of combinations of n objects taken r at a time is denoted by $C(n, r)$. In our example,

$$C(7, 2) = \frac{P(7, 2)}{2!} \text{ and } C(7, 3) = \frac{P(7, 3)}{3!}. \text{ In general,}$$

$$C(n, r) = \frac{P(n, r)}{r!}$$

Now, can you help Ben Ezra find how many different planetary conjunctions are possible? To do so, we need to find $C(7, 2) + C(7, 3) + C(7, 4) + \cdots + C(7, 7)$. If you arrive at a total of 120, you are on the way to understanding the formula for combinations.

Here is another way of thinking about the concept itself. $C(n, r)$ actually counts the number of subsets of r objects that can be made from a set of n objects. Thus, $C(4, 2)$ counts all the subsets of 2 objects that can be formed from a set of 4 objects. (If the set is $\{a, b, c, d\}$, the subsets are $\{a, b\}$, $\{a, c\}$, $\{a, d\}$, $\{b, c\}$, $\{b, d\}$, and $\{c, d\}$, a total of 6.) By the formula, $C(4, 2) = \frac{P(4, 2)}{2!} = \frac{12}{2} = 6$.
Now, you have both the concept and the formula for combinations!

In Section 9.2, we found the number of ordered arrangements that are possible with n distinguishable objects. Sometimes we may wish to count the number of subsets of these objects that can be selected if we *disregard the order* in which the objects are selected. Such subsets are called **combinations.** We use the symbol $C(n, r)$ to denote the number of combinations of r objects that can be formed from a set of n objects. The symbols $_nC_r$, $C_{n,r}$, C_r^n, and $\binom{n}{r}$ are also used to represent $C(n, r)$.

EXAMPLE 1   How many different sums of money can be made from a set of coins consisting of a penny, a nickel, and a dime if exactly 2 coins are selected?

Solution Because the **order** in which we select the coins is **not** important, the question asked is equivalent to finding $C(3, 2)$, the number of combinations of 2 things that can be formed using a set of 3 things. One of the sums is 6¢ (it makes no difference whether the penny is selected first and then the nickel, or vice versa), the second sum is 11¢, and the third sum is 15¢. Hence, $C(3, 2)$, the number of combinations of 3 objects taken 2 at a time, is 3.

EXAMPLE 2 Consider the set $S = \{a, b, c, d\}$.

(a) How many combinations of 2 elements are possible using elements of the set S?

(b) How many permutations of 2 elements are possible using elements of the set S?

(c) How many subsets of 2 elements does the set S have?

Solution
(a) The 6 possible combinations are shown in Table 9.2. Hence, $C(4, 2) = 6$.

(b) $P(4, 2) = 4 \times 3 = 12$. The 12 permutations are shown in the table.

(c) This problem is equivalent to finding the number of combinations that can be made from 4 objects using 2 at a time; hence, the answer is 6, as in part (a).

Table 9.2

Combinations	Permutations
ab	ab, ba
ac	ac, ca
ad	ad, da
bc	bc, cb
bd	bd, db
cd	cd, dc

We can see from the table in Example 2 that every combination determines 2! permutations, so $P(4, 2) = 2! \cdot C(4, 2)$. We use a similar argument to solve Example 3.

EXAMPLE 3 How many sets of 3 letters can be made from the English alphabet?

Solution Here we want to find $C(26, 3)$. One of the possible combinations is, for example, $\{A, B, C\}$. This choice determines $3! = 6$ permutations (ABC, ACB, BAC, BCA, CAB, CBA). If we were to make a table similar to the one in Example 2, we would see that to each combination there corresponds $3! = 6$ permutations. Hence, there are 6 times as many permutations as there are combinations. That is, $P(26, 3) = 6 \cdot C(26, 3)$; but $P(26, 3) = 26 \times 25 \times 24 = 15,600$, so $15,600 = 6 \times C(26, 3)$ or $C(26, 3) = 2600$.

The number of ways in which we can select a combination of r objects from a set of n objects is $C(n, r)$. The r objects in any one of these combinations can be arranged (permuted) in $r!$ ways. By the SCP, the total number of permutations is $r! \times C(n, r)$; but this number is $P(n, r)$. Hence,

$$P(n, r) = (r!)C(n, r)$$

so:

> The number of combinations of n objects, r at a time:
>
> $$C(n, r) = \frac{P(n, r)}{r!} \qquad 1 \le r \le n$$

The following useful form of the formula for $C(n, r)$ is obtained in the next example:

$$C(n, r) = \frac{n!}{r!(n - r)!}$$

EXAMPLE 4   Show that $C(n, r)$ has the form given above.

Solution   We know that

$$C(n, r) = \frac{P(n, r)}{r!} \quad \text{and} \quad P(n, r) = \frac{n!}{(n - r)!}$$

Thus, by substituting for $P(n, r)$ we obtain

$$C(n, r) = \frac{P(n, r)}{r!} = \frac{n!}{(n - r)!} \div r! = \frac{n!}{r!(n - r)!}$$

as given.   ∎

The meaning of $C(n, r)$ can also be stated in terms of a set of n elements: $C(n, r)$ is the number of subsets of r elements each that can be formed from a set of n elements. Note that this is just a repetition of the statement made at the beginning of this section.

EXAMPLE 5   How many subsets of *at least* 3 elements can be formed from a set of 4 elements?

Solution   If we wish to have *at least* 3 elements in the subset, we can have either 3 or 4 elements. Using the preceding statement, the number of subsets of 3 elements that can be formed from a set of 4 elements is

$$C(4, 3) = \frac{4!}{3!1!} = 4$$

and the number of subsets of 4 elements that can be formed from a set of 4 elements is

$$C(4, 4) = \frac{4!}{4!0!} = 1.$$

Thus, the number of subsets of at least 3 elements that can be formed from a set of 4 elements is $4 + 1 = 5$. (Try it with the set $\{a, b, c, d\}$.)

EXAMPLE 5 Compute:

(a) $C(26, 3)$ (b) $C(8, 2)$

Solution (a) From the second formula for $C(n, r)$, we get

$$C(26, 3) = \frac{26!}{3!23!} = \frac{26 \times 25 \times 24 \times 23!}{3!23!} = 2600$$

(b) Similarly,

$$C(8, 2) = \frac{8!}{2!6!} = \frac{8 \times 7 \times 6!}{2!6!} = 28$$

You can make your work easier by noting possible cancellations, as in the solution for Example 6.

EXAMPLE 7 How many different 2-card hands can be obtained from an ordinary deck of 52 cards?

Solution The question asked is equivalent to, "How many combinations are there of 52 elements, 2 at a time?" Using the first formula for $C(n, r)$, we find

$$C(52, 2) = \frac{P(52, 2)}{2!} = \frac{52 \cdot 51}{2 \cdot 1} = 1326$$

Suppose you are asked to find the number of combinations of 10 objects, 8 at a time. You can see that if you take away any combination of 8 of the objects, a combination of 2 of the objects is left. This shows that $C(10, 8) = C(10, 2)$. This result can be verified directly as follows:

$$C(10, 8) = \frac{P(10, 8)}{8!} = \frac{10 \cdot 9 \cdot 8 \cdot 7 \cdot 6 \cdot 5 \cdot 4 \cdot 3}{8 \cdot 7 \cdot 6 \cdot 5 \cdot 4 \cdot 3 \cdot 2 \cdot 1} = \frac{10 \cdot 9}{2 \cdot 1}$$

and

$$C(10, 2) = \frac{P(10, 2)}{2!} = \frac{10 \cdot 9}{2 \cdot 1}$$

Therefore,

$$C(10, 8) = C(10, 2)$$

In general,

$$C(n, r) = C(n, n - r)$$

The second formula for $C(n, r)$, which was verified in Example 4, makes this obvious because

$$C(n, n - r) = \frac{n!}{(n - r)![n - (n - r)]!}$$

$$= \frac{n!}{(n - r)!r!} = C(n, r)$$

EXAMPLE 8   Romano's Restaurant offers the pizza menu shown in the margin. Find how many different pizzas you can order.

(a) With 1 item   (b) With 2 items
(c) With 3 items   (d) With 4 items

Solution   (a) Because there are exactly 6 different items available, there are 6 different pizzas with 1 item. Notice that if you use the formula for $C(6, 1)$, it gives $\frac{6}{1} = 6$.

(b) The order in which the items are added is not important. (If you order pepperoni and onion, you get the same pizza as if you order onion and pepperoni.) Thus, we need to find the number of combinations of 6 things, 2 at a time:

$$C(6, 2) = \frac{P(6, 2)}{2!} = \frac{6 \cdot 5}{1 \cdot 2} = 15$$

(c) Here, we need $C(6, 3)$:

$$C(6, 3) = \frac{P(6, 3)}{3!} = \frac{6 \cdot 5 \cdot 4}{3 \cdot 2 \cdot 1} = 20$$

(d) Here, the answer is $C(6, 4)$, which is the same as $C(6, 2) = 15$.

Some calculators have a $C(n, r)$ or $_nC_r$ key. By following the instructions for the calculator, you can calculate answers to many of the following problems without actually performing all the detailed arithmetic.

ROMANO'S

Greek - Italian Restaurant

Menu For Lunch & Take Out

555-6666

PIZZA

OUR SPECIAL DOUGH LIGHT AND CRISPY
TO YOUR EXPECTATION   ONE-SIZE ONLY
10"-6 PIECES
PLAIN CHEESE 5.95
ANY 1 ITEM 6.95
ANY 2 COMBINATIONS 7.95
ANY 3 COMBINATIONS 8.95
SPECIAL (All Items) 9.95

ITEMS

PEPPERONI, ONION, PEPPERS, MUSHROOMS,
SAUSAGE, AND MEATBALL

SOFT DRINKS

	Sm.	Lg.
COKE, 7-UP	.75	.95
TAB, ROOT BEER	.75	.95
COFFEE or ICE TEA		.95

DESSERTS

Try Our Delicious Homemade Desserts
RICE PUDDING 1.50
GALACTOBURICO 1.50
Greek Custard with Fillo
BAKLAVA 2.50
Walnuts, Honey, and Fillo
BOUGATZA 2.50
Walnuts, Honey, Cinnamon, and Fillo
SPUMONI 2.50
Italian-style Ice Cream

Exercise 9.3

In problems 1–6, evaluate each of the following:

1. $C(5, 2)$ and $P(5, 2)$
2. $C(6, 4)$ and $P(6, 4)$
3. $C(7, 3)$ and $P(7, 3)$
4. $C(5, 0)$ and $P(5, 0)$
5. $C(9, 6)$ and $P(9, 6)$
6. $C(7, 0)$ and $P(7, 0)$

In problems 7–10, find the number of combinations that can be made from:

7. 5 objects taken 4 at a time
8. 9 objects taken 3 at a time
9. 10 objects taken 2 at a time
10. 12 objects taken 3 at a time

11. How many subsets of 2 elements can be made from a set of 8 elements?
12. How many subsets of 5 elements can be made from a set of 7 elements?
13. How many different 8-element subsets can be made from a set of 12 elements?
14. How many different 10 element subsets can be made from a set of 15 elements?
15. Let T be a set of 10 elements.
    (a) How many subsets of 3 elements does T have?
    (b) How many subsets of less than 3 elements does T have?
    (c) How many subsets of no elements does T have?
    (d) How many subsets of more than 9 elements does T have?

16. How many different sums of money can be formed from a penny, a nickel, a dime, a quarter, and a half-dollar, if exactly 3 coins are to be used?
17. Rework problem 16 if 4 coins are to be used.
18. Rework problem 16 if at least 2 coins are to be used.
19. Let $A = \{1, 2, 3, 4, 5\}$.
    (a) How many subsets of 3 elements does the set A have?
    (b) How many subsets of A have no more than 3 elements?

20. If 20 people all shake hands with each other, how many handshakes are there?
21. The Greek alphabet has 24 letters. In how many ways can 3 different Greek letters be selected if the order does not matter?
22. The Mathematics Department is sending 5 of its 10 members to a meeting. In how may ways can the 5 members be selected?
23. A committee is to consist of 3 members. If there are 4 men and 6 women available to serve on this committee, how many different committees can be formed?

24. The Book-of-the-Month Club offers a choice of 3 books from a list of 40. How many different selections of 3 books each can be made from this list?

25. How many different 5-card poker hands are there in a deck of 52 cards?

26. A restaurant offers 8 different kinds of sandwiches. In how many ways could you select 2 different kinds?

27. The U.S. Senate has 100 members. How many different 5-member committees can be formed from the Senate?

28. In how many ways can a committee of 7 be formed from a group of 12 eligible people?

29. Johnny has a $1 bill, a $5 bill, a $10 bill, and a $20 bill in his pocket. How many different sums of money can Johnny make with these bills if he uses at least 1 bill each time?

30. Desi has 6 coins: a penny, a nickel, a dime, a quarter, a half-dollar, and a dollar. How many different sums of money can Desi form by using 2 of these coins?

31. Refer to problem 30. How many different sums of money can Desi form if she uses at least 1 coin each time?

32. How many different committees can be formed from 8 people if each committee must consist of at least 3 people?

33. In how many ways can 8 people be divided into 2 equal groups?

34. How many diagonals does a polygon of:
    (a) 8 sides have? (A diagonal is a line segment joining two nonadjacent vertices.)
    (b) n sides have?
    [*Hint:* Think of *all* the lines joining the vertices two at a time. How many of these lines are sides and not diagonals?]

*I*n Other Words

35. Write in your own words the difference between a permutation of 3 objects and a combination of 3 objects.

36. If you knew that a *combination* for your locker was 1, 2, 3,
    (a) Would this combination necessarily open the locker?
    (b) What are the permutations of 1, 2, 3? Would one of these open the locker? Explain.

37. Discuss why a *combination lock* should really be called a *permutation lock*.

38. Consider $P(n, r)$ and $C(n, r)$.
    (a) Discuss the conditions under which $P(n, r) = C(n, r)$ and explain why.
    (b) Is $P(n, r)$ greater than or less than $C(n, r)$? Explain.

Using Your Knowledge

Figure 9.9 shows the famous Pascal's Triangle mentioned in the Discovery section of Exercise 1.2. The Triangle actually counts the number of subsets of k elements that can be made from a set of n elements, that is, C (n, k). If you consider n to be the row number and k the diagonal number, you can find C (5, 2) by going to the fifth row, second diagonal. The answer will be 10. Note that the value 10 is obtained by adding the 4 and 6 above 10 in the triangle. Similarly, the 5 in the fifth row, first diagonal is found by adding the 1 and 4 above 5 in the preceding row.

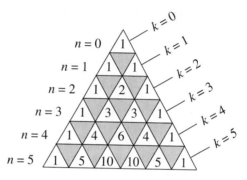

FIGURE 9.9

39. Construct the next two rows of Pascal's Triangle.
40. Use Pascal's Triangle to find:
    (a) $C(6, 4)$ (b) $C(7, 3)$
41. You might have learned in algebra that:

$$(a + b)^0 = \qquad\qquad \mathbf{1}$$
$$(a + b)^1 = \qquad\qquad \mathbf{1}a + \mathbf{1}b$$
$$(a + b)^2 = \qquad \mathbf{1}a^2 + \mathbf{2}ab + \mathbf{1}b^2$$
$$(a + b)^3 = \mathbf{1}a^3 + \mathbf{3}a^2b + \mathbf{3}ab^2 + \mathbf{1}b^3$$

Compare Pascal's Triangle with the given expressions, then find:
(a) $(a + b)^4$ (b) $(a + b)^5$

42. Use Pascal's Triangle to find $(a + b)^6$.

Discovery

Suppose a fair coin is flipped 5 times in succession. How many different outcomes are possible? Since the coin can fall in either of 2 ways (heads or tails), the number of different outcomes is $2^5 = 32$.

In how many different ways can the outcome be 2 heads and 3 tails? If you think a moment, you will realize that the answer is the number of combinations of 5 things, 2 at a time. Look at the 5 tosses and determine in how many ways you can select 2 of them, the order being unimportant.) Thus, the correct answer is

$$C(5, 2) = \frac{5 \cdot 4}{2 \cdot 1} = 10$$

See if you can discover the answers to the following questions:

43. In how many different ways can the outcome be 0 heads and 5 tails? We can call this number $C(5, 0)$.
44. Rework problem 43 for 1 head and 4 tails.
45. Rework problem 43 for 3 heads and 2 tails.
46. Rework problem 43 for 4 heads and 1 tail.
47. Rework problem 43 for 5 heads and 0 tails.
48. Add the answer we found for 2 heads and 3 tails and your answers for problems 43–47. You should come out with

$$C(5, 0) + C(5, 1) + C(5, 2) + C(5, 3) + C(5, 4) + C(5, 5) = 32$$

    Explain why.

49. The result of problem 48 is a special case of the general result

$$C(n, 0) + C(n, 1) + C(n, 2) + \cdots + C(n, n) = 2^n$$

    Can you tell why this must be a correct result? [*Hint:*   Think of the coin being flipped n times.]

Calculator Corner

Some calculators can evaluate $C(n, r)$. To do this, you must enter n and r using special keys, say, $\boxed{a}$ and $\boxed{b}$, on your calculator. Thus, to evaluate $C(26, 3)$, as in Example 6(a), we press $\boxed{26}$ $\boxed{a}$ $\boxed{3}$ $\boxed{b}$ $\boxed{2nd}$ $\boxed{_nC_r}$. As before, the answer is 2600.

1. Check the answers to Examples 6, 7, and 8 using your calculator.

Computer Corner

Two programs in the appendix deal with combinations. The Permutations and Combinations Formula Program will actually calculate $C(n, r)$ and give the answer in scientific notation if the numbers are large. The Combinations of r Items from n Items Program will actually display (in set notation) the combinations of a set of n items when r items are selected, provided you actually list the n elements in the original set.

1. Check the answers to Examples 6, 7, and 8 using the first program.

2. Check the combinations listed in Table 9.2,. Example 2, using the second program.

9.4   MISCELLANEOUS COUNTING METHODS

GETTING STARTED

"COUNTING" ON WINNING THE LOTTERY

In Section 9.1 we asked the question "Why does it seem so difficult to win the lottery?" The answer, we have found, is because there are so many possible *permutations* or so many *combinations* depending on the game you play. For example, suppose you play a lottery in which you pick 4 digits and you win if the digits are drawn in the exact order you have chosen. To find your chances of winning, you must find in how many ways you can select the four digits. Using the sequential counting principle, the number of ways in which we can fill the four boxes

☐ ☐ ☐ ☐

using ten digits (0 to 9) to fill each box, is:

$\boxed{10} \times \boxed{10} \times \boxed{10} \times \boxed{10}$

or 10,000 ways. Only one number will win, so your chances are 1 in 10,000. (If you pick 1,345 and the number selected is 5,431 you are out of luck.) Here we used the SCP as our counting method.

    You can also play this game by selecting the 24-way box. In this case, you select a set of four numbers and win if the numbers come out in *any order*. How many ways can you win now? Since there are $P(4, 4)$ or 24 ways of permuting the four numbers you choose, your chances are increased to 24 in 10,000. Here we used permutations as our counting method.

    Other lottery games are even more challenging. For example, in many state lotteries you are to pick six different numbers from a set of 49 numbers. You win the jackpot if you match *(in any order)* the six winning lottery numbers. How many chances of winning do you have now? To find out, you must find the number of ways in which 6 numbers can be selected from a set of 49 numbers when the order is not important; that is, we must find $C(49, 6)$. If you have a calculator, or if you are patient, you can compute $C(49, 6)$ and obtain 13,983,816. Your chances are only 1 in almost 14 million. Here we used combinations as our counting method.

    The examples and problems in this section will use the SCP, permutations, and combinations. The question you must consider is when to use which method. We will begin this section by showing you a diagram that may help you to make this choice.

In the preceding sections, we discussed the use of the sequential counting principle (SCP), permutations, and combinations in simple counting problems. Very often, the most difficult step in dealing with a counting problem is to decide which method or formula to use. We shall try to help you with this step in the following discussion.

A. *Permutations and Combinations*

As you recall, if the problem involves two or more events that are to occur in succession, you must use the SCP. For problems that involve the choosing of *r* items from a set of *n* different items, with no repetitions allowed, remember the diagram shown in Figure 9.10.

FIGURE 9.10

The next example will help to clarify this idea.

EXAMPLE 1   An employment agency has listed 5 highly skilled workers. Find in how many ways 2 of these workers can be selected:

(a) If the first one is to be a foreman and the second one is to be a helper.
(b) If they are simply to be sent to do a job.

Solution   In both parts of this problem, 2 workers are to be selected from 5.

(a) If the first worker is to be foreman and the second a helper, then the *order* in which they are picked is important. Hence, we must use *permutations*. The answer is

$$P(5, 2) = 5 \cdot 4 = 20$$

(b) Here the order is *not* important. (It makes no difference if Joe and Sally, or Sally and Joe are picked; both will be sent to the job.) Thus, we must use *combinations,* and the answer is

$$C(5, 2) = \frac{5 \cdot 4}{2 \cdot 1} = 10$$

∎

Sometimes, we must combine more than one principle in solving a counting problem. We illustrate this in the next example.

EXAMPLE 2   A television network has 6 different half-hour programs during prime time (7 P.M. to 10 P.M.). If you want to watch 3 programs in one evening:

(a) How many choices do you have?
(b) If exactly one of the programs must be after 9 P.M., how many choices do you have?

Solution In this problem, you can choose the programs, but you must watch them at the times when they are presented. No permutations are allowed. Thus, to answer the questions, we must use combinations.

(a) Here, we simply need to select 3 of the 6 programs. This means

$$C(6, 3) = \frac{6 \cdot 5 \cdot 4}{3 \cdot 2 \cdot 1} = 20 \text{ choices}$$

(b) We divide the problem into two parts:

1. Select 1 program after 9 P.M. There are 2 choices.
2. Select 2 other programs from 4 to before 9 P.M. There are

$$C(4, 2) = \frac{4 \cdot 3}{2 \cdot 1} = 6 \text{ choices}$$

Now we use the SCP to combine the two sets of choices. This gives

$$6 \cdot 2 = 12 \text{ choices}$$

∎

EXAMPLE 3 Here is another view of the television problem. A local station manager has 10 different half-hour programs available and needs to schedule 6 of them in the hours from 7 P.M. to 10 P.M. The station manager feels that 4 of the programs are unsuitable for showing before 9 P.M., but is obligated to show 2 of these sometime during the evening. How many choices does this leave for the evening's schedule?

Solution We divide this problem into two parts, as we did in Example 2(b). Here, however, the station manager can control the order as well as the choice of programs. Therefore, this problem requires permutations.

1. For the hours from 7 P.M. to 9 P.M., there are 6 programs available. Since the order of showing has to be considered, the number of choices is $P(6, 4) = 6 \cdot 5 \cdot 4 \cdot 3 = 360$.
2. For the hour from 9 P.M. to 10 P.M., there are 4 programs, of which 2 must be selected. The number of choices is $P(4, 2) = 4 \cdot 3 = 12$.

Now, we can use the SCP to give us the total number of choices, which is $360 \cdot 12 = 4320$. (Pity the poor station manager!)

∎

EXAMPLE 4 Roy and Rosie are eating out at an oriental restaurant. They select a special family dinner that allows an individual choice of 1 of 2 soups, 1 entree from 10 items in group A, 1 entree from 9 items in group B, and an individual choice of 1 of 4 desserts. How many different possibilities are there?

Solution We consider two cases:

1. Roy picks an entree from group A and Rosie picks one from group B. Thus, Roy has a choice of 2 soups, 10 entrees, and 4 desserts, so by the

SCP, he has $2 \cdot 10 \cdot 4 = 80$ choices. At the same time, Rosie has a choice of 2 soups, 9 entrees, and 4 desserts, so she has $2 \cdot 9 \cdot 4 = 72$ choices. Hence, by the SCP, together they have $80 \cdot 72 = 5760$ different choices available.

2. Roy picks an entree from group B and Rosie picks one from group A. This simply exchanges the choices we found in case 1, so the number of choices for both is again 5760.

Thus, the total number of possibilities is $2 \cdot 5760 = 11,520$. ∎

B. *Permutations of Non-Distinct Objects*

In these examples, all the objects considered were distinct (you could tell them apart). Here is a different type of problem. If you go to Madison, Wisconsin, and look at the white pages of the phone book, you might find that the last name listed is Hero Zzyzzx (pronounced "Ziz-icks"). Can we find in how many different ways the letters in Mr. Zzyzzx's last name can be arranged? Before tackling this problem, let us look at a simpler one. It is conceivable that no one calls Mr. Zzyzzx by his proper last name; perhaps he is named zzx (zicks) for short. In how many different ways can the letters in the name zzx be arranged? To do this problem, we first rewrite the name as $z_1 z_2 x$ so that we now have three distinct things. Then we look at all the possible arrangements of z_1, z_2, and x. After this step, we erase the subscripts and look at the arrangements again. Table 9.3 shows the two sets of arrangements. Notice that with the subscripts we have 3 distinct objects, which can be ordered in $P(3, 3) = 3! = 6$ ways. The second half of the table, with the subscripts erased, shows that two permutations of z_1, z_2, and x, in which the 2 z's are simply interchanged, become identical. Hence, to find the number of distinct arrangements without subscripts, we must divide the number with subscripts by the number of ways in which the identical letters can be permuted. Because there are 2 z's, they can be permuted in 2! ways, so the number of arrangements of zzx is

$$\frac{3!}{2!} = 3$$

Table 9.3

With Subscripts		Without Subscripts	
z_1z_2x	z_2z_1x	zzx	zzx
z_1xz_2	z_2xz_1	zxz	zxz
xz_1z_2	xz_2z_1	xzz	xzz

A similar argument leads to the general result. Suppose that a set of n objects consists of r different types, objects of the same type being indistinguishable. If there are n_1 objects of type 1, n_2 objects of type 2, . . . , n_r objects of type r, then the total number of *distinct* arrangements of the n objects is

$$\frac{n!}{n_1!n_2! \cdots n_r!}$$

With this formula, we can find the number of distinct arrangements of the letters in the name Zzyzzx. We regard the Z and the z as distinct, so there are 6 letters, 1 Z, 3 z's, 1 y, and 1 x. The formula gives

$$\frac{6!}{1!3!1!1!} = 6 \cdot 5 \cdot 4 = 120$$

EXAMPLE 5   In how many different ways can the letters in the name Minnie be arranged?

Solution   There is a total of $n = 6$ letters in the name: one M, two i's, two n's, and one e. Thus, $n_1 = 1$, $n_2 = 2$, $n_3 = 2$, and $n_4 = 1$. Hence, the number of distinct arrangements is

$$\frac{6!}{1!2!2!1!} = \frac{6 \cdot 5 \cdot 4 \cdot 3 \cdot 2 \cdot 1}{1 \cdot 1 \cdot 2 \cdot 1 \cdot 2 \cdot 1} = 180$$

■

EXAMPLE 6   The last name in the San Francisco phone book used to be (are you ready?) Zachary Zzzzzzzzzra. (Please, don't ask how to pronounce it!) In how many distinguishable ways can the letters in Zzzzzzzzzra be arranged?

Solution   Here, $n = 11$, $n_1 = 1$ (there is one Z), $n_2 = 8$ (there are 8 z's), $n_3 = 1$ (there is one r), and $n_4 = 1$ (there is one a). Thus, the number of distinct arrangements is

$$\frac{11!}{1!8!1!1!} = 11 \cdot 10 \cdot 9 = 990$$

■

Exercise 9.4

A.   1. Three cards are dealt in succession and without replacement from a standard deck of 52 cards.
(a) In how many different orders can the cards be dealt?
(b) How many different 3-card hands are possible?
2. An employment agency has 6 temporary workers.
(a) In how many ways could 4 of them be assigned to the research department?
(b) In how many ways could 3 of them be assigned to 3 different companies?

3. The playbook for the quarterback of the Dallas Cowboys contains 50 plays.

   (a) In how many ways could the quarterback select 3 plays to use in succession in the next 3 downs?

   (b) In how many ways could he select a set of 3 plays to study?

4. A student must take 3 different courses on Mondays. In how many ways can the student do this:

   (a) If there are 6 different courses, all available at each of the 3 hours 8 A.M., 9 A.M., and 10 A.M.?

   (b) If only 1 of these courses is available each hour between 8 A.M. and 2 P.M. (6 hours)?

5. Rework problem 4(b) if the student wants to keep the hour from 12 noon to 1 P.M. free for lunch.

6. A student wishes to schedule mathematics, English, and science. These classes are available every hour between 9 A.M. and noon (3 hours).

   (a) How many different schedules are possible?

   (b) How many schedules are possible if this student wants to take mathematics at 11 A.M. with his favorite instructor, Mr. B.?

7. Peter must select 3 electives from a group of 7 courses.

   (a) In how many ways can Peter do this?

   (b) If all 7 of these courses are available each of the 4 hours from 8 A.M. to noon, from how many different schedules (hours and what course at each hour) can Peter choose?

Table 9.4

Area	Courses
I	2
II	50
III	20
IV	40
V	100

8. At the University of South Florida, a student must take at least 2 courses from each of 5 different areas in order to satisfy the general distribution requirement. Each of the areas has the number of courses indicated in Table 9.4.

   (a) If Sandy has satisfied all the requirements except for area V, and she wishes to take 3 courses in this area, how many choices does she have?

   (b) Bill has already satisfied his requirements in areas I, II, and III. Now he wishes to take the minimum number of courses in areas IV and V. How many choices does he have?

9. A class consists of 14 boys and 10 girls. They want to elect officers so that the president and secretary are girls, and the vice-president and treasurer are boys.

   (a) How many possibilities are there?

   (b) How many are there if 2 of the boys refuse to participate?

10. A company has 6 officers and 4 directors (10 different people). In how many ways can a committee of 4 be selected from these 10 people so that:
    (a) 2 members are officers and 2 are directors?
    (b) 3 members are officers and 1 is a director?
    (c) All the members are officers?
    (d) There are no restrictions?

11. There are 4 vacancies on the scholarship committee at a certain university. In order to balance the men and women on the committee, 1 woman and 3 men are to be appointed. In how many ways can this be done if there are:
    (a) 7 men and 8 women available to serve?
    (b) 5 men and 2 women available to serve?

12. Romano's Restaurant has the menu shown in Example 8 of Section 9.3. In how many ways can a meal consisting of a pizza with 3 toppings, 2 beverages, and a dessert be chosen? The menu shows that there are 6 toppings for the pizza, 6 beverages, and 5 desserts offered.

B. 13. How many distinct arrangements can be made with the letters in the word TALLAHASSEE?

14. How many distinct arrangements can be made with the letters in the word MISSISSIPPI?

15. Do you know what a *palindrome* is? It is a word or phrase with the same spelling when written forward or backward. The longest single-word palindrome in the English language is the word REDIVIDER. How many distinct arrangements can be made with the letters in this word?

16. There is a place in Morocco with a name that has 8 vowels in a row in its spelling! Do you know what place this is? It is spelled IJOUAOUOUENE. How many distinct arrangements can be made with the letters in this name?

17. A contractor needs to buy 7 electronic components from 3 different subcontractors. The contractor wants to buy 2 of the components from the first subcontractor, 3 from the second, and 2 from the third. In how many ways can this be done?

18. An advertiser has a contract for 20 weeks that provides 3 different ads each week. If it is decided that in no 2 weeks will the same 3 ads be shown, how many different ads are necessary? [*Hint:* You need to find the least n such that $C(n, 3) \geq 20$.]

19. A cable television network wishes to show 5 movies every day for 3 weeks (21 days) without having to show the same 5 movies any 2 days in the 3 weeks. What is the least number of movies the network must have in order to do this? [See the hint in problem 18.]

20. Repeat problem 19 if the network wants to show the movies for 8 weeks.

21. Polly needs to take biology, English, and history. All of these are available every hour between 9 A.M. and 3 P.M. (6 hours). If Polly must schedule 2 of these courses between 9 A.M. and 1 P.M. and 1 course between 1 P.M. and 3 P.M., how many schedules (hours and what course each hour) are available to her?

22. Roy must elect 3 courses from among 4 courses in group I and 3 courses in group II. If he must take at least 1 of his 3 electives from each group, how many choices does he have? [*Hint:* First find how many choices he has if he elects only 1 course from group I. Then find how many choices he has if he elects 2 courses from group I. Since he must do one or the other of these, the final answer is the sum of the two answers.]

*I*n Other Words

23. Describe in your own words how you would decide which of the formulas to use (SCP, permutations, combinations) in a counting problem.

24. Which formula would you use in a counting problem involving indistinguishable objects. Explain.

Using Your Knowledge

Do you know an easy way of finding how many positive integers are exact divisors of a given positive integer? For example, how many exact divisors does 4,500 have? The easy way to answer this question is to write 4,500 first as a product of its prime divisors. We find that

$$4,500 = 2^2 3^2 5^3$$

Now you can see that every exact divisor of 4,500 must be of the form $2^a 3^b 5^c$, where a is 0, 1, or 2; b is 0, 1, or 2; and c is 0, 1, 2, or 3. Because there are 3 choices for a, 3 choices for b, and 4 choices for c, the SCP tells us that the number of exact divisors of 4,500 is $3 \cdot 3 \cdot 4 = 36$. Notice that the exponents in the prime factorization of 4500 are 2, 2, and 3 and the number of exact divisors is the product $(2 + 1)(2 + 1)(3 + 1)$. Try this out for a small number, say, 12, where you can check the answer by writing out all the exact divisors.

25. How many exact divisors does 144 have?

26. How many exact divisors does 2,520 have?

27. If the integer $N = 2^a 3^b 5^c 7^d$, how many exact divisors does N have?

28. How many exact divisors does the number $2^4 3^2 7^3$ have?

Chapter 9 Summary

Section	Item	Meaning	Example
9.1	SCP	Sequential counting principle: If one thing can occur in m ways and a second thing can then occur in n ways, and a third thing can occur in r ways, and so on, then the sequence of things can occur in $m \times n \times r \times \cdots$ ways.	If there are 3 roads to go to the beach and 2 dates are available, then you have $3 \times 2 = 6$ different choices.
9.2	Permutation	An ordered arrangement of n distinguishable objects, taken r at a time and with no repetitions	
9.2	$n!$ (n factorial)	$n(n-1)(n-2) \cdots \cdot 3 \cdot 2 \cdot 1$	$3! = 3 \cdot 2 \cdot 1 = 6$
9.2.	$P(n, r)$	$n(n-1)(n-2) \cdots \cdot (n-r+1)$ or $\dfrac{n!}{(n-r)!}$	$P(6, 2) = \dfrac{6!}{(6-2)!}$
9.2	0!	1	
9.2	Complementary counting principle	$n(A) = n(\mathcal{U}) - n(A')$	
9.2	Additive counting principle	$n(A \cup B) = n(A) + n(B) - n(A \cap B)$	
9.3	Combination	A selection of r objects without regard to order, taken from a set of n distinguishable objects	
9.3	$C(n, r)$	$\dfrac{n!}{r!(n-r)!} = \dfrac{P(n, r)}{r!}$	$C(6, 2) = \dfrac{6!}{2!4!}$
9.4	Permutations of a set of n objects, not all different	$\dfrac{n!}{n_2! n_2! \cdots \cdot n_r!}$	The number of arrangements of the letters aabbbc is $\dfrac{6!}{2!3!1!}$

Research Questions

Sources of information for these questions can be found in the Bibliography at the end of the book.

1. Who introduced the symbol $n!$, in what work, and why?
2. Write a report about the journal that Leibniz helped establish, the position he attained at the journal, and his mathematical achievements.
3. Research and write a paper on Leibniz's life, giving particular emphasis to *De Ars Combinatoria,* one of his works.

4. Write a report about Ben Ezra and his contributions to combinatorics.
5. This man rediscovered Euclid's 32nd proposition, invented the first calculating machine at the age of 18, and, inspired by a persistent toothache, became a successful researcher of the properties of the cycloid (a geometric curve). Find out who this mathematician was and write a paper detailing the events mentioned.

Chapter 9 Practice Test

1. A student wants to take two courses, A and B, both of which are available at 9, 10, and 11 A.M. Make a tree diagram to show all the possible schedules for that student. Use a notation like $(A, 9)$ to mean course A at 9 A.M., $(B, 11)$ to mean course B at 11 A.M., and so on.
2. A restaurant offers a choice of 2 soups, 3 entrees, and 5 desserts. How many different meals consisting of a soup, an entree, and a dessert are possible?
3. Suppose that one of two dice is black and the other is red.
   (a) If we distinguish the result of a toss of the two dice by both numbers and colors, how many different results are possible?
   (b) In how many ways could you get a sum of 5?
4. Two cards are drawn in succession and without replacement from a standard deck of 52 cards. In how many ways could these be a black jack and a red card, in that order?
5. An airline has 3 flights from city A to city B and 5 flights from city B to city C. In how many ways could you fly from city A to city C using this airline?
6. Compute:
   (a) 7!   (b) $\dfrac{7!}{4!}$
7. Compute:
   (a) $3! \times 4!$ (b) $3! + 4!$
8. Find:
   (a) $P(5, 5)$ (b) $P(6, 6)$
9. Find:
   (a) $P(8, 2)$ (b) $P(7, 3)$
10. In how many ways can 4 people be arranged in a row for a group picture?
11. Three married couples are posing for a group picture. They are to be seated in a row of 6 chairs, with each husband and wife together. In how many ways can this be done? *Hint:* First count the number of ways in which the couples can be arranged.
12. Bobby has 6 pigeons: 2 white, 2 gray, and 2 gray and white. In how many ways can Bobby select 3 of his pigeons and include exactly 1 white bird?
13. How many counting numbers less than 50 are divisible by 2 or 5?

14. How many different sums of money can be made from a set of coins consisting of a penny, a nickel, a dime, and a quarter if exactly 2 coins are selected?

15. Find:
    (a) $C(5, 2)$ (b) $C(6, 4)$

16. Find:
    (a) $C(6, 0)$ (b) $\dfrac{C(5, 4)}{C(5, 3)}$

17. How many subsets of 3 elements does the set $\{a, b, c, d, e, f\}$ have?

18. A student wants to schedule mathematics, English, science, and economics. These 4 classes are available every hour between 8 A.M. and noon (4 hours). How many different schedules are possible?

19. Two cards are drawn in succession and without replacement from a standard deck of 52 cards. How many different sets of 2 cards are possible?

20. Billy has 5 coins: a penny, a nickel, a dime, a quarter, and a half-dollar. How many different sums of money can Billy form by using 1, 2, or 3 of these coins?

21. On a certain night, there are 8 half-hour programs scheduled on one television station. If you want to watch 4 of these programs, how many choices do you have?

22. How many distinct arrangements can you make with the letters in the word BOOGABOO?

23. How many distinct arrangements can be made with the letters in the palindrome MADAM I'M ADAM? (Disregard the apostrophe.)

24. The A-1 Company needs 3 skilled employees, 1 to be a foreman and 2 to be helpers. If the company has 5 competent applicants, in how many ways can the employees be selected?

25. One of the biggest trading sprees on record (to that date) on the New York Stock Exchange occurred on August 26, 1982. On this day, 1977 stocks were traded, for a volume of 137,350,000 shares. Of the 1977 stocks traded, 1189 advanced (a), 460 declined (d), and 328 were unchanged (n). Suppose at the end of the day, you marked a, d, or n after each stock traded. How many distinct arrangements of all the a's, d's, and n's are possible? (Do not try to simplify your answer.)

CHAPTER PREVIEW

In this chapter we will study probability, the science of determining the likelihood or chance that an event will occur.

The study of probability dates back to the Assyrians and Sumerians who had games similar to dice. The Egyptians even had dice-like objects called *tali* made from the heel bone of an animal, polished and engraved so that when thrown they could land on any of four different sides with different probabilities, since the talus were not uniformly shaped. In Section 10.1 we shall study how to assign probabilities to an event. We will then use the ideas we studied in Chapter 9 (tree diagrams, the sequential counting principle, permutations, and combinations) to handle more complex problems and then study some of the theories and formulas used to facilitate the computations in probability. Because probability is heavily dependent on arithmetic, the absence of these formulas and methods long hampered the development of the theory of probability. It was not until the contributions of Pascal, Fermat, and Laplace that the theory was fully developed.

Sections 10.4 and 10.5 are devoted to the study of conditional probability and independent events, ideas that are used in medicine, law, and insurance.

We end the chapter by studying odds and mathematical expectation. If your state has a lottery, you can verify the odds of the game and the probability of obtaining different prizes. But our applications of mathematical expectation are not limited to gambling. We also use the idea as a management tool to determine which way to proceed when confronted with different business decisions involving outcomes with given probabilities, and consider the results that can be expected when these outcomes occur.

Probability

THE HUMAN SIDE OF MATHEMATICS

Blaise Pascal is undoubtedly one of the greatest might-have-beens in the history of mathematics. His most original contribution was in the theory of probability but this notoriety was shared by the famous French mathematician, Pierre Fermat. Although Pascal did first-rate mathematics, he was distracted by philosophical subtleties, and buried his talent in searching for answers to unanswerable questions.

Born in the French province of Auvergne in June of 1623, Pascal moved with his father and sisters to Paris when Blaise was 7 years old. The boy was blessed with a brilliant mind, and at the age of 12 plunged into the study of geometry, even proving a few theorems on his own without any book to help.

By the age of 17, Pascal had written an amazing essay on the conic sections, including new and deep theorems on the properties of these curves. So profound was this work, that René Descartes could not

Blaise Pascal (1623–1662)
It is truth very certain that, when it is not in our power to determine what is true, we ought to follow what is most probable.

René Descartes

believe it had been done so by anyone so young.

At the age of 18, Pascal had invented the world's first calculating machine, and had begun to work in physics and mechanics. But he continued his scientific work for only a few years, quitting at the age of 27 to devote himself to religious contemplation.

He lapsed into mathematics only a few times after this. He was 31 when the Chevalier de Méré proposed to him a problem on the division of the pot in an unfinished gambling game. Pascal wrote to Fermat about the problem, and in the ensuing correspondence these two men shared equally in establishing basic results in the theory of probability.

Looking Ahead: Pascal and Fermat were not the first to delve into matters of probability theory. However, mathematicians' interest in this field grew because of their writings and prompted the thorough development of the theories contained in this chapter.

10.1   SAMPLE SPACES AND PROBABILITY

"Tonight Show" host Jay Leno (right) talks with actor Jason Priestly

GETTING STARTED

PROBABILITY AND THE TONIGHT SHOW

Which is more probable, appearing on the "Tonight Show" or winning the jackpot in your state lottery with a single ticket? (If there is no lottery in your state, the probability of winning it is, of course, 0.) According to a book called *What Are the Chances* the probability of appearing on the "Tonight Show" is 1 in 490,000, that is $\frac{1}{490,000}$. What is the probability of winning the jackpot in your state lottery? In most lotteries you buy a $1 ticket and pick six numbers from 1 to 49. (In California you pick numbers from 1 to 53.) If you match all six numbers, you win the jackpot. How probable is that? Since there is only one set of winning numbers and $C(49, 6)$ possible number combinations, your probability is 1 in $C(49, 6)$, that is, $\frac{1}{13,983,816}$. It is much more probable that you will appear on the "Tonight Show"! If you are playing the California lottery, the probability that you hold a winning ticket is even smaller, since there are more possible number combinations, namely, $C(53, 6)$ instead of $C(49, 6)$. This makes the probability of winning the California jackpot 1 in 22,957,480.

Probability theory was developed by mathematicians studying gambling games. In 1654, Antoine Gombaud, better known as the Chevalier de Méré, offered even money that in four rolls of a die, at least one 6 would come up. He reasoned that since the chance that a 6 will come up when a die is thrown is $\frac{1}{6}$, in four rolls the chances of getting at least one 6 should equal $\frac{4}{6} = \frac{2}{3}$. Do you think he was right? You will be able to give the answer after you read this section!

The WIZARD OF ID by permission of Johnny Hart and Creator's Syndicate, Inc.

We often hear such statements as, "It will probably be a hot day tomorrow," "I have a good chance of getting a B in this course," and "If a penny is tossed, there is a 50–50 chance that it will come up heads." Each of us has a sort of intuitive feeling as to what such a statement means, but it is not easy to give an exact mathematical formulation of this meaning. The objective of *probability theory* is to make such statements precise by giving them numerical measures.

The theory of probability is an important tool in the solution of many problems of the modern world. Although the most obvious applications are in gambling games, important applications occur in many situations involving an element of uncertainty. Probability theory is used to estimate whether a missile will hit its target, to determine premiums on insurance policies, and to make important business decisions such as where to locate a supermarket and how many checkout clerks to employ so that customers will not be kept waiting in line too long. Various sampling techniques, which are used in opinion polls and in the quality control of mass-produced items, are based on the theory of probability.

We want the **probability** of a given event to be a mathematical estimate of the likelihood that this event will occur. The following examples show how a probability may be assigned to a given event.

EXAMPLE 1   A fair coin is tossed; find the probability of a head coming up.

Solution   At this time we are unable to solve this problem because we have not even defined the term *probability*. However, our intuition tells us the following:

1. When a fair coin is tossed, it may turn up in either of 2 ways. Assuming that the coin will not stand on edge, heads or tails are the only 2 possible **outcomes.**

2. If the coin is balanced (and this is what we mean by saying "the coin is fair"), the 2 outcomes are considered **equally likely.**

3. The probability of obtaining heads when a fair coin is tossed, denoted by $P(H)$, is 1 out of 2. That is, $P(H) = \frac{1}{2}$. ■

A. *Sample Spaces and Probability*

Activities such as tossing a coin (as in Example 1), drawing a card from a deck, or rolling a pair of dice are called **experiments.** The set $\mathcal{U}$ of all possible outcomes for an experiment is called the **sample space** for the experiment. These terms are illustrated in Table 10.1 on the following page.

Returning to Example 1, we see that the set of all possible outcomes for the experiment is $\mathcal{U} = \{H, T\}$. But there are only two subsets of $\mathcal{U}$ that can occur, namely, $\{H\}$ and $\{T\}$, and each of these is called an **event.** If heads come up, that is, if the event $E = \{H\}$ occurs, we say that we have a **favorable outcome,** or a **success.** Since there are **two** equally likely events in $\mathcal{U}$, and **one** of these is E, we assign the value $\frac{1}{2}$ to the event E.

Table 10.1 *Experiments and Sample Spaces*

Experiment	Possible Outcomes	Sample Space $\mathcal{U}$
A penny is tossed.	Heads or tails are equally likely outcomes.	$\{H, T\}$
There are 3 beige and 3 red balls in a box; 1 ball is drawn at random.	A beige or a red ball is equally likely to be drawn.	$\{b_1, b_2, b_3, r_1, r_2, r_3\}$
A penny and a nickel are tossed.	**Penny** **Nickel** H H H T T H T T	$\{(H, H), (H, T),$ $(T, H), (T, T)\}$
One die is rolled.	The numbers from 1 to 6 are all equally likely outcomes.	$\{1, 2, 3, 4, 5, 6\}$
The pointer is spun:	The pointer is equally likely to point to 1, 2, 3, or 4.	$\{1, 2, 3, 4\}$
An integer between 1 and 50 (inclusive) is selected at random.	The integers from 1 to 50 are all equally likely to be selected.	$\{1, 2, 3, \ldots, 50\}$

We now expand upon the problem discussed in Example 1. Suppose that the coin is tossed 3 times. Can we find the probability that 3 heads appear? As before, we proceed in three steps:

1. The set of all possible outcomes for this experiment can be found by drawing a tree diagram as shown in Figure 10.1 (page 701). As you can see, the possibilities for the first toss are labeled H and T, and likewise for the other two tosses. The number of outcomes is 8.

2. The 8 outcomes are equally likely.

3. We conclude that the probability of getting 3 heads, denoted by $P(HHH)$,* is 1 out of 8; that is, $P(HHH) = \frac{1}{8}$.

---

* Technically, we should write $P(\{HHH\})$ instead of $P(HHH)$. However, we shall write $P(HHH)$ whenever the meaning is clear.

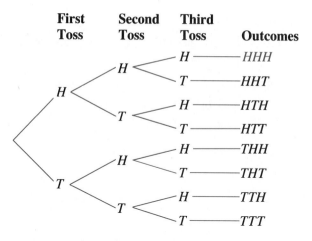

| First Toss | Second Toss | Third Toss | Outcomes |

FIGURE 10.1 *Tree diagram*

If we want to know the probability of getting **at least** 2 heads, the 4 outcomes *HHH*, *HHT*, *HTH*, and *THH* are favorable, so the probability of getting at least 2 heads is $\frac{4}{8} = \frac{1}{2}$.

In examples such as these, in which all the possible outcomes are equally likely, the task of finding the probability of any event E can be simplified by using the following definition:

Definition 10.1

Suppose an experiment has $n(\mathcal{U})$ possible outcomes, **all equally likely.** Suppose further that the event E occurs in $n(E)$ of these outcomes. Then $P(E)$, the **probability** of event E, is given by

$$P(E) = \frac{\text{Number of favorable outcomes}}{\text{Number of possible outcomes}} = \frac{n(E)}{n(\mathcal{U})} \qquad (1)$$

We illustrate the use of equation (1) in the following examples. Note that $0 \le P(E) \le 1$ because $0 \le n(E) \le n(\mathcal{U})$.

Problem Solving:	**Computing Probability**
	There are 75 possible numbers in Bingo. Find the probability that the first number selected is:
	(a) number 25 (b) number 80 (c) an odd number (d) a number less than 80
1. Read the problem. **2. Select the unknown.**	We want to find the probability of four events (a), (b), (c), and (d).

3. Think of a plan.

We have to find out how many outcomes are possible when the first number is selected and in how many ways each of the four given events (a), (b), (c), and (d) can occur.

If you select a number from a group of 75 numbers, there are 75 equally likely outcomes; that is, the universal set is

$$\mathcal{U} = \{1, 2, 3, \ldots, 75\} \quad \text{and} \quad n(\mathcal{U}) = 75.$$

Let T be: number 25 is selected.
Let E be: number 80 is selected.
Let O be: an odd number is selected.
Let L be: a number less than 80 is selected.

4. Use Definition 10.1 to find the probability of each event.

In how many ways can you

(a) select number 25?

(a) There is only one way of selecting number 25, thus

$$P(T) = \frac{n(T)}{n(\mathcal{U})} = \frac{1}{75}.$$

(b) select number 80?

(b) There is no way number 80 can be selected, thus, $P(E) = \frac{0}{75} = 0$. This event is *impossible*.

(c) select an odd number?

(c) There are 38 odd numbers that are less than 76, thus, $P(O) = \frac{38}{75}$.

(d) select a number that is less than 80?

(d) All 75 numbers in Bingo are less than 80, thus, $P(L) = \frac{75}{75} = 1$. We say that this event is *certain*.

5. Verify the solution.

Are all probabilities between 0 and 1 inclusive?

TRY EXAMPLE 2 NOW.

Cover the solution, write your own, and then check your work.

EXAMPLE 2　A single die is rolled. Find the probability of obtaining

(a) a number greater than 4
(b) an odd number

Solution　(a) Let E be the event in which a number greater than 4 appears. When a die is rolled, there are 6 equally likely outcomes, so that $n(\mathcal{U}) = 6$. Two of these outcomes (5 and 6) are in E, that is, $n(E) = 2$. Hence,

$$P(E) = \frac{n(E)}{n(\mathcal{U})} = \frac{2}{6} = \frac{1}{3}$$

(b) Let O be the event in which an odd number appears. Three outcomes (1, 3, 5) are in O. Thus, $P(O) = \frac{3}{6} = \frac{1}{2}$.

EXAMPLE 3 Ten balls numbered from 1 to 10 are placed in an urn. If 1 ball is selected at random, find the probability that:

(a) An even-numbered ball is selected (event E)
(b) Ball number 3 is chosen (event T)
(c) Ball number 3 is not chosen (event T')

Solution (a) There are 5 outcomes (2, 4, 6, 8, 10) in E out of 10 equally likely outcomes. Hence,

$$P(E) = \tfrac{5}{10} = \tfrac{1}{2}$$

(b) There is only 1 outcome (3) in the event T out of 10 equally likely outcomes. Thus, $P(T) = \tfrac{1}{10}$.
(c) There are 9 outcomes (all except the 3) in T' out of the 10 possible outcomes. Hence, $P(T') = \tfrac{9}{10}$. ∎

In Example 3 we found $P(T) = \tfrac{1}{10}$ and $P(T') = \tfrac{9}{10}$, so that $P(T') = 1 - P(T)$. This is a general result because $T \cup T' = \mathcal{U}$ and $T \cap T' = \emptyset$. Thus,

$$n(T \cup T') = n(T) + n(T') = n(\mathcal{U})$$

Therefore,

$$\frac{n(T)}{n(\mathcal{U})} + \frac{n(T')}{n(\mathcal{U})} = \frac{n(\mathcal{U})}{n(\mathcal{U})}$$

or, by Definition 10.1,

$$P(T) + P(T') = 1$$

and

$$P(T') = 1 - P(T)$$

The next example illustrates the use of this idea.

EXAMPLE 4 A coin is thrown 3 times. Find the probability of obtaining at least 1 head.

Solution Let E be the event that we obtain at least 1 head. Then E' is the event that we obtain 0 heads; that is, that we obtain 3 tails. From the above discussion, $P(E) = 1 - P(E')$. Here, $P(E')$ is the same as $P(TTT) = \tfrac{1}{8}$; hence, $P(E) = 1 - P(TTT) = 1 - \tfrac{1}{8} = \tfrac{7}{8}$. ∎

EXAMPLE 5 The science of heredity uses the theory of probability to determine the likelihood of obtaining flowers of a specified color when cross-breeding. Suppose we represent with letters the genes that determine the color of an offspring

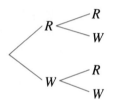

FIGURE 10.2

flower. For example, a white offspring has genes WW, a red offspring has genes RR, and a pink offspring has genes RW or WR. When we cross-breed 2 pink flowers, each plant contributes one of its color genes to each of its offspring. The tree diagram in Figure 10.2 shows the 4 possibilities. Assuming that these possibilities are all equally likely, what is the probability of obtaining:

(a) A white flower?
(b) A pink flower?
(c) A red flower?

Solution (a) We see from the tree diagram that the probability of obtaining a white flower (WW) is $\frac{1}{4}$.
(b) The probability of obtaining a pink flower (RW or WR) is $\frac{2}{4} = \frac{1}{2}$.
(c) The probability of obtaining a red flower (RR) is $\frac{1}{4}$. ∎

EXAMPLE 6 A light die and a dark die are rolled. Find:

(a) The sample space for this experiment
(b) The probability that the sum of the two numbers coming up is 12

Solution (a) Figure 10.3 shows the 36 possible outcomes. The sample space for this experiment is given as follows, where the number appearing first is the number on the dark die:

$$\begin{bmatrix}
(1, 1) & (1, 2) & (1, 3) & (1, 4) & (1, 5) & (1, 6)\\
(2, 1) & (2, 2) & (2, 3) & (2, 4) & (2, 5) & (2, 6)\\
(3, 1) & (3, 2) & (3, 3) & (3, 4) & (3, 5) & (3, 6)\\
(4, 1) & (4, 2) & (4, 3) & (4, 4) & (4, 5) & (4, 6)\\
(5, 1) & (5, 2) & (5, 3) & (5, 4) & (5, 5) & (5, 6)\\
(6, 1) & (6, 2) & (6, 3) & (6, 4) & (6, 5) & (6, 6)
\end{bmatrix}$$

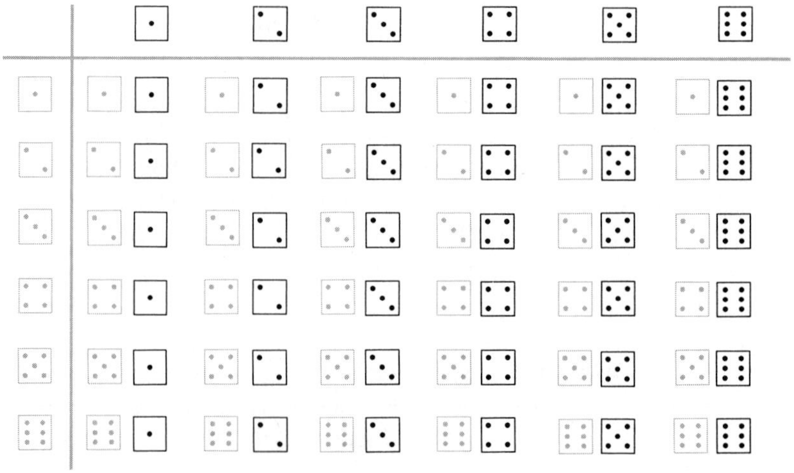

FIGURE 10.3

(b) The probability that the sum of the two numbers coming up is 12 is $\frac{1}{36}$, because there is only 1 favorable case, $(6, 6)$, and there are 36 possible outcomes, all equally likely.

■

EXAMPLE 7   Find the probability of getting a king when drawing 1 card at random from a standard deck of 52 playing cards.

Solution   A standard deck of playing cards consists of 4 suits (clubs, diamonds, hearts, and spades) of 13 cards each. The clubs and spades are printed in black; the diamonds and hearts are printed in red. Each suit contains 9 cards numbered from 2 to 10, an ace, and 3 picture cards: a jack, a queen, and a king. Since 4 of the 52 cards are kings, the probability of drawing a king is

$$\frac{4}{52} = \frac{1}{13}.$$

■

B. *Events That Are Not Equally Likely*

Thus far, we have considered only experiments with equally likely outcomes. Now we look at a procedure that can be used to compute probabilities of events when the outcomes are not all equally likely. We proceed in three steps:

1. We determine $\mathcal{U}$, the sample space — that is, the set of all possible outcomes for the given experiment.
2. We assign a positive number (weight) to each element of $\mathcal{U}$. (We try to assign this weight so that it measures the relative likelihood that this outcome will actually occur.)
3. Let $w(E)$ be the sum of the weights of the elements in E, and let $w(\mathcal{U})$ be the sum of the weights of the elements in $\mathcal{U}$. The probability of the event E is

$$P(E) = \frac{w(E)}{w(\mathcal{U})}$$

EXAMPLE 8   Suppose there is a race between two horses, A and B. If A is twice as likely to win as B, what is the probability that A wins the race?

Solution   1. $\mathcal{U}$, the sample space is $\{A \text{ wins}, B \text{ wins}\}$.
2. Because A is twice as likely to win as B, we assign a weight of 2 to $\{A \text{ wins}\}$ and 1 to $\{B \text{ wins}\}$.
3. The weight of event E $(= \{A \text{ wins}\})$ is $W(E) = 2$, and the sum of all the weights is $w(\mathcal{U}) = 3$. Thus,

$$P(E) = \frac{w(E)}{w(\mathcal{U})} = \frac{2}{3}$$

■

EXAMPLE 9   An accident is twice as likely to occur at noon as at 3 P.M., and 7 times as likely to occur at 6 P.M. as at 3 P.M. If an accident does occur at one of these hours, what is the probability that it occurs at noon?

Solution   1. Let N, T, and S be the events that the accident occurs at noon, at 3 P.M., and at 6 P.M., respectively. The sample space is $\mathcal{U} = \{N, T, S\}$.
2. Because event N is twice as likely as event T, and event S is 7 times as likely as event T, we assign a weight of 2 to N, 1 to T, and 7 to S.
3. The sum of all the weights is $1 + 2 + 7 = 10$, so

$$P(N) = \tfrac{2}{10} = \tfrac{1}{5} \qquad\qquad\blacksquare$$

Exercise 10.1

A.   On a single toss of a die, what is the probability of obtaining the following?

1. The number 5
2. An even number
3. A number greater than 4
4. A number less than 5

A single ball is taken at random from an urn containing 10 balls numbered 1 through 10. What is the probability of obtaining the following?

5. Ball number 8
6. An even-numbered ball
7. A ball different from 5
8. A ball whose number is less than 10
9. A ball numbered 12
10. A ball that is either less than 5 or odd

In problems 11–16, assume that a single card is drawn from a well-shuffled deck of 52 cards. Find the probability that:

11. An ace is drawn.
12. The king of spades is drawn.
13. A spade is drawn.
14. One of the picture cards (jack, queen, or king) is drawn.
15. A picture card or a spade is drawn.
16. A red card or a picture card is drawn.
17. An executive has to visit one of his five plants for an inspection. If these plants are numbered 1, 2, 3, 4, 5 and if he is to select the plant he will visit at random, find the probability that:
    (a) He will visit plant number 1.
    (b) He will visit an odd-numbered plant.
    (c) He will not visit plant number 4.

18. Four fair coins are tossed.
    (a) Draw a tree diagram to show all the possible outcomes.
    (b) Find the probability that 2 or more heads come up.
    (c) Find the probability that exactly 1 head comes up.

19. A disk is divided into 3 equal parts numbered 1, 2, and 3, respectively (see the figure in the margin). After the disk is spun and comes to a stop, a fixed pointer will be pointing to one of the three numbers. Suppose that the disk is spun once.
    (a) Find the probability that the disk stops on the number 3.
    (b) Find the probability that the disk stops on an even number.

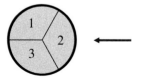

Many companies send packages from one location to another using delivery services such as Airborne and Federal Express. Assume that a person can select from 8 such delivery services A, B, C, D, E, F, G, and H. If one of the services is to be selected at random to mail a package, answer problems 20–23.

20. Find the probability that company A is selected.

21. Find the probability that company G is selected.

22. Find the probability that company C is not used to mail the package

23. Find the probability that one of the first three companies is selected.

24. The genetic code of an organism is the self-reproducing record of the protein pattern in that organism. This code is formed by groups of small molecules that can be of 4 kinds: adenine (A), cytosine (C), guanine (G), and thymine (T).
    (a) Draw a tree diagram to find all possible groups of 2 molecules. [*Note*: It is possible for both molecules to be of the same kind.]
    (b) Assume that all the outcomes in part (a) are equally likely. Find the probability of obtaining 2 adenine molecules in a row.
    (c) Find the probability of obtaining a guanine molecule and a cytosine molecule, in that order.
    (d) Find the probability of obtaining two cytosine molecules in a row.

25. In a survey conducted on a Friday at Quick Shop Supermarket, it was found that 650 of 850 people who entered the supermarket bought at least 1 item. Find the probability that a person entering the supermarket on Friday will purchase:
    (a) At least 1 item
    (b) No item

26. Two common sources of nicotine are cigarettes and cigars. Suppose that 35 percent of the adults in the United States smoke cigarettes but not cigars and 10 percent smoke both cigarettes and cigars. Find the probability that a randomly selected adult does not smoke cigarettes. [*Hint*: Draw a Venn diagram.]

Table 10.2

Salary	Sex M	F	Totals
Low	40	200	240
Average	300	160	460
High	500	300	800
Totals	840	660	1500

Use Table 10.2 in problems 27–30. The table gives the numbers of males and females in a survey falling into various salary classifications. On the basis of the information in the table, find the probability that a person selected at random from those surveyed:

27. (a) is a female   (b) is a male

28. (a) has a high income   (b) has a low income

29. Is a female with
    (a) an average income   (b) a high income

30. Is a male with
    (a) a low income   (b) a high income

In problems 31–35, find the probability of obtaining the following on a single toss of a pair of dice, one red and one white (see Example 6):

31. A sum of 7

32. A sum of 2

33. The same number on both dice

34. Different numbers on the two dice

35. An even number for the sum

B. Use the procedure in Example 8 to solve the following problems:

36. Stock A is twice as likely to rise in price as stock B or C, while B is as likely to rise in price as C. If it is known that exactly one of the stocks will rise in price, what is the probability that:
    (a) A will rise   (b) B will rise   (c) C will rise
        in price?   in price?   in price?

37. A die is loaded in such a way that the probability of a particular number turning up is proportional to the number of dots showing. Thus, a 6 is three times as likely as a 2 and six times as likely as a 1. Find the probability that:
    (a) The number 3 will turn up.
    (b) An even number will turn up.
    (c) A number greater than 4 will turn up.

38. Three horses, A, B, and C, are in a race. Horse A is twice as likely to win the race as horse B, and horse B is twice as likely to win as horse C. Find the probability that:
    (a) A wins.   (b) B wins.   (c) C wins.

39. In a certain experiment, the event A can occur, or the event B can occur, or C the experiment fails. Event A is given a weight of 5, B is given a weight of 3, and C is given a weight of 2. Assuming these weights are correct, find the probability that:
    (a) A occurs.   (b) B occurs.   (c) C occurs.

40. The weather forecaster predicts that it is $1\frac{1}{2}$ times as likely for it to be sunny than cloudy tomorrow, and 3 times as likely for it to be sunny than rainy. Based on these predictions, what is the probability that tomorrow will be:
    (a) Sunny?   (b) Cloudy?   (c) Rainy?

In Other Words

41. Explain in your own words what is meant by a probability experiment and the corresponding sample space. Give an example.

42. Explain under what circumstances the probability formula

$$P(E) = \frac{n(E)}{n(\mathcal{U})}$$

    does *not* apply. Give an example.

Using Your Knowledge

Do you have to have surgery soon? The chances are that you will have no trouble at all! Table 10.3 gives the statistics for the numbers of certain operations and the number of successes in a recent year. On the basis of these statistics, estimate the following probabilities.

43. The probability of a gallbladder operation being successful.

44. The probability of an appendectomy being successful.

45. The probability of a hernia operation being successful.

Table 10.3

Type	Number of Operations	Number of Successes
Gallbladder	472,000	465,300
Appendectomy	784,000	781,000
Hernia	508,000	506,000

10.2   COUNTING TECHNIQUES AND PROBABILITY

Poker Improbabilities

Have you ever played poker? Scarne's *Complete Guide to Gambling* claims that 95 out of 100 adults have played the game! In his book, *Poker Stories* (1896) John F. B. Lillard tells the story of a professional gambler stopping for a beer at a saloon in Butte, Montana. As luck would have it, a poker game was

in progress, so the hustler decided to join in and make some money. After playing for a while, the hustler dealt himself four aces. Do you know the probability of getting 4 aces in a poker hand? Since there are four aces in a deck, there is only one way of getting four aces but the fifth card can be any of the 48 remaining; hence, there are $1 \cdot C(48, 1) = 48$ ways of getting four aces of the $C(52, 5) = 2,598,960$ possible poker hands (see Example 6 for the computation). Thus, the probability of 4 aces in poker is only

$$\frac{48}{2,598,960} = \frac{1}{54,145}.$$

Assured of winning, the hustler made a fair-sized bet that forced every player to drop out, except for one old stalwart with gray whiskers and a deadpan poker face. The old cowboy didn't blink, he merely shoved all his chips into the pot and called. The hustler showed his four aces and reached for the pot.

"Not so fast, sonny," said the cowboy, laying down three clubs and two diamonds. (Can you find the probability of getting three clubs and two diamonds? It is

$$\frac{C(13, 3) \cdot C(13, 2)}{C(52, 5)} = \frac{22,308}{2,598,960}.$$

"What do you mean, not so fast?" the hustler said. "My four aces have a lower probability and they should win."

"Of course they should—ord'narily," the cowboy said, "But in this town a Lollapalooza beats anythin', and that's what I've got, three clubs and two diamonds, a Lollapalooza."

The hustler knew he had just been out-hustled, but he figured he could still change his "luck." On the next deal, the hustler dealt himself a Lollapalooza and gave four aces to the old cowboy with the gray whiskers. Again he made a fair-sized bet and again the old cowboy stayed while the rest dropped out. The hustler pushed all his chips to the center of the table. The cowboy called again.

"Well," the hustler said grinning, "This time I can't lose. Seems I've got the Lollapalooza!"

But the old cowboy was already bellied-up to the table, raking in the pot. "Sorry, pardner," he said, as the hustler looked on, "Only one Lollapalooza per night!"

In this section, we shall use the SCP, permutations, and combinations to find the probability of many events, including different poker hands.

The counting techniques that we studied in Chapter 9 play a key role in many probability problems. In this section, we illustrate how these techniques are used in such problems.

A. *Using Tree Diagrams*

EXAMPLE 1 Have you heard of the witches of Wall Street? These are people who use astrology, tarot cards, or other supernatural means to predict whether a given stock will go up, go down, or stay unchanged. Not being witches, we assume that a stock is equally likely to go up, go down, or stay unchanged. A broker selects two stocks at random from the New York Stock Exchange list.

(a) What is the probability that both stocks go up?

(b) What is the probability that both stocks go down?

(c) What is the probability that one stock goes up and one down?

Solution   In order to find the total number of equally likely possibilities for the two stocks, we draw the tree diagram shown in Figure 10.4.

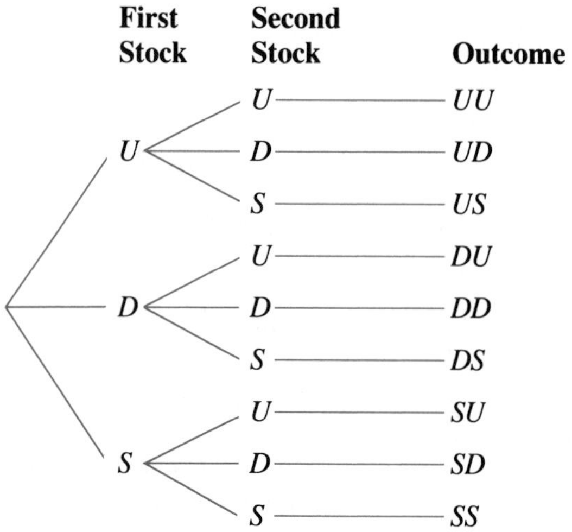

First Stock	Second Stock	Outcome

FIGURE 10.4

(a) There is only 1 outcome (*UU*) out of 9 in which both stocks go up. Thus, the probability that both stocks go up is $\frac{1}{9}$.

(b) There is only 1 outcome (*DD*) in which both stocks go down, so the probability that both go down is $\frac{1}{9}$.

(c) There are 2 outcomes (*UD*, *DU*) in which one stock goes up and one down. Hence, the probability of this event is $\frac{2}{9}$.

(Notice that the tree diagram shows that there are 4 outcomes in which one stock stays unchanged and the other goes either up or down. The probability of this event is thus $\frac{4}{9}$.)

■

B. *Using Permutations and Combinations*

In many games of chance, probability is used to determine payoffs. For example, a slot machine has 3 dials with 20 symbols on each dial, as listed in Table 10.4. In the next example, we shall find the probability of getting certain arrangements of these symbols on the 3 dials.

Table 10.4

Symbol	Dial 1	2	3
Bar	1	3	1
Bell	1	3	3
Cherry	7	7	0
Lemon	3	0	4
Orange	3	6	7
Plum	5	1	5

EXAMPLE 2   Refer to the slot machine and to Table 10.4 to answer these questions:

(a) What is the probability of getting 3 bars?

(b) What is the probability of getting 3 bells?

(c) What is the probability of getting 3 oranges?

(d) What is the probability of getting 3 plums?

(e) Based on your answers to these questions, which payoff should be the greatest and which should be the least?

Solution (a) We make 3 boxes representing the 3 dials:

☐ ☐ ☐

There are 20 choices for each of the boxes (each dial has 20 symbols), so we enter a 20 in each box:

20 20 20

The total number of possibilities is $20 \times 20 \times 20 = 8000$. Now, the number of ways to get 3 bars is $1 \times 3 \times 1 = 3$, because the first dial has 1 bar, the second has 3 bars, and the third has 1 bar. Thus,

$$P(3 \text{ bars}) = \frac{\text{Number of favorable cases}}{\text{Number of possible outcomes}} = \frac{3}{8000}$$

(b) The number of ways of getting 3 bells is $1 \times 3 \times 3 = 9$. Thus,

$$P(3 \text{ bells}) = \frac{9}{8000}$$

(c) The number of ways of getting 3 oranges is $3 \times 6 \times 7 = 126$. Thus,

$$P(3 \text{ oranges}) = \frac{126}{8000} = \frac{63}{4000}$$

(d) The number of ways of getting 3 plums is $5 \times 1 \times 5 = 25$. Thus,

$$P(3 \text{ plums}) = \frac{25}{8000} = \frac{1}{320}$$

(e) Since 3 bars is the outcome with the lowest probability and 3 oranges is the outcome with the highest probability, the greatest payoff should be for 3 bars and the least for 3 oranges. (This is how payoffs are actually determined.)

■

EXAMPLE 3 Suppose you are one of a committee of ten people, of whom two are to be chosen for a particular task. If these are selected by just drawing names out of a hat, what is the probability that you will be one of the two selected?

Solution It is easy to calculate the probability that you will not be selected. Since there are 9 people not including you, there are $P(9, 2)$ ways of selecting two not including you. Also there are $P(10, 2)$ ways of selecting two people from the entire ten. Hence, the probability P' that you will *not* be selected is

$$P' = \frac{P(9, 2)}{P(10, 2)} = \frac{9 \times 8}{10 \times 9} = \frac{4}{5}$$

So the probability that you *will* be selected is

$$P = 1 - P' = \frac{1}{5}$$ ∎

The next example deals with a problem involving ordinary playing cards. Note that in solving part (a), you can use combinations, permutations, or the SCP. The important thing is to be consistent in the computation.

EXAMPLE 4   Two cards are drawn in succession from an ordinary deck of 52 cards. Find the probability that:

(a) The cards are both aces.
(b) An ace and a king, in that order, are obtained.

Solution   (a) Here, the order is not important because we are simply interested in getting 2 aces. We can find this probability by using combinations. The number of ways to draw 2 aces is $C(4, 2)$, because there are 4 aces and we want a combination of any 2 of them. The number of combinations of 2 cards picked from the deck of 52 cards is $C(52, 2)$. Thus, the probability of both cards being aces is

$$\frac{C(4, 2)}{C(52, 2)} = \frac{P(4, 2)}{2!} \div \frac{P(52, 2)}{2!} = \frac{P(4, 2)}{P(52, 2)} = \frac{4 \cdot 3}{52 \cdot 51} = \frac{1}{221}$$

We can also find the probability using permutations. The number of ways to draw two aces is $P(4, 2)$ and the number of ways of picking 2 cards from 52 is $P(52, 2)$

By the SCP, there are 4 ways of drawing the first ace and 3 for the second, out of 52 choices for the first card and 51 for the second.

(b) In this part of the problem, we want to consider the order in which the 2 cards are drawn, so we use permutations. The number of ways of selecting an ace is $P(4, 1)$ and the number of ways of selecting a king is $P(4, 1)$. By the SCP, the number of ways of doing these two things in succession is $P(4, 1)P(4, 1)$. The total number of ways of drawing 2 cards is $P(52, 2)$, so the probability of drawing an ace and a king, in that order, is

$$\frac{P(4, 1)P(4, 1)}{P(52, 2)} = \frac{4 \cdot 4}{52 \cdot 51} = \frac{4}{663}$$ ∎

In part (a) of Example 4, we found that

$$\frac{C(4,2)}{C(52, 2)} = \frac{P(4, 2)}{P(52, 2)}$$

This equation is a special case of a general result that can be obtained as follows:

$$\frac{C(m, r)}{C(n, r)} = C(m, r) \div C(n, r)$$

$$= \frac{P(m, r)}{r!} \div \frac{P(n, r)}{r!}$$

$$= \frac{P(m, r)}{r!} \times \frac{r!}{P(n, r)} = \frac{P(m, r)}{P(n, r)}$$

EXAMPLE 5   Suppose we take one suit, say, the 13 hearts, out of a standard deck of 52 cards. Shuffle the 13 hearts and then draw 3 of them. What is the probability that none of the 3 will be an ace, king, queen, or jack?

Solution   Here the order does not matter, so we use combinations. The number of combinations of 13 things taken 3 at a time is $C(13, 3)$. There are 9 cards not including the ace, king, queen, or jack, and the number of combinations of these taken 3 at a time is $C(9, 3)$. Thus, the required probability is

$$\underbrace{\frac{C(9, 3)}{C(13, 3)} = \frac{P(9, 3)}{P(13, 3)}}_{\text{Using Permutations}} = \underbrace{\frac{9 \cdot 8 \cdot 7}{13 \cdot 12 \cdot 11}}_{\text{Using the SCP}} = \frac{42}{143}$$

In Example 5, because we are taking 3 cards from both the 13 hearts and the 9 cards, we could use either combinations or permutations. The next example is one that requires the use of combinations.

EXAMPLE 6   A poker hand consists of 5 cards. What is the probability of getting a hand of 4 aces and a king?

Solution   Here, the order is not to be considered because any order of getting the aces and the king will result in a hand that consists of 4 aces and a king. Now, the number of ways in which 4 aces can be selected is $C(4, 4)$, and the number of ways in which 1 king can be selected is $C(4, 1)$. Hence, by the sequential counting principle (SCP), the number of ways of getting 4 aces and a king is $C(4, 4)C(4, 1)$. Furthermore, the total number of 5-card hands is $C(52, 5)$, so the required probability is

$$\frac{C(4, 4)C(4, 1)}{C(52, 5)} = \frac{1 \cdot 4}{C(52, 5)}$$

Since

$$C(52, 5) = \frac{52 \cdot 51 \cdot 50 \cdot 49 \cdot 48}{5 \cdot 4 \cdot 3 \cdot 2 \cdot 1} = 2,598,960$$

the probability of getting 4 aces and a king is

$$\frac{C(4, 4)C(4, 1)}{C(52, 5)} = \frac{4}{2,598,960} = \frac{1}{649,740}$$

which is very small indeed!   ∎

EXAMPLE 7   Five cards are drawn from a standard deck. What is the probability of getting exactly one ace and no picture cards?

Solution   Since there are 4 aces, the number of ways of getting exactly 1 ace is $C(4, 1)$. There are 36 cards that are not aces or picture cards. The number of ways of getting 4 of these is $C(36, 4)$. Thus, the number of ways of getting 1 ace and 4 of the 36 cards is, by the sequential counting principle (SCP),

$$C(4, 1)C(36, 4).$$

The total number of ways that 5 cards can be drawn from the entire deck is $C(52, 5)$, so the required probability is

$$\frac{C(4, 1)C(36, 4)}{C(52, 5)} = \frac{4 \cdot 36 \cdot 35 \cdot 34 \cdot 33}{4 \cdot 3 \cdot 2 \cdot 1 \cdot C(52, 5)}$$

$$= \frac{235,620}{2,598,960} \quad \text{(See Example 6)}$$

$$= \frac{33}{364}   \quad\quad ∎$$

Do we always use the SCP and/or a permutation formula and/or a combination in solving a probability problem? Not necessarily; sometimes it is easier to look at the actual possible outcomes or to reason the problem out directly. This is illustrated in the next example.

EXAMPLE 8   A careless clerk was supposed to mail 3 bills to 3 customers. He addressed 3 envelopes but absent-mindedly paid no attention to which bill he put in which envelope.

(a) What is the probability that exactly 1 of the customers received the proper bill?
(b) What is the probability that exactly 2 of the customers received the proper bills?

Solution   In Table 10.5 the headings C_1, C_2, and C_3 represent the customers, and the numbers 1, 2, and 3 below represent the bills received by the customers. Therefore, the rows represent the possible outcomes.

(a) The table shows that there are 6 possibilities and 3 cases in which exactly 1 (that is, 1 and only 1) of the customers received the proper bill. Thus, the required probability is

$$P = \tfrac{3}{6} = \tfrac{1}{2}$$

Table 10.5

C_1	C_2	C_3	
1	2	3	
①	3	2	←Favorable
2	1	③	←Favorable
2	3	1	
3	1	2	
3	②	1	←Favorable

(b) Here the probability is 0, because if 2 customers received their proper bills, then the third one did also. This means that there is no case in which 2 and only 2 received the proper bills.

∎

In Example 8, if there were 4 customers and 4 bills, then there would be a total of $P(4, 4) = 24$ cases in all. (This is just the number of ways in which the bills could be permuted.) You can see that it would be quite cumbersome to list all these cases. Instead, let us draw a tree showing the possible favorable cases if 1 customer, C_1, receives the proper bill (see Figure 10.5). This shows the 1 under C_1; then C_2 can have only the 3 or the 4. If C_2 has the 3, then C_3 must have the 4 and C_4 the 2. (Otherwise more than 1 customer would receive the proper bill.) If C_2 has the 4, then C_3 must have the 2 and C_4 the 3. These are the only 2 favorable cases possible if C_1 gets bill 1. The same argument holds if one of the other customers gets the proper bill; there are just 2 ways in which none of the other customers gets a proper bill. Since there are 4 customers, the SCP shows that there are only $4 \times 2 = 8$ favorable cases. Thus, the probability that exactly 1 of the customers gets the proper bill is $\frac{8}{24} = \frac{1}{3}$.

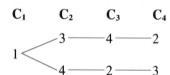

FIGURE 10.5

Exercise 10.2 _____

A. 1. A man has 3 pairs of shoes, 2 suits, and 3 shirts. If he picks a pair of shoes, a suit, and a shirt at random, what is the probability that he picks his favorite shoes, suit, and shirt?

2. At the end of a meal in a restaurant, a person wants to have pie à la mode (pie topped with ice cream) for dessert. There are 5 flavors of ice cream—chocolate, vanilla, strawberry, peach, and coffee—and there are 2 kinds of pie—apple and cherry. If the waiter picks the pie and ice cream at random, what is the probability that the person will get apple pie with vanilla ice cream?

3. A fair die is rolled 3 times in succession. What is the probability that even numbers come up all 3 times?

B. 4. Jim belongs to a club of 40 members. A committee of three is to be selected at random from the 40 members. Find the probability that Jim is one of the three selected.

5. Helen and Patty both belong to a club of 25 members. A committee of 4 is to be selected at random from the 25 members. Find the probability that both Helen and Patty will be selected.

6. Two cards are drawn at random, in succession and without replacement, from a deck of 52 cards.
   (a) Find the number of ways in which the ace of spades and a king can be selected, in that order.
   (b) What is the probability of drawing the ace of spades and a king, in that order?

7. Mr. C. Nile and Mr. D. Mented agreed to meet at 8:00 P.M. in one of the Spanish restaurants in Ybor City. They were both punctual, and they both remembered the date agreed upon. Unfortunately, they forgot to specify the name of the restaurant. If there are 5 Spanish restaurants in Ybor City, and the two men each go to one of these, find the probability that:

   (a) They meet each other.   (b) They miss each other.

8. P.U. University offers 100 courses, 25 of which are mathematics. All of these courses are available each hour, and a counselor randomly selects 4 different courses to be taken by a student. Find the probability that the selection will not include a mathematics course. (Do not simplify your answer.)

9. A piggy bank contains 2 quarters, 3 nickels, and 2 dimes. A person takes 2 coins at random from this bank. Label the coins Q_1, Q_2, N_1, N_2, N_3, D_1, D_2 so that they may all be regarded as different. Then find the probability that the value of the 2 coins selected is:
   (a) 35¢   (b) 50¢

10. A committee of 2 is chosen at random from a population of 5 men and 6 women. What is the probability that the committee will consist of 1 man and 1 woman?

In problems 11–15, assume that 2 cards are drawn in succession and without replacement from an ordinary deck of 52 cards. Find the probability that:

11. Two kings are obtained   12. Two spades are obtained.

13. A spade and a king other than the king of spades (in that order) are obtained.

14. A spade and a king other than the king of spades (not necessarily in that order) are obtained.

15. Two red cards are obtained.

In problems 16 and 17, assume that there is an urn containing five $50 bills, four $20 bills, three $10 bills, two $5 bills, and one $1 bill, and the bills all have different serial numbers so that they can be distinguished from each other. A person reaches into the urn and withdraws one bill and then another.

16. (a) In how many ways can two $20 bills be withdrawn?
    (b) How many different outcomes are possible?
    (c) What is the probability of selecting two $20 bills?

17. (a) In how many ways can a $50 bill and a $10 bill be selected, in that order?
    (b) What is the probability of selecting a $50 bill and a $10 bill, in that order?
    (c) What is the probability of selecting two bills, one of which is a $50 bill and the other a $10 bill?

18. Two percent of the auto tires manufactured by a company are defective. If two tires are randomly selected from a week's production, find the probability that neither is defective.

19. For the data in problem 18, find the probability that at least one of the two selected tires is defective.

20. A box contains 10 computer disks, of which 2 are defective. If 2 disks are randomly selected from the box, find the probability that both are defective.

21. A survey showed that 10 percent of high school football players later played football in college. Of these, 5 percent went on to play professional football. Find the probability that a randomly selected high school football player will play both collegiate and professional football.

22. An urn contains 5 white balls and 3 black balls. Two balls are drawn at random from this urn. Find the probability that:
    (a) Both balls are white.   (b) Both balls are black.
    (c) One ball is white and the other is black.

23. In this problem, do not simplify your answers. What is the probability that a 5-card poker hand will contain:
    (a) 2 kings, 2 aces, and 1 other card?
    (b) 3 kings and 2 aces?
    (c) 4 cards of a kind (same face values)?

24. A box of light bulbs contains 95 good bulbs and 5 bad ones. If 3 bulbs are selected at random from the box, what is the probability that 2 are good and 1 is bad?

25. A plumbing company needs to hire 2 plumbers. Five people (4 men and 1 woman) apply for the job. Since they are all equally qualified, the selection is made at random (2 names are pulled out of a hat). What is the probability that the woman is hired?

26. Low-calorie food is required to contain no more than 40 calories per serving. The Food and Drug Administration (FDA) suspects that a certain company is marketing illegally labeled low-calorie food. If an inspector selects 3 cans at random from a shelf holding 10 cans (3 legally labeled and 7 illegally labeled), what is the probability that:
    (a) All 3 cans selected are legally labeled?
    (b) Only 2 of the cans are legally labeled?

In problems 27–32 a poker hand consisting of 5 cards is drawn. Find the probability of obtaining:

27. a royal flush (ten, jack, queen, king, ace of the same suit).
28. a straight flush (five consecutive cards of the same suit).
29. four of a kind (four cards of the same face value).
30. a full house (one pair and one triple of the same face value).
31. a flush (five cards of the same suit but not a straight or royal flush).
32. a straight (five consecutive cards, not all of the same suit).

In Other Words

A mathematician, a statistician, and a fool observed ten tosses of a coin. Heads came up 10 times. Do you agree or disagree with statements 33–35? Explain why.

33. Tails are "due." Bet on tails.
34. Heads are "hot." Bet on heads.
35. It is a random fluke. Don't bet.

36. Explain which strategy you think
    (a) the statistician would pick.
    (b) the mathematician would pick.
    (c) the fool will pick.

    If you do this right, you would have answered the classic riddle, "How do you tell the difference between a mathematician, a statistician, and a fool?"

Using Your Knowledge

Have you heard of Dr. Spock? (No, not Mr. Spock with the pointy ears in "Star Trek.") Benjamin Spock, a famous pediatrician, was accused of violating the Selective Service Act by encouraging resistance to the Vietnam War. In his trial, the defense challenged the legality of the method used to select the jury. In the Boston District Court, jurors were selected in three stages, as follows:

37. The clerk of the court selects 300 names at random from the Boston city directory. If the directory lists 76,000 names (40,000 women and 36,000 men), what is the probability of selecting 150 men and 150 women? (Do not simplify.)
38. The 300 names are placed in a box, and the names of 30 potential jurors are drawn. If the names in the box correspond to 160 women and 140 men, find the probability that 15 men and 15 women are selected. (Do not simplify.)
39. The subgroup of 30 is called a *venire*. From the venire, 12 jurors are selected. If the venire consists of 16 women and 14 men, what is the probability that the final jury consists of 6 men and 6 women? (Do not simplify.)

By the way, it was shown that the Spock trial judge selected only about 14.6% women, while his colleagues selected about 29% women. This showed that the trial judge systematically reduced the proportion of women and had not selected a jury legally.

Calculator Corner

You can use a calculator to compute expressions such as $C(52, 5)$ in Example 6. To do this, enter

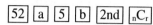

10.3 COMPUTATION OF PROBABILITIES

GETTING STARTED

ADVERTISING AND PROBABILITY

Does advertising influence a consumer's decision when buying a car? A car dealership conducted a survey of people inquiring about a new model car. Of the people surveyed, 45% had seen an advertisement for the car in the paper, 50% eventually bought a car, and 25% had neither seen the ad nor did they buy a car. What is the probability that a person selected at random from the survey read the ad and bought a car?

At this time, we are unable to answer this question. However, let us assume that 100 persons were surveyed. If we follow the information in the problem:

> 45 had seen the ad (S)
> 50 bought a car (B)
> 25 neither saw the ad nor bought a car ($S' \cap B'$)

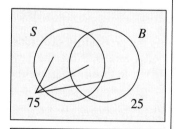

We can draw a Venn diagram using the sets S and B. Since 25 persons neither saw the ad nor bought the car, we place 25 persons outside both circles. This means that we must have 75 persons in $S \cup B$. Since S must have 45 persons and B 50 ($45 + 50 = 95$), there must be 20 persons in $S \cap B$ as shown in the next diagram. Thus, the number of persons that saw the ad and bought a car is 20.

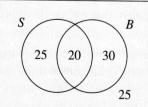

If we generalize this idea to probability (see Example 3), the probability that a person selected at random read the ad and bought a car is 20%. Compare this with the probability that a person bought a car. Do you think that seeing the ad made a lot of difference?

In this section we will formalize some of the ideas we have used. What do you think the probability for an impossible event should be? What about the probability of an event that is certain to occur? The answers to these questions are given in properties 1 and 2 that follow. We will use these properties to solve many of the examples in this section.

In this section we give four formulas, or properties, that are useful in the computation of probabilities. The letters E, A, and B stand for events in a sample space $\mathcal{U}$.

> **Property 1**
>
> $$P(E) = 0 \quad \text{if and only if} \quad E = \emptyset \tag{1}$$

Property 1 states that an **impossible event** has a probability 0. The next example illustrates this idea.

EXAMPLE 1   A die is tossed. What is the probability that a 7 turns up?

Solution   The sample space for this experiment is

$$\mathcal{U} = \{1, 2, 3, 4, 5, 6\}$$

so it is impossible for a 7 to come up. Thus, $P(7) = 0$.   ∎

> **Property 2**
>
> $$0 \leq P(E) \leq 1 \tag{2}$$

Property 2 says that the probability of any event is a number between 0 and 1, inclusive. This follows because the number of favorable cases cannot be less than 0 or more than the total number of possible cases. Thus, $P(E) = 1$ means that the event E is *certain* to occur.

> **Property 3**
>
> $$P(A \cup B) = P(A) + P(B) - P(A \cap B) \tag{3}$$

Equation (3) says that the probability of A *or* B is the probability of A plus the probability of B, decreased by the probability of A *and* B. Note the key words "*or*" and "*and*." The subtraction of $P(A \cap B)$ is to ensure that events belonging to both A *and* B are not counted twice.

EXAMPLE 2   A penny and a nickel are tossed. What is the probability that one *or* the other of the coins will turn up heads?

Solution   If we use subscripts p and n for penny and nickel, respectively, we can list the possible cases as follows: (H_p, H_n), (H_p, T_n), (T_p, H_n), (T_p, T_n). Since there are 3 favorable cases out of the 4 possible,

$$P(H_p \cup H_n) = \tfrac{3}{4}$$

We can check that equation (3) gives

$$P(H_p \cup H_n) = P(H_p) + P(H_n) - P(H_p \cap H_n)$$
$$= \tfrac{1}{2} + \tfrac{1}{2} - \tfrac{1}{4} = \tfrac{3}{4}$$

as before.

■

EXAMPLE 3 A card is drawn from a pack of 52 playing cards. Find the probability that the card is either an ace or a red card.

Solution Let A be the event in which the card drawn is an ace, and let R be the event in which the card drawn is red. Then by equation (3),

$$P(A \cup R) = P(A) + P(R) - P(A \cap R).$$

Now, $P(A) = \tfrac{4}{52}$, $P(R) = \tfrac{26}{52}$, and $P(A \cap R) = \tfrac{2}{52}$, so

$$P(A \cup R) = \tfrac{4}{52} + \tfrac{26}{52} - \tfrac{2}{52} = \tfrac{7}{13}.$$

■

Equation (3), in case all outcomes in the sample space are equally likely, is derived from the fact that

$$P(E) = \frac{n(E)}{n(\mathcal{U})}$$

Hence,

$$P(A \cup B) = \frac{n(A \cup B)}{n(\mathcal{U})} = \frac{n(A) + n(B) - n(A \cap B)}{n(\mathcal{U})} \qquad \text{See Section 10.5.}$$

$$= \frac{n(A)}{n(\mathcal{U})} + \frac{n(B)}{n(\mathcal{U})} - \frac{n(A \cap B)}{n(\mathcal{U})}$$

$$= P(A) + P(B) - P(A \cap B)$$

If the outcomes are not equally likely (see Section 10.1), then the same result follows by replacing $n(E)$ and $n(\mathcal{U})$ by $w(E)$ and $w(\mathcal{U})$, where these mean the sum of the weights of the outcomes in E and $\mathcal{U}$, respectively.

EXAMPLE 4 An urn contains 5 red, 2 black, and 3 yellow balls. Find the probability that a ball selected at random from the urn will be red or yellow.

Solution By equation (3),

$$P(R \cup Y) = P(R) + P(Y) - P(R \cap Y)$$
$$= \tfrac{5}{10} + \tfrac{3}{10} - 0 = \tfrac{4}{5}$$

■

In Example 4, notice that $P(R \cap Y) = 0$. This means the events of selecting a red ball and selecting a yellow ball cannot occur simultaneously, so that $R \cap Y = \emptyset$. We say that A and B are **mutually exclusive** if $A \cap B = \emptyset$. For any two mutually exclusive events A and B, it follows that $P(A \cap B) = 0$, and equation (3) becomes

---

Property 4

$$P(A \cup B) = P(A) + P(B) \quad \text{if} \quad P(A \cap B) = 0 \tag{4}$$

EXAMPLE 5   Show that the events R and Y of Example 4 are mutually exclusive.

Solution   Because $P(R \cap Y) = 0$, $R \cap Y = \emptyset$ (property 1), so R and Y are mutually exclusive.

■

EXAMPLE 6   In a game of blackjack (also called twenty-one), a player and the dealer each get 2 cards. Let A and B be the events defined as follows:

  A: The player gets an ace and a face card for 21 points.
  B: The dealer gets an ace and a 10 for 21 points.

Are A and B mutually exclusive events?

Solution   No; both player and dealer can get 21 points. (In the game of blackjack, 21 points wins, and in most casinos, the dealer would be the winner with this tie score.)

■

EXAMPLE 7   The video games that you can attach to your television set have both audio and video. It is estimated that the probability of the audio being defective is 0.03, the probability of at least one or the other (audio or video) being defective is 0.04, but the probability of both being defective is only 0.01. What is the probability that the video is defective?

Solution   We let S stand for the event that the audio is defective and V for the event that the video is defective. Then, using formula (3), with $P(S) = 0.03$, $P(S \cup V) = 0.04$, and $P(S \cap V) = 0.01$, we get

$$P(S \cup V) = P(S) + P(V) - P(S \cap V)$$

so that

$$0.04 = 0.03 + P(V) - 0.01$$

Thus,

$$P(V) = 0.02$$

■

We have used the formula $P(T') = 1 - P(T)$ to calculate the probability of the complement of an event. For example, if the probability that it will rain today is $\frac{1}{4}$, the probability that it will not rain today is $\frac{3}{4} = 1 - \frac{1}{4}$, and if the probability of a stock going up in price is $\frac{3}{8}$, the probability that the stock will not go up in price is $\frac{5}{8} = 1 - \frac{3}{8}$. We now illustrate how this property is used in the field of life insurance.

Table 10.6 *Table of Mortality for 100,000 Americans*

Age in Years	Number Alive	Age in Years	Number Alive	Age in Years	Number Alive
10	100,000	40	78,100	70	38,600
15	96,300	45	74,200	75	26,200
20	92,600	50	69,800	80	14,500
25	89,000	55	64,600	85	5,500
30	85,400	60	57,900	90	850
35	81,800	65	49,300	95	3

Table 10.6 is a **mortality table** for 100,000 people. According to this table, of 100,000 people alive at age 10, some 96,300 were alive at age 15; but only 3 were alive at age 95. A table like this is used to calculate a portion of the premium on life insurance policies. We use this table in the next example.

EXAMPLE 8   Find the probability that a person who is alive at age 20:

(a) Will still be alive at age 70
(b) Will not be alive at age 70

Solution   (a) Based on Table 10.6 the probability that a person alive at 20 is still alive at 70 is given by

$$P(\text{Being alive at } 70) = \frac{\text{Number alive at } 70}{\text{Number alive at } 20}$$

$$= \frac{38,600}{92,600} = \frac{193}{463}$$

(b) Using formula (4), we find that the probability of the person not being alive at 70 is

$$1 - \frac{193}{463} = \frac{270}{463}$$

Exercise 10.3

In problems 1–4, find the answer to the given question, and indicate which of the four properties given in this section you used.

1. A die is thrown. Find the probability that the number that turns up is a 0.
2. A die is thrown. Find the probability that an odd or an even number comes up.
3. Two dice are thrown. Find the probability that the sum of the two faces that turn up is between 0 and 13.

4. An absent-minded professor wished to mail 3 report cards to 3 of his students. He addressed 3 envelopes but, unfortunately, did not pay any attention to which card he put in which envelope. What is the probability that exactly 2 students receive their own report cards? (Assume that all 3 envelopes were delivered.)

A single ball is drawn from an urn containing ten balls numbered 1 through 10. In problems 5–8, find the probability that the ball chosen is:

5. An even-numbered ball or a ball with a number greater than 7

6. An odd-numbered ball or a ball with a number less than 5

7. An even-numbered ball or an odd-numbered ball

8. A ball with a number that is greater than 7 or less than 5

In problems 9–13, a single card is drawn from a deck of 52 cards. Find the probability that the card chosen is:

9. The king of hearts or a spade

10. The ace of hearts or an ace

11. The ace of diamonds or a diamond

12. The ace of clubs or a black card

13. The king of hearts or a picture card (jack, queen, or king)

14. The U.S. Weather Service reports that in a certain northern city it rains 40 days and snows 50 days in the winter. However, it rains and snows on only 10 of those days. Based on this information, what is the probability that it will rain or snow in that city on a particular winter day? (Assume there are 90 days of winter.)

15. Among the first 50 stocks listed in the New York Stock Exchange transactions on a certain day (as reported in the *Wall Street Journal*), there were 26 stocks that went down, 15 that went up, and 9 that remained unchanged. Based on this information, find the probability that a stock selected at random from this list would not have remained unchanged.

Table 10.7

Table 10.7 shows the probability that there is a given number of people waiting in line at a checkout register at Dear's Department Store. In problems 16–20, find the probability of having:

Number of Persons in Line	Probability
0	0.10
1	0.15
2	0.20
3	0.35
4 or more	0.20

16. Exactly 2 persons in line

17. More than 3 persons in line

18. At least 1 person in line

19. More than 3 persons or fewer than 2 persons in line

20. More than 2 persons or fewer than 3 persons in line

In solving problems 21–25, refer to Table 10.6.

21. What is the probability that a person who is alive at age 20 will not be alive at age 65?

22. What is the probability that a person who is alive at age 25 will be alive at age 70?

23. What is the probability that a person who is alive at age 25 will not be alive at age 70?

24. What is the probability that a person who is alive at age 55 will live 80 more years? (Assume that none of the persons in the table attained 100 years of age.)

25. What is the probability that a person who is alive at 55 will live less than 80 more years? (See problem 24.)

Problems 26–30 refer to Table 10.8. This table shows the number of correctly and incorrectly filled out tax forms obtained from a random sample of 100 returns examined by the Internal Revenue Service (IRS) in a recent year.

Table 10.8

	Short form (1040A)	Long Form (1040)		
	No Itemized Deductions	No Itemized Deductions	Itemized Deductions	Totals
Correct	15	40	10	65
Incorrect	5	20	10	35
Totals	20	60	20	100

26. Find the probability that a form was a long form (1040) or an incorrectly filled out form.

27. Find the probability that a form had no itemized deductions and was correctly filled out.

28. Find the probability that a form was not filled out incorrectly.

29. Find the probability that a form was not a short form (1040A).

30. Find the probability that a form was a long form (1040) with no itemized deductions and filled out incorrectly.

31. A traffic light follows the pattern green, yellow, red for 60, 5, and 20 seconds, respectively. What is the probability that a driver approaching this light will find it green or yellow?

32. A driver approaching the green light decides to go ahead through the intersection whether the light changes or not. If it takes the driver 6 seconds to get through the intersection, what is the probability that the driver makes it through the intersection before the light turns red? See problem 31.

*I*n Other Words

33. Explain, in your own words, the meaning of an event's probability being 0.

34. Explain, in your own words, the meaning of an event's probability being 1.

35. Explain, in your own words, the circumstances under which you can use the formula $P(A \cup B) = P(A) + P(B)$.

36. Explain why the probability of an event cannot be negative.

Using Your Knowledge

In this section we learned how to use a mortality table to calculate the probability that a person alive at a certain age will be alive at a later age. There are other tables that give the probabilities of different events. For example, many mortgage companies use a credit-scoring table to estimate the likelihood that an applicant will repay a loan. One such table appears below.

Table 10.9 *A Hypothetical Credit-Scoring Table*

Age	Under 25 (12 pts)	25–29 (5 pts)	30–34 (0 pts)	35–39 (1 pt)	40–44 (18 pts)	45–49 (22 pts)	50 + (31 pts)
Time at Address	1 yr or less (9 pts)	1–2 yr (0 pts)	2–3 yr (5 pts)	3–5 yr (0 pts)	5–9 yr (5 pts)	10 yr + (21 pts)	
Age of Auto	None (0 pts)	0–1 yr (12 pts)	2 yr (16 pts)	3–4 yr (13 pts)	5–7 yr (3 pts)	8 yr + (0 pts)	
Monthly Auto Payment	None (18 pts)	$1–$80 (6 pts)	$81–$99 (1 pt)	$100–$139 (4 pts)	$140 + (0 pts)		
Housing Cost	$1–$125 (0 pts)	$126 – $274 (10 pts)	$275 + (12 pts)	Owns clear (12 pts)	Lives with relatives (24 pts)		
Checking and Savings Accounts	Both (15 pts)	Checking only (2 pts)	Savings only (2 pts)	Neither (0 pts)			
Finance Company Reference	Yes (0 pts)	No (15 pts)					
Major Credit Cards	None (0 pts)	1 (5 pts)	2 + (15 pts)				
Ratio of Debt to Income	No debts (41 pts)	1–5% (16 pts)	6–15% (20 pts)	16% + (0 pts)			

In Table 10.9 your score depends on the number of points you get on the eight tabulated items. To obtain your score, you add the scores (shown in color) on the individual items. For example, if your age is 21, you get 12 points. If you have lived at your present address for less than a year, you get 9 more points. Moreover, if your car is 2 years old, you get another 16 points. So far, your score is 12 + 9 + 16. This should give you the idea.

A lender using the scoring table selects a cutoff point from a table, such as Table 10.10 that gauges the probability that an applicant will repay a loan.

Table 10.10

Total Score	Probability of Repayment
60	0.70
65	0.74
70	0.78
75	0.81
80	0.84
85	0.87
90	0.89
95	0.91
100	0.92
105	0.93
110	0.94
115	0.95
120	0.955
125	0.96
130	0.9625

37. John Dough, 27 years old, living for 3 years at his present address, has a 2-year-old automobile on which he pays $200 monthly. He pays $130 per month for his apartment and has no savings account, but he does have a checking account. He has no finance company reference. He has one major credit card, and his debt-to-income ratio is 12%. Based on the credit-scoring table, what is the probability that Mr. Dough will repay a loan?

38. What is the probability in problem 37 if John sells his car and rides the bus to work?

39. Find the probability that you will repay a loan, based on the information in the table.

Discovery

The Venn diagrams we studied in Chapter 1 can often be used to find the probability of an event by showing the number of elements in the universal set and the number of elements corresponding to the event under consideration. For example, if there are 100 employees in a certain firm and it is known that 82 are males (M), 9 are clerk typists (C), and 2 of these clerk typists are male, we can draw a diagram corresponding to this situation as shown in Figure 10.6. From this diagram, we can conclude that

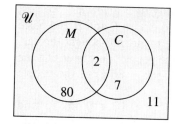

FIGURE 10.6

$$P(M) = \frac{82}{100} \qquad P(C) = \frac{9}{100} \qquad P(M \cap C) = \frac{2}{100}$$

$$P(M \cup C) = \frac{82}{100} + \frac{9}{100} - \frac{2}{100} = \frac{89}{100}$$

Using this technique, solve the following problems.

In problems 40–42, assume that of the 100 persons in a company, 70 are married, 80 are college graduates, and 60 are both married and college graduates. Find the probability that if a person is selected at random from this group, the person will be:

40. Married and a college graduate

41. Married or a college graduate

42. Not married and not a college graduate

In a recent election, voters were asked to vote on two issues, A and B. A Gallup poll indicated that of 1000 eligible voters, 600 persons voted in favor of A, 500 persons voted in favor of B, 200 persons voted in favor of both A and B, and 50 persons voted against both issues. If an eligible voter is selected at random, find the probability that the voter:

43. Voted for A but not B

44. Voted for B but not A

45. Voted for both A and B

46. Voted against both A and B

47. Did not vote at all

10.4   CONDITIONAL PROBABILITY

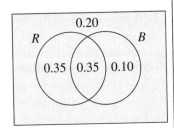

GETTING STARTED

SURVEYS AND CONDITIONAL PROBABILITY

Have you been in a car dealership and seen consumer magazines that rank different automobiles? If you were the manager of a dealership, you would like to know if people who read the reports in *Consumer Reports* or *Car and Driver* are more likely to buy your model of car. The first step would be to conduct a survey of potential buyers. Suppose results of such a survey are as follows:

70% of the people read the report (R)
45% bought a car (B)
20% neither read the report nor bought a car

We want to find the effect of reading the report (R) on buying the car (B). Thus, we must compare the probability that the person bought a car $P(B)$ with the probability that the person bought the car given that the person read the report, denoted by $P(B \mid R)$ and read as "the probability of B given R." We first make a Venn diagram of the situation. We label two circles R and B and place 20%, the percentage of people that neither read the report nor bought the car, outside these two circles. This means that 80% of the people must be inside the two circles. But 70% + 45% = 115%, so 35% (115% − 80%) of the people must be in $B \cap R$ as shown.

We can see from the diagram that $P(B) = 0.35 + 0.10 = 0.45$. To find $P(B \mid R)$, we have to look at all the people that bought a car *given* that they read the report; that is, we must look inside the circle labeled R. Inside this circle, 35% of the people out of 70% bought a car; that is,

$$P(B \mid R) = \frac{P(B \cap R)}{P(R)} = \frac{0.35}{0.35 + 0.35} = \frac{0.35}{0.70} = 0.50$$

Thus, $P(B) = 0.45$ and $P(B \mid R) = 0.50$, which means that people are more likely to buy the dealer's car if they have read the article. For this reason many dealers give copies of consumer magazine articles to potential customers. In this section we shall study *conditional* probability, that is, probabilities computed using a subset of the sample space.

The WIZARD OF ID by permission of Johnny Hart and Creator's Syndicate, Inc.

As the *Wizard of Id* cartoon shows, it is sometimes the case that in considering the probability of an event A, we obtain additional information that may suggest a "revision" of the probability of A. For example, assume that in Getwell Hospital 70 of the patients have lung cancer (C), 60 of the patients smoke (S), and 50 have cancer and smoke. If there are 100 patients in the hospital, and 1 is selected at random, then $P(C) = \frac{70}{100}$ and $P(S) = \frac{60}{100}$. But suppose a patient selected at random tells you that he or she smokes. What is the probability that this patient has cancer? In other words, what is the probability that a patient has cancer, given that the patient smokes? The expression "given that the patient smokes" means that we must restrict our attention to those patients who smoke. We have thus added a **restrictive condition** to the problem. Essentially, the condition that the person smokes requires that we use S as our sample space.

To compute $P(C \mid S)$ (read, "the probability of C, given S"), we recall that there are 50 favorable outcomes (people who have lung cancer and smoke) and 60 elements in the new sample space (people who smoke). Hence, $P(C \mid S) = \frac{50}{60} = \frac{5}{6}$.

We note that

$$P(C \mid S) = \frac{n(C \cap S)}{n(S)}$$

$$= \frac{n(C \cap S)/n(\mathcal{U})}{n(S)/n(\mathcal{U})} = \frac{P(C \cap S)}{P(S)}$$

This discussion suggests the next definition.

Definition 10.2

If A and B are events in a sample space $\mathcal{U}$ and $P(B) \neq 0$, the *conditional probability of A, given B*, is denoted by $P(A \mid B)$ and is defined by

$$P(A \mid B) = \frac{P(A \cap B)}{P(B)} \tag{1}$$

Notice that the conditional probability of A, given B, results in a new sample space consisting of the elements in $\mathcal{U}$ for which B occurs. This gives rise to a second method of handling conditional probability, as illustrated in the following examples.

EXAMPLE 1   A die is thrown. Find the probability that a 3 came up if it is known that an odd number turned up.

Solution   *Method 1.*   Let T be the event in which a 3 turns up and Q be the event in which an odd number turns up. By equation (1),

$$P(T \mid Q) = \frac{P(T \cap Q)}{P(Q)} = \frac{\frac{1}{6}}{\frac{3}{6}} = \frac{1}{3}$$

Method 2.   We know that an odd number turned up, so our new sample space is $\mathcal{U} = \{1, 3, 5\}$. Only one outcome (3) is favorable, so

$$P(T \mid Q) = \tfrac{1}{3}.$$ ∎

EXAMPLE 2   A coin is thrown; then a die is tossed. Find the probability of obtaining a 6, given that heads came up.

Solution   *Method 1.*   Let S be the event in which a 6 turns up, and let H be the event in which heads come up.

$$P(S \mid H) = \frac{P(S \cap H)}{P(H)} = \frac{\frac{1}{12}}{\frac{1}{2}} = \frac{1}{12} \cdot 2 = \frac{1}{6}$$

Method 2.   We know that heads came up, so our new sample space is $\mathcal{U} = \{(H, 1), (H, 2), (H, 3), (H, 4), (H, 5), (H, 6)\}$. Only one outcome is favorable, $(H, 6)$, so $P(S \mid H) = \tfrac{1}{6}$.   ∎

EXAMPLE 3   Two dice were thrown, and a friend tells us that the numbers that came up were different. Find the probability that the sum of the two numbers was 4.

Solution   *Method 1.*   Let D be the event in which the two dice show different numbers, and let F be the event in which the sum is 4. By equation (1),

$$P(F \mid D) = \frac{P(F \cap D)}{P(D)}$$

Now, $P(F \cap D) = \tfrac{2}{36}$, because there are two outcomes, $(3, 1)$ and $(1, 3)$, in which the sum is 4 and the numbers are different, and there are 36 possible outcomes. Furthermore,

$$P(D) = \frac{36 - 6}{36} = \frac{30}{36}$$

so

$$P(F \mid D) = \frac{P(F \cap D)}{P(D)} = \frac{\frac{2}{36}}{\frac{30}{36}} = \frac{1}{15}$$

Method 2. We know that the numbers on the two dice were different, so we have $36 - 6 = 30$ (36 outcomes minus 6 that show the same number on both dice) elements in our sample space. Of these, only two, $(3, 1)$ and $(1, 3)$, are favorable. Hence, $P(F \mid D) = \frac{2}{30} = \frac{1}{15}$. ∎

EXAMPLE 4   Two dice are thrown and a friend tells you that the first die shows a 6. Find the probability that the sum of the numbers showing on the two dice is 7.

Solution   *Method 1.* Let S_1 be the event in which the first die shows a 6, and let S_2 be the event in which the sum is 7. Then

$$P(S_2 \mid S_1) = \frac{P(S_2 \cap S_1)}{P(S_1)} = \frac{\frac{1}{36}}{\frac{6}{36}} = \frac{1}{6}$$

Method 2. We know that a 6 came up on the first die, so our new sample space is $\mathcal{U} = \{(6, 1), (6, 2), (6, 3), (6, 4), (6, 5), (6, 6)\}$. Hence, $P(S_1 \mid S_2) = \frac{1}{6}$, because there is only one favorable outcome, $(6, 1)$. ∎

EXAMPLE 5   Suppose we represent with the letters B and b the genes that determine the color of a person's eyes. If the person has two b genes, the person has blue eyes; otherwise, the person has brown eyes. If it is known that a man has brown eyes, what is the probability that he has two B genes? (Assume that both genes are equally likely to occur.)

Solution   The tree diagram for the four possibilities appears in Figure 10.7.

Method 1. Let T be the event in which the man has two B genes, and let B be the event in which the man has brown eyes. By Definition 10.2

$$P(T \mid B) = \frac{P(T \cap B)}{P(B)} = \frac{\frac{1}{4}}{\frac{3}{4}} = \frac{1}{3}$$

Method 2. It is known that the man has brown eyes, so we consider the three outcomes corresponding to these cases (BB, Bb, bB). Because only one of these equally likely outcomes (BB) is favorable, the probability that a man has two B genes if it is known that he has brown eyes is $\frac{1}{3}$.

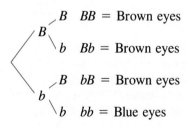

FIGURE 10.7   ∎

Table 10.11 *Strokes per 1000 People*

Blood Pressure	Ages 45–74
Normal	8
Borderline	14
High	31

Other important applications also make use of conditional probability. For example, the Framingham Heart Disease Study began in 1948 and focused on strokes and heart failure. Table 10.11, based on this study, shows the number of strokes per 1000 people for various conditions. As you can see, the incidence of stroke for people aged 45–74 increases almost fourfold as blood pressure goes from normal to high (from 8 per 1000 to 31 per 1000). Note that the numbers in the body of the table are all per 1000. This means that the table is actually giving us approximate conditional probabilities; we can interpret the last number in the table, 31, as meaning that the probability that a person has a stroke, given that this person has high blood pressure and is in the age group 45–74, is about $\frac{31}{1000}$. We look at some other aspects of this study in the next example.

EXAMPLE 6   Assume the numbers in Table 10.11 are accurate, and find the probability that:

(a) A person in the 45–74 age group has a stroke, given that the person has normal blood pressure.

(b) A person in the 45–74 age group has a stroke, given that the person has either normal or borderline blood pressure.

(c) A person in the 45–74 age group has a stroke.

(d) If a person in the 45–74 age group has a stroke, what is the probability that the person has normal blood pressure?

Solution   (a) This probability can be read directly from the table; it is $\frac{8}{1000}$.

(b) Here we have two mutually exclusive sets, those with normal blood pressure and those with borderline blood pressure. Hence, the required probability is the sum of the probabilities for the two sets, that is,

$$\frac{8}{1000} + \frac{14}{1000} = \frac{22}{1000} = \frac{11}{500}$$

(c) The idea is similar to that in part (b); there are three mutually exclusive sets, so the required probability is the sum of the probabilities for the three sets, that is,

$$\frac{8}{1000} + \frac{14}{1000} + \frac{31}{1000} = \frac{53}{1000}$$

(d) Here we know the person has a stroke, so we can use the idea of conditional probability. The population for this condition consists of the $8 + 14 + 31 = 53$ people who have a stroke. Of these, 8 have normal blood pressure. Thus, the required probability is $\frac{8}{53}$.

Exercise 10.4

1. A die was thrown. Find the probability that a 5 came up if it is known that an even number turned up.

2. A coin was thrown; then a die was tossed. Find the probability of obtaining a 7, given that tails came up.

3. Two dice were thrown, and a friend tells us that the numbers that came up were identical. Find the probability that the sum of the two numbers was:
   (a) 8   (b) 9
   (c) An even number   (d) An odd number

4. Referring to Example 5 of this section, find the probability that a person has two *b* genes, given that the person has:
   (a) Brown eyes   (b) Blue eyes

5. For a family with 2 children, the sample space indicating boy (*B*) or girl (*G*) is *BB, BG, GB, GG*. If each of the outcomes is equally likely, find the probability that the family has 2 boys if it is known that the first child is a boy.

6. A family has 3 children. If each of the outcomes in the sample space is equally likely, find the probability that the family has 3 girls if its known that:
   (a) The first child is a girl   (b) The first child is a boy

7. Referring to problem 6, find the probability that the family has exactly 2 girls if it is known that the first child is a girl.

8. Table 10.12 gives the approximate number of suicides per 100,000 persons, classified according to country and age for one year:
   Based on the table, find the probability that:
   (a) A person between 25 and 44 years of age committed suicide, if it is known that the person lived in the United States
   (b) A person between 25 and 44 years of age committed suicide, if it is known that the person lived in Canada
   (c) A person committed suicide, given that the person lived in Germany

Table 10.12

Country	Age 15–24	25–44	45–64	65 or over
United States	10	20	30	40
Canada	10	15	13	14
Germany	20	30	50	50

9. The personnel director of Gadget Manufacturing Company has compiled Table 10.13, which shows the percentage of men and women employees who were absent the indicated number of days. Suppose there are as many women as men employees.

Table 10.13

Sex	0	1–5	6–10	11 or more	Total
			Absences (Days)		
Men	20%	40%	40%	0	100%
Women	20%	20%	20%	40%	100%

(a) Find the probability that an employee missed 6–10 days, given that the employee is a woman.
(b) Find the probability that an employee is a woman, given that the employee missed 6–10 days.

10. Table 10.14 describes the student population in a large college.

Table 10.14

	Freshman (%)	Sophomore (%)	Junior (%)	Senior (%)
Male	25	13	12	10
Female	15	10	8	7

(a) Find the probability that a randomly selected student is female.
(b) Find the probability that a randomly selected student is a junior.
(c) If the selected student is a junior, find the probability that the student is female.

11. An examination of Professor X's records for the last ten years shows the following distribution of grades in his courses.

(a) If one of Professor X's students is randomly selected, what is the probability that the student received neither an A nor a B?
(b) If 200 of Professor X's students were selected, how many would be expected to have received a B or a D?

Grade	Percentage of all grades
A	15
B	30
C	40
D	10
F	5

(c) If it is known that one of Professor X's students did not get a C or a D, what is the probability that the student received a B?

In problems 12–14, assume that 2 cards are drawn in succession and without replacement from a standard deck of 52 cards. Find the probability that:

12. The second card is the ace of hearts, if it is known that the first card was the ace of spades.

13. The second card is a king, if it is known that the first card was a king.

14. The second card is a 7, if it is known that the first card was a 6.

Table 10.15

Industry	Low	High
Computers	5	10
Petroleum	20	15

The Merrilee Brokerage House studied two groups of industries (computers and petroleum) and rated them as low risks or high risks, as shown in Table 10.15. Use this information in problems 15 and 16.

15. If a person selected one of these stocks at random (i.e., each stock has probability $\frac{1}{50}$ of being selected), find the probability that the person selected a computer stock, given that the person selected a low-risk stock.

16. If a person selected one of the stocks at random, find the probability that the person selected a petroleum stock, given that the person selected a high-risk stock.

17. A stock market analyst figures the probabilities that two related stocks, A and B, will go up in price. She finds the probability that A will go up to be 0.6 and the probability that both stocks will go up to be 0.4. What should be her estimate of the probability that stock B goes up, given that stock A does go up?

18. The Florida Tourist Commission estimates that a person visiting Florida will visit Disney World, Busch Gardens, or both with probabilities 0.5, 0.3, and 0.2, respectively. Find the probability that a person visiting Florida will visit Busch Gardens, given that the person did visit Disney World.

19. A recent survey of 400 instructors at a major university revealed the data shown in Table 10.16. Based on the data, what is the probability that:
    (a) An instructor received a good evaluation, given that the instructor was tenured?
    (b) An instructor received a good evaluation?

Table 10.16

	Good Evaluations	Poor Evaluations
Tenured	72	168
Nontenured	84	76

20. Referring to the data in problem 19, find the probability that:
    (a) An instructor received a poor evaluation, given that the instructor was tenured.
    (b) An instructor received a poor evaluation.

21. Billy was taking a history test, and his memory started playing tricks on him. He needed the date when Columbus reached America, and he remembered that it was 1492 or 1294 or 1249 or 1429, but was not sure which. Then he remembered that the number formed by the first three digits was not divisible by 3. What is the probability that he guessed the right date? [*Hint*: Recall that a number is divisible by 3 if the sum of its digits is divisible by 3. Use this information to find which dates this leaves Billy to choose from.]

22. Nancy was asked to guess at a preselected number between 1 and 50 (inclusive). By asking questions first, Nancy learned that the number was divisible by 2 and/or by 3. What is the probability that Nancy guessed the right number after correctly using her information? [*Hint*: Eliminate the numbers that are not divisible by 2 or by 3. This eliminates all the odd numbers that are not multiples of 3.]

23. A doctor for a pharmaceutical company treats 100 patients with an experimental drug and another 100 patients with a conventional drug. The results of the experiment are given in Table 10.17. What is the probability that:
    (a) a patient chosen at random from the group of 200 patients has improved, $P(I)$?
    (b) a patient taking the experimental drug has improved, $P(I \mid E)$?

Table 10.17

	Improved (*I*)	**Same (*S*)**
Experimental (*E*)	70	30
Conventional (*C*)	65	35

24. The University Apartments has 1000 units classified by size and location as shown in Table 10.18. What is the probability of selecting at random:
    (a) a first-floor apartment?
    (b) a first-floor, three-bedroom apartment?
    (c) a second-floor apartment, given that it is a one-bedroom?
    (d) a two-or three-bedroom apartment, given that it is located on the first floor?

Table 10.18

	Bedrooms		
	One	**Two**	**Three**
First Floor	20%	30%	10%
Second Floor	15%	20%	5%

In Other Words

25. Of the two methods of solving conditional probability problems, which do you prefer? Why?
26. Can you find two events A and B so that $P(A|B) = P(A)$? What is the relationship between A and B? Explain.

Using Your Knowledge

The Statistical Abstracts of the United States gives the number of crime victims per 1000 persons, 12 years old and over, as shown in Table 10.19. Use the information in this table to do the following problems:

27. (a) Find the probability that the victim of one of the three types of crime was a male.
   (b) Find the probability that the victim of one of the three types of crime was a female.
   (c) Considering your answers to parts (a) and (b), which sex would you say is more likely to be the victim of one of these three types of crime?

Table 10.19

Sex	Robbery	Assault	Personal Larceny
Male	5	18	52
Female	2	9	42

28. If it is known that an assault was committed:
   (a) What is the probability that the victim was a male?
   (b) What is the probability that the victim was a female?

29. If it is known that the victim was a female, what is the probability that the crime was assault?

30. If it is known that the victim was a male, what is the probability that the crime was robbery?

10.5 INDEPENDENT EVENTS

GETTING STARTED

PROBABILITIES IN BINGO AND BIRTHDAYS

Have you played Bingo lately? The world's biggest Bingo contest was held in Cherokee, North Carolina, and offered a $200,000 prize to any player who could fill a 24-number card by the 48th number called (there are 75 possible numbers in Bingo). What is the probability that you would win this game? The

A water tower advertises bingo on a Florida Seminole Indian reservation

probability that any given number on your 24 number card is drawn is $\frac{48}{75}$, the probability of drawing a second number on your card is $\frac{47}{74}$, and so on. To win, you must get *all* 24 numbers on your card within 48 draws. The probability is:

$$\frac{48}{75} \cdot \frac{47}{74} \cdot \frac{46}{73} \cdot \cdot \cdot \cdot \cdot \frac{25}{52} = \frac{1}{799,399}.$$

Note that we have multiplied the individual probabilities to find the final answer. In this section, we shall study *independent* events. If two events A and B are independent, $P(A \cap B) = P(A) \cdot P(B)$.

A classical use of this formula is the birthday problem. Given a group of people, what is $P(L)$, the probability that *at least* two people have the same birthday? It is easier to find $P(L')$, the probability that *no* two people have the same birthday, and then compute $P(L) = 1 - P(L')$. Assuming that all birthdays are equally likely, the probability that a second person's birthday is different from the first is $\frac{364}{365}$, the probability that a third person has a different birthday from the other two is $\frac{363}{365}$, and the probability that an *n*th person has a different birthday from all others is

$$\frac{365 - n + 1}{365}$$

Thus,

$$P(L) = 1 - \frac{364}{365} \cdot \frac{363}{365} \cdot \frac{362}{365} \cdot \cdot \cdot \cdot \cdot \frac{365 - n + 1}{365}$$

Now, we compute some of these probabilities and give some others. When $n = 2$,

$$P(L) = 1 - \frac{364}{365} \approx 1 - 0.997 = 0.003$$

When $n = 3$,

$$P(L) = 1 - \frac{364}{365} \cdot \frac{363}{365} \approx 1 - 0.992 = 0.008$$

When $n = 10$, $P(L) = 0.117$, when $n = 22$, $P(L) = 0.476$, and when n is 23, $P(L) = 0.507$. Thus, with 22 people in a room, the probability that at least two have the same birthday is slightly under $\frac{1}{2}$; add one more person and it becomes slightly better than $\frac{1}{2}$.

One of the more important concepts in probability is that of *independence*. In this section we shall define what we mean when we say that two events are independent. For example, the probability of obtaining a sum of 7 when two dice are thrown *and* it is known that the first die shows a 6 is $\frac{1}{6}$, that is, $P(S|6) = \frac{1}{6}$. It is of interest that the probability of obtaining a 7 when two dice are thrown is also $\frac{1}{6}$, so $P(S|6) = P(S)$. This means that the additional information that a 6 came up on the first die does not affect the probability of the sum being 7. It can happen, in general, that the probability of an event A is not affected by the occurence or nonoccurrence of a second event B. Hence, we state the following definition:

Definition 10.3 — Two events A and B are said to be **independent** if and only if

$$P(A|B) = P(A) \tag{1}$$

If A and B are independent, we may substitute $P(A)$ for $P(A|B)$ in the equation

$$P(A|B) = \frac{P(A \cap B)}{P(B)} \quad \text{See equation (1), Section 10.4}$$

to obtain

$$P(A) = \frac{P(A \cap B)}{P(B)}$$

Then, multiplying by $P(B)$, we get

$$P(A \cap B) = P(A) \cdot P(B)$$

Consequently, we see that an equivalent definition of independence is as follows:

Definition 10.4 — Two events A and B are **independent** if and only if

$$P(A \cap B) = P(A) \cdot P(B) \tag{2}$$

A. *Independent Events*

The preceding ideas can be applied to experiments involving more than two events. We define **independent events** to be such that the occurrence or nonoccurrence of any one of these events does not affect the probability of any other. The most important result for applications is that if n events E_1, $E_2, \ldots, E_n$ are known to be independent, then the following multiplication rule holds:

$$P(E_1 \cap E_2 \cap E_3 \cap \cdots \cap E_n) = P(E_1) \cdot P(E_2) \cdot \cdots \cdot P(E_n) \tag{3}$$

The next examples illustrate these ideas.

EXAMPLE 1 Two coins are tossed. Let E_1 be the event in which the first coin comes up tails, and let E_2 be the event in which the second coin comes up heads. Are E_1 and E_2 independent?

Solution Because $P(E_1 \cap E_2) = \frac{1}{4}$, $P(E_1) = \frac{1}{2}$, $P(E_2) = \frac{1}{2}$, and $\frac{1}{2} \cdot \frac{1}{2} = \frac{1}{4}$, we see that $P(E_1 \cap E_2) = P(E_1) \cdot P(E_2)$. Hence, E_1 and E_2 are independent. ∎

EXAMPLE 2   We have two urns, I and II. Urn I contains 2 red and 3 black balls, while urn II contains 3 red and 2 black balls. A ball is drawn at random from each urn. What is the probability that both balls are black?

Solution   Let $P(B_1)$ be the probability of drawing a black ball from urn I, and let $P(B_2)$ be the probability of drawing a black ball from urn II. Clearly, B_1 and B_2 are independent events. Thus, $P(B_1) = \frac{3}{5}$ and $P(B_2) = \frac{2}{5}$, so $P(B_1 \cap B_2) = \frac{3}{5} \cdot \frac{2}{5} = \frac{6}{25}$.   ∎

EXAMPLE 3   Bob is taking math, Spanish, and English. He estimates that his probabilities of receiving an A in these courses are $\frac{1}{10}$, $\frac{3}{10}$, and $\frac{7}{10}$, respectively. If he assumes that the grades can be regarded as independent events, find the probability that Bob makes:

(a) All A's (event A)   (b) No A's (event N)
(c) Exactly two A's (event T)

Solution   (a) $P(A) = P(M) \cdot P(S) \cdot P(E) = \frac{1}{10} \cdot \frac{3}{10} \cdot \frac{7}{10} = \frac{21}{1000}$, where M is the event in which he makes an A in math, S is the event in which he makes an A in Spanish, and E is the event in which he makes an A in English. (See the tree diagram in Figure 10.8.

(b) $P(N) = P(M') \cdot P(S') \cdot P(E') = \frac{9}{10} \cdot \frac{7}{10} \cdot \frac{3}{10} = \frac{189}{1000}$

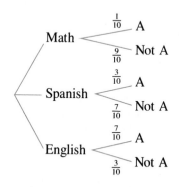

(c) There are three ways of getting exactly two A's:

1. Getting A's in math and Spanish and not in English: The probability of this event is

$$P(M) \cdot P(S) \cdot P(E') = \frac{1}{10} \cdot \frac{3}{10} \cdot \frac{3}{10} = \frac{9}{1000}$$

2. Getting A's in math and English and not in Spanish: The probability of this event is

$$P(M) \cdot P(S') \cdot P(E) = \frac{1}{10} \cdot \frac{7}{10} \cdot \frac{7}{10} = \frac{49}{1000}$$

3. Getting A's in Spanish and English and not in math: The probability of this event is

$$P(M') \cdot P(S) \cdot P(E) = \frac{9}{10} \cdot \frac{3}{10} \cdot \frac{7}{10} = \frac{189}{1000}$$

Since the three events we have just considered are mutually exclusive, the probability of getting exactly two A's is the sum of the probabilities we calculated. Thus,

$$P(T) = \frac{9}{1000} + \frac{49}{1000} + \frac{189}{1000} = \frac{247}{1000}$$ ∎

FIGURE 10.8

EXAMPLE 4 Do you recall our mentioning the witches of Wall Street? (See Example 1 of Section 10.2.) The witches in this case are persons who claim that they use occult powers to predict the behavior of stocks on the stock market. One of the most famous of the witches claims to have a 70% accuracy record. A stockbroker selects 3 stocks at random from the New York Stock Exchange listing and asks this witch to predict their behavior. Assuming that the 70% accuracy claim is valid, find the probability that the witch will:

(a) Correctly predict the behavior of all 3 stocks

(b) Incorrectly predict the behavior of all 3 stocks

(c) Correctly predict the behavior of exactly 2 of the 3 stocks

Solution (a) The probability of correctly predicting the behavior of all 3 stocks is the product

$$(0.70)(0.70)(0.70) = 0.343$$

(b) The probability of incorrectly predicting the behavior of all 3 stocks is the product

$$(0.30)(0.30)(0.30) = 0.027$$

(c) The probability of correctly predicting the behavior of 2 specific stocks and incorrectly predicting the behavior of the third stock is the product

$$(0.70)(0.70)(0.30) = 0.147$$

Because there are 3 ways of selecting the 2 specific stocks, we use the SCP and multiply the last result by 3. Thus, the probability of correctly predicting the behavior of exactly 2 of the stocks is

$$(3)(0.147) = 0.441$$

You can visualize the calculations in Example 4(c) by looking at the tree diagram in Figure 10.9, where C represents a correct prediction and I represents an incorrect prediction. Each branch is labeled with the probability of the event it represents. Note that if you find and add the probabilities at the ends of all the branches, the sum will be 1.

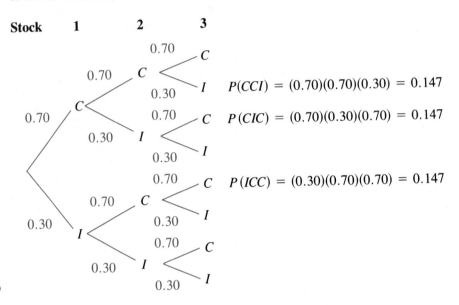

FIGURE 10.9

B. Stochastic Processes

A **stochastic process** is a sequence of experiments in which the outcome of each experiment depends on chance. For example, the repeated tossing of a coin or of a die is a stochastic process. Tossing a coin and then rolling a die would also be an example of a stochastic process.

In the case of repeated tosses of a coin, we assume that on each toss there are two possible outcomes, each with probability $\frac{1}{2}$. If the coin is tossed twice, we can construct a tree diagram corresponding to this sequence of experiments (see Figure 10.10).

First Toss	Second Toss	Final Outcome	Probability
	$P(H\mid H)$ H	(H, H)	$P(H \cap H) = \frac{1}{2} \times \frac{1}{2} = \frac{1}{4}$
$P(H)$ H	$\frac{1}{2}$		
$\frac{1}{2}$ $P(T\mid H)$	$\frac{1}{2}$ T	(H, T)	$P(H \cap T) = \frac{1}{2} \times \frac{1}{2} = \frac{1}{4}$
	$P(H\mid T)$ H	(T, H)	$P(T \cap H) = \frac{1}{2} \times \frac{1}{2} = \frac{1}{4}$
$\frac{1}{2}$	$\frac{1}{2}$		
$P(T)$ T	$\frac{1}{2}$ T	(T, T)	$P(T \cap T) = \frac{1}{2} \times \frac{1}{2} = \frac{1}{4}$
	$P(T\mid T)$		

FIGURE 10.10

As you can see from Figure 10.10 we have put on each branch the probability of the event corresponding to that branch. To obtain the probability of, say, a tail and then a head, $P(T \cap H)$, we multiply the probabilities on each of the branches going along the path that leads from the start to the final outcome, as indicated in the figure. This multiplication gives $(\frac{1}{2})(\frac{1}{2}) = \frac{1}{4}$, in agreement with the results we have previously obtained.

It is possible to show, by means of the sequential counting principle, that the terminal probabilities are always correctly obtained by using this multiplication technique. Notice that Figure 10.10 illustrates the fact that, for example,

$$P(H \cap T) = P(H \mid T) \cdot P(T)$$

and

$$P(T \cap T) = P(T \mid T) \cdot P(T)$$

EXAMPLE 5   A coin and a die are tossed. What is the probability of getting a head and a 5?

Solution   Since the outcomes depend only on chance, this is a stochastic process for which the multiplication procedure can be used. Since the probability of getting a head on the coin is $\frac{1}{2}$, and the probability of getting a 5 on the die is $\frac{1}{6}$, the probability of getting a head and a 5 is

$$P(H, 5) = \frac{1}{2} \times \frac{1}{6} = \frac{1}{12}$$

∎

EXAMPLE 6   Jim has two coins, one fair (F) and the other unbalanced (U) so that the probability of its coming up heads is $\frac{2}{3}$. He picks up one of the coins, tosses it and it comes up heads. What is the probability that the outcome came from the unbalanced coin?

Solution   We draw a tree diagram as shown in Figure 10.11. The probabilities at the ends of the branches are obtained by the multiplication technique. The starred probabilities (*) may be taken as weights for the corresponding events. Thus, the required probability is

$$\frac{\frac{2}{6}}{\frac{1}{4} + \frac{2}{6}} = \frac{4}{7}$$

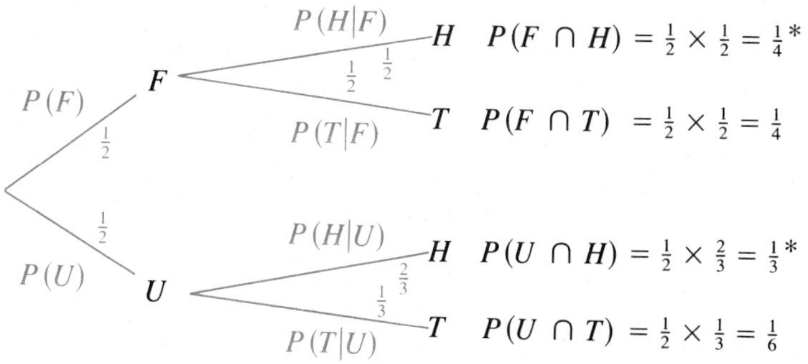

$P(H \mid F)$ — H $P(F \cap H) = \frac{1}{2} \times \frac{1}{2} = \frac{1}{4}$*

$P(F)$ F $\frac{1}{2}$ $\frac{1}{2}$

$\frac{1}{2}$

$P(T \mid F)$ — T $P(F \cap T) = \frac{1}{2} \times \frac{1}{2} = \frac{1}{4}$

$\frac{1}{2}$

$P(H \mid U)$ — H $P(U \cap H) = \frac{1}{2} \times \frac{2}{3} = \frac{1}{3}$*

$P(U)$ U $\frac{2}{3}$ $\frac{1}{3}$

FIGURE 10.11

$P(T \mid U)$ — T $P(U \cap T) = \frac{1}{2} \times \frac{1}{3} = \frac{1}{6}$

The required probability can also be found by using the equation

$$P(U \mid H) = \frac{P(U \cap H)}{P(U)} = \frac{\frac{1}{3}}{\frac{1}{4} + \frac{1}{3}} = \frac{4}{7}$$

■

EXAMPLE 7   Referring to Table 10.6 (page 725), find the probability that 2 men who are 50 and 55 years old, respectively, will both be alive at age 70.

Solution   The probability that a 50-year-old man lives to 70 is $\frac{386}{698} = \frac{193}{349}$, and the probability that a 55-year-old man lives to 70 is $\frac{386}{646} = \frac{193}{323}$. Thus, the probability that both men live to 70 is

$$\frac{193}{349} \times \frac{193}{323} = \frac{37{,}249}{112{,}727} \approx 0.33$$

■

Exercise 10.5

A.   1. Two coins are tossed. Let E_1 be the event in which the first coin comes up heads, and let E_2 be the event in which the second coin comes up tails. Are E_1 and E_2 independent?

2. A bubble gum machine has 50 cherry-flavored gums, 20 grape-flavored gums, and 30 licorice-flavored gums; while a second machine has 40 cherry, 50 grape, and 10 licorice. A gum is drawn at random from each machine. Find the probability that:
   (a) Both gums are cherry flavored.
   (b) Both gums are licorice flavored.
   (c) The gum from the first machine is cherry flavored, and the one from the second machine is grape flavored.

3. A radio repair shop has estimated the probability that a radio sent to their shop has a bad tube is $\frac{1}{4}$, the probability that the radio has a bad rectifier is $\frac{1}{8}$, and the probability that it has a bad capacitor is $\frac{1}{3}$. If we assume that tubes, rectifiers, and capacitors are independent, find the probability that:
   (a) A tube, a capacitor, and a rectifier are bad in a radio sent to the shop
   (b) A tube and a rectifier are bad in a radio sent to the shop
   (c) None of the three parts (tubes, capacitors, and rectifiers) is bad

4. Table 10.20 gives the kinds of stock available in three brokerage houses, H_1, H_2, and H_3. A brokerage house is selected at random, and one type of stock is selected. Find the probability that the stock is:
   (a) A petroleum stock
   (b) A computer stock

Table 10.20

	Petroleum	Computers
H_1	3	2
H_2	2	3
H_3	2	2

5. A coin is tossed 3 times. Find the probability of obtaining:
   (a) Heads on the first and last toss, and tails on the second toss
   (b) At least 2 heads
   (c) At most 2 heads

6. A die is rolled 3 times. Find the probability of obtaining:
   (a) An odd number each time
   (b) Two odd numbers first and an even one on the last roll
   (c) At least two odd numbers

7. A card is drawn from an ordinary deck of 52 cards, and the result is recorded on paper. The card is then returned to the deck and another card is drawn and recorded. Find the probability that:
   (a) The first card is a spade.
   (b) The second card is a spade.
   (c) Both cards are spades.
   (d) Neither card is a spade.

8. Rework problem 7, assuming that the 2 cards are drawn in succession and without replacement. [*Hint*: Make a tree diagram and assign probabilities to each of the branches.]

9. A family has 3 children. Let M be the event, "the family has at most 1 girl," and let B be the event, "the family has children of both sexes." Find:
   (a) $P(M)$ (b) $P(B)$ (c) $P(B \cap M)$
   (d) Determine whether B and M are independent.

10. Two cards are drawn in succession and without replacement from an ordinary deck of 52 cards. What is the probability that:
    (a) The first card is a king and the second card is an ace?
    (b) Both cards are aces?
    (c) Neither card is an ace?
    (d) Exactly 1 card is an ace?

11. A company has estimated that the probabilities of success for 3 products introduced in the market are $\frac{1}{4}$, $\frac{2}{3}$, and $\frac{1}{2}$, respectively. Assuming independence, find:
    (a) The probability that the 3 products are successful
    (b) The probability that none of the products is successful

12. In problem 11, find the probability that exactly 1 product is successful.

13. A coin is tossed. If heads come up, a die is rolled; but if tails come up, the coin is thrown again. Find the probability of obtaining:
    (a) 2 tails
    (b) Heads and the number 6
    (c) Heads and an even number

14. In a survey of 100 persons, the data in Table 10.21 were obtained.
    (a) Are S and L independent?
    (b) Are S' and L' independent?

    Table 10.21

	Lung Cancer (L)	No Lung Cancer (L')
Smoker (S)	42	28
Nonsmoker (S')	18	12

15. Referring to Table 10.6 (page 725), find the probability that two persons, one 30 years old and the other 40 years old, will live to be 60.

16. In problem 15, find the probability that both persons will live to be 70.

17. The *Apollo* module has five components: the main engine, the propulsion system, the command service module, the lunar excursion module (LEM), and the LEM engine. If each of the systems is considered independent of the others and the probability that each of the systems performs satisfactorily is 0.90, what is the probability that all the systems will perform satisfactorily?

18. A die is loaded so that 1, 2, 3, and 4 each has probability $\frac{1}{8}$ of coming up while 5 and 6 each has a probability $\frac{1}{4}$ of coming up. Consider the events $A = \{1, 3, 5\}$ and $B = \{2, 4, 5\}$. Determine whether A and B are independent.

19. On one of the experimental flights of the space shuttle *Columbia,* the mission was cut short due to a malfunction of a battery aboard the ship. The batteries in the *Columbia* are guaranteed to have a failure rate of only 1 in 20. The system of 3 batteries is designed to operate as long as any one of the batteries functions properly. Find the probability that:
    (a) All 3 batteries fail.
    (b) Exactly 2 fail.

20. In a certain city, the probability of catching a burglar is 0.30, and the probability of convicting a caught burglar is 0.60. Find the probability that a burglar will be caught and convicted.

21. In Example 4, what is the probability of the witch predicting correctly the behavior of 1 of the stocks and incorrectly predicting the behavior of the other 2?

22. In Example 4, suppose the broker had selected 4 stocks. What is the probability that the witch would give a correct prediction for 2 of the stocks and an incorrect prediction for the other 2 stocks?

B. 23. Three boxes, labeled A, B, and C, contain 1 red and 2 black balls, 2 red and 1 black ball, and 1 red and 1 black ball, respectively. First a box is selected at random, and then a ball is drawn at random from that box. Find the probability that the ball is red. [*Hint*: Draw a tree diagram, assign the probabilities to the separate branches, and compute the terminal probabilities by using the multiplication technique. Then add the terminal probabilities for all the outcomes in which the ball is red.]

24. There are 3 filing cabinets, each with 2 drawers. All the drawers contain letters. In one cabinet, both drawers contain airmail letters; in a second cabinet, both drawers contain ordinary letters; and in the third cabinet, one drawer contains airmail and the other contains ordinary letters. A cabinet is selected at random, and then a drawer is picked at random from this cabinet. When the drawer is opened, it is found to contain airmail letters. What is the probability that the other drawer of this cabinet also contains airmail letters? [*Hint*: Use the same procedure as in problem 23.]

25. John has 2 coins, one fair and the other unbalanced so that the probability of its coming up heads is $\frac{3}{4}$. He picks one of the coins at random, tosses it, and it comes up heads. What is the probability that he picked the unbalanced coin?

26. A box contains 3 green balls and 2 yellow balls. Two balls are drawn at random in succession and without replacement. If the second ball is yellow, what is the probability that the first one is green?

In Other Words

27. (a) Explain, in your own words, what is meant by the statement: "Two events A and B are independent."
    (b) If A and B are independent events and you know $P(A)$ and $P(B)$, how can you calculate $P(A \cap B)$?

28. In Getting Started we found the probability that at least two people have the same birthday. Is this the same as finding the probability that another person has the same birthday as you do? Explain.

Using Your Knowledge

Suppose a fair coin is flipped 10 times in succession. What is the probability that exactly 4 of the flips will turn up heads? This is a problem in which repeated trials of the same experiment are made, and the probability of success is the same for each of the trials. This type of procedure is often called a **Bernoulli trial,** *and the final probability is known as a* **binomial probability.**

Let us see if we can discover how to calculate such a probability. We represent the 10 flips and one possible success like this:

$$
\begin{array}{cccccccccc}
\text{H} & \text{T} & \text{T} & \text{H} & \text{H} & \text{T} & \text{T} & \text{T} & \text{H} & \text{T} \\
1 & 2 & 3 & 4 & 5 & 6 & 7 & 8 & 9 & 10
\end{array}
$$

Because each flip is independent of the others, the probability of getting the particular sequence shown is $(\frac{1}{2})^{10}$. All we need do now is find in how many ways we can succeed, that is, in how many ways we can get exactly 4 heads. But this is the same as the number of ways we can select 4 of the 10 flips — that is, C(10, 4). The successful ways of getting 4 heads are all mutually exclusive, so the probability of getting exactly 4 heads is

$$\frac{C(10, 4)}{2^{10}}$$

Let us suppose now that the coin is biased so that the probability of heads on any one toss is p and the probability of tails is q = 1 − p. The probability of getting the arrangement we have shown is now $p^4 q^6$. (Why?) Hence, the probability of getting exactly 4 heads is

$$C(10, 4)p^4 q^6$$

You should be able to convince yourself that if n is the number of trials, p is the probability of success in each trial, and q = 1 − p is the probability of failure, then the probability of exactly x successes is

$$C(n, x)p^x q^{n-x}$$

29. Suppose that a fair coin is tossed 50 times in succession. What is the probability of getting exactly 25 heads? (Do not multiply out your answer.)

30. If a fair coin is tossed 6 times in succession, what is the probability of getting at least 3 heads?

31. Suppose that the coin in problem 30 is biased 2 to 1 in favor of heads. Can you calculate the probability of getting at least 3 heads?

32. Suppose that a fair coin is tossed an even number of times, 2, 4, 6, ... What happens to the probability of getting heads in exactly half the tosses as the number of tosses increases?

33. A fair die is tossed 5 times in succession. What is the probability of getting exactly two 3's?

34. In problem 33, what is the probability of obtaining at least two 3's?

Discovery

$$A \text{———} S_1 \text{———} S_2 \text{———} B$$

FIGURE 10.12

Suppose you have two switches, S_1 and S_2, installed in series in an electrical circuit, and these switches have probabilities $P(S_1) = \frac{9}{10}$ and $P(S_2) = \frac{8}{10}$ of working. As you can see from Figure 10.12, the probability that the circuit works is the probability that S_1 and S_2 work, that is,

$$P(S_1) \cdot P(S_2) = \frac{9}{10} \times \frac{8}{10} = \frac{72}{100}$$

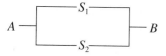

FIGURE 10.13

If the same two switches are installed in parallel (see Figure 10.13), then we can calculate the probability that the circuit works by first calculating the probability that it does not work:

The probability that S_1 fails is $1 - \frac{9}{10} = \frac{1}{10}$.

The probability that S_2 fails is $1 - \frac{8}{10} = \frac{2}{10}$.

The probability that both S_1 and S_2 fails is $\frac{1}{10} \times \frac{2}{10} = \frac{2}{100}$.

Thus, the probability that the circuit works is $1 - \frac{2}{100} = \frac{98}{100}$. By comparing the probability that a series circuit works $(\frac{72}{100})$ with the probability that a parallel circuit works $(\frac{98}{100})$, we can see that it is better to install switches in parallel.

35. What is the probability that a series circuit with three switches, S_1, S_2, and S_3, with probabilities $\frac{1}{3}$, $\frac{1}{2}$, and $\frac{3}{4}$ of working will work?

36. What is the probability if the switches are installed in parallel?

We have just seen that, under certain circumstances, it is better to install parallel rather than series circuits to obtain maximum reliability. However, in the case of security systems, independent components in series are the most reliable. For example, the soldier in the picture is guarding a triple-threat security system that uses voice patterns, fingerprints, and handwriting to screen persons entering a maximum security area. Here is how the system operates: To enter a secure area, a person must pass through a room that has a door at each end and contains three small booths. In the first booth, the person punches in his or her four-digit identification number. This causes the machine inside the booth to intone four words, which the person must repeat. If the voice pattern matches the pattern that goes with the identification number, the machine says, "Thank you," and the person goes to the next booth. After en-

A Pease Air Force Base guard and the triple-threat security system—who goes there?

tering his or her number there, the person signs his or her name on a Mylar sheet. If the signature is acceptable, the machine flashes a green light and the person goes to the third booth. There, he or she punches in the identification number once more, and then pokes a finger into a slot, fingerprint down. If a yellow light flashes, "IDENTITY VERIFIED," the door opens and the person can enter the high-security area.

37. If each of the machines is 98% reliable, what is the probability that a person fools the first machine?
38. What is the probability that a person fools the first two machines?
39. What is the probability that a person fools all three machines?
40. Based on your answer to problem 39, how would you rate the reliability of this security system?

10.6 ODDS AND MATHEMATICAL EXPECTATION

GETTING STARTED

LOTTERY ODDS

Look at the information on the lottery ticket below. The odds of winning the first prize by picking 6 out of 6 numbers (there are 49 numbers to pick from) are said to be 1 : 13,983,816. But in Section 10.1 we found that the *probability* of winning the first prize is $\frac{1}{13,983,816}$. Isn't there a difference between odds and probability? Of course there is! What most state lotteries report as *odds* are actually the *probabilities* of winning. To explain further, the **probability** of an event is a fraction whose numerator is the number of times the event can

PRIZE DIVISIONS AND ODDS OF WINNING

MATCHING NUMBERS	ODDS
6 of 6 numbers	1 in 13,983,816
5 of 6 numbers	1 in 54,200.84
4 of 6 numbers	1 in 1,032.4
3 of 6 numbers	1 in 56.66
Overall Odds	1 in 53.66

occur and whose denominator is the total number of possibilities in the sample space. Thus, if we throw a die, the probability of getting a number greater than 4 is $\frac{2}{6}$, since there are two favorable outcomes of numbers greater than 4 (5 and 6) out of 6 total possibilities (1, 2, 3, 4, 5, and 6.) The **odds** in favor of an event are defined as the **ratio** of favorable to unfavorable occurrences for the event. Thus, the odds for getting a number greater than 4 are **2 to 4,** since there are 2 favorable outcomes (5 and 6) and 4 unfavorable ones (1, 2, 3, and 4.) These odds are sometimes written as 2 : 4 (read "2 to 4"). Now, back to the lottery ticket on page 752. Since the probability of winning the first prize is $\frac{1}{13,983,816}$ the odds for winning the first prize are 1 : 13,983,815 not 1 : 13,983,816.

Here are some probabilities. What are the corresponding odds?

Probability of:	Odds in Favor
getting married if you are 18 or older is 0.64 having 3 or more children is 0.11 developing high blood pressure is $\frac{2}{5}$ getting accepted to medical school is $\frac{6}{10}$ never eating candy is $\frac{1}{33}$	64 : 36

Note that if the odds for the event are 64 to 36, the probability of the event should be

$$\frac{64}{64 + 36} = \frac{64}{100} = 0.64.$$

We shall study more about the relationship between odds and probability in this section.

In this chapter we have several times used games of chance to illustrate the concepts of probability. In connection with these games, one often encounters such statements as "the odds are 1 to 5 for throwing a 1 with a die" or "the odds are 12 to 1 against picking an ace from a deck of cards." When a person gives you 1 to 5 odds for throwing a 1 with a die, it usually means that if a 1 does occur, you pay $5, and that the person pays $1 in case a 1 does not occur. These statements simply compare the number of favorable outcomes to the number of unfavorable outcomes. Thus, odds of 1 to 5 mean that there are 5 times as many unfavorable as favorable outcomes.

A. *Odds*

Definition 10.5

If an event E is such that the total number of favorable outcomes is f and the total number of unfavorable outcomes is u, the **the odds in favor of E are f to u.**

For instance, there are 4 aces in a standard deck of 52 cards. Thus, if a single card is drawn from the deck, there are 4 ways of getting an ace (favorable) and 48 ways of not getting an ace (unfavorable). Thus, the odds in favor of drawing an ace are 4 to 48, or 1 to 12.

favorable   unfavorable

EXAMPLE 1   A die is rolled. What odds should a person give:

(a) In favor of 1 turning up?
(b) Against a 1 turning up?

Solution   (a) In this case, there is one favorable outcome, so $f = 1$, and there are 5 unfavorable outcomes, so $u = 5$. Thus, the odds are 1 to 5.

(b) There are 5 ways in which a 1 does not turn up (favorable) and 1 way in which a 1 turns up (unfavorable), so the odds against a 1 turning up are 5 to 1.   ∎

EXAMPLE 2   A horse named Camarero has a record of 73 wins and 4 losses. Based on this record, what is the probability of a win for this horse?

Solution   Here, $f = 73$, $u = 4$, and the probability is

$$\frac{f}{f + u} = \frac{73}{73 + 4} = \frac{73}{77}$$ ∎

If n is the total number of possible outcomes, and f and u are as before, then we know that

$$P(E) = \frac{f}{n} \quad \text{and} \quad P(\text{Not } E) = \frac{u}{n}$$

Therefore,

$$\frac{P(E)}{P(\text{Not } E)} = \frac{f/n}{u/n} = \frac{f}{u}$$

Thus, an equivalent definition of odds in favor of the event E is

$$P(E) \quad \text{to} \quad P(\text{Not } E)$$

or, since $P(\text{Not } E) = 1 - P(E)$,

$$P(E) \quad \text{to} \quad 1 - P(E)$$

In the case of the die in Example 1(a), the odds are $\frac{1}{6}$ to $\frac{5}{6}$, which is the same as 1 to 5. Note that if $P(E)$ and $P(\text{Not } E)$ are expressed as fractions with the same denominator, you can just compare the numerators. For example, if $P(E) = \frac{2}{7}$, then $P(\text{Not } E) = 1 - \frac{2}{7} = \frac{5}{7}$, so the odds in favor of E are 2 to 5.

EXAMPLE 3   A horse named Blue Bonnet has won 5 of her last 8 races and is thus assigned a probability of $\frac{5}{8}$ of winning her 9th race. Assuming this probability is correct, what are the odds *against* Blue Bonnet winning that race?

Solution   Since $P(\text{Winning}) = \frac{5}{8}$, we know that $P(\text{Not winning}) = 1 - \frac{5}{8} = \frac{3}{8}$. Thus, the odds in favor of Blue Bonnet are 5 to 3, and the odds *against* her are 3 to 5.   ∎

EXAMPLE 4   The Florida lottery prints 250 million tickets for each game. The prizes and the number of instant winning tickets are shown in the first two columns of Table 10.22. Entry tickets are to be sent to the Lottery Department for drawings in which 14 big prizes are awarded (see columns 3 and 4 in the table).

Table 10.22

Prize	Number of Winners	Prize	Number of Winners
Entry	1,000,000	$10,000	4 per game
Free ticket	25,000,000	$15,000	4 per game
$ 2	25,000,000	$25,000	2 per game
$ 5	5,000,000	$50,000	2 per game
$ 25	416,666	$1,000,000	2 per game
$ 50	208,333		
$5000	3,125		

If you buy a single Florida lottery ticket, what is the probability that you win $50? What are the odds in favor of this?

Solution   According to Table 10.22, of the 250 million tickets printed, 208,333 win $50. Therefore, the probability of your winning $50 with 1 ticket is

$$\frac{208,333}{250,000,000} \approx \frac{1}{1200}$$

Since $1 - \frac{1}{1200} = \frac{1199}{1200}$, the odds in favor of your winning $50 are 1 to 1199.   ∎

B. *Expected Value*

In many games of chance, we are concerned with betting. Suppose that a given event E has probability $P(E) = f/n$ of occurring and $P(\text{Not } E) = u/n$ of not occurring. If we now agree to pay f dollars if E does not occur in exchange for receiving u dollars if E does occur, then we can calculate our "expected average winnings" by multiplying $P(E)$ (the approximate proportion of the times we win) by u (the amount we win each time). Similarly, our losses will be $P(\text{Not } E) \times f$, because we lose f dollars approximately $P(\text{Not } E)$ of the times. If the bet is to be fair, the average net winnings should be 0. Let us see if this is the case. Our net winnings will be

$$P(E) \times u - P(\text{Not } E) \times f = \frac{f}{n} \times u - \frac{u}{n} \times f$$

$$= \frac{fu - uf}{n} = 0$$

as they should be. Since the odds in favor of E are f to u, we state the following definition:

Definition 10.6

Fair Bet

If the probability that event E will occur is f/n and the probability that E will not occur is u/n, where n is the total number of possible outcomes, then odds of f to u in favor of E occurring constitute a **fair bet.**

EXAMPLE 5   A woman bets that she can throw a 7 in one throw of a pair of dice. What odds should she give for the bet to be fair?

Solution $P(7) = \frac{6}{36} = \frac{1}{6}$. Here $1 = f$ and $f + u = 6$, so $u = 5$. Hence, the odds should be 1 to 5.

Sometimes we wish to compute the *expected value*, or *mathematical expectation*, of a game. For example, if a woman wins $6 when she obtains a 1 in a single throw of a die and loses $12 for any other number, our intuition tells us that if she plays the game many times, she will win $6 one-sixth of the time and she will lose $12 five-sixths of the time. We might then expect her to gain $(\$6)(\frac{1}{6}) - (\$12)(\frac{5}{6}) = -\$9$; that is, to lose $9 per try on the average.

For another example, if a fair die is thrown 600 times, we would expect $(\frac{1}{6})(600) = 100$ ones to appear. This does not mean that exactly 100 ones *will appear*, but that this is the *expected average* number of ones for this experiment. In fact, if the number of ones were far away from 100, we would have good reason to doubt the honesty of the die.

Definition 10.7

Expected Value

If the k possible outcomes of an experiment are assigned the values a_1, a_2, . . . , a_k and they occur with probabilities p_1, p_2, . . . , p_k, respectively, then the **expected value** of the experiment is given by

$$E = a_1 p_1 + a_2 p_2 + a_3 p_3 + \cdots + a_k p_k$$

A casino game called Keno is played with 80 balls numbered 1 through 80. Twenty winning balls are chosen at random. A popular bet is the $2, 10-number bet in which you select 10 numbers and the casino will pay you, say, $4, if exactly five of the numbers you picked match 5 of the 20 that were selected. What is the probability of that happening?

There are 80 numbers altogether, 10 you pick and 70 you do not. There are $C(10, 5)$ ways to pick the 5 matching numbers from your 10. That leaves $C(70, 15)$ for the numbers you do not pick.

Thus, the number of ways of matching 5 numbers from the 10 is

$$C(10, 5) \cdot C(70, 15)$$

The number of combinations when 20 balls are picked from 80 is $C(80, 20)$. Thus,

$$P(\text{match } 5) = \frac{C(10, 5) \cdot C(70, 15)}{C(80, 20)} = 0.0514277$$

Here are the payoffs and probabilities for a $2, 10-number bet.

Match	Pays	Probability
5	$ 4	0.0514277
6	$ 40	0.0114794
7	$ 280	0.0016111
8	$ 1,800	0.0001354
9	$ 8,000	0.0000061
10	$50,000	0.0000001

Problem Solving: Mathematical Expectation

1. Read the problem.

Find the mathematical expectation for a $2, 10-number bet in Keno.

2. Select the unknown.

We want to find the mathematical expectation of a $2 bet.

3. Think of a plan.
Find how much you can expect to get if you match 5, 6, 7, 8, 9, or 10 numbers. Subtract the $2 cost of the ticket.

To find how much you can expect to get for matching 5, 6, 7, 8, 9, or 10 numbers, we multiply the payoffs by their probability and add to get your winnings. Then, subtract $2.

4. Use the table to find the expected value of the winnings if
you match 5 numbers.
you match 6 numbers
you match 7 numbers
you match 8 numbers
you match 9 numbers
you match 10 numbers

Here are those amounts rounded off to two decimal places.

$4 \cdot 0.0514277$ = $0.21
$40 \cdot 0.0114794$ = $0.46
$280 \cdot 0.0016111$ = $0.45
$1,800 \cdot 0.0001354$ = $0.24
$8,000 \cdot 0.0000061$ = $0.05
$50,000 \cdot 0.0000001$ = $0.01
$1.42

Subtract the cost of the $2 ticket to find E.	$E = \$1.42 - \$2.00 = -\$0.58$
5. Verify the solution.	Do this with a calculator!
TRY EXAMPLE 6 NOW.	Cover the solution, write your own, and then check your work.

EXAMPLE 6   A die is thrown. If an even number comes up, a person receives $10; otherwise, the person loses $20. Find the expected value of this game.

Solution   We let $a_1 = \$10$ and $a_2 = -\$20$. Now $p_1 = \frac{3}{6} = \frac{1}{2}$ and $p_2 = \frac{1}{2}$, so $E = (\$10)(\frac{1}{2}) - (\$20)(\frac{1}{2}) = -\$5$.   ∎

In Example 6, the player is expected to lose $5 per game in the long run; so we say that this game is not fair.

Definition 10.8   A game is **fair** if its expected value is 0.

EXAMPLE 7   A coin is thrown. If heads come up, we win $1; if tails come up, we lose $1. In this a fair game?

Solution   Here, $a_1 = \$1$, $a_2 = -\$1$, and $p_1 = p_2 = \frac{1}{2}$, so $E = (1)(\frac{1}{2}) - 1(\frac{1}{2}) = 0$. Thus, by Definition 10.8, the game is fair.   ∎

EXAMPLE 8   A die is thrown. A person receives double the number of dollars corresponding to the dots on the face that turns up. How much should a player pay for playing in order to make this a fair game?

Solution   The player can win $2, $4, $6, $8, $10, $12, each with probability $\frac{1}{6}$, so expected winnings (the player does not lose) are $E = 2(\frac{1}{6}) + 4(\frac{1}{6}) + 6(\frac{1}{6}) + 8(\frac{1}{6}) + 10(\frac{1}{6}) + 12(\frac{1}{6}) = \frac{42}{6} = \$7$. A person paying $7 can expect winnings of 0. Thus, $7 is a fair price to pay for playing this game.   ∎

EXAMPLE 9   Dear's Department Store wishes to open a new store in one of two locations. It is estimated that if the first location is chosen, the store will make a profit of $100,000 per year if successful and will lose $50,000 per year otherwise. For the second location, it is estimated that the annual profit will be $150,000 if successful; otherwise, the annual loss will be $80,000. If the probability of success at each location is $\frac{3}{4}$, which location should be chosen in order to maximize the expected profit?

Solution For the first location, $a_1 = \$100,000$, $p_1 = \frac{3}{4}$, $a_2 = -\$50,000$, and $p_2 = \frac{1}{4}$. Thus, the expected profit is

$$E_1 = \$100,000(\tfrac{3}{4}) - \$50,000(\tfrac{1}{4}) = \$75,000 - \$12,500 = \$62,500$$

For the second location, $a_1 = \$150,000$, $p_1 = \frac{3}{4}$, $a_2 = -\$80,000$, and $p_2 = \frac{1}{4}$. Thus, the expected profit is

$$E_2 = \$150,000(\tfrac{3}{4}) - \$80,000(\tfrac{1}{4}) = \$112,500 - \$20,000 = \$92,500$$

The expected profit from the second location ($92,500) is greater than that for the first location ($62,500), so the second location should be chosen. ∎

Decision problems that depend on mathematical expectation require three things for their solution: *options*, *values*, and *probabilities*. In Example 9 we have the information given in Table 10.23. With this information we can find the expected value for each option and hence make the desired decision.

Table 10.23

	Options			
	Site 1		Site 2	
Values	$100,000	−$50,000	$150,000	−$80,000
Probabilities	$\frac{3}{4}$	$\frac{1}{4}$	$\frac{3}{4}$	$\frac{1}{4}$

Exercise 10.6

A. In problems 1–7, find the odds in favor of obtaining:

1. A 2 in one throw of a single die
2. An even number in one throw of a single die
3. An ace when drawing 1 card from an ordinary deck of 52 cards
4. A red card when drawing 1 card from an ordinary deck of 52 cards
5. 2 tails when an ordinary coin is thrown twice
6. At least 1 tail when an ordinary coin is thrown twice
7. A vowel when 1 letter is chosen at random from among the 26 letters of the English alphabet

In problems 8–12, find the odds against obtaining:

8. A 4 in one throw of a single die
9. An odd number in one throw of a single die
10. The king of spades when drawing 1 card from an ordinary deck of 52 cards
11. One of the picture cards (jack, queen, king) when drawing 1 card from an ordinary deck of 52 cards

12. At most 1 tail when an ordinary coin is thrown twice

13. If you buy 1 Florida lottery ticket, what is the probability of your winning $5, according to Table 10.22? What are the odds in favor of your winning $5?

14. If you buy 1 Florida lottery ticket, what is the probability of your winning $5,000, according to Table 10.22? What are the odds in favor of your winning $5,000?

15. If the correct odds in favor of Johnny winning a race are 3 to 2, what is the probability that Johnny wins?

The information for problems 16–25 was taken from the book *What Are the Chances* by Siskin, Staller, and Rorvik. Find the missing number(s).

Event	Probability	Odds
16. Being the victim of a serious crime in your lifetime.	$\frac{1}{20}$	?
17. Being the victim of a serious crime in San Antonio, where there are 630 violent crimes per 100,000 population.	?	?
18. Having complications during surgery in June.	?	1 to 4
19. Having complications during surgery in July when new interns and residents are brought in.	$\frac{1}{2}$	?
20. Having high cholesterol levels.	$\frac{1}{4}$	?
21. Publishing one of the ten bestselling novels of the year.	?	10 to 4867
22. Getting rich by hard work.	?	41 to 9
23. Being a top executive of a major company without going to college.	?	3 to 21
24. Completing 4 years of college.	0.19	?
25. Growing up being incompetent in math.	0.33	?

B. 26. A coin is thrown twice. If heads come up either time, we get $2; but if heads do not occur, we lose $4. What is the expected value of this game?

27. Two dice are thrown. If the sum of the dots showing is even, we get $10; otherwise, we lose $20. What is the expected value of this game?

28. A die is thrown. A person receives the number of dollars corresponding to the dots on the face that turns up. How much should a player pay in order to make this game fair?

29. In a recent charity raffle, there were 10,000 tickets in all. If the grand prize was a Lincoln Continental (priced at $21,500), what is a fair price to pay for a ticket?

30. If in problem 29 the charity paid $20,000 for the Lincoln and they wished to make a profit of $10,000 from the raffle, for how much should each ticket sell?

31. A man offers to bet $3 against $5 that he can roll a 7 on one throw of his pair of dice. If he wins fairly consistently, are his dice fair? Explain.

32. Louie gets an "Entry" ticket in the Florida lottery and offers to sell it to you for $10. Refer to Table 10.22 on page 755 and determine whether this is a fair price. Explain.

33. If in Example 9 of this section the probabilities of success in the first and second locations are $\frac{2}{3}$ and $\frac{2}{5}$, respectively, what location should be chosen in order to have a maximum expected profit? See Table 10.23.

34. Gadget Manufacturing Company is debating whether to continue or discontinue an advertising campaign for a new product. Their research department has predicted the gain or loss to be derived from the decision to continue or discontinue the campaign, as summarized in Table 10.24. If the president of the firm assigns odds of 4 to 1 in favor of the success of the advertising campaign, find:
    (a) The expected value for the company if the advertising campaign is continued
    (b) The expected value for the company if the advertising campaign is discontinued
    (c) The best decision based on the answers to parts (a) and (b)

    Table 10.24

Advertising Campaign	Successful	Unsuccessful
Continue	$20,000	−$10,000
Discontinue	$30,000	5,000

35. Repeat problem 34 if the president of the firm assigns odds of 4 to 1 against the success of the advertising campaign.

In Other Words

36. Explain the difference between "the probability of an event" and "the odds in favor of an event."

37. Explain why betting in Keno is not a fair bet.

38. Explain in your own words what information is needed in order to solve a decision problem that depends on mathematical expectation.

Using Your Knowledge

The graph shows the probabilities that a baseball team that is ahead by 1, 2, 3, 4, 5, or 6 runs after a certain number of innings goes on to win the game. As you can see, if a team is leading by 1 run at the end of the first inning, the probability that this team wins is about 0.62. If a team is ahead by 2 runs at the end of the first inning, then the probability of this team's winning the game is about 0.72.

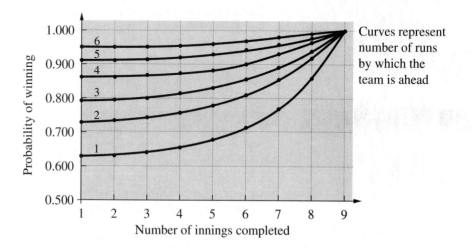

Suppose a team is ahead by 1 run at the end of the first inning. The probability that this team wins the game is

$$0.62 = \frac{62}{100} = \frac{31}{50}$$

Therefore, the odds in favor of this team winning the game should be 31 to 19. Use the graph shown above to solve the following problems.

39. Find the probability that a team leading by 2 runs at the end of the sixth inning:
    (a) Wins the game
    (b) Loses the game

40. For the same situation as in problem 39, find:
    (a) The odds in favor of this team winning the game
    (b) The odds against this team winning the game

41. At the end of the sixth inning, a team is ahead by 4 runs. A man offers to bet $10 on this team. How much money should be put up against his $10 to make a fair bet?

Discovery

In American roulette, the wheel has 38 compartments, 2 of which, the 0 and 00, are colored green. The rest of the compartments are numbered from 1 through 36, and half of them are red and the other half black. The wheel is spun in one direction, and a small ivory ball is spun in the other direction. If the wheel is fair, all the compartments are equally likely and hence the ball has probability $\frac{1}{38}$ of landing in any particular one of them. If a player bets, say, $1, on a given number, and the ball comes to rest on that number, the player receives from the croupier 36 times his or her stake, that is, $36. In this case, the player wins $35 with probability $\frac{1}{38}$ and loses $1 with probability $\frac{37}{38}$. The expected value of this game is

$$E = \$35(\tfrac{1}{38}) - \$1(\tfrac{37}{38}) = -\tfrac{\$1}{19} = -5\tfrac{5}{19} \text{ cents}$$

This may be interpreted to mean that in the long run, for every dollar that we bet in roulette, we are expected to lose $5\frac{5}{19}¢$.

A second way to play roulette is to bet on red or black. Suppose a player bets $1 on red. If the ball stops on a red number (there are 18 of them), the player receives twice his or her stake, thus winning $1. If a black number comes up, the player loses his or her stake. If a 0 or 00 turns up, then the wheel is spun again until it stops on a number different from 0 and 00. If this is black, the player loses the $1, but if it is red, the player receives only the original stake (gaining nothing).

42. Can you discover what is the expected value of this game?
43. If we place 50¢ on red and 50¢ on black, what will be the expected value of the game? [*Hint:* The answer is not 0.]

Chapter 10 Summary

Section	Item	Meaning	Example
10.1A	Experiment	An activity	Tossing a coin, drawing a card from a deck
10.1A	Sample space	The set of all possible outcomes for an experiment	The sample space for tossing a coin is $\{H, T\}$
10.1A	$P(E)$	The probability of event E, $P(E) = \dfrac{n(E)}{n(\mathcal{U})}$	When tossing a coin, the probability of tails is $P(T) = \frac{1}{2}$.
10.1A	$P(T')$	$1 - P(T)$	The probability of a 3 when rolling a die is $\frac{1}{6}$. The probability of not rolling a 3 is $\frac{5}{6}$.

Section	Item	Meaning	Example
10.3	$P(E) = 0$	E is an impossible event.	Rolling a 7 on a die
10.3	$P(E) = 1$	E is a certain event.	Rolling less than 7 on a die
10.3	$P(A \cup B)$	$P(A) + P(B) - P(A \cap B)$	
10.3	Mutually exclusive events	The two events cannot occur simultaneously, $P(A \cap B) = 0$.	Throwing a 5 and a 6 on one throw of a die
10.4	$P(A\|B)$, the probability of A, given B	$\dfrac{P(A \cap B)}{P(B)}$	
10.5	Independent events	$P(A \cap B) = P(A) \cdot P(B)$	Throwing a 6 with a die and tails with a coin are independent events.
10.5A	$P(E_1 \cap E_2 \cap ... \cap E_n)$	$P(E_1) \cdot P(E_2) \cdot \; ... \; \cdot P(E_n)$, when the events are independent	
10.5B	Stochastic process	A sequence of experiments in which the outcome of each experiment depends on chance	
10.6A	Odds in favor	The ratio of favorable to unfavorable occurrences	The odds for a 3 when tossing a die are 1 to 5.
10.6B	Expected value	$E = a_1 p_1 + a_2 p_2 + \cdots + a_n p_n$, where the a's are the values that occur with probability p_1, p_2, and so on	

Research Questions

Sources of information for these questions can be found in the Bibliography at the end of the book.

1. Write a report about Antoine Gombaud, the Chevalier de Méré, and the gambling problem he proposed to Pascal.

2. Find out and write a report about the correspondence between Pascal and Fermat and its influence in the development of the theory of probability.

3. Find the name, author, and year of publication of the first work on the mathematical treatment of probability.

4. The Arts Conjectandi was published in 1713 after the death of its author, a brilliant member of a mathematical family. Write a paragraph detailing the circumstances under which the book was published, its contents, and a genealogical table of the family.

5. The theory of probability was studied by the Russian mathematicians P. L. Chebyshev, A. A. Markov, and Andrei Nikolaevich Kolmogorov. Write a paragraph about their contributions to probability.

6. He was the examiner of Napoleon and later his interior minister, senator, and count. He was also the author of *Theorie Analytique des Probabilites*. Who was this mathematician and what were his contributions to probability?

7. Probability theory contains several paradoxes, among them the Petersburg paradox. Write a paper explaining this paradox and telling what mathematicians tried to solve it.

8. Find out how insurance companies use mortality tables to establish the cost of life insurance premiums.

9. Investigate and write several paragraphs about three areas that use probability (weather, sports, and genetics, for example).

10. Find out what the Needle problem is.

Chapter 10 Practice Test

1. A single fair die is tossed. Find:
   (a) The probability of obtaining a number different from 7
   (b) The probability of obtaining a number greater than 2

2. A box contains 2 red balls, marked R_1 and R_2, and 3 white balls, marked W_1, W_2, and W_3. If 2 balls are drawn in succession and without replacement from this box, find the number of elements in the sample space for this experiment. (We are interested in which balls are drawn and the order in which they are drawn.)

3. A box contains 5 balls numbered from 1 to 5. If a ball is taken at random from the box, find the probability that it is:
   (a) An even-numbered ball
   (b) Ball number 2
   (c) Not ball number 2

4. Two cards are drawn at random and without replacement from a standard deck of 52 cards. Find:
   (a) The probability that both cards are red
   (b) The probability that neither card is an ace

5. A card is drawn at random from a standard deck of 52 cards and then replaced. Then a second card is drawn. Find:
   (a) The probability that both cards are red
   (b) The probability that neither card is red

6. A fair coin is tossed 5 times. What is the probability of obtaining at least 1 head?

7. An urn contains 5 white, 3 black, and 2 red balls. Find the probability of obtaining the following in a single draw:
   (a) A white or a black ball
   (b) A ball that is not red

8. A student estimates that the probability of his passing math or English is 0.9, the probability of his passing English is 0.8, but the probability of passing both is 0.6. What should be his estimate of the probability of passing math?

9. Three cards are drawn in succession and without replacement from a standard deck of 52 cards. What is the probability that they are all face cards (jack, queen, king)?

10. Two dice are rolled. Find the probability that the sum turning up is 11, given that the first die showed a 5.

11. Two dice are rolled. Find the probability that the sum turning up is 11, given that the second die showed an even number.

12. Two dice are rolled. Find the probability that:
    (a) They show a sum of 10.
    (b) The first die comes up an odd number.
    (c) Are these two events independent? Explain.

13. A certain drug used to reduce hypertension (high blood pressure) produces side effects in 4% of the patients. Three patients who have taken the drug are selected at random. Find the probability that:
    (a) They all had side effects.
    (b) None of them had side effects.

14. Roland has to take an English course and a history course, both of which are available at 8 A.M., 9 A.M., and 3 P.M. If Roland picks a schedule at random, what is the probability that he will have English at 8 A.M. and history at 3 P.M.?

15. The probability that a cassette tape is defect-free is 0.97. If 2 tapes are selected at random, what is the probability that both are defective?

16. A card is selected at random from a deck of 52 cards. What are the odds in favor of the card being:
    (a) A king?   (b) Not a king?

17. The probability of an event is $\frac{3}{7}$. Find:
    (a) The odds in favor of this event occurring
    (b) The odds against this event occurring

18. The odds in favor of an event occurring are 3 to 7.
    (a) What are the odds against this event occurring?
    (b) What is the probability that the event will not occur?

19. A coin is tossed twice. If exactly 1 head comes up, we receive $5, and if 2 tails come up, we receive $5; otherwise, we get nothing. How much should we be willing to pay in order to play this game?

20. The probabilities of being an "instant winner" of $2, $5, $25, or $50 in the Florida lottery are $\frac{1}{10}$, $\frac{1}{50}$, $\frac{1}{600}$, and $\frac{1}{1200}$, respectively. What is the mathematical expectation of being an "instant winner"?

Americans are fascinated by numbers. Consider the *Guinness Book of World Records*, almanacs, surveys, and so on. But what are the meanings of all of these numbers, and how can we interpret them? In this chapter we discuss different ways of organizing and reporting data. The simplest way is to use the **frequency distribution** of Section 11.1, a type of table that tells us how many objects of different types we have in each of several categories. Such a distribution can then be represented by a graph called a **histogram**.

When we want to describe an entire sample or population by a number, we use an **average**. The three most common averages are the **mean,** the **median,** and the **mode**. Each of these averages, which are studied in Section 11.2, uses one number to try to tell us where the "middle" of a set of data is. However, averages cannot tell us how far data values are spread out away from this "middle." For this we use the **range** and the **standard deviation**. Using means, standard deviations, and *z***-scores** we can compute precisely how far from the "middle" we are. These topics are covered in Sections 11.3 and 11.4.

In real life, newspapers and magazines present data using many varieties of graphs including line, bar, and circle graphs. We study these in Section 11.5.

An important aspect of statistics is predicting the likelihood of future outcomes based on the numbers or data gathered from earlier observations. For example, can you predict winning Olympic times based on athletes' past performances, or the incidence of cancer based on exposure to ultraviolet sunlight? We will make predictions and study **scattergrams** and **correlations** in the last two sections of the chapter.

Statistics

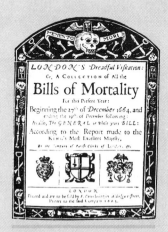

**THE HUMAN SIDE
OF MATHEMATICS**

Statistical analysis emerged in London, where in 1662 John Graunt published a remarkable book, *Natural and Political Observations upon the Bills of Mortality*.

At that time, the population of London had already reached approximately 100,000. Overcrowding, the difficulties of obtaining even the daily necessities of life, the prevalence of disease, and the many plague years all combined to make Londoners exceedingly interested in reports of births and deaths. After the great plague in 1603, these reports, which had appeared only sporadically before, became regular weekly publications. The causes of death (weird diseases such as jawfaln, King's-Evil, planet, and

Presented as "London's dreadful visitation," the Bills of Mortality *provided an annual accounting of deaths in seventeenth century London*

Let the world be our laboratory and let us gather statistics on what occurs therein.

Morris Kline

tissick) were reported in the *Bills of Mortality*, published regularly starting in 1629.

After this perhaps morbid beginning for statistical analysis, many mathematicians, among them such famous ones as Laplace (1749–1827) and Gauss (1777–1855), made important contributions to the basic ideas of statistics. Furthermore, the analysis of numerical data is fundamental in so many different fields that one could make a long list of scientists in such areas as biology, geology, genetics, and evolution who contributed greatly to this study. The well-known names of Charles Darwin (1809–1882), Gregor Mendel (1822–1884), and Karl Pearson (1857–1936) would surely be included in this list.

11.1   FREQUENCY DISTRIBUTIONS

GETTING STARTED

COMPARISON SHOPPING FOR JEANS

A buyer for a large department store wanted to compare prices of high-quality jeans for men and women. One way to do this is to look in a consumer magazine at the 15 best-rated jeans for men and women and their prices. The actual prices appear below. How can we organize the information so that we can make meaningful comparisons? Let us look at prices for women's jeans.

Women's Jeans		Men's Jeans	
Sears Jeans That Fit	$⑲+	Wrangler Prorodeo	$20
Wrangler Prorodeo	26	Wrangler American Hero	17
Chic Heavenly Blues	48+	Levi's 509	31
P.S. Gitano	21	Wrangler Rustler	15
Gap Straight Leg	30	J.C. Penney Long Haul	23+
Lee Easy Rider	33	Guess/Georges Marciano	㊅⓪
L. L. Bean Stretch	36	Wrangler American Hero	23
Lands' End Square Rigger	26+	Levi's 550	45
L. L. Bean Double L	27	Lands' End Square Rigger	20+
Levi's 501	35	Levi's 501	34
Lee Relaxed Rider	29	Gap Tapered Leg	34
Calvin Klein	㊾㋜	L. L. Bean Double L	27
Levi's 902	34	Sears Roebucks	⑭+
Bonjour	20	Gap Easy Fit	32
Gap Classic Contour	30	Lee Riders Straightleg	20

Since these prices range from $52 to $19, we will break them into three **classes** (you could as easily make it 4 or 5) of **width**

$$\frac{52 - 19}{3} = \frac{33}{3} = 11.$$

The **lower limits** for our classes will be 19, 19 + 11 = 30, and 30 + 11 = 41, as shown in the table. The corresponding **upper limits** are 29, 40, and 51. Notice that there is a gap between the end of one class and the beginning of the next (from 29 to 30, for example). We can fix this by making the upper limits of the classes 30, 41, and 52 (instead of 29, 40, and 51). See **step 1** in the table. Now, in which class will the $30 price go? Unless otherwise specified, data values falling on class upper limits are included in the next *higher* class.

	Step 1		Step 2	Step 3
Lower Limit		Upper Limit	Tally	Frequency
19	–	30	||||| ||	7
30	–	41	|||||		6
41	–	52*	||	2

*Note that 52 *must* go in the third class.

With this convention we can tally the prices falling in each class (**step 2**) and note their frequency (**step 3**). We can then make a picture of this information, called a **histogram,** in which each of the classes is represented by a bar whose width is 11 units, the **class width,** and whose height is given by the **frequency** as shown in Figure 11.1. Note that this histogram does not show the lower and upper limits. Rather, each class is described by a single value called its **midpoint**. Sometimes the lower and upper limits are shown as well.

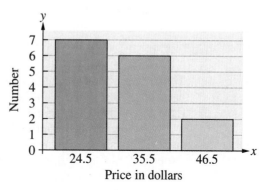

FIGURE 11.1

The word *statistics* brings to the minds of most people an image of a mass of numerical data. To a statistician, **statistics** means the analysis of these data and the deduction of logical conclusions from them. It is in this sense that the science of statistics is one of the most important branches of applied mathematics.

Today, we know that statistics are used throughout industry in the manufacture of goods, in the study of wages and work conditions, in insurance and investments, and in many other ways. No one can look through a newspaper or a news magazine without seeing evidence of the impact of statistics on our daily lives. We are constantly exhorted to buy this and not to buy that, to read this magazine, to see that movie, to eat certain foods, and not to smoke cigarettes—all on the basis of statistical evidence that seems to show the desirability of following this advice.

A. *Frequency Distributions*

Let us look at a statistics problem that should interest a teacher and a class who might wonder how well they are learning a certain subject. Out of 10 possible points, the class of 25 students made the following scores:

6	5	4	0	9
2	0	8	8	1
10	6	8	5	5
8	7	9	10	9
6	5	8	4	7

This listing shows at once that there were some good scores and some poor ones; but, because the scores are not arranged in any particular order, it is difficult to conclude anything else from the list.

A **frequency distribution** is often a suitable way of organizing a list of numbers to show what patterns may be present. First, the scores from 0 through 10 are listed in order in a column (see Table 11.1). Then, by going through the original list in the order in which it is given, we can make tally marks on the appropriate lines of our table. Finally, in a third column we can list the number of times that each score occurs; this number is the **frequency** of the score.

It is now easier to see that a score of 8 occurred more times than any other number. This score was made by

$$\frac{5}{25} = \frac{1}{5} = 20\% \text{ of the students}$$

Ten of the students, or 40% of the class, received scores of 8 or better. Only 6, or 24%, received scores less than 5.

If there are very many items in a set of numerical data, then it is usually necessary to shorten the frequency distribution by grouping the data into intervals. For instance, in the preceding distribution we can group the scores in intervals of 2 to obtain the listing in Table 11.2.

Table 11.1 *Frequency Distribution*

Score	Tally Marks	Frequency
0	II	2
1	I	1
2	I	1
3		0
4	II	2
5	IIII	4
6	III	3
7	II	2
8	THL	5
9	III	3
10	II	2
		25 Total

Table 11.2 *Frequency Distribution with Grouped Data*

Score	Frequency
0–1	3
2–3	1
4–5	6
6–7	5
8–9	8
10–11	2

Of course, some of the detailed information in the first table has been lost in the second table, but for some purposes a condensed table may furnish all the information that is required.

B. *Histograms*

It is also possible to present the information contained in Table 11.1 by means of a special type of graph, called a **histogram,** consisting of vertical bars with no space between bars. In the histogram of Figure 11.2, the units on the *y* axis represent the frequencies, while those on the *x* axis indicate the scores.

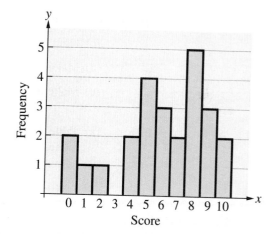

FIGURE 11.2

Histogram for Table 11.1

C. *Frequency Polygons*

From the histogram in Figure 11.2 we can construct a **frequency polygon** (or line graph) by connecting the midpoints of the tops of the bars, as shown in Figure 11.3. It is customary to extend the graph to the base line (*x* axis) using the midpoints of the extended intervals at both ends. This "ties the graph down," but has no predictive significance.

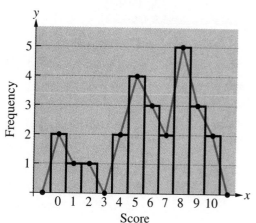

FIGURE 11.3

Frequency polygon

EXAMPLE 1   The following list gives the hourly wages of a group of 30 workers who are performing similar tasks, but, because of differences in seniority and skill, are paid at different rates.

$8.00	$7.90	$8.00	$8.10	$7.90	$7.90
7.90	7.80	7.90	8.00	7.80	8.00
8.10	7.70	7.90	7.80	8.10	8.00
8.00	8.10	8.20	7.80	8.20	8.10
7.70	8.00	7.80	7.70	7.80	8.00

(a) Make a frequency distribution of these rates.

(b) What is the most frequent rate?

(c) How many workers are being paid less than $8.00/hr?

(d) Make a histogram of the wage rate distribution.

(e) Make a frequency polygon of the distribution.

Solution   (a) Table 11.3 lists the wage rates from the lowest ($7.70) to the highest ($8.20). We tally these from the given data and thus obtain the desired frequency distribution.

(b) From the frequency distribution, we read off the most frequent rate to be $8.00/hr.

(c) Again, we read from the frequency distribution that 15 workers are being paid less than $8.00/hr.

(d) The desired histogram appears in Figure 11.4.

(e) The figure also shows the frequency polygon.

Table 11.3

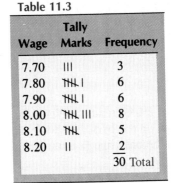

Wage	Tally Marks	Frequency
7.70	|||	3
7.80	ℍℍ		6
7.90	ℍℍ		6
8.00	ℍℍ |||	8
8.10	ℍℍ	5
8.20	||	2
		30 Total

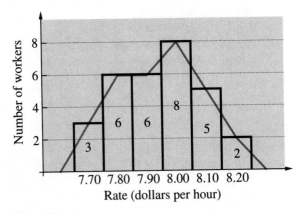

FIGURE 11.4

In making a frequency distribution where the data are to be grouped, we use the following procedure.

1. Decide on the number of classes into which the data are to be grouped. This depends on the number of items that have to be grouped but is usually between 3 and 15.

   (a) The **width** of each class is given by:

   $$\textbf{class width} \approx \frac{\text{largest data value} - \text{smallest data value}}{\text{desired number of classes}}$$

   $\approx$ means "approximately." If you want the class width to be a whole number, round **up** to the nearest whole number

   (b) The lowest and highest values in each class are called the **lower class limit** and **upper class limit,** respectively. Note that the difference between the lower class limit of one class and that of the next should be the class width.

   (c) The center of the class is called the **midpoint**.

   (d) To make sure that the bars in a histogram touch we can:
      (i) use the half-way points between the upper limit of one class and the lower limit of the next class, the **class boundaries,** as the end-points of the bars, or
      (ii) use the upper class limit of the first class as the lower class limit of the second class and stipulate that values falling on class limits will be included in the next higher class.

2. Sort or tally the data into the appropriate classes.

3. Count the number of items in each class.

4. Display the results in a table.

5. If desired, make a histogram and/or frequency polygon of the distribution.

By following this procedure in the next two examples, you will see that it is really not very difficult to tabulate a frequency distribution and construct a histogram or frequency polygon.

Problem Solving:	**Making Histograms**
	Make a frequency distribution with three classes and construct the corresponding histogram for the men's jeans prices shown in the Getting Started section.
1. Read the problem.	We want to make a frequency distribution and then a histogram for the men's jeans' prices.

2. Select the unknown.

3. Think of a plan.

4. Use the procedure we have studied to carry out the plan.
What is the class width?
What are the class limits?
What are the class boundaries?
Are these boundaries convenient for this problem?

Make the frequency distribution.

Draw the histogram.

We need to create three classes and determine their frequencies.

We have to find the class width and class limits, then tabulate and graph the data.

Since the highest price is 60 and the lowest 14, the class width will be:

$$\frac{60 - 14}{3} = 15.3$$

which is rounded **up** to 16. The lower limits for our classes will be 14, 30, and 46, making the upper limits 29, 45, and 61. Thus, the class boundaries will be the halfway points between 29 and 30 (29.5), 45 and 46 (45.5), and 45.5 + 16 = 61.5. However, these boundaries are not convenient or natural, so we choose to make our class limits 14 to 30, 30 to 46, and 46 to 62. The tallies, frequencies, and histogram are shown.

Lower Limit		Upper Limit	Tally	Frequency
14	–	30	THL IIII	9
30	–	46	THL	5
46	–	62	I	1

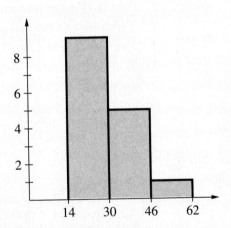

5. Verify the solution.

TRY EXAMPLE 2 NOW.   Cover the solution, write your own, and then check your work.

EXAMPLE 2 In a study of voter turnout in 20 cities with populations of over 100,000 in the United States, the following data were found:

Turnout Rate as a Percent of the Voting Age Population

85.2	72.4	81.2	62.8	71.6
72.1	87.2	76.6	58.5	70.0
76.5	74.1	70.0	80.3	65.9
74.9	70.8	67.0	72.5	73.1

Inspection of the data shows that the smallest number is 58.5 and the largest is 87.2. This time we go from 55 to 90, with the convenient class width of 5 units.

(a) Make a frequency distribution of the data on voting rate (r) using a class interval of 5%, so that the classes will be $55 < r \leq 60, 60 < r \leq 65, \ldots, 85 < r \leq 90$.

(b) Make a histogram and a frequency polygon of this distribution.

(c) In what percent of the cities was the voting rate greater than 80%?

(d) In what percent was the voting rate less than or equal to 70%?

Solution (a) The required frequency distribution appears in Table 11.4. (You should check this table.)

(b) The histogram and frequency polygon are shown in Figure 11.5. These are constructed from the frequency distribution, just as before with ungrouped data.

(c) In 4 out of 20 cities, the voting rate was greater than 80%. Thus, the required percent is $\frac{4}{20} = 20\%$.

(d) In 6 out of 20 cities, the voting rate was less than or equal to 70%. Thus, in 30% of the cities, no more than 70% of the voting age population voted.

FIGURE 11.5

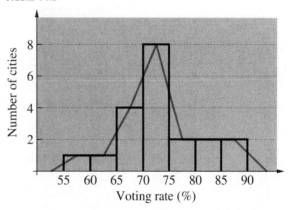

Table 11.4

Voting Rate $r\%$	Tally Marks	Frequency
$55 < r \leq 60$	I	1
$60 < r \leq 65$	I	1
$65 < r \leq 70$	IIII	4
$70 < r \leq 75$	THL III	8
$75 < r \leq 80$	II	2
$80 < r \leq 85$	II	2
$85 < r \leq 90$	II	2

Exercise 11.1 _____

A. 1. Thirty students were asked to list the television programs each had watched during the preceding week. From this list, the number of hours each had spent watching television during the week was calculated. The results are displayed in the following list:

1	5	4	7	10	8	2	3	9	6
6	12	8	14	3	4	8	7	2	1
0	3	5	8	10	12	0	15	1	4

(a) Make a frequency distribution of the number of hours of television watching per student. Label the three columns "Number of hours," "Tally marks," and "Frequency."
(b) What is the most frequent number of hours per student?
(c) How many students watched television more than 10 hr?
(d) How many students watched television 5 hr or less?
(e) What percent of the students watched television more than 7 hr?

B. 2. Prepare a histogram for the data obtained in problem 1(a).

3. Have you read in the newspapers or magazines about cases in which individuals became so disgusted with the amount of time they had to wait to see a doctor or a dentist that they sued for lost wages? The waiting times for 50 patients are given in Table 11.5.

Table 11.5

Waiting Time t min	Number of Patients
$0 < t \leq 3.5$	10
$3.5 < t \leq 7.0$	8
$7.0 < t \leq 10.5$	6
$10.5 < t \leq 14.0$	16
$14.0 < t \leq 17.5$	6
$17.5 < t \leq 21.0$	4

(a) Make a histogram for this set of data.
(b) What percent of the patients waited 7.0 min or less?
(c) What percent of the patients had to wait more than 10.5 min?

Table 11.6

Score	Frequency
-3	0
-2	1
-1	1
0	13
$+1$	19
$+2$	11
$+3$	5

4. General Foods Corporation, in testing a new product, which they called Solid H, had 50 people (25 men and 25 women selected at random) taste the product and indicate their reaction on the picture ballot shown. The

Please check the box under the picture which expresses how you feel toward the product which you have just tasted.

boxes on the ballot were then assigned scores of $+3$, $+2$, $+1$, 0, -1, -2, -3 in order from left to right. Table 11.6 shows the frequency for this taste test. (Incidentally, no significant difference was found between the men's and women's reactions.)

(a) Make a histogram of these data.

(b) What percent of the tasters liked Solid H?

(c) What percent were undecided?

5. Would you like to be a writer? Look at the following list of authors whose books were published at the age given:

	Age
Allen Dulles *(The Boer War: A History)*	8
Hilda Conkling *(Poems by a Little Girl)*	9
Betty Thorpe *(Fioretta)*	10
Nathalia Crane *(Janitor's Boys)*	10
David Statler *(Roaring Guns)*	9
Erlin Hogan *(The Four Funny Men)*	8
Minou Drouet *(First Poems)*	8
Dorothy Straight *(How the World Began)*	6
Kali Diana Grosvenor *(Poems by Kali)*	7
Benjamin Friedman *(The Ridiculous Book)*	9

(a) Make a frequency distribution showing the number of authors for each age.

(b) Make a histogram for the distribution in part (a).

(c) What percent of the authors were less than 8 years old when they published their first books?

6. How tall are you? Here are 10 famous people and their heights:

	Height (in.)
Honoré de Balzac (French novelist)	62
Napoleon Bonaparte (French emperor)	66
Yuri Gagarin (Soviet cosmonaut)	62
Hirohito (Japanese emperor)	65
Nikita Khrushchev (Soviet leader)	63
James Madison (U.S. president)	64
Margaret Mead (U.S. anthropologist)	62
Pablo Picasso (Spanish painter)	64
Mickey Rooney (U.S. actor)	63
Tutankhamen (Egyptian king)	66

(a) Make a frequency distribution showing the number of people for each height.

(b) Make a histogram for the distribution in part (a).

7. Here are 25 stocks listed on the New York Stock Exchange and their closing prices at the end of a recent year:

American Express	$20\frac{1}{2}$	Hewlett Packard	57
American Realty	$5\frac{3}{4}$	Inland Steel	$21\frac{5}{8}$
Canadian Pacific	$15\frac{3}{8}$	Kellogg	$65\frac{3}{8}$
Chase Manhattan	$17\frac{1}{4}$	McDermott	$17\frac{1}{8}$
Chrysler Corporation	$11\frac{3}{4}$	Pepsico	$33\frac{7}{8}$
Continental Bank	$9\frac{3}{8}$	Phillips Petroleum	24
Delta Airlines	$66\frac{1}{8}$	Reynolds Aluminum	55
Exxon	$60\frac{7}{8}$	Sears	$37\frac{7}{8}$
Ford Motor	$28\frac{1}{8}$	Sun Company	$37\frac{7}{8}$
General Dynamics	$53\frac{1}{4}$	Texaco	$61\frac{1}{4}$
General Motors	$28\frac{7}{8}$	Transamerica	$39\frac{7}{8}$
Goodrich	42	Union Pacific	$51\frac{3}{4}$
		U.S. Air	$12\frac{1}{8}$

(a) Make a frequency distribution of these stocks, grouped in intervals of $10. The first two lines of your table should look like this:

Price	Tally Marks	Frequency
$0 < P \leq 10$	II	2
$10 < P \leq 20$	IIII	5

(b) What is the most frequent price interval for these stocks?

(c) How many of the stocks sold for more than $40 per share?

(d) How many of the stocks sold for $30 or less per share?

(e) What percent of the stocks sold for prices between 20\frac{1}{8}$ and $30 per share?

(f) What percent of the stocks sold for $20 or less per share?

8. Make a histogram for the data obtained in problem 7(a).

C. 9. Do you know that certain isotopes (different forms) of the elements are used in nuclear reactors and for medical purposes such as the treatment of cancer? At the present time, about 1400 isotopes have been observed, but, of these, only 332 occur naturally. The table lists the number of elements having 1–10 naturally occurring isotopes. For instance, there are 22 elements having only 1 such isotope, but only 1 element having the maximum number, 10. Make a histogram and a frequency polygon for these data.

Number of Naturally Occurring Isotopes	Number of Elements	Number of Naturally Occurring Isotopes	Number of Elements
1	22	6	9
2	21	7	11
3	9	8	3
4	6	9	1
5	7	10	1

10. Twenty apprentices were asked to measure the diameter of a steel rod with a micrometer (an instrument that can measure to thousandths of an inch). Here are their results (in inches):

0.254	0.245	0.253	0.251
0.249	0.252	0.251	0.252
0.247	0.251	0.250	0.247
0.251	0.249	0.246	0.249
0.250	0.248	0.249	0.253

(a) Make a frequency distribution of these measurements.
(b) What single measurement has as many measurements above it as below it?
(c) What percent of the measurements are between 0.249 and 0.251 in., inclusive?
(d) What would you take as the best estimate of the diameter? Why?

11. Here is a quotation from *Robinson Crusoe,* which many of you probably have read:

> Upon the whole, here was an undoubted testimony that there was scarce any condition in the world so miserable, but was something negative or something positive, to be thankful for in it. . . .

(a) There are 151 letters in this quotation. Make a frequency distribution of the 151 letters.
(b) What letter occurs most frequently?
(c) What percent of the letters are vowels?

12. Four coins were tossed 32 times, and each time the number of heads occurring was recorded, as follows:

1	2	2	1	2	1	2	3
2	3	0	3	4	3	3	4
3	1	3	2	1	2	2	1
2	3	2	1	2	0	1	2

Label three columns "Number of heads," "Tally," and "Frequency," and prepare a frequency distribution for these data.

13. (a) Make a histogram for the data in problem 12.
    (b) Now make a frequency polygon for the data of problem 12.

14. A high school class was asked to roll dice 3000 times. The sums of the top faces of the dice, the frequency of these sums, and the theoretical number of times the sums should have occurred appear in Table 11.7. Make a histogram for these data showing the actual frequency with a solid line and the theoretical frequency with a dotted line (perhaps of a different color).

Table 11.7

Sum	Actual Frequency	Theoretical Frequency
2	79	83
3	152	167
4	252	250
5	312	333
6	431	417
7	494	500
8	465	417
9	338	333
10	267	250
11	129	167
12	91	83

15. In a study of air pollution in a certain city, the concentration of sulfur dioxide in the air (in parts per million) was obtained for 30 days:

0.04	0.17	0.18	0.13	0.10	0.07
0.09	0.16	0.20	0.22	0.06	0.05
0.08	0.05	0.11	0.07	0.09	0.07
0.08	0.02	0.08	0.08	0.18	0.01
0.03	0.06	0.12	0.01	0.11	0.04

(a) Make a frequency distribution for these data grouped in the intervals 0.00–0.04, 0.05–0.09, 0.10–0.14, 0.15–0.19, 0.20–0.24.
(b) For what percent of the time was the concentration of sulfur dioxide more than 0.14 part per million?

16. Make a histogram and a frequency polygon for the data in problem 15.

17. Here are the minimum weekly salaries (rounded to the nearest hundred dollars) for persons engaged in film production:

$7800	$5200	$4600	$1900	$1800	$1600
$1500	$1400	$800	$700	$700	$600

(a) Make a frequency distribution using 4 classes with the upper class limit of the first class as the lower class limit of the second.
(b) Make a histogram and a frequency polygon from your frequency distribution.

18. The following numbers represent the salaries of the 15 best paid players in the National Hockey League (in thousands of dollars):

$2,000 $1,500 $950 $700 $600
$550 $510 $510 $500 $485
$475 $467 $446 $425 $425

(a) Make a frequency distribution using 4 classes with the upper class limit of the first class as the lower class limit of the second.

(b) Make a histogram and a frequency polygon from your frequency distribution.

19. Here are the salaries of the 25 best paid baseball players in 1947 (in thousands of dollars):

$90 $75 $65 $60 $44 $30 $30 $28 $26 $25
$23 $23 $20 $20 $20 $20 $20 $20 $20 $20
$20 $20 $20 $20 $20

(a) Make a frequency distribution using 5 classes with the upper class limit of the first class as the lower class limit of the second.

(b) Make a histogram and a frequency polygon from your frequency distribution.

20. Are the weights of players in different football teams very different? The chart shows the weight (wt) of the Chicago Bears and the San Francisco 49ers.

(a) Make frequency tables and histograms for each of the two teams using six classes.

(b) Can you tell if either team seems to have heavier players?

CHICAGO BEARS

No.	Player	P	Ht.	Wt.	Exp.	No.	Player	P	Ht.	Wt.	Exp.
4	Jim Harbaugh	QB	6-3	220	5	37	Maurice Douglass	CB	5-11	200	6
6	Kevin Butler	K	6-1	190	7	49	David Tate	S	6-0	177	4
8	Maury Buford	P	6-0	198	10	50	Mike Singletary	LB	6-0	230	11
10	Peter Tom Willis	QB	6-2	200	2	51	Jim Morrissey	LB	6-3	227	7
17	Chris Gardocki	P/K	6-1	180	R	53	Dante Jones	LB	6-1	236	4
20	Mark Carrier	S	6-1	180	2	55	John Roper	LB	6-1	228	3
21	Donnell Woolford	CB	5-9	187	3	57	Tom Thayer	G	6-4	270	7
22	Johnny Bailey	RB	5-8	180	2	58	Mike Stonebreaker	LB	6-0	226	R
23	Shaun Gayle	S	5-11	194	8	59	Ron Rivera	LB	6-3	240	8
25	Brad Muster	FB	6-3	231	4	60	Stan Thomas	T	6-5	302	R
26	John Mangum	CB	5-10	173	2	62	Mark Bortz	G	6-6	272	9
29	Dennis Gentry	WR	5-8	180	10	63	Jay Hilgenberg	C	6-3	260	11
30	James Rouse	FB	6-0	220	2	67	Jerry Fontenot	C	6-3	272	3
31	Mark Green	RB	5-11	195	3	71	James Williams	DE	6-7	305	R
32	Lemuel Stinson	CB	5-9	159	4	72	Wiliam Perry	DT	6-2	360	7
33	Darren Lewis	RB	5-10	219	R	73	John Wojciechowski	G	6-4	270	5
35	Neal Anderson	RB	5-11	210	6	75	Ron Mattes	T	6-6	300	6
36	Markus Paul	S	6-2	199	3	76	Steve McMichael	DT	6-2	268	12

No.	Player	P	Ht.	Wt.	Exp.	No.	Player	P	Ht.	Wt.	Exp.
78	Keith Van Horne	T	6-6	283	11	88	Glen Kozlowski	WR	6-1	205	3
80	James Thornton	TE	6-2	242	4	93	Trace Armstrong	DE	6-4	259	3
81	Anthony Morgan	WR	6-1	195	R	95	Richard Dent	DE	6-5	268	9
82	Wendell Davis	WR	5-11	188	4	96	Tim Ryan	DT	6-4	268	2
85	Keith Jennings	TE	6-4	251	1	97	Chris Zorich	DT	6-1	267	R
87	Tom Waddell	WR	6-1	180	2						

SAN FRANCISCO 49ERS

No.	Player	P	Ht.	Wt.	Exp.	No.	Player	P	Ht.	Wt.	Exp.
4	Joe Prokop	P	6-2	225	6	67	Roy Foster	G	6-4	290	10
6	Mike Cofer	K	6-1	160	4	69	Tom Neville	G	6-5	298	4
8	Steve Young	QB	6-2	200	7	72	Frank Pollack	T-G	6-5	285	2
13	Steve Bono	QB	6-4	215	7	74	Steve Wallace	T	6-5	276	6
14	Bill Musgrave	QB	6-2	196	R	78	Pierce Holt	DE	6-4	280	4
22	Todd Bowles	FS	6-2	205	6	79	Harris Barton	G-T	6-4	280	5
23	Spencer Tillman	RB	5-11	206	5	80	Jerry Rice	WR	6-2	200	7
24	Harry Sydney	FB	6-0	217	5	81	Jamie Williams	TE	6-4	245	9
29	Don Griffin	CB	6-0	176	6	82	John Taylor	WR	6-1	185	5
30	Keith Henderson	RB	6-1	220	3	84	Brent Jones	TE	6-4	230	5
35	Dexter Carter	RB	5-9	170	2	86	Sanjay Beach	WR	6-1	190	1
36	Merton Hanks	CB	6-2	185	R	88	Mike Sherrard	WR	6-2	187	3
40	Johnnie Jackson	FS	6-1	204	3	89	Wesley Walls	TE	6-5	246	3
41	David Whitmore	FS	6-0	235	2	90	Darin Jordan	LB	6-2	245	2
43	David Waymer	FS	6-1	188	12	91	Larry Roberts	DE	6-3	275	6
44	Tom Rathman	FB	6-1	232	6	92	Tim Harris	LB	6-6	258	6
45	Kevin Lewis	CB	5-11	173	2	93	Greg Joelson	DE	6-3	270	1
53	Bill Romanowski	LB	6-4	231	4	94	Charles Haley	LB	6-5	230	6
54	Mitch Donahue	LB	6-2	254	R	95	Michael Carter	NT	6-2	285	8
59	Keith DeLong	LB	6-2	235	3	96	Dennis Brown	DE	6-4	290	2
60	Chuck Thomas	C	6-3	280	6	97	Ted Washington	NT	6-4	299	R
61	Jesse Sapolu	C	6-4	260	6	98	Antonio Goss	LB	6-4	228	3
62	Guy McIntyre	G	6-3	265	8	99	Mike Walter	LB	6-3	238	9
64	Jim Burt	NT	6-1	270	11						

21. Are you looking for a printer for your computer? Here are the list prices (in dollars) of the 15 best rated dot-matrix printers:

$500 $300 $475 $280 $550 $265 $300 $310
$250 $240 $300 $250 $190 $290 $180

(a) Find the class width using five classes.

(b) Make a frequency table with the five classes showing the class boundaries and frequencies.

(c) Make a histogram showing the boundaries.

22. One of the top-grossing film of all times is "E.T.: The Extra Terrestrial" with $367.7 million grossed by 1991. But which films are the losers? Here are the amounts lost by the 10 biggest movie failures (in millions):

$35 $25 $23.3 $20 $20
$18.5 $17 $16.6 $15 $14

(a) Find the class width using three classes.
(b) Make a frequency table with the three classes showing the class boundaries and frequencies.
(c) Make a histogram showing the boundaries.

23. Do you think you're getting old? Still, you're probably not nearly as old as Shigechiyo Izumi, of Japan, who almost made it to 121 years. Here are the authenticated ages of the 25 oldest people, rounded to the nearest year.

121	115	115	114	113	113	113	113	112
112	112	112	112	111	111	111	111	111
111	110	110	110	110	110	109		

(a) Find the class width using five classes.
(b) Make a frequency table with the five classes showing the class boundaries and frequencies.
(c) Make a histogram showing the boundaries.

In Other Words

24. When making a histogram, why is it necessary to make the class boundaries the end-points of the bar?

25. Explain the difference between class limits and class boundaries.

26. A survey of the weight of 200 persons and a histogram of the last digit of each weight show that 0 occurred 130 times and 5 occurred 123 times. What might be wrong with the survey?

Using Your Knowledge

Around 1940 it was estimated that it would require approximately 10 years of computation to find the value of the number π (pi) to 1000 decimal places. But in the early 1960s a computer calculated the value of π to more than 100,000 decimal places in less than 9 hr! Since then, several hundred thousand decimal places for π have been calculated. Here are the first 40 decimal places of π:

3.14159 26535 89793 23846 26433 83279 50288 41971

27. Make a frequency distribution of the digits after the decimal point. List the digits from 0 to 9 in your first column.

28. What are the most and the least frequently occurring digits?

Mathematicians are interested in knowing whether the digits all occur with the same frequency. This question can hardly be answered with so few decimal places. However, you should notice that only two of the digits occur with a frequency more than one unit away from what you should expect in 40 decimal places.

Discovery

In this section we have shown an honest way of depicting statistical data by means of a histogram. But you can lie with statistics! Here is how. In a newspaper ad for a certain magazine, the circulation of the magazine was as shown. The height of the bars in the diagram seem to indicate that sales in the first 9 months were tripled by the first quarter of the next year (a whopping 200% rise in sales!).

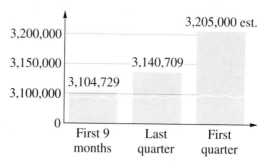

29. Can you discover what was the approximate jump in sales from the first 9 months to the first quarter of the next year?

30. Can you discover what was the approximate percent rise in sales?

31. Can you discover what is wrong with the graph?

11.2   MEASURES OF CENTRAL TENDENCY: THE MEAN, MEDIAN, AND MODE

GETTING STARTED

TONGUE TWISTER AVERAGES

Is there a relationship between the number of words in a tongue twister and the difficulty in reciting it? Shown in the table are several tongue twisters and the percentage of successful attempts out of 30 total attempts at reciting each. What is the average number of words in each? It depends on what you mean by average.

Phrase	Success Rate	Words
"The seething sea ceaseth and thus the seething sea sufficeth us"	3%	11
"The sixth sick sheik's sixth sheep's sick"	30%	7
"The Leith police dismisseth us"	67%	5
"Sixty-six sick chicks"	77%	4
"Toy boat" (said five times fast)	67%	10

"Tie twine to three tree twigs"	80%	6
"She sells seashells by the seashore"	83%	6
"Long slim slick sycamore saplings"	87%	5
"How much wood could a woodchuck chuck if a woodchuck could chuck wood?"	80%	13
"Peter Piper . . ." (you know this one)	57%	35
"Three new blue beans in a new-blown bladder"	90%	9
"Twixt six thick thumbs stick six thick sticks"	93%	8
"Better baby buggy bumpers"	97%	4

Let us arrange the number of words in each twister in ascending order.

4 4 5 5 6 6 $\boxed{7}$ 8 9 10 11 13 35

The easiest average to compute is the **mode,** the value occurring most often. We see that 4, 5, and 6 are modes for these numbers; they occur twice each. If Peter Piper were replaced by "Zack zapped Zeus zinc," the most common number of words (the **mode**) would then be 4.

Another type of average is the **median,** the middle value of an ordered set of numbers (there are as many values above as below the median). In this case, the median number of words is 7.

Finally, we can look at the **mean** number of words in each tongue-twister. We do this by adding the number of words in each and dividing by the total number of tongue twisters. The mean is:

$$\frac{11 + 7 + 5 + 4 + 10 + 6 + 6 + 5 + 13 + 35 + 9 + 8 + 4}{13}$$

$$= \frac{123}{13} = 9.5$$

So, what is the **average** number of words in these tongue twisters? Either 4, 5, 6, 7, or 9.5. Which of the numbers do you think is most representative? In this section we shall study three types of **averages:** the mean, the median, and the mode and how they can be used in different situations.

Alberto and Barney have just gotten back their test papers. There are 9 questions and each one counted 10 points. Their scores are given in the following table.

	Question									
	1	2	3	4	5	6	7	8	9	Total
Alberto	10	7	10	7	7	10	9	10	2	72
Barney	10	8	10	7	7	7	10	7	7	73

Table 11.8 *Frequency*

Score	Alberto	Barney
2	1	0
7	3	5
8	0	1
9	1	0
10	4	3

Who do you think wrote a better paper? As you can see, Alberto's **average** score is $\frac{72}{9} = 8$, and Barney's **average** score is $\frac{73}{9} = 8.1$. Barney clearly has the higher average and concludes that he wrote the better paper. Do you agree?

Alberto does not agree, because he did as well as or better than Barney on 6 of the 9 questions. Alberto thinks that Barney's higher average does not tell the whole story, so he tries something else. First, he makes a frequency distribution of the two sets of scores, as shown in Table 11.8.

Upon inspecting this list, Alberto says, "I did better than you did, Barney, because I scored 10 more often than any other number, and you scored 7 more often than any other number." Would you agree with Alberto?

The average score that we first gave is called the *mean*. It is the one that most of us think of as the average.

Definition 11.1

> The **mean** of a set of numbers is the sum of the numbers divided by the number of elements in the set. The mean is usually denoted by the symbol $\overline{x}$ (read, "*x* bar").

Reprinted with special permission of North America Syndicate, Inc.

Alberto used a different kind of measure that is really not an average at all. The measure he used is called the *mode*.

Definition 11.2

> The **mode** of a set of numbers is that number of the set that occurs most often.

If no number in the set occurs more than once, then there is no mode. However, if several numbers all occur an equal number of times and more than all the rest, then all of these several numbers are modes. Thus, it is possible for a set of numbers to have more than one mode.

The mean and the mode are useful because they give an indication of a sort of center of the set. For this reason they are called **measures of central tendency**.

EXAMPLE 1   Ten golf professionals playing a certain course scored 69, 71, 72, 68, 69, 73, 71, 70, 69, and 68. Find:

(a) The mean (average) of these scores
(b) The mode of these scores

Solution   (a) $\bar{x} = \dfrac{69 + 71 + 72 + 68 + 69 + 73 + 71 + 70 + 69 + 68}{10} = \dfrac{700}{10}$

$$= 70$$

(b) The score that occurred most often is 69 (three times). Hence, the mode is 69. ∎

There is a third commonly used measure of central tendency, called the *median*.

| Definition 11.3 | The **median** of a set of numbers is the middle number when the numbers are arranged in order of magnitude. If there is no single middle number, then the median is the mean (average) of the two middle numbers. |

Let us list Alberto's and Barney's scores in order of magnitude:

Table 11.9

Alberto	2	7	7	7	⑨	10	10	10	10
Barney	7	7	7	7	⑦	8	10	10	10

Measure	Alberto	Barney
Mean	8	8.1
Mode	10	7
Median	9	7

The median is circled in each case.

Now, look at the three measures we have found for the scores in Table 11.9. The mode and the median in this case would appear to some people to be evidence that perhaps Alberto did write a better paper than Barney.

EXAMPLE 2   Have you been exercising lately? You must exercise if you want to keep your weight down. Here are 10 different activities with the corresponding hourly energy expenditures (in calories) for a 150-lb person:

Fencing	300	Square dancing	350
Golf	250	Squash	600
Running	900	Swimming	300
Sitting	100	Volleyball	350
Standing	150	Wood chopping	400

(a) Find the mean of these numbers.
(b) Find the median number of calories spent in these activities.
(c) Find the mode of these numbers.

Solution   (a) The mean is obtained by adding all the numbers and dividing the sum by 10. The sum of the numbers in the first column is 1700, and the sum of the numbers in the second column is 2000. Thus, the mean is

$$\frac{1700 + 2000}{10} = 370 \text{ calories per hour}$$

(b) To find the median, we must first arrange the numbers in order of magnitude, as follows:

Sitting	100
Standing	150
Golf	250
Fencing	300
Swimming	300
Square dancing	350
Volleyball	350
Wood chopping	400
Squash	600
Running	900

$\leftarrow$ Median $= \dfrac{300 + 350}{2} = 325$

Since we have an even number of items, the median is the average of the two middle items.

(c) The mode is the number with the greatest frequency if there is one such number. In this case, the numbers 300 and 350 both occur twice, while all other numbers occur just once. Thus, there are two modes, 300 and 350.

EXAMPLE 3   For the frequency distribution of wage rates given in Example 1 of Section 11.1, find:

(a) The mean rate   (b) The mode   (c) The median rate

Solution   (a) We refer to the table on page 774 and make the calculation shown in Table 11.10, finding the mean rate to be $7.94/hr.

(b) The mode is the most frequent rate, $8.00/hr.

(c) Since 15 workers get $7.90 or less and the other 15 get $8.00 or more per hour, the median rate is the mean of $7.90 and $8.00, that is, $7.95/hr.

Table 11.10

Wage Rate	Frequency	Frequency × Rate
7.70	3	23.10
7.80	6	46.80
7.90	6	47.40
8.00	8	64.00
8.10	5	40.50
8.20	2	16.40
	30	30)238.20
		7.94 = $\bar{x}$

EXAMPLE 4   The table shows the distribution of scores made by a large number of students taking a five-question true-false test.

(a) What was the median score?
(b) What was the mean score?

Score (Number Correct)	Proportion of Students
0	0.05
1	0.05
2	0.10
3	0.35
4	0.25
5	0.20

Solution   (a) The table gives the proportion of students making each score, so the sum of these proportions must be 1. To find the median (the middle value) we add the proportions starting from the top until we get a sum of 0.5 or more. This occurs when we add the first four items. Thus the median score is 3.

(b) To find the mean score, we add the products of the scores and their proportions as follows:

$$0 \times 0.05 = 0$$
$$1 \times 0.05 = 0.05$$
$$2 \times 0.10 = 0.20$$
$$3 \times 0.35 = 1.05$$
$$4 \times 0.25 = 1.00$$
$$\underline{5 \times 0.20 = 1.00}$$
$$Sum = 3.30$$

Since the sum of the proportions is 1, the mean score is 3.30.   ∎

EXAMPLE 5   In a physics class, half the students scored 80 on a mid-term exam. Most of the remaining students scored 70 except for a few who scored 20. Which of the following statements is true?

(a) The mean and the median are the same.
(b) The mean and the mode are the same.
(c) The mean is less than the median.
(d) The mean is greater than the median.

Solution   Since half the students scored 80 and the next best score was 70, the median score on the mid-term is 75 (midway between 80 and 70). Also, not all of the remaining students scored 70, so the mean is less than 75. Thus, statement (c) is correct.   ∎

EXAMPLE 6   The following chart shows the distribution of scores on a placement test for students at South High School. In the chart x is the score and y is the frequency. Which of the following statements is true?

(a) The mode and the mean are the same.
(b) The mode and the median are the same.
(c) The median is less than the mode.
(d) The median is greater than the mode.

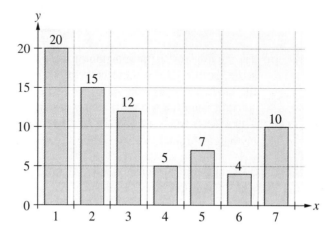

Solution   The chart shows that the mode is $x = 1$. It also shows that more than 20 students scored higher than 1. Hence the median must be greater than 1, and therefore statement (d) is correct. ∎

In this section, we introduced three **measures of central tendency**. Here is how they compare:

1. The **mean** (arithmetic average) is the most commonly used of the three measures. A set of data always has a unique mean, and this mean takes account of each item of the data. On the negative side, finding the mean takes the most calculation of the three measures. Another bad feature of the mean is its sensitivity to extreme values. For instance, the mean of the data 2, 4, 6, 8 is $\frac{20}{4} = 5$, but the mean of 2, 4, 6, 28 is $\frac{40}{4} = 10$, a shift of 5 units toward the extreme value 28.

2. The **mode** has the advantage of requiring no calculation. However, the mode may not exist, as in the case of the data 2, 4, 6, 8. On the other hand, the mode may be most useful. For example, suppose a shoe manufacturer surveys 100 women to see which of three styles, A, B, or C, of shoes each one prefers and finds style A selected by 30 women, style B by 50, and style C by 20. The mode is 50 and there is not much doubt about which style the manufacturer will feature.

3. The **median** always exists and is unique, as in the case of the mean. However, the median requires very little computation and is not sensitive to extreme values. Of course, in order to find the median, the data must be arranged in order of magnitude, which may not be practical for large sets of data. But the most important disadvantage of the median is its failure to take account of each item of data. Hence, in many statistical problems, the median is not a reliable measure.

Exercise 11.2

1. Find the mean and the median for each set of numbers:
    (a) 1, 5, 9, 13, 17
    (b) 1, 3, 9, 27, 81
    (c) 1, 4, 9, 16, 25
    (d) For which of these sets are the mean and the median the same? Which measure is the same for all three sets? Which (if any) of the sets has a mode?

2. Show that the median of the set of numbers 1, 2, 4, 8, 16, 32 is 6. How does this compare with the mean?

3. Out of 10 possible points, a class of 20 students made the following test scores:

    0, 0, 1, 2, 4, 5, 5, 6, 6, 6, 7, 8, 8, 8, 8, 9, 9, 9, 10, 10

    Find the mean, the median, and the mode. Which of these three measures do you think is the least representative of the set of scores?

4. Find the mean and the median of the set of numbers:

    0, 3, 26, 43, 45, 60, 72, 75, 79, 82, 83

5. An instructor gave a short test to a class of 25 students and found the scores on the basis of 10 to be as follows:

Score	3	4	5	6	7	8	9	10
Number of Students	2	1	3	2	6	4	4	3

The instructor asked two students, Agnes and Betty, to calculate the average score. Agnes made the calculation

$$\frac{3 + 4 + 5 + 6 + 7 + 8 + 9 + 10}{8} = \frac{52}{8} = 6.5$$

and said the average score is 6.5. Betty calculated a *weighted average* by multiplying each score by the number of students attaining that score, adding the results, and dividing by the total number of students as shown.

$$\frac{2 \cdot 3 + 1 \cdot 4 + 3 \cdot 5 + 2 \cdot 6 + 6 \cdot 7 + 4 \cdot 8 + 4 \cdot 9 + 3 \cdot 10}{25}$$

$$= \frac{177}{25} = 7.08$$

She then said the average was 7.08. Who is correct, Agnes or Betty? Why?

6. An investor bought 150 shares of Fly-Hi Airlines stock. He paid $60 per share for 50 shares, $50 per share for 60 shares, and $75 per share for 40 shares. What was his average cost per share? (Compare problem 5.)

7. Make a frequency distribution of the number of letters per word in the following quotation: "For seven days seven priests with seven trumpets invested Jericho, and on the seventh day they encompassed the city seven times."
   (a) Find the mode(s) of the number of letters per word.
   (b) Find the median. (You can use your frequency distribution to do this.)
   (c) Find the mean of the number of letters per word.
   (d) Do you think your answers would give a good indication of the average length of words in ordinary English writing? Why?

8. Here are the temperatures at 1-hr intervals in Denver, Colorado, from 1 P.M. on a certain day to 9 A.M. the next day:

1 P.M.	90	8 P.M.	81	3 A.M.	66
2 P.M.	91	9 P.M.	79	4 A.M.	65
3 P.M.	92	10 P.M.	76	5 A.M.	66
4 P.M.	92	11 P.M.	74	6 A.M.	64
5 P.M.	91	12 M	71	7 A.M	64
6 P.M.	89	1 A.M.	71	8 A.M	71
7 P.M.	86	2 A.M.	69	9 A.M	75

   (a) What was the mean temperature? The median temperature?
   (b) What was the mean temperature from 1 P.M. to 9 P.M.? The median temperature?
   (c) What was the mean temperature from midnight to 6 A.M.? The median temperature?

9. Suppose that a dime and a nickel are tossed. They can fall in four different ways: (H, H), (H, T), (T, H), (T, T), where we agree to let the first letter indicate how the dime falls and the second letter, the nickel. How many tosses do you think it would take, on the average, to get all four possibilities at least once? A good way to find out is by experimenting. Take a dime and a nickel and toss them to get your data. You can keep track of what happens with a frequency distribution. For example, on the

first trial it took 11 tosses to get all four possibilities (H, H), (H, T), (T, H), (T, T). You can keep track of what happens with a frequency distribution like this one:

	Trial 1	Trial 2	Trial 3
(H, H)	I	I	IIII I
(H, T)	I	I	III
(T, H)	IIII	I	III
(T, T)	IIII I	IIII	I
	11	7	12 (etc.)

You will need to make tally marks in the trials column until there is at least one mark for each possibility. Then write the total number of tosses at the bottom of the column. A new column will be needed for each trial, of course. Do 20 trials.

(a) When you finish the 20 trials, make a frequency distribution of the number of tosses required to give all four possibilities.

(b) Use the frequency distribution you obtained in part (a) to find the median number of tosses.

(c) Find the mean number of tosses needed to obtain all four possibilities.

10. The mean score on a test taken by 20 students is 75; what is the sum of the 20 test scores?

11. A mathematics professor lost a test paper belonging to one of her students. She remembered that the mean score for the class of 20 was 81, and that the sum of the 19 other scores was 1560. What was the grade on the paper she lost?

12. If in problem 11 the mean was 82, and the sum of the 19 other scores was still 1560, what was the grade on the lost paper?

13. The mean salary for the 20 workers in company A is $90 per week, while in company B the mean salary for its 30 workers is $80 per week. If the two companies merge, what is the mean salary for the 50 employees of the new company?

14. A student has a mean score of 88 on five tests taken. What score must he obtain on his next test to have a mean (average) score of 80 on all six tests?

15. The table below shows the distribution of families by income in a particular urban area.

Annual Income ($)	Proportion of Families	Annual Income ($)	Proportion of Families
0–9,999	0.02	35,000–49,999	0.10
10,000–14,999	0.09	50,000–79,999	0.07
15,000–19,999	0.25	80,000–119,999	0.05
20,000–24,999	0.30	120,000+	0.01
25,000–34,999	0.11		

(a) What proportion of the familes have income of at least $25,000?

(b) What is the median income range?

(c) Find the mean of the lower income levels in the left-hand column.

(d) Find the amount below which 36% of the families have lower incomes.

16. In a history test given to 100 students, 50 earned scores of 80 or more. Of the other students, 40 earned scores between 60 and 75, and the other ten earned scores between 10 and 40. Which one of the following statements is true about the distribution of scores?

(a) The mean and the median are the same.

(b) The mean is less than the median.

(c) The median is less than the mean.

17. In a mathematics test given to 50 students, 25 earned scores of 90. Most of the other students scored 80, and the remaining students scored 30. Which of the following statements is true about the distribution of scores?

(a) The mode is the same as the mean.

(b) The median is greater than the mean.

(c) The mode is greater than the mean.

(d) The mean is greater than the median.

18. The graph below shows the distribution of scores on a placement test given to juniors at West High School. Which of the following statements applies to this distribution?

(a) The mode and the mean are the same.

(b) The mode is greater than the mean.

(c) The mode and the median are the same.

(d) The mode is less than the median.

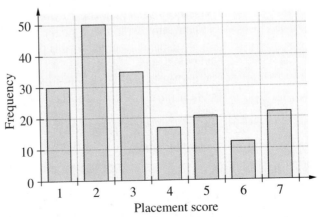

19. One hundred students took a math test. None of the students scored over 95 or less than 50. Which of the following is the most reasonable estimate of the mean (average) score?

(a) 80   (b) 60   (c) 70   (d) 55

20. Gretchen owns five $5000 municipal bonds. Each quarter, she receives the following interest payments: $81.25, $112.50, $118.75, $125.00, and $137.50. Which of the following is the most reasonable estimate of the mean (average) interest payment?
    (a) $108   (b) $116   (c) $120   (d) $105

*I*n Other Words

21. Explain in your own words what is meant by the median of a set of scores. Is the median a good measure of a set of scores?

22. What is meant by the mode of a set of scores? Is this a good measure? If so, for what purpose? Give an example.

Using Your Knowledge

*Have you ever been in the checkout line at a supermarket or department store for so long that you were tempted to walk out? There is a mathematical theory called **queuing** (pronounced, "cueing") theory that studies ways in which lines at supermarkets, department stores, and so on, can be reduced to a minimum. The following problems show how a store manager can estimate the average number of people waiting at a particular counter.*

23. Suppose that in a 5-min interval customers arrive as indicated in Table 11.11. (Arrival time is assumed to be at the beginning of each minute.) In the first minute, A and B arrive. During the second minute, B moves to the head of the line (A was gone because it took 1 min to serve him), and C and D arrive, and so on. From the figure, find:
    (a) The average (mean) number of people in line
    (b) The mode of the number of people in line

Table 11.11

Time	Customers
1	A, B
2	C, D
3	
4	E, F
5	

Table 11.12

Time	Customers
1	A
2	B
3	C, D, E
4	F
5	

24. Use the ideas of problem 23 and suppose that the list of arrivals is as shown in Table 11.12. (Assume it takes 1 min to serve the first customer in line and that customer leaves immediately.)
    (a) Draw a diagram showing the line during each of the first 5 min.
    (b) Find the mean of the number of people in line during the 5 min.
    (c) Find the mode of the number of people in line.

Discovery

We have just studied three measures of central tendency: the mean, the median, and the mode. All these measures are frequently called averages. Suppose that the chart below shows the salaries at Scrooge Manufacturing Company.

Boss	Boss' son	Boss' assistant	Boss' secretaries	Workers
$100,000	$50,000	$25,000	$10,000	$6,000 each

25. Scrooge claims that the workers should not unionize; after all, he says, the average salary is $21,000. Can you discover what average this is?

26. Manny Chevitz, the union leader, claims that Scrooge Manufacturing really needs a union. Just look at their salaries! A meager $6000 on the average. Can you discover what average he means?

27. B. Crooked, the politician, wants both union and management support. He says that the workers are about average as far as salary is concerned. You can figure it out. The company's average salary is $8000. Can you discover what average B. Crooked has in mind?

Calculator Corner

If you have a calculator with $\boxed{\Sigma +}$ *(read, "sigma plus") and* $\boxed{\overline{x}}$ *keys, you are in luck. The calculation for the mean is automatically done for you. First, place the calculator in the statistics mode (press* $\boxed{\text{mode}}$ $\boxed{\text{stat}}$ *or* $\boxed{\text{2nd}}$ $\boxed{\text{stat}}$ *).*
To find the mean of the numbers in Example 2, enter $\boxed{300}$ $\boxed{\Sigma +}$ $\boxed{250}$ $\boxed{\Sigma +}$ $\boxed{900}$ $\boxed{\Sigma +}$ $\boxed{100}$ $\boxed{\Sigma +}$ $\boxed{150}$ $\boxed{\Sigma +}$ $\boxed{350}$ $\boxed{\Sigma +}$ $\boxed{600}$ $\boxed{\Sigma +}$ $\boxed{300}$ $\boxed{\Sigma +}$ $\boxed{350}$ $\boxed{\Sigma +}$ $\boxed{400}$ $\boxed{\Sigma +}$ $\boxed{\text{2nd}}$ $\boxed{\overline{x}}$
The display gives the mean $\overline{x} = 370$.

Computer Corner

The mean, median, and mode of a list of numbers can be found using the Mean, Median, and Mode Program found in the Programs in BASIC appendix. Simply enter the numbers and press return.

11.3 MEASURES OF DISPERSION: THE RANGE AND STANDARD DEVIATION

TV Guide *and local newspaper listings offer viewers a daily menu of what's on television—some hot, some not*

GETTING STARTED

RATINGS DEVIATIONS FOR MOVIES AND T.V.

Which programs get the best television ratings, weekly series or movies? The ratings for the ten best series and ten best movies according to the *Top 10 Almanac* are shown in Table 11.13. If you were a manufacturer selling your product to consumers, would you buy television advertisement time during a series or during a movie? Before you make up your mind, look at Table 11.13 and note that the series ratings **range** from 18 to 24 (6 points) while the movies **range** from 19 to 25 (also 6 points). Since the range is the same in both distributions, we might look next at the mean rating in each category. But the mean is 21 in both cases. What else can we look at to try to determine the best air time for an advertiser? There is a measurement that indicates how the data differs from the mean, and it is called the **standard deviation (s)**. The standard deviation, like the range, is a measure of the spread of data. To obtain the standard deviation of a set of numbers, start by computing the difference between each measurement and the mean, that is $x - \bar{x}$, as shown in Table 11.14 for the movie ratings data.

Table 11.13

| | Ratings | |
Rank	Series	Movies
1	24	25
2	23	23
3	23	22
4	22	21
5	21	21
6	20	20
7	20	20
8	20	20
9	19	19
10	18	19
Total	210	210

Table 11.14

Rank	Movie Ratings (x)	$x - \bar{x}$	$(x - \bar{x})^2$
1	25	$25 - 21 = 4$	16
2	23	$23 - 21 = 2$	4
3	22	$22 - 21 = 1$	1
4	21	$21 - 21 = 0$	0
5	21	$21 - 21 = 0$	0
6	20	$20 - 21 = -1$	1
7	20	$20 - 21 = -1$	1
8	20	$20 - 21 = -1$	1
9	19	$19 - 21 = -2$	4
10	19	$19 - 21 = -2$	4
Total	210		32

Unfortunately, if we add the $x - \bar{x}$ values, we get a sum of 0. (This will always be true when finding standard deviations. Can you figure out why?) Therefore, we square each $x - \bar{x}$ value before we do the addition, and then arrive at a sum of 32. If we were looking at the entire population of movies on T.V., we would then divide this number by the population size to get a type of "average squared difference" of ratings from the mean. However, this sample does not include the entire population so, as a rule, we divide instead by one less than our sample (here, that number is $10 - 1 = 9$) to make the final value of our standard deviation a bit larger. Doing this we then have $s^2 = \frac{32}{9}$, whose units are squared ratings points. What kind of unit is that? To return to rating points, we need to take the square root of $\frac{32}{9}$ obtaining

$$s = \sqrt{\frac{32}{9}} \quad \text{or} \quad \frac{4\sqrt{2}}{3}$$

(remember that $\sqrt{32} = \sqrt{16 \cdot 2} = 4\sqrt{2}$). A calculator or square root table will yield $s = 1.89$. For the series data, $s = 1.94$ (try it), which means that series ratings are slightly more dispersed or spread out. You might like advertising time during movies because their ratings are "closer" together and slightly less variable.

   In this section you will learn how to find the range and calculate the standard deviation of a set of sample data.

Most of the time we want to know more about a set of numbers than we can learn from a measure of central tendency. For instance, the two sets of numbers {3, 5, 7} and {0, 5, 10} both have the same mean and the same median, 5, but the two sets of numbers are quite different. Clearly, some information about how the numbers vary will be useful in describing the set.

   A number that describes how the numbers of a set are spread out, or dispersed, is called a **measure of dispersion**. A very simple example of such a measure is the range.

Definition 11.4

The **range** of a set of numbers is the difference between the greatest and the least of the numbers in the set.

   The two sets {3, 5, 7} and {0, 5, 10} have ranges $7 - 3 = 4$ and $10 - 0 = 10$, respectively. Because the range is determined by only two numbers of the set, you can see that it gives us very little information about the other numbers of the set. The range actually gives us only a general notion of the spread of the given data.

   Another measure of dispersion is called the **standard deviation**. It is the most commonly used of these measures, and the only additional one that we shall consider. The easiest way to define the standard deviation is by means of a formula.

Definition 11.5

Let a set of n numbers be denoted by $x_1, x_2, x_3, \ldots, x_n$, and let the mean of these numbers be denoted by $\bar{x}$. Then the **standard deviation** s is given by

$$s = \sqrt{\frac{(x_1 - \bar{x})^2 + (x_2 - \bar{x})^2 + (x_3 - \bar{x})^2 + \cdots + (x_n - \bar{x})^2}{n - 1}}$$

If the standard deviation is to be calculated for an entire population, then the sum of the squared differences is divided by n, the size of the entire population. For a sample drawn from a population (as in this book), $n - 1$ is used, where n is the sample size.

In order to find the standard deviation, we have to find:

1. The mean, $\bar{x}$, of the set of numbers
2. The difference (deviation) between each number of the set and the mean
3. The squares of these deviations
4. The sum of the squared deviations divided by $n - 1$
5. The square root of this quotient, which is the number s

The last four steps motivate the name **root-mean-square deviation,** which is often used for the standard deviation. As we shall learn, the number s gives a good indication of how the data are spread about the mean.

EXAMPLE 1 The ages of 5 schoolchildren were found to be 7, 9, 10, 11, and 13. Find the standard deviation s for this set of ages.

Solution We follow the five steps given above, as shown in Table 11.15.

Table 11.15 *Calculation of the Standard Deviation*

Age	Difference from Mean	Square of Difference
x	$x - \bar{x}$	$(x - \bar{x})^2$
7	-3	9
9	-1	1
10	0	0
11	1	1
13	3	9
50 Sum of ages		20 Sum of squares
$\bar{x} = \frac{50}{5} = 10$ Mean of ages		$\frac{20}{5-1} = 5$

1. The mean of the five ages is

$$\bar{x} = \frac{7 + 9 + 10 + 11 + 13}{5} = \frac{50}{5} = 10 \quad \text{(column 1)}$$

2. We now find the difference (deviation) between each number and the mean (column 2).
3. We square the numbers in column 2 to get column 3.
4. We find the sum of the squares in column 3 divided by $5 - 1$.

$$\frac{9 + 1 + 0 + 1 + 9}{5 - 1} = \frac{20}{5 - 1} = 5$$

5. The standard deviation is the square root of the number found in step 4. Thus, $s = \sqrt{5} \approx 2.2$. Note that $\sqrt{5}$ can be found from a table or with a calculator.   ∎

The number s, although it seems complicated to compute, is a most useful number to know. In many practical applications, about 68% of the data are within 1 standard deviation from the mean. That is, 68% of the numbers lie between $\bar{x} - s$ and $\bar{x} + s$. Also, about 95% of the data are within 2 standard deviations from the mean; that is, 95% of the numbers lie between $\bar{x} - 2s$ and $\bar{x} + 2s$.

For example, if the mean of a set of 1000 numbers is 200 and the standard deviation is 25, then approximately 680 of the numbers lie between 175 and 225, and all but about 50 of the numbers lie between 150 and 250. Thus, even with no further information, the number s gives a fair idea of how the data are spread about the mean. These ideas are discussed more fully in Section 11.4.

EXAMPLE 2   A consumer group checks the price of 1 dozen large eggs at 11 chain stores, with the following results:

Store Number	1	2	3	4	5	6	7	8	9	10	11
Price (cents)	70	68	72	60	63	75	66	65	72	69	68

Find the mean, median, mode, and standard deviation. What percent of the data are within 1 standard deviation from the mean?

Solution   In Table 11.16 the data are arranged in order of magnitude. The mean is found to be 68¢. The median is the middle price 68¢. The modes are 68¢ and 72¢. The calculation of the standard deviation is shown in the table. The result is $s = 4.3$. To find the percent of the data within 1 standard deviation from the mean, we first find $\bar{x} - s = 63.7$ and $\bar{x} + s = 72.3$. By examining the data, we see that eight of the prices are between these two numbers. Thus, 73% of the prices are within 1 standard deviation from the mean price.

Note that you are not expected to calculate square roots. Use Table I in the back of the book or a calculator. We will give both forms of the answer, as $\sqrt{18.8}$ and 4.3, in the answer section.

Table 11.16

x	$x - \bar{x}$	$(x - \bar{x})^2$
60	-8	64
63	-5	25
65	-3	9
66	-2	4
68	0	0
68	0	0
69	1	1
70	2	4
72	4	16
72	4	16
75	7	49
748		188

$$\bar{x} = \frac{748}{11} = 68 \qquad \frac{188}{10} = 18.8$$

$$s = \sqrt{18.8} \approx 4.3$$

Exercise 11.3

In problems 1–10:

(a) State the range.   (b) Find the standard deviation s.

1. 3, 5, 8, 13, 21
2. 1, 4, 9, 16, 25
3. 5, 10, 15, 20, 25
4. 6, 9, 12, 15, 18
5. 5, 6, 7, 8, 9
6. 4, 6, 8, 10, 12
7. 5, 9, 1, 3, 8, 7, 2
8. 2, 0, 4, 6, 8, 10, 8, 2
9. $-3, -2, -1, 0, 1, 2, 3$
10. $-6, -4, -2, 0, 2, 4, 6$

11. Out of 10 possible points, a class of 20 students made the following test scores:

    0, 0, 1, 2, 4, 4, 5, 6, 6, 6, 7, 8, 8, 8, 8, 9, 9, 9, 10, 10

    (a) What is the mode?   (b) What is the median?
    (c) What is the mean?   (d) Calculate the standard deviation.
    (e) What percent of the scores lie within 1 standard deviation from the mean?
    (f) What percent of the scores lie within 2 standard deviations from the mean?

12. Suppose that the 4 students who scored lowest on the test in problem 11 dropped the course. Answer the same question as in problem 11 for the remaining students.

13. Elmer Duffer plays golf on a par 75 course that is really too tough for him. His scores in his last 10 games are 103, 110, 113, 102, 105, 110, 111, 110, 106, 110.
    (a) What is Elmer's mode?
    (b) What is his median score?
    (c) What is his mean score?
    (d) Calculate the standard deviation of his scores.
    (e) Which of his scores are more than 1 standard deviation from his mean score? What percent of the games is this?

14. Answer the same questions as in problem 13 for the lowest 8 of Elmer's 10 scores.

15. The daily number of pounds of garbage for six different households were as follows:

    6, 2, 17, 3, 5, 9

    Find the range, mean, and standard deviation of the weights.

16. The carry on luggage weight (in pounds) for a random sample of 10 passengers during a domestic flight were as follows:

    30, 30, 32, 35, 37, 40, 40, 40, 42, 44

    Find the range, mean, and standard deviation of the weights.

17. The response time of six emergency fire calls were measured to the nearest minute and found to be 6, 7, 9, 12, 3, 5. Find the range, mean, and standard deviation for the calls.

18. From 1918 to 1931 Babe Ruth was the American League home run champion 12 times (he did not win in 1922 and 1925). The number of home runs he hit to earn the titles were

11	29	54	59	41	46
47	60	54	46	49	46

    Find the range, mean, and standard deviation for the number of home runs.

In Other Words

19. Suppose the standard deviation of a set of numbers is 0. What does this tell you about the numbers? Explain.

20. Two classes, each with 100 students, took an examination with maximum possible score 100. In the first class, the mean score was 75 and the standard deviation was 5. In the second class, the mean score was 70 and the standard deviation was 15. Which of the two classes do you think had more scores of 90 or better? Why?

Using Your Knowledge

A *binomial experiment* is one that consists of a number of identical trials, each trial having only two possible outcomes (like tossing a coin that must fall heads or tails). Let us consider one of the outcomes as a success and the other as a failure. If p is the probability of success, then $1 - p$ is the probability of failure.

Suppose the experiment consists of n trials; then the theoretical expected number of successes is pn. For instance, if the experiment consists of tossing a fair coin 100 times, then the expected number of heads is $(\frac{1}{2})(100) = 50$. This means that if the experiment of tossing the coin 100 times is repeated many times, then the average number of heads is theoretically 50. In general, if a binomial experiment is repeated many times, then the theoretical mean (average) number of successes is pn, where p is the probability of success in one trial and n is the number of trials in the experiment.

If we let P_k denote the probability of k successes and $n - k$ failures in a binomial experiment with n trials, then the set of numbers $P_0, P_1, P_2, \ldots, P_n$ constitutes a *binomial frequency distribution*. The following simple formula has been obtained for the standard deviation of such a distribution:

$$s = \sqrt{np(1 - p)}$$

For example, if the experiment consists of tossing a fair coin 10,000 times and tallying the number of heads, then n = 10,000, $p = \frac{1}{2}$, $\bar{x} = 5000$, and

$$s = \sqrt{10,000(\tfrac{1}{2})(1 - \tfrac{1}{2})} = \sqrt{2500} = 50$$

If this experiment (tossing the coin 10,000 times) were repeated many times, then we would expect the average number of heads to be close to 5000. Although we are not justified in expecting the number of heads in any one experiment to be exactly 5000, we may expect that about 68% of the time the number of heads will be between 4950 and 5050.

21. If a fair die is rolled, the probability that it comes up 2 is $\frac{1}{6}$ and the probability that it comes up not 2 is $\frac{5}{6}$. If we regard 2 as a success and any other number as a failure, what is the standard deviation for the experiment of rolling the die 180 times?

22. Suppose that in rolling a die we regard a 3 or a 4 as a success and any other number as a failure. What is the standard deviation for the experiment of rolling the die 18 times? How far away from the mean would the number of successes have to be before you became suspicious of the die's honesty?

23. Suppose a die is loaded so that the probability that a 6 comes up is $\frac{1}{4}$. If we regard a 6 as a success and any other number as a failure, what is the standard deviation for the experiment of rolling the die 400 times?

Calculator Corner

If you have a calculator with a $\boxed{\sigma_{n-1}}$ *key, it will compute the standard deviation for a set of data at the push of a button. For example, to find the standard deviation of Example 1, set the calculator in the statistics mode and enter*

$$\boxed{7}\ \boxed{\Sigma+}\ \boxed{9}\ \boxed{\Sigma+}\ \boxed{10}\ \boxed{\Sigma+}\ \boxed{11}\ \boxed{\Sigma+}\ \boxed{13}\ \boxed{2nd}\ \boxed{\sigma_{n-1}}$$

The result is given as 2.2.

Computer Corner

To find the standard deviation of a set of numbers requires some tedious calculations. The Standard Deviation, Range, and Mean Program will do it for you. As a matter of fact, since you need the mean to find the standard deviation, the program will also give you the mean (and the range, in case you need it). You need only press RETURN (ENTER) after each entry. When all entries are in, press RETURN (ENTER) one more time, and the mean, range, and standard deviation will be displayed.

11.4 THE NORMAL DISTRIBUTION: A PROBLEM-SOLVING TOOL

Colleges and universities use the Scholastic Aptitude Test (SAT) as a standardized measure of how well prepared students are to do college-level work

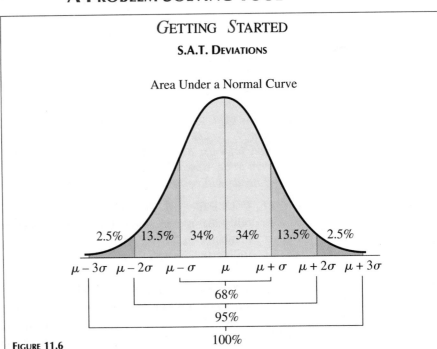

GETTING STARTED

S.A.T. DEVIATIONS

Area Under a Normal Curve

FIGURE 11.6

Do you remember your S.A.T. verbal and math scores? In a recent year, the mean score for the verbal portion was μ (read, "mu") = 425 with a standard deviation of σ (read, "sigma") = 110, while the math scores had a mean of 475 and a standard deviation of 125. Suppose you scored 536 on the verbal portion and your friend scored 600 on the math portion. Which is the better score? It might not be the 600! To be able to compare scores, we must learn about the **normal curve** shown in Figure 11.6. This bell-shaped curve has four important properties: 1. It is smooth and symmetric (if you fold the graph in half along the center line, the two parts of the curve coincide exactly). 2. Its highest point occurs over the mean μ of the entire population. 3. The curve levels out and approaches the x axis but never touches it. 4. The total area under any normal curve is 1 and the proportion of data values between one, two, and three standard deviations to either side of the mean is as shown. (Some books give these values as 34.1%, 13.6%, and 2.15%, we use 34%, 13.5%, and 2.5% for convenience.)

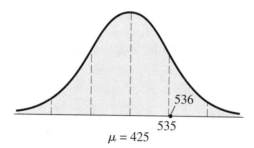

FIGURE 11.7

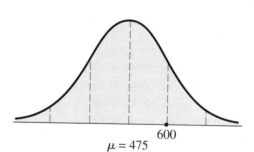

FIGURE 11.8

Now, for the rest of the story. If we assume that scores on the verbal and mathematical portions of the S.A.T. are normally distributed and have the means and standard deviations mentioned, we can label the curves in Figures 11.7 and 11.8 with their respective means, $\mu = 425$ and 475. In Figure 11.7, one standard deviation to the right of the mean will have value $\mu + \sigma$ or $425 + 110 = 535$, while in Figure 11.8 one standard deviation to the right of the 475 mean will be 600 (475 + 125). Now, a score of 536 on the verbal will be slightly to the right of one standard deviation (535), while a score of 600 on the math will be **exactly** one standard deviation from the mean. Believe it or not, a 536 verbal score is comparatively better than a 600 math score!

The normal distribution we have mentioned is an example of a continuous probability distribution studied by the French mathematician Abraham De Moivre and the German mathematician Carl Gauss (as a matter of fact, normal distributions are sometimes called Gaussian distributions in his honor). First, we must learn to recognize normal distributions.

A. *The Normal Distribution*

Look at the curves in Figure 11.9. They are **not** normal distributions! (a) is not symmetric, (b) is not bellshaped, (c) crosses the *x* axis, and (d) has tails turning up away from the *x* axis. We show some normal curves in Example 1.

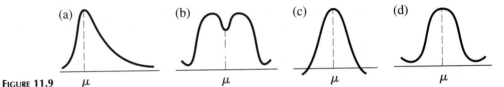

FIGURE 11.9

EXAMPLE 1   Consider the normal curves in Figure 11.10.

(a) What is the mean for *A*?   (b) What is the mean for *B*?
(c) What is the standard deviation for *A*?
(d) What is the standard deviation for *B*?
(e) What percent of the values would you expect to lie between −3 and −1 in *B*?
(f) What percent of the values would you expect to lie between 0 and 1 in *A*?

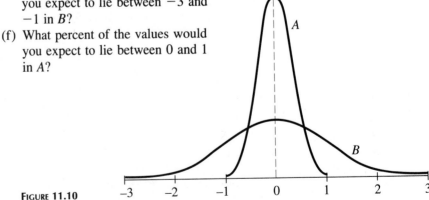

FIGURE 11.10

Solution   (a) The mean for *A* is 0 (under the highest point).

(b) The mean for *B* is also 0.

(c) The interval from 0 to 1 must have 3 standard deviations, so each of them must be $\frac{1}{3}$ unit.

(d) The standard deviation for *B* is 1 (there are 3 to the right of 0).

(e) Since there are two standard deviations between -3 and -1, $2.5\% + 13.5\% = 16\%$ of the values would be in that region. (Refer to Figure 11.6 for the values.)

(f) Half of the values should be between 0 and 1. ∎

Problem Solving: The Normal Distribution

Refer to the S.A.T. data given in Getting Started and Figure 11.6.

(a) What percent of the scores would you expect to be under 425 on the verbal portion of the S.A.T.?

(b) What percent of the scores would you expect to be between 350 and 475 on the mathematics portion of the S.A.T.?

(c) If 1000 students took the S.A.T., how many students should score more than 725 on the mathematics portion of the S.A.T.?

1. Read the problem.

2. Select the unknown. Where do you find the different percents under the normal curve?

We are asked several questions about S.A.T. scores. There are two things that are essential: the information in Figure 11.6 (Memorize it!) and the corresponding information given in Figures 11.7 and 11.8.

3. Think of a plan. Look at Figure 11.6. What percent of the values:

(a) are to the left of μ?

(b) are between $\mu - \sigma$ and μ?

(c) are to the right of $\mu + \sigma$?

If we examine Figure 11.6, we will see that:

50% of the values are to the left of μ

34% of the values are between $\mu - \sigma$ and μ and $13.5\% + 2.5\% = 16\%$ of the values are to the right of $\mu + \sigma$. Thus,

4. Use the values shown in Figures 11.7 and 11.8 to answer the questions.

5. Verify the solution.

(a) In Figure 11.7 $\mu = 425$, so we expect 50% of the scores to be to the left of μ and to be less than 425 on the verbal portion.

(b) In Figure 11.8 $\mu = 475$ and $\mu - \sigma = 350$. Thus, 34% of the scores are between $\mu - \sigma = 350$ and $\mu = 475$.

(c) In Figure 11.8 16% of the values are to the right of $\mu + \sigma$. Since 16% of $1000 = 160$, 160 students should score higher than 725 on the mathematics portion.

TRY EXAMPLE 2 NOW.

Cover the solution, write your own, and then check your work.

EXAMPLE 2   The heights of 1000 girls are measured and found to be normally distributed, with a mean of 64 in. and a standard deviation of 2 in.

(a) About how many of the girls are over 68 in. tall?
(b) About how many are between 60 and 64 in. tall?
(c) About how many are between 62 and 66 in. tall?

Solution   We refer to Figure 11.6 for the required percentages.

(a) Because 68 in. is 2 standard deviations above the mean, about 2.5%, or 25, of the girls are over 68 in. tall.
(b) We see that 64 in. is the mean, and 60 in. is exactly 2 standard deviations below the mean; hence, we add 13.5% and 34% to find that 47.5%, or 475, girls are between 60 and 64 in. tall.
(c) Because 62 in. is 1 standard deviation below the mean, and 66 in. is 1 standard deviation above the mean, we add 34% and 34% to find that about 68%, or 680, girls will be between these two heights.   ■

EXAMPLE 3   A standardized reading comprehension test is given to 10,000 high school students. The scores are found to be normally distributed, with a mean of 500 and a standard deviation of 60. If a score below 440 is considered to indicate a serious reading deficiency, about how many of the students are rated as seriously deficient in reading comprehension?

Solution   Since 440 is exactly 1 standard deviation below the mean, scores below 440 are more than 1 standard deviation below the mean. By referring to the percentages in Figure 11.6 we see that we must add 13.5% and 2.5% to get the total percentage of students who scored more than 1 standard deviation below the mean. Thus, 16% of the 10,000 students, or 1600, are rated as seriously deficient in reading comprehension.   ■

In Getting Started, we were able to compare two scores on two different tests by referring to the normal curve. Now, suppose Rudy earned a score of 80 on his American history test and a score of 80 on his geometry test. Which of these is the better score? Without additional information, we cannot answer this question. However, if we are told that the mean score in the American history test was 60, with a standard deviation of 25.5, and the mean score in the geometry test was 70, with a standard deviation of 14.5, then we can use a technique similar to the one used in Getting Started to compare Rudy's two scores.

B. *z-Scores*

In order to make a valid comparison, we have to restate the scores on a common scale. A score on this scale is known as a **standardized score,** or a *z*-**score.**

Definition 11.6 ━━━

If x is a given score and μ and σ are the mean and standard deviation of the entire set of scores, then the **corresponding z-score** is

$$z = \frac{x - \mu}{\sigma}$$

Since the numerator of z is the difference between x and the mean, *the z-score gives the number of standard deviations that x is from the mean.*

EXAMPLE 4 Compare Rudy's scores in American history and geometry, given all the preceding information.

Solution Rudy's z-scores are

American history: $z = \dfrac{80 - 60}{25.5} = 0.78$

Geometry: $\qquad z = \dfrac{80 - 70}{14.5} = 0.69$

Thus, Rudy did better in American history than in geometry. ∎

C. *Distribution of z-Scores*

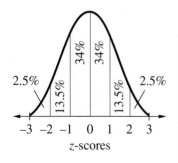

FIGURE 11.11
Distribution of z-scores

For a normal distribution of scores, if we subtract μ from each score, the resulting numbers will have a mean of 0. If we then divide each number by the standard deviation σ, the resulting numbers will have a standard deviation of 1. Thus, the z-scores are distributed as shown in Figure 11.11. For instance, 34% of the z-scores lie between 0 and 1, 13.5% between 1 and 2, and 2.5% are greater than 2. For such a distribution of scores, the probabilities of randomly selecting z-scores between 0 and a given point to the right of 0 have been calculated and appear in tables such as Table II in the back of the book. To read the probability that a score falls between 0 and 0.25 standard deviation above the mean, we go down the column under z to 0.2 and then across to the column under 5; the number there is 0.099, the desired probability.

EXAMPLE 5 For a certain normally distributed set of data, the mean is $\mu = 100$ and the standard deviation is 15. Find the probability that a randomly selected item of the data falls between 100 and 120.

Solution 1. We first find the z-score for 120:

$$z = \frac{x - \mu}{\sigma} = \frac{120 - 100}{15} = \frac{4}{3} \approx 1.33$$

2. We then refer to Table II and read down the column under z to the number 1.3 and then across the column under 3 to read the desired probability, 0.408. ∎

EXAMPLE 6   Refer to Table II. In the column under 5 and across from 2.0, the entry 0.480 appears. What does this mean?

Solution   This means that if an item is selected at random from a normally distributed set of data, the probability that this item is within 2.05 standard deviations from the mean is 0.480.

■

EXAMPLE 7   Referring to Example 5, find the probability that a randomly selected item is less than 110.

Solution   The probability that a randomly selected item of the data is less than 100 is 50% because 50% of the scores are to the left of the mean.

To find the probability that a randomly selected item is less than 110, we can find the probability that the item is between 100 and 110 and add this probability to 50% = 0.50.

1. The z-score for 110 is

$$z = \frac{x - \mu}{\sigma} = \frac{110 - 100}{15} \approx 0.66$$

2. The value by 0.6 and under 6 in Table II is 0.245. Thus, the probability that a randomly selected item of the data is less than 110 is

$$0.50 + 0.245 = 0.745.$$

■

Exercise 11.4

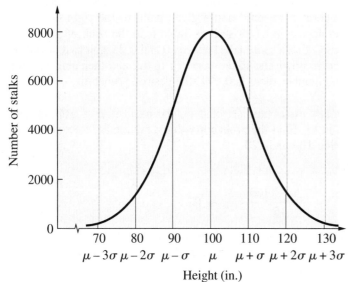

Height (in.)

Farmer Brown's corn

A. 1. Farmer Brown has planted a field of experimental corn. By judicious sampling, it is estimated that there are about 20,000 plants and that a graph of their heights looks like that shown in the figure.
    (a) What is the mean height of farmer Brown's corn?
    (b) What is the standard deviation from the mean?
    (c) What percent of the cornstalks are between 90 and 110 in. tall?
    (d) About how many stalks are between 80 and 90 in. tall?

2. Suppose you were informed that the annual income of lawyers is normally distributed, with a mean of $40,000 and a standard deviation of $10,000.

   (a) What would you estimate for the percent of lawyers with incomes over $50,000?

   (b) What percent of lawyers would you estimate have an annual income of less than $20,000?

   (c) If a lawyer were selected at random, what would be the probability that his or her annual income is more than $60,000?

   (d) If the information given here were correct, would you think it very likely that 50% of all lawyers have annual incomes of over $50,000? Why?

3. Part of a test given to young children consists of putting together a simple jigsaw puzzle. Suppose that such a puzzle is given to 1000 children, each child is timed, and a graph of the times is made. Suppose the graph is a normal curve with a mean time of 120 sec and a standard deviation of 15 sec.

   (a) About how many of the children finished the puzzle in less than 90 sec?

   (b) How many took more than 150 sec?

   (c) If you rated as "average" all the children within 1 standard deviation from the mean, how many children would fall into this classification?

4. For a certain standardized placement test, it was found that the scores were normally distributed, with a mean of 200 and a standard deviation of 30. Suppose this test is given to 1000 students.

   (a) How many are expected to make scores between 170 and 230?

   (b) How many are expected to score above 260?

   (c) What is the expected range of all the scores?

5. A psychology teacher gave an objective-type test to a class of 500 students, and after seeing the results, decided that the scores were normally distributed. The mean score was 50, and the standard deviation was 10. The teacher assigned a grade of A to all scores of 70 or over, B to scores of 60 to 69, C to scores 40 to 59, D to scores of 30 to 39, and F to scores below 30. About how many of each grade did the teacher assign?

6. In a study of 100 common stocks, it was found that the annual dividend rates were normally distributed, with a mean of 4.0% and a standard deviation of 0.5%.

   (a) About how many of these stocks do you think paid dividends of over 5%?

   (b) About how many paid between 3 and 5%?

   (c) If you picked one of these stocks at random, what do you think would be the probability that it paid at least 4.5%?

7. The lifetimes of a random sample of 200 automobile tires were found to be normally distributed, with a mean of 26,000 mi and a standard deviation of 2500 mi. About how many of these tires gave out before 21,000 mi?

8. Suppose that 100 measurements of the specific gravity of copper gave a mean of 8.8 with a standard deviation of 0.2. Between what limits did about 95% of the measurements fall?

9. Suppose that 10 measurements of the length of a wooden beam have a mean of 20 ft and a standard deviation of 0.5 in. Between what limits do almost all the measurements fall?

10. An experiment consists of tossing 100 dimes repeatedly and noting the number of heads each time. The graph of the number of heads turns out to be very nearly a normal curve, with a mean of 50 and a standard deviation of 5.
    (a) Within what limits would you expect the number of heads to be 95% of the time?
    (b) What percent of the time would you expect the number of heads to be between 45 and 55?
    (c) Suppose that a particular one of the dimes arouses your suspicion by turning up heads too often. You toss this dime 100 times. How many times will it have to turn up heads in order for you to be almost 100% certain that it is not a fair coin? [*Hint:* Almost all the data in a normal distribution fall within 3 standard deviations of the mean.]

11. The purchasing director of Druid Enterprises is considering the purchase of 8000 ball bearings. The purchase is dependent on receiving at least a dozen ball bearings that will last 40 days. If the manufacturer claims that the lifetime of each ball bearing is 30 days, with a standard deviation of 5 days, what will be the decision of the purchasing director and why?

12. The Department of Transportation (DOT) counted the number of vehicles using a certain road for a period of 50 days. The mean number of vehicles using the road was 350 and the standard deviation was 10.
    (a) How many days was the road used by more than 360 vehicles?
    (b) How many days was the number of vehicles using the road between 340 and 380?
    (c) What is the least number of vehicles you would expect on this road on any given day?
    (d) What is the highest number of vehicles you would expect on this road on any given day?

13. In a recent year, the scores on the mathematics portion of the Scholastic Aptitude Test (S.A.T.) had a 455 mean and a 112 standard deviation. This same year, the mathematics portion of the American College Test (A.C.T.) had a mean of 17.3 and a standard deviation of 7.9. A student scored 570 on the S.A.T. while another student made a 25 score on the A.C.T. Which student has the higher score relative to his or her test?

14. Suppose you are the manager of a cereal packing company. Every box must contain at least 16 ounces of cereal. Your packing machine has a normal distribution for the weights of the cereal with a standard deviation of 0.05 ounces and a mean equal to the setting on the machine. What will you make this setting to ensure that all of the packages contain at least 16 ounces of cereal?

B. 15. In a certain normal distribution of scores, the mean is 5 and the standard deviation is 1.25. Find the z-score corresponding to a score of:
(a) 6   (b) 7   (c) 7.5

16. In a certain normal distribution of scores, the mean is 10 and the standard deviation is 2. Find the z-score corresponding to a score of:
(a) 11   (b) 13   (c) 14.2

17. Gretchen scored 85 on a test in German and also on a test in English. If the mean in the German test was 75, with a standard deviation of 20, and the mean in the English test was 80, with a standard deviation of 15, which of Gretchen's 85's was the better score?

18. Juan scored 88 on a Spanish test and 90 on an algebra test. If the mean on the Spanish test was 78, with a standard deviation of 7.5, and the mean on the algebra test was 82, with a standard deviation of 6.5, which of Juan's scores was the better score?

C. In problems 19–23 assume a normally distributed set of test scores with a mean of $\mu = 100$ and a standard deviation of 15.

19. Find the probability that a person selected at random will have a score between:
(a) 100 and 110   (b) 100 and 130

20. Find the probability that a person selected at random will have a score between 80 and 120. [*Hint:* In Example 5, we found the probability that the score is between 100 and 120 to be 0.408. The probability that the score is between 80 and 100 is also 0.408. (Recall the symmetry of the normal curve.)]

21. Find the probability that a person selected at random will have a score
(a) between 55 and 145   (b) less than 60

22. Find the probability that a person selected at random will have a score
(a) between 75 and 100   (b) more than 80

23. Find the probability that a person selected at random will have a score between 110 and 130. [*Hint:* In problem 19 you found the probability that the score will be between 100 and 110 and the probability that the score will be between 100 and 130. You should be able to see how to combine these two results to get the desired probability.]

24. In problem 10, it was noted that the distribution of heads if 100 dimes are tossed repeatedly is approximately a normal distribution, with a mean of 50 and a standard deviation of 5. Find the probability of getting 60 heads if 100 fair coins are tossed. [*Hint:*   To use the normal curve, consider 60 to be between 59.5 and 60.5 and proceed as in problem 23. This will give a very good approximation and is much easier to calculate than the exact probability, which is $C(100, 60) \cdot 2^{100}$.]

25. The heights of the male students in a large college were found to be normally distributed, with a mean of 5 ft 7 in. and a standard deviation of 3 in. Suppose these students are to be divided into five equal-sized groups according to height. Approximately what is the height of the shortest student in the tallest group?

26. If 10 of the boys who show up for the basketball team are over 6 ft 3 in. tall, about how many male students are there in the college mentioned in problem 25?

In Other Words

27. Can you have two normal curves with the same mean and different standard deviations? Explain and make a sketch.

28. Can you have two normal curves with the same standard deviation and different means? Explain and make a sketch.

29. If you have two normal curves, is it true that the curve with the larger mean must also have the larger standard deviation? Explain your answer.

30. Explain in your own words the meaning of a z-score.

Using Your Knowledge

*z-scores provide a way of making comparisons among different sets of data. To compare scores within one set of data, we use a measurement called a **percentile**. Percentiles are used extensively in educational measurements and enable us to convert raw scores into meaningful comparative scores. If you take an exam and are told that you scored in the 95th percentile, it does not mean that you scored 95% on the exam, but rather that you scored higher than 95% of the persons taking the exam. The formula used to find the percentile corresponding to a particular score is as follows:*

$$\text{Percentile of score } x = \frac{\text{Number of scores less than } x}{\text{Total number of scores}} \cdot 100$$

Thus, if 80 students take a test, and 50 students score less than you do, you will be in the $\frac{50}{80} \cdot 100 = 62.5$ percentile. Use this knowledge to solve the following problems.

31. A student took a test in a class of 50 students, and 40 of the students scored less than she did. What was her percentile?

32. A student took a test in a class of 80, and only 9 students scored better than he did. What was his percentile?

33. The scores in a class were as follows:

    83, 85, 90, 90, 92, 93, 97, 97, 98, 100

    (a) What percentile corresponds to a score of 90?
    (b) What percentile corresponds to a score of 97?
    (c) What percentile corresponds to a score of 100?
    (d) What percentile corresponds to a score of 83?

34. The scores on a placement test were scaled so that some of the scores and the corresponding percentiles were as follows:

Score	Percentile
119	98
150	85
130	72
90	50
60	26
30	10
20	1

    What percent of the scores fell between 30 and 90? *Hint:* Look at the definition of the percentile. The percentile gives the percent of what?

Discovery

We have discovered that we can make fairly accurate predictions about the dispersion of the measurements in a normal distribution. For instance, 68% of the measurements fall between $\mu - \sigma$ and $\mu + \sigma$, 95% between $\mu - 2\sigma$ and $\mu + 2\sigma$, and nearly 100% between $\mu - 3\sigma$ and $\mu + 3\sigma$. But what can we say in case the distribution is not normal?

The great Russian mathematician, Pafnuti Lvovich Chebyshev (1821–1894), discovered the following remarkable result:

Chebyshev's Theorem

For any distribution with a finite number N of measurements and for any h such that $h > 1$, the number of measurements within h standard deviations of the mean is **at least** equal to

$$\left(1 - \frac{1}{h^2}\right)N$$

For example, if $h = 2$, *then* $1 - (1/h^2) = \frac{3}{4}$, *so that at least* $\frac{3}{4}N$, *or 75%, of the measurements fall between* $\mu - 2\sigma$ *and* $\mu + 2\sigma$. *This is not as large a percentage as for a normal distribution, but the amazing thing is that this result holds for any kind of distribution at all—as long as there is only a finite number of measurements!*

Suppose we have 20 numbers with a mean of 8 and a standard deviation of 2. How many of the numbers can we **guarantee** *fall between 2 and 14? Because 2 and 14 are each 3 standard deviations from the mean, we take* h = 3 *in Chebyshev's theorem and obtain*

$$\left(1 - \frac{1}{3^2}\right)(20) = \frac{160}{9} \approx 17.8$$

Thus, the theorem guarantees that at least 18 of the 20 numbers fall between 2 and 14.

In the same way, by taking h = 1.5, *we find that*

$$\left(1 - \frac{1}{1.5^2}\right)(20) = \left(\frac{5}{9}\right)(20) \approx 11.1$$

Hence, we can guarantee that at least 12 of the 20 numbers fall within 1.5 standard deviations from the mean, that is, between 5 and 11.

You should notice that Chebyshev's theorem makes no claim at all for the case where h ≤ 1.

35. If 100 measurements have a mean of 50 and a standard deviation of 5, can you discover how many of the measurements must be between:
    (a) 40 and 60?   (b) 35 and 65?   (c) 43 and 57?

36. Can you discover the smallest value of h that is large enough to guarantee that of a set of measurements at least:
    (a) 96% will be within h standard deviations from the mean?
    (b) 91% will be within h standard deviations from the mean?
    (c) 64% will be within h standard deviations from the mean?

37. Find the mean and the standard deviation of the following numbers: 1, 1, 1, 2, 6, 10, 11, 11, 11. How many of these numbers lie within 1 standard deviation from the mean? How many lie within 2 standard deviations from the mean? How do these results compare with those predicted by Chebyshev's theorem?

38. Do you think it is possible for all the items in an entire population to be *less* than 1 standard deviation from the mean? Can you discover how to justify your answer? [*Hint:* The formula for the standard deviation shows that $n\sigma^2 = (x_1 - \overline{x})^2 + (x_2 - \overline{x})^2 + \cdots + (x_n - \overline{x})^2$.]

39. Can Chebyshev's theorem be used to find the percentage of the measurements that must fall between 2 and 3 standard deviations from the mean? What can you say about this percentage?

Calculator Corner

You can find the probability that a randomly selected item will fall between the mean and a given z-score by using the $\boxed{R(t)}$ *key on your calculator. Thus, to find the probability that a randomly selected item falls between the mean and a score of 120, as in Example 2, place the calculator in the statistics mode and press*

$\boxed{120}$ $\boxed{-}$ $\boxed{100}$ $\boxed{=}$ $\boxed{\div}$ $\boxed{15}$ $\boxed{=}$ $\boxed{2nd}$ $\boxed{R(t)}$

The result is given as 0.40878. Note that there is a slight difference (due to rounding) between this answer and the one in the text.

1–5.   Use a calculator to rework problems 19–24 in Exercise 11.4.

11.5 STATISTICAL GRAPHS: A PROBLEM-SOLVING TOOL

Running on empty: A recent survey indicated that 91% of female respondents do not stop for gas until their tanks are nearly empty

GETTING STARTED

GASSING UP AND PIE CHARTS

Americans are often fascinated with numbers. Many of the facts of American life are expressed in books such as *The First Really Important Survey of American Habits, The Top 10 Almanac, The Day America Told the Truth, The Great Divide,* and *On an Average Day.* These books are devoted to surveys of American habits using numbers, tables, and graphs. For example, do you gas up your car when is it $\frac{3}{4}$ full, $\frac{1}{2}$ empty, $\frac{3}{4}$ empty, or almost empty? As you would expect, different age groups of different sexes behave differently. Thus, 2%, 42%, 38%, and 18% of males in the 21–34 age group fill their tanks when they are $\frac{3}{4}$ full, $\frac{1}{2}$ empty, $\frac{3}{4}$ empty, or almost empty, respectively. For females, the corresponding percentages are 1%, 2%, 6%, and 91%. Why do you think this difference exists? Whatever the reason, we could compare the data better if the information were contained in a table with a caption and column heading. (See Table 11.17.)

Table 11.17 enables us instantly to compare differences based on sex. We can also show the division of a total quantity (100%) into its components parts

Table 11.17

Percent of People That Gas up Car When It Is:								
Age	3/4 Full		1/2 Empty		3/4 Empty		Almost Empty	
	Male	Female	Male	Female	Male	Female	Male	Female
21–34	2	1	42	2	38	6	18	91

by using a **circle graph** or **pie chart**. If we are interested only in a rough sketch, we use the four-step procedure shown in Figure 11.12. Now, here is a word of caution. Mathematicians and statisticians use the starting point shown in Step 4 and move *counterclockwise*. (See Figure 11.13a.) Computer-generated pie charts start at the 12 o'clock point and move *clockwise*. (See Figure 11.13b.) Both are correct, and both methods are used in this book.

Step 1. Make a circle.

Step 2. Divide it into 2 equal parts.

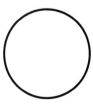

Step 3. Subdivide each of the 2 parts into 5 equal parts.

Step 4. Each of the subdivisions represents $\frac{1}{10}$, or 10%.

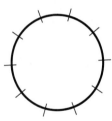

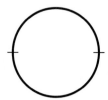

FIGURE 11.12

Percent of males gassing car when it is:

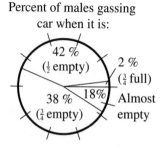

FIGURE 11.13a

Percent of females gassing car when it is:

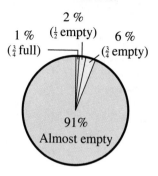

FIGURE 11.13b

A graph of a set of data can often provide information at a glance that might be difficult and less impressive to glean from a table of numbers. No table of numbers would make the visual impact created by the graph in Figure 11.14, for example.

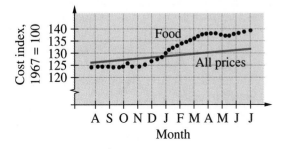

FIGURE 11.14
The high cost of eating

FIGURE 11.15

It is almost always possible to alter the appearance of a graph to make things seem better than they are. For instance, Figure 11.15 is a portion of Figure 11.14, but with a compressed vertical scale. Obviously, things look better on this graph! Can you see why an economist might feel it politically advantageous to publish one of these graphs rather than the other?

A. *Line Graphs*

The construction of line graphs is similar to the type of graphing we did in Chapter 6. As before, we draw two perpendicular lines called **axes**. The horizontal line is still the *x* **axis** and the vertical line the *y* **axis**. Each of these lines have equally spaced points with numbers or other identifying information assigned to them. For example, the number on the *x* axis may represent the number of hours a person has worked while those on the *y* axis may indicate the earnings for that person. We make our first line graph next.

EXAMPLE 1   Construct a line graph for the following data:

	Unemployment Rate	
	Women	**Men**
January	6.4%	5.3%
February	8.0%	7.6%
March	6.0%	5.1%

Solution   In Figure 11.16 we start by making a time scale and labeling the points Jan., Feb., and Mar. (Time is usually shown on the *x* axis.) We then label the *y* axis with the percents from 1 to 9.

To graph the point corresponding to the unemployment rate for women in Jan., go to Jan. on the horizontal scale and move 6.4 units up. The point is marked in color on the graph. Now, go to Feb. on the horizontal axis and move 8.0 units up. Make a dot. Finally, starting at Mar., go 6 units up and mark the point. Now, join all three points with 2 line segments. Note that we made a grid of horizontal and vertical lines to make the work easier to read. The same result can be obtained by doing the graph on graph paper. We use a similar procedure to add the men (shown in color).

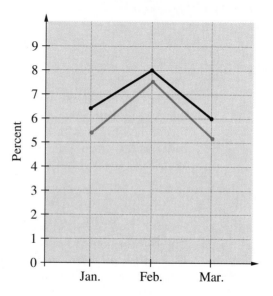

FIGURE 11.16

B. *Bar Graphs*

Newspapers and magazines often publish **bar graphs** of the type shown in Figure 11.17. These graphs again have the advantage of displaying the data in a form that is easy to understand. It would be difficult for most people to obtain the same information from a table of numbers. As in the case of line graphs, bar graphs may also be made to distort the truth. For example, consider the two graphs in Figures 11.18 and 11.19. The graph in Figure 11.18 does not have the bars starting at 0, so it gives a somewhat exaggerated picture of the proportion of gasoline saved at lower speeds, even though the numerical data are the same for both graphs. The graph in Figure 11.19 gives a correct picture of the proportion of gasoline saved. Why do you think the first bar graph rather than the second would be published?

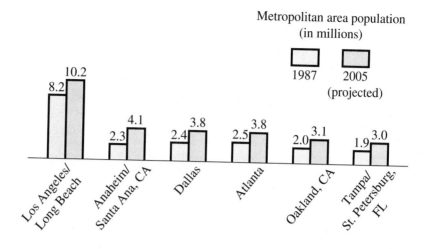

FIGURE 11.17

Bar graph showing metropolitan areas that will gain more than 1 million residents by the year 2005

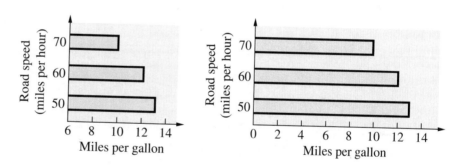

FIGURE 11.18   **FIGURE 11.19**

EXAMPLE 2   In a recent poll the features patrons liked in a restaurant were listed as follows:

Self-service salad bar	57%
Varied portion sizes	47%
More varied menu	42%
All-you-can-eat specials	37%
Self-service soup bar	30%

Use horizontal bars to make a bar graph of this information.

Solution   We label the *x* axis with percents equally spaced and at intervals of 10. However, since the highest percent used in the problem is 57, we can shorten the *x* axis and stop at 60%. Find the points on the graph just as you did for the line graphs, but instead of connecting the dots with a line, draw a bar as in Figure 11.20. The labels can be placed alongside the vertical axis or inside the bars as shown.

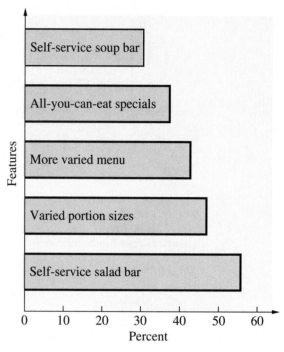

FIGURE **11.20**

C. *Circle Graphs*

Graphs like those in Figures 11.21 and 11.22 are called **circle graphs,** or **pie charts**. Such graphs are a very popular means of displaying data, and they are also susceptible to being drawn to make things look better than they are. For

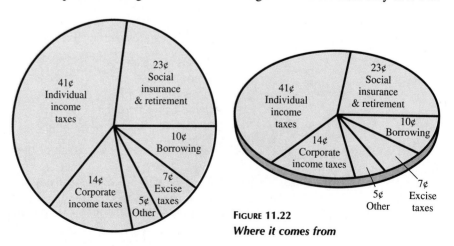

FIGURE **11.21**
Circle graph

FIGURE **11.22**
Where it comes from

instance, compare the graph in Figure 11.21 with the version of the same data that was published by the Internal Revenue Service. Does the visual impression of Figure 11.22 make you feel that individual income taxes are not quite so large a chunk of federal income as Figure 11.21 indicates?

Circle graphs are quite easy to draw if you know how to use a simple compass and a protractor. For the graph in Figure 11.21, which shows where the typical dollar of federal money comes from, 23¢ is 23% of a dollar. The entire circle corresponds to 360°, so you would use 23% of 360°, or 82.8° ≈ 83°, for the slice that represents 23¢, and likewise for the other slices. This is the most accurate and honest way to present data on a circle graph.

EXAMPLE 3 A marketing executive for a food manufacturer wants to show that food is an important part of a family budget. She finds out that the typical budget is as follows:

Monthly Family Budget

Savings	$ 300
Housing	500
Clothing	200
Food	800
Other	200
Total	$2000

Make a circle graph for this data.

Solution First determine what *percent* of the total amount each of the items represents.

$$\text{Savings} \quad \frac{300}{2000} = \frac{3}{20} = 15\%$$

$$\text{Housing} \quad \frac{500}{2000} = \frac{1}{4} = 25\%$$

$$\text{Clothing} \quad \frac{200}{2000} = \frac{1}{10} = 10\%$$

$$\text{Food} \quad \frac{800}{2000} = \frac{2}{5} = 40\%$$

$$\text{Other} \quad \frac{200}{2000} = \frac{1}{10} = 10\%$$

Then, find out how many degrees each slice covers.

$$15\% \text{ of } 360° = 0.15 \times 360° = 54°$$
$$25\% \text{ of } 360° = 0.25 \times 360° = 90°$$
$$10\% \text{ of } 360° = 0.10 \times 360° = 36°$$
$$40\% \text{ of } 360° = 0.40 \times 360° = 144°$$
$$10\% \text{ of } 360° = 0.10 \times 360° = 36°$$

Now, measure the required number of degrees with a protractor and label each of the slices as shown in Figure 11.23. As a check, make sure the sum of the percentages is 100 and the sum of the degrees for the slices is 360.

Monthly Family Budget

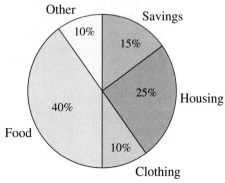

FIGURE 11.23

Exercise 11.5

In problems 1–6, make a line graph for the given data.

A. 1. Rice consumed per capita in the U.S.

1970	6.7 lbs	1985	9.1 lbs
1975	7.6 lbs	1990	16.6 lbs
1980	9.5 lbs		

2. Daily calories needed to maintain weight for females aged:

11–14	2200 calories	23–50	2000 calories
15–18	2100 calories	51–75	1800 calories
19–22	2050 calories	75+	1500 calories

3. Percent of married couples with and without children:

	1960	1970	1980	1990
With children	44%	40%	31%	27%
Without children	30%	30%	30%	30%

4. Percent of males squeezing the toothpaste tube from top or bottom:

Age	Bottom	Top
21–34	37	63
35–44	33	67
45–54	10	90
55+	10	90

5. Percent of females squeezing the toothpaste tube from top or bottom:

Age	Bottom	Top
21–34	33	67
35–44	43	57
45–54	30	70
55+	45	55

6. Projected percent of age ranges in the U.S.

	1950	1990	2010	2030	2050
Under 14	27%	22%	18%	19%	19%
15–64	65%	66%	68%	62%	62%
65+	8%	12%	13%	20%	19%

B. Draw a bar graph based on the data provided.

7. According to Merrill Lynch Relocation Management, Inc., hundreds of people accepted a transfer from their company. Here are the numbers of employees relocated in various industries.

Industry	Number
Computers	803
Petroleum	324
Transportation	271
Public utilities	265
Retail/Wholesale	231

Use horizontal bars to make a graph of this information.

8. A manager in the food industry had to predict food consumption trends for the year 2000. Here is the data.

Food	Increase in Average Consumption by 2000
Fish	44%
Fresh vegetables	35%
Fresh fruits	23%
Beef	30%
Pork	12%
Poultry	7%

(a) Use horizontal bars to make a graph of this information.
(b) If you wish to be in a growing business, which industry would you choose to own or manage in the year 2000? Which business would you avoid?

9. The personnel department of a major corporation was asked to make a vertical bar graph indicating the percent of salary to be replaced by pension and social security income for married persons who worked for 40 years. Here is the information supplied by the Bureau of Labor Statistics.

Salary at Time of Retirement	Percent Received from Pension and Social Security
$20,000	93%
$30,000	74%
$40,000	64%

(a) Make the graph.
(b) If you retired at $20,000, what amount would you expect from your pension and Social Security?

10. A recent survey of 5000 households showed that more people planned to make major purchases this year. Here are the percents.

	Bought Last Year	Plan to Buy This Year
Home	3.6%	5.0%
Car	8.6%	11.3%
Appliance	27.1%	43.2%

Use side-by-side vertical bars comparing the percent of consumers planning to buy each of the items with the percent who bought them last year.

11. In a survey conducted by *Chain Store Age,* respondents indicated where their 35 mm cameras were bought. Some of the responses were as follows:

Source of Purchase	This Year	Two Years Ago
Discount stores	18.6%	23.7%
Sears	11.4%	6.2%
Department stores	15.7%	4.1%
Specialty stores	30.0%	29.9%

(a) Use side-by-side vertical bars comparing the given percents during the specified time periods.
(b) Based on the graph, where do most people now buy their 35 mm cameras?
(c) Based on the graph, which store category lost the most sales in the two-year interval?
(d) Based on the graph, which stores would you say had the most consistent camera sales over the two year period?

12. In another survey conducted by *Chain Store Age*, respondents indicated which store provided the best value for home electronics. Here are some of the results.

Source for Best Values	Last Year	This Year
Department stores	15%	20%
Electronic stores	31%	20%
Sears	17%	14%
Discount stores	8%	10%

(a) Use the same horizontal bars to include each of the four categories for the given time periods.

(b) Based on the graph, which stores provided the best value for home electronics?

C. In problems 13–18 make a circle graph for the data.

13. Have you been to a meeting lately? Here are the number of hours per week spent in meetings by chief marketing executives.

Hours	Percent	Hours	Percent
Fewer than 5	2	20–24	22
5–9	10	25–29	16
10–14	17	29+	17
15–19	16		

14. Clairol, Inc. reports that the percentage of industry sales for favorite hair colorings are as follows:

Blond	40%
Brunette	38%
Red	13%
Black	8%
Other	1%

15. Have you looked in your refrigerator and found some UFOs (unidentified food objects)? The makers of Saran Wrap found out the following information from survey respondents:

9% don't have leftovers
61% have leftovers that are 6 days or less
23% have leftovers that are 1–4 weeks old
5% have leftovers that are more than 4 weeks old
2% don't know

16. Where do you think you use the most water in the home? According to *National Wildlife Magazine*, the percents of water used in different parts of the home is as follows:

Toilet	40%	Laundry	12%
Shower/bath	20%	Kitchen	10%
Bathroom sink	15%	Outside	3%

17. What are you recording on your VCR? A survey by the A.C. Nielsen company indicated the percent of taping sources were as follows:

Pay services	10%	Major networks	66%
Basic cable	7%	Independent networks	13%
PBS	4%		

18. How often do you wash your car? Here are the results of a survey of 1000 drivers.

220 wash them weekly	230 wash them once a month
180 wash them every 2 weeks	370 never wash them!

19. The National Restaurant Association surveyed 500 customers at fast-food restaurants serving breakfast and compiled the following figures:

Who Eats Breakfast Out?

Age	Number	Age	Number
18–24	80	50–64	90
25–34	130	65+	50
35–49	150		

(a) Make a circle graph for this data.

(b) If you were the manager of a fast-food restaurant serving breakfast, what age group would you cater to?

20. Where does money used for advertising go? For every dollar spent in advertising:

17 cents go to newspapers	6 cents go to magazines
21 cents go to television	3 cents go to business publications
16 cents go to direct mail	20 cents go to other sources
7 cents go to radio	

Make a circle graph for this data.

21. A company specializing in leisure products surveyed 500 people and found out their favorite activities were as follows:

75 read	60 had family fun
250 watched T.V.	65 had other activities
50 watched movies	

Make a circle graph for this data.

22. According to *Pizza Today*, sales of pizza by the "big 5" were as follows:

Godfather's	$250 million	Little Caesar's	$1 billion
Pizza Hut	$3 billion	Pantera's	$350 million
Domino's	$2 billion		

Make a circle graph for this data. *Hint:* 1 billion = 1000 million.

23. The U.S. Department of Labor updated its theoretical budget for a retired couple. The high budget for such a couple is apportioned approximately as follows:

Food	22%	Medical care	6%
Housing	35%	Other family costs	7%
Transportation	11%	Miscellaneous	7%
Clothing	6%	Income taxes	3%
Personal care	3%		

Make a circle graph to show this budget.

24. The pie chart shown here appeared side-by-side with the one in Figure 11.22. Make a circle graph to represent the same data. Compare the impression made by your circle graph with the pie chart.

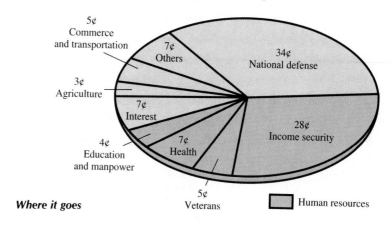

Where it goes

25. According to an advertisement for a color television, the top six brands of television sets were voted as best by the following percentages of about 2700 people:

Brand	1	2	3	4	5	6
Percent	50.1	21.1	8.8	8.5	5.8	5.7

(a) Make a circle graph to illustrate this information.
(b) Make a bar graph for the same data.
(c) Which of these do you think makes the stronger impression? Why?

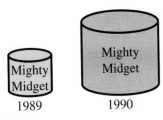

1989   1990

FIGURE 11.24

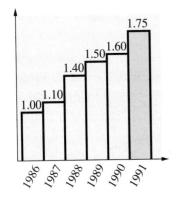

FIGURE 11.25

26. A survey made by the University of Michigan's Institute for Social Research showed that many of the women surveyed really enjoy keeping house. The survey found that about 67% of the women who responded had an unqualified liking for housework, while only 4% had an unqualified dislike for housework. Make a bar graph to illustrate these data.

27. The Mighty Midget Canning Company wants to impress the public with the growth of Mighty Midget business, which they claim has doubled over the previous year. They publish the pictorial graph shown in Figure 11.24.
    (a) Can you see something wrong with this? [*Hint:* Your mind compares the volumes pictured here. The volume of a cylinder is $\pi r^2 h$. What happens if you double the radius r and the height h?]
    (b) Draw a bar graph that correctly represents the situation.

28. The U.B. Wary Company wants to give its stockholders a very strong impression of the rapid rate at which earnings have grown and prints the histogram shown in Figure 11.25 in its annual report. Redraw this graph to give a more honest impression.

29. Do you know that playing golf is not a particularly good way to lose weight? Here is the calorie consumption per hour for five popular activities. Make a bar graph with horizontal bars, with each bar identified at the left side of your graph.

Activity	Calories Consumed per Hour
Bicycling (15 mi/hr)	730
Running (6 mi/hr)	700
Swimming (40 yd/min)	550
Walking (4 mi/hr)	330
Golf (walking and carrying your clubs)	300

(These figures apply to a person weighing 150 lb; you have to add or subtract 10% for each 15-lb difference in weight.)

30. Women are generally lighter than men, so they require fewer calories per day. Here are three occupations and their energy-per-day requirements. Make a vertical bar graph with the bars for male and female side-by-side for comparison. On the average, about what percent more calories does the male require than the female for these three occupations?

Occupation	Calories per Day
University student, male	2960
University student, female	2300
Laboratory technician, male	2850
Laboratory technician, female	2100
Office worker, male	2500
Office worker, female	1900

31. Although the best a cold remedy can do is ease the discomfort (without curing the cold), the relief seems to be worth plenty to victims. Here is how people in the United States spent money on cold remedies in a recent year. Make a bar graph with the horizontal bars to represent the data. Be sure to identify the bars.

Cold Remedy	Millions Spent
Cough drops and sore throat remedies	$130
Nasal sprays, drops, and vaporizers	$160
Aspirin substitutes	$275
Cold and cough syrups	$310
Aspirin	$575

32. The more you learn, the more you earn! Here are the median incomes by educational attainment for persons 25 years or older:

Level of Education	Women	Men
Less than 8 years	$9,800	$14,600
8 years	$10,800	$16,800
High school (1–3 years)	$11,800	$19,100
High school (4 years)	$14,600	$23,300
College (1–3 years)	$17,000	$25,800
College (4 or more years)	$21,900	$33,900

Make a side-by-side vertical bar graph for these data. Find the women's income as a percent of men's in each category.

33. The chart shows the annual sales for the ABC Bookstore for the years 1981–1990.
    (a) Approximately what were the sales in 1984?
    (b) When did the sales seem to start leveling off?

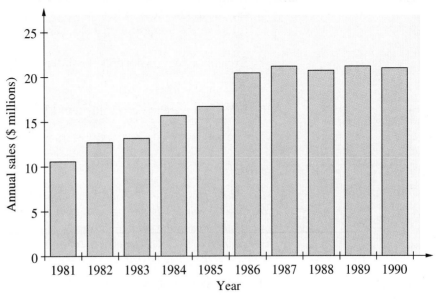

34. The circle graph shows Harry's time allotment for Mondays, Wednesdays, and Fridays. What percent of the time is Harry allowing for classes and study?

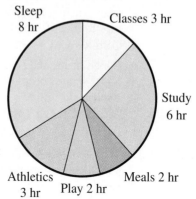

Sleep 8 hr

Classes 3 hr

Study 6 hr

Meals 2 hr

Athletics 3 hr   Play 2 hr

*I*n Other Words

You are the manager of a store whose sales (in millions) for January, February, and March were $20, $21, and $23 million, respectively.

35. Explain how you would make a line graph that would:
    (a) Make sales look better.
    (b) Make sales look flat.

36. Explain how you would make a bar graph that would:
    (a) Make sales look better.
    (b) Give the impression that sales are not increasing.

37. Explain in your own words the difference between a bar graph and a histogram.

38. When is a pie chart especially useful?

Discovery

Misleading graphs can be used in statistics to accomplish whatever deception you have in mind. The two graphs shown in Figure 11.26, for example, give exactly the same information. However, the graph on the left seems to indicate a steep increase in government payrolls, while the graph on the right shows the stability of the same payrolls!

39. Can you discover what is wrong?

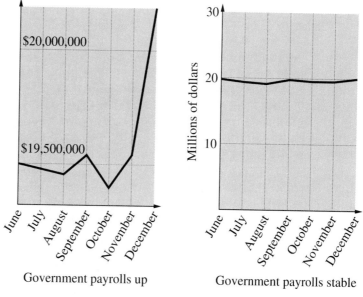

Government payrolls up   Government payrolls stable

FIGURE 11.26

11.6 MAKING PREDICTIONS

GETTING STARTED

OLYMPIC PREDICTIONS

Table 11.18 gives the winning times (in seconds) for the women's 200-m dash in the Olympic Games from 1948 to 1984. The points in Figure 11.27 are the graphs of the corresponding number pairs (1948, 24.4), (1952, 23.7), and so

Table 11.18

Year	Time (sec)
1948	24.4
1952	23.7
1956	23.4
1960	23.2
1964	23.0
1968	22.5
1972	22.4
1976	22.37
1980	(No U.S. participation)
1984	21.81

Jackie Joyner Kersee brought home the gold from the women's heptathlon at the 1988 Summer Olympics in Seoul, Korea

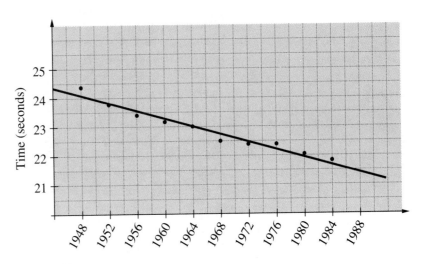

FIGURE 11.27

on. As you can see, the points do not lie on a straight line. However, we can draw a straight line that goes "between" the points and seems to fit the data fairly well. Such a line has been drawn in Figure 11.27. Statisticians sometimes use lines like this to make predictions of unknown results. For example, the winning time for this event in the 1988 Olympics as indicated by the line in the graph is about 21.4 sec. The actual winning time (made by Florence Griffith Joyner of the United States) was 21.34 sec. (The time predicted by the graph is less than $\frac{3}{10}$ of 1% in error!) In this section we will show you how to make predictions by drawing lines to fit given data.

How do we draw a line to fit data such as that in Table 11.18? One way is just to use our best visual judgment, but a better way is to calculate a *least-squares line*. If we have n points, say, (x_1, y_1), (x_2, y_2), . . . , (x_n, y_n), in the xy plane, a line $y = mx + b$ is called the **least-squares line** for these points if the sum of the squares of the differences between the actual y values of the points and the corresponding y values on the line is as small as possible. The line in Figure 11.27 is the least-squares line for the data in Table 11.18. If you have a calculator and wish to know the details of determining a least-squares line, then you should read the Using Your Knowledge section of Exercise 11.6.

EXAMPLE 1   Table 11.19 gives the winning times in seconds for the men's 100-m freestyle swim in the Olympic Games from 1960 to 1984. Make a graph of these data, then draw a line "between" the points and predict the winning time for this event in the 1988 Olympics.

Solution The required graph is shown in the figure below. The line in this figure is the least-squares line for the given data. From this line, we can read the predicted time for the 1988 Olympics as about 48.3 sec. The actual winning time was 48.63 sec, so the predicted time is off by less than 0.7%.

Table 11.19

Year	Time (sec)
1960	55.2
1964	53.4
1968	52.2
1972	51.22
1976	49.99
1980	50.40
1984	49.80

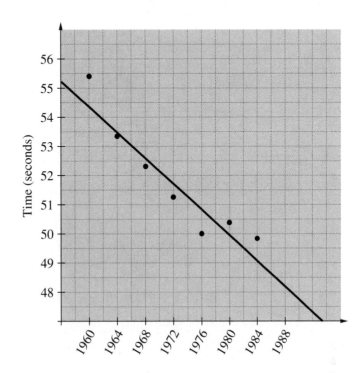

Another way in which statisticians make predictions is based on a **sampling procedure**. The idea is quite simple. The statistician takes data from a **random sample** of the population and assumes that the entire population behaves in the same way as the sample. The difficulties lie in making certain that the sample is actually random and represents the population in a satisfactory manner. We shall not discuss the different ways in which a sample is selected, but only mention that one of these ways uses a table of random numbers. (Such tables can be generated by a computer.)

EXAMPLE 2 A certain school has 3000 students. A random sample of 50 students is selected and asked to name their favorite track and field event. If 10 of these students name the 100-m dash, how many students in the school would you expect to have the same favorite event?

Solution We would expect $\frac{10}{50}$, or 20%, of the student body to favor the 100-m dash. Thus, the required number is 20% of 3000 or $(0.20)(3000) = 600$.

EXAMPLE 3   In a certain county, 15% of the eleventh-grade students failed a required literacy test. If 60 of the eleventh-grade students in this county were selected at random, how many of these would we expect to have failed the test?

Solution   We would expect 15% of the 60 students to have failed the test; that is, $(0.15)(60) = 9$ students.   ■

Exercise 11.6

In problems 1–3, each table gives the winning results in an Olympic event from 1960 to 1984. Make a graph of the data. Draw the best line that you can "between" the points, and predict the results for the 1988 Olympics.

1. Men's 400-m hurdles, time in seconds

Year	1960	1964	1968	1972	1976	1980	1984
Time	49.3	49.6	48.1	47.8	47.6	48.7	47.8

2. Women's 100-m freestyle swimming, time in seconds

Year	1960	1964	1968	1972	1976	1980	1984
Time	61.2	59.5	60.0	58.6	55.7	54.8	55.9

3. Women's running high jump, height in inches

Year	1960	1964	1968	1972	1976	1980	1984
Height	72.75	74.75	71.75	75.63	76.00	77.50	79.50

4. The following table shows the world records for the men's mile run since 1965. The times are the number of seconds over 3 min. Make a graph of the data. Draw the best line that you can "between" the points, and predict when the mile will first be run in 3 min and 45 sec.

Year	1965	1966	1967	1975	1980	1981	1985
Time	53.6	51.3	51.1	49.4	48.8	47.3	46.3

5. In the Shell Marathon a Japanese experimental vehicle achieved the equivalent of 6,409 miles per gallon! Of course, the mileage you get depends on your speed. The table shows the speed in miles per hour (x) and the distance (y) a car ran on 1 gallon of gas.

x	30	35	40	45	50	55	60	65
y	34	31	32	30	29	30	28	27

(a) Make a graph of these data.
(b) Draw a line between the points and predict how many miles per gallon you would get if your speed were 70 miles per hour.

6. The table shows the number (x) of television ads Top Flight Auto ran during a certain week and the number (y) of cars they sold during the same week.

x	3	10	0	7	13	8	14
y	7	15	10	8	14	10	20

(a) Make a graph of these data.
(b) If the management decides that they can afford only 6 ads per week, can you predict how many cars would be sold?

7. Does the number of student absences in a course influence the number of failures? The table shows the average number (x) of absences per student in a certain course and the number (y) of students failing the course.

x	5	7	2	4	3
y	16	20	9	12	10

(a) Make a graph of these data.
(b) Can you predict how many students would fail the course if the average number of absences per student were 6?

8. The manager of the concession stand at a baseball stadium is trying to predict the number of hot dogs that must be bought for an upcoming game. The number x (thousands) of advance tickets sold and the number y

(thousands) of hot dogs sold the day of the game for the last 5 games are shown.

x	23	32	19	29	20
y	16	23	13	22	16

If advance ticket sales are 26,000 tickets, how many hot dogs should the concessionaire buy?

9. In the school of Example 2, of the 50 students selected at random, 12 said they preferred their hamburgers plain. How many of the 3000 students in the school would you expect to prefer their hamburgers plain?

10. A state welfare department selected 150 people at random from its welfare roll of 10,000 people. Upon investigation, it was found that 9 of the 150 had gotten on the welfare roll through fraud. About how many of the 10,000 people on the roll would you expect to be guilty of fraud?

11. An automobile tire manufacturer selected a random sample of 150 tires from a batch of 10,000 tires. It was found that 3 of the 150 tires were defective. How many of the 10,000 tires should the manufacturer expect to be defective?

12. An automobile manufacturer selected a random sample of 150 cars that it manufactured and found a defective steering assembly in 5 of the 150 cars. If the manufacturer had turned out 5000 cars under the same conditions, how many of these should he expect to have defective steering assemblies?

13. The best shooting percentage for one basketball season is 0.727 and belongs to Wilt Chamberlain. If he attempted 586 baskets, how many would you expect him to make?

14. A recent study indicates that 9 out of 50 males and 19 out of 50 females squeeze their toothpaste tube from the bottom. If a group of 200 males and 200 females is chosen, how many males and how many females would you expect to be squeezing the toothpaste tube from the bottom?

15. Can you predict the weather? Groundhogs are supposed to be able to! On February 2 of every year several famous groundhogs emerge from hibernation. If they see their shadow, that means six more weeks of winter. Here are the records of six famous groundhogs for a period of years.

Punxsutawney Phil (15 years)	10 right, 5 wrong
Sun Prairie (7 years)	3 right, 4 wrong
West Orange, NJ (13 years)	7 right, 6 wrong
Staten Island, NY (7 years)	6 right, 1 wrong
Lilburn, GA (7 years)	6 right, 1 wrong
Chicago (6 years)	1 right, 5 wrong

If these six groundhogs predict the weather for the next 20 years, how many times would you expect:
(a) Punxsutawney Phil to be right?
(b) Sun Prairie to be right?
(c) West Orange to be wrong?
(d) Staten Island to be wrong?
(e) Lilburn to be wrong?
(f) Chicago to be right?

16. The graph represents the average monthly temperature for the first six months of the year. What would you predict to be the increase in the average temperature from February to May?

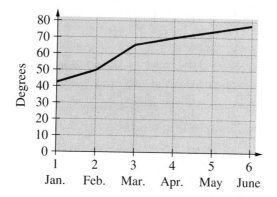

17. The publisher of a science fiction magazine wants to determine which features of the magazine are the most popular with its readers and decides to make a survey. Which of the following procedures would be the most appropriate for obtaining a statistically unbiased sample?
(a) Survey the first 100 subscribers from an alphabetical listing of all the subscribers
(b) Survey a random sample of people from the telephone directory.
(c) Have the readers voluntarily mail in their preferences.
(d) Survey a random sample of readers from a list of all subscribers.

18. A tax committee in a small city wants to estimate the average county tax paid by the citizens of their city and decides to make a survey. Which of the following procedures would be the most appropriate for obtaining a statistically unbiased sample?
(a) Survey all the residents of one section of the city.
(b) Survey a random sample of people at the largest shopping mall in the city.
(c) Survey a random sample of all the people in the city.
(d) Survey all the people who work for the largest employer in the city.

*I*n Other Words

19. To make predictions, statisticians take data from a random sample. Discuss why the following procedures might not yield a random sample of the population of California.
    (a) Every third woman shopper on Rodeo Drive is selected.
    (b) Every third man in Berkeley is selected.
    (c) Select every third person leaving a baseball game in Oakland.

20. If you use a sampling procedure to make a prediction, what do you assume about the sample? How can you make sure that you have a satisfactory sample?

Using Your Knowledge

In this section we described what is meant by a least-squares line to fit a given set of points. In order to facilitate writing the formulas for the calculation of such a line, we shall use the summation symbol Σ to indicate a sum. For example, if we have a number of x *values, then* Σ x *stands for the sum of these values. Similarly,* Σ x² *stands for the sum of the squares of the* x *values. Thus, if the* x *values are 1, 2, 3, 4, then* Σ x = 1 + 2 + 3 + 4 = 10 *and* Σ x² = 1 + 4 + 9 + 16 = 30.

Although the derivation of the least-squares formula is too advanced to be given here, the formulas themselves are not difficult to describe. Suppose we want the least-squares line for n *given points,* $(x_1, y_1), (x_2, y_2), \ldots, (x_n, y_n)$. *If the equation of this line is*

$$y = mx + b \tag{1}$$

then

$$m = \frac{n(\Sigma\ xy) - (\Sigma\ x)(\Sigma\ y)}{n(\Sigma\ x^2) - (\Sigma\ x)^2} \tag{2}$$

and

$$b = \frac{(\Sigma\ x^2)(\Sigma\ y) - (\Sigma\ x)(\Sigma\ xy)}{n(\Sigma\ x^2) - (\Sigma\ x)^2} \tag{3}$$

To use these formulas efficiently, we make a table with the headings x, y, x², *and* xy, *as shown in Table 11.20. The first two columns simply list the* x's *and* y's, *the third column lists the* x²'s, *and the last column gives the* xy *products. After filling out the table, we add the four columns to get* Σ x, Σ y, Σ x², *and* Σ xy, *the four sums that are required in equations (2) and (3).*

We illlustrate the calculation of the least-squares line for the data for the women's 200-m dash given at the beginning of this section. To simplify the arithmetic, we designate the successive Olympics starting with 1948 as 1, 2, 3, . . . ; these are the x *values. For the* y *values, we take the number of seconds over 20. Then our calculations are as shown in the table.*

Table 11.20

x	y	x^2	xy
1	4.4	1	4.4
2	3.7	4	7.4
3	3.4	9	10.2
4	3.2	16	12.8
5	3.0	25	15.0
6	2.5	36	15.0
7	2.4	49	16.8
8	2.37	64	18.96
10	1.81	100	18.1
46	26.78	304	118.66

We have thus found Σ x = 46, Σ y = 26.78, Σ x^2 = 304, *and* Σ xy = 118.66, *and we are ready to use equations (2) and (3). Since there are nine points,* n = 9, *and we get*

$$m = \frac{(9)(118.66) - (46)(26.78)}{(9)(304) - (46)^2} = -0.264$$

$$b = \frac{(304)(26.78) - (46)(118.66)}{(9)(304) - (46)^2} = 4.327$$

(These answers are rounded to three decimal places.) The required line has the equation, given by equation (1),

$$y = -0.264x + 4.327$$

If we put x = 9 *in this equation, we get* y = 1.951 $\approx$ 1.95. *Thus, the predicted winning time for the 1980 Olympics is 20 + 1.95, or about 22 sec. (Of course, you must not carry this type of prediction too far, because after about 36 Olympics, the winner would reach the finish line before she started the race!)*

21. Find the least-squares line for the data in Example 1. Let x be the number of the Olympics with 1960 as number 1, and let the y values be the number of seconds over 50.

22. Find the least-squares line for problem 1, Exercise 11.6.

23. Find the least-squares line for problem 2, Exercise 11.6.

24. Find the least-squares line for problem 3, Exercise 11.6.

25. Find the least-squares line for problem 4, Exercise 11.6. [*Hint:* Let x be the number of years after 1965 and let y be the number of seconds over 45.]

11.7   SCATTERGRAMS AND CORRELATION

CORRELATION OF CANCER TO SOLAR RADIATION

You have probably heard the expression "What does that have to do with the price of tea in China?" In many practical applications of mathematics such as business, medicine, social sciences, and economics we find pairs of variables that have to be considered simultaneously. (Perhaps tea production and tea prices!) In general, we are looking for certain "patterns" or "co-relations." For example, in Norway, the annual herring catch has dwindled from more than a million tons to less than 4,000 and the rates of breast and colon cancer have nearly doubled. Is there a connection? Is there a relationship between herring catch and cancer? Yes, if you consider the fact that herring is rich in vitamin D, a nutrient that you can get from sunlight, and there is not too much sunlight in Norway! If this were the case, people living in sunny areas, where they receive greater amounts of sunlight, and hence more vitamin D, should have less breast and colon cancer. Drs. Frank and Cedric Garland have shown during the past decade that a population's vitamin D intake can be a predictor of breast and colon cancer. How can they make this claim? They looked at the number of deaths per 1000 women in places where there was not too much sunlight (say, New York, Chicago, and Boston) and the number of deaths per thousand in sunny places (Las Vegas, Honolulu, and Phoenix, for example). The graph of the results, called a **scattergram,** is shown. As you can see, the

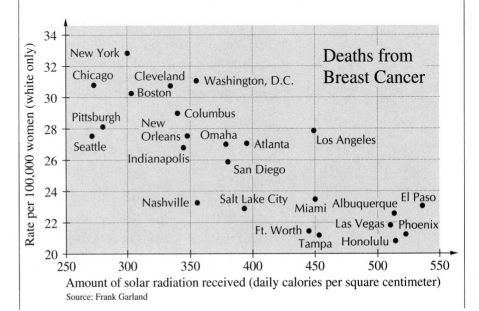

Source: Frank Garland

sunnier it is, the fewer deaths from breast cancer there are. We say that there is a **negative correlation** between the amount of solar radiation (sunshine) received and the number of breast cancer deaths. On the other hand, there is a **positive correlation** (not shown) between the amount of solar radiation received and the number of skin cancers. In this section we will study positive and negative correlations.

Twenty students tried out for the basketball team at West Side High. The coach listed their heights and weights as in Table 11.21. We have graphed the ordered pairs (Height, Weight) as shown in Figure 11.28. This type of graph, the scattered set of points, is called a **scattergram**. The scattergram indicates how the height and weight are related. As you might expect, in any group of boys (or girls) the greater height would usually correspond to the greater weight.

The line drawn "between" the points in Figure 11.28 is the least-squares line for the data in Table 11.21. Notice that most of the points lie close to the line. Because this line slopes upward, we say that the scattergram shows a **positive correlation** between the heights and the weights of the 20 students.

Three kinds of correlation are possible. The scattergrams in Figure 11.29 illustrate typical cases. A good illustration of a negative correlation appears in Example 1 of Section 11.6.

Table 11.21

Height (in.)	Weight (lb)	Height (in.)	Weight (lb)
61.4	106	68.9	147
62.6	108	68.9	152
63.0	101	69.3	143
63.4	114	69.7	143
63.8	112	70.1	150
65.7	123	70.9	147
66.1	121	70.9	163
67.3	136	72.8	158
67.7	143	72.8	165
68.1	143	73.2	163

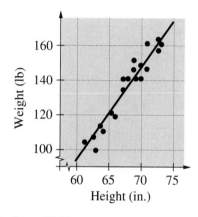

FIGURE 11.28

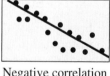

Positive correlation
(Line slopes upward)

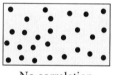

Negative correlation
(Line slopes downward)

No correlation
(No particular pattern)

FIGURE 11.29

EXAMPLE 1   Ten students were selected at random and a comparison was made of their high
school grade-point averages (GPA) and their grade-point averages at the end of
their freshman year in college (see Table 11.22). Make a scattergram and decide what kind of correlation is present.

Solution   We graph the given ordered pairs as shown in the scattergram below. This scattergram indicates a positive correlation between the high school and college
GPAs. Are you surprised?

Table 11.22

High School GPA	College GPA
2.2	2.0
2.4	2.0
2.5	2.7
2.7	2.3
2.9	3.0
3.0	2.5
3.2	2.8
3.5	3.4
3.9	4.0
4.0	3.9

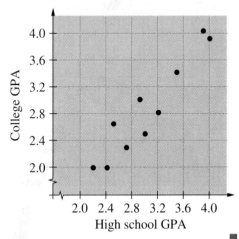

Exercise 11.7

In problems 1–8, state what kind of correlation you would expect in a scattergram for the indicated ordered pairs.

1. (Length of person's leg, Person's height)
2. (Outdoor temperature, Cost of air conditioning a house)
3. (Student's weight, Student's score on math test)
4. (Person's salary, Cost of person's home)
5. (Altitude, Atmospheric pressure)
6. (Weight of auto, Miles per gallon of fuel)
7. (Student's score on college aptitude test, Student's GPA)
8. (Speed of auto, Miles per gallon)

In problems 9–16, make a scattergram for the given data, and state what kind
of correlation is present.

9.

x	2	4	7	3	1	5	8	10	6	9
y	1	3	8	4	2	2	6	7	6	4

10.

x	9	10	8	8	6	4	5	5	3	2
y	4	2	3	6	4	8	7	5	8	10

11. The following table gives the weights and the highway miles per gallon for eight automobiles:

Weight (lb)	2800	1900	2000	3300	3100	2900	4000	2600
Miles per Gallon	19	34	28	19	24	23	16	24

12. The following table gives the scores of 10 students on an English exam and their corresponding scores on an economics exam:

English	50	95	55	20	85	75	45	20	80	90
Economics	75	95	70	35	70	80	40	15	60	90

13. Here are some recent statistics on years of schooling successfully completed and average annual salaries for men over 25:

Years of School	8	12	15	16
Average Salary	$16,800	$23,300	$25,800	$33,900

14. The following table gives the gain in reading speed for students in a speed-reading program:

Weeks in Program	2	3	3	4	5	6	8	9
Speed Gain (Words per Minute)	40	60	80	100	110	150	190	220

15. A student was curious about the effect of antifreeze on the freezing point of a water–antifreeze mixture. He went to the chemistry lab, where he made the measurements in the following table:

Percent Antifreeze (By Volume)	10	20	30	40	50
Freezing Point (Degrees C)	−4	−10	−20	−24	−36

16. The following table gives the heights of students and their corresponding scores on an English test:

Height (in.)	62	67	70	64	72	68	65	61	73	67
Test Score	85	60	75	70	95	35	60	80	45	100

17. The power chart shows the number of power outages experienced by the Central Power Company during the twelve weeks starting June 1.

    (a) During which week was there no outage?

    (b) Which week had the greatest number of outages?

    (c) When did a decline in the number of outages seem to start?

    (d) Is any kind of correlation shown by the chart?

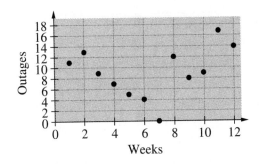

18. The chart shows the hours studied by ten students and the grades they received on an examination.

    (a) What kind of correlation (if any) is shown here?

    (b) If a student studied for 12 hours, about what grade would you expect him to make?

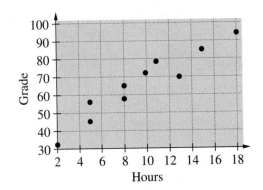

In Other Words

19. During the past 10 years there has been a positive correlation between the number of cars with air bags sold in Florida and the number of traffic accidents.
    (a) Do air bags cause traffic accidents?
    (b) What other factors may cause traffic accidents and the number of cars with air bags to increase together?
20. Describe what happens to the related items of data if the corresponding scattergram shows
    (a) A positive correlation
    (b) A negative correlation

Using Your Knowledge

(The following discussion requires a comprehension of the material in the Using Your Knowledge section of Exercise 11.6.)

*In order to describe how good the correlation is for a given set of ordered pairs, Karl Pearson introduced a measure called a **correlation coefficient**. In order to calculate this coefficient, we need exactly the quantities that we use to find the least-squares line in addition to one more sum,* $\Sigma\ y^2$, *the sum of the squares of the y's. In terms of these quantities, the correlation coefficient r is given by the formula*

$$r = \frac{n(\Sigma\ xy) - (\Sigma\ x)(\Sigma\ y)}{\sqrt{n(\Sigma\ x^2) - (\Sigma\ x)^2}\ \sqrt{n(\Sigma\ y^2) - (\Sigma\ y)^2}} \tag{1}$$

If you have calculated the least-squares line, then the formula for r is quite easy to use in spite of its forbidding appearance.

Pearson devised his formula so that $-1 \le r \le 1$, *with a value of r close to 1 meaning that there is a high positive correlation, and a value of r close to* -1 *meaning that there is a high negative correlation. It is usually agreed that a value of r between* -0.2 *and 0.2 indicates an insignificant correlation.*

We illustrate the use of equation (1) by calculating r for the data we used to find a least squares line in the Using Your Knowledge section of Exercise 11.6. By adding the squares of the y values, we obtain $\Sigma\ y^2 = 84.75$ *(rounded to two places), and from Table 11.20 on page 843,* $\Sigma\ x = 46$, $\Sigma\ y = 26.78$, $\Sigma\ x^2 = 304$, $\Sigma\ xy = 118.66$, *and* n = 9 *(the number of ordered pairs). By substituting into equation (1), we get*

$$r = \frac{(9)(118.66) - (46)(26.78)}{\sqrt{(9)(304) - (46)^2}\ \sqrt{(9)(84.75) - (26.78)^2}}$$

$$= \frac{-163.94}{\sqrt{620}\ \sqrt{45.58}} \approx -0.98$$

Thus, we have just found that there is a very high negative correlation between the x's and y's. This means that the data are very closely described by the least-squares line we found earlier.

You should not assume that there is any cause-and-effect relationship between two variables simply because the correlation is high. A classic example of a high positive correlation is that of the number of storks found in English villages and the number of babies born in these villages. Do you think there is a cause-and-effect relationship here?

Use your calculator to find the correlation coefficient for the following problems in Exercise 11.7.

21. problem 11   22. problem 12   23. problem 13
24. problem 15   25. problem 16

Chapter 11 Summary

Section	Item	Meaning	Example
11.1A	Frequency distribution	A way of organizing a list of numbers	
11.1A	Frequency	Number of times an entry occurs	
11.1B	Histogram	A special type of graph consisting of vertical bars with no space between the bars	
11.1C	Frequency polygon	A line graph connecting the midpoints of the tops of the bars in a histogram	
11.2	Mean, $\bar{x}$	The sum of the scores divided by the number of scores	The mean of 3, 7, and 8 is 6.
11.2	Mode	The number that occurs most often	The mode of 1, 2, 2, and 3 is 2.
11.2	Median	If the numbers are arranged in order of magnitude for an odd number of scores, the median is the middle number; for an even number of scores, the median is the average of the two middle numbers.	Median ↓ 1 3 ⑧ 15 19 1 2 5 9 11 18 $\dfrac{5+9}{2} = 7 \leftarrow$ Median

Section	Item	Meaning	Example
11.3	Range	The difference between the greatest and the least numbers in a set	The range of 2, 8, and 19 is 17.
11.3	Standard deviation, s	$\sqrt{\dfrac{(x_1 - \bar{x})^2 + \cdots + (x_n - \bar{x})^2}{n-1}}$, where $\bar{x}$ is the mean and n is the number of items	
11.5	z-Score	$z = \dfrac{x - \bar{x}}{s}$, where x is a score, $\bar{x}$ is the mean, and s is the standard deviation	

Research Questions

Sources of information for most of these questions can be found in the Bibliography at the end of the book.

1. Go to the library, look through newspapers and magazines, and find some examples of histograms, line, bar, and circle graphs. Are there any distortions in the drawings? Discuss your findings.

2. Write a brief report about the contents of John Graunt's *Bills of Mortality*.

3. Write a paragraph on how statistics are used in different sports.

4. Write a report on how surveys are used to determine the ratings and rankings of television programs by such organizations as A. C. Nielsen.

5. Discuss the Harris and Gallup polls and the techniques used in their surveys.

6. Prepare a report or an exhibit of how statistics are used in medicine, psychology, and/or business.

7. Discuss the life and work of Adolph Quetelet (1796–1894).

8. Research and write a report on how Gregor Mendel (1822–1884), Sir Francis Galton (1822–1911), and Florence Nightingale (1820–1910) used statistics in their work.

9. Look at the scattergram in Getting Started, Section 11.7. Find out the average daily amount of solar radiation in your area, then make a prediction about the rate of breast cancer mortality per 100,000 women in your area.

Chapter 11 Practice Test

The following scores were made on a scholastic aptitude test by a group of 25 high school seniors:

85	65	89	83	98
67	88	87	88	90
95	77	91	73	88
99	67	91	72	86
79	83	61	70	75

Use these data for problems 1–3.

1. Group the scores into intervals of $60 < s \leq 65$, $65 < s \leq 70$, $70 < s \leq 75$, and so on. Then make a frequency distribution with this grouping.

2. Make a histogram for the frequency distribution in problem 1.

3. Make a frequency polygon for the distribution in problem 1.

4. During a certain week, the following maximum temperatures (in degrees Fahrenheit) were recorded in a large eastern city: 78, 82, 82, 71, 69, 73, 70.

   (a) Find the mean of these temperatures.

   (b) Find the mode of the temperature readings.

   (c) Find the median high temperature for the week.

5. (a) Find the range of temperatures in problem 4.

   (b) Find the standard deviation of the temperatures in problem 4.

6. A fair coin is tossed 256 times. If this experiment is repeated many times, the numbers of heads will form an approximately normal distribution, with a mean of 128 and a standard deviation of 8.

   (a) Within what limits may we be almost 100% confident that the total number of heads in 256 tosses will lie?

   (b) What is the probability that heads will occur fewer than 112 times?

7. A normal distribution consists of 1000 scores, with a mean of 100 and a standard deviation of 20.

   (a) About how many of the scores are above 140?

   (b) About how many scores are below 80?

   (c) About how many scores are between 60 and 80?

8. A testing program shows that the breaking points of fishing lines made from a certain plastic fiber are normally distributed, with a mean of 10 lb and a standard deviation of 1 lb.

   (a) What is the probability that one of these lines selected at random has a breaking point of more than 10 lb?

   (b) What is the probability that one of these lines selected at random has a breaking point of less than 8 lb?

9. On a multiple-choice test taken by 1000 students, the scores were normally distributed, with a mean of 50 and a standard deviation of 5. Find the z-score corresponding to a score of:

   (a) 58

   (b) 62

10. Agnes scored 88 on a French test and 90 on a psychology test. The mean score in the French test was 76, with a standard deviation of 18, and the mean in the psychology test was 80, with a standard deviation of 16. If the scores were normally distributed, which of Agnes' scores was the better score?

11. With the data given in problem 9, find the probability that a randomly selected student will have a score between 50 and 62. (Use Table II in the back of the book.)

12. Here is a list of 5 of the most active stocks on the New York Stock Exchange on February 19, 1988. Make a bar graph of the yield rates of these stocks.

Stock	Price ($)	Dividend ($)	Yield Rate (%)
Fed DS	$60\frac{1}{4}$	1.48	2.5
Ford M	$44\frac{3}{4}$	2.00	4.5
Noes Ut	$20\frac{3}{4}$	1.76	8.5
Exxon	$42\frac{3}{4}$	2.00	4.7
Gen El	$43\frac{1}{4}$	1.40	3.2

13. Here are the amounts (to the nearest billion) the federal government has spent on education for selected years.

1984	1988	1989	1990
17	21	24	26

   (a) Make a line graph for this information.

   (b) Use your graph to estimate how much was spent on education in 1986.

14. In a recent poll, the features that patrons liked in a restaurant were listed as follows:

Low-calorie entrees	67%
Varied portion sizes	47%
Cholesterol-free entrees	52%
All-you-can-eat specials	27%
Self-service soup bar	35%

Use horizontal bars and make a bar graph of this information.

15. The typical family budget is as follows:

Monthly Family Budget

Savings	$ 200
Housing	600
Clothing	300
Food	800
Other	100
Total	$2000

Make a circle graph for these data.

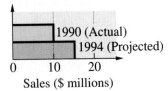

16. The bar graph in the figure in the margin shows the 1990 sales and the projected 1994 sales of the Wesellum Corporation. Read the graph, and estimate the percent increase that was projected for 1994 over 1990.

17. The testing department of Circle Tire Company checks a random sample of 150 of a certain type of tire that the company makes and finds a defective tread on 3 of these tires. In a batch of 10,000 of these tires, how many are expected to have defective treads?

18. In a large county, 50,000 high school students took a reading comprehension test, and 4000 of these students got a rating of excellent. In a random sample of 100 of these students, how many should be expected to have gotten an excellent rating on this test?

19. Graph the 5 points given in the table below. Draw the best line you can "between" these points, and estimate the value of y for $x = 7$.

x	1	2	3	4	5
y	10.2	7.6	5.8	4.4	2.0

20. What kind of correlation would you expect for the indicated ordered pairs?
    (a) (Value of a family's home, Family's annual income)
    (b) (Number of hours of training, Number of minutes in which runner can do the mile run)
    (c) (Person's shoe size, Person's salary)
    (d) (Number of children getting polio immunization, Number of children contracting polio)

Do you know the difference between **simple** and **compound** interest, or how to use percents to figure out sales taxes or discounts? As an informed consumer, you should be aware of these topics, but if you are not, we shall discuss them in Section 12.1. What about your credit cards? How much interest do you pay on them? What is their annual fee? Can you get some cards **without** an annual fee? Credit cards and other types of credit such as **revolving charge accounts** and **add-on interest** are studied in Section 12.2

As a consumer, you do have certain rights regarding credit purchases. In Section 12.3 we discuss the **Truth-in-Lending Act,** its provisions and the benefits afforded you as a consumer under the Act. Finally, Section 12.4 discusses the American dream: buying a house. We start by discussing how much you can afford, how much of a down payment you should make, the different types of loans available to you, and how monthly payments are estimated. We also discuss an expense often overlooked when buying a home: the closing costs. What do they entail and when do they have to be paid? If you study this section you will gain a wealth of information regarding the mechanics and strategies for buying a home.

Consumer Mathematics

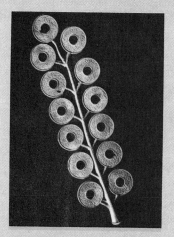

Have you ever wished for a money tree? The picture shows an East Indian money tree. The tin coins, used by the people of the Malay Peninsula in the nineteenth century, were broken off as needed.

The first coins were probably made about 2500 years ago in Lydia, now part of western Turkey. The coins were of a natural mixture of gold and silver called *electrum*, and they were stamped with a design showing that the king guaranteed them to be of uniform size. These coins were accepted by traders as a convenient medium of exchange and inspired other countries to make their own coins. According to many historians, coins were also independently invented in China and India.

The first paper money was used in China about 1400 years ago. Marco Polo, who traveled in China in the 1200s, was amazed to see the Chinese people using paper money instead of coins. However, Europeans were skeptical about a piece of paper having any value, and it was not until the 17th century, when banks began to issue paper bills (called *bank notes*) to depositors and borrowers, that paper money was accepted.

In the American colonies, several kinds of paper money were circulated. Some of this money was in the form of bills of credit issued by the individual colonies, and some, backed by real estate, was issued by the newly established land banks. During the Revolutionary War, the Continental Congress printed money that was called *Continental currency*. Unfortunately, this currency was overissued and soon became worthless.

Until 1863, most of the currency in the United States consisted of notes issued by various state banks. Then, Congress established national banks with the authority to issue bank notes. By taxing all new issues of state bank notes, they forced such notes out of existence. In 1913, the Federal Reserve System was established and Federal Reserve notes gradually replaced national bank notes and became the official currency of the United States.

12.1   INTEREST

GETTING STARTED

SIMPLE AND COMPOUND INTEREST

Do you know the difference between simple and compound interest? First, you should know that **interest** is the amount paid for using borrowed money. When you deposit money in a savings account, buy a certificate of deposit, or loan money to someone, the person or institution receiving the money will pay you **interest** for the use of your money. On the other hand, if you borrow money from a bank, you must pay interest for the money you borrow. How is interest computed? It depends! **Simple interest (I)** depends on the **principal P** (the amount borrowed or invested), the **interest rate r** (the portion of the principal charged for using the principal and usually expressed as a percent) and the **time** or **term t,** the period (in years) during which the borrower or investor has the use of all or part of the money. To calculate simple interest, we use the formula:

$$I = Prt$$

Now, suppose you invest $1000 at 6% simple interest for one year. Here $P = \$1000$, $r = 6\% = 0.06$, and $t = 1$. Thus,

$$I = \$1000 \times 0.06 \times 1 = \$60$$

At the end of the year, you get your $1000 back plus $60 in interest, that is, $1000 + $60 = $1060.

But suppose you invest the $1000 at the same nominal rate of 6% and the interest is **compounded** quarterly. How much money would you get at the end of the year? Let us write the information in a table.

Quarter	Interest	New Principal
1st	$\$1000 \times 0.06 \times \frac{1}{4} = \$15$	$\$1000 + \$15.00 = \$1015.00$
2nd	$\$1015 \times 0.06 \times \frac{1}{4} = \$15.23$	$\$1015 + \$15.23 = \$1030.23$
3rd	$\$1030.23 \times 0.06 \times \frac{1}{4} = \$15.45$	$\$1030.23 + \$15.45 = \$1045.68$
4th	$\$1045.68 \times 0.06 \times \frac{1}{4} = \$15.69$	$\$1045.68 + \$15.69 = \$1061.37$

Thus, at the end of the year, you get $1061.37. which is $1.37 more than the simple interest amount.

In this section we shall discuss simple and compound interest and its applications.

There are many consumer problems that you will probably encounter and that will directly affect your personal finances. Some of these problems involve calculating best buys, checking credit account statements, comparing interest rates, using credit cards, and purchasing a home or a car. In this chapter, we have tried to discuss most of these problems.

Realistic problems of these types are usually solved with the aid of a calculator. Hence, the examples show how a calculator can be used to obtain the answer. Of course, a calculator is not absolutely necessary; it is just a tool to help you do the arithmetic faster and easier. If you choose to use a calculator, we recommend one that is based on *algebraic logic*. You can tell if your calculator uses algebraic logic by doing the calculation: $2 + 3 \times 4$. Press $\boxed{2}$ $\boxed{+}$ $\boxed{3}$ $\boxed{\times}$ $\boxed{4}$ $\boxed{=}$. If the display shows 14, the logic is algebraic. If it shows 20, the calculator does not use the algebraic order of operations that gives priority to multiplication and division, and you should refer to your owner's manual to determine how to proceed.

A. *Simple Interest*

How much would you get if you received 12% interest on $1 million for 10 years? The answer depends on how this interest is calculated!

Reprinted with special permission of King Features Syndicate, Inc.

The **simple interest** for 1 year at the rate r on a principal P is just the principal times the rate—that is, Pr. The simple interest for t years is thus obtained by multiplying by t. This means that the formula for calculating the simple interest I on a principal P at the rate r for t years is

$$I = Prt$$

Notice that in the calculation of simple interest, the principal is just the original principal; the periodic interest does *not* earn further interest. Thus, if you receive 12% interest ($r = 12\% = 0.12$) on $1 million ($P = \$1,000,000$) for 10 years ($t = 10$), the simple interest is

$$
\begin{aligned}
I &= \overbrace{P}^{} \times \overbrace{r}^{} \times \overbrace{t}^{} \\
&= 1{,}000{,}000 \times 0.12 \times 10 \text{ dollars} \\
&= 1{,}200{,}000 \quad \text{dollars}
\end{aligned}
$$

Of course, at the end of the 10 years, you would also get your $1 million back, so you would receive $1,000,000 + $1,200,000 = $2,200,000 at simple interest. The final amount A is given as $A = P + I$.

However, if your annual interest were calculated on your original principal *plus* all previously earned interest—that is, if your interest were **compounded annually**—you would receive the much greater amount of $3,105,848 (to the nearest dollar). We will discuss compound interest later in this section.

As a consumer, you will be interested in three important applications of simple interest: loans and deposits, taxes, and discounts. We consider these applications next.

Of course, you know that borrowing money from (or depositing money in) a bank or lending institution involves interest. Here is an example.

EXAMPLE 1   A loan company charges 32% simple interest for a 2-year, $600 loan.

(a) What is the total interest on this loan?
(b) What is the interest for 3 months?
(c) What is the total amount A that must be paid to the loan company at the end of 2 years?

Solution   (a) The interest is given by $I = Prt$, where $P = 600$, $r = 32\% = 0.32$, and $t = 2$. Thus,

$$I = 600 \times 0.32 \times 2 = 384$$

On a calculator with a percent key $\boxed{\%}$, press

$$\boxed{6}\ \boxed{0}\ \boxed{0}\ \boxed{\times}\ \boxed{3}\ \boxed{2}\ \boxed{\%}\ \boxed{\times}\ \boxed{2}\ \boxed{=}$$

The interest for the 2 years is $384.

(b) Here, $P = 600$, $r = 32\% = 0.32$, and $t = \frac{3}{12} = \frac{1}{4}$, because 3 months is $\frac{3}{12}$ of a year. Thus,

$$
\begin{aligned}
I &= 600 \times 0.32 \times \tfrac{1}{4} \\
&= 600 \times 0.08 \qquad 0.32 \times \tfrac{1}{4} = 0.08 \\
&= 48.00
\end{aligned}
$$

The interest for 3 months is $48.

(c) At the end of 2 years, the loan company must be paid the original $600 plus the interest of $384; that is,

$$A = 600 + 384 = 984$$

The company must be paid $984.   ∎

B. *Taxes*

You have probably heard the saying, "There is nothing certain but death and taxes." Here is a simple problem "it is certain" you can do.

EXAMPLE 2   A state has a 6% sales tax. Mary Rios buys an item priced at $84.

(a) What is the sales tax on this item?
(b) What is Mary's total cost for this item?

Solution   (a) The sales tax S is simply 6% of 84; that is,

$$S = 0.06 \times 84 = 5.04$$

The tax is $5.04.

(b) The total cost is the price, $84, plus the tax:

$$\$84 + \$5.04 = \$89.04$$

A calculator with a percent key $\boxed{\%}$ will give the total cost automatically if you press $\boxed{8}\,\boxed{4}\,\boxed{+}\,\boxed{6}\,\boxed{\%}\,\boxed{=}$.

■

C. *Discounts*

In Examples 1 and 2, the consumer had to pay interest or taxes. But there is some hope! Sometimes, you can obtain a discount on certain purchases. Such a discount is usually stated as a percent. For instance, the coupon shown in the margin would entitle you to a 20% discount on certain purchases.

EXAMPLE 3   Ralph McWaters purchased a $42 item and used his coupon to get 20% off.

(a) How much was his discount?
(b) How much did he have to pay for the item?

Solution   (a) His discount d was 20% of 42:

$$d = 0.20 \times 42 = \$8.40$$

(b) Since he had a discount of $8.40, he had to pay

$$\$42 - \$8.40 = \$33.60$$

for the item. A calculator with a percent key $\boxed{\%}$ will obtain the final price if you press $\boxed{4}\,\boxed{2}\,\boxed{-}\,\boxed{2}\,\boxed{0}\,\boxed{\%}\,\boxed{=}$.

■

D. *Compound Interest*

As we mentioned earlier, when interest is **compounded,** the interest is calculated not only on the original principal but also on the earned interest. For example, if you deposit $1000 in a savings account that pays 6% interest compounded annually, then in the first year, the account will earn interest calculated as

$$I = Prt$$
$$= \$1000 \times 0.06 \times 1 = \$60.00$$

If you make no withdrawal, then at the beginning of the second year the accumulated amount will be

$$\$1000 + \$60 = \$1060$$

which is the new principal. In the second year, this new principal will earn interest

$$I = Prt$$
$$= \$1060 \times 0.06 \times 1 = \$63.60$$

Thus, at the beginning of the third year, the accumulated amount will be

$$\$1060 + \$63.60 = \$1123.60$$

and so on.

You can see that when interest is compounded, the earned interest increases each year ($60, $63.60, and so on, in the preceding illustration). This is because the interest at the end of a year is calculated on the accumulated amount (principal plus interest) at the beginning of that year. Piecewise calculation of the accumulated amount is a very time-consuming procedure, but it can be avoided by developing a general formula for the amount A_n accumulated after n interest periods and the use of special tables. To develop the formula for A_n, we let I be the compound interest, P be the original principal, i be the rate per period, and A_1 be the compound amount at the end of the first period:

$$I = Pi \qquad \text{Interest for the first period}$$
$$A_1 = P + I$$
$$= P + Pi \qquad \text{Substitute } Pi \text{ for } I.$$
$$= P(1 + i) \qquad \text{Use the distributive property.}$$

After the end of the second period, the compound amount A_2 is

$$A_2 = A_1 + A_1 i$$
$$= A_1(1 + i) \qquad \text{Use the distributive property.}$$
$$= P(1 + i)(1 + i) \qquad \text{Substitute } P(1 + i) \text{ for } A_1.$$
$$= P(1 + i)^2 \qquad \text{Substitute } (1 + i)^2 \text{ for } (1 + i)(1 + i).$$

If we continue this procedure, after n periods, A_n will be

$$A_n = P(1 + i)^n$$

Thus, if we deposit $1 at 6% compounded annually for 20 years,

$$A_{20} = \$1(1 + 0.06)^{20}$$

Fortunately, there are tables that give the value of the accumulated amount for a $1 initial deposit at compound interest i for n time periods. Table 12.1 is such a table. To find the value of the accumulated amount $(1 + 0.06)^{20}$ in Table 12.1, we go down the column headed n until we reach 20, and then go across to the column headed 6%. The accumulated amount given there is

$3.2071. If we wish to know the accumulated amount for an original deposit of $1000 instead of $1, we simply multiply the $3.2071 by 1000 to obtain $3207.10.

In using Table 12.1 there is one word of warning: *The entries in this table have been rounded to four decimal places from more accurate values.* Consequently, you should not expect answers to be accurate to more than the number of digits in the table entry. If more accuracy is needed, you must use a table with more decimal places or a calculator.

Many financial transactions call for interest to be compounded more often than once a year. In such cases, the interest rate is customarily stated as a

Table 12.1 *Amount (in dollars) to Which $1 Will Grow in n Periods Under Compound Interest*

n	1%	2%	3%	4%	5%	6%
1	1.0100	1.0200	1.0300	1.0400	1.0500	1.0600
2	1.0201	1.0404	1.0609	1.0816	1.1025	1.1236
3	1.0303	1.0612	1.0927	1.1249	1.1576	1.1910
4	1.0406	1.0824	1.1255	1.1699	1.2155	1.2625
5	1.0510	1.1041	1.1593	1.2167	1.2763	1.3382
6	1.0615	1.1262	1.1941	1.2653	1.3401	1.4185
7	1.0721	1.1487	1.2299	1.3159	1.4071	1.5036
8	1.0829	1.1717	1.2668	1.3686	1.4775	1.5938
9	1.0937	1.1951	1.3048	1.4233	1.5513	1.6895
10	1.1046	1.2190	1.3439	1.4802	1.6289	1.7908
11	1.1157	1.2434	1.3842	1.5395	1.7103	1.8983
12	1.1268	1.2682	1.4258	1.6010	1.7959	2.0122
13	1.1381	1.2936	1.4685	1.6651	1.8856	2.1329
14	1.1495	1.3195	1.5126	1.7317	1.9799	2.2609
15	1.1610	1.3459	1.5580	1.8009	2.0789	2.3966
16	1.1726	1.3728	1.6047	1.8730	2.1829	2.5404
17	1.1843	1.4002	1.6528	1.9479	2.2920	2.6928
18	1.1961	1.4282	1.7024	2.0258	2.4066	2.8543
19	1.2081	1.4568	1.7535	2.1068	2.5270	3.0256
20	1.2202	1.4859	1.8061	2.1911	2.6533	3.2071
21	1.2324	1.5157	1.8603	2.2788	2.7860	3.3996
22	1.2447	1.5460	1.9161	2.3699	2.9253	3.6035
23	1.2572	1.5769	1.9736	2.4647	3.0715	3.8198
24	1.2697	1.6084	2.0328	2.5633	3.2251	4.0489
30	1.3478	1.8114	2.4273	3.2434	4.3219	5.7434
36	1.4308	2.0399	2.8983	4.1039	5.7918	8.1473
42	1.5188	2.2972	3.4607	5.1928	7.7616	11.5570
48	1.6122	2.5870	4.1323	6.5705	10.4013	16.3939

Table 12.1 *(cont.)*

n	7%	8%	9%	10%	11%	12%
1	1.0700	1.0800	1.0900	1.1000	1.1100	1.1200
2	1.1449	1.1664	1.1881	1.2100	1.2321	1.2544
3	1.2250	1.2597	1.2950	1.3310	1.3676	1.4049
4	1.3108	1.3605	1.4116	1.4641	1.5181	1.5735
5	1.4026	1.4693	1.5386	1.6105	1.6851	1.7623
6	1.5007	1.5869	1.6771	1.7716	1.8704	1.9738
7	1.6058	1.7138	1.8280	1.9487	2.0762	2.2107
8	1.7182	1.8509	1.9926	2.1436	2.3045	2.4760
9	1.8385	1.9990	2.1719	2.3579	2.5580	2.7731
10	1.9672	2.1589	2.3674	2.5937	2.8394	3.1058
11	2.1049	2.3316	2.5804	2.8531	3.1518	3.4785
12	2.2522	2.5182	2.8127	3.1384	3.4985	3.8960
13	2.4098	2.7196	3.0658	3.4523	3.8833	4.3635
14	2.5785	2.9372	3.3417	3.7975	4.3104	4.8871
15	2.7590	3.1722	3.6425	4.1772	4.7846	5.4736
16	2.9522	3.4259	3.9703	4.5950	5.3109	6.1304
17	3.1588	3.7000	4.3276	5.0545	5.8951	6.8660
18	3.3799	3.9960	4.7171	5.5599	6.5436	7.6900
19	3.6165	4.3157	5.1417	6.1159	7.2633	8.6128
20	3.8697	4.6610	5.6044	6.7275	8.0623	9.6403
21	4.1406	5.0338	6.1088	7.4002	8.9492	10.8038
22	4.4304	5.4365	6.6586	8.1403	9.9336	12.1003
23	4.7405	5.8715	7.2579	8.9543	11.0263	13.5523
24	5.0724	6.3412	7.9111	9.8497	12.2392	15.1786
30	7.6123	10.0627	13.2677	17.4494	22.8923	29.9599
36	11.4239	15.9682	22.2512	30.9127	42.8181	59.1356
42	17.1443	25.3395	37.3175	54.7637	80.0876	116.7231
48	25.7289	40.2106	62.5852	97.0172	149.7970	230.3908

nominal annual rate, it being understood that the actual rate per interest period is the nominal rate divided by the number of periods per year. For instance, if interest is at 18%, compounded monthly, then the actual interest rate is $\frac{18}{12}\% = 1.5\%$ per month, because there are 12 months in a year.

EXAMPLE 4 Find the accumulated amount and the interest earned for:

(a) $8000 at 8% compounded annually for 5 years
(b) $3500 at 12% compounded semiannually for 10 years

Solution (a) In Table 12.1, we go down the column under *n* until we come to 5 and then across to the column under 8%. The number there is 1.4693. Hence, the accumulated amount will be

$$\$8000 \times 1.4693 = \$11{,}754 \quad \text{to the nearest dollar}$$

The interest earned is the difference between the \$11,754 and the original deposit, that is, \$11,754 − \$8000 = \$3754.

(b) Because *semiannually* means twice a year, interest is compounded every 6 months, and the actual rate per interest period is the nominal rate, 12% divided by 2, or 6%. In 10 years, there are 2 × 10 = 20 interest periods. Hence, we go down the column under *n* until we come to 20 and then across to the column headed 6% to find the accumulated amount 3.2071. Since this is the amount for \$1, we multiply by \$3500 to get

$$\$3500 \times 3.2071 = \$11{,}225 \quad \text{to the nearest dollar}$$

The amount of interest earned is \$11,225 − \$3500 = \$7725. ∎

Exercise 12.1

A. In problems 1–10, find the simple interest.

	Principal	Rate	Time
1.	\$3,000	8%	1 year
2.	\$4,500	7%	1 year
3.	\$2,000	9%	3 years
4.	\$6,200	8%	4 years
5.	\$4,000	10%	6 months
6.	\$6,000	12%	4 months
7.	\$2,500	10%	3 months
8.	\$12,000	9%	1 month
9.	\$16,000	7%	5 months
10.	\$30,000	8%	2 months

B. 11. The state sales tax in Florida is 6%. Desiree Cole bought \$40.20 worth of merchandise.
(a) What was the tax on this purchase?
(b) What was the total price of the purchase?

12. The state sales tax in Alabama is 4%. Beto Frias bought a refrigerator priced at \$666.
(a) What was the sales tax on this refrigerator?
(b) How much was the total price of the purchase?

13. Have you seen the FICA (Federal Insurance Contribution Act, better known as Social Security) deduction taken from your paycheck? For 1989, the FICA tax rate was 7.51% of your annual salary. Find the FICA tax for a person earning $24,000 a year.

14. It was projected that the FICA tax for 1990 and subsequent years would be 7.65% of your annual salary. Walter Snyder makes $30,000 a year. What would his FICA tax deduction be based on this rate?

According to the instructions for figuring a single person's estimated federal income tax for a recent year, the tax was 15% of the taxable income if that income was between $0 and $20,350. If the taxable income was between $20,350 and $49,300, then the tax was $3052.50 plus 28% of the amount over $20,350. Use this information in problems 15 and 16.

15. Mabelle was single and had a taxable income of $25,850. How much was her estimated income tax?

16. Bob was single and had a taxable income of $9500. What was his estimated income tax?

C. 17. An article selling for $200 was discounted 20%.

(a) What was the amount of the deduction?

(b) What was the final cost after the discount?

(c) If the sales tax was 5%, what was the final cost after the discount and including the sales tax?

18. A Sealy mattress sells regularly for $240. It is offered on sale at 50% off.

(a) What is the amount of the discount?

(b) What is the price after the discount?

(c) If the sales tax rate is 6%, what is the total price of the mattress after the discount and including the sales tax?

19. A jewelry store is selling rings at a 25% discount. If the original price of a ring was $500:

(a) What is the amount of the discount?

(b) What is the price of the ring after the discount?

20. If you have a Magic Kingdom Club Card from Disneyland, Howard Johnson's offers a 10% discount on double rooms. A family stayed at Howard Johnson's for 4 days. The rate per day was $45.

(a) What was the price of the room for the 4 days?

(b) What was the amount of the discount?

(c) If the sales tax rate was 6%, what was the total bill?

21. Some oil companies are offering a 5% discount on the gasoline you buy if you pay cash. Anita Gonzalez filled her gas tank, and the pump registered $14.20.
    (a) If she paid cash, what was the amount of her discount?
    (b) What did she pay after her discount?

22. U-Mart had bicycles selling regularly for $120. The bicycles were put on sale at 20% off. The manager found that some of the bicycles were dented or scratched, and offered an additional 10% discount.
    (a) What was the price of a dented bicycle after the two discounts? (Careful! This is not a 30% discount, but 20%, followed by 10%.)
    (b) Would it be better to take the 20% discount followed by the 10% discount, or to take a single 28% discount?

D. In problems 23–26, use Table 12.1 to find the final accumulated amount and the total interest if interest is compounded annually. (Answers to nearest five digits.)

23. $100 at 6% for 8 years

24. $1000 at 9% for 11 years

25. $2580 at 12% for 9 years

26. $6230 at 11% for 12 years

In problems 27–32, use Table 12.1 to find the final accumulated amount and the total interest. (Give answers to the same number of digits as the table entry.)

27. $12,000 at 10% compounded semiannually for 8 years

28. $15,000 at 14% compounded semiannually for 10 years

29. $20,000 at 8% compounded quarterly for 3 years

30. $30,000 at 12% compounded quarterly for 4 years

31. $40,000 at 20% compounded semiannually for 24 years

32. $50,000 at 16% compounded semiannually for 15 years

33. When a child is born, grandparents sometimes deposit a certain amount of money that can be used to send the child to college. Mary and John Glendale deposited $1000 when their granddaughter Anna was born. The account was paying 6% compounded annually.
    (a) How much money will there be in the account when Anna becomes 18 years old?
    (b) How much money would there be in the account after 18 years if the interest had been compounded semiannually?

34. When Natasha was born, her mother deposited $100 in an account paying 6% compounded annually. After 10 years, the money was transferred into another account paying 10% compounded semiannually.
    (a) How much money was in the account after the first 10 years?
    (b) How much money was in the account at the end of 18 years? (Give answers to the nearest cent.)

35. Jack loaned Janie $3000. She promised to repay the $3000 plus interest at 10% compounded annually at the end of 3 years.
    (a) How much did she have to pay Jack at the end of 3 years?
    (b) How much interest did she pay?

36. Bank *A* pays 8% interest compounded quarterly, while bank *B* pays 10% compounded semiannually. If $1000 was deposited in each bank, how much money would there be at the end of 5 years in the:
    (a) Bank *A* account?   (b) Bank *B* account?
    (c) In which bank would you deposit your money?

37. How much more would there be at the end of 5 years if $1000 were invested at 12% compounded quarterly rather than semiannually?

38. Suppose you can invest $1000 in a fund that pays 6% compounded annually or into a fund that pays 6.5% annually, but does not reinvest the interest. How long would it be before the accumulated interest in the first fund exceeds the total interest paid out by the second fund? Make a table to show what happens and explain.

In Other Words

39. Discuss the difference between simple and compound interest.

40. If you increase the price of a product by 10% and then decrease that price by 10%, would the new price be the same as the original price? Explain.

Using Your Knowledge

*You may have noticed banks advertising various **effective** annual interest rates. Do you know what an effective annual interest rate is? It is the simple interest rate that would result in the same total amount of interest as the compound rate yields in 1 year. For example, if interest is at 6% compounded quarterly, then a table shows that a $1 deposit would accumulate to $1.0614 in 1 year. (Use $n = 4$ and a periodic rate of $1\frac{1}{2}\%$; see Table 12.3.) Thus, the interest is $0.0614 and, because the initial deposit is $1, the effective annual rate is 0.0614, or 6.14%.*

You can see now that an easy way to find the effective annual rate is to look in a table for the accumulated amount of $1. If the nominal rate is r% *and interest is compounded* k *times a year, then you will find the required entry by going down the column under* n *until you come to* k *and then across to the column under* r/k%. *By subtracting 1 from this entry, you obtain the desired effective rate. Tables 12.2, 12.3, and 12.4 give some selected values from compound interest rates.*

Table 12.2 *Accumulated Amount of $1 for* n *Periods*

Periodic Rate	3%	$4\frac{1}{2}\%$	6%	$7\frac{1}{2}\%$	9%
$n = 2$	1.0609	1.0920	1.1236	1.1556	1.1881

Table 12.3 *Accumulated Amount of $1 for n Periods*

Periodic Rate	$1\frac{1}{4}$%	$1\frac{1}{2}$%	$1\frac{3}{4}$%	2%	$2\frac{1}{4}$%
$n = 4$	1.0509	1.0614	1.0719	1.0824	1.0931

Table 12.4 *Accumulated Amount of $1 for n Periods*

Periodic Rate	$\frac{1}{2}$%	$\frac{3}{4}$%	1%	$1\frac{1}{4}$%	$1\frac{1}{2}$%
$n = 12$	1.0617	1.0938	1.1268	1.1607	1.1956

Find the effective annual rate for each of the following:

41. 6%, compounded semiannually
42. 6%, compounded monthly
43. 8%, compounded quarterly
44. 12%, compounded monthly

45. 9%, compounded quarterly
46. 15%, compounded semiannually
47. 18%, compounded monthly
48. 15%, compounded monthly

Calculator Corner

What happens if you do not have Table 12.1? Use a calculator, of course. If your calculator has a $\boxed{y^x}$ key (a power key), then the quantity $(1.06)^{20}$ can be obtained by pressing

$$\boxed{1}\;\boxed{.}\;\boxed{0}\;\boxed{6}\;\boxed{y^x}\;\boxed{2}\;\boxed{0}\;\boxed{=}$$

This time the accumulated amount is given to nine decimal places!

12.2 CONSUMER CREDIT

GETTING STARTED

EVERYTHING YOU ALWAYS WANTED TO KNOW ABOUT CREDIT CARDS

Do you have a credit card or are you planning to get one soon? You can save money if you know the **interest rate** (the percent you pay on the card balance), the **annual fee** (the amount paid for the privilege of having the card), and the **grace period** (the interest-free period between purchases and billing given to consumers who pay off their balances entirely) on your cards. The interest rate can be **fixed** or **variable** (dependent on the amount you owe or some standard such as the **prime rate**, the rate banks charge their best customers). How can you save money? First, you can get a card with no annual fee for a savings of $20 to $50. Next, you can eliminate interest payments by paying off your entire balance each month. Note that if a balance of *any amount* is carried over from the previous month, most banks will charge interest from the date of each new purchase, even *before* the monthly statement arrives.

The type of card you should have to maximize savings depends on your monthly balance. If you plan to pay your balance in full each month, the annual fee is the largest expense. Get a card with no annual fee and the longest grace period available. If you plan to have a high monthly balance, choose a card with a low interest rate. (For example, if your average balance is $1000, you will pay $180 annually on an 18% card but only $120 on a 12% card, a potential savings of $180 − $120, or $60.) Now, suppose you already have a credit card. How can you decide your best course of action? Follow these steps:

1. Find the annual fee and interest rate on your card.

2. Look at your past statements and find your average monthly balance.

3. Figure your annual cost by multiplying the interest rate by the monthly balance and add the annual fee.

Here is an example. Suppose you have a card with a $25 annual fee and an 18% interest rate. If the average monthly balance on your card is $500 and you can get a card with a 14% interest rate and no annual fee, you will be saving 4% of $500 or $20 in interest and the $25 annual fee, a total of $45. On the other hand, if your annual fee is $20 and your interest rate is 14%, changing to another card with no annual fee and 19% interest makes no sense. (You pay 14% of $500, or $70, plus the $20 fee, $90 in all with the first card and 19% of $500 or $95 with the other.) How do you find the interest rate and annual fee on credit cards? Find a consumer magazine or an organization (such as BankCard Holders of America) that publishes the latest information regarding annual fees and interest rates for credit cards.

To obtain a credit card, you have to meet requirements set by the institution that issues the card. These requirements will vary but are illustrated in the following example.

Company *A* will issue a credit card to an applicant that meets the following requirements:

1. The applicant must have a good credit rating*.

2. If single, the applicant must have a gross annual income of at least $30,000.

3. If married, the couple's combined gross annual income must be at least $40,000.

---

* Your credit rating is usually determined by a credit bureau, an organization that tracks the history of an individual's spending and repayment habits.

EXAMPLE 1 Using the above requirements, determine which of the following applicants qualifies for a credit card from company A.

(a) Annie Jones is single, has a good credit rating, and earns $25,000 per year.

(b) John Smith has an excellent credit rating, and earns $35,000 per year. His wife has no paying job.

(c) Don and Daryl Barnes each earn $24,000 per year and have a good credit rating.

(d) Bill Spender is single, earns $40,000 per year, and has only a fair credit rating.

Solution Only Don and Daryl Barnes meet the requirements of company A. They have a good credit rating and their combined annual income is $48,000. ∎

As we have mentioned, one of the costs associated with credit cards is the **finance charge** that is collected if you decide to pay for your purchases later than the allowed payment (grace) period. Usually, if the entire balance is paid within a certain time (25–30 days), there is no charge. However, if you want more time, then you will have to pay the finance charge computed at the rate printed on the monthly statement you receive from the company issuing the card. Figure 12.1 shows the top portion of such a statement. As you can see, the periodic rate (monthly) is 1.5%. This rate is used to calculate the charge on $600. Where does the $600 come from? The back of the statement indicates that "The Finance Charge is computed on the Average Daily Balance, which is

FIGURE 12.1

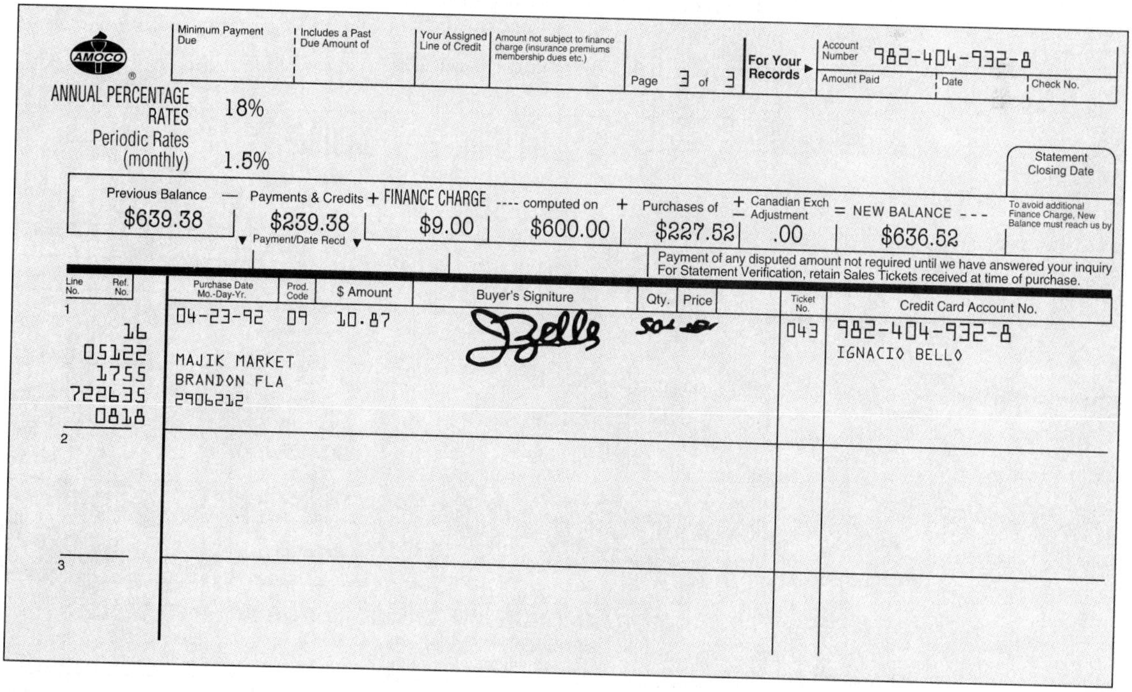

the sum of the Daily Balances divided by the number of days in the Billing Period." Fortunately, the computer calculated this average daily balance and came out with the correct amount. In Example 2, we shall verify only the finance charge.

EXAMPLE 2   Find the finance charge (interest) to be paid on the statement in Figure 12.1 if the monthly rate is 1.5% computed on the average daily balance of $600.

Solution   The finance charge is 1.5% of $600, that is,

$$0.015 \times \$600 = \$9.00$$
∎

Next, let us look at a different problem. Suppose you wish to obtain a credit card. First, you have to make an application to the issuing bank for such a card. If your application is accepted, then you must pay a fee. (Some credit unions and banks issue cards free.) After some time, the card finally arrives in the mail. Now, suppose you wish to use your card at a restaurant where these cards are accepted. Instead of collecting cash, the cashier will place your card in a stamping machine that will print on a receipt certain information that is on the card: the card number, your name, and the expiration date of the card; it will also print the name and identification numbers of the restaurant as well as the date of the transaction. The cashier will then write the amount of the purchase on the receipt and add the applicable tax. You will sign the receipt and be given a copy for your records. Figure 12.2 shows such a receipt.

At the end of the billing period, a statement is sent to you. If the balance due is $10 or less, you must pay the account *in full*. Otherwise, you must make a minimum payment of $10 or 5% of the balance due, *whichever is greater*. (Terms vary from one bank to another.)

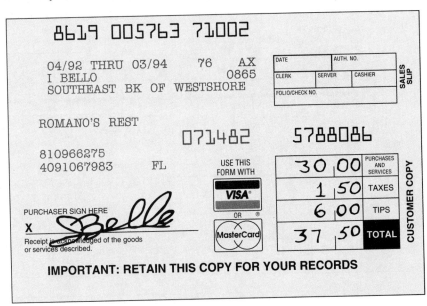

FIGURE 12.2

EXAMPLE 3   The customer who signed the receipt in Figure 12.2 received a statement at the end of the month. The new balance was listed as $37.50. Find:

(a) The minimum payment due
(b) The finance charge that will be due the next month if only the minimum payment is made now

Solution   (a) Because the new balance is $37.50 and 5% of $37.50 is $1.875, the minimum payment is $10. (Remember, you pay $10 or 5% of the new balance, whichever is greater.)

(b) After paying the $10, the customer's new balance is

$$\$37.50 - \$10 = \$27.50$$

The finance charge is 1.5% of $27.50, or

$$0.015 \times 27.50 = \$0.4125$$

Thus, if no additional credit card purchases are made, the finance charge will be $0.41.

◼

Many large department stores prefer to handle their own credit card business and therefore do not accept bank credit cards. This procedure offers two main advantages to the stores:

1. The stores save the commission on sales that the national credit card companies charge for their services.
2. The interest (finance charges) collected from their customers is a welcome source of revenue to the stores.

Most charge accounts at department stores are called **revolving charge accounts**. Although the operational procedure of these accounts is similar to that employed by the national credit card companies, there may be some differences between them.

1. The interest for revolving charge accounts is $1\frac{1}{2}$% per month on the unpaid balance for balances under $500. If the balance is over $500, some accounts charge only 1% interest per month on the amount over $500.
2. The minimum monthly payment may be established by the department store, and it may or may not be similar to that of the national credit card companies.

EXAMPLE 4   Mary Lewis received her statement from Sears, where she has a revolving charge account. Her previous balance was $225.59, and she charged an additional $18.72 to her account. Find:

(a) The finance charge for the month (Sears charges interest on the average daily balance as described in the form shown in Figure 12.3 on the following page.)
(b) The new balance
(c) The minimum monthly payment

Sears | REVOLVING CHARGE ACCOUNT

SEARS, ROEBUCK AND CO.

Please return this portion with your payment. You may pay at any Sears Store, or by mail. **Please allow 5 days to assure processing by the Billing Date.**

Please mention this number when ordering or writing.

97 11234 56789 7

MS MARY LEWIS
1234 MAIN ST
ANYWHERE IL 60606

Amount Due

INSTAL.PMT.   NONE DUE

NEW BALANCE

$ _____
AMOUNT PAID

PLEASE DIRECT INQUIRIES TO YOUR NEAREST SEARS STORE AND REFER TO THIS STATEMENT WHEN MAKING AN INQUIRY.

DATE Mo. Day	Reference Number	TRANSACTION DESCRIPTION See reverse side for a more detailed description of the department numbers indicated below.	CHARGES	PAYMENTS AND CREDITS
		FINANCE CHARGE ON AVG DAILY BAL OF $222.99	3.34	
0608	TPBT	MENS WORK & SPORTSWEAR 41	18.72	

ACCOUNT NUMBER	BILLING DATE	PREVIOUS BALANCE	NEW BALANCE	MINIMUM PAYMENT
97 11234 56789 7	JULY 06 1992	$ 225.59	$	$

If the *FINANCE CHARGE* exceeds 50¢, the *ANNUAL PERCENTAGE RATE* is 18% of the AVERAGE DAILY BALANCE excluding any purchases added during the monthly billing period and excluding any unpaid Finance Charge.

To avoid a Finance Charge next month, pay this amount within 30 days from Billing Date.

If you prefer to pay in installments, pay this amount or more within 30 days from Billing Date. The sooner you pay and the more you pay, the smaller your Finance Charge.

NOTICE: See reverse side for important information.

Thank You for Shopping at Sears

14351-610 Rev. 7/74

R

On a Sears Revolving Charge Account your monthly payments decrease as your account balance decreases . . . and, likewise your monthly payments increases as your account balance increases. Payments are flexible with your balance, as shown on the table below. Any premiums for Group Insurance, for which you may have contracted, other than Accidental Death and Disability Insurance, are in addition to your minimum monthly payments.

New Balance	Minimum Payment
$ .01 to $ 10.00	Balance
10.01 to 200.00	$10.00
200.01 to 250.00	15.00
250.01 to 300.00	20.00
300.01 to 350.00	25.00
350.01 to 400.00	30.00
400.01 to 450.00	35.00
450.01 to 500.00	40.00
Over $500.00	1/10 of New Bal.

FIGURE 12.3

Courtesy of Sears, Roebuck and Co.

Solution   (a) Since the average daily balance was $222.99, the finance
charge is $1\frac{1}{2}\%$ (18% annual rate) of the $222.99, that is,

$$0.015 \times \$222.99 = \$3.34$$

(b) The new balance is calculated as follows:

Previous balance	$225.59
Finance charge	3.34
New purchases	18.72
New balance	$247.65

(c) The minimum monthly payment is found by using the
information given at the bottom of Figure 12.3. (This is a
copy of the table that appears on the back of the statement.)
Because the new balance is between $200.01 and $250, the
minimum payment is $15.   ■

Some stores charge interest on the unpaid balance. How do we find the
new balance under this method? The next example will tell you.

EXAMPLE 5   Ms. Spoto received a statement from a department store where she has a
charge account. Her previous balance was $280. She made a $20 payment and
charged an additional $30.12 to her account. If the store charges 1.5% of the
unpaid balance, find:

(a) The finance charge
(b) The new balance

Solution   (a) The unpaid balance is $280 − $20 = $260, so the finance
charge is 1.5% of $260, which is $0.015 \times 260 = \$3.90$.

(b) The new balance is computed as follows:

Unpaid balance	$260.00
Finance charge	3.90
Purchases	30.12
New balance	$294.02

                                                                           ■

There is another way of charging interest when consumers buy on credit,
the **add-on interest** used by furniture stores, appliance stores, and car dealers.
For example, suppose you wish to buy some furniture costing $2500 and you
make a $500 down payment. The amount to be financed is $2000. If the store
charges a 10% add-on rate for 5 years (60 monthly payments), the interest will
be

$$I = Prt$$
$$= \$2000 \times 0.10 \times 5 = \$1000$$

Thus, the total amount to be paid is $2000 + $1000 = $3000. The monthly payment is found by dividing this total by the number of payments:

$$\text{Monthly payment} = \frac{\$3000}{60} = \$50$$

Note that the add-on interest is charged on the *entire* $2000 for the 5 years, but the customer does *not* have the full use of the entire amount for the 5 years. It would be fairer to charge interest on the *unpaid balance only*.

EXAMPLE 6   A used car costing $8500 can be bought with $2500 down and a 12% add-on interest rate to be paid in 48 monthly installments. Find:

(a) The total interest charged
(b) The monthly payment

Solution   (a) The amount to be financed is $8500 − $2500 = $6000. The interest is 12% of $6000 for 4 years. Thus,

$$\text{Interest} = 0.12 \times \$6000 \times 4 = \$2880$$

(b) Total amount owed = $6000 + $2880 = $8880

$$\text{Monthly payment} = \frac{\$8880}{48} = \$185$$

Exercise 12.2

1. Chad and Susan Johnson are married and have a good credit rating. Chad earns $25,000 per year. What is the least that Susan must earn for the couple to qualify for a card from Company A? (See Example 1.)

2. Jim and Alice Brown are married and have an excellent credit rating. They both work and earn the same salaries. What is the least that each salary must be for the Browns to qualify for a card from Company A? (See Example 1.)

In problems 3–7, find the new balance, assuming that the bank charges $1\frac{1}{2}\%$ per month on the unpaid balance.

	Previous Balance	Payment	New Purchases
3.	$100	$ 10	$50
4.	$300	$190	$25
5.	$134.39	$ 25	$73.98
6.	$145.96	$ 55	$44.97
7.	$378.93	$ 75	$248.99

In problems 8–17, (a) find the finance charge for the month, (b) the new balance, and (c) the minimum monthly payment using the following rates and payments table.

Monthly Rate	Unpaid Balance	New Balance	Minimum Payment
$1\frac{1}{2}\%$	Up to $500	Under $200	$10
1%	Over $500	Over $200	5% of new balance

	Previous Balance	New Purchases		Previous Balance	New Purchases
8.	$50.40	$173	9.	$85	$150
10.	$154	$75	11.	$344	$60
12.	$666.80	$53.49	13.	$80.45	$98.73
14.	$34.97	$50	15.	$55.90	$35.99
16.	$98.56	$45.01	17.	$34.76	$87.53

18. Phyllis Phillips has a revolving charge account that charges a finance charge on the unpaid balance using the following schedule:

$1\frac{1}{2}\%$ per month of that portion of the balance up to $300
1% per month on that portion of the balance over $300

If the previous month's balance was $685, find the finance charge.

19. Daisy Rose has a credit card that charges a finance charge on the previous balance according to the following schedule:

2% per month on balances up to $100
$1\frac{1}{2}\%$ per month on balances between $100 and $200
1% per month on balances of $200 or over

If the previous month's balance was $190, find the finance charge.

20. Mr. Dan Dapper received a statement from his clothing store showing a finance charge of $1.50 on a previous balance of $100. Find the monthly finance charge rate.

21. Paul Peters received a statement from the ABC Department Store showing a previous balance of $90. If the ABC store's finance charges are 1.5% on the previous balance, find the finance charge for the month.

22. In problem 21, if the monthly rate were 1.25%, what would be the finance charge for the month?

23. A $9000 car can be purchased with $1600 down, the balance plus a 9% add-on interest rate to be paid in 36 monthly installments. Find:
(a) The total interest charged
(b) The monthly payment, rounded to the nearest dollar

24. The Ortegas move into their first apartment and decide to buy furniture priced at $400 with $40 down, the balance plus 10% add-on interest to be paid in monthly installments in 1 year. Find:
    (a) The total interest charged

    (b) The monthly payment

25. Wayne Sierpinski wishes to buy a stove and a refrigerator from an appliance dealer. The cost of the two items is $2400, and Wayne pays $400 down and finances the balance at 15% add-on interest to be paid in 18 monthly installments. Find:
    (a) The total interest charged
    (b) The monthly payment, to the nearest dollar

26. Bill Seeker bought a boat costing $8500 with $1500 down, the balance plus add-on interest to be paid in 36 monthly installments. If the add-on interest rate was 18%, find:
    (a) The total interest charged
    (b) The monthly payment, to the nearest dollar

27. Felicia Johnson bought a freezer costing $500 on the following terms: $100 down and the balance plus a 10% add-on interest rate to be paid in 18 monthly installments. Find:
    (a) The total interest to be paid by Ms. Johnson
    (b) The amount of her monthly payment, to the nearest dollar

28. Cissie owes $1000 to a department store that charges a monthly interest rate of 1.5% on the unpaid balance.
    (i) Cissie considers paying off this debt at the rate of $200 at the end of each month for 5 months and then paying off the balance at the end of the 6th month.
    (ii) She also considers making payments of $200 plus the month's interest at the end of each month for 5 months.

    Make a table showing the monthly payments and the interest under each scheme. How much would Cissie save by using her second scheme? How do you account for this savings? Explain fully.

In Other Words

29. An article in *Money* magazine states, "If you pay in full each month, you can get the most from the grace period by making big credit purchases just after your statement closing date and paying your bill on time at the last minute." Explain why.

30. The same article says to "buy bigger ticket items toward the end of the billing cycle and pay as much of the bill as possible as soon as you get your bill." Explain why.

Using Your Knowledge

A table shows that a monthly payment of $61 (to the nearest dollar) for 18 months will repay $1000 with interest at 1% per month on the unpaid balance. Can we find the equivalent add-on interest rate? Yes; here is how to do it. Eighteen payments of $61 make a total of $1098 (18 × $61), which shows that the total interest paid is $98. Since this is the interest for 18 months ($1\frac{1}{2}$, or $\frac{3}{2}$, years), the equivalent add-on interest rate is

$$\frac{98}{(1000)(\frac{3}{2})} = \frac{98}{1500} = 0.065$$

or 6.5%, to the nearest tenth of a percent.

A table shows that the following monthly installment payments will repay $1000 in the stated term and at the stated rate of interest on the unpaid balance. Find the equivalent add-on interest rate to the nearest tenth of a percent.

	Monthly Payment	Term	Rate per Month on Unpaid Balance
31.	$47	2 years	1%
32.	$64	18 months	$1\frac{1}{2}\%$
33.	$50	2 years	$1\frac{1}{2}\%$
34.	$48	2 years	$1\frac{1}{4}\%$

12.3 ANNUAL PERCENTAGE RATE (APR) AND THE RULE OF 78

GETTING STARTED

TRUTH-IN-LENDING: APR TO Z

In the preceding section we studied several types of consumer credit: credit cards, revolving charges, and add-on interest. Before 1969, it was almost impossible to compare the different types of credit accounts available to consumers. In an effort to standardize the credit industry, the government enacted the federal Truth-in-Lending Act of 1969. A key feature of this law is the inclusion of the **total payment,** the **amount financed,** and the **finance charges** in credit contracts. In conjunction with this law, the Board of Governors of the Federal Reserve System issued Regulation Z requiring all lenders who make consumer loans to disclose certain information regarding the cost of consumer credit.

How can we compare loans? To do so, two items are of crucial importance: the **finance charge** and the **annual percentage rate** (APR). A look at annual percentage rates will enable us to compare different credit options. For example, suppose you can borrow $200 for a year at 8% add-on, or get the same $200 by paying $17.95 each month. Which is the better deal? In the first instance, you borrow $200 at 8% add-on, which means that you pay 8% of $200 or $16 in finance charges. The charge you pay per $100 financed is: $\frac{16}{200} \times 100 = \$8$. On the other hand, if you pay $17.95 per month for 12 months, you pay a total of $215.40. Here the finance charge per $100 financed is: $\frac{15.40}{200} \times 100 = \$7.70$. Obviously, the second loan is a better deal. Can we find the APR for each loan? To help in doing so, tables have been prepared so that we can translate the finance charge per $100 to the APR. (See Table 12.5 that follows.) In this section we shall discuss the APR and one of the methods that will enable you to get a refund on your interest in case you decide to pay off your loan early.

As you have seen in Sections 12.1 and 12.2, there are many ways of stating the interest rates used to compute credit costs. A few examples are 12% *simple interest,* 12% *compounded annually,* 12% *add-on interest,* and 1% *per month on the unpaid balance.* How can you compare various credit costs? Without some help, it is difficult to do this. In response, Congress enacted the Truth-in-Lending Act on July 1, 1969. This law helps the consumer to know exactly what credit costs. Under this law, all sellers (car dealers, banks, credit card companies, and so on) must disclose to the consumer two items:

1. The finance charge
2. The *annual percentage rate* (APR)

A. *APR*

Recall that the finance charge is the total dollar amount you are charged for credit. It includes interest and other charges such as service charges, loan and finder's fees, credit-related insurance, and appraisal fees. The **annual percentage rate (APR)** is the charge for credit stated as a percent.

Table 12.5 *True Annual Interest Rate (APR)*

Number of Payments	14%	14½%	15%	15½%	16%	16½%	17%	17½%	18%
6	$ 4.12	$ 4.27	$ 4.42	$ 4.57	$ 4.72	$ 4.87	$ 5.02	$ 5.17	$ 5.32
12	7.74	8.03	8.31	8.59	8.88	9.16	9.45	9.73	10.02
18	11.45	11.87	12.29	12.72	13.14	13.57	13.99	14.42	14.85
24	15.23	15.80	16.37	16.94	17.51	18.09	18.66	19.24	19.82
30	19.10	19.81	20.54	21.26	21.99	22.72	23.45	24.18	24.92
36	23.04	23.92	24.80	25.68	26.57	27.46	28.35	29.25	30.15
42	27.06	28.10	29.15	30.19	31.25	32.31	33.37	34.44	35.51
48	31.17	32.37	33.59	34.81	36.03	37.27	38.50	39.75	41.00

Note: Numbers in body of table are finance charges per $100 of amount financed.

In general, the lowest APR corresponds to the best credit buy, regardless of the amount borrowed or the period of time for repayment. For example, suppose you borrow $100 for a year and pay a finance charge of $8. If you keep the entire $100 for the whole year and then pay $108 all at one time, then you are paying an APR of 8%. On the other hand, if you repay the $100 plus the $8 finance charge in 12 equal monthly payments (8% add-on), you do not really have the use of the $100 for the whole year. What, in this case, is your APR? The formulas needed to compute the APR are rather complicated, and as a consequence, tables such as Table 12.5 have been constructed to help you find the APR. These tables are based on the cost per $100 of the amount financed. To use Table 12.5, you must first find the finance charge per $1 of the amount financed and then multiply by 100. Thus, to find the APR on the $100 borrowed at 8% add-on interest and repaid in 12 equal payments of $9, we first find the finance charge per $100 as follows:

1. The finance charge is $108 − $100 = $8

2. The charge per $100 financed is

$$\frac{\text{Finance charge}}{\text{Amount financed}} \times 100 = \frac{\$8}{\$100} \times 100 = \$8$$

Since there are 12 payments, we look across the row labeled 12 in Table 12.5 until we find the number closest to $8. This number is $8.03. We then read the heading of the column in which the $8.03 appears to obtain the APR. In our case, the heading is $14\frac{1}{2}\%$. Thus, the 8% add-on rate is equivalent to a $14\frac{1}{2}\%$ APR. (Of course, Table 12.5 will give the APR only to the nearest $\frac{1}{2}\%$.)

EXAMPLE 1 Mary Lewis bought some furniture that cost $1400. She paid $200 down and agreed to pay the balance in 30 monthly installments of $48.80 each. What was the APR for her purchase?

Solution We first find the finance charge per $100 as follows:

Payments:	30 × 48.80 = $1464
Amount financed:	−1200
Finance charge:	$ 264

Finance charge per $100: $\dfrac{\$264}{\$1200} \times 100 = \$22$

We now turn to Table 12.5 and read across the row labeled 30 (the number of payments) until we find the number closest to $22. This number is $21.99. We then read the column heading to obtain the APR, 16%. ∎

B. *The Rule of 78*

In all the preceding examples, we have assumed that the consumer will faithfully make the payments until the debt is satisfied. But what if you wish to pay in full before the final due date? (Perhaps your rich aunt gave you some money.) In many cases, you are entitled to a partial refund of the finance charge! The problem is to find how much you should get back. One way of calculating the refund is to use the **rule of 78**. This rule assumes that the final payment includes a portion, say, a, of the finance charge, the payment before that includes $2a$ of the finance charge, the second from the final payment includes $3a$ of the finance charge, and so on. If the total number of payments is 12, then the finance charge is paid off by the sum of $a + 2a + 3a + 4a + 5a + 6a + 7a + 8a + 9a + 10a + 11a + 12a = 78a$ dollars. If the finance charge is F, then we see that

$$78a = F$$

so $a = \frac{1}{78}F$. This is the reason for the name, "rule of 78". Now, suppose you borrow $1000 for 1 year at 8% add-on interest. The interest is $80, and the monthly payment is one-twelfth of $1080, that is, $90. If you wish to pay off the loan at the end of 6 months, are you entitled to a refund of half of the $80 interest charge? Not according to the rule of 78. Your remaining finance charge payments, according to this rule, are

$$\tfrac{1}{78}F + \tfrac{2}{78}F + \tfrac{3}{78}F + \tfrac{4}{78}F + \tfrac{5}{78}F + \tfrac{6}{78}F = \tfrac{21}{78}F$$

Since $F = \$80$, you are entitled to a refund of $\frac{21}{78} \times 80$, or $21.54. There are six payments of $90 each for a total of $540, so you would need to pay $540 − $21.54 = $518.46 to cover the balance of the loan.

Notice that to obtain the numerator of the fraction $\frac{21}{78}$, we had to add $1 + 2 + 3 + 4 + 5 + 6$. If there were n payments remaining, then to find the numerator we would have to add

$$1 + 2 + 3 + \cdots + (n - 2) + (n - 1) + n$$

There is an easy way to do this. Let us call the sum S. Then we can write S twice, once forwards and once backwards:

$$S = 1 + \quad 2 \quad + \quad 3 \quad + \cdots + (n - 2) + (n - 1) + n$$
$$S = n + (n - 1) + (n - 2) + \cdots + \quad 3 \quad + \quad 2 \quad + 1$$

If we add these two lines, we get

$$2S = (n + 1) + (n + 1) + (n + 1) + \cdots + (n + 1) + (n + 1) + (n + 1)$$

and, because there are n terms on the right,

$$2S = n(n + 1)$$
$$S = \frac{n(n + 1)}{2}$$

Thus, for $n = 6$, we obtain

$$S = \frac{6 \times (6 + 1)}{2} = \frac{6 \times 7}{2} = 21$$

as before. For $n = 12$, we find $S = (12 \times 13)/2 = 78$, which again agrees with our previous result.

Now suppose the loan is for 15 months, and you wish to pay off in full after 10 payments, so that there are 5 payments remaining. By arguing in the same way as for the 12-month loan, you can see that you are entitled to a refund of a fraction a/b of the finance charge, where the numerator is

$$a = 1 + 2 + 3 + 4 + 5 = \frac{5 \times 6}{2} = 15$$

and the denominator is

$$b = 1 + 2 + 3 + \cdots + 15 = \frac{15 \times 16}{2} = 120$$

Thus, you are entitled to $\frac{15}{120} = \frac{1}{8}$ of the total finance charge.

In general, if the loan calls for a total of n payments and the loan is paid off with r payments remaining, then the unearned interest is a fraction a/b of the total finance charge, with the numerator

$$a = 1 + 2 + 3 + \cdots + r = \frac{r(r + 1)}{2}$$

and the denominator

$$b = 1 + 2 + 3 + \cdots + n = \frac{n(n + 1)}{2}$$

Thus,

$$\frac{a}{b} = \frac{r(r + 1)}{n(n + 1)} \quad \text{The 2's cancel.}$$

and the unearned interest is given by

$$\frac{r(r + 1)}{n(n + 1)} \times F$$

where F is the finance charge. For example, if an 18-month loan is paid off with 6 payments remaining, the amount of unearned interest is

$$\frac{6 \times 7}{18 \times 19} \times F = \frac{7}{57}F$$

Although the denominator is no longer 78 (except for a 12-payment loan), the rule is still called the rule of 78.

EXAMPLE 2   Cal Olleb purchased a television set on a 15-month installment plan that included a $60 finance charge and called for payments of $25 monthly. If Cal decided to pay off the loan at the end of the eighth month, find:

(a) The amount of the interest refund using the rule of 78
(b) The amount needed to pay off the loan

Solution   (a) Here, $n = 15$ and $r = 7$. We substitute into the formula to obtain

$$\frac{7 \times 8}{15 \times 16} \times \$60 = \frac{7}{30} \times \$60 = \$14$$

(b) There are 7 payments of $25 each left, that is, $175. Thus, Cal needs

$$\$175 - \$14 = \$161$$

to pay off the loan.   ∎

Exercise 12.3

A. In problems 1–10, find the APR.

	Amount Financed	Finance Charge	Number of Payments
1.	$2500	$194	12
2.	$2000	$166	12
3.	$1500	$264	24
4.	$3500	$675	24
5.	$1500	$210	18
6.	$4500	$1364	36
7.	$4500	$1570	48
8.	$4000	$170.80	6
9.	$5000	$1800	48
10.	$4000	$908.80	30

B. In problems 11–15, find the unearned finance charge and the amount needed to pay off the loan.

	Finance Charge	Number of Payments	Frequency	Amount	Number of Payments Remaining
11.	$15.60	12	Monthly	$25	4
12.	$23.40	12	Monthly	$35	5
13.	$31.20	12	Monthly	$45	6
14.	$52.00	18	Weekly	$10	9
15.	$58.50	20	Weekly	$10	5

16. Alfreda Brown bought a car costing $6500 with $500 down and the rest to be paid in 48 equal installments of $173.
    (a) What was the finance charge?
    (b) What was the APR?

17. Gerardo Norega bought a dinette set for $300, which he paid in 12 monthly payments of $27.
    (a) What was the finance charge?
    (b) What was the APR on this sale?

18. Yu-Feng Liang bought a car for $6500. He made a down payment of $1000 and paid off the balance in 48 monthly payments of $159 each.
    (a) What was the finance charge?
    (b) What was the APR?

19. A used sailboat is selling for $1500. The owner wants $500 down and 18 monthly payments of $63.
    (a) What finance charge does the owner have in mind?
    (b) What is the APR for this transaction?

20. Natasha Gagarin paid $195 interest on a $2000 purchase. If she made 12 equal monthly payments to pay off the account, what was the APR for this purchase?

21. Virginia Osterman bought a television set on a 12-month installment plan that included a $31.20 finance charge and called for payments of $50 per month. If she decided to pay the full balance at the end of the eighth month, find:
    (a) The interest refund
    (b) The amount needed to pay off the loan

22. Marie Siciliano bought a washing machine on a 12-month installment plan that included a finance charge of $46.80 and called for a monthly payment of $70. If Marie wanted to pay off the loan after 7 months, find:
    (a) The interest refund
    (b) The amount needed to pay off the loan

23. A couple buys furniture priced at $800 with $80 down and the balance to be paid at 10% add-on interest. If the loan is to be repaid in 12 equal monthly payments, find:
    (a) The finance charge   (b) The monthly payment
    (c) The interest refund if they decide to pay off the loan after 8 months
    (d) The amount needed to pay off the loan

24. Dan Leizack is buying a video recorder that costs $1200. He paid $200 down and financed the balance at 15% add-on interest to be repaid in 18 monthly payments. Find:
    (a) The finance charge   (b) The monthly payment
    (c) The interest refund if he pays off the loan after 9 months
    (d) The amount needed to pay off the loan

25. Joe Clemente bought a stereo costing $1000 with $200 down and 10% add-on interest to be paid in 18 equal monthly installments. Find:
    (a) The finance charge   (b) The monthly payment
    (c) The interest refund if he pays off the loan after 15 months
    (d) The amount needed to pay off the loan

*I*n Other Words

26. Do you think the rule of 78 gives the debtor a fair break? In your own words, explain why or why not.

Using Your Knowledge

Approximating the APR by formula

The APR for the loans just discussed can also be approximated (however, not within the $\frac{1}{4}$ of 1% accuracy required by Regulation Z*) by using the following formula:

$$\text{APR} = \frac{2mI}{P(n+1)}$$

Where

  m is the number of payment periods per year,
  I is the interest (or finance charge),
  P is the principal (amount financed), and
  n is the number of periodic payments to be made.

Thus, in Example 1, m = 12, I = $264, P = $1200, n = 30, *and*

$$\text{APR} = \frac{2mI}{P(n+1)} = \frac{2 \times 12 \times 264}{1200 \times 31} = 17\%$$

In problems 27–36, use the APR formula to find the APR in the specified problem. In each case, state the difference between the two answers.

27. problem 1   28. problem 2
29. problem 3   30. problem 4
31. problem 5   32. problem 6
33. problem 7   34. problem 8
35. problem 9   36. problem 10

---

*Regulation Z limits the use of this formula for approximating APRs to the "exceptional instance where circumstances may leave a creditor with no alternative."

12.4 BUYING A HOUSE

GETTING STARTED

HOUSES: HOW MUCH DOWN? HOW MUCH A MONTH?

As for most people, the single largest credit purchase (and investment) of your life will be buying a house. This purchase will require many decisions in what may be unfamiliar areas. In this section, we will try to help you make these decisions wisely. The first question is: how much house can you afford? Look at the rules at the top of the next page to figure this out. Next, what type of loans are available? See the discussion after Example 1 and in the Using Your Knowledge section of Exercise 12.4. The information there is accurate, except for the rates. What will be the difference in the monthly payment amount if the interest rate is 1 percent higher? From Table 12.6, shown later in this section, you can see that for each $1000 borrowed, the payment difference between a 7%, 30-year loan (first row, last column) and an 8% loan (third row, last column) is $7.32 − $6.64 = $0.68. Now, this does not seem like much, but if you are borrowing $100,000, the difference in payment will be $68! Can you figure out how much the payment difference per $1000 will be on a 30-year loan if the rate is lowered from 13% to 12%? (Current rates are about 9% lower than those appearing in the Using Your Knowledge section of Exercise 12.4.) Of course, your monthly payment should not be the only consideration when buying a house. You must consider the amount of **down payment** required, the **interest rate,** the number of **years taken to pay off** the loan, if there are any **penalties** for prepayment (paying the loan early), the **loan application fee** covering the cost of appraisal and credit report ($250–$300), and one of the most overlooked items when buying a home: the **closing costs.** These may include, but not be limited to, any or all of the following. **Points:** These are fees lenders charge to increase profits. **Each point is equivalent to 1% of the loan amount,** so if you are borrowing $80,000 and you are paying 1 point, you have to pay $800 at closing. **Loan origination fee:** Typically, this is 1% of the loan amount ($700 on a $70,000 loan).

Private Mortgage Insurance (PMI): Insurance is required if your down payment is less than 20% of the purchase price. Fees vary, but typically first year premiums are 1% of the loan amount for a 5% down payment, 0.4% with a 10% down payment, and 0.3% with a 15% down payment, plus a monthly fee. You must prepay the first year's premium at closing or can decide to make a lump sum payment of 2.95% of the mortgage amount if you put 10% down or 2.30% with a 15% down payment.

What else must be paid at closing? First monthly mortgage payment, title search and title insurance, property survey, deed recording, document preparation, homeowners insurance, prorated property taxes, and lawyers' fees. These expenses can add $2000–$4000 to the immediate price of the home. In this section you will learn more of the details!

Many home owners will say that buying a house is both a harrowing experience and a rewarding one at the same time

One of the first, if not the first, decision you must make when buying a house is how much to spend. Certain rules of thumb are sometimes used as guides in helping a family decide what price home to buy. Here are three such rules.

> 1. Spend no more than 2 to $2\frac{1}{2}$ times your annual income.
> 2. Limit housing expenses to 1 week's pay out of each month's gross pay (before deductions).
> 3. Do not let the amount of the monthly payment of principal, interest, taxes, and insurance exceed 28% of your monthly gross pay.

EXAMPLE 1

John and Pat Harrell earn $35,000 annually. Can they afford an $80,000 home with a $60,000 mortgage that requires monthly payments of $710 including principal, interest, taxes, and insurance (PITI)?

Solution

Here are the maximum amounts they can spend according to the three criteria given above:

1. $2.5 \times \$35,000 = \$87,500$

2. If the Harrells earn $35,000 annually, in 1 week they earn

$$\frac{\$35,000}{52} = \$673.08$$

3. The Harrells' gross pay is $35,000. Their monthly gross pay is

$$\frac{\$35000}{12} = \$2916.67 \text{ per month}$$

and 28% of $2916.67 = $816.67.

Thus, the Harrells qualify under the first and third criteria, but not under the second. Of course, they must have the $20,000 down payment!　∎

Now that you know how much house you can afford, you need to borrow money to buy it. How do you do that? By getting a **mortgage loan,** a contract in which the lender agrees to lend you money to buy a specific house or property. The contract creates a lien (a charge against the property making it security for payment) and you, in turn, agree to repay the money according to the terms of the contract. There are many different types of mortgage loan plans (see the Using Your Knowledge section of Exercise 12.4) but we shall discuss only two of these: **conventional loans** and **Federal Housing Authority (FHA) loans**.

Conventional loans are arranged between you and a private lender. In these loans, the **amount of the down payment,** the **repayment period,** and the **interest rate** are agreed on by the **borrower** and the **lender**. The lender usually requires taxes and insurance to be paid in advance through a reserve **(escrow)** account. Lenders sometimes require borrowers to pay for private mortgage insurance (PMI) if the down payment is less than 20% of the loan amount. In addition, they may require that the buyer:

1. Be steadily employed and a resident of the state in which the property is located
2. Have enough savings to make one or two mortgage payments
3. Have the necessary down payment in hand (not borrowed)

Maximum amounts for conventional loans are set by individual lenders. Loans up to 80% of the value of the property are quite common, and loans of 90 to 95% can often be obtained.

FHA loans are made by private lenders and are insured by the Federal Housing Administration. The FHA does *not* make loans; it simply insures the lender against loss in case you, the borrower, fail to repay the loan in full. To pay expenses and to cover this insurance, the FHA charges (at closing) an insurance premium of 3.8% of the loan for 30-year loans, 2.4% on 15-year loans, or an additional 0.5% is added to the interest rate to pay the insurance. To qualify for an FHA loan, a buyer must have:

1. A total housing expense less than 29% of the buyer's gross income
2. Total monthly payments (all debts with 12 or more payments plus total housing expenses) less than 41% of the gross income.

Interest rates on these loans are usually 1 or 2 percentage points lower than conventional loan rates. The FHA loan maximum for a single-family dwelling depends on its location but cannot exceed $101,250. Down payments are as follows:

1. 3% of the first $25,000, plus 5% of the balance over $25,000, up to the maximum loan amount
2. A minimum of 3% down is required.

Walden Savings & Loan		
Your neighborhood lender		
Mortgage Rates		
Loan	Int. Rate	APR
30–year fixed	8.45%	8.99%
15–year fixed	8.05%	8.69%
1–year adjust.	5.50%	7.06%
FHA 30–year fixed	6.75%	

EXAMPLE 2   A family wishes to buy a $64,000 house.

(a) If a lender is willing to loan them 90% of the price of the house, what will be the amount of the loan?
(b) What will be the down payment with that loan?
(c) If they decide to obtain an FHA loan instead, what will be the minimum down payment?
(d) What will be the maximum FHA loan they can get?

Solution   (a) 90% of $64,000 = $57,600
(b) $64,000 − $57,600 = $6400 (= 10% of $64,000)

(c) With an FHA loan, the family will have to pay down 3% of $25,000 plus 5% of the amount over $25,000 ($64,000 − $25,000 = $39,000). Thus, the minimum down payment is computed as follows:

$$3\% \text{ of } \$25,000 = \$\ 750$$
$$5\% \text{ of } \$39,000 = \underline{\$1950}$$
$$\text{Total minimum down payment} = \$2700$$

(d) $64,000 − $2700 = $61,300

The last item we shall discuss in connection with mortgages is the **actual amount** of the monthly payment. This amount depends on three factors:

1. The amount borrowed
2. The interest rate
3. The number of years taken to pay off the loan

Table 12.6 shows the monthly payments for $1000 borrowed at various rates and for various times. To figure the actual monthly payment, find the appro-

Table 12.6 *Monthly Payments for Each $1000 Borrowed*

Interest Rate	Payment Period				
	10 years	15 years	20 years	25 years	30 years
7%	11.60	8.97	7.75	7.05	6.64
$7\frac{1}{2}\%$	11.86	9.26	8.04	7.37	6.98
8%	12.12	9.54	8.35	7.70	7.32
$8\frac{1}{2}\%$	12.38	9.83	8.66	8.04	7.67
9%	12.67	10.14	9.00	8.39	8.05
$9\frac{1}{2}\%$	12.94	10.44	9.32	8.74	8.41
10%	13.22	10.75	9.65	9.09	8.78
$10\frac{1}{2}\%$	13.49	11.05	9.98	9.44	9.15
11%	13.78	11.37	10.32	9.80	9.52
$11\frac{1}{2}\%$	14.06	11.68	10.66	10.16	9.90
12%	14.35	12.00	11.01	10.53	10.29
$12\frac{1}{2}\%$	14.64	12.33	11.36	10.90	10.67
13%	14.93	12.65	11.72	11.28	11.06
$13\frac{1}{2}\%$	15.23	12.98	12.07	11.66	11.45
14%	15.53	13.32	12.44	12.04	11.85
$14\frac{1}{2}\%$	15.83	13.66	12.80	12.42	12.25
15%	16.13	14.00	13.17	12.81	12.64
$15\frac{1}{2}\%$	16.44	14.34	13.54	13.20	13.05
16%	16.75	14.69	13.91	13.59	13.45
$16\frac{1}{2}\%$	17.06	15.04	14.29	13.98	13.85
17%	17.38	15.39	14.67	14.38	14.26

priate interest rate and the payment period, and then multiply the amount shown in the table by the number of thousands of dollars borrowed. Thus, to figure the monthly payment on a $40,000 mortgage at 10% for 30 years, look down the column for 30 years until you come to the row labeled 10%. The amount per $1000 is $8.78. Multiply this amount by 40 (there are 40 thousands in $40,000) to obtain $351.20 for the required monthly payment.

EXAMPLE 3   Athanassio and Gregoria Pappas wish to obtain a 30-year loan to buy a $50,000 house.

(a) If they can get a loan of 95% of the value of the house, what is the amount of the loan?

(b) What will be the down payment with that loan?

(c) If the interest rate is 11%, what will be the monthly payment?

(d) What will be the minimum down payment with an FHA loan?

(e) If the FHA loan carries 9% interest, what will be the monthly payment?

Solution   (a) 95% of $50,000 = $47,500

(b) $50,000 − $47,500 = $2500

(c) We read from Table 12.6 that the amount per $1000 on a 30-year loan at 11% is $9.52. Thus, the monthly payment will be

$$47.5 \times \$9.52 = \$452.20$$ The mortgage loan is for 47.5 thousands

(d) With an FHA loan, the minimum down payment is

$$
\begin{array}{r}
3\% \text{ of } \$25{,}000 = \$\ 750 \\
\text{plus } 5\% \text{ of } \$25{,}000 = \underline{\$1250} \\
\$2000
\end{array}
$$

(e) In Table 12.6, we find the amount per $1000 on a 30-year loan at 9% to be $8.05. The amount to be financed is $48,000 ($50,000 − $2000). Thus, the monthly payment will be

$$48 \times \$8.05 = \$386.40$$

Note: This is not the entire payment, because for an FHA loan, interest and taxes must be added to this amount.

Exercise 12.4 _____

1. A family has a $40,000 annual salary. Can they afford an $80,000 house with a $70,000 mortgage requiring payments of $750 per month, including principal, interest, taxes, and insurance?
   (a) Use the first criterion given in the text.
   (b) Use the second criterion given in the text.
   (c) Use the third criterion given in the text.

2. A family earns $36,000 annually. Can they afford a $95,000 house with a $60,000 mortgage requiring monthly payments of $570, including principal, interest, taxes, and insurance?
   (a) Use the first criterion given in the text.
   (b) Use the second criterion given in the text.
   (c) Use the third criterion given in the text.

3. The Browning family wants to buy a $77,000 house.
   (a) If they can get a loan of 80% of the value of the house, what is the amount of the loan?
   (b) What will be the down payment on this loan?
   (c) If they decide to obtain an FHA loan, what will be the down payment? (Do not forget that the maximum FHA loan for this location is $67,500.)

4. The Scotdale family wants to buy a $60,000 house.
   (a) If they can get a loan of 95% of the purchase price, what will be the amount of the loan?
   (b) What will be the down payment with this loan?
   (c) If they use an FHA loan, what will be the down payment?

In problems 5–10, find the total monthly payment, including taxes and insurance, for the given mortgage loans.

	Amount	Rate	Time (Years)	Annual Taxes	Annual Insurance
5.	$30,000	8%	20	$400	$160
6.	$40,000	$8\frac{1}{2}\%$	30	$600	$180
7.	$45,000	9%	25	$540	$210
8.	$50,000	$9\frac{1}{2}\%$	20	$720	$240
9.	$73,000	10%	30	$840	$380
10.	$80,000	$10\frac{1}{2}\%$	15	$1000	$390

11. The Aikido family wants to obtain a conventional loan for 30 years at 11%. Suppose they find a lender that will loan them 95% for the $60,000

house they have selected, and their taxes and insurance amount to $1500 a year.
(a) What will be their down payment on the loan?
(b) What will be their total monthly payment, including taxes and insurance?

12. The Perez family is planning to buy a $90,000 house. Suppose they get a loan of 80% of the price of the house, and this is a 25-year loan at 10%.
(a) What will be their down payment on the loan?
(b) If their taxes and insurance amount to $810 annually, what will be their monthly payment, including taxes and insurance?

13. The Green family obtained a 30-year FHA loan at 12% to buy a $75,000 house. They made the minimum required down payment, and their taxes and insurance amounted to $360 annually.
(a) What was their down payment?
(b) What was their total monthly payment?

14. A family was planning to buy a $95,000 house with an FHA loan carrying $9\frac{1}{2}\%$ interest over a 20-year period. If they could get the largest possible loan, $75,000 for this location, and their taxes and insurance amounted to $1200 annually, find:
(a) Their down payment
(b) Their total monthly payment

15. The Bixley family has a $50,000 mortgage loan at 10% for 30 years.
(a) What is their monthly mortgage payment?
(b) How many payments will they have to make in all?
(c) What is the total amount they will pay for principal and interest?
(d) What is the total interest they will pay?
(e) If their loan was 80% of the price of the house, is the price more or less than the total interest?

16. The Peminides have a $35,000 mortgage loan at 9% for 30 years.
(a) What is their monthly mortgage payment?
(b) How many payments will they have to make in all?
(c) What is the total amount they will pay for principal and interest?
(d) If their loan was 80% of the price of the house, is the price more or less than the total interest?

17. If you think house prices are high, we have bad news! The costs we have mentioned in the text are not all-inclusive. As we mentioned, you also have to pay **closing costs**. These costs include various fees and are usually paid at the time of closing—that is, when the final mortgage contract is signed. They are in addition to the agreed-upon down payment. Here are

some typical closing costs for a $50,000 house with the buyer making a 20% down payment.

Credit report fee	$ 45
$\frac{3}{12}$ estimated taxes of $600	$150 To escrow account
Insurance premium for 1 year	$300
$\frac{2}{12}$ insurance premium	$ 50 To escrow account
Title insurance	$220
Mortgage recording fee	$ 20
Loan fee, 1 point (1% of loan amount)	$?
Total closing costs	

(a) What would be the total cash payment, down payment plus closing costs, at the time of closing?

(b) If the buyer had to make escrow account deposits each month for taxes and insurance, what would be the combined monthly payment under mortgage terms of 14% for 30 years?

(c) Suppose the lender agreed to add the closing costs to the loan amount instead of asking for cash. What would be the combined monthly payment with the same terms as in part (b)?

18. Here are some different closing costs for a $75,000 house with a 10% down payment.

Credit report fee	$ 45
Mortgage recording fee	$ 15
Lot survey	$250
Loan fee (1.5 percent of loan amount)	$?
Insurance premium for 1 year	$210
Total closing costs	

(a) What would be the total cash payment, down payment plus closing costs, at the time of closing?

(b) If no escrow account was required, what would be the monthly payment for a 25-year, 10% loan?

(c) If the lender added the closing costs to the loan amount instead of asking for cash, what would be the monthly payment under the same terms as in part (b)?

19. Here are some closing costs for a $120,000 home with 20% down.

Credit fee	$ 45
Mortgage recording fee	$ 25
Plot plan	$250
1 point loan fee	$?
Title insurance	$350
Total closing costs	

(a) Find the cash payment, down payment plus closing costs, at the time of closing.

(b) If the buyer had to make escrow account deposits each month for $1200 taxes and insurance, what would be the combined monthly payment under mortgage terms of 9% for 30 years?

(c) Suppose the lender agrees to add the closing costs to the loan amount instead of asking for cash. What would be the combined monthly payment with the same terms as in part (b)?

20. Here are some closing costs for a $150,000 home with 25% down.

Credit fee	$ 45
Mortgage recording fee	$ 25
Lot survey	$300
$1\frac{1}{2}$ point loan fee	$?
Title insurance	$420
Total closing costs	

(a) Find the cash payment, down payment plus closing costs, at the time of closing.

(b) If the buyer had to make escrow account deposits each month for $1500 taxes and insurance, what would be the combined monthly payment under mortgage terms of 8% for 20 years?

(c) Suppose the lender agrees to add the closing costs to the loan amount instead of asking for cash. What would be the combined monthly payment with the same terms as in part (b)?

The following information will be used in problems 21–22.

Closing costs for an $84,000 house with a 10% down payment:

2 points	2% of loan contract
Appraisal and credit report	$235 conventional loan ($200 FHA)
Recording fee	$25
Title insurance	$295

21. Assume you are getting a 15-year conventional loan with a 10% interest rate. Use the given information to find:

(a) The total cash payment, down payment plus closing costs, at the time of closing

(b) The monthly payment (assuming no escrow account)

22. Assume you are getting a 30-year FHA loan with an 8% interest rate. Use the given information to find:

(a) The total cash payment, down payment plus closing costs, at the time of closing

(b) The monthly payment (assuming no escrow account)

In Other Words

23. Write in your own words the advantages and disadvantages of an FHA loan.

24. Write in your own words the advantages and disadvantages of a conventional loan.

25. Suppose you buy a $100,000 home and finance it at 9% for 30 years. Which is greater, the price of the house or the interest you pay on the loan? Answer the same question for a $50,000 home. Explain your answers.

Using Your Knowledge

There are so many different types of loans available that we cannot discuss all the possible financing alternatives you may have when you buy a house. The accompanying information derived from Money *magazine might help you to make some sense out of the existing confusion. Most of the types of loans mentioned are still used, but interest rates are 9% **lower** in many cases!*

A Gallery of Loans

This chart will help you shop for the housing loan that's best for you. Your choice should be determined by your income and your expectations about inflation and interest rates. As they rise and fall, so will rates for inflation-indexed and adjustable-rate mortgages. Fixed-rate loans don't fluctuate, but they can be expensive. All of the loans listed are widely available, except for the adjustable-balance mortgages. They have been offered so far only in Utah, but they may become more common in the future if inflation worsens.

Type of Loan	Typical Minimum Down Payment	Initial Interest Rate (Rates Vary)	Interest Rate After Five Years	Who Should Consider
Fixed rate Conventional	10%	16% to 17%	Unchanged	High-income people who believe interest rates won't drop much
Graduated payment	5%	16% to 17%	Unchanged	People who feel certain their incomes will rise substantially
Growing equity	10%	14% to 16%	Unchanged	Borrowers who can afford high payments and want to pay off their loans early

Type of Loan	Typical Minimum Down Payment	Initial Interest Rate (Rates Vary)	Interest Rate After Five Years	Who Should Consider
Zero interest rate	30%	0	0	Same as above
Adjustable rate Typical adjustable rate	10%	15% to $16\frac{1}{2}$%	Unknown	People who expect interest rates to drop
Dual rate	10%	15 to $16\frac{1}{2}$%	Unknown	Borrowers who, in return for lower monthly payments, are willing to give some of their equity to lenders if interest rates rise
Balloon payment	20%	12% to 16%	Loan is usually repaid by then	Borrowers who believe they'll be able to refinance their loans at lower rates in the future
Equity sharing Shared equity	10%	16% to 17%	Unchanged	People who are willing to give investors part of their houses' tax benefits and future appreciation in return for help in raising down payments and making monthly loan payments
Partnership mortgage	10%	16% to 17%	Unchanged	Low-income people who are willing to give investors most of the tax deductions a home generates and some of the future appreciation in exchange for down payments and help in monthly payments
Inflation indexed Adjustable balance	10%	$10\frac{1}{2}$%	Unknown	Borrowers who are confident that their incomes will keep pace with inflation

26. Find out the current rates for the type of loans in the chart.

Chapter 12 Summary

Section	Item	Meaning	Example
12.1A	$I = Prt$	Simple interest equals Prt, where P is principal, r is rate, and t is time.	The interest on a \$500 2-year loan at 12% is $I = 500 \cdot 0.12 \cdot 2 = \$120$.
12.1A	$A = P + I$	Amount equals principal plus interest.	
12.1D	$A_n = P(1 + i)^n$	Compound amount equals $P(1 + i)^n$, where P is principal, i is rate per period, and n is the number of periods.	
12.3A	APR	Annual percentage rate	
12.3B	Rule of 78	The unearned interest rate on a loan of n periods with r remaining periods is $$\frac{r(r + 1)}{n(n + 1)} \times F$$ where F is the finance charge.	

Research Questions

Sources of information for these questions can be found in the Bibliography at the end of the book.

1. Go to an encyclopedia and write a report about the origin of coins citing places, peoples, and dates.

2. Write a report about the origin of paper money citing places, peoples, and dates.

3. Write a brief report about continental currency.

4. Find out and report about the Federal Reserve System and its relationship to the printing and control of money in the United States.

5. Go to a bank or a savings and loan and research their requirements for getting a mortgage loan. Write out all of these requirements.

Chapter 12 Practice Test

1. The Ready-Money Loan Company charges 28% simple interest (annual) for a 2-year, $800 loan. Find:

   (a) The total interest on this loan

   (b) The interest for 3 months

   (c) The total amount to be paid to the loan company at the end of 2 years

2. A state has a 6% sales tax.

   (a) What is the sales tax on a microwave oven priced at $360?

   (b) What is the total cost of this oven?

3. In a sale, a store offers a 20% discount on a freezer chest that is normally priced at $390.

   (a) How much is the discount?

   (b) What is the sale price of the freezer?

4. Here is a portion of a compound interest table to use in this problem:

Amount (in dollars) to Which $1 Will Grow in n Periods Under Compound Interest

n	2%	4%	6%	8%	10%
1	1.0200	1.0400	1.0600	1.0800	1.1000
2	1.0404	1.0609	1.1236	1.1664	1.2100
3	1.0612	1.1249	1.1910	1.2597	1.3310
4	1.0824	1.1699	1.2625	1.3605	1.4641
5	1.1041	1.2167	1.3382	1.4693	1.6105
6	1.1262	1.2653	1.4185	1.5869	1.7716
7	1.1487	1.3159	1.5036	1.7138	1.9487
8	1.1717	1.3686	1.5938	1.8509	2.1436

Find the accumulated amount and the interest earned for:

(a) $100 at 8% compounded semiannually for 2 years

(b) $100 at 8% compounded quarterly for 2 years

5. A credit card holder is obligated to pay the balance in full if it is less than $10. Otherwise, the minimum payment is $10 or 5% of the balance, whichever is more. Suppose that a customer received a statement listing the balance as $185.76.

   (a) Find the minimum payment due.

   (b) The finance charge is 1.5% per month. What will be the amount of this charge on the next statement if the customer makes only the minimum payment?

6. JoAnn Jones received a statement showing that she owed a balance of $179.64 to a department store where she had a revolving charge account. JoAnn made a payment of $50 and charged an additional $23.50. If the store charges 1.5% per month on the unpaid balance, find:

   (a) The finance charge for the month

   (b) The new balance

7. A car costing $6500 can be bought with $1500 down and a 12% add-on interest to be paid in 48 equal monthly installments.
   (a) What is the total interest charge?
   (b) What is the monthly payment?

8. Here is a table for you to use in this problem:

   True Annual Interest Rate for a 12-Payment Plan

	14%	$14\frac{1}{2}$%	15%	$15\frac{1}{2}$%	16%
Finance Charge (Per $100 of the amount financed)	7.74	8.03	8.31	8.59	8.88

   Sam Bearss borrows $200 and agrees to pay $18.10 per month for 12 months.

   (a) What is the APR for this transaction?

   (b) If Sam decided to pay off the balance of the loan after 5 months (with 7 payments remaining), use the rule of 78 to find the amount of the interest refund.

   (c) Find the amount needed to pay off the loan.

9. The Mendoza family wants to buy a $50,000 house.

   (a) If a bank was willing to loan them 75% of the price of the house, what would be the amount of the loan?

   (b) What would be the down payment for this house?

   (c) If they decided to obtain an FHA loan instead, what would be the minimum down payment? (Assume that the FHA requires a down payment of 3% of the first $25,000 and 5% of the balance up to a maximum loan amount of $67,500.)

   (d) What would be the maximum FHA loan they could get?

10. Refer to problem 9. Suppose the Mendoza family contracted for a 15-year mortgage at 12% with the bank that loaned them 75% of the price of the

house. What is their monthly payment for principal and interest? (Use the table below.)

Monthly Payment ($) for Each $1000 Borrowed

Rate	10 years	15 years	20 years
11%	13.78	11.37	10.32
12%	14.35	12.00	11.01
13%	14.93	12.65	11.72

How do you measure length, volume, and weight? If you go to a supermarket to buy tape, soda, and cheese you can find out. The length of a roll of Scotch tape is 36 yards or 32.9 meters, soda can be bought in quart or liter bottles, and cheese is sold by the pound or kilogram. (Read the labels!) Clearly, two measurement systems exist side by side in the United States. The U.S. customary system measures these items in yards, quarts, and pounds and the international metric system uses meters, liters, and kilograms.

The metric system has seen steady use in the United States. In science, medicine, and manufacturing the system is predominant. As a matter of fact, the Trade Act of 1988 calls for the federal government to adopt metric specifications by December 31, 1992, and mandates the Commerce Department to oversee the program.

In Section 13.1 we shall familiarize ourselves with the types of measurements used in different situations involving lengths, volumes, and weights as well as the conversions that can be made within the metric system. The computations involved are always easy. They entail only multiplication or division by the appropriate power of 10.

There is one more measurement that needs to be discussed: temperature. In the U.S. system temperature is measured in degrees Fahrenheit; in the metric system it is measured in degrees Celsius. We compare these two scales and give the appropriate conversion formulas in Section 13.2.

Finally, most people think that changing from the U.S. to the metric system would involve constant conversions from one system to the other. This is not so! When you buy soda in a 2 liter bottle you need not convert it to quarts! But, in case the urge is irresistible, we show how to convert from the metric to the U.S. system and vice versa in Section 13.3.

The Metric System

**John Quincy Adams
(1767–1848)**
The Metropolitan Museum of Art, Gift of I. N. Phelps Stokes, E. S. Hawes, A. M. Hawes, and M. H. Hawes, 1937.

THE HUMAN SIDE
OF MATHEMATICS

In his report to the Congress as James Monroe's secretary of state in 1821, John Quincy Adams said:

Weights and measures may be ranked among the necessaries of life to every individual of human society. They enter into the economical arrangements and daily concerns of every family. They are necessary to every occupation of human industry; to the distribution and security of every species of property; to every transaction of trade and commerce. . . . The knowledge of them, as in established use, is among the first elements of education, and is often learned by those who learn nothing else, not even to read and write.

Early Babylonian and Egyptian records and the Bible indicate that length was first measured with the forearm, hand, or finger, and time was measured by the periods of the sun, moon, and stars. To measure capacities of containers, they were filled with plant seeds, which were then counted to obtain the volume. As civilizations developed numeration systems, it became possible to create weights and measures to suit trade and commerce, land division, taxation, and science.

The measurement system used in the U.S is the one brought by the colonists from England. These measures originated in a variety of cultures, and evolved into the *inch*, *foot*, and *yard* through a complicated transformation not yet fully understood.

In 1790, the French Academy of Sciences created a system of weights and measures that was both simple and scientific. In this metric system, measures for volume and weight were derived from the unit of length, which was selected to be a portion of the circumference of the Earth. Thus, the basic units were related to each other and to nature. Moreover, the larger and smaller versions of these units were obtained by multiplying or dividing by powers of 10, so that a simple shifting of the decimal point avoided all the awkward conversions of the English system.

13.1   THE METRIC SYSTEM

The bottle of wine holds 750 ml. The wedge of cheese weighs about 250 g.

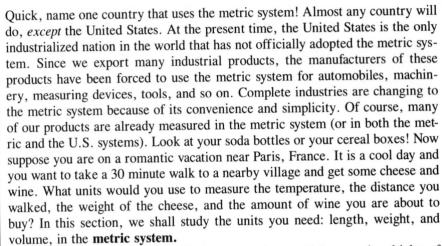

GETTING STARTED

INCHING TOWARD THE METRIC SYSTEM

Quick, name one country that uses the metric system! Almost any country will do, *except* the United States. At the present time, the United States is the only industrialized nation in the world that has not officially adopted the metric system. Since we export many industrial products, the manufacturers of these products have been forced to use the metric system for automobiles, machinery, measuring devices, tools, and so on. Complete industries are changing to the metric system because of its convenience and simplicity. Of course, many of our products are already measured in the metric system (or in both the metric and the U.S. systems). Look at your soda bottles or your cereal boxes! Now suppose you are on a romantic vacation near Paris, France. It is a cool day and you want to take a 30 minute walk to a nearby village and get some cheese and wine. What units would you use to measure the temperature, the distance you walked, the weight of the cheese, and the amount of wine you are about to buy? In this section, we shall study the units you need: length, weight, and volume, in the **metric system.**

The metric system is a **decimal** system using multiples or submultiples of ten, eliminating the difficult calculations encountered in the U.S. customary system. (For example, do you know how many feet there are in 2 miles or how many rods in a furlong?) Moreover, all metric measurements are derived from a single base unit, the meter. Other basic units are then derived from the meter. For example, a **liter** is the volume of a cube 10 centimeters on each edge while the **kilogram** is the mass of one liter of water at constant temperature. Clearly, the metric system is much more standardized than the U.S. system. Some of the measures from which the U.S. system is derived are the **cubit,** the length of the forearm from the elbow to the tip of the middle finger (about 18 inches); the **foot,** equivalent to 12 thumb-widths, called "uncias" (the Roman word for $\frac{1}{12}$); and the **mile,** called "milia passuum" by the Romans and equivalent to 1000 paces. All of these measurements were dependent on whose **cubit, foot,** or **paces** were used.

Weights and measures were among the earliest tools invented by humans. Rudimentary measures for constructing dwellings, fashioning clothing, and bartering food were used in many primitive societies. At first, people naturally used parts of their bodies as measuring instruments. Thus, the length of a human *foot,* or the circumference of a person's waist (*gird* in Saxon, later evolving into *yard*) were used as standards of measurement. Later, when means for weighing objects were invented, seeds and stones served as standard weights. For instance, the *carat,* a unit still used for measuring precious stones such as diamonds, was derived from the weight of the carob seed.

Peanuts. Reprinted by permission of UFS, Inc.

In an effort to standardize measurements, the National Assembly of France in 1790 requested the French Academy of Sciences to "deduce an invariable standard for all the measures and all the weights." The result was the metric system.

In 1960, the General Conference on Weights and Measures adopted a revised and simplified version of the metric system, the **International System of Units,** which is now called **SI** (after the French name, *Le Système International d'Unités*). The SI is the system that we study in the following pages.

A. *Metric Units*

The metric system is a decimal system of weights and measures. The basic units in the metric system are:

1. The **meter** (the unit of length, a little longer than a yard)
2. The **liter** (the unit of volume or capacity, a little more than a quart)
3. The **gram** (the unit of weight, about the weight of a regular paper clip)
4. The **second** (the unit of time)

A meter is a little longer than a yard

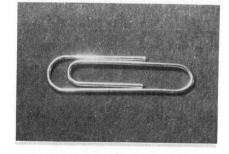

A gram is about the weight of a paper clip

A liter is a little more than a quart

Multiples and subdivisions of the basic units are given in powers of ten. The prefixes shown below in boldface are commonly used in everyday life and we shall study them in this chapter. Note the abbreviations in parentheses. It is customary to use these prefix abbreviations only with the abbreviations of the units themselves. For example, kg means kilograms, ml means milliliters, and so on.

kilo (k)	hecto (h)	deka (dk)	Standard Unit	deci (d)	centi (c)	milli (m)
1000 units	100 units	10 units	1 unit	0.1 units	0.01 units	0.001 units

Now, to convert from one unit to another, we can substitute the correct equivalence. This is equivalent to multiplying or dividing by the appropriate power of ten. For example, to find out how many meters there are in 5 km, that is, to find 5 km = _____ m, we write

$$1 \text{ km} = 1000 \text{ m}$$

$$5 \text{ km} = 5 \cdot 1000 = 5000 \text{ m}$$

Similarly,

$$1 \text{ ml} = 0.001 \text{ liter}$$

$$750 \text{ ml} = 750 \cdot 0.001 \text{ l} = 0.750 \text{ l}$$

EXAMPLE 1   Fill in the blanks with the appropriate numbers.

(a) 1.2 m = _____ cm
(b) 2 l = _____ ml
(c) 1 g = _____ kg

Solution   (a) Since 1 m = 100 cm, to change from meters to centimeters we multiply by 100, that is, move the decimal *two* places to the right. Thus, 1.2 m = 1.2 × 100 cm = <u>120</u> cm

(b) Since a liter is 1000 ml, 2 liters = 2 · 1000 ml = <u>2000</u> ml

(c) One kilogram = 1000 grams; thus, $1 \text{ g} = \dfrac{1}{1000} \text{ kg} = \underline{0.001} \text{ kg}$.   ∎

B. *Which Unit to Use*

Let us see how the metric system would relate to you. You are probably accustomed to seeing carpet sold by the square yard. In the metric system, it would be sold by the square *meter*. In stating traveling distances, you now use miles; in the metric system, you would use *kilometers*. Smaller dimensions, such as tool sizes, would be measured in *centimeters* or in *millimeters*. While studying the following examples remember that:

1 quart (qt)	is about	1 liter (l)
1 inch (in.)	is about	2.5 centimeters (cm)
1 kilogram (kg)	is about	2.2 pounds (lb)
1 ounce (oz)	is about	28 grams (g)

EXAMPLE 2   What metric unit should be used for the following products?

(a) A glue stick weighing about 1/4 oz
(b) A small ruler about 6 in. long
(c) A half gallon of milk

Solution   (a) The ounce is a small unit of weight, so use grams.
(b) 6 in. is a short length, so use centimeters.
(c) A half gallon is 2 quarts, so use liters.

■

C. *Length (Linear Measure)*

As we indicated, the standard metric unit of length is the **meter.** The meter (39.37 in.) is a little longer than a yard and was originally defined to be 1 ten-millionth of the distance from the North Pole to the Equator. However, the 1960 conference redefined it in terms of the wavelength of the orange-red line in the spectrum of krypton-86. This definition makes it easy for any scientific laboratory in the world to reproduce the length of the meter.

A yard is divided into 36 equal parts (inches), whereas a meter is divided into 100 equal parts (centimeters). The centimeter is about 0.4 in., and the inch is about 2.5 cm. To give you an idea of the relative lengths of the inch and the centimeter, here are two line segments 1 in. and 1 cm long, respectively:

——————————— 1 in.

———— 1 cm

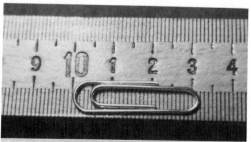

A paper clip is about 3 cm long

From these comparisons of the inch and the centimeter, you can probably see that in the metric system we measure small distances (the length of a pencil, the width of a book, your height) in centimeters. For long distances, we use the kilometer. The kilometer is about 0.6 mi, and the mile is about 1.6 km. If you recall that **kilo** means **1000,** then you know that a kilometer is 1000 m. Table 13.1 shows the relationships among some metric units of length. Notice that the prefixes are the familiar ones we already mentioned. The abbreviations for the more commonly used units are in boldface type.

Table 13.1

kilometer	hectometer	dekameter	meter	decimeter	centimeter	millimeter
km	hm	dkm	**m**	dm	**cm**	**mm**
1000 m	100 m	10 m	1 m	0.1 m	0.01 m	0.001 m

As you can see from the table, each metric unit of length is a multiple or a submultiple of the basic unit, the meter. Thus, to change from one unit to another, we simply substitute the correct equivalence. This is equivalent to multiplying or dividing by the correct power of ten. For example, if we wish to know how many centimeters there are in 3 km, we proceed as follows:

$$1 \text{ kilometer} = 1000 \text{ m}$$
$$= 1000 \times (100 \text{ cm})$$
$$= 100,000 \text{ cm}$$

Hence, 3 km is 300,000 cm.

Another way to change from one unit to another is to notice that **a shift of one place to the right in Table 13.1 moves the decimal point one place to the right,** and **a shift of one place to the left moves the decimal point one place to the left.** Thus, to change 3 km to centimeters, a shift of five places to the right in the table, we move the decimal point in the 3 five places to the right to obtain 300,000 cm. Similarly, to change 256 mm to meters, a shift of three places to the left in the table, we move the decimal point in the 256 three places to the left to get 256 mm = 0.256 m.

EXAMPLE 3   (a) The height of a basketball player is 205 cm. How many meters is that?

(b) The display screen on a pocket calculator is 65 mm long. How many centimeters is that?

Solution   (a) From Table 13.1, we see that

$$1 \text{ cm} = 0.01 \text{ m}$$

Thus,

$$205 \text{ cm} = 205 \times 0.01 \text{ m} = 2.05 \text{ m}$$

Note that to go from cm to m in Table 13.1, we move 2 places left. Thus, to change 205 cm to meters, move the decimal two places left in 205, obtaining 2.05 m as before.

(b) Table 13.1 shows that to go from mm to cm, we move the decimal point one place to the left. Hence,

$$65 \text{ mm} = 6.5 \text{ cm}.$$

As Example 3 illustrates, a change from one metric unit of length to another requires us to move the decimal point the correct number of places: to the **right** if converting to a **smaller** unit, or to the **left** if converting to a **larger** unit.

D. *Volume (Capacity) Units*

The standard metric unit of volume (or capacity) is the liter. Table 13.2 shows the relationships among the various units. As before, the abbreviations in boldface are for the most commonly used units.

Table 13.2

kiloliter	hectoliter	dekaliter	liter	deciliter	centiliter	milliliter
kl	hl	dkl	**l**	dl	cl	**ml**
1000 liters	100 liters	10 liters	1 liter	0.1 liter	0.01 liter	0.001 liter

EXAMPLE 4   (a) A soft drink bottle contains 0.946 liter. How many milliliters is that?

(b) To make six 250-ml servings of ice cream, how many liters of ice cream are required?

Solution   (a) Table 13.2 shows that there are 1000 ml in 1 l. Thus,

$$0.946 \text{ liter} = 0.946 \times 1000 \text{ ml} = 946 \text{ ml}$$

Note that to go from l to ml in Table 13.2, we must move 3 places right. Thus, 0.946 l = 946 ml

(b) The six servings would require

$$6 \times 250 \text{ ml} = 1500 \text{ ml}$$

Since 1 ml = 0.001 l, we just move the decimal point three places left in 1500. Thus, 1.5 liters are required.

E. *Units of Weight*

Many people use the words *mass* and *weight* as though they were synonyms, but the two concepts are entirely different. The **mass** of an object is the *quantity of matter* in the object. The **weight** of the object is the *force* with which the Earth pulls on it. To measure your weight, you can stand on a spring scale; but to measure your mass, you would have to sit on a balance scale and be balanced against some standard masses. Suppose you are on the moon. The gravitational pull of the moon is only one-sixth the gravitational pull of the Earth. Thus, if your Earth weight were 150 lb, your moon weight would be only one-sixth of that, or 25 lb. However, your mass on the moon is exactly the same as it is on the Earth.

A spring scale with 1 kg of apples

The basic unit of *mass* is the gram, originally defined to be the *mass* of 1 cubic centimeter of water. However, for most everyday affairs, the gram is simply regarded as the basic unit *weight;* it is the *weight* of a cubic centimeter of water under certain standard conditions on the surface of the Earth. (This does not apply to scientific work, where a separate unit of weight must be defined.) The gram is used to weigh small objects. For example, a candy bar, the contents of a tuna fish can, and your breakfast cereal are suitably weighed in grams. Very small objects, such as pills, are weighed in milligrams. For heavier objects, we use the kilogram. Thus, we would buy meat, vegetables, and coffee in kilograms. A kilogram is about 2.2 lb, and a pound is about 0.45 kg. Table 13.3 gives the relationships among the customary metric units of weight. As before, the abbreviations for the most commonly used units are in boldface type.

Table 13.3

kilogram	hectogram	dekagram	gram	decigram	centigram	milligram
kg	hg	dkg	**g**	dg	cg	**mg**
1000 g	100 g	10 g	1 g	0.1 g	0.01 g	0.001 g

EXAMPLE 5   (a) A box of Kellogg's Kenmei Rice Bran weighs 629 grams. How many kilograms is that?

(b) A certain antacid stomach tablet contains about 250 mg of calcium carbonate. What fraction of a gram is that?

Solution   (a) Table 13.3 shows that

$$1 \text{ kg} = 1000 \text{ g}$$

so that

$$1 \text{ g} = 0.001 \text{ kg}$$

Thus,

$$629 \text{ g} = 629 \times 0.001 \text{ kg} = 0.629 \text{ kg}$$

Note that to go from g to kg in Table 13.3 we must move 3 places left; thus, 629 grams = 0.629 kg.

(b) From Table 13.3, we see that

$$1 \text{ mg} = 0.001 \text{ g}$$

Thus,

$$250 \text{ mg} = 250 \times 0.001 \text{ g} = 0.25 \text{ g} = \frac{1}{4} \text{ g}$$

Exercise 13.1

A. 1. Fill in the blanks with the appropriate number:
   (a) 1 kiloliter = _____ liters
   (b) 1 milligram = _____ grams
   (c) 1 meter = _____ centimeters
   (d) 1 kilometer = _____ meters

B. 2. Indicate the appropriate metric units for each of the following items:
   (a) A quart of vinegar   (b) A 100-lb bag of cement
   (c) $\frac{1}{4}$-in.-wide tape   (d) 14-in. shoelaces
   (e) A 2-oz candy bar

In problems 3–8 select the answer that is most nearly correct.

3. The height of a professional basketball player is:
   (a) 200 mm   (b) 200 m   (c) 200 cm

4. The dimensions of the living room in an ordinary home are:
   (a) 4m by 5m   (b) 4 cm by 5 cm   (c) 4 mm by 5 mm

5. The diameter of an aspirin tablet is:
   (a) 1 cm   (b) 1 mm   (c) 1 m

6. The length of the 100-yd dash is about:
   (a) 100 cm   (b) 100 mm   (c) 100 m

7. The weight of an average human male is:
   (a) 70 kg   (b) 70 g   (c) 70 mg

8. The length of an ordinary lead pencil is:
   (a) 19 mm   (b) 19 cm   (c) 19 m

C. In problems 9 and 10, fill in the blank with the correct numbers.

9. (a) 8 km = _____ m   (b) 4 m = _____ cm
   (c) 3409 cm = _____ m   (d) 49.4 mm = _____ cm

10. (a) 8413 mm = _____ m   (b) 7.3 m = _____ mm
    (c) 319 mm = _____ m   (d) 758 m = _____ km

11. A bed is 210 cm long. How many meters is that?

12. The diameter of a vitamin C tablet is 6 mm. How many centimeters is that?

13. The length of a certain race is 1.5 km. How many meters is that?

14. The depth of a swimming pool is 1.6 m. How many centimeters is that?

15. Dr. James Strange of the University of South Florida wishes to explore Mount Ararat in Turkey searching for Noah's ark. According to the book of Genesis, the dimensions of the ark are as given below. If a cubit is 52.5 cm, give each dimension in meters.
    (a) Length, 300 cubits   (b) Breadth, 50 cubits
    (c) Height, 30 cubits

D. 16. Fill in the blanks with the correct numbers.
    (a) 6.3 kl = _____ liters   (b) 72.3 ml = _____ liters
    (c) 1.3 l = _____ ml   (d) 3479 ml = _____ kl

17. Since a liter is the volume of a cube that is 10 cm on each edge, the volume of a cube that is 1 m on each edge is how many liters?

18. A person drank 60 ml of milk. Is that more or less than half a liter of milk?

19. Sea water contains 3.5 g of salt per liter. How many grams of salt are there in 1000 ml of sea water?

20. Hydrogen weighs about 0.0001 g per milliliter. How much would 1 liter of hydrogen weigh?

21. A liter is equivalent to 1000 cm^3. How many liters of liquid will a rectangular container 50 cm long and 20 cm wide hold when filled to a depth of 10 cm?

22. A gallon of gas is about 3.8 liters. An American car takes about 20 gal of gas. How many liters is that?

23. A certain medicine has 20 ml of medication per liter of solution. How many milliliters of solution are needed to obtain 5 ml of medication?

24. A tanker truck delivers 10 kl of gasoline to a service station.
    (a) How many liters is that?
    (b) If 100 liters is about 26.4 gal, how many gallons were delivered?

E. In problems 25 and 26, fill in the blanks with the correct numbers.

25. (a) 14 kg = _____ g   (b) 4.8 kg = _____ g
    (c) 2.8 g = _____ kg   (d) 3.9 g = _____ mg

26. (a) 37 mg = _____ g   (b) 49 mg = _____ kg
    (c) 41 g = _____ kg   (d) 3978 g = _____ kg

27. A gram is the weight of 1 cubic centimeter (cm^3) of water (under certain standard conditions). What is the weight of 1 liter of water? (See problem 17.)

In problems 28 and 29, select the answer that is most nearly correct.

28. The amount of milk in a quart carton is about:
    (a) 100 ml   (b) 1 liter   (c) 1 kl

29. The water needed to fill a 1 liter bottle weighs:
    (a) 0.5 kg   (b) 1 kg   (c) 2 kg

In Other Words

30. Describe in your own words how the units of length (the meter), weight (the gram), and volume (the liter) are defined.

Using Your Knowledge

31. The *humerus* is the bone in a person's upper arm. With this bone as a clue, an anthropologist can tell about how tall a person was. If the bone is that of a female, then the height of the person is about

(2.75 × Humerus length) + 71.48 cm

Suppose the humerus of a female was found to be 31 cm long. About how tall was the person?

In problems 32 and 33, match each item in the first column with an appropriate measure in the second column.

32. (i) A letter-size sheet of paper
    (ii) A newspaper
    (iii) A credit card
    (iv) A regular bank check
    (v) A postage stamp

    (a) 20 × 25 mm
    (b) 54 × 86 mm
    (c) 70 × 150 mm
    (d) 21.5 × 28 cm
    (e) 35 × 56 cm

33. (i) A person
    (ii) A book
    (iii) A small automobile
    (iv) A common pin
    (v) An orange

    (a) 80 mg
    (b) 68 g
    (c) 1 kg
    (d) 72 kg
    (e) 1000 kg

Discovery

34. Here is a problem just for fun: One glass is half full of wine. A second glass, which is twice the size of the first glass, is one-quarter full of wine. Both glasses are filled with water, and the contents are then mixed in a third container. Can you discover what part of the total mixture is wine?

35. Millie's Tavern is a peculiar place indeed. Her liters of wine contain only 400 ml, and she insists on calling them "Millie liters"! Moreover, she has quite a time measuring her wine, since she has only a very large pitcher and two small glasses that hold 500 ml and 300 ml, respectively. Can you discover how Millie measures her Millie liter (400-ml) drinks using the two glasses and the pitcher?

36. Barely a half block from Millie's Tavern, there is a dairy called the Half-and-Half, not because they sell this product, but because they give you only half of what you pay for, cleverly keeping the other half. In this dairy, a liter of milk gets you only 500 ml. Can you discover how they measure their liters (500 ml) if they have only a large pitcher and two glasses that hold 300 and 700 ml, respectively?

13.2   CELSIUS AND FAHRENHEIT TEMPERATURES

Some thermometers give the conversion formulas we use

GETTING STARTED

U.S. AND METRIC TEMPERATURES

The thermometer shows both the Fahrenheit scale and the scale used in the metric system, the Celsius or Centigrade scale. What is the relationship between the two? You might know that water freezes at 0°C (read, "0 degrees Celsius"), which is equivalent to 32°F (read, "32 degrees Fahrenheit"). Also, water boils at 100°C or 212°F. Can we derive the relationship between the two scales with this information? If we assume that the relationship is **linear,** and we consider points of the form (F, C), where F is the temperature in Fahrenheit degrees and C is the temperature in Celsius degrees, we know that the line relating the temperatures goes through the points (0, 32) and (100, 212). Thus, the **slope** of the line is

$$m = \frac{100 - 0}{212 - 32} = \frac{100}{180} = \frac{5}{9}$$

Now, using the **point-slope** formula $y - y_1 = m(x - x_1)$ with $y = C$, $x = F$, and $(x_1, y_1) = (32, 0)$, we have

$$C - 0 = \frac{5}{9}(F - 32) \text{ or } C = \frac{5(F - 32)}{9}$$

Now, if the temperature is 41°F, the corresponding Celsius temperature is

$$C = \frac{5(41 - 32)}{9} = \frac{5(9)}{9} = 5°C$$

If you solve for F in the equation

$$C = \frac{5(F - 32)}{9}$$

you will find that

$$F = \frac{9C}{5} + 32$$

In this section we shall study how these two formulas are used to convert between the Fahrenheit and Celsius temperature scales.

We have now discussed length, volume, and weight. What about temperature? The temperature scale we normally use was invented by Gabriel Robert Fahrenheit. As we have mentioned in Getting Started, in the **Fahrenheit** scale, the boiling point of water is 212°F, and the freezing point of water is 32°F. The temperature scale was modified by Anders Celsius, who avoided the

LUTHER

By Brumsic Brandon, Jr.

awkward numbers 32 and 212. In the **Celsius** scale, the freezing and boiling points of water are 0°C and 100°C, respectively. Because this scale is based on the number 100, it is sometimes called the **centigrade** scale. Figure 13.1 shows the comparison between the two scales.

The formulas for converting from one scale to the other were derived in Getting Started. They are displayed here for easy reference.

$$C = \frac{5(F - 32)}{9} \qquad F = \frac{9C}{5} + 32$$

Note that there are 100 Celsius degrees and 180 Fahrenheit degrees between the freezing and boiling points of water (Figure 13.1). Therefore, any piece of the temperature scale has $\frac{100}{180} = \frac{5}{9}$ as many Celsius as Fahrenheit degrees. If we subtract 32 from the Fahrenheit reading to bring the freezing point back to 0, then the Celsius reading must be given by $C = \frac{5}{9}(F - 32)$. Similar reasoning leads to the formula $F = \frac{9}{5}C + 32$.

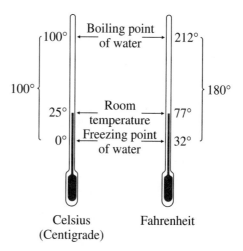

FIGURE 13.1

EXAMPLE 1   Desi had the flu. Her temperature was 104°F. What is that on the Celsius scale?

Solution   We replace F by 104 in the formula

$$C = \frac{5(F - 32)}{9} \quad \text{to get} \quad C = \frac{5(104 - 32)}{9} = \frac{5(72)}{9} = 40$$

Thus, her temperature was 40°C.   ■

EXAMPLE 2   The melting point of gold is 1000°C. What is that on the Fahrenheit scale?

Solution   We substitute 1000 for C in the formula

$$F = \frac{9C}{5} + 32$$

to find

$$F = \frac{9(1000)}{5} + 32$$

$$= 1800 + 32 = 1832$$

Hence, the melting point of gold is 1832°F.   ■

Exercise 13.2

In problems 1–10, fill in the blanks with the correct numbers.

1. 59°F = _____ °C   2. 113°F = _____ °C
3. 86°F = _____ °C   4. −4°F = _____ °C
5. −22°F = _____ °C   6. 0°F = _____ °C
7. 10°C = _____ °F   8. 25°C = _____ °F
9. −10°C = _____ °F   10. −15°C = _____ °F

11. In an Air Force experiment, heavily clothed men endured temperatures of 500°F. How many degrees Celsius is that?

12. The temperature in Death Valley has been recorded at 131°F. How many degrees Celsius is that?

13. A temperature of 41°C is a dangerously high body temperature for a human being. How many degrees Fahrenheit is that?

14. For a very short time in September 1933, the temperature in Coimbra, Portugal, rose to 70°C. What is that on the Fahrenheit scale?

15. The average normal human body temperature is 98.6°F. What is that on the Celsius scale?

16. Tungsten, which is used for the filament in electric light bulbs, has a melting point of 3410°C. What is that on the Fahrenheit scale?

17. What Celsius temperatures should we use for the following?
    (a) Cool to 41°F
    (b) Boil at 212°F

18. During the second quarter of the 1981 NFL play-off game in Cincinnati, the wind–chill factor reached −58°F. (It got worse later.) What is the equivalent Celsius wind–chill factor?

19. Dry ice changes from a solid to a vapor at −78°C. Express this temperature in degrees Fahrenheit.

In Other Words

20. What do you think are the advantages of the Celsius temperature scale over the Fahrenheit scale?

Using Your Knowledge

Refer to the thermometer shown at the beginning of this section to find the approximate Celsius temperatures.

21. On a very cold morning when the temperature was 25°F below zero.

22. On a mild spring day when the temperature was 68°F.

23. Of a child with body temperature of 97.5°F.

Discovery

In 1848, Lord Kelvin, a British physicist, proposed using a Celsius scale in which temperatures were moved downward so that 0°K (read, "0 degrees Kelvin") would be the temperature at which all molecular motion was believed to cease (also called absolute zero). This point occurred at −273.15°C. In the Kelvin scale water boils at 373.15°K and it freezes at 273.15°K.

24. Can you use points of the form (C, K) to discover a relationship between the Celsius and Kelvin scales? [*Hint:* Use the points (373.15, 100) and (273.15, 0) and use a procedure similar to the one used in Getting Started.]

Computer Corner

Converting temperatures from Celsius to Fahrenheit or vice versa is a matter of using the formulas given in the text. The Temperature Converter Program in the Programs in BASIC appendix can do it for you! You simply enter the temperature followed by a C for Celsius or an F for Fahrenheit and the program does the rest.

13.3   CONVERT IF YOU MUST

GETTING STARTED

METRIC ADAGES

What do you think would happen if the U.S. adopted the metric system right this minute? Many people believe that they would have to be making conversions from U.S. to metric and from metric to U.S. constantly. This is just not true! For example, you probably buy soda or spring water in 1- and 2-liter bottles, but this does not require that you convert liters to quarts. You might have a foreign car that is totally metric, but you do not need to convert tire or engine sizes to the U.S. system. However, if you insist on converting, here are a few items you may want to convert to the metric system first. Table 13.4 will help.

1. A miss is as good as ＿＿ km.
   (a mile)
2. I wouldn't touch it with a ＿＿ -m pole.
   (10-ft)
3. He was so stubborn he wouldn't give ＿＿ cm.
   (an inch)
4. Walk ＿＿ km in my moccasins.
   (a mile)
5. ＿＿ grams of prevention is worth ＿＿ kilograms of cure.
   (An ounce)   (a pound)

Table 13.4 *U.S. Units and Metric Equivalents**

1 in. = 2.54 cm†	1 cm ≈ 0.394 in.
1 yd ≈ 0.914 m	1 m ≈ 1.09 yd
1 mi ≈ 1.61 km	1 km ≈ 0.621 mi
1 lb ≈ 0.454 kg	1 kg ≈ 2.20 lb
1 qt ≈ 0.946 liter	1 liter ≈ 1.06 qt

*The symbol ≈ means "is approximately equal to."
† The inch is legally defined to be *exactly* 2.54 cm.

The preceding sections of this chapter have clearly shown the advantages of the metric system. Despite these advantages, many people are still opposed to changing to this system of measurement. Most of these people think that if the metric system is put into effect, then they must continually convert U.S. (formerly called English) units into metric units, and vice versa. Nothing is further from the truth! Once you learn to "think metric," you will usually not have to make conversions between the U.S. and metric systems. However, in case you occasionally must make such conversions, Table 13.4 should prove helpful.

As you can see from Table 13.4 with the exception of the inches to centimeters conversion, the relationships are all approximate. Some of these num-

TIGER

Reprinted with special permission of King Features Syndicate, Inc.

bers are stated with two decimal places and some with three. The reason is that these numbers are either the results of certain measurements or else are rounded-off approximations to the true values. For example, when we say that a yard is 0.914 m, we are giving the result to the nearest thousandth of a meter; the actual equivalence is between 0.9135 and 0.9145. Thus, in calculations with the numbers in the table, we must use the round-off rules and the rules for approximate numbers given in Section 4.5.

Let us look at the conversion from centimeters to inches. We have the exact equivalence 1 in. = 2.54 cm. To express centimeters in terms of inches, we must divide by 2.54 to get

$$\frac{1}{2.54} \text{ in.} = \frac{2.54}{2.54} \text{ cm}$$

or

$$\text{cm} = \frac{1}{2.54} \text{ in.}$$

If we carry out this division, we find

$$\frac{1}{2.54} = 0.3937007 \ldots$$

which, rounded off to three decimal places, gives the result in the table, 0.394.

Problem Solving:	**U.S. to Metric and Metric to U.S. Conversions**

Use Table 13.4 to convert:

    (a) 10 inches to centimeters   (b) 3 meters to yards
    (c) 8 miles to kilometers   (d) 9 kilograms to pounds
    (e) 2 quarts to liters

1. Read the problem
2. Select the unknown

We have to convert inches to centimeters, meters to yards, miles to kilometers, kilograms to pounds, and quarts to liters.

3. Think of a plan

We use Table 13.4 to find the proper conversions.

4. Use the table to determine the proper substitution for finding the required equivalent measure.

(a) Since 1 inch = 2.54 cm

$$10 \text{ inches} = 10 \cdot 2.54 \text{ cm}$$
$$= 25.4 \text{ cm}$$

(b)   1 meter = 1.09 yd
Thus,   3 meters = 3 · 1.09 yd
$$= 3.27 \text{ yd}$$

(c)   1 mile = 1.61 km
Hence,   8 miles = 8 · 1.61 km
$$= 12.9 \text{ km}$$
(Rounded from 12.88 km)

(d)   1 kg = 2.2 lb
So,   9 kg = 9 · 2.2 lb
$$= 19.8 \text{ lbs}$$

(e)   1 qt = 0.946 liter
Thus,   2 qts = 2 · 0.946 liter
$$= 1.90 \text{ liters (Rounded from 1.892 liters)}$$

5. Verify your answers. Did you use the correct procedure when rounding off answers?

If you do not remember how to round numbers or how to determine the number of significant digits in a decimal, review Section 4.5 before you go on!

TRY EXAMPLE 1 NOW.

Cover the solution, write your own, and then check your work.

EXAMPLE 1   The record distance reached by a boomerang before it starts to return to the thrower is about 90 yd (to the nearest yard). How many meters is that?

Solution   From Table 13.4, we see that 1 yd ≈ 0.914 m. Thus, we must multiply 90 by 0.914, giving 82.26. Since the 90 yd is correct to the nearest yard, the 90 has two significant digits and our answer must be rounded to two significant digits. Hence, we see that 90. yd ≈ 82 m. (Note that we have followed the custom of putting a decimal point after an integer with terminal 0's when all the 0's are significant.)   ■

EXAMPLE 2   How many grams are there in an ounce?

Solution   From Table 13.4, we see that 1 lb ≈ 0.454 kg. Since there are 16 oz in a pound and 1000 g in a kilogram, we have

$$16 \text{ oz} \approx 454 \text{ g}$$

$$1 \text{ oz} \approx \frac{454}{16} \text{ g}$$

If we divide 454 by 16, we get 28.375, but this must be rounded to three significant digits because there are only three significant digits in 0.454. Therefore,

$$1 \text{ oz} \approx 28.4 \text{ g}$$

■

EXAMPLE 3 The maximum speed limit on many highways is 55 mi/hr. How many kilometers per hour (km/hr) is this? (Assume the 55 to be exact.)

Solution From Table 13.4, we have 1 mi ≈ 1.61 km. Thus, we multiply 1.61 by 55 to get 88.55. This result must be rounded to agree with the three significant digits in the 1.61. Therefore,

$$55 \text{ mi/hr} \approx 88.6 \text{ km/hr}$$

■

EXAMPLE 4 The top speed of a certain European car is 200 km/hr. How many miles per hour is this? (Assume the 200 to be exact.)

Solution
$$1 \text{ km} \approx 0.621 \text{ mi}$$
$$200 \text{ km} \approx 200 \times 0.621 \text{ mi}$$
$$\approx 124 \text{ mi (Rounded from 124.2)}$$

Thus, 200 km/hr is equivalent to 124 mi/hr.

■

EXAMPLE 5 Mary bought 3 qt of milk. How many liters of milk is this?

Solution
$$1 \text{ qt} \approx 0.946 \text{ liter}$$
$$3 \text{ qt} \approx 3 \times 0.946 \text{ liter}$$
$$\approx 2.84 \text{ liters (Rounded from 2.838)}$$

■

Finally, here is a conversion that you probably see almost every day: gallons to liters, or liters to gallons. As you can see from the brochure shown on the next page, 1 gal is about 3.7854 liters, and 4 liters is a little more than 1 gal. A more precise relationship is:

$$1 \text{ liter} \approx 0.2642172 \text{ gal}$$
$$1 \text{ gal} \approx 3.785412 \text{ liters}$$

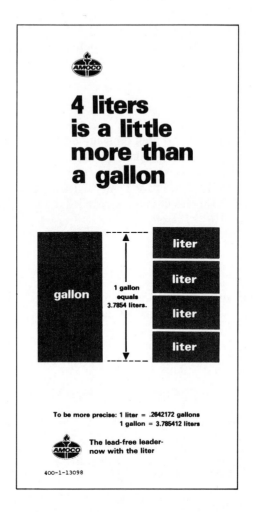

Suppose you fill your tank, and it takes 38 liters of gasoline. To the nearest tenth of a gallon, how many gallons of gas would that be? We write

$$38 \textbf{ liters} \approx (38)(\textbf{0.2642172 gal})$$
$$\approx 10.040254 \text{ gal}$$
$$\approx 10.0 \text{ gal}$$

EXAMPLE 6   The gas tank of a car has a capacity of 13.2 gal. To the nearest liter, how many liters is that?

Solution   We write

$$13.2 \textbf{ gal} \approx (13.2)(\textbf{3.785412 liters})$$
$$\approx 49.967438 \text{ liters}$$
$$\approx 50 \text{ liters}$$

Exercise 13.3 _____

In problems 1–28, use Table 13.4 to fill in the blank with the appropriate number. (Assume the given numbers are all exact.)

1. 8 in. = _____ cm
2. 5.2 in. = _____ cm
3. 12 cm = _____ in.
4. 25 cm = _____ in.
5. 51 yd = _____ m
6. 1.2 yd = _____ m
7. 3.7 m = _____ yd
8. 4.5 m = _____ yd
9. 4 mi = _____ km
10. 6.1 mi = _____ km
11. 3.7 km = _____ mi
12. 14 km = _____ mi
13. 6 lb = _____ kg
14. 8 lb = _____ kg
15. 5 kg = _____ lb
16. 1.2 kg = _____ lb
17. 5 qt = _____ liters
18. 6.1 qt = _____ liters
19. 8.1 liters = _____ qt
20. 11 liters = _____ qt
21. 75 cm = _____ ft
22. 800 m = _____ ft
23. 1 in.^{3} = _____ cm^3
    (to the nearest hundredth)
24. 1 cm^3 = _____ in.^{3}
    (to the nearest hundredth)
25. 2 yd = _____ cm
26. 3 yd = _____ cm
27. 78 cm = _____ yd
28. 100 cm = _____ yd

In the remaining problems, use Table 13.4 and assume the given numbers are exact.

29. The speed limit is 40 mi/hr. How many kilometers per hour is that? (Answer to the nearest kilometer per hour.)

30. Find the distance (to the nearest kilometer) from Tampa, Florida, to:
    (a) Zephyrhills, Florida, 22 mi
    (b) Ocala, Florida, 93 mi

31. The longest field goal in National Football League competition was 63 yd. How many meters is that?

32. The *U.S.S. New Jersey* is the longest battleship, measuring 296 yd long. How many meters is that?

33. Mount Everest is 8848 m high. How many feet is that?

34. The screen of a television set measures 24 in. diagonally. How many centimeters is that?

35. The largest omelet ever made weighed 1234 lb. How many kilograms is that?

36. Miss Helge Anderson of Sweden has been drinking 20 qt of water per day since 1922. How many liters per day is that?

37. The longest street in the world is Figueroa Street in Los Angeles. This street is 30 mi long. How many kilometers is that?

38. A car is traveling 125 km/hr. How many miles per hour is that?

39. The maximum allowable weight for a flyweight wrestler is 52 kg. How many pounds is that?

40. The largest car ever built was the Bugatti Royale, type 41, with an eight-cylinder engine of 12.7-liter capacity. How many quarts is this?

41. Two adjacent sides of a rectangle are measured and found to be 52.3 and 96.84 m long, respectively. How many meters long is the perimeter of the rectangle?

42. A rectangle is measured and found to be 21.5 ft by 32.63 ft. How many meters long is the perimeter?

43. A road sign warns of a bridge with a safe load of 14 tons. A metric ton is 1000 kg (very close to 2200 lb). What is the safe load of the bridge in metric tons? Answer to the nearest tenth.

44. Another road sign warns of a bridge with a safe load of 15 tons. What is this safe load in metric tons? (See problem 43.)

45. The Pontiac 1000 had a highway mileage estimated to be 40 mi/gal. To the nearest tenth, how many kilometers per liter is that?

*I*n Other Words

46. Discuss three reasons why it is easier to measure distances in the metric system than in the U.S. customary system.

Using Your Knowledge

47. A Boeing 747 requires about 1900 m for a takeoff runway. About how many miles is this?

48. A fully loaded Boeing 747 weighs about 320,000 kg. About how many tons is this? (1 ton = 2000 lb)

49. The longest recorded distance for throwing (and catching) a raw hen's egg without breaking it is 316 ft $5\frac{3}{4}$ in. About how many meters is this?

50. The largest champagne bottle made is called a *Nebuchadnezzar;* it holds 16 liters. How many gallons is this?

51. In 1954, the winner of the Miss World contest had the Junoesque measurements 40–26–38. These measurements are in inches. What would they be in centimeters.

52. An 1878 bottle (1 liter) of Chartreuse (a liqueur) sold for $42. About how much per ounce is this?

53. You have probably heard the expression, "Hang in there!" Well, Rudy Kishazy did just that. He hung onto a glider that took off from Mount Blanc and landed 35 minutes later at Servoz, France, a distance of 15 mi. How many kilometers is that?

54. Romantic young ladies always dream about that knight in shining armor, but do you know what is the longest recorded ride in full armor? It is 146 mi. How many kilometers is that? (By the way, Dick Brown took the ride on June 12–15, 1973.)

55. Do you get thirsty on a hot summer day? Of course, you do! But nothing compares with the unquenchable thirst of Miss Helge Anderson of Sweden. She has been drinking 40 pt of water every day since 1922. About how many liters of water per day is that? (Remember that 2 pt = 1 qt.)

56. Do you know how to knit? If you do, you might try to equal the feat of Mrs. Gwen Mathewman of Yorkshire, England. In 1974, she knitted 836 garments. How much wool do you think she used? An unbelievable 9770 oz! How many grams is that?

57. What did you have for breakfast today? An omelet? We'll bet that you couldn't eat the largest omelet ever made—it weighed 1234 lb. About how many grams is that?

Discovery

58. Are you puzzled by the material in this chapter? We hope not, for here is a "cross-number" puzzle that will amuse you. See if you can discover all the correct numbers.

Across

1. 3 g + 125 mg = _____ mg
2. 2000 g − 0.275 kg = _____ g
5. 13.2 g − 0.65 g = _____ cg
7. 180 g + 200 dg = _____ dkg
8. 11 dg + 13 cg = _____ cg
9. 100 dg = _____ g
10. 10.22 hg − 0.938 kg = _____ g
12. 50 dg + 120 cg − 2075 mg = _____ mg
13. 2.5 kg = _____ g

Down

1. 55 kg − 20 kg = _____ hg
3. 60 dkg − 0.1 kg = _____ g
4. 3.5 g + 40 dg = _____ dg
6. 510,000 g = _____ kg
7. 1.133 g − 0.915 g = _____ mg
8. 110,500 mg + 3500 mg = _____ g
9. 1200 cg = _____ g
11. 4.20 dg = _____ mg

Note: The prefixes hecto (h), deka (da), and deci (d) are not as commonly used as the others in the puzzle, but they are (SI).

Solve like a crossword puzzle except that numbers replace words. Be sure to express answers in the indicated units.

Chapter 13 Summary

Section	Item	Meaning	Example
13.1A	kilo (k)	One thousand	1 kilometer = 1000 meters
13.1A	hecto (h)	One hundred	1 hectogram = 100 grams
13.1A	deka (dk)	Ten	1 dekaliter = 10 liters
13.1A	deci (d)	One-tenth	1 decimeter = 0.1 meter
13.1A	centi (c)	One-hundredth	1 centigram = 0.01 gram
13.1A	milli (m)	One-thousandth	1 millimeter = 0.001 meter
13.1C	kilometer (km)	1000 meters	
13.1C	hectometer (hm)	100 meters	
13.1C	dekameter (dkm)	10 meters	
13.1C	meter (m)	Basic unit of length	
13.1C	decimeter (dm)	0.1 meter	
13.1C	centimeter (cm)	0.01 meter	
13.1C	millimeter (mm)	0.001 meter	
13.1D	kiloliter (kl)	1000 liters	
13.1D	hectoliter (hl)	100 liters	
13.1D	dekaliter (dkl)	10 liters	
13.1D	liter (l)	Basic unit of volume	
13.1D	deciliter (dl)	0.1 liter	
13.1D	centiliter (cl)	0.01 liter	
13.1D	milliliter (ml)	0.001 liter	
13.1E	kilogram (kg)	1000 grams	
13.1E	hectogram (hg)	100 grams	
13.1E	dekagram (dkg)	10 grams	
13.1E	gram (g)	Basic unit of weight	

Section	Item	Meaning	Example
13.1E	decigram (dg)	0.1 gram	
13.1E	centigram (cg)	0.01 gram	
13.1E	milligram (mg)	0.001 gram	
13.2	$C = \dfrac{5(F - 32)}{9}$	Formula to convert Fahrenheit to Celsius degrees	
13.2	$F = \dfrac{9C}{5} + 32$	Formula to convert Celsius to Fahrenheit degrees	

Research Questions

Sources of information for these questions can be found in the Bibliography at the end of the book.

1. Go to an encyclopedia or other source and write a paper citing the advantages of the metric system of measure over the U.S. customary system. How many countries, other than the U.S., are **not** using the metric system?

2. Find the origins of the words *inch, foot, yard, carat, cubit, furlong, fathom, league* and state what type of measurement each represents.

3. Write a brief report about the SI system of measurement, its inception, and the standards for length, weight, and volume.

4. Investigate and trace the development of the metric system in Europe and the efforts to use this system in the U.S.

5. Write a report on Isaac Asimov's book, *Asimov on Numbers,* concentrating on Chapter 10, which deals with prefixes and extent of measurability of length, mass, and time.

Chapter 13 Practice Test

1. Write the power of 10 that corresponds to the following prefixes:
   (a) centi   (b) milli   (c) kilo

2. A person is buying some paint to paint a house. In the metric system, the paint would be measured in which of the following?
   (a) Grams   (b) Centimeters   (c) Liters

3. A fruit market sells oranges by weight. In the metric system, the oranges should be weighed in which of the following units?
   (a) Liters   (b) Kilograms   (c) Meters

4. A steel rod is $\frac{3}{4}$ m long. How many centimeters is that?
5. A racetrack is 0.9 km long. How many meters is that?
6. The sides of a triangle are 3 cm, 4 cm, and 6 cm long, respectively. What are these lengths in millimeters?
7. A piece of a straight line is 0.082 m long. How many millimeters is that?
8. A water tank holds 8.3 kl of water. How many liters is that?
9. A bottle with a capacity of 92 cl holds how many liters?
10. A small container holds 19 ml of liquid. How many centiliters is that?
11. A liter of wine will fill about ten large wine glasses. How many milliliters does one of these glasses hold?
12. A 1-carat diamond weighs 0.2 g. How many milligrams will a 2-carat diamond weigh?
13. A market prices onions at $1 per kilogram. How many cents per gram is that?
14. Convert 275 mg to kilograms.
15. A person bought a 250-g can of tuna fish. How many kilograms is that?
16. A baby weighed 4.1 kg at birth. How many grams is that?
17. The temperature in San Francisco was 77°F. What is that in degrees Celsius?
18. The temperature in New York was 20°C. What is that in degrees Fahrenheit?

In problems 19–25, assume the given numbers are exact.
19. In some Canadian towns, the posted speed limit is 40 km/hr. How many miles per hour is this?
20. A woman weighs 52 kg. How many pounds is this?
21. A wine bottle contains 750 ml of wine.
    (a) How many liters is this?   (b) How many quarts?
22. The sides of a triangle are found to be 152, 178, and 135 m long. How many kilometers long is the perimeter of the triangle?
23. The side of a square is 3.5 in. long. How many centimeters long is the perimeter of the square?
24. The sides of a triangle are measured to be 16.3, 18.9, and 15.46 cm long, respectively. How many centimeters long is the perimeter of the triangle?
25. Which of the following is most nearly correct? Ten inches is about:
    (a) 30 cm   (b) 25 cm   (c) 20 cm

CHAPTER
PREVIEW

In the last few years millions of **personal computers (PCs)** have been sold to individuals, businesses, schools, and universities. Computers are used to make bus, class, and work schedules; route traffic and phone calls; and to calculate tuition and bank fees. Most people who own computers use software programs called **applications.** For example, a **word processing** application enables you to write documents, a **spreadsheet** application can perform intricate calculations, and a **drawing** application may let you draw in your computer.

In this chapter we want to help you take advantage of the capabilities of your computer. To communicate with a computer we first need a programming **language,** and the proliferation of languages and "dialects" of these languages has been dramatic. Recently, a new language called QBASIC has become standard with computers whose operating systems, usually called DOS, use a version whose number is 5.0 or higher. QBASIC is also available for Macintosh computers. But, there is a price to pay for all the conveniences: not all languages are exactly alike. Thus, we have tried to introduce the **commands** that are common to most languages. When there are exceptions, we have tried to note them, but when in doubt, read your programming manual.

We start the chapter by familiarizing you with the terminology and the basics of programming. The PRINT command is introduced in Section 14.1 followed by LET and END, which are given in 14.2. We then discuss READ, DATA, GOTO, and INPUT commands in Section 14.3. We end the chapter by discussing the IF. . .THEN. . . (Section 14.4) and the FOR and NEXT commands (Section 14.5).

Computers

Grace Murray Hopper

THE HUMAN SIDE OF MATHEMATICS

The programming used in early computers was as primitive as the machines in which it ran. Machines such as Harvard's Mark I, a five-ton mass of relays, switches, shafts, and gears, received instructions from spools of punched paper tape and worked mostly in machine code, binary digits corresponding to a computer's circuit.

One frustrated programmer, Grace Murray Hopper, was not satisfied with the progress being made. Hopper was accustomed to being in the vanguard. She had grown up fascinated by things mechanical. After graduating from Vassar College in 1928, she earned a Ph.D in mathematics from Yale.

In 1944, Hopper was commissioned as a Lieutenant in the U.S. Naval Reserve. Later, she joined the programming team assigned to the Mark I. Because the Mark I was assigned to compute ballistic firing tables, it had some mathematical operations wired into it, but Hopper discovered that the machine required a subroutine, a tool that has become one of the fundamental elements of modern programming. Later, Grace Hopper and her colleagues christened

another aspect of computing. On a muggy, summer afternoon while running tests on the Mark I at Harvard University, a mysterious malfunction brought the computer to a screeching halt. Further investigation revealed the remains of a moth trapped in one of the thousands of mechanical relays in the computer. They extracted the dead moth with tweezers and meticulously taped it into the log book that they kept. (See photo on page 932) The accompanying notation recorded the "first actual case of bug being found," and thus was born the term "debugging the computer."

A civilian again in 1949, Hopper joined the Eckert-Mauchly Computer Corporation builders of the Universal Automatic Computer, or UNIVAC. There, her efforts to ease the programmer's burden led Hopper to the study of Short Code, a computer language translator that turned a program into machine code one line at a time. She also set up a library of standardized subroutines for the UNIVAC, the first computer to be manufactured and sold in significant quantities, thanks in great part to the work of this amazing individual, Grace Murray Hopper.

14.1   GETTING STARTED WITH COMPUTERS

The **first generation** of modern computers started with ENIAC (Electronic Numerical Integrator and Computer) and was followed by a **second generation** (transistors replacing tubes) as well as a **third** (using integrated circuits) and a **fourth** (with miniaturized memory chips). Personal computers (PC for short) belong to the fourth generation and the fifth generation will be in the realm of artificial intelligence (AI).

A. *The Components*

A typical personal computer has components that include:

1. A **keyboard** (to enter information and instructions)
2. A **video monitor** (to view the instructions and results)
3. One or more **disk drives** (to store information permanently or to enter additional instructions)
4. A **system unit** (into which the other three components are plugged) housing the **central processing unit (CPU)**

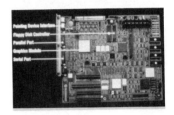

When you turn on a computer, a quartz clock in the CPU emits a reset signal that clears the computer of all instructions and gets it ready to "boot," a process so named because the computer pulls itself up "by its own bootstraps." At this point, the computer will give itself a checkup by whirring, moaning, and groaning for a short time. (Some computers display on the screen the status of the equipment checked. If a specific part is functional, the display will sometimes say PASS next to the name of the part.) And then . . . nothing! (If a floppy disk is being used, some models display a screen message saying that floppy A—that is, disk drive A—is not ready and that there is a disk read error.) Why? Because we have not given the computer any specific instructions as to how to proceed. How do we do that? Let us start all over again. If your computer has a hard drive, the C drive, the instructions may be in the computer and the monitor will probably show the **C prompt** C>_ .

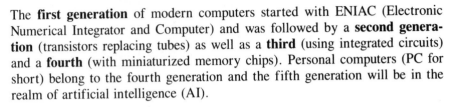

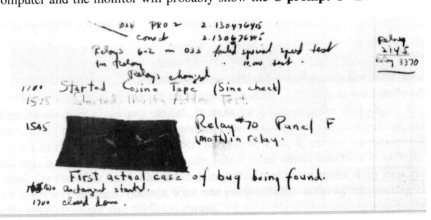

Barely discernable under the discolored tape in a mid-1940s log book are the remains of the first "computer bug," an actual moth found trapped between points at a mechanical relay in the Mark I computer at Harvard University

B. *Getting Restarted*

This time, before we start, place the disk operating **system diskette, DOS** (or a copy of it), with its label up, in drive A (the left or top drive if there are two). Now, turn on the computer. After checking itself, the computer will beep and will ask you to enter a new time and date. You must do so using the format 1-2-93 or 1/2/93 for the date and then pressing the ENTER or RETURN key ⏎. The time used in most computers is a 24-hour system, so 4:30 in the afternoon is written as 16:30. To type the colon (:), you have to press the up-arrow key ↑ and : (abbreviated as SHIFT + :) as on a regular typewriter. Now that you know how, here is a little secret: You can by-pass entering the date and time by simply pressing ⏎ twice. The make and model of your computer, the version of the instructions (program) in the system disk (something like 1.1, 2.3, or 3.3), and the copyright holder for the **disk operating system (DOS)** being used will then appear on the screen. The computer is now ready and the next line will say

> A>_

This means that your system program is on, and drive A is waiting for action.

C. *Back to Basics*

We can find out what programs, or **files,** are on the system disk by asking the computer for a **directory.** Type DIR and press ⏎. A list of all the files will appear on the screen. Two of these, BASIC and BASICA (which has more features), enable the computer to speak in the BASIC language. But how do we get started? Type:

> QBASIC ⏎ or BASICA ⏎

which means, "Load the program named QBASIC or BASICA from the diskette in drive A."

If You Are Using BASICA or GW-BASIC

The monitor indicates the type of Basica being used (BASIC VER. 4.02 or GW-BASIC 4.1), the copyright holder, the memory available (62426 bytes free, for example), and the word OK, which means the computer is now really ready for BASIC. The little dash or blinking box after the OK is called a **cursor** and it tells us where anything we type will appear on the screen. To make sure we have a clean

If You Are Using QBASIC

The program opens a window with two options: Press ⏎, the ENTER key, to see the survival guide (which you should do some other time) or remove the QBASIC program diskette, insert the QBASIC Help diskette in drive A, and press ESC to clear the dialog box. A new **View Window** (UNTITLED) appears. Note the **Menu Bar** at the top of the window. It is activated by pressing the ALT key, then

start, we want to erase all prior programs that may be somewhere in the machine. Type NEW and press ⏎, the RETURN, or ENTER key. Type CLS and press ⏎ to clear the screen. Look at the bottom of the screen. 1LIST, 2RUN, 3LOAD″, 4SAVE″ mean that if you press F1, it will **list** the steps on your program; if you press F2, it will **run** your program; if you press F3 and write the name of your program, it will **load** it; and if you press F4 and write the name of your program, it will **save** it.

pressing one of the highlighted letters (**F** for File, **E** for Exit, **V** for **V**iew, and so on) selects a menu, or you can press → ⏎. To make sure you have a new window, type ALT F N, then type CLS ⏎ to clear the **output** screen. Now look at the bottom of the screen. The **commands** for the **View Window** are shown. For example, pressing Shift + F1 = Help, and pressing F5 = Run. In QBASIC, the program is in the **View Window** but the answer, or **output,** appears on a separate **output screen.**

What do we want to do next? Whatever it is, we have to use the BASIC language to communicate with the computer. The set of instructions we give the computer is called a **program,** and the writing of these instructions is called **programming.** Let us write a very simple program as an introduction to BASIC. Type the following line:

```
10  PRINT "I AM GLAD TO MEET YOU."
```

Hold it. Do *not* press the ⏎ yet! First, if you made a keyboarding error, do not worry. Use the backspace key ← as your eraser. Each time you press the ← key, the character to the left of the cursor will be erased. If your mistake was at the beginning of the line, erase to that point and retype. (If you hold the backspace key down for a few seconds, it may wipe out the entire line.) Now, study carefully what you typed.

1. Is everything after the word PRINT inside quotations?
2. Is all the punctuation correct?
3. Do you have any misspelled words you wish to change?

If everything is satisfactory, press ⏎. The cursor will move to the left margin to let you know your instructions have been entered. (By now, you should have noticed that instructions are entered by pressing the ⏎ key. We shall omit this step from now on.) But what if you find an error after the instructions are entered? In BASICA, retype the entire line correctly. When you type ⏎, the old line will be replaced by the new one. Finally, you have to tell **(command)** the computer to **execute,** or **run,** your program. Type RUN and press ⏎, or press F5 in QBASIC. If you have been careful, the computer will display

```
I AM GLAD TO MEET YOU.
```

EXAMPLE 1   What will be printed if you run the following programs?

(a) 10   PRINT I AM A PROGRAMMER NOW.
(b) 20   PRINT I AM A PROGRAMMER NOW."
(c) 30   PRINT "I AM A PROGRAMMER NOW.'"
(d) 40   PRINT "I AM A PROGRAMMER NOW."

Solution   (a) Five 0's will print. There are no quotation marks after the
word PRINT, so each word will be interpreted as a variable
starting with a 0 value.
(b) Five 0's will print. Again, there are no quotations after
PRINT.
(c) I AM A PROGRAMMER NOW.' Since the computer prints
everything between the quotation marks, it will print the
extra ' (apostrophe) at the end of the sentence.
(d) I AM A PROGRAMMER NOW.

■

You can print numbers, words, and characters in the same program, as shown
in the next example.

EXAMPLE 2   What will happen if you run the following program?

```
10   PRINT   "5 - 3"
20   PRINT   "IS"
30   PRINT   5 - 3
40   PRINT   "THAT IS, 5 - 3 =" 5 - 3
```

Solution
```
5 - 3
IS
2
THAT IS, 5 - 3 = 2.
```

Line 40 combines the printing of words and numbers. It prints the statement
inside the quotes, and then prints the indicated difference $5 - 3$ or 2 outside
the quotation marks.

■

We can even play music on a computer! But you have to know the sound of the
musical notes and the **PLAY** command. For example, type

```
10   PLAY   "ABCDEFG"
RUN
```

What happened?
We now combine the **PRINT** and **PLAY** commands in Example 3.

EXAMPLE 3   What happens if you run the following program?

```
10   PLAY "CCDCFE"
20   PRINT "HAPPY BIRTHDAY"
```

Solution   The computer plays the notes CCDCFE (Happy birthday to you) and then prints HAPPY BIRTHDAY. But wait, there is no "TO YOU" in the printing, can we add it to the program? Of course, type the new line

```
30  PRINT "TO YOU"
```

When run, this program will play CCDCFE (Happy birthday to you) and print

```
HAPPY BIRTHDAY
TO YOU
```
∎

A last word of wisdom: Always remove the diskette(s) before turning off the system—or the disk might end up with some of its files erased, unreadable, or unusable.

Exercise 14.1

A. 1. Name the main characteristic of second-generation computers.
   2. Name the main characteristic of third-generation computers.
   3. Name the main characteristic of fourth-generation computers.
   4. To what computer generation do personal computers belong?
   5. Name four components of a typical personal computer.

B. 6. Write two different ways in which you can enter the date June 8, 1998, in a personal computer.
   7. Write two different ways in which you can enter the date August 4, 1997, in a personal computer.
   8. Suppose it is 9 o'clock in the morning and you want to enter this time into your computer. What would you type?
   9. Suppose it is 8 o'clock in the evening and you want to enter this time into your computer. What would you type?
   10. What does the abbreviation DOS stand for?

C. 11. What happens if you type DIR and press ⏎ ?
   12. After typing DIR and pressing ⏎ , the screen showed

```
MICKEY
MINNIE
GOOFY
```

You want to use the Goofy program. What do you have to do?

   13. Suppose you type

```
I DO NOT MAKE MISTE_
```

The cursor is right after the E. How would you erase the E?

   14. Suppose you write the following program:

```
10  PRINT "I DO NOT MAKE MISTEAKS"
```

Then you press the $\leftarrow$ key. In BASICA, how would you correct the misspelled word without using the $\leftarrow$ key?

In problems 15–20, what will be printed if you run the given program?

15. `10   PRINT WE NEED QUOTATION MARKS AT THE END"`

16. `20   PRINT 'WE NEED QUOTATION MARKS AT THE END'`

17. `30   PRINT "WE NEED QUOTATION MARKS AT THE END"`

18. `10   PRINT I AM A PROGRAMMER`
    `10   PRINT I AM A PROGRAMMER"`

19. `20   PRINT "I KNOW THE ANSWER"`
    `20   PRINT I KNOW THE ANSWER`

20. `30   PRINT THIS IS THE END"`
    `30   PRINT "THIS IS THE END"`

21. Write a program that prints the following:

    ```
    5 + 3
    IS
    8
    THAT IS, 5 + 3 = 8
    ```

22. Write a program that prints the following:

    ```
    6/3
    IS
    2
    THAT IS, 6 ÷ 3 = 2
    ```

23. Write a program that prints the following:

    ```
    ##########
    #        #
    ##########
    ```

24. Write a program that prints the following:

    ```
          *****
        *       *
      *   ^   ^   *
    *     o   o     *
      *     +     *
        *  ___  *
          *   *
          *****
    ```

25. A student works the following hours during successive days of the week: 3, 5, 5, 4, 3. Write a program that will calculate and print the total number of hours worked for the week as shown.

    `TOTAL HOURS WORKED: 20`

26. Change the program in problem 25 so that it lists the number of hours worked each day and then the total hours. The first and last lines should look like this:

    ```
    MONDAY: 3
    TOTAL HOURS WORKED: 20
    ```

27. What happens if you run the program

    `10   PLAY "EDCDEEEP8DDDP4EGG"`

    Note that P8 and P4 represent pauses in the playing of the music.

28. Modify the program in problem 21 so that it plays the song and writes the lyrics to it using three lines.

In Other Words

29. What does the command **NEW** do and why is it used?

30. Explain the differences in the procedure to use the commands **NEW** and **RUN** in BASIC and QBASIC.

31. What is the difference between the commands **NEW** and **CLS**?

14.2   PROGRAMMING A COMPUTER

GETTING STARTED

WHAT IS THE TEMPERATURE?

We have already discussed the rules of arithmetic (Chapter 4) and generalized them to algebra (Chapter 5). During this process, we learned the **order** in which operations involving real numbers could be formed. In this section, we shall go through a similar process by first discussing mathematical operations and the order in which they are executed by the computer. We then study two new important commands: LET and END. An **assignment** statement such as LET is used to **assign** a value, say, 5, to a variable, say, A. This is done by writing

LET A = 5

Variables can be single letters (A, B, X), a letter and a single digit (A1, B2, X3), or two letters (AA, AB, or AX). How do we use LET and PRINT statements? As you recall, the formula to convert degrees Celsius to degrees Fahrenheit is:

$$F = \frac{9}{5}C + 32$$

Here is a program that will convert temperatures from Celsius to Fahrenheit. The first line of the program is an optional line. It is simply a remark (REM, for short) and does not affect the program at all, but merely reminds programmers what the program does.

```
10   REM *CELSIUS TO FAHRENHEIT CONVERTER*
20   LET C = 15                Assigns 15 to C
30   LET F = (9/5)*C + 32    Assigns (9/5)*C + 32 to F
40   PRINT C; "DEGREES (C) = "F;"DEGREES (F)"
```

Can you figure out what the last line did? It printed C, then printed DEGREES (C) = and the value of F followed by DEGREES (F). We will talk more about these types of programs in Section 14.2.

Now that you know how to load BASIC (or QBASIC), we will discuss how to communicate with your computer in this language by using a **program,** which is a list of instructions that can be stored in the computer to be executed, or run. The writing of these instructions is called **programming.** Always remember that a computer has no mind of its own; it will do exactly what you instruct it to do (which in many cases may *not* be what you really intend it to do). Just remember that every detail is important. A misspelled word or a misplaced comma can upset an entire program. Mistakes in a program are called **bugs** and locating and correcting these errors is called **debugging.**

Several languages have been designed to fill various programming needs. Some of these languages are:

ALGOL	**ALG**orithm-**O**riented **L**anguage
BASIC	**B**eginner's **A**ll-purpose **S**ymbolic **I**nstruction **C**ode
COBOL	**CO**mmon **B**usiness-**O**riented **L**anguage
FORTRAN	**FOR**mula **TRAN**slation
LISP	**LIS**t **P**rocessing
PASCAL	Named after the French mathematician Blaise Pascal
C	Designed by Dennis Ritchie of Bell Telephone Company to improve an earlier language developed by Ken Thompson and named—you guessed it—B!

For now, we shall concentrate on BASIC, one of the easiest languages to use because it is so close to ordinary English that it is almost self-explanatory. Where shall we start? With the mathematical operations, of course.

A. *Mathematical Operations*

In BASIC, the symbols for the mathematical operations are:

Symbol	Meaning	Example	
+	Plus	3 + 5	
−	Minus	3 − 5	
*	Times	3 * 5	3 times 5
/	Divided by	3 / 5	3 divided by 5
^	With exponent	3 ^ 5	3^5 or 3 with exponent 5

[*Note:* Some systems use ** and other systems use the upward-pointing arrow for exponentiation.]

Parentheses are used just as in ordinary mathematical notation. For example, in BASIC, the expression $4 \times 3^2 - (8 + 9)(5 \div 12)^4$ would appear as follows:

```
4*3^2-(8+9)*(5/12)^4
```

You can remember this order
by memorizing:
Please
Excuse
My **D**ear
Aunt **S**ally

The *order of operations* is exactly as in algebra, from left to right:

1. Operations inside **p**arentheses are done first.
2. **E**xponentiation precedes the other operations.
3. **M**ultiplications and **d**ivisions are done next.
4. **A**dditions and **s**ubtractions are done last.

Thus, $4 + 3 \cdot 5$ will give $4 + 15 = 19$, since $3 \cdot 5$ is done first. Parentheses can be used to make sure calculations are done in the order you want. For example, to add $4 + 3$ first in $4 + 3 \cdot 5$, you should write $(4 + 3) \cdot 5$. Then the result will be $7 \cdot 5 = 35$.

EXAMPLE 1   Write in BASIC:

(a) $4(2 + 3)$ (b) $5^2 + 12^2$ (c) $8 \div (3^4 - 4^3)$

Solution   (a) `4*(2 + 3)`   (b) `5^2+12^2`   (c) `8/(3^4-4^3)`   ∎

EXAMPLE 2   Evaluate:

(a) `(16/4)^3`   (b) `2^3+3^2`   (c) `(2*5)^3`

Solution   (a) $(16 \div 4)^3 = 4^3 = 64$ (b) $2^3 + 3^2 = 8 + 9 = 17$
(c) $(2 \times 5)^3 = 10^3 = 1000$ ∎

If you want the computer to perform some mathematical operations or run a program that will do a certain task, you must type commands at the keyboard. In BASIC, a program consists of a set of lines that are called *statements*. A **statement** is an expression or an instruction that is meaningful to the computer. Each statement is preceded by a **line number** and followed by a **keyword (command)** that tells the computer what type of operation is to be performed. If a statement is too long for a single line, it may be split into two statements with another number assigned to the second line. If more lines are needed, they must be treated in the same manner.

Each instruction that tells a computer to do something is called a **command.** You can include several commands in one line, but they must be separated by colons (:). We shall now consider three simple commands: LET, PRINT, and END.

B. *The LET, PRINT, and END Commands*

A command such as LET A = 5 tells the computer to assign the name A to a storage space and to store 5 in that space. Unless a later command changes this, the computer will use the number 5 for the letter A in each calculation it is instructed to perform with A. (You can actually shorten things by simply writing A = 5; the LET is optional but it helps to identify the program line where A is given a value.)

As you have seen, the PRINT command means exactly what it says. If you type the commands LET A = 5 and then PRINT A, the computer will display the number 5. If you type PRINT A$^\wedge$2, it will display 25 (the square of the number in storage space A), and it will keep the number 5 in storage space A. If you type only PRINT 5$^\wedge$2, the computer will again display 25, but it will not store a number anywhere. Note that a variable such as A can have only *one* value at a time. Thus, if you write 10 LET A = 5 and later 60 LET A = 40, the value of A is now 40 and the old value is lost.

Finally, to tell the computer it has come to the end of a program, enter a line number (some fussy programmers use nines, for example, 9, 99, or 999) and the word END.

EXAMPLE 3 What will be the output if the following program is run?

```
10   LET  A=5
20   LET  B=2
30   LET  C=3
40   LET  X=A*B
50   LET  Y=A*B+C
60   LET  Z=Y-A^B
70   LET  W=B/A+C^3
80   PRINT X; Y; Z; W
90   END
```

Solution We type in the word RUN (no line number is needed), and the computer will display the values it calculated for X, Y, Z, and W. The last three lines of the completed and run program would look like this:

```
RUN
10      13       -12      27.4
OK   Some computers omit the OK
```

This means that X = 10, Y = 13, Z = -12, and W = 27.4. (You can check these answers by doing the computations indicated on lines 40, 50, 60, and 70.) The effect of the semicolon separating the variables in line 80 is to make the answers appear next to each other. If you wanted the answers displayed on separate lines, you would type a separate PRINT command for each of the variables X, Y, Z, and W. The OK on the third line tells us that the computer is ready for further instructions. ∎

Study Example 3 carefully to see what the computer was instructed to do. In the first three lines, it was commanded to store the numbers 5, 2, and 3 in spaces named A, B, and C, respectively. Then it was instructed to calculate $A \times B = 5 \times 2$, $A \times B + C = 5 \times 2 + 3$, $(A \times B + C) - A^B = (5 \times 2 + 3) - 5^2$, and $B/A + C^3 = \frac{2}{5} + 3^3$ and assign the resulting values to the variables X, Y, Z, and W, respectively. Then it was commanded to print the answers next to each other. If we had entered commas, the answers would be spaced differently.

To illustrate the difference in how output will be spaced depending on whether commas or semicolons are used, type the following:

```
10   PRINT "THESE NUMBERS ARE PRINTED USING COMMAS"
20   PRINT 1, 2, 3
30   PRINT "THESE NUMBERS ARE PRINTED USING SEMICOLONS"
40   PRINT 1; 2; 3

RUN
```

You should get a result that looks like this:

```
THESE NUMBERS ARE PRINTED USING COMMAS
 1                             2                             3
THESE NUMBERS ARE PRINTED USING SEMICOLONS
 1      2      3
```

Since many computers use only capital letters, we have used capital letters throughout our programs. It is very important to distinguish the number 0 (zero) from the letter "oh" (O) and the number 1 (one) from lowercase "el" (l). The computer has separate keys for these symbols.

A computer that is equipped to use BASIC will always execute your commands in the order in which they are numbered. This is the reason for numbering the lines 10, 20, 30, and so on. If you find you have left out an instruction, you can insert it by using an intermediate line number and typing a line at the end without having to retype the entire program. For instance, suppose that in Example 3, the instruction in line 50 had been omitted. In line 60 we have

```
LET Z=Y-A^B
```

but Y was not defined, so when we type in RUN, the computer will automatically assign the value 0 to Y and thus give a different value for Z. We can correct this by simply typing the line

```
45   LET Y=A*B+C
```

at the end of the program. (Recall that in BASIC if you type in an incorrect instruction, you can correct it just by typing a new line with the same line number and the correct instruction. The computer will automatically replace the original line with the new one.)

EXAMPLE 4   What number will the computer display for the following program?

```
10   LET X=2
20   LET Y=4*X^3-3*X^2+10*X-156
30   PRINT Y
40   END

RUN
```

Solution Since the computer does exponentiation first, multiplication and division second, and addition and subtraction last, the program asks for the value of

$$4(2^3) - 3(2^2) + (10)(2) - 156 = 32 - 12 + 20 - 156 = -116$$

Thus, the printout will be -116.

■

In a sequence of multiplications and divisions, the operations will be done in the order in which they occur from left to right, unless parentheses indicate otherwise.

EXAMPLE 5 Justify the two answers given for the following program:

```
10    LET X=2*3/12*4
20    LET Y=2*3/(12*4)
30    PRINT X; Y
40    END

RUN
2     .125
OK
```

Solution In doing the calculation called for in line 10, the computer would first multiply 2 times 3, to get 6. It would then divide 6 by 12, to get 0.5. Then it would multiply 0.5 by 4 to get the answer 2.

In doing the calculation called for in line 20, the computer would multiply 2 times 3 and 12 times 4, getting 6 and 48, respectively. Then it would divide 6 by 48 to get 0.125.

■

Can you determine the printout for the next program?

```
10    LET X=(6+2*3)/6*4
20    LET Y=6+2*3/(6*4)
30    PRINT X+Y; X-Y; X*Y
40    END

RUN
```

If you got the answers 14.25, 1.75, and 50, then you are beginning to understand the order of operations and the LET and PRINT commands.

Note that the printouts in the above examples were just numbers, identified only if you go back and see what you asked the computer to do. You can label the answers in the printout by using the PRINT statement and quotation marks. (Some systems use single rather than double quotation marks.) This is done by modifying the PRINT commands in the preceding program to match those shown below. The semicolon after the item in quotation marks in line

30, for example, causes the computer to print the equation X + Y = 14.25 without any extra space after the equals sign.

```
30   PRINT "X+Y="; X+Y
40   PRINT "X-Y="; X-Y
50   PRINT "X*Y="; X*Y
60   END

RUN
X+Y=14.25
X-Y=1.75
X*Y=50
```

Note: With a single PRINT command you can ask the computer to print out more than one item, but in that case the items must be separated by semicolons or commas in the PRINT line of your program. Thus, lines 30, 40, and 50 could be made into one line reading like this:

```
25   PRINT "X+Y="; X+Y, "X-Y="; X-Y, "X*Y="; X*Y
```

When line 25 is RUN, we get

```
X + Y = 14.25            X - Y = 1.75            X * Y = 50
```

C. *String Variables*

Your computer keyboard contains letters, numbers, and punctuation marks called **characters** (A, #, and 8, for example). A **string** is a single character or series of characters written (strung) together to form a word, numbers, or sequence of symbols. To assign a value to a string variable, the variable must be followed by a dollar ($) sign and the characters that make up the string must be enclosed by quotation marks. The variable used may be a letter (A$ or B$), a letter and a single digit (A1$ or B2$), or two letters (AA$ or AB$). Some forms of BASIC even let you use words like **first$** for the variable. Now, let us look at this program:

```
10   LET A$="DEAR STUDENT:"
20   LET B$=" YOU MISSED YOUR TEST"
30   PRINT A$
40   PRINT B$
50   PRINT A$+B$
60   END
```

The output will be:

```
DEAR STUDENT:
YOU MISSED YOUR TEST
DEAR STUDENT: YOU MISSED YOUR TEST
```

Note that line 50 attaches A$ to B$. An extra space was left after the first quotation mark in line 20; otherwise line 50 would print as

```
DEAR STUDENT:YOU MISSED YOUR TEST
```

EXAMPLE 6   What will be printed if the following program is run?

```
10   LET A=8
20   LET A$="EIGHT"
30   PRINT "CALL ME AT"A
40   PRINT "CALL ME AT "A$
50   PRINT A "IS A GOOD TIME TO CALL."
60   PRINT A$" IS A GOOD TIME TO CALL."
70   PRINT "CALL ME AT" A "TOMORROW."
80   PRINT "CALL ME AT "A$" TOMORROW."
90   END
```

Solution   Before we show the output, examine each line. We have provided extra spaces in certain places so that the output will be properly printed.

Line 30:   There is no space between the last quotation mark and A.
Line 40:   There is an extra space before the last quotation mark so that the words in lines 20 and 40 are separated by a space when printed.
Line 60:   An extra space is needed after the opening quotes.
Line 70:   No extra spaces are needed.
Line 80:   An extra space is needed at the end of the first quote and at the beginning of the second set of quotes.

Here is the output.

```
CALL ME AT 8
CALL ME AT EIGHT
8 IS A GOOD TIME TO CALL.
EIGHT IS A GOOD TIME TO CALL.
CALL ME AT 8 TOMORROW.
CALL ME AT EIGHT TOMORROW.
```

Exercise 14.2

A.   In problems 1–8, write each expression in BASIC.

1. $(3 + 4) \div (5 + 9)$ 2. $(5 - 2)(7 + 8)$ 3. $3^2 + 4^2$
4. $2 \times 3 \div 4 \times 6$ 5. $2(3^3) - 5(4^2)$ 6. $3(2^5) - 2(3^4)$
7. $\dfrac{5 \times 8}{6 \times 9}$ 8. $\dfrac{6 - 2}{5 \times 4}$

In problems 9–18, evaluate the given BASIC expression.

9. 4+8/2-24/6   10. 3*4-2   11. (4+8)/2-24/6
12. 3*4-2*3   13. 2^3+3*2^2   14. 3*5^2-4*5
15. 3*4/6*8   16. 3*4/(6*8)   17. 4*5^3
18. (4*5)^3

B. In problems 19–26, determine what would be printed if the given program were run:

19.
```
10   LET X=456-241+612
20   LET Y=.62/(.31+.93)
30   LET Z=2^3-6
40   PRINT X; Y; Z
50   PRINT 2*X; Y^Z
60   END
```

20.
```
10   LET X=1+2*3/6*5
20   LET Y=1+2*3/(6*5)
30   LET Z=(1+2)*3/6*5
40   LET W=(1+2)*3/(6*5)
50   PRINT X; Y; Z; W
60   END
```

21.
```
10   LET A=3
20   LET B=2
30   LET X=A^B+B^A
40   PRINT "A="; A,  "B="; B,  "X="; X
50   END
```

22.
```
10   LET X=10/2.5
20   LET Y=X^2
30   LET Z=1*2*3*4
40   LET W=3*Z-2*Y
50   PRINT "W="; W
60   END
```

23.
```
10   LET A=2
20   LET B=3
20   LET B=4
30   LET X=A*B+A^B
40   PRINT "A="; A,  "B="; B,  "X="; X
50   END
```

24.
```
10   LET X=20/2.5
20   LET Y=X^2
30   LET Z=1*2*3*4*5
30   LET Z=1*2*3*4
40   LET W=2*Z-5*Y
50   PRINT "W="; W
```

25.
```
10   LET X=12.5/2.5
20   LET Z=2*3*8
30   LET W=X+Y+Z
40   PRINT "W="; W
50   END
```

26.
```
10   LET A=4
20   LET B=2
30   LET X=A^B+C
40   PRINT "X=",  X
50   END
```

The spirals in the daisy shown here are seen as two distinct sets radiating clockwise and counterclockwise, with each set always made up of a predetermined number of spirals. Most daisies have 21 and 34, adjacent numbers in the Fibonacci sequence.

27. Write a BASIC program that will calculate and print the sum of the first four counting numbers. Run your program if a computer is available.

28. Write a BASIC program that will calculate and print the sum of the squares of the first four counting numbers. Run your program if a computer is available.

29. The Fibonacci sequence is a sequence of numbers that starts with 1, 1, 2. Each following term is the sum of the two terms that precede it. Thus, the fourth term is $1 + 2$, or 3, and the fifth term is $2 + 3$, or 5. Write a BASIC program that will compute and print the first eight terms of the sequence. Start with

```
10   LET A=1
20   LET B=1
30   LET C=A+B
```

Run your program if a computer is available.

C. 30. Write a three-line program with output

```
TO BE OR NOT TO BE
THAT IS THE QUESTION
```

using "TO BE" as a string variable. (Do not use END as a line.)

31. Write a three-line program with output

```
IT IS NOT WHETHER YOU WIN OR LOSE THAT COUNTS.
IT IS WHETHER I WIN OR LOSE THAT COUNTS.
```

using "WIN OR LOSE THAT COUNTS" as a string variable. (Do not use END as a line.)

32. Consider the program:

```
10   LET W1$="EVERYBODY "
20   LET W2$="LOVES"
30   LET W3$="SOMEBODY"
40   LET W4$="SOMETIME"
```

Add a line with a PRINT statement using the four string variables to generate the output:

```
SOMEBODY LOVES EVERYBODY SOMETIME
```

33. Consider the program:

```
10   LET Q1$="IT IS NOT WHETHER YOU"
20   LET Q2$=" WIN OR LOSE THAT COUNTS "
30   LET Q3$="IT IS WHETHER I"
```

Add two lines with PRINT statements using the three string variables to generate the output

```
IT IS NOT WHETHER YOU WIN OR LOSE THAT COUNTS
IT IS WHETHER I WIN OR LOSE THAT COUNTS
```

Using Your Knowledge

We have discussed how to edit a line using two different methods:

1. *Pressing the backspace key (which will erase any symbols to its left)*
2. *Retyping the line number we wish to edit and writing the information correctly*

There is a third method of editing lines: using the EDIT command. You may have heard the story of a retraction that was to appear in a newspaper. The headline to be edited on the computer was:

    10 PRINT "MR. X IS A SOP ON THE POLICE FORCE."

We wish to change this line so that when printed it will read:

    MR. X IS A COP ON THE POLICE FORCE

To do this, type:

    EDIT   10   Remember to hit the ⏎ key.

We get a flashing cursor under the 1 in 10. Since we want to change the S in the word SOP, press the right arrow key ⟶ and make the cursor stop under the S. Press the key that says Del *, and the S will be deleted. Now, to insert C, the correct letter, press* Ins *and the letter C. What is the rest of the story? The programmer in the newspaper did not know about the EDIT command and tried to retype the line correctly. It now read:*

    10 PRINT "MR. X IS A COP ON THE POLICE FARCE."

34. Give the steps needed to use the EDIT command in fixing the new line 10.

14.3 THE READ, DATA, GOTO, AND INPUT COMMANDS

GETTING STARTED

READ THE DATA AND GOTO INPUT

In the previous Getting Started, we discussed a program that converted temperatures from Celsius to Fahrenheit. Unfortunately, if we wish to convert 20°C, 25°C, and 30°C to Fahrenheit, we would have to retype line 20 three times and run the program three times. Wouldn't it be nice if we could type the program once and get our three answers? Fortunately, the READ, DATA, and GOTO commands can do this for us. Let us see how by studying the program.

Meteorologists for the U.S. Weather Service use sophisticated computers to track weather systems and predict their future courses

```
10   REM *CELSIUS TO FAHRENHEIT CONVERTER*
20   LET C=15              Assigns 15 to C
30   LET F=(9/5)*C+32      Assigns (9/5)*C + 32 to F
40   PRINT C; "DEGREES (C)=" F; "DEGREES (F)"
```

We need a way of letting C = 20 and finding F, then letting C = 25 and finding the next F, and finally letting C = 30 and finding the last F. To accomplish this, we use a new line 20 that commands the computer to read the value of C. But where from? The next DATA line, line 30, tells the computer that the values to be read are 20, 25, and 30. As before, line 50 tells the computer to print the information we want. If you run this program, however, it will only give the value of F when C = 20. We need to tell the computer that after printing the value of F when C = 20, it has to start over again. How do we do that? Add line 60 GOTO 10. Do it and see the results!

```
10   REM *CELSIUS TO FAHRENHEIT CONVERTER*
20   READ C                Tells the computer to read C
30   DATA 20, 25, 30       Tells the computer the values to be read
40   LET F=(9/5)*C+32      Assigns (9/5)*C + 32 to F
50   PRINT C; "DEGREES (C)=" F; "DEGREES (F)"
```

In this section, we shall study the commands we have mentioned: READ, DATA, and GOTO plus the INPUT command.

One of the important characteristics of the digital computer is that it can be programmed to do various types of repetitive calculations. The READ, DATA, and GOTO commands are often used in problems that require repetitive calculations.

A. *The READ, DATA, and GOTO Commands*

The READ command makes the computer read one or more numbers from a DATA statement. On lines between the READ and DATA statements, the computer can be commanded to perform various operations with these numbers. The GOTO command tells the computer to go to the line whose number is specified in the command. For instance, GOTO 20 instructs the computer to go to line 20. The GOTO command plays an important role in a READ and DATA program; it instructs the computer to return to the READ command, pick the next number(s) from the DATA line, and continue the execution of the program by moving to line 30. All of this is illustrated by the following program.

```
10   PRINT "A", "B", "A/B"
20   READ A, B
30   PRINT A, B, A/B
40   GOTO 20
50   DATA 1, 2, 3, 4, 5, 8, 9, 15
60   END
```

```
RUN
A    B    A/B
1    2    .5
3    4    .75
5    8    .625
9    15   .6
OUT OF DATA IN 20
```

This is one of many error messages the computer can send. There are 75 more.

Line 10 of this program simply furnishes headings for the table that is to be printed out. The READ command in line 20 tells the computer to take the first two numbers in the DATA line (line 50) and call the first number A and the second B. Line 30 instructs the computer to print the numbers A and B and their quotient A/B. The GOTO command in line 40 tells the computer to go back to line 20 and READ the next two numbers in the DATA line for A and B. The first time line 20 is executed, the computer takes A = 1, B = 2 (the first two numbers in the DATA line) and then finds their quotient and prints the values of A, B, and A/B as instructed by line 30. The second time line 20 is executed, the computer takes the next two numbers, A = 3, B = 4, from the DATA line and then goes to line 30 as before. This procedure is continued until the data are exhausted. The output is displayed as shown and the computer displays OUT OF DATA IN 20 when it has used all the numbers on the DATA line. The program may be ended in this way if we wish. If we have more data to run with the same program, we simply retype line 50 with the new data and then type RUN. The computer executes the program all over again but now with the new data. Note that DATA lines can go anywhere in the program. When a READ command is read, the computer will automatically search the program for the data to be read.

The items in lines 10 and 30 are separated by commas. This is to give proper spacing between the items enclosed by quotation marks in line 10 and correspondingly in line 30. For most systems, the use of commas divides the page into five zones of 14 spaces each and a sixth zone 10 spaces wide. Each item is typed out in a separate zone. You should check the spacing for the system you are using.

A root of a number such as the square root, the cube root, the fourth root, and so on, is indicated by using the exponents 1/2, 1/3, 1/4, and so on. Thus, $2^{(1/7)}$ stands for the number that gives 2 when raised to the seventh power; that is, $2^{(1/7)}$ is the seventh root of 2. If we write a fractional exponent such as 2/3, we mean to take the cube root and square the result. For instance, $8^{(2/3)}$ is 4. You can check this by taking the cube root of 8, which is 2, and then squaring to get 4. This convention is used in the next example.

EXAMPLE 1   Explain the printout for the following program:

```
10    READ B
20    LET X=5^(1/B)
30    PRINT "B="; B, "5^(1/B)="; X
40    GOTO 10
```

```
50   DATA 2, 3, 4, 5, 6
60   END

RUN
B=2          5^(1/B)=2.236068
B=3          5^(1/B)=1.709976
B=4          5^(1/B)=1.495349
B=5          5^(1/B)=1.37973
B=6          5^(1/B)=1.30766
OUT OF DATA IN 10
```

Solution   When line 10 is executed for the first time, the computer takes B = 2, the first number in line 50. It then goes to line 20 and calculates 5^(1/2), that is, the square root of 5, which it calls X. Next, it prints B=2 and 5^(1/B)=2.236068, according to the instruction in line 30. Line 40 tells the computer to return to line 10. The second time line 10 is executed, the computer takes B = 3, the second number in line 50. It then repeats the calculation called for in line 20, this time finding the cube root of 5 and calling that X. The printout is similar to that in the first stage. This procedure is repeated until all the numbers in line 50 are used. The program computes in succession the square root, the cube root, the fourth root, the fifth root, and the sixth root of 5.

∎

EXAMPLE 2   The five roots obtained in Example 1 may be rounded to three decimal places and checked for accuracy by raising each to the power corresponding to the root and comparing with 5. Thus, 2.236 would be squared, 1.710 would be cubed, and so on. Write a program to calculate the required powers of these decimals.

Solution
```
10   READ A, B
20   PRINT A^B
30   GOTO 10
40   DATA 2.236, 2, 1.710, 3, 1.495, 4, 1.380, 5, 1.308, 6
50   END
```

If this program is run, the resulting five powers are found to be 4.999696, 5.000211, 4.995337, 5.0049, and 5.007794. (Final digits may be different because of computer rounding.)

∎

Note that no expression involving a calculation, not even anything as simple as 1 + 2 or 1/2, is permitted in the DATA statement. For a number such as 1/3, you have to use .33333333.

B. *The INPUT Command*

We have already mentioned that the power of the computer lies in its tremendous ability to perform repetitive tasks at amazing speeds. So far, however, the commands we have learned are run once, and a particular answer is obtained. The next command will enable us to use the same program to **input** as much information as we wish and see the computer's subsequent output.

The INPUT statement allows you to assign data to letters (variables) from the keyboard. When the INPUT command is executed, the computer displays a question mark indicating that it is waiting for data to be input and the ENTER key to be pressed. Here is a very simple program to demonstrate the INPUT command:

```
10   PRINT "TYPE ANY NUMBER"
20   INPUT A

RUN
```

The printout will be:

```
TYPE ANY NUMBER
?_
```

The question mark tells you the computer is waiting! Type in any number and press ↵ . The computer prints the number. Some give the OK sign. An incorrect response, however, will cause the message "Redo from start" and a new request to be displayed. (Try entering n.) The language BASICA takes a shortcut by combining the INPUT and PRINT statements. Change line 10 to

```
10   INPUT "TYPE ANY NUMBER";A
```

Delete line 20 by typing

```
20    ↵

RUN
```

The printout is now

```
TYPE ANY NUMBER?_
```

If you type a number, some computers say OK. Great. We get the same result, but saved one line of typing and one line on the printout. Let us use these ideas to modify the program in Example 2. Instead of having to read the data in line 40, we write

```
10   INPUT A, B
20   PRINT A^B
30   GOTO 10

RUN
```

The computer shows us the customary question mark (our turn). Now, enter the first pair of numbers on the data line 2.236, 2, and ↵ . The answer 4.999696 appears on the next line. If we enter the next pair of numbers on line 40, 1.710, 3, and ↵ , we get the next answer, 5.000211. In this manner, we can get all the answers in Example 2, and as many more as we wish to run.

There is only one problem. We have not instructed the computer to END the program. It keeps asking for more pairs of numbers. How can we stop it? Press $\boxed{\text{Ctrl}}$ and $\boxed{\text{Scroll Lock}}$ simultaneously (or $\boxed{\text{Ctrl}}$ and $\boxed{\text{C}}$ or $\boxed{\text{Ctrl}}$ and $\boxed{\text{Break}}$). We finally get a break! We are in charge again.

EXAMPLE 3   Use the INPUT statement to obtain the first line of the printout in Example 1.

Solution

```
10   INPUT B
20   LET X=5^(1/B)
30   PRINT "B="; B, "5^(1/B)="; X
40   GOTO 10
50   END
```

If you RUN the program, the ? will ask for a number. Enter 2 and the result will be just like the first line of the printout of Example 1. Since line 40 tells the computer to go back to 10, the program is repeated automatically (you do not have to type RUN). Unfortunately, we are in an infinite loop (from line 10 to line 40 and back again). The computer does not get to line 50 so that it can END. As before, press $\boxed{\text{Ctrl}}$ and $\boxed{\text{C}}$ to break out of the loop. Note that in line 30, there is a comma after the second B so that the printout is not crowded. (Try it using a semicolon.) Here is one last piece of advice. If you ran this program several times, you might want to "erase" the screen somewhere along the line. You can do this by typing CLS and pressing $\boxed{\leftarrow}$. ∎

Exercise 14.3

A. In problems 1–6, determine what would be printed if the given program were run.

```
1. 10   READ A, B
   20   PRINT A; B; (A+B)/2
   30   GOTO 10
   40   DATA 5, 7, 25, 35, 40, 48
   50   END
```

```
2. 10   READ A, B, C
   20   PRINT (A+B+C)/3
   30   GOTO 10
   40   DATA 75, 80, 64, 90, 100, 62
   50   END
```

```
3. 10   READ P
   20   PRINT "1.05*"; P; "="; 1.05*P
   30   GOTO 10
   40   DATA 500, 750, 1500, 2000
   50   END
```

```
4. 10   PRINT "A", "A^2", "A^3"
   20   READ A
   30   PRINT A, A^2, A^3
   40   GOTO 20
   50   DATA 1, 2, 3, 4, 5
   60   END
```

```
5. 10   PRINT "X", "Y"
   20   READ X
   30   LET Y=X^2+3*X−1
   40   PRINT X, Y
   50   GOTO 20
   60   DATA −3, −2, −1, 0, 1, 2, 3
   70   END
```

```
6. 10   PRINT "X", "Y"
   20   READ X
   30   LET Y=X^3−X^2
   40   PRINT X, Y
   50   GOTO 20
   60   DATA −2, −1, 0, 1, 2
   70   END
```

7. Write a program that computes and prints a table of the fourth powers of the integers from 1 to 8. The first lines of your table should look like this:

```
N   N^4
1   1
2   16
3   81
```

Run your program if a computer is available.

8. The "triangular" numbers are the integers obtained by starting with 1, which is the first triangular number; adding 2 to get 3, the second triangular number; then adding 3 to get 6, the third triangular number; and so on. The $(n + 1)$th triangular number is obtained by adding $n + 1$ to the nth triangular number. Write a program that will compute and print a table of the first 10 triangular numbers. Make your printout start like this:

```
N   NTH TRIANG. NO.
1   1
2   3
3   6
```

Run your program if a computer is available.

1   3   6   10

Can you see why they are called triangular numbers?

9. A formula obtained in algebra for the sum of the squares of the first N positive integers is $S = N(N + 1)(2N + 1)/6$. Write a program that will

compute and print a table of the values of S for the first 10 positive integers. Your table should start like this:

```
N   S
1   1
2   5
3   14
```

Run your program if a computer is available.

10. A formula obtained in algebra for the sum of the cubes of the first N positive integers is $S = N^2(N + 1)^2/4$. Write a program that will compute and print the sum of the cubes of the first 10 positive integers. Run your program if a computer is available.

B. In problems 11–16, use the INPUT statement to modify the indicated program so that the first line of the new printout is the same as before.

   11. problem 1   12. problem 2
   13. problem 3   14. problem 4
   15. problem 5   16. problem 6

17. Use the INPUT statement to modify the program in problem 8 so that the first line of the new printout is the same as before.

18. Use the INPUT statement to modify the program in problem 9 so that the first line of the new printout is the same as before.

19. Use the INPUT statement to write a program to calculate the area of a rectangle. [*Hint:* The area A of a rectangle is found by multiplying its length L by its width W. Run your program if a computer is available.]

20. Use the INPUT statement to write a program to calculate the area of a triangle. [*Hint:* The area A of a triangle is found by multiplying its base B by its height H and dividing this product by 2. Run your program if a computer is available.]

C. Applications. Problems 21–24 will apply the concepts studied to write programs you may use in everyday life.

   21. Write a program that will use the READ and DATA statements to compute your weekly wages at $7 per hour for 38 hours using line 10 as your first line.

   ```
   10   READ N$, rate, hours
   ```

   22. Modify the program in problem 21 so that it will calculate the wages for three workers, C. Chen, D. Drawdy, and E. Eisenstein whose hourly rates are $8, $7, and $11 and who worked 35, 38, and 40 hours, respectively.

23. Getting Started for Section 8.1 shows how fast calories are burned when performing different activities. Assuming that cycling, jogging, and swimming burn 250, 650, and 300 calories per hour, respectively, and that a person loses one pound when 3500 calories are burned, write a program that allows the user to input the number of hours spent on each of these activities and then calculates the number of pounds lost. Lines 10, 20, and 30 should be INPUT lines for the number of hours spent on cycling, jogging, and swimming.

24. When performing aerobic exercises, the highest heart rate p for a person whose age is A is given by $p = 190 - A$. (See Example 6, Section 6.6.) Write a program that asks for the name N$ and age A of a person and that, when the information is entered, prints:

```
(N$) YOUR MAXIMUM ALLOWED HEART RATE IS (P)
```

In Other Words

25. What happens if the computer is given an incorrect response to an INPUT statement?

26. What happens in a program if all the DATA have been read and another item is requested by a READ statement?

Using Your Knowledge

In problems 27–33 let us try to use most of the material we have studied to construct a useful program that would compute class averages.

27. The first line, line 10, should have the output:

```
NAME                CLASS AVERAGE
```

What should this line be?

28. Line 20 should be able to READ the students' scores for 3 quizzes and 3 exams given. If ST$ is the string variable to be used and Q1, Q2, Q3, E1, E2, and E3 are the grades, what should line 20 be?

29. The next line, line 30, should add the points for each student to obtain T. But there is one twist. Exam scores are worth twice as much as quiz grades. Now, let line 30 define T.

30. Line 40 should find the average A. Note that there were 3 quizzes and 3 exams, but the exams are worth twice as much as the quizzes. To find the average A, by what number should you divide T? [*Hint:* Let the line be identical to your answer.]

31. Now we are ready to print. Line 50 should print the students' names (ST$) and their averages A.

32. Now, we need to start all over again. What should line 60 read so that the process is started again?

33. What else do we need? The names of the students and the DATA lines for each student. Here are the grades; you do the DATA lines as 70, 80, and 90.

```
70   A. AARON, 80, 92, 78, 68, 72, 90
80   B. BAKER, 50, 74, 82, 91, 83, 70
90   B. HAMILTON, 95, 93, 98, 100, 72, 84
```

Now, run it and see!

14.4 THE IF . . . THEN . . .
COMMAND

GETTING STARTED

DECISIONS, DECISIONS, DECISIONS

One of the most interesting and important features of the modern digital computer is its ability to make decisions. In BASIC, a computer is asked to make a decision by means of the IF. . . THEN. . . command. A mathematical statement using equality or inequality signs is inserted after the word IF and a command is inserted after the word THEN. *If the statement following the IF is* true, *the computer will go to the line named after the THEN. If the statement is* not true, t*he computer will simply go on to the next command in the usual numerical order.*

The IF. . . THEN. . . statement is often used with the GOTO statement implied. Thus, we can type

```
10   IF A=5 THEN GOTO 50
```

or the shorter version

```
10   IF A=5 THEN 50
```

Let us use the IF. . . THEN. . . statement to find out if a given number is a solution of the equation $3x - 2 = x + 6$. Our program will ask us for a number (line 10), lets us examine the equation (line 20), prints the bad news (line 30), tells the computer to go start again (line 40), and if the correct number is entered, lets us know that the number is the solution (line 50). We then end the problem using line 60.

```
10   INPUT "TYPE A NUMBER"; x
20   IF 3*x-2=x+6 THEN 50
30   PRINT x; "IS NOT THE SOLUTION"
40   GOTO 10
50   PRINT x; "IS THE SOLUTION"
60   END
```

We will study the IF. . . THEN. . . statement in this section.

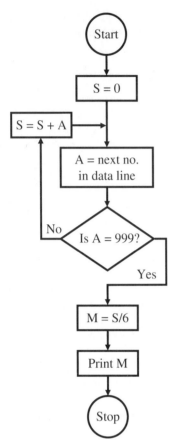

FIGURE **14.1**

Now, let us use all this information to construct a program that finds the average of six numbers, say, 0.121, 0.156, 0.162, 0.170, 0.135, and 0.174. The arithmetic involved is simple: Add the numbers and divide by 6. To tell the computer to get the sum S of the six numbers, we start with a sum of 0 and add the first number 0.121. The sum S is 0.121. Now, we add the next number, 0.156, to this sum, obtaining the new sum $S = 0.121 + 0.156 = 0.277$. We then get the next number, 0.162, and add it to 0.277. To do this we must tell the computer to **initialize** the value of S at $S = 0$ (see line 10 of the following program), then read some data (lines 20 and 60), and continue to add new values of A to the sum (lines 40 and 50). How do we tell the computer to stop? We throw in a "flag," a number that tells the computer we are finished (the 999 in line 30). This number is written in the DATA line, and when it is reached, the computer is told to calculate the answer S/6, call it M (line 70), and then print it in the form "AVERAGE =" (line 80). Here is the program:

```
10    LET S=0
20    READ A
30    IF A=999 THEN 70
40    LET S=S+A
50    GOTO 20
60    DATA .121, .156, .162, .170, .135, .174, 999
70    LET M=S/6
80    PRINT "AVERAGE=" ; M
90    END

RUN
AVERAGE = .153
```

A quicker way of doing this is to type:

```
10    INPUT "WRITE THE NUMBERS A, B, C, D, E, F TO
      AVERAGE"; A, B, C, D, E, F
20    LET M=(A+B+C+D+E+F)/6
30    PRINT "AVERAGE ="; M
```

If you then input the numbers shown above in the DATA line, the answer AVERAGE = 0.153 is displayed.

The diagram in Figure 14.1 is called a **flowchart** and illustrates the way in which a portion of the preceding program is recycled. The diamond-shaped decision box creates a loop in the flowchart, and the corresponding part of the program is called a **loop.** Loops are quite useful in programs that require recycling a set of operations.

EXAMPLE 1	Determine what will be printed if the following program is run:

```
10    LET A=0
20    READ B
30    IF B=9999 THEN 90
40    IF B>A THEN 60
```

```
50   GOTO 20
60   LET A=B
70   GOTO 20
80   DATA 761, 325, 671, 892, 346, 9999
90   PRINT A
95   END
```

Solution   In the first stage, the computer reads B = 761 ≠ 9999, so it goes to line 40. There it finds the IF statement to be true (761 > 0), and is instructed to go to line 60. Line 60 tells the computer to replace the current value of A by the current value of B. Thus, the new value of A is 761. Next, the computer goes to line 70, then to line 20 and reads the next value of B, 325 ≠ 9999. This time, the IF statement in line 40 is *not* true (325 ≯ 761), so the computer then continues its normal flow to line 50 and so back to line 20. Notice that the current value of A is replaced by the current value of B only when B is greater than A. The procedure continues through the first five numbers in the DATA line, at which time the value of A is 892, the largest number encountered so far. Then the computer reads 9999 from the DATA line, and line 30 tells it to go to line 90, where it is instructed to print the current value of A. This ends the program. The final printout is, of course, the largest of the first five numbers in the DATA line, 892. The 9999 was simply the "flag" (not one of the data numbers) used to stop the program. This little trick avoids the OUT OF DATA IN 20 error message. ∎

The general form of the IF. . . THEN. . . instruction is

IF [relationship] THEN [statement]

The following relational symbols are permitted in the relationship:

=	Equals
<	Is less than
>	Is greater than
<=	Is less than or equal to
>=	Is greater than or equal to
<>	Is not equal to

The following instruction illustrates a correct usage of these symbols:

30   IF (A^2+B^2)>=C^2 THEN 45

If the current value of $(A^2 + B^2)$ is greater than or equal to the current value of C^2, the computer goes to line 45; but if the current value of $(A^2 + B^2)$ is less than the current value of C^2, the computer proceeds to the next line in normal numerical order.

In BASIC, the symbol SQR(X) causes the computer to calculate the square root of X. Any positive number (or 0) may be used for X, and the computer will calculate the nonnegative square root.

EXAMPLE 2   Determine what will be printed if the following program is run:

```
10   LET X=1
20   PRINT X; SQR(X)
30   LET X=X+1
40   IF X>10 THEN 60
50   GOTO 20
60   END
```

Solution   In the first stage, the computer prints 1 and its square root. Line 30 instructs the computer to replace the current value of X (which is 1) by X + 1 (which is 2). (The equal sign on line 30 tells the computer to replace the variable to the left of the equal sign with the value on the right.) Since the IF statement in line 40 is not true, the computer goes to line 50, which returns it to line 20 and makes it print out 2 and its square root. This procedure is repeated, at each stage the value of X being increased by 1, until the computer comes to X = 11. Then the IF statement in line 40 is true, and the computer goes to line 60, which ends the program. The printout will thus be a two-column array with the integers from 1 to 10 in the first column and decimal values for their respective square roots in the second column.   ∎

Another important special function is symbolized by INT(X), which stands for the greatest integer that is less than or equal to X. If X is an integer, then INT(X) = X. For example, INT(5) = 5, INT(−3) = −3, and INT(0) = 0. If X is not an integer, however, INT(X) is the integer that just precedes X (is to the left of X) on the number line. Thus, for positive X, INT(3.571) = 3, INT(4.3172) = 4, and INT(0.678) = 0. For negative X INT(−2.18) = −3 and INT(−1.98) = −2. (See Figure 14.2.)

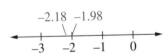

EXAMPLE 3   What will be the printout if the following program is run?

```
10   LET A=A+5
20   PRINT A; INT(SQR(A))
30   IF A>25 THEN 50
40   GOTO 10
50   END
```

Solution   Since SQR(5) is a number between 2 and 3, INT(SQR(5)) = 2. If you follow the loop in this program, you will see that the printout is a two-column array:

```
 5   2
10   3
15   3
20   4
25   5
30   5
```

∎

The next example gives an interesting application of both INT(X) and SQR(X) in finding all the exact divisors of a given integer. These numbers are then printed as factor pairs.

EXAMPLE 4   Give the printout of the following program if it were run:

```
10   LET A=42
20   LET D=1
30   LET Q=A/D
40   IF Q=INT(Q) THEN 70
50   LET D=D+1
60   GOTO 25
25   IF D>SQR(A) THEN 90   ← Notice the convenience of not
70   PRINT D; Q                having to retype the program
80   GOTO 50                   over again because of an omitted
90   END                       command.
```

Solution   The program is designed to find all the divisors of the number specified in line 10. Notice that line 40 instructs the computer to print out the divisor D and the quotient Q only if Q is an integer. That is, the computer finds and prints the **factor pairs** of A. Thus, it only needs to check for divisors from 1 to the square root of A (see line 25). The output is as follows:

```
1    42
2    21
3    14
6     7
```

Exercise 14.4 _____

1. Describe what would be printed if the following program were run. You need not do the calculation called for in line 20.

```
10   LET X=1
20   PRINT X; X^(1/3)
30   LET X=X+1
40   IF X>100 THEN 60
50   GOTO 20
60   END
```

2. Determine what the following program will accomplish. You need not compute the actual numbers that are printed out.

```
10   LET A=1
20   LET B=A^4
30   LET A=A+1
40   IF B<=100000 THEN 20
50   PRINT A-1; B
60   END
```

3. Determine what would be printed if the following program were run:

```
10   READ A, B
20   PRINT A; B; INT(A/B)
30   GOTO 10
40   DATA 9, 4, 100, 32, 500, 45
50   END
```

4. Determine what would be printed if the following program were run:

```
10   READ A, B
20   IF A=99 THEN 70
30   LET C=SQR(A^2+B^2)
40   PRINT A; B; C
50   GOTO 10
60   DATA 3, 4, 5, 12, 20, 21, 99, 1
70   END
```

5. Determine what would be printed if the following program were run using 48 for the first number and 60 for the second:

```
10   INPUT "FIRST NUMBER"; F
20   INPUT "SECOND NUMBER"; S
30   P=F*S
40   R=INT(F/S)
50   R=F-S*R
60   F=S
70   S=R
80   IF R<>0 THEN 40
90   PRINT "THE GCF IS"; F
100  PRINT "THE LCM IS"; P/F
110  END
```

6. Determine what would be printed if the following program were run using $2.58 for the cost and $3.00 for the amount tendered:

```
10   INPUT "COST OF ITEM $"; I
20   I=INT(100*I+.5)
30   INPUT "AMOUNT TENDERED $"; A
40   A=INT(100*A+.5)
50   IF I>A THEN PRINT "YOU DID NOT GIVE ME ENOUGH MONEY!": GOTO 170
60   IF I=A THEN PRINT "THANK YOU. THERE IS NO CHANGE.": GOTO 170
70   C=A-I
80   D=INT(C/100): C=C-100*D
90   Q=INT(C/25): C=C-25*Q
100  DI=INT(C/10): C=C-10*DI
110  N=INT(C/5): C=C-5*N
120  P=C
130  PRINT "YOUR CHANGE IS", "DOLLARS", "QUARTERS", "DIMES"
140  PRINT "     ", D, Q, DI
150  PRINT, "NICKELS", "PENNIES"
160  PRINT, N, P
170  END
```

7. Write a program that will find and print the smallest positive integer whose fifth power is greater than 100,000. Run your program if a computer is available.

8. Write a program that will calculate and print a table of the first 10 positive integers and their respective fourth roots. Do not use the READ, DATA type of program. Run your program if a computer is available.

9. If \$1 is invested in a savings account that earns interest at the rate R compounded annually, the total amount, A dollars, at the end of N years is given by $A = (1 + R)^N$. Write a program that finds and prints the number of years it takes for money to double at interest rates of 4, 5, 6, 7, and 8%. This means to find the smallest integer N for which $(1 + R)^N \geq 2$ and $R = 0.04, 0.05, 0.06, 0.07,$ and 0.08. Ask the computer to print a two-column table with headings R and N. Run your program if a computer is available.

10. We know that the sum of the probabilities of all the possible outcomes of an experiment is 1. However, the probabilities may be given as rounded decimal approximations, so there may be round-off errors. For example, to three decimal places, the probabilities of getting 0, 1, 2, 3, 4, or 5 heads when a fair coin is tossed five times are 0.031, 0.156, 0.312, 0.312, 0.156, and 0.031, respectively (see Chapter 10). The maximum rounding error in each of these numbers is 0.0005. Hence, the sum, say S, has a maximum rounding error 6×0.0005, or 0.003, and we should be willing to accept a sum that is within 0.003 of the correct value, that is, if the absolute value of $1 - S$ is less than or equal to 0.003. In BASIC, the symbol ABS(X) stands for the absolute value of X. Write a program that will add up the six given probabilities and print the message "OK" if the sum is acceptable, that is, if ABS($1-S$)≤0.003, and the message "SORRY" otherwise. Run your program if a computer is available.

11. Repeat problem 10 for N probabilities, $p_1, p_2, \ldots, p_N$, with the requirement that ABS($1-S$) be less than or equal to $0.0005N$. You can do this with a READ, DATA type program, where the first instruction is LET $N=$____. Write $p_1, p_2, \ldots, p_N$ for the probabilities in the DATA line. It is then understood that the appropriate data will be entered when the numerical values are given and before the program is run. Run the program if a computer is available.

12. It is known that if M and N are two positive integers with $M > N$, then the numbers $2MN$, $M^2 - N^2$, and $M^2 + N^2$ are integers that can be taken as the measures of the three sides of a right triangle. Thus, you can show that $(2MN)^2 + (M^2 - N^2)^2 = (M^2 + N^2)^2$. Write a program that will compute and print out the sides for all possible right triangles for $M = 2,$ 3, 4, and 5. For convenience, let $A = 2MN$, $B = M^2 - N^2$, and $C = M^2 + N^2$. Your table should start like this:

A	B	C
4	3	5
6	8	10
12	5	13

We have used $M = 2, N = 1$ in the first line; $M = 3, N = 1$ in the second line; and $M = 3, N = 2$ in the third line. Run the program if a computer is available.

In Other Words

The following questions refer to the "square root" program in Example 2.

13. When the computer executes line 20, what value is stored for X?
14. Explain what happens when line 30 is reached.
15. Explain what a "loop" is and determine how many times the computer will go through the loop in the program and why.
16. Explain why the computer does not indefinitely continue computing square roots then modify one line in the program so that the computer will be able to find $\sqrt{50}$.

Using Your Knowledge

Suppose you deposit $1000 for 1 year in a savings account that pays 5% interest compounded monthly. The banker who credits your account at the end of each month would be interested in the following program, which calculates and prints the interest and the new amount (principal plus interest) for the first month:

```
10   LET A=1000
20   LET B=100*.05*A/12
30   LET I=.01*INT(B+.5)
40   LET A=A+I
50   PRINT I; A
60   END
```

Lines 20 and 30 of this program involve the simple but clever little trick that is used to round off the interest to the nearest cent. This trick becomes clear if you carry out the computation of the interest. The actual interest is

$$0.05 \times 1000 \div 12 = 4.166666. . .$$

The banker wants to round this to 4.17, which we can do by inspection; but remember that the computer must be instructed how to do this. We first multiply the interest by 100 to get 416.6666. . . . Then we add 0.5 to get 417.1666. . . . Next, we find INT(417.1666. . .), which is 417, and finally we multiply by 0.01 to get 4.17. The remainder of the program should offer no difficulty.

Notice that by changing line 10 to let A be any desired amount, this same program can be used over and over for all the accounts that carry the same interest rate, 5% compounded monthly. Remember that a modern computer can do thousands of additions in a fraction of a second; hence, the apparent added complication needed to round off properly would not increase appreciably the time taken by the computer to run the program.

17. Modify the above program to take account of an initial deposit of $5000 and an interest rate of $5\frac{1}{4}\%$ compounded monthly.

18. Repeat problem 17 if the interest is compounded daily (365 days in a year).

19. Determine what the following program will print if it is run:

```
 10   PRINT "N", "I", "A"
 20   PRINT 0, 0, 1000
 30   LET A=1000
 40   LET N=0
 50   LET B=100*.05*A/12
 60   LET I=.01*INT(B+.5)
 70   LET A=A+I
 80   LET N=N+1
 90   IF N>12 THEN 120
100   PRINT N, I, A
110   GOTO 50
120   END
```

Discovery

A **perfect number** is a positive integer that is equal to the sum of its proper divisors. (Recall that a proper divisor is an exact divisor that is less than the number itself.) The smallest perfect number is 6, as you can easily verify. No odd perfect number has ever been found, and mathematicians are convinced that there is none; but no one has been able to prove this. The following program will discover the next even perfect number after 6. See if you can follow through and convince yourself of this fact. [Hint: Try taking P = 2 instead of 8 and carry out the instructions in the program. The printout should be the number 6.]

```
 10   LET P=8
 20   LET S=0
 30   LET D=1
 40   LET Q=P/D
 50   IF Q<>INT(Q) THEN 70
 60   LET S=S+D
 70   LET D=D+1
 80   IF D>=P THEN 100
 90   GOTO 40
100   IF S=P THEN 130
110   LET P=P+2
120   GOTO 20
130   PRINT P; "IS THE NEXT PERFECT NUMBER."
140   END
```

20. Can you discover what modification to make in the above program if you were trying to find an odd perfect number?

21. Can you make a flowchart for the above program?

14.5   THE FOR AND NEXT COMMANDS

GETTING STARTED

RECYCLING NUMBERS

When a set of calculations is to be recycled several times, the FOR and NEXT commands are frequently more convenient and result in a shorter program than one constructed with the IF. . . THEN. . . command. The FOR line could have the form

```
20   FOR K=1 TO 8
```

which tells us the starting point and the ending point of the count. The NEXT line would then be of the form

```
50   NEXT K
```

Notice that the same letter, K, is used as in the FOR line. These two lines would cause the program steps between lines 20 and 50 to be performed eight times. Here, the starting value of K is 1, and with no further instruction in the FOR line, the computer automatically increases the value of K by 1 each time it goes to the NEXT line. Thus, the program calls for *eight* loops. In this section, we shall study the FOR and NEXT commands in more detail.

We start by discussing a program that illustrates how the FOR and NEXT commands are used to calculate 8! (read "eight factorial") where 8! = $1 \times 2 \times 3 \times 4 \times 5 \times 6 \times 7 \times 8$.

```
10   LET F=1
20   FOR K=1 TO 8
30   LET F=F*K
40   NEXT K
50   PRINT "FACTORIAL 8 = "; F
60   END
```

In this program, line 20 tells the computer to execute a loop eight times using K = 1, 2, 3, 4, 5, 6, 7, 8 in succession and doing whatever it is instructed to do between this line and the command NEXT, which closes the loop. If the program is run, the computer will automatically calculate $1 \times 1 = 1$, $1 \times 2 = 2$, $2 \times 3 = 6$, $6 \times 4 = 24$, . . . , $5040 \times 8 = 40{,}320$ in succession, which exhausts the K. The computer will then go to line 50, print the message FACTORIAL 8 = 40320, and end the program.

In executing the command FOR K = _____ TO _____, the computer will use a *step size* of 1 unless it is instructed to do otherwise. The next examples illustrate the flexibility of the FOR command.

___

EXAMPLE 1 Write a program that will add the odd integers from 1 to 13 and print the sum.

Solution

```
10   LET S=0
20   FOR K=1 TO 13 STEP 2
30   LET S=S+K
40   NEXT K
50   PRINT S
60   END
```

Notice that line 20 specifies a step size of 2. Thus, the computer will increase the value of K by 2 each time and use K = 1, 3, 5, 7, 9, 11, and 13 in succession.

∎

The blanks in the command FOR K = ＿＿ TO ＿＿ STEP ＿＿ may be filled by numbers or expressions that are evaluated in other parts of the program. For instance, the following are acceptable:

```
FOR K=5 TO 12.5 STEP .5
FOR K=15 TO -7 STEP -2.56
FOR K=N TO N+1 STEP .01*J        ← Here, the N and J would be
                                    evaluated in other parts of
                                    the program.
```

___

EXAMPLE 2 If you ran the program in Example 1, you would find the printout to be the number 49, which is 7^2. Since the program added the first seven odd positive integers, you might be curious about this coincidence and want to experiment a little. Write a program that will add the first N odd positive integers for N = 10, 15, 20, and 30, and print out N, the sum S, and SQR(S).

Solution

```
10   PRINT "N", "S", "SQR(S)"
20   READ N
30   LET S=0
40   FOR K=1 to 2*N-1 STEP 2      ← Recall that the Nth odd
50   LET S=S+K                       positive integer is 2N - 1.
60   NEXT K
70   PRINT N, S, SQR(S)
80   GOTO 20
90   DATA 10, 15, 20, 30
95   END
```

If you run this program, the printout will be as follows:

```
N    S     SQR(S)
10   100   10
15   225   15
20   400   20
30   900   30
OUT OF DATA IN 20
```

∎

Although we have considered only the most elementary features of BASIC, the ten commands that we have discussed can be used to write many interesting and useful programs. A brief summary of these ten commands is given in Table 14.1.

Table 14.1

Command	Example	What It Does
LET	LET A=5+2^3	Makes assignments and computations
PRINT	PRINT ''A=''; A	Prints messages and results
END	END	Ends a program
READ	READ X, Y, Z	Enters numbers from DATA line
DATA	DATA 2, 4, -7, 3.14	Stores data for READ line
GOTO	GOTO 40	Transfers computer to another line
INPUT	INPUT A	Assigns data to letters
IF. . . THEN. . .	IF K>8 THEN 90	Makes and acts on a decision
FOR	FOR J=1 TO 15	Starts a loop
NEXT	NEXT J	Closes a loop

Exercise 14.5

In problems 1–6, figure out what would be printed if the program were run.

```
1. 10   LET S=0
   20   FOR K=1 TO 5
   30   LET S=S+K^2
   40   PRINT S
   50   NEXT K
   60   END
```

```
2. 10   LET S=0
   20   FOR K=1 TO 11 STEP 2
   30   LET S=S+K^2
   40   NEXT K
   50   PRINT S
   60   END
```

```
3. 10   LET P=1
   20   FOR K=2 TO 10 STEP 2
   30   LET P=P*K
   40   NEXT K
   50   PRINT P
   60   END
```

```
4. 10   LET P=1
   20   FOR K=2 TO 6 STEP 2
   30   LET P=P*K
   40   NEXT K
   50   PRINT SQR(P)
   60   END
```

```
5. 10    READ N                    6. 10    PRINT "N", "F"
   20    LET P=1                      20    READ N
   30    FOR K=1 TO N STEP 2          30    LET F=1
   40    LET P=P*K                    40    FOR K=1 TO N
   50    NEXT K                       50    LET F=F*K
   60    PRINT N; P                   60    NEXT K
   70    DATA 5, 9, 11                70    PRINT N, F
   80    GOTO 10                      80    DATA 3, 5, 8
   90    END                          90    GOTO 20
                                      95    END
```

7. Here is part of a payroll calculation for three employees. It is assumed that time-and-a-half is paid for work over 40 hr per week. Use the following notation:

I for employee's identification number
R for hourly rate of pay
H for hours worked
P for gross pay

Determine what the printout would be if the program were run.

```
10    PRINT "I", "R", "H", "P"
20    FOR K=1 TO 3
30    READ I, R, H
40    IF H>40 THEN 70
50    LET P=R*H
60    GOTO 80
70    LET P=R*40+1.5*R*(H-40)
80    PRINT I, R, H, P
90    NEXT K
95    DATA 001, 4.00, 42, 002, 3.75, 39, 003, 3.50, 45
99    END
```

8. Suppose the total tax that the employer in problem 7 must withhold for various purposes comes to 10% of each employee's gross pay. Modify the program given in problem 7 so that it will calculate and print out (on a line with the employee number, I) the gross pay P, the tax T, and the net pay N.

9. Write a program that will compute and print out all the divisors of 36. You can use the instruction FOR K=1 TO 6. Do you see why? Run your program if a computer is available.

10. Write a program that will print out a table of the positive integers from 1 to 20 and their respective cube roots. Run your program if a computer is available.

11. Write a program that will print out a table of the even integers from 2 to 20 and their respective fifth powers. Run your program if a computer is available.

12. Write a program that will print out a table of the square roots of the numbers from 1 to 2 in steps of 0.1. Run your program if a computer is available.

In Other Words

13. What does the FOR command do?
14. What does the NEXT command do?
15. What happens if a FOR or NEXT command is used in a program without the other?
16. If a loop begins with FOR k = m TO n STEP r
    (a) Under what conditions will the loop be executed?
    (b) Under what conditions will the loop not be executed?

Using Your Knowledge

Suppose you deposit $100 at the beginning of each month in a bank account that pays 5% interest compounded monthly. The following program will print out the number of the month, the month's interest, and the accumulated amount A at the end of each month for 1 year. The program assumes that the bank will round off to cents in the usual way. (For an explanation of line 50, see the Using Your Knowledge section of Exercise 14.4.) Use the following notation:

N = *Number of month*
I = *Interest for the month*
A = *Accumulation at the end of the month*

```
 10  PRINT "N", "I", "A"
 20  LET A=0
 30  LET N=0
 40  FOR K=1 TO 12
 50  LET B=100*.05*(A+100)/12
 60  LET I=.01*INT(B+.5)
 70  LET A=A+I+100
 80  LET N=N+1
 90  PRINT N, I, A
100  NEXT K
110  END
```

Check this program for the first two or three values of K to assure yourself that it does what it is supposed to do. Run the program if a computer is available.

17. Suppose you wanted to continue the deposits for a second year and would like to compare the figures for the second year with those for the first year. How would you modify the program to give you these figures?

18. How would you modify the program if the interest rate were $5\frac{1}{4}\%$ compounded monthly?

19. Suppose you borrow $500 to pay for some wheels and you agree to repay the loan at the rate of $50 per month beginning 1 month after you get the money. Each $50 payment is to include interest on the unpaid balance at the rate of 1% per month. The final payment will be a partial payment (that is, less than $50) 1 month after the last full payment. Write a program that will calculate the total number of payments, the amount of the last payment, and the total amount of interest on the loan. (Since you do not know ahead of time how many payments are required, you will not want to use the FOR, NEXT type of program.)

Discovery

*In the Discovery section of Exercise 14.4, we gave a program to find a perfect number. If a number is not perfect, it is classified as **deficient** if the sum of its proper divisors is less than the number itself; it is classified as **abundant** if the sum of its proper divisors is greater than the number itself. To discover whether a given integer, say, 18, is deficient, abundant, or perfect, we can use the following program:*

```
10   LET N=18
20   LET S=0
30   FOR K=1 TO INT(N/2)
40   LET Q=N/K
50   IF Q<>INT(Q) THEN 70
60   LET S=S+K
70   NEXT K
80   IF S<N THEN 110
90   IF S>N THEN 130
100  IF S=N THEN 150
110  PRINT N; "IS DEFICIENT."
120  GOTO 160
130  PRINT N; "IS ABUNDANT."
140  GOTO 160
150  PRINT N; "IS PERFECT."
160  END
```

20. Check through this program to see if it will actually classify 18 correctly. You do not need a computer to do this.

Working problems 21–24 will offer some help for you in finding deficient, abundant, and perfect numbers.

21. Start your program with an instruction to print three columns labeled D, A, and P. This will give you appropriate headings for your table.

22. Modify the program given on the previous page by replacing the three PRINT instructions with one print line. If you use quotes with an empty space between them, the computer will move over one column before printing the value of N.

23. Your program should have two FOR, NEXT loops in it, with the above program as the "inner" loop. What are the lines in these loops?

24. Write a program that will classify all the integers from 2 to 30 as deficient (D), abundant (A), or perfect (P). GOOD LUCK!

Chapter 14 Summary

Section	Item	Meaning	Example
14.2A	*	Times	4*6 (4 times 6)
14.2A	/	Divided by	4/6 (4 divided by 6)
14.2A	^	With exponent	4^6 (4^6)
14.2B	LET	Makes assignments and computations	LET A=3+4^2
14.2B	PRINT	Prints messages and results	PRINT "A="; 7 prints A = 7
14.2B	END	Ends a program	
14.3A	READ	Enters numbers from DATA line	READ X, Y, Z
14.3A	DATA	Stores data for READ line	DATA 3, 5, 6.5, –2
14.3A	GOTO	Transfers program flow to another line	GOTO 20
14.3B	INPUT	Assigns data to letters	INPUT A
14.4	IF. . . THEN. . .	Makes and acts on a decision	IF A>B, THEN 90 If A is greater than B, the computer will go to line 90.
14.4	SQR(X)	The square root of X	SQR(16) The computer will calculate $\sqrt{16}$.
14.4	INT(X)	The greatest integer in X	INT(5)=5, INT(4.5)=4, INT(–3.5)=–4

Section	Item	Meaning	Example
14.4	ABS(X)	The absolute value of X	ABS(-3.2)=3.2
14.5	FOR	Starts a loop	FOR M=1 TO 5
14.5	NEXT	Closes a loop	NEXT M

Research Questions

Sources of information for these questions can be found in the Bibliography at the end of the book.

Note: Completion of all questions in this section will provide a historical perspective of the development of computers.

1. In 1930, Vannevar Bush ushered in the computer age. Write a report on Vannevar Bush, the machine he built, and the type of algebra used by one of his students, Claude Shannon, in improving the design of the machine.

2. In 1936, Alan Turing published *On Computable Numbers*. Find out about the computer Turing designed and his work for British intelligence in trying to break the scrambled messages of Enigma, and write a report on your findings.

3. In 1941, Konrad Zuse designed and built the first general purpose computer. Write a report on this development including the name of the computer and its successors.

4. In 1944, Howard Aiken designed his own computer. Find out and report on the name of the computer, the major corporation that backed him on this endeavor, and how later, because of the competition with Aiken, this corporation became one of the largest computer manufacturers in the world.

5. In 1945, John von Neumann outlined the critical elements of a computer system. Write a report on von Neumann's contributions to the development of computers.

6. In 1946, J. Preper Eckert and John Mauchly unveiled the first large-scale electronic digital computer. Write a report on these two men and the computer they developed.

7. In 1951, LEO, the first business computer, was completed. Find out about this computer and what LEO stands for, and then write a report on your findings.

8. In 1977, three mass-market computers emerged. Write a report on these computers and the companies that produced them.

9. Write a report on the significance of microchips to computers.

10. Write a report on the latest developments in computer technology.

Chapter 14 Practice Test

1. Suppose you are about to write line 80 of your program. You want your computer to write the phrase

```
THE ANSWER IS . . .
```

What instructions would you give the computer?

2. Write in BASIC:
   (a) $4(2 + 5^2) \div 8$ (b) $3^2 - 3 \cdot 2^3$

3. Evaluate:
   (a) $(15/3)^2$ (b) 2^4-3^3 (c) $3*4/2-1$

In problems 4–12, determine what the printout would be if the given BASIC program were run.

4.
```
10   LET A=5
20   LET B=12
30   LET C=SQR(A^2+B^2)
40   PRINT 2*A; 2*B; 2*C
50   END
```

5.
```
10   LET X=9
20   LET Y=3*X
30   LET Z=Y^(1/3)
40   LET U=Y-2*X/Z
50   PRINT U
60   END
```

6.
```
10   READ X
20   LET Y=3*X-2*X^2
30   PRINT X; Y
40   GOTO 10
50   DATA 1, 2, 3
60   END
```

7. Use the INPUT statement to obtain the first line of the printout in problem 6.

8.
```
5    LET A=0
10   READ B
20   LET A=A+B
30   PRINT A
40   GOTO 10
50   DATA 1, 2, 3, 4, 5
60   END
```

9.
```
10   LET A=1
20   READ B
30   IF B=999 THEN 80
40   IF A>B THEN 60
50   LET A=B
60   GOTO 20
70   DATA 25, 2001, 3260, 437, 500, 64, 999
80   PRINT A
90   END
```

10.
```
10   FOR K=1 TO 4
20   LET B=2^K
30   PRINT B
40   NEXT K
50   END
```

11.
```
10   LET S=0
20   FOR K=1 TO 10
30   LET S=S+K
40   NEXT K
50   PRINT S
60   END
```

12.
```
10   LET A=18
20   FOR K=1 TO 9
30   LET B=18/K
40   IF B=INT(B) THEN 60
50   GOTO 70
60   PRINT K
70   NEXT K
80   END
```

13. Write a BASIC program that will compute and print out the value of $\sqrt{(38)^2 - 4(13)(17)}$.

14. Write a READ, DATA program that will compute and print out the cube roots of 20, 30, 38, and 42, and that will not print out an OUT OF DATA message.

15. Write a FOR, NEXT program that will print out a table of the fifth roots of the odd integers from 1 to 15.

Programs in BASIC

In this Appendix you will find programs that will help you do exercises throughout this text. They are all written in the computer language BASIC but you do not need to know how to program in BASIC to use these programs on your computer. You must, however, be careful to retype them exactly as they are printed here. If you would like more background in BASIC, or if you are already familiar with the language but could use a refresher, we suggest that you review Chapter 14 before going on. There are some advanced commands in these programs that may not be discussed in the chapter. Several of them are explained briefly below:

A$	Read, "A string," a type of variable that can be assigned to indicate letters, words, and/or combinations of letters, numbers, spaces, and other characters
DIM	Establishes the number of DIMensions and the number of elements per dimension in numeric and string arrays
INKEY$	Checks the keyboard looking for a pressed key
INSTR	Used to search for one STRing INside another string
LEN	Measures the LENgth of strings by counting the number of characters enclosed in quotes or assigned to string variables
LOCATE	Controls the cursor, placing it on a specific row and column on the screen
VAL	Converts numbers written as strings into their numeric value

For a nearly exhaustive list of commands used in BASIC, see David A. Lien, *The BASIC Handbook*, 3rd edition, published by Compusoft.

STATEMENT GENERATOR PROGRAM

This program will find a statement with a given truth table.

```
10 PRINT "PUT CAPS LOCK ON PLEASE"
20 INPUT "HOW MANY VARIABLES (<5) ";N:CLS:FOR I=1 TO N:PRINT "P";I;"    ";:NEXT
30 PRINT "DESIRED TRUTH VALUE       DESIRED CONJUNCTION "
40 FOR I=1 TO 70:PRINT "=";:NEXT:DIM B$(2^N,N+2) :PRINT
50 FOR I=1 TO N :T=0:A$="T" :FOR J=1 TO 2^N:K=2^N/2^I:T=T+1
60 IF  T>K  AND A$="T" THEN A$="F" :T=1
70 IF T>K AND A$="F" THEN A$="T" :T=1
80 LOCATE J+3,7*I-5 :PRINT A$:B$(J,I)=A$:NEXT J:NEXT I
90 FOR J=1 TO 2^N:LOCATE J+3,30:INPUT "> ";B$(J,N+1):LOCATE J+3,30:PRINT " "
100 LOCATE J+3,40
110 IF B$(J,N+1)="F" THEN X$="~"
120  X$=X$+"("
130 FOR I=1 TO N -1  :IF B$(J,I)="F" THEN X$=X$+"~"
140 X$=X$+"P"+STR$(I)+" ^ "  :NEXT
150 I=N :IF B$(J,I)="F" THEN X$=X$+"~"
160 X$=X$+"P"+STR$(I)+")":PRINT X$:B$(J,N+2)=X$:X$="":NEXT J
170 INPUT "PRESS RETURN FOR FUNCTION ";X$:F=0
180 FOR I=1 TO 2^N-1:IF B$(I,N+1) = "T" THEN PRINT B$(I,N+2);" v ";:F=1
190 NEXT :IF B$(2^N,N+1) ="T" THEN PRINT B$(2^N,N+2):F=1
200 IF F=0 THEN PRINT "P1~P1" :PRINT
210 INPUT "RUN AGAIN (Y/N) ";A$:IF A$="Y" THEN RUN
```

POWER SET PROGRAM

This program will list all the subsets (the power set) of a set, provided you enter the number of elements in the set and the elements themselves.

```
10 INPUT "NUMBER OF ELEMENTS ";N:DIM A$(N):DIM B(N):S$="("
20 FOR I= 1 TO N:PRINT "ENTER ELEMENT ";I;:INPUT A$(I):NEXT:CLS
30 FOR I=1 TO N:S$=S$+A$(I)+" ":NEXT:S$=S$+")":PRINT "THE POWER SET OF ";S$;"="
40 PRINT "(( ) ";:FOR I=1 TO 2^N-1:J=1
50 IF B(J)=1 THEN B(J)=0:J=J+1 :GOTO 50
60 B(J)=1 :S$="":S$="("
70 FOR K=1 TO N
80 IF B(K)=1 THEN S$=S$+A$(K)+ " "
90 NEXT
100 S$=S$+")":PRINT S$;" ";
110 NEXT
120 PRINT ")"
130 INPUT "RUN AGAIN (Y/N) ";A$ :IF A$="Y" THEN RUN
```

CONVERTING FROM BASE 10 PROGRAM

This program will convert a number from base 10 to base X ($X < 11$).

```
5 PRINT "PUT CAPS LOCK ON "
10 CLS:PRINT "METHOD OF SUCCESSIVE APPROXIMATIONS -CHANGE OF BASE"
20 INPUT "ENTER NUMBER IN BASE TEN ";N :INPUT "CHANGE TO WHAT BASE (<11) ";K
30 PRINT:PRINT K;"|> ";N :T=N
40 L=INT(N/K):R=N-L*K :N=L
50 IF L<K THEN PRINT TAB(7);L;TAB(20);R:GOTO 70
60 PRINT K;"|> ";N;TAB(20);R :X$=RIGHT$(STR$(R),1)+X$:GOTO 40
70 X$=RIGHT$(STR$(L),1)+RIGHT$(STR$(R),1)+X$
80 PRINT "THUS , ";T;" = ";X$;" BASE ";K
90  PRINT :INPUT "RUN AGAIN (Y/N) ";A$:IF A$="Y" THEN RUN
```

A2

CONVERTING TO BASE 10 PROGRAM

This program will convert a number from base X ($X < 11$) to base 10.

```
5 PRINT "PUT CAPS LOCK ON PLEASE"
10 CLS:PRINT "CHANGE FROM A BASE X (X<11) TO BASE 10"
15 INPUT "ENTER THE BASE OF THE NUMBER ";B
20 INPUT "ENTER NUMBER PLEASE ";X$  :K=LEN(X$):S$=X$
22 FOR I=1 TO K
24 S= VAL(RIGHT$(X$,1)):X$=LEFT$(X$,K-I)
26 T=S*B^(I-1)+T
30 NEXT
40 PRINT S$;" BASE ";B ;"  = ";T;"  BASE 10"
50 INPUT "RUN AGAIN (Y/N) ";X$:IF X$="Y" THEN RUN
```

BASE CONVERTER PROGRAM (X, Y < 11)

This program will convert a number from base X to base Y, provided X and Y are less than 11.

```
5 PRINT "PUT CAPS LOCK ON PLEASE"
10 CLS:PRINT "CHANGE FROM BASE X TO BASE Y (X AND Y <11)"
20 INPUT "ENTER THE ORIGINAL BASE OF THE NUMBER ";B
30 INPUT "ENTER NUMBER PLEASE ";X$  :K=LEN(X$):S$=X$
40 FOR I=1 TO K
50 S= VAL(RIGHT$(X$,1)):X$=LEFT$(X$,K-I)
60 T=S*B^(I-1)+T
70 NEXT
80 N=T : INPUT "CHANGE TO WHAT BASE ";K  :X$=""
90 L=INT(N/K):R=N-L*K :N=L
100 IF L<K THEN GOTO 120
110 X$=RIGHT$(STR$(R),1)+X$:GOTO 90
120 X$=RIGHT$(STR$(L),1)+RIGHT$(STR$(R),1)+X$
130 PRINT "THUS , ";S$;"  IN BASE ";B;"  = " ;X$;" BASE ";K
140 PRINT :INPUT "RUN AGAIN (Y/N) ";A$:IF A$="Y" THEN RUN
```

BASE CONVERTER PROGRAM (X, Y < 17)

This program will convert a number from base X to base Y, provided X and Y are less than 17.

```
10 DIM A$(16):FOR I=0 TO 9 :A$(I)=RIGHT$(STR$(I),1):NEXT
20 A$(10)="A":A$(11)="B":A$(12)="C":A$(13)="D":A$(14)="E":A$(15)="F":A$(16)="G"
30 CLS:PRINT "CHANGE FROM BASE X TO BASE Y (X,Y <17)"
40 INPUT "ENTER THE ORIGINAL BASE OF THE NUMBER ";B
50 INPUT "ENTER NUMBER IN THE ORIGINAL BASE PLEASE ";X$:A$=X$:K=LEN(X$):S$=X$
60 FOR I=1 TO K
70 S$= RIGHT$(X$,1):X$=LEFT$(X$,K-I)
80 S=VAL(S$):FOR J=10 TO 16 :IF S$=A$(J) THEN S=J
90 NEXT
100 T=S*B^(I-1)+T
110 NEXT
120 N=T : INPUT "CHANGE TO WHAT BASE ";K  :X$=""
130 L=INT(N/K):R=N-L*K :N=L
140 IF L<K THEN GOTO 160
150 X$=RIGHT$(STR$(R),1)+X$:GOTO 130
160 X$=A$(L)+A$(R)+X$
170 PRINT "THUS , ";A$;"  IN BASE ";B;"  = " ;X$;" BASE ";K
180 PRINT :INPUT "RUN AGAIN (Y/N) ";A$:IF A$="Y" THEN RUN
```

A3

PRIME SEARCHER PROGRAM

This program will search and display all the prime numbers up to the number you desire.

```
10 CLS:PRINT "SEARCH FOR PRIMES : I WILL LIST ALL PRIMES UP TO THE"
20 INPUT "NUMBER YOU WOULD LIKE TO TEST UP TO ";N
30 CLS:DIM A(N)
40 FOR I=2 TO INT(N^.5)
50 IF A(I)<>0 THEN GOTO 70
60 FOR K=2 TO INT(N/I) :A(I*K)=1:NEXT
70 NEXT
80 CLS: FOR I= 2 TO N
90 IF A(I)=0 THEN PRINT TAB(L*7);I; :L=L+1
100 IF L=10 THEN PRINT :L=0    :C=C+1
110 IF C=20 THEN INPUT "PRESS RETURN FOR MORE ";A$:CLS:C=0
120 NEXT
130 PRINT:PRINT "THATS ALL"
140 INPUT "RUN AGAIN (Y/N) ";A$:IF A$="Y" THEN RUN
```

SIEVE OF ERATOSTHENES PROGRAM

This program will write the numbers up to 320 on the screen and then create a Sieve of Eratosthenes before your own eyes. The program eliminates the multiples of 2, 3, and so on, leaving only primes displayed on the screen.

```
10 CLS:PRINT "SEARCH FOR PRIMES BY SIEVE METHOD "   :DIM A$(320)
20 FOR I=2 TO 320 :A$(I) =RIGHT$(STR$(I),LEN(STR$(I))-1):NEXT:J=1
30 FOR S=2 TO INT(320^.5)
31 IF A$(S)= "   " THEN GOTO  110
40 FOR I=2 TO 320
50 IF J=16 THEN J=0:PRINT
60 PRINT TAB(J*5);A$(I); :FOR K=1 TO 200:NEXT
70 J=J+1
80 NEXT
95 LOCATE 23,5:PRINT"CROSSING OUT MULTIPLES OF ";S
96 FOR K=2*S TO 320 STEP S:A$(K)="   ":NEXT
100 LOCATE 2,1
110 LOCATE 2,1 : J=1:NEXT
120 LOCATE 23,5:PRINT "                                           "
121 INPUT "RUN AGAIN (Y/N) ";A$:IF A$="Y"  THEN RUN
```

PRIME FACTORIZATION PROGRAM

This program will factor any number into a product of primes.

```
10 CLS:PRINT "FACTOR A NUMBER INTO A PRODUCT OF PRIMES" :K=0
20 INPUT "ENTER NUMBER PLEASE ";N
30 IF N=1 THEN PRINT N;"=" ;1 :GOTO 90
40 PRINT N;"= ";
50 FOR I=2 TO N
60 IF K=0 AND INT(N/I)*I=N THEN PRINT I; :K=1:N=N/I:GOTO 50
70 IF INT(N/I)*I =N THEN PRINT "*";I; :N=N/I :GOTO 50
80 NEXT
90 PRINT
100 INPUT "RUN AGAIN (Y/N) ";A$:IF A$="Y" THEN RUN
```

GCF FINDER PROGRAM

This program will find the GCF of two integers. Make sure you enter the larger of the two integers first.

```
10 PRINT "FIND THE GREATEST COMMON FACTOR  OF TWO INTEGERS"
20 INPUT "ENTER LARGEST INTEGER ";B:INPUT "ENTER SMALLEST INTEGER ";C
30 L=B:S=C:LR=S
40 Q=INT(B/C):R=B-Q*C
50 IF R=0 THEN GCF=LR :GOTO 70
60 LR=R :B=C:C=R :GOTO 40
70 PRINT "THE GREATEST COMMON FACTOR  OF ";L;" AND ";S;" IS
80 PRINT LR
90 INPUT "RUN AGAIN (Y/N) ";A$:IF A$="Y" THEN RUN
```

REDUCING FRACTIONS

This program will reduce a proper or improper fraction, provided you enter its numerator and denominator.

```
10 H=0:CLS:PRINT "REDUCE A PROPER OR IMPROPER FRACTION "
20 INPUT "ENTER NUMERATOR   ";B:INPUT "ENTER DENOMINATOR    ";C
30 L=B:S=C:LR=B :IF C>B THEN H=B:B=C:C=H
40 Q=INT(B/C):R=B-Q*C
50 IF R=0 THEN GCD=LR :GOTO 70
60 LR=R :B=C:C=R :GOTO 40
70  B=L/LR:C=S/LR
80 IF B>C THEN I= INT(B/C) :B=B-I*C
90 PRINT L;TAB(15);B
100 IF I<>0 THEN PRINT "------  =";TAB(10);I;
102 IF I=0 THEN PRINT "------  =";
110 PRINT TAB(15);"------"
120 PRINT     S;TAB(15);C
130 INPUT " RUN AGAIN (Y/N) ";A$ :IF A$ ="Y" THEN RUN
```

LCM FINDER PROGRAM

This program will find the LCM of several numbers, provided you enter the numbers.

```
10 R=0:CLS:PRINT "FIND THE LCM":INPUT "HOW MANY NUMBERS ";N:DIM A(N)
20 FOR I=1 TO N:PRINT "NUMBER ";I;:INPUT"";A(I):NEXT:J=2:LM =1
30 PRINT "THE LCM OF ";:FOR I=1 TO N:PRINT A(I);:IF R<A(I) THEN R=A(I)
40 NEXT
50 FOR I=1 TO N
60 IF (INT(A(I)/J)*J=A(I)) AND (T=0) THEN T=T+1:A(I)=A(I)/J:L=I:GOTO 80
70 IF (INT(A(I)/J)*J=A(I)) THEN A(I)=A(I)/J :T=T+1
80 NEXT
100 LM=LM*J:IF T<=1 THEN A(L)=A(L)*J :LM=LM/J:J=J+1
110 T=0:L=0   :IF J<> R THEN GOTO 50
130 PRINT "IS : ";:FOR I=1 TO N :LM=LM*A(I):NEXT:PRINT LM
140 INPUT "RUN AGAIN (Y/N) ";A$: IF A$= "Y" THEN RUN
```

ADDITION OF FRACTIONS PROGRAM

This program will add or subtract fractions if you enter their numerators and denominators. Answers are not reduced.

```
10 CLS:R=0:PRINT "ADD OR SUBTRACT FRACTIONS :NOTE 3/5  - 2/5  = 3/5 + (-2)/5"
20 PRINT "ENTER (-A)/B FOR -  A/B":INPUT "HOW MANY FRACTIONS ";N
25 DIM A(N),B(N),C(N)
30 FOR I=1 TO N:PRINT "NUMERATOR ";I;:INPUT"";B(I): PRINT "DENOMINATOR ";I;
35 INPUT "";A(I):C(I)=A(I):NEXT:J=2:LM=1
40 FOR I=1 TO N:IF R<A(I) THEN R=A(I)
50 NEXT
60 FOR I=1 TO N
70 IF (INT(A(I)/J)*J=A(I)) AND (T=0) THEN T=T+1:A(I)=A(I)/J:L=I:GOTO 90
80 IF (INT(A(I)/J)*J=A(I)) THEN A(I)=A(I)/J :T=T+1
90 NEXT
100 LM=LM*J:IF T<=1 THEN A(L)=A(L)*J : LM=LM/J:J=J+1
110 T=0:L=0   :IF J<> R THEN GOTO 60
120 FOR I=1 TO N :LM=LM*A(I):NEXT:FOR I=1 TO N:T=B(I)*LM/C(I)+T:NEXT
122 FOR I=1 TO N-1:PRINT B(I);"/";C(I);" + ";:NEXT:PRINT B(N);"/";C(N);" ="
130 PRINT T;"/";LM
140 INPUT "RUN AGAIN (Y/N) ";A$:IF A$="Y" THEN RUN
```

ADDITION OF FRACTIONS (REDUCED) PROGRAM

This program will add or subtract several fractions and then reduce the answer. The program asks for the numerator and denominator of each of the fractions involved.

```
10 CLS:R=0:PRINT "ADD OR SUBTRACT FRACTIONS :NOTE 3/5  - 2/5  = 3/5 + (-2)/5"
20 PRINT "ENTER (-A)/B FOR -  A/B":INPUT "HOW MANY FRACTIONS ";N
30 DIM A(N),B(N),C(N)
40 FOR I=1 TO N:PRINT "NUMERATOR ";I;:INPUT"";B(I): PRINT "DENOMINATOR ";I;
50 INPUT "";A(I):C(I)=A(I):NEXT:J=2:LM=1
60 FOR I=1 TO N:IF R<A(I) THEN R=A(I)
70 NEXT
80 FOR I=1 TO N
90 IF (INT(A(I)/J)*J=A(I)) AND (T=0) THEN T=T+1:A(I)=A(I)/J:L=I:GOTO 110
100 IF (INT(A(I)/J)*J=A(I)) THEN A(I)=A(I)/J :T=T+1
110 NEXT
120 LM=LM*J:IF T<=1 THEN A(L)=A(L)*J : LM=LM/J:J=J+1
130 T=0:L=0   :IF J<> R THEN GOTO 80
140 FOR I=1 TO N :LM=LM*A(I):NEXT:FOR I=1 TO N:T=B(I)*LM/C(I)+T:NEXT
150 FOR I=1 TO N-1:PRINT B(I);"/";C(I);" + ";:NEXT:PRINT B(N);"/";C(N);" ="
160 H=0:B=T:C=LM:I=0
170 L=B:S=C:LR=B :IF C>B THEN H=B:B=C:C=H
180 Q=INT(B/C):R=B-Q*C
190 IF R=0 THEN GCD=LR :GOTO 210
200 LR=R :B=C:C=R  :GOTO 180
210  B=L/LR:C=S/LR
220 IF B>C THEN I= INT(B/C) :B=B-I*C
230 PRINT L;TAB(15);B
240 IF I<>0 THEN PRINT "------  =";TAB(10);I;
250 IF I=0 THEN PRINT "------  =";
260 PRINT TAB(15);"------"
270 PRINT    S;TAB(15);C
280 INPUT "RUN AGAIN (Y/N) ";A$:IF A$="Y" THEN RUN
```

FACTORIAL PROGRAM FOR LARGE *n*

This program will calculate *n*! for large *n*. The answer will be displayed on the screen.

```
10 DIM A(300) ,B(10) :CLS:PRINT "CALCULATE FACTORIALS "
20 INPUT "ENTER NUMBER ";A$    :K=LEN(A$)
30 FOR I=1 TO K  :A(I)=VAL(MID$(A$,K-I+1,1)):NEXT
40 FOR I=     VAL(A$)-1  TO 2 STEP -1
50 FOR J=1 TO K:A(J)=A(J)*I:NEXT
60 FOR J=1 TO K:C=INT(A(J)/10):A(J+1)=A(J+1)+C:A(J)=A(J) MOD 10    :NEXT
80 IF A(K+1)<>0 THEN K=K+1
85 IF A(K)>10 THEN A(K+1)=INT(A(K)/10):A(K)=A(K) MOD 10 :K=K+1:GOTO 85
90 NEXT
92 FOR I=K TO 1 STEP -1:X$=X$+RIGHT$(STR$(A(I)),1):NEXT
100 PRINT X$
110 INPUT "RUN AGAIN (Y/N) ";A$:IF A$="Y" THEN RUN
```

FACTORIAL PROGRAM ($n < 30$)

This program will calculate $n!$ for a given n. If n is large, the answer is given in scientific notation.

```
10 CLS :PRINT " FIND THE FACTORIAL OF AN INTEGER " :J=1
20 INPUT "ENTER NUMBER ";N :FOR I=2 TO N:J=J*I:NEXT
30 PRINT N;" FACTORIAL IS ";J
40 INPUT "RUN AGAIN (Y/N) ";A$:IF A$="Y" THEN RUN
```

MATRIX ADDITION OR SUBTRACTION PROGRAM

This program will add (enter a 1) or subtract (enter a 2) two matrices, provided you enter the number of rows and columns and all the entries for each matrix.

```
10 CLS:M=1:PRINT "ADD OR SUBTRACT MATRICES ":INPUT "NUMBER OF ROWS ";R
20 INPUT "NUMBER OF COLUMNS ";C:G=4:PRINT"PRESS 1 FOR ADD, PRESS 2 FOR SUBTRACT"
30 DIM A(R,C),B(R,C)
40 G=VAL(INKEY$):IF G<>1 AND G<>2 THEN GOTO 40
50 CLS:PRINT"ENTER MATRIX A ":IF G=2 THEN M=-1
60 FOR I=1 TO R:FOR J=1 TO C:LOCATE 2,3 :PRINT "ENTRY IN ROW ";I;"COLUMN ";J
70 LOCATE 2+I,J*5 :INPUT;" ",A(I,J) :NEXT J:PRINT:NEXT I :PRINT
80 PRINT "ENTER MATRIX B"
90 FOR I=1 TO R:FOR J=1 TO C:LOCATE 3+R,3 :PRINT "ENTRY IN ROW ";I;"COLUMN ";J
100 LOCATE  4+R+I,J*5 :INPUT;" ",B(I,J) :NEXT J:PRINT:NEXT I :PRINT
110 FOR I=1 TO R:FOR J=1 TO C:A(I,J)=A(I,J)+M*B(I,J):NEXT J:NEXT I
120 PRINT :PRINT"THE RESULTING MATRIX IS ":LOCATE 5+2*R,2
130 FOR I=1 TO R:FOR J=1 TO C:LOCATE 7+2*R+I,5*J:PRINT A(I,J):NEXT J:NEXT I
140 INPUT "RUN AGAIN (Y/N) ";A$:IF A$="Y" THEN RUN
```

MATRIX MULTIPLICATION PROGRAM

This program will multiply two matrices, provided you enter the number of rows and columns and all the entries for each matrix.

```
10 CLS:M=1:PRINT "MULTIPLY TWO MATRICES":INPUT "NUMBER OF ROWS A";R
20 INPUT "NUMBER OF COLUMNS A";C:INPUT"NUMBER OF COLUMNS B ";B  :CLS
30 DIM A(R,C),B(C,B),C(R,B)
40 CLS:PRINT"ENTER MATRIX A "
50 FOR I=1 TO R:FOR J=1 TO C:LOCATE 2,3 :PRINT "ENTRY IN ROW ";I;"COLUMN ";J
60 LOCATE 2+I,J*5 :INPUT;" ",A(I,J) :NEXT J:PRINT:NEXT I :PRINT
70 PRINT "ENTER MATRIX B"
80 FOR I=1 TO C:FOR J=1 TO B:LOCATE 3+R,3 :PRINT "ENTRY IN ROW ";I;"COLUMN ";J
90 LOCATE  4+R+I,J*5 :INPUT;" ",B(I,J) :NEXT J:PRINT:NEXT I :PRINT
100 FOR I=1 TO R:FOR J=1 TO B:FOR K=1 TO C:C(I,J)=C(I,J)+A(I,K)*B(K,J)
110 NEXT K:NEXT J:NEXT I
120 PRINT :PRINT"THE RESULTING MATRIX IS ":LOCATE 6+2*R,2
130 FOR I=1 TO R:FOR J=1 TO B:LOCATE 8+2*R+I,5*J:PRINT C(I,J):NEXT J:NEXT I
140 INPUT "RUN AGAIN (Y/N) ";A$:IF A$="Y" THEN RUN
```

DETERMINANTS PROGRAM

This program will calculate the determinant of a 2 × 2 or 3 × 3 matrix, provided you enter the matrix.

```
10 CLS:PRINT "CALCULATE THE DETERMINANT OF A 2X2 OR 3X3 MATRIX "
20 INPUT "NUMBER OF ROWS";R:CLS:DIM A(3,3):IF R=2 THEN A(3,3)=1
40 PRINT"ENTER MATRIX A "
50 FOR I=1 TO R:FOR J=1 TO R:LOCATE 2,3 :PRINT "ENTRY IN ROW ";I;"COLUMN ";J
60 LOCATE 2+I,J*5 :INPUT;" ",A(I,J) :NEXT J:PRINT:NEXT I :PRINT
70 D=A(1,1)*A(2,2)*A(3,3)+A(1,2)*A(2,3)*A(3,1)+A(1,3)*A(2,1)*A(3,2)
80 D=D-A(3,1)*A(2,2)*A(1,3)-A(3,2)*A(2,3)*A(1,1)-A(3,3)*A(2,1)*A(1,2)
90 PRINT:PRINT "THE DETERMINANT IS ";D
140 INPUT "RUN AGAIN (Y/N) ";A$:IF A$="Y" THEN RUN
```

PERMUTATIONS AND COMBINATIONS FORMULA PROGRAM

This program will find the number of combinations and permutations of n objects taken r at a time.

```
10 CLS:PRINT "PERMUTATIONS  P(n,r) AND COMBINATIONS C(n,r)"
20 INPUT "NUMBER OF ITEMS (n) ";N
30 INPUT "NUMBER OF THINGS TO BE TAKEN AT A TIME (r) ";R
40 K= N-R+1 :P=1 :S=1
50 FOR I=N-R+1 TO N:P=P*I:NEXT
55 FOR I=2 TO R :S=S*I:NEXT
60 PRINT "P(";N;",";R;") = ";P
65 PRINT "C(";N;",";R;") =";P/S
70 INPUT "RUN AGAIN (Y/N) ";A$:IF A$="Y" THEN RUN
```

COMBINATIONS OF *r* ITEMS FROM *n* ITEMS PROGRAM

This program will list as a set all possible combinations of r items picked from a set of n items. You must enter the number of items to be picked and the set from which you wish to pick them.

```
10 CLS:PRINT "FIND ALL COMBINATIONS OF R ITEMS TAKEN FROM A SET OF N ITEMS "
20 INPUT "HOW MANY ITEMS TO BE PICKED ";R:INPUT "HOW MANY ITEMS TO PICK FROM";N
30 DIM A$(N),B(N):FOR I= 1 TO N:PRINT "ENTER ELEMENT ";I;:INPUT A$(I):NEXT:CLS
40 FOR I=1 TO N:S$=S$+A$(I)+" ":NEXT:PRINT "THE COMBINATIONS ARE:"
50 FOR I=1 TO 2^N-1:J=1
60 IF B(J)=1 THEN B(J)=0:J=J+1 :GOTO 60
70 B(J)=1 :S$="":S$="(" :L=0:FOR K=1 TO N:L=L+B(K):NEXT K
80 IF L<> R THEN GOTO 130
90 FOR K=1 TO N
100 IF B(K)=1 THEN S$=S$+A$(K)+ " "
110 NEXT
120 S$=S$+")":PRINT S$;" ";
130 NEXT :PRINT
140 INPUT "RUN AGAIN (Y/N) ";A$ :IF A$="Y" THEN RUN
```

DISTANCE BETWEEN TWO POINTS PROGRAM

This program will find the distance between (x_1, y_1) and (x_2, y_2). You must enter each of the four numbers separately.

```
10 CLS:PRINT "CALCULATE THE DISTANCE BETWEEN TWO POINTS"
12 PRINT "ENTER FIRST POINT ":INPUT "X1= ";X1:INPUT "Y1= ";Y1
14 PRINT "ENTER SECOND POINT ":INPUT "X2= ";X2:INPUT "Y2= ";Y2
16 T=(X2-X1)^2 +(Y2-Y1)^2
18 FOR I=INT(T^.5+1 ) TO 1 STEP -1  :IF INT(T/I^2)*I^2=T THEN GOTO 20
19 NEXT
20 IF I=1 THEN PRINT "SQRT(";T;") = ";T^.5 :GOTO 25
22 PRINT I"*SQRT(";T/I^2;") = ";T^.5
25 INPUT "RUN AGAIN (Y/N) ";A$ :IF A$="Y" THEN RUN
```

TEMPERATURE CONVERTER PROGRAM

This program will convert temperatures from Fahrenheit to Celsius (centigrade) and vice versa. Make sure you enter F or C following the temperature you wish to convert.

```
10 CLS:PRINT "FAHRENHEIT TO CELSIUS  OR  CELSIUS TO FAHRENHEIT  CONVERTER "
20 PRINT "ENTER TEMPERATURE FOLLOWED BY C FOR CELSIUS OR F FOR FAHRENHEIT"
30 INPUT " ";A$ :A=VAL(A$):IF INSTR(A$,"C")=0 THEN GOTO 50
40 F=9*A/5+32 :PRINT A;" C  = ";F;" F":GOTO 60
50 C=(A -32)*5/9: PRINT A ;"F = ";C;" C"
60 INPUT "RUN AGAIN (Y/N) ";A$:IF A$="Y" THEN RUN
10 CLS:PRINT "FAHRENHEIT TO CELSIUS  OR  CELSIUS TO FAHRENHEIT  CONVERTER "
20 PRINT "ENTER TEMPERATURE FOLLOWED BY C FOR CELSIUS OR F FOR FAHRENHEIT"
30 INPUT " ";A$ :A=VAL(A$):IF INSTR(A$,"C")=0 THEN GOTO 50
40 F=9*A/5+32 :PRINT A;" C  = ";F;" F":GOTO 60
50 C=(A -32)*5/9: PRINT A ;"F = ";C;" C"
60 INPUT "RUN AGAIN (Y/N) ";A$:IF A$="Y" THEN RUN
10 CLS:PRINT "FAHRENHEIT TO CELSIUS  OR  CELSIUS TO FAHRENHEIT  CONVERTER "
20 PRINT "ENTER TEMPERATURE FOLLOWED BY C FOR CELSIUS OR F FOR FAHRENHEIT"
30 INPUT " ";A$ :A=VAL(A$):IF INSTR(A$,"C")=0 THEN GOTO 50
40 F=9*A/5+32 :PRINT A;" C  = ";F;" F":GOTO 60
50 C=(A -32)*5/9: PRINT A ;"F = ";C;" C"
60 INPUT "RUN AGAIN (Y/N) ";A$:IF A$="Y" THEN RUN
```

INVERSE FINDER PROGRAM

This program will find the inverse of a 2×2 or 3×3 matrix when the matrix is entered.

```
10 DIM A(10),B(10):CLS:PRINT "FIND INVERSE OF 2X2 OR 3X3 MATRIX":PRINT
20 K=1:INPUT "NUMBER OF ROWS ";N:IF N=2 THEN B(9)=1
30 FOR I=1 TO N:FOR J=1 TO N :LOCATE 5,1:PRINT "INPUT ENTRY ROW ";I;"COLUMN ";J
40 LOCATE I+7,J*10:INPUT " ",B(K ):K=K+1:NEXT J:IF N=2 THEN K=K+1
50 NEXT I
60 A(1)=B(5)*B(9)-B(8)*B(6):A(2)=B(7)*B(6)-B(4)*B(9):A(3)=B(4)*B(8)-B(7)*B(5)
70 A(4)=B(8)*B(3)-B(2)*B(9):A(5)=B(1)*B(9)-B(7)*B(3):A(6)=B(7)*B(2)-B(1)*B(8)
80 A(7)=B(2)*B(6)-B(5)*B(3):A(8)=B(4)*B(3)-B(1)*B(6):A(9)=B(1)*B(5)-B(4)*B(2)
90 D=A(1)*B(1)+A(2)*B(2)+A(3)*B(3):IF D=0 THEN PRINT "NO INVERSE DET.0":GOTO 160
100 C=A(2):A(2)=A(4):A(4)=C:C=A(3):A(3)=A(7):A(7)=C:C=A(6):A(6)=A(8):A(8)=C
110 K=1:PRINT:PRINT "INVERSE IS":FOR I=1 TO N:FOR J=1 TO N:LOCATE I+14,J*15
120  IF INT(A(K)/D)*D=A(K) THEN PRINT A(K)/D :GOTO 140
130 PRINT A(K);"/";D
140 K=K+1:NEXT J :IF N=2 THEN K=K+1
150 NEXT I
160 INPUT "RUN AGAIN (Y/N) ";A$:IF A$="Y" THEN RUN
```

MATRIX REDUCTION PROGRAM

This program will reduce a matrix to a desired form if you enter the number of rows and columns and the elements of the matrix.

```
10 CLS:PRINT"THIS PROGRAM WILL MANUALLY ROW REDUCE A MATRIX"
20 INPUT "NUMBER ROWS ";N:INPUT "NUMBER COLUMNS ";M:DIM A(N,M,2)
30 FOR I=1 TO N:FOR J=1 TO M:LOCATE 4,6 :PRINT "ENTER ROW ";I;"COLUMN ";J
40 LOCATE I+5,J*9:INPUT"",A$:A(I,J,1)=VAL(A$):A(I,J,2)=1:X=INSTR(A$,"/")
50 IF X<>0 THEN B$=RIGHT$(A$,LEN(A$)-X):A(I,J,2)=VAL(B$)
60 NEXT J:NEXT I
70 PRINT "1 ADD A TIMES ROW I TO ROW J":PRINT"2 MULTIPLY A TIMES ROW I"
80 PRINT "3 SWAP ROW I WITH ROW J":INPUT "ENTER 1,2 OR 3 AND RETURN ";C$
85 C=VAL(C$):IF C$="" THEN RUN "MENU"
90 IF C=3 THEN INPUT "I ";I:INPUT "J ";J :GOTO 140
100 INPUT "A ";A$:X=INSTR(A$,"/"):T=VAL(A$):B=1:IF X= 0 THEN GOTO 120
110 B=VAL(RIGHT$(A$,LEN(A$)-X))
120 INPUT "I ";I:P=I:IF C=1 THEN INPUT "J ";J :P=J:GOTO 160
130 FOR K=1 TO M:A(I,K,1)=A(I,K,1)*T:A(I,K,2)=A(I,K,2)*B:NEXT K :GOTO 180
140 FOR K=1 TO M:FOR H= 1 TO 2:C=A(I,K,H):A(I,K,H)=A(J,K,H):A(J,K,H)=C
150 NEXT H:NEXT K :GOTO 220
160 FOR K=1 TO M:A(J,K,1)=A(J,K,1)*A(I,K,2)*B+A(I,K,1)*A(J,K,2)*T
170 A(J,K,2)=A(J,K,2)*A(I,K,2)*B:NEXT K
180 FOR J=1 TO M:IF A(P,J,1) =0 THEN  A(P,J,2)=1
190 FOR K=A(P,J,1) TO 2 STEP -1:T=A(P,J,1):B=A(P,J,2)
200 IF (INT(T/K)*K=T AND INT(B/K)*K=B) THEN T=T/K:B=B/K:A(P,J,1)=T:A(P,J,2)=B
210 NEXT K :NEXT J
220 CLS:FOR I=1 TO N:FOR J=1 TO M:LOCATE I+5,J*9:T=A(I,J,1):B=A(I,J,2)
230 IF B=1 THEN PRINT T ELSE B$=STR$(B):A$=STR$(T)+"/"+B$:PRINT A$
240 NEXT J:NEXT I :PRINT :PRINT:GOTO 70
```

SOLVING SYSTEMS OF EQUATIONS

This program will solve a system of two or three linear equations when you enter the coefficients of the variables and the numerical part of each equation. Recall that for an equation such as $x + y = 3$, you must enter a coefficient of 1 for x and y. The numerical value is 3.

```
10 A$(1)="X  +":A$(2)="Y  +":A$(3)="Z":CLS:PRINT "SOLVE SYSTEM OF EQUATIONS "
20 INPUT "NUMBER OF EQUATIONS (2 OR 3) ";N:K=1:IF N=2 THEN B(9)=1:A$(2)="Y"
30 FOR I=1 TO N:FOR J=1 TO N :LOCATE 5,1:PRINT "INPUT ENTRY ROW ";I;"COLUMN ";J
40 LOCATE I+7,J*10+4:PRINT A$(J):LOCATE I+7,J*10:INPUT " ",B(K ):K=K+1:NEXT J
50 LOCATE I+7,J*10+8:INPUT "=  ",C(I):IF N=2 THEN K=K+1
60 NEXT I:FOR I=1 TO 9:D(I)=B(I):NEXT:A$(1)="X":A$(2)="Y":GOSUB 100:D1=D
70 IF D=0 THEN PRINT "I CAN'T SOLVE THIS ONE " :GOTO 120
80 FOR I=1 TO 3:B(I)=C(1):B(I+3)=C(2):B(I+6)=C(3):GOSUB 100:T(I)=D:NEXT
90 FOR I=1 TO N :PRINT A$(I);"=";T(I)/D1:NEXT:GOTO 120
100 A(1)=B(5)*B(9)-B(8)*B(6):A(2)=B(7)*B(6)-B(4)*B(9):A(3)=B(4)*B(8)-B(7)*B(5)
110 D=0:D=A(1)*B(1)+A(2)*B(2)+A(3)*B(3):FOR J=1 TO 9:B(J)=D(J):NEXT:RETURN
120 INPUT "RUN AGAIN (Y/N) ";A$:IF A$="Y" THEN RUN
```

SOLVING QUADRATIC EQUATIONS BY FORMULA

This program will solve any quadratic equation using the quadratic formula. You enter the coefficients of x^2 and x and the numerical term.

```
10 CLS:PRINT "QUADRATIC FORMULA PROGRAM " :A$(1)="X^2 +":A$(2)="X +":P=1
20 FOR I=1 TO 3:LOCATE 4,9*I+3:PRINT A$(I):LOCATE 4,9*I:INPUT "",A(I):NEXT
30 LOCATE 4,9*I-3:PRINT " =  0":PRINT:PRINT:D=A(2)^2-4*A(1)*A(3):B=A(2)
40 FOR I=INT(ABS(D)^.5)+1 TO 2 STEP -1:IF INT(D/I^2)*I^2=D THEN P=I:I=0
50 NEXT :D=D/P^2 :S=2*A(1):FOR I=S TO 2 STEP -1:V=INT(S/I):W=INT(B/I):T=INT(P/I)
60 IF V*I=S AND W*I=B AND  T*I=P THEN S=V:B=W:P=T
70 NEXT : IF D=0 THEN PRINT "X= " ;-1*B;"/";S ;"   = ";-1*B/S:GOTO 140
80 IF D< 0 THEN D=-1*D:GOTO 120
90 PRINT "X= (";-1*B;" + ";P;" SQRT(";D;")  ) / ";S;"   = ";(-1*B+P*D^.5)/S
100 PRINT "X= (";-1*B;" - ";P;" SQRT(";D;")  ) / ";S;"   = ";(-1*B-P*D^.5)/S
110 GOTO 140
120 PRINT "X= (";-1*B;" + ";P;" i SQRT(";D;")  ) / "; S
130 PRINT "X= (";-1*B;" - ";P;" i SQRT(";D;")  ) / ";S
140 PRINT :INPUT "RUN AGAIN (Y/N) ";A$:IF A$="Y" THEN  RUN
```

EQUATION OF A LINE PROGRAM

This program will find the equation of a line, given a point and the slope of the line. You must enter the point as an ordered pair of numbers (x_1, y_1).

```
10 LINE INPUT "ENTER POINT '(X,Y)' OR SLOPE M ";A$ :R= INSTR(A$,"/")
20 LINE INPUT "ENTER POINT '(X,Y)' OR SLOPE M ";B$ :S=INSTR(B$,"/")
30 X=INSTR(A$,"(" ):Y=INSTR(B$,"(") :Z=INSTR(A$,","):W=INSTR(B$,",")
40 IF X=0 OR Y=0 THEN GOTO 130
50 X1=VAL(RIGHT$(A$,LEN(A$)-1)):Y1=VAL(RIGHT$(A$,LEN(A$)-Z))
60 X2=VAL(RIGHT$(B$,LEN(B$)-1)):Y2=VAL(RIGHT$(B$,LEN(B$)-W)):MT=Y2-Y1:MB=X2-X1
70 IF MB<0 THEN MT=-1*MT:MB=-1*MB
80 H=ABS(MT):K=MT:J=MB:IF MB=0 THEN PRINT "X= ";X2 :GOTO 170
90 B=Y1-MT*X1/MB:IF MT=0 THEN PRINT   "Y= ";Y1 :GOTO 170
100 FOR I=H TO 2 STEP -1:IF INT(K/I)*I=K AND INT(J/I)*I=J THEN MT=K/I:MB=J/I
110 NEXT:IF MB=1 THEN PRINT"Y= ";MT;"X +";B ELSE PRINT"Y= (";MT;"/";MB;") X +";B
120 GOTO 170
130 IF X<>0 THEN X1=VAL(RIGHT$(A$,LEN(A$)-1)):Y1=VAL(RIGHT$(A$,LEN(A$)-Z)):P$=B$
140 IF Y<>0 THEN X1=VAL(RIGHT$(B$,LEN(B$)-1)):Y1=VAL(RIGHT$(B$,LEN(B$)-W)):P$=A$
150 MT=VAL(P$):K=R+S:MB=1:IF K<>0 THEN MB=VAL(RIGHT$(P$,LEN(P$)-K))
160 GOTO 70
170 INPUT "RUN AGAIN (Y/N) ";A$:IF A$="Y" THEN RUN
```

MEAN, MEDIAN, AND MODE PROGRAM

This program will find the mean, median, and mode of a set of numbers. Press RETURN (ENTER) after each entry. When all entries are completed, press ENTER again.

```
10 DIM A(200),C(200)
20 PRINT"THIS PROGRAM FINDS THE MEAN ,MEDIAN AND MODE OF A LIST OF NUMBERS"
30 PRINT"ENTER NUMBER PRESS RETURN. WHEN DONE JUST PRESS RETURN"
40 INPUT"NUMBER AND RETURN OR JUST RETURN ";N$:P=VAL(N$)
50 T=T+P:F=F+1:IF N$="" THEN 120
60 FOR I=1 TO K
70 IF A(I)=P THEN C(I)=C(I)+1 :GOTO 100
80 NEXT I
90 K=K+1:A(K)=P:C(K)=1
100 IF C(I)>L THEN L=C(I)
110 GOTO 40
120 FOR I=1 TO K:FOR J=I+1 TO K
130 IF A(I)>=A(J) THEN B=A(I):A(I)=A(J):A(J)=B:B=C(I):C(I)=C(J):C(J)=B
140 NEXT J,I
150 PRINT"*******************************************"
160 PRINT"MEAN IS ";T/(F-1):M=INT((F-1)/2)+1
170 IF (F-1)/2 =(M-1) THEN A$="E":M1=(F-1)/2:GOTO 190
180 A$="O"
190 FOR I=1 TO K:C=C+C(I)
200 IF A$="O" AND C>=M THEN M=A(I):GOTO 240
210 IF A$="E" AND C>M1 THEN M=A(I):GOTO 240
220 IF A$="E" AND C=M1 THEN M=(A(I)+A(I+1))/2:GOTO 240
230 NEXT
240 PRINT "MEDIAN IS ";M
250 IF L=1 THEN PRINT"NO MODE ":GOTO 290
260 PRINT"MODE IS ";
270 FOR I=1 TO K :IF C(I)=L THEN PRINT"   ";A(I)
280 NEXT
290 PRINT"*******************************************"
300 INPUT"RUN AGAIN (Y/N) ";A$:IF A$="Y" THEN RUN
```

This program will find the standard deviation, range, and mean of a set of numbers. Press RETURN (ENTER) after each entry. When all entries are completed, press ENTER again.

```
10 DIM A(200)
20 PRINT"   <<<< STANDARD DEVIATION AND RANGE PROGRAM >>>>"
30 PRINT"ENTER NUMBER AND PRESS RETURN OR JUST PRESS RETURN WHEN DONE"
40 INPUT "NUMBER ";N$:IF N$="" THEN 100
50 IF K=0 THEN L=VAL(N$):U=VAL(N$)
60 K=K+1 :T=T+VAL(N$):A(K)=VAL(N$)
70 IF A(K)>U THEN U=A(K)
80 IF A(K)<L THEN L=A(K)
90 GOTO 40
100 PRINT"*****************************************"
110 M=T/K :T=0 :R=U-L
120 PRINT" MEAN IS                  "; M
130 PRINT" RANGE IS                 "; R
140 FOR I=1 TO K
150 T= T+(A(I)-M)^2
160 NEXT
170 T=T/(K-1) :S=T^.5
180 PRINT" STANDARD DEVIATION IS ";S
190 PRINT"*****************************************"
200 INPUT "RUN AGAIN (Y/N) ";A$
210 IF A$="Y" THEN RUN
1000 RUN"menu"
```

A12

Answers to Odd-Numbered Problems

## CHAPTER 1

Exercise 1.1

1. Not well defined
3. Well defined
5. Well defined
7. Not well defined
9. (a) Incorrect (b) Correct (c) Incorrect
   (d) Correct (e) Incorrect
11. $\in$
13. $\notin$
15. The set consisting of the first and the last letters of the English alphabet.
17. The set consisting of the names of the first biblical man and woman.
19. The set of counting numbers from 1 to 7.
21. The set of odd counting numbers from 1 to 51.
23. The set of counting numbers starting with 1 and then adding 3 successively until the number 25 is obtained.
25. {Dioxin, Xylene}
27. {1, 2, 3, 4, 5, 6, 7}
29. {0, 1, 2, 3, 4, 5, 6, 7}
31. {4, 5, 6, 7}
33. $\emptyset$ or {}
35. {4, 5, 6, . . .}
37. {5, 10, 15, . . .}
39. $\emptyset$ or {}
41. {1, 2}
43. {2, 4, 6, 8}
45. {WangB, Gull}
47. {ENSCO, WDigit1, TexAir}
49. {WhrEnf, EchBg}
51. $\{x \mid x$ is a stock whose last price was between 3 and 10$\}$
53. $\{x \mid x$ is a stock whose last price was greater than 20$\}$
55. {M, I, S, P}
57. $\{\frac{1}{1}, \frac{1}{2}, \frac{1}{3}, \ldots, \frac{1}{n}, \ldots\}$
59. Only the set in problem 58 is empty.
61. Sets A and B are not equal.
63. Sets A and B are equal.
65. (a) = (b) $\neq$ (c) $\neq$
67. $A = C$ is true. The other statements are false.
69. The set of all good students is not well defined because the meaning of the word "good" is not agreed upon by everyone. Answers to the second question may vary.
71. (a) If $g \in S$, then Gepetto shaves himself, which contradicts the statement that Gepetto shaves all those men and only those men who do not shave themselves. Therefore, $g \notin S$.
    (b) If $g \in D$, then Gepetto does not shave himself, and so by the same statement he does shave himself. Thus, there is again a contradiction and $g \notin D$.
73. The word "non-self-descriptive" cannot be classified in either way without having a contradiction.
75. $n + 1$

Exercise 1.2

1. $\emptyset$, {a}, {b}, {a, b}   The first three are proper subsets.
3. $\emptyset$, {1}, {2}, {3}, {4}, {1, 2}, {1, 3}, {1, 4}, {2, 3}, {2, 4}, {3, 4}, {1, 2, 3} {1, 2, 4}, {1, 3, 4}, {2, 3, 4}, {1, 2, 3, 4}   All but the last of these are proper subsets.

A13

5. Ø, {1}, {2}, {1, 2}   The first three are proper subsets.

7. 2^4 or 16

9. 2^{10} or 1024

11. 5

13. 6

15. Yes. Every set is a subset of itself.

17. B ⊂ A

19. ⊂

21. ⊄

23. ⊂

25. The different sums that you can select correspond to the sets: Ø, {n}, {d}, {q}, {n, d}, {n, q}, {d, q}, {n, d, q}. If you must use at least one coin, then there are 7 choices.

27. 8

29. 3

31. (a) 5 (b) 10 (c) 10

33. 8

35. Every set is a subset of itself.

37. The empty set is a proper subset of every non-empty set.

39. Every set is a subset of the corresponding universal set.

41. {Alpine, Hindu, Mediterranean, Nordic}

43. {African Negroes, Negritos, Oceanic Negroes}

45. {Mediterranean, Hindu}

47. For $n = 3$, the numbers are 1, 3, 3, 1. For $n = 4$, the numbers are 1, 4, 6, 4, 1 and $t = 16$. For $n = 5$, the numbers are 1, 5, 10, 10, 5, 1 and $t = 32$.

49. $\dbinom{n+1}{k} = \dbinom{n}{k-1} + \dbinom{n}{k}$

Exercise 1.3

1. (a) {1, 3, 4} (b) {1} (c) {1, 6}

3. (a) {1, 3, 4} (b) {1, 2, 3, 4, 5, 6}

5. {1, 2, 3, 4, 5, 6, 7}

7. {1}

9. (a) {c} (b) Ø

11. (a) Correct (b) Incorrect

13. (a) Correct (b) Correct

15. (a) {b, d, f} (b) {a, c}

17. (a) Ø (b) {a, b, c, d, f}

19. (a) {c, e} (b) {a, b, c, d, f}

21. (a) {b, d, f} (b) {a, c}

23. (a) {a, b, c, d, e, f} (b) {c, e}

25. (a) {b, d, f} (b) {a, c}

27. (a) {2, 3} (b) {2, 3}

29. $\mathcal{U}$

31. Ø

33. A

35. Ø

37. A

39. {1, 2, 3, 4, 5}

41. {Beauty, Consideration, Kindliness, Friendliness, Helpfulness, Loyalty}

43. {Intelligence, Cheerfulness, Congeniality}

45. {Intelligence, Cheerfulness}

47. {Is aware of others, Follows up on action}

49. {Follows up on action}

51. (a) F (b) M

53. (a) Male employees who work in the data processing department.

   (b) Female employees who are under 21.

55. $D \cap S$

57. $M \cap D$

59. Male employees or employees who are 21 or over.

61. (a) The set of full-time employees who do shop work. {04, 08}

   (b) The set of part-time employees who do outdoor field work or indoor office work. {02, 05, 07}

63. A and B have no elements in common.

65. All elements of A are elements of B, and all elements of B are elements of A.

67. (a) & (b) The set of characteristics that are in both columns of the table.

   (c) The set of characteristics that appear in either column of the table.

   (d) $G' = $ {Short, Short neck}

   (e) $O' = $ {Tall, Long neck}

69. {Sunbeam snakes}   71. {7, 9} is correct   73. $2n - 1$ for $n \geq 2$

Exercise 1.4

1.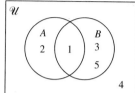

3.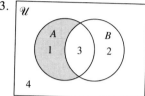

5.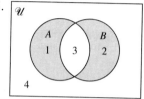

7.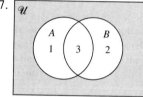

9. Region 1   11. Ø
15. Regions 1, 4, 5, 6, 7

13. Regions 4, 5, 7
17. Region 8

19.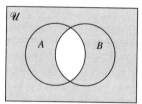

21.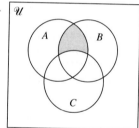

23.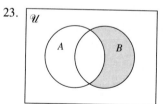

25.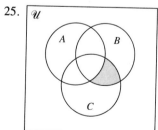

27.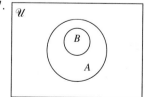

29.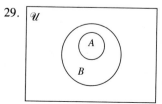

31. (a) Both $A \cup (B \cup C)$ and $(A \cup B) \cup C$ correspond to regions 1, 2, 3, 4, 5, 6, 7. This verifies the given equality.
   (b) Both $A \cap (B \cap C)$ and $(A \cap B) \cap C$ correspond to region 7. This verifies the given equality.

35. $A \cap B$ corresponds to regions 3, 7.

33. (a) $A \cup A'$ corresponds to regions 1, 2, 3, 4, 5, 6, 7, 8. Therefore, $A \cup A' = \mathcal{U}$.
   (b) Since A and A' have no region in common, $A \cap A' = \varnothing$.
   (c) $A - B$ corresponds to regions 1 and 5 and $A \cap B'$ also corresponds to regions 1 and 5. Thus $A - B = A \cap B'$.

37. (a) A = {a, b c, e}, B = {a, b, g, h}, $\mathcal{U}$ = {a, b, c, d, e, f, g, h}
   (b) A $\cup$ B = {a, b, c, e, g, h}
   (c) (A $\cap$ B)$'$ = {c, d, e, f, g, h}

39.

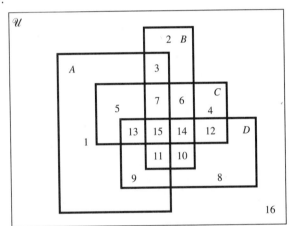

41. Arizona, California, Florida, Texas

43. The set of elements common to A and B.
47. False   49. False

53. No, because the B− person does not have the A antigen.
57. 16 or 2^4

45. The set of elements in $\mathcal{U}$ and not in either A or C.
51. An AB$^+$ person who has all three antigens and thus may receive blood from any person.
55. No, because the O$^-$ does not have the Rh antigen.

59. (a) Region 11   (b) Regions 8 and 16

Exercise 1.5

1. 30
5. 40 people subscribe to both.
9. (a) 22   (b) 36   (c) 6
13. 200
17. $450
21. (a) 120   (b) 80   (c) 50
25. (a) 73   (b) 55   (c) 91   (d) 38   (e) 5

3. 20
7. (a) None   (b) 10   (c) 10
11. (a) $120,000   (b) $510,000   (c) $1,305,000
15. (a) 5   (b) 30   (c) 20
19. 28
23. (a) 80   (b) 120   (c) 50
27. False. A counterexample is $A = \{1, 2\}$, $B = \{m, n\}$.

29. False. A counterexample is $A = \{1, 2\}$, $B = \{1, 2, 3\}$.

33. 16 different subsets

31. The Venn diagram shows that with the added information, the statistics in the cartoon are possible.

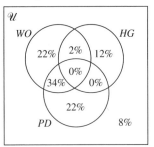

Exercise 1.6

1. The following correspondence shows that sets N and O are equivalent.

$$
\begin{array}{ccccc}
1 & 2 & 3 & \cdots & n & \cdots \\
\updownarrow & \updownarrow & \updownarrow & & \updownarrow & \\
1 & 3 & 5 & \cdots & 2n - 1 & \cdots
\end{array}
$$

3. The following correspondence shows that sets E and G are equivalent.

$$
\begin{array}{ccccc}
2 & 4 & 6 & \cdots & 2n & \cdots \\
\updownarrow & \updownarrow & \updownarrow & & \updownarrow & \\
102 & 104 & 106 & \cdots & 100 + 2n & \cdots
\end{array}
$$

5. The following correspondence shows that sets G and T are equivalent.

$$
\begin{array}{ccccc}
202 & 204 & 206 \cdots & 200 + 2n & \cdots \\
\updownarrow & \updownarrow & \updownarrow & \updownarrow & \\
302 & 304 & 306 \cdots & 300 + 2n & \cdots
\end{array}
$$

7. The following correspondence shows that sets P and Q are equivalent.

$$
\begin{array}{cccc}
2 & 4 & 8 & 12 \\
\updownarrow & \updownarrow & \updownarrow & \updownarrow \\
6 & 12 & 24 & 36
\end{array}
$$

9. The following correspondence shows that sets I^- and N are equivalent.

$$
\begin{array}{ccccc}
-1 & -2 & -3 \cdots & -n & \cdots \\
\updownarrow & \updownarrow & \updownarrow & \updownarrow & \\
1 & 2 & 3 \cdots & n & \cdots
\end{array}
$$

11. $n(A) = 26$

15. $n(E) = \aleph_0$

13. $n(C) = 50$

17. The set $\{100, 200, 300, \ldots\}$ can be put into one-to-one correspondence with a subset of itself, $\{200, 300, 400, \ldots\}$. This shows that the set is infinite.

19. The set $\{\frac{1}{3}, \frac{2}{3}, \frac{3}{3}, \ldots\}$ can be put into one-to-one correspondence with a subset of itself, $\{\frac{2}{3}, \frac{3}{3}, \frac{4}{3}, \ldots\}$, which shows the set is infinite.

21. Sets B and D are equal and equivalent.

23. Set A is neither equal nor equivalent to any of the other sets.

25. $\aleph_0$

27. $\aleph_0$

29. (a) $\frac{7}{9}$ and $\frac{8}{9}$ (b) $\frac{1}{3} + \frac{2}{9} + \frac{4}{27} + \frac{8}{81} + \cdots$ The sum gets closer and closer to 1.

31. To room 223.

33. Rooms $1, 3, 5, \ldots, 2n + 1, \ldots$

35. To room 666.

Chapter 1 Practice Test

1. $\{3, 4, 5, 6, 7, 8, 9\}$

2. (a) The set of vowels in the English alphabet: $\{x \mid x$ is a vowel in the English alphabet$\}$.
   (b) This is the set of even counting numbers less than 10: $\{x \mid x$ is an even counting number less than 10$\}$

3. The proper subsets are $\emptyset$, $\{\$\}$, $\{¢\}$, $\{\%\}$, $\{\$, ¢\}$ $\{\$, \%\}$, $\{¢, \%\}$.

4. (a) Both blanks take the symbol $\in$.
   (b) First blank takes $\in$; second blank takes $\notin$.

5. (a) First blank takes $\in$; second blank takes $\notin$.
   (b) Both blanks take the symbol $\in$.

6. (a) $\{King\}$ (b) $\emptyset$ (c) $\{Queen\}$ (d) $\{Queen\}$

7. (a) $\{Ace, Queen, Jack\}$ (b) $\{King\}$

8. The shaded region in the diagram on the left corresponds to $A - B$. The darker region in the diagram on the right corresponds to $A \cap B'$. This shows that $A - B = A \cap B'$.

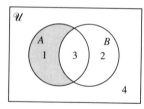 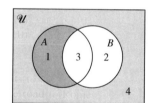

9. The darker region in the diagram corresponds to the set $A \cap B \cap C'$.

10. (a) Regions 1, 2, 5 (b) Regions 2, 3, 4, 6, 8

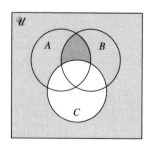

11. $(A \cap B) \cup C$ corresponds to regions 3, 4, 5, 6, 7 and $(A \cup C) \cap (B \cup C)$ corresponds to the same regions. This verifies the equation
    $(A \cap B) \cup C = (A \cup C) \cap (B \cup C)$.

12. $(A \cap B)'$ and $A' \cup B'$ both correspond to regions 1, 2, 3, 4, 6, 8. This verifies the equation $(A \cap B)' = A' \cup B'$.

13. Part b is correct.

14. None of these.

15. (a) $\notin$ (b) $\in$ (c) $\notin$

16. (a) $=$ (b) $\neq$

17. (a) $=$ (b) $\neq$

18. (a) 60 (b) 55

19. (a) 5 (b) 43

20. $B - A$ or $B \cap A'$ or $A' \cap B$

21. (a) 55 (b) 30 (c) 45

22. (a) 47 (b) 12 (c) 26 (d) 3 (e) 10

23. Statement (b) is correct.

24. Statement (c) is correct.

25. Statement (c) is correct.

26. The following correspondence shows that the two sets have the same cardinal number.

$$
\begin{array}{cccc}
1 & 3 & \dots 2n-1 & \dots \\
\updownarrow & \updownarrow & \updownarrow & \\
2 & 4 & \dots \quad 2n & \dots
\end{array}
$$

27. The following correspondence shows that the two sets are equivalent,

$$
\begin{array}{cccc}
1 & 2 & \dots \; n & \dots \\
\updownarrow & \updownarrow & \updownarrow & \\
4 & 16 & \dots (2n)^2 & \dots
\end{array}
$$

28. 12

29. $\aleph_0$

30. A one-to-one correspondence can be set up between the given set

$\left\{ \dfrac{1}{2}, \dfrac{1}{3}, \dfrac{1}{4}, \dots, \dfrac{1}{n}, \dots \right\}$ and a subset of itself $\left\{ \dfrac{1}{3}, \dfrac{1}{4}, \dfrac{1}{5}, \dots, \dfrac{1}{n+1}, \dots \right\}$, so the given set is infinite.

CHAPTER 2

Exercise 2.1

1. Not a statement.

3. A compound statement with the components: Jane is taking an English course. She has four themes to write.

5. Not a statement.

7. A compound statement with the components: Students at Ohio State University are required to take a course in history. Students at Ohio State University are required to take a course in economics.

9. $a \wedge f$ 11. $d \vee f$ 13. $b \wedge p$

15. $a \vee m$ 17. $p \wedge q$ 19. $\sim p \wedge \sim q$

21. Dagwood loves Blondie, or Blondie does not love Dagwood.

23. Dagwood loves Blondie but Blondie does not love Dagwood.

25. It is not the case that Dagwood and Blondie love each other.

27. Bill's store is not making a good profit.

29. My dog is not a spaniel.

31. I like to work overtime.

33. These two are negations of each other.

35. Some men are not mortal.

37. All basketball players are 6 feet tall.

39. He is not bald and he does not have a 10-inch forehead.

41. No circles are round.

43. Nobody up there loves me.

45. Somebody does not like to go on a trip.

47. Some persons occupying your covered auto are not insured.

49. All expenses are subject to the 2% limit.

51. Statement (d)

53. $(d \wedge p) \vee r$

55. $r \wedge (t \vee g)$

57. (a) The diagram is neither a rectangle nor a square.
(b) The diagram is a square or not a rectangle.
(c) The diagram is a square and a rectangle.

Exercise 2.2

1. Today is Friday or Monday.
5. He is a gentleman or a scholar.
9. $g \wedge s$

13. $\sim q \wedge p$
17. $p \vee q$, true.
21. $\sim q \wedge \sim p$, false.
25. $(g \vee j) \wedge \sim (g \wedge j)$, true.
29. $\sim[(i \wedge a) \vee p]$ or $\sim(i \wedge a) \wedge \sim p$ or $(\sim i \vee \sim a) \wedge \sim p$
33. $(i \vee d) \wedge (f \vee g \vee t)$
37. Only Boris.
41. 0 is less than or equal to 3.

45. I will not go fishing or the sun is not shining. This would be true if either or both of the components, "I will not go fishing" and "The sun is not shining" are true.

3. Today is not Friday.
7. He is a gentleman and a scholar.
11. (a) $p \wedge q$ (b) $p \vee q$ (c) Statement (a) is false. Statement (b) is true.

15. $p \vee q$
19. $\sim p \wedge \sim q$, false.
23. $g \vee \sim j$, false.
27. $b \vee c \vee (s \wedge e)$
31. No.

35. $i \vee r \vee p$
39. 7 is greater than or equal to 5.
43. $\frac{1}{2}$ is greater than $\frac{1}{8}$.
47. $\{(e \wedge g) \vee a] \wedge h \wedge (c \vee n \vee \sim t)$

49.

g	s	(a) $g \wedge s$	(b) $g \vee s$	(c) $\sim g \vee \sim s$	(d) $\sim g \wedge \sim s$
T	T	T	T	F	F
T	F	F	T	T	F
F	T	F	T	T	F
F	F	F	F	T	T

51. The table for problem 49 shows that if any two of the statements are true, then the remaining two are false. Note that the table shows the only possible pairs that can be simultaneously true.

53. The same table shows that (a) and (c) always have opposite truth values, and this is also the case for (b) and (d). If (a) is true, then (b) is true, but if (a) is false, then (b) can be true or false.

Exercise 2.3

1.

		1	2	4	3
p	q	p	$\vee$	$\sim q$	

p	q	$p \vee \sim q$	
T	T	**T**	F
T	F	**T**	T
F	T	**F**	F
F	F	**T**	T

3.

p	q	$\sim p \wedge q$	
		1	2	3	4
T	T	F	**F**
T	F	F	**F**
F	T	T	**T**
F	F	T	**F**

5.

p	q	$\sim(p \vee \sim q)$		
		1	2	5	4	3
T	T	**F**	T	F
T	F	**F**	T	T
F	T	**T**	F	F
F	F	**F**	T	T

7.

p	q	$\sim(\sim p \wedge q)$			
		1	2	6	3	5	4
T	T	**T**	F	F	F
T	F	**T**	F	F	T
F	T	**T**	T	F	F
F	F	**F**	T	T	T

9.

1	2	3	6	4	5
p	*q*	\multicolumn{4}{c}{$(p \wedge q) \vee (\sim p \wedge q)$}

p	*q*				
T	T	T	**T**	F	F
T	F	F	**F**	F	F
F	T	F	**T**	T	T
F	F	F	**F**	T	F

11.

1	2	3	5	4
p	*q*	*r*	\multicolumn{2}{c}{$p \wedge (q \vee r)$}

p	*q*	*r*		
T	T	T	**T**	T
T	T	F	**T**	T
T	F	T	**T**	T
T	F	F	**F**	F
F	T	T	**F**	T
F	T	F	**F**	T
F	F	T	**F**	T
F	F	F	**F**	F

13.

1	2	3	4	7	6	5
p	*q*	*r*	\multicolumn{4}{c}{$(p \vee q) \vee (r \wedge \sim q)$}

p	*q*	*r*				
T	T	T	T	**T**	F	F
T	T	F	T	**T**	F	F
T	F	T	T	**T**	T	T
T	F	F	T	**T**	F	T
F	T	T	T	**T**	F	F
F	T	F	T	**T**	F	F
F	F	T	F	**T**	T	T
F	F	F	F	**F**	F	T

15. (a) True when *p* and *q* are both true.
(b) False if at least one of *p* and *q* is false.
(c) True if at least one of *p* and *q* is true.
(d) False only if both *p* and *q* are false.

17.

1	2	3	5	4	6	8	7
p	*q*	*r*	\multicolumn{2}{c}{$p \vee (q \wedge r)$}	\multicolumn{3}{c}{$(p \vee q) \wedge (p \vee r)$}

p	*q*	*r*					
T	T	T	T	T	T	T	T
T	T	F	T	F	T	T	T
T	F	T	T	F	T	T	T
T	F	F	T	F	T	T	T
F	T	T	T	T	T	T	T
F	T	F	F	F	T	F	F
F	F	T	F	F	F	F	T
F	F	F	F	F	F	F	F

Columns 5 and 8 of the above truth table show that the two statements have the same truth values, so they are equivalent.

19.

1	2	4	3	5	7	6
p	*q*	\multicolumn{2}{c}{$\sim(p \vee q)$}	\multicolumn{3}{c}{$\sim p \wedge \sim q$}

p	*q*					
T	T	F	T	F	F	F
T	F	F	T	F	F	T
F	T	F	T	T	F	F
F	F	T	F	T	T	T

Columns 4 and 7 of the table show that the two statements have the same truth values, so they are equivalent.

21.

1	2	3	5	4	6
p	*q*	\multicolumn{3}{c}{$(p \wedge q) \vee \sim p$}	$q \vee \sim p$

p	*q*				
T	T	T	T	F	T
T	F	F	F	F	F
F	T	F	T	T	T
F	F	F	T	T	T

Columns 5 and 6 of the table show that the two statements have the same truth values, so they are equivalent.

23. (a) $p \wedge q$ is true only when both p and q are true. This gives the truth values TFFF. $p \wedge \sim q$ is true only when p is true and q is false, giving the truth values FTFF. $\sim p \wedge q$ is true only when p is false and q is true. This gives the truth values FFTF. $\sim p \wedge \sim q$ is true only when p and q are both false, giving the truth values FFFT. Thus verifies the table.

   (b) $p \wedge q$ is true only in the first row and $\sim p \wedge \sim q$ is true only the last row. So $(p \wedge q) \vee (\sim p \wedge \sim q)$ has the truth values TFFT.

   (c) $(p \wedge \sim q) \vee (\sim p \wedge q)$ has truth values FTTF. $(p \wedge \sim q) \vee (\sim p \vee q) \vee (\sim p \wedge \sim q)$ has truth values FTTT. $\sim(p \wedge q)$ is a simpler statement with truth values FTTT.

25. (a) True if Billy does go to the zoo and does feed peanuts to the elephants or the monkeys.

   (b) True if one of the following is true:

     (i) I file the report and pay the tax.

     (ii) I file the report, do not pay the tax and go to jail.

     (iii) I do not file the report and do go to jail.

27.

1	2	3	4
p	q	$(p \wedge q)$	$* \; p$
T	T	T	F
T	F	F	F
F	T	F	T
F	F	F	T

29.

1	2	3	5	4
p	q	$(p \wedge q)$	$*$	$\sim p$
T	T	T	F	F
T	F	T	F	F
F	T	T	F	T
F	F	F	F	T

31.

1	2	4	3	5
p	q	$(p \wedge$	$\sim q)$	$@ \; q$
T	T	F	F	T
T	F	T	T	T
F	T	F	F	T
F	F	F	T	T

33. $\sim p \wedge \sim q$ 35. $p \vee q$

37. Statement d.

39. None are eligible.

41. We will not pay for damage due to wear or we will not pay for damage due to tear.

43. You may not deduct travel expenses and you may not deduct political contributions.

45. The statement is true only if Lizzie does go to campus and either studies at the library or attends a class.

47. $e \wedge c \wedge f$

49. $e \wedge f$

51. Fish.

Exercise 2.4

1.

1	2	3	5	4	6
p	q	$\sim q$	$\rightarrow$	$\sim p$	$p \rightarrow q$
T	T	F	T	F	T
T	F	T	F	F	F
F	T	F	T	T	T
F	F	T	T	T	T

Columns 5 and 6 are identical, so $\sim q \rightarrow \sim p$ is equivalent to $p \rightarrow q$.

3.

1	2	3	4	5
p	q	$\sim p$	$\rightarrow q$	$p \vee q$
T	T	F	T	T
T	F	F	T	T
F	T	T	T	T
F	F	T	F	F

Since Columns 4 and 5 are identical, $\sim p \rightarrow q$ and $p \vee q$ are equivalent.

5. F

9. x may be any number.

13. It is false whenever the antecedent, "You've got the time," is true, and the consequent, "We've got the beer," is false.

15.

1	2	3	4	6	5
p	q	r		$p \to q \leftrightarrow p \lor r$	
T	T	T	T	T	T
T	T	F	T	T	T
T	F	T	F	F	T
T	F	F	F	F	T
F	T	T	T	T	T
F	T	F	T	F	F
F	F	T	T	T	T
F	F	F	T	F	F

19. The final columns in the tables in problems 17 and 18 are identical, so the two statements are equivalent.

23. $\sim q \to \sim p$

27. $\sim b \to \sim s$

31. $\sim o \lor g$ Eva does not have a day off, or she would go to the beach.

35. If it is a dog, then it is a mammal.

39. If it is a rectangle with perpendicular diagonals, then it is a square.

41.

1	2	4	3	6	5
p	q	$\sim(p \to q)$		$p \land \sim q$	
T	T	F	T	F	F
T	F	T	F	T	T
F	T	F	T	F	F
F	F	F	T	F	T

Since columns 4 and 6 are identical, $\sim(p \to q)$ and $p \land \sim q$ are equivalent.

43. Johnny does not play quarterback and his team does not lose.

47. Evel Knievel is careless, but he will not lose his life.

51. If Joe had not had an accident, then he could get car insurance.

55. (a) $f \to a$ (b) $p \to t$

59. Joe can retire at age 65 without breaking his promise if he is not in good health or if they have more than $600,000 in savings.

7. T

11. x may be any number except 4.

17.

1	2	3	5	4
p	q	r	$p \to (q \land r)$	
T	T	T	T	T
T	T	F	F	F
T	F	T	F	F
T	F	F	F	F
F	T	T	T	T
F	T	F	T	F
F	F	T	T	F
F	F	F	T	F

21. $p \to q$

25. $q \to \sim p$

29. $\sim a \lor b$ The temperature is not above 80°, or I would go to the beach.

33. You do not have the time or we got the beer.

37. If it is a man, then it is created equal.

45. I kiss you once, but I do not kiss you again.

49. If Johnny plays quarterback, then his team wins.

53. No

57. The statement $\sim q \to \sim p$ is: "If you do not cut the dangerous emissions caused by your driving, then you do not switch from a car that gets 25 miles per gallon to one that gets 50 miles per gallon." This is true if the statement given in the problem is true.

61. Statement (d).

63. Statement (d).

67. The student has to take the placement examination only if the student has satisfied the freshman requirements (perhaps by advanced courses in high school) and is being admitted to sophomore standing, but is entering college for the first time.

71. No. It only says that an adjustment will be made if a report is made in 10 days.

65. No. $p \rightarrow q$ is true if p is false and q is either true or false.

69. $r \rightarrow a$

Exercise 2.5

1. If n is divisible by 2, then n is an even number.
5. $q \rightarrow p$.

9. If the measure gets a two-thirds vote, then it carries.

13. If birds are of a feather, then they flock together.
17. $p \leftrightarrow s$
19. (a) Converse: If you are not strong, then you do not eat your spinach.
   Inverse: If you eat your spinach, then you are strong.
   Contrapositive: If you are strong, then you eat your spinach.
   (b) Converse: If you are strong, then you eat your spinach.
   Inverse: If you do not eat your spinach, then you are not strong.
   Contrapositive: If you are not strong, then you do not eat your spinach.
   (c) Converse: If you eat your spinach, then you are strong.
   Inverse: If you are not strong, then you do not each your spinach.
   Contrapositive: If you do not eat your spinach, then you are not strong.
21. If the square of an integer is divisible by 4, the integer is even. True.
25. If you pass this course, then you get passing grades on all the tests. False.
29. If a person does not want to improve the world, then the person is not a radical.

33. (a) $f \rightarrow \sim r$ (b) $r \rightarrow \sim f$
   (c) If you need to report the income, then you rented your vacation home for 15 or more days a year.

37. (a) $k \rightarrow p$ (b) $k \leftrightarrow p$ (c) $p \rightarrow k$
41. Equivalence (c).

3. $q \rightarrow p$.
7. If one is a mathematics major, then one takes calculus.
11. If we have a stable economy, then we have low unemployment.
15.

			Converse	Inverse
p	q	$p \rightarrow q$	$q \rightarrow p$	$\sim p \rightarrow \sim q$
T	T	T	T	T
T	F	F	T	T
F	T	T	F	F
F	F	T	T	T

The converse, $q \rightarrow p$, is true except when q is true and p is false (third row). The inverse, $\sim p \rightarrow \sim q$, is true except when p is true and q is false (third row). Thus, the converse and the inverse have the same truth values, and hence are equivalent.

23. If I am neat and well dressed, then I can get a date. False.
27. If we cannot find a cure for cancer, then the research is inadequately funded.
31. (a) $u \rightarrow a$
   (b) If you use this box, then your recent scores were earned after October 1.
35. (a) If you are under 18, then you are not admitted without parent or guardian.
   (b) If you are admitted without parent or guardian, then you are not under 18.
39. (a) $b \leftrightarrow c$ (b) $b \rightarrow c$ (c) $c \rightarrow b$
43. Statement (b).

45. (a) Every even integer is twice another integer.
 (b) If two integers are equal, then their squares are equal.
 (c) $(2k)^2 = (2k) \times (2k) = 2 \times 2 \times k \times k = 4k^2$
 (d) $n^2 = 4k^2 = 2 \times 2k^2$, so n^2 is even.

47. "For q to be true, it is necessary for p to be true," means that q cannot be true if p is not true. It does not mean that q is true if p is true. For example, for an integer n to be divisible by 4, it is necessary for n to be even, but that is not sufficient. (6 is even but not divisible by 4.) "For q to be true, it is sufficient for p to be true." means that q is true if p is true. For an integer to be divisible by 4, it is sufficient for the integer to be the square of an even integer. (Look at problem 45.) However, this is not a necessary condition. (12 is divisible by 4, but 12 is not the square of any integer.)

49. Answers may vary. Here are two examples.
 i. To freeze water, it is necessary that the temperature be below 0° C.
 ii. To be admitted to a college, it is necessary for you to satisfy the entrance requirements.

51. The contrapositive of $\sim q \rightarrow \sim p$ is $p \rightarrow q$.

53. The inverse of $p \rightarrow q$ is $\sim p \rightarrow \sim q$, and the contrapositive of $\sim p \rightarrow \sim q$ is $q \rightarrow p$.

55. $(\sim r \wedge \sim s) \vee (p \vee q) \Leftrightarrow (r \vee s) \rightarrow (p \vee q)$
 is true because
 $(r \vee s) \rightarrow (p \vee q) \Leftrightarrow \sim (r \vee s) \vee (p \vee q) \Leftrightarrow$
 $(\sim r \wedge \sim s) \vee (p \vee q).$

57. The direct statement.

59. The contrapositive.

Exercise 2.6

1.

1	**2**	**3**	**4**
p	q	$(p \wedge q) \rightarrow p$	
T	T	T	T
T	F	F	T
F	T	F	T
F	F	F	T

Column 3 is the conjunction of columns 1 and 2, so has T only in the first row, where both p and q are T. Therefore, column 4 is all Ts, which shows that $(p \wedge q) \rightarrow p$ is a tautology.

3.

1	**3**	**2**
p	$p \leftrightarrow \sim p$	
T	F	F
F	F	T

Since column 3 is all F's, the statement $p \leftrightarrow \sim p$ is a contradiction.

5. A contradiction. 7. A tautology. 9. u implies v and w implies v.

11.

p	q
T	F
F	T

The table shows the only cases that can arise. If p is true, then q is false, and if q is true, then p is false. Thus, neither one implies the other.

13.

p	q
T	T
T	F
F	F

The table shows the only cases that can arise. If p is true, then q can be true or false. Thus, p does not imply q. If q is true, then p is true. Thus, q implies p.

15.

p	*q*
T	T
T	F
F	F

The table shows the only cases that can arise. If *p* is true, then *q* can be true or false, so *p* does not imply *q*. If *q* is true, then *p* is true, so *q* implies *p*.

19. Statements (a), (b), (d), and (e) can all be true at the same time, or statements (b), (c), (d), and (f) can all be true at the same time.

23. Equivalent.

27. The truth values for $p \to q$ are TFTT. If the F case is missing, so that $p \to q$ is a tautology, then $p \Rightarrow q$.

31. (a) $Q \cap R'$. (b) $(P \cap Q) \cap R'$.

35. Here is a diagram for the statement $p \lor q$.

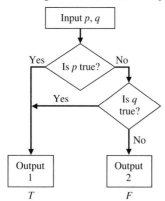

17.

p	*q*
T	T
T	F
F	F

The table shows the only cases that can arise. If *p* is true then *q* can be true or false, so *p* does not imply *q*. If *q* is true, then *p* is true, so *q* implies *p*.

21.

1	2	3	4	6	5
p	*q*	($\sim p$	$\land$ *q*) $\to$	(p	$\to$ *q*)
T	T	F	F	T	T
T	F	F	F	T	F
F	T	T	T	T	T
F	F	T	F	T	T

Since column 6 is all T's, the first statement, $\sim p \land q$, implies the second, $p \to q$.

25. The second statement implies the first.

29. By definition, the statement $p \to q$ is true when p is false. Hence, a false statement implies any statement.

33. Output 1 is T and Output 2 is F.

Exercise 2.7

1. Premises: "No misers are generous," and "Some old people are not generous." Conclusion: "Some old people are misers."

5. Premises: "No kitten that loves fish is unteachable," and "No kitten without a tail will play with a gorilla." Conclusion: "No unteachable kitten will play with a gorilla."

3. Premises: "All diligent students get A's," and "All lazy students are not successful." Conclusion: "All diligent students are lazy."

7. Valid

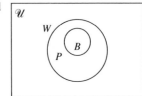

9. Invalid

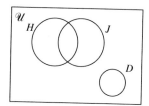

11. Valid

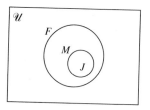

13. Invalid

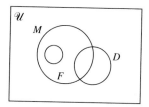

15. Invalid

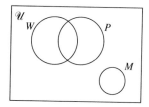

17. Invalid

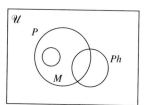

19. Valid

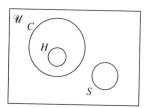

21. Invalid

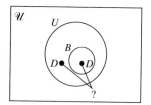

23. Invalid

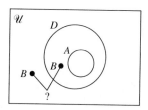

25. Invalid

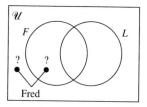

27. Statement (b) can be logically deduced.

29. (a) Yes. An argument is valid if and only if the conclusion is true whenever all the premises are true.
   (b) No. By the preceding statement, if the premises are all true and the conclusion is false, then the argument is invalid.

33. The conclusion is true.

31. No. It may be that the conclusion does not follow from the premises. See Example 2 of this section.

35. Valid

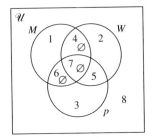

37. Invalid

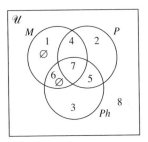

39. Invalid

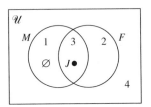

41. Invalid

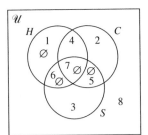

43. Valid

45. Only the first conclusion is valid.

Exercise 2.8

1. $e \rightarrow p$
     $\sim e$
     ∴ $\sim p$
     Invalid

3. $s \rightarrow e$
     $\sim e$
     ∴ $\sim s$
     Valid

5.
$$\frac{g}{\therefore \ g \wedge r}$$
Invalid

9.
$$\begin{array}{c} t \rightarrow b \\ t \\ \hline \therefore \ b \end{array}$$
Valid

13.
$$\begin{array}{c} m \rightarrow e \\ \sim m \\ \hline \therefore \ \sim e \end{array}$$
Invalid

17. Valid.
21. Valid.
25. s
29. All romances are well written.
33. Conclusion (c).
37. None of these.
41. "Affirming the consequent" means that the "then" statement is affirmed and the "if" statement is taken as a valid conclusion. This is a fallacy because $p \rightarrow q$ is true if p is false and q is either true or false.

7.
$$\begin{array}{c} w \rightarrow m \\ \sim w \rightarrow g \\ \hline \therefore \ m \vee g \end{array}$$
Valid

11.
$$\begin{array}{c} s \rightarrow f \\ s \\ \hline \therefore f \end{array}$$
Valid

15.
$$\begin{array}{c} f \rightarrow s \\ \sim f \\ \hline \therefore \ \sim s \end{array}$$
Invalid

19. Invalid.
23. $p \rightarrow r$.
27. q
31. Aardvarks do not vote.
35. Statement (b).
39. You read X magazine
43. Kittens that will play with a gorilla do not have green eyes. (Or the equivalent: No kitten with green eyes will play with a gorilla.)

Exercise 2.9

1.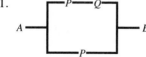

3.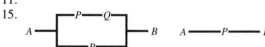

5.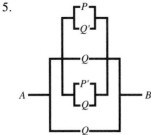

7.

9.
13.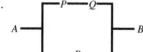

11.
15.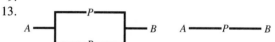

17. $A \longrightarrow P \longrightarrow Q' \longrightarrow B$

19. $A \longrightarrow P \longrightarrow Q' \longrightarrow B$

21. In a circuit with switches P and Q in series, current will flow if and only if both switches are closed. This corresponds to the statement $p \wedge q$, which is true if and only if p and q are both true.

25. The final output voltage is low (0) when the input voltages corresponding to P and Q are both low (0) or both high (1); the output voltage is high (1) in the other cases.

23. The final output voltage is low (0) except when the input voltage corresponding to P is high (1) and that corresponding to Q is low (0).

Chapter 2 Practice Test

1. (b), (c), (d), and (e) are statements. Each is either true or false. (a) is not a statement because people do not agree on what is good. (f) is a question, so is neither true nor false.

2. (a) d: The number of years is divisible by 4. p: The year is a presidential election year. The logical connective is *if . . . then . . . . $d \to p$.*
   (b) b: I love Bill. $\sim m$: Bill does not love me. The logical connective is *and. $b \wedge \sim m$.*
   (c) e: A candidate is elected president of the United States. m: He receives a majority of the electoral college votes. The logical connective is *if and only if. $e \leftrightarrow m$.*
   (d) s: Janet can make sense out of symbolic logic. f: She fails this course. The logical connective is *or. $s \vee f$.*
   (e) s: Janet can make sense out of symbolic logic. The logical modifier is *not. $\sim s$*

3. (a) It is not the case the he is a gentleman and a scholar.
   (b) He is not a gentleman, but he is a scholar.

4. (a) I will go neither to the beach nor to the movies.
   (b) I will either not stay in my room or not do my homework.
   (c) Pluto is a planet.

5. (a) Some cats are not felines.
   (b) No dog is well trained.
   (c) Some dogs are afraid of a mouse.

6. (a) Joey does not study, but he will not fail this course.
   (b) Sally does not study hard, but she gets an A in this course.

7. (a) $p \leftrightarrow q$ (b) $p \wedge q$ (c) $\sim p$ (d) $p \to q$
   (e) $p \vee q$

8.

1	2	3	7	4	6	5
p	q	$(p \vee q)$	$\wedge$	$(\sim p$	$\vee$	$\sim q)$
T	T	T	F	F	F	F
T	F	T	T	F	T	T
F	T	T	T	T	T	F
F	F	F	F	T	T	T

9.

1	2	3	5	4
p	q	$(p \vee q)$	$\to$	$\sim p$
T	T	T	F	F
T	F	T	F	F
F	T	T	T	T
F	F	F	T	T

10. Statement (b).

11. When at least one of the statements "Sally is naturally beautiful," and "Sally knows how to use makeup," is true.

12. The premise, "$2 + 2 = 5$," is false, so the statement (a conditional) is true.

14. (a) If you make a golf score of 62 again, then you made it once.
    (b) If you did not make a golf score of 62 once, then you will not make it again.
    (c) If you do not make a golf score of 62 again, then you did not make it once.

16. (a) $b \rightarrow c$ (b) $c \rightarrow b$ (c) $b \leftrightarrow c$

18. Only statement (b).

20. Nothing in the premises tells whether S (for Sally) goes inside the circle L or not. Thus, the argument is invalid.

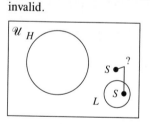

13.

1	2	3	6	5	4
p	q	$(p \rightarrow q)$	$\leftrightarrow$	$(q$	$\vee$	$\sim p)$
T	T	T	T	T	F
T	F	F	T	F	F
F	T	T	T	T	T
F	F	T	T	T	T

15. (a) $m \rightarrow p$ (b) $p \rightarrow m$ (c) $p \leftrightarrow m$

17. (b) implies (a); (b) implies (c); (c) implies (a).

19. Nothing in the premises tells whether the J (for John) is inside or outside of the circle H. Thus, the argument is invalid.

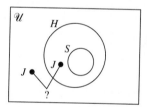

21. With s for "He is a student," and h for "He studies hard," the argument can be symbolized and a truth table constructed.

$$s \rightarrow h$$
$$\underline{\sim s}$$
$$\therefore \sim h$$

		Prem.	Prem.	Concl.
s	h	$s \rightarrow h$	$\sim s$	$\sim h$
T	T	T	F	F
T	F	F	F	T
F	T	T	T	F	← Premises T, Conclusion F
F	F	T	T	T

In the third row of the table, both premises are true and the conclusion is false, so the argument is invalid.

22. With f for "Sally is a loafer," and h for "Sally works hard," the argument can be symbolized and a truth table constructed.

			Prem.	Prem.	Concl.	
$f \to \sim h$						
$\sim h$	f	h	$f \to \sim h$	$\sim h$	f	
$\therefore f$						
	T	T	F	F	T	
	T	F	T	T	T	
	F	T	T	F	F	
	F	F	T	T	F	← Premises T, Conclusion F

In the fourth row of the truth table, the premises are both true and the conclusion is false, so the argument is invalid.

23. With w for "You win the race," and r for "You are a good runner," the argument can be symbolized and a truth table constructed.

			Prem.	Prem.	Concl.
$w \to r$					
w	r	w	$w \to r$	w	r
$\therefore r$					
	T	T	T	T	T
	T	F	T	F	T
	F	T	F	T	F
	F	F	T	F	F

The first row of the table is the only row where the premises are both true. In this row the conclusion is also true, so the argument is valid.

24. Suppose that p, q, and r are all true. Then, the first premise, $p \to q$, is true because p and q are both true. The second premise, $\sim q \to \sim r$ is also true, because $\sim q$ is false. However, the conclusion, $p \to \sim r$ is false, because p is true and $\sim r$ is false. In this case, the premises are both true and the conclusion is false. Thus, the argument is invalid. (If you constructed a truth table, the first row would correspond to the preceding statements.)

25. Since $p \to q$ is equivalent to $\sim p \vee q$, and $\sim p \to \sim q$ is equivalent to $p \vee \sim q$, the given statement is equivalent to $(\sim p \vee q) \wedge (p \vee \sim q)$. Thus, the following is the corresponding switching circuit.

CHAPTER 3

Exercise 3.1

1. ∩∩||||

3. 9∩∩∩∩||

5. 9999∩∩∩ |||
   9999 ||

7. 113

9. 322

11. 11,232

13. ∩∩∩ ||||
    + ∩∩ |||
    ∩∩∩∩∩||||||||

15.   9999∩∩∩ || → 999∩
      -   9∩∩∩∩||| -   ∩∩|

    →99∩∩∩∩∩∩∩∩∩∩||||||||||
      -                 ∩∩|
    99∩∩∩∩∩∩∩∩ |||||||||

17. \1   40
    \2   80
    \4   160
    \8   320
    ‾‾‾‾‾‾‾‾
    15   600

21. 18   32
     9   64*
     4   128
     2   256
     1   512*
        ‾‾‾‾‾
         576*

25. ▼▼▼▼▼▼ ▼

29. ▼▼ ▼▼▼

33. ▼ ▼▼ ⟨▼▼▼

37. 192

41.   ⟨⟨⟨▼▼
      + ⟨⟨⟨⟨▼▼▼
      ‾‾‾‾‾‾‾‾‾‾‾‾‾‾‾‾‾‾
        ⟨⟨⟨⟨⟨⟨⟨▼▼▼▼▼ = ▼ ⟨▼▼▼▼▼

45. 126

49. 90,405

53. CXLV

57. 8

61. No. C is more than two steps larger than I, so this subtraction is not allowed. I may be subtracted from V or X only.

65. The Egyptian system was based on 10 and the Babylonian on 60. The Egyptian system was not a positional system; it depended essentially on the addition of the symbol values. The Babylonian system used spacing to change symbol values.

69. Assume the answer is 3. $3 + (\frac{2}{3})(3) = 5$. $5 - (\frac{1}{3})(5) = \frac{10}{3}$ and $10 \div \frac{10}{3} = 3$. Therefore, the correct answer is $3 \times 3 = 9$.

19.   1   51
     \2   102
     \4   204
      8   408
    \16   816
     ‾‾‾‾‾‾‾‾‾
     22 1122

23. 12   51
     6   102
     3   204*
     1   408*
        ‾‾‾‾‾
         612*

27. ⟨⟨⟨ ▼▼

31. ▼▼▼▼ ⟨▼▼▼▼▼▼▼▼

35. 92

39. 4322

43.   ▼▼ ⟨▼▼▼
     + ▼ ▼▼▼▼▼▼▼▼
     ‾‾‾‾‾‾‾‾‾‾‾‾‾‾‾‾‾‾‾‾‾‾‾‾‾‾
     ▼▼▼ ⟨▼▼▼▼▼▼▼▼▼▼▼▼▼ = ▼▼▼ ⟨⟨▼

47. 42,000

51. LXXII

55. X̄X̄X̄ĪĪDIII

59. 4

63. The Babylonian system is a base 60 system and our decimal system is a base 10 system. Another important difference is the lack of a symbol for zero in the Babylonian system. The Babylonian system was not a good place system, it depended on spacing. The symbol for 1 was the same as that for 60, and only the spacing could show which was intended.

67. Assume the answer is 6. $6 + (\frac{1}{6})(6) = 7$, and $21 \div 7 = 3$. Hence, the correct answer is $3 \times 6 = 18$.

71. $n = 8$.

Exercise 3.2

1. $(4 \times 10^2) + (3 \times 10) + (2 \times 10^0)$

5. $(1 \times 10^4) + (2 \times 10^3) + (3 \times 10^2) + (4 \times 10) + (9 \times 10^0)$

9. 45

13. 748,308

17.   23 $(2 \times 10) + (3 \times 10^0)$
    +13 $(1 \times 10) + (3 \times 10^0)$
    ‾‾‾‾   ‾‾‾‾‾‾‾‾‾‾‾‾‾‾‾‾‾‾‾‾‾‾‾‾‾‾‾‾
     36     $(3 \times 10) + (6 \times 10^0)$

3. $(2 \times 10^3) + (3 \times 10^2) + (7 \times 10^0)$

7. 1

11. 9071

15. 4,000,031

19.   71 $(7 \times 10) + (1 \times 10^0)$
    +23 $(2 \times 10) + (3 \times 10^0)$
    ‾‾‾‾   ‾‾‾‾‾‾‾‾‾‾‾‾‾‾‾‾‾‾‾‾‾‾‾‾‾‾‾‾
     94     $(9 \times 10) + (4 \times 10^0)$

21. $\begin{array}{r} 76 \\ -54 \\ \hline 22 \end{array}$ $\begin{array}{l}(7 \times 10) + (6 \times 10^0) \\ (-)(5 \times 10) + (4 \times 10^0) \\ \hline (2 \times 10) + (2 \times 10^0)\end{array}$

23. $\begin{array}{r} 84 \\ -31 \\ \hline 53 \end{array}$ $\begin{array}{l}(8 \times 10) + (4 \times 10^0) \\ (-)(3 \times 10) + (1 \times 10^0) \\ \hline (5 \times 10) + (3 \times 10^0)\end{array}$

25. 7^{11}

27. 6^{40}

29. 6^7

31. 6^{12}

33. 5^{12}

35. 10^{30}

37. $\begin{array}{r} 25 \\ \times 51 \\ \hline 25 \\ 125 \\ \hline 1275 \end{array}$ $\begin{array}{l}(2 \times 10) + (5 \times 10^0) \\ \times \quad (5 \times 10) + (1 \times 10^0) \\ \hline (2 \times 10) + (5 \times 10^0) \\ (10 \times 10^2) + (25 \times 10) \\ \hline 10^3 + (27 \times 10) + (5 \times 10^0)\end{array}$

$$= (1 \times 10^3) + (2 \times 10^2) + (7 \times 10) + (5 \times 10^0) = 1275$$

39. $\begin{array}{r} 62 \\ \times 25 \\ \hline 310 \\ 124 \\ \hline 1550 \end{array}$ $\begin{array}{l}(6 \times 10) + (\ 2 \times 10^0) \\ \times \quad (2 \times 10) + (\ 5 \times 10^0) \\ \hline (30 \times 10) + (10 \times 10^0) \\ (12 \times 10^2) + (\ 4 \times 10) \\ \hline (12 \times 10^2) + (34 \times 10) + (\ 1 \times 10)\end{array}$

$$= (1 \times 10^3) + (5 \times 10^2) + (5 \times 10) = 1550$$

41. $\begin{array}{r} 8 \\ 8)\overline{64} \\ 64 \\ \hline 0 \end{array}$ $8 \times 10^0 \overline{)\,(6 \times 10) + (4 \times 10^0)}$
  $\underline{(6 \times 10) + (4 \times 10^0)}$
  0

43. $\begin{array}{r} 12 \\ 6)\overline{72} \\ 6 \\ \hline 12 \\ 12 \\ \hline 0 \end{array}$ $(6 \times 10^0) \overline{)\,(7 \times 10) + (2 \times 10^0)}$
  $\underline{(6 \times 10)}$
  $(1 \times 10) + (2 \times 10^0)$
  $\underline{(1 \times 10) + (2 \times 10^0)}$
  0

45. 3×10^5

47. 9×10^9

49. 2×10^8

51. You must add the exponents to obtain a^{m+n}.

53. You must multiply the exponent m by n to obtain a^{mn}.

55. There were 137,256 on the road to Rome.

Exercise 3.3

1. 22_{three}

3. 31_{four}

5. (*******) *******; 17_{eight}

7. (*******) (*******) *; 21_{seven}

9. 22

11. 139

13. 27

15. 291

17. 30_{five}

19. 11100_{two}

21. $19_{sixteen}$

23. 41_{six}

25. 121_{seven}

27. 46_{eight}

29. $5BB_{sixteen}$

31. $73 = 1001001_{two} = 111_{eight}$

33. One of the meanings of binary is "based on two". The prefix *bi-* means "two".

35. Hexadecimal means "based on 16". The prefix *hexa-* means "six".

37. The trick works because the columns correspond to the binary digits in the number. For instance, $6 = 110_{two}$ and this corresponds to the number $6 = 2 + 4$, the numbers that head columns B and C. Note that 6 occurs in columns B and C, but not in A.

39. Use the same procedure as for the numbers from 1 to 7, but with five columns instead of three.

Calculator Corner

1. 13
5. 1914

3. 113
7. 2620

Exercise 3.4

1. 67_8
5. 110101_2
9. 37_{16}
13. 10010101_2
17. 411_8
21. $365 = 555_8 = 16D_{16}$
25. HELP, I AM LOST. H $\leftrightarrow$ 72, E $\leftrightarrow$ 69, L $\leftrightarrow$ 76,
     P $\leftrightarrow$ 80 I $\leftrightarrow$ 73, A $\leftrightarrow$ 65, M $\leftrightarrow$ 77, O $\leftrightarrow$ 79,
     S $\leftrightarrow$ 83, T $\leftrightarrow$ 84

3. 155_8
7. 11000110_2
11. $6D_{16}$
15. 11111001101_2
19. $15F_{16}$
23. HELLO. H $\leftrightarrow$ 72, E $\leftrightarrow$ 69, L $\leftrightarrow$ 76, O $\leftrightarrow$ 79

27. Use the given table to find the binary equivalent of each of the base 4 digits:

3	1	2
$\downarrow$	$\downarrow$	$\downarrow$
11	01	10

This shows that $312_4 = 110110_2$.

29. 1233_4
33. 55
37. 011111_2

31. 61_8
35. 000001_2

Exercise 3.5

1. 1001_2
5. 10010_2
9. 1_2
13. 10010_2
17. 110111_2
21. 100_2 R 10_2

3. 10011_2
7. 101_2
11. 1010_2
15. 101101_2
19. 110_2 R 1_2
23. 1011_2 R 100_2

25. In base 2, there are only two digits, 0 and 1. The addition and multiplication tables are much simpler than in the decimal system.

		Binary	Decimal	Hexadecimal
27.	A	01000001	65	41
29.	Q	01010001	81	51
31.	X	01011000	88	58

33.

Hexadecimal	Binary	Letter
48	01001000	H
45	01000101	E
4C	01001100	L
50	01010000	P

Exercise 3.6

1. 600_8

3. 10112_8

5. 432_8

7. 7154_8

9. 507_8

11. 2306_8

13. 35_8 R 4_8

15. 250_8 R 5_8

17. 417_{16}

19. $9B8_{16}$

21. $A367_{16}$

23. $4A451_{16}$

25. Answers may vary. The main reason is that there are only two digits in the binary system contrasted with 16 digits in the hexadecimal system.

27. 2.625

29. 2.125

31. 58.75

Chapter 3 Practice Test

1. (a) ∩ ∩ ∩ ||| (b) 9999∩ ∩ |||
   ∩ ∩ ∩   999∩ ||

2. (a) 23 (b) 121

3. (a) ▼ ▼▼▼ (b) ‹▼▼ ‹▼▼▼▼▼

4. (a) 82 (b) 131

5. (a)
\1	21	(b) 23	(21)
\2	42	11	(42)
\4	84	5	(84)
8	168	2	168
\16	336	1	(336)
	483		483

6. (a) LIII (b) XLII (c) $\overline{\text{XXII}}$

7. (a) 67 (b) 48,000

8. (a) $(2 \times 10^3) + (5 \times 10^2) + (0 \times 10) + (7 \times 10^0)$

   (b) $(1 \times 10^2) + (8 \times 10) + (9 \times 10^0)$

9. (a) 3702 (b) 59,040

10. (a)
$$\begin{array}{ll} 75 & (7 \times 10) + 5 \\ +32 & +(3 \times 10) + 2 \\ \hline 107 & (10 \times 10) + 7 \\ & = (1 \times 10^2) + 7 \\ & = 107 \end{array}$$
   (b)
$$\begin{array}{ll} 56 & (5 \times 10) + 6 \\ -24 & (-)(2 \times 10) + 4 \\ \hline 32 & (3 \times 10) + 2 \\ & = 32 \end{array}$$

11. (a) $3^4 \times 3^8 = 3^{4+8} = 3^{12}$ (b) $2^9 \div 2^3 = 2^{9-3} = 2^6$

12. (a)
$$\begin{array}{ll} 83 & (8 \times 10) + 3 \\ \times 21 & \times (2 \times 10) + 1 \\ \hline 83 & (8 \times 10) + 3 \\ 166 & (16 \times 10^2) + (6 \times 10) \\ \hline 1743 & (16 \times 10^2) + (14 \times 10) + 3 \end{array}$$
$$= (1 \times 10^3) + (6 \times 10^2) + (1 \times 10^2) + (4 \times 10) + 3$$
$$= (1 \times 10^3) + (7 \times 10^2) + (4 \times 10) + 3 = 1743$$

   (b)
$$\begin{array}{l} 7R5 \\ 7)\overline{54} \\ \underline{49} \\ 5 \end{array}$$
$$\begin{array}{l} (7 \times 10^0) \text{ R } (5 \times 10^0) \\ 7 \times 10^0)\overline{(5 \times 10) + (4 \times 10^0)} \\ \underline{(4 \times 10) + (9 \times 10^0)} \\ (5 \times 10^0) \end{array}$$

13. (a) 35 (b) 48 (c) 13

14. (a) 106 (b) 2604

15. (a) 113_5 (b) 53_6

16. (a) 100111_2 (b) 1000001111_2

17. (a) 57_8 (b) $2F_{16}$

18. (a) 135_8 (b) 11010111_2

19. (a) $5D_{16}$ (B) 1010111101_2
21. (a) 10010_2 (b) 110_2
23. (a) 700_8 (b) 233_8
25. (a) 319_{16} (b) $A1EC_{16}$

20. (a) 53_8 (b) 17_{16}
22. (a) 100111_2 (b) 111_2 R 1_2
24. (a) 564_8 (b) 77_8

CHAPTER 4

Exercise 4.1

1. For identification only.

3. A cardinal number.

5. The "First" is for identification; the "one" is an ordinal number.

7.

$\times$	1	2	3	4 . . .
1	1	2	3	4 . . .
2	2	4	6	8 . . .
3	3	6	9	12 . . .
4	4	8	12	16 . . .
.	.	.	.	. . . .
.	.	.	.	. . . .
.	.	.	.	. . . .

   (a) Yes. Multiplication associates a unique result with each pair of elements of N.
   (b) Yes. The result of multiplying any two natural numbers is always a natural number.
   (c) Yes. For any two natural numbers a, b, a $\times$ b = b $\times$ a.

9. $4(3 + 8) = 4 \times 3 + 4 \times 8 = 12 + 32 = 44$

11. $8(3 + 8) = 8 \times 3 + 8 \times 8 = 24 + 64 = 88$

13. $6 \cdot 17 = 6(10 + 7) = 6 \times 10 + 6 \times 7 = 60 + 42 = 102$

15. $7 \cdot 23 = 7(20 + 3) = 7 \times 20 + 7 \times 3 = 140 + 21 = 161$

17. Yes to both questions. Adding or multiplying two even, natural numbers yields another even, natural number.

19. (a) Yes. The operation * associates a unique result with each pair of elements of A.
   (b) Yes. The result of the operation * is an element of A.
   (c) Yes. The table is symmetric to a diagonal from upper left to lower right. Thus, if x and y are any two elements of A, then $x * y = y * x$.
   (d) Yes. You can check that if x, y, z are any three elements of A, $x * (y * z) = (x * y) *z$. For example, $a * (c * b) = a * b = c$ and $(a * c) * b = a * b = c$. (The table gives $c * b = b$ and $a * c = a$.)

21. (a) The commutative property of addition.
   (b) The associative property of addition.

23. (a) The distributive property of multiplication over addition.
   (b) The commutative property of addition.

25. (a) The distributive property of multiplication over addition.
   (b) The commutative property of multiplication.

27. (a) The distributive property of multiplication over addition.
   (b) The commutative property of multiplication.

29. (a) The commutative property of multiplication.
   (b) The distributive property of multiplication over addition.

31. (a) The commutative property of addition.
   (b) The commutative property of multiplication.

33. The commutative and the associative properties of addition.

35. 6

37. 3

39. 9

41. The commutative and associative properties of multiplication.

43. No. For example, $2 + (6 \times 3) = 2 + 18 = 20$, but $(2 + 6) \times (2 + 3) = 8 \times 5 = 40$.

45. No. For example, $12 - (2 \times 3) = 12 - 6 = 6$, but $(12 - 2) \times (12 - 3) = 10 \times 9 = 90$.

47. Let $n(A) = a$ and $n(B) = b$. Form the Cartesian product $A \times B$, and define $ab = n(A \times B)$

49. Let $n(A) = a$, $n(B) = b$ and $n(C) = c$. Form the Cartesian products $(A \times B) \times C$ and $A \times (B \times C)$. Since these two sets have the same number of elements, $(ab)c = a(bc)$. (See problem 47.)

Exercise 4.2

1. 51 52 ⑤3 54 55 56 57 58 ⑤9 60

   ⑥1 62 63 64 65 66 ⑥7 68 69 70

   ⑦1 72 ⑦3 74 75 76 77 78 ⑦9 80

   81 82 ⑧3 84 85 86 87 88 ⑧9 90

   91 92 93 94 95 96 ⑨7 98 99 100

   The primes in the table are circled.

3. 6

5. 4

7. (a) 2 and 3

   (b) No. If any pair of consecutive counting numbers greater than 2 is selected, one of the pair must be an even number (divisible by 2) and hence, not a prime.

9. (a) The product part of m is exactly divisible by 2, so that m divided by 2 would have a remainder of 1.

   9b) The product part of m is exactly divisible by 3, so that m divided by 3 would have a remainder of 1.

   (c) and (d) Exactly the same reasoning as in parts (a) and (b) applies here. If m is divided by any prime from 2 to P, there is remainder of 1.

   (e) Because P was assumed to be the largest prime.

   (f) Because m is not divisible by any of the primes from 2 to P.

11. 1, 2, 5, 10, 25, 50.

13. 1, 2, 4, 8, 16, 32, 64, 128

15. 1, 7, 11, 13, 77, 91, 143, 1001

17. 41 is a prime.

19. $91 = 7 \times 13$

21. $148 = 2^2 \times 37$

23. 490

25. 1200

27. (a) Divisible by 3 and by 5.

   (b) Divisible by 2, by 3 and by 5.

   (c) Divisible by 2, by 3 and by 5.

29. Three: 2, 11, and 22

31. 27

33. Relatively prime.

35. 47

37. Relatively prime.

39. 20

41. $\frac{31}{44}$

43. $\frac{3}{14}$

45. $\frac{1}{4}$

47. LCM = 165; $\frac{14}{165}$

49. LCM = 992; $\frac{101}{992}$

51. LCM = 720; $\frac{7}{720}$

53. LCM = 180; $\frac{31}{180}$

55. LCM = 167,580; $\frac{281}{33516}$

57. $2\frac{5}{8}$ cups

59. $35\frac{3}{8}$ ft

61. $84\frac{5}{8}$ ft

63. $\frac{3}{5}$

65. $\frac{1}{2}$

67. $\frac{3}{20}$

71. (a) $100 = 3 + 97 = 11 + 89 = 17 + 83 = 29 + 71 = 41 + 59$.

   (b) $200 = 3 + 197 = 7 + 193 = 19 + 181 = 37 + 163 = 43 + 157 = 61 + 139 = 73 + 127 = 97 + 103$.

75. The largest prime that you need to try is 13, because the next prime is 17 and $17^2 = 289$ which is greater than 211.

79. Since 999 and 99 and 9 are all divisible by 9, only the sum

$$2 \times 1 + 8 \times 1 + 5 \times 1 + 3$$

which is exactly the sum of the digits, needs to be checked. If this sum is divisible by 9, the original number is divisible by 9 and not otherwise.

81. (a) Divisible by 4, not by 8.
   (b) Divisible by 4 and by 8.
   (c) Divisible by 4 and by 8.
   (d) Divisible by 4, not by 8.

85. $496 = 1 + 2 + 4 + 8 + 16 + 31 + 62 + 124 + 248$

69. $\frac{3}{10}$

73. The number 1 has only one divisor, itself. It is not a prime because a prime must have *two distinct* divisors, 1 and itself. It is not a composite number because it has only one divisor.

77. All the other digits are multiples of 3, so their sum is divisible by 3. Thus, only the sum of 2 and 7 needs to be checked.

83. None of the numbers 1, 2, 3, 4, 5 is the sum of its proper divisors. Therefore, 6 is the smallest perfect number.

87. All primes are deficient because they have only 1 as a proper divisor.

Exercise 4.3

1.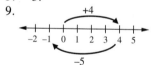

5. -3.

9.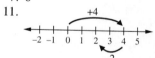

13.

3.

7. 8

11.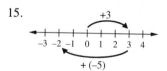

15.

17. $3 + (-8) = -5$

21. $-5 + (-2) = -7$

25. $-3 + (+4) = 1$

29. (a) -15 (b) -72

33. (a) -60 (b) -60

37. (a) -27 (b) 4

41. 10

45. 11,800

49. Step 1. m is assumed to be a multiplicative identity.
   Step 3. 1 is a multiplicative identity.
   Step 4. Both m and 1 equal $m \cdot 1$.

19. $3 + (-4) = -1$

23. $5 + (+6) = 11$

27. $-5 + (+3) = -2$

31. (a) -20 (b) -39

35. A negative, even integer.

39. (a) -9 (b) -5

43. -5

47. 20 km

51. Step 1. By the definition of subtraction.
   Step 3. By the associative property of addition.
   Step 5. 0 is the additive identity.

53. (b) adding a (c) identity   (e) q
     (f) identity . . . unique

55. Step 1. 0 is the additive identity.
     Step 3. By the distributive property.
     Step 5. The additive identity (0) is unique.

57. The product of two positive numbers is a positive number.

59. The product of two negative numbers is a positive number.

61. -3

63. 0

Exercise 4.4

1. Numerator 3, denominator 4.   3. Numerator 3, denominator -5.
5. $\frac{17}{41} = \frac{289}{697}$ 7. $\frac{11}{91} = \frac{253}{2093}$ 9. $\frac{5}{2}$ 11. $\frac{7}{16}$ 13. $\frac{15}{14}$ 15. $\frac{2}{3}$ 17. $\frac{14}{18}$ 19. $\frac{11}{18}$ 21. $\frac{16}{63}$
23. $\frac{19}{12}$ 25. $\frac{176}{323}$ 27. $\frac{2}{63}$ 29. $-\frac{1}{12}$ 31. $\frac{62}{323}$ 33. $\frac{2}{3}$ 35. $\frac{21}{8}$ 37. $\frac{56}{27}$ 39. $\frac{18}{77}$ 41. $\frac{9}{14}$
43. $-\frac{1}{6}$ 45. $\frac{1}{8}$ 47. $\frac{1}{4}$ 49. $\frac{49}{80}$ 51.   16   53. $\frac{3}{2}$ 55. $\frac{2}{5}$ 57. $1\frac{9}{14}$ 59. $\frac{2}{7}$ 61. $3\frac{5}{12}$
63. $\frac{3}{7}$ 65. $-\frac{3}{4}$ 67. -18 69. $-\frac{4}{5}$ 71. -30 73. $7\frac{1}{8}$ 75. $2\frac{5}{8}$ 77. 0   79. $-\frac{2}{9}$
81. $-5\frac{3}{4}$ 83. 3   85. $1\frac{5}{16}$ lb   87. $\frac{1}{2}$ 89. $4\frac{9}{10}$ 91. $12\frac{1}{10}$
93. If $\frac{0}{0} = n$, then $0 = 0 \times n = 0$ no matter what value is assigned to n. Thus, $\frac{0}{0}$ cannot be uniquely defined.

95. 126 mi

97. 3 in.

99. $\frac{5}{1} \frac{5}{2} \frac{5}{3} \frac{5}{4} \frac{5}{5} \frac{5}{6} \frac{5}{7} \frac{5}{8} \frac{5}{9} \cdots$
     $\frac{6}{1} \frac{6}{2} \frac{6}{3} \frac{6}{4} \frac{6}{5} \frac{6}{6} \frac{6}{7} \frac{6}{8} \frac{6}{9} \cdots$

101. $\frac{2}{2} = 1, \frac{4}{2} = 2, \frac{3}{3} = 1, \frac{2}{4} = \frac{1}{2}$ and these have already been caught in the one-to-one correspondence.

103. Neither. The two sets have the same cardinal number.

Exercise 4.5

1. $6 \times 10^2 + 9 \times 10 + 2 + 8 \times 10^{-2} + 7 \times 10^{-3}$
3. $1 \times 10^{-3} + 7 \times 10^{-5}$
5. 5020.39
7. 0.004702
9. 9.35×10^2
11. 1.2×10^{-3}
13. 86,400
15. 0.00671
17. 2×10^{-8}
19. 6.82×10^{-1}
21. 3×10^{-2}
23. 4×10^{25}
25. 2×10^3
27. 3×10^8
29. 31
31. (a) 4.74   (b) -4.74
33. (a) -4.158 (b) -5.864
35. (a) 0.045   (b) 0.128
37. (a) -0.05 (b) 0.02
39. $3831.88 (millions)
41. 21 cents
43. Harry lost $9.25
     George lost $16.50
45. $176
47. 3300 oz
49. 392.5 mi
51. $14,422,500
53. 1.26×10^{19}
55. 59.26
57. 78
59. Answers may vary.
61. $11

Exercise 4.6

1. 0.9
3. 1.1
5. 0.17
7. 1.21
9. 0.003
11. 1.243
13. 0.6
15. 0.5625
17. 0.625
19. 0.714285 . . .

21. 0.266 . . .
25. 0.1875
29. 0.00992
33. 0.$\overline{64}$
37. 0.21$\overline{5}$
41. 5.$\overline{07}$
45. $\frac{31}{99}$
49. $\dfrac{229}{99}$
53. $\dfrac{14}{11}$
57. $\dfrac{224}{1111}$
61. 0.009
65. 0.3415
69. 345%
73. 900.3%
77. 60%
81. 9.1
85. 125%
89. (a) 64.5 (b) 39
93. 445,000,000 (to the nearest million)
97. 35
101. 10%
105. Net loss of $18

23. 7.142857 . . .
27. 0.015625
31. 0.$\overline{5}$
35. 0.$\overline{235}$
39. 0.079$\overline{35}$
43. $\frac{8}{9}$
47. $\frac{38}{333}$
51. $\dfrac{137}{111}$
55. $\dfrac{151}{330}$
59. 0.29
63. 0.4569
67. 0.000234
71. 56.7%
75. 0.45%
79. 83.3%
83. 33$\frac{1}{3}$%
87. 50.4%
91. $10.81
95. 20%
99. 29%
103. 25.3 mi/gal
107. $\frac{4}{9}$

Exercise 4.7

1. Irrational   3. Irrational 5. Rational 7. Rational 9. Rational 11. Rational
13. Irrational 15. Rational 17. Irrational 19. Rational 21. 4 23. 8 25. 9
27. -13 29. 14 31. -9 33. $<$ 35. $<$ 37. $=$ 39. $<$ 41. $<$ 43. $=$
45. $=$ 47. 0.315 (Other answers are possible.)
49. 0.311212345 . . . (Other answers are possible.)
53. 0.101101001000 . . . (Other answers are possible.)
57. 0.5101001000 . . . (Other answers are possible.)
61. 0.21 $<$ 0.2121 $<$ 0.21211 $<$ 0.212112111 . . .
         $<$ 0.21212
65. 163 mi
69. A rational number can be expressed as a terminating
    decimal or as a nonterminating, repeating decimal.
    An irrational number cannot be expressed this way.
73. $h = 3$

51. 0.1011 (Other answers are possible.)
55. $\frac{7}{22}$ (Other answers are possible.)
59. $\frac{11}{18}$ (Other answers are possible.)
63. 3.09

67. 31
71. $(OB)^2 = 1^2 + (\sqrt{5})^2 = 1 + 5 = 6$,
    so that $OB = \sqrt{6}$.

Exercise 4.8

1. $3\sqrt{10}$
5. $6\sqrt{5}$
9. $8\sqrt{6}$
13. $\frac{3\sqrt{7}}{7}$
17. $\sqrt{2}$

3. Simplest form.
7. $10\sqrt{2}$
11. $14\sqrt{3}$
15. $-\frac{\sqrt{10}}{5}$
19. $\frac{\sqrt{3}}{7}$

21. $\frac{2\sqrt{3}}{3}$

23. $\frac{2\sqrt{2}}{7}$

25. $\frac{3}{5}$

27. $\frac{4\sqrt{10}}{25}$

29. $5\sqrt{10}$

31. $\sqrt{14}$

33. $\frac{1}{5}$

35. $\frac{\sqrt{6}}{2}$

37. $3\sqrt{3}$

39. $9\sqrt{5}$

41. 5

43. 5

45. $5\sqrt{7}$

47. $-7\sqrt{7}$

49. $-8\sqrt{5}$

51. $20\sqrt{41}$ m

53. $\frac{5\sqrt{2}}{4}$ sec

55. 20%

57. 7i

59. $3\sqrt{7}\,i$

61. 10i

63. $i5\sqrt{2}$

65. $i10\sqrt{2}$

67. $i4\sqrt{3}$

69. Check *Pure Imaginary* and *Complex*.

71. Check *Real* and *Complex*.

73. Check *Pure Imaginary* and *Complex*.

75. Check *Whole numbers, Integers, Rational numbers, Real numbers,* and *Complex numbers.*

77. Check *Natural numbers, Whole numbers, Integers, Rational numbers, Real numbers,* and *Complex numbers.*

79. Check *Complex numbers* only.

81. Try an example. Suppose $a = -2$ and $b = -3$. Then, by definition, $\sqrt{-2} = i\sqrt{2}$ and $\sqrt{-3} = i\sqrt{3}$, so that $\sqrt{-2}\cdot\sqrt{-3} = (i\sqrt{2})(i\sqrt{3}) = i^2\sqrt{6} = -\sqrt{6}$. Does this agree with what you would get by using $\sqrt{a}\cdot\sqrt{b} = \sqrt{ab}$?

83. $6\frac{4}{13} = 6.31$ (Calculator gives 6.32.)

85. $9\frac{4}{19} = 9.21$ (Calculator gives 9.22.)

87. $(7 + 13i) + (11 + 6i) = (7 + 11) + (13 + 6)i$ $= 18 + 19i$

89. $(7 + \sqrt{12}i) - (5 - \sqrt{3}i) =$ $(7 - 5) + (\sqrt{12} + \sqrt{3})i = 2 + 3\sqrt{3}i$ (Note that $\sqrt{12} = \sqrt{4 \times 3} = 2\sqrt{3}$.)

Exercise 4.9

1. (a) $a_1 = 7$ (b) $d = 6$ (c) $a_{10} = 61$ (d) $a_n = 6n + 1$

3. (a) $a_1 = 43$ (b) $d = -9$ (c) $a_{10} = -38$ (d) $a_n = 52 - 9n$

5. (a) $a_1 = 2$ (b) $d = -5$ (c) $a_{10} = -43$ (d) $a_n = 7 - 5n$

7. (a) $a_1 = -\frac{5}{6}$ (b) $d = \frac{1}{2}$ (c) $a_{10} = \frac{11}{3}$ (d) $a_n = \frac{n}{2} - \frac{4}{3}$, or $\frac{3n - 8}{6}$

9. (a) $a_1 = 0.6$ (b) $d = -0.4$ (c) $a_{10} = -3$ (d) $a_n = 1 - 0.4n$

11. $S_{10} = 340$, $S_n = n(3n + 4)$

13. $S_{10} = 25$, $S_n = \frac{n}{2}(95 - 9n)$

15. $S_{10} = -205$, $S_n = \frac{n}{2}(9 - 5n)$

17. $S_{10} = 14\frac{1}{6}$, $S_n = \frac{n}{12}(3n - 13)$

19. $S_{10} = -12$, $S_n = \frac{n}{5}(4 - n)$

21. (a) $a_1 = 3$ (b) $r = 2$ (c) $a_{10} = 1536$ (d) $a_n = 3 \cdot 2^{n-1}$

23. (a) $a_1 = \frac{1}{3}$ (b) $r = 3$ (c) $a_{10} = 6561$ (d) $a_n = 3^{n-2}$

25. (a) $a_1 = 16$ (b) $r = -\frac{1}{4}$ (c) $a_{10} = -\frac{1}{16384}$ (d) $a_n = \frac{(-1)^{n-1}}{4^{n-3}}$

27. $S_{10} = 3(2^{10} - 1)$, $S_n = 3(2^n - 1)$

29. $S_{10} = \frac{1}{6}(3^{10} - 1)$, $S_n = \frac{1}{6}(3^n - 1)$

31. $S_{10} = \frac{4^{10} - 1}{5 \cdot 4^7}$, $S_n = \frac{4^n - (-1)^n}{5 \cdot 4^{n-3}}$

33. $S = 12$

35. $S = -16$

37. $S = \frac{7}{9}$

39. $\frac{208}{99}$

41. (a) \$1,020   (b) \$18,000

43. (a) \$95   (b) \$8,625

45. \$610.51

47. If n is an even number, there are $n/2$ pairs and the sum of each pair is $(n + 1)$. The total sum is $n(n + 1)/2$. If n is an odd number, find the sum of the first $(n - 1)$ terms. The preceding formula gives $n(n - 1)/2$. Then adding n, the omitted term, gives the sum $n(n + 1)/2$, as before.

49. In an arithmetic sequence, each term after the first is obtained by adding the constant difference d to the preceding term. In a geometric sequence, each term after the first is obtained by multiplying the preceding term by the constant ratio r.

51. Neither

53. $a_2 + a_3 = a_4$

Chapter 4 Practice Test

1. (a) Ordinal number   (b) Cardinal number
   (c) Identification

2. (a) Yes. All the table entries are elements of the set A.
   (b) Yes. The table is symmetric to the diagonal from upper left to lower right. This means that if x and y are any two elements of A, then $x * y = y * x$.

3. (a) The commutative property of addition.
   (b) The distributive property of multiplication over addition.
   (c) The commutative property of multiplication.

4. $2^2 \times 5 \times 61$.

5. Composite $(143 = 11 \times 13)$

6. (a) 436 and 1530 are divisible by 2.
   (b) 387 and 1530 are divisible by 3.
   (c) 2345 and 1530 are divisible by 5.

7. GCF$(216, 254) = 2$. $\frac{216}{254} = \frac{108}{127}$

8. LCM$(18, 54, 60) = 540$. $\frac{1}{18} + \frac{1}{54} - \frac{1}{60} = \frac{31}{540}$

9. $\frac{1}{8}$

10. (a) $8 - 19 = 8 + (-19) = -11$
    (b) $8 - (-19) = 8 + (+19) = 27$
    (c) $-8 - 19 = -8 + (-19) = -27$
    (d) $-8 - (-19) = -8 + (+19) = 11$

11. 56,000

12. $\frac{12}{16}$

13. (a) $\frac{3}{2}$ (b) $-\frac{7}{4}$ (c) $\frac{8}{21}$ (d) $-\frac{1}{8}$

14. (a) $-\frac{35}{128}$ (b) $\frac{14}{5}$

15. (a) $2 \times 10 + 3 + 5 \times 10^{-1} + 8 \times 10^{-3}$
    (b) 803.04.

16. 4.8×10^{-1}

17. (a) 9.53 (b) 4.63 (c) 1.943 (d) 5.6

18. 44.6 cm

19. 4731.1 ft^2

20. (a) 0.75 (b) 0.0666 . . .

21. (a) $\frac{4}{33}$ (b) $\frac{239}{90}$

22. (a) 0.21 (b) 0.0935 (c) 0.0026

23. (a) 52% (b) 276.5% (c) 60% (d) 18.2%

24. 79.17%

25. 26.7 million

26. (a) Rational (b) Irrational (c) Rational
    (d) Rational (e) Irrational (f) Irrational

27. (a) 0.24 (Other answers are possible.)
    (b) 0.23456 . . . (Other answers are possible.)

28. 12.6 in.

29. 9.39 cm

30. (a) $4\sqrt{6}$ (b) $\sqrt{58}$ is in simplest form.

31. (a) $\frac{2\sqrt{5}}{5}$ (b) $\frac{4\sqrt{3}}{7}$

32. (a) $4\sqrt{3}$ (b) $2\sqrt{2}$

33. (a) $\sqrt{10}$ (b) $2\sqrt{2}$

34. (a) $6i$ (b) $\sqrt{43}i$

35. (a) Check *Complex numbers*.
    (b) Check *Pure imaginary numbers* and *Complex numbers*.
    (c) Check *Real numbers* and *Complex numbers*.
    (d) Check *Pure imaginary numbers* and *Complex numbers*.

36. (a) Check *Natural numbers, Integers, Rational numbers, Real numbers,* and *Complex numbers*.
    (b) Check *Complex numbers*.
    (c) Check *Irrational numbers, Real numbers,* and *Complex numbers*.
    (d) Check *Complex numbers*.

37. (a) A geometric sequence.
    (b) An arithmetic sequence.
39. $\frac{31}{16}$

38. 270

40. (a) $\frac{4}{9}$　(b) $\frac{7}{33}$　(c) $\frac{23}{9}$

CHAPTER 5

Exercise 5.1

1. -2 and 0 are solutions.
5. {2}
9. Ø
13. {1, 2, 3, 4, 5}
17. Ø
21. {4}
25. {-1}
29. {2, 3, 4, . . .}
33. {0}
37. Yes
41. 1 cm per sec.
45. 6 cm long.

49. No. For example, the replacement set for the equation $x - 1 = 0$ may be given as the set {0, 2, 4, 6}. None of these elements are solutions of the equation.
53. $202
57. 14 dimes, 6 quarters.

3. 3 and 1 are solutions.
7. {1, 2, 3, . . .}
11. {1, 2, 3}
15. {1, 2, 3, 4, 5, 7, 8, 9, . . .}
19. {23}
23. {. . . , -2, -1, 0, 1, 2, . . .}
27. {3, 4, 5, . . .}
31. Ø
35. {. . . , 4, 5, 6, 7}
39. 150
43. 32° F
47. The replacement set for an equation is the set of numbers that the variable may assume for a given problem.
51. $110

55. 78 in. or 6 ft 6 in.
59. 84 years.

Exercise 5.2

1. 2
5. $x = 3$
9. $x = 9$
13. $x = 2$
17. $x = \frac{3}{2}$
21. $x = \frac{15}{4}$ or $3\frac{3}{4}$
25. $x = 10$
29. $\{x \mid x < 4\}$
33. $\{x \mid x > 3\}$
37. $\{x \mid x > -4\}$
41. $\{x \mid x \le -9\}$
45. $\{x \mid x > -4\}$
49. Ø
53. $\{x \mid x > -2\}$
57. $\{x \mid x \le -4\}$
61. 10%
65. 200
69. 67%
73. $20 < t < 40$
77. $2 \le e \le 7$
81. 625

3. $x = 5$
7. $x = 2$
11. $x = 1$
15. $n = 6$
19. $x = 12$
23. $x = \frac{10}{7}$ or $1\frac{3}{7}$
27. $p = 4$
31. $\{x \mid x > 3\}$
35. $\{x \mid x \ge -2\}$
39. $\{x \mid x \le -2\}$
43. $\{x \mid x > 3\}$
47. $\{x \mid x \le -\frac{2}{3}\}$
51. $\{x \mid x \le 2\}$
55. $\{x \mid x \le \frac{2}{5}\}$
59. 32
63. 12.5%
67. 671 billion barrels.
71. The $100 price.
75. $s > 23,000$
79. 250
83. 50 minutes

Exercise 5.3

1.

3.

5.

7.

9.

11.

13.

15.

17.

19.

21. The solution set is Ø.

23.

25.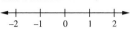

27. (a) All the real numbers between -1 and $+2$ including the 2 but not the -1.
   (b) All the real numbers between -1 and $+2$ including the -1 but not the 2.
   (c) All the real numbers between -1 and $+2$, not including the endpoints.
   (d) All the real numbers between -1 and $+2$ including the end points.

29. $(-\infty, 5)$

31. $(9, +\infty)$

33. $[-4, -1)$

35. $[-1, 10]$

37. $305_9 = 503_7$

39. $102_7 = 201_5$ and $204_7 = 402_5$

Exercise 5.4

1. $\{-1, 0, 1, 2, 3, 4\}$

3. $\{3, 4, 5, 6\}$

5. $\{2\}$

7. $\{\ldots, -8, -7, -6, 6, 7, 8, \ldots\}$

9.

11. Ø

13.

15.

17. Ø

19.

21.

23.

25.

27. (a) $\{x \mid x < 1 \text{ or } x > 4\}$ (b) $\{x \mid x \leq 1 \text{ or } x > 4\}$
   (c) $\{x \mid x \leq 1 \text{ or } x \geq 4\}$ (d) $\{x \mid x < 1 \text{ or } x \geq 4\}$

29. Let j inches be Joe's height. Then $j = 60$.

31. Let f inches be Frank's height and s inches be Sam's height. Then $f = s - 3$

33. Let s be Sam's height. Then $s = 77$.

35. Bill is taller than 74 in. (6 ft 2 in.)

Exercise 5.5

1. 10

3. $\frac{1}{8}$

5. 3

7. 2

9. -8

11. 2 and $\frac{5}{3}$ are solutions.

13. $\{0\}$

15. $\{-5, 5\}$

17. $\{\ldots, -3, -2, -1, 1, 2, 3, \ldots\}$

19. No interval.

21. In interval notation: $[-4, 4]$

23. In interval notation: $(-4, 2)$

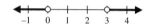

25. In interval notation: $(-\infty, -1]$ and $[1, +\infty)$

27. In interval notation: $(-\infty, -1)$ and $(3, +\infty)$

29. In interval notation: $(-2, 2)$

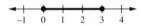

31. In interval notation: $(-\infty, -2]$ and $[2, +\infty)$

33. In interval notation: $[0, 3]$

35. In interval notation: $(-\infty, 0)$ and $(3, +\infty)$

37. Any amount between $450 and $550, inclusive.

39. Yes

41. "The absolute value of x is less than a." is equivalent to "x is between $-a$ and a."

Exercise 5.6

1. $(x + 2)(x + 4)$ 3. $(x - 4)(x + 3)$ 5. $(x + 9)(x - 2)$ 7. $(x - 5)^2$ 9. $(x + 5)^2$

11. -3 and 2   13. -1 and 3   15. $\{2, 4\}$ 17. $\{-2, 3\}$ 19. $\{-1, 0, 1\}$

21. $\{-2, \frac{1}{2}\}$ 23. $\{-4, 4\}$ 25. $\{-5, 5\}$ 27. $\{-\frac{3}{2}, \frac{8}{5}, 2\}$ 29. $\{-6, 6\}$ 31. $\{3, 9\}$

33. $\{-2, 10\}$ 35. $\{-20, 1\}$ 37. $\{-3, 4\}$ 39. $\{-\frac{5}{2}, 1\}$ 41. $\{-\frac{7}{2}, 1\}$

43. $\left\{\dfrac{-5 - \sqrt{13}}{2}, \dfrac{-5 + \sqrt{13}}{2}\right\}$

45. $\left\{\dfrac{4 - \sqrt{6}}{5}, \dfrac{4 + \sqrt{6}}{5}\right\}$

47. $\left\{\dfrac{3 - \sqrt{2}}{7}, \dfrac{3 + \sqrt{2}}{7}\right\}$

49. $\left\{\dfrac{1 - i}{3}, \dfrac{1 + i}{3}\right\}$

51. $\left\{\dfrac{-1 - i}{2}, \dfrac{-1 + i}{2}\right\}$

53. $\left\{\dfrac{-2 - i}{2}, \dfrac{-2 + i}{2}\right\}$

55.
$$(2ax + b)^2 = (2ax + b)(2ax + b) = 2ax(2ax + b) + b(2ax + b)$$
$$= (4a^2x^2 + 2abx) + (2abx + b^2)$$
$$= 4a^2x^2 + 4abx + b^2$$

which is the left side of the equation, as stated. If we subtract b from both sides of the equation,

$$2ax + b = \pm\sqrt{b^2 - 4ac}$$

we get

$$2ax = -b \pm \sqrt{b^2 - 4ac}$$

If we divide both sides of this last equation by $2a$, we get the quadratic formula as given.

57. 6 cm, 8 cm, and 10 cm

59. 5 in., 12 in., and 13 in.

61. If $b^2 - 4ac = 0$, the two answers coincide. The only solution is $\dfrac{-b}{2a}$.

63. If $b^2 - 4ac < 0$, the two solutions are the imaginary numbers

$$\frac{-b \pm i\sqrt{4ac - b^2}}{2a}$$

65. 1.3 sec

67. 7225

Exercise 5.7

1. $4m = m + 18$
3. $10x + (x - 3) = 26(x - 3)$
5. $4x + 5 = 29, x = 6$
7. $3x + 8 = 29, x = 7$
9. $3x - 2 = 16, x = 6$
11. $2x^2 = 2x + 12, x = -2$ or 3
13. $\frac{1}{3}x^2 - 2 = 10, x = -6$ or 6
15. 2.71 million lb
17. Russia has 6575 ships and Japan has 8851 ships.
19. 130
21. 14% per yr
23. (a) 204 mi (b) The mileage rate
25. 10%
27. 30 mph
29. 76.5 ft
31. 0.6 sec
33. 20 mph
35. 4 and 5
37. 36
39. You should try to determine what is the unknown, that is, what is wanted.
41. 5.22 yr
43. If M were greater than G, then y would be negative, which is unrealistic.

Exercise 5.8

1. 7000 to 2000; 7000 : 2000; $\frac{7000}{2000}$
3. 70 to 4260; 70 : 4260; $\frac{70}{4260}$
5. $\frac{10}{3}$
7. 17
9. (a) 6 cents (b) 5 cents (c) White Magic
11. $x = 12$
13. $x = 6$
15. $x = 24$
17. $\frac{9}{2}$
19. 6
21. 66.5 in.
23. 2.81
25. 2650
27. (a) $R = kt$ (b) k = 45 (c) 2.4 min
29. (a) $T = kh^3$ (b) $k = \frac{1}{1750} = 0.0005714$ (c) 241
31. (a) $f = k/d$ (b) $k = 4$ (c) 16
33. 10.8 in.^{3}
35. A ratio is simply a fraction such as a/b. A proportion is an equation between two ratios such as $a/b = c/d$.

Chapter 5 Practice Test

1. (a) $x = -5$ (b) $x = 13$
2. (a) $\{0, 1, 2, 3, \ldots\}$ (b) $\{-1, 0, 1, 2, 3 \ldots\}$
3. $x = 4$
4. $\{x \mid x \geq -3\}$
5. (a)
6. (a)

(b)

(b) The solution set is empty.

7.

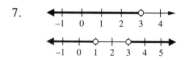

8. $x = \pm 3$.

9.

10.

11.

12.

13.

14. (a) $(x + 1)(x + 2)$ (b) $(x + 1)(x - 4)$

15. (a) $x = -2$ or $x = 1$ (b) $x = 0$ or $x = 1$

16. $x = -5$ or $x = -2$

17. $x = -2$ or $x = 5$

18. $x = -\frac{5}{2}$ or $x = 1$

19. $x = -2$ or $x = \frac{1}{3}$

20. (a) $x = \pm\frac{4}{3}$ (b) $x = \pm\frac{2}{5}$

21. 8 cm, 15 cm, 17 cm

22. $10x + y = 5(x + y)$

23. 200 mi

24. 7 and 8

25. 4 and 5

26. (a) 801 to 688; 801 : 688; $\frac{801}{688}$ (b) $\frac{801}{1990}$

27. 17

28. (a) $6\frac{1}{4}$ ¢ per oz for the 8 oz box; $6\frac{1}{3}$ ¢ per oz for the 12 oz box

(b) The 8 oz box

29. 5

30. (a) $\dfrac{x}{8} = \dfrac{9}{5}$ (b) 14.4 ft long

31. (a) $C = kx^2$ (b) $k = \frac{1}{225}$ (c) $144

32. (a) $t = k/I$ (b) $k = 10$ (c) $\frac{1}{60}$ sec

CHAPTER 6

Exercise 6.1

1. Domain: {1, 2, 3}. Range: {2, 3, 4}

3. Domain: {1, 2, 3}. Range: {1, 2, 3,}

5. Domain: $\{x \,|\, x$ is a real number}. Range: $\{y \,|\, y$ is a real number}.

7. Domain: $\{x \,|\, x$ is a real number}. Range: $\{y \,|\, y$ is a real number}.

9. Domain: $\{x \,|\, x$ is a real number}. Range: $\{y \,|\, y \geq 0\}$.

11. Domain: $\{x \,|\, x \geq 0\}$. Range: $\{y \,|\, y$ is a real number}.

13. Domain: $\{x \,|\, x \neq 0\}$. Range: $\{y \,|\, y \neq 0\}$.

15. Domain: {−1, 0, 1, 2}. Range: {−2, 0, 2, 4}. Ordered pairs: (−1, −2), (0, 0), (1, 2), (2, 4).

17. Domain: {0, 1, 2, 3, 4}. Range: {−3, −1, 1, 3, 5}. Ordered pairs: (0, −3), (1, −1), (2, 1), (3, 3), (4, 5).

19. Domain: {0, 1, 4, 9, 16, 25}.
Range: {0, 1, 2, 3, 4, 5}
Ordered pairs: (0, 0), (1, 1), (4, 2), (9, 3), (16, 4), (25, 5).

21. Domain: {1, 2, 3}. Range: {2, 3, 4}
Ordered pairs: (1, 2), (1, 3), (1, 4), (2, 3), (2, 4), (3, 4).

23. This is a function because one real value of y corresponds to each real value of x.

25. This is not a function because two values of y correspond to each positive value of x.

27. This is a function because one real y value corresponds to each x value in the domain.

29. This is a function because one real value of y corresponds to each real value of x.

31. (a) 1   (b) 7   (c) −5

33. (a) 0   (b) 2   (c) 5

35. (a) $3x + 3h + 1$ (b) $3h$ (c) 3

37. $g(x) = x^2$. Missing numbers: $\frac{1}{16}$, 4.41, ± 8

39. (a) 1   (b) −5   (c) 15

41. (a) 140 beats per min.   (b) 130 beats per min.

43. (a) 160 lb   (b) 78 in.

45. (a) 639 lb per sq ft.   6390 lb per sq ft.
49. 777,600 Joules
53. (a) This is not a function because there are two values of y for each value of $x > -1$. Domain: $\{x \mid x \geq -1\}$
    (b) This is a function because there is just one value of y for each value of x in the domain, $\{x \mid x \geq 0\}$.
57. $c = f(x) = 4(x - 40)$
61. An equivalence relation.
65. An equivalence relation.

47. (a) 144 ft (b) 400 ft
51. 2592 Newtons
55. $g(x) = \sqrt{x - 1}$ is real if and only if $x \geq 1$. Thus, we would exclude all values of x less than 1 if g is to have real values.

59. $f(t) = 16t^2$
63. An equivalence relation.

Exercise 6.2

1.
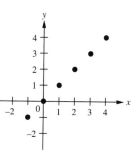

3.
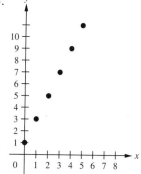

5.
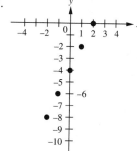

7.
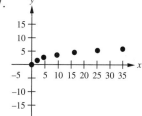

9.
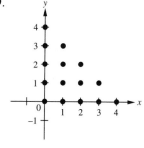

11.
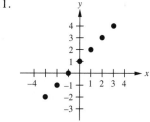

13.

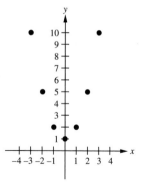

15.

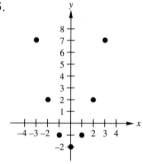

17.

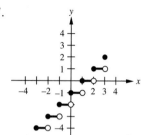

19. (a) $h(x) = 2.89 + 70.64$ (b) $h(34) = 168.9$ cm, or about 169cm

21. (a)$F(x) = 10x + 20$ (b) $F(8) = 100$; $100

23. (a) $V = 10,000 - 2000t$
    (b)

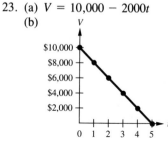

25. (a)

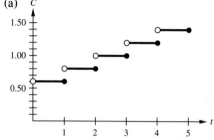

(b) More than 12 but not more than 13 min.

27. No. For a relation to be a function, there must be just one y-value for each x-value in the domain. A relation is not restricted in this manner.

29. For the graph to be that of a function, there must be only one y-value for each x-value in the domain. This means that no vertical line can cut the graph in more than one point.

31. Since the postage is 29 cents for the first ounce or fraction thereof, the first three entries are 29. Then, 23 cents is added for each additional ounce or fraction thereof, so the next two entries are 52, and the last entry is 75.

Weight (oz)	Postage (¢)
$\frac{1}{2}$	29
$\frac{3}{4}$	29
1	29
$1\frac{1}{2}$	52
2	52
$2\frac{1}{4}$	75

33. Here is the graph of the postage function given by $p(x) = 29 - 23[\![1 - x]\!]$, $0 < x \le 11$.

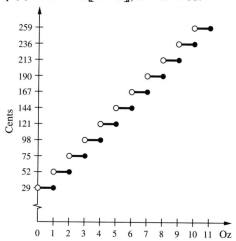

35. $C(t) = 0.36 - 0.28[\![1 - t]\!]$
For $0 < t \le 1$, $[\![1 - t]\!] = 0$, so that $C(t) = 0.36$
For $1 < t \le 2$, $[\![1 - t]\!] = -1$, so that $C(t) = 0.64$
For $2 < t \le 3$, $[\![1 - t]\!] = -2$, so that $C(t) = 0.92$
For $3 < t \le 4$, $[\![1 - t]\!] = -3$, so that $C(t) = 1.20$
This verifies the formula.

37. $f(x) = \sqrt{x}$ 39. 10,000 units

Exercise 6.3

1. 4

3.
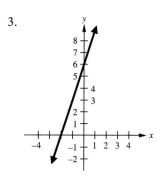

5.

7.

9.

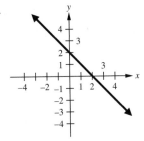

11.

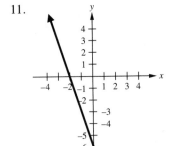

13.

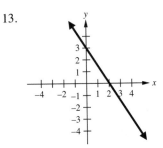

15.

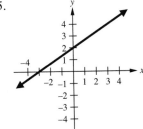

17.

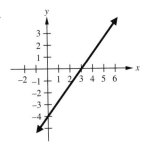

19. 5 units

21. $\sqrt{73} \approx 8.54$ units

23. $\sqrt{58} \approx 7.62$ units

25. 2 units

27. 4 units

29. Not a right triangle; scalene.

31. A right triangle; isosceles.

33. (a) $E(x) = 500 + 25x$,   (b)
    $S(x) = 1000 + 20x$

(c) The cost is the same for 100 persons.

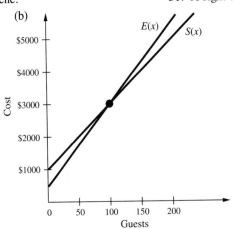

35. (a)

t	$C(t)$
$0 < t \le 1$	\$1.16
$1 < t \le 2$	\$1.81
$2 < t \le 3$	\$2.46
$3 < t \le 4$	\$3.11
$4 < t \le 5$	\$3.76

(b)

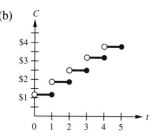

37. Use the distance formula to find the square of the length of each side of the triangle:

$$(AB)^2 = (a_1 - b_1)^2 + (a_2 - b_2)^2$$
$$(AC)^2 = (a_1 - c_1)^2 + (a_2 - c_2)^2$$
$$(BC)^2 = (b_1 - c_1)^2 + (b_2 - c_2)^2$$

The triangle is a right triangle if and only if one of these squares equals the sum of the other two squares. So we can check this.

39. See the Problem Solving procedure following Example 1 and follow it step by step for $x = c$.

41. See the answer for problem 3.

43. See the answer for problem 9.

45. See the answer for problem 11.

47. See the answer for problem 13.

49. See the answer for problem 15.

51. See the answer for problem 17.

Exercise 6.4

1. $m = 1$

3. $m = -1$

5. $m = -\frac{1}{8}$

7. $m = \frac{1}{4}$

9. $m = 0$

11. $y = \frac{1}{2}x + \frac{3}{2}$

13. $y = -x + 6$

15. $y = 5$

17. (a) $m = 1$ (b) $b = 2$

19. (a) $m = \frac{4}{3}$ (b) $b = 0$

21. (a) $m = -1$ (b) $b = 14$

23. (a) $m = 0$ (b) $b = 6$

25. (a) The slope is not defined. (b) The line does not intersect the y-axis.

27. $3x - y = 4$

29. $x + y = 5$

31. $10x - y = 0$

33. $w = 5h - 176$

35. $w = 5h - 187$

37. Parallel

39. Not parallel

41. Parallel

43. $4x - y = 6$

45. (a) $5x - 2y = 10$ (b) $x + 2y = 3$
(c) $2x + y = 2$ (d) $5x - 4y = 1$

47. For the first line, $m_1 = 2$ and for the second line $m_2 = -\frac{415}{790}$. Since $m_2 \ne -\dfrac{1}{m_1}$, the lines are not perpendicular.

49. If (x_1, y_1) and (x_2, y_2) are any two distinct points on a horizontal line, $y_1 = y_2$ and $x_1 \ne x_2$. Thus, the slope is $m = \dfrac{y_2 - y_1}{x_2 - x_1} = \dfrac{0}{x_2 - x_1} = 0$.

51.

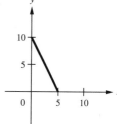

53. The point (5, 0) corresponds to buying 5 units of food, spending all his money on food.

57. The equation of the line through (0, 0) and (20, 10) is $2y = x$. The equation of the line through (35, 0) and (40, 15) is $y = 3x - 105$. Solving this pair of equations gives $x = 42$, $y = 21$. Thus, the treasure is located at the intersection of 42nd St. East and 21st Avenue North.

55. $y = 2x + 2000$

Exercise 6.5

1. (1, 2)
5. $(2, -\frac{1}{2})$
9. (4, 2)
13. No solution.
17. $(2, -\frac{1}{2})$
21. $(-2, \frac{1}{2})$
25. $(\frac{2}{3}, \frac{5}{6})$
29. $u = -\frac{5}{2}, v = 6$

3. (3, −4)
7. (1, 2)
11. (3, −4)
15. (1, 2)
19. (−3, 10)
23. (2, −5)
27. No solution
31. (a) 100   (b)
    (c) Company A

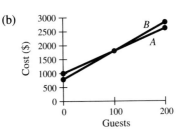

33. 4   35. 5
37. Step 1. Graph the two equations. The graphs will be straight lines.
Step 2. If the lines are not parallel or coincident, read the coordinates of the point of intersection. This is the solution.
Step 3. Check the solution in the given equations.
If the lines are parallel, there is no solution. If the lines are coincident, all points on the line satisfy both equations.
39. 33 nickels, 13 dimes   41. 250
43. 100 adult, 200 children's tickets

Exercise 6.6

1.

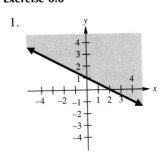

3.

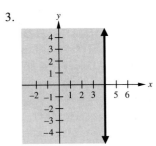

5.

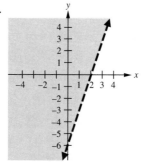

7.

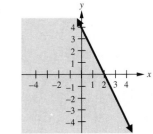

9.

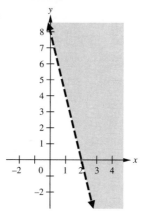

11.

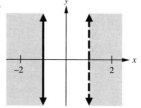

13.

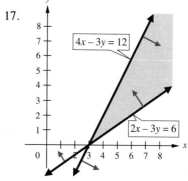

15.

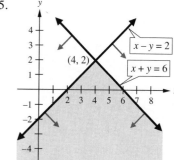

17.

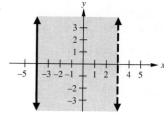

19.

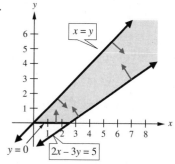

21.

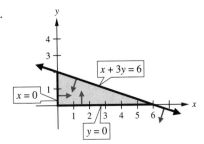

23.

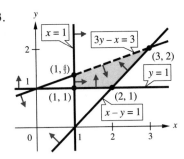

25.

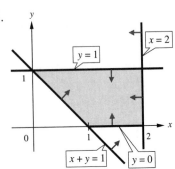

27. Conditions (b).

29. Conditions (a).

31. The region shown in (b).

33.

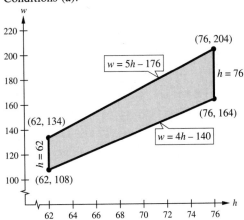

35. Suppose $c \neq 0$.
   Step 1. Find the intercepts of the line $ax + by = c$.
   Step 2. Draw a dashed line through these intercepts.
   Step 3. Substitute $(0, 0)$ into the equation. This gives zero for the left side.
   Step 4. If $c > 0$, shade the region opposite the origin. If $c < 0$, shade the region on the origin side of the line.

36. Suppose $c = 0$.
Step 1. Draw the line $ax + by = 0$. This line goes through the origin and the point $(b, -a)$.
Step 2. Substitute (a, b) into the left side. This gives $a^2 + b^2 > 0$, so shade the region that is on the same side of the line as the point (a, b).

37. The graph would show $x = k$ as a solid line with the region to the right of this line as the shaded region.

39. The possible pairs of integers are $(4, 2)$, $(5, 2)$, $(5, 3)$, $(5, 4)$, $(6, 2)$, $(6, 3)$, and $(7, 2)$.

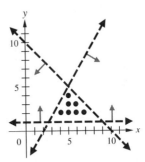

41. Cutting up the 2-inch square by connecting the midpoints of the opposite sides gives four smaller squares, each 1 inch on a side. Since there are five points, at least two of them must be inside or on the perimeter of one of the four small squares. The diagonal of this small square is $\sqrt{1^2 + 1^2} = \sqrt{2}$, so the two points cannot be more than $\sqrt{2}$ inches apart.

43. Leave everything as in the given flowchart except for interchanging the shading instructions at the end, so that if the answer to the question, "Is $c > 0$?" is "No", the half-plane not containing the origin will be shaded, and if the answer is "Yes", then the half-plane containing the origin will be shaded.

Exercise 6.7

1. Minimum value 3 at $(1, 1)$.
5. Minimum value 6 at $(2, 2)$.
9. 80 cars and 20 trucks.
13. 3 oz of X and 2 oz of Y.
17. 500 boxes of oranges, 100 boxes of grapefruit, and 200 boxes of tangerines.
21. (a) 6 oz of each juice (b) 42 cents (c) 30 units A, 30 units C, 12 units D.
25. (c) The least amount that Gary can bet for a net gain of $100 is $1500 on the champion to win and $800 on the challenger to win, for a total of $2300.

3. Minimum value 2 at $(\frac{1}{3}, \frac{2}{3})$.
7. Maximum value 10 at $(2, 4)$.
11. 50 tablets in each bottle.
15. 100 batches from I and 10 batches from II.
19. 2 shrubs and 3 trees.

23. Wording will vary.

Chapter 6 Practice Test

1. Domain: $\{0, 2, 3, 5\}$; range: $\{-1, 2, 3, 4\}$

3. Domain: $\{1, 2, 3, 4\}$; range: $\{1, 2, 3, 4\}$
5. (a) 0 (b) 0 (c) 6

2. Domain: the set of all real numbers; range: the set of all real numbers
4. Functions: b and c
6. 203 mi

7.

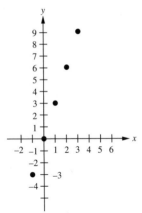

8.

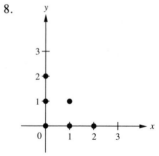

9.

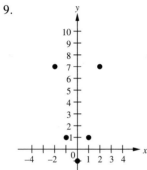

10.

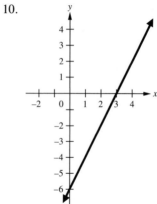

11.

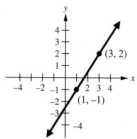

12. (a) 5 units   (b) 10 units

13. It is a right triangle.

14. (a) $\frac{1}{10}$ (b) $x - 10y = 29$

15. (a) $y = -2x + 5$ (b) $y = -4x + 2$; $m = -4$, $b = 2$

16. (a) Not parallel; intersect at $(\frac{1}{6}, \frac{2}{3})$ (b) Parallel lines

17. $2x - 3y = 8$

18. $(5, -3)$

19.

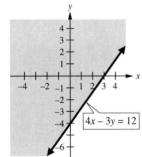

$4x - 3y = 12$

20.

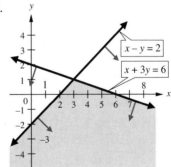

$x - y = 2$

$x + 3y = 6$

21.

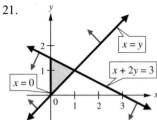

$x = y$

$x + 2y = 3$

$x = 0$

22. The two equations represent the same line. Solution set: $\{(a, 2a - 3) \mid a$ is a real number$)$

23. Maximum value 16 at (0, 8)

24. Minimum value −6 at (3, 0)

25. Run machine A 30 hr and machine B 10 hr

CHAPTER 7

Exercise 7.1

1. (a)    (b)    (c) P ●———————● Q

3. The segment $\overleftrightarrow{BC}$ 5. The ray $\overrightarrow{AD}$ 7. The segment $\overrightarrow{AD}$ 9. The segment $\overrightarrow{AD}$

11. Ø   13. The point C 15. Six; AB, AC, AD, BC, BD, CD 17. Four; ABC, ABD, ACD, BCD 19. (a) AB, AC, AD, BC, BD, CD (c) AB and CD; AC and BD; AD and BC (c) No   21. True   23. True   25. True   27. False   29. False   31. Collinear   33. Coplanar   35. Yes   37. Line BD

39. (a)The three points must be collinear and the distance from P to R must be the sum of the distances from P to Q and from Q to R.
(b)$PR = PQ + QR$
(c)P–Q–R or R–Q–P

41. $AC = AB \cup BC$; $BC = AC - AB$

43. Point, line, and plane

45. The ray may have its endpoint only in common with the plane, or it may have some other single point in common with the plane, or it may lie entirely in the plane.

47. 190

49. $\frac{1}{2}n(n - 1)$

51. $\frac{1}{6}n(n - 1)(n - 2)$

53.   i. There are exactly four points.
     ii. Each pair of points lies on exactly one line.
     iii. Every line passes through exactly two points.

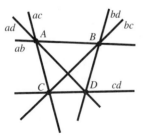

(a) There are exactly six lines.
(b) Exactly three lines pass through each point.
(c) Corresponding to each line, there is exactly one other line not passing through the same points.

55. Yes. Just change the wording in the solution to problem 52 to correspond:
     (a) Denote the clubs by *a, b, c, d* (property i). Denote the common members by *ab, ac, ad, bc, bd, cd* (property ii). None of these members can be in another club because each pair of clubs has only one member in common. Therefore, there are at least six members. Now suppose there is another member, say *xy*. Then *xy* must be in two of the clubs *a, b, c, d* (property iii), so *xy* must be one of the members already listed (property ii). Thus, there are exactly six members.
     (b) This can be seen from the listing in part (a): club *a*, members *ab, ac, ad*; club *b*, members *ab, bc, bd*; club *c*, members *ac, bc, cd*; club *d*, members *ad, bd, cd*.
     (c) This can also be seen from the listing in part (a). For instance, the only member not in the same club with *ab* is *cd*.

Exercise 7.2

1. (a) $\angle BAC$ (b) $\angle \beta$ 3. $\angle BAC, \angle CAD, \angle DAE, \angle EAF$ 5. $\angle BAE, \angle CAE,$
   $\angle CAF$ 7. (a) $\angle DAE$ (b) $\angle CAD$ 9. (a) $\angle DAF$ (b) $\angle BAE$ 11. $35°$
   13. $15°$ 15. $\angle B$ 17. $110°$ 19. $20°$ 21. $220°$ 23. (a) $150°$ (b) $30°$
   (c) $150°$ 25. $\angle C, \angle E, \angle A, \angle G$ 27. (a) $49°$ (b) $139°$ 29. 16
   31. $x = 15$; $35°$ and $145°$ 33. $x = 10$; $30°$ and $60°$ 35. (a) $30°$ (b) $180°$
   37. $90°$ 39. $25°$
41. (a) $m\angle A + m\angle B = 180°$ Angles A and B form a straight angle.
     (b) $m\angle C + m\angle B = 180°$ Angles C and B form a straight angle.
     (c) $m\angle A + m\angle B = m\angle C + m\angle B$ Both sides equal 180°.
     (d) $m\angle A = m\angle C$ Subtract $m\angle B$ from both sides.

43. (a) One of the usual meanings of *acute* is "sharp" or "intense." Thus "an acute pain" means "a sharp or intense pain."
    (b) One of the ordinary meanings of *obtuse* is "dull." Thus, "obtuse intelligence" means "dull intelligence" or "stupidity."

47. N 50° W

45. The sum of the angles is 0.2° too large.

49. 360 − 40 = 320, so the navigator's bearing would be 320°.

Exercise 7.3

1. (a)   (b)

3. (a) *C, D, G, I, J, L, M, N, O, P, S, U, V, W, Z*
   (b) *B, D, O*

5. (a) *D, O*   (b) *A, E, F, H, K, Q*
9. Parallelogram
13. Trapezoid
17. Scalene, right
21. Isosceles, acute
25. (a) (b) (c)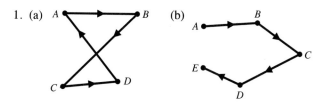

7. Convex
11. Rectangle
15. Parallelogram
19. Scalene, acute
23. Scalene, obtuse
27. (a) (b) 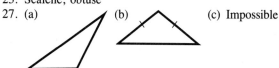 (c) Impossible

29. (a) $m\angle A = m\angle B = 50°$, $m\angle C = 80°$.
    (b) $m\angle A = m\angle B = 40°$, $m\angle C = 100°$.
33. 2160°
37. 135°
41. (a) $E \subset I$ and $(I \cup S) = T \subset P$
    (b)

31. 30°

35. 108°
39. 144°
43.

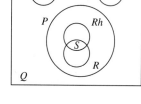

45. (a) No   (b) No   (c) Yes

47. The opposite sides of the rectangle are equal and the diagonal is common to both triangles, so the SSS statement applies. (The angles opposite the diagonal are both right angles and the opposite sides of the rectangle are parallel, so the SAS and the ASA statements also apply.)

49. The sum of the measures of the three angles is 180°. Thus, if two angles of one triangle are equal to the corresponding two angles of the second triangle, then the third angles are equal and the ASA statement applies.

51. $n = 6$

53. $n = 5$

55. $360 \div 25$ is not a whole number.

Exercise 7.4

1. (a) and (c)
5. $x = 5\frac{1}{3}$, $y = 6\frac{2}{3}$
9. $1\frac{1}{3}$
13. 8 in., 12 in., and 16 in.
17. 25 ft. The two triangles are similar because the corresponding angles are equal.
21. The corresponding angles of the two triangles are equal.
25. $x = 3$, $y = 4.5$
29. Because PQ is parallel to AB.

33. The numerators of the two fractions are equal, so the denominators must also be equal.

3. (a) and (c)
7. 14
11. $5\frac{1}{4}$ cm, $3\frac{1}{2}$ cm
15. $18\frac{3}{4}$ ft
19. 600 m

23. Answers will vary.

27. 125 ft
31. AC corresponds to PC and BC corresponds to QC in the similar triangles, so these corresponding sides must be proportional.
35. Triangle ABC is similar to triangle PQC, and triangle PQC is congruent to triangle $A_1B_1C_1$.

Exercise 7.5

1. 65 cm
5. 184.6 m
9. 30 cm
13. 90 ft
17. $7\pi \approx 22.0$ m
21. $3\pi \approx 9.42$ cm
25. $61\pi \approx 192$ cm
29. $8\pi \approx 25.1$ ft
33. $\dfrac{7}{\pi} \approx 2.23$ cm
37. About 15,500,000 (rounded from 15,520,000)
41. A bicycle tire.

45. Draw two perpendicular diameters. Then bisect the arcs that join successive points where these diameters intersect the circumference. The midpoints of the arcs and the ends of the two diameters are the vertices of the octagon.

3. 12.6 yd
7. 57.2 in.
11. 10 ft
15. 716 by 518 ft
19. $20\pi \approx 62.8$ ft
23. $9\pi \approx 28.3$ yd
27. $16\pi \approx 50.2$ cm
31. $d = 15$ cm, $r = 7.5$ cm
35. $\dfrac{4.125}{\pi} \approx 1.31$ in.
39. $16\pi \approx 50.2$ yd
43. The worn tire has a smaller circumference, so will turn more times per mile.

Exercise 7.6

1. 15 in.^{2}
5. 24 ft^2
9. $800 + 50\pi \approx 957$ cm^2
13. $18 - \frac{9}{2}\pi \approx 3.87$ cm^2

3. 15 in.^{2}
7. 30 ft^2
11. $64 + 32\pi \approx 164$ cm^2
15. $\frac{25}{4}\pi \approx 19.6$ ft^2

17. 8 ft

19. 15 in.

21. $600

23. The side opposite the base is 12 ft and the other two sides are each 10 ft long.

25. 6400 yd²

27. 18 ft

29. 96 ft

31. 16π cm²

33. 12 in. wide and 18 in. long

35. $3\frac{1}{2}$ ft by $4\frac{1}{2}$ ft

37. Let ABC be an equilateral triangle of side s. Let D be the midpoint of the base AB. Draw the line CD. Triangles ADC and BDC are congruent by the SSS statement, so that $\angle ADC = \angle BDC$. Since the two angles are supplementary, each must be a right angle. Thus, triangle ADC is a right triangle. Let the length of CD be h. Then,

$$h^2 + \left(\frac{s}{2}\right)^2 = s^2$$

which gives

$$h^2 = \frac{3s^2}{4} \text{ and } h = \frac{s\sqrt{3}}{2}.$$

The area of the triangle is

$$A = \frac{1}{2}bh = \frac{1}{2}(s)(\frac{s\sqrt{3}}{2}) = s^2 \cdot \frac{\sqrt{3}}{4}.$$

39. (a) The area is multiplied by 4. (b) The area is multiplied by 9. (c) The area is multiplied by k^2.

41. The area of the circle is larger by about 6.8 cm².

43. The hypotenuse of the cut out triangle is the side x of the octagon. Thus, $x = s\sqrt{2}$. One side of the original square consists of one side of the octagon plus two sides of cut out triangles, so that

$$2s + s\sqrt{2} = a \text{ and } s = \frac{a}{2 + \sqrt{2}} = \frac{2 - \sqrt{2}}{2}a.$$

45. (a) in.² and cm² (b) mi² and km² (c) and (d) yd² and m²

47. (a) $2\frac{2}{3}$ (b) $42

49. (a) 15 (b) $60

51. (a) 2.49 ¢/in.² (b) 2.36 ¢/in.² (c) The 10-in. pie.

53. The area of the triangle taken away is Wx and the area of the triangle added on is hy. Since $hy = Wx$, the area of the new rectangle is equal to the area of the original one.

Exercise 7.7

1. (a) A, B, C, D, E (b) $AB, AC, AD, AE, BC, BE, CD, CE, DE$

3. $ABCD$

5.

7.

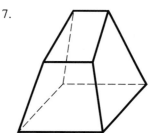

9. (a) The volume is multiplied by 8. (b) The volume is multiplied by 27.

11. (a) 1600 in.^{3} (b) 880 in.^{2}

13. (a) $V = 264x^3$ (b) $S = 240x^2$

15. 50 in.^{3}

17. 32 in.^{3}

19. 1.5

21. (a) $V = 225\pi \approx 707$ in.^{3}
      $S = 140\pi \approx 440$ in.^{2}
   (b) $V = \frac{225}{3}\pi \approx 236$ in.^{3}
      $S = (25 + 5\sqrt{106})\pi \approx 240$ in.^{2}

23. (a) $V = 36\pi \approx 113$ ft^3,
      $S = 42\pi \approx 132$ ft^2
   (b) $V = 12\pi \approx 37.7$ ft^3,
      $S = 24\pi \approx 75.4$ ft^2

25. $288\pi \approx 904$ in.^{3}

27. $2{,}536{,}456\pi \approx 7{,}960{,}000$ ft^3

29. $1024\pi \approx 3220$ m^3

31. $r = 381$ cm, $h = 10.16$ cm, $V \approx 147.5\pi \approx 463$ cm^3, The can holds about 463 gm.

33. (a) Baseball: $S_1 = \frac{81}{\pi} \approx 25.8$ in.^{2}, $V_1 = \frac{243}{2\pi^2} \approx 12.3$ in.^{3} (b) $\frac{S_1}{S_3} \approx \frac{9}{100}$ (c) $\frac{V_1}{V_2} = \frac{1}{27}$

   Soccer ball: $S_2 = \frac{729}{\pi} \approx 232$ in.^{2}, $V_2 = \frac{6561}{2\pi^2} \approx 333$ in.^{3}

   Basketball: $S_3 = \frac{900}{\pi} \approx 287$ in.^{2}, $V_3 = \frac{4500}{\pi^2} \approx 456$ in.^{3}

35. (a) $\frac{6561}{2\pi^2} \approx 333$ in.^{3} (b) About 15.66 lb.

37. (a) 1428 in.^{3} (b) 730 in.^{2} (c) 32,000

39. Answers will vary.

41. No. This is true only if the length of the radius is more than three units.

43. Since the sum of the face angles at a vertex must be less than 360°, three, four or five equilateral triangles, three squares or three pentagons can be put together at any vertex. There are no other possibilities, so only the five regular polyhedrons listed are possible.

45. Figure   F   V   E
    7.99(II)   6   8   12 $F + V = 14 = E + 2$
    7.99(III) 6   5   9 $F + V = 11 = E + 2$
    7.99(IV)   7   10 15 $F + V = 17 = E + 2$
    7.100   5   6   9 $F + V = 11 = E + 2$
    7.101   6   6   10 $F + V = 12 = E + 2$
    Thus, Euler's formula is $F + V = E + 2$.

Exercise 7.8

1. (a) 3 (b) 0 (c) This network is traversable; all three vertices are possible starting points.

3. (a) 3 (B, D, and E) (b) 2(A and C)
   (c) Traversable; start at either A or C.

5. (a) 1 (A only) (b) 4(B, C, D, E) (c) Not traversable; it has more than 2 odd vertices.

7. (a) 5 (A, C, D, E, G) (b) 2 (B, F)
   (c) Traversable; start at B or F.

9. (a) 1, the vertex of the pyramid.
   (b) 4, the vertices of the base.
   (c) Not traversable; it has more than 2 odd vertices.

11. Think of each region as a vertex with the individual line segments in its boundary as the number of paths to the vertex. The boundary of region A has four segments, so the corresponding vertex would be even. The boundary of region B has five segments, so the corresponding vertex would be odd. The boundary of region C has four segments, so the corresponding vertex would be even. The boundary of region D has five segments, so the corresponding vertex would be odd. The boundary of region E has 10 segments, so the corresponding vertex would be even. Thus, the network would have two odd vertices (B and D). By starting in region B or D, it is possible to draw a simple connected broken line that crosses each line segment exactly once.

13. Region A has three doorways, so the corresponding vertex would be odd. Regions B, C, D and the outside each has two doorways, so the corresponding vertices would be even. Region F has three doorways, so the corresponding vertex would be odd. There are two odd vertices, A and F. By starting in either of these rooms and ending in the other, it is possible for a walk to pass through each doorway exactly once. It is not possible to start and end outside.

17. All the rooms and the outside have an even number of doorways, so the corresponding network would have no odd vertices. The walk can start in any room or outside and end in the same place and pass through each doorway exactly once.

21. Room A and the outside D each have three doorways. Thus, the corresponding network has two odd vertices. By starting in A and ending in D (or vice versa), a walk could pass through each doorway exactly once. It is not possible start and end in D. (See the traversability rules.)

25. V: 3, R: 2; A: 3

29. V: 2, R: 3; A: 3

15. A and D have three doorways and the other rooms and the outside each have an even number of doorways. Thus, the corresponding network would have two odd vertices. By starting in either A or D and ending in the other, it is possible for a walk to pass through each doorway exactly once. It is not possible to start and end outside.

19. Rooms B and D have three doorways, so the corresponding network would have two odd vertices. The walk can start in either B or D and end in the other one, passing through each doorway exactly once. It is not possible to start and end outside.

23. Since each arc has two endpoints, the total number of endpoints must be even. An odd vertex accounts for an odd number of endpoints, while an even vertex accounts for an even number of endpoints. Thus, there must be an even number of odd vertices.

27. V: 5, R: 2; A: 5

31. V: 6, R: 3; A: 7 Numbers 25–32 all fit Euler's formula, $V + R = A + 2$.

Chapter 7 Practice Test

1. (a) $\overrightarrow{XY}$ (b) Point Y (c) $\overleftrightarrow{WZ}$
3. (a) $\overleftrightarrow{AD}$, $\overleftrightarrow{BE}$, and $\overleftrightarrow{CF}$, $\overleftrightarrow{EF}$ and $\overleftrightarrow{BC}$, $\overleftrightarrow{DE}$ and $\overleftrightarrow{AB}$, $\overleftrightarrow{DF}$ and $\overleftrightarrow{AC}$

2. Six; $\overleftrightarrow{AB}$, $\overleftrightarrow{AC}$, $\overleftrightarrow{AD}$, $\overleftrightarrow{BC}$, $\overleftrightarrow{BD}$, and $\overleftrightarrow{CD}$. No.
4. No; skew lines are not parallel and do not intersect, so they are not coplanar.

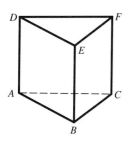

(b) $\overleftrightarrow{AB}$ and $\overleftrightarrow{CF}$, $\overleftrightarrow{AB}$ and $\overleftrightarrow{DF}$, $\overleftrightarrow{AB}$ and $\overleftrightarrow{EF}$, $\overleftrightarrow{BC}$ and $\overleftrightarrow{AD}$, $\overleftrightarrow{BC}$ and $\overleftrightarrow{DE}$, $\overleftrightarrow{BC}$ and $\overleftrightarrow{DF}$, $\overleftrightarrow{AC}$ and $\overleftrightarrow{BE}$, $\overleftrightarrow{AC}$ and $\overleftrightarrow{DE}$, $\overleftrightarrow{AC}$ and $\overleftrightarrow{EF}$, $\overleftrightarrow{DE}$ and $\overleftrightarrow{CF}$, $\overleftrightarrow{EF}$ and $\overleftrightarrow{AD}$, $\overleftrightarrow{DF}$ and $\overleftrightarrow{BE}$

(c) $\overleftrightarrow{AB}$, $\overleftrightarrow{AC}$, and $\overleftrightarrow{AD}$; $\overleftrightarrow{AD}$, $\overleftrightarrow{DE}$, and $\overleftrightarrow{DF}$; $\overleftrightarrow{BE}$, $\overleftrightarrow{AB}$, and $\overleftrightarrow{BC}$; $\overleftrightarrow{BE}$, $\overleftrightarrow{EF}$, and $\overleftrightarrow{ED}$; $\overleftrightarrow{CF}$, $\overleftrightarrow{AC}$, and $\overleftrightarrow{BC}$; $\overleftrightarrow{CF}$, $\overleftrightarrow{EF}$, and $\overleftrightarrow{DF}$

5. (a) 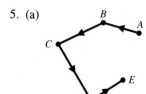 (b)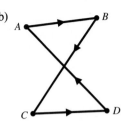

6. (a) 120° (b) 60°

7. $m\angle A = 135°$, $m\angle B = 45°$

8. (a) $m\angle C = 130°$ (b) $m\angle E = 50°$
(c) $m\angle D = 130°$

9. (a) $m\angle C = 99°$ (b) $m\angle A = m\angle B = 72°$,
$m\angle C = 36°$

10. $m\angle A = 72°$, $m\angle B = 18°$

11. (a) 140° (b) 144°

12. 20 yd by 40 yd

13. $XZ = 6$ in., $YZ = 4\frac{1}{2}$ in.

14. $2\sqrt{2}\pi$ cm

15. $(2\pi - 4)$ cm²   16. $\dfrac{11}{\pi}$ in.   17. 15 ft²   18. 85 ft   19. $12 + \dfrac{9\pi}{8} \approx 15.5$ ft²

20. $4 - \pi \approx 0.86$ in.² 21. 62 ft²   22. 4 in   23. $2\sqrt{3}$ in.   24. 10 in.   25. $\dfrac{3\sqrt{3}}{2\pi}$ 26. 30 ft³   27. 10 ft³

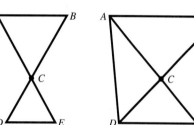

Traversable   Not traversable

CHAPTER 8

Exercise 8.1

1. (a) $\begin{bmatrix} 8 & 4 \\ 0 & -4 \end{bmatrix}$ (b) $\begin{bmatrix} 6 & -12 \\ -9 & -3 \end{bmatrix}$ (c) $\begin{bmatrix} 5 & 1 \\ -1 & -1 \end{bmatrix}$ 3. (a) $\begin{bmatrix} 3 & 10 \\ 5 & 0 \end{bmatrix}$ (b) $\begin{bmatrix} -3 & 0 \\ 1 & 0 \end{bmatrix}$

5. (a) $\begin{bmatrix} 0 & 13 \\ 8 & -3 \end{bmatrix}$ (b) $\begin{bmatrix} -1 & -21 \\ -12 & -4 \end{bmatrix}$

7. (a) $\begin{bmatrix} 0 & 1 & 3 \\ 7 & 3 & -3 \\ 4 & 3 & 0 \end{bmatrix}$ (b) $\begin{bmatrix} 2 & -3 & 1 \\ -1 & -3 & -1 \\ 4 & 1 & 2 \end{bmatrix}$ (c) $\begin{bmatrix} 1 & 0 & -1 \\ 2 & 2 & -6 \\ 1 & 5 & 1 \end{bmatrix}$

9. (a) $\begin{bmatrix} -1 & 4 & 7 \\ 18 & 9 & -7 \\ 8 & 7 & -1 \end{bmatrix}$ (b) $\begin{bmatrix} -5 & 8 & -1 \\ 6 & 9 & 1 \\ -8 & -1 & -5 \end{bmatrix}$ 11. (a) $\begin{bmatrix} 3 & -1 & 0 \\ 7 & 4 & -14 \\ 6 & 12 & 3 \end{bmatrix}$ (b) $\begin{bmatrix} -1 & 1 & 4 \\ 5 & 1 & 3 \\ 3 & -2 & -1 \end{bmatrix}$

13. $\begin{bmatrix} 3 & 0 & 3 \\ 10 & 4 & 2 \\ 4 & -1 & 2 \end{bmatrix}$ 15. $\begin{bmatrix} 7 & -6 & 7 \\ 4 & -3 & 0 \\ 1 & -3 & 5 \end{bmatrix}$

17. $\begin{bmatrix} -19 & -3 & -2 \\ 4 & 2 & 12 \\ -7 & 3 & 6 \end{bmatrix}$

19. $\begin{bmatrix} -15 & -9 & 2 \\ -2 & -5 & 10 \\ -10 & 1 & 9 \end{bmatrix}$

21. $I^2 = I$

23. $BA = I$

25. $BA = I$

27. $BA = I$

29. No; the matrices could not be conformable for both orders of multiplication.

33. (a)
	E	M	L
Armchairs	20	15	10
Rockers	12	8	5

(b)
	E	M	L
Armchairs	120	90	60
Rockers	72	48	30

35.
	E	M	L
Armchairs	30	15	10
Rockers	12	28	0

37.
	July	Aug.	Sept.	Oct.	Nov.
Bolts	650	1300	2100	2600	2400
Clamps	400	800	1400	1600	1800
Screws	1200	2400	4100	4800	5100

39. (a) $C^2 = \begin{bmatrix} 2 & 0 & 0 \\ 0 & 1 & 1 \\ 0 & 1 & 1 \end{bmatrix}$

(b) It means that Tom can communicate with himself by 2 two-step communications.

(c) Two. The 1 in the second row, third column, means that Dick can communicate with Harry by a two-step communication. The 1 in the third row, second column means that Harry can communicate with Dick by a two-step communication.

41. If we do a "row-column" multiplication the result will be the matrix

$$\begin{bmatrix} -2 \cdot & -2 & 0 \\ 0 & 4 & 4 \end{bmatrix}$$

As the figure shows, the multiplication rotated the triangle about the y axis and doubled the length of each side.

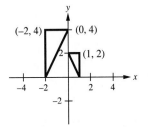

43. Reflects (a, b) across the y axis

45. Rotates (a, b) 180° around the origin

47.

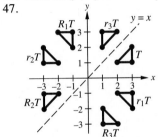

49. Yes; the sum of two 2×2 matrices is a 2×2 matrix.

51. Yes; the 2×2 zero matrix

53. Yes

55. Suppose A has an inverse, say $B = \begin{bmatrix} x & y \\ z & w \end{bmatrix}$. Then, $AB = \begin{bmatrix} 1 & 2 \\ 0 & 0 \end{bmatrix} \begin{bmatrix} x & y \\ z & w \end{bmatrix} = \begin{bmatrix} x + 2z & y + 2w \\ 0 & 0 \end{bmatrix}$. Since there are no values of x, y, z, w to make this last matrix the identity matrix, A has no inverse.

Exercise 8.2

1. $x = 1, y = 2, z = 0$

3. $x = -1, y = -1, z = 3$

5. $x = -2, y = -1, z = 3$

7. No solution

9. $x = 1 - k, y = 2, z = k$, where k is any real number

13. 8 type I, 10 type II, 12 type III

15. 50% type I, 25% type II, 25% type III

17. The matrix in (a) is singular. The matrices in (b) and (c) are nonsingular.

Exercise 8.3

1. $\begin{bmatrix} -\frac{5}{2} & 2 \\ \frac{3}{2} & -1 \end{bmatrix}$

3. $\begin{bmatrix} \frac{1}{9} & \frac{1}{18} \\ -\frac{4}{9} & \frac{5}{18} \end{bmatrix}$

5. No inverse

7. $\begin{bmatrix} -1 & 0 \\ 0 & -1 \end{bmatrix}$

9. $x = -3, y = 5$

11. $x = 3, y = 2$

13. Yes, they are inverses of each other.

15. Yes, they are inverses of each other.

17. $\begin{bmatrix} -1 & 4 & 2 \\ -1 & 4 & 1 \\ -1 & 3 & 1 \end{bmatrix}$

19. $\begin{bmatrix} -\frac{3}{2} & \frac{7}{2} & -\frac{5}{2} \\ \frac{1}{2} & -\frac{1}{2} & \frac{1}{2} \\ -1 & 2 & -1 \end{bmatrix}$

23. $x = 2, y = 1, z = -3$

25. $x = -1, y = 3, z = 5$

27. (a) TO ERR IS HUMAN
    (b) The encoded message is
    $30. -37.19.0.7. -2.13. -4.3. -43.35. -7.$

29. To do this problem, consider the possibility of having an m by n unit matrix if $m \neq n$.

Exercise 8.4

1. 4

3. 11

5. 3

7. 7

9. 5

11. 9

13. 1

15. 2

17. 11

19. 10

21. 1

23. 12

25. 6

27. 4

29.

$\otimes$	1	2	3	4	5	6	7	8	9	10	11	12
1	1	2	3	4	5	6	7	8	9	10	11	12
2	2	4	6	8	10	12	2	4	6	8	10	12
3	3	6	9	12	3	6	9	12	3	6	9	12
4	4	8	12	4	8	12	4	8	12	4	8	12
5	5	10	3	8	1	6	11	4	9	2	7	12
6	6	12	6	12	6	12	6	12	6	12	6	12
7	7	2	9	4	11	6	1	8	3	10	5	12
8	8	4	12	8	4	12	8	4	12	8	4	12
9	9	6	3	12	9	6	3	12	9	6	3	12
10	10	8	6	4	2	12	10	8	6	4	2	12
11	11	10	9	8	7	6	5	4	3	2	1	12
12	12	12	12	12	12	12	12	12	12	12	12	12

31. 3   33. 11
35. 4   37. 8
39. Impossible
41. (a)

$\oplus$	I	II	III	IV	V	VI	VII	VIII
I	II	III	IV	V	VI	VII	VIII	I
II	III	IV	V	VI	VII	VIII	I	II
III	IV	V	VI	VII	VIII	I	II	III
IV	V	VI	VII	VIII	I	II	III	IV
V	VI	VII	VIII	I	II	III	IV	V
VI	VII	VIII	I	II	III	IV	V	VI
VII	VIII	I	II	III	IV	V	VI	VII
VIII	I	II	III	IV	V	VI	VII	VIII

(b) The set {I, II, III, IV, V, VI, VII, VIII} is closed under the operation of clock arithmetic addition because the addition of any two elements of the set always yields another element of the set. (Only elements of the set appear in the table.)

43. No. The element VIII (which corresponds to zero) appears in every row and in every column of the table. This means that if any element, say A, of the set is selected, there is another element B such that $A \oplus B$ = VIII. (You can check this in the table.)

45. (a) If $a \otimes b = 12$, then a is a divisor of 12 or b is a divisor of 12.
    (b) The product of 12 and any of the integers from 1 to 12 is 12. Besides these, the following pairs have a product of 12: 2 and 6, 3 and 4, 3 and 8, 4 and 6, 4 and 9, 6 and 6, 6 and 8, 6 and 10. (See the table in problem 29.)

47.

$\oplus$	0	1	2	3	4
0	0	1	2	3	4
1	1	2	3	4	0
2	2	3	4	0	1
3	3	4	0	1	2
4	4	0	1	2	3

48. Yes

Exercise 8.5

1. False   3. False   5. False   7. 2 (mod 5)   9. 4 (mod 5)   11. 3 (mod 5)
13. 1 (mod 5)   15. 3 (mod 5)   17. 3 (mod 5)   19. 0   21. 0   23. 1   25. 2
27. 2   29. 2   31. 3   33. 2   35. Yes   37. Yes; 1   39. Wednesday
41. Saturday   43. Friday
45.

+	0	1	2	3
0	0	1	2	3
1	1	2	3	0
2	2	3	0	1
3	3	0	1	2

47. The 0005234983 is correct. Dividing 523498 by 7 leaves a remainder of 3, not 1.
51. 2

49. 5

53. 1

55. The (5, 3) design is the same as the (5, 2) design in the figure in the text.

57. The (19, 17) and the (19, 9) designs are the same.

59. $m = 9$

Exercise 8.6

1. (a) a (b) c (c) b

3. (a) a (b) a (c) Yes

5. (a) c (b) c (c) Yes

7. Yes; if $x \in S$ and $y \in S$, then $(x @ y) \in S$.

9. (a) Yes; if a and b are natural numbers, then a F $b = a$, which is a natural number.
   (b) Yes; a F $(b$ F $c) = a$ F $b = a$ and $(a$ F $b)$ F c $= a$ F $c = a$. Thus, a F $(b$ F $C) = (a$ F $b)$ F c.
   (c) No; if $a \neq b$, then a F $b = a$ and b F $a = b$, so that a F $b \neq b$ F a.

11. (a) No; for example, $3 + 5 = 8$, which is not an odd number.
    (b) Yes; the product of two odd numbers is an odd number.
    (c) Yes; the sum of two even numbers is an even number.
    (d) Yes; the product of two even numbers is an even number.

13.

$\cap$	$\emptyset$	$\{a\}$	$\{b\}$	$\{a, b\}$
$\emptyset$	$\emptyset$	$\emptyset$	$\emptyset$	$\emptyset$
$\{a\}$	$\emptyset$	$\{a\}$	$\emptyset$	$\{a\}$
$\{b\}$	$\emptyset$	$\emptyset$	$\{b\}$	$\{b\}$
$\{a, b\}$	$\emptyset$	$\{a\}$	$\{b\}$	$\{a, b\}$

15. (a) Ø   (b) Ø   (c) Yes

17. Yes; all elements in the table are elements of S.

19. (a)

L	1	2	3	4
1	1	2	3	4
2	2	2	3	4
3	3	3	3	4
4	4	4	4	4

(b) 1

21. (a) No inverse   (b) No inverse   (c) No inverse
    (d) 4

23. Yes; 1

25. (a) The identity element is A, because for every B that is a subset of A, $A \cap B = B \cap A = B$
    (b) No; there is no other identity element.

27. Yes; the identity element is 0.

29. (a) 3   (b) 4

31. If a, b, c are real numbers, then a F $(b$ L $c) = a$ and $(a$ F $b)$ L $(a$ F $c) = a$ L $a = a$. Thus, this distributive property holds.

33. Yes

35. Yes

37. Check to see that $a ◆ b$ is always an element of S.

39. Check the table to see if there is an element e in S such that the column under e is identical to the column at the far left and the row opposite e is identical to the top row. If there is, then e is the identity element. If there is no such element, then there is no identity element.

41. $6 \times 9999 = 6(10,000 - 1) = 600000 - 6$
    $= 59,994$

43. $7 \times 59 = 7(60 - 1) = 420 - 7 = 413$

45. $4 \times 9995 = 4(10,000 - 5) = 40,000 - 20$
    $= 39,980$

47. Here are the steps:

Think of a number:	x
Add 3 to it:	$x + 3$
Triple the result:	$3x + 9$
Subtract 9:	$3x$
Divide by the number with which you started, x:	3

Exercise 8.7

1. Yes (actually, a commutative group)
5. No; no identity element
9. No; no multiplicative inverses
13. No; no multiplicative inverse for 0
17. No; no multiplicative inverses
21. You have to check that $x * (y * z) = (x * y) * z$ for all possible values of x, y, z from the set $\{a, b, c\}$. If you had to check all possible cases, there would be 27 of these because each of the 3 places has three possible values. However, since the operation has the commutative property, the number of cases to be checked is greatly reduced. Think about it.
25. No; matrix multiplication is not commutative.

27.

C	1	2	3	4	5	6
1	1	2	3	4	5	6
2	2	1	4	3	6	5
3	3	6	5	2	1	4
4	4	5	6	1	2	3
5	5	4	1	6	3	2
6	6	3	2	5	4	1

3. No; no multiplicative inverses
7. No; no multiplicative inverses
11. Yes
15. No; no identity element
19. No; no multiplicative inverses
23. The system is a commutative group. It satisfies all the requirements of Definition 8.19.

29. The set is a group under the operation C.

Exercise 8.8

1. Strictly determined. Optimal pure strategy: Row player should play row 1, column player should play column 1. Value = 4.
5. Strictly determined. Optimal pure strategy: Row player should play row 1, column player should play column 3. Value = 4.
9. No saddle point. Row player should play row 1 five-sixths of the time and row 2 one-sixth of the time.
13. Optimum row strategy: Play row 1 one-fourth of the time, row 2 three-fourths of the time, do not play row 3. Value = 3.
17. Ann's optimum strategy: Buy no bonds, buy stocks with five-sevenths and money market funds with two-sevenths of her investment. Her expected return would be $11\frac{3}{7}\%$.

3. Not strictly determined.

7. Strictly determined. Optimal pure strategy: Row player should play row 3, column player should play column 3. Value = 4.
11. No saddle point. Row player should play row 1 one-sixth of the time and row 2 five-sixths of the time.
15. Study 2 hr, one-half the time and 4 hours, one-half the time.

19. Station R should price its gasoline at $1 four-fifths of the time.

21. (a)

	Young	Old
Performance	70%	20%
Safety	40%	80%

(b) 4/9 Performance
5/9 Safety

23.

		Freeze	
		Yes	No
Water	Yes	6000	−400
	No	−4000	4000

Optimum strategy: Water $\frac{5}{9}$ of the time; don't water $\frac{4}{9}$ of the time. Expected value $= \frac{\$14000}{9} \approx \$1556$.

25. If row i dominates row j, this means that in the long run playing row i is more profitable than playing row j. Thus, row j may be eliminated from the row player's options.

27. Row 1

29. Send poems $\frac{5}{8}$ of the time and candy $\frac{3}{8}$ of the time. Do not send flowers.

Chapter 8 Practice Test

1. $x = 3, y = 4$

2. $AB = BA = \begin{bmatrix} 1 & 0 \\ 0 & 1 \end{bmatrix}$

3. $[20\ 25\ 10] \begin{bmatrix} 1 & 2 & 1 & 1 \\ 1 & 3 & 2 & 1 \\ 4 & 4 & 2 & 2 \end{bmatrix} = \begin{matrix} \text{Frames} & \text{Wheels} & \text{Chains} & \text{Paint} \\ [\ 85 & 155 & 90 & 65\ ] \end{matrix}$

4. Type I, $5.25; type II, $7.00; type III, $14.50

5. $\begin{bmatrix} 10 & -3 & 2 \\ -8 & -11 & 12 \\ 5 & -4 & 7 \end{bmatrix}$

6. $\begin{bmatrix} 0 & 1 & 1 \\ 6 & 2 & 1 \\ 5 & 3 & 1 \end{bmatrix}$

7. $AB = \begin{bmatrix} -3 & 4 & -1 \\ -5 & 5 & -1 \\ -2 & 11 & -4 \end{bmatrix}$; $BA = \begin{bmatrix} -2 & -1 & 1 \\ 6 & -5 & 9 \\ 2 & -3 & 5 \end{bmatrix}$

8. $\begin{bmatrix} 11 & 5 & 2 \\ 17 & 13 & 9 \\ 23 & 14 & 9 \end{bmatrix}$

9. $AA^{-1} = \begin{bmatrix} 1 & 0 & 0 \\ 0 & 1 & 0 \\ 0 & 0 & 1 \end{bmatrix}$

10. $\begin{bmatrix} \frac{1}{5} & \frac{1}{5} \\ \frac{2}{5} & -\frac{3}{5} \end{bmatrix}$

11. $x = -1, y = -2, z = 3$

12. $\frac{1}{4} \begin{bmatrix} 5 & -1 & -1 \\ -8 & 0 & 4 \\ -6 & 2 & 2 \end{bmatrix} \begin{bmatrix} 1 \\ 9 \\ 0 \end{bmatrix} = \frac{1}{4} \begin{bmatrix} -4 \\ -8 \\ 12 \end{bmatrix} = \begin{bmatrix} -1 \\ -2 \\ 3 \end{bmatrix}$

13. $x = -2, y = 7, z = 1$

14. $\begin{bmatrix} -1 & -1 & 2 \\ 0 & -1 & 2 \\ -2 & -4 & 7 \end{bmatrix}$

15. $\begin{bmatrix} -1 & -1 & 2 \\ 0 & -1 & 2 \\ -2 & -4 & 7 \end{bmatrix} \begin{bmatrix} 5 \\ 7 \\ 5 \end{bmatrix} = \begin{bmatrix} -2 \\ 3 \\ -3 \end{bmatrix}$

16. $\begin{bmatrix} 3 & 3 & 3 & | & 1 & 0 & 0 \\ 4 & 2 & 0 & | & 0 & 1 & 0 \\ 3 & 3 & 3 & | & 0 & 0 & 1 \end{bmatrix} \sim \begin{bmatrix} 3 & 3 & 3 & | & 1 & 0 & 0 \\ 4 & 2 & 0 & | & 0 & 1 & 0 \\ 0 & 0 & 0 & | & -1 & 0 & 1 \end{bmatrix}$

$$R_3 - R_1 \rightarrow R_3$$

The three O's in the third row show that no row operations can reduce the given matrix to the identity matrix. Thus, the given matrix has no inverse.

17. 40 nickels, 50 dimes, 32 quarters

19. The system has no solution.

18. $x = -\frac{1}{2}$, $y = 0$, $z = 2$

20. $x = -\dfrac{k + 1}{6}$, $y = \dfrac{4 - 2k}{3}$, $z = k$, where k is any real number

21. (a) 2 (b) 5 (c) 6 (d) 5

23. (a) True (b) True (c) False

25. (a) $n = 2 + 7k$, k any integer (b) $n = 6 + 7k$, k any integer

27. Yes. All the entries in the table are elements of S.

29. Yes. The table is symmetrical to the diagonal from upper left to lower right.

31. (a) # (b) ¢ (c) % (d) $

33. Yes. $a\ S\ (b\ L\ c) = b\ L\ c$ and $(a\ S\ b)\ L\ (a\ S\ c) = b\ L\ c$. Therefore, S is distributive over L.

35. Yes. The system has the five properties (closure, associative, identity, inverse, and commutative), so the system is a commutative group.

37. Yes. The system has the six properties (closure, associative, commutative, identity, distributive of multiplication over addition, and inverses, except there is no inverse for 0 with respect to multiplication), so the system is a field.

39. No. The element 0 has no inverse.

41. Not strictly determined.

43. Strictly determined. Value = 2.

45. (a)

	H	C
This Year H	0.6	0.4
Next Year C	0.3	0.7

(b) 50%

22. (a) 3 (b) 12 (c) 9 (d) No solution

24. (a) 0 (b) 2 (c) 3 (d) 4

26. (a) $n = 2 + 3k$, k any integer (b) $n = 1 + 3k$, k any integer

28. (a) # (b) # (c) %

30. The identity element is #.

32. (a) No identity element (b) No (c) Not commutative

34. $a\ L\ (b\ S\ c) = a\ L\ c$ and $(a\ L\ b)\ S\ (a\ L\ c) = a\ L\ c$. Thus, L is distributive over S.

36. Yes. The same explanation as for problem 35.

38. Yes. All the requirements of Definition 8.19 are satisfied.

40. Yes. All the requirements of Definition 8.20 are satisfied.

42. Strictly determined. Value = 1.

44. Optimum strategy: Row player should play row 1. Column player should play column 2. Payoff for the row player is −6.

CHAPTER 9

Exercise 9.1

1. 8 different outfits

3. 8 different outcomes.

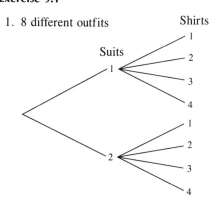

5. (a) 9 (b) 126 (c) 25 7. (a) 12 (b) 144 9. 30 11. 17,576 13. 378
15. 16 17. 90 19. 900,000,000 21. 59,280 23. 80 25. 152 27. 5760
29. 3840
31. $(a, @), (a, \&), (a, \%), (b, @), (b, \&), (b, \%), (c, @), (c, \&), (c, \%), (@, a),$
$(\&, a), (\%, a), (@, b), (\&, b), (\%, b), (@, c), (\&, c), (\%, c)$
33. If a single event can occur in m ways or in n ways, then the total number of ways in which the event can occur is $m + n$. (Assume no duplications)   35. 24
37. There are not enough different sets of initials for 27,000 people, so at least two people must have the same set of initials   39. 144
41. It will point to 3 if no slippage occurs.

Exercise 9.2

1. 24 3. 720 5. 120 7. 40,320 9. 362,880 11. 990 13. 126 15. 90
17. 10 19. 20,160 21. 120 23. 5040 25. 1716 27. 650 29. 60 31. 9
33. 31 35. 1 37. 57 39. 60
41. $n! = n \times (n - 1)!$ for $n > 1$. This formula holds for $n = 1$ only if 0! is defined to be 1.
The formula $P(n, r) = \dfrac{n!}{(n - r)!}$ holds for $r = n$, only if 0! is defined to be 1.
45. 120
49. $(n - 1)!$

43. The number of elements in the union of two sets is the sum of the number of elements in each of the sets diminished by the number of elements common to the two sets.

47. 3, including a possible tie for fourth place.
51. 4

Exercise 9.3

1. $C(5, 2) = 10, P(5, 2) = 20$
5. $C(9, 6) = 84, P(9, 6) = 60,480$
9. $C(10, 2) = 45$
13. $C(12,8) = 495$
17. $C(5, 4) = 5$
21. $C(24, 3) = 2024$
25. $C(52, 5) = 2,598,960$
29. 15
33. $C(8, 4) = 70$

37. The order of the numbers is important, so a permutation is being used.
41. (a) $(a + b)^4 = a^4 + 4a^3b + 6a^2b^2 + 4ab^3 + b^4$
(b) $(a + b)^5 = a^5 + 5a^4b + 10a^3b^2 + 10a^2b^3 + 5ab^4 + b^5$
45. $C(5, 3) = 10$
49. The left side is the sum of the number of ways in which there could be 0 heads and n tails, 1 head and $n - 1$ tails, 2 heads and $n - 2$ tails, and so on, to n heads and 0 tails. The right side is exactly the number of ways in which n coins can fall either heads or tails. Thus, the two sides are equal.

3. $C(7, 3) = 35, P(7, 3) = 210$
7. $C(5, 4) = 5$
11. $C(8, 2) = 28$
15. (a) 120 (b) 56 (c) 1 (d) 1
19. (a) $C(5, 3) = 10$ (b) 26
23. $C(10, 3) = 120$
27. $C(100, 5) = 75,287,520$
31. 63
35. Answers will vary; the important difference is that permutations take account of order and combinations do not.
39. $n = 6$: 1 6 15 20 15 6 1
$n = 7$: 1 7 21 35 35 21 7 1
43. $C(5, 0) = 1$

47. $C(5, 5) = 1$

Exercise 9.4

1. (a) $P(52, 3) = 132,600$ (b) $C(52, 3) = 22,100$

5. $C(5, 3) = 10$
9. (a) $P(10, 2)P(14, 2) = 16,380$
   (b) $P(10, 2)P(12, 2) = 11,880$
13. $831,600$
17. $C(7, 2)C(5, 3)C(2, 2) = 210$
21. $C(4, 2)P(3, 2)C(2, 1) = 72$
25. 15

3. (a) $50 \times 50 \times 50 = 125,000$
   (b) $C(50, 3) = 19,600$
7. (a) $C(7, 3) = 35$ (b) $P(7, 4) = 840$
11. (a) $C(7, 3)C(8, 1) = 280$
    (b) $C(5, 3)C(2, 1) = 20$
15. $22,680$
19. $C(n, 5) = 21$ for $n = 7$
23. Answers will vary.
27. $(a + 1)(b + 1)(c + 1)(d + 1)$

Chapter 9 Practice Test

1.

2. 30

3. (a) 36   (b) 4
5. 15
7. (a) 144   (b) 30
9. (a) 56   (b) 210
11. 48
13. 29
15. (a) 10   (b) 15
17. 20
19. 1326
21. 70
23. 34,650
25. $\frac{1977!}{1189!460!328!}$

4. 52
6. (a) 5040   (b) 210
8. (a) 120   (b) 720
10. 24
12. 72
14. 6
16. (a) 1   (b) 1/2
18. 24
20. 25
22. 840
24. 30

CHAPTER 10

Exercise 10.1

1. $\frac{1}{6}$ 3. $\frac{1}{3}$ 5. $\frac{1}{10}$ 7. $\frac{9}{10}$ 9. 0   11. $\frac{1}{13}$ 13. $\frac{1}{4}$ 15. $\frac{11}{26}$ 17. (a) $\frac{1}{5}$ (b) $\frac{3}{5}$ (c) $\frac{4}{5}$
19. (a) $\frac{1}{3}$ (b) $\frac{1}{3}$ 21. $\frac{1}{8}$ 23. $\frac{3}{8}$ 25. (a) $\frac{13}{17}$ (b) $\frac{4}{17}$ 27. (a) $\frac{11}{25}$ (b) $\frac{14}{25}$
29. (a) $\frac{8}{75}$ (b) $\frac{1}{3}$ 31. $\frac{1}{6}$ 33. $\frac{1}{6}$ 35. $\frac{1}{2}$ 37. (a) $\frac{1}{7}$ (b) $\frac{4}{7}$ (c) $\frac{11}{21}$
39. (a) $\frac{1}{2}$ (b) $\frac{3}{10}$ (c) $\frac{1}{5}$
41. Answers will vary. Tossing a coin is a simple probability experiment. The sample space is the set of all the possible results.
45. $\frac{253}{254}$ or about 0.996

43. $\frac{4653}{4720}$ or about 0.986

Exercise 10.2

1. $\frac{1}{18}$

3. $\frac{1}{8}$

5. $\frac{P(4,2)P(23,2)}{P(25,4)} = \frac{1}{50}$

7. (a) $\frac{1}{5}$ (b) $\frac{4}{5}$

9. (a) $\frac{4}{21}$ (b) $\frac{1}{21}$

11. $\frac{P(4,2)}{P(52,2)} = \frac{1}{221}$

13. $\frac{13 \times 3}{52 \times 51} = \frac{1}{68}$

15. $\frac{P(26,2)}{P(52,2)} = \frac{25}{102}$

17. (a) 15 (b) $\frac{5 \times 3}{15 \times 14} = \frac{1}{14}$ (c) $\frac{1}{7}$

19. 0.0396

21. 0.005

23. (a) $\frac{C(4,2)C(4,2)C(44,1)}{C(52,5)}$ (b) $\frac{C(4,3)C(4,2)}{C(52,5)}$ (c) $\frac{C(13,1)C(48,1)}{C(52,5)}$

25. $\frac{2}{5}$

27. $\frac{4}{C(52,5)} = \frac{1}{649740} \cong 0.0000015$

29. $\frac{13 \times 48}{C(52,5)} = \frac{1}{4165} \approx 0.00024$

31. $\frac{4 \times [C(13,5) - 10]}{C(52,5)} = \frac{5148 - 40}{C(52,5)} = \frac{1277}{649740} \approx 0.0020$

33. No. The coin is probably weighted to come up heads. Bet on heads.

35. No. The coin is probably weighted to come up heads. Bet on heads.

37. $\dfrac{C(40{,}000, 150)C(36{,}000, 150)}{C(76{,}000, 300)}$

39. $\dfrac{C(16, 6)C(14, 6)}{C(30, 12)}$

Exercise 10.3

1. 0; property (1) 3. 1; property (2) 5. $\frac{3}{5}$ 7. 1 9. $\frac{7}{26}$ 11. $\frac{1}{4}$ 13. $\frac{3}{13}$ 15. $\frac{41}{50}$

17. 0.2 19. 0.45 21. $\frac{433}{926}$ 23. $\frac{252}{445}$ 25. 1 27. $\frac{11}{20}$ 29. $\frac{4}{5}$ 31. $\frac{13}{17}$

33. If the probability of an event is 0, then the event cannot occur.

35. If $P(A \cap B) = 0$, that is, A and B have no common elements, then $P(A \cup B) = P(A) + P(B)$.

37. About 0.83.

39. Answers will vary.

41. $\frac{9}{10}$

43. $\frac{2}{5}$

45. $\frac{1}{5}$

47. $\frac{1}{20}$

Exercise 10.4

1. 0 3. (a) $\frac{1}{6}$ (b) 0 (c) 1 (d) 0 5. $\frac{1}{2}$ 7. $\frac{1}{2}$ 9. (a) $\frac{1}{5}$ (b) $\frac{1}{3}$

11. (a) $\frac{11}{20}$ (b) 80 (c) $\frac{3}{5}$ 13. $\frac{1}{17}$ 15. $\frac{1}{5}$ 17. $\frac{P(a \cap b)}{P(a)} = \frac{2}{3}$ 19. (a) $\frac{3}{10}$ (b) $\frac{39}{100}$ 21. $\frac{1}{3}$

23. (a) $\frac{27}{40}$ (b) $\frac{7}{10}$ 24. Answers will vary. 27. (a) $\frac{75}{128}$ (b) $\frac{53}{128}$ (c) Male 29. $\frac{9}{53}$

Exercise 10.5

1. Yes 3. (a) $\frac{1}{96}$ (b) $\frac{1}{48}$ (c) $\frac{7}{16}$ 5. (a) $\frac{1}{8}$ (b) $\frac{1}{2}$ (c) $\frac{7}{8}$

7. (a) $\frac{1}{4}$ (b) $\frac{1}{4}$ (c) $\frac{1}{16}$ (d) $\frac{9}{16}$ 9. (a) $\frac{1}{2}$ (b) $\frac{3}{4}$ (c) $\frac{3}{8}$ (d) They are independent.

11. (a) $\frac{1}{12}$ (b) $\frac{1}{8}$ 13. (a) $\frac{1}{4}$ (b) $\frac{1}{12}$ (c) $\frac{1}{4}$ 15. About 0.503 17. About 0.59

19. (a) $\frac{1}{8000}$ (b) $\frac{57}{8000}$ 21. 0.189 23. $\frac{1}{2}$

25. $\frac{3}{5}$ Hint: Draw a tree and use the final probabilities as weights for the two possibilities.

27. (a) The probability of one of the events does not depend on the probability of the other event. The occurrence or non-occurrence of one of the events does not affect the occurrence or non-occurrence of the other event.

(b) Find the product $P(A)P(B)$.

29. $\frac{C(50,25)}{2^{50}}$

31. $1 - \left[C(6,0)\left(\frac{1}{3}\right)^6 + C(6,1)\left(\frac{1}{3}\right)^5\left(\frac{2}{3}\right) + C(6,2)\left(\frac{1}{3}\right)^4\left(\frac{2}{3}\right)^2 \right] = \frac{656}{729}$

33. $C(5,2)\left(\frac{1}{6}\right)^2\left(\frac{5}{6}\right)^3 = \frac{625}{3888}$

35. $\frac{1}{8}$

37. 0.02

39. 0.000008

Exercise 10.6

1. 1 to 5   3. 1 to 12   5. 1 to 3   7. 5 to 21   9. 1 to 1   11. 10 to 3
13. $\frac{1}{50}$; 1 to 49   15. $\frac{3}{5}$ 17. $\frac{63}{10000}$; 63 to 9937   19. 1 to 1   21. $\frac{10}{4877}$ 23. $\frac{1}{8}$
25. 33 to 67   27. −$5   29. $2.15   31. No
33. Build at the first location and make $50,000.

35. (a) −$4000   (b) $10,000
    (c) Discontinue the campaign.

37. The mathematical expectation is that you lose $0.58 per $2 bet.

39. (a) 0.80   (b) 0.20

41. Odds against you are 9 to 1, so put up $1 for each $9. Thus, you should bet (1/9)($10) or about $1.11 to make the bet fair.

43. If ball stops on red or black, you break even. If ball stops on 0 or 00 and then on red or black, you lose 50 cents. Thus, the expected value is $-(\$0.50)(\frac{2}{38})(\frac{36}{38}) = -\frac{\$9}{361} \approx -\$0.025$

Chapter 10 Practice Test

1. (a) 1   (b) $\frac{2}{3}$ 2. 20   3. (a) $\frac{2}{5}$ (b) $\frac{1}{5}$ (c) $\frac{4}{5}$ 4. (a) $\frac{25}{102}$ (b) $\frac{188}{221}$
5. (a) $\frac{1}{4}$ (b) $\frac{1}{4}$ 6. $\frac{31}{32}$ 7. (a) $\frac{4}{5}$ (b) $\frac{4}{5}$ 8. 0.7   9. $\frac{11}{1105}$ 10. $\frac{1}{6}$ 11. $\frac{1}{18}$
12. (a) $\frac{1}{12}$ (b) $\frac{1}{2}$ (c) No. $P(A \cap B) = \frac{1}{36} \neq P(A)P(B)$
13. (a) 0.000064   (b) 0.884736   14. $\frac{1}{6}$ 15. 0.0009   16. (a) 1 to 12   (b) 12 to 1
17. (a) 3 to 4   (b) 4 to 3   18. (a) 7 to 3   (b) $\frac{7}{10}$ 19. $3.75   20. $38\frac{1}{3}$ cents

CHAPTER 11

Exercise 11.1

1. (a)

Number of Hours	Tally Marks	Frequency
0	II	2
1	III	3
2	II	2
3	III	3
4	III	3
5	II	2
6	II	2
7	II	2
8	IIII	4
9	I	1
10	II	2
11		0
12	II	2
13		0
14	I	1
15	I	1

(b) 8   (c) 4   (d) 15   (e) 36.7%

3. (a)

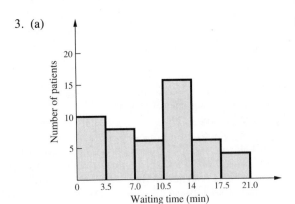

(b) 36%   (c) 52%

5. (a)

Age	Talley Marks	Frequency
6			1
7			1
8					3
9					3
10				2

(b)

(c) 20%

7. (a)

Price	Tally Marks	Frequency
$0 < P \leq 10$	||	2
$10 < P \leq 20$	ЖИТ	5
$20 < P \leq 30$	ЖИТ	5
$30 < P \leq 40$	||||	4
$40 < P \leq 50$			1
$50 < P \leq 60$	||||	4
$60 < P \leq 70$	||||	4

(b) There is no most frequent price interval. Five sold between $10 and $20, and five sold between $20 and $30.

(c) 9   (d) 12   (e) 20%   (f) 28%

9.

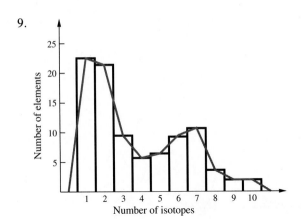

11. (a)

Letter	Frequency	Letter	Frequency
a	10	n	13
b	4	o	14
c	3	p	2
d	4	q	0
e	18	r	7
f	2	s	10
g	3	t	17
h	9	u	5
i	12	v	2
j	0	w	5
k	1	x	0
l	4	y	2
m	4	z	0

(b) e   (c) 39.1%

13.

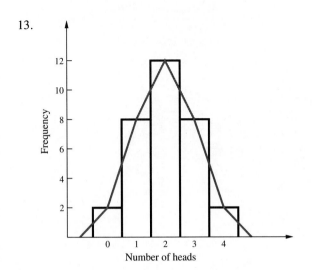

15. (a)

Concentration	Tally Marks	Frequency
0.00–0.04	JHT I	6
0.05–0.09	JHT JHT III	13
0.10–0.14	JHT	5
0.15–0.19	IIII	4
0.20–0.24	II	2

(b) 20%

17. (a)

Weekly Salary	Tally Marks	Frequency
600–2400	JHT IIII	9
2400–4200		0
4200–6000	II	2
6000–7800	I	1

(b)

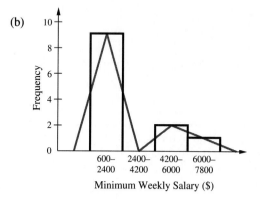

19. (a)

Salary (×1000)	Tally Marks	Frequency
20–34	JHT JHT JHT JHT	20
34–48	I	1
48–62	I	1
62–76	II	2
76–90	I	1

(b)

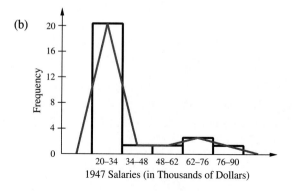

21. (a) $74   (b)

Price	Tally Marks	Frequency
180–254	JHT	5
254–328	JHT II	7
328–402		0
402–476	I	1
476–550	II	2

(c)

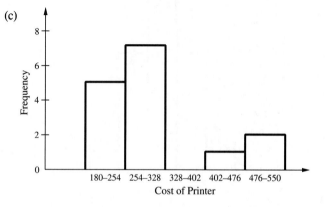

23. (a) 3 years

(b)

Age	Tally Marks	Frequency
109–112	JHT JHT II	12
112–115	JHT JHT	10
115–118	II	2
118–121		0
121–124	I	1

(c)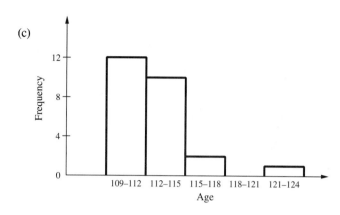

25. The upper- and lower-class limits, respectively, are the least and the greatest values in that class. Each class boundary is the midpoint between the upper limit of the respective class and the lower limit of the next class.

29. 100,271

31. In each case, most of the bar is omitted.

27.

Digit	Frequency
0	1
1	4
2	5
3	6
4	4
5	4
6	3
7	3
8	5
9	5

Exercise 11.2

1. (a) Mean = 9; median = 9 (b) Mean = 24.2; median = 9 (c) Mean = 11; median = 9 (d) Mean = median for part (a) only. Median = 9 for all three. None has a mode.

3. Mean = 6.05; median = 6.5; mode = 8; the mode is the least representative.

5. Betty is correct. She took account of the number of students making each score, and Agnes did not.

7.

Number of Letters	Frequency
2	1
3	5
4	4
5	5
6	0
7	3
8	2
9	0
10	0
11	1

(a) 3 and 5 (b) 5 (c) 5.05
(d) No; there is too much repetition.

9. (b)–(c) Answers will vary, but should be approx. 8.

13. $84 per week

17. Statements (b) and (c) are both true

21. The median of a set of scores is the middle number (if there is one) when the scores are arranged in order of magnitude. If there is no middle number, the median is the average of the two middle numbers. The median is not a good measure as it gives no indication of how the scores are spread.

25. The mean

11. 60

15. (a) 0.34   (b) 25,000–$34,999   (c) $39,444
    (d) $20,000

19. 70

23. (a) 2.4   (b) 2

27. The mean of a secretary's and a worker's salaries.

Exercise 11.3

1. (a) 18   (b) 7.21

5. (a) 4   (b) 1.58

9. (a) 6   (b) 2.16

13. (a) 110   (b) 110   (c) 108   (d) 3.71   (e) 102, 103, 113; 30%

17. Range 9, mean, 7, standard deviation $\sqrt{10} \approx 3.16$

21. 5

3. (a) 20   (b) 7.91

7. (a) 8   (b) 3.11

11. (a) 8   (b) 6.5   (c) 6   (d) 3.23   (e) 70%
    (f) 100%

15. Range 15, mean 7, standard deviation $\sqrt{30} \approx 5.48$.

19. The numbers are all the same. If zero is the standard deviation, then $(x - \bar{x})^2 = 0$ for all x in the set.

23. 8.66

Exercise 11.4

1. (a) 100 in.   (b) 10 in.   (c) 68%   (d) 2700

5. A, 12 or 13; B, 68 or 67; C, 340; D, 68 or 67; F, 12 or 13

9. 19 ft $10\frac{1}{2}$ in. and 20 ft $1\frac{1}{2}$ in.

13. The SAT score is the higher.

17. The German test score.

21. (a) 0.998   (b) 0.004

25. 5 ft $9\frac{1}{2}$ in.

29. No. If curve A in Figure 11.10 is moved two units to the right, this would be an example. The standard deviation for A would be 1/3 unit and that for B would be 1 unit, while the mean for A would be 2 and that for B would be 0.

3. (a) 25   (b) 25   (c) 680

7. 5

11. The purchasing director will decide to buy. If the lifetimes are normally distributed, $2\frac{1}{2}$ % will last 40 or more days. Thus, of the 8000, about 200 would last 40 or more days.

15. (a) 0.8   (b) 1.6   (c) 2

19. (a) 0.249   (b) 0.477

23. 0.228

27. Yes. See Figure 11.10. Here both curves have the mean 0. The standard deviation for A is 1/3 unit while that for B is 1 unit.

31. 80

33. (a) 20 (b) 60 (c) 90 (d) 0
37. $\bar{x} = 6$, $s = 4.77$. Three lie within one standard deviation from the mean, and all nine lie within 2 standard deviations from the mean. The theorem makes no prediction for 1 standard deviation, it predicts 75% for 2 standard deviations.

35. (a) 75 (b) 89 (c) 49
39. No. It cannot exceed 25%.

Exercise 11.5

1.
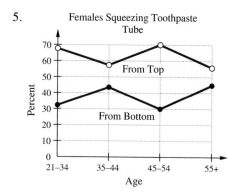

3.
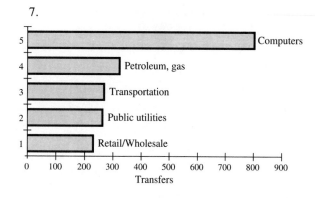

5.

7.

9. (a)
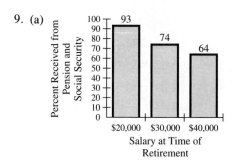

(b) $18,600

11. (a)
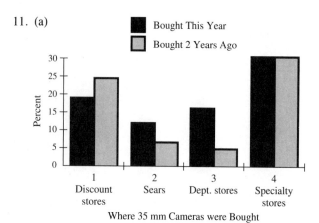

Where 35 mm Cameras were Bought

(b) At specialty stores. (c) Department stores. (d) The specialty stores.

13.
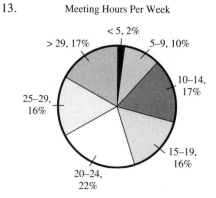

15.
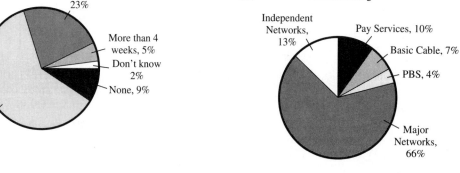

17.
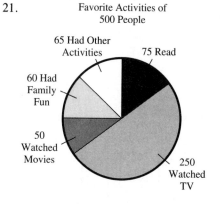

19. (a)

21.

23.

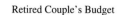

Retired Couple's Budget

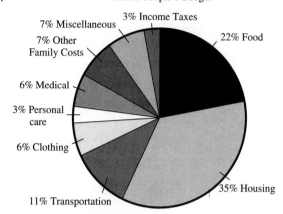

7% Miscellaneous

3% Income Taxes

7% Other Family Costs

22% Food

6% Medical

3% Personal care

6% Clothing

11% Transportation

35% Housing

25. (a)

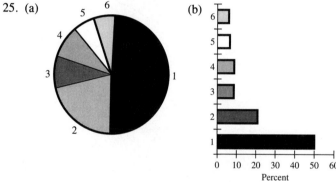

(b)

(c) The circle graph. The area corresponding to Brand 1 overshadows all the rest of the chart.

Percent

27. (a) Yes, to give a correct visual impression, only the height should be doubled. If both the height and the radius are doubled, the volume is multiplied by 8.

(b)

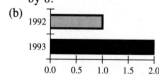

1992

1993

0.0　0.5　1.0　1.5　2.0

29.　Golf (Walking and Carrying Your Clubs)

Walking (4 MPH)

Swimming (40 Yd/Min)

Running (6 MPH)

Bicycling (15 MPH)

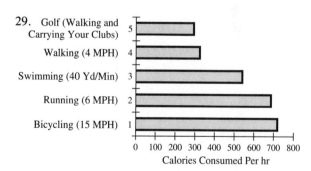

0　100　200　300　400　500　600　700　800

Calories Consumed Per hr

31.

Aspirin

Cold and Cough Syrups

Aspirin Substitutes

Nasal Sprays, Drops, and Vaporizers

Cough Drops and Sore Throat Remedies

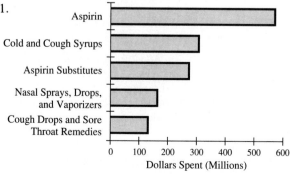

0　100　200　300　400　500　600

Dollars Spent (Millions)

33. (a) $16,000,000 (b) In 1986.

37. The area of the bar in a bar graph indicates the amount of the item that is graphed. For this reason the bars are usually shaded. In a histogram, the height of the bar corresponds to the frequency of the item in question and there is no space between the bars.

35. (a) Use a large scale on the vertical axis.
    (b) Use a very small scale on the vertical axis.

39. The graph on the right has a very much compressed vertical scale which diminishes the visual effect of each increase or decrease.

Exercise 11.6

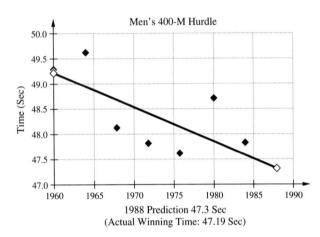

1988 Prediction 47.3 Sec
(Actual Winning Time: 47.19 Sec)

3.

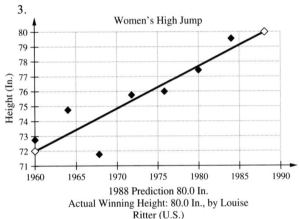

1988 Prediction 80.0 In.
Actual Winning Height: 80.0 In., by Louise Ritter (U.S.)

5. (a)

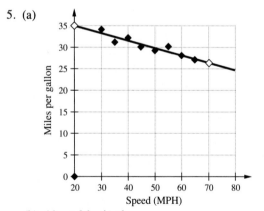

(b) About 26 mi/gal.
9. 720 11. 200   13. About 426

17. Procedure (d)

7. (a)

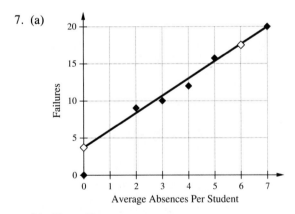

(b) About 18
15. (a) About 13 (b) About 9 (c) About 9
    (d) About 3 (e) About 3 (f) About 3
19. (a) The women who shop in Rodeo Drive are not necessarily a good representation of the entire population of California.
    (b) The same can be said of the male population of Berkeley.
    (b) The same can be said of the people attending an Oakland baseball game.

21. $y = -0.872x + 5.231$

23. $y = -1.057x + 12.186$, where x is the number of the Olympics with 1960 as number 1, and $y = t - 50$.

25. $y = -0.293x + 7.368$, where $x = $ year $- 1965$, $y = t - 45$

Exercise 11.7

1. Positive

3. None

5. Negative

7. Positive

9. Positive correlation

11. Negative correlation

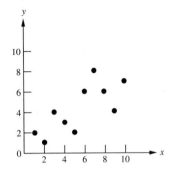

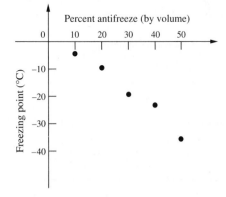

13. Positive correlation

15. Negative correlation

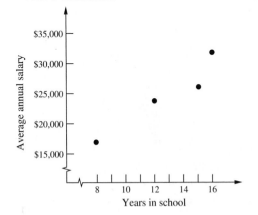

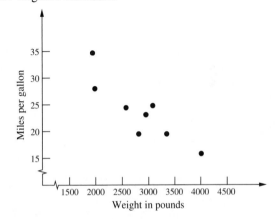

17. (a) The 7th (b) The 11th (c) After the 2nd week (d) No

19. (a) No (b) Answers may vary. It is possible that the number of cars with air bags being sold is increasing at a rate that makes them representative of the entire population of cars.

21. $r = -0.89$

23. $r = 0.93$

25. $r = -0.21$

Chapter 11 Practice Test

1.

Score	Tally Marks	Frequency
$60 < s \le 65$	II	2
$65 < s \le 70$	III	3
$70 < s \le 75$	III	3
$75 < s \le 80$	II	2
$80 < s \le 85$	III	3
$85 < s \le 90$	JHT II	7
$90 < s \le 95$	III	3
$95 < s \le 100$	II	2

2. and 3.

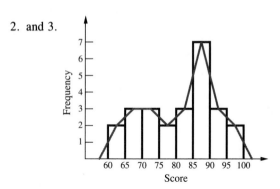

4. (a) 75 (b) 82 (c) 73
5. (a) 13 (b) 5.60
6. (a) 104–152 (b) 0.025
7. (a) 25 (b) 160 (c) 135
8. (a) 0.5 (b) 0.025
9. (a) 1.6 (b) 2.4
10. The score in French was the better score.
11. 0.492
12.

Fed DS — 2.5%
Ford M — 4.5%
Noes UT — 8.5%
Exxon — 4.7%
Gen El — 3.2%

13. (a)

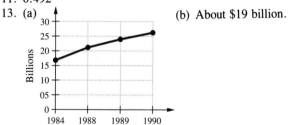

(b) About $19 billion.

14.

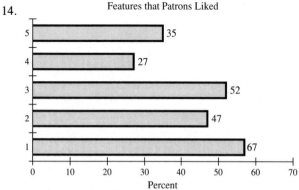

Features that Patrons Liked

5 — 35
4 — 27
3 — 52
2 — 47
1 — 67

1 Low calorie entrees
2 Varied portion sizes
3 Cholesterol-free entrees
4 All-you-can-eat specials
5 Self-service soup bar

15.

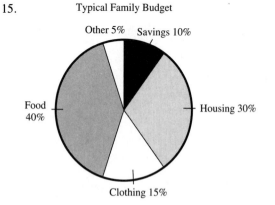

Typical Family Budget

Other 5%   Savings 10%
Food 40%   Housing 30%
Clothing 15%

16. About 50%
18. About 8
20. (a) Positive (b) Positive (c) None (d) Negative

17. About 200
19. For $x = 7$, $y \approx -1.8$.

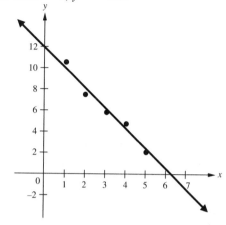

CHAPTER 12

Exercise 12.1

1. $240
5. $200
9. $466.67
13. $1802.40
17. (a) $40 (b) $160 (c) 168
21. (a) $0.71 (b) $13.49
25. $7154.60; $4574.60
29. $25,364; $5364
33. (a) $2854.30 (b) $2898.30
37. $15.30

3. $540
7. $62.50
11. (a) $2.41 (b) $42.61
15. $4592.50
19. (a) $125 (b) $375
23. $159.38; $59.38
27. $26,195; $14,195
31. $3,880,690; $3,840,690
35. (a) $3993 (b) $993
39. Simple interest means that the interest itself does not earn additional interest. Compound interest means that the interest earns interest at the same rate. For instance, $100 at 10% simple interest would earn $20 in two years, while $100 at 10% compounded annually would earn $21 in two years.

41. 6.09%
45. 9.31%

43. 8.24%
47. 19.56%

Exercise 12.2

1. $15,000 per year
5. $185.01
9. (a) $1.28 (b) $236.28 (c) $11.81
13. (a) $1.21 (b) $180.39 (c) $10.00
17. (a) $0.52 (b) $122.81 (c) $10.00
21. $1.35
25. (a) $450 (b) $136

3. $141.35
7. $557.48
11. (a) $5.16 (b) $409.16 (c) $20.46
15. (a) $0.84 (b) $92.73 (c) $10.00
19. $2.85
23. (a) $1998 (b) $261
27. (a) $60 (b) $26

29. This procedure gives the longest possible time between the purchase date and the date when payment
must be made to avoid a finance charge.
33. 10%

31. 6.4%

Exercise 12.3

1. 14%
5. 17%
9. 16%
13. (a) $8.40   (b) $261.60
17. (a) $24   (b) $14\frac{1}{2}$%
21. (a) $4   (b) $196
25. (a) $120   (b) $51.11   (c) $4.21   (d) $149.12
29. 16.9% (0.9% more than aswer to problem 3).
33. 17.1% (1.6% more than answer to problem 7).

3. 16%
7. $15\frac{1}{2}$%
11. (a) $2   (b) $98
15. (a) $4.18   (b) $45.82
19. (a) $134   (b) $16\frac{1}{2}$%
23. (a) $72   (b) $66   (c) $9.23   (d) $254.77
27. 14.3% (0.3% more than aswer to problem 1).
31. 17.7% (0.7% more than answer to problem 5).
35. 17.6% (1.6% more than answer to problem 9).

Exercise 12.4

1. (a) Yes   (b) Yes   (c) Yes
5. $297.17
9. $742.61
13. (a) $3250   (b) $768.31

17. (a) $11,185   (b) $549   (c)   (c) $563.04
21. (a) $10,467   (b) $812.70
25. On a loan of $100,000 at 9% for 30 years, the total
interest will be $189,800, which is more than the
price of the house. On a $50,000 loan under the
same terms, the total interest will be $94,900, which
is more than the price of the house.

3. (a) $61,600   (b) $15,400   (c) $9500
7. $440.05
11. (a) $3000   (b) $667.64
15. (a) $439   (b) 360   (c) $158,040   (d) $108,040
    (e) Less
19. (a) $25,630   (b) $872.80   (c) $885.92
23. Answers will vary.

Chapter 12 Practice Test

1. (a) $448   (b) $56   (c) $1248
3. (a) $78   (b) $312
5. (a) $10   (b) $2.64
7. (a) $2400   (b) $154.17
9. (a) $37,500   (b) $12,500   (c) $2000   (d) $48,000

2. (a) $21.60   (b) $381.60
4. (a) $116.99; $16.99   (b) $117.17; $17.17
6. (a) $1.94   (b) $155.08
8. (a) $15\frac{1}{2}$%   (b) $6.17   (c) $120.53
10. $450

CHAPTER 13

Exercise 13.1

1. (a) 1000   (b) 0.001   (c) 100   (d) 1000
5. Answer (a)
9. (a) 8000   (b) 400   (c) 34.09   (d) 4.94
13. 1500
17. 1000

3. Answer (c)
7. Answer (a)
11. 2.1
15. (a) 157.5 m   (b) 26.25 m   (c) 15.75 m
19. 3.5

21. 10
25. (a) 14,000   (b) 4800   (c) 0.0028   (d) 3900
29. Answer (b)
33. i and d; ii and c; iii and e; iv and a; v and b

23. 250
27. 1000 g
31. About 157 cm
35. (1) Fill the 300 ml glass and empty it into the 500 ml glass.
    (2) Fill the 300 ml glass from the pitcher again and use the glass to fill the 500 ml glass. (This leaves 100 ml in the 300 ml glass.)
    (3) Empty the 500 ml glass into the pitcher and then empty the 300 ml glass into the 500 ml glass.
    (4) Fill the 300 ml glass from the pitcher and empty the glass into the 500 ml glass. This gives 400 ml of wine in the 500 ml glass.

Exercise 13.2

1. 15   3. 30   5. −30   7. 50   9. 14   11. 260   13. 105.8   15. 37° C
17. (a) 5° C   (b) 100° C   19. −108.4° F   21. −32° C   23. 36° C

Exercise 13.3

1. 20.32   3. 4.73   5. 46.6   7. 4.03   9. 6.44   11. 2.30   13. 2.72   15. 11.0
17. 4.73   19. 8.59   21. 2.46   23. 16.39   25. 183   27. 0.854   29. 64 km/hr
31. 58   33. 28,900   35. 560   37. 48   39. 114   41. 298   43. 12.7   45. 17.0
47. 1.18   49. 96.5   51. 101.6−66.0−96.52   53. About 24   55. About 19
57. About 560,000

Chapter 13 Practice Test

1. (a) 10^{-2} (b) 10^{-3} (c) 10^3
3. (b) Kilograms
5. 900
7. 82
9. 0.92
11. 100
13. $\frac{1}{10}$
15. 0.250
17. 25° C
19. 24.8 (or 25) mi/hr
21. (a) 0.75   (b) 0.795
23. 35.56
25. (b) 25 cm

2. (c) Liters
4. 75
6. 30 mm, 40 mm, and 60 mm, respectively.
8. 8300
10. 1.9
12. 400
14. 0.000275 kg
16. 4100
18. 68° F
20. 114
22. 0.465
24. 50.7

CHAPTER 14

Exercise 14.1

1. Transistors replaced tubes.
5. Keyboard, video monitor, disk drives, system unit.
9. 20:00

3. Used miniaturized memory chips.
7. 8-4-97 or 8/4/97
11. A list of all the files on the disk

13. Press the ⏎ backspace key

15. Six 0's are printed (syntax error in 10).

17. WE NEED QUOTATION MARKS AT THE END

19. Four 0's are printed.

21.
```
10  PRINT "5 + 3"
20  PRINT "IS"
30  PRINT 5 + 3
40  PRINT "THAT IS, 5 + 3 =" ; 5 + 3
```

23.
```
10  PRINT  "##########"
20  PRINT  "#        #"
30  PRINT  "##########"
```

25. `10  PRINT "TOTAL HOURS WORKED:" 3 + 5 + 5 + 4 + 3`

27. It plays "Mary Had a Little Lamb."

29. It erases all prior programs in the machine.

31. NEW clears the computer memory; CLS clears only the screen.

Exercise 14.2

1. $(3+4)/(5+9)$ 3. $3\wedge 2+4\wedge 2$ 5. $2*3\wedge 3-5*4\wedge 2$ 7. $5*8/(6*9)$ 9. 4 11. 2

13. 20 15. 16 17. 500

19.
```
827     0.5     2
1654    0.25
```

21. A=3 B=2 X=17

23. A=2 B=4 X=24

25. W=53

27.
```
10  LET S=1+2+3+4
20  PRINT S
30  END
```

29.
```
10   LET A=1
20   LET B=1
30   LET C=A+B
40   LET D=B+C
50   LET E=C+D
60   LET F=D+E
70   LET G=E+F
80   LET H=F+G
90   PRINT A; B; C; D
100  PRINT E; F; G; H
110  END
```

31.
```
10  LET A$=" WIN OR LOSE THAT COUNTS"
20  PRINT "IT IS NOT WHETHER YOU" A$
30  PRINT "IT IS WHETHER I" A$
```

33.
```
40  PRINT Q1$ + Q2$
50  PRINT Q3$ + Q2$
```

Exercise 14.3

1.
```
5    7    6
25   35   30
40   48   44
OUT OF DATA IN 10
```

3. 1.05*500=525
    1.05*750=787.5
    1.05*1500=1575
    1.05*2000=2100
    OUT OF DATA IN 10

5.
X	Y
−3	−1
−2	−3
−1	−3
0	−1
1	3
2	9
3	17

OUT OF DATA IN 20

7.
```
10   PRINT "N", "N^4"
20   READ N
30   LET F=N^4
40   PRINT N, F
50   GOTO 20
60   DATA 1, 2, 3, 4, 5, 6, 7, 8
70   END
```

9.
```
10   PRINT "N", "S"
20   READ N
30   LET S=N*(N+1)*(2*N+1)/6
40   PRINT N, S
50   GOTO 20
60   DATA 1, 2, 3, 4, 5, 6, 7, 8, 9, 10
70   END
```

11.
```
10   INPUT A,B
20   PRINT A;B;(A+B)/2
30   GOTO 10
40   END
```

13.
```
10   INPUT P
20   PRINT "1.05*";P;"=";1.05*P
30   GOTO 10
40   END
```

15.
```
10   INPUT X
20   PRINT "X", "Y"
30   LET Y=X^2+3*X−1
40   PRINT X,Y
50   GOTO 10
60   END
```

17.
```
10   INPUT N
20   PRINT "N", "NTH TRIANG.  NO."
30   LET T=T+N
40   PRINT N, T
50   GOTO 10
60   END
```

19.
```
10   INPUT "WHAT IS THE LENGTH";L
20   INPUT "WHAT IS THE WIDTH";W
30   LET A=W*L
40   PRINT "THE AREA OF THE RECTANGLE IS";A
50   END
```

21.
```
10   READ n$, rate, hours
20   PRINT n$, "$" hours*rate
30   DATA "YOUR NAME", 7, 38
```

23.
```
10   INPUT "ENTER NUMBER OF HOURS CYCLING",CYCLING
20   INPUT "ENTER NUMBER OF HOUR JOGGING",JOGGING
30   INPUT "ENTER NUMBER OF HOURS SWIMMING',SWIMMING
40   LET POUNDS = (250*CYCLING + 650*JOGGING + 300*SWIMMING)/3500
50   PRINT "NUMBER OF POUNDS LOST=";POUNDS
```

25. You get the message "?REDO FROM START"

27. 10 PRINT "NAME", "CLASS AVERAGE"

29. 30 LET T = (Q1 + Q2 + Q3) + 2*(E1 + E2 + E3)

31. 50 PRINT ST$, A

33.
```
70   DATA A.AARON, 80, 92, 78, 68, 72, 90
80   DATA B.BAKER, 50, 74, 82, 91, 83, 70
90   DATA B.HAMILTON, 95, 93, 98, 100, 72, 84
```

Exercise 14.4

1. Would print out X and $\sqrt[3]{X}$ for X = 1, 2, 3, . . . , 100.

3.
```
9      4     2
100    32    3
500    45    11
OUT OF DATA IN 10
```

5.
```
FIRST NUMBER? 48
SECOND NUMBER? 60
THE GCF IS 12
THE LCM IS 240
```

7.
```
10 LET A=1
20 LET A=A+1
30 LET B=A^5
40 IF B<=100000 THEN 20
50 PRINT A; B
60 END
```

9.
```
10 PRINT "R", "N"
20 READ R
30 IF R=1 THEN 120
40 LET N=1
50 LET A=(1 + R)^N
60 IF A>=2 THEN 90
70 LET N=N+1
80 GOTO 50
90 PRINT R, N
100 GOTO 20
110 DATA.04, .05, .06, .07, .08, 1
120 END
```

11.
```
10 LET N=  (value to be entered)
20 LET S=0
30 READ P
40 IF P=2 THEN 80
50 LET S=S+P
60 GOTO 30
70 DATA p1, p2, . . . pN, 2
80 IF ABS(1-S)<=.0005*N THEN 110
90 PRINT "SORRY"
100 GOTO 120
110 PRINT "OK"
120 END
```

13. 1

15. A *loop* is a repetitive process that performs the same task each time, but with different numbers. The program will go through the loop 11 times. After the last time ($x = 11$), the program ends.

17.
```
10 LET A=5000
20 LET B=100*.0525*A/12
30 LET I=.01*INT(B+.5)
40 LET A=A+I
50 PRINT I; A
60 END
```

19. This program will print out a three-column table giving the number of the month, the interest, and the new amount at the end of the month for 12 months for an initial deposit of $1000 at 5% compounded monthly. If the program is run, the following table will be printed out:

```
N    I      A
0    0      1000
1    4.17   1004.17
2    4.18   1008.35
3    4.2    1012.55
4    4.22   1016.77
5    4.24   1021.01
6    4.25   1025.26
7    4.27   1029.53
8    4.29   1033.82
9    4.31   1038.13
10   4.33   1042.46
11   4.34   1046.8
12   4.36   1051.16
```

21.

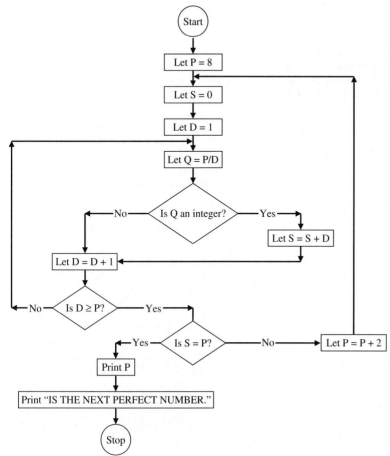

Exercise 14.5

1. 1
    5
    14
    30
    55

3. 3840

5. 5   15
    9   945
    11   10395
    OUT OF DATA IN 10

7. | I | R | H | P |
    |---|------|----|--------|
    | 1 | 4 | 42 | 172 |
    | 2 | 3.75 | 39 | 146.25 |
    | 3 | 3.5 | 45 | 166.25 |

9.
```
10 LET A=36
20 FOR K=1 TO 6
30 LET Q=A/K
40 IF Q=INT(Q) THEN 60
50 GOTO 70
60 PRINT K; Q
70 NEXT K
80 END
```

11.
```
10 PRINT "N", "FIFTH POWER"
20 FOR K=2 TO 20 STEP 2
30 LET F=K^5
40 PRINT K, F
50 NEXT K
60 END
```

13. It tells us the starting and ending points of a count, setting the parameters for a loop.

15. An error message will appear (FOR WITHOUT NEXT).

17. In line 40, change the 12 to 24. No other changes are necessary.

19.
```
10 LET B=500
20 LET N=0
30 LET J=.01*INT(B+.5)
40 LET P=50-J
50 IF P>=B THEN 90
60 LET N=N+1
70 LET B=B-P
80 GOTO 30
90 LET R=B+J
100 LET I=N*50+R-500
110 PRINT N; R; I
120 END
```

21. The first line should be the instruction: PRINT "D", "A", "P"

23. The outer loop starts with FOR n = 2 TO 30 and ends with NEXT n. The inner loop starts with FOR k = 1 TO INT(n/2) and ends with NEXT k.

Chapter 14 Practice Test

1. 80 PRINT "THE ANSWER IS..."

2. (a) $4*(2+5^2)/8$ (b) 3^2-3*2^3

3. (a) 25   (b) -11 (c) 5

4. 10   24   26

5. 21

6.
```
1    1
2   -2
3   -9
OUT OF DATA IN 10
```

7.
```
10 INPUT X
20 LET Y=3*X-2*X^2
30 PRINT X;Y
40 GOTO 10
50 END
```

8.
```
1
3
6
10
15
OUT OF DATA IN 10
```

9. 3260

10.
```
2
4
8
16
```

11. 55

12.
```
1
2
3
6
9
```

13.
```
10 LET A=SQR(38^2-4*13*17)
20 PRINT A
30 END
```

14.
```
PRINT "N", "CUBE ROOT"
20 READ N
30 IF N=99 THEN 80
40 LET C=N^(1/3)
50 PRINT N, C
60 GOTO 20
70 DATA 20, 30, 38, 42, 99
80 END
```

15.
```
10 PRINT "N", "FIFTH ROOT"
20 FOR K=1 TO 15 STEP 2
30 LET F=K^(1/5)
40 PRINT K, F
50 NEXT K
60 END
```

Research Bibliography

The entries in this bibliography provide a first resource for investigating the Research Questions that appear at the end of each chapter in the text. Many of these books will also contain their own bibliographies which you can use for an even more thorough information search. Also, using your library's card catalog system, be sure to look under subject as well as title listings to gain a better idea of the resources that your library has available even beyond the specific titles listed here.

Bell, E. T. *Men of Mathematics*. New York: Simon and Schuster, 1965.

Billstein, R. *et al. A Problem Solving Approach to Mathematics,* 4th ed. Redwood City, CA: Benjamin Cummings Publishing Company, 1990.

Brewer, James W. and Martha K. Smith, ed. "Emmy Noether, A Tribute to Her Life and Work." *Pure and Applied Mathematics,* 69, Marcel Dehker,   1981.

Burton, David. *The History of Math: An Introduction,* 2d ed. Dubuque, IA: Wm. C. Brown Publishers, 1991.

Copi, I. *Introduction to Logic,* 6th ed. New York: Macmillan, 1982.

Constable, George, ed. *Understanding Computers*. Alexandria, VA: Time-Life Books, 1985.

Eves, Howard. *An Introduction to the History of Mathematics,* 4th ed. New York: Holt, Rinehart and Winston, 1976.

Kahane, Howard. *Logic and Philosophy: A Modern Introduction,* 6th ed. Belmont, CA: Wadsworth Publishing, 1990.

Krause, Eugene. *Mathematics for Elementary Teachers,* 2d ed. Lexington, MA: D. C. Heath and Company, 1991.

Lien, David A. *Learning IBM Basic,* Rev. Ed. San Diego, CA: Compusoft Publishing, 1986.

Newman, James. *The World of Mathematics,* 4 Vols. New York: Simon and Schuster, 1956.

Osen, Lynn M. *Women in Mathematics,* Cambridge, MA: MIT Press, 1974.

Pedoe, Don. *The Gentle Art of Mathematics,* New York: Collier Books, 1963.

Perl, Teri H. *Math Equals*. Reading, MA: Addison-Wesley, 1978.

Presley, Brice. *A Guide to Programming the IBM Personal Computers,* 2d ed. New York: Delmar Publishers, 1985.

Schneider, David L. *A Brief Course in Microsoft QBASIC*. San Francisco: Dellen Publishing, 1991.

Chapter 1

Page 3, David Eugene Smith Collection, Rare Book and Manuscript Library, Columbia University; *Page 43,* Harvey Reid, Woodpecker Records, photo by Nancy Moulton; *Page 53,* NASA.

Chapter 2

Page 63, © Topham/The Image Works; *Page 93 (top),* Photo Researchers/Spencer Grant; *Page 116,* P. Sach.

Chapter 3

Page 150, Cliches des Musees Nationauex, France; *Page 154,* Lee Boltin Picture Library; *Page 160,* Bridgeman/Art Resource, NY; *Page 161,* Photo Researchers/Charles Cocaine; *Page 168,* Creative Publications; *Page 170,* Creative Publications; *Page 176,* NASA/Rainbow; *Page 188,* Phoebe Apperson Hearst Museum of Anthropology, University of California/Berkeley.

Chapter 4

Page 201, David Eugene Smith Collection, Rare Book and Manuscript Library, Columbia University; *Page 210,* Courtesy of Amdahl Corporation, Sunnyvale, CA; *Page 226,* © Antman/The Image Works; *Page 239,* Tony Stone Worldwide/Hugh Sitton; *Page 300,* Photo Researchers/Guy Sauvage Van-dystadt.

Chapter 5

Page 317, The Bettmann Archive; *Page 318,* Animals Animals/© Stephen Dalton; *Page 325,* © Daemmrich/The Image Works; *Page 347,* Tony Stone Worldwide/Charles Gupton; *Page 363 (top left),* Thomas A. Ploch, *(bottom)* NASA; *Page 375,* P. Sach.

Chapter 6

Page 389, Culver Pictures, Inc.; *Page 390,* Reproduced by permission of J. C. Penney Co, Inc. 1992; *Page 395,* Tony Stone Worldwide/Lori Adamski Peek; *Page 410,* Fundamental Photographs/Richard Megna; *Page 460,* P. Sach.

Chapter 7

Page 467, The Bettmann Archive; *Page 477,* Tony Stone Worldwide/Hideo Kurihara; *Page 487,* Bruce Iverson; *Page 511,* Culver Pictures, Inc; *Page 533,* H. Armstrong Roberts; *Page 537,* Representation of Rubik's Cube™ is by permission of Seven Towns Ltd., Seven Towns Ltd. owns the trademark of Rubik™ and Rubik's Cube™.

Chapter 8

Page 561, Historical Pictures/Stock Montage; *Page 578,* illustration by John Tenniel from *The Complete Illustrated Works of Lewis Carroll,* Chancellor Press, London, 1982.